Better Homes and Gardens®

New Cook Book

16TH EDITION

HOUGHTON MIFFLIN HARCOURT
BOSTON • NEW YORK

Meredith Corporation

Gayle Goodson Butler
Executive Vice President, Editor in Chief
Better Homes and Gardens® Magazine

Better Homes and Gardens® New Cook Book

Editor: Jan Miller

Project Editor: Shelli McConnell, Purple Pear Publishing, Inc.

Contributing Editors: Lisa Appleton, Carlos Acevedo, Ellen Boeke, Carrie Boyd, Jessica Christensen, Diana McMillen, Annie Peterson, Mary Williams

Contributing Copy Editor and Proofreader: Gretchen Kauffman, Angela Renkoski

Contributing Art Director, Photography: Stephanie Hunter

Test Kitchen Director: Lynn Blanchard

Test Kitchen Product Supervisor: Colleen Weeden

Test Kitchen Culinary Professionals: Sarah Brekke, Carla Christian, R.D.; Juliana Hale; Sammy Mila; Jill Moberly; Lori Wilson

Contributing Photographers: Karla Conrad, Jason Donnelly, Jacob Fox, Andy Lyons

Contributing Stylists: Greg Luna, Main Dish Media, Sue Mitchell, Dianna Nolin, Jennifer Peterson, Charlie Worthington

Administrative Assistants: Barb Allen, Ann Schill, Marlene Todd

Special Interest Media

Editorial Director: James D. Blume

Editorial Director, Food: Jennifer Dorland Darling

Art Director: Gene Rauch

Houghton Mifflin Harcourt

Publisher: Natalie Chapman

Editorial Director: Cindy Kitchel

Executive Editor: Anne Ficklen

Editorial Associate: Molly Aronica

Managing Editor: Marina Padakis Lowry

Production Director: Tom Hyland

Design Director: Ken Carlson, Waterbury Publications, Inc.

Associate Design Director: Doug Samuelson, Waterbury Publications, Inc.

Production Assistant: Mindy Samuelson, Waterbury Publications, Inc.

Our seal assures you that every recipe in *Better Homes and Gardens® New Cook Book* has been tested in the Better Homes and Gardens® Test Kitchen. This means that each recipe is practical and reliable and meets our high standards of taste appeal. We guarantee your satisfaction with this book for as long as you own it.

www.hmhco.com

Library of Congress Cataloging-in-Publication Data

New cook book. — 16th edition.
pages cm.
Includes index.
ISBN 978-0-544-71446-5 (comb bound);
ISBN 978-0-544-30798-8 (ebk)
1. Cooking. I. Better homes and gardens.
TX714.N468 2014
641.5—dc23
2014012314

Book design by Waterbury Publications, Inc., Des Moines, Iowa.

Printed in China

SCP 10 9 8 7 6 5
4500683247

contents

making good recipes great

I love this book! Working on this new edition has allowed me to engage in some passionate conversations with so many people about cooking. I'm often asked who decides if a recipe is good enough to be published in the *Better Homes and Gardens® New Cook Book*. The answer is simple. It takes a team to make sure that an individual recipe meets our expectations—and the Better Homes and Gardens® Test Kitchen staff plays a key role. These food professionals take their jobs seriously because they know how important it is to you to cook delicious food—and to do it well. So as we tested and tasted the recipes for this book, we talked about what you may experience at home. From ingredients to mixing to doneness questions, we worked through them all to make sure you have the same success in your kitchen as we have in ours.

The brand-new Cook's Secret pages in this edition bring our Test Kitchen into your home. For each chapter, we selected a classic recipe—and some variations and accompaniments, too—and defined the steps that are key to their success. Our team not only shows you the steps for HOW to prepare these recipes, but we've also included the WHYS behind what we do to transform a good recipe to great.

We've also added a new Holiday Favorites chapter. We know how important this book is for helping you create Thanksgiving dinner and special celebrations, so this chapter includes the delicious traditions that fill your table at those memorable times. The renewed interest in home gardening, farmer's markets, and sustainability has demanded an updated Canning and Freezing chapter dedicated to the do-it-yourself craft of food preservation. The love and appreciation for eating fresh all year is growing too, so the Vegetables & Fruits chapter features a beautiful new produce guide and creative ways to eat your veggies and fruits.

As we update each edition, there is always at least one recipe that surprises me—for this edition it was Chocolate Chip Cookies. It's a beloved recipe we thought was perfect until we started talking about it. I discovered our editors and Test Kitchen staff all used the recipe, but each had tweaked it a bit. We also decided we wished the cookie would stay fresh longer when stored. I'm pleased to say the refreshed Chocolate Chip Cookies recipe is a keeper! Take a peek at the Cook's Secret pages (240–241). I hope you're as happy with each bite of this made-new classic as we are!

I would love to hear what you think about our new features! Send me a note at spoon@meredith.com.

Here's to happy moments in your kitchen!

Jan Miller

Jan Miller

cooking basics

knives

This chapter opens with the topic of knives for a reason—they're a major player in kitchen success.

You can make do without a lot of kitchen gadgets and appliances, but a good set of knives is almost invaluable. Although high-quality cutlery can be expensive, if you invest in the best set you can afford, then hand-wash and dry and keep them professionally sharpened, your knives will last for years. Choose knives that feel balanced and comfortable in your hand. Good, practical knives have high-carbon, stainless-steel blades.

NECESSITIES

1 SERRATED BREAD KNIFE: Use a sawing motion with a serrated blade to cut through crusty breads and tender cakes.

2 CHEF'S KNIFE: Slice, dice, chop, and mince with this all-purpose wedge-shape blade.

3 UTILITY KNIFE: The thin, ultrasharp blade is perfect for delicate tasks, such as cutting fish, soft fruits, and cheeses.

4 SCISSORS: Keep a pair solely for the kitchen. Use for everything from opening packages to cutting chicken and snipping fresh herbs—you'll wonder how you ever lived without it.

5 PARING KNIFE: This small knife is ideal for coring, peeling, and cutting. Keep a few on hand so you'll always have a clean one to reach for as you cook.

USEFUL EXTRAS

6 CARVING KNIFE: Slicing meats is simple with this long, thin-bladed knife.

7 TOMATO KNIFE: Ever try to slice a tomato and have the pulp squeeze out all over the counter? That won't happen with this knife—its scalloped edge cleanly slices through the soft skin of tomatoes and other fruits and vegetables.

8 SANTOKU KNIFE: Hollowed-out impressions in the Japanese-style blade minimize sticking, making the knife versatile in your kitchen.

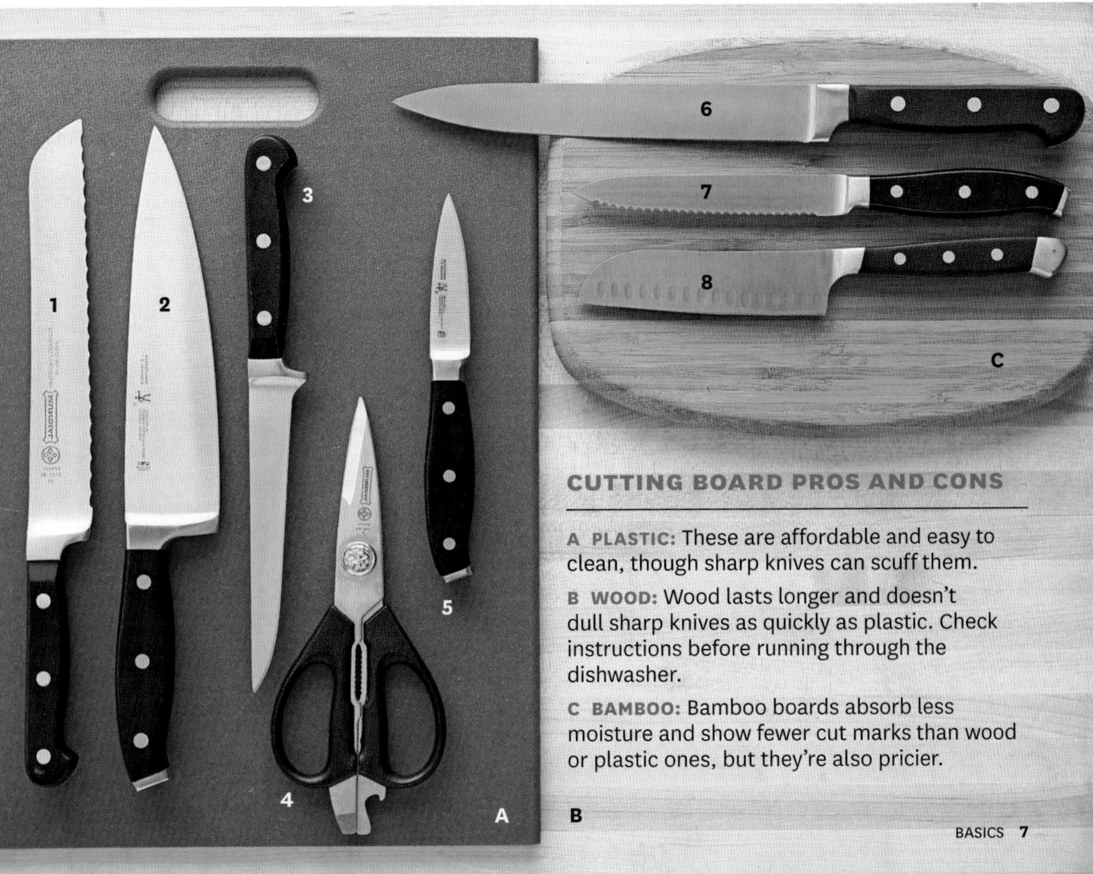

CUTTING BOARD PROS AND CONS

A PLASTIC: These are affordable and easy to clean, though sharp knives can scuff them.

B WOOD: Wood lasts longer and doesn't dull sharp knives as quickly as plastic. Check instructions before running through the dishwasher.

C BAMBOO: Bamboo boards absorb less moisture and show fewer cut marks than wood or plastic ones, but they're also pricier.

kitchen toolbox

These go-to tools make it easier for you to cook more good things more often.

NECESSITIES

1 LARGE LIQUID MEASURES: With the 8-cup measure, you can measure large amounts of liquids and measure multiple liquids together. Also use them to hold ingredients while you prepare other foods.

2, 3 SMALL LIQUID MEASURES: The 1-cup and 2-cup measures are a must for any kitchen.

4 GRADUATED MEASURING CUPS: Use these only for dry ingredients, such as flour and sugar, and soft solids, such as shortening. They're also known as dry measuring cups.

5 KITCHEN TONGS: Toss a salad, serve spaghetti, flip cutlets in a frying pan, and snag pickles out of the jar with this handy tool.

6 CAN OPENER: A no-brainer—just remember that after opening a can, handle the lid with caution; it can be as sharp as a knife.

7 MEASURING SPOONS: Use these spoons for both dry and liquid ingredients.

8 HEAT-RESISTANT TONGS: An alternative to No. 5, these offer two advantages: They stay cooler than all-metal tongs and are friendlier to nonstick cookware.

9 VEGETABLE PEELER: Its obvious function is to remove the skin from vegetables, but it can also make long shavings of cheese and strips of citrus peel for cooking and garnishing.

10 SILICONE SCRAPERS: These tools mix, stir, and fold ingredients and scrape up every bit of whatever is in your bowl, jar, or pan. They're heat-resistant too.

11 TURNER/SPATULA: Flip and serve anything grilled, broiled, baked, or pan-fried.

12 EGG SEPARATOR: This gadget cradles the yolk over a cup that catches the white. If you don't have one, crack the egg into a bowl and gently scoop up the yolk with your hand, allowing the white to run through your fingers.

13 WOODEN SPOONS: Stirring thick batter and dough is an easy task for these sturdy spoons. Because they're made of wood, they stay cool and don't scratch nonstick cookware.

14 WIRE WHISK: This tool is a must for beating eggs and other ingredients. Also use it for smoothing out lumpy sauces.

15 BOX GRATER: The sides with the larger slits or holes are for shredding foods; the sides with the smaller slits or holes are for grating foods.

16 COLANDER: Use to drain boiled foods or pasta and to hold foods while rinsing.

USEFUL EXTRAS

17 MEAT MALLET: The smooth side flattens meat; the spiked side flattens and tenderizes.

18 MORTAR AND PESTLE: Crush herbs and spices to boost their fresh flavors when cooking.

19, 20 POTATO MASHERS: Use one of these low-tech tools to achieve fluffy mashed potatoes.

21 FINE-MESH SIEVE: When straining foods that have fine particles, use this instead of a colander. You can also use it for sifting.

22 CHEESE SLICER: Most have an adjustable wire to define thickness of slices.

23 CITRUS JUICER: Choose one with a sieve to easily strain pulp and seeds. If you don't have one, use a fork. While gently squeezing fruit, lift and lower the fork to extract juice into a bowl.

24, 25 HANDHELD GRATERS: These are especially handy when you want to grate or shred a food directly over a pan, plate, or bowl.

26 PASTRY BLENDER: Pie and biscuit bakers use this time-honored gadget to cut butter or shortening into flour into small pieces for masterfully flaky results.

27 PASTRY BRUSH: Use this to grease a baking pan and brush barbecue sauce on meat (as directed in recipes). Also brush butter on sheets of phyllo dough and glazes on baked goods.

28 SLOTTED SPOON: This spoon is useful for removing solids from liquids, such as vegetables from a broth. Use it for stirring too.

29 ROLLING PIN: This helps you roll out everything from piecrusts and puff pastry to pizza and cookie dough. Although rolling pins can be made of a variety of materials, the Test Kitchen pros prefer those made of wood.

30 PIZZA CUTTER: Whether you like slices or squares, this lets you cut pizza your way.

31 KITCHEN TIMER: Keep track of the minutes with this classic wind-up timer. To get timings down to the second, go with a digital model.

1
2
3
4
5
6
7
8
9
10
11
12
13
14
15
16
17
18
19
20
21
22
23
24
25
26
27
28
29
30
31

1
2
3
4
5
6
7

cookware

If you buy good-quality pans, these workhorses will serve you well for many, many years.

NECESSITIES

1 LARGE NONSTICK SKILLET WITH SLOPED SIDES: The sides allow for easier tossing and flipping of foods you're preparing. The nonstick coating allows you to cook with less fat.

2 POT: Cook pasta and make big batches of broth, soup, stew, and chili in this vessel. Look for one with a volume of 6 to 8 quarts.

3 MEDIUM SAUCEPAN: Saucepans have tall straight sides with tight-fitting lids. A midsize saucepan (2 quarts) works well for tasks such as making sauces and cooking rice.

4 LARGE SAUCEPAN: A large saucepan holds 3 to 4 quarts and is perfect for small-batch soups and stews.

5 SMALL SAUCEPAN: Use the smallest saucepan (1 to 1½ quarts) for small-volume tasks, such as melting chocolate and butter.

6 LARGE STRAIGHT-SIDED SKILLET (WITH LID): Sometimes called a sauté pan, this straight-sided skillet is often interchangeable with a slope-sided skillet. However, with its lid, this one works better for braising meats, such as bone-in chicken, on the stove top. Either can handle most pan-frying jobs.

7 DUTCH OVEN: With this stove-top-to-oven pot, you can brown foods and bake them in the same vessel. The one shown is made of porcelain enamel-coated cast iron. A 4- to 6-quart size with a lid will handle many jobs.

METAL MATTERS

Choosing the best metal for your pans is important for successful, delicious results.

Pans are made in a variety of metals. Heavy stainless-steel pans, enameled cast-iron pans, hard-anondized aluminum pans, and tri-ply pans are all good choices for the home cook. Note that some recipes, such as those for puddings and custards, call specifically for a heavy saucepan. In this case, any of these types of pan may be used.

USEFUL EXTRAS

1 OMELET PAN: The nonstick surface and sloped sides make folding the eggs and sliding omelets from pan to plate a cinch.

2 WOK: Whether it has a flat or rounded bottom, the wok's deep, sloped sides help keep the bite-size pieces of food in the pan while stir-frying.

3 GRILL PAN: Get the appealing grill marks and low-fat results of grilling without having to stand outside. The grooves in the heavy stove-top pan allow fat to drain off the food.

4 GRIDDLE PAN: Make Saturday morning breakfast—bacon, eggs, and pancakes—on this flat, low-rim pan.

1

2

3

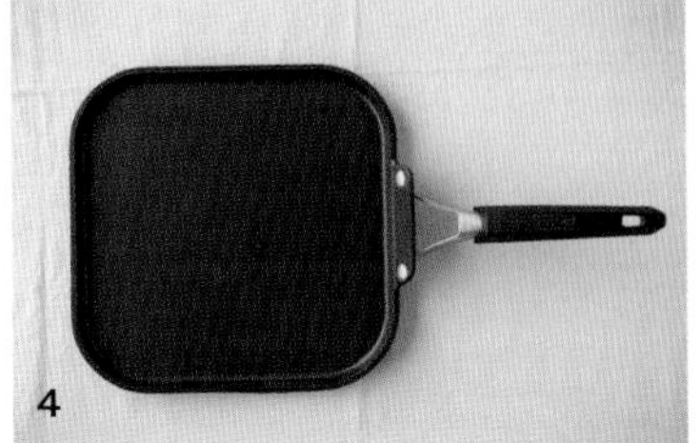

4

1
2
3
4
5
6
7
8

bakeware

With just a few essentials, you can bake all kinds of pies, tarts, cakes, cookies, breads, and casseroles.

PAN OR DISH—WHAT'S WHAT

In this book, a baking pan refers to a metal container, and a baking dish means an oven-safe glass or ceramic vessel.

BAKING PANS (METAL): Aluminum—nonstick or not—is a great choice for baking pans. It's lightweight and conducts heat well for even baking and browning. Also use aluminum or other metal baking pans when broiling; high temperatures might cause glass or ceramic to shatter.

BAKING DISHES (GLASS OR CERAMIC): Use when called for and when baking egg dishes and acidic foods, such as tomatoes and lemons. Metal pans can cause these foods to discolor.

NECESSITIES (see page 12)

1 LOAF PAN: You will need at least one if you're a fan of zucchini or banana bread or meat loaf. The most common size is 8×4×2 inches, though the larger 9×5×3-inch pan comes in handy too.

2 ROUND CASSEROLE DISH: Sized in 1½, 2, or 3 quarts, these usually come with a lid. If you don't have a lid, use foil to cover the dish.

3 PIE PLATE: The pie recipes in this book call for 9-inch pie plates; they can be made of glass, ceramic, stoneware, aluminum, or tin.

4 ROUND CAKE PANS: Though two will do for baking standard birthday cakes, fancier recipes often call for three pans. Choose pans with an 8- or 9-inch diameter that are 1½ inches deep.

5 RECTANGULAR AND SQUARE PANS AND DISHES: Stock up on rectangular (9×13×2-inch) and square (8×8×2-inch or 9×9×2-inch) baking pans, as well as rectangular (3-quart) and square (2-quart) baking dishes for lasagna, casseroles, brownies, cakes, bars, and more.

6 JELLY-ROLL PAN: You might never make a jelly roll, but you still need this 15×10×1-inch pan for other treats, such as bar cookies and brownies.

7 COOKIE SHEET: This low- or no-sided pan allows heat to circulate around the cookies.

8 MUFFIN PAN: Though many recipes yield more than 12 cupcakes, that's how many cups you'll find in a standard muffin pan. Bake in batches or buy two pans. Mini muffin pans also come in handy for baking small tassie-style cookies.

USEFUL EXTRAS (see below)

1 TUBE PAN: Also called an angel food cake pan, this has a hollow center tube that ensures even baking; most have a removable bottom.

2 RAMEKINS: Use these for cooking custards and other individual desserts. They're also great for holding prepped and measured ingredients to have them ready to add in a quick-moving recipe.

3 TART PANS WITH REMOVABLE BOTTOMS: These help you bake beautiful tarts with fancifully fluted sides and move them easily from pan to serving plate. They come in a variety of sizes.

4 SPRINGFORM PAN: This pan has a latch that springs open, making it easy to remove its sides from a baked dessert, such as cheesecake. When a recipe calls for this pan, don't even think of substituting another—you'll be hard-pressed to get your dessert out of the pan.

5 FLUTED TUBE PAN: These pans add depth and texture to pound cakes and coffee cakes.

6 SOUFFLÉ DISH: Steep, straight sides help soufflés rise to the occasion. You'll also find this dish surprisingly versatile for making other desserts and for serving side dishes.

cooking techniques & tips

From ingredient know-how to cooking methods, you'll find the help and hints you need to successfuly prepare all of the recipes in this book.

COOKING METHODS

These cooking terms appear often in our recipes. Here's what they mean.

1 SAUTÉ: From the French word *sautér* ("to jump"), sauté means to cook and stir foods in a small amount of fat or oil over fairly high heat in an open shallow pan. It's best to cut food into uniform-size pieces to ensure even cooking.

2 STIR-FRY: This is a method of quickly cooking small, uniform pieces of food in a little hot oil in a wok or large skillet over medium-high heat. Stir foods constantly to prevent burning. This technique is usually used to cook vegetables and to prepare many Asian-style dishes.

3 STEAM: Food is placed in a steamer basket, set over boiling water, and covered. In this relatively fast cooking method, steam from boiling water cooks the food, usually vegetables, while helping to retain color and nutrients.

4 BROIL: Food is cooked below direct, dry heat. To broil, position the broiler pan and its rack so the surface of the food (not the rack) is the specified distance from the heat source. Before heating the broiler, use a ruler to measure the distance in a cold oven.

5 PAN-FRY: This refers to cooking food, often lightly coated or breaded, in a skillet with a small amount of hot fat or oil. The surface of the food should brown and, if coated, become crisp. Thin cuts of fish and chicken work well for pan-frying.

6 ROAST: With this method, food is cooked with dry heat, uncovered, in an oven. Roasting works best with tender meats that have internal or surface fat to keep them moist. Large items, such as turkey and beef roasts, are often placed on a rack in a roasting pan to allow the melted fat to drip away.

BROIL, ROAST, OR BRAISE?

To learn which cooking methods best suit each cut of meat, check out the photos on pages 376–377, 394–395, and 404.

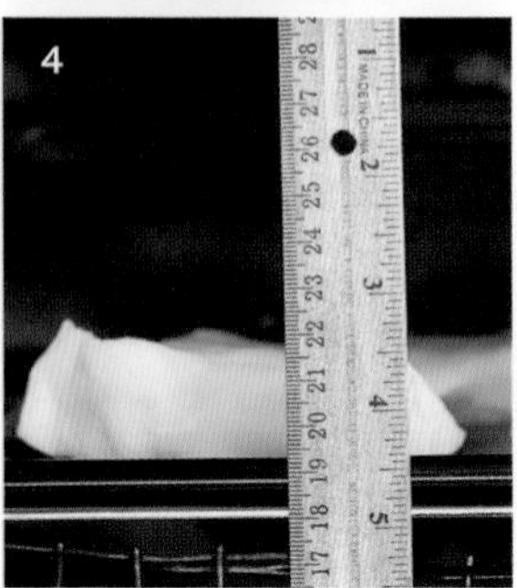

USING THE MICROWAVE

Use your microwave to help you get a few key ingredients recipe-ready in seconds.

SOFTENING BUTTER: To quickly soften butter, put it in a microwave-safe dish; microwave on 30% power for 15 seconds. Check and repeat if necessary. If you accidentally melt the butter, start over with another stick—do not use melted butter in place of softened butter.

MELTING BUTTER: Slice the butter into ½-inch-thick pieces and arrange evenly in a microwave-safe dish. Cover the dish with a plain white paper towel. Microwave at 70% power for 30 seconds, checking and stirring every 5 to 10 seconds. Do this until evenly melted; avoid burning the butter.

SOFTENING CREAM CHEESE: Microwave, uncovered, in a microwave-safe bowl on 100% power. Allow 10 to 20 seconds for 3 to 8 ounces. Let stand before using.

SOFTENING TORTILLAS: Before microwaving, place tortillas between plain white paper towels. Microwave on 100% power for 20 to 40 seconds.

MELTING CHOCOLATE OR CANDY COATING: In a small microwave-safe bowl microwave 1 cup semisweet or milk chocolate pieces or 1 ounce chopped unsweetened or semisweet chocolate, uncovered, on 70% power for 1 minute; stir. Microwave at the same power for 1 to 1½ minutes more, stirring every 15 seconds until chocolate is melted and smooth.

THERMOMETERS

For safety and delicious results when cooking, rely on an accurate thermometer.

1 DIAL OVEN-SAFE MEAT THERMOMETER: Use this thermometer for larger cuts of meat, such as roasts. Insert it into meat before roasting. This thermometer is left in the meat throughout the cooking time.

2 INSTANT-READ THERMOMETER: This dial or digital thermometer gives an internal reading within seconds. Don't leave this thermometer in the food while cooking, unless your model is designed for this.

3 CANDY THERMOMETER: Marked with candy-making stages, this thermometer can measure extra-high temperatures. Most have a clip that attaches to the pan. For more information, see page 177.

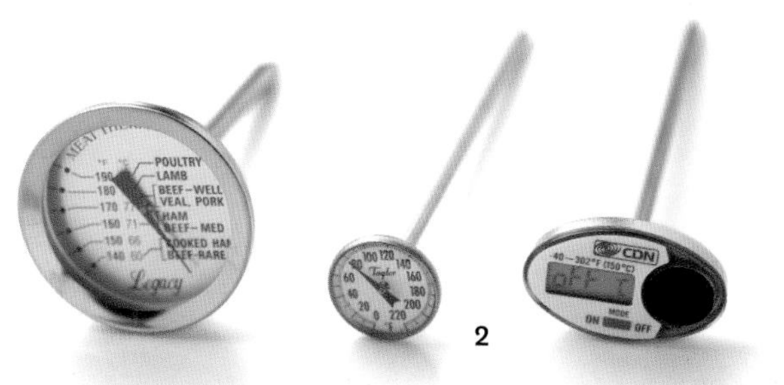

1 2 3

CUTTING 101

JULIENNE
Cut food into matchlike sticks by slicing the food into 2×¼-inch pieces. Stack and cut slices lengthwise into ⅛- to ¼-inch-wide strips.

Most of the recipes in this book call for food to be ***chopped****. This term refers to cutting up food into small, irregular pieces.*

CUBE
Use a chef's knife to cut foods into uniform pieces that are about ½ inch on all sides.

DICE
Use a chef's knife to cut foods into pieces that are ⅛ to ¼ inch on all sides.

WEDGE
Cut your food, flat side down, at an angle on a cutting board.

standard mixing methods

Doughs and batters are not all created equal. Although most recipes call for a mixture of the same basic ingredients—flour, sugar, fat, milk, and eggs—the manner in which you combine them (as well as the ratio used) creates a variety of textures. With baking, you'll likely use one of these mixing methods to get the job done.

BUTTER-STYLE CAKES METHOD (CREAMING)

Most butter-base cakes call for this method of beating the butter first, then slowly beating in sugar, and later eggs, one at a time, to work in as much air as possible. Flour and liquid are added alternately in batches to evenly incorporate each addition. First add some of the flour and limit the mixing after the first addition of liquid. Once liquid is combined with flour, gluten begins to develop and overmixing will cause toughness.

1. CREAMING
Start by beating softened butter to incorporate air. Beat sugar into mixture in small batches.

2. ADD EGGS
Beat in eggs, one at a time, to further incorporate air into the butter mixture.

3. ALTERNATELY ADD FLOUR
Start by beating about one-third or one-fourth of the flour mixture into the butter mixture until combined.

4. ALTERNATELY ADD LIQUID
After the first flour addition, add a portion of the liquid. Beat just until combined. Repeat alternating until all the flour and liquid are added.

QUICK BREAD METHOD

Most muffin and quick bread recipes use this simple method. Dry and wet ingredients are combined in two bowls. The wet ingredients are added to the dry ingredients all at once and stirred just until combined. The stirring is so brief—to avoid toughness—that the batter will be lumpy.

1. MIX DRY INGREDIENTS
Thoroughly whisk together all dry ingredients—such as flour, baking powder, salt, and/or spices—in a large bowl so they are well blended.

2. MIX WET INGREDIENTS
In a separate bowl stir to combine wet ingredients—such as eggs, milk, oil, butter, zucchini, pumpkin, and banana.

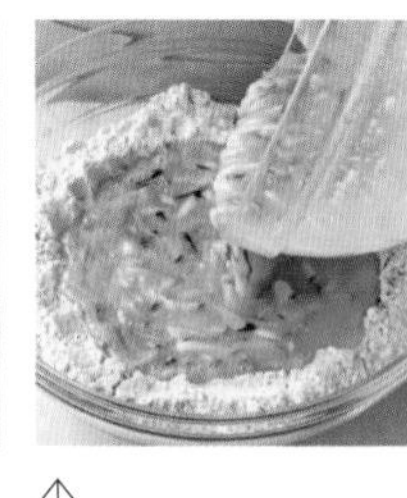

3. ADD WET TO DRY
Press dry ingredients against the sides of the bowl to create a well (indentation) in the center. Pour wet ingredients into the well.

4. MIX
Stir the wet and dry ingredients together just until the two are combined; some flour lumps will remain. Overmixing may cause toughness from excess gluten.

BISCUIT/PIECRUST METHOD

Biscuits and piecrust rely on pockets of fat in the dough mixture to create tender flakiness. These pockets are formed by cutting fat and flour together to create small pieces of flour-coated fat before the liquid is added.

1. CUT IN FAT
Use a pastry blender to cut cold fat into flour until it is the size of peas.

2. SCRAPE AS NEEDED
Use a butter knife to clean off the pastry blender as necessary.

3. WET INGREDIENTS
For biscuits, add the wet ingredients all at once to a well in the flour. For piecrust, add liquid gradually.

4. MIX TOGETHER
Stir the wet and dry ingredients just until all is moistened.

FOLDING METHOD

Folding calls for mixing light ingredients (such as beaten egg whites) with heavier mixtures without decreasing the volume of the egg whites. Starting at the back of the bowl, cut down vertically through the mixture with a spatula and sweep under the mixture and back up the nearest side of the bowl.

1. BEAT EGG WHITES
Start by beating egg whites until stiff peaks form.

2. LIGHTEN MIXTURE
Fold in some of the egg whites by cutting down vertically and sweeping back up the side.

3. ADD MIXTURE
Pour the lightened mixture into the remaining beaten egg whites.

4. FOLD
Continue cutting down with spatula and sweeping back up and over. Mixture will be light and airy.

STIR-TOGETHER METHOD

Instead of adding wet ingredients to dry all at once or beating the batter with an electric mixer, this simple method calls for stirring in ingredients, one at a time, with a wooden spoon.

1. COMBINE WET
Begin by combining fat and liquid.

2. ADD FLOUR
Other ingredients, such as flour or sugar, are stirred in all at once.

3. ADD EGGS
Ingredients, such as eggs, are stirred in one at a time.

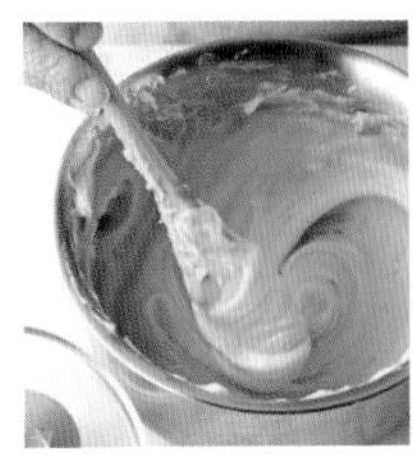

4. FINISH
The mixture should be thickened and smooth.

measuring

Knowing how to measure ingredients properly is key to recipe success.

When it comes to measuring, what you use is most important: Use liquid measuring cups for liquid ingredients and graduated measuring cups for dry ingredients. Find information on these and other measuring tools on page 8.

MEASURING DRY INGREDIENTS

Before measuring a dry ingredient, such as flour, stir it in its original container. Using a large spoon, fill the measuring cup without shaking or packing (see photo, top). With the back edge of a knife blade or with the flat edge of a spatula, level off the excess into a bowl you're not using for the recipe (see photo, center) or back into the container. Pack brown sugar into a dry measuring cup. Use your fingers to press it firmly into the cup (see photo, bottom).

MEASURING LIQUID INGREDIENTS

Pour the liquid into a liquid measuring cup set on a level surface. To confirm the measurement, bend down so your eye is level with the markings on the sides of the cup. When measuring 1 tablespoon or less, fill the appropriate-size measuring spoon to the rim without letting liquid spill over.

EXTRA KNOW-HOW

BUTTER, BLOCK-STYLE CREAM CHEESE, AND SHORTENING: These ingredients have measurement markings on the wrapper. Make sure the wrapper is on straight and cut the wrapper at the appropriate measure. If your cream cheese or shortening doesn't have a wrapper with markings, spoon it into a graduated measuring cup. Pack it firmly into the cup and level off the top.

STICKY LIQUIDS: For syrups, molasses, and other sticky liquids, spray the liquid measure with nonstick cooking spray before measuring so the liquid will slip right out.

WEIGHTS AND MEASURES

Tablespoon Math

3 teaspoons = 1 tablespoon
4 tablespoons = ¼ cup
5 tablespoons + 1 teaspoon = ⅓ cup
8 tablespoons = ½ cup
10 tablespoons + 2 teaspoons = ⅔ cup
12 tablespoons = ¾ cup
16 tablespoons = 1 cup

Measure	Equivalent Measure	Equivalent Ounces
1 tablespoon		½ fluid ounce
1 cup	½ pint	8 fluid ounces
2 cups	1 pint	16 fluid ounces
2 pints (4 cups)	1 quart	32 fluid ounces
4 quarts (16 cups)	1 gallon	128 fluid ounces

ingredients to know

Every cook needs to know these important things about these key ingredients.

THICKENERS

Flour and cornstarch are the most common thickeners. Here's how to use each to thicken 1 cup sauce (medium thickness): In a jar with a screw-top lid combine 2 tablespoons flour with ¼ cup cold water OR 1 tablespoon cornstarch with 1 tablespoon cold water. Shake the starch-water mixture in the jar until thoroughly combined. Stir the mixture into the sauce to be thickened; cook and stir over medium heat until thickened and bubbly. To be sure the starch is completely cooked, cook and stir a flour-thickened sauce 1 minute more and a cornstarch-thickened sauce 2 minutes more.

LEAVENERS: BAKING POWDER AND BAKING SODA

Baking powder and baking soda are often used together in baking recipes as leaveners. Baking powder is double-acting, releasing gas when it becomes wet and gas when exposed to heat. Baking soda is an alkali and is used when acid ingredients (such as buttermilk and molasses) are included in recipes. Baking soda and the acid react as soon as a liquid is added, so any recipe that uses only soda should be baked immediately. Baking soda and powder are not interchangeable; do not sub one for the other.

USE LEMON JUICE OR VINEGAR TO MAKE SOUR MILK

SOUR MILK

For baking recipes that call for buttermilk, you can use sour milk as a substitute. To make 1 cup sour milk, place 1 tablespoon lemon juice or vinegar in a glass measuring cup. Add enough milk to make 1 cup total liquid; stir. Let the mixture stand for 5 minutes before using it in a recipe.

VANILLA BEANS

Vanilla bean pods should not be eaten; rather, the tiny, dark seeds inside are used to bring intense vanilla flavor to a recipe. To remove seeds, cut the pod lengthwise with a paring knife and scrape out the tiny seeds. If you do not have a vanilla bean on hand, you can substitute vanilla extract: 1 vanilla bean = 1 tablespon vanilla extract.

CITRUS ZESTING, PEELING, AND SECTIONING

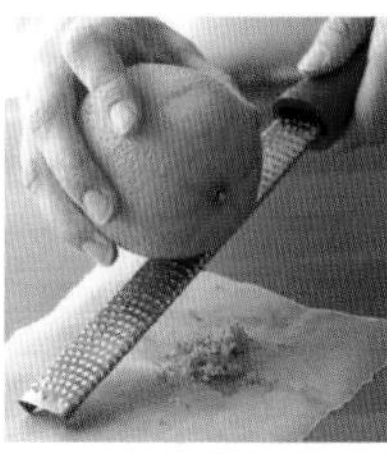

CITRUS ZEST
To remove zest, draw the fruit across a fruit zester or grater; avoid the bitter white membrane (the pith).

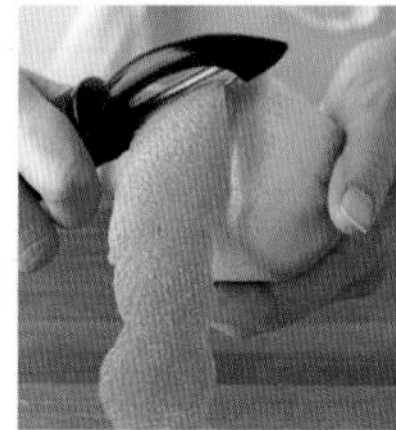

PEELING CITRUS
You can use a vegetable peeler, as shown, to cut the outer layer of skin from the fruit. If you don't have a peeler, use a paring knife.

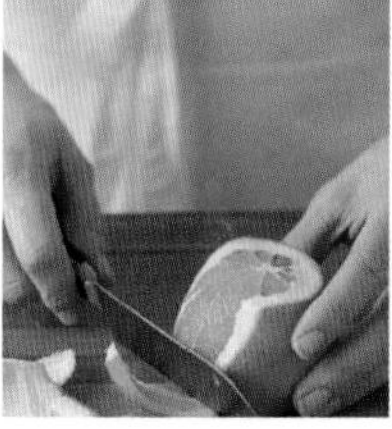

SECTIONING CITRUS
1. Cut off a slice from both ends of the fruit. Cut away the peel and the white part of the rind, working from top to bottom.

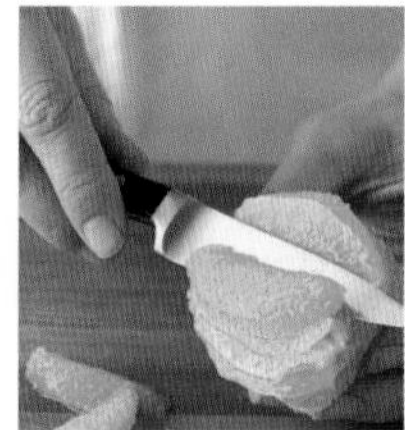

2. Tip the fruit to its side and cut into the center between one section and the membrane. Cut along the other side of section next to membrane to free the section.

Here is more ingredient know-how to ensure cooking success!

EGGS

Eggs play a key role in many recipes. Follow these tips to make the most of this ingredient.

Before adding eggs in a recipe, crack them into a separate bowl to ensure no eggshells get into your finished food. To crack an egg, tap it firmly on a flat countertop or on the rim of a bowl. If a shell piece gets in the raw egg, use a spoon to fish it out. When separating yolk and white, use an egg separator (see photo, above, and page 8).

PASTEURIZING EGG WHITES: For food safety, when preparing recipes that use raw egg whites, use purchased pasteurized egg whites. Or follow these steps to pasteurize:

- In a small saucepan stir together 2 egg whites, 2 tablespoons granulated sugar, 1 teaspoon water, and 1/8 teaspoon cream of tartar just until combined but not foamy. Heat and stir over low heat until mixture registers 160°F. You might see a few small bits of cooked white in the mixture.
- Remove from heat and place saucepan in a large bowl half-filled with ice water (see photo, above). Stir 2 minutes to cool mixture quickly.

EGG EQUIVALENTS

Recipes in this cookbook were developed and tested using large eggs. If you purchase eggs in other sizes, adjust the number you use to ensure success when preparing baked goods, soufflés, egg-thickened sauces, and recipes in which egg binds ingredients. For most other recipes, egg size isn't critical.

Large Eggs	Other Size Equivalents
1 large egg	1 jumbo, 1 extra-large, 1 medium, or 1 small egg
2 large eggs	2 jumbo, 2 extra-large, 2 medium, or 3 small eggs
3 large eggs	2 jumbo, 3 extra-large, 3 medium, or 4 small eggs
4 large eggs	3 jumbo, 4 extra-large, 5 medium, or 5 small eggs
5 large eggs	4 jumbo, 4 extra-large, 6 medium, or 7 small eggs
6 large eggs	5 jumbo, 5 extra-large, 7 medium, or 8 small eggs

EGG MATH

1 medium egg = 3 tablespoons
1 large egg = 3½ tablespoons
1 extra-large egg = 4 tablespoons

BEATING EGGS AND EGG WHITES STEP-BY-STEP

1. For a lightly beaten egg, use a fork to beat a whole egg. It's ready when it's pale yellow with no streaks of white or yolk.

2. For beaten egg yolks, beat on high speed about 5 minutes or until they are thick and have a lemon color.

3. For soft peaks, beat the egg whites with a mixer on medium speed until peaks form with tips that curl when the beaters are lifted.

4. For stiff peaks, beat on high speed until egg whites form peaks with tips that stand straight when the beaters are lifted. Take care not to overbeat egg whites—they can get lumpy and won't blend well with other ingredients.

FINELY CHOPPED

CHOPPED

COURSELY CHOPPED

WHOLE NUT

CRACKER CRUMBS

SOFT BREAD CRUMBS

FINE DRY BREAD CRUMBS

PANKO CRUMBS

NUTS

CHOPPING NUTS: Many types of nuts can be purchased chopped. If you buy nuts whole, you can chop them the size your recipe specifies.

- Coarsely chopped nuts are large irregular pieces that are more than ¼ inch in size.
- Chopped nuts are medium irregular pieces about ¼ inch in size.
- Finely chopped nuts are small irregular pieces that are about ⅛ inch in size.

GRINDING NUTS: Use a blender or food processor to grind nuts, adding 1 tablespoon of the sugar or flour called for in the recipe for each cup of nuts to help absorb some of the oil. Use a start-and-stop motion to prevent overprocessing the nuts.

TOASTING NUTS, SEEDS, AND COCONUT: To toast whole nuts or large pieces, spread them in a shallow pan. Bake in a 350°F oven for 5 to 10 minutes, shaking the pan once or twice. Toast coconut the same way, but watch closely to avoid burning it. Toast finely chopped or ground nuts or seeds in a dry skillet over medium heat. Stir often so nuts don't burn.

REMOVING SKINS

Hazelnuts come swathed in papery skin that is typically removed. To do this, toast whole nuts as above, then rub the warm nuts in a dry dish towel until skins come loose.

CUBES AND CRUMBS

CRACKER CRUMBS: For 1 cup of crumbs, you will need about 28 saltine crackers, 14 graham crackers, or 24 rich round crackers. To make the crumbs, place the crackers in a food processor fitted with the blade attachment. Process using on/off pulses until crumbs are desired consistency.

SOFT (FRESH) BREAD CRUMBS: Cut bread into cubes and process as you would cracker crumbs. Use 1 slice of fresh bread for every ¾ cup crumbs.

FINE DRY BREAD CRUMBS: First, make dry bread cubes (see below). Process the cubes as you would cracker crumbs. One slice of bread yields ¼ cup fine dry crumbs. Or purchase panko.

WHEN TO USE SOFT OR DRY CRUMBS: Dry bread crumbs and cracker crumbs are usually used for breading foods that are to be fried. Soft bread crumbs tend to be used for crispy toppings on casseroles and as filler in ground meat dishes, such as meat loaf and meatballs.

DRY BREAD CUBES: Often called for in stuffing and casserole recipes, dry bread cubes can be made from just about any type of bread. To make, stack a few slices and cut the bread into ½-inch-wide strips using a serrated knife. Cut strips crosswise into ½-inch cubes. Preheat the oven to 300°F. Arrange cubes in a single layer on a baking pan. Bake for 10 to 15 minutes or until golden, stirring once or twice; let cool.

CRUMBS ON CALL

if your bread has turned the corner from fresh to dry, freeze it. That way you'll have some bread to thaw and make into dry crumbs or cubes as needed.

pantry primer

Consider your pantry more of a strategy than a place in your kitchen. A well-stocked pantry will make your cooking life a lot easier.

A pantry is anywhere you would store food, from the cupboard to the refrigerator and the freezer. A well-stocked pantry helps eliminate time-wasting extra trips to the grocery store. Even if you do have to run to the store for fresh meat or produce, it minimizes time spent hunting for staples on every trip. These lists show basic ingredients that are often used in recipes in this book. They're also ingredients that keep relatively well if stored correctly (see storage information on the inside back cover). Tailor your pantry according to foods you and your family love and fill it with recipe ingredients you use again and again. You'll be surprised how much easier it is to motivate yourself to cook a meal—even on the busiest weeknight.

MUST-HAVES

1. BAKING POWDER
2. VANILLA
3. SALT
4. EGGS
5. ONIONS
6. GARLIC CLOVES
7. CANOLA OR OTHER NEUTRAL OIL
8. BUTTER
9. OLIVE OIL
10. ALL-PURPOSE FLOUR
11. GRANULATED SUGAR
12. BROWN SUGAR
13. CRACKED BLACK PEPPER

PERSONALIZE YOUR PANTRY

Make your pantry work for you. Here and on pages 24–25 are lists of suggested foods to help you maintain a hardworking pantry. Within each category, choose what works for you! Select the types of beans you use most, the frozen vegetables your family loves, the dried pastas you reach for over and over, and the spices that are your go-to favorites.

GOOD TO HAVE

1. PASTA
2. BEANS (GARBANZO, KIDNEY, WHITE, PINTO, AND/OR BLACK; CANNED OR DRIED)
3. DICED TOMATOES
4. MARINARA SAUCE
5. FINE DRY BREAD CRUMBS OR PANKO
6. CHUNKY SALSA
7. COUSCOUS
8. HONEY
9. WHOLE WHEAT FLOUR
10. CORNMEAL
11. COCONUT MILK
12. COCOA POWDER
13. CORNSTARCH
14. YEAST
15. BALSAMIC, RED WINE, OR CIDER VINEGAR
16. RAISINS (OR OTHER DRIED FRUIT, SUCH AS APRICOTS, CHERRIES, AND CRANBERRIES)
17. SHREDDED UNSWEETENED COCONUT
18. CHICKEN BROTH (REDUCED-SODIUM WHEN POSSIBLE)
19. TUNA
20. KETCHUP
21. TOMATO PASTE
22. RAMEN NOODLES OR EGG NOODLES
23. RICE
24. OATS
25. POTATOES

FRIDGE FAVORITES

1. TORTILLAS
2. LEMONS
3. LOW-FAT MILK
4. OLIVES
5. PREMADE PIZZA DOUGH
6. SWEET PEPPERS
7. SOY SAUCE
8. DIJON-STYLE MUSTARD
9. PLAIN LOW-FAT YOGURT
10. FETA CHEESE
11. PEANUT BUTTER
12. SALAD GREENS
13. CARROTS
14. CELERY
15. CREAM CHEESE
16. MUSHROOMS
17. BACON
18. GRATED PARMESAN CHEESE
19. SHREDDED ITALIAN CHEESE BLEND
20. SHREDDED MEXICAN-STYLE FOUR-CHEESE BLEND

SPICES & HERBS

1. CURRY POWDER
2. CRUSHED RED PEPPER
3. DRIED THYME
4. CAYENNE PEPPER
5. GROUND CUMIN

1 2 3 4 5

FREEZER FAVORITES

1. FROZEN BERRIES (BLUEBERRIES, STRAWBERRIES, AND/OR MIXED BERRIES)
2. FROZEN CORN
3. FROZEN SPINACH
4. FROZEN PEAS
5. FROZEN VEGETABLE BLENDS (OR OTHER FROZEN VEGETABLES, SUCH AS PEPPERS AND BROCCOLI)
6. SHRIMP
7. BONELESS, SKINLESS CHICKEN BREAST HALVES
8. WHOLE WHEAT SANDWICH BREAD
9. WALNUTS, ALMONDS, PEANUTS, AND/OR PECANS
10. GROUND BEEF
11. GROUND TURKEY
12. ITALIAN SAUSAGE
13. ROLLS, PITA BREAD, AND/OR BAGUETTE

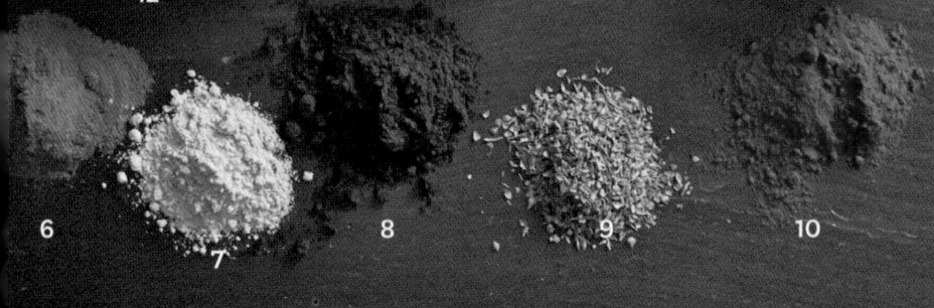

SPICES & HERBS

6. GROUND CINNAMON
7. GROUND GINGER
8. GROUND CLOVES
9. DRIED OREGANO
10. CHILI POWDER

spices

Spices—the seeds, bark, fruit, or flowers of a plant—add layers of flavor to your cooking. The more you cook, the more you'll love using them.

GARLIC

Although you can purchase minced garlic by the jar, you will get the best flavor if you use a fresh bulb.

- Pick firm and plump bulbs; the skin should be papery and dry.

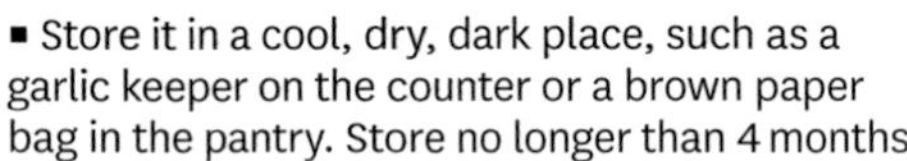

- Store it in a cool, dry, dark place, such as a garlic keeper on the counter or a brown paper bag in the pantry. Store no longer than 4 months.
- Leave bulbs whole so that individual cloves won't dry too quickly.
- For minced garlic, remove the cloves from the head. Peel away the papery skin and finely mince with a sharp knife or use a garlic press.

GARLIC MATH

1 bulb of garlic = between 10 and 20 cloves
1 clove of garlic = ½ teaspoon minced or ⅛ teaspoon garlic powder

PEPPER

PEPPERCORNS: Because pepper can lose flavor after it is ground, many cooks prefer to purchase whole peppercorns and grind them as needed. To do this, you need a pepper mill; most come with settings that allow coarse to finely ground pepper.

CRACKED BLACK PEPPER: Cracked whole peppercorns add texture and bite to rubs and classic dishes such as steak au poivre.

GROUND BLACK PEPPER: Black pepper may be purchased in coarse-ground and regular ground varieties. A smaller grind is called for when the peppery notes are meant to blend more seamlessly with the other flavors.

HERB AND SPICE SWAPS

If you find yourself lacking a particular herb or spice called for in a recipe, there's usually another choice that can be successfully substituted. Here are some easy swaps to use in popular styles of ethnic cooking.

Don't have	Swap with
MEXICAN	
Chili powder	Combine oregano, cumin, and either red pepper flakes or hot sauce.
Cilantro	Though it won't replace the flavor, Italian parsley or basil will add freshness to your dish.
Cumin	Coriander
ITALIAN	
Basil	Oregano
Fennel	Anise seeds
Garlic	Garlic powder
Oregano	Marjoram or thyme
GREEK	
Bay leaf	Thyme
Marjoram	Oregano or sage
Rosemary	Savory or thyme
Dill	Tarragon
INDIAN	
Cardamom	Equal parts cloves and cinnamon
Cinnamon	Mace, allspice, or a smaller amount of nutmeg
Curry powder	Use a blend of turmeric, ginger, black pepper, coriander, cumin, and chili powder.

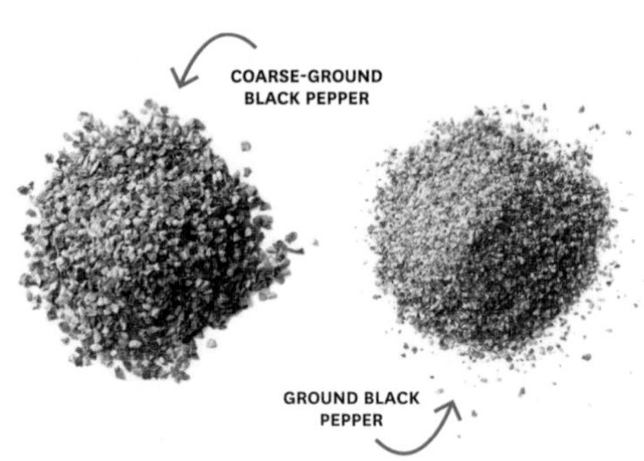

SPICES

Here are popular spices and top forms to use them in. Note that some cooks prefer buying spices in their whole form and crushing or grinding them for the most intense flavor.

1. **CINNAMON STICKS:** Use to infuse hot drinks with cinnamon flavor.
2. **GROUND CINNAMON:** meats, breads, desserts
3. **CARDAMOM PODS**
4. **GROUND CARDAMOM:** curried dishes, baked goods
5. **CAYENNE PEPPER:** stews, barbecue rubs and sauces, egg and cheese dishes
6. **CHILI POWDER**
7. **GROUND CHIPOTLE CHILE POWDER:** stews, marinades, meats
8. **GROUND CLOVES**
9. **WHOLE CLOVES:** meats, desserts, spiced beverages
10. **CUMIN SEEDS**
11. **GROUND CUMIN:** meats, poultry, soups, stews
12. **CURRY POWDER:** meats, sauces, stews
13. **FENNEL SEEDS:** meat, sausage, poultry, breads, sauces
14. **WHOLE NUTMEG**
15. **GROUND NUTMEG:** baked goods, white sauces, custard
16. **GROUND MUSTARD:** salad dressings, egg and cheese dishes
17. **MUSTARD SEEDS:** pickling, relishes
18. **GROUND GINGER:** marinades, baked goods
19. **CRYSTALLIZED GINGER:** Add as a finishing touch to desserts.
20. **PAPRIKA:** meat, fish, chicken, egg dishes
21. **FRESH GINGER:** stir-fries, soups, sauces, beverages

herbs

It's amazing how a simple dose of something green can add so much fresh flavor to your cooking.

USING DRIED HERBS FOR FRESH

Some recipes specify using fresh herbs. However, sometimes fresh herbs aren't available, or it just isn't practical to buy a bunch when only a teaspoon is needed. In such cases, dried herbs can usually be substituted. To do so, use one-third the amount of dried herb for the fresh herb called for in the recipe. (For example, substitute 1 teaspoon of a dried herb for 1 tablespoon of a fresh herb.) When substituting a ground herb for dried leaf herb, use about half of the amount of the dried leaf herb called for in the recipe.

Store whole, dried herbs and spices for 1 to 2 years. Store ground spices and herbs for up to 6 months.

USING DRIED HERBS

Before using a dried herb in any recipe, crush with a mortar and pestle to release the aromatic oils and bring out the flavor. If you don't have this utensil, place the dried herb in the palm of your hand and press and rub it with your thumb or rub the herbs between your thumb and two fingers.

FRESH HERB POINTERS

1. STRIPPING
To remove leaves from the herb's stem, hold onto the stem with one hand and strip the leaves into a bowl, using the thumb and forefinger of the other hand.

2. SNIPPING
To cut large leaves, place them in a measuring cup or bowl and snip them with kitchen shears. Use quick, short strokes. For herbs with tough stems, such as rosemary, strip leaves from the stem first.

3. CHIFFONADE
The term literally means "made of rags," but in herb-speak, it refers to herbs cut into strips or shreds. To do this, roll up larger leaves and cut across the roll.

4. STORING
To store fresh herbs, cut ½ inch from the bottom of stems; stand them in a jar with water. Loosely cover leaves with a plastic bag. Store the herbs in the refrigerator (except basil, which should be stored at room temperature).

BOUQUET GARNI

A bouquet garni (boo-KAY gar-NEE) is a French term for a group of fresh and/or dried herbs tied together or bundled in cheesecloth to flavor a recipe and then remove for a pristine appearance. To make one, use several layers of 100%-cotton cheesecloth. Tie the cheesecloth closed with kitchen string to form a bag.

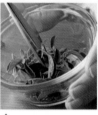

FRESH HERBS

Here are some of the most commonly used culinary herbs, along with foods they complement particularly well.

1. **SAGE:** poultry, sausage, pork, stuffing, vegetables
2. **TARRAGON:** poultry, fish, grilled meats, vinaigrettes
3. **THYME:** chicken, beef, vegetables, sauces
4. **ROSEMARY:** lamb, pork, fish, breads
5. **ITALIAN (FLAT-LEAF) PARSLEY:** almost any dish
6. **BASIL:** sauces, salads, tomato dishes, pesto
7. **MARJORAM:** lamb, veal, vegetables
8. **MINT:** salads, marinades, dressings; also an edible garnish for desserts
9. **DILL:** fish, seafood, vegetables, pickles
10. **CHIVES:** eggs, salad dressings, potatoes, seafood
11. **CURLY-LEAF PARSLEY:** interchangeable with Italian parsley
12. **OREGANO:** pizza, pasta, bean soups, sauces, pasta salads
13. **CILANTRO:** Asian, Indian, Mexican cuisines

food safety

The pleasure of cooking for friends and family comes with the responsibility of making sure everything you serve is safe to eat.

TEMPERATURE TIPS

You cannot see, taste, or smell most bacteria that cause food borne illnesses, so it's wise to prevent the bacteria from growing in the first place. A key step in doing this is to keep hot foods hot and cold foods cold. Store cold foods at 40°F or below and serve hot foods immediately or keep them at 140°F or above. It's between these temperatures that illness-causing bacteria thrive and multiply.

DON'T CROSS-CONTAMINATE

Cross-contamination occurs when ready-to-eat foods pick up bacteria from other foods, unclean hands, cutting boards, knives, and other utensils. To avoid cross-contamination, keep raw meat, poultry, eggs, fish, shellfish, and the juices away from other foods. Follow these guidelines.

- Keep raw meat, poultry, fish, and shellfish separate from other foods in your grocery cart and shopping bags.
- Once home, store raw meat, poultry, fish, and shellfish in sealed containers or plastic bags so the juices don't drip onto other foods. Place whole roasts and poultry on a tray or pan that's large enough to catch any juices that might leak.
- If possible, purchase two cutting boards. Use one only for raw meats, poultry, fish, and shellfish. Use the other for ready-to-eat foods, such as breads and vegetables.
- Don't wash raw beef, pork, lamb, poultry, and veal before cooking. Rinsing these foods poses a risk of cross-contamination with other foods and utensils in the kitchen. Bacteria that might be present are destroyed with proper cooking.
- Place cooked foods on a clean plate. Never reuse the unwashed dish that held the raw meat, poultry, fish, or shellfish.
- Keep your hands and all surfaces and utensils that come into contact with food clean.

SAFE FOOD TEMPERATURES

Always use a food thermometer to ensure that food has reached a high enough temperature to destroy harmful bacteria. Here are USDA recommended minimum internal temperatures for meats and other foods.

Food	Final Doneness Temperature
Beef, lamb, and veal steaks, chops, and roasts	145°F
Hamburger, meat loaf, ground pork, veal, and lamb	160°F
Pork chops, ribs, and roasts	145°F
Egg dishes	160°F
Leftovers	165°F
Stuffing and casseroles	165°F
Chicken and turkey	
breast	165°F
ground	165°F
whole bird, legs, thighs, and wings	165°F
Duck and goose	180°F

THE TWO-HOUR TIME LIMIT

To make sure leftovers stay bacteria-free, refrigerate them immediately after the meal is finished. Discard any food that has been left out for more than 2 hours (1 hour if the temperature is higher than 80°F).

QUESTIONS? ASK THE REGULATORS

For the latest information on ever-changing food safety regulations and precautions call or go to

- The USDA Meat and Poultry Hotline at 888-674-6854
- The U.S. FDA Center for Food Safety and Applied Nutrition Outreach Center at 888-723-3366
- foodsafety.gov.

freezing foods

Good foods successfully stored in the freezer are culinary gifts to open and enjoy when you need them most.

COLD ENOUGH

Check the temperature of your freezer to ensure it maintains the proper temperature for food storage. Freezers should maintain a temp of 0°F.

COOL IT, STORE IT, FREEZE IT

To keep bacteria from growing, foods that are to be frozen must be cooled quickly first. To freeze soups and stews, see page 567. To freeze other foods, divide them into small portions in shallow containers. Arrange containers in a single layer in freezer to allow cold air to circulate around packages until frozen. Stack after completely frozen. These vessels are best for freezer-bound foods:

FREEZER-SAFE CONTAINERS: Look for a phrase or an icon on the label or container bottom indicating they are designed for freezer use.

BAKING DISHES: Use freezer-to-oven or freezer-to-microwave dishes and cover them with plastic freezer wrap or heavy-duty foil.*

GLASS JARS WITH TIGHT-FITTING LIDS: All major brands of canning jars are acceptable for use in the refrigerator and freezer. Leave headspace in the jar for the food to expand if you plan to freeze liquids or semiliquids.

SELF-SEALING STORAGE BAGS AND PLASTIC WRAP: Buy products made for freezer use.

HEAVY-DUTY FOIL: Regular foil won't make the cut when it comes to storing foods in the freezer.*

***NOTE:** Foods that contain acidic ingredients, such as tomatoes, should not be wrapped and stored in foil. To freeze dishes with acidic ingredients, wrap the food in plastic wrap first; cover with foil. Remove plastic before heating.

LABEL IT

Take a moment to label foods before storing them. Use a wax crayon or waterproof marking pen to note the name of the food item or recipe, the quantity, the date it was frozen, and any special information about its use.

THAW SAFELY

Thawing foods properly is another piece of the food-safety puzzle. These are key concepts:

- Thaw foods in the refrigerator, not at room temperature (a few exceptions include breads and sweets that specifically call for thawing at room temperature). Make sure that thawing foods don't drip onto other foods.
- Some foods can be successfully thawed in a microwave. Follow the manufacturer's instructions and cook the food immediately after thawing.
- You can also thaw food by placing it in a leakproof plastic bag and immersing it in cold tap water in the sink, changing the water every half hour to keep it cold. When changing the water, flip the bag if it's not fully submerged. Cook food immediately after thawing.

REHEAT THOROUGHLY

Reheat food to a safe internal temperature before serving.

- Bring sauces, soups, and gravies to a rolling boil in a covered saucepan; stir occasionally.
- Heat leftovers to 165°F.
- See "Thaw Safely," above, for helpful thawing tips.

FOODS NOT TO FREEZE

These foods lose flavor, texture, and overall quality when frozen, so it is not recommended.

- Battered and fried foods
- Cooked egg whites and yolks, as well as icings made with egg whites
- Cottage and ricotta cheeses
- Custard and cream pies and desserts with cream fillings
- Soups and stews made with potatoes, which can darken and become mushy
- Stews thickened with cornstarch or flour
- Sour cream, mayonnaise, and salad dressings
- Stuffed chops and chicken breasts
- Whole eggs in the shell, raw or cooked

eating healthy

Eating well means eating foods you enjoy as well as foods that are good for you. Follow these guidelines to make sure you are getting the most benefit from what you eat.

YOUR PLATE

The USDA's MyPlate nutrition tool (choosemyplate.gov) uses a plate divided into quadrants as a guide when putting together healthful meals (see photo, below). Half the plate is made up of fruits and vegetables; the other half is divided between grains and protein. A glass or bowl can be added to the meal to include dairy foods such as milk or yogurt. As you plan your own meals, use this info as a guide.

FOOD GROUP BREAKDOWN

The recommended number of servings for adults and the amount of food that counts as a serving are listed for each food group.

FRUITS

Amount You Need Each Day
1½ to 2 cups or equivalent
What is a cup or equivalent of fruit?
1 cup fresh fruit
1 large banana
32 grapes
8 large strawberries
1 large orange or peach
1 cup fruit juice
½ cup dried fruit

VEGETABLES

Amount You Need Each Day
2½ to 3 cups or equivalent
What is a cup or equivalent of vegetables?
1 cup raw or cooked vegetables
2 cups raw spinach
1 large sweet potato
1 medium regular potato
1 large ear sweet corn
12 baby carrots

GRAINS

Number of Servings You Need Each Day
5 to 8 (with half being whole grain choices)
What is a serving of grains?
1 slice bread
1 to 1¼ cups ready-to-eat cereal
½ cup cooked rice, pasta, or cereal
1 6-inch tortilla

PROTEIN

Number of Servings You Need Each Day
5 to 6 ounces or equivalent
What is a serving of protein?
1 ounce cooked meat, poultry, or fish
1 egg
½ ounce nuts or seeds
1 tablespoon peanut butter
¼ cup cooked dried beans or shelled edamame
¼ cup tofu
1 ounce tempeh
2 tablespoons hummus

DAIRY

Amount You Need Each Day
3 cups or equivalent
What is a cup or equivalent of dairy?
1 cup milk
1 cup fresh or frozen yogurt

1 cup calcium-fortified soymilk
1½ ounces unprocessed cheese
2 cups cottage cheese
1 cup pudding made with milk

FATS AND OILS

Although fats and oils are not a food group, they provide essential nutrients. Generally, adults can allow 5 to 6 teaspoons fats and oils per day in a healthy diet. Many people are able to consume enough fat in the foods they eat, but if you aren't, adding foods with healthy fats can benefit your health.

What counts as a teaspoon or equivalent of fat?

1 teaspoon vegetable oil (such as canola, olive, or peanut)
8 large olives
⅙ of an avocado
1½ teaspoons peanut butter or almond butter
⅓ ounce peanuts, almonds, or mixed nuts
1 tablespoon regular Italian dressing

NUTRITION INFORMATION GUIDE

To help you watch your nutrient intake, each recipe in this book includes a nutrition analysis for a single serving. Here's an example.

PER 3 SHRIMP: 473 cal., 15 g total fat (3 g sat. fat), 65 mg chol., 1,533 mg sodium, 60 g carb., 5 g fiber, 18 g pro.
EXCHANGES: 1½ Vegetable, 3½ Starch, 1 Lean Meat, 2 Fat

Read what each of the labels refers to and use the guidelines to help you make smart food choices at every meal.

CAL. Total calories per serving. The estimated calorie requirements per day are based on age and gender. For example, the requirement for moderately active women between the ages of 31 and 50 is 2,000 calories; for moderately active men in that age group, the number is 2,400 to 2,600.

TOTAL FAT The amount of all types of fat per serving, which includes saturated, polyunsaturated, monounsaturated, and trans fats. For a healthy diet, strive to keep total fat between 20 percent to 35 percent of daily calorie intake.

SAT. FAT Saturated fat per serving. Limit saturated fat to 10 percent of daily calories.

CHOL. Cholesterol per serving. Limit this to 300 milligrams per day.

SODIUM Sodium per serving. Based on the Dietary Guidelines for Americans, keep sodium less than 2,300 milligrams per day.

CARB. Carbohydrate per serving. Strive to consume carbohydrate from unrefined sources such as whole grains. If you consume foods and beverages high in added sugars, you tend to consume more calories, which may lead to weight gain.

FIBER Total fiber per serving. This includes soluble and insoluble fiber. Strive to get 25 to 30 grams of fiber per day.

PRO. Protein per serving. Look for lean meats and poultry. And vary your protein sources with fish, beans, peas, nuts, and seeds.

HOW WE TEST AND CALCULATE NUTRITION ANALYSES

To determine nutritional values in each recipe, the Better Homes and Gardens® Test Kitchen uses nutrition analysis software. When looking at the analyses, keep these factors in mind:

- When milk is a recipe ingredient, the analysis is calculated using 2 percent (reduced-fat) milk.
- When an egg is a recipe ingredient, large eggs are used in testing and in the analysis.
- When vegetable oil is listed in the ingredient list of a recipe, any neutral oil may be used in testing: corn, safflower, or canola. Recipes that require olive oil will specifically call for it.
- When onions are an ingredient, yellow onions are used in testing and in the analysis.
- When an ingredient is listed as optional, such as a garnish, it is not included in the analysis.
- When ingredient choices appear, the first choice is used to calculate the analysis.
- When there is a range in the number of servings (4 to 6 servings), the first (smaller) number is used.
- For marinade, it is assumed most of the marinade is discarded.
- Most of the time margarine is an acceptable substitution for butter in cooking. Use butter only for all baking recipes and for recipes specifying butter.
- Diabetic exchanges, listed with the analysis for each recipe, are based on the exchange list from the Academy of Nutrition and Dietetics and the American Diabetes Association.

LOOK FOR THESE ICONS

If you are searching for a specific type of recipe, use these icons to find what you are looking for.

BEST-LOVED Favorite takes on the classics

FAST Preparation takes 30 minutes or less

LOW-CALORIE Main dishes fewer than 400 calories, side dishes fewer than 250 calories, snacks fewer than 150 calories, and desserts fewer than 200 calories

table setting 101

Placing flatware properly on the table shows guests you care about presentation and their ease and enjoyment.

1 CASUAL MEALS: This simple setting is perfect for everyday lunches and dinners. Having soup? Simply place the bowl on the plate. This setting can also be used for casual entertaining for close friends and family.

2 INFORMAL DINNERS AND LUNCHEONS: This setting adds a wineglass and a bread and/or salad plate. Use it for a special brunch, ladies' luncheon, and a celebratory dinner at home.

3 FORMAL MEALS: This setting is for holiday meals and formal entertaining. Before serving dessert, clear all unnecessary plates, utensils, and glasses.

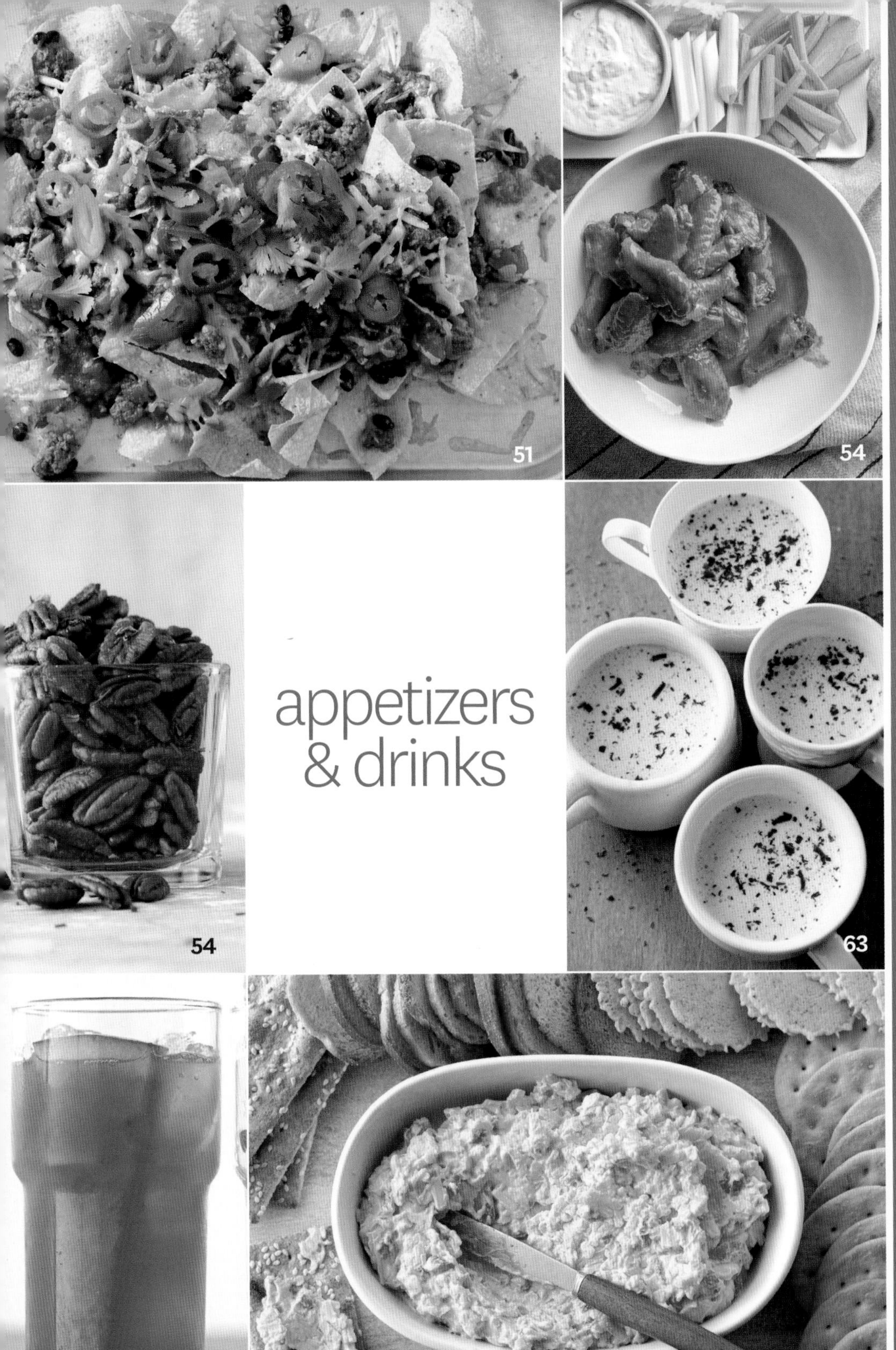

appetizers & drinks

appetizers & drinks

Casual appetizer parties are among the easiest and most enjoyable gatherings. Here's how to pull one off.

MENU PLANNER

- Choose a combination of crowd-pleasing recipes you feel confident serving plus a new one or two to create a little buzz come party time.
- Anchor your appetizer buffet with one or two hearty bites, such as cocktail meatballs, fondue, and/or chicken drumettes.
- Don't knock yourself out—complement the recipes you choose to cook with foods that require little or no prep, such as a cheese tray or a platter of cured meats.
- Relax. Keep in mind that many party foods taste better when served closer to room temperature than piping hot or ice cold. That means you don't have to rush foods from oven or fridge to the table. However, perishable foods should not stand at room temperature longer than 2 hours.

DRINK PLANNER

- Rather than offering a full bar, consider serving one stylish cocktail or punch plus beer, wine, and plenty of nonalcoholic beverages. That way, you won't need to mix drinks all night.
- Plan on serving one 750-milliliter bottle of wine for every two guests. Chill more white wines than you think you'll need. Generally, inexpensive and moderately priced wines that have been chilled can be returned to room-temperature storage without damage.
- Allow 12 ounces of beer per guest for every half hour to an hour of party time.
- Purchase about 1 pound of ice per guest. Store it in coolers during the party.

A SATISFYING SOIREE

This chart gives you an idea of how much food to make or purchase. In general, plan on about 12 appetizer servings per person for cocktail parties. Purchase more food than you think you'll need—keep no-prep items such as cured meats and cheeses in the fridge to bring out if necessary.

Food	Per Guest	For 12	For 24	For 48
Chicken wings	2	2 pounds	4 pounds	8 pounds
Cocktail meatballs	2	1 pound	2 pounds	4 pounds
Crackers	4	8 ounces	1 pound	2 pounds
Dips/Spreads	2 tablespoons	1½ cups	3 cups	6 cups
Fondue/Chili con Queso	¼ cup	3 cups	6 cups	12 cups
Nuts	1 ounce	12 ounces	1½ pounds	3 pounds
Shrimp (large)	4	1 pound	2 pounds	4 pounds
Stuffed mushrooms	2	1 pound	2 pounds	4 pounds
Veggie dippers	2 pieces	24 pieces	48 pieces	96 pieces

DISH IT OUT—AGAIN AND AGAIN

Be sure to have almost twice as many glasses and appetizer plates on hand as there are guests.

Crab Dip, page 43

root vegetable chips

The Secret: For the best baked veggie chips, a two-step baking process—much like the double-frying method for french fries—brings out the earthy flavor of root vegetables and gives them a crispy crunch.

ROOT VEGETABLE CHIPS POINTERS

1. THIN, THIN, THIN
Use a mandoline to slice the veggies to 1/16 inch thick. Small, thin pieces have a lot of surface area and will be quick to lose any remaining moisture in the oven. Low moisture means crispy chips.

↓

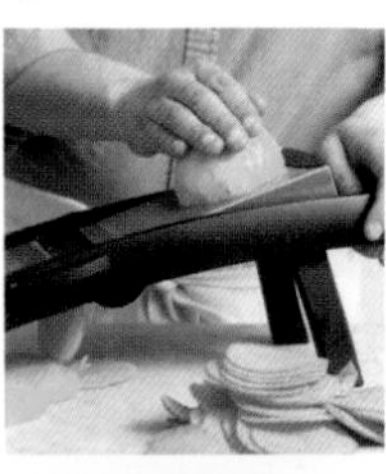

↑

2. DRY, DRY, DRY
Sandwich slices of beets between paper towels; press to remove as much liquid as possible. You want the interiors of the sliced veggies as they bake to be dry by the time the crust forms on the exteriors.

LOW-CALORIE

Baked Root Vegetable Chips

PREP: 15 MINUTES **BAKE:** 14 MINUTES AT 375°F **STAND:** 5 MINUTES **COOL:** 5 MINUTES **MAKES:** 4 SERVINGS

- **Nonstick cooking spray**
- **2 sweet potatoes, purple beets, or golden beets, peeled**
- **1/4 teaspoon salt**
- **1/4 teaspoon black pepper**

1 Preheat oven to 375°F. Lightly coat two large baking sheets with cooking spray; set aside.

2 Use a mandoline to slice vegetables 1/16 inch thick. If using beets, place slices between sheets of paper towels; press firmly to remove excess liquid. Arrange vegetable slices in a single layer on the prepared baking sheets. Coat vegetable slices with cooking spray; sprinkle with salt and pepper.

3 Bake for 10 minutes. Remove baking sheets from oven; let stand for 5 minutes. Return baking sheets to oven. Bake for 4 to 8 minutes more,* or until the center of each chip no longer looks wet. Transfer chips to paper towels. Let cool for 5 minutes to crisp the chips. Store cooled chips in an airtight container at room temperature for up to 24 hours. If necessary, recrisp the chips by baking them in a 325°F oven for 3 to 4 minutes.

***NOTE:** Remove pan and check chips for doneness every minute after 4 minutes to avoid burning.

PER SERVING: 57 cal., 0 g total fat, 0 mg chol., 181 mg sodium, 13 g carb., 2 g fiber, 1 g pro. **EXCHANGES:** 1 Starch

ROOT, ROOT, ROOT!

Because root vegetables are relatively low in moisture compared to other veggies, they are perfect for baked chips. Use sweet potatoes or beets—red and gold varieties both work well.

kale chips

The Secret: A little oil massage is all it takes to transform kale from bitter and tough to soft and sweet. Finish off the chips with a short stay in the oven and they will practically dissolve in your mouth.

LOW-CALORIE

Peppered Kale Chips

PREP: 10 MINUTES **BAKE:** 22 MINUTES AT 300°F **MAKES:** 2 CUPS

- 12 **ounces fresh kale (1 bunch)**
- 1 **tablespoon olive oil**
- ¼ **teaspoon salt**
- ¼ **teaspoon coarsely ground black pepper**
- ⅛ **teaspoon cayenne pepper (optional)**

1 Preheat oven to 300°F. Line two large baking sheets with parchment paper; set aside.

2 Remove and discard thick stems from kale. Tear leaves into bite-size pieces. Rinse and dry kale pieces in a salad spinner or pat them dry with paper towels.

3 In a large bowl combine kale, oil, salt, black pepper, and, if desired, cayenne pepper. Use your hands to massage the oil and seasonings into the kale until thoroughly coated.

4 Arrange kale pieces in a single layer on the prepared baking sheets. Bake for 20 minutes. Stir gently. Bake for 2 to 4 minutes more or until dry and crisp (check chips frequently to make sure they do not burn). Store cooled chips in an airtight container at room temperature for up to 24 hours. If necessary, recrisp the chips by baking them in a 325°F oven for 3 to 4 minutes.

PER ½ CUP: 72 cal., 4 g total fat (1 g sat. fat), 0 mg chol., 178 mg sodium, 8 g carb., 2 g fiber, 4 g pro.
EXCHANGES: 1½ Vegetable, ½ Fat

KALE'S THE QUEEN

Kale, the queen of leafy greens, is a member of the cabbage family. Look for curly-leaf (shown here) and Tuscan or dinosaur varieties in your grocery store.

KALE CHIPS STEP-BY-STEP

1. BITE-SIZE
Think about potato chips and tear your leaves into similar-size pieces. Holding each leaf at the base of the stem, tear leafy portions away from the thick stem.

↓

↑

2. DRY, DRY, DRY
Use a salad spinner to completely dry leaves. If you don't have a spinner, dry the leaves between paper towels. If the kale is wet, the oil won't adhere and the chips won't crisp.

↑

3. AH, MASSAGE
Use your hands to massage the oil and spices onto the leaves. This helps break down the cellulose structure of the kale and brings out its flavor. The leaves will darken and wilt slightly.

LOW-CALORIE

Marinated Olives

PREP: 10 MINUTES **CHILL:** 2 DAYS **STAND:** 1 HOUR
MAKES: 8 TO 10 SERVINGS

- **2 cups black and/or green olives, pitted, rinsed, and drained**
- **½ cup extra virgin olive oil**
- **2 3×½-inch strips of lemon peel**
- **½ cup lemon juice**
- **4 to 6 cloves garlic, sliced**
- **2 teaspoons snipped fresh oregano or 1 teaspoon dried oregano, crushed**
- **1 bay leaf**
- **½ teaspoon crushed red pepper**

1 In a 1-quart jar with a screw-top lid combine olives, olive oil, lemon peel, lemon juice, garlic, oregano, bay leaf, and red pepper. Cover and shake to coat olives with marinade. Refrigerate for 2 days, shaking jar occasionally.

2 Before serving, let stand at room temperature for 1 to 2 hours. Remove olives from marinade. Store in the refrigerator for up to 2 weeks.

PER ¼ CUP: 70 cal., 7 g total fat (1 g sat. fat), 0 mg chol., 293 mg sodium, 3 g carb., 1 g fiber, 0 g pro. EXCHANGES: 1½ Fat

THE ART OF ANTIPASTO

If you're short on time, head to your favorite gourmet market or Italian grocery store. Creating a beautiful antipasto platter is more about savvy selecting and artful arranging than complicated, all-day cooking.

CURED MEATS: At the meat counter, select very thinly sliced cured meats, such as prosciutto, capocollo, and salami.
GIARDINIERA: Take these brined Italian veggies from the jar into a strainer to a pretty bowl.
OLIVES: Serve the Marinated Olives (above) or select a few varieties and mix them.
ROASTED RED AND YELLOW PEPPERS AND/OR MARINATED ARTICHOKE HEARTS: Buy in jars, drain, and place in a bowl with a baby arugula garnish.
CAPRESE: Arrange slices of fresh mozzarella and roma tomatoes in a dish. Top with fresh basil leaves. If desired, serve a quality olive oil and/or balsamic vinegar on the side.
CHEESE: Select one big-flavored blue cheese or a selection of sliced or cubed cheeses. See page 49 for more about cheese.
BREAD: Whether ciabatta, a baguette, or a country-style loaf, buy plenty of bread to accompany all the goodies you have laid out.

LOW-CALORIE

Bruschetta

PREP: 30 MINUTES **BROIL:** 2 MINUTES PER BATCH
MAKES: 36 APPETIZERS

- **3 tablespoons olive oil**
- **1 tablespoon snipped fresh chives**
- **1 tablespoon snipped fresh basil**
- **1 tablespoon lemon juice**
- **1 clove garlic, minced**
- **2 cups chopped, seeded roma, yellow, and/or cherry tomatoes**
- **½ cup finely chopped red onion**
- **Salt**
- **Freshly ground black pepper**
- **1 8-ounce loaf baguette-style French bread**
- **Snipped fresh basil (optional)**

1 Preheat broiler. In a medium bowl stir together 1 tablespoon of the olive oil, the chives, 1 tablespoon basil, lemon juice, and garlic. Stir in tomatoes and onion. Season to taste with salt and pepper; set aside.

2 Cut the bread into 36 slices; arrange on two large baking sheets. Lightly brush one side of each slice with some of the remaining 2 tablespoons olive oil. Broil bread, one sheet at a time, 3 to 4 inches from the heat for 2 to 3 minutes or until toasted, turning once.*

3 To serve, with a slotted spoon, spoon tomato mixture onto the oiled side of each toast slice. If desired, garnish with additional fresh basil. Serve within 30 minutes.

***NOTE:** Bread slices may be toasted up to 1 day ahead. Store in an airtight container at room temperature.

SEAFOOD BRUSCHETTA: Prepare as directed, except decrease tomatoes to 1 cup. Add 6 ounces lump crabmeat or 6 ounces peeled, deveined cooked shrimp, coarsely chopped; and 1 tablespoon snipped fresh dill weed to the tomato mixture.

WHITE BEAN BRUSCHETTA: Prepare as directed, except substitute snipped fresh thyme for the chives and snipped fresh oregano for the basil. Decrease tomatoes to 1 cup. Add one 15-ounce can cannellini beans (white kidney beans), rinsed and drained, to the tomato mixture. Drizzle assembled toasts with an additional 2 tablespoons olive oil. Garnish with additional snipped fresh thyme or oregano.

PER APPETIZER PLAIN, SEAFOOD, OR WHITE BEAN VARIATIONS: 31 cal., 1 g total fat (0 g sat. fat), 0 mg chol., 50 mg sodium, 4 g carb., 0 g fiber, 1 g pro. EXCHANGES: ½ Starch

BRUSCHETTA

8 to try

CONFETTI: Substitute ranch dressing for the mayonnaise and stir ¼ cup finely chopped red and/or green sweet peppers into yolk mixture. Garnish with additional chopped sweet peppers.

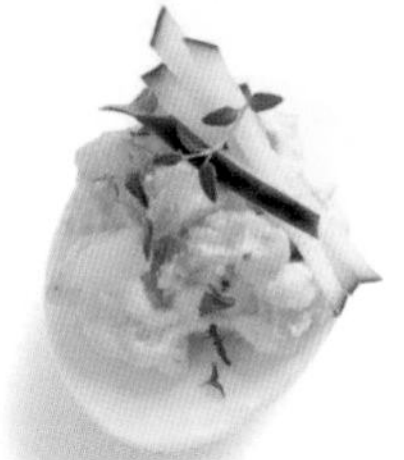

CUCUMBER-SHRIMP: Substitute 1 teaspoon lemon juice for the vinegar and stir ¼ cup chopped cooked shrimp and 1 teaspoon fresh thyme into yolk mixture. Garnish with finely chopped cucumber and thyme leaves.

FAST LOW-CALORIE

Deviled Eggs

PREP: 25 MINUTES **MAKES:** 12 SERVINGS

- **6 Hard-Cooked Eggs (page 130), peeled**
- **¼ cup mayonnaise**
- **1 teaspoon yellow mustard**
- **1 teaspoon vinegar**
- **Paprika and/or parsley sprigs (optional)**

1 Halve hard-cooked eggs lengthwise and remove yolks. Set whites aside. Place yolks in a small bowl; mash with a fork. Add mayonnaise, mustard, and vinegar; mix well. If desired, season with *salt* and *black pepper.* Stuff egg white halves with yolk mixture. Cover and chill until serving time (up to 24 hours). If desired, garnish with paprika and/or parsley.

PER DEVILED EGG HALF: 72 cal., 6 g total fat (1 g sat. fat), 109 mg chol., 62 mg sodium, 0 g carb., 0 g fiber, 3 g pro.
EXCHANGES: ½ Medium-Fat Meat, 1 Fat

MESH OR MASH?

If you are particular about how smooth your filling is, push the yolks through a fine-mesh sieve. The sieve creates a very fine-texture yolk to stir into your remaining filling ingredients. If you like a chunkier filling, use a fork to mash to the desired texture.

SMOKED SALMON: Stir 1 tablespoon snipped fresh chives into yolk mixture. Top each egg with a few strips of lox-style smoked salmon, a little sour cream, and additional snipped chives.

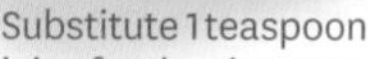

HAM AND ASPARAGUS: Substitute 1 teaspoon lemon juice for the vinegar and stir ¼ cup chopped cooked asparagus and 1 tablespoon diced cooked ham into yolk mixture.

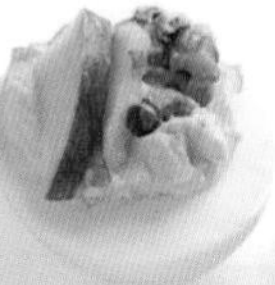

BLUE CHEESE, APPLE, AND WALNUT: Stir ¼ cup chopped or thinly sliced red or green apple, 1 tablespoon crumbled blue cheese, and 1 tablespoon chopped toasted walnuts (see tip, page 21) into the yolk mixture.

MEXICAN-STYLE: Substitute Mexican-style sour cream dip for the mayonnaise and stir ¼ cup chopped avocado and 1 tablespoon snipped fresh cilantro into the yolk mixture. Top with additional cilantro and avocado.

BACON AND BASIL: Stir 2 slices bacon, crisp-cooked and crumbled; 2 tablespoons chopped fresh tomato; and 1 tablespoon snipped fresh basil into yolk mixture. Garnish with additional tomato and basil leaves.

GREEK-STYLE: Stir 2 tablespoons crumbled feta cheese, 1 tablespoon chopped pitted Kalamata olives, and 2 teaspoons snipped fresh oregano into yolk mixture. Top with additional olives, feta cheese, and oregano.

Creamy Dip for Fruit

PREP: 15 MINUTES **CHILL:** 60 MINUTES
MAKES: 2 CUPS

- **1 8-ounce package cream cheese,* softened**
- **1 8-ounce carton sour cream***
- **1/4 cup packed brown sugar**
- **1 teaspoon vanilla**
- **2 to 3 tablespoons milk**
- **Assorted fruit, such as cherries, sliced apple, pear, banana, and/or strawberries**

1 In a small mixing bowl beat the cream cheese with an electric mixer on low speed until smooth. Gradually add the sour cream, beating until combined. Add the brown sugar and vanilla; beat just until combined. Stir in enough milk to make dipping consistency. Cover; chill at least 60 minutes before serving. Serve with assorted fruit.

***NOTE:** For a lighter version of the dip, use reduced-fat cream cheese and substitute 2/3 cup plain low-fat yogurt for the sour cream.

SPICE DIP: Prepare as directed, except add 1/2 teaspoon ground cinnamon or pumpkin pie spice.

PER 1/4 CUP PLAIN OR SPICE VARIATION: 181 cal., 15 g total fat (9 g sat. fat), 46 mg chol., 117 mg sodium, 9 g carb., 0 g fiber, 2 g pro. EXCHANGES: 1/2 Other Carb., 3 Fat

CREAMY MARSHMALLOW DIP: Prepare as directed, except omit brown sugar and stir in one 7-ounce jar marshmallow crème.

PER 1/4 CUP: 234 cal., 15 g total fat (9 g sat. fat), 46 mg chol., 135 mg sodium, 22 g carb., 0 g fiber, 3 g pro. EXCHANGES: 1 1/2 Other Carb., 3 Fat

LOW-CALORIE

Dill Dip

PREP: 10 MINUTES **CHILL:** 1 TO 24 HOURS
MAKES: ABOUT 2 CUPS

- **1 8-ounce package cream cheese, softened**
- **1 8-ounce carton sour cream**
- **2 tablespoons finely chopped green onion (1)**
- **2 tablespoons snipped fresh dill weed or 2 teaspoons dried dill weed**
- **1/2 teaspoon seasoned salt or salt**
- **Milk (optional)**
- **Assorted vegetable dippers, crackers, and/or potato chips**

1 In a medium mixing bowl beat cream cheese, sour cream, green onion, dill, and seasoned salt with an electric mixer on low speed until fluffy. Cover and chill for 1 to 24 hours. If dip thickens after chilling, stir in 1 to 2 tablespoons milk. Serve with vegetable dippers, crackers, and/or chips.

CREAMY BLUE CHEESE DIP: Prepare as directed, except omit dill and seasoned salt. Stir 1/2 cup crumbled blue cheese and 1/3 cup chopped toasted walnuts into cream cheese mixture.

SPINACH-DILL DIP: Prepare as directed, except stir half of a 10-ounce package frozen chopped spinach, thawed and well drained, into the beaten cream cheese mixture.

PER 1 TABLESPOON PLAIN, BLUE CHEESE, OR SPINACH VARIATIONS: 38 cal., 4 g total fat (2 g sat. fat), 11 mg chol., 52 mg sodium, 1 g carb., 0 g fiber, 1 g pro. EXCHANGES: 1 Fat

LOW-CALORIE

Crab Dip *(photo, page 37)*

PREP: 20 MINUTES **CHILL:** 2 TO 24 HOURS
MAKES: 1 1/3 CUPS

- **1 cup cooked crabmeat or one 6-ounce can crabmeat, drained, flaked, and cartilage removed**
- **1/2 cup mayonnaise**
- **1/2 cup sour cream**
- **2 tablespoons finely chopped red onion or green onion**
- **1 tablespoon snipped fresh dill weed or 1 teaspoon dried dill weed**
- **1 teaspoon finely shredded lemon peel or lime peel**
- **1 teaspoon lemon juice or lime juice**
- **Several dashes bottled hot pepper sauce**
- **Dash cayenne pepper (optional)**
- **Assorted crackers and/or vegetable dippers**

1 In a small bowl stir together crabmeat, mayonnaise, sour cream, the 2 tablespoons onion, dill, lemon peel, lemon juice, hot pepper sauce, and, if desired, cayenne pepper. Season to taste with *salt* and *black pepper*.

2 Transfer dip to a serving dish. Cover and chill for 2 to 24 hours. If desired, garnish with additional finely chopped red or green onion. Serve with crackers and/or vegetable dippers.

PER ABOUT 2 TABLESPOONS: 117 cal., 11 g fat (3 g sat. fat), 26 mg chol., 145 mg sodium, 1 g carb., 0 g fiber, 4 g pro. EXCHANGES: 1/2 Lean Meat, 2 Fat

CRAB TARTLETS: Prepare as directed through Step 1. Spoon dip into 30 miniature phyllo dough shells (two 2.1-ounce packages); serve cold. Or place filled shells on a large baking sheet. Bake in a 350°F oven for 5 to 8 minutes or until heated through. Makes 30 tartlets.

PER TARTLET: 62 cal., 5 g total fat (1 g sat. fat), 9 mg chol., 58 mg sodium, 3 g carb., 0 g fiber, 2 g pro. EXCHANGES: 1 Fat

LOW-CALORIE

Chunky Guacamole

PREP: 20 MINUTES **CHILL:** 1 HOUR **MAKES:** 2 CUPS

- **2/3 cup finely chopped, seeded roma tomatoes (2 medium)**
- **1 to 2 tablespoons finely chopped red onion**
- **1 to 2 cloves garlic, minced**
- **2 tablespoons lime juice**
- **1 tablespoon olive oil**
- **1/4 teaspoon salt**
- **1/8 teaspoon black pepper**
- **2 ripe avocados, halved, seeded, peeled, and coarsely mashed (see photos 1 and 2, below)**
- **Tortilla chips**

1 In a medium bowl combine tomatoes, red onion, garlic, lime juice, olive oil, salt, and pepper. Gently stir in mashed avocados. Cover the surface with plastic wrap. Chill for up to 1 hour. Serve with tortilla chips.

PER 2 TABLESPOONS: 48 cal., 5 g total fat (1 g sat. fat), 0 mg chol., 39 mg sodium, 3 g carb., 1 g fiber, 1 g pro.
EXCHANGES: 1 Fat

MASHING AVOCADOS STEP-BY-STEP

1. Cut the avocado lengthwise around the seed. Twist the halves apart. Use a small spoon to scoop around the seed to remove it.

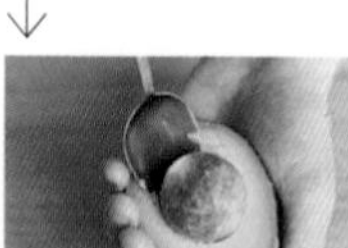

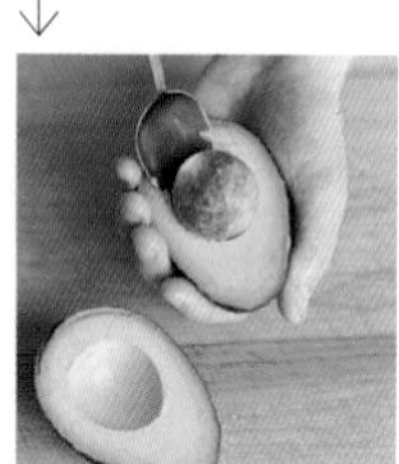

2. Scoop out the avocado flesh and place it in a resealable plastic bag; seal bag. Use your hands to mash the avocado to the desired texture. Squeeze the avocado into bowl with tomato mixture.

WORKING WITH CHILE PEPPERS

Chile peppers contain volatile oils that can burn your skin and eyes. These oils are released when the chiles are cut. When working with chiles, wear plastic or rubber gloves. If your bare hands do touch the cut peppers, wash your hands and nails well with soap and warm water.

CHUNKY GUACAMOLE

FAST LOW-CALORIE

Fresh Tomato Salsa

START TO FINISH: 30 MINUTES **MAKES:** 3 CUPS

- **6 roma tomatoes, coarsely chopped**
- **1 small red onion, coarsely chopped**
- **1 large fresh poblano chile pepper, seeded and coarsely chopped (see tip, left)**
- **1 to 2 large fresh jalapeño chile peppers, seeded and coarsely chopped (see tip, left)**
- **2 tablespoons lime juice**
- **1 tablespoon canola oil or vegetable oil**
- **1 teaspoon cumin seeds, toasted and ground,* or 1/2 teaspoon ground cumin**
- **1 teaspoon coriander seeds, toasted and ground,* or 1/2 teaspoon ground coriander**
- **1/2 teaspoon kosher salt or salt**
- **1/4 teaspoon black pepper**

1 In a food processor combine all ingredients. Cover; process with on/off turns until finely chopped. Cover and chill up to 3 days.

***NOTE:** To toast seeds, in a dry, small skillet heat the cumin and coriander seeds over medium-low heat for 1 to 2 minutes or until lightly toasted, shaking skillet occasionally. Remove seeds from heat; allow to cool before grinding with a spice grinder or a mortar and pestle.

PER 1/4 CUP: 28 cal., 1 g total fat, (0 g sat. fat), 0 mg chol., 84 mg sodium, 4 g carb., 1 g fiber, 1 g pro.
EXCHANGES: 1/2 Vegetable

HUMMUS

FAST LOW-CALORIE

Hummus

START TO FINISH: 15 MINUTES
MAKES: ABOUT 1¾ CUPS

- **1 15-ounce can garbanzo beans (chickpeas), rinsed and drained**
- **1 clove garlic, minced**
- **¼ cup tahini (sesame seed paste)**
- **¼ cup lemon juice**
- **¼ cup olive oil**
- **½ teaspoon salt**
- **¼ teaspoon paprika**
- **Stir-ins such as ¼ cup sliced green onions, ¼ cup crumbled feta cheese, ⅓ cup chopped ripe olives or Kalamata olives, ⅓ cup chopped roasted red sweet peppers, 2 to 3 chopped chipotle peppers, 1 tablespoon snipped fresh dill weed, and/or ¼ cup purchased basil pesto (optional)**
- **1 tablespoon snipped fresh parsley**
- **2 to 3 teaspoons olive oil (optional)**
- **2 tablespoons pine nuts, toasted (see tip, page 21) (optional)**
- **Toasted pita wedges or vegetable dippers**

1 In a blender or food processor combine garbanzo beans, garlic, tahini, lemon juice, the ¼ cup oil, salt, and paprika. Cover and blend or process until smooth, scraping sides as necessary.

2 If desired, add one or more stir-ins. Spoon hummus into a serving dish. Top with parsley. If desired, drizzle with 2 to 3 teaspoons oil and sprinkle with pine nuts. Serve with pita wedges or vegetable dippers.

PER 2 TABLESPOONS: 97 cal., 6 g total fat (1 g sat. fat), 0 mg chol., 176 mg sodium, 8 g carb., 2 g fiber, 2 g pro. EXCHANGES: ½ Starch, 1 Fat

Mexican Seven-Layer Dip

PREP: 20 MINUTES **CHILL:** 4 TO 24 HOURS
MAKES: 16 SERVINGS

- **1 16-ounce can refried beans**
- **½ cup bottled salsa**
- **1 7-ounce package refrigerated avocado dip (guacamole)**
- **1 8-ounce carton sour cream**
- **1 cup shredded cheddar cheese (4 ounces)**
- **¼ cup sliced green onions (2)**
- **¼ cup sliced pitted ripe olives**
- **1 cup chopped, seeded tomato (1 large)**
- **8 cups tortilla chips or crackers**

1 In a medium bowl combine refried beans and salsa; spread onto a 12-inch platter or in a 2-quart rectangular baking dish. Carefully layer guacamole and sour cream over bean mixture. Top with cheese, green onions, and olives. Cover and chill for 4 to 24 hours. Before serving, sprinkle with tomato. Serve with tortilla chips.

PER ¼ CUP DIP AND ½ CUP CHIPS: 179 cal., 11 g total fat (4 g sat. fat), 15 mg chol., 340 mg sodium, 16 g carb., 3 g fiber, 5 g pro. EXCHANGES: 1 Starch, 2 Fat

BEST-LOVED LOW-CALORIE

Smoky Cheese Ball

PREP: 30 MINUTES **STAND:** 45 MINUTES
CHILL: 4 TO 24 HOURS **MAKES:** 3½ CUPS

- **2 8-ounce packages cream cheese**
- **2 cups finely shredded smoked cheddar, Swiss, or Gouda cheese (8 ounces)**
- **½ cup butter**
- **2 tablespoons milk**
- **2 teaspoons steak sauce**
- **1 cup finely chopped toasted nuts (see tip, page 21)**
- **Assorted crackers**

1 In a medium mixing bowl let cream cheese, cheddar cheese, and butter stand at room temperature for 30 minutes. Add milk and steak sauce; beat until fluffy. Cover and chill for 4 to 24 hours.

2 Shape mixture into a ball; roll in nuts. Let stand for 15 minutes. Serve with crackers.

PER 1 TABLESPOON: 73 cal., 7 g total fat (4 g sat. fat), 18 mg chol., 66 mg sodium, 1 g carb., 0 g fiber, 2 g pro. EXCHANGES: 1½ Fat

LOW-CALORIE

Pimiento Cheese *(photo, page 35)*

PREP: 10 MINUTES **CHILL:** 4 TO 24 HOURS
MAKES: 2¼ CUPS

- **3 cups shredded cheddar cheese (12 ounces)**
- **⅔ cup mayonnaise**
- **1 4-ounce jar sliced pimientos, drained and chopped**
- **1 teaspoon Worcestershire sauce**
- **1 teaspoon yellow mustard**
- **¼ teaspoon garlic powder**
- **Assorted crackers**

1 In a large bowl stir together cheese, mayonnaise, pimientos, Worcestershire, mustard, and garlic powder, mashing mixture with the back of a spoon as you mix (mixture will be chunky). Transfer to a serving bowl. Cover with plastic wrap and chill for 4 to 24 hours. Serve as a spread with crackers.

PER 2 TABLESPOONS: 137 cal., 13 g total fat (5 g sat. fat), 23 mg chol., 169 mg sodium, 1 g carb., 0 g fiber, 5 g pro.
EXCHANGES: ½ High-Fat Meat, 1 Fat

BEEF AND PICKLE CHEESE: Prepare as directed, except omit the pimientos, Worcestershire, and mustard. Substitute Monterey Jack cheese for the cheddar cheese. Add one 3-ounce package cream cheese, softened; ½ cup chopped dill pickle; and ½ cup chopped dried beef or boiled ham (about 2½ ounces) to cheese mixture. If desired, serve with melba toasts or rye crackers.

PER 2 TABLESPOONS: 114 cal., 10 g total fat (4 g sat. fat), 21 mg chol., 231 mg sodium, 0 g carb., 0 g fiber, 5 g pro.
EXCHANGES: ½ High-Fat Meat, 1½ Fat

Brie en Croûte

PREP: 30 MINUTES **BAKE:** 20 MINUTES AT 400°F
STAND: 10 MINUTES **MAKES:** 2 ROUNDS (12 SERVINGS)

- **½ of a 17.3-ounce package frozen puff pastry sheets, thawed (1 sheet)**
- **2 tablespoons jalapeño pepper jelly, apple jelly, or apricot jelly**
- **2 4.5-ounce rounds Brie or Camembert cheese**
- **2 tablespoons chopped nuts, toasted (see tip, page 21)**
- **1 egg, slightly beaten**
- **1 tablespoon water**
- **Apple and/or pear slices (optional)**

1 Preheat oven to 400°F. Grease a baking sheet; set aside. Unfold pastry on a lightly floured surface; roll into a 16×10-inch rectangle. Cut into two 8-inch circles (see photo 1, right); reserve trimmings.

2 Spread jelly over top of each cheese round. Sprinkle with nuts; lightly press nuts into jelly.

3 Combine egg and water; set aside. Place pastry circles over cheese rounds. Invert rounds and pastry. Brush edges of circles with a little of the egg mixture. Bring edges of pastry up and over cheese rounds, pleating and pinching edges to cover and seal. Trim excess pastry (see photo 2, below). Place rounds, smooth sides up, on prepared baking sheet. Brush egg mixture over tops and sides. Cut small slits for steam to escape. Using hors d'oeuvre cutters, cut shapes from reserved pastry. Brush shapes with egg mixture; place on top of rounds.

4 Bake for 20 to 25 minutes or until pastry is deep golden brown. Let stand for 10 to 20 minutes before serving. If desired, serve with apple and/or pear slices.

PER SERVING: 207 cal., 15 g total fat (6 g sat. fat), 37 mg chol., 192 mg sodium, 12 g carb., 0 g fiber, 7 g pro.
EXCHANGES: ½ Starch, ½ Other Carb., ½ Lean Meat, 2½ Fat

BRIE EN CROÛTE WITH APRICOTS AND ALMONDS: Prepare as directed, except substitute 2 tablespoons apricot preserves for the jelly and substitute ½ cup chopped almonds and ⅓ cup finely snipped dried apricots for the 2 tablespoons chopped nuts.

PER SERVING: 229 cal., 16 g total fat (6 g sat. fat), 37 mg chol., 192 mg sodium, 14 g carb., 1 g fiber, 7 g pro.
EXCHANGES: ½ Starch, ½ Other Carb., 1 Lean Meat, 3 Fat

BRIE EN CROÛTE STEP-BY-STEP

1. Using an 8-inch round cake pan as a guide, cut two circles from the pastry.

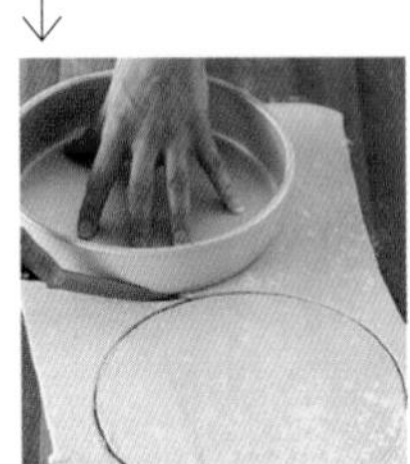

2. Carefully bring the pastry up and over each cheese round, pleating the edges as necessary to fit over top of cheese round. Use kitchen shears to trim excess pastry from pleats and create an even thickness.

Asiago-Artichoke Dip

PREP: 20 MINUTES **BAKE:** 30 MINUTES AT 350°F
STAND: 15 MINUTES **MAKES:** 3 CUPS

- **1 14-ounce can artichoke hearts, rinsed and drained**
- **2 ounces thinly sliced prosciutto or 2 slices bacon**
- **1 cup arugula or fresh spinach, chopped**
- **1 8-ounce carton sour cream**
- **3 tablespoons all-purpose flour**
- **½ cup mayonnaise**
- **½ cup bottled roasted red sweet peppers, drained and finely chopped**
- **¾ cup finely shredded Asiago cheese or Parmesan cheese (3 ounces)**
- **¼ cup thinly sliced green onions (2)**
- **Thinly sliced prosciutto or bacon, cut up and crisp-cooked (optional)**
- **Assorted crackers, pita chips, flatbread, and/or toasted baguette slices**

1 Preheat oven to 350°F. Place artichoke hearts in a fine-mesh sieve. To remove excess liquid, firmly press on artichoke hearts with paper towels. Chop artichoke hearts; set aside.

2 Cut the 2 ounces prosciutto crosswise into thin strips; separate strips. In a medium skillet cook and stir prosciutto over medium heat about 2 minutes or until slightly crisp; add arugula. Cook and stir 1 minute more; set aside.

3 In a large bowl stir together sour cream and flour. Stir in mayonnaise and roasted peppers. Stir in artichokes, ½ cup of the cheese, the green onions, and the arugula mixture. Transfer to an ungreased 9-inch pie plate or casserole dish. Sprinkle with the remaining ¼ cup cheese.

4 Bake, uncovered, about 30 minutes or until edges are light brown and mixture is hot in center. Let stand for 15 minutes before serving. If desired, sprinkle with crisp-cooked prosciutto and additional Asiago cheese. Serve with crackers.

PER ¼ CUP: 155 cal., 14 g total fat (5 g sat. fat), 24 mg chol., 341 mg sodium, 4 g carb., 1 g fiber, 4 g pro.
EXCHANGES: ½ Vegetable, ½ Lean Meat, 2½ Fat

LIGHT ASIAGO-ARTICHOKE DIP: Prepare as directed, except omit prosciutto and omit Step 2. Increase arugula to 2 cups. Substitute light sour cream for the sour cream and reduced-fat mayonnaise for the mayonnaise. Omit the ¼ cup finely shredded Asiago cheese sprinkled on top. Serve with vegetable dippers.

PER ¼ CUP: 93 cal., 7 g total fat (3 g sat. fat), 15 mg chol., 192 mg sodium, 6 g carb., 1 g fiber, 2 g pro.
EXCHANGES: 1 Vegetable, 1 Fat

SEMIHARD
1
2
3
4
5
HARD
1
2
3
4

BLUE
1
2
3
4
SOFT-
RIPENED
1
2
SEMISOFT
1
2
3
4

FRESH
1
2
3
4
5

cheese 101

SEMIHARD

Semihard (or semifirm) cheeses have more moisture than hard cheeses, but they have a slightly smoother texture. They're often used in cooking because they melt well. Choose longer-aged semihard cheeses for bolder and more complex flavors. To store semihard cheeses, wrap them in waxed paper and place in an airtight container.

1. Cheddar
2. White cheddar
3. Gruyère
4. Gouda
5. Swiss

HARD

Great for grating, hard cheeses have been aged to remove moisture and allow the salt in the cheese to crystallize. This is what gives these cheeses their sharp flavor and slightly granular texture. Because they do not need to breathe, hard cheeses can be wrapped tightly in plastic wrap in an airtight container for storage.

1. Asiago
2. Manchego
3. Pecorino-Romano
4. Parmigiano-Reggiano

BLUE

Blue cheeses contain blue veins created by the addition of mold during the cheesemaking process. Softer blue cheeses can be used for spreading and melt well in cooking. Slice and serve higher-end, drier blues for eating out of hand. Wrap blue cheeses in foil or waxed paper, then in plastic wrap.

1. Blue cheese
2. Gorgonzola
3. Roquefort
4. Stilton

SOFT-RIPENED

Soft-ripened cheeses have a smooth interior and thin, bloomy rind. Brie and Camembert have very similar flavors and can be used interchangeably in recipes. However, Camembert typically has a slightly stronger flavor and firmer texture than Brie. Store soft-ripened cheeses wrapped in waxed paper, which allows them to breathe.

1. Brie
2. Camembert

SEMISOFT

Semisoft cheeses have a high moisture content; their pliable texture makes them easy to slice and tuck into cold sandwiches. To store semisoft cheeses, wrap in waxed paper and place in an airtight container.

1. Fontina
2. Monterey Jack
3. Muenster
4. Havarti

FRESH

Terrific in salads and quick-cooking dishes, these unaged cheeses have a high moisture content, soft texture, and flavors that range from mild to tangy. Store, tightly covered, in their original containers (and original liquid if applicable) for up to 5 days.

1. Chèvre
2. Feta
3. Fresh mozzarella
4. Mascarpone
5. Ricotta

PARTY CHEESE

Follow these tips to design a fascinating cheese tray for appetizer parties.

- Serve three to five different cheeses and purchase 3 to 4 ounces per guest.
- Vary the textures and flavors, serving at least one semisoft cheese, one soft-ripened or blue cheese, and a firm cheese.
- Vary the cheeses by milk source, choosing at least one each of goat's, cow's, and sheep's milk. If you go to a cheese shop, the cheese monger can let you taste the differences among them.
- Because most cheeses taste best at room temperature, arrange the tray and set it out for 30 minutes before serving.
- Serve with crackers and/or breads and easy accompaniments such as olives and nuts or dried or fresh fruits.

BEST-LOVED

Swiss Fondue

PREP: 30 MINUTES **STAND:** 30 MINUTES
BAKE: 5 MINUTES AT 350°F **MAKES:** 4 CUPS

- **20 ounces Gruyère, Emmental, or Swiss cheese, shredded (5 cups)**
- **1 clove garlic, halved**
- **3 tablespoons all-purpose flour**
- **3 to 4 ounces French bread, herb bread, or rye bread, cut into 1-inch cubes, and/or 4 cups vegetables (such as broccoli florets, cauliflower florets, tiny new potatoes, and/or cherry tomatoes)**
- **1½ cups dry white wine**
- **¼ cup milk**
- **1 tablespoon cognac or brandy (optional)**
- **1 teaspoon Dijon-style mustard**
- **⅛ teaspoon ground nutmeg**

1 Let shredded cheese stand at room temperature for 30 minutes. Meanwhile, rub inside of a fondue pot with garlic; discard garlic. Set pan aside. Toss cheese with flour; set aside.

2 Preheat oven to 350°F. Place bread cubes on a baking sheet. Bake for 5 to 7 minutes or until crisp and toasted; set aside. To precook vegetables, in a large saucepan bring a small amount of water to boiling; add broccoli or cauliflower florets. Simmer, covered, about 3 minutes or until crisp-tender. Drain and rinse with cold water; set aside. To cook potatoes, simmer, covered, for 10 to 12 minutes or until tender.

3 In a large saucepan heat wine over medium heat until small bubbles rise to the surface. Just before wine boils, reduce heat to medium-low and stir in the cheese mixture, a little at a time, whisking constantly and making sure cheese is melted before adding more. Gradually stir in milk. Cook and stir until bubbles begin to form.

4 If desired, stir in cognac. Stir in mustard, and nutmeg. Transfer cheese mixture to a fondue pot. Keep mixture bubbling gently over a fondue burner. (Mixture thickens if it cools; if mixture becomes too thick, reheat and stir in a little more milk.) Serve with toasted bread cubes and/or vegetables.

PER ¼ CUP: 188 cal., 12 g total fat (7 g sat. fat), 39 mg chol., 164 mg sodium, 5 g carb., 0 g fiber, 11 g pro.
EXCHANGES: 1½ High-Fat Meat

FAST LOW-CALORIE

Chile con Queso

START TO FINISH: 20 MINUTES **MAKES:** 2⅔ CUPS

- **½ cup finely chopped onion (1 medium)**
- **1 tablespoon butter**
- **1⅓ cups chopped, seeded tomatoes (about 2 medium)**
- **1 4-ounce can diced green chiles**
- **½ teaspoon ground cumin**
- **2 ounces Monterey Jack cheese with jalapeño peppers, shredded (½ cup)**
- **1 teaspoon cornstarch**
- **1 8-ounce package cream cheese, cubed**
- **Tortilla chips or corn chips**

1 In a medium saucepan cook onion in butter until tender. Stir in tomatoes, undrained chiles, and cumin. Heat to boiling; reduce heat. Simmer, uncovered, for 10 minutes, stirring occasionally.

2 Toss shredded cheese with cornstarch. Gradually add cheese mixture to saucepan, stirring until cheese melts. Gradually add the cream cheese, stirring until cheese melts and is smooth; heat through. Serve with chips.

SLOW COOKER DIRECTIONS: Prepare as directed. Transfer mixture to a 1½- or 2-quart slow cooker. Keep warm on low-heat setting, if available, up to 2 hours, stirring occasionally.

ROASTED POBLANO CHILE CON QUESO: Preheat oven to 425°F. Quarter 2 fresh poblano chile peppers lengthwise; remove stems, seeds, and membranes (see tip, page 44). Place pepper pieces, cut sides down, on a foil-lined baking sheet. Bake for 20 to 25 minutes or until peppers are charred and very tender. Bring the foil up around peppers and fold edges together to enclose. Let stand about 15 minutes or until cool enough to handle. Use a sharp knife to loosen edges of the skins; gently pull off the skin in strips and discard. Finely chop peppers. Prepare Chili con Queso as directed, except substitute the finely chopped poblano peppers for the canned diced green chiles.

PER 2 TABLESPOONS PLAIN OR ROASTED POBLANO VARIATION: 58 cal., 5 g total fat (3 g sat. fat), 16 mg chol., 79 mg sodium, 5 g carb., 0 g fiber, 2 g pro. EXCHANGES: 1 Fat

Nachos

PREP: 15 MINUTES **BAKE:** 20 MINUTES AT 350°F
MAKES: 8 SERVINGS

- **8 cups tortilla chips**
- **1 pound ground beef**
- **1 15-ounce can black beans or pinto beans, rinsed and drained**
- **1 cup bottled chunky salsa**
- **1½ cups shredded Monterey Jack cheese with jalapeño peppers, cheddar cheese, Colby and Monterey Jack cheese, and/or Mexican cheese blend (6 ounces)**
- **Optional toppings such as thinly sliced green onion, snipped fresh cilantro, seeded and chopped fresh jalapeño pepper (see tip, page 44), pickled jalapeño slices, sour cream, and/or bottled chunky salsa**

1 Preheat oven to 350°F. Spread two-thirds of the tortilla chips on an 11- or 12-inch ovenproof platter or pizza pan; set aside.

2 In a large skillet cook ground beef over medium heat until browned. Drain off fat.

3 Add the beans and the 1 cup salsa to the beef. Spoon about two-thirds of the beef mixture over chips. Sprinkle with 1 cup of the cheese. Bake about 10 minutes or until cheese melts. Remove from oven. Top with remaining chips, beef mixture, and cheese. Bake about 10 minutes more or until cheese melts.

4 If desired, top with green onion, cilantro, jalapeño pepper, pickled jalapeño slices, sour cream, and/or additional salsa.

PER SERVING: 417 cal., 25 g total fat (10 g sat. fat), 63 mg chol., 615 mg sodium, 29 g carb., 4 g fiber, 21 g pro.
EXCHANGES: 2 Starch, 2 Medium-Fat Meat, 2½ Fat

MEATLESS NACHOS: Prepare as directed, except omit beef and skip Step 2. Add another 15-ounce can black beans or pinto beans, rinsed and drained, to the bean mixture.

PER SERVING: 314 cal., 14 g total fat (5 g sat. fat), 22 mg chol., 746 mg sodium, 37 g carb., 7 g fiber, 14 g pro.
EXCHANGES: 2½ Starch, 1 Lean Meat, 2 Fat

CHICKEN NACHOS: Prepare as directed, except substitute 1 pound skinless, boneless chicken breast, cut into bite-size pieces, for the ground beef in Step 2. Cook chicken pieces until they are no longer pink. Continue as directed.

PER SERVING: 337 cal., 15 g total fat (6 g sat. fat), 59 mg chol., 643 mg sodium, 29 g carb., 4 g fiber, 23 g pro..
EXCHANGES: 2 Starch, 2½ Lean Meat, 2 Fat

LOW-CALORIE

Stuffed Mushrooms

PREP: 20 MINUTES **BAKE:** 17 MINUTES AT 425°F
MAKES: 24 MUSHROOMS

- **24 large fresh mushrooms, about 2 inches in diameter**
- **½ cup seasoned fine dry bread crumbs**
- **⅓ cup grated Parmesan cheese**
- **⅓ cup sour cream**
- **2 cloves garlic, minced**
- **2 tablespoons snipped fresh Italian parsley**
- **¼ teaspoon black pepper**
- **Nonstick cooking spray**

1 Preheat oven to 425°F. Clean mushrooms. Remove stems from mushrooms; discard stems. Place mushroom caps, stem sides up, in a 15×10×1-inch baking pan; set aside.

2 In a small bowl stir together bread crumbs, Parmesan cheese, sour cream, garlic, parsley, and pepper. Spoon mixture into mushroom caps. Lightly coat mushrooms with nonstick cooking spray. Bake, uncovered, for 17 to 20 minutes or until light brown and heated through.

PER MUSHROOM: 25 cal., 1 g fat (1 g sat. fat), 2 mg chol., 64 mg sodium, 2 g carb., 0 g fiber, 1 g pro. **EXCHANGES:** ½ Fat

BACON-CHEDDAR-STUFFED MUSHROOMS: Prepare as directed, except stir 4 slices bacon, crisp-cooked and crumbled, and ½ cup shredded cheddar cheese (2 ounces) into the filling.

PER MUSHROOM: 42 cal., 3 g total fat (1 g sat. fat), 6 mg chol., 110 mg sodium, 2 g carb., 0 g fiber, 3 g pro.
EXCHANGES: ½ High-Fat Meat

BLUE CHEESE- AND WALNUT-STUFFED MUSHROOMS: Prepare as directed, except stir ½ cup crumbled blue cheese (2 ounces) and ¼ cup chopped toasted walnuts (see tip, page 21) into the filling.

PER MUSHROOM: 43 cal., 3 g total fat (1 g sat. fat), 5 mg chol., 103 mg sodium, 3 g carb., 0 g fiber, 2 g pro. **EXCHANGES:** 1 Fat

BEST-LOVED LOW-CALORIE

Potato Skins

PREP: 20 MINUTES **BAKE:** 50 MINUTES AT 425°F
MAKES: 24 WEDGES

- **6 large baking potatoes (such as russet)**
- **1 tablespoon vegetable oil**
- **1 to 1½ teaspoons chili powder**
- **Several drops bottled hot pepper sauce**
- **Salt**
- **8 slices crisp-cooked bacon, crumbled**
- **⅔ cup finely chopped tomato (1 medium)**
- **2 tablespoons finely chopped green onion (1)**
- **1 cup shredded cheddar cheese (4 ounces)**
- **½ cup sour cream**

1 Preheat oven to 425°F. Scrub potatoes and prick with a fork. Bake for 40 to 45 minutes or until tender; let cool.

2 Cut each potato lengthwise into four wedges. Carefully scoop out the inside of each potato wedge, leaving a ¼-inch shell. Cover and chill the leftover white portion of the potato for another use.

3 Line a large baking sheet with foil; set aside. In a small bowl combine the oil, chili powder, and hot pepper sauce. Using a pastry brush, brush the insides of the potato wedges with the oil mixture. Sprinkle with salt. Place the potato wedges in a single layer on the prepared baking sheet. Sprinkle wedges with bacon, tomato, and green onion; top with cheese.

4 Bake about 10 minutes more or until cheese melts and potatoes are heated through. Serve with sour cream.

MAKE-AHEAD DIRECTIONS: Prepare as directed through Step 3. Cover; chill potato wedges for up to 24 hours. Uncover and bake as directed.

PER 2 WEDGES: 64 cal., 4 g total fat (2 g sat. fat), 10 mg chol., 146 mg sodium, 4 g carb., 1 g fiber, 3 g pro. **EXCHANGES:** 1 Fat

LOW-CALORIE

Zesty Shrimp Cocktail

PREP: 25 MINUTES **CHILL:** 2 HOURS TO OVERNIGHT
MAKES: 8 TO 10 SERVINGS

- **1½ pounds fresh or frozen large shrimp in shells**
- **¾ cup bottled chili sauce**
- **2 tablespoons lemon juice**
- **2 tablespoons thinly sliced green onion (1)**
- **1 tablespoon prepared horseradish**
- **2 teaspoons Worcestershire sauce**
- **Several dashes bottled hot pepper sauce**

1 Thaw shrimp if frozen. Peel and devein shrimp (see photos 1–3, page 311). Cook shrimp in lightly salted boiling water for 1 to 3 minutes or until shrimp turn opaque, stirring occasionally. Rinse in a colander under cold running water; drain again. Chill for 2 hours or overnight.

2 For sauce, in a small bowl stir together chili sauce, lemon juice, green onion, horseradish, Worcestershire sauce, and hot pepper sauce. Cover and chill until serving time. (Sauce can be stored in an airtight container in the refrigerator for up to 2 weeks.) Serve shrimp with sauce.

PER SERVING: 84 cal., 0 g total fat, 103 mg chol., 383 mg sodium, 8 g carb., 0 g fiber, 13 g pro.
EXCHANGES: ½ Other Carb., 2 Lean Meat

SHRIMP AND AVOCADO COCKTAIL: Prepare shrimp and sauce as directed. To serve, line 8 to 10 chilled martini glasses or individual plates with mixed torn salad greens. Halve, seed, peel, and dice 2 avocados and arrange on greens. Peel and section 1 medium orange (or use half of an 11-ounce can mandarin orange sections, drained); arrange in glasses. Toss the shrimp with the sauce and place in glasses. Garnish with lime wedges.

PER SERVING: 149 cal., 6 g total fat (1 g sat. fat), 103 mg chol., 388 mg sodium, 13 g carb., 3 g fiber, 14 g pro.
EXCHANGES: 1 Vegetable, 1/2 Other Carb., 2 Lean Meat, 1 1/2 Fat

BEST-LOVED

Gingery Apricot-Glazed Pork Ribs

PREP: 35 MINUTES **MARINATE:** 6 TO 24 HOURS
BAKE: 75 MINUTES AT 350°F **MAKES:** 14 TO 16 SERVINGS

- **4 pounds pork loin back ribs, halved across the bones***
- **1 cup finely chopped onion (1 large)**
- **2/3 cup dry sherry**
- **1/2 cup rice vinegar**
- **1/2 cup soy sauce**
- **1/4 cup finely chopped fresh ginger**
- **2 tablespoons finely chopped garlic (about 12 cloves)**
- **1 teaspoon black pepper**
- **2/3 cup apricot preserves**
- **3 tablespoons spicy brown mustard**
- **1 tablespoon toasted sesame oil**
- **1/4 teaspoon cayenne pepper**
- **1 tablespoon toasted sesame seeds**

PORK RIBS STEP-BY-STEP

1. Place the ribs, bone sides up, onto a cutting board. Using a sharp knife, slice between each bone.

2. Place the ribs in a sturdy resealable plastic bag set in a shallow dish. Pour marinade over the ribs. Seal bag and turn to thoroughly coat each rib.

GINGERY APRICOT-GLAZED PORK RIBS

1 Trim fat from ribs. Cut ribs into single-rib portions (see photo 1, left). Place rib pieces in a large resealable plastic bag set in a shallow dish. For marinade, in a medium bowl combine onion, sherry, vinegar, soy sauce, ginger, garlic, and black pepper. Pour over ribs; seal bag and turn to coat ribs (see photo 2, left). Marinate in the refrigerator for 6 to 24 hours, turning bag occasionally.

2 Preheat oven to 350°F. Drain rib pieces, reserving 1/4 cup of the marinade. Arrange rib pieces, meaty sides up, in a shallow roasting pan. Roast, uncovered, about 1 hour or until tender.

3 Meanwhile, in a small saucepan combine apricot preserves, mustard, oil, and cayenne pepper. Add the reserved marinade. Bring to boiling; reduce heat. Simmer, uncovered, for 3 minutes.

4 Brush ribs generously with sauce. Bake, uncovered, for 15 minutes, brushing once or twice with sauce during baking. Sprinkle with sesame seeds before serving. If desired, heat remaining sauce; serve with ribs.

***NOTE:** Ask your butcher to cut ribs in half across the bones.

PER SERVING: 292 cal., 20 g total fat (7 g sat. fat), 65 mg chol., 262 mg sodium, 12 g carb., 0 g fiber, 13 g pro.
EXCHANGES: 1 Other Carb., 2 Medium-Fat Meat, 2 Fat

Buffalo Chicken Wings

PREP: 25 MINUTES **BROIL:** 20 MINUTES PER BATCH
MAKES: 12 SERVINGS

- **1 8-ounce carton sour cream**
- **1 cup mayonnaise**
- **1 cup crumbled blue cheese (4 ounces)**
- **1/4 cup thinly sliced green onions (2)**
- **2 cloves garlic, minced**
- **1 cup Louisiana hot sauce**
- **6 tablespoons butter, melted**
- **2 tablespoons cider vinegar**
- **24 chicken wings (about 5 pounds)**

1 In a medium bowl stir together the sour cream, mayonnaise, blue cheese, green onions, garlic, 1/2 teaspoon *salt,* and 1/2 teaspoon *black pepper.* Cover and chill until serving time.

2 Preheat broiler. In a very large bowl combine the hot sauce, butter, and vinegar; reserve 1 cup. Cut off and discard tips of chicken wings. Cut wings at joints to form 48 pieces (see photo 1, below). Add wing pieces to the remaining sauce mixture in bowl; toss to coat.

3 Arrange half of the chicken wing pieces on the unheated rack of a broiler pan. Broil 4 to 5 inches from the heat for 10 minutes. Turn wings. Broil about 10 minutes more or until tender and brown. Place broiled wings in a clean very large bowl; cover to keep warm. Repeat with remaining chicken wing pieces. Add reserved 1 cup sauce to the broiled wings (see photo 2, below); toss to coat. Transfer to a serving platter. Serve with sour cream mixture and *celery* and/or *carrot sticks.*

PER SERVING: 456 cal., 40 g total fat (14 g sat. fat), 98 mg chol., 1,473 mg sodium, 2 g carb., 0 g fiber, 22 g pro.
EXCHANGES: 1/2 Vegetable, 3 Medium-Fat Meat, 5 Fat

CHICKEN WINGS STEP-BY-STEP

1. Using a chef's knife, cut off and discard the tips from the chicken wings. Cut rest of the wings at the joints to make two pieces each.

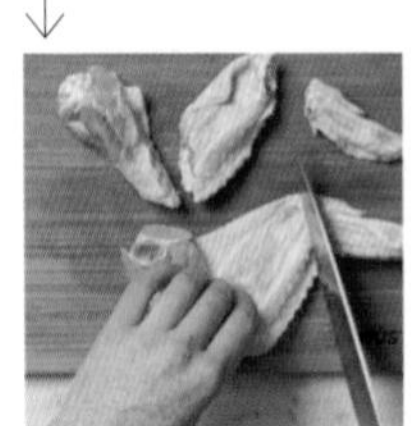

2. Pour the remaining sauce over the hot broiled wings. Toss to coat the wings well. Serve immediately while hot.

BUFFALO CHICKEN WINGS

FAST

Savory Nuts *(photo, page 35)*

PREP: 10 MINUTES **BAKE:** 12 MINUTES AT 350°F
MAKES: 2 CUPS

- **2 cups whole almonds, pecan halves, and/or cashews**
- **2 tablespoons Worcestershire-style marinade for chicken or bottled Italian vinaigrette salad dressing**
- **1 tablespoon olive oil**
- **2 teaspoons snipped fresh thyme or 1/2 teaspoon dried thyme, crushed**
- **1 teaspoon snipped fresh rosemary or 1/4 teaspoon dried rosemary, crushed**
- **1/8 teaspoon cayenne pepper**

1 Preheat oven to 350°F. Line a 13×9×2-inch baking pan with foil; lightly grease. Spread nuts in an even layer in the prepared pan. In a small bowl combine marinade, oil, thyme, rosemary, 1/4 teaspoon *salt,* and cayenne pepper. Drizzle over nuts; toss gently to coat.

2 Bake for 12 to 15 minutes or until toasted, stirring occasionally. Spread nuts on a sheet of foil; cool completely. Store in an airtight container at room temperature up to 3 weeks.

PER 1/4 CUP: 242 cal., 19 g total fat (1 g sat. fat), 0 mg chol., 132 mg sodium, 8 g carb., 4 g fiber, 8 g pro.
EXCHANGES: 1/2 Carb., 1 High-Fat Meat, 2 Fat

make it mine

Party Mix

Partygoers have munched on nut-and-cereal mixes for decades. Customize the classic party mix with a few updated flourishes as well as the basic ingredients you like best.

PREP: 20 MINUTES
BAKE: 45 MINUTES AT 250°F
MAKES: 16 TO 18 CUPS

- **5 cups CRUNCHY TREAT**
- **4 cups round toasted oat cereal**
- **3 cups WHOLE NUTS**
- **8 cups CEREAL**
- **1 cup butter**
- **¼ cup Worcestershire sauce**
- **SEASONING**
- **Several drops bottled hot pepper sauce (optional)**

1 Preheat oven to 250°F. In a roasting pan* combine desired Crunchy Treat, round toasted oat cereal, Nuts, and Cereal; set aside.

2 In a small saucepan heat and stir butter, Worcestershire sauce, Seasonings, and, if desired, bottled hot pepper sauce, until butter melts. Drizzle butter mixture over cereal mixture; stir gently to coat.

3 Bake for 45 minutes, stirring every 15 minutes. Spread on a large piece of foil to cool. Store in an airtight container at room temperature for up to 2 weeks or in the freezer for up to 3 months.

***NOTE:** If you don't have a roasting pan big enough to hold the party mix, purchase a large disposable roasting pan.

CRUNCHY TREAT
(pick one or more)

Bagel crisps
Cheese crackers
Corn chips
Fish-shape crackers
Oyster crackers
Pretzel sticks
Small pretzel twists or squares
Sesame sticks
Thin wheat crackers
Wasabi peas

WHOLE NUTS *(pick one)*

Almonds
Cashews
Hazelnuts
Mixed nuts
Peanuts
Pecans
Soy nuts
Walnuts

CEREAL *(pick one or more)*

Bite-size corn, rice, or wheat square cereal
Crispy corn and rice cereal
Puffed corn cereal
Sweetened oat square cereal

SEASONING *(pick one)*

BARBECUE: 1 teaspoon garlic powder plus 1 teaspoon onion powder; substitute ½ cup barbecue sauce for Worcestershire sauce

CAJUN: 1 tablespoon Cajun seasoning plus 1 teaspoon garlic powder

ITALIAN: ½ cup grated Parmesan cheese plus 1 teaspoon garlic powder; substitute bottled Italian vinaigrette for the Worcestershire sauce

RANCH: One 1-ounce package ranch salad dressing mix

TACO: One 1-ounce package taco seasoning mix plus 1 teaspoon ground cumin

LOW-CALORIE

Chimichurri Shrimp Spring Rolls

PREP: 30 MINUTES **STAND:** 15 MINUTES
MAKES: 10 SPRING ROLLS

- **1 recipe Chimichurri Sauce**
- **4 ounces cooked shrimp, peeled, deveined, and chopped**
- **1 cup shredded romaine lettuce**
- **3/4 cup packaged coarsely shredded carrots**
- **1/2 cup fresh cilantro leaves**
- **1/2 cup fresh mint leaves**
- **2 green onions, cut into thin bite-size strips**
- **1 ounce dried rice vermicelli noodles**
- **10 8-inch rice papers**
- **10 sprigs fresh Italian parsley or cilantro**
- **Soy sauce (optional)**
- **Sesame seeds (optional)**

1 Prepare Chimichurri Sauce. In a medium bowl combine the sauce, shrimp, lettuce, carrots, cilantro, mint, and green onions. Let stand for 15 to 30 minutes to allow shrimp and vegetables to soften slightly and absorb flavor from the sauce, stirring occasionally.

2 Meanwhile, in a medium saucepan cook the vermicelli in lightly salted boiling water for 3 minutes or just until tender; drain. Rinse under cold water; drain well. Use kitchen shears to snip the noodles into small pieces; set aside.

3 To assemble, pour warm water into a shallow pot or pie plate. Carefully dip a rice paper into the water (see photo 1, below); transfer to a clean round dinner plate. Let stand for several seconds to soften. Place a parsley or cilantro sprig just below the center of the paper. Spoon about 1/3 cup of the shrimp mixture onto sprig. Arrange some of the vermicelli noodles across mixture (see photo 2, below). Tightly roll up rice paper from the bottom, tucking in sides as you roll (see photo 3, below). If desired, add another parsley or cilantro sprig to rice paper as you roll (see photo 4, below).

4 Repeat with the remaining rice papers, parsley sprigs, shrimp mixture, and noodles. If desired, serve spring rolls with soy sauce sprinkled with sesame seeds for dipping.

CHIMICHURRI SAUCE: In a blender or food processor combine 1½ cups lightly packed fresh Italian parsley; 1/4 cup olive oil; 1/4 cup rice vinegar; 4 to 6 cloves garlic, minced; 1/4 teaspoon salt; 1/4 teaspoon black pepper; and 1/4 teaspoon crushed red pepper. Cover and blend or process with several on/off pulses until chopped but not pureed.

VEGETARIAN SPRING ROLLS: Prepare as directed, except omit shrimp and substitute 3/4 cup diced firm tofu (fresh bean curd).

MAKE-AHEAD DIRECTIONS: Prepare as directed. Layer spring rolls between damp paper towels in an airtight container. Store in the refrigerator for up to 4 hours.

PER SPRING ROLL SHRIMP OR VEGETARIAN VARIATION: 128 cal., 6 g total fat (1 g sat. fat), 22 mg chol., 312 mg sodium, 15 g carb., 2 g fiber, 4 g pro. EXCHANGES: 1 Starch, 1 Fat

SPRING ROLLS STEP-BY-STEP

1. Find a shallow pot or pie plate that has a bigger diameter than the rice paper. Fill it with warm water. Dip the rice paper in the warm water.

2. Carefully transfer the rice paper to a large plate and let it absorb the water and soften. Arrange filling ingredients across the bottom third of the rice paper.

3. Fold the bottom edge of the rice paper over the filling and roll it over. Tuck in the sides of the rice paper to enclose the filling.

4. For a decorative look, you can add a parsley or cilantro sprig to the rice paper. Continue rolling, sealing the rice paper to itself.

BEST-LOVED LOW-CALORIE

Asian Dumplings with Pickled Ginger Drizzle

PREP: 50 MINUTES **COOK:** 6 MINUTES
MAKES: 28 TO 30 DUMPLINGS

2 cups chopped napa cabbage
1 teaspoon salt
1 tablespoon snipped fresh cilantro
2 teaspoons toasted sesame oil
2 teaspoons soy sauce
2 teaspoons rice wine
2 tablespoons thinly sliced green onion (1)
1 small serrano chile pepper, seeded and finely chopped (see tip, page 44)
1 teaspoon grated fresh ginger
1/4 teaspoon hot chili-flavor oil
8 ounces ground raw turkey breast
28 to 30 round wonton wrappers (3½-inch diameter)
Nonstick cooking spray
1 recipe Pickled Ginger Drizzle

1 For filling, in a small bowl combine the cabbage and salt; toss to combine. Let cabbage stand at room temperature for 30 minutes. Transfer cabbage to a fine-mesh sieve; press cabbage firmly to remove all excess liquid. Transfer cabbage to a medium bowl. Add cilantro, sesame oil, soy sauce, rice wine, green onion, serrano chile pepper, ginger, and hot chili oil; toss well to combine. Stir in ground turkey breast until combined.

2 For dumplings, line a baking sheet with waxed paper; set aside. Spoon a scant 1 tablespoon filling onto center of 1 wonton wrapper. (Cover remaining wrappers with a damp cloth to keep them from drying out.) Lightly brush edges of wrapper with water, fold dumpling in half, and press edges together (see photos 1 and 2, below). Repeat with remaining filling and wrappers. Arrange the dumplings, sealed edges up, about ½ inch apart on the prepared baking sheet.

3 Cut a piece of parchment paper to fit inside a steamer basket. Line steamer basket with parchment. Lightly spray parchment with cooking spray. Arrange dumplings in a single layer in steamer basket (in batches if necessary).

4 Set steamer basket in a wok or large pot over, but not touching, boiling water. Cover and steam about 6 minutes or until dumplings reach 165°F (check with an instant-read thermometer inserted into filling). Remove dumplings and arrange on a serving platter. Serve warm drizzled with Pickled Ginger Drizzle.

PICKLED GINGER DRIZZLE: In a screw-top jar combine ⅓ cup canola oil; 2 tablespoons white wine vinegar; 2 tablespoons soy sauce; 1 small fresh jalapeno chile pepper, seeded and finely chopped (see tip, page 44); 1 tablespoon sugar; 1 tablespoon liquid from jar of pickled ginger; 1 tablespoon finely chopped pickled ginger; 1 tablespoon lime juice; and 2 teaspoons sesame oil. Cover and shake well.

MAKE-AHEAD DIRECTIONS: Prepare Pickled Ginger Drizzle as directed. Store in refrigerator for up to 3 days. Shake well before serving.

PER 2 DUMPLINGS: 133 cal., 7 g total fat (1 g sat. fat), 9 mg chol., 528 mg sodium, 12 g carb., 0 g fiber, 6 g pro.
EXCHANGES: ½ Starch, ½ Lean Meat, 1 Fat

DUMPLINGS STEP-BY-STEP

1. Spoon a scant tablespoon filling in the center of each wrapper. Don't overfill. Brush water on the edge of the wrapper around filling.

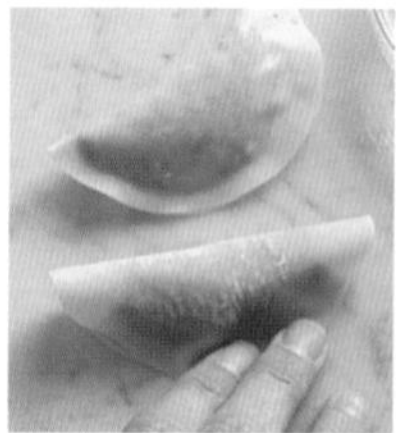

2. Fold the wrapper in half over the filling.

BEST-LOVED FAST LOW-CALORIE

California Sushi Rolls

START TO FINISH: 30 MINUTES **MAKES:** 12 PIECES

2 8-inch square sheets nori (seaweed)
1 recipe Sushi Rice Filling
Desired fillings (such as small carrot, zucchini, or cucumber sticks; avocado slices; canned crabmeat; smoked salmon (lox style); and/or small cooked shrimp, peeled and deveined)
1 recipe Honey-Ginger Sauce

1 Lay nori on a sushi mat lined with plastic wrap; with damp fingers, spread 1 cup of the Sushi Rice Filling over each sheet to within 1 inch of one edge (see photo 1, below). Arrange desired fillings crosswise just off the center of the rice (see photo 2, below).

2 Roll nori toward the unfilled edge. (For a tight, even roll, place your hands under the edge of the mat closest to you. While carefully lifting the edge of the nori, roll it away from you.) Brush unfilled edge with water and seal to top of roll (see photo 3, below).

3 Cut each roll into six pieces; arrange on a platter. Serve with Honey-Ginger Sauce.

SUSHI RICE FILLING: In a fine-mesh sieve wash ½ cup short grain rice under running water, rubbing grains together with your fingers. In a small saucepan combine rice and ¾ cup cold water. Bring to boiling; reduce heat. Simmer, covered, for 15 minutes (rice should be sticky). Remove from heat. In a small bowl stir together 2 teaspoons rice vinegar, 1 teaspoon sugar, and ½ teaspoon salt. Stir vinegar mixture into rice in saucepan; cover and cool about 45 minutes or until room temperature.

HONEY-GINGER SAUCE: In a small saucepan combine ⅓ cup honey; ¼ cup water; 2 tablespoons plum sauce; 2 tablespoons soy sauce; and a 1- to 2-inch piece fresh ginger, peeled and thinly sliced. Bring to boiling, stirring frequently; reduce heat. Simmer, uncovered, for 15 to 20 minutes or until slightly thickened, stirring occasionally. Strain into a small bowl; cool. Cover and chill.

PER PIECE: 73 cal., 0 g total fat, 1 mg chol., 293 mg sodium, 17 g carb., 1 g fiber, 1 g pro. EXCHANGES: 1 Starch

SUSHI ROLLS STEP-BY-STEP

1. Press small handfuls of the sticky rice evenly over the nori. Dip your fingers in water to keep the rice from sticking to you.

2. Just off-center and opposite the unfilled edge of the nori, arrange the filling ingredients crosswise on rice.

3. Use the sushi mat to lift and roll the nori toward the unfilled edge. Roll as tightly as you can. Wet the edge of the nori with water for a good seal.

drinks

Here's how to make everything you drink—from your morning cup of joe to your favorite nightcap—more dashing and delicious.

JAVA JIVE

Most coffee lovers are quite particular about their brew. Key into these concepts to make it *your* way:

- The longer the beans are roasted, the darker they get. Choose light beans for lighter flavor, darker beans for stronger flavor.
- Ground coffee loses its freshness quickly, so it's best to purchase beans whole and grind them fresh each time you make coffee.
- Whole beans stay fresh about a week, so buy only what you'll need for the week. Store beans at room temperature in an airtight container.
- Follow manufacturer's guidelines for your coffee maker for fine or coarse grind. Coffee too coarsely ground can result in weak flavor; if it's too finely ground, it can taste bitter and clog the filter.

COFFEE-MAKING EQUIPMENT

Automatic drip coffeemakers and single-cup brewers are convenient, make reliably good coffee, and offer a plethora of options. But coffee lovers often prefer to use a manual coffee cone dripper or a French press. These let you control the temperature of the water used to brew the coffee. A few hints:

- For each 6-ounce cup, use ¾ cup fresh, cold water and 1 to 2 tablespoons ground coffee, depending on how strong you like your brew.
- For manual coffee cone drippers, bring water to a full boil. Take the kettle off the heat and pause for a moment before pouring the water into the coffee. Water just under boiling (195°F to 205°F) best releases coffee's flavorful compounds.
- To use a French press, measure coffee into the carafe. Heat water as for a manual drip maker. Pour water over coffee; place lid on carafe. Wait for 4 minutes; slowly press plunger to bottom of carafe to trap the grounds; serve.

TEA FOR YOU

Tea is available in bags or in loose-leaf form. Loose-leaf tea requires an infuser (such as a tea ball or spoon) or a strainer; bags do not.

HOT TEA: Use 1 bag or about 1 teaspoon loose-leaf tea per cup. Bring fresh, cool water to a full boil. If using loose-leaf tea, place it into an infuser. Warm the teapot by filling it with boiling water; let it stand a minute until pot is warmed. Empty the pot. Place infuser or tea bag(s) into the pot. (If not using an infuser or bag(s), place tea directly into pot.) Add more boiling water; cover pot and let steep for 3 to 5 minutes. Remove bag(s) or infuser and pour into teacup(s) or pour loose tea through a strainer into teacup(s).

TRADITIONAL ICED TEA: Using 4 cups of water and 4 to 8 teaspoons loose tea or 4 to 8 tea bags, prepare tea as above. Steep as directed; remove bags and let tea cool for 2 hours at room temperature. Serve over ice; refrigerate leftover tea.

REFRIGERATOR-BREWED TEA: Place 6 to 8 tea bags in 1½ quarts cold water; cover. Let "brew" in the refrigerator about 24 hours. Remove tea bags and serve tea over ice. In a hurry? Use instant tea or "cold brew" tea bags according to package directions.

A French press produces a richly textured coffee rife with natural oils. Some sediment will remain in the coffee—fans of the French press feel this adds character to the brew.

LOW-CALORIE

Iced Green Tea

PREP: 25 MINUTES **MAKES:** 12 SERVINGS

- **12 cups water**
- **1/4 to 1/2 cup sugar**
- **3 inches fresh ginger, peeled and thinly sliced**
- **12 green tea bags**
- **Ice cubes**

1 In a large saucepan combine water, sugar, and ginger. Bring to boiling; reduce heat. Simmer, covered, for 5 minutes. Remove from heat. Add tea bags; cover and let stand for 3 minutes. Remove and discard tea bags. Strain ginger from tea; discard ginger. Transfer tea to a 2-gallon pitcher or punch bowl. Cover; cool for several hours. If desired, chill. Serve tea in tall glasses over ice.

PER 8 OUNCES: 18 cal., 0 g total fat, 0 mg chol., 8 mg sodium, 5 g carb., 0 g fiber, 0 g pro. EXCHANGES: Free

POMEGRANATE ICED GREEN TEA: Prepare as directed, except stir one 15.2-ounce bottle (1 3/4 cups) pomegranate juice into the tea mixture after straining ginger from tea. Makes 14 servings.

PER 8 OUNCES: 32 cal., 0 g fat, 0 mg chol., 10 mg sodium, 8 carb., 0 g fiber, 0 g pro. EXCHANGES: 1/2 Other Carb.

FAST LOW-CALORIE

Chai

START TO FINISH: 15 MINUTES **MAKES:** 2 SERVINGS

- **1 cup water**
- **2 black tea bags, such as orange pekoe, English breakfast, Lapsang Souchong, or Darjeeling**
- **1 3-inch piece stick cinnamon**
- **1 cup milk**
- **2 tablespoons raw sugar, granulated sugar, or honey**
- **1 teaspoon vanilla**
- **1/4 teaspoon ground ginger**
- **1/8 teaspoon ground cardamom**

1 In a small saucepan combine water, tea bags, and cinnamon stick. Bring to boiling. Remove from heat. Cover and let stand for 5 minutes. Remove and discard tea bags and cinnamon stick.

2 Whisk the milk, sugar, vanilla, ginger, and cardamom into tea. Heat and stir over medium heat just until heated through (do not boil).

PER 8 OUNCES: 122 cal., 2 g total fat (2 g sat. fat), 10 mg chol., 55 mg sodium, 20 g carb., 1 g fiber, 4 g pro.
EXCHANGES: 1/2 Milk, 1 Other Carb., 1/2 Fat

BEST-LOVED FAST LOW-CALORIE

Mocha Coffee Cooler

START TO FINISH: 5 MINUTES **MAKES:** 4 SERVINGS

- **1 cup strong coffee, chilled**
- **1 cup half-and-half, light cream, or milk**
- **3 tablespoons chocolate-flavor syrup**
- **2 tablespoons sugar**
- **1 cup ice cubes**
- **Additional chocolate-flavor syrup (optional)**
- **Crushed chocolate-covered coffee beans (optional)**

1 In a blender combine coffee, half-and-half, chocolate syrup, and sugar. Cover and blend until combined. Add ice cubes; cover and blend until nearly smooth. If desired, drizzle chocolate syrup around insides of glasses. Pour coffee mixture into glasses. If desired, top with crushed coffee beans.

PER 7 OUNCES: 142 cal., 7 g total fat (4 g sat. fat), 22 mg chol., 36 mg sodium, 18 g carb., 0 g fiber, 2 g pro.
EXCHANGES: 1 Other Carb., 1 1/2 Fat

FAST LOW-CALORIE

Vanilla Café Latte

START TO FINISH: 10 MINUTES **MAKES:** 1 SERVING

- **1/4 cup hot espresso or hot strong coffee**
- **2 teaspoons vanilla beverage-flavoring syrup or 1 teaspoon sugar and 1/4 teaspoon vanilla**
- **2 to 3 tablespoons steamed milk**
- **2 tablespoons frothed milk***
- **Ground cinnamon or grated chocolate**

1 Pull the espresso or pour the coffee into a mug or cup. Stir in vanilla syrup. Add steamed milk and top with frothed milk. Sprinkle with cinnamon.

***NOTE:** To make frothed milk, use the steam wand on your espresso machine to steam and froth the milk. Or place hot, but not boiling, milk in a blender. Cover and blend until froth forms on top of the milk. Or place the hot milk in a deep bowl and use an immersion blender to blend the milk until froth forms on top.

PER 4 OUNCES: 55 cal., 1 g total fat (1 g sat. fat), 5 mg chol., 26 mg sodium, 9 g carb., 0 g fiber, 2 g pro.
EXCHANGES: 1/2 Other Carb.

BEST-LOVED

Eggnog

PREP: 15 MINUTES **CHILL:** 4 TO 24 HOURS
MAKES: 7 SERVINGS

- **4 egg yolks, lightly beaten**
- **2 cups milk**
- **⅓ cup sugar**
- **1 cup whipping cream**
- **2 tablespoons (1 ounce) light rum**
- **2 tablespoons (1 ounce) bourbon**
- **1 teaspoon vanilla**
- **Ground nutmeg**

1 In a large heavy saucepan stir together yolks, milk, and sugar (see photo 1, below). Cook and stir over medium heat until milk mixture just coats a metal spoon (see photo 2, below); do not let boil. Place pan in a sink or bowl of ice water; stir for 2 minutes. Stir in cream, rum, bourbon, and vanilla. Cover and chill for 4 to 24 hours. Serve in glasses. Sprinkle with nutmeg.

PER 4 OUNCES: 241 cal., 17 g total fat (10 g sat. fat), 172 mg chol., 46 mg sodium, 14 g carb., 0 g fiber, 5 g pro.
EXCHANGES: 1 Other Carb., ½ Lean Meat, 3½ Fat

LOWER-FAT EGGNOG: Prepare as directed, except omit whipping cream and use 3 cups milk.

PER 4 OUNCES: 141 cal., 5 g total fat (2 g sat. fat), 128 mg chol., 48 mg sodium, 15 g carb., 0 g fiber, 5 g pro.
EXCHANGES: 1 Other Carb., ½ Lean Meat, 1½ Fat

ALCOHOL-FREE EGGNOG: Prepare as directed, except omit the rum and bourbon and increase the milk to 2⅓ cups.

PER 4 OUNCES: 229 cal., 15 g total fat (10 g sat. fat), 173 mg chol., 51 mg sodium, 15 g carb., 0 g fiber, 5 g pro.
EXCHANGES: 1 Other Carb., ½ Lean Meat, 3 Fat

EGGNOG STEP-BY-STEP

1. Pour lightly beaten egg yolks into saucepan. Add the milk and sugar and use a whisk to combine them well.

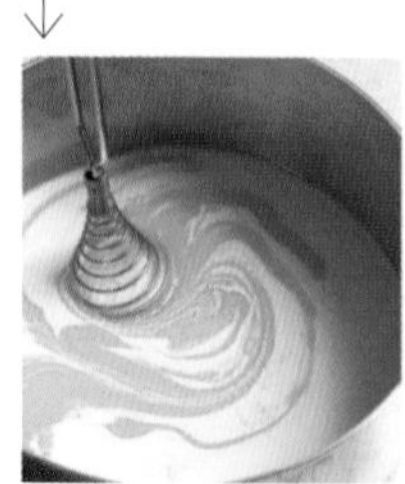

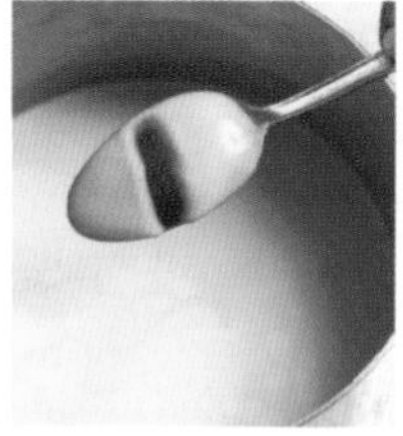

2. You are making a custard base for the eggnog. Cook and stir milk mixture over medium heat. It's ready when you can dip a spoon in it and swipe your finger across the back, leaving a line.

EGGNOG

FAST

Hot Chocolate Mix

START TO FINISH: 15 MINUTES
MAKES: 16 CUPS MIX (ENOUGH FOR 32 SERVINGS)

- **1 25.6-ounce package nonfat dry milk powder**
- **1 16-ounce jar powdered nondairy creamer**
- **1 8-ounce container unsweetened cocoa powder, sifted**
- **2 cups powdered sugar**
- **Tiny marshmallows (optional)**

1 In an extra-large bowl combine dry milk powder, nondairy creamer, cocoa powder, and powdered sugar. Store in a tightly covered container for up to 3 months.

2 For one serving, place ½ cup of the mix in a mug or cup and add ½ cup boiling water. If desired, top with marshmallows.

PER 6 OUNCES: 197 cal., 5 g total fat (4 g sat. fat), 4 mg chol., 126 mg sodium, 30 g carb., 2 g fiber, 9 g pro.
EXCHANGES: 1 Milk, 1 Other Carb., 1 Fat

MALTED HOT CHOCOLATE MIX: Prepare as directed, except add one 13-ounce jar malted milk powder to the dry mix. Makes about 18 cups mix (enough for 36 servings).

PER 6 OUNCES: 219 cal., 5 g total fat (4 g sat. fat), 6 mg chol., 154 mg sodium, 34 g carb., 2 g fiber, 10 g pro.
EXCHANGES: 1 Milk, 1½ Other Carb., 1 Fat

FAST

Hot Chocolate

START TO FINISH: 15 MINUTES **MAKES:** 6 SERVINGS

- **2 ounces semisweet chocolate, coarsely chopped, or 1/3 cup semisweet chocolate pieces**
- **1/3 cup sugar**
- **4 cups milk**
- **1 tablespoon instant coffee crystals (optional)**
- **Whipped cream or tiny marshmallows (optional)**

1 In a medium saucepan combine chocolate, sugar, and 1/2 cup of the milk. Cook and stir over medium heat until mixture comes just to boiling. Stir in remaining milk and, if desired, coffee crystals; heat through but do not boil. Remove from heat.

2 If desired, beat mixture with an immersion blender or wire whisk until frothy. Serve in mugs. If desired, top with whipped cream.

PER 6 OUNCES: 170 cal., 6 g total fat (4 g sat. fat), 13 mg chol., 68 mg sodium, 25 g carb., 1 g fiber, 6 g pro.
EXCHANGES: 1/2 Milk, 1 Other Carb., 1 Fat

BEST-LOVED FAST

White Hot Chocolate *(photo, page 35)*

START TO FINISH: 20 MINUTES **MAKES:** 4 SERVINGS

- **3 ounces white baking chocolate with cocoa butter, chopped**
- **2 cups milk, half-and-half, or light cream**
- **1/3 cup hot strong coffee**
- **1/2 teaspoon vanilla**
- **Grated nutmeg or chocolate-flavor sprinkles (optional)**
- **Grated white and/or dark chocolate**

1 In a medium saucepan combine white chocolate and 1/3 cup of the milk. Cook and stir over low heat until chocolate melts. Add remaining milk. Stir until heated through. Add coffee and vanilla. Serve in mugs. If desired, sprinkle with nutmeg and grated chocolate.

PER 5 1/2 OUNCES: 184 cal., 9 g total fat (6 g sat. fat), 14 mg chol., 73 mg sodium, 18 g carb., 0 g fiber, 6 g pro.
EXCHANGES: 1/2 Milk, 1/2 Other Carb., 1 1/2 Fat

BEST-LOVED FAST LOW-CALORIE

Hot Spiced Cider

START TO FINISH: 20 MINUTES **MAKES:** 8 SERVINGS

- **8 cups apple cider or apple juice**
- **1/4 cup packed brown sugar**
- **6 inches stick cinnamon**
- **1 teaspoon whole allspice**
- **1 teaspoon whole cloves**
- **2 3×3/4-inch strips orange peel**
- **8 orange wedges (optional)**

1 In a large saucepan combine cider and brown sugar. For spice bag, place cinnamon stick, allspice, cloves, and orange peel in the center of a double-thick, 6-inch square of 100% cotton cheesecloth (see photo 1, below). Tie closed with clean cotton kitchen string (see photo 2, below). Add bag to the saucepan. Bring to boiling; reduce heat. Simmer, covered, for 10 minutes. Remove and discard spice bag. Serve cider in mugs. If desired, garnish with orange wedges.

PER 8 OUNCES: 143 cal., 0 g total fat, 0 mg chol., 13 mg sodium, 35 g carb., 1 g fiber, 0 g pro. EXCHANGES: 2 Other Carb.

MAKING A SPICE BAG STEP-BY-STEP

1. Layer two 6-inch squares of cheesecloth on a work surface. Pile the stick cinnamon, allspice, cloves, and orange peel in the middle of the cheesecloth.

2. Gather the edges of the cheesecloth up around the spices to make a bundle. Tie the bundle closed with cotton kitchen string.

8 to try

FAST LOW-CALORIE

Basic Smoothie

This Basic Smoothie is a simple starting place to create an array of sipping treats. If you use frozen fruit, you might not need as much ice for creamy, cold results.

START TO FINISH: 10 MINUTES
MAKES: 2 SERVINGS

- **⅔ cup plain yogurt**
- **½ cup orange juice or orange juice blend**
- **2 tablespoons honey or sugar**
- **¼ teaspoon vanilla**
- **1 cup small ice cubes or crushed ice**

1 In a blender combine yogurt, orange juice, honey, vanilla, and ice cubes. Cover and blend until nearly smooth. Serve in tall glasses and garnish as desired.

PER 8 OUNCES: 147 cal., 1 g total fat (1 g sat. fat), 5 mg chol., 61 mg sodium, 30 g carb., 0 g fiber, 5 g pro. EXCHANGES: ½ Milk, 1½ Other Carb.

SMOOTHIE SAVVY

You can do more than change up the fruit and juice in your smoothie.

1 To bump up the fiber and make your smoothie more healthful, add 1 or 2 tablespoons chia seeds, flaxseeds, or unsalted pumpkin seeds (pepitas). The pepitas add a nice chewy dimension to the smoothie, too, because they don't get completely ground up.
2 Opt for Greek yogurt instead of regular yogurt. It's thicker, so it adds more body to the smoothie. It also contributes a lot more protein.
3 Spice it up with a little ground cinnamon, unsweetened cocoa powder, ground ginger, or vanilla.

BANANA-BLUEBERRY: Substitute blueberry yogurt for the plain yogurt; add half a ripe banana and ½ cup fresh or frozen blueberries.

MANGO: Add ½ cup chopped fresh or frozen mango.

MOCHA: Substitute coffee-flavor yogurt for the plain yogurt, milk for the orange juice, and chocolate-flavor syrup for the honey.

BERRY: Add ½ cup halved fresh strawberries or fresh raspberries.

ORANGE DREAM: Substitute orange yogurt for the plain yogurt and add ½ cup mandarin orange sections.

PEANUT BUTTER-BANANA: Substitute vanilla yogurt for the plain yogurt and milk for the orange juice; add half a ripe banana and 2 tablespoons creamy peanut butter.

PEACH: Add 1 cup frozen peach slices and omit the ice.

POMEGRANATE: Substitute pomegranate juice for the orange juice.

BEST-LOVED FAST

Milk Shakes

START TO FINISH: 5 MINUTES **MAKES:** 2 SERVINGS

- **1 pint vanilla ice cream**
- **½ to ¾ cup milk**
- **2 tablespoons malted milk powder (optional)**

1 In a blender combine ice cream, milk, and, if desired, malted milk powder. Cover and blend until smooth.

PER 8 OUNCES: 329 cal., 17 g total fat (11 g sat. fat), 68 mg chol., 140 mg sodium, 37 g carb., 1 g fiber, 7 g pro.
EXCHANGES: 1 Milk, 1½ Other Carb., 3 Fat

FRUITY MILK SHAKES: Prepare as directed, except add 2 cups sliced fresh or frozen fruit, such as peeled peaches, strawberries, mango, and/or whole blueberries. Omit the malted milk powder. Makes 3 servings.

PER 8 OUNCES: 259 cal., 12 g total fat (7 g sat. fat), 45 mg chol., 93 mg sodium, 34 g carb., 2 g fiber, 6 g pro.
EXCHANGES: ½ Fruit, ½ Milk, 1½ Other Carb., 2 Fat

PEANUT BUTTER-BANANA SHAKES: Prepare as directed, except increase milk to 1 cup and add 1 medium ripe banana, sliced, and 3 tablespoons creamy peanut butter with the milk. If desired, substitute chocolate ice cream for the vanilla ice cream. To make a malt, use chocolate malted milk powder rather than plain. Makes 3 servings.

PER 8 OUNCES: 368 cal., 20 g total fat (9 g sat. fat), 49 mg chol., 184 mg sodium, 39 g carb., 3 g fiber, 10 g pro.
EXCHANGES: ½ Fruit, 1 Milk, 1½ Other Carb., 4 Fat

FAST

Lemonade

START TO FINISH: 20 MINUTES **MAKES:** 4 SERVINGS

- **3 cups cold water**
- **1 cup lemon juice (5 to 6 lemons)**
- **¾ cup sugar**
- **Lemon slices**

1 In a 1½-quart pitcher stir together the water, lemon juice, and sugar until sugar dissolves. If desired, chill in the refrigerator. Serve in glasses over *ice*. Garnish with lemon slices.

RASPBERRY LEMONADE: Prepare as directed, except add puree: Place 1 cup fresh raspberries in a blender or food processor; cover and blend or process until pureed. Press mixture through a fine-mesh sieve; discard seeds. Add strained puree to pitcher. If desired, add additional sugar. Garnish with fresh raspberries.

PER 8 OUNCES PLAIN OR RASPBERRY VARIATION: 163 cal., 0 g total fat, 0 mg chol., 6 mg sodium, 44 g carb., 1 g fiber, 0 g pro. EXCHANGES: 3 Other Carb.

FAST LOW-CALORIE

Watermelon Agua Fresca *(photo, page 35)*

START TO FINISH: 25 MINUTES **MAKES:** 8 SERVINGS

- **1 6- to 8-pound seedless watermelon**
- **2 cups cold water**
- **2 tablespoons lime juice**
- **2 tablespoons honey**
- **Ice cubes**
- **Watermelon wedges (optional)**
- **Lime wedges (optional)**
- **Honey (optional)**

1 Cut the rind from the whole watermelon; discard rind. Cut the flesh into 2-inch cubes (13 cups).

2 In a blender combine about one-third of the watermelon cubes and ⅔ cup of the water. Cover and blend until smooth. Strain through a fine-mesh sieve into a large pitcher or large glass jar; discard solids. Repeat twice, using remaining watermelon and water.

3 Stir lime juice and the 2 tablespoons honey into strained watermelon mixture. Serve in ice-filled glasses. If desired, garnish with watermelon wedges or lime wedges and drizzle with additional honey.

PER 8 OUNCES: 70 cal., 0 g total fat, 0 mg chol., 4 mg sodium, 18 g carb., 1 g fiber, 1 g pro. EXCHANGES: 1 Fruit

FLAVORED WATERS

Bottled water is available in an array of flavors, but it's easy to create your own. Add fresh herbs or pieces of fruit to plain water or carbonated water for fresh flavor. **FOR FRUIT- AND HERB-INFUSED WATER:** Place a cup of sliced fruit and herbs (any combo) in a quart jar. Crush the fruit and herbs lightly and fill the jar with water. Cover and chill to let flavors infuse. If desired, strain the fruit from the water or simply put a straw in the jar. **FLAVOR COMBOS:** strawberry-basil, cherry-lime, orange-lemon-lime, strawberry-orange, pomegranate-blueberry, ginger-lime, watermelon-mint

↑

THE SHAKE
The shaker is imperative to margs on the rocks and ranges in size from small (8 ounces) to large (28 ounces). Fill your shaker with the ice to chill the container; add the juice and liquor. Cover and shake VIGOROUSLY about 10 seconds. 1 Mississippi, 2 Mississippi . . .

RIM IT
Whether you serve your margarita on the rocks or blended, rimming the edge of the glass finishes the drink. Use lime wedges to wet the glass edge. Then dip the rim in coarse salt in a pie plate or other shallow dish.

↓

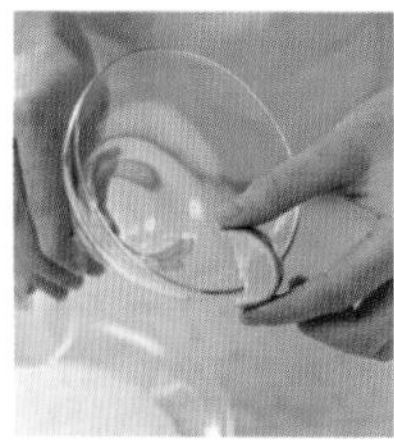

FAST

margaritas

The Secret: Whether you prefer your margarita blended or on the rocks, we have a perfect formula for you.

START TO FINISH: 5 MINUTES **MAKES:** 2 SERVINGS

2 parts tequila, 1 part lime juice, 1 part orange liqueur

- **Lime wedge**
- **Coarse salt**
- **1 cup ice cubes**
- **½ cup (4 ounces) silver or gold tequila**
- **¼ cup (2 ounces) lime juice**
- **¼ cup (2 ounces) orange liqueur**
- **Ice cubes**
- **Lime wedges or slices**

1 Rub the lime wedge around the rims of two 6- to 8-ounce rocks glasses. Dip the rims into a dish of coarse salt to coat; set aside. Add ice cubes to cocktail shaker; combine tequila, lime juice, and orange liqueur. Add to shaker; cover and shake until very cold. Strain liquid into prepared glasses filled with additional ice. Garnish with lime wedges.

Frozen limeade concentrate and the correct amount of ice are KEY.

PER 4 OUNCES: 216 cal., 0 g total fat, 0 mg chol., 586 mg sodium, 13 g carb., 0 g fiber, 0 g pro.
EXCHANGES: ½ Starch, 4 Fat

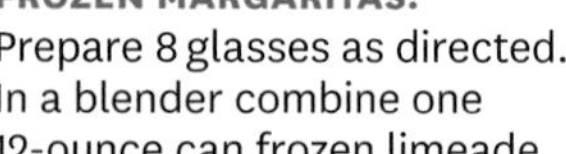

FROZEN MARGARITAS: Prepare 8 glasses as directed. In a blender combine one 12-ounce can frozen limeade concentrate, ⅔ cup silver or gold tequila, and ½ cup orange liqueur. Cover and blend until combined. With blender running, add 4 cups ices cubes, 1 cup at a time, blending until mixture becomes slushy. Pour into prepared glasses. Makes 8 servings.

PER 4 OUNCES: 188 cal., 0 g total fat, 0 mg chol., 585 mg sodium, 32 g carb., 0g fiber, 0 g pro.
EXCHANGES: 2 Starch, 1 Fat

LIME MATH: For the best flavor, fresh lime juice is hard to top. A medium lime should yield 2 tablespoons juice and about 1½ teaspoons finely shredded lime peel.

BIG BATCH

Make it easy! If you're entertaining a crowd and go for margaritas on the rocks, multiply the basic recipe by 4 and chill. Don't add ice to your pitcher—instead, pour mixture into ice-filled glasses to serve.

ORANGE LIQUEUR

The classic margarita includes an orange liqueur. Use any of the three shown above.

GRAND MARNIER: A cognac that adds a little more sweetness.

COINTREAU: A French Triple Sec using sour and sweet orange peels.

TRIPLE SEC: Meaning “triple distilled,” a clear strong liqueur made with Curaçao orange peels.

TEQUILA

GOLD TEQUILA: May be an aged tequila or an unaged silver tequila that has been flavored and colored with caramel. Bottom line—smoother and sweeter margarita.

SILVER TEQUILA: A clear spirit that may be 100% agave or a blend of agave and other spirits *(mixto)*. Aged for zero to 60 days, it’s cheaper and used for blending in drinks.

SPARKLING GOLDEN SANGRIA

Sparkling Golden Sangria

PREP: 20 MINUTES **CHILL:** 1 TO 24 HOURS
MAKES: 8 SERVINGS

- **3 cups white grape juice, chilled**
- **½ cup (4 ounces) orange liqueur**
- **¼ cup superfine or granulated sugar**
- **3 tablespoons honey**
- **1 medium nectarine, pitted and sliced**
- **1 navel orange, halved and thinly sliced**
- **¾ cup fresh or frozen sweet cherries, pitted and halved, or canned mandarin orange sections, drained**
- **¾ cup fresh golden or red raspberries**
- **½ cup fresh basil leaves**
- **½ cup fresh mint leaves**
- **1 750-milliliter bottle sparkling white wine, chilled**

1 In a large pitcher or glass jar combine grape juice, orange liqueur, sugar, and honey, stirring until sugar and honey dissolve. Stir in nectarine, orange, cherries, raspberries, basil, and mint. Chill for 1 hour or up to 24 hours, stirring occasionally. Just before serving, add sparkling wine to fruit mixture. Serve in glasses over *ice*.

PER 1¼ CUPS: 248 cal., 0 g total fat, 0 mg chol., 10 mg sodium, 43 g carb., 2 g fiber, 1 g pro. EXCHANGES: 1½ Fruit, 1 Other Carb., 2 Fat

NONALCOHOLIC SPARKLING SANGRIA: Prepare as directed, except substitute orange juice for the orange liqueur and sparkling water or club soda for the sparkling white wine.

PER 1¼ CUPS: 148 cal., 0 g total fat, 0 mg chol., 10 mg sodium, 37 g carb., 2 g fiber, 1 g pro. EXCHANGES: 1½ Fruit, 1 Starch

Sweet Cherry Sangria

PREP: 20 MINUTES **CHILL:** 4 TO 24 HOURS
MAKES: 8 TO 10 SERVINGS

- **1 750-milliliter bottle red wine, such as Beaujolais or Zinfandel**
- **4 cups freshly squeezed orange juice (about 12 oranges)**
- **1½ cups fresh dark sweet cherries, pitted and halved**
- **¾ cup (6 ounces) cherry beverage-flavoring syrup**
- **½ cup (4 ounces) orange liqueur**

1 In a large pitcher stir together wine, orange juice, cherries, cherry flavoring syrup, and orange liqueur. Cover and chill for 4 to 24 hours to blend flavors. Serve in glasses over *ice*.

PER 8 OUNCES: 274 cal., 0 g total fat, 0 mg chol., 13 mg sodium, 45 g carb., 1 g fiber, 1 g pro. EXCHANGES: 3 Other Carb., 2 Fat

BEST-LOVED FAST

Summer Fruit Daiquiries

START TO FINISH: 15 MINUTES
MAKES: 6 TO 8 SERVINGS

- **3 cups fresh or frozen peeled peach slices, thawed; fresh or frozen strawberries, thawed; fresh or frozen cubed mango, thawed; or cubed, seeded watermelon**
- **½ of a 12-ounce can (¾ cup) frozen limeade or lemonade concentrate, thawed**
- **¼ cup (2 ounces) light rum or orange juice**
- **2 tablespoons powdered sugar**
- **2 to 3 cups ice cubes**
- **Fresh peach chunks, small fresh strawberries, mango cubes, or watermelon cubes (optional)**

1 In a blender combine the 3 cups fruit, the limeade concentrate, rum, and powdered sugar. Cover and blend until smooth. With blender running, gradually add ice cubes through opening in lid until mixture is desired thickness. Serve in glasses. If desired, garnish with fruit pieces threaded on wooden skewers.

PER 4 TO 5 OUNCES: 131 cal., 0 g total fat, 0 mg chol., 0 mg sodium, 28 g carb., 1 g fiber, 1 g pro. EXCHANGES: ½ Fruit, 1½ Other Carb., ½ Fat

EIGHT POPULAR WINES

Pair these eight easy-to-find wines with our tasty food suggestions.

REDS

CABERNET SAUVIGNON: Bold and full, with cassis, black cherry, and sometimes cedarlike flavors. Pair with grilled and broiled steaks and lamb.

MERLOT: A soft and fruity wine, often less mouth-drying (tannic) than Cabernet Sauvignon. Try with beef, pork, burgers, red-sauced pasta, and pizza.

PINOT NOIR: A silky, elegant wine with bright, red-fruit flavors and sometimes earthy, smoky notes. Enjoy with salmon, poultry, and meat dishes, especially those featuring mushrooms.

SHIRAZ/SYRAH: Full-bodied, with vivid plum and black-fruit flavors and often smoky, spicy notes. Pair with lamb, pizza, burgers, and barbecue.

WHITES

CHARDONNAY: Exhibits pear, apple, and/or tropical fruit notes. Some are rich and buttery, sometimes with strong oak nuances. Enjoy with creamy pasta, seafood, and roast chicken.

PINOT GRIGIO: Light bodied, with mild peach and citrus notes. Try with light fish and chicken dishes.

RIESLING: Bright and fruity, ranges from sweet to dry and often has floral, peach, and citrus tones. Pair with pork, ham, chicken, and spicy foods.

SAUVIGNON BLANC: Bright and citrusy, often with grassy or herblike aromas. Enjoy with chicken and fish flavored with tomatoes, herbs, and/or feta cheese.

make it mine

Party Punch

One beautiful punch and ice decorations let you wow a crowd.

PREP: 15 MINUTES **CHILL:** 4 HOURS
MAKES: 16 TO 18 SERVINGS (ABOUT 8 OUNCES EACH)

- **4 cups water**
- **1 12-ounce can FROZEN JUICE CONCENTRATE, thawed**
- **1 cup sugar**
- **2½ cups JUICE BLEND, chilled**
- **1 2-liter bottle CARBONATED BEVERAGE, chilled**
- **Ice Cups, Ice Ring, or ice cubes**
- **1 cup STIR-IN (optional)**

1 In a large pitcher or bowl combine the water and desired Frozen Juice Concentrate. Add sugar; stir until dissolved. Cover and chill at least 4 hours.

2 To serve, pour juice mixture into a very large punch bowl. Stir in Juice Blend. Slowly stir in Carbonated Beverage. Add Ice Cups and, if desired, Stir-In.

ICE CUPS: Place 12 silicone cupcake cups on a large rimmed baking pan. Place whole or sliced fruit, fresh herb leaves, and thin citrus slices in cups. Pour club soda or lemon-lime carbonated beverage around fruit to fill cups. (Leave some fruit sticking out.) Freeze several hours or until firm. To unmold, peel molds off of ice cups. Transfer desired number of ice cups to the punch bowl. Place any remaining ice cups in a large resealable plastic bag; seal. Store in the freezer until ready to use.

ICE RING: Place 2 to 3 cups whole or sliced fruit, fresh mint leaves, and citrus peel curls in a fluted tube pan. Fill and freeze as directed for Ice Cups. To unmold, dip bottom of the pan in warm water for a few seconds. Invert over a large plate, tapping on bottom of pan to release the ring. Place in punch bowl.

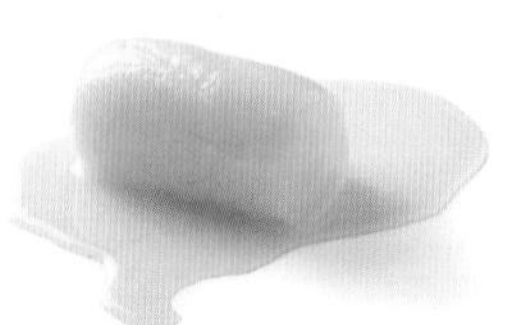

FROZEN JUICE CONCENTRATE *(pick one)*

Cranberry
Lemonade
Limeade
Orange
Pineapple

JUICE BLEND *(pick one)*

Cranberry-apple
Pineapple-orange-banana
Pink grapefruit
Pomegranate
Raspberry
Strawberry

CARBONATED BEVERAGE *(pick one)*

Cream soda
Ginger ale
Lemon-lime carbonated beverage
Orange carbonated beverage
Strawberry carbonated beverage

STIR-IN *(pick one)*

Citrus fruit slices
Kiwifruit slices
Rum, vodka, gin, bourbon, or tequila
Sherbet or sorbet
Sliced fresh strawberries

FAST

Mojito

START TO FINISH: 10 MINUTES **MAKES:** 1 SERVING

- **8 large or 10 to 12 small fresh mint leaves**
- **1 tablespoon fresh lime juice**
- **2 to 3 teaspoons superfine sugar**
- **Ice cubes**
- **3 tablespoons light rum**
- **½ cup club soda, chilled**
- **1 sugarcane stalk (optional)**
- **1 lime wedge**
- **1 to 2 mint sprigs (optional)**

1 In a tall glass combine mint leaves, lime juice, and sugar. Use a muddler or the back of a spoon to crush mint against the side of the glass until the mint is pulverized and sugar dissolves.

2 Fill glass three-quarters full with ice. Add rum and top with club soda. If desired, stir with a sugarcane stalk, swizzle stick, or cocktail spoon to combine. Squeeze and drop in lime wedge; stir again. If desired, garnish with mint sprigs.

PER 6 OUNCES: 140 cal., 0 g fat, 0 mg chol., 29 mg sodium, 12 g carb., 1 g fiber, 0 g pro. EXCHANGES: ½ Other Carb., 2 Fat

FAST

Piña Colada

START TO FINISH: 10 MINUTES **MAKES:** 4 SERVINGS

- **½ cup (4 ounces) cream of coconut**
- **1 8-ounce can crushed pineapple (juice pack), undrained**
- **⅓ cup (about 3 ounces) dark or light rum**
- **1 tablespoon lemon or lime juice**
- **4 cups ice cubes**

1 In a blender combine cream of coconut, pineapple, rum, and lemon juice. Cover and blend until smooth. With blender running, gradually add ice cubes through opening in lid until smooth. Serve in glasses.

PER 8 OUNCES: 210 cal., 6 g fat (6 g sat. fat), 0 mg chol., 14 mg sodium, 29 g carb., 1 g fiber, 1 g pro.
EXCHANGES: 2 Other Carb., 2 Fat

THE MUDDLER

The Mojito gets its characteristic minty flavor from muddling fresh mint leaves. Muddlers are often shaped like a bat with a flat end that is used to press herbs to release their oils. Make a few gentle twists with the muddler to soften and bruise the leaves. If you don't have a muddler, use the handle of a wooden spoon.

classic cocktails

Sidecar

If desired, wet the rim of a chilled glass with water. Dip the rim into a dish of superfine sugar to coat; set aside. In a cocktail shaker combine 1/4 cup (2 ounces) brandy, 2 tablespoons (1 ounce) lemon juice, and 2 tablespoons (1 ounce) orange liqueur. Add ice cubes; cover and shake until very cold. Strain liquid into prepared glass or a glass filled with additional ice cubes. Garnish with a lemon peel twist. Makes 1 serving.

PER SERVING: 234 cal., 0 g total fat, 0 mg chol., 1 mg sodium, 12 g carb., 0 g fiber, 0 g pro. **EXCHANGES:** 1/2 Starch, 4 Fat

Martini

Thread 2 olives on a cocktail pick; set aside. In a cocktail shaker combine 1/4 cup (2 ounces) gin or vodka and 1 1/2 teaspoon (1/4 ounce) dry vermouth. Add ice cubes; cover and shake until very cold. Strain liquid into a martini glass. Garnish with olives and/or a lemon twist. Makes 1 serving.

PER SERVING: 145 cal., 1 g total fat (0 sat. fat), 0 mg chol., 85 mg sodium, 1 g carb., 0 g fiber, 0 g pro. **EXCHANGES:** 3 Fat

Vodka Gimlet

In a cocktail shaker combine 3 tablespoons (1 1/2 ounces) vodka or gin and 1 tablespoon (1/2 ounce) lime juice. Add ice cubes; cover and shake until very cold. Strain liquid into an ice-filled glass. If desired, garnish with lime slices. Makes 1 serving.

PER SERVING: 98 cal., 0 g total fat, 0 mg chol., 0 mg sodium, 1 g carb., 0 g fiber, 0 g pro. **EXCHANGES:** 2 Fat

Whiskey Sour

In a rocks glass combine 1/4 cup (2 ounces) bourbon, 2 tablespoons (1 ounce) lime juice, 2 tablespoons (1 ounce) lemon juice, and 1 tablespoon sugar. Stir until sugar dissolves. Add ice cubes. If desired, garnish with an orange slice and a maraschino cherry. Makes 1 serving.

PER SERVING: 205 cal., 0 g total fat, 0 mg chol., 1 mg sodium, 17 g carb., 0 g fiber, 0 g pro. **EXCHANGES:** 1 Carb., 3 Fat

Cosmopolitan

In a cocktail shaker combine 1/4 cup (2 ounces) vodka, 2 tablespoons (1 ounce) orange liqueur, 2 tablespoons (1 ounce) cranberry juice, and 1 tablespoon (1/2 ounce) lime juice. Add ice cubes; cover and shake until very cold. Strain liquid into a chilled glass. If desired, garnish with lime peel twist. Makes 1 serving.

PER SERVING: 232 cal., 0 g total fat, 0 mg chol., 1 mg sodium, 15 g carb., 0 g fiber, 0 g pro. **EXCHANGES:** 1 Other Carb., 3 1/2 Fat

Manhattan

In a cocktail shaker combine 1/4 cup (2 ounces) bourbon, 1 tablespoon (1/2 ounce) vermouth, and a dash bitters. Add ice cubes; cover and shake until very cold. Strain liquid into a chilled glass or an ice-filled glass. Garnish with a maraschino cherry. Makes 1 serving.

PER SERVING: 163 cal., 0 g total fat, 0 mg chol., 5 mg sodium, 5 g carb., 0 g fiber, 0 g pro. **EXCHANGES:** 2 1/2 Fat

beans, rice & grains

beans, rice & grains

Learn how these hearty ingredients can bring texture, flavor, and more nutrition to your diet.

BEAN TALK

High in fiber and phytonutrients and low in fat and saturated fat, beans and other legumes are inexpensive, easy-to-enjoy superfoods. Beans are a good source of vitamins and minerals.

STORING BEANS: Placed in an airtight container in a cool, dry, dark place, beans can be stored up to 1 year. However, the older they are, the longer they need to cook. For this reason, do not combine new packages of beans with older.

A RICE PRIMER

Here's a sampling of the rice varieties that will go with almost anything you serve.

ARBORIO RICE: As it cooks, this short grain white rice releases starch, creating a creamy texture. It's often used for making risotto.

AROMATIC RICE: Great for adding fragrance to meals, varieties include basmati, jasmine, and Texmati. Aromas range from flowers and nuts to popped corn.

BROWN RICE: Pleasantly chewy and nutlike in flavor, this rice retains the bran around the rice kernel. The longer cooking time pays off in nutritious goodness.

CONVERTED RICE: Also referred to as parboiled rice, this rice has been steamed, pressure-cooked, and dried before packaging. The process helps the nutrients stay within the grain and reduces surface starch, which keeps the rice from sticking together and helps retain a firm texture while cooking.

INSTANT AND QUICK-COOKING RICE: These are partially or fully cooked and dried before packaging, giving the rice a short cooking time.

WHITE RICE: White rice has had the bran and germ removed and is available in short, medium, and long grain varieties. The shorter the grain, the more likely the rice will stick together when cooked.

WILD RICE: Actually a marsh grass, not a grain, wild rice has a nutty flavor.

WHOLE GRAIN GOODNESS

Grains that have not been refined are known as whole grains. Because they have not had the germ and bran removed, whole grains retain more nutrients than refined grains. They are especially good sources of fiber, which research suggests can reduce the risk of heart disease and help maintain a healthy weight. To integrate whole grains into your diet, reach for brown rice as well as these and other whole grains.

BARLEY: Pleasantly chewy and mild in flavor, barley is one of the oldest grains and one of the richest sources of soluble and insoluble fiber.

BULGUR: These are wheat kernels that have been boiled, dried, and cracked. With a tender, chewy texture and earthy flavor, bulgur is very high in fiber and rich in iron, phosphorus, zinc, manganese, selenium, and magnesium.

FARRO: Nutty and chewy, this Italian staple is high in protein and fiber. Semi-pearled and pearled farro cook faster than the whole grain.

MILLET: Cook and use this tiny grain like rice or use in baked goods. It's a good source of manganese, magnesium, and phosphorus.

QUINOA: Containing more protein than any other grain, quinoa is slightly chewy with a light, delicate flavor and texture.

SPELT: A distant cousin of wheat, spelt has a richer flavor, more of many nutrients, and higher protein content than wheat.

WHEAT BERRIES: These whole, unprocessed kernels of wheat are slightly sweet and have a nutty flavor and pleasantly chewy texture.

beans, rice & grains guide

Good value, good nutrition, long shelf life—no wonder these ingredients endure as cornerstones to many satisfying meals.

BEANS, PEAS, AND LENTILS

Black beans · Black-eyed peas · Cranberry beans

Fava beans (broad beans) · Garbanzo beans (chickpeas) · Great Northern beans

Lima beans, baby · Lima beans, Christmas (calico) · Lima beans, large (butter beans)

Navy or pea beans · Pinto beans · Red beans

Red kidney beans · Soybeans (dried) · Soybeans (edamame —fresh green sweet)

Green split peas · Yellow split peas · Brown lentils

French lentils · Red lentils · Yellow lentils

RICE

Arborio rice · Basmati rice · Regular brown rice

Instant white rice · Long grain white rice · Wild rice

GRAINS

Barley, pearl · Buckwheat groats · Bulgur

Cracked wheat · Farina · Farro

Hominy grits · Millet · Oats (rolled, regular)

Oats (steel-cut) · Quinoa · Spelt

Wheat berries · Wheat bran · Wheat germ (toasted)

CUBAN RED BEANS AND RICE

LOW-CALORIE

Cuban Red Beans and Rice

START TO FINISH: 35 MINUTES
MAKES: 4 MAIN-DISH SERVINGS

- **1 large sweet onion, cut into thin wedges**
- **1 cup chopped green or red sweet pepper (1 large)**
- **4 cloves garlic, minced**
- **1 tablespoon canola oil**
- **½ cup snipped fresh cilantro**
- **½ teaspoon dried oregano, crushed**
- **½ teaspoon ground cumin**
- **¼ teaspoon black pepper**
- **2 15- to 16-ounce cans pinto beans and/or red kidney beans, rinsed and drained**
- **1 cup vegetable broth**
- **¼ cup lime juice**
- **2 cups hot cooked brown rice**
- **Lime wedges and/or small hot chile peppers (see tip, page 44) (optional)**

1 In a large saucepan cook onion, sweet pepper, and garlic in hot oil over medium heat for 5 to 7 minutes or until tender, stirring occasionally. Add ¼ cup of the cilantro, the oregano, cumin, and black pepper. Cook and stir for 1 minute.

2 Add beans and broth. Bring to boiling; reduce heat. Simmer, uncovered, for 15 to 20 minutes or until liquid is thickened to desired consistency. Stir in the lime juice. Prepare rice according to package directions. Serve beans over rice and sprinkle with the remaining cilantro. If desired, serve with lime wedges and/or hot chile peppers.

PER 1 CUP + ½ CUP RICE: 369 cal., 6 g total fat (1 g sat. fat), 0 mg chol., 933 mg sodium, 67 g carb., 13 g fiber, 17 g pro.
EXCHANGES: ½ Vegetable, 4½ Starch, ½ Lean Meat

Classic Baked Beans

PREP: 20 MINUTES **BAKE:** 45 MINUTES AT 350°F
MAKES: 8 SIDE-DISH SERVINGS

- **6 slices bacon**
- **½ cup chopped onion**
- **1 15- to 16-ounce can butter beans, rinsed and drained**
- **1 15- to 16-ounce can pork and beans in tomato sauce**
- **1 15- to 16-ounce can kidney or pinto beans, rinsed and drained**
- **½ cup packed brown sugar**
- **⅓ cup ketchup**
- **2 tablespoons Worcestershire sauce**

1 Preheat oven to 350°F. In a very large skillet cook bacon over medium heat until crisp. Drain on paper towels, reserving 2 tablespoons drippings in skillet. Crumble bacon and set aside. Add onion to reserved drippings; cook and stir over medium heat about 4 minutes or until onion is tender.

2 In a 2-quart casserole combine butter beans, pork and beans in tomato sauce, kidney beans, brown sugar, ketchup, and Worcestershire sauce. Stir in the bacon and onion mixture. Bake, covered, about 45 minutes or until bubbly around the edges.

SLOW COOKER DIRECTIONS: Double the recipe ingredients. Prepare bacon and onion as directed. In a 4- to 5-quart slow cooker combine beans, brown sugar, ketchup, and Worcestershire sauce. Stir in bacon and onion mixture. Cover and cook on low-heat setting for 5 to 6 hours or on high-heat setting for 2½ to 3 hours.

PER 1 CUP: 259 cal., 6 g total fat, (2 g sat. fat), 13 mg chol., 788 mg sodium, 42 g carb., 7 g fiber, 10 g pro.
EXCHANGES: 1½ Starch, 1 Other Carb., 1 Lean Meat, ½ Fat

baked beans with bacon

The Secret: Adding traditional, flavorful baked bean ingredients (think molasses and brown sugar) AFTER the beans are cooked to a tender bite makes all the difference.

PREP: 30 MINUTES **STAND:** 60 MINUTES **COOK:** 60 MINUTES
BAKE: 90 MINUTES AT 300°F **MAKES:** 10 SIDE-DISH SERVINGS

- **1 pound dried navy beans or Great Northern beans (2⅓ cups)**
- **16 cups water**
- **4 ounces bacon or pancetta, chopped**
- **1 cup chopped onion (1 large)**
- **¼ cup packed brown sugar**
- **⅓ cup molasses or pure maple syrup**
- **¼ cup Worcestershire sauce**
- **1½ teaspoons dry mustard**
- **½ teaspoon salt**
- **¼ teaspoon black pepper**
- **4 ounces bacon or pancetta, chopped, crisp-cooked, drained, and crumbled (optional)**

1 Sort through and rinse beans. In a 4- to 5-quart oven-going Dutch oven combine beans and 8 cups of the water. Bring to boiling; reduce heat. Simmer, uncovered, for 2 minutes. Remove from heat. Cover and let stand for 60 minutes. (Or place beans in water in Dutch oven. Cover and let soak in a cool place overnight.) Drain and rinse the beans.

2 Return beans to Dutch oven. Stir in the remaining 8 cups fresh water. Bring to boiling; reduce heat. Cover and simmer for 60 to 90 minutes or until beans are tender, stirring occasionally. Drain beans, reserving liquid.

3 Preheat oven to 300°F. In the same Dutch oven cook the 4 ounces bacon and the onion over medium heat until bacon is slightly crisp and onion is tender, stirring occasionally. Add brown sugar; cook and stir until sugar dissolves. Stir in molasses, Worcestershire sauce, dry mustard, salt, and pepper. Stir in drained beans and 1¼ cups of the reserved bean liquid.

4 Cover and bake beans for 60 minutes. Uncover and bake for 30 to 45 minutes or until desired consistency, stirring occasionally. Beans will thicken slightly as they cool. If necessary, stir in additional reserved bean liquid. If desired, sprinkle with additional cooked bacon.

PER ½ CUP: 267 cal., 6 g total fat (2 g sat. fat), 8 mg chol., 282 mg sodium, 43 g carb., 11 g fiber, 12 g pro.
EXCHANGES: 2 Starch, 1 Other Carb., 1 Medium-Fat Meat

BAKED BEANS STEP-BY-STEP

1. DO THE SORT-AND-RINSE STEP
Beans can be dirty. Sort through the package of beans and remove any twigs, pebbles, and broken or shriveled beans. Rinse thoroughly in a colander.

2. WHY SOAK?
Soaking dried beans helps the beans soften slightly, allowing them to cook quicker. Water starts to seep into the bean where it was attached to the plant. Small spot, long process. Soak beans overnight or use the universal quick-soak method in the recipe.

3. DUMP THE SOAKING LIQUID
Beans will plump slightly after soaking. After you drain the beans, toss the soaking liquid. There's really no reason to keep it. And your GI tract will thank you!

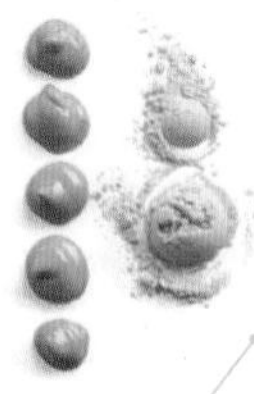

Dry mustard has a stronger flavor than prepared mustard. If you need to swap, use 4½ teaspoons yellow mustard.

SWEET & SASSY

Molasses and brown sugar are traditionally used to sweeten a pot of baked beans. Although they offer a sweet, almost smoky flavor, they are acidic ingredients. The calcium in each helps keep the beans firm, so while you are baking the beans to develop the flavor, they are not turning to mush. We added maple syrup as an option to molasses. It has less calcium, so watch more carefully and check the texture while baking.

3. AFTER 60 MINUTES
Because the beans are pretty tender when we add the sauce ingredients, the first hour in the oven allows them to absorb that great molasses-y flavor.

4. NOW FOR CONSISTENCY
How much time your beans spend in the oven for the last cooking time is up to you. Baking them with the lid off allows the excess liquid to evaporate and the sauce to thicken. When the beans are as saucy or as thick as you like, they're ready to serve!

MAKE IT MEATY

If bacon seems too ho-hum for you and pancetta isn't your thing, you can stir in 1 to 1½ cups of any variety of cooked smoked meats when you stir in the molasses and remaining ingredients. Try chopped ham, sliced link polish sausage, kielbasa, Andouille sausage, turkey link sausage, or chopped smoked pork hocks.

BEST-LOVED FAST LOW-CALORIE

Succotash

START TO FINISH: 25 MINUTES
MAKES: 6 SIDE-DISH SERVINGS

- **2 cups frozen lima beans**
- **2 tablespoons butter**
- **2 cups fresh corn kernels or frozen whole kernel corn**
- **¼ teaspoon salt**
- **⅛ teaspoon black pepper**
- **¼ cup whipping cream**
- **¼ cup diced cooked ham or crumbled, crisp-cooked bacon**

1 Cook lima beans according to package directions; drain and set aside.

2 Melt butter in a large skillet over medium heat. Add corn, salt, and pepper. Cook and stir for 2 minutes. Add drained beans. Cook and stir 1 minute more.

3 Add whipping cream and ham. Bring to boiling; reduce heat. Simmer, uncovered, about 2 minutes or until cream thickens slightly. If desired, sprinkle with additional pepper.

PER ½ CUP: 182 cal., 9 g total fat (5 g sat. fat), 27 mg chol., 207 mg sodium, 22 g carb., 4 g fiber, 6 g pro.
EXCHANGES: 1 Vegetable, 1 Starch, 1½ Fat

FAST

Falafels

START TO FINISH: 25 MINUTES
MAKES: 4 MAIN-DISH SERVINGS

- **1 15-ounce can garbanzo beans (chickpeas), rinsed and drained**
- **¼ cup purchased coarsely shredded carrot**
- **2 tablespoons all-purpose flour**
- **2 tablespoons snipped fresh parsley**
- **3 tablespoons olive oil**
- **3 cloves garlic, halved**
- **1 teaspoon ground coriander**
- **½ teaspoon ground cumin**
- **½ cup mayonnaise**
- **1 clove garlic, minced**
- **¼ teaspoon cayenne pepper**
- **4 pita bread rounds**
- **1 cup fresh spinach leaves, shredded**

1 In a food processor combine beans, carrot, flour, parsley, 1 tablespoon of oil, halved garlic, coriander, cumin, ½ teaspoon *salt,* and ⅛ teaspoon *black pepper.* Cover; process until chopped and mixture holds together.

2 Shape mixture into four 3-inch patties. In a large skillet heat the remaining 2 tablespoons oil over medium-high heat. Add the patties. Cook for 2 to 3 minutes per side or until browned and heated through.

3 In a bowl stir together mayonnaise, minced garlic, and cayenne pepper. Spread mixture on pita rounds. Top with patties and spinach.

PER PATTY: 607 cal., 34 g total fat (6 g sat. fat), 10 mg chol., 1,093 mg sodium, 63 g carb., 7 g fiber, 12 g pro.
EXCHANGES: 4 Starch, 6 Fat

DRIED OR CANNED BEANS

Yes, you can use canned beans for dried—here's how to do the math:

- One pound (2¼ to 2½ cups) of dried, uncooked beans yields 6 to 7 cups cooked beans. One 15-ounce can of beans equals about 1¾ cups drained beans. Use 3½ to four 15-ounce cans for each pound of dried beans.
- Be sure to drain and rinse the canned beans under cold running water to eliminate the salty liquid.

Black Bean-Chipotle Burgers

PREP: 35 MINUTES **CHILL:** 60 MINUTES
COOK: 10 MINUTES **MAKES:** 4 BURGERS

- **1 15-ounce can black beans, rinsed and drained**
- **½ cup frozen whole kernel corn, thawed**
- **1 cup corn chips, finely crushed**
- **½ cup cooked brown rice**
- **¼ cup finely chopped red onion**
- **¼ cup bottled chunky salsa**
- **½ to 1 teaspoon finely chopped canned chipotle peppers in adobo sauce (see tip, page 44)**
- **½ teaspoon ground cumin**
- **1 clove garlic, minced**
- **1 tablespoon olive oil**
- **Finely shredded green cabbage**
- **4 tostada shells, heated according to package directions**
- **Bottled chunky salsa, sour cream, fresh cilantro leaves, crumbled queso fresco, and/or avocado slices**

1 In a medium bowl mash half of the beans with potato masher or pastry blender until well mashed (see photo 1, below). Stir in remaining beans, corn, corn chips, rice, onion, the ¼ cup salsa, chipotle peppers, cumin, and garlic.

2 Shape mixture into four 3½-inch patties, about ¾ inch thick (see photo 2, below). Place patties on a tray; cover and chill at least 60 minutes before cooking.

3 Brush both sides of patties with olive oil. Cook in a very large skillet or on a griddle over medium heat about 10 minutes or until heated through, turning once.*

4 Place some shredded cabbage on each tostada shell. Place the burgers on the cabbage and top with additional salsa, sour cream, cilantro, cheese, and/or avocado slices.

***BROILER DIRECTIONS:** Preheat broiler. Place patties on the unheated rack of a broiler pan. Broil 4 inches from heat about 10 minutes or until heated through, turning once.

PER BURGER: 362 cal., 17 g total fat (3 g sat. fat), 6 mg chol., 600 mg sodium, 46 g carb., 9 g fiber, 14 g pro.
EXCHANGES: ½ Vegetable, 3 Starch, ½ Lean Meat, 3 Fat

BLACK BEAN-CHIPOTLE BURGERS STEP-BY-STEP

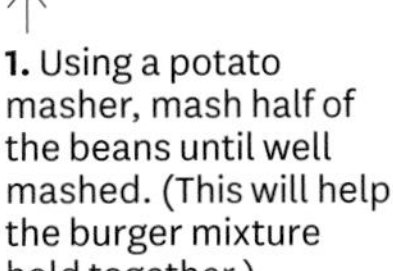

1. Using a potato masher, mash half of the beans until well mashed. (This will help the burger mixture hold together.)

2. Use a measuring cup to uniformly shape the bean mixture into 3½-inch patties.

Refried Beans

PREP: 20 MINUTES **STAND:** 60 MINUTES
COOK: 2 HOURS 30 MINUTES
MAKES: 4 SIDE-DISH SERVINGS

- **8 ounces dried pinto beans (about 1¼ cups)**
- **8 cups water**
- **½ teaspoon salt**
- **2 tablespoons bacon drippings or olive oil**
- **2 cloves garlic, minced**
- **Black pepper**

1 Rinse beans. In a large saucepan or Dutch oven combine beans and 4 cups of the water. Bring to boiling; reduce heat. Simmer, covered, for 2 minutes. Remove from heat. Cover and let stand for 60 minutes (see photo 2, page 78). (Or place beans in water in pan. Cover and let soak in a cool place overnight.) Drain and rinse the beans.

2 In same saucepan or Dutch oven combine beans, remaining 4 cups fresh water, and the salt. Bring to boiling; reduce heat. Simmer, covered, for 2½ to 3 hours or until beans are very tender. Drain beans, reserving liquid.

3 In a large heavy skillet heat bacon drippings. Stir in garlic. Add beans; mash thoroughly with a potato masher. Stir in enough of the cooking liquid (about ¼ cup) to make a pastelike mixture. Cook, uncovered, over low heat for 8 to 10 minutes or until thick, stirring often. Season to taste with additional salt and black pepper.

PER ½ CUP: 257 cal., 7 g total fat (3 g sat. fat), 6 mg chol., 321 mg sodium, 36 g carb., 9 g fiber, 12 g pro.
EXCHANGES: 2½ Starch, ½ Lean Meat, 1 Fat

GINGERED VEGETABLE-TOFU STIR-FRY

LOW-CALORIE

Gingered Vegetable-Tofu Stir-Fry

START TO FINISH: 45 MINUTES
MAKES: 4 MAIN-DISH SERVINGS

- **3/4 cup water**
- **1/4 cup dry sherry, dry white wine, or chicken broth**
- **3 tablespoons soy sauce**
- **1 tablespoon cornstarch**
- **1/2 teaspoon sugar**
- **1 tablespoon olive oil**
- **2 teaspoons grated fresh ginger**
- **1 pound fresh asparagus, cut into 1-inch pieces (2 1/2 cups), or one 10-ounce package frozen cut asparagus, thawed and well drained**
- **1 small yellow summer squash, halved lengthwise and sliced (1 1/4 cups)**
- **1/4 cup sliced green onions (2)**
- **12 ounces extra-firm tofu (fresh bean curd), cut into 1/2-inch cubes and patted dry with paper towels (2 cups)**
- **1/2 cup chopped toasted almonds**
- **2 cups hot cooked brown rice**

1 For sauce, in a bowl mix water, dry sherry, soy sauce, cornstarch, and sugar; set aside.

2 Pour the olive oil into a wok or large skillet (add more oil as necessary during cooking). Preheat the wok or large skillet over medium-high heat. Stir-fry the ginger in hot oil for 15 seconds. Add the fresh asparagus (if using) and squash; stir-fry for 3 minutes. Add the thawed asparagus (if using) and green onions; stir-fry for 1 to 2 minutes more or until the asparagus is crisp-tender. Remove vegetables from wok.

3 Add tofu to hot wok or skillet. Carefully stir-fry for 2 to 3 minutes or until lightly browned. Remove from wok. Stir sauce; add to hot wok. Cook and stir until thickened and bubbly. Return cooked vegetables and tofu to wok. Stir all ingredients together to coat with sauce. Cover; cook about 1 minute more or until heated through. Stir in almonds. Serve over rice.

PER 1 CUP STIR-FRY + 1/2 CUP RICE: 329 cal., 13 g total fat (1 g sat. fat), 0 mg chol., 836 mg sodium, 37 g carb., 6 g fiber, 15 g pro. **EXCHANGES:** 1 Vegetable, 1 1/2 Starch, 1/2 Other Carb., 1 1/2 Lean Meat, 1 1/2 Fat

FAST LOW-CALORIE

Tofu and Mushrooms on Greens

START TO FINISH: 30 MINUTES
MAKES: 4 MAIN-DISH SERVINGS

- **8 ounces button and/or cremini mushrooms, quartered**
- **3 cloves garlic, minced**
- **2 tablespoons olive oil**
- **1 tablespoon butter**
- **1 tablespoon snipped fresh thyme or 1 teaspoon dried thyme, crushed**
- **1/4 teaspoon salt**
- **1/8 teaspoon black pepper**
- **12 ounces tofu (fresh bean curd), drained and cut into 1/2-inch-thick slices**
- **1/4 cup balsamic vinegar**
- **6 cups torn mixed greens**
- **1/4 cup crumbled herbed feta cheese**
- **Toasted baguette-style French bread slices**

1 In a large skillet cook mushrooms and garlic in hot olive oil and butter over medium heat until mushrooms are tender and liquid evaporates. Stir in thyme, salt, and pepper. Remove from skillet; keep warm.

2 Lightly season tofu slices with additional salt and pepper. In same skillet cook tofu, half at a time if necessary, over medium-high heat for 3 to 4 minutes or until lightly browned and heated through, turning once. Remove from skillet. Add balsamic vinegar to skillet; bring to boiling. Boil gently 1 minute. Remove from heat.

3 Serve tofu on greens on serving plates. Drizzle with the balsamic vinegar. Top tofu with mushrooms and cheese. Serve with bread.

PER SERVING: 271 cal., 13 g total fat (4 g sat. fat), 9 mg chol., 415 mg sodium, 28 g carb., 3 g fiber, 11 g pro.
EXCHANGES: 1 1/2 Vegetable, 1 1/2 Starch, 1/2 Lean Meat, 2 Fat

Spanish Rice

PREP: 25 MINUTES **COOK:** 27 MINUTES
STAND: 5 MINUTES **MAKES:** 6 SIDE-DISH SERVINGS

- **4 ounces bacon, chopped (about 4 slices)**
- **1 cup coarsely chopped onion (1 large)**
- **¾ cup chopped green sweet pepper (1 medium)**
- **1 clove garlic, minced**
- **1 14.5-ounce can diced tomatoes, undrained**
- **½ teaspoon black pepper**
- **¼ teaspoon cayenne pepper**
- **1 cup uncooked jasmine rice or long grain rice**
- **2 teaspoons olive oil**
- **½ teaspoon salt**
- **2 cups water**
- **¼ cup halved pitted green olives (optional)**
- **1 cup shredded cheddar cheese (4 ounces)**

1 In a large skillet cook bacon until crisp. Remove bacon from skillet; drain on paper towels. Remove all but 1 tablespoon bacon drippings from the skillet. Add onion, sweet pepper, and garlic. Cook and stir over medium heat for 7 to 10 minutes or until tender. Add undrained tomatoes, black pepper, and cayenne pepper. Bring to boiling; reduce heat. Simmer, covered, for 20 minutes.

2 Meanwhile, in a medium saucepan stir together rice, oil, and salt. Add the water. Bring to boiling. Reduce heat to low and simmer, covered, about 15 minutes or until rice is tender.

3 Add the cooked rice, cooked bacon, and, if desired, olives to skillet. Top with cheese. Cover and let stand about 5 minutes or until the cheese melts.

PER ⅔ CUP: 273 cal., 12 g total fat (6 g sat. fat), 28 mg chol., 577 mg sodium, 32 g carb., 2 g fiber, 9 g pro.
EXCHANGES: ½ Vegetable, 2 Starch, 2 Fat

cook's secrets

fried rice

The Secret: Cold, cold, cold! The best fried rice starts with chilled cooked long grain white rice.

START TO FINISH: 30 MINUTES **MAKES:** 6 SIDE-DISH SERVINGS

- **2 eggs**
- **1 teaspoon soy sauce**
- **1 teaspoon toasted sesame or vegetable oil**
- **1 clove garlic, minced**
- **1 tablespoon vegetable oil**
- **½ cup thinly bias-sliced celery (1 stalk)**
- **¾ cup sliced fresh mushrooms**
- **2 cups chilled cooked long grain white rice***
- **½ cup julienned carrots or packaged fresh julienned carrots**
- **½ cup frozen peas**
- **2 tablespoons soy sauce**
- **¼ cup sliced green onions**

To get the best flavor, use toasted sesame oil rather than the light-color, untoasted sesame oil. If you rarely use it, keep it in the fridge so it doesn't become rancid.

1 In a small bowl lightly beat eggs and 1 teaspoon soy sauce; set aside.

2 Pour 1 teaspoon sesame oil into a wok or large skillet. Preheat over medium heat. Add garlic and cook 30 seconds. Add egg mixture and cook, without stirring, until set. Turn egg and cook until just set. Remove egg and slice (see photos 1 and 2, left). Remove wok from the heat.

3 Pour 1 tablespoon vegetable oil into the wok (add more oil as necessary during cooking). Heat over medium-high heat. Stir-fry celery in hot oil for 1 minute. Add mushrooms; stir-fry for 1 to 2 minutes or until vegetables are crisp-tender.

4 Add cold rice, carrots, and peas. Pour 2 tablespoons soy sauce over all. Cook and stir over medium-high heat for 4 to 6 minutes or until heated through. Add sliced eggs and green onions; cook and stir 1 minute more or until heated through.

***NOTE:** For cooked white rice, in a medium saucepan bring 2 cups water and ¼ teaspoon salt to a full boil. Slowly add 1 cup long grain rice. Reduce the heat and cover the saucepan with a tight-fitting lid. Cook about 15 minutes or until the rice is tender and the water is absorbed. Remove the pan from the heat and let stand, covered, for 5 minutes. Fluff rice; chill.

PER ½ CUP: 140 cal., 5 g total fat (1 g sat. fat), 71 mg chol., 409 mg sodium, 18 g carb., 2 g fiber, g pro. EXCHANGES: 1 Starch, ½ Lean Meat, 1 Fat

FRIED RICE POINTERS

1. EGG PERFECTION
A restaurantworthy fried rice includes perfectly done eggs. Cook the egg over medium-high heat, tilting the pan to spread the egg in an even layer. Cook, without stirring, for 30 seconds until the egg sets.

2. EGGS-ACTLY RIGHT
Use a spatula to turn the egg and cook until just set. The egg will look dry and slightly shiny.

3. ROLL IT
Turn the egg out onto a cutting board, roll it up, and cut it into thin slices.

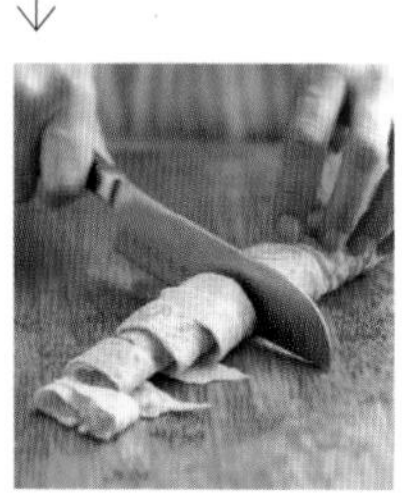

WOK OR NOT

The shape of a wok is designed to spread heat evenly while cooking over high heat for short periods of time. Round- and flat-bottom woks are available in various materials: aluminum, stainless steel, and carbon steel. If you don't own a wok, you can use a large skillet.

For fast rice, chill one 8.5-ounce package cooked white rice and add it here.

↑

4. WHY SO COLD? Adding cold rice gives you the best-textured fried rice. Once rice is cooked and chilled, the long starch chains in rice (amylose) link tightly together and harden. When it is reheated, the rice will not turn to mush. You may have to break up larger clumps of rice to stir in the remaining ingredients.

5. HEAT THROUGH After adding the veggies and the eggs, you really are just heating through. Don't get carried away and cook for longer timings than specified in the recipe.

MAKE IT A MAIN DISH

Add a healthful protein and this recipe easily goes from 6 serve-alongs to 4 main-dish servings. Pick what's in your pantry or what your family prefers. Stir your selection in with the rice and finish the recipe as directed. Here are suggested amounts:

- 12 ounces peeled and deveined fully cooked shrimp
- 12 ounces chopped cooked chicken or pork
- 8 ounces extra-firm tofu, cut into ¾-inch cubes

make it mine

Rice Pilaf

Take a look in your fridge and cupboard. Chances are you have the ingredients you need to create a rice pilaf to complement whatever you plan to serve for dinner.

PREP: 15 MINUTES
COOK: 15 TO 45 MINUTES
MAKES: 4 TO 6 SIDE-DISH SERVINGS

- RICE or GRAIN
- 2 cloves garlic, minced
- 2 tablespoons butter
- 1 14.5-ounce can reduced-sodium chicken broth
- 1/4 cup DRIED FRUIT (optional)
- 1/4 cup CHOPPED VEGETABLE
- 1/4 cup LIQUID
- 1 to 2 teaspoons FRESH HERB or 1/4 teaspoon DRIED HERB
- 1/2 cup STIR-IN

1 In a medium saucepan cook and stir the uncooked Rice or Grain and garlic in hot butter for 3 minutes.* Carefully stir in chicken broth, Dried Fruit (if desired), Chopped Vegetable, Liquid, and Dried Herb (if using). Bring mixture to boiling; reduce heat. Simmer, covered, for specified time (see timings, right) or until rice is tender and liquid is absorbed. Add Stir-In and Fresh Herb (if using).

***NOTE:** This step lightly toasts the rice or grain. Toasting helps the rice or grain absorb liquid better.

FINAL STEP IN RICE COOKING

Once rice is done, avoid overstirring the mixture. Instead, fluff the cooked rice with a fork so it stays light and doesn't clump.

RICE OR GRAIN *(pick one)*
- 3/4 cup long grain rice or basmati rice (Cook 15 to 20 minutes)
- 1/2 cup wild rice plus 1/3 cup regular barley (Cook 45 to 50 minutes)

DRIED FRUIT *(pick one)*
- Cherries
- Cranberries
- Raisins
- Snipped apricots

CHOPPED VEGETABLE *(pick one)*
- Carrots
- Celery
- Mushrooms
- Sweet peppers
- Zucchini

LIQUID *(pick one)*
- Apple juice
- Dry white wine
- Water

FRESH OR DRIED HERB *(pick one)*
- Basil
- Oregano
- Thyme

STIR-IN *(pick one)*
- Crumbled crisp-cooked bacon
- Sliced green onions
- Toasted chopped almonds, pecans, pine nuts or walnuts (see tip, page 21)

8 to try

Risotto

Make this delectable creamy Italian-style rice dish or switch up its flavor eight ways with the addition of meat, vegetables, and/or herbs.

START TO FINISH: 40 MINUTES
MAKES: 6 SIDE-DISH SERVINGS

- **1/2 cup chopped onion (1 medium)**
- **2 cloves garlic, minced**
- **2 tablespoons olive oil**
- **1 cup uncooked arborio rice**
- **2 14.5-ounce cans reduced-sodium chicken broth**
- **1/4 cup grated Parmesan cheese**
- **Finely shredded lemon peel (optional)**

1 In a 3-quart saucepan cook onion and garlic in hot oil over medium heat for 3 to 5 minutes or until onion is tender, stirring occasionally. Add the rice and cook for 3 to 5 minutes or until rice is golden brown, stirring frequently (see photo 1, below).

2 Meanwhile, in a 1½-quart saucepan bring broth to boiling; reduce heat. Cover and keep broth simmering. Carefully stir 1/2 cup of the broth into the rice mixture. Cook over medium heat until liquid is absorbed, stirring frequently. Continue adding broth, 1/2 cup at a time, stirring frequently until the broth has been absorbed (see photo 2, below). Rice should be tender and creamy (should take 20 to 25 minutes).

3 Stir in cheese; heat through. If desired, sprinkle with lemon peel. Serve immediately.

THE TRICK TO CREAMY RISOTTO

Don't be tempted to skip toasting the rice. This step helps give risotto its texture.

1 Brown the rice in olive oil with the onions and garlic in saucepan.

2 Toasted rice absorbs broth better than plain rice as it's cooked and stirred, resulting in the creamiest risotto.

VEGETABLE: Add 1 cup frozen peas and 1/4 cup shredded carrot with the final 1/2 cup broth. Add 2 cups shredded fresh spinach, and 1 tablespoon snipped fresh thyme with cheese.

CHICKEN AND PROSCIUTTO: Stir in 1 cup shredded roasted chicken and 1/4 cup small strips prosciutto with final 1/2 cup broth. Top with 2 tablespoons blue cheese.

EDAMAME: Cook 1 cup frozen shelled sweet soybeans (edamame) according to package directions. Stir edamame into rice with the final 1/2 cup broth. Sprinkle with crisp-cooked bacon.

CORN AND TOMATOES: Stir in 1 cup fresh or frozen corn, 1/3 cup snipped dried tomatoes (oil pack), and 1 tablespoon snipped fresh oregano with the final 1/2 cup broth.

FARRO: Substitute 1 cup pearled farro for the rice.

SHRIMP: Stir 1½ cups cooked, peeled shrimp into mixture with final 1/2 cup broth. Sprinkle with lemon peel.

CARAMELIZED ONIONS: While risotto cooks, in large skillet heat 1 tablespoon olive oil. Add 2 cups sliced, halved onions; cover and cook over medium-low heat 15 minutes. Uncover; cook 10 to 15 minutes more or until onions are browned, stirring frequently. Stir onions and 1 cup small pieces cooked asparagus into rice with final 1/2 cup broth.

MUSHROOMS: Add 1/4 cup dried porcini mushrooms to broth. Bring to boiling; reduce heat. Simmer, covered, 5 minutes. Strain through fine-mesh sieve; chop mushrooms. Return broth to saucepan; add 2 tablespoons butter to oil. Cook 2 cups quartered fresh cremini mushrooms with onion. Stir in mushrooms with last broth addition.

BEST-LOVED LOW-CALORIE

Baked Cheese Grits

PREP: 15 MINUTES **BAKE:** 25 MINUTES AT 325°F
STAND: 5 MINUTES
MAKES: 4 OR 5 SIDE-DISH SERVINGS

- **2 cups chicken broth**
- **½ cup quick-cooking grits**
- **1 egg, lightly beaten**
- **1 cup shredded cheddar cheese (4 ounces)**
- **2 tablespoons sliced green onion (1)**
- **1 tablespoon butter**
- **½ cup chopped fresh tomato (optional)**
- **1 tablespoon snipped fresh cilantro (optional)**

1 Preheat oven to 325°F. In medium saucepan bring broth to boiling. Slowly add grits, stirring constantly. Gradually stir about ½ cup of the hot mixture into egg. Return egg mixture to saucepan; stir to combine. Remove saucepan from heat. Stir cheese, green onion, and butter into grits until cheese and butter melts.

2 Pour grits mixture into an ungreased 1-quart casserole dish. Bake, uncovered, for 25 to 30 minutes or until knife inserted near center comes out clean. Let stand 5 minutes before serving. If desired, top with the chopped tomato and cilantro.

PER ⅔ CUP: 238 cal., 14 g total fat (8 g sat. fat), 91 mg chol., 694 mg sodium, 17 g carb., 0 g fiber, 11 g pro.
EXCHANGES: 1 Starch, 1 High-Fat Meat, 1 Fat

LOW-CALORIE

Polenta

PREP: 15 MINUTES **COOK:** 25 MINUTES
MAKES: 6 SIDE-DISH SERVINGS

- **2½ cups water***
- **1 cup coarse-ground yellow cornmeal****
- **1 cup cold water***
- **1 teaspoon salt**

1 In a medium saucepan bring the 2½ cups water to boiling. Meanwhile, in a bowl stir together cornmeal, 1 cup cold water, and salt.

2 Slowly add cornmeal mixture to boiling water, stirring constantly. Cook and stir until mixture returns to boiling. Reduce heat to medium-low; cook for 25 to 30 minutes or until mixture is very thick and tender, stirring frequently and adjusting heat as needed to maintain slow boil. Spoon polenta into bowls.

***NOTE:** For added flavor, use chicken broth in place of the water and omit the salt.

****TO USE REGULAR CORNMEAL:** Increase water in saucepan to 2¾ cups; cook and stir just 10 to 15 minutes after mixture boils in Step 2.

OPTIONAL STIR-INS:
- Decrease salt to ½ teaspoon and stir in ½ cup shredded Parmesan, Romano, or Fontina cheese (2 ounces) after cooking.
- Stir in 2 tablespoons snipped fresh basil or Italian parsley, or 1 teaspoon snipped fresh oregano or thyme after cooking.
- Decrease salt to ½ teaspoon and stir in 2 tablespoons butter after cooking.

FIRM POLENTA: Prepare as directed, except pour the cooked polenta into a 9-inch pie plate, spreading evenly. Let stand, uncovered, for 30 minutes. Cover and chill for at least 1 hour or until firm. Preheat oven to 350°F. Bake polenta, uncovered, about 25 minutes or until heated through. Let stand on a wire rack for 5 minutes. Cut into 6 wedges to serve.

PER ½ CUP PLAIN OR WEDGE FIRM POLENTA: 85 cal., 0 g total fat, 0 mg chol., 390 mg sodium, 18 g carb., 1 g fiber, 2 g pro. EXCHANGES: 1 Starch

FRIED POLENTA: Prepare as directed, except pour the cooked polenta into a 7½×3½×2-inch loaf pan or 8×4×2-inch loaf pan; cool. Cover and chill for at least 4 hours or overnight. Run a thin metal spatula around the edges of the pan. Remove polenta loaf from the pan and cut crosswise into 12 slices. In a large skillet or on a griddle heat 1 tablespoon butter over medium-high heat. Reduce heat to medium. Cook half of the polenta slices for 16 to 20 minutes or until brown and crisp, turning once halfway through cooking. Repeat with remaining slices, adding 1 tablespoon butter to skillet before adding polenta slices. If desired, serve with additional butter and honey or maple-flavor syrup.

PER 2 SLICES: 119 cal., 4 g total fat (2 g sat. fat), 10 mg chol., 418 mg sodium, 18 g carb., 1 g fiber, 2 g pro.
EXCHANGES: 1 Starch

GRITS, POLENTA, AND CORNMEAL

All three of these whole grains start with dried corn. Grits and polenta differ in their corn content. The corn used for grits is one that results in a creamy, mushy cooked texture. In contrast, polenta is made from corn that has a coarser texture when cooked. Cornmeal is dried corn ground into a fine, medium, or coarse texture. Can't find exactly what you need at the supermarket? Coarse-ground cornmeal works as a substitute for any of them—just cook until thickened.

ROASTED VEGETABLES WITH POLENTA

LOW-CALORIE

Roasted Vegetables with Polenta

PREP: 20 MINUTES **ROAST:** 15 MINUTES AT 425°F
MAKES: 6 SIDE-DISH SERVINGS

- **6 cups vegetables, such as trimmed asparagus, thick slices red or green sweet peppers, sliced zucchini, quartered mushrooms, and/or red onion slices**
- **¼ cup olive oil**
- **¼ teaspoon salt**
- **1 recipe Polenta (page 88) or one 16-ounce tube refrigerated cooked polenta**
- **Shredded Parmesan cheese**

1 Preheat oven to 425°F. In a shallow roasting pan combine vegetables, olive oil, and salt; toss to coat vegetables. Roast, uncovered, for 15 to 20 minutes or until vegetables are just tender, stirring once.

2 Meanwhile, prepare Polenta. (Or slice refrigerated polenta and heat in skillet according to package directions.)

3 To serve, spoon polenta into a shallow bowl. Spoon roasted vegetables on top of the polenta. Serve with Parmesan cheese.

PER ⅔ CUP VEGETABLES + ½ CUP POLENTA: 222 cal., 11 g total fat (2 g sat. fat), 4 mg chol., 560 mg sodium, 25 g carb., 4 g fiber, 6 g pro. EXCHANGES: 1 Vegetable, 1½ Starch, 2 Fat

LOW-CALORIE

Squash, Corn, and Barley Succotash

START TO FINISH: 60 MINUTES
MAKES: 12 SIDE-DISH SERVINGS

- **4 cups water**
- **½ cup regular barley**
- **1 teaspoon salt**
- **1 tablespoon olive oil**
- **1 cup finely chopped onion**
- **1 2-pound butternut squash, peeled, seeded, and cut into ½-inch cubes (about 4 cups)**
- **1 cup reduced-sodium chicken broth**
- **¼ teaspoon black pepper**
- **⅛ teaspoon dried thyme, crushed**
- **1 16-ounce package (about 3 cups) frozen whole kernel corn**
- **¼ cup snipped fresh parsley**

1 In a medium saucepan bring water to boiling. Add barley and ½ teaspoon of the salt. Return to boiling; reduce heat. Cover and simmer about 40 minutes or until barley is tender, stirring occasionally. Drain; set aside.

2 Meanwhile, in a very large skillet heat oil over medium-high heat. Add onion; cook and stir about 5 minutes or until tender. Stir in the remaining ½ teaspoon salt, squash, broth, pepper, and thyme. Bring to boiling; reduce heat. Cover and simmer for 10 to 15 minutes or until squash is just tender. Stir in corn; cover and cook 5 minutes more. Stir in barley and parsley; heat through.

PER ⅔ CUP: 106 cal., 2 g total fat (0 g sat. fat), 0 mg chol., 250 mg sodium, 22 g carb., 4 g fiber, 3 g pro.
EXCHANGES: 1 Vegetable, 1 Starch

SQUASH, CORN, AND BARLEY SUCCOTASH

BABY SPINACH, COUSCOUS, AND BULGUR PLATTER

LOW-CALORIE

Baby Spinach, Couscous, and Bulgur Platter

PREP: 30 MINUTES **CHILL:** 2 TO 24 HOURS
MAKES: 4 MAIN-DISH SERVINGS

- **2 cups vegetable broth or water**
- **½ cup bulgur**
- **½ teaspoon ground cumin**
- **¼ teaspoon sea salt or salt**
- **⅛ teaspoon black pepper**
- **½ cup quick-cooking couscous**
- **1 15-ounce can garbanzo beans (chickpeas), rinsed and drained**
- **1 recipe Yogurt-Mint Salad Dressing**
- **5 cups prewashed packaged baby spinach or torn spinach**
- **1 cup coarsely chopped apple**
- **½ of a small red onion, thinly sliced and separated into rings**

1 In a medium saucepan combine the broth, bulgur, cumin, salt, and black pepper. Bring to boiling; reduce heat. Simmer, covered, about 10 minutes or until the bulgur is nearly tender. Remove from heat; stir in couscous. Cover and let stand for 5 minutes.

2 Using a fork, fluff grain mixture. Transfer to a large bowl; cool slightly. Stir in garbanzo beans. Cover; chill 2 to 24 hours. Meanwhile, prepare Yogurt-Mint Salad Dressing.

3 To serve, arrange spinach on serving platter or in bowls. Spoon grain mixture over spinach. Top with apple and onion. Drizzle with dressing.

YOGURT-MINT SALAD DRESSING: In a small bowl combine ⅔ cup plain yogurt; ⅓ cup bottled red wine vinaigrette salad dressing; 2 tablespoons snipped fresh mint, cilantro, or Italian parsley; and ¼ teaspoon crushed red pepper. Serve immediately or cover and chill up to 1 week. Stir before serving.

PER 1 CUP SPINACH + 1 CUP GRAIN MIXTURE: 354 cal., 9 g total fat (1 g sat. fat), 2 mg chol., 1,318 mg sodium, 58 g carb., 10 g fiber, 13 g pro. **EXCHANGES:** 1 Vegetable, 3½ Starch, 1 Fat

Squash-Mushroom and Farro Stuffing

PREP: 40 MINUTES
ROAST: 25 MINUTES AT 425°F/20 MINUTES AT 350°F
MAKES: 10 SIDE-DISH SERVINGS

- **½ of a medium butternut squash, peeled, seeded, and cut into ½-inch cubes (1 pound or 2¾ cups)**
- **2 tablespoons olive oil**
- **3 cups halved fresh cremini and/or button mushrooms (if mushrooms are small, leave whole)**
- **6 cups water**
- **1½ cups pearled farro**
- **4 ounces thick-sliced pancetta, chopped**
- **¾ cup coarsely chopped onion (1 large)**
- **½ cup thinly sliced celery (1 stalk)**
- **3 cloves garlic, minced**
- **¾ cup dry white wine**
- **½ cup half-and-half or light cream**
- **1 tablespoon snipped fresh thyme or 1 teaspoon dried thyme, crushed**
- **2 teaspoons snipped fresh rosemary or ½ teaspoon dried rosemary, crushed**
- **¾ teaspoon salt**
- **¼ teaspoon black pepper**
- **½ cup finely shredded Asiago cheese (2 ounces)**

1 Preheat oven to 425°F. Line a shallow baking pan with foil. In a large bowl toss squash with 1 tablespoon of the oil. Transfer squash to prepared pan. Roast for 10 minutes. Stir squash and push to one side of the pan. Toss mushrooms with remaining 1 tablespoon olive oil. Place mushrooms on other side of pan. Roast about 15 minutes or until squash is just tender and mushrooms are roasted. Reduce oven temperature to 350°F.

2 Meanwhile, in a large saucepan bring the water to boiling; add farro. Return to boiling; reduce heat. Simmer, covered, for 25 to 30 minutes or until just tender; drain.

3 For stuffing, in a very large skillet cook and stir pancetta over medium-high heat until crisp. Using slotted spoon, transfer pancetta to paper towels to drain. Add onion, celery, and garlic to drippings in skillet. Cook over medium heat about 3 minutes or until vegetables are tender, stirring occasionally. Stir in wine, half-and-half, thyme, rosemary, salt, and pepper. Bring to boiling. Add squash to skillet and mash slightly to a saucelike consistency. Stir in cheese until it melts. Stir in drained farro, mushrooms, and pancetta, tossing to combine. Transfer to buttered 2-quart casserole or baking dish; cover with foil. Bake 20 minutes or until heated.

PER ¾ CUP: 251 cal., 10 g total fat (4 g sat. fat), 14 mg chol., 334 mg sodium, 28 g carb., 3 g fiber, 10 g pro.
EXCHANGES: 1½ Vegetable, 1½ Starch, 1½ Fat

LOW-CALORIE

Creamy Farro-Smothered Portobellos

(photo, page 73)

PREP: 20 MINUTES **COOK:** 20 MINUTES
MAKES: 6 MAIN-DISH SERVINGS

- **3 cups reduced-sodium vegetable broth**
- **1 cup pearled or semipearled farro**
- **6 5-inch fresh portobello mushrooms, stems and gills removed**
- **Nonstick cooking spray**
- **2 cups chopped fresh Swiss chard**
- **¼ cup snipped dried tomatoes (not oil pack)**
- **2 teaspoons snipped fresh thyme or ½ teaspoon dried thyme, crushed**
- **4 ounces soft goat cheese (chèvre), cut up**
- **¼ cup finely shredded or shaved Parmesan cheese (1 ounce)**
- **¼ cup sliced green onion tops**
- **Black pepper**

1 In a medium saucepan bring broth to boiling; stir in farro. Return to boiling; reduce heat. Simmer, covered, for 15 minutes.

2 Meanwhile, lightly coat both sides of mushrooms with cooking spray. Preheat a grill pan over medium heat. Add mushrooms; cook for 8 to 10 minutes or until tender, turning once.

3 Stir Swiss chard, dried tomatoes, and thyme into farro. Cook, covered, for 5 to 10 minutes more or until farro is tender. Remove from heat. Stir in goat cheese until it melts.

4 To serve, place mushrooms, stemmed sides up, on a serving platter. Spoon farro mixture over mushrooms. Sprinkle with Parmesan cheese, green onion tops, and pepper.

PER MUSHROOM: 215 cal., 6 g total fat (4 g sat. fat), 12 mg chol., 482 mg sodium, 28 g carb., 3 g fiber, 12 g pro.
EXCHANGES: 1 Vegetable, 1½ Starch, 1 Medium-Fat Meat

TABBOULEH

BEST-LOVED LOW-CALORIE

Tabbouleh

PREP: 25 MINUTES **CHILL:** 4 TO 24 HOURS
MAKES: 5 SIDE-DISH SERVINGS

- **¾ cup bulgur**
- **¾ cup chopped cucumber**
- **½ cup snipped fresh parsley**
- **¼ cup thinly sliced green onions (2)**
- **1 tablespoon snipped fresh mint**
- **2 tablespoons water**
- **3 tablespoons vegetable oil**
- **3 tablespoons lemon juice**
- **¼ teaspoon salt**
- **¾ cup chopped tomato**
- **4 lettuce leaves**
- **Lemon slices and/or mint sprigs (optional)**

1 Place bulgur in a colander; rinse with cold water. In a large bowl combine bulgur, cucumber, parsley, green onions, and mint.

2 For dressing, in a screw-top jar combine water, oil, lemon juice, and salt. Cover and shake well. Drizzle dressing over bulgur mixture; toss to coat. Cover and chill for 4 to 24 hours. Just before serving, stir tomato into bulgur mixture. Serve in a lettuce-lined bowl and, if desired, garnish with lemon slices and/or mint sprigs.

PER 1 CUP: 161 cal., 9 g total fat (1 g sat. fat), 0 mg chol., 128 mg sodium, 20 g carb., 5 g fiber, 3 g pro.
EXCHANGES: ½ Vegetable, 1 Starch, 1½ Fat

BEST-LOVED

Greek Quinoa and Avocados

PREP: 20 MINUTES **COOK:** 15 MINUTES
MAKES: 4 SIDE-DISH SERVINGS

- **½ cup quinoa, rinsed and drained**
- **1 cup water**
- **2 roma tomatoes, seeded and chopped**
- **½ cup shredded fresh spinach**
- **⅓ cup finely chopped red onion**
- **2 tablespoons lemon juice**
- **2 tablespoons olive oil**
- **Spinach leaves**
- **2 ripe avocados, halved, seeded, peeled, and sliced***
- **⅓ cup crumbled feta cheese**

1 In a small saucepan combine quinoa and water. Bring to boiling; reduce heat. Simmer, covered, about 15 minutes or until liquid is absorbed. Place quinoa in a medium bowl.

2 Add tomatoes, shredded spinach, and onion to quinoa; stir to combine. In small bowl whisk together lemon juice, olive oil, and ½ teaspoon *salt*. Add to quinoa mixture; toss to coat.

3 Place spinach leaves on plates. Arrange avocado slices on top of spinach. Spoon quinoa mixture over avocados. Sprinkle with feta.

***NOTE:** Brush avocado slices with additional lemon juice to prevent discoloring.

PER 1⅓ CUPS: 300 cal., 21 g total fat (4 g sat. fat), 11 mg chol., 456 mg sodium, 24 g carb., 7 g fiber, 7 g pro.
EXCHANGES: 1½ Vegetable, 1 Starch, 4 Fat

LOW-CALORIE

Peppers Stuffed with Quinoa and Spinach

PREP: 25 MINUTES **COOK:** 12 MINUTES
BAKE: 40 MINUTES AT 400°F
MAKES: 6 MAIN-DISH SERVINGS

- **1 14.5-ounce can vegetable broth**
- **⅓ cup quick-cooking barley**
- **⅓ cup quinoa, rinsed and drained**
- **2 tablespoons olive oil**
- **½ cup chopped onion (1 medium)**
- **2 cloves garlic, minced**
- **2 cups sliced fresh mushrooms**
- **¼ teaspoon salt**
- **¼ teaspoon black pepper**
- **1 14.5-ounce can diced tomatoes, drained**
- **½ of a 10-ounce package frozen chopped spinach, thawed and well drained, or 3 cups fresh spinach**
- **1¼ cups shredded Monterey Jack cheese with jalapeño peppers or Monterey Jack cheese (5 ounces)**
- **3 large red sweet peppers**
- **Salt and black pepper**

1 Preheat oven to 400°F. In a medium saucepan bring broth to boiling. Add barley and quinoa. Return to boiling; reduce heat. Cook, covered, about 12 minutes or until tender. Drain, reserving ⅓ cup cooking liquid; set aside.

2 In a large skillet heat oil over medium heat. Add onion and garlic. Cook and stir for 2 minutes. Add mushrooms. Cook and stir for 4 to 5 minutes more or until mushrooms and onion are tender. Stir in salt and black pepper, drained tomatoes, and spinach. Stir in the quinoa mixture and ½ cup of the cheese. Remove from heat.

3 Cut peppers in half lengthwise; remove and discard seeds and membranes. Sprinkle insides of peppers lightly with additional salt and black pepper. Fill pepper halves with quinoa mixture. Place peppers, filled sides up, in a 3-quart rectangular baking dish. Pour reserved cooking liquid into dish around peppers.

4 Bake, covered, for 30 minutes. Uncover; top each with remaining cheese. Bake, uncovered, about 10 minutes or until peppers are crisp-tender and cheese is browned.

PER PEPPER HALF: 253 cal., 13 g total fat (5 g sat. fat), 21 mg chol., 641 mg sodium, 24 g carb., 5 g fiber, 11 g pro.
EXCHANGES: 2 Vegetable, 1 Starch, ½ Lean Meat, 2 Fat

COOKING GRAINS

Pour the called-for amount of water into a medium saucepan. Bring the water to a full boil, unless the chart specifies otherwise. If desired, add 1/4 teaspoon salt to the water. Slowly add the grain and return to boiling; reduce heat. Simmer, covered, for the time specified or until most of the water is absorbed and grain is tender.

Grain	Amount of Grain	Amount of Water	Cooking Directions	Yield
Barley, quick-cooking pearl	1¼ cups	2 cups	Simmer, covered, for 10 to 12 minutes. Drain if necessary.	3 cups
Barley, regular pearl	¾ cup	3 cups	Simmer, covered, about 45 minutes. Drain if necessary.	3 cups
Buckwheat groats or kasha	⅔ cup	1½ cups	Add to cold water. Bring to boiling. Simmer, covered, for 6 to 8 minutes.	2¼ cups
Bulgur	1 cup	2 cups	Add to cold water. Bring to boiling. Simmer, covered, about 15 minutes.	3 cups
Farina, quick-cooking	¾ cup	3½ cups	Simmer, uncovered, for 2 to 3 minutes, stirring constantly.	3½ cups
Farro, pearled	1 cup	3 cups	Combine farro and water in saucepan. Bring to boiling. Simmer, covered, for 25 to 30 minutes. Drain if necessary.	2½ cups
Hominy grits, quick-cooking	¾ cup	3 cups	Simmer, covered, about 5 minutes, stirring occasionally.	3 cups
Millet	¾ cup	2 cups	Simmer, covered, for 15 to 20 minutes. Let stand, covered, for 5 minutes.	3 cups
Oats, rolled, quick-cooking	1½ cups	3 cups	Simmer, uncovered, for 1 minute. Let stand, covered, for 3 minutes.	3 cups
Oats, rolled, regular	1⅔ cups	3 cups	Simmer, uncovered, for 5 to 7 minutes. Let stand, covered, for 3 minutes.	3 cups
Oats, steel-cut	1⅓ cups	4 cups	Cook in large saucepan. Add ½ teaspoon salt. Simmer, covered, for 25 to 30 minutes.	4 cups
Quinoa	¾ cup	1½ cups	Rinse well. Simmer, covered, about 15 minutes. Drain if necessary.	1¾ cups
Rice, black	1 cup	1¾ cups	Combine black rice and water in saucepan. Bring to boiling. Simmer, covered, for 30 minutes.	3 cups
Rice, long grain, white	1 cup	2 cups	Simmer, covered, about 15 minutes. Let stand, covered, for 5 minutes.	2 cups
Rice, red	1 cup	1½ cups	Combine red rice and water in saucepan. Bring to boiling. Simmer, covered, for 20 minutes. Remove from heat; let stand 10 minutes.	2½ cups
Rice, regular, brown	1 cup	2 cups	Simmer, covered, about 45 minutes. Let stand, covered, for 5 minutes.	3 cups
Rice, wild	1 cup	2 cups	Rinse well. Simmer, covered, about 40 minutes or until most of the water is absorbed. Drain if necessary.	3 cups
Rye berries	¾ cup	2½ cups	Simmer, covered, about 60 minutes; drain. (Or soak berries in 2½ cups water in the refrigerator for 6 to 24 hours. Do not drain. Bring to boiling; reduce heat. Simmer, covered, for 30 minutes.)	2 cups
Spelt	1 cup	3 cups	Simmer, covered, for 50 to 60 minutes.	2½ cups
Wheat, cracked	⅔ cup	1½ cups	Add to cold water. Bring to boiling. Simmer, covered, for 12 to 15 minutes. Let stand, covered, for 5 minutes.	1¾ cups
Wheat berries	¾ cup	2½ cups	Simmer, covered, for 45 to 60 minutes; drain. (Or soak and cook as for rye berries.)	2 cups

COOKING DRIED BEANS, LENTILS, AND SPLIT PEAS

Rinse beans, lentils, or split peas. (See special cooking instructions below for black-eyed peas, fava beans, lentils, and split peas.) In a large Dutch oven combine 1 pound beans and 8 cups cold water. Bring to boiling; reduce heat. Simmer for 2 minutes. Remove from heat. Cover and let stand for 60 minutes. (Or omit cooking step and soak beans in cold water overnight in a covered Dutch oven.) Drain and rinse. In the same Dutch oven combine beans and 8 cups fresh water. Bring to boiling; reduce heat. Simmer, covered, for time listed below or until beans are tender, stirring occasionally. Cooking time depends on the dryness of the beans.

Variety	Amount	Appearance (see photo, page 76)	Cooking Time	Yield
Black beans	1 pound	Small, black, oval	60 to 90 minutes	6 cups
Black-eyed peas	1 pound	Small, cream color, oval (one side has a black oval with a cream-color dot in the center)	Do not presoak. Simmer, covered, for 45 to 60 minutes.	7 cups
Cranberry beans	1 pound	Small, tan color with specks and streaks of burgundy, oval	75 to 90 minutes	7 cups
Fava or broad beans	1 pound	Large, brown, flat oval	Follow these soaking directions instead of those above: Bring beans to boiling; simmer, covered, 15 to 30 minutes to soften skins. Let stand 60 minutes. Drain and peel. To cook, combine peeled beans and 8 cups fresh water. Bring to boiling; simmer, covered, for 45 to 50 minutes or until tender.	6 cups
Garbanzo beans (chickpeas)	1 pound	Medium, yellow or golden, round and irregular	90 minutes to 2 hours	6¼ cups
Great Northern beans	1 pound	Small to medium, white, oval shape	60 to 90 minutes	7 cups
Kidney beans, red	1 pound	Medium to large, brownish red, kidney shape	60 to 90 minutes	6⅔ cups
Lentils, brown, French, red, or yellow	1 pound	Tiny, disk shape	Do not presoak. Use 5 cups water. Simmer brown, French, and yellow lentils, covered, 25 to 30 minutes; simmer red, covered, 5 to 10 minutes.	7 cups
Lima beans, baby	1 pound	Small, off-white, wide oval	45 to 60 minutes	6½ cups
Lima beans, Christmas (calico)	1 pound	Medium, burgundy and cream color, wide oval	45 to 60 minutes	6½ cups
Lima beans, large (butter beans)	1 pound	Medium, off-white, wide oval	60 to 75 minutes	6½ cups
Navy or pea beans	1 pound	Small, off-white, oval	60 to 90 minutes	6¼ cups
Pinto beans	1 pound	Small, tan color with brown specks, oval	75 to 90 minutes	6½ cups
Red beans	1 pound	Small, dark red, oval	60 to 90 minutes	6½ cups
Soybeans	1 pound	Small, cream color, oval	3 to 3½ hours	7 cups
Split peas	1 pound	Tiny, green or yellow, disk shape	Do not presoak. Use 5 cups water. Simmer, covered, about 45 minutes.	5½ cups

breads

breads

Homemade breads are among the most gratifying items you can bake. And, yes, you can do it. These tips will help you get the hang of bread making.

LEAVENER LOGIC

- Active dry yeast (used in this book) feeds on sugar in the dough to make carbon dioxide. It works slowly and develops flavor in dough as breads rise. Store any opened yeast in the refrigerator; use before the expiration date.
- Baking soda and baking powder work fast and are used in quick breads and muffins. Baking soda reacts immediately with acidic ingredients, such as buttermilk, sour cream, brown sugar, and lemon juice, so be sure to bake batters with baking soda immediately. Do not substitute baking powder for baking soda or vice versa. Store both in a cool, dry place.

MEASURING THE FLOUR

Most flours are presifted, so sifting is not necessary. Before measuring, stir the flour in the container to loosen it. Over the flour container or sack, lightly spoon flour into a dry measuring cup until it overflows; use the flat side of a knife to level the flour even with the top of the cup. Don't shake or tap the cup; this will cause the flour to settle.

YEAST BREAD HINTS

- Yeast dough needs to rise in a warm (80°F to 85°F), draft-free place. An unheated oven with a bowl of warm water on the rack below works well. (See "Perfect Proofing," page 111.)
- Place the dough in a greased bowl that's twice its size. Cover the bowl with plastic wrap sprayed with cooking spray or a towel.
- Dough should double in size in its first rise. In its second rise, if it's in a pan, don't let the shaped dough rise above the top of the pan. It will rise more as it bakes due to "oven spring," a boost in rising caused by the oven's heat.
- A baked loaf sounds hollow when tapped lightly with your fingers. If it's browning too fast but doesn't sound hollow, loosely tent the loaf with foil. Yeast breads containing sugar or butter often need this step.
- Store yeast breads at room temperature because they become stale quickly when chilled.
- If bread has cheese or meat in it, enjoy what you want the day it's baked and freeze the rest.

QUICK BREAD HINTS

Quick breads don't use yeast to help them rise. They use faster leaveners such as baking soda and baking powder.

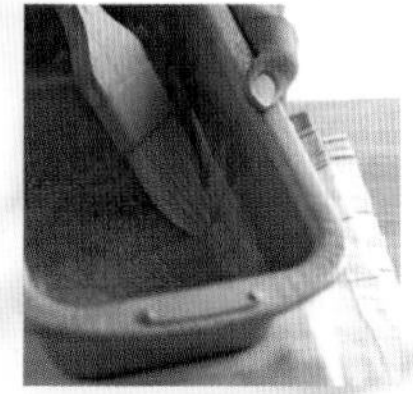

GREASE PANS: Dip a brush in shortening; lightly coat the bottom and ½ inch up sides of the pan, making sure to get into the corners. Do not grease all the way up the sides because batter needs to cling to ungreased pan sides as it rises.

CHECK DONENESS: Peek at quick bread loaves 10 to 15 minutes before minimum baking time to see if they're browning too quickly. If they are, cover them loosely with foil.

REMOVE FROM PAN: Run a thin-bladed knife around loaf edges to loosen it; turn loaf out onto a wire rack.

COOL AND STORE: For best flavor and easy slicing, wrap cooled bread in foil or plastic wrap and store overnight at room temperature.

FREEZE FOR LATER: To freeze quick bread loaves, place cooled loaves in freezer containers or bags and freeze up to 3 months.

Mixed-Grain Bread, page 101

PREPARING BREAD STEP-BY-STEP

1. ACTIVATING YEAST
Check the date first to make sure it has not expired. Yeast needs a warm liquid to get it going so it will do its job and make bread rise. However, it's sensitive. If the liquid is too hot, it can kill the yeast. Use an instant-read thermometer to make sure the liquid is between 120°F–130°F.

2. MIXING DOUGH
The dough gets too stiff for a mixer, so you'll need to stir in as much of the remaining flour as you can with a wooden spoon. Stir until dough looks ropey and pulls away from sides of the bowl.

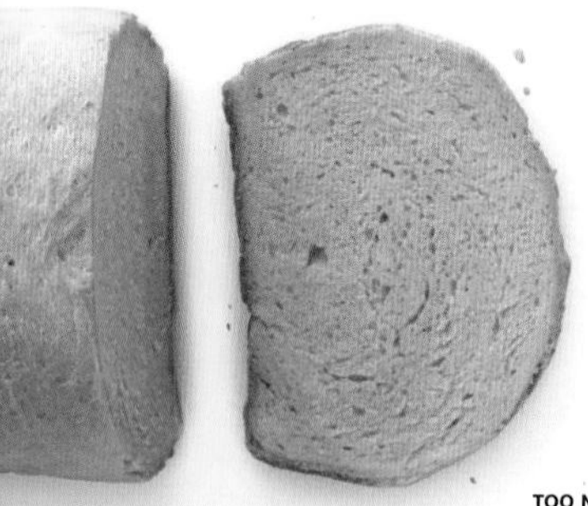

TOO MUCH FLOUR! TIGHT CRUMB TEXTURE

white bread

The Secret: It's all in the kneading. You have to know when to stop: Add just a few tablespoons too much flour and your loaf goes from tender to tuggy. We'll show you!

LOW-CALORIE

PREP: 30 MINUTES **RISE:** 75 MINUTES **REST:** 10 MINUTES
BAKE: 35 MINUTES AT 375°F **MAKES:** 2 LOAVES (24 SLICES)

- **5¾ to 6¼ cups all-purpose flour**
- **1 package active dry yeast**
- **2¼ cups milk or buttermilk**
- **2 tablespoons sugar**
- **1 tablespoon butter**
- **1½ teaspoons salt**

Use bleached or unbleached all-purpose flour or bread flour; the protein content makes for the best structure for yeast bread.

1 In a large mixing bowl combine 2½ cups of the flour and the yeast; set aside. In a medium saucepan heat and stir milk, sugar, butter, and salt just until warm (120°F to 130°F) and butter almost melts. Add milk mixture to flour mixture. Beat with an electric mixer on low speed for 30 seconds, scraping sides of bowl constantly. Beat on high speed for 3 minutes. Using a wooden spoon, stir in as much of the remaining flour as you can (see photo 2, left).

2 Turn dough out onto a lightly floured surface. Knead in enough of the remaining flour to make a moderately stiff dough that is smooth and elastic (6 to 8 minutes total; see photo 3, page 99). Shape dough into a ball. Place in a lightly greased bowl, turning to grease surface of dough. Cover; let rise in a warm place (see "Perfect Proofing," page 111) until double in size (45 to 60 minutes).

3 Punch dough down (see photo 5, page 99). Turn dough out onto a lightly floured surface. Divide in half. Cover dough; let rest for 10 minutes. Meanwhile, lightly grease two 8×4×2-inch loaf pans.

4 Shape each dough half into a loaf by patting or rolling (see photos 1 and 2, page 101). To shape dough by patting, gently pat and pinch each half of dough into a loaf shape, tucking edges underneath. To shape dough by rolling, on a lightly floured surface roll each half of dough into a 12×8-inch rectangle. Tightly roll up, starting from a short side, sealing seams with fingertips.

5 Place the shaped dough halves in the prepared pans, seam sides down. Cover and let rise in a warm place until nearly double in size (about 30 minutes).

6 Preheat oven to 375°F. Bake for 35 to 40 minutes or until bread sounds hollow when lightly tapped (if necessary, cover loosely with foil the last 5 to 10 minutes of baking to prevent overbrowning). Immediately remove bread from pans. Cool completely on wire racks.

WHOLE WHEAT BREAD: Prepare as directed, except decrease all-purpose flour to 3¾ to 4¼ cups and stir in 2 cups whole wheat flour after beating the mixture for 3 minutes in Step 1.

PER SLICE PLAIN OR WHOLE WHEAT VARIATION: 130 cal., 1 g total fat (1 g sat. fat), 3 mg chol., 159 mg sodium, 25 g carb., 1 g fiber, 4 g pro.
EXCHANGES: 1½ Starch

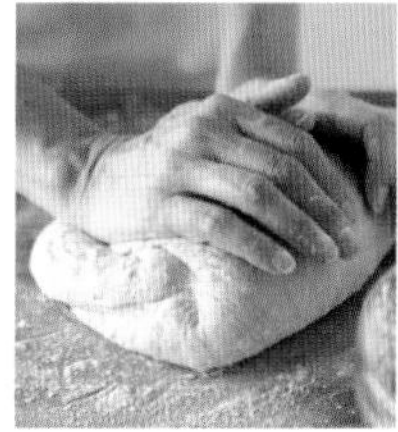

3. KNEAD IT
To knead dough, fold it over and push with the heel of your hand. Turn the dough a quarter turn and repeat until dough is moderately stiff—set a timer for 6 minutes and knead until the dough is smooth but elastic. Shoot for the minimum amount of flour, gradually adding more flour as you knead.

4. PROOF IN A POKE
The dough is ready to shape when it has proofed, or risen, sufficiently. It's ready when indentations stay after two fingers are pressed ½ inch into the center of the dough.

5. PUNCH IT DOWN
Punch the dough in the center with your fist. Pull the edges in and away from the sides of the bowl.

THE RIGHT STIFFNESS

Knead the dough until it is the stiffness specified in the recipes in this chapter. Each recipe offers approximate kneading times. The following terms are used to describe the stiffness you need to achieve:

SOFT DOUGH: Extremely sticky; used for breads that don't require kneading
MODERATELY SOFT DOUGH: Slightly sticky but smooth; used for rich, sweet breads
MODERATELY STIFF DOUGH: Slightly firm to the touch but not sticky; for nonsweet breads
STIFF DOUGH: Firm to the touch; holds its shape after 8 to 10 minutes of kneading

LOW-CALORIE

Potato Bread *(photo, page 95)*

PREP: 55 MINUTES **RISE:** 90 MINUTES
REST: 10 MINUTES **BAKE:** 35 MINUTES AT 375°F
MAKES: 2 LOAVES (24 SLICES)

- **1 large russet or long white potato (about 10 ounces)**
- **2 cups water**
- **1/4 cup butter, cut up**
- **1 1/2 teaspoons salt**
- **4 1/2 to 4 3/4 cups all-purpose flour**
- **2 packages active dry yeast**
- **2 eggs**

1 Peel and cube potato. In a saucepan combine potato and the water. Bring to boiling; reduce heat. Simmer, covered, for 12 to 15 minutes or until very tender. Drain, reserving 1 cup of hot cooking liquid. Set liquid aside. Mash potato with a potato masher (should have 1 cup); set aside.

2 In a small bowl combine reserved cooking liquid, butter, and salt. Cool to 120°F to 130°F.

3 In a large mixing bowl combine 2 cups of the flour and the yeast. Add reserved cooking liquid mixture and the eggs. Beat with electric mixer on low to medium speed for 30 seconds, scraping sides of bowl constantly. Beat on high speed for 3 minutes. Using a wooden spoon, stir in mashed potatoes and as much of the remaining flour as you can (see photo 2, page 98).

4 Turn dough out onto a lightly floured surface. Knead in enough of the remaining flour to make a moderately stiff dough that is smooth and elastic (6 to 8 minutes total; see photo 3, page 99). Shape dough into a ball. Place in a lightly greased bowl, turning to grease surface of dough. Cover; let rise in a warm place until double in size (1 to 1 1/2 hours).

5 Punch dough down (see photo 5, page 99). Turn dough out onto lightly floured surface. Divide in half. Cover; let rest for 10 minutes. Meanwhile, lightly grease two 8×4×2-inch loaf pans.

6 Shape each dough half into a loaf by patting or rolling (see photos 1 and 2, page 101). Place loaves in prepared pans. Lightly sprinkle tops with additional all-purpose flour. Cover; let rise until nearly double in size (30 to 40 minutes).

7 Preheat oven to 375°F. Bake for 35 to 40 minutes or until bread sounds hollow when lightly tapped. (If necessary, cover loosely with foil the last 15 minutes of baking to prevent overbrowning.) Cool on wire racks.

POTATO ROLLS: Prepare as directed through Step 5, except grease two large baking sheets. Divide each half of dough into 12 pieces. Shape pieces into balls. Lightly dip tops in flour. Arrange balls 1 1/2 inches apart on prepared baking sheets. Bake for 20 to 25 minutes or until golden. Cool on wire racks. Makes 24 rolls.

PER SLICE OR ROLL: 119 cal., 3 g total fat (1 g sat. fat), 23 mg chol., 167 mg sodium, 20 g carb., 1 g fiber, 3 g pro. EXCHANGES: 1 Starch, 1/2 Fat

BEST-LOVED

Golden Wheat Bread

PREP: 40 MINUTES **RISE:** 105 MINUTES
REST: 10 MINUTES **BAKE:** 55 MINUTES AT 350°F
MAKES: 2 LOAVES (24 SLICES)

- **2 packages active dry yeast**
- **1/2 cup warm water (105°F to 115°F)**
- **2 cups milk**
- **1/2 cup shortening**
- **3/4 cup packed brown sugar**
- **2 cups whole wheat flour**
- **1 egg, lightly beaten**
- **1 1/2 teaspoons salt**
- **4 3/4 to 5 1/4 cups bread flour**

1 In a small bowl dissolve yeast in the warm water; set aside. In a saucepan bring milk just to a simmer; remove from heat. Pour milk into a large mixing bowl. Whisk in shortening and brown sugar until shortening melts. Whisk in whole wheat flour. Cool to lukewarm (105°F to 115°F). Stir in yeast mixture, egg, and salt. Using a wooden spoon, stir in as much of the bread flour as you can (see photo 2, page 98).

2 Turn dough out onto a lightly floured surface. Knead in enough remaining bread flour to make a moderately stiff dough that is smooth and elastic (6 to 8 minutes total; see photo 3, page 99). Shape dough into a ball. Place in a lightly greased bowl, turning to grease surface of dough. Cover; let rise in a warm place until double in size (1 1/4 to 1 1/2 hours).

3 Punch dough down (see photo 5, page 99). Turn out onto a lightly floured surface. Divide in half. Cover; let rest for 10 minutes. Meanwhile, lightly grease two 9×5×3-inch loaf pans.

4 Shape each dough half into a loaf by patting or rolling (see photos 1 and 2, page 101). Place shaped dough halves in prepared pans. Cover; let rise in a warm place until nearly double in size (about 30 minutes).

5 Preheat oven to 350°F. Bake for 30 minutes; cover loosely with foil to prevent overbrowning. Bake about 25 minutes more or until an instant-read thermometer inserted into the center of the bread registers 210°F.* Immediately remove bread from pans. Cool on wire racks.

***NOTE:** This bread will not sound hollow when tapped, so it is necessary to take an internal temperature reading to ensure that it is done.

PER SLICE: 210 cal., 5 g total fat (1 g sat. fat), 10 mg chol., 160 mg sodium, 35 g carb., 2 g fiber, 6 g pro.
EXCHANGES: 2 Starch, ½ Other Carb., ½ Fat

Mixed-Grain Bread

PREP: 30 MINUTES **RISE:** 90 MINUTES
REST: 10 MINUTES **BAKE:** 30 MINUTES AT 375°F
MAKES: 2 LOAVES (24 SLICES)

3½ to 4 cups all-purpose flour
2 packages active dry yeast
1½ cups milk
½ cup cracked wheat
¼ cup cornmeal
¼ cup packed brown sugar
3 tablespoons vegetable oil
2 teaspoons salt
1½ cups whole wheat flour
½ cup rolled oats

1 In a large mixing bowl combine 2 cups of the all-purpose flour and the yeast; set aside. In a medium saucepan combine milk, ¾ cup *water,* cracked wheat, cornmeal, brown sugar, oil, and salt. Heat and stir over medium-low heat just until warm (120°F to 130°F). Add milk mixture to flour mixture. Beat with an electric mixer on low to medium speed 30 seconds, scraping sides of bowl constantly. Beat on high speed for 3 minutes. Using a wooden spoon, stir in whole wheat flour, rolled oats, and as much of the remaining all-purpose flour as you can.

SHAPING DOUGH STEP-BY-STEP

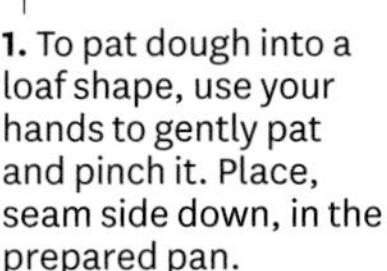

1. To pat dough into a loaf shape, use your hands to gently pat and pinch it. Place, seam side down, in the prepared pan.

2. To shape by rolling, roll dough into a 12×8-inch rectangle. Tightly roll up rectangle, starting from a short side. Pinch seam to seal.

MIXED-GRAIN BREAD

2 Turn dough out onto a lightly floured surface. Knead in enough of the remaining all-purpose flour to make a moderately stiff dough that is almost smooth and elastic (6 to 8 minutes total; see photo 3, page 99). Shape dough into a ball. Place in a lightly greased bowl, turning to grease surface of dough. Cover; let rise in a warm place until double in size (about 1 hour).

3 Punch dough down (see photo 5, page 99). Turn out onto a lightly floured surface. Divide in half. Cover; let rest for 10 minutes. Meanwhile, lightly grease two 8×4×2-inch loaf pans.

4 Shape each dough half into a loaf by patting or rolling (see photos 1 and 2, left). Place loaves in prepared pans. Cover; let rise in warm place until nearly double in size (about 30 minutes).

5 Preheat oven to 375°F. Brush loaf tops with additional water; sprinkle with additional rolled oats. Bake for 30 to 35 minutes or until bread sounds hollow when lightly tapped. (If necessary, cover loosely with foil the last 10 minutes of baking to prevent overbrowning.) Immediately remove bread from pans. Cool on wire racks.

PER SLICE: 157 cal., 3 g total fat (0 g sat. fat), 1 mg chol., 203 mg sodium, 29 g carb., 3 g fiber, 5 g pro.
EXCHANGES: 2 Starch

MIXED-GRAIN SEED BREAD: Prepare as directed, except add ¼ cup sunflower kernels, ¼ cup millet or sesame seeds, and 2 tablespoons poppy seeds with the rolled oats.

PER SLICE: 177 cal., 4 g total fat (1 g sat. fat), 1 mg chol., 203 mg sodium, 31 g carb., 3 g fiber, 5 g pro. EXCHANGES: 2 Starch, ½ Fat

Mock Sourdough Bread

PREP: 45 MINUTES **RISE:** 75 MINUTES
REST: 10 MINUTES **BAKE:** 30 MINUTES AT 375°F
MAKES: 2 LOAVES (24 SLICES)

- **6¾ to 7¼ cups all-purpose flour**
- **1 package active dry yeast**
- **1½ cups water**
- **3 tablespoons sugar**
- **3 tablespoons vegetable oil**
- **2 teaspoons salt**
- **1 6-ounce carton (⅔ cup) plain yogurt**
- **2 tablespoons lemon juice**

1 In a large mixing bowl combine 2½ cups of the flour and the yeast; set aside. In a medium saucepan heat and stir the water, sugar, oil, and salt just until warm (120°F to 130°F). Add water mixture to flour mixture along with the yogurt and lemon juice. Beat with an electric mixer on low speed for 30 seconds, scraping sides of bowl constantly. Beat on high speed for 3 minutes. Using a wooden spoon, stir in as much of the remaining flour as you can.

2 Turn dough out onto a lightly floured surface. Knead in enough of the remaining flour to make a moderately stiff dough that is smooth and elastic (6 to 8 minutes total; see photo 3, page 99). Shape dough into a ball. Place in a lightly greased bowl, turning to grease surface of dough. Cover; let rise in a warm place until double in size (45 to 60 minutes).

3 Punch dough down (see photo 5, page 99). Turn out onto a lightly floured surface. Divide in half. Cover; let rest for 10 minutes. Meanwhile, lightly grease a baking sheet.

4 Shape each dough half by gently pulling it into a ball, tucking edges underneath. Place dough rounds on prepared baking sheet. Flatten each round slightly to about 6 inches in diameter. Using a sharp knife, lightly score loaf tops in a crisscross pattern. Cover; let rise in a warm place until nearly double in size (about 30 minutes).

5 Preheat oven to 375°F. Bake for 30 to 35 minutes or until bread sounds hollow when lightly tapped. (An instant-read thermometer should register at least 200°F when inserted into centers of loaves.) (If necessary, cover loosely with foil the last 10 minutes of baking to prevent overbrowning.) Immediately remove bread from baking sheets. Cool on wire racks.

PER SLICE: 155 cal., 2 g total fat (0 g sat. fat), 0 mg chol., 200 mg sodium, 29 g carb., 1 g fiber, 4 g pro.
EXCHANGES: 2 Starch

LOW-CALORIE

Caraway-Rye Bread

PREP: 40 MINUTES **RISE:** 90 MINUTES
REST: 10 MINUTES **BAKE:** 30 MINUTES AT 375°F
MAKES: 2 LOAVES (24 SLICES)

- **4 to 4½ cups bread flour**
- **1 package active dry yeast**
- **2 cups warm water (120°F to 130°F)**
- **¼ cup packed brown sugar**
- **2 tablespoons vegetable oil**
- **1½ teaspoons salt**
- **1½ cups rye flour**
- **1 tablespoon caraway seeds**
- **2 teaspoons milk**

1 In a large mixing bowl stir together 2¾ cups of the bread flour and the yeast. Add the warm water, brown sugar, oil, and salt. Beat with an electric mixer on low speed for 30 seconds, scraping sides of bowl constantly. Beat on high speed for 3 minutes. Using a wooden spoon, stir in rye flour, caraway seeds, and as much of the remaining bread flour as you can.

2 Turn dough out onto a lightly floured surface. Knead in enough remaining bread flour to make a moderately stiff dough that is smooth and elastic (6 to 8 minutes total; see photo 3, page 99). Shape dough into a ball. Place in a lightly greased bowl, turning to grease surface of dough. Cover; let rise in a warm place until double in size (about 1 hour).

3 Punch dough down (see photo 5, page 99). Turn dough out onto a lightly floured surface. Divide dough in half. Cover; let rest 10 minutes. Meanwhile, lightly grease a baking sheet; sprinkle baking sheet with *cornmeal.*

4 Shape each dough half by gently pulling it into a ball, tucking edges under. Place dough rounds on prepared baking sheet. Flatten each dough round slightly to about 6 inches in diameter. (Or shape each dough half into a loaf shape by patting or rolling [see photos 1 and 2, page 101]. Place in two greased 8×4×2-inch loaf pans.) If desired, lightly score loaf tops using a sharp knife. Cover and let rise in a warm place until nearly double (30 to 45 minutes).

5 Preheat oven to 375°F. Brush loaf tops with milk. Bake for 30 to 35 minutes or until deep golden brown and bread sounds hollow when lightly tapped. Remove from baking sheet (or pans). Cool on wire racks.

PEASANT RYE BREAD: Prepare as directed, except substitute ¼ cup yellow cornmeal and ¼ cup whole bran cereal for ½ cup rye flour.

PER SLICE FOR CARAWAY-RYE OR PEASANT RYE VARIATION: 126 cal., 2 g total fat (0 g sat. fat), 0 mg chol., 148 mg sodium, 24 g carb., 2 g fiber, 4 g pro. EXCHANGES: 1½ Starch

LOW-CALORIE

Best Basic Challah

PREP: 60 MINUTES **RISE:** 90 MINUTES
REST: 10 MINUTES **BAKE:** 30 MINUTES AT 350°F
MAKES: 3 LOAVES (36 SLICES)

- **1¾ cups warm water (105°F to 115°F)**
- **½ cup honey**
- **2 packages active dry yeast**
- **4 eggs, lightly beaten**
- **½ cup butter, melted and cooled**
- **1 tablespoon salt**
- **7½ to 8 cups bread flour or 8 to 8½ cups all-purpose flour**
- **1 egg, lightly beaten**
- **1 tablespoon water**

1 In a large bowl stir together the 1¾ cups warm water, the honey, and yeast. Let stand about 10 minutes or until foamy. Using a wooden spoon, stir in the 4 eggs, the melted butter, and salt. Gradually stir in as much of the flour as you can.

2 Turn dough out onto a lightly floured surface. Knead in enough of the remaining flour to make a moderately soft dough that is smooth and elastic (5 to 7 minutes total; see photo 3, page 99). Shape dough into a ball. Place in a lightly greased bowl, turning to grease surface of dough. Cover; let rise in a warm place until double in size (1 to 1½ hours).

3 Punch dough down (see photo 5, page 99). Turn dough out onto a lightly floured surface. Divide into six portions. Cover; let rest for 10 minutes. Meanwhile, lightly grease a large baking sheet; set aside.

4 Divide each portion into thirds (18 portions total). Gently roll each third into an 18-inch-long rope. Place three ropes on the prepared baking sheet 1 inch apart; braid. Repeat with another 3 ropes to make another braid. Brush one side of a braid with water; lightly press the two braids together to make a double-braided loaf. Repeat with the remaining portions of dough to make two more double-braided loaves. Cover and let rise in a warm place until nearly double in size (about 30 minutes).

5 Preheat oven to 350°F. In a small bowl combine the 1 egg and the 1 tablespoon water; brush over braids. Bake for 30 to 35 minutes or until loaves sound hollow when lightly tapped.* Immediately remove loaves from baking sheet. Cool on wire racks.

***NOTE:** For an extra-shiny, glossy look, remove loaves from oven and immediately brush with additional egg mixture.

PER SLICE: 113 cal., 3 g total fat (1 g sat. fat), 27 mg chol., 167 mg sodium, 19 g carb., 1 g fiber, 3 g pro.
EXCHANGES: 1 Starch, ½ Fat

LOW-CALORIE

French Bread

PREP: 40 MINUTES **RISE:** 95 MINUTES
REST: 10 MINUTES **BAKE:** 35 MINUTES AT 375°F
MAKES: 2 LOAVES (28 SLICES)

- **5½ to 6 cups all-purpose flour**
- **2 packages active dry yeast**
- **1½ teaspoons salt**
- **2 cups warm water (120°F to 130°F)**
- **Cornmeal**
- **1 egg white, slightly beaten**
- **1 tablespoon water**

1 In a large mixing bowl combine 2 cups of the flour, the yeast, and salt. Add the 2 cups warm water. Beat with an electric mixer on low speed for 30 seconds, scraping sides of bowl constantly. Beat on high speed for 3 minutes. Using a wooden spoon, stir in as much of the remaining flour as you can.

2 Turn dough out onto a lightly floured surface. Knead in enough remaining flour to make a stiff dough that is smooth and elastic (8 to 10 minutes total; see photo 3, page 99). Shape dough into a ball. Place in a lightly greased bowl, turning to grease surface of dough. Cover; let rise in a warm place until double in size (about 1 hour).

3 Punch dough down (see photo 5, page 99). Turn dough out onto a lightly floured surface. Divide in half. Cover; let rest for 10 minutes. Meanwhile, lightly grease a baking sheet; sprinkle baking sheet with cornmeal.

4 Roll each dough half into a 15×10-inch rectangle. Tightly roll up, starting from a long side; seal well. If desired, pinch and slightly pull to taper loaves. Place loaves, seam sides down, on prepared baking sheet. In a small bowl stir together egg white and the 1 tablespoon water. Brush some of the egg white mixture over loaf tops. Let rise until nearly double in size (35 to 45 minutes).

5 Preheat oven to 375°F. Using a sharp knife, make three or four ¼-inch-deep diagonal cuts across each loaf top. Bake for 20 minutes. Brush again with egg white mixture. Bake for 15 to 20 minutes more or until bread sounds hollow when lightly tapped. Immediately remove loaves from baking sheet. Cool on wire racks.

PER SLICE: 92 cal., 0 g total fat, 0 mg chol., 128 mg sodium, 19 g carb., 1 g fiber, 3 g pro. **EXCHANGES:** 1 Starch

FAST

Garlic Bread

PREP: 15 MINUTES **BAKE:** 12 MINUTES AT 400°F
MAKES: 12 SERVINGS

- **1 16-ounce baguette-style French bread**
- **½ cup butter, softened**
- **½ teaspoon garlic salt**

1 Preheat oven to 400°F. Using a serrated knife, cut bread in half horizontally.

2 In a small bowl stir together butter and garlic salt. Spread mixture on cut sides of bread halves. Reassemble loaf and wrap tightly in heavy foil.

3 Bake for 12 to 15 minutes or until heated through. (To broil, place bread on a baking sheet, spread sides up. Broil 4 to 5 inches from the heat for 3 to 4 minutes or until toasted.)

ROASTED GARLIC BREAD: Preheat oven to 425°F. Using a sharp knife, cut ½ inch off the tops of 2 whole garlic bulbs to expose the ends of the individual cloves. Leaving garlic bulbs whole, remove any loose, papery outer layers. Place garlic bulbs in a shallow baking dish. Drizzle with 2 teaspoons olive oil. Cover with foil. Roast for 25 to 35 minutes or until garlic cloves are soft when gently squeezed. When cool enough to handle, squeeze garlic out of the bulbs. In a small bowl stir together ½ cup butter, softened, and the roasted garlic. Spread mixture on bread. Bake or broil as directed.

PER SERVING PLAIN OR ROASTED VARIATION: 177 cal., 8 g total fat (5 g sat. fat), 20 mg chol., 340 mg sodium, 21 g carb., 1 g fiber, 5 g pro. **EXCHANGES:** 1½ Starch, 1½ Fat

HERBED GARLIC BREAD: In a food processor combine 6 cloves garlic, ¼ cup packed fresh basil leaves, 2 tablespoons fresh Italian parsley leaves, 1 tablespoon fresh oregano leaves, ¼ teaspoon salt, and ¼ teaspoon black pepper. Cover and pulse until chopped. Add ½ cup butter, softened, and 2 tablespoons olive oil. Cover and pulse until combined. Spread mixture on bread. Bake or broil as directed.

PER SERVING: 200 cal., 11 g total fat (5 g sat. fat), 20 mg chol., 349 mg sodium, 22 g carb., 1 g fiber, 5 g pro.
EXCHANGES: 1½ Starch, 2 Fat

CHEDDAR-BACON LOAF: In a small bowl combine ½ cup butter, softened; 1 cup shredded sharp cheddar cheese (4 ounces); 6 slices bacon, crisp-cooked and crumbled; ¼ cup sliced green onions (2); 2 teaspoons yellow mustard; and 1 teaspoon lemon juice. Spread mixture on bread. Bake or broil as directed.

PER SERVING: 237 cal., 13 g total fat (8 g sat. fat), 35 mg chol., 462 mg sodium, 22 g carb., 1 g fiber, 8 g pro.
EXCHANGES: 1½ Starch, ½ High-Fat Meat, 1½ Fat

No-Knead Bread

PREP: 20 MINUTES **REST:** 4 TO 24 HOURS + 15 MINUTES **RISE:** 60 MINUTES
BAKE: 40 MINUTES AT 450°F
MAKES: 1 LOAF (10 SLICES)

- **3 cups all-purpose flour**
- **1½ teaspoons salt**
- **¼ teaspoon active dry yeast**
- **1⅔ cups warm water (120°F to 130°F)**
- **5 tablespoons all-purpose flour**
- **1 to 2 tablespoons yellow cornmeal**

1 In a large bowl combine the 3 cups flour, the salt, and yeast. Add the warm water. Stir until flour mixture is moistened (dough will be very sticky and soft). Cover; let rest at room temperature for 4 to 24 hours.

2 Generously sprinkle ¼ cup of the additional flour on a large piece of parchment paper. Turn dough out onto floured paper (see photo 1, below). Sprinkle top of dough mixture lightly with the remaining 1 tablespoon additional flour; using a large spatula, gently fold dough over onto itself (see photo 2, below). Cover; let rest for 15 minutes.

3 Grease a 5- to 6-quart Dutch oven or heavy pot with a diameter of 8½ to 9½ inches; sprinkle cornmeal over bottom and about 2 inches up the sides, tilting pan to coat. Gently turn dough into prepared Dutch oven,* using a spatula to help scrape dough off the paper (some dough may remain on the paper; dough may not fill bottom of pan) (see photo 3, below). Cover; let rise at room temperature until dough has risen by about 1 inch in the pan (1 to 2 hours).

4 Preheat oven to 450°F. Cover Dutch oven with a lid or foil; bake for 25 minutes. Uncover; bake about 15 minutes more or until top is golden brown. Immediately remove bread from pan. Cool completely on wire rack.

***NOTE:** Use a baking sheet to support dough when turning it into the Dutch oven.

PER SLICE: 154 cal., 0 g total fat, 0 mg chol., 351 mg sodium, 32 g carb., 1 g fiber, 4 g pro. **EXCHANGES:** 1 Starch

NO-KNEAD BREAD STEP-BY-STEP

1. The dough for this bread is very soft, so it doesn't get kneaded, but it does need a little more flour worked in. Use a stiff spatula to scrape dough onto floured parchment.

2. Sprinkle the top of the dough with flour. Use the spatula to lift and fold the dough over. You don't want to overwork the dough (as with kneading).

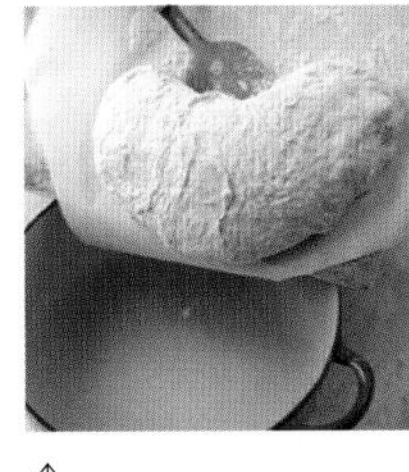

3. Slide a baking sheet under the parchment to support it. Hold the paper in place with your thumb and scrape dough off paper into the prepared Dutch oven.

NO-KNEAD FOCACCIA

No-Knead Focaccia

PREP: 20 MINUTES **REST:** 2 HOURS
RISE: 90 MINUTES **BAKE:** 30 MINUTES AT 400°F
MAKES: 12 SERVINGS

- **4 cups all-purpose flour**
- **½ teaspoon active dry yeast**
- **1½ teaspoons salt**
- **1⅔ cups warm water (120°F to 130°F)**
- **6 tablespoons roasted, salted pumpkin seeds (pepitas), chopped oil-packed dried tomatoes, and/or chopped pitted Kalamata olives**
- **1 tablespoon olive oil**
- **¼ teaspoon coarse salt**
- **¼ teaspoon smoked paprika**

1 In a large bowl combine 3 cups of the flour, the yeast, and 1½ teaspoons salt. Add the warm water. Stir until flour mixture is moistened. (The dough will be sticky and soft.) Cover bowl with waxed paper; let rest at room temperature for 2 hours.

2 Grease a 15×10×1-inch baking pan; set aside. Using a fork, stir the remaining 1 cup flour into the dough. Gather dough with your hands. Place dough in the prepared pan. Using a rubber spatula coated with *nonstick cooking spray,* gently spread dough evenly in pan (dough will be sticky). Coat a piece of plastic wrap with cooking spray; cover dough with plastic wrap, coated side down. Let rise at room temperature for 90 minutes to 2 hours or until puffy.

3 Preheat oven to 400°F. Uncover dough. Sprinkle pumpkin seeds, dried tomatoes, and/or olives over surface of dough. Brush lightly with olive oil. Sprinkle with coarse salt and paprika. Bake, uncovered, about 30 minutes or until golden brown. Cool slightly in pan on wire rack. Serve warm.

PER SERVING: 203 cal., 5 g total fat (1 g sat. fat), 0 mg chol., 341 mg sodium, 33 g carb., 2 g fiber, 6 g pro.
EXCHANGES: 2 Starch, ½ Fat

Multigrain Rolls *(photo, page 95)*

PREP: 45 MINUTES **RISE:** 90 MINUTES
REST: 10 MINUTES **BAKE:** 12 MINUTES AT 375°F
MAKES: 18 ROLLS

- **3¾ to 4¼ cups all-purpose flour**
- **2 packages active dry yeast**
- **1½ cups milk**
- **⅓ cup honey**
- **¼ cup butter, cut up**
- **2 teaspoons salt**
- **2 eggs**
- **⅔ cup whole wheat flour**
- **½ cup rye flour**
- **½ cup quick-cooking rolled oats**
- **⅓ cup toasted wheat germ**
- **1 tablespoon cornmeal**
- **1 egg, lightly beaten**
- **Sesame seeds, poppy seeds, and/or cornmeal**

1 In a large mixing bowl combine 2 cups of the all-purpose flour and the yeast; set aside. In medium saucepan heat and stir milk, honey, butter, and salt just until warm (120°F to 130°F) and butter almost melts (see photo 1, page 98). Add to flour mixture with the 2 eggs. Beat with an electric mixer on medium speed for 30 seconds, scraping sides of bowl constantly. Beat on high speed for 3 minutes. Using a wooden spoon, stir in whole wheat and rye flours, oats, wheat germ, and cornmeal. Stir in as much remaining all-purpose flour as you can.

2 Turn dough out onto a lightly floured surface. Knead in enough of the remaining all-purpose flour to make a moderately stiff dough that is smooth and elastic (6 to 8 minutes total; see photo 3, page 99). Shape dough into a ball. Place in a lightly greased bowl, turning to grease surface of dough. Cover; let rise in a warm place until double in size (1 to 1½ hours).

3 Punch dough down (see photo 5, page 99). Turn dough out onto a lightly floured surface. Divide dough into six portions. Cover; let rest for 10 minutes. Meanwhile, lightly grease two large baking sheets. Lightly sprinkle greased baking sheets with additional cornmeal or quick-cooking rolled oats.

4 Divide each portion of dough into thirds (18 portions total). Shape each third into a ball by pulling dough and pinching underneath. Flatten and pull each ball to form a 4×2-inch oval. Place on prepared baking sheets. Using kitchen shears, make three slanted cuts about ¾ inch deep on both long sides of each oval for a feathered look. Cover; let rise in a warm place until nearly double in size (30 to 45 minutes).

5 Preheat oven to 375°F. In a small bowl combine beaten egg with 1 tablespoon *water.* Brush tops of rolls with egg mixture. Sprinkle with sesame seeds, poppy seeds, and/or additional cornmeal. Bake for 12 to 15 minutes or until golden. Cool on wire racks.

PER ROLL: 211 cal., 5 g total fat (2 g sat. fat), 44 mg chol., 298 mg sodium, 36 g carb., 2 g fiber, 7 g pro.
EXCHANGES: 2½ Starch, ½ Fat

LOW-CALORIE

Pull-Apart Cornmeal Dinner Rolls

PREP: 30 MINUTES **RISE:** 90 MINUTES
REST: 10 MINUTES **BAKE:** 12 MINUTES AT 400°F
MAKES: 32 ROLLS

- **1 cup milk**
- **¼ cup sugar**
- **¼ cup butter, cut up**
- **¼ cup yellow cornmeal**
- **1 teaspoon salt**
- **1 package active dry yeast**
- **¼ cup warm water (105°F to 115°F)**
- **1 egg, lightly beaten**
- **3¾ to 4¼ cups all-purpose flour**
- **2 tablespoons butter, melted**
- **1 to 2 tablespoons yellow cornmeal**

1 In a small saucepan heat and stir milk, sugar, the ¼ cup butter, ¼ cup cornmeal, and the salt just until warm (105°F to 115°F) and butter almost melts. In a large bowl dissolve yeast in the warm water. Add warm milk mixture and egg. Using a wooden spoon, stir in enough flour to make a soft dough.

2 Turn dough out onto a lightly floured surface. Knead in enough of the remaining flour to make a moderately soft dough that is smooth and elastic (about 3 minutes total; see photo 3, page 99). Shape dough into a ball. Place in a lightly greased bowl, turning to grease surface of dough. Cover; let rise in a warm place until double in size (about 1 hour).

3 Punch dough down (see photo 5, page 99). Turn dough out onto a lightly floured surface. Cover and let rest for 10 minutes. Meanwhile, grease a 15×10×1-inch baking pan.

4 Roll or pat dough into a 10×8-inch rectangle. Cut into 2½×1-inch strips. Arrange strips in prepared pan, leaving about ¼ inch between each strip. Cover; let rise in warm place until nearly double in size (about 30 minutes).

5 Preheat oven to 400°F. Brush rolls with melted butter. Sprinkle with 1 to 2 tablespoons cornmeal. Bake 12 to 15 minutes or until golden. Cool slightly. Remove from pan; serve warm.

PARMESAN-HERB DINNER ROLLS: Prepare rolls as directed, except add ½ teaspoon dried rosemary, crushed, or 1 teaspoon dried thyme or oregano, crushed, to saucepan with the milk mixture in Step 1. Brush rolls with butter and sprinkle with 2 tablespoons grated Parmesan cheese instead of cornmeal. Bake as directed.

MAKE-AHEAD DIRECTIONS: Prepare as directed through Step 4, except do not let rolls rise in the pan. Cover pan and refrigerate for up to 24 hours. Let rolls stand for 30 minutes at room temperature before baking. Bake as directed.

PER ROLL PLAIN OR PARMESAN-HERB VARIATION: 90 cal., 3 g total fat (2 g sat. fat), 13 mg chol., 94 mg sodium, 14 g carb., 1 g fiber, 2 g pro. EXCHANGES: 1 Starch, ½ Fat

BEST-LOVED LOW-CALORIE

Overnight Refrigerator Rolls

PREP: 35 MINUTES **CHILL:** OVERNIGHT
REST: 10 MINUTES **RISE:** 45 MINUTES
BAKE: 12 MINUTES AT 375°F **MAKES:** 24 ROLLS

- **1¼ cups warm water (105°F to 115°F)**
- **1 package active dry yeast**
- **4 to 4¼ cups all-purpose flour**
- **⅓ cup butter, melted, or vegetable oil**
- **⅓ cup sugar**
- **1 teaspoon salt**
- **1 egg**
- **Nonstick cooking spray**
- **2 tablespoons butter, melted (optional)**

1 In a large mixing bowl combine warm water and yeast. Stir to dissolve yeast. Add 1½ cups of the flour, ⅓ cup melted butter, the sugar, salt, and egg. Beat with an electric mixer on low speed for 1 minute, scraping sides of bowl constantly.

2 Using a wooden spoon, stir in enough of the remaining flour to make a soft dough that just starts to pull away from sides of bowl (dough will be slightly sticky). Coat a 3-quart covered container with cooking spray. Place dough in container, turning to grease surface of dough. Cover and refrigerate overnight.

3 Punch dough down (see photo 5, page 99). Turn dough out onto a lightly floured surface. Divide in half. Cover and let rest for 10 minutes. Meanwhile, lightly grease a 13×9×2-inch baking pan or baking sheets.

4 Shape dough into 24 balls or desired rolls (be careful not to overwork dough; it becomes stickier the more you work with it). Place rolls in prepared baking pan or 2 to 3 inches apart on baking sheets. Cover; let rise in a warm place until nearly double in size (about 45 minutes).

5 Preheat oven to 375°F. Bake about 20 minutes for pan rolls or for 12 to 15 minutes for individual rolls or until golden. Remove rolls from pans. If desired, brush tops of rolls with melted butter. Serve warm.

BUTTERHORN ROLLS: On a lightly floured surface roll each dough half into a 10-inch circle. If desired, brush with melted butter. Cut each dough circle into 12 wedges. To shape rolls, begin at wide end of each wedge and loosely roll toward the point. Place, point sides down, 2 to 3 inches apart on prepared baking sheets. Makes 24 rolls.

PARKER HOUSE ROLLS: On a lightly floured surface roll each dough half until ¼ inch thick. Cut dough with a floured 2½-inch round cutter. Brush with melted butter. Using the dull edge of a table knife, make an off-center crease in each round. Fold each round along the crease. Press the folded edge firmly. Place, larger halves up, 2 to 3 inches apart on prepared baking sheets. Makes 24 rolls.

PER ROLL PLAIN, BUTTERHORN, OR PARKER HOUSE VARIATIONS: 113 cal., 3 g total fat (2 g sat. fat), 16 mg chol., 119 mg sodium, 19 g carb., 1 g fiber, 3 g pro. EXCHANGES: 1 Starch, ½ Fat

ROSETTES: Divide each dough half into 16 pieces. On a lightly floured surface roll each piece into a 12-inch-long rope. Tie each rope in a loose knot, leaving two long ends. Tuck top end under knot and bottom end into the top center. Place 2 to 3 inches apart on prepared baking sheets. Makes 32 rolls.

PER ROLL: 85 cal., 2 g total fat (1 g sat. fat), 12 mg chol., 89 mg sodium, 14 g carb., 0 g fiber, 2 g pro. EXCHANGES: 1 Starch, ½ Fat

HAMBURGER OR FRANKFURTER BUNS: Divide dough into 12 pieces. Cover and let rest for 10 minutes. For hamburger buns, shape each piece into a ball, tucking edges under. Place on a greased baking sheet. Using your fingers, slightly flatten balls to 4 inches in diameter. For frankfurter buns, shape each portion into a roll about 5½ inches long, tapering ends. Place 2 to 3 inches apart on prepared baking sheets. Makes 12 buns.

PER BUN: 226 cal., 6 g total fat (3 g sat. fat), 31 mg chol., 238 mg sodium, 38 g carb., 1 g fiber, 5 g pro. EXCHANGES: 2½ Starch, 1 Fat

ADD SOME TEXTURE AND FLAVOR

Before baking rolls, brush tops with melted butter. Sprinkle tops with sesame seeds, poppy seeds, or a combination of both. You could add lemon-pepper seasoning to the seeds for additional flavor. Or sprinkle rolls with a mixture of yellow cornmeal and grated Parmesan cheese.

cook's secrets

CINNAMON ROLL POINTERS

1. WATCH YOUR TEMP
This is where you can really blow it! If you heat the milk mixture beyond 130°F, you might kill the yeast, and nothing you do from this point will matter. Be gentle with your heat and use a candy or instant-read thermometer to check your temp in the pan. If you need a visual clue: When the butter is almost melted, you're ready to remove the mixture from the heat.

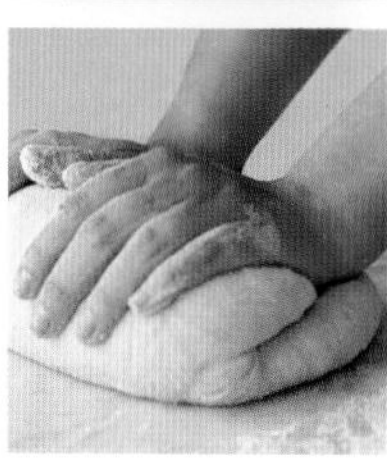

2. NEED TO KNEAD
Kneading dough is important to the texture of the rolls. On a floured surface fold dough in half and push down and away with the heels of your hands. Turn the dough; repeat. Keep folding, pushing, and turning the dough, adding small amounts of flour to keep dough from sticking. After 3 to 5 minutes, the dough should be smooth and slightly sticky (if you press into dough, it springs back).

potato cinnamon rolls

The Secret: You'll never know these light, fluffy rolls are made with potato. Yep! Mashed potato adds moisture and structure without contributing to the development of gluten.

PREP: 45 MINUTES **RISE:** 75 MINUTES **REST:** 10 MINUTES
BAKE: 25 MINUTES AT 375°F **COOL:** 10 MINUTES **MAKES:** 12 ROLLS

The amount of water that flour will absorb varies—it depends on the type of flour, the amount of protein in the flour, and how much moisture is in the air. To avoid tough rolls, use the lesser amount of flour in the range and gradually work toward the greater amount as you knead.

- **4¼ to 4¾ cups all-purpose flour**
- **1 package active dry yeast**
- **1 cup milk**
- **1 cup mashed, cooked potato***
- **⅓ cup butter, cut up**
- **⅓ cup granulated sugar**
- **1 teaspoon salt**
- **2 eggs**
- **½ cup packed brown sugar**
- **1 tablespoon ground cinnamon**
- **¼ cup butter, softened**
- **1 recipe Vanilla Icing, Cream Cheese Icing, or Browned Butter Icing (page 113)**

1 In a large mixing bowl combine 1½ cups of the flour and the yeast; set aside. In a saucepan heat and stir milk, potato, ⅓ cup butter, granulated sugar, and salt just until warm (120°F to 130°F) and butter almost melts; add to flour mixture along with the eggs. Beat with an electric mixer on low speed for 30 seconds, scraping sides of bowl. Beat on high speed for 3 minutes. Stir in as much of the remaining flour as you can.

2 Turn dough out onto a lightly floured surface. Knead in enough of the remaining flour to make a moderately soft dough that is smooth and elastic (3 to 5 minutes total; see photo 2, left). Shape dough into a ball. Place in a lightly greased bowl; turn to grease surface of the dough. Cover; let rise in a warm place until double in size (45 to 60 minutes).

3 Punch dough down. Turn out onto a lightly floured surface. Cover; let rest for 10 minutes. Meanwhile, lightly grease a 13×9×2-inch baking pan; set aside. For filling, in a small bowl stir together brown sugar and cinnamon; set aside.

4 Roll dough into an 18×12-inch rectangle. Spread ¼ cup butter over dough and sprinkle with filling, leaving 1 inch unfilled along one of the long sides. Roll up rectangle, starting from the filled long side (see photo 8, page 111); pinch dough to seal seam. Slice into 12 equal pieces (see photo 11, page 111). Arrange in the prepared pan. Cover; let rise in a warm place until nearly double in size (about 30 minutes).

5 Preheat oven to 375°F. Bake for 25 to 30 minutes or until golden. Cool in pan on a wire rack for 10 minutes; remove from pan. Drizzle or spread with icing. Serve warm.

*MASHED POTATO IN A HURRY

Scrub a 10-ounce potato (leave the skin on). Prick it with a fork. Microwave on 100% power (high) about 7 minutes or until tender. Halve potato and scoop pulp out of skin into a small bowl; discard skin. Mash pulp with a potato masher or an electric mixer on low speed. Measure 1 cup mashed potato.

3. PERFECT PROOFING
Stop guessing; here's the perfect warm place for letting your dough rise. Boil some water in a 2-cup glass measure. Cover dough with a kitchen towel and place it in a cold oven or the microwave with the steaming water in the 2-cup measure. Shut the door and let the dough rise for the amount of time specified in the recipe.

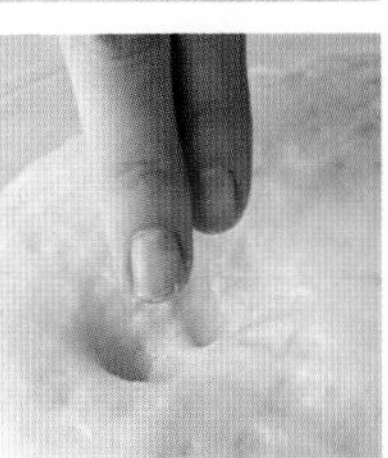

4. THE TWO-FINGER TEST
After letting the dough rise for 45 minutes, look to see if it has nearly doubled in size. If so, gently press two fingers into the surface of the dough. If the indentations remain, the dough has risen adequately. If not, let it go 15 more minutes and recheck.

5. THE PUNCH
This is the best part of making homemade dough! Punch your fist into the center of the dough to deflate it. This is important so your dough does not have big pockets of air as you roll it out. Let the dough stand for 10 minutes to relax the gluten, making the dough easier to roll out.

6. THE RIGHT RECTANGLE
Achieving an 18×12-inch rectangle is key to making evenly shaped rolls. The hardest part is making four good corners. Alternate rolling dough from the center to the edges with rolling dough from the center to the corners diagonally.

7. SQUARE CORNERS
You may have to gently lift and pull the corners to shape them—just don't stretch and tear the dough.

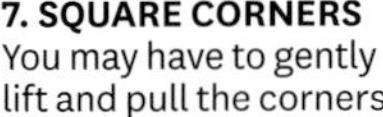

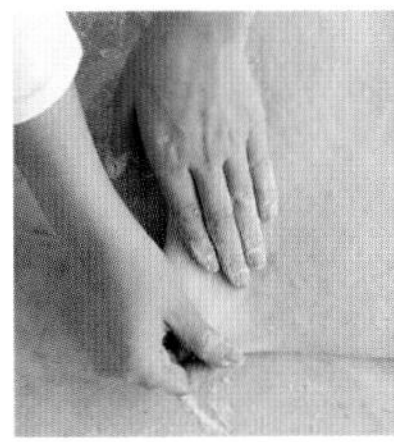

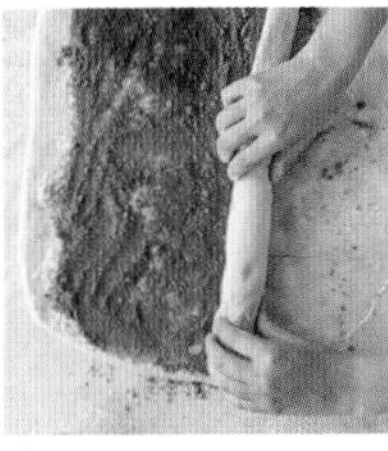

8. ROLL IT UP
Gently roll the dough into a spiral, starting with a long side. You may have to guide the roll along, moving your hands from one end of the dough to another, to get an even roll.

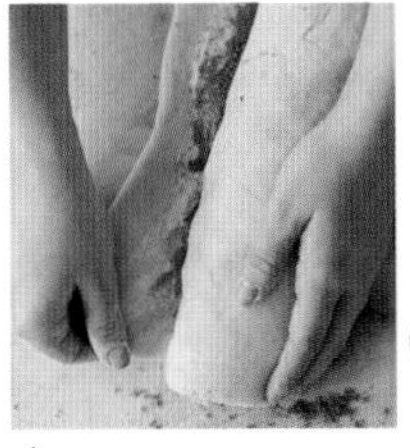

9. EVEN IT UP
Gently pull the corners so they're square and even. This makes it easier to use the entire roll of dough without trimming.

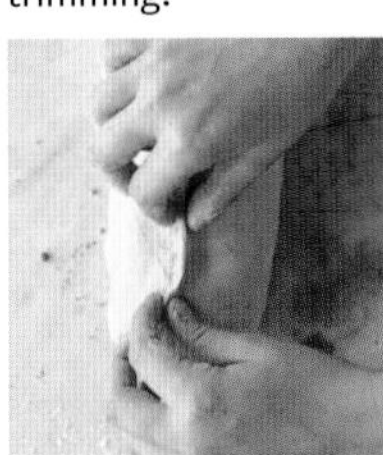

10. THE PINCH
Using your index finger and thumb, pinch the seam to seal the edges.

11. STRING'S THE THING
If you're not a confident cutter, use a ruler to make sure you find the exact midpoint of the dough log. Cut the log in half using a serrated knife or kitchen string (these items won't squish the spiral). Place a loop of string around the log and pull the ends of the string in opposite directions to cut through the dough.

YEAST: IT'S NOT SO SCARY

ACTIVE DRY YEAST: Active dry yeast comes in packets and larger jars. It's mixed with flour or dissolved in warm liquid before use. Check the expiration date!
QUICK-RISING YEAST: Also called fast-rising or instant yeast, this more active yeast cuts the rise time by about one-third. It can be substituted for active dry yeast except in recipes requiring the dough to rise in the refrigerator or when using sourdough starter.

cook's secrets

CINNAMON ROLL COFFEE CAKE

For a fun (and easy) spin on the traditional rolls, shape the dough into two big rolls.

1. CUT IT LENGTHWISE
Prepare and roll up dough log as directed in Step 4, page 110, except cut rolled dough log in half lengthwise.

2. START A SPIRAL
Line two baking sheets with parchment paper. In the center of each baking sheet coil one dough half, cut sides up, to form a snail shape.

3. TUCK & BAKE
Tuck ends under and let rolls rise on baking sheets as directed. Bake in a preheated 350°F oven for 30 minutes or until golden, covering edges with foil if necessary to prevent overbrowning.

iced over!

Frosting slathered on top or a light drizzle of icing? Try one of these sweet toppings.

VANILLA ICING: In a small bowl stir together 1½ cups powdered sugar, ½ teaspoon vanilla, and enough milk (4 to 6 tablespoons) to reach drizzling consistency.

PER ROLL WITH VANILLA ICING: 396 cal., 11 g total fat (6 g sat. fat), 61 mg chol., 283 mg sodium, 68 g carb., 2 g fiber, 7 g pro. EXCHANGES: 2 Starch, 2½ Other Carb., 2 Fat

CREAM CHEESE ICING: In a medium mixing bowl beat one 3-ounce package softened cream cheese with 2 tablespoons softened butter and 1 teaspoon vanilla with an electric mixer on medium speed until combined. Gradually beat in 2½ cups powdered sugar until smooth. Beat in milk, 1 teaspoon at a time, to reach spreading consistency.

PER ROLL WITH CREAM CHEESE ICING: 472 cal., 15 g total fat (9 g sat. fat), 69 mg chol., 339 mg sodium, 78 g carb., 2 g fiber, 7 g pro. EXCHANGES: 2 Starch, 3 Other Carb., 3 Fat

BROWNED BUTTER ICING: In a small saucepan heat ¾ cup butter over low heat until melted. Continue heating until butter turns a delicate light brown, stirring occasionally. Remove from heat. In a large mixing bowl combine 3 cups powdered sugar, 2 tablespoons milk, and 1 teaspoon vanilla. Add the browned butter. Beat with an electric mixer on low speed until combined. Beat on medium to high speed, adding milk, 1 teaspoon at a time, to reach spreading consistency.

PER ROLL WITH BROWNED BUTTER ICING: 553 cal., 22 g total fat (14 g sat. fat), 87 mg chol., 402 mg sodium, 82 g carb., 2 g fiber, 7 g pro. EXCHANGES: 2½ Starch, 3 Other Carb., 4 Fat

change them up!

If you are a sticky bun fan, give the Caramel-Pecan variation a try. Or go fruity—pears make an easy sub for the apples as does any dried fruit.

CARAMEL-PECAN ROLLS: Prepare as directed on page 110 through Step 3, except for filling. In a small saucepan combine ⅔ cup packed brown sugar, ¼ cup butter, and 2 tablespoons light-color corn syrup. Stir over medium heat until combined. Spread mixture in prepared pan. Sprinkle ⅔ cup toasted chopped pecans over butter mixture; set aside. Continue with Step 4, placing rolls on top of pecan mixture in pan. After baking, immediately invert rolls onto a serving platter. Omit the icing.

PER ROLL: 465 cal., 19 g total fat (9 g sat. fat), 67 mg chol., 338 mg sodium, 68 g carb., 2 g fiber, 8 g pro. EXCHANGES: 2½ Starch, 2 Other Carb., 3 Fat

APPLE-RAISIN ROLLS: Prepare as directed on page 110 through Step 4, except instead of using brown sugar and cinnamon for filling, stir together ⅓ cup granulated sugar, ⅓ cup chopped dried apples, ¼ cup raisins, and 2 teaspoons apple pie spice. If desired, omit icing.

PER ROLL: 332 cal., 11 g total fat (6 g sat. fat), 56 mg chol., 298 mg sodium, 52 g carb., 2 g fiber, 7 g pro. EXCHANGES: ½ Fruit, 2½ Starch, ½ Other Carb., 1½ Fat

MAKE AHEAD

Prepare the basic recipe on page 110 through Step 4, except don't let the rolls rise after shaping. Cover loosely with oiled waxed paper and with plastic wrap. Chill for 2 to 24 hours. Before baking, let chilled rolls stand, covered, for 30 minutes at room temperature. Uncover and bake as directed.

Easy Cinnamon Rolls

PREP: 25 MINUTES **RISE:** 60 MINUTES
BAKE: 25 MINUTES AT 375°F **STAND:** 5 MINUTES
MAKES: 16 ROLLS

- **½ cup packed brown sugar**
- **1 tablespoon ground cinnamon**
- **2 16-ounce loaves frozen white bread dough or sweet roll dough, thawed**
- **3 tablespoons butter, melted**
- **¾ cup raisins (optional)**
- **1 recipe Vanilla Icing**

1 Grease a 13×9×2-inch baking pan; set aside. In a small bowl stir together brown sugar and cinnamon; set aside. On a lightly floured surface roll each loaf of dough into a 12×8-inch rectangle, stopping occasionally to let dough relax if necessary. Brush with melted butter; sprinkle with brown sugar mixture. If desired, sprinkle with raisins.

2 Starting from a short side, roll up each dough rectangle. Pinch dough to seal seams. Slice each roll into eight equal pieces. Arrange in prepared pan. Cover; let rise in a warm place until nearly double (about 1 hour).

3 Preheat oven to 375°F. Break any surface bubbles in rolls with a greased toothpick. Bake for 25 to 30 minutes or until rolls are golden and sound hollow when tapped. (If necessary, cover rolls with foil the last 10 minutes of baking to prevent overbrowning.) Let stand in pan on a wire rack for 5 minutes; remove from pan. Drizzle with Vanilla Icing. Serve warm.

VANILLA ICING: In a small bowl stir together 1½ cups powdered sugar, ½ teaspoon vanilla, and enough milk (2 to 3 tablespoons) to reach drizzling consistency.

MAKE-AHEAD DIRECTIONS: Prepare as directed through Step 2. Cover with oiled waxed paper, then with plastic wrap. Chill for 2 hours or up to 24 hours. Before baking, let rolls stand, covered, for 1 hour at room temperature. Uncover and bake as directed.

PER ROLL: 235 cal., 4 g total fat (1 g sat. fat), 6 mg chol., 284 mg sodium, 45 g carb., 1 g fiber, 3 g pro.
EXCHANGES: 1 Starch, 2 Other Carb., ½ Fat

EASY CARAMEL-PECAN ROLLS: Prepare as directed, except generously grease the pan and line with parchment paper or nonstick foil. Stir together 1¼ cups powdered sugar and ⅓ cup whipping cream; pour evenly into the prepared pan, spreading gently. Sprinkle 1 cup chopped pecans over mixture. Continue as directed.

PER ROLL: 336 cal., 11 g total fat (3 g sat. fat), 13 mg chol., 286 mg sodium, 55 g carb., 1 g fiber, 4 g pro.
EXCHANGES: 1 Starch, 2½ Other Carb., 2 Fat

Monkey Bread

PREP: 20 MINUTES **RISE:** OVERNIGHT
BAKE: 40 MINUTES AT 350°F **STAND:** 1 MINUTE
MAKES: 24 ROLLS

- **1 36.5-ounce package frozen cinnamon sweet roll dough or orange sweet roll dough (12 rolls)**
- **½ cup chopped pecans**
- **⅓ cup butter, melted**
- **¾ cup sugar**
- **¼ cup caramel-flavor ice cream topping**

1 The night before, place frozen rolls about 2 inches apart on a large greased cookie sheet. Discard frosting packets or reserve for another use. Cover rolls with lightly greased plastic wrap. Refrigerate overnight to let dough thaw and begin to rise.

2 Preheat oven to 350°F. Generously grease a 10-inch fluted tube pan. Sprinkle ¼ cup of the pecans in the bottom of the pan.

3 Cut each roll in half. Dip each roll half into melted butter; roll in sugar. Layer coated roll halves in the prepared pan. Drizzle with any remaining butter; sprinkle with any remaining sugar. Sprinkle the remaining ¼ cup pecans on top. Drizzle ice cream topping over all.

4 Place pan on a baking sheet. Bake for 40 to 45 minutes or until golden brown. Let stand for 1 minute. Invert onto a large serving platter. Spoon any topping and nuts that remain in pan onto rolls. Cool slightly. Serve warm.

PER ROLL: 171 cal., 6 g total fat (2 g sat. fat), 7 mg chol., 150 mg sodium, 26 g carb., 1 g fiber, 2 g pro.
EXCHANGES: ½ Starch, 1½ Other Carb., 1 Fat

TAKE A SHORTCUT

Frozen bread dough or sweet roll dough lets you take a big shortcut while still producing a home-baked breakfast treat. Keep a package or two in your freezer to save time and effort. Sweet roll dough is especially good for making monkey bread because you only have to halve the rolls to get pull-apart results.

BEST-LOVED

Orange Bowknots

PREP: 45 MINUTES **RISE:** 90 MINUTES
REST: 10 MINUTES **BAKE:** 12 MINUTES AT 375°F
MAKES: 24 ROLLS

- **6 to 6½ cups all-purpose flour**
- **1 package active dry yeast**
- **1¼ cups milk**
- **½ cup butter, margarine, or shortening**
- **⅓ cup granulated sugar**
- **½ teaspoon salt**
- **2 eggs**
- **2 tablespoons finely shredded orange peel**
- **¼ cup orange juice**
- **1 recipe Orange Icing**

1 In a large mixing bowl combine 2 cups of the flour and the yeast; set aside. In a medium saucepan heat and stir the milk, butter, granulated sugar, and salt just until warm (120°F to 130°F) and butter almost melts; add to flour mixture along with eggs. Beat with an electric mixer on low speed for 30 seconds, scraping sides of bowl constantly. Beat on high speed for 3 minutes. Using a wooden spoon, stir in orange peel, orange juice, and as much of the remaining flour as you can.

2 Turn dough out onto a lightly floured surface. Knead in enough of the remaining flour to make a moderately soft dough that is smooth and elastic (3 to 5 minutes total; see photo 3, page 99). Shape dough into a ball. Place in a lightly greased bowl, turning to grease surface of dough. Cover; let rise in a warm place until double in size (about 1 hour).

3 Punch dough down (see photo 5, page 99). Turn out onto a lightly floured surface. Divide in half. Cover and let rest 10 minutes. Lightly grease two large baking sheets; set aside.

4 Roll each dough half into a 12×7-inch rectangle. Cut each rectangle into twelve 7-inch-long strips. Tie each strip loosely in a knot. Place knots 2 inches apart on prepared baking sheets. Cover; let rise in a warm place until nearly double in size (about 30 minutes).

5 Preheat oven to 375°F. Bake for 12 to 14 minutes or until golden. Immediately remove from baking sheets. Cool on wire racks. Drizzle with Orange Icing.

ORANGE ICING: In a medium bowl combine 1½ cups powdered sugar, 1½ teaspoons finely shredded orange peel, and enough orange juice (2 to 3 tablespoons) to reach drizzling consistency.

PER ROLL: 203 cal., 5 g total fat (3 g sat. fat), 29 mg chol., 88 mg sodium, 35 g carb., 1 g fiber, 4 g pro.
EXCHANGES: 1½ Starch, ½ Other Carb., 1 Fat

Corn Bread

PREP: 15 MINUTES **BAKE:** 20 MINUTES AT 400°F
MAKES: 9 SERVINGS

- **1 cup cornmeal**
- **¾ cup all-purpose flour**
- **2 to 4 tablespoons sugar**
- **2½ teaspoons baking powder**
- **½ teaspoon salt**
- **1 cup milk**
- **2 eggs**
- **¼ cup butter, melted**

1 Preheat oven to 400°F. Grease an 8×8×2-inch square or 9×1½-inch round baking pan; set aside. In a medium bowl stir together cornmeal, flour, sugar, baking powder, and salt; set aside.

2 In a small bowl whisk together the milk, eggs, and butter. Add milk mixture all at once to cornmeal mixture. Stir just until moistened. Pour batter into the prepared pan.

3 Bake about 20 minutes or until edges are golden brown. Cool slightly; serve warm.

STONE-GROUND CORN BREAD: Prepare as directed, except substitute ½ cup stone-ground yellow cornmeal for ½ cup yellow cornmeal.

PER SERVING PLAIN OR STONE-GROUND VARIATION: 173 cal., 7 g total fat (4 g sat. fat), 63 mg chol., 298 mg sodium, 23 g carb., 1 g fiber, 5 g pro. EXCHANGES: 1½ Other Carb., 1 Fat

QUICK SEED BREAD

CORN MUFFINS: Prepare as directed, except spoon batter into 12 greased 2½-inch muffin cups, filling cups two-thirds full. Bake in a preheated 400°F oven about 15 minutes or until edges are golden brown. Makes 12 muffins.

SKILLET CORN BREAD: Prepare as directed, except place 9-inch cast-iron skillet in oven with butter; when butter melts, swirl to coat pan; pour butter into milk mixture. Continue as directed, working quickly so batter goes into hot skillet. Bake as directed. Makes 12 wedges.

PER MUFFIN OR WEDGE: 130 cal., 6 g total fat (3 g sat. fat), 47 mg chol., 224 mg sodium, 17 g carb., 1 g fiber, 3 g pro.
EXCHANGES: 1 Starch, 1 Fat

Quick Seed Bread

PREP: 20 MINUTES **BAKE:** 45 MINUTES AT 350°F
COOL: 10 MINUTES **STAND:** OVERNIGHT
MAKES: 1 LOAF (14 SLICES)

- 1½ **cups all-purpose flour**
- ½ **cup whole wheat flour**
- ¾ **cup packed brown sugar**
- ½ **cup dry-roasted sunflower kernels**
- ⅓ **cup flaxseed meal**
- 2 **tablespoons sesame seeds**
- 2 **tablespoons poppy seeds**
- 1 **teaspoon baking powder**
- ½ **teaspoon baking soda**
- 1 **egg**
- 1¼ **cups buttermilk or sour milk (see tip, page 19)**
- ¼ **cup vegetable oil**
- 4 **teaspoons sesame seeds, poppy seeds, and/or dry-roasted sunflower kernels**

1 Preheat oven to 350°F. Grease the bottom and ½ inch up sides of a 9×5×3-inch loaf pan (see photo, page 97); set aside.

2 In a large bowl stir together the flours, brown sugar, ½ cup sunflower kernels, flaxseed meal, the 2 tablespoons sesame seeds, the 2 tablespoons poppy seeds, the baking powder, baking soda, and ½ teaspoon *salt*. Make a well in center of the flour mixture; set aside. In a medium bowl beat egg with a fork; stir in buttermilk and oil. Add egg mixture all at once to flour mixture. Stir just until moistened (batter should be lumpy). Spread into prepared pan. Sprinkle with the 4 teaspoons seeds.

3 Bake for 45 to 55 minutes or until a wooden toothpick inserted near the center comes out clean. Cool in pan on a wire rack for 10 minutes. Remove from pan. Cool completely on wire rack. Wrap and store overnight before slicing.

PER SLICE: 216 cal., 10 g total fat (1 g sat. fat), 16 mg chol., 180 mg sodium, 28 g carb., 2 g fiber, 5 g pro.
EXCHANGES: 2 Starch, 1½ Fat

CREAM CHEESE RIBBON PUMPKIN BREAD

BEST-LOVED

Pumpkin Bread

PREP: 20 MINUTES **BAKE:** 55 MINUTES AT 350°F
COOL: 10 MINUTES **STAND:** OVERNIGHT
MAKES: 2 LOAVES (32 SLICES)

- **3 cups sugar**
- **1 cup vegetable oil**
- **4 eggs**
- **3⅓ cups all-purpose flour**
- **2 teaspoons baking soda**
- **1½ teaspoons salt**
- **1 teaspoon ground cinnamon**
- **1 teaspoon ground nutmeg**
- **⅔ cup water**
- **1 15-ounce can pumpkin**

1 Preheat oven to 350°F. Grease the bottom and ½ inch up sides of two 9×5×3-inch, three 8×4×2-inch, or four 7½×3½×2-inch loaf pans (see photo, page 97); set aside. In a mixing bowl beat sugar and oil with an electric mixer on medium speed. Add eggs; beat well.

2 In a large bowl combine flour, baking soda, salt, cinnamon, and nutmeg. Add flour mixture and the water alternately to sugar mixture, beating on low speed after each addition just until combined. Beat in pumpkin. Spoon batter into prepared pans.

3 Bake for 55 to 60 minutes for the 9×5 loaves, 45 to 50 for the 8×4 loaves, 40 to 45 minutes for the 7½×3 loaves, or until a wooden toothpick inserted near centers comes out clean. Cool in pans on a wire rack for 10 minutes. Remove from pans. Cool completely on wire rack. Wrap and store overnight before slicing.

PER SLICE: 195 cal., 8 g total fat (1 g sat. fat), 26 mg chol., 198 mg sodium, 30 g carb., 1 g fiber, 2 g pro.
EXCHANGES: ½ Starch, 1½ Other Carb., 1½ Fat

CREAM CHEESE RIBBON PUMPKIN BREAD: Prepare as directed in Step 1, except use three 8×4×2-inch pans. In a medium mixing bowl beat together half of an 8-ounce package cream cheese, softened, and ¼ cup sugar with an electric mixer on medium speed until combined. Beat in ½ cup sour cream, 1 egg, and 1 tablespoon milk. Stir in 3 tablespoons finely chopped crystallized ginger; set aside. Prepare batter as directed. Pour 1½ cups batter into each prepared pan. Divide cream cheese mixture evenly among pans. Spoon remaining batter over cream cheese mixture; spread evenly. Bake for 60 to 65 minutes or until cracks on tops of loaves appear dry. Cool as directed; wrap and refrigerate overnight before slicing. Let stand at room temperature for 1 hour before serving.

PER SLICE: 223 cal., 10 g total fat (2 g sat. fat), 39 mg chol., 214 mg sodium, 32 g carb., 1 g fiber, 3 g pro.
EXCHANGES: ½ Starch, 1½ Other Carb., 2 Fat

Cinnamon-Nut Bread

PREP: 30 MINUTES **BAKE:** 55 MINUTES AT 350°F
COOL: 10 MINUTES **STAND:** OVERNIGHT
MAKES: 14 SERVINGS

- **1⅓ cups sugar**
- **½ cup finely chopped toasted pecans or walnuts (see tip, page 21)**
- **2 teaspoons ground cinnamon**
- **2 cups all-purpose flour**
- **1 teaspoon baking powder**
- **½ teaspoon salt**
- **1 egg**
- **1 cup milk**
- **⅓ cup vegetable oil**

1 Preheat oven to 350°F. Grease and flour the bottom and ½ inch up the sides of a 9×5×3-inch loaf pan (see photo, page 97); set aside. In a small bowl stir together ⅓ cup of the sugar, the pecans, and cinnamon; set aside.

2 In a large bowl stir together the remaining 1 cup sugar, the flour, baking powder, and salt. In a medium bowl beat egg with a fork; stir in milk and oil. Add egg mixture all at once to flour mixture. Stir just until moistened (batter should be lumpy).

3 Spoon half of the batter into prepared pan. Sprinkle with half of the cinnamon mixture. Repeat with remaining batter and cinnamon mixture (see photo 1, below). Using a table knife or thin metal spatula, cut down through batter and pull up in a circular motion to marble the cinnamon mixture (see photo 2, below).

4 Bake for 55 to 60 minutes or until a wooden toothpick inserted near the center comes out clean. Cool in pan on a wire rack for 10 minutes. Remove from pan. Cool completely on wire rack. Wrap and store overnight before slicing.

PER SERVING: 227 cal., 9 g total fat (1 g sat. fat), 17 mg chol., 122 mg sodium, 35 g carb., 1 g fiber, 3 g pro.
EXCHANGES: ½ Starch, 1½ Other Carb., 2 Fat

CRANBERRY-NUT BREAD: Prepare as directed, except fold 1 cup coarsely chopped cranberries into batter.

BLUEBERRY-NUT BREAD: Prepare as directed, except fold 1 cup fresh blueberries into batter.

PER SLICE CRANBERRY OR BLUEBERRY VARIATION: 233 cal., 9 g total fat (1 g sat. fat), 17 mg chol., 122 mg sodium, 36 g carb., 1 g fiber, 3 g pro. EXCHANGES: 1 Starch, 1½ Other Carb., 2 Fat

CINNAMON-NUT BREAD STEP-BY-STEP

1. Pour the remaining half of the batter over the cinnamon mixture in the pan.

2. To swirl cinnamon mixture throughout the batter, use a table knife or thin spatula to cut down through the batter. Pull the batter up and over in a circular motion. Repeat in different areas of the batter.

Zucchini Bread

PREP: 25 MINUTES **BAKE:** 55 MINUTES AT 350°F
COOL: 10 MINUTES **STAND:** OVERNIGHT
MAKES: 2 LOAVES (28 SLICES)

- **3 cups all-purpose flour**
- **1 tablespoon baking powder**
- **1½ teaspoons ground cinnamon**
- **1 teaspoon salt**
- **2 eggs, lightly beaten**
- **2 cups sugar**
- **2½ cups coarsely shredded, unpeeled zucchini**
- **1 cup vegetable oil**
- **2 teaspoons vanilla**
- **1 cup chopped walnuts or pecans (optional)**
- **⅔ cup raisins (optional)**

1 Preheat oven to 350°F. Grease bottom and ½ inch up sides of two 8×4×2-inch loaf pans (see photo, page 97); set aside. In a large bowl stir together the flour, baking powder, cinnamon, and salt. Make a well in center of flour mixture; set aside.

2 In a medium bowl combine eggs, sugar, shredded zucchini, oil, and vanilla. Add zucchini mixture all at once to flour mixture. Stir just until moistened (batter should be lumpy). If desired, fold in nuts and raisins. Spoon batter into prepared pans.

3 Bake about 55 minutes or until a wooden toothpick inserted near centers comes out clean. Cool in pans on a wire rack for 10 minutes. Remove from pans. Cool completely on wire rack. Wrap in foil or plastic wrap and store overnight before slicing.

PER SLICE: 181 cal., 8 g total fat (1 g sat. fat), 15 mg chol., 115 mg sodium, 25 g carb., 1 g fiber, 2 g pro.
EXCHANGES: ½ Starch, 1 Other Carb., 1½ Fat

BANANA BREAD

BEST-LOVED

Banana Bread

PREP: 25 MINUTES **BAKE:** 70 MINUTES AT 350°F
COOL: 10 MINUTES **STAND:** OVERNIGHT
MAKES: 1 LOAF (16 SLICES)

- **5 medium bananas (unpeeled)**
- **2 cups all-purpose flour**
- **1½ teaspoons baking powder**
- **1 teaspoon ground cinnamon**
- **½ teaspoon baking soda**
- **¼ teaspoon salt**
- **¼ teaspoon ground ginger**
- **¼ teaspoon ground nutmeg**
- **2 eggs, lightly beaten**
- **1 cup sugar**
- **½ cup vegetable oil or melted butter**
- **¼ cup chopped walnuts**
- **1 recipe Streusel-Nut Topping (optional)**

1 Preheat oven to 350°F. Line a 15×10×1-inch baking pan with foil. Arrange bananas in the pan. Prick banana skins with the tines of a fork at 1-inch intervals. Bake for 15 minutes. Cool bananas in baking pan. Grease bottom and ½ inch up the sides of one 9×5×3-inch or two 7½×3½×2-inch loaf pans (see photo 2, right). Set pan(s) aside. In a large bowl combine flour, baking powder, cinnamon, baking soda, salt, ginger, and nutmeg. Make a well in center of flour mixture; set aside.

2 In a medium bowl stir together eggs, sugar, and oil; set aside. Using a small sharp knife, split the banana peels. Measure 1½ cups of the roasted bananas (gently press the roasted bananas into measuring cups). Stir into egg mixture. Add egg mixture all at once to flour mixture. Stir just until moistened (batter should be lumpy). Fold in walnuts. Spoon batter into prepared pan(s). If desired, sprinkle Streusel-Nut Topping over batter.

3 Bake for 50 to 55 minutes for the 9×5 loaf or 40 to 45 minutes for the 7½×3½ loaves or until a wooden toothpick inserted near center(s) comes out clean. (If necessary to prevent overbrowning, cover bread loosely with foil for the last 15 minutes of baking.) Cool in pan(s) on a wire rack for 10 minutes. Remove from pan(s). Cool completely on rack. Wrap in foil or plastic wrap and store overnight before slicing.*

***NOTE:** The quick bread's texture will be more evenly moist and less crumbly after standing.

BLUEBERRY-COCONUT BANANA BREAD: Prepare as directed, except toss ½ cup fresh or frozen blueberries in 1 tablespoon all-purpose flour; fold into batter with the walnuts. Sprinkle an additional ¼ cup fresh or frozen blueberries on top of batter in pan(s). If using the topping, add ¼ cup flaked coconut to the topping.

PER SLICE PLAIN OR BLUEBERRY-COCONUT VARIATION: 220 cal., 9 g total fat (1 g sat. fat), 23 mg chol., 131 mg sodium, 34 g carb., 2 g fiber, 3 g pro. EXCHANGES: 1 Starch, 1 Other Carb., 2 Fat

STREUSEL-NUT TOPPING: In a small bowl combine 3 tablespoons packed brown sugar and 2 tablespoons all-purpose flour. Using a pastry blender, cut in 4 teaspoons butter until mixture resembles coarse crumbs. Stir in ¼ cup chopped walnuts.

BANANA BREAD STEP-BY-STEP

1. Roasting the bananas concentrates the flavor, making it more intense and sweet.

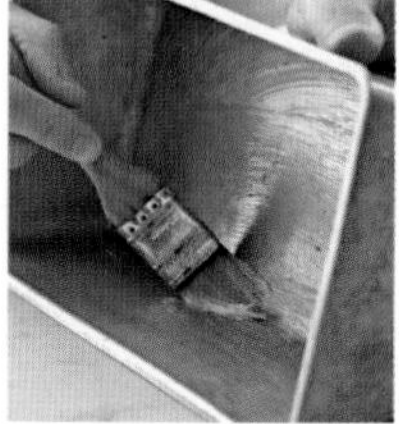

2. Brush the bottom and just ½ inch up the sides of the loaf pan. This lets the batter cling to the sides of the pan as it rises, but you can still easily loosen the bread to remove it from the pan.

make it mine

Muffins

First decide whether you want a sweet or savory treat. Then choose your muffin ingredients accordingly.

PREP: 20 MINUTES
BAKE: 15 MINUTES AT 400°F
COOL: 5 MINUTES **MAKES:** 12 MUFFINS

- **FLOUR**
- **1/4 cup granulated sugar or packed brown sugar**
- **1 1/2 teaspoons baking powder**
- **1/2 teaspoon baking soda**
- **1/4 teaspoon salt**
- **2 eggs, lightly beaten**
- **LIQUID**
- **3/4 cup buttermilk, sour milk (see tip, page 19), or milk**
- **2 tablespoons butter, melted, or vegetable oil**
- **STIR-IN**
- **TOPPING (optional)**

1 Preheat oven to 400°F. Grease twelve 2 1/2-inch muffin cups; set aside. In a medium bowl stir together the Flour, sugar, baking powder, baking soda, and salt. Make a well in center of flour mixture; set aside.

2 In a bowl combine eggs, Liquid, buttermilk, and butter. Add egg mixture all at once to flour mixture. Stir just until moistened (batter should be lumpy). Fold in Stir-In.

3 Spoon batter into prepared muffin cups, filling each half to two-thirds full. If desired, sprinkle Topping over batter in cups.

4 Bake for 15 to 18 minutes or until golden. Cool in muffin cups on a wire rack for 5 minutes. Remove from muffin cups; serve warm.

CHIP TOPPING: Crush 1 cup of your favorite flavor potato chips or dry cereal flakes; measure about 1/3 cup crushed.

STREUSEL TOPPING: In a small bowl stir together 3 tablespoons all-purpose flour, 3 tablespoons packed brown sugar, and 1/4 teaspoon ground cinnamon or ground ginger. Cut in 2 tablespoons butter until mixture resembles coarse crumbs. If desired, stir in 2 tablespoons chopped nuts and 2 tablespoons coconut.

FLOUR *(pick one)*

2 cups all-purpose flour
1 1/3 cups all-purpose flour and 3/4 cup buckwheat flour
1 1/3 cups all-purpose flour and 3/4 cup quick-cooking oats
1 cup all-purpose flour and 1 cup yellow cornmeal
1 cup all-purpose flour and 1 cup rye flour
1/2 cup all-purpose flour and 1 1/2 cups whole wheat flour

LIQUID *(pick one)*

SAVORY OPTIONS
3/4 cup ricotta cheese
3/4 cup sour cream
3/4 cup plain yogurt
3/4 cup finely shredded unpeeled zucchini

SWEET OPTIONS
3/4 cup applesauce
3/4 cup canned pumpkin
3/4 cup lemon curd

STIR-IN *(pick one)*

SAVORY OPTIONS
2 to 4 tablespoons thinly sliced green onions
2 to 4 tablespoons finely chopped sweet pepper
2 to 4 tablespoons crumbled crisp-cooked bacon
2 tablespoons grated Parmesan cheese

SWEET OPTIONS
3/4 cup fresh or frozen blueberries
1/3 cup dried fruit (blueberries; raisins; chopped cranberries or cherries; snipped dates, apricots, or figs)

TOPPING *(pick one)*

SAVORY OPTION
Chip Topping (left)

SWEET OPTION
Streusel Topping (left)

DOUBLE-CHOCOLATE MUFFINS

Double-Chocolate Muffins

PREP: 15 MINUTES **BAKE:** 18 MINUTES AT 375°F
COOL: 5 MINUTES **MAKES:** 12 MUFFINS

- **1¼ cups all-purpose flour**
- **½ cup granulated sugar**
- **⅓ cup packed brown sugar**
- **¼ cup unsweetened cocoa powder**
- **2 teaspoons baking powder**
- **¼ teaspoon baking soda**
- **½ teaspoon salt**
- **1 cup miniature semisweet chocolate pieces**
- **½ cup vegetable oil**
- **½ cup milk**
- **1 egg**

1 Preheat oven to 375°F. Grease twelve 2½-inch muffin cups or line with paper bake cups; set aside. In a medium bowl combine flour, granulated sugar, brown sugar, cocoa powder, baking powder, baking soda, and salt. Stir in chocolate pieces. Make a well in center of flour mixture; set aside.

2 In a small bowl whisk together the oil, milk, and egg. Add oil mixture all at once to the flour mixture. Stir just until moistened.

3 Spoon batter into prepared muffin cups, filling each two-thirds full. Bake for 18 to 20 minutes or until edges are firm (tops will be slightly rounded, but because this muffin is so rich, they will flatten as they cool). Cool in muffin cups on a wire rack for 5 minutes. Remove from muffin cups; serve warm.

PER MUFFIN: 295 cal., 15 g total fat (4 g sat. fat), 19 mg chol., 148 mg sodium, 38 g carb., 2 g fiber, 3 g pro.
EXCHANGES: 1 Starch, 1½ Other Carb., 3 Fat

Bran Cereal Muffins

PREP: 15 MINUTES **BAKE:** 20 MINUTES AT 400°F
COOL: 5 MINUTES **MAKES:** 24 MUFFINS

- **1 cup boiling water**
- **3 cups whole bran cereal (not flakes)**
- **2½ cups all-purpose flour**
- **½ cup granulated sugar**
- **½ cup packed brown sugar**
- **2 teaspoons baking powder**
- **1 teaspoon ground cinnamon (optional)**
- **½ teaspoon baking soda**
- **½ teaspoon salt**
- **2 eggs**
- **2 cups buttermilk or sour milk (see tip, page 19)**
- **½ cup vegetable oil**

1 Preheat oven to 400°F. Grease twenty-four 2½-inch muffin cups or line with paper bake cups; set aside. In a medium bowl pour boiling water over cereal. Stir to combine; set aside.

2 In another medium bowl combine flour, granulated sugar, brown sugar, baking powder, cinnamon (if desired), baking soda, and salt. In a large bowl combine eggs, buttermilk, and oil. Stir cereal and flour mixture into buttermilk mixture just until moistened.

3 Spoon batter into prepared muffin cups, filling each three-fourths full. Bake about 20 minutes or until a wooden toothpick inserted in centers comes out clean. Cool in muffin cups on a wire rack for 5 minutes. Remove from muffin cups; serve warm.

PER MUFFIN: 162 cal., 5 g total fat (1 g sat. fat), 18 mg chol., 201 mg sodium, 29 g carb., 5 g fiber, 3 g pro.
EXCHANGES: ½ Starch, 1½ Other Carb., 1 Fat

STIR IT EASY

After adding the liquids to the flour mixture, stir just until the dry ingredients are moist. The batter will look lumpy with little bits of flour. Do not overmix.

8 to try

Flaky Biscuits

PREP: 15 MINUTES
BAKE: 10 MINUTES AT 450°F
MAKES: 12 BISCUITS

- **3 cups all-purpose flour**
- **1 tablespoon baking powder**
- **1 tablespoon sugar**
- **1 teaspoon salt**
- **¾ teaspoon cream of tartar**
- **¾ cup butter or ½ cup butter and ¼ cup shortening**
- **1 cup milk**

1 Preheat oven to 450°F. In a large bowl combine flour, baking powder, sugar, salt, and cream of tartar. Using a pastry blender, cut in butter until mixture resembles coarse crumbs. Make a well in center of flour mixture. Add milk all at once. Using a fork, stir just until mixture is moistened.

2 Turn dough out onto a lightly floured surface. Knead dough by folding and gently pressing it just until dough holds together. Pat or lightly roll dough until ¾ inch thick. Cut dough with a floured 2½-inch biscuit cutter;* reroll scraps as necessary and dip cutter into flour between cuts.

3 Place dough circles 1 inch apart on an ungreased baking sheet. If desired, brush with additional milk. Bake for 10 to 14 minutes or until golden. Remove biscuits from baking sheet and serve warm.

***NOTE:** Alternately, roll dough into a circle; cut into wedges. Or roll it into a rectangle; cut into strips or squares.

DROP BISCUITS: Prepare as directed through Step 1, except increase the milk to 1¼ cups. Using a large spoon, drop dough into 12 mounds onto a greased baking sheet. Bake as directed.

BUTTERMILK BISCUITS: Prepare as directed, except for rolled-dough biscuits substitute 1¼ cups buttermilk or sour milk (see tip, page 19) for the 1 cup milk. For drop biscuits, substitute 1½ cups buttermilk or sour milk for the 1¼ cups milk.

PER BISCUIT FOR PLAIN, DROP, OR BUTTERMILK VARIATIONS: 231 cal., 12 g total fat (7 g sat. fat), 32 mg chol., 427 mg sodium, 26 g carb., 1 g fiber, 4 g pro. EXCHANGES: 1½ Starch, 2 Fat

GREEK: Stir ½ cup crumbled feta cheese, ⅓ cup chopped Kalamata olives, and ⅓ cup snipped dried tomatoes (not oil-packed) into flour mixture.

CHILE CHEESE: Stir 2 tablespoons chopped chipotle peppers in adobo sauce and 1 cup shredded cheddar cheese into the milk.

CHEDDAR AND PROSCIUTTO: Stir ¾ cup shredded white cheddar, ⅓ cup sliced green onions, and 2 tablespoons chopped prosciutto into flour mixture.

GARLIC AND HERB: Stir 3 to 4 cloves minced roasted garlic and 1 tablespoon snipped fresh thyme into the milk.

BACON AND BLUE CHEESE: Stir ½ cup crumbled blue cheese and 2 slices crumbled cooked bacon into flour mixture.

PEPPER-PARMESAN: Stir 1 cup shredded Parmesan cheese and 2 teaspoons cracked black pepper into flour mixture. Sprinkle cut biscuits with Parmesan.

CHOCOLATE CHIP-ORANGE: Stir ⅓ cup mini semisweet chocolate pieces and 2 teaspoons shredded orange peel into flour. Sprinkle cut biscuits with sugar.

CINNAMON AND RAISIN: Use 2 tablespoons sugar in biscuits. Stir ⅓ cup raisins and 1 teaspoon cinnamon into flour mixture. Sprinkle cut biscuits with cinnamon-sugar.

CHERRY SCONES

Scones

PREP: 20 MINUTES **BAKE:** 12 MINUTES AT 400°F
MAKES: 12 SCONES

- **2½ cups all-purpose flour**
- **2 tablespoons sugar**
- **1 tablespoon baking powder**
- **⅓ cup butter**
- **2 eggs, beaten**
- **¾ cup whipping cream**
- **½ cup dried currants or snipped raisins**

1 Preheat oven to 400°F. In a large bowl combine flour, 2 tablespoons sugar, baking powder, and ¼ teaspoon *salt*. Using a pastry blender, cut in butter until mixture resembles coarse crumbs. Make a well in center of flour mixture; set aside.

2 In a medium bowl combine eggs, the ¾ cup whipping cream, and the currants. Add egg mixture all at once to flour mixture. Using a fork, stir just until moistened.

3 Turn dough out onto a lightly floured surface. Knead dough by folding and gently pressing it for 10 to 12 strokes or until dough is nearly smooth. Divide in half. Pat or lightly roll each dough half into a 6-inch circle. Cut each circle into six wedges.

4 Place dough wedges 2 inches apart on an ungreased baking sheet. Brush wedges with additional whipping cream or *milk* and sprinkle with *coarse sugar*. Bake for 12 to 14 minutes or until golden. Remove scones from baking sheet; serve warm.

CHERRY SCONES: Prepare as directed, except omit the currants. In a small bowl pour enough boiling water over ½ cup snipped dried red tart cherries to cover. Let stand for 5 minutes; drain well. Stir drained cherries and ¼ teaspoon almond extract in with the egg mixture.

CHOCOLATE CHIP SCONES: Prepare as directed, except add ⅛ teaspoon ground cinnamon to flour mixture and substitute ½ cup miniature semisweet chocolate pieces for currants.

ORANGE SCONES: Prepare as directed, except omit the currants and stir in 1½ teaspoons finely shredded orange peel with egg mixture. Bake as directed. For icing, combine 1 cup powdered sugar, 1 tablespoon orange juice, and ¼ teaspoon vanilla; stir in additional orange juice, 1 teaspoon at a time, to reach drizzling consistency. Drizzle over scones.

PER SCONE PLAIN, CHERRY, CHOCOLATE CHIP, OR ORANGE VARIATIONS: 237 cal., 12 g total fat (7 g sat. fat), 71 mg chol., 164 mg sodium, 28 g carb., 1 g fiber, 4 g pro.
EXCHANGES: 1 Starch, 1 Other Carb., 2 Fat

Popovers

PREP: 10 MINUTES **BAKE:** 35 MINUTES AT 400°F
MAKES: 6 POPOVERS

- **1 tablespoon shortening**
- **2 eggs, lightly beaten**
- **1 cup milk**
- **1 tablespoon vegetable oil**
- **1 cup all-purpose flour**

1 Preheat oven to 400°F. Using ½ teaspoon shortening for each cup, grease the bottoms and sides of six popover pan cups or six 6-ounce custard cups. (Place the custard cups, if using, in a 15×10×1-inch baking pan; set aside.)

2 In a medium bowl use a wire whisk to beat eggs, milk, and oil until combined. Add flour and ½ teaspoon *salt;* beat until smooth. Fill the prepared cups half full with batter. Bake about 35 minutes or until very firm.

3 Immediately after removing from oven, prick each popover to let steam escape. Turn off oven. For crisper popovers, return popovers to oven for 5 to 10 minutes or until desired crispness is reached. Remove popovers from cups; serve immediately.

ASIAGO POPOVERS: Prepare as directed, except add 2 tablespoons grated Asiago or Parmesan cheese with the flour.

PER POPOVER PLAIN OR ASIAGO VARIATION: 158 cal., 7 g total fat (2 g sat. fat), 74 mg chol., 234 mg sodium, 18 g carb., 1 g fiber, 6 g pro. EXCHANGES: 1 Starch, 1 Fat

breakfasts & brunches

breakfasts & brunches

Great morning meals are a much-loved highlight of home cooking. These tips will help you start your days in delicious style.

COOKING BREAKFAST MEATS

PORK BACON: Follow package directions for the stove top or microwave oven. To bake, preheat oven to 400°F. Place bacon slices side by side on a rack in a foil-lined shallow baking pan with sides. Bake for 18 to 21 minutes or until bacon is crisp-cooked. Drain well on paper towels.

UNCOOKED SAUSAGE PATTIES: To fry, place ½-inch-thick sausage patties in an unheated skillet and cook over medium-low heat about 12 minutes or until centers are no longer pink, turning once. Drain the sausage patties on paper towels. To bake, preheat oven to 400°F. Arrange ½-inch-thick patties on a rack in a shallow baking pan with sides. Bake for 18 to 20 minutes or until centers are no longer pink and the internal temperature registers 160°F on an instant-read thermometer. Drain on paper towels.

UNCOOKED SAUSAGE LINKS: To fry, place sausage links in an unheated skillet; cook over medium-low heat for 14 to 16 minutes or until centers are no longer pink, turning frequently to brown evenly. Drain on paper towels. To bake, preheat oven to 375°F. Place uncooked links in a shallow baking pan with sides. Bake for 16 to 18 minutes or until centers are no longer pink, turning once. Drain on paper towels.

ALL ABOUT EGGS

Select, store, and handle your morning mainstays with perfection.

- When purchasing eggs, select clean fresh eggs from a refrigerated display case. Avoid eggs that are cracked or leaking; they might have become contaminated with harmful bacteria.
- Keep eggs in their cartons and store on an inside shelf in the refrigerator for up to 5 weeks after packing date. The packing date is represented by a number from 1 to 365 stamped on the carton, with 1 representing January 1 and 365 representing December 31.
- When separating eggs, use an egg separator to avoid contaminating egg with any bacteria on the shell. Avoid getting any shell in raw eggs.
- Wash your hands, utensils, and countertop after working with raw eggs.
- Serve hot egg dishes promptly and chill leftovers quickly. Refrigerate cold dishes immediately after preparation.
- For more information about handling eggs safely, call the U.S. Department of Agriculture Meat and Poultry Hotline at 888/674-6854.

STORING EGGS

Type of egg	Storage
Raw eggs in shell	Refrigerate up to 5 weeks; do not freeze.
Raw egg whites	Refrigerate, tightly covered, up to 4 days; freeze up to 1 year.
Raw whole egg yolks	Cover with water. Refrigerate, tightly covered, up to 2 days; do not freeze.
Hard-cooked eggs in shell	Refrigerate up to 7 days; do not freeze.

HOTCAKES (AND HOT WAFFLES)

When cooking for a crowd, you can keep finished pancakes and waffles warm while you're cooking the rest of the batch. Place the pancakes or waffles in a single layer on a baking sheet. Place the baking sheet in a preheated warm oven (200°F to 250°F) up to 15 or 20 minutes.

FREEZING COFFEE CAKES

Leftover coffee cake freezes well. Wrap in freezer wrap and freeze for up to 1 month. Thaw at room temperature for 1 hour. If desired, wrap in foil and reheat in a preheated 350°F oven for 10 to 15 minutes.

scrambled eggs

The Secret: Lift and fold, lift and fold. For the fluffiest, lightest scrambled eggs, the key is in the wrist. Resist the stir and embrace the fold.

SCRAMBLED EGG POINTERS

1. WHY WHISK?
Vigorously whisking the egg mixture incorporates air and helps give the scrambled eggs a light and fluffy texture.

2. LET THEM SIT FIRST
After you pour the eggs into the heated skillet, let them sit for 20 to 30 seconds or until the eggs begin to set on the bottom. Resist the urge to stir! Let ribbons of cooked egg begin to form before you put your spatula to work.

↓

↑

3. LIFT & FOLD
Lift and fold the cooked egg toward the center, allowing uncooked eggs to flow under the spatula. Repeat lifting and folding until eggs are just set and still appear slightly wet.

FAST LOW-CALORIE

Fast Scrambled Eggs

START TO FINISH: 10 MINUTES **MAKES:** 3 SERVINGS

- **6 eggs**
- **1/3 cup milk, half-and-half, or light cream**
- **1/4 teaspoon salt**
- **Dash black pepper**
- **1 tablespoon butter or margarine**

1 In a medium bowl whisk together eggs, milk, salt, and pepper. In a large skillet melt butter over medium heat; pour in egg mixture. Cook over medium heat, without stirring, until mixture begins to set on the bottom and around edges.

2 With a spatula or large spoon, lift and fold the partially cooked egg mixture so the uncooked portion flows underneath (see photo 2, left). Continue cooking over medium heat for 2 to 3 minutes or until egg mixture is cooked through but is still glossy and moist (see photo 3, left). Immediately remove skillet from heat.

PER SERVING: 191 cal., 14 g total fat (6 g sat. fat), 435 mg chol., 372 mg sodium, 2 g carb., 0 g fiber, 14 g pro. EXCHANGES: 2 Medium-Fat Meat, 1 Fat

MEAT-LOVER'S SCRAMBLED EGGS: Omit butter. In the skillet cook and stir 3 slices bacon, chopped, and 4 ounces bulk pork sausage over medium heat until bacon is crisp and sausage is browned. Drain, reserving 1 tablespoon drippings in skillet; set meat aside. Prepare egg mixture and cook in drippings. Sprinkle with bacon, sausage, and 1/3 cup chopped cooked ham or Polish sausage. Continue cooking as directed.

PER SERVING: 378 cal., 29 g total fat (10 g sat. fat), 474 mg chol., 972 mg sodium, 3 g carb., 0 g fiber, 25 g pro. EXCHANGES: 3½ Medium-Fat Meat, 2½ Fat

CHEESE-AND-ONION SCRAMBLED EGGS: Prepare as directed, except cook 2 tablespoons sliced green onion (1) in the butter for 30 seconds; add egg mixture and continue as directed. After eggs begin to set, fold in 1/2 cup shredded cheddar, mozzarella, or Monterey Jack cheese with jalapeño peppers (2 ounces).

PER SERVING: 268 cal., 21 g total fat (10 g sat. fat), 455 mg chol., 490 mg sodium, 3 g carb., 0 g fiber, 18 g pro. EXCHANGES: 2½ Medium-Fat Meat, 2 Fat

EGG MATH

Eggs come in a variety of sizes: medium, large, and extra-large. One medium egg contains about 3 tablespoons of liquid, large eggs are approximately 3½ tablespoons volume, and extra-large eggs contain about 4 tablespoons volume. The Test Kitchen uses large eggs when testing all recipes.

MUSHROOM SCRAMBLED EGGS: Prepare as directed, except increase the butter to 2 tablespoons. Cook 1½ cups sliced fresh mushrooms and 1 tablespoon chopped onion in the butter. Add 1 tablespoon snipped fresh parsley, ½ teaspoon dry mustard, and ¼ teaspoon Worcestershire sauce to beaten egg mixture. Add egg mixture to skillet and continue as directed.

PER SERVING: 239 cal., 18 g total fat (8 g sat. fat), 446 mg chol., 407 mg sodium, 4 g carb., 1 g fiber, 15 g pro. **EXCHANGES:** ½ Vegetable, 2 Medium-Fat Meat, 1½ Fat

DENVER SCRAMBLED EGGS: Prepare as directed, except omit salt and increase butter to 2 tablespoons. In the skillet cook 1 cup sliced fresh mushrooms, ⅓ cup diced cooked ham, ¼ cup chopped onion, and 2 tablespoons finely chopped green sweet pepper in the butter. Add egg mixture to skillet and continue as directed.

PER SERVING: 263 cal., 20 g total fat (9 g sat. fat), 454 mg chol., 404 mg sodium, 5 g carb., 1 g fiber, 17 g pro. **EXCHANGES:** ½ Vegetable, 2 Medium-Fat Meat, 2 Fat

LOW-FAT SCRAMBLED EGGS: Prepare as directed, except substitute 3 whole eggs and 5 egg whites for the 6 whole eggs. Substitute fat-free milk for the milk. Omit the butter and coat a nonstick skillet with nonstick cooking spray before cooking the egg mixture as directed.

PER SERVING: 107 cal., 5 g total fat (2 g sat. fat), 212 mg chol., 367 mg sodium, 2 g carb., 0 g fiber, 13 g pro. **EXCHANGES:** 2 Lean Meat

DENVER SCRAMBLED EGGS

PUT IT TO USE!

If you need breakfast on the run, make your scrambled eggs portable with these easy ideas.

BURRITOS: Simply roll up scrambled eggs, a little shredded cheese, and salsa in a flour tortilla. This makes a great breakfast to go!

PANINI: Sandwich scrambled eggs between bread along with sliced prosciutto or ham and a few basil leaves. Press with a panini press or toast on a griddle.

PIZZA: Start with a purchased pizza crust and top with scrambled eggs and your favorite toppings. Bake according to package directions.

cook's secrets

cooking eggs

Whether cooking sunny-side-up eggs for breakfast or boiling hard-cooked eggs as an ingredient in a recipe, everything you need to know for perfectly done eggs is right here.

HARD-COOKED EGG POINTERS

1. BOILING EGGS
Place eggs in the bottom of a large saucepan. They should be in a single layer. Add enough cold water to cover them by 1 inch.

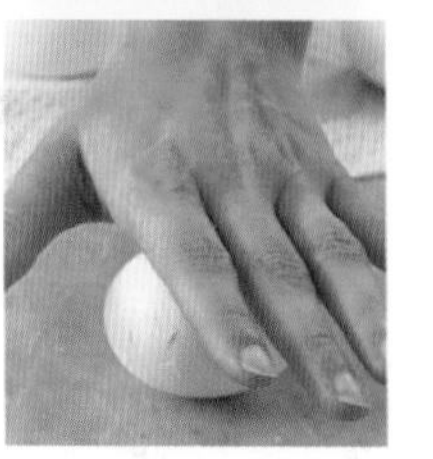

2. GIVE IT A ROLL
To peel cooled eggs more easily, lightly tap egg on the countertop. Gently roll the egg under your palm against the countertop to completely crack the shell.

When making hard-cooked eggs, use eggs that are a week old for easiest peeling, then run under cold water after cooking to peel.

FAST LOW-CALORIE

Hard-Cooked Eggs

START TO FINISH: 25 MINUTES **MAKES:** 6 EGGS

- **6 large eggs***
- **Cold water**

1 Place eggs in a single layer in a large saucepan (do not stack eggs). Add enough cold water to cover the eggs by 1 inch (see photo 1, left). Bring to a rapid boil over high heat (water will have large rapidly breaking bubbles). Remove from heat, cover, and let eggs stand for 15 minutes;* drain.

2 Run cold water over the eggs or place them in ice water until cool enough to handle; drain.

3 To peel eggs, gently tap each egg on the countertop. Roll the eggs between the palms of your hands or against the countertop (see photo 2, left). Peel off the eggshells, starting at the large ends.

***NOTE:** If you use extra-large eggs, let eggs stand in the boiled water for 18 minutes.

PER EGG: 78 cal., 5 g total fat (2 g sat. fat), 212 mg chol., 62 mg sodium, 1 g carb., 0 g fiber, 6 g pro.
EXCHANGES: 1 Medium-Fat Meat

FAST LOW-CALORIE

Poached Eggs

START TO FINISH: 10 MINUTES **MAKES:** 4 EGGS

- **4 cups water**
- **1 tablespoon vinegar**
- **4 eggs**
- **Salt and black pepper**

1 Add water to a large skillet; add vinegar. Bring the vinegar mixture to boiling; reduce heat to simmering (bubbles should begin to break the surface of the mixture).

2 Break an egg into a custard cup or small bowl and slip egg into the simmering water (see photo 1, page 131). Repeat with remaining eggs, allowing each egg an equal amount of space in the water-vinegar mixture.

3 Simmer eggs, uncovered, for 3 to 5 minutes or until whites are completely set and yolks begin to thicken but are not hard. Remove eggs (see photo 2, page 131). Season to taste with salt and pepper.

PAN-POACHED EGGS: Lightly grease cups of an egg-poaching pan. Place cups into bottom pan over boiling water (follow manufacturer's directions); reduce heat to simmering. Break an egg into a custard cup or small bowl. Carefully slide egg into a poaching cup. Repeat with remaining eggs. Cover; cook for 4 to 6 minutes or until the whites are completely set and

POACHER

Although a special pan is not essential to achieving the perfect poached egg, it makes the job easier and the eggs more uniformly shaped.

yolks begin to thicken but are not hard. Run a knife around edges to loosen eggs. Invert cups to remove eggs.

MAKE-AHEAD DIRECTIONS: Prepare as directed. Place cooked eggs in a bowl of cold water. Cover and chill for up to 1 hour. To reheat eggs, in a saucepan bring water to simmering. Using a slotted spoon, slip eggs into the simmering water and heat about 2 minutes. Remove with a slotted spoon.

PER EGG: 73 cal., 5 g total fat (2 g sat. fat), 212 mg chol., 273 mg sodium, 1 g carb., 0 g fiber, 6 g pro.
EXCHANGES: 1 Medium-Fat Meat

These make-ahead directions come in handy if you're making Eggs Benedict (page 132) for a crowd.

POACHED EGG POINTERS

1. SLIP THEM IN
Break one egg at a time into a custard cup. Hold the lip of the cup close to the simmering vinegar mixture and slip the egg in.

2. DRAIN WELL
When the eggs are cooked, use a slotted spoon to remove them from the skillet so the liquid drains away.

FAST LOW-CALORIE

Fried Eggs

START TO FINISH: 10 MINUTES **MAKES:** 4 EGGS

- 2 **teaspoons butter or margarine, or nonstick cooking spray**
- 4 **eggs**
- **Salt (optional)**
- **Black pepper (optional)**

1 In a large skillet melt butter over medium heat (see photo 1, below). (Or coat an unheated skillet with nonstick cooking spray.) Break eggs into skillet. If desired, sprinkle with salt and pepper. Reduce heat to low; cook eggs for 3 to 4 minutes or until whites are completely set and yolks start to thicken.

2 For fried eggs over-easy or over-hard, when the whites are completely set and the yolks start to thicken, turn the eggs (see photo 2, below) and cook 30 seconds more (over easy) or 1 minute more (over hard).

STEAM-BASTED FRIED EGGS: Prepare as directed, except when egg edges turn white, add 1 tablespoon water (see photo 3, below). Cover skillet and cook eggs for 3 to 4 minutes or until yolks begin to thicken but are not hard (see photo 4, below).

PER EGG: 88 cal., 7 g total fat (3 g sat. fat), 217 mg chol., 84 mg sodium, 0 g carb., 0 g fiber, 6 g pro.
EXCHANGES: 1 Medium-Fat Meat, ½ Fat

FRIED EGGS STEP-BY-STEP

1. Make sure the skillet is hot. Add the butter to the hot skillet. Let it melt and swirl to coat the bottom of the pan.

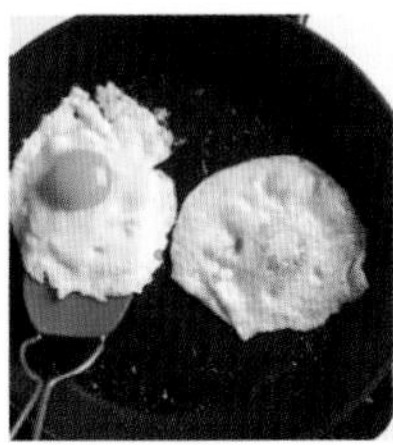

2. For over-easy or over-hard eggs, gently turn the eggs over after the whites have almost completely set. It helps to have a thin spatula for this delicate task.

3. For prettier eggs, cook the tops with steam; do not turn eggs. Add 1 tablespoon water to the skillet. Cover the skillet.

4. A glass lid is best for covering the skillet so you can see when the yolks are set and start to thicken but are still a little runny.

SALMON BENEDICT

BEST-LOVED FAST LOW-CALORIE

Eggs Benedict

START TO FINISH: 25 MINUTES **MAKES:** 4 SERVINGS

- **1 recipe Poached Eggs (page 130)**
- **1 recipe Mock Hollandaise Sauce**
- **2 English muffins, split**
- **4 slices Canadian-style bacon**
- **Cracked black pepper**

1 Prepare Poached Eggs. Remove eggs from skillet with a slotted spoon and place them in a large pan of warm water to keep them warm. Prepare the Mock Hollandaise Sauce.

2 Preheat broiler. Place muffin halves, cut sides up, on a baking sheet. Broil 3 to 4 inches from the heat about 2 minutes or until browned. Top each muffin half with a slice of Canadian-style bacon; broil about 1 minute more or until bacon is heated.

3 To serve, top each bacon-topped muffin half with an egg. Spoon Mock Hollandaise Sauce over eggs. Sprinkle with pepper.

MOCK HOLLANDAISE SAUCE: In a small saucepan combine 1/3 cup sour cream, 1/3 cup mayonnaise, 2 teaspoons lemon juice, and 2 teaspoons yellow mustard. Cook and stir over medium-low heat until warm. If desired, stir in a little milk to thin.

PER SERVING: 346 cal., 25 g total fat (7 g sat. fat), 240 mg chol., 885 mg sodium, 14 g carb., 1 g fiber, 14 g pro.
EXCHANGES: 1 Starch, 1½ High-Fat Meat, 2½ Fat

SALMON BENEDICT: Prepare as directed, except spread 1 tablespoon softened tub-style cream cheese with herbs on each toasted English muffin half. Substitute 4 ounces thinly sliced smoked salmon (lox-style) for the Canadian-style bacon. If desired, stir 1 tablespoon drained capers and 1/2 teaspoon dried dill weed into the Mock Hollandaise Sauce. If desired, sprinkle with additional dill weed.

PER SERVING: 391 cal., 30 g total fat (10 g sat. fat), 248 mg chol., 1,161 mg sodium, 15 mg carb., 1 g fiber, 15 g pro.
EXCHANGES: 1 Starch, 1½ High-Fat Meat, 3½ Fat

REUBEN BENEDICT: Prepare as directed, except substitute 4 slices marble rye or rye bread for the English muffins and thinly sliced corned beef for the Canadian-style bacon. Divide 1/2 cup rinsed and drained sauerkraut evenly over the corned beef. Stir 1/2 cup shredded Swiss cheese into the Mock Hollandaise Sauce.

PER SERVING: 461 cal., 34 g total fat (11 g sat. fat), 269 mg chol., 1,160 mg sodium, 19 mg carb., 3 g fiber, 19 g pro.
EXCHANGES: 1 Starch, 2 High-Fat Meat, 3½ Fat

BEST-LOVED LOW-CALORIE

Breakfast Pizza

PREP: 25 MINUTES **BAKE:** 20 MINUTES AT 375°F
MAKES: 10 SERVINGS

- **1 16-ounce loaf frozen whole wheat bread dough, thawed**
- **1 cup halved zucchini slices and/or green or red sweet pepper pieces**
- **1 cup sliced fresh mushrooms**
- **1/4 teaspoon crushed red pepper (optional)**
- **1 tablespoon vegetable oil**
- **8 eggs**
- **1/2 cup milk**
- **1 tablespoon butter or margarine**
- **1½ cups shredded cheddar and/or mozzarella cheese (6 ounces)**
- **2 slices bacon, crisp-cooked, drained, and crumbled**
- **Bottled salsa (optional)**

1 Grease a 13-inch pizza pan; set aside. Preheat oven to 375°F. On a lightly floured surface roll bread dough into a 14-inch circle. If dough is difficult to roll out, stop and let it rest a few minutes. Transfer dough to prepared pan. Build up edges slightly. Prick dough generously with a fork. Bake for 15 to 20 minutes or until light brown.

2 Meanwhile, in a large skillet cook zucchini, mushrooms, and, if desired, crushed red pepper in hot oil about 5 minutes or until vegetables are almost tender. Remove zucchini mixture and drain.

3 In a medium bowl beat together eggs and milk. In the same skillet melt butter over medium heat; pour in egg mixture. Cook, without stirring, until mixture begins to set on the bottom and around edges. Using a large spatula, lift and fold partially cooked eggs so uncooked portion flows underneath (see photo 2, page 128). Continue cooking over medium heat for 2 to 3 minutes or until egg mixture is cooked through but is still glossy and moist (see photo 3, page 128). Remove from heat.

4 Sprinkle half of the shredded cheese over the hot crust. Top with scrambled eggs, zucchini mixture, bacon, and remaining cheese. Bake for 5 to 8 minutes more or until cheese melts. Cut into 10 slices. If desired, serve with salsa.

PER SLICE: 283 cal., 15 g total fat (6 g sat. fat), 193 mg chol., 465 mg sodium, 23 g carb., 2 g fiber, 16 g pro.
EXCHANGES: 1½ Starch, 1½ Lean Meat, 2 Fat

SAUSAGE-MUSHROOM BREAKFAST PIZZA: Prepare as directed, except omit zucchini, crushed red pepper, oil, and bacon. After preparing crust, in a large skillet cook 8 ounces bulk pork sausage or Italian sausage and the mushrooms until meat is browned; remove from skillet and drain. Continue as directed in Steps 3 and 4, substituting the sausage mixture for the zucchini mixture and bacon.

PER SLICE: 330 cal., 19 g total fat (8 g sat. fat), 207 mg chol., 571 mg sodium, 23 g carb., 2 g fiber, 19 g pro.
EXCHANGES: 1½ Starch, 2 Lean Meat, 2½ Fat

EASY BREAKFAST PIZZA: Prepare as directed, except omit the bread dough and Step 1. Substitute one 12-inch Italian bread shell (such as Boboli) and continue as directed, baking as directed on the bread shell package. Or substitute one 13.8-ounce package refrigerated pizza dough, baking filled crust as directed on the package.

PER SLICE: 287 cal., 16 g total fat (6 g sat. fat), 196 mg chol., 462 mg sodium, 22 g carb., 0 g fiber, 16 g pro.
EXCHANGES: 1½ Starch, 1½ Lean Meat, 2 Fat

BEST-LOVED LOW-CALORIE

Farmer's Casserole

PREP: 25 MINUTES **BAKE:** 40 MINUTES AT 350°F
STAND: 5 MINUTES **MAKES:** 6 SERVINGS

- **Nonstick cooking spray**
- **3 cups frozen shredded hash brown potatoes**
- **¾ cup shredded Monterey Jack cheese with jalapeño peppers or shredded cheddar cheese (3 ounces)**
- **1 cup diced cooked ham, cooked breakfast sausage, or Canadian-style bacon**

BREAKFAST PIZZA

- **¼ cup sliced green onions (2)**
- **4 eggs, beaten, or 1 cup refrigerated or frozen egg product, thawed**
- **1½ cups milk or one 12-ounce can evaporated milk or evaporated fat-free milk**
- **⅛ teaspoon salt**
- **⅛ teaspoon black pepper**

1 Preheat oven to 350°F. Coat a 2-quart square baking dish with nonstick cooking spray. Arrange hash brown potatoes evenly in the dish. Sprinkle with cheese, ham, and green onions.

2 In a medium bowl combine eggs, milk, salt, and pepper. Pour egg mixture over layers in dish.

3 Bake, uncovered, for 40 to 45 minutes or until a knife inserted near the center comes out clean. Let stand for 5 minutes before serving.

FARMER'S CASSEROLE FOR 12: Prepare as directed, except double all ingredients and use a 3-quart rectangular baking dish. Preheat oven to 350°F. Bake, uncovered, for 45 to 55 minutes or until a knife inserted near the center comes out clean. Let stand for 5 minutes before serving. Makes 12 servings.

MAKE-AHEAD DIRECTIONS: Prepare as directed through Step 2. Cover and chill for up to 24 hours. Preheat oven to 350°F. Bake, uncovered, for 50 to 55 minutes or until a knife inserted near the center comes out clean. Let stand for 5 minutes before serving.

PER PIECE: 263 cal., 12 g total fat (6 g sat. fat), 175 mg chol., 589 mg sodium, 22 g carb., 2 g fiber, 17 g pro.
EXCHANGES: 1½ Starch, 2 Lean Meat, 1 Fat

OVERNIGHT BREAKFAST PIE

LOW-CALORIE

Overnight Breakfast Pie

PREP: 20 MINUTES **CHILL:** 2 TO 24 HOURS
BAKE: 50 MINUTES AT 325°F **MAKES:** 6 TO 8 SERVINGS

- **8 slices bacon**
- **1/2 cup panko bread crumbs**
- **5 eggs**
- **2 1/2 cups frozen shredded hash brown potatoes**
- **1 cup shredded Swiss cheese (4 ounces)**
- **1/2 cup cottage cheese**
- **1/3 cup milk**
- **1/4 cup chopped green onions (2)**
- **1/2 teaspoon salt**
- **1/4 teaspoon black pepper**
- **4 drops bottled hot pepper sauce**

1 In a large skillet cook bacon over medium heat until crisp. Drain bacon on paper towels, reserving 1 tablespoon drippings in skillet. Crumble bacon; set aside. Stir bread crumbs into the reserved drippings. Transfer to a small bowl; cover and chill until needed.

2 Lightly grease a 9-inch pie plate; set aside. In a medium bowl beat eggs with a fork until foamy. Stir in crumbled bacon, potatoes, Swiss cheese, cottage cheese, milk, chopped green onions, salt, pepper, and hot pepper sauce. Pour mixture into prepared pie plate. Cover and chill for 2 to 24 hours.

3 Preheat oven to 325°F. Sprinkle pie with bread crumb mixture. Bake, uncovered, about 50 minutes or until a knife inserted in the center comes out clean. If desired, garnish with *sliced green onions*. Cut into wedges.

PER WEDGE: 324 cal., 17 g total fat (7 g sat. fat), 210 mg chol., 640 mg sodium, 22 g carb., 2 g fiber, 20 g pro.
EXCHANGES: 1½ Starch, 2 Medium-Fat Meat, 1 Fat

Quiche Lorraine

PREP: 40 MINUTES **BAKE:** 13 MINUTES AT 450°F/ 45 MINUTES AT 325°F **STAND:** 10 MINUTES
MAKES: 6 SERVINGS

- **1 recipe Pastry for Single-Crust Pie (page 440)**
- **8 slices bacon**
- **1 medium onion, thinly sliced**
- **4 eggs, lightly beaten**
- **1 cup half-and-half or light cream**
- **3/4 cup milk**
- **1/4 teaspoon salt**
- **Pinch freshly grated nutmeg or dash ground nutmeg**
- **1 1/2 cups shredded Swiss cheese (6 ounces)**
- **1 tablespoon all-purpose flour**

1 Preheat oven to 450°F. Prepare Pastry for Single-Crust Pie, fluting the edges high to contain filling. Line the unpricked pastry shell with a double thickness of heavy foil. Bake for 8 minutes; remove foil. Bake for 5 to 6 minutes more or until pastry is set and light brown. Remove from oven. Reduce oven temperature to 325°F. (Pastry shell should still be hot when filling is added; do not partially bake pastry shell ahead of time.)

2 Meanwhile, in a large skillet cook bacon until crisp. Drain, reserving 2 tablespoons of the drippings. Crumble bacon finely; set aside. Cook onion in reserved drippings over medium heat about 5 minutes or until tender but not browned; drain.

3 In a medium bowl whisk together eggs, half-and-half, milk, salt, and nutmeg until well mixed. Stir in crumbled bacon and onion. In another medium bowl combine shredded cheese and flour; toss until flour coats cheese (see photo 2, page 135). Add to egg mixture; mix well.

4 Carefully pour egg mixture into the hot baked pastry shell (to minimize spilling, place the pastry shell on the oven rack and pour egg mixture into pastry shell). To prevent overbrowning, cover edge of crust with foil (see photo 3, page 135). Bake for 45 to 55 minutes or until a knife inserted near the center comes out clean (see photo 4, page 135). Let stand for 10 minutes. Cut into wedges.

PER WEDGE: 591 cal., 42 g total fat (19 g sat. fat), 204 mg chol., 684 mg sodium, 32 g carb., 1 g fiber, 22 g pro.
EXCHANGES: 1½ Starch, ½ Other Carb., 2½ High-Fat Meat, 4 Fat

VEGGIE QUICHE: Prepare as directed, except omit the bacon. Cook 1½ cups finely chopped vegetables (such as kale, Brussels sprouts, and/or fresh cremini mushrooms) with the onion in 2 tablespoons olive oil. Substitute dilled Havarti cheese for the Swiss cheese. Top quiche with a mixture of ½ cup quartered cherry tomatoes, 2 tablespoons snipped fresh parsley, and 1 to 2 teaspoons finely shredded lemon peel.

PER WEDGE: 515 cal., 37 g total fat (16 g sat. fat), 182 mg chol., 581 mg sodium, 32 g carb., 2 g fiber, 16 g pro.
EXCHANGES: ½ Vegetable, 1½ Starch, ½ Other Carb., 1½ Medium-Fat Meat, 5½ Fat

ITALIAN QUICHE: Prepare as directed, except substitute 6 ounces pancetta, cut into strips, for the bacon. After cooking pancetta until crisp, set aside ¼ cup of the strips for the top. Stir one 6-ounce jar marinated artichoke hearts, drained and coarsely chopped, into the egg mixture; substitute 1 tablespoon snipped fresh oregano or 1 teaspoon dried Italian seasoning, crushed, for the nutmeg; and substitute Fontina cheese for the Swiss cheese. Before serving, top with the reserved pancetta.

SMOKY QUICHE: Prepare as directed, except use apple-smoked bacon and substitute smoked paprika for the nutmeg. Substitute 6 ounces smoked cheddar cheese for the Swiss cheese. Garnish with fresh cilantro sprigs.

PER WEDGE ITALIAN OR SMOKY VARIATION: 601 cal., 43 g total fat (20 g sat. fat), 205 mg chol., 1,107 mg sodium, 31 g carb., 1 g fiber, 23 g pro. EXCHANGES: 1½ Starch, ½ Other Carb., 2½ High-Fat Meat, 4 Fat

FAST LOW-CALORIE

Frittata

START TO FINISH: 25 MINUTES **MAKES:** 4 SERVINGS

- **8 eggs, lightly beaten**
- **1 tablespoon snipped fresh basil or 1 teaspoon dried basil, crushed**
- **¼ teaspoon salt**
- **¼ teaspoon black pepper**
- **2 tablespoons olive oil**
- **1½ cups chopped fresh vegetables, such as summer squash, broccoli, roma tomatoes, and/or sweet peppers**
- **⅓ cup thinly sliced green onions (3)**
- **½ cup chopped cooked ham, kielbasa, chicken, or turkey; or crumbled cooked pork sausage**
- **½ cup shredded cheddar, Monterey Jack, or Swiss cheese (2 ounces)**

1 In a medium bowl combine eggs, basil, salt, and pepper; set aside. Heat oil in a large broilerproof skillet; add vegetables and green onions. Cook, uncovered, over medium heat about 5 minutes or until vegetables are crisp-tender, stirring occasionally. Stir in meat.

2 Pour egg mixture into skillet. Cook over medium heat. As mixture sets, run a spatula around edge of skillet, lifting egg mixture so uncooked portion flows underneath. Continue cooking and lifting until almost set (surface will be moist). Sprinkle with cheese.

3 Preheat broiler. Place skillet under broiler 4 to 5 inches from heat. Broil for 1 to 2 minutes or until top is just set and cheese melts.

PER SERVING: 297 cal., 23 g total fat (8 g sat. fat), 448 mg chol., 596 mg sodium, 4 g carb., 1 g fiber, 20 g pro.
EXCHANGES: 3 Medium-Fat Meat, 1½ Fat

QUICHE LORRAINE STEP-BY-STEP

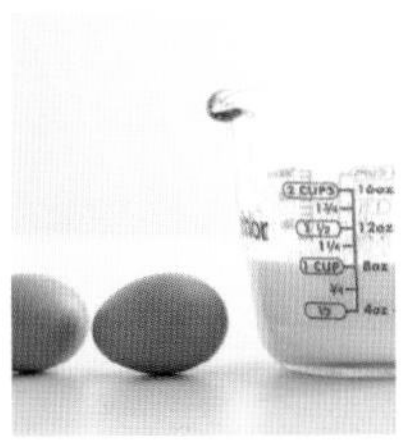

1. The right ratio of milk to eggs is what allows the egg mixture to set up nicely without becoming tough and rubbery.

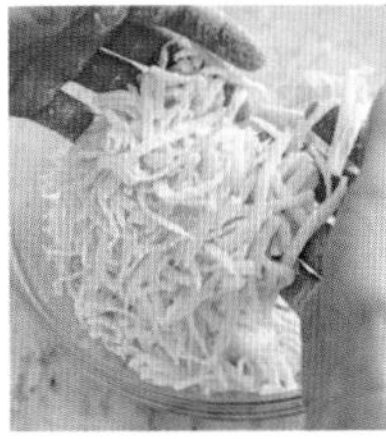

2. Use your fingers to evenly toss the flour with the cheese. This helps the cheese bind with the egg mixture and keeps the cheese evenly dispersed.

3. Make a crust shield. Fold a 12-inch foil square into fourths. Cut an arc 3½ inches from the folded point. Unfold; loosely place foil over the crust.

4. To test for doneness, insert a knife near the center of the quiche. The quiche is done when the knife comes out clean.

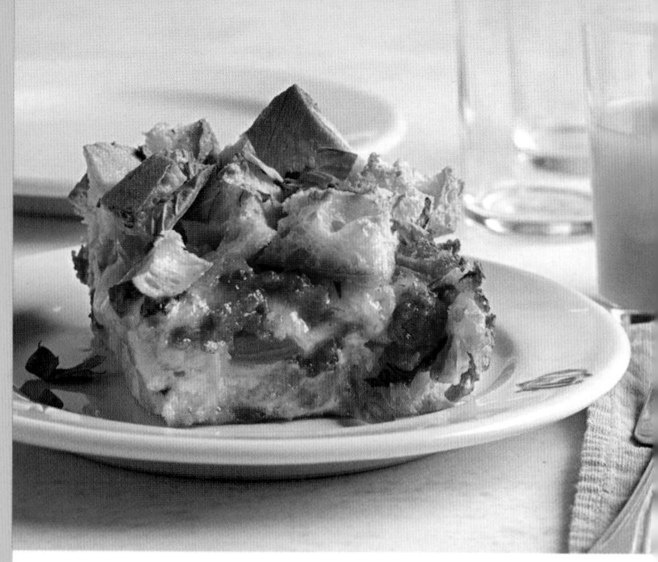

Egg Casserole

Round up a handful of your favorite ingredients and you'll be 20 minutes away from popping a colorful casserole into the oven—or into the fridge to bake up to a day later.

PREP: 20 MINUTES
BAKE: 45 MINUTES AT 325°F
STAND: 10 MINUTES **MAKES:** 6 SERVINGS

- 4 to 5 cups BREAD CUBES*
- MEAT
- VEGETABLE
- 4 to 6 ounces SHREDDED CHEESE
- 4 eggs, lightly beaten
- 1½ cups DAIRY
- SEASONING

1 Preheat oven to 325°F. Grease a 2-quart square baking dish. Spread half of the Bread Cubes in the dish. Add Meat, Vegetable, and Shredded Cheese. Top with the remaining Bread Cubes.

2 In a bowl whisk together eggs, Dairy, and Seasoning. Evenly pour over the layers in the dish.

3 Bake, uncovered, about 45 minutes or until a knife inserted near the center comes out clean. Let stand for 10 minutes before serving.

***NOTE:** To make bread cubes, stack several slices of bread. Cut into strips. Cut stacked strips crosswise into cubes.

MAKE-AHEAD DIRECTIONS: Prepare as directed through Step 2. Cover and refrigerate for 2 to 24 hours. Bake, uncovered, in a preheated 350°F oven for 60 to 65 minutes or until a knife inserted near the center comes out clean. Let stand for 10 minutes before serving.

BREAD CUBES *(pick one)*

- Baguette-style French bread
- English muffins
- Pumpernickel
- Rye bread
- White or wheat bread

MEAT *(pick one)*

- 6 slices bacon, crisp-cooked, drained, and crumbled
- 5 ounces chopped Canadian-style bacon
- One 6-ounce can lump crabmeat, drained and flaked
- 2 cups cubed cooked ham or cubed smoked turkey
- 8 ounces cooked bulk pork sausage

VEGETABLE *(pick one)*

- 1½ cups blanched cut-up asparagus or broccoli florets
- 1 cup frozen hash brown potatoes
- ½ cup canned sliced mushrooms
- 1 cup fresh or frozen chopped spinach (thawed and squeezed dry if frozen)
- ¾ cup chopped sweet pepper

SHREDDED CHEESE *(pick one)*

- Cheddar
- Italian blend
- Monterey Jack
- Swiss

DAIRY *(pick one)*

- Half-and-half
- Milk
- ½ cup sour cream plus 1 cup milk

SEASONING *(pick one)*

- 1 tablespoon Dijon-style or coarse-grain mustard
- 1 teaspoon dried dill weed
- 2 cloves garlic, minced
- ¼ cup sliced green onions
- 1 tablespoon snipped fresh Italian parsley or basil

BEST-LOVED

Cheese Soufflé

PREP: 50 MINUTES **BAKE:** 40 MINUTES AT 350°F
MAKES: 4 SERVINGS

- **4 egg yolks**
- **4 egg whites**
- **¼ cup butter or margarine**
- **¼ cup all-purpose flour**
- **¼ teaspoon dry mustard**
- **Dash cayenne pepper**
- **1 cup milk**
- **2 cups shredded cheddar, Colby, Havarti, and/or process Swiss cheese (8 ounces)**

1 Allow the egg yolks and egg whites to stand at room temperature for 30 minutes.

2 Preheat oven to 350°F. For cheese sauce, in a medium saucepan melt butter; stir in flour, dry mustard, and cayenne pepper. Add milk all at once. Cook and stir over medium heat until thickened and bubbly. Remove from heat. Add cheese, a little at a time, stirring until cheese melts (see photo 1, below). In a medium bowl beat egg yolks with a whisk until combined. Slowly add cheese sauce to egg yolks, whisking constantly (see photo 2, below); cool slightly.

3 In a large mixing bowl beat egg whites with an electric mixer on medium to high speed until stiff peaks form (tips stand straight). Gently fold about 1 cup of the stiffly beaten egg whites into cheese sauce (see photo 3, below). Gradually pour cheese sauce over remaining stiffly beaten egg whites, folding to combine. Pour into an ungreased 2-quart soufflé dish.

4 Bake about 40 minutes or until a knife inserted near center comes out clean. Serve immediately.

PER SERVING: 459 cal., 36 g total fat (22 g sat. fat), 305 mg chol., 521 mg sodium, 10 g carb., 0 g fiber, 23 g pro.
EXCHANGES: ½ Starch, 3 Medium-Fat Meat, 4 Fat

CHEESE SOUFFLÉ STEP-BY-STEP

1. Add the cheese in small increments, stirring with a whisk after each addition. This ensures that the cheese melts completely and smoothly.

2. Very gradually add the hot cheese sauce to the egg yolks while constantly whisking. If you add the sauce all at once, the eggs are likely to "cook" and curdle.

3. To ensure the soufflé hits its maximum height, stir a cup of the whites into the cheese sauce. Pour the lightened sauce over remaining whites; fold to combine uniformly.

8 to try

FAST LOW-CALORIE

French Omelet

Omelets are an endlessly versatile dish. Enjoy the Filled French Omelets with the fillings shown here any time of day.

START TO FINISH: 10 MINUTES
MAKES: 1 OMELET

- **2 eggs or 4 egg whites**
- **2 tablespoons water**
- **1/8 teaspoon salt**
- **Dash black pepper**
- **1 tablespoon butter or margarine**

1 In a small bowl combine eggs, water, salt, and pepper. Using a fork, beat until combined but not frothy. Heat a small nonstick skillet with flared sides over medium-high heat until skillet is hot.

2 Melt butter in skillet. Add egg mixture to skillet; reduce heat to medium. Immediately begin stirring eggs gently but continuously with a heat-resistant spatula until mixture resembles small pieces of cooked egg surrounded by liquid egg. Stop stirring. Cook for 30 to 60 seconds more or until eggs are set and shiny.

3 With a spatula, lift and fold an edge of the omelet about a third of the way toward the center. Fold the opposite omelet edge toward the center and transfer to a warm plate. If making more than one omelet, cover each with foil to keep it warm while preparing the additional omelets.

PER OMELET: 245 cal., 21 g total fat (10 g sat. fat), 454 mg chol., 513 mg sodium, 1 g carb., 0 g fiber, 13 g pro. EXCHANGES: 2 Medium-Fat Meat, 2 Fat

FILLED FRENCH OMELET: Prepare one of the fillings at right. For one omelet, if using fresh vegetables (1/3 to 1/2 cup chopped or sliced mushrooms, onion, sweet pepper, asparagus, or potatoes), cook vegetables in 1 teaspoon butter or vegetable oil in a skillet. If called for, add 1/8 to 1/4 teaspoon herb to egg mixture. Use 2 to 3 tablespoons shredded cheese and 1/3 to 1/2 cup cooked meat. Spoon filling across the center of omelet before Step 3. If desired, sprinkle top of omelet with additional cheese.

POTATO-BACON: Cook frozen diced hash brown potatoes and chopped bacon in oil. Add to omelet; add shredded cheddar cheese.

ASPARAGUS-HAM: Add dill weed to eggs; fill with chopped cooked asparagus, cooked ham or prosciutto, and shredded Parmesan.

BEAN-SALSA: Fill with black beans, salsa, and shredded Monterey Jack cheese.

SPINACH-FETA: Fill with shredded fresh spinach and crumbled feta cheese.

CHEESE-MUSHROOM: Cook sliced fresh mushrooms in butter; add to omelet. Add shredded cheddar cheese.

SHRIMP-AVOCADO: Fill with whole or chopped cooked shrimp, sliced avocado, and fresh cilantro sprigs.

DENVER: Cook chopped green and/or red sweet pepper, onion, and basil in butter; stir in chopped cooked ham.

ITALIAN: Fill with cooked Italian sausage, chopped roasted red sweet peppers, and torn provolone cheese.

FAST LOW-CALORIE

Buttermilk Pancakes

START TO FINISH: 25 MINUTES
MAKES: 12 STANDARD-SIZE PANCAKES OR 40 MINI PANCAKES

- **1¾ cups all-purpose flour**
- **2 tablespoons granulated sugar**
- **2 teaspoons baking powder**
- **½ teaspoon baking soda**
- **¼ teaspoon salt**
- **1 egg, lightly beaten**
- **1½ cups buttermilk or sour milk (see tip, page 19)**
- **3 tablespoons vegetable oil**
- **Desired fruit option (optional)***

1 In a large bowl stir together flour, granulated sugar, baking powder, baking soda, and salt. In another bowl use a fork to combine egg, buttermilk, and oil. Add egg mixture all at once to flour mixture. Stir just until moistened (batter should be slightly lumpy) (see photo 1, below). If desired, stir in desired fruit option.

2 For standard-size pancakes, pour about ¼ cup batter onto a hot, lightly greased griddle or heavy skillet (see photo 2, below). Spread batter if necessary. For mini pancakes, use about 1 tablespoon batter. Cook over medium heat for 1 to 2 minutes on each side or until pancakes are golden brown; turn over when surfaces are bubbly and edges are slightly dry (see photo 3, below). Serve warm. If desired, top with *butter* and desired *syrup*.

PANCAKES: Prepare as directed, except substitute milk for buttermilk, increase baking powder to 1 tablespoon, and omit baking soda.

WHOLE WHEAT PANCAKES: Prepare as directed, except substitute whole wheat flour for the all-purpose flour and packed brown sugar for the granulated sugar.

BUCKWHEAT PANCAKES: Prepare as directed, except use ¾ cup all-purpose flour and add 1 cup buckwheat flour.

CORNMEAL PANCAKES: Prepare as directed, except use 1¼ cups all-purpose flour and add ½ cup cornmeal.

PER STANDARD-SIZE BUTTERMILK, PLAIN, WHOLE WHEAT, BUCKWHEAT, OR CORNMEAL VARIATIONS: 123 cal., 4 g total fat (1 g sat. fat), 19 mg chol., 179 mg sodium, 18 g carb., 0 g fiber, 3 g pro. EXCHANGES: 1 Starch, 1 Fat

***FRUIT OPTIONS:** If desired, stir one of the following fruits into the pancake batter in Step 1: ½ cup chopped fresh apple, apricot, peach, nectarine, or pear; ½ cup fresh or frozen blueberries; or ¼ cup chopped dried apple, pear, apricot, raisins, currants, dates, cranberries, blueberries, cherries, or mixed fruit.

GRIDDLE KNOW-HOW

A light coating of nonstick cooking spray or vegetable oil (or some bacon drippings) on your skillet helps prevent sticking. If the surface is nonstick, however, you may not need to grease it at all. The real key is to make sure the skillet is hot enough before adding the batter. A drop of water flicked on the surface should sputter and dance across the skillet.

PANCAKES STEP-BY-STEP

1. When stirring the wet ingredients into flour mixture, the batter should be slightly lumpy. Do not overmix or the pancakes will be tough.

2. Pour batter onto a hot griddle or skillet, using a scoop or ¼-cup measuring cup.

3. The pancakes are ready to turn when the top surfaces are bubbly and the edges look slightly dry.

hash browns

The Secret: Excess water is the enemy! The secret to crispy-outside, tender-inside hash browns is to remove as much moisture from the shredded potatoes as possible.

HASH BROWN POINTERS

1. EVEN UP
Once the butter foams, the oil and butter are hot. Sprinkle the dried shredded potatoes in an even layer in the bottom of the skillet. Gently press with the back of a spatula to form a cake.

2. GO FOR GOLD
After cooking about 12 minutes, carefully lift up a section of the potatoes. If they are golden brown, they're ready to flip.

3. THE FLIP
To keep hash browns in one piece, first invert a baking sheet to cover the skillet. Invert them together so the potatoes end up on the baking sheet. Slide the potatoes back to the skillet to finish cooking the other side.

LOW-CALORIE

Perfect Hash Browns

PREP: 20 MINUTES **COOK:** 20 MINUTES **MAKES:** 6 SERVINGS

- **1¼ pounds russet potatoes**
- **¼ teaspoon salt**
- **⅛ teaspoon black pepper**
- **1 to 2 tablespoons olive oil**
- **1 tablespoon butter**
- **Paprika (optional)**

This combo is ideal for frying. Butter gives great flavor, but the milk solids burn at a high temperature. Combining butter with oil protects the milk solids and allows you to fry at a higher temperature, ensuring delicious, crispy potatoes.

1 Peel potatoes. Coarsely shred potatoes using a handheld shredder or a food processor with a coarse shredding blade.

2 Place shredded potatoes in a large bowl. Add enough cool water to cover potatoes; stir well. Drain in a colander set in a sink. Repeat rinsing and draining two or three times until water runs clear. Drain again, pressing out as much water as you can with a rubber spatula. Line a salad spinner with paper towels; add potatoes and spin. Repeat if necessary until potatoes are dry. Transfer potatoes to a large bowl. Sprinkle potatoes with salt and pepper, tossing to combine.

3 In a large nonstick skillet* heat 1 tablespoon of the oil and the butter over medium-high heat until butter foams. Add potatoes to the skillet, spreading into an even layer. Gently press with the back of a spatula (see photo 1, left). Reduce heat to medium. Cook, without stirring, about 12 minutes or until the bottom is golden brown and crisp (see photo 2, left).

4 Invert a baking sheet or plate over the top of the skillet. Carefully invert the skillet with the baking sheet to transfer the potatoes to the baking sheet (see photo 3, left). If necessary, add the remaining 1 tablespoon oil to the skillet. Using the baking sheet, slide the potatoes back into the skillet, uncooked side down. Cook, without stirring, about 8 minutes more or until the bottom is golden brown. If desired, sprinkle with paprika before serving.

***NOTE:** A skillet with flared sides works best.

MAKE-AHEAD DIRECTIONS: Shred potatoes as directed in Step 1. Place shredded potatoes in a bowl of cool water. Chill in the refrigerator overnight. Continue as directed in Step 2.

PER SERVING: 110 cal., 4 g total fat (2 g sat. fat), 5 mg chol., 120 mg sodium, 17 g carb., 1 g fiber, 2 g pro.
EXCHANGES: 1 Starch, ½ Fat

THE RIGHT STUFF!

Follow these tips for great hash browns:

THE SPUD: Russets are the best choice. Their dry, slightly mealy texture helps hash browns stay intact and gives them a fluffy interior.

THE SHRED: Use the coarse-grate side of a box grater. Finely grated potatoes cause hash browns to retain moisture and end up mushy. A food processor works too.

THE DUNK: We said water was the enemy, but in this step it's your friend. The dunk and rinse are important to keep your potatoes from oxidizing and turning color. It also rinses extra starch from the potatoes so they aren't gummy when you fry them.

THE SPIN: A salad spinner—the ultimate tool to remove water—is crucial to drying your potatoes. If you don't have one, pressing the potato pieces with paper towels will work. Be patient and thorough in your drying—drier potatoes brown much better.

BEST-LOVED FAST LOW-CALORIE

Waffles

PREP: 15 MINUTES **BAKE:** PER WAFFLE BAKER DIRECTIONS **MAKES:** 12 TO 16 (4-INCH) WAFFLES

- **1¾ cups all-purpose flour**
- **2 tablespoons sugar**
- **1 tablespoon baking powder**
- **¼ teaspoon salt**
- **2 eggs**
- **1¾ cups milk**
- **½ cup vegetable oil or butter, melted**
- **1 teaspoon vanilla**

1 In a medium bowl stir together flour, sugar, baking powder, and salt. Make a well in the center of the flour mixture; set aside.

2 In another medium bowl beat eggs lightly; stir in milk, oil, and vanilla. Add egg mixture all at once to the flour mixture. Stir just until moistened (batter should be slightly lumpy).

3 Add batter to a preheated, lightly greased waffle baker according to manufacturer's directions (use a regular or Belgian waffle baker) (see photo 1, below). Close lid quickly; do not open until done. Bake according to manufacturer's directions. When done, use a fork to lift waffle off grid (see photo 2, below). Repeat with remaining batter. Serve warm.

BUTTERMILK WAFFLES: Prepare as directed, except reduce baking powder to 1 teaspoon and add ½ teaspoon baking soda. Substitute 2 cups buttermilk or sour milk (see tip, page 19) for milk.

CORNMEAL WAFFLES: Prepare as directed, except decrease flour to 1 cup and add 1 cup cornmeal to the flour mixture.

WAFFLES STEP-BY-STEP

1. Add batter to the center of a hot waffle baker. Don't fill the grids completely; the batter will spread to the edges when the lid is shut.

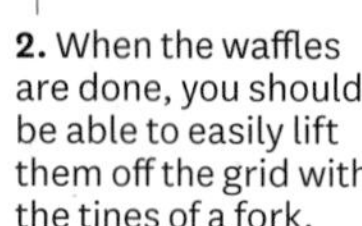

2. When the waffles are done, you should be able to easily lift them off the grid with the tines of a fork.

GINGERBREAD WAFFLES: Prepare as directed, except increase flour to 2 cups and omit the sugar. Add ½ teaspoon ground ginger, ½ teaspoon ground cinnamon, and ¼ teaspoon ground cloves to the flour mixture. Add 2 tablespoons molasses to the egg mixture.

PER WAFFLE PLAIN, BUTTERMILK, CORNMEAL, OR GINGERBREAD VARIATIONS: 185 cal., 11 g total fat (1 g sat. fat), 38 mg chol., 135 mg sodium, 18 g carb., 0 g fiber, 4 g pro.
EXCHANGES: 1 Starch, 2 Fat

CHOCOLATE WAFFLES: Prepare as directed, except decrease flour to 1½ cups, increase sugar to ¼ cup, and add ⅓ cup unsweetened cocoa powder to the flour mixture. Fold ¼ cup miniature semisweet chocolate pieces into the batter. (You might need to lightly coat the waffle baker with nonstick cooking spray between each waffle to prevent sticking.)

PER WAFFLE: 216 cal., 12 g total fat (2 g sat. fat), 38 mg chol., 136 mg sodium, 22 g carb., 1 g fiber, 5 g pro.
EXCHANGES: 1 Starch, ½ Other Carb., 2 Fat

ADDITIONS: Fold one of the following into the batter: ½ cup raisins or finely snipped dried fruit; ½ cup fresh or frozen blueberries, raspberries, or blackberries; ½ cup finely chopped nuts (toasted if desired); ½ cup chopped banana; ½ cup crumbled cooked bacon; ½ cup shredded cheddar cheese; or ¼ cup shredded coconut.

Caramel-Pecan French Toast

PREP: 20 MINUTES **CHILL:** 2 TO 24 HOURS
BAKE: 30 MINUTES AT 350°F **STAND:** 10 MINUTES
MAKES: 8 SERVINGS

- **1 cup packed brown sugar**
- **½ cup butter**
- **2 tablespoons light-color corn syrup**
- **1 cup chopped pecans, toasted (see tip, page 21)**
- **16 ½-inch-thick slices French bread**
- **6 eggs, lightly beaten**
- **1½ cups milk**
- **1 teaspoon vanilla**
- **1 tablespoon granulated sugar**
- **1½ teaspoons ground cinnamon**
- **¼ teaspoon ground nutmeg**
- **Raspberries, maple syrup, and/or chopped pecans, toasted (optional)**

1 In a medium saucepan combine brown sugar, butter, and corn syrup. Cook and stir until butter melts and brown sugar dissolves. Pour into a 3-quart rectangular baking dish. Sprinkle with ½ cup of the pecans.

2 Arrange half of the bread slices in a single layer in the baking dish. Sprinkle with remaining pecans; top with remaining bread slices.

3 In a medium bowl whisk together eggs, milk, and vanilla. Gradually pour egg mixture over bread; press lightly with the back of a large spoon to moisten bread. In a small bowl stir together granulated sugar, cinnamon, and nutmeg; sprinkle over bread. Cover and chill for 2 to 24 hours.

4 Preheat oven to 350°F. Bake, uncovered, for 30 to 40 minutes or until lightly browned. Let stand for 10 minutes before serving. To serve, invert French toast onto a large serving platter. If desired, serve with raspberries, maple syrup, and/or additional pecans.

PER 2 SLICES: 579 cal., 27 g total fat (10 g sat. fat), 193 mg chol., 579 mg sodium, 72 g carb., 3 g fiber, 15 g pro.
EXCHANGES: 2 Starch, 3 Other Carb., 1 Medium-Fat Meat, 4 Fat

CARAMEL-PECAN FRENCH TOAST

FAST

French Toast

PREP: 10 MINUTES **COOK:** 4 MINUTES PER SLICE
MAKES: 4 SERVINGS

- **4 eggs, lightly beaten**
- **1 cup milk**
- **2 tablespoons sugar**
- **2 teaspoons vanilla**
- **½ teaspoon finely shredded orange peel (optional)**
- **½ teaspoon ground cinnamon (optional)**
- **¼ teaspoon ground nutmeg (optional)**
- **8 slices Texas toast or ½-inch-thick slices country Italian bread or rich egg bread (challah or brioche)**
- **2 tablespoons butter or margarine**
- **Maple-flavor syrup (optional)**

1 In a shallow bowl beat together eggs, milk, sugar, vanilla, and, if desired, orange peel, cinnamon, and/or nutmeg. Dip bread slices into egg mixture, coating both sides (let soak in egg mixture about 10 seconds per side).

2 In a skillet or on a griddle melt 1 tablespoon of the butter over medium heat; add half of the bread slices and cook for 2 to 3 minutes on each side or until golden brown. Repeat with remaining butter and bread slices. Serve warm. If desired, serve with syrup.

PER 2 SLICES: 410 cal., 17 g total fat (7 g sat. fat), 272 mg chol., 530 mg sodium, 48 g carb., 2 g fiber, 16 g pro.
EXCHANGES: 3 Starch, 1 Medium-Fat Meat, 2 Fat

BEST-LOVED LOW-CALORIE

Crepes

START TO FINISH: 40 MINUTES
MAKES: 16 TO 18 CREPES

- **2 eggs, beaten**
- **1½ cups milk**
- **1 cup all-purpose flour**
- **1 tablespoon vegetable oil**
- **¼ teaspoon salt**

1 In a medium mixing bowl combine eggs, milk, flour, oil, and salt; whisk until smooth.

2 Heat a lightly greased 6-inch skillet over medium-high heat; remove from heat. Spoon in 2 tablespoons batter; lift and tilt skillet to spread batter evenly. Return to heat; cook for 1 to 2 minutes or until browned on one side only. (Or cook on a crepemaker according to manufacturer's directions.) Invert over paper towels; remove crepe. Repeat with remaining batter, greasing skillet occasionally. If crepes are browning too quickly, reduce heat to medium.

PER CREPE: 56 cal., 2 g total fat (0 g sat. fat), 25 mg chol., 56 mg sodium, 7 g carb., 0 g fiber, 2 g pro.
EXCHANGES: ½ Starch, ½ Fat

CHOCOLATE-HAZELNUT CREPES: Prepare as directed, except for each crepe spread unbrowned side with 1 tablespoon chocolate-hazelnut spread. Sprinkle 1 tablespoon chopped, toasted hazelnuts along one edge of crepe; roll up from the filled edge.

PER CREPE: 201 cal., 12 g total fat (3 g sat. fat), 25 mg chol., 64 mg sodium, 19 g carb., 1 g fiber, 5 g pro.
EXCHANGES: 1 Starch, 2 Fat

STRAWBERRY-CREAM CHEESE CREPES: Prepare as directed, except for each crepe spread unbrowned side of a cooled crepe with 2 tablespoons whipped cream cheese. Arrange ¼ cup sliced fresh strawberries along one edge of crepe. Drizzle with 1 teaspoon honey; roll up from the filled edge.

PER CREPE: 149 cal., 8 g total fat (4 g sat. fat), 45 mg chol., 147 mg sodium, 17 g carb., 1 g fiber, 4 g pro.
EXCHANGES: 1 Starch, 1½ Fat

Blueberry Buckle

PREP: 20 MINUTES **BAKE:** 50 MINUTES AT 350°F
MAKES: 9 SERVINGS

- **2 cups all-purpose flour**
- **2½ teaspoons baking powder**
- **¼ teaspoon salt**
- **½ cup shortening**
- **¾ cup sugar**
- **1 egg**
- **½ cup milk**
- **2 cups fresh or frozen blueberries**
- **½ cup all-purpose flour**
- **½ cup sugar**
- **½ teaspoon ground cinnamon**
- **¼ cup butter**

1 Preheat oven to 350°F. Grease bottom and ½ inch up sides of a 9×9×2-inch or 8×8×2-inch baking pan; set aside. In a medium bowl combine the 2 cups flour, baking powder, and salt; set aside.

2 In a medium mixing bowl beat shortening with an electric mixer on medium speed for 30 seconds. Add the ¾ cup sugar. Beat on medium to high speed until light and fluffy. Add egg; beat well. Add flour mixture and milk alternately to beaten egg mixture; beat until smooth after each addition.

3 Spread batter in prepared pan. Sprinkle with blueberries. In another bowl combine the ½ cup flour, the ½ cup sugar, and cinnamon. Using a pastry blender, cut in butter until mixture resembles coarse crumbs; sprinkle over blueberries. Bake for 50 to 60 minutes or until golden. Serve warm.

RASPBERRY BUCKLE: Prepare as directed, except substitute fresh or frozen red raspberries for the blueberries.

PER SERVING BLUEBERRY OR RASPBERRY VARIATION: 411 cal., 17 g total fat (6 g sat. fat), 38 mg chol., 182 mg sodium, 60 g carb., 2 g fiber, 5 g pro. EXCHANGES: 2 Starch, 2 Carb., 3 Fat

BEST-LOVED

Cake Doughnuts

PREP: 45 MINUTES **CHILL:** 2 TO 4 HOURS
COOK: 2 MINUTES PER BATCH
MAKES: ABOUT 16 DOUGHNUTS AND HOLES

- **4 cups all-purpose flour**
- **2 teaspoons baking powder**
- **¼ teaspoon salt**
- **2 eggs**
- **1¼ cups granulated sugar**
- **1 teaspoon vanilla**
- **⅔ cup milk**
- **¼ cup butter, melted**
- **Vegetable oil or shortening for deep-fat frying**
- **Powdered sugar, granulated sugar, Chocolate Glaze, or Powdered Sugar Icing (page 173)**

1 In a medium bowl combine the flour, baking powder, and salt; set aside. In a large mixing bowl combine eggs, 1¼ cups granulated sugar, and the vanilla; beat with an electric mixer on medium speed for 3 minutes or until thick. In a small bowl combine the milk and melted butter.

2 Add flour mixture and milk mixture alternately to egg mixture, beating on low speed after each addition until just combined. Cover and chill dough for 2 to 4 hours.

3 On a well-floured surface roll dough to ½-inch thickness (do not stir in additional flour) (see photo 1, below). Cut dough with a floured 2½-inch doughnut cutter (see photo 2, below), dipping cutter into flour between cuts. Reroll dough as necessary.

4 Fry 2 or 3 doughnuts and holes at a time in deep hot oil (365°F) for 2 to 3 minutes or until doughnuts are golden brown, turning once. Remove with a slotted spoon (see photo 3, below) and drain on paper towels. Repeat with remaining dough. Cool doughnuts slightly and coat with powdered sugar or granulated sugar, or dip tops in Chocolate Glaze (see photo 4, below) or Powdered Sugar Icing.

PER DOUGHNUT AND HOLE WITH POWDERED SUGAR: 342 cal., 18 g total fat (3 g sat. fat), 35 mg chol., 100 mg sodium, 42 g carb., 1 g fiber, 4 g pro. EXCHANGES: 1 Starch, 2 Other Carb., 3½ Fat

SPICED DOUGHNUTS: Prepare as directed, except add 1 teaspoon ground cinnamon, ½ teaspoon ground ginger, and ⅛ teaspoon ground cloves to the flour mixture and coat warm doughnuts in a mixture of ⅔ cup granulated sugar and ½ teaspoon ground cinnamon.

PER DOUGHNUT AND HOLE: 368 cal., 18 g total fat (3 g sat. fat), 35 mg chol., 100 mg sodium, 49 mg carb., 1 g fiber, 4 g pro. EXCHANGES: 1 Starch, 2 Other Carb., 3½ Fat

CAKE DOUGHNUTS

CHOCOLATE GLAZE: In a small saucepan melt 3 ounces unsweetened chocolate, chopped, and 3 tablespoons butter over low heat. Remove from heat. Stir in 3 cups powdered sugar and 1½ teaspoons vanilla. Stir in 4 to 5 tablespoons warm water until glaze coats the back of a spoon.

TWO-BITE TREATS

Remove doughnut holes from the cutter; do not reroll. Fry them with doughnuts for tasty bites.

CAKE DOUGHNUTS STEP-BY-STEP

1. Roll out dough on a generously floured surface so dough doesn't stick.

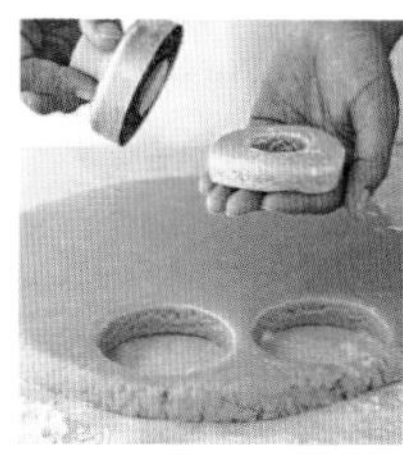
2. Dip cutter into flour between cuts to prevent dough from sticking to the cutter.

3. Use a slotted spoon to turn and remove doughnuts; allow excess oil to drain into pan before moving doughnuts to paper towels.

4. If glazing doughnuts, dip tops halfway in glaze. Allow to dry on a wire rack.

BEST-LOVED

Chocolate-Pecan Coffee Cake

PREP: 30 MINUTES **BAKE:** 55 MINUTES AT 325°F
COOL: 20 MINUTES **MAKES:** 12 SERVINGS

- **½ cup butter, softened**
- **1 cup granulated sugar**
- **2 teaspoons baking powder**
- **½ teaspoon baking soda**
- **¼ teaspoon salt**
- **2 eggs**
- **1 teaspoon vanilla**
- **2¼ cups all-purpose flour**
- **1 8-ounce carton sour cream**
- **1 recipe Coconut-Pecan Topping**

1 Preheat oven to 325°F. Grease and flour a 10-inch fluted tube pan; set aside. In a large mixing bowl beat butter with an electric mixer on medium to high speed for 30 seconds. Add granulated sugar, baking powder, baking soda, and salt. Beat until well combined, scraping sides of bowl occasionally. Add eggs, one at a time, beating well after each addition. Beat in vanilla. Add flour and sour cream alternately to butter mixture, beating on low speed after each addition just until combined.

2 Sprinkle half of the Coconut-Pecan Topping into the prepared pan. Spoon half of the cake batter in mounds over the coconut topping. Carefully spread to an even layer. Sprinkle with remaining coconut topping. Spoon in remaining cake batter and spread to an even layer.

3 Bake for 55 to 65 minutes or until a long wooden skewer inserted near the center comes out clean. Cool on a wire rack for 20 minutes. Invert cake and remove pan. Serve warm.

COCONUT-PECAN TOPPING: In a large bowl combine 1 cup all-purpose flour, 1 cup packed brown sugar, and 1 teaspoon ground cinnamon. Cut in ½ cup cold butter, cut up, until mixture resembles coarse crumbs; stir in ¾ cup semisweet chocolate pieces, ½ cup flaked coconut, and ½ cup chopped pecans.

PER SERVING: 550 cal., 28 g total fat (16 g sat. fat), 86 mg chol., 297 mg sodium, 71 g carb., 2 g fiber, 6 g pro.
EXCHANGES: 2 Starch, 3 Other Carb., 5 Fat

FAST LOW-CALORIE

Cranberry-Almond Cereal Mix

PREP: 10 MINUTES **COOK:** 8 MINUTES
MAKES: 4⅓ CUPS

- **1 cup regular rolled oats**
- **1 cup quick-cooking barley**
- **1 cup bulgur or cracked wheat**
- **1 cup dried cranberries, raisins, and/or snipped dried apricots**
- **¾ cup sliced almonds, toasted (see tip, page 21)**
- **⅓ cup sugar**
- **1 tablespoon ground cinnamon**
- **¼ teaspoon salt**
- **Milk (optional)**

1 In an airtight container stir together oats, barley, bulgur, cranberries, almonds, sugar, cinnamon, and salt. Cover and seal. Store at room temperature for up to 2 months or freeze for up to 6 months.

MICROWAVE DIRECTIONS: For one breakfast serving, in a microwave-safe 1-quart bowl combine ¾ cup water and ⅓ cup cereal mix. Microwave, uncovered, on 50% power (medium) for 8 to 11 minutes or until cereal reaches desired consistency, stirring once. Stir before serving. If desired, serve with milk.

PER ⅓ CUP: 201 cal., 4 g total fat (0 g sat. fat), 0 mg chol., 47 mg sodium, 39 g carb., 6 g fiber, 6 g pro.
EXCHANGES: ½ Fruit, 1½ Starch, ½ Other Carb.

Fruit and Nut Granola

PREP: 15 MINUTES **BAKE:** 20 MINUTES AT 300°F
MAKES: 7 CUPS

- **4 cups regular rolled oats**
- **1 cup coarsely chopped pecans or slivered or sliced almonds**
- **⅔ cup packed brown sugar**
- **2 teaspoons ground cinnamon**
- **⅛ teaspoon salt**
- **⅛ teaspoon ground allspice or nutmeg**
- **½ cup butter**
- **¼ cup honey**
- **1 cup dried fruit (such as raisins, golden raisins, currants, snipped tart red cherries, blueberries, cranberries, snipped apricots, snipped apples, and/or snipped dates)**
- **Plain or vanilla yogurt (optional)**

FRUIT AND NUT GRANOLA

1 Preheat oven to 300°F. Lightly grease a 15×10×1-inch baking pan; set aside. In a large bowl combine the oats, pecans, brown sugar, cinnamon, salt, and allspice; set aside.

2 In a small saucepan heat butter and honey over medium heat until butter melts, stirring occasionally. Drizzle over the oats mixture; toss to coat. Spread evenly into the prepared pan.

3 Bake about 20 minutes or until light brown, stirring after 10 minutes. Remove from oven. Stir in dried fruit.

4 Spread granola on a large piece of foil to cool. Store at room temperature in an airtight container for up to 5 days. (Or place in freezer bags and freeze for up to 2 months.) If desired, serve with yogurt.

PER ½ CUP: 373 cal., 15 g fat (5 g sat. fat), 17 mg chol., 84 mg sodium, 54 g carb., 6 g fiber, 9 g pro.
EXCHANGES: ½ Fruit, 2 Starch, 1 Other Carb., 2½ Fat

OH, HONEY!

Honey flavors vary from delicate to robust depending on what flowers the bees have available for sipping. Switch up the flavor of your granola with a different variety of honey. Try clover, orange blossom, buckwheat, wildflower, or blueberry. Or use maple-flavor syrup instead of any honey.

LOW-CALORIE

Steel-Cut Oatmeal

PREP: 10 MINUTES **COOK:** 25 MINUTES
MAKES: 6 SERVINGS

- 4 **cups water**
- ½ **teaspoon salt**
- 1⅓ **cups steel-cut oats**
- **Toppings (optional)**

1 In a large saucepan bring water and salt to boiling. Stir in oats. Cover and simmer for 25 to 30 minutes or until oats are just tender and liquid is nearly absorbed. Serve warm in bowls. If desired, add toppings.

SLOW COOKER OATMEAL: In a 3½- or 4-quart slow cooker combine 6 cups water, 2 cups steel-cut oats, and 1 teaspoon salt. Cover and cook on low-heat setting for 6 to 7 hours or on high-heat setting for 3 to 3½ hours. Serve as directed. Makes 9 servings.

MAKE-AHEAD DIRECTIONS: Prepare oatmeal as directed. Place cooked oatmeal in an airtight container and chill for up to 3 days. Place ⅔ cup chilled cooked oatmeal in a microwave-safe bowl. Microwave, covered with waxed paper, on 100% power (high) for 50 to 60 seconds or until heated, stirring once. Serve as directed.

PER ⅔ CUP (WITHOUT TOPPINGS): 142 cal., 3 g total fat (0 g sat. fat), 0 mg chol., 199 mg sodium, 24 g carb., 4 g fiber, 6 g pro. EXCHANGES: 1½ Starch, ½ Fat

TOPPINGS: Top warm oatmeal with dried fruit (sweet cherries, raisins, tropical fruit bits, chopped dates, snipped apricots); chopped nuts (almonds, pecans, walnuts, hazelnuts); shredded or flaked coconut; brown sugar; pure maple syrup; and/or milk, half-and-half, or light cream.

LOW-CALORIE

Coconut-Chia Oat Squares

PREP: 20 MINUTES **BAKE:** 18 MINUTES AT 325°F
MAKES: 3½ CUPS

- **Nonstick cooking spray**
- 1 **cup rolled oats**
- ½ **cup oat bran**
- ½ **cup flaked or shredded coconut**
- ⅓ **cup packed brown sugar**
- ¼ **cup whole wheat flour**
- 3 **tablespoons almond butter or peanut butter**
- 2 **tablespoons water**
- 1 **tablespoon honey**
- ⅛ **teaspoon baking soda**

COCONUT-CHIA OAT SQUARES

- ⅛ **teaspoon salt**
- ⅛ **teaspoon coconut extract**
- 2 **tablespoons chia seeds**

1 Preheat oven to 325°F. Coat a 15×10×1-inch baking pan with cooking spray; set aside. Place oats, oat bran, shredded coconut, brown sugar, and flour in a food processor. Cover and process until finely ground. Add almond butter, the water, honey, baking soda, salt, and coconut extract. Cover and process until combined. Transfer mixture to a large bowl. Stir in chia seeds (mixture will be crumbly).

2 Using the bottom of a measuring cup, press oat mixture firmly into the prepared baking pan (mixture will be pressed thin in the pan). Bake for 18 to 20 minutes or until golden brown. Cool in pan on a wire rack (mixture will crisp as it cools).

3 Use a table knife or small metal spatula to release the oat mixture from the pan. Break mixture into small bite-size pieces (about ¾-inch pieces). Store at room temperature in an airtight container for up to 1 week.

PER HEAPING ½ CUP: 296 cal., 10 g total fat (3 g sat. fat), 0 mg chol., 116 mg sodium, 48 g carb., 8 g fiber, 9 g pro. EXCHANGES: 2 Starch, 1 Other Carb., 1½ Fat

cakes & frostings

ANGEL FOOD, CHIFFON & SPONGE CAKES

BUTTER OR SHORTENING CAKES

CHOCOLATE CAKES

CUPCAKES & CAKE POPS

FROSTINGS, FILLINGS, GLAZES & TOPPERS

FROSTINGS, FILLINGS, GLAZES & TOPPERS *(continued)*

FRUIT & VEGETABLE CAKES

POUND & TUBE CAKES

TIPS

cakes & frostings

With these essentials, you can craft flawless cakes—from simple to simply spectacular.

THE BEST PAN FOR THE JOB

Pans come in a variety of materials. A superb all-around choice is the simple, sturdy single-wall aluminum pan, with or without nonstick coating. Lightweight and a good conductor of heat, it ensures even baking and browning. With all pans, keep these things in mind.

- Shiny baking pans reflect heat, producing cakes with golden, delicate crusts.
- Dark- or dull-finish pans and glass dishes absorb heat, increasing browning. (If they brown your cakes too much, reduce oven temperature by 25°F; check doneness 3 to 5 minutes early.)

DON'T GET STUCK

Removing a cake from the pan is a make-or-break moment. Use one of these ways to ensure cakes will slip out easily when the time comes.

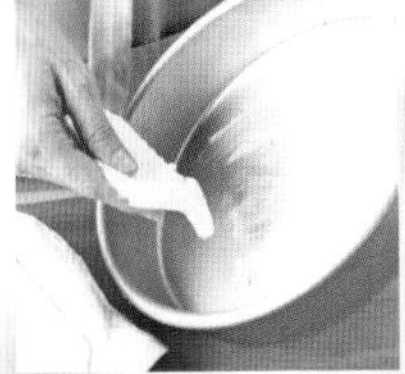

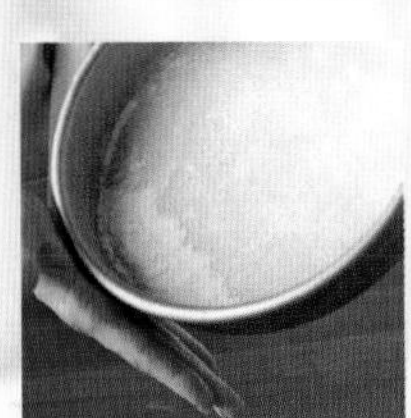

- Grease and lightly flour. Unless a recipe says otherwise, use a paper towel or pastry brush to evenly spread shortening or butter on bottom, sides, and corners of a pan. Sprinkle a little flour into the pan; tap so flour covers all greased surfaces. Tap out any extra flour. For chocolate cakes, you can use cocoa powder instead of flour.
- Use nonstick spray. As an alternative to shortening or butter, apply nonstick cooking spray; flour as directed.
- Line the pan. If a recipe calls for waxed or parchment paper, place the pan on the paper and trace around its base with a pencil. Cut just inside the traced line; line the bottom of a lightly greased pan with the paper, smoothing out any wrinkles or bubbles. Unless otherwise specified, grease and flour lined pan as directed.

NICELY DONE!

Never underestimate the importance of the proper oven temperature to get your cake done just right.

- Always fully preheat the oven before baking.
- Use a reliable oven thermometer to ensure your oven is accurately calibrated.

DONENESS TESTS: Once the minimum baking time is reached, use the doneness test most appropriate for the type of cake you're baking.

- For butter-style cakes (those with beaten butter and sugar in the batter): Insert a wooden toothpick near the center of the cake. If toothpick comes out clean (with only a crumb or two on it), the cake is done. If there is any wet batter on it, bake the cake for a few minutes more and test in a new spot with a new toothpick.
- For foam cakes (such as angel food, sponge, and chiffon): Touch the top lightly with your finger. If the top springs back, the cake is done.

Poppy Seed Cake, page 165

cook's secrets

white cake

The Secret: What makes a good cake great? Setting your timer to beat the butter and sugar together for at least 3 minutes. The height and texture of your cake depend on it!

PREP: 55 MINUTES **BAKE:** 30 MINUTES AT 350°F **COOL:** 60 MINUTES
MAKES: 12 SERVINGS

- **4 egg whites**
- **2 cups all-purpose flour**
- **1 teaspoon baking powder**
- **½ teaspoon baking soda**
- **½ teaspoon salt**
- **½ cup butter or shortening, softened**
- **1¾ cups sugar**
- **1 teaspoon vanilla**
- **1⅓ cups buttermilk or sour milk (see tip, page 19)**

As your kitchen warms, butter might go from soft to melty. In order to incorporate as much air into the batter as possible, butter should be softened without signs of melting. Liquid bubbles won't hold air.

1 Allow egg whites to stand at room temperature for 30 minutes. Meanwhile, grease and lightly flour two 9×1½-inch or 8×1½-inch round cake pans or grease one 13×9×2-inch baking pan; set pan(s) aside. In a medium bowl stir together flour, baking powder, baking soda, and salt; set aside.

2 Preheat oven to 350°F. In a large mixing bowl beat butter with an electric mixer on medium to high speed for 30 seconds. Add sugar and vanilla; beat on medium speed for 3 to 5 minutes or until light. Add egg whites, one at a time, beating well after each addition. Add flour mixture and buttermilk alternately, beating on low speed after each addition just until combined. Spread batter evenly into prepared pan(s).

3 Bake for 30 to 35 minutes or until a wooden toothpick inserted near center(s) comes out clean. Cool cake layers in pans on wire racks for 10 minutes. Remove layers from pans; cool thoroughly on racks. Or place the 13×9×2-inch cake in pan on a wire rack; cool thoroughly. Frost with desired frosting (see pages 172–174).

PER SERVING: 275 cal., 8 g total fat (5 g sat. fat), 21 mg chol., 271 mg sodium, 47 g carb., 1 g fiber, 4 g pro.
EXCHANGES: 1 Starch, 2 Carb., 1½ Fat

CAKE POINTERS

1. BEAT IT
This is it—the most important step when making a "shortened" (or creamed) cake. Beat the fat and sugar together for 3 to 5 minutes. DON'T cut this short! Tiny air bubbles are created and trapped in the mixture, acting as a leavener along with the baking powder and soda in this recipe. Preserving these bubbles is essential to having a light and fluffy crumb texture.

2. EGGS, 1 AT A TIME
Add egg whites, one at a time, beating after each until integrated. The protein in the egg whites helps create structure around the air bubbles to reinforce the texture.

REMOVING CAKES FROM PANS STEP-BY-STEP

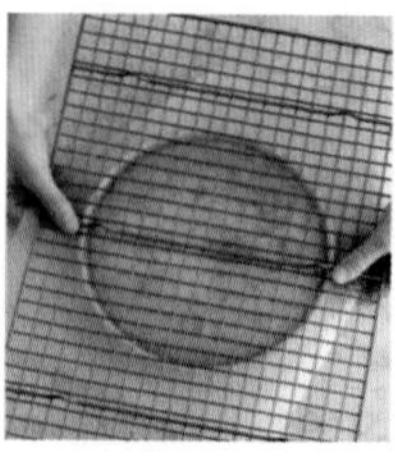

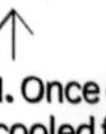

1. Once cake layers have cooled for 10 minutes ONLY, run a thin metal spatula or knife around the edges of the cake pan. Place a cooling rack over top.

2. Invert the pan with the rack so the pan ends up on top. Shake gently to loosen cake layer from the pan.

3. If you lined the bottom of the cake layer with paper, carefully remove the paper, pulling slowly and gently.

↑

3. ADVICE ON MIXING
When adding milk and the dry ingredients alternately, gluten can develop. Too much gluten makes for a tough cake. If you add more of the flour first, it will be coated with the butter and protected from gluten development. Once you add milk, gluten might form. Try not to overmix at this point and beat on low speed. Batter may look curdled at certain times through this step. Never fear.

4. GENTLY, GENTLY
Plan to end with the last of your milk instead of the last of your flour, beating on low JUST until combined.

↑

5. EVEN UP
Pour batter evenly between prepared pans. Using a metal spatula, smooth tops before baking.

PREPARING PANS

With the exception of angel food and chiffon cakes, most cakes require pans to be greased and floured. For a quick brush-on: Stir together 1/4 cup vegetable oil, 1/4 cup shortening, and 1/4 cup flour. Use this for recipes that call for greased and floured pans. The mixture may be stored in a covered container in the refrigerator for up to one month. If you're still leery about getting your cake out of your pan in one piece, line the bottom of the pan with waxed or parchment paper as directed on page 151. Grease the paper with brush-on mixture and flour.

fill & frost

The Secret: The crumb coat will save you from crumbs in your frosting and tears in your cake layers. Check out the details below. Pick your favorite flavor of Butter Frosting, page 172 to frost this cake.

FROSTING A LAYER CAKE STEP-BY-STEP

1. FIRST LAYER
Place the first cake layer on a pedestal or cake plate. For quick cleanup, tuck small pieces of waxed paper around and under the cake. Spread ½ cup frosting evenly over surface to ¼ inch of the edge.

2. TOP OFF
If necessary, use a serrated knife to trim the rounded surface off the cake layer. Place the second cake layer on top of the frosting. Center the cake, aligning the edges of the cakes.

3. CRUMB COAT
Here's the key to frosting perfection! Spread a very thin coat of frosting over the entire cake to seal in the crumbs and fill in any imperfections. Allow the crumb coat to dry before finishing frosting the cake. Using the thin metal spatula, frost cake with the remaining frosting. Push the frosting onto the sides of the cake without moving the spatula back and forth.

FINISH IT!

STRIPES
Using a straight metal spatula and starting at the base of the cake, pull the spatula straight up toward the top of the cake. Repeat until you've covered the entire cake.

ROSES
Place your remaining frosting in a pastry bag fitted with a large star tip and pipe rose circles around the cake. You can decide how large or small and how closely spaced they are.

PETALS
Place your frosting in a pastry bag with an open tip or transfer frosting to a gallon resealable plastic bag and cut off a corner. Pipe three dots of frosting of similar size in a row from top to bottom. Using a rounded knife or thin metal spatula, place the tip in the center of the frosting dot and pull the frosting horizontally to one side; repeat.

FILLING FLAVORS

Add a little flavor surprise to your layer cake. Instead of using frosting between the two cake layers, spread (from left, below) approximately ½ to ⅔ cup jam or preserves; lemon, orange, or lime curd; or chocolate-hazelnut spread.

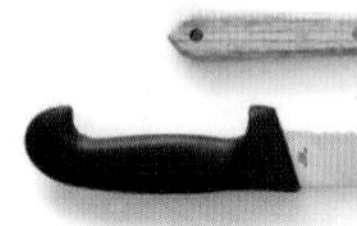

FROSTING TOOLS

Two of the best tools to have are a thin straight or offset metal spatula and a long serrated knife. The thin metal spatula comes in many sizes; if you don't feel like a pro, choose a smaller spatula. A LONG serrated knife is best for making cake layers even and trimming when necessary.

Yellow Cake

PREP: 50 MINUTES **BAKE:** 20 MINUTES AT 375°F
COOL: 60 MINUTES **MAKES:** 12 SERVINGS

- **¾ cup butter**
- **3 eggs**
- **2½ cups all-purpose flour**
- **2½ teaspoons baking powder**
- **½ teaspoon salt**
- **1¾ cups sugar**
- **1½ teaspoons vanilla**
- **1¼ cups milk**

1 Allow butter and eggs to stand at room temperature for 30 minutes. Meanwhile, grease and lightly flour two 9×1½-inch or 8×1½-inch round cake pans or grease one 13×9×2-inch baking pan; set pan(s) aside. In a medium bowl stir together flour, baking powder, and salt; set flour mixture aside.

2 Preheat oven to 375°F. In a large mixing bowl beat butter with an electric mixer on medium to high speed for 30 seconds. Gradually add sugar, about ¼ cup at a time, beating on medium speed until well combined. Scrape sides of bowl; beat for 2 minutes more. Add eggs, one at a time, beating well after each addition. Beat in vanilla. Add flour mixture and milk alternately to butter mixture, beating on low speed after each addition just until combined. Spread batter evenly into the prepared pan(s).

3 Bake for 20 to 25 minutes for 9-inch pans, 30 to 35 minutes for 8-inch pans, 25 to 30 minutes for 13×9×2-inch pan, or until a wooden toothpick inserted near center(s) comes out clean. Cool cake layers in pans on wire racks for 10 minutes. Remove layers from pans; cool thoroughly on wire racks. Or place the 13×9×2-inch cake in pan on a wire rack; cool thoroughly. Frost with desired frosting (see recipes, pages 172–174).

CITRUS YELLOW CAKE: Prepare as directed, except stir 2 teaspoons finely shredded orange peel or lemon peel into batter.

PER SERVING PLAIN OR CITRUS VARIATION: 342 cal., 14 g total fat (8 g sat. fat), 885 mg chol., 257 mg sodium, 51 g carb., 1 g fiber, 5 g pro. EXCHANGES: 1½ Starch, 2 Other Carb., 2½ Fat

CHOOSING A CAKE PLATE

Layer cakes presented on pedestal cake stands always look spectacular, but if you don't have one, use any flat, round platter or plate. You will want the platter to be at least an inch larger in diameter than the cake. Also be sure it has a flat surface with no rim so the cake will be level.

BEST-LOVED

Chocolate Cake

PREP: 60 MINUTES **BAKE:** 35 MINUTES AT 350°F
COOL: 60 MINUTES **MAKES:** 12 SERVINGS

- **¾ cup butter**
- **3 eggs**
- **2 cups all-purpose flour**
- **¾ cup unsweetened cocoa powder**
- **1 teaspoon baking soda**
- **¾ teaspoon baking powder**
- **½ teaspoon salt**
- **2 cups sugar**
- **2 teaspoons vanilla**
- **1½ cups milk**

1 Allow butter and eggs to stand at room temperature for 30 minutes. Meanwhile, lightly grease the bottoms of two 8×8×2-inch square or 9×1½-inch round cake pans. Line bottoms of pans with waxed paper; grease and lightly flour pans. Or grease one 13×9×2-inch baking pan. Set pan(s) aside. In a medium bowl stir together flour, cocoa powder, baking soda, baking powder, and salt; set aside.

2 Preheat oven to 350°F. In a large mixing bowl beat butter with an electric mixer on medium to high speed for 30 seconds. Gradually add sugar, ¼ cup at a time, beating on medium speed until well combined. Scrape sides of bowl; beat for 2 minutes more. Add eggs, one at a time, beating well after each addition. Beat in vanilla. Add flour mixture and milk alternately, beating on low speed after each addition just until combined. Beat on medium to high speed for 20 seconds more. Spread batter evenly into prepared pan(s).

3 Bake for 35 to 40 minutes for 8-inch pans and 13×9×2-inch pan, or 30 to 35 minutes for 9-inch pans, or until a wooden toothpick inserted near center(s) comes out clean. Cool cake layers in pans on wire racks for 10 minutes. Remove layers from pans; peel off waxed paper. Cool thoroughly on wire racks. Or place 13×9×2-inch cake in pan on a wire rack; cool thoroughly. Frost with desired frosting (see recipes, pages 172–174).

DEVIL'S FOOD CAKE: Prepare as directed, except omit baking powder and increase baking soda to 1¼ teaspoons.

PER SERVING PLAIN OR DEVIL'S FOOD VARIATION: 354 cal., 14 g total fat (9 g sat. fat), 86 mg chol., 330 mg sodium, 54 g carb., 2 g fiber, 6 g pro. EXCHANGES: 2 Starch, 1½ Other Carb., 2½ Fat

German Chocolate Cake

PREP: 60 MINUTES **BAKE:** 35 MINUTES AT 350°F
COOL: 60 MINUTES **MAKES:** 12 SERVINGS

- **1 4-ounce package sweet baking chocolate, chopped**
- **1½ cups milk**
- **¾ cup butter**
- **3 eggs**
- **2 cups all-purpose flour**
- **1 teaspoon baking soda**
- **¾ teaspoon baking powder**
- **½ teaspoon salt**
- **1¾ cups sugar**
- **2 teaspoons vanilla**
- **1 recipe Coconut-Pecan Frosting**

1 In a small saucepan combine chocolate and milk. Cook and stir over low heat until melted; set aside to cool.

2 Allow butter and eggs to stand at room temperature for 30 minutes. Meanwhile, lightly grease the bottoms of two 8×8×2-inch square or 9×1½-inch round cake pans. Line bottoms of pans with waxed paper; grease and lightly flour pans. Or grease one 13×9×2-inch baking pan. Set pan(s) aside. In a medium bowl stir together flour, baking soda, baking powder, and salt; set aside.

3 Preheat oven to 350°F. In a large mixing bowl beat butter with an electric mixer on medium to high speed for 30 seconds. Gradually add sugar, about ¼ cup at a time, beating on medium speed until well combined. Scrape sides of bowl; beat on medium speed for 2 minutes more. Add eggs, one at a time, beating well after each addition. Beat in vanilla. Add flour mixture and chocolate mixture alternately, beating on low speed after each addition just until combined. Beat on medium to high speed for 20 seconds more. Spread batter evenly into prepared pan(s).

4 Bake for 35 to 40 minutes for 8-inch pans, 30 to 35 minutes for 9-inch pans, 40 to 45 minutes for 13×9×2-inch pan, or until a wooden toothpick inserted near the center(s) comes out clean. Cool cake layers in pans on wire racks for 10 minutes. Remove layers from pans; peel off waxed paper. Cool thoroughly on wire racks. Or place 13×9×2-inch cake in pan on a wire rack; cool thoroughly.

5 Spread Coconut-Pecan Frosting over the top of each layer; stack the layers on a cake plate. Or spread Coconut-Pecan Frosting over the top of the 13×9-inch cake.

COCONUT-PECAN FROSTING: In a medium saucepan combine 4 egg yolks, one 12-ounce can evaporated milk, 1½ cups sugar, and ½ cup butter. Cook and stir over medium heat for 20 to 25 minutes or until thickened and mixture coats back of a metal spoon. Remove from heat; stir in one 7-ounce package flaked coconut and 1 cup chopped pecans. Cover and cool thoroughly before using to frost cake.

PER SERVING: 730 cal., 39 g total fat (21 g sat. fat), 170 mg chol., 514 mg sodium, 91 g carb., 4 g fiber, 10 g pro.
EXCHANGES: 2 Starch, 4 Other Carb., ½ Medium-Fat Meat, 6½ Fat

MAKE A CAKE ANY SIZE YOU WANT

If you want to make a cake of a different size or shape than the one specified in the recipe, no problem! Make one large cake or your favorite-size cupcakes using the baking times below as a guide. Baking times will vary with different cake batters. Be sure to test the cake at the minimum baking time.

2½-inch cupcakes, 15 to 20 minutes

13×9×2-inch baking pan, 30 to 35 minutes

Fluted tube pan, 40 to 45 minutes

Jumbo 3½-inch cupcakes, 20 to 25 minutes

9×1½-inch round pans, 25 to 30 minutes
8×1½-inch round pans, 30 to 35 minutes

STRAWBERRY CUPCAKES

Strawberry Cake

PREP: 15 MINUTES **BAKE:** 30 MINUTES AT 350°F
COOL: 60 MINUTES **MAKES:** 15 SERVINGS

- **1 10-ounce pouch or 16-ounce container frozen strawberries in syrup, thawed**
- **1 package 2-layer-size white cake mix**
- **½ of an 8-ounce package cream cheese, softened**
- **¼ cup butter, softened**
- **1 teaspoon vanilla**
- **4 cups powdered sugar**
- **1 to 2 drops red food coloring (optional)**

1 Preheat oven to 350°F. Grease a 13×9×2-inch baking pan; set pan aside. Drain strawberries, reserving 3 tablespoons syrup for frosting. Add enough water to remaining syrup to equal ¾ cup. Prepare cake mix according to package directions, substituting the syrup-water mixture for the liquid called for on the package; stir in all of the strawberries. (Batter will be thick.) Spread batter into the prepared pan.

2 Bake for 30 to 35 minutes or until a wooden toothpick inserted near the center comes out clean. Cool thoroughly in pan on a wire rack.

3 For frosting, in a mixing bowl beat cream cheese, butter, vanilla, and reserved syrup with an electric mixer on medium speed until fluffy. Gradually beat in powdered sugar. If desired, beat in food coloring. Spread over cooled cake.

PER SERVING: 345 cal., 11 g total fat (4 g sat. fat), 16 mg chol., 287 mg sodium, 63 g carb., 0 g fiber, 3 g pro.
EXCHANGES: 1 Starch, 3 Other Carb., 2 Fat

STRAWBERRY CUPCAKES: Grease and flour twenty-four 2½-inch muffin cups or line with paper bake cups. Prepare batter as directed. Fill muffin cups two-thirds full with batter. Bake about 18 minutes or until a wooden toothpick inserted in centers comes out clean. Cool in muffin cups on wire racks for 5 minutes. Remove from cups; cool thoroughly on wire racks. Pipe or spread frosting on cupcakes. Makes 24 cupcakes.

PER CUPCAKE: 216 cal., 7 g total fat (3 g sat. fat), 10 mg chol., 179 mg sodium, 40 g carb., 0 g fiber, 2 g pro.
EXCHANGES: 2½ Other Carb., 1½ Fat

Mississippi Mud Cake

PREP: 15 MINUTES **BAKE:** 30 MINUTES AT 350°F
STAND: 15 MINUTES **MAKES:** 12 SERVINGS

- **1 package 2-layer-size chocolate cake mix**
- **1¼ cups water**
- **⅓ cup vegetable oil**
- **⅓ cup creamy peanut butter**
- **3 eggs**
- **1 cup semisweet chocolate pieces**
- **1 cup tiny marshmallows**
- **1 16-ounce can chocolate fudge frosting**
- **1 cup chopped cocktail peanuts**

1 Preheat the oven to 350°F. Grease and lightly flour a 13×9×2-inch baking pan; set aside.

2 In a large mixing bowl combine cake mix, water, oil, peanut butter, and eggs. Beat with an electric mixer on low speed just until combined. Beat on medium speed for 2 minutes. Fold in chocolate pieces. Spread batter into the prepared pan.

3 Bake for 30 to 35 minutes or until a wooden toothpick inserted near center comes out clean. Sprinkle marshmallows over hot cake; let stand for 15 minutes. Drop spoonfuls of frosting over cake; spread evenly. Sprinkle with peanuts.

PER SERVING: 592 cal., 31 g total fat (8 g sat. fat), 53 mg chol., 484 mg sodium, 73 g carb., 4 g fiber, 9 g pro.
EXCHANGES: 3 Starch, 2 Other Carb., 5½ Fat

FROSTING CUPCAKES

To pipe frosting on a cupcake, fill a pastry bag fitted with a large round or star tip with frosting. Hold the tip perpendicular to the top of the cupcake and starting at the outside edge, pipe the frosting around the edge of the cupcake. Without stopping, continue to pipe frosting in overlapping, concentric circles to cover the cupcake. Piping usually requires more frosting than spreading the frosting over the cupcakes.

BEST-LOVED

Italian Cream Cake

PREP: 60 MINUTES **BAKE:** 35 MINUTES AT 350°F
COOL: 60 MINUTES **MAKES:** 16 SERVINGS

- **5 eggs**
- **½ cup butter**
- **2 cups all-purpose flour**
- **1 teaspoon baking soda**
- **½ cup shortening**
- **2 cups sugar**
- **1 teaspoon vanilla**
- **1 cup buttermilk or sour milk (see tip, page 19)**
- **1 cup flaked coconut**
- **1¼ cup finely chopped pecans, toasted (see tip, page 21)**
- **1 recipe Cream Cheese Frosting (page 173)**

1 Separate eggs. Allow egg yolks, egg whites, and butter to stand at room temperature for 30 minutes. Meanwhile, grease and flour three 8×1½-inch or 9×1½-inch round cake pans; set pans aside. In a medium bowl combine flour and baking soda; set aside.

2 Preheat oven to 350°F. In a very large mixing bowl beat butter and shortening with electric mixer on medium to high speed for 30 seconds. Add sugar; beat until well combined. Add egg yolks and vanilla; beat on medium speed until combined. Add flour mixture and buttermilk alternately to butter mixture, beating on low speed after each addition just until combined. Fold in coconut and ½ cup of the pecans.

3 Thoroughly wash beaters. In a mixing bowl beat egg whites until stiff peaks form (tips stand straight; see photo 2, page 170). Fold about one-third of the egg whites into cake batter to lighten it. Fold in remaining whites. Spread batter evenly into the prepared pans.

4 Bake about 35 minutes for 8-inch pans, about 25 minutes for 9-inch pans, or until a wooden toothpick inserted near centers comes out clean. Cool cake layers in pans on wire racks for 10 minutes. Remove layers from pans. Cool thoroughly on wire racks.

5 Place one cake layer, bottom side up, on plate. Spread with ½ cup Cream Cheese Frosting; sprinkle with ¼ cup nuts. Top with second layer, bottom side down. Spread with ½ cup frosting; sprinkle with ¼ cup nuts. Top with remaining layer, bottom side up; spread top and sides of cake with remaining frosting. Sprinkle remaining nuts around top edge of cake. Store in refrigerator for up to 2 days.

PER SERVING: 644 cal., 33 g total fat (15 g sat. fat), 112 mg chol., 262 mg sodium, 84 g carb., 2 g fiber, 6 g pro.
EXCHANGES: 2 Starch, 3½ Other Carb., 6 Fat

BEST-LOVED

Carrot Cake

PREP: 30 MINUTES **BAKE:** 35 MINUTES AT 350°F
COOL: 2 HOURS **MAKES:** 12 SERVINGS

- **4 eggs**
- **2 cups all-purpose flour**
- **2 cups sugar**
- **2 teaspoons baking powder**
- **1 teaspoon ground cinnamon (optional)**
- **½ teaspoon salt**
- **½ teaspoon baking soda**
- **3 cups finely shredded carrots (lightly packed)**
- **¾ cup vegetable oil**
- **1 recipe Cream Cheese Frosting (page 173)**
- **½ cup finely chopped pecans, toasted (see tip, page 21) (optional)**

1 Allow eggs to stand at room temperature for 30 minutes. Meanwhile, grease two 8×1½-inch round cake pans. Line bottoms of pans with waxed paper; grease the paper. Set pans aside.

2 Preheat oven to 350°F. In a large bowl stir together flour, sugar, baking powder, cinnamon (if desired), salt, and baking soda; set aside.

3 In another bowl lightly beat eggs; add carrots and oil. Add egg mixture to flour mixture. Stir until combined. Pour batter into the prepared pans.

4 Bake for 35 to 40 minutes or until a wooden toothpick inserted near centers comes out clean. Cool cake layers in pans on wire racks for 10 minutes. Remove layers from pans; peel off waxed paper. Cool thoroughly on wire racks.

5 Frost cake with Cream Cheese Frosting. If desired, lightly press chopped pecans onto sides of cake and pipe additional Cream Cheese Frosting around top edge of cake. Cover and store cake in the refrigerator for up to 3 days.

GINGER-CARROT CAKE: Prepare as directed, except don't add the cinnamon; add 2 teaspoons grated fresh ginger or ¾ teaspoon ground ginger with the eggs, carrot, and oil.

PER SERVING PLAIN OR GINGER VARIATION: 711 cal., 30 g total fat (10 g sat. fat), 112 mg chol., 350 mg sodium, 108 g carb., 1 g fiber, 6 g pro. EXCHANGES: 2 Starch, 5 Other Carb., 5½ Fat

FINELY MEANS FINELY

The carrots need to be finely shredded to release the proper amount of moisture into the batter. Use a food processor to quickly shred them.

APPLE CAKE WITH BUTTERY CARAMEL SAUCE

Apple Cake with Buttery Caramel Sauce

PREP: 35 MINUTES **BAKE:** 45 MINUTES AT 350°F
COOL: 45 MINUTES **MAKES:** 16 SERVINGS

2 cups all-purpose flour
1 teaspoon baking powder
½ teaspoon salt
½ teaspoon ground nutmeg
½ teaspoon ground cinnamon
¼ teaspoon baking soda
½ cup butter, softened
2 cups granulated sugar
2 eggs
6 cups coarsely chopped, unpeeled cooking apples (about 5 to 6 medium apples)
1 cup chopped walnuts
1 recipe Buttery Caramel Sauce

1 Preheat oven to 350°F. Grease a 13×9×2-inch baking pan; set pan aside. In a medium bowl stir together the flour, baking powder, salt, nutmeg, cinnamon, and baking soda; set aside.

2 In a very large mixing bowl beat butter with an electric mixer on medium to high speed for 30 seconds. Add granulated sugar, ¼ cup at a time, beating on medium speed until combined. Scrape sides of bowl; beat for 2 minutes more. Add eggs, one at a time, beating well after each addition. Add flour mixture to butter mixture, beating on low speed just until combined. Fold in apples and walnuts (batter will be thick). Spread batter into prepared baking pan.

3 Bake for 45 to 50 minutes or until a wooden toothpick inserted near the center comes out clean. Cool in pan on a wire rack for 45 minutes. Serve warm with Buttery Caramel Sauce.

BUTTERY CARAMEL SAUCE: In a small saucepan melt ⅓ cup butter over medium heat. Stir in ⅓ cup granulated sugar, ⅓ cup packed brown sugar, and ⅓ cup whipping cream. Bring to boiling, stirring constantly. Remove from heat; stir in ½ teaspoon vanilla. Serve warm.

MAKE-AHEAD DIRECTIONS: Cool cake; cover cake pan with foil and freeze for up to 1 month. Thaw covered cake in the refrigerator overnight. Reheat cake, covered, in a preheated 325°F oven about 30 minutes or until warm. Sauce can be covered and refrigerated for up to 1 week. Reheat in a saucepan over medium heat.

PER SERVING: 369 cal., 17 g total fat (8 g sat. fat), 59 mg chol., 188 mg sodium, 23 g carb., 2 g fiber, 4 g pro.
EXCHANGES: 1 Starch, 2½ Other Carb., 3 Fat

Gingerbread

PREP: 20 MINUTES **BAKE:** 20 MINUTES AT 325°F
COOL: 30 MINUTES **MAKES:** 9 SERVINGS

1¼ cups all-purpose flour
¾ teaspoon ground ginger
½ teaspoon baking soda
½ teaspoon baking powder
½ teaspoon ground cinnamon
¼ teaspoon salt
¼ teaspoon ground cloves
¼ cup sour cream
3 tablespoons strong brewed coffee, cooled, or milk
⅓ cup butter, softened
¼ cup packed brown sugar
1 egg
½ cup molasses
Sifted powdered sugar
Sweetened Whipped Cream (page 270) (optional)

1 Preheat oven to 325°F. Lightly grease a 9×9×2-inch baking pan; set pan aside.

2 In a small bowl stir together flour, ginger, baking soda, baking powder, cinnamon, salt, and cloves; set flour mixture aside. In another small bowl stir together sour cream and the cooled coffee; set aside.

3 In a medium mixing bowl beat butter and brown sugar with an electric mixer on medium speed until light. Add egg, beating on medium speed until combined. Gradually add molasses, beating until smooth. Add flour mixture and sour cream mixture alternately, beating on low speed after each addition just until combined. Beat on high speed for 20 seconds more. Spread batter into the prepared pan.

4 Bake for 20 to 25 minutes or until a wooden toothpick inserted near the center comes out clean (cake might dip slightly in center). Cool in pan on a wire rack for 30 minutes. Sift powdered sugar over cake. If desired, serve with Sweetened Whipped Cream.

PER SERVING: 224 cal., 9 g total fat (5 g sat. fat), 44 mg chol., 217 mg sodium, 35 g carb., 1 g fiber, 3 g pro.
EXCHANGES: 1 Starch, 1½ Other Carb., 1½ Fat

BEST-LOVED

Oatmeal Cake

PREP: 40 MINUTES **BAKE:** 30 MINUTES AT 350°F
BROIL: 3 MINUTES **COOL:** 30 MINUTES
MAKES: 16 SERVINGS

- **2¼ cups water**
- **1½ cups rolled oats**
- **½ cup butter, cut up**
- **3 eggs, lightly beaten**
- **1½ cups packed brown sugar**
- **1¼ cups whole wheat flour**
- **1 cup all-purpose flour**
- **1½ teaspoons baking soda**
- **1½ teaspoons ground cinnamon**
- **¾ teaspoon salt**
- **¾ teaspoon ground nutmeg**
- **½ cup butter, cut up**
- **1⅓ cups packed brown sugar**
- **½ cup half-and-half, light cream, or evaporated milk**
- **2 cups flaked coconut**
- **1 cup chopped pecans**
- **1 teaspoon vanilla**

1 Preheat oven to 350°F. Lightly grease the bottom of a 13×9×2-inch baking pan; set aside.

2 In a large saucepan bring water to boiling. Add oats and ½ cup butter. Reduce heat to low; cook for 5 minutes to soften the oats, stirring occasionally. Remove from heat; set aside.

3 In a large bowl stir together the eggs and the 1½ cups brown sugar; set aside. In a medium bowl stir together the whole wheat flour, all-purpose flour, baking soda, cinnamon, salt, and nutmeg. Using a wooden spoon, stir oat mixture into egg mixture until combined. Fold in flour mixture just until moistened. (Batter will be thick.) Spread batter into the prepared pan.

4 Bake for 30 to 35 minutes or until a wooden toothpick inserted near the center comes out clean. Transfer to a wire rack. Preheat broiler.

OATMEAL CAKE

5 Meanwhile, in a medium saucepan melt ½ cup butter. Stir in the 1⅓ cups brown sugar and the half-and-half until combined. Remove from heat. Stir in coconut, pecans, and vanilla; mix well. Spoon coconut mixture over hot cake.

6 Broil 4 to 5 inches from the heat for 3 to 4 minutes or until topping is bubbly and begins to brown, watching closely. Cool in pan on a wire rack at least 30 minutes before serving. Serve warm or at room temperature.

PER SERVING: 481 cal., 24 g total fat (13 g sat. fat), 68 mg chol., 397 mg sodium, 64 g carb., 4 g fiber, 6 g pro.
EXCHANGES: 1½ Starch, 2½ Other Carb., 4½ Fat

PICK A PAN

Every cake has been tested in the pan sizes listed in the recipe. If you don't have a pan of the specified size, use this chart as a guide for substituting pans. Measure the batter in a 4-cup or larger liquid measuring cup and choose the pan that will hold no more than one-half to two-thirds of the pan volume. Refer to the tip on page 156 for baking times.

Pan size	Pan volume
8×1½-inch round	4 cups
9×1½-inch round	6 cups
8×8×2-inch	8 cups
13×9×2-inch	14 cups
15×10×1-inch	10 cups
10-inch fluted tube pan	12 cups
10-inch tube pan	16 cups
2½-inch muffin cup	½ cup

PINEAPPLE UPSIDE-DOWN CAKE

Pineapple Upside-Down Cake

PREP: 25 MINUTES **BAKE:** 30 MINUTES AT 350°F
COOL: 35 MINUTES **MAKES:** 8 SERVINGS

- **1/4 cup butter, cut up**
- **1/2 cup packed brown sugar**
- **1 8-ounce can pineapple tidbits, drained**
- **1/2 cup chopped pecans, toasted (see tip, page 21)**
- **1 1/3 cups all-purpose flour**
- **2/3 cup granulated sugar**
- **2 teaspoons baking powder**
- **1/4 teaspoon salt**
- **1/4 teaspoon ground ginger**
- **2/3 cup milk**
- **1/4 cup butter, softened**
- **1 egg**
- **1 teaspoon vanilla**

1 Preheat oven to 350°F. Place 1/4 cup butter in a 9×1 1/2-inch round cake pan. Place pan in oven until butter melts. Stir in brown sugar. Arrange pineapple and pecans in pan; set aside.

2 In a medium mixing bowl stir together flour, granulated sugar, baking powder, salt, and ginger. Add milk, 1/4 cup softened butter, the egg, and vanilla. Beat with an electric mixer on low speed until combined. Beat on medium speed for 1 minute (batter might still be lumpy). Spread batter into the prepared pan.

3 Bake for 30 to 35 minutes or until a wooden toothpick inserted near center comes out clean. Cool in pan on wire rack for 5 minutes. Loosen sides of cake; invert onto plate. Cool for 30 minutes; serve warm.

PER SERVING: 380 cal., 18 g total fat (8 g sat. fat), 59 mg chol., 236 mg sodium, 53 g carb., 1 g fiber, 4 g pro.
EXCHANGES: 1 Starch, 2 1/2 Carb., 3 1/2 Fat

CRANBERRY-WALNUT UPSIDE-DOWN CAKE: Prepare as directed, except stir 2 tablespoons orange juice into the melted butter and brown sugar mixture. Substitute 2/3 cup dried cranberries for the pineapple. Before using, place cranberries in a small bowl, add boiling water to cover, and let stand for 5 minutes; drain. Substitute chopped toasted walnuts for the pecans.

CHERRY-PECAN UPSIDE-DOWN CAKE: Prepare as directed, except stir 2 tablespoons orange juice into the melted butter and brown sugar mixture. Substitute 2/3 cup dried cherries for the pineapple. Before using, place cherries in a small bowl, add boiling water to cover, and let stand for 5 minutes; drain.

PER SERVING CRANBERRY-WALNUT OR CHERRY-PECAN VARIATIONS: 397 cal., 18 g total fat (8 g sat. fat), 59 mg chol., 236 mg sodium, 57 g carb., 2 g fiber, 5 g pro.
EXCHANGES: 1 Starch, 3 Other Carb., 3 1/2 Fat

HAWAIIAN UPSIDE-DOWN CAKE: Prepare as directed, except stir 1 tablespoon rum or 1 tablespoon water plus a few drops rum extract into the melted butter and brown sugar mixture. Substitute chopped toasted macadamia nuts for the pecans and add 2 tablespoons toasted flaked coconut to pan with the nuts.

PER SERVING: 405 cal., 20 g total fat (9 g sat. fat), 59 mg chol., 242 mg sodium, 54 g carb., 2 g fiber, 5 g pro.
EXCHANGES: 1 Starch, 2 1/2 Other Carb., 4 Fat

Busy-Day Cake *(photo, page 149)*

PREP: 25 MINUTES **BAKE:** 30 MINUTES AT 350°F
COOL: 40 MINUTES **MAKES:** 8 SERVINGS

- **1 1/3 cups all-purpose flour**
- **2/3 cup sugar**
- **2 teaspoons baking powder**
- **2/3 cup milk**
- **1/4 cup butter, softened**
- **1 egg**
- **1 teaspoon vanilla**
- **3 cups assorted fresh berries**
- **Sweetened Whipped Cream (page 270) (optional)**

1 Preheat oven to 350°F. Grease and lightly flour an 8×1 1/2-inch round cake pan; set aside.

2 In a medium mixing bowl combine flour, sugar, and baking powder. Add milk, butter, egg, and vanilla. Beat with an electric mixer on low speed until combined. Beat on medium speed for 1 minute. Spread into prepared pan.

3 Bake about 30 minutes or until a wooden toothpick inserted near center comes out clean. Cool cake in pan on a wire rack for 10 minutes. Loosen sides of cake; invert onto plate. Cool for 30 minutes; serve warm with berries and, if desired, Sweetened Whipped Cream.

PER SERVING: 346 cal., 18 g total fat (11 g sat. fat), 84 mg chol., 130 mg sodium, 42 g carb., 2 g fiber, 5 g pro.
EXCHANGES: 1½ Starch, 1½ Other Carb., 3 Fat

Rhubarb Cake

PREP: 25 MINUTES **BAKE:** 40 MINUTES AT 350°F
COOL: 30 MINUTES **MAKES:** 15 SERVINGS

- **½ cup butter, softened**
- **1½ cups packed brown sugar**
- **¼ teaspoon salt**
- **2 eggs**
- **1 teaspoon vanilla**
- **1 cup buttermilk or sour milk (see tip, page, 19)**
- **1 teaspoon baking soda**
- **2 cups all-purpose flour**
- **1½ cups sliced fresh rhubarb or chopped frozen unsweetened rhubarb**
- **½ cup chopped pecans, toasted (see tip, page 21)**
- **½ cup granulated sugar**
- **1 teaspoon ground cinnamon**
- **2 tablespoons butter**

1 Preheat oven to 350°F. Grease and flour a 13×9×2-inch baking pan; set aside. In a large mixing bowl beat the ½ cup butter with an electric mixer on medium to high speed for 30 seconds. Add brown sugar and salt; beat until light and fluffy. Beat in eggs and vanilla. In a bowl combine buttermilk and baking soda. Add flour and buttermilk mixture alternately to butter mixture, beating on low speed after each addition just until combined. Fold in rhubarb and pecans. Spread batter into prepared pan.

2 In a small bowl combine granulated sugar and cinnamon. Using a pastry blender or fork, cut in the 2 tablespoons butter until mixture resembles coarse crumbs. Sprinkle sugar mixture evenly over batter.

3 Bake for 40 to 45 minutes or until a wooden toothpick inserted in the center comes out clean. Cool in pan on a wire rack at least 30 minutes before serving.

PER SERVING: 283 cal., 11 g total fat (5 g sat. fat), 49 mg chol., 211 mg sodium, 43 g carb., 1 g fiber, 4 g pro.
EXCHANGES: 1 Starch, 2 Other Carb., 2 Fat

Lemonade Cake

PREP: 45 MINUTES **BAKE:** 30 MINUTES AT 350°F
COOL: 60 MINUTES **MAKES:** 15 SERVINGS

- **⅓ cup butter**
- **3 eggs**
- **2¼ cups all-purpose flour**
- **1 teaspoon baking powder**
- **½ teaspoon baking soda**
- **½ teaspoon salt**
- **1⅓ cups granulated sugar**
- **¼ cup frozen lemonade concentrate, thawed**
- **1 teaspoon vanilla**
- **1¼ cups buttermilk or sour milk (see tip, page 19)**
- **Yellow food coloring (optional)**
- **1 recipe Lemon Butter Frosting**
- **Lemon peel strips (optional)**

1 Allow butter and eggs to stand at room temperature for 30 minutes. Meanwhile, grease a 13×9×2-inch baking pan; set aside. In a medium bowl stir together flour, baking powder, baking soda, and salt; set aside.

2 Preheat oven to 350°F. In a large mixing bowl beat butter with an electric mixer on medium to high speed for 30 seconds. Gradually add granulated sugar, about ¼ cup at a time, beating on medium speed until well combined. Scrape sides of bowl; beat for 2 minutes more. Add eggs, one at a time, beating well after each addition. Beat in lemonade concentrate and vanilla. Add flour mixture and buttermilk alternately, beating on low speed after each addition just until combined. If desired, stir in a few drops of yellow food coloring. Spread batter into the prepared pan.

3 Bake for 30 to 35 minutes or until top springs back when lightly touched. Cool thoroughly in pan on a wire rack. Spread cake with Lemon Butter Frosting. If desired, garnish with strips of lemon peel.

LEMON BUTTER FROSTING: In a large mixing bowl beat ⅓ cup softened butter with an electric mixer on medium speed until smooth. Gradually add 1 cup powdered sugar, beating well. Beat in ⅓ cup frozen lemonade concentrate, thawed, and ½ teaspoon vanilla. Gradually beat in 3 cups additional powdered sugar. Beat in additional frozen lemonade concentrate (1 to 2 teaspoons), thawed, to reach spreading consistency.

PER SERVING: 380 cal., 10 g total fat (6 g sat. fat), 65 mg chol., 238 mg sodium, 71 g carb., 1 g fiber, 4 g pro.
EXCHANGES: 1 Starch, 4 Other Carb., 2 Fat

make it mine

Snack Cake

Whether you need something to tote to potlucks or to reward hungry kids after school, here's one cake recipe you can customize in countless ways.

PREP: 15 MINUTES
BAKE: 35 MINUTES AT 350°F
COOL: 60 MINUTES **MAKES:** 12 SERVINGS

- FLOUR
- SWEETENER
- **1 teaspoon baking soda**
- **½ teaspoon baking powder**
- **½ teaspoon salt**
- LIQUID
- **⅔ cup vegetable oil**
- FLAVORING
- **2 eggs**
- **½ cup** SPRINKLE
- **½ recipe Powdered Sugar Icing (page 173) (optional)**

1 Preheat oven to 350°F. Grease a 13×9×2-inch baking pan; set aside. In a very large mixing bowl stir together Flour, dry Sweetener (if using), baking soda, baking powder, and salt. Add the Liquid, vegetable oil, liquid Sweetener (if using), and Flavoring. Beat with an electric mixer on low to medium speed until combined. Beat in eggs. Scrape sides of bowl; continue beating on medium speed for 2 minutes more. Spread batter into the prepared pan.

2 Bake for 20 minutes. Top evenly with Sprinkle. Bake about 15 minutes more or until top springs back when lightly touched and a wooden toothpick inserted near the center comes out clean. Cool thoroughly in pan on a wire rack. If desired, drizzle Powdered Sugar Icing over cake.

FLOUR *(pick one)*

- **2 cups all-purpose flour and 1 cup unsweetened cocoa powder**
- **3 cups all-purpose flour**
- **2 cups all-purpose flour and 1 cup whole wheat flour**
- **3 cups cake flour**

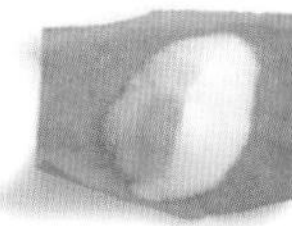

SWEETENER *(pick one)*

- **2 cups granulated sugar**
- **1 cup granulated sugar and 1 cup packed brown sugar**
- **1½ cups granulated sugar and ½ cup honey**
- **1½ cups granulated sugar and ½ cup molasses**

LIQUID *(pick one)*

- **1 cup buttermilk and ½ cup water**
- **1½ cups milk**
- **1 cup milk and ½ cup orange juice**
- **one 6-ounce carton plain yogurt and ½ cup water**

FLAVORING *(pick one)*

- **½ teaspoon almond extract**
- **2 teaspoons instant espresso powder or coffee crystals**
- **½ teaspoon peppermint extract**
- **1 teaspoon finely shredded citrus peel (orange, tangerine, lemon, or lime)**
- **1 teaspoon vanilla**

SPRINKLE *(pick one or more)*

- **Semisweet chocolate pieces, miniature semisweet chocolate pieces, milk chocolate pieces, peanut butter pieces, or dark chocolate pieces**
- **Flaked coconut**
- **Chopped toasted nuts (pecans, walnuts, hazelnuts, almonds, or macadamia nuts)**
- **Dried fruit (tart red cherries, raisins, cranberries, snipped apricots)**

SOUR CREAM POUND CAKE

Sour Cream Pound Cake

PREP: 55 MINUTES **BAKE:** 60 MINUTES AT 325°F
COOL: 60 MINUTES **MAKES:** 10 SERVINGS

- **1/2 cup butter**
- **3 eggs**
- **1/2 cup sour cream**
- **1 1/2 cups all-purpose flour**
- **1/4 teaspoon baking powder**
- **1/8 teaspoon baking soda**
- **1 cup sugar**
- **1/2 teaspoon vanilla**
- **Sweetened Whipped Cream (page 270) (optional)**
- **Fresh raspberries, blueberries, and/or strawberries (optional)**

1 Allow butter, eggs, and sour cream to stand at room temperature for 30 minutes. Meanwhile, grease and lightly flour a 9×5×3-inch loaf pan; set aside. In a bowl stir together flour, baking powder, and baking soda; set aside.

2 Preheat the oven to 325°F. In a large mixing bowl beat butter with an electric mixer on medium to high speed for 30 seconds. Gradually add sugar, beating about 10 minutes or until light and fluffy. Beat in vanilla. Add eggs, one at a time, beating 1 minute after each addition and scraping sides of bowl frequently. Add flour mixture and sour cream alternately to butter mixture, beating on low to medium speed after each addition just until combined. Pour batter into the prepared pan.

3 Bake for 60 to 75 minutes or until a wooden toothpick inserted near the center comes out clean. Cool cake in pan on a wire rack for 10 minutes. Remove from pan; cool thoroughly on rack. If desired, serve with Sweetened Whipped Cream and fresh berries.

PER SERVING: 268 cal., 13 g total fat (7 g sat. fat), 93 mg chol., 116 mg sodium, 35 g carb., 1 g fiber, 4 g pro.
EXCHANGES: 1 Starch, 1 1/2 Other Carb., 2 1/2 Fat

BEST-LOVED

Poppy Seed Cake *(photo, page 151)*

PREP: 15 MINUTES **BAKE:** 65 MINUTES AT 325°F
COOL: 60 MINUTES **MAKES:** 16 SERVINGS

- **3 cups all-purpose flour**
- **2 1/4 cups sugar**
- **1 1/2 teaspoons baking powder**
- **1 1/2 teaspoons salt**
- **3 eggs, lightly beaten**
- **1 1/2 cups milk**
- **1/2 cup vegetable oil**
- **1/2 cup butter, melted and cooled**
- **4 teaspoons poppy seeds**
- **1 1/2 teaspoons almond extract**
- **1 1/2 teaspoons butter flavoring**
- **1 1/2 teaspoons vanilla**
- **1 recipe Orange Glaze**

1 Preheat oven to 325°F. Generously grease and flour a 10-inch fluted tube pan; set aside. In a large mixing bowl stir together flour, sugar, baking powder, and salt; set aside.

2 In a medium bowl combine eggs, milk, oil, butter, poppy seeds, almond extract, butter flavoring, and vanilla. Add egg mixture all at once to flour mixture. Beat with an electric mixer on medium to high speed for 2 minutes. Spoon batter into prepared pan; spread evenly.

3 Bake about 65 minutes or until a wooden toothpick inserted near the center comes out clean. Cool in pan on a wire rack for 10 minutes. Remove cake from pan. Generously brush Orange Glaze over top and sides of warm cake. Cool thoroughly on wire rack.

ORANGE GLAZE: In a small saucepan combine 3/4 cup sugar and 1/4 cup orange juice. Heat and stir just until sugar dissolves. Remove from heat. Stir in 1/2 teaspoon almond extract and 1/2 teaspoon vanilla.

PER SERVING: 377 cal., 14 g total fat (5 g sat. fat), 57 mg chol., 316 mg sodium, 58 g carb., 1 g fiber, 5 g pro.
EXCHANGES: 1 1/2 Starch, 2 1/2 Other Carb., 2 1/2 Fat

BEST-LOVED

Marbled Chocolate-Peanut Butter Cake *(photo, page 149)*

PREP: 30 MINUTES **BAKE:** 60 MINUTES AT 350°F
COOL: 60 MINUTES **MAKES:** 12 SERVINGS

- **3 cups all-purpose flour**
- **4 teaspoons baking powder**
- **½ teaspoon baking soda**
- **½ teaspoon salt**
- **1 cup butter, softened**
- **2½ cups granulated sugar**
- **3 eggs**
- **1 8-ounce carton sour cream**
- **2 teaspoons vanilla**
- **1¼ cups milk**
- **4 ounces bittersweet chocolate, melted and cooled**
- **¾ cup creamy peanut butter**
- **1 recipe Peanut Butter Glaze**

1 Preheat oven to 350°F. Grease and flour a 10-inch fluted tube pan; set aside. In a medium bowl stir together flour, baking powder, baking soda, and salt; set aside.

2 In a very large mixing bowl beat butter with an electric mixer on low to medium speed for 30 seconds. Gradually add granulated sugar, beating until combined. Add eggs, one at a time, beating for 1 minute after each addition and scraping bowl frequently. Beat in sour cream and vanilla. Add flour mixture and milk alternately, beating on low to medium speed after each addition just until combined.

3 Transfer half (3½ cups) of the batter to a medium bowl; stir in melted chocolate. Stir peanut butter into remaining batter.

4 Using a separate large spoon for each batter, alternately drop spoonfuls of chocolate batter and peanut butter batter into the prepared pan. Using a table knife or thin metal spatula, gently cut through batters to swirl them together (do not overmix).

5 Bake about 60 minutes or until a wooden toothpick inserted near the center comes out clean. Cool cake in pan on a wire rack for 15 minutes. Remove cake from pan; cool thoroughly on wire rack. Drizzle Peanut Butter Glaze over cake.

PEANUT BUTTER GLAZE: In a small bowl stir together 1¼ cups powdered sugar, ⅓ cup creamy peanut butter, and enough milk (4 to 5 tablespoons) to make glaze a thick drizzling consistency.

PER SERVING: 716 cal., 36 g fat (17 g sat. fat), 100 mg chol., 602 mg sodium, 91 g carb., 3 g fiber, 13 g pro.
EXCHANGES: 1½ Starch, 4½ Other Carb., 1 Lean Meat, 6½ Fat

Mini Flourless Chocolate Cakes

PREP: 15 MINUTES **BAKE:** 20 MINUTES AT 350°F
COOL: 30 MINUTES **MAKES:** 6 MINI CAKES

- **Nonstick cooking spray**
- **4 eggs**
- **8 ounces bittersweet or semisweet chocolate, chopped**
- **½ cup butter**
- **¼ cup granulated sugar**
- **1 teaspoon vanilla**
- **2 teaspoons powdered sugar**
- **Sweetened Whipped Cream (page 270) (optional)**
- **Fresh raspberries or small fresh strawberries (optional)**

1 Allow eggs to stand at room temperature for 30 minutes. Meanwhile, lightly coat six 6-ounce custard cups with cooking spray. Place the prepared custard cups in a 15×10×1-inch baking pan; set aside.

2 Preheat oven to 350°F. Place chocolate and butter in a medium microwave-safe bowl. Microwave on 50% power (medium) about 1½ minutes or until melted and smooth, stirring every 30 seconds. Set chocolate mixture aside.

3 In a medium mixing bowl beat eggs and sugar with an electric mixer on high speed for 5 minutes. Beat in vanilla. Fold the egg mixture into the chocolate mixture, about one-third at a time, until thoroughly combined. Spoon about ⅔ cup batter into each prepared custard cup.

4 Bake for 20 to 25 minutes or just until set. Cool cakes in cups on a wire rack for 30 minutes before serving. Sprinkle cakes with powdered sugar. Serve warm in custard cups. If desired, garnish each cake with Sweetened Whipped Cream and fresh berries.

PER MINI CAKE: 410 cal., 33 g total fat (19 g sat. fat), 166 mg chol., 183 mg sodium, 30 g carb., 3 g fiber, 6 g pro.
EXCHANGES: 2 Other Carb., 1 Medium-Fat Meat, 5½ Fat

SUPER TOPPER

For a special occasion or any time you want an over-the-top dessert, skip the Peanut Butter Glaze. Instead, serve slices of Marbled Chocolate-Peanut Butter Cake with Salted Caramel Sauce (page 291).

Layered Ice Cream Cake

PREP: 30 MINUTES **BAKE:** 15 MINUTES AT 350°F
COOL: 60 MINUTES **FREEZE:** 4 TO 6 HOURS
STAND: 10 MINUTES **MAKES:** 16 SERVINGS

- **1 package 2-layer-size chocolate or white cake mix**
- **½ gallon strawberry or other desired-flavor ice cream, softened**
- **1 8-ounce package cream cheese, softened**
- **½ cup powdered sugar**
- **¼ cup milk**
- **1 teaspoon vanilla**
- **1 16-ounce container frozen whipped dessert topping, thawed**
- **Multicolored sprinkles (optional)**

1 Preheat oven to 350°F. Grease and flour three 9×1½-inch round cake pans; set aside. Prepare cake mix according to package directions. Spread batter evenly into prepared pans. Bake for 15 to 18 minutes or until tops spring back when lightly touched. Cool in pans on wire racks for 10 minutes. Remove cake layers from pans; cool thoroughly on wire racks.

2 To assemble, place one cake layer on the bottom of a 9-inch springform pan (if necessary, trim to fit); add sides of pan. Spoon half of the ice cream onto cake layer in pan; spread evenly (see photo 1, below). Top with another cake layer. Spread remaining ice cream over cake layer in pan. Top with remaining cake layer. Cover with plastic wrap; freeze for 3 to 4 hours or until firm.

3 For frosting, in a large mixing bowl beat cream cheese, powdered sugar, milk, and vanilla with an electric mixer on medium to high speed until light and fluffy. Stir in a small amount of whipped topping to lighten. Fold in remaining whipped topping.

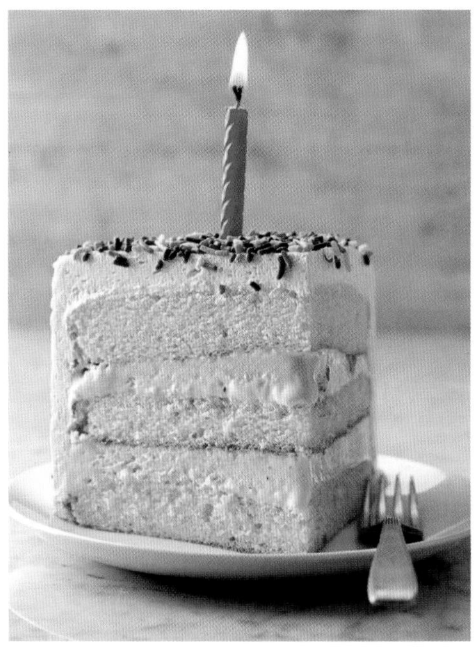

4 Remove plastic wrap from cake. Remove sides of pan. Using a wide spatula, transfer cake from pan bottom to a serving plate. Spread top and sides of cake with frosting (see photo 2, below). If desired, reserve some of the frosting to pipe around edge of cake. Freeze, uncovered, for 1 to 2 hours or until firm. Cover with plastic wrap and freeze for up to 1 month.

5 To serve, let stand at room temperature for 10 to 15 minutes. If desired, sprinkle with multicolored sprinkles. Cut into wedges.

PER SERVING: 481 cal., 26 g total fat (14 g sat. fat), 88 mg chol., 321 mg sodium, 55 g carb., 1 g fiber, 6 g pro.
EXCHANGES: 2 Starch, 1½ Other Carb., 5 Fat

LAYERED ICE CREAM CAKE STEP-BY-STEP

1. Cover the top of the cake layer with scoops of the softened ice cream. Use the back of a metal spoon to spread the ice cream into an even layer.

2. Before frosting the frozen cake, run a long metal spatula around the edge to make the ice cream layers even with the cake layers. If necessary, let the cake stand a few minutes to soften the ice cream just a little.

WHY A SPRINGFORM PAN?

A springform pan holds the cake and ice cream layers in place until frozen. But if you don't have one, you can still make this cake. Place two of the layers on a large baking sheet and spread the ice cream over each. Freeze for 30 to 60 minutes or until firm. Stack the frozen layers on a cake plate. Prepare the frosting as directed in Step 3 and freeze and serve as directed.

Hot Cocoa Brownie Cake with Marshmallow Frosting

PREP: 30 MINUTES **BAKE:** ACCORDING TO PACKAGE DIRECTIONS/7 MINUTES AT 450°F **COOL:** 90 MINUTES **CHILL:** 30 MINUTES **MAKES:** 10 SERVINGS

1 18.3-ounce package brownie mix
1/3 cup whipping cream
4 ounces semisweet chocolate, chopped
1 recipe Marshmallow Frosting
Unsweetened cocoa powder (optional)

1 Preheat oven to 350°F. Grease and flour a 9×1½-inch round cake pan; set aside.

2 Prepare brownie mix according to package directions. Pour into the prepared pan. Bake according to the package directions for a 9×9-inch square pan. Cool thoroughly on a wire rack. Remove brownie from pan. Place cooled brownie on a baking sheet.

3 Meanwhile, in a small saucepan bring cream just to boiling over medium-high heat. Remove from heat. Add chocolate (do not stir). Let stand for 5 minutes. Stir until smooth. Spread chocolate evenly over top of brownie. Chill for 30 minutes.

4 Preheat oven to 450°F. Prepare Marshmallow Frosting. Spread Marshmallow Frosting over top of brownie to cover chocolate layer.

5 Bake about 7 minutes or until frosting is lightly browned. Cool thoroughly on a wire rack. If desired, sift cocoa powder over top.

MARSHMALLOW FROSTING: In the top of a 2-quart double boiler combine ¾ cup sugar, 3 tablespoons cold water, 1 egg white, and ¼ teaspoon cream of tartar. Beat with an electric mixer on low speed for 30 seconds. Place the double boiler top over boiling water (upper pan should not the touch water). Cook, beating constantly with the electric mixer on high speed, until stiff peaks form (tips stand straight), about 13 minutes. Remove the pan from heat. Beat in 1 teaspoon vanilla.

PER SERVING: 354 cal., 10 g total fat (6 g sat. fat), 11 mg chol., 173 mg sodium, 63 g carb., 2 g fiber, 3 g pro.
EXCHANGES: 4 Other Carb., 2 Fat

SERVING AND STORING CAKE

To enjoy cakes at their yummiest best, follow these tips.

- Allow cakes frosted with butter-type frosting to stand about an hour before slicing to let the frosting set.
- Assemble cakes that are filled or frosted with whipped cream no more than 2 hours before serving to prevent them from becoming soggy.
- Use a thin-bladed knife to cut cake. Run the knife under hot water and wipe dry before the first cut and between the subsequent cuts.
- Most cakes can be covered and stored at room temperature for 2 to 3 days. If you don't have a cake cover, invert a large bowl over the cake. Directly covering a cake with plastic wrap will mar the frosting.
- If a cake filling or frosting contains whipped cream, cream cheese, sour cream, or eggs, store the cake, covered, in the refrigerator.
- To freeze cake, place the cooled, unfrosted layers on a baking sheet and freeze until firm. Transfer frozen layers to large freezer bags or wrap and seal in freezer wrap. Freeze for up to 4 months. Thaw cake at room temperature before frosting.
- Cakes that are served directly from pans can be covered and frozen in the pans. Frost these cakes after thawing.

BEST-LOVED

Cream-Filled Cake Roll

PREP: 60 MINUTES **BAKE:** 12 MINUTES AT 375°F
COOL: 60 MINUTES **MAKES:** 10 SLICES

- **4 eggs**
- **½ cup all-purpose flour**
- **1 teaspoon baking powder**
- **½ teaspoon vanilla**
- **⅓ cup granulated sugar**
- **½ cup granulated sugar**
- **Powdered sugar**
- **1 recipe desired filling**

1 Separate eggs. Allow egg whites and yolks to stand at room temperature for 30 minutes. Meanwhile, grease a 15×10×1-inch baking pan. Line bottom of pan with waxed paper or parchment paper; grease paper. Set pan aside. In a medium bowl stir together flour and baking powder; set aside.

2 Preheat oven to 375°F. In a medium mixing bowl beat egg yolks and vanilla with an electric mixer on high speed about 5 minutes or until thick and lemon color. Gradually beat in the ⅓ cup granulated sugar, beating on high speed until sugar is almost dissolved.

3 Thoroughly wash beaters. In another bowl beat egg whites on medium speed until soft peaks form (tips curl; see photo, page 170). Gradually beat in the ½ cup granulated sugar, beating until stiff peaks form (tips stand straight; see photo, page 170). Fold yolk mixture into beaten whites. Sprinkle flour mixture over egg mixture; fold in gently just until combined. Spread batter evenly in the prepared pan.

4 Bake for 12 to 15 minutes or until top springs back when lightly touched. Immediately loosen cake edge from pan and turn cake out onto a towel sprinkled with powdered sugar. Remove waxed paper. Roll towel and cake into a spiral, starting from a short side of the cake. Cool on a wire rack for at least 60 minutes. Meanwhile, prepare desired filling.

5 Unroll cake; remove towel. Spread cake with desired filling to within 1 inch of edges. Roll up cake; trim ends. Cover; chill for up to 6 hours.

STRAWBERRY-CREAM FILLING: In a medium mixing bowl beat ¾ cup whipping cream, 1 tablespoon granulated sugar, and ½ teaspoon vanilla with an electric mixer on medium speed until soft peaks form (tips curl). Fold in 1 cup chopped strawberries. Sprinkle filled cake with powdered sugar.

LEMON-CREAM FILLING: In a medium mixing bowl beat one 3-ounce package cream cheese, softened, with an electric mixer on medium speed until smooth. Beat in ¼ cup purchased lemon curd. In another mixing bowl beat ½ cup whipping cream with the mixer on high speed until soft peaks form (tips curl); fold into cream cheese mixture. If desired, for icing, in a small bowl stir together ¾ cup powdered sugar, ½ teaspoon finely shredded lemon peel, and 1 tablespoon lemon juice; drizzle over cake.

PER SLICE: 219 cal., 10 g total fat (5 g sat. fat), 116 mg chol., 90 mg sodium, 30 g carb., 1 g fiber, 4 g pro.
EXCHANGES: 1 Starch, 1 Other Carb., 2 Fat

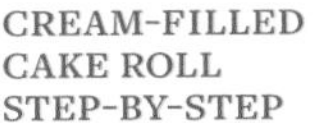

CREAM-FILLED CAKE ROLL STEP-BY-STEP

1. Gently roll the hot cake and towel into a spiral; let cake cool. This prevents cake from cracking when filled and rolled later.

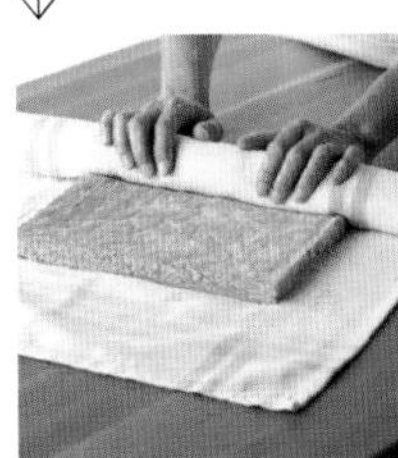

2. Unroll cake, remove towel, and spread filling over cake, leaving a 1-inch border around the edge. The border will fill as you reroll the cake.

Chocolate-Espresso Chiffon Cake

PREP: 60 MINUTES **BAKE:** 60 MINUTES AT 325°F
COOL: 2 HOURS **MAKES:** 14 SERVINGS

- **8 eggs**
- **2 cups all-purpose flour**
- **1½ cups sugar**
- **1 tablespoon baking powder**
- **1 teaspoon salt**
- **4 teaspoons instant espresso coffee powder or instant coffee crystals**
- **¾ cup water**
- **½ cup vegetable oil**
- **1 teaspoon vanilla**
- **3 ounces bittersweet chocolate, grated**
- **½ teaspoon cream of tartar**
- **1 recipe Espresso Whipped Cream**

1 Separate eggs; discard three of the egg yolks. Allow egg yolks and whites to stand at room temperature for 30 minutes. In a large mixing bowl stir together flour, sugar, baking powder, and salt. Make a well in center of flour mixture. Dissolve espresso in the water.

2 Preheat oven to 325°F. Add oil, the five yolks, espresso, and vanilla to flour mixture. Beat with an electric mixer on low speed until combined. Beat on medium to high speed for 4 to 5 minutes or until smooth. Fold in chocolate.

3 Thoroughly wash beaters. In a very large mixing bowl beat whites and cream of tartar on medium speed until stiff peaks form (tips stand straight; see photo 2, below). Pour batter in a thin stream over beaten egg whites; fold in gently. Pour into ungreased 10-inch tube pan.

4 Bake for 60 to 70 minutes or until top springs back when lightly touched. Immediately invert cake; cool thoroughly in pan. Loosen sides of cake from pan; remove cake. Serve with Espresso Whipped Cream.

ESPRESSO WHIPPED CREAM: In a chilled mixing bowl beat 1 cup whipping cream, 1 tablespoon sugar, ½ to 1 teaspoon instant espresso coffee powder or instant coffee crystals, and ½ teaspoon vanilla with an electric mixer on medium speed until soft peaks form (tips curl).

PER SERVING: 342 cal., 18 g total fat (7 g sat. fat), 99 mg chol., 286 mg sodium, 41 g carb., 1 g fiber, 6 g pro.
EXCHANGES: 2 Starch, ½ Other Carb., 3 Fat

LOW-CALORIE

Angel Food Cake

PREP: 50 MINUTES **BAKE:** 40 MINUTES AT 350°F
COOL: 2 HOURS **MAKES:** 12 SERVINGS

- **1½ cups egg whites (10 to 12 large eggs)**
- **1½ cups sifted powdered sugar**
- **1 cup sifted cake flour or sifted all-purpose flour**
- **1½ teaspoons cream of tartar**
- **1 teaspoon vanilla**
- **1 cup granulated sugar**
- **1 recipe Powdered Sugar Icing (page 173) (optional)**

1 In a very large mixing bowl allow egg whites to stand at room temperature for 30 minutes. Meanwhile, sift powdered sugar and flour together three times; set aside.

ANGEL FOOD CAKE STEP-BY-STEP

1. Using a very clean bowl and beaters, beat egg white mixture until soft peaks form (tips of mixture curl slightly when beaters are lifted).

2. Continue beating while adding sugar a little at a time. Beat until stiff peaks form (tips stand straight when beaters are lifted). Be careful not to overbeat.

3. To fold in flour, cut down through the beaten whites with a rubber spatula; scrape across the bottom of the bowl, bringing spatula up and over.

4. To eliminate large bubbles or pockets of air, gently cut through batter in the pan with a thin metal spatula or table knife.

ANGEL FOOD CAKE

2 Adjust the baking rack to the lowest position in oven. Preheat oven to 350°F. Add cream of tartar and vanilla to egg whites. Beat with an electric mixer on medium speed until soft peaks form (tips curl; see photo 1, page 170). Gradually add granulated sugar, about 2 tablespoons at a time, beating until stiff peaks form (tips stand straight; see photo 2, page 170).

3 Sift about one-fourth of the flour mixture over the beaten egg whites; fold in gently (see photo 3, page 170). (If the bowl is too full, transfer to a larger bowl.) Repeat, folding in remaining flour mixture by fourths. Pour into an ungreased 10-inch tube pan. Gently cut through batter to remove any large air pockets (see photo 4, page 170).

4 Bake on the lowest rack for 40 to 45 minutes or until top springs back when lightly touched. Immediately invert cake; cool thoroughly in the pan. Loosen sides of cake from pan; remove cake from pan. Place cake on platter. If desired, spoon Powdered Sugar Icing over top.

CHOCOLATE ANGEL FOOD CAKE: Prepare as directed, except sift 1/4 cup unsweetened cocoa powder with the flour mixture.

HONEY ANGEL FOOD CAKE: Prepare as above, except in Step 2 after beating egg white mixture to soft peaks, gradually pour 1/4 cup honey in a thin stream over the egg white mixture and reduce granulated sugar to 1/2 cup.

PER SERVING PLAIN, CHOCOLATE, OR HONEY VARIATIONS: 172 cal., 0 g total fat, 0 mg chol., 51 mg sodium, 39 g carb., 0 g fiber, 4 g pro. EXCHANGES: 2 1/2 Other Carb., 1/2 Lean Meat

NOT A SPECK OF FAT

When making angel food, chiffon, and sponge cakes, beating egg whites is crucial to achieving the correct volume and texture. Even a tiny bit of fat from the yolks or less-than-clean bowls or beaters can make beating whites difficult if not impossible. Before you start, be sure the bowl and beaters are clean. Cold eggs are easier to separate than room-temperature ones; let the whites stand at room temperature for 30 minutes after separating them. If you used the beaters to beat yolks, be sure to wash them again with soap and water before beating the whites.

8 to try

ALMOND: Substitute ½ teaspoon almond extract for the vanilla. Top cake with toasted sliced almonds.

DARK CHOCOLATE: Substitute ½ cup unsweetened cocoa powder for ½ cup of the powdered sugar.

BEST-LOVED

Butter Frosting

Butter Frosting is the go-to frosting for cakes and cupcakes. Flavored with vanilla, it works for just about any cake. Add variety with these combos.

START TO FINISH: 20 MINUTES
MAKES: ABOUT 4½ CUPS

- **¾ cup butter, softened**
- **8 cups powdered sugar (about 2 pounds)**
- **⅓ cup milk**
- **2 teaspoons vanilla**
- **Milk**
- **Food coloring (optional)**

1 In a very large mixing bowl beat butter with an electric mixer on medium speed until smooth. Gradually add 2 cups of the powdered sugar, beating well. Slowly beat in ⅓ cup milk and the vanilla. Gradually beat in remaining powdered sugar. Beat in enough additional milk to reach spreading consistency. If desired, tint with food coloring. (This frosts tops and sides of two 8- or 9-inch layers or about 30 cupcakes. Halve the recipe to frost a 13×9×2-inch cake.) (To decorate cakes or to pipe frosting on cupcakes, double the recipe. Store extra frosting in a tightly covered container in the refrigerator for up to 3 days.)

PER 1/12 OF RECIPE: 401 cal., 12 g total fat (7 g sat. fat), 31 mg chol., 85 mg sodium, 76 g carb., 0 g fiber, 0 g pro. **EXCHANGES:** 5 Other Carb., 2½ Fat

PEANUT BUTTER: Beat ½ cup peanut butter into butter before adding powdered sugar. Sprinkle cake with chopped peanuts.

STRAWBERRY: Beat ⅓ cup strawberry jam into butter before adding powdered sugar. Garnish cake with fresh strawberries.

CITRUS: Substitute lemon or orange juice for the milk; add ½ teaspoon finely shredded lemon or orange peel. Top cake with additional lemon or orange peel.

MILK CHOCOLATE: Melt 1 cup milk chocolate pieces and beat into the butter before adding powdered sugar. Top cake with chocolate curls.

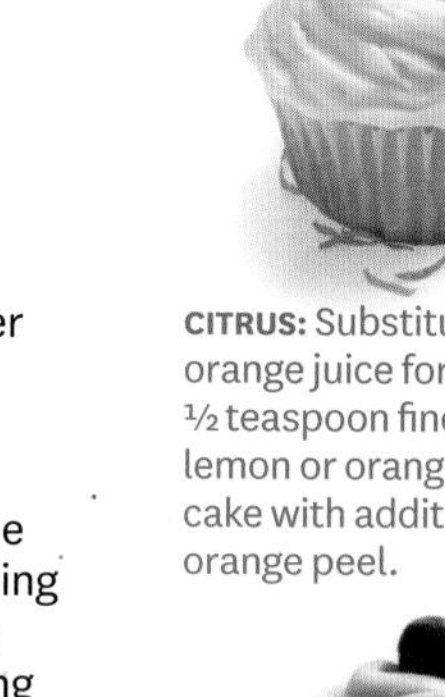

COFFEE: Add 1 tablespoon instant espresso coffee powder or instant coffee crystals or substitute strong brewed coffee for the milk. Garnish with chocolate-covered coffee beans.

PEPPERMINT: Substitute ½ teaspoon peppermint extract for the vanilla; if desired, tint pink with red food coloring. Sprinkle top with crushed peppermint candies; press additional candies on sides of cake.

FAST LOW-CALORIE

Powdered Sugar Icing

START TO FINISH: 10 MINUTES **MAKES:** ½ CUP

- **1 cup powdered sugar**
- **¼ teaspoon vanilla**
- **1 tablespoon milk or orange juice**
- **Milk**

1 In a small bowl combine powdered sugar, vanilla, and 1 tablespoon milk. Stir in additional milk, 1 teaspoon at a time, until icing reaches desired consistency. (This makes enough to drizzle over one 10-inch tube cake.)

CHOCOLATE POWDERED SUGAR ICING: Prepare as above, except add 2 tablespoons unsweetened cocoa powder to the powdered sugar and use milk, not orange juice.

PER 1/12 OF RECIPE PLAIN OR CHOCOLATE VARIATION: 40 cal., 0 g total fat, 0 mg chol., 1 mg sodium, 10 g carb., 0 g fiber, 0 g pro. EXCHANGES: ½ Other Carb.

FAST

Meringue Frosting

START TO FINISH: 25 MINUTES
MAKES: ABOUT 5 CUPS

- **1½ cups granulated sugar**
- **⅓ cup cold water**
- **2 egg whites**
- **¼ teaspoon cream of tartar**
- **1 teaspoon vanilla**

1 In a 3-quart top of a double boiler combine sugar, water, egg whites, and cream of tartar. Beat with an electric mixer on low speed for 30 seconds.

2 Place the pan over boiling water (upper pan should not touch the water). Cook, beating constantly with the electric mixer on high speed, for 10 to 13 minutes or until an instant-read thermometer registers 160°F when inserted in the mixture, stopping beaters and quickly scraping bottom and sides of pan every 5 minutes to prevent sticking. Remove pan from the heat; add vanilla. Beat about 1 minute more or until frosting is fluffy and holds soft peaks. (This frosts tops and sides of two 8- or 9-inch cake layers or one 10-inch tube cake.) Store frosted cake in the refrigerator and serve the same day it is made.

PER 1/12 OF RECIPE: 101 cal., 0 g total fat, 0 mg chol., 9 mg sodium, 25 g carb., 0 g fiber, 1 g pro. EXCHANGES: 1½ Other Carb.

FAST

Creamy White Frosting

START TO FINISH: 25 MINUTES
MAKES: ABOUT 3 CUPS

- **1 cup shortening**
- **1½ teaspoons vanilla**
- **½ teaspoon almond extract**
- **1 pound powdered sugar (about 4 cups)**
- **3 to 4 tablespoons milk**

1 In a large mixing bowl beat shortening, vanilla, and almond extract with an electric mixer on medium speed for 30 seconds. Slowly add about half of the powdered sugar, beating well. Add 2 tablespoons of the milk. Gradually beat in remaining powdered sugar and enough remaining milk to reach spreading consistency. (This frosts the tops and sides of two 8- or 9-inch cake layers. Halve the recipe to frost a 13×9×2-inch cake.) You can freeze this frosting in a freezer container for up to 3 months; thaw at room temperature before using.

PER 1/12 OF RECIPE: 298 cal., 16 g total fat (4 g sat. fat), 0 mg chol., 2 mg sodium, 38 g carb., 0 g fiber, 0 g pro. EXCHANGES: 2½ Other Carb., 3 Fat

FAST

Cream Cheese Frosting

START TO FINISH: 20 MINUTES
MAKES: ABOUT 3½ CUPS

- **1 8-ounce package cream cheese, softened**
- **½ cup butter, softened**
- **2 teaspoons vanilla**
- **5½ to 6 cups powdered sugar**

1 In a large mixing bowl beat cream cheese, butter, and vanilla with an electric mixer on medium speed until light and fluffy. Gradually beat in powdered sugar to reach spreading consistency. (This frosts tops and sides of two 8- or 9-inch layers. Halve the recipe to frost a 13×9×2-inch cake.) Cover and store the frosted cake in refrigerator.

COCOA-CREAM CHEESE FROSTING: Prepare as directed, except beat ½ cup unsweetened cocoa powder into the cream cheese mixture and reduce powdered sugar to 5 to 5½ cups.

PER 1/12 OF RECIPE PLAIN OR COCOA VARIATION: 348 cal., 14 g total fat (9 g sat. fat), 41 mg chol., 116 mg sodium, 56 g carb., 0 g fiber, 1 g pro. EXCHANGES: 3½ Other Carb., 3 Fat

FAST

Browned Butter Frosting

START TO FINISH: 20 MINUTES **MAKES:** 3 CUPS

- **¾ cup butter, cut up**
- **6 cups powdered sugar**
- **4 to 5 tablespoons milk**
- **2 teaspoons vanilla**

1 In a small saucepan heat butter over low heat until melted. Continue heating until butter turns a light golden brown. Remove from heat. In a large mixing bowl combine powdered sugar, 4 tablespoons of the milk, and the vanilla. Add browned butter. Beat with an electric mixer on low speed until combined. Beat on medium to high speed, adding additional milk, if necessary, to reach spreading consistency. (This frosts the tops and sides of two 8- or 9-inch cake layers.)

PER 1/12 OF RECIPE: 340 cal., 12 g total fat (7 g sat. fat), 31 mg chol., 85 mg sodium, 60 g carb., 0 g fiber, 0 g pro. **EXCHANGES:** 4 Other Carb., 2½ Fat

FAST

No-Cook Fudge Frosting

START TO FINISH: 15 MINUTES **MAKES:** 4½ CUPS

- **8 cups powdered sugar (about 2 pounds)**
- **1 cup unsweetened cocoa powder**
- **1 cup butter, softened**
- **⅔ cup boiling water**
- **2 teaspoons vanilla**
- **Boiling water**

1 In a large mixing bowl combine powdered sugar and cocoa powder. Add butter, the ⅔ cup boiling water, and the vanilla. Beat with an electric mixer on low speed until combined. Beat for 1 minute on medium speed. If necessary, cool for 20 minutes or until frosting is spreading consistency. If frosting is too thick, add boiling water, 1 tablespoon at a time, until frosting reaches spreading consistency. (This frosts tops and sides of two 8- or 9-inch cake layers. Halve the recipe to frost a 13×9×2-inch cake.)

PER 1/12 OF RECIPE: 447 cal., 16 g total fat (10 g sat. fat), 41 mg chol., 112 mg sodium, 79 g carb., 2 g fiber, 1 g pro. **EXCHANGES:** 5½ Other Carb., 3 Fat

FAST

Chocolate-Sour Cream Frosting

START TO FINISH: 20 MINUTES **MAKES:** 4½ CUPS

- **2 cups semisweet chocolate pieces**
- **½ cup butter**
- **1 8-ounce carton sour cream**
- **4½ cups powdered sugar**

1 In a large saucepan melt chocolate and butter over low heat until melted, stirring frequently. Cool for 5 minutes. Stir in sour cream. Gradually add powdered sugar, beating with a wooden spoon until smooth. (This frosts tops and sides of two 8- or 9-inch cake layers. Halve the recipe to frost a 13×9×2-inch cake.) Cover and store frosted cake in the refrigerator.

CHOCOLATE-MINT SOUR CREAM FROSTING: Prepare as directed, except stir in ½ teaspoon mint extract with the sour cream.

PER 1/12 OF RECIPE PLAIN OR MINT VARIATION: 415 cal., 20 g total fat (12 g sat. fat), 30 mg chol., 73 mg sodium, 63 g carb., 2 g fiber, 2 g pro. **EXCHANGES:** 4 Other Carb., 4 Fat

Ganache

START TO FINISH: 35 MINUTES **MAKES:** 2 CUPS

- **1 cup whipping cream**
- **12 ounces milk chocolate, semisweet chocolate, or bittersweet chocolate, chopped**

1 In a medium saucepan bring whipping cream just to boiling over medium-high heat. Remove from heat. Add chocolate (do not stir). Let stand for 5 minutes. Stir until smooth. Cool for 15 minutes. (This frosts tops and sides of an 8- or 9-inch cake layer.)

PER 1/12 OF RECIPE: 220 cal., 16 g total fat (10 g sat. fat), 34 mg chol., 36 mg sodium, 17 g carb., 0 g fiber, 3 g pro. **EXCHANGES:** 1 Other Carb., 3 Fat

candies

candies

Candy recipes range from super simple to a little bit tricky. All are within any cook's reach with the right equipment, ingredients, and know-how.

ESSENTIAL EQUIPMENT

Using the right equipment helps ensure that your candy will be a success.

PAN SIZE: Recipes in this chapter include a recommended saucepan size. This is key. If your pan is too small, the candy mixture can boil over, which is dangerous. If it's too large, the mixture spreads too thinly and might not cover the thermometer bulb. Use high-quality, heavy saucepans.

THERMOMETER: Although not all candies call for using a thermometer, many candies are much easier to make with one. Choose a thermometer that's easy to read and clips to the side of the pan. Check the thermometer for accuracy each time you prepare candy. To do this, submerge the tip in boiling water for a few minutes. It should register 212°F (at sea level). If it registers above or below this temperature, add or subtract the number of degrees it is above or below 212°F from the temperature specified in the recipe; cook to the adjusted temperature.

SPOONS: Use long-handled wooden or high-heat-resistant spoons when stirring hot candy mixtures. Standard metal spoons become too hot to handle.

INGREDIENT KNOW-HOW

- Use the exact ingredients specified in the recipe; for example, if the recipe calls for butter, don't substitute margarine.
- Measure and prepare all ingredients before you start—candy making moves quickly. For example, once your peanut brittle mixture has reached the right temperature, you don't want to hunt down the baking soda required in the next step.
- Measure all ingredients accurately and do not halve or double candy recipes.

COOKING BASICS

Follow these tips to ensure success at key points in the candy-making process, from getting ready to cook the mixture through cooling it.

- If a recipe calls for buttering the sides of the pan, do so to help prevent the mixture from boiling over and to prevent crystales from forming on the sides of the pan.
- When you combine the sugar with the other ingredients, gently stir to make sure the sugar thoroughly dissolves as you bring the mixture to a boil.
- When using a candy thermometer, clip the thermometer onto the pan after the sugar dissolves. Make sure the bulb or tip doesn't touch the bottom of the pan and that it's completely covered with the bubbling candy mixture—not just with foam (see photo, below).

- Boil candy mixtures at a moderate, steady rate (bubbles should form over the entire surface of the mixture). If a recipe suggests a range-top heat setting, use this as a guide because the actual temperatures of heat settings vary with models.
- When cooling candy, such as fudge, be sure the thermometer bulb is covered with the candy mixture for an accurate reading. If it isn't covered, carefully prop up the saucepan with a folded hot pad.

KEEP IT FRESH

Follow storage guidelines for each recipe. Avoid storing different types of candies in the same container. Candies can trade flavors, and one candy can change the consistency of another.

Peanut Brittle, page 185

fudge

The Secret: Managing the sugar crystals is key—large crystals mean you end up with a coarse, grainy fudge; small crystals make for a smooth, silky bite.

FUDGE POINTERS

1. BUTTER UP
First things first. Using a pastry brush, butter the foil-lined pan. This makes it easy to pull the foil away from your candy.

2. MORE BUTTER!
Same pastry brush, more butter. This step is imperative. Brushing the saucepan makes it difficult for the fudge to boil over and may prevent crystals from clinging to the side of the pan.

3. CREAM, NOT MILK
Unlike milk, half-and half is less likely to curdle, so light cream is often used in fudge recipes. Stir this mixture without a candy thermometer in the pan until it just boils.

Corn syrup is your partner in the pursuit of a creamy, smooth fudge. In fudge recipes corn syrup interferes with sugar crystal formation.

PREP: 15 MINUTES **COOK:** 20 MINUTES
COOL: 50 MINUTES **MAKES:** ABOUT 1¼ POUNDS (18 PIECES)

- **2 cups sugar**
- **¾ cup half-and-half or light cream**
- **2 ounces unsweetened chocolate, cut up**
- **1 teaspoon light-color corn syrup**
- **⅛ teaspoon salt**
- **2 tablespoons butter**
- **1 teaspoon vanilla**
- **½ cup chopped nuts (optional)**

1 Line an 8×4×2-inch loaf pan with foil, extending the foil over the edges of the pan. Butter the foil; set pan aside.

2 Butter the sides of a 2-quart heavy saucepan. In the saucepan combine sugar, half-and-half, chocolate, corn syrup, and salt. Cook and stir over medium heat until mixture boils. Clip a candy thermometer to the side of the pan. Reduce heat to medium-low; continue boiling at a moderate, steady rate, stirring occasionally, until thermometer registers 236°F, soft-ball stage (20 to 25 minutes). Adjust heat as necessary to maintain a steady boil.

3 Remove saucepan from heat. Add butter and vanilla, but do not stir. Cool mixture, without stirring, to 110°F (50 to 60 minutes). If necessary, prop saucepan so the bulb of the thermometer is covered with the candy mixture. Remove thermometer from saucepan. Beat mixture vigorously with a clean wooden spoon until candy just begins to thicken. If desired, add nuts. Continue beating until the fudge just starts to lose its gloss (6 to 8 minutes total).

4 Immediately spread fudge evenly in the prepared pan. Score into squares while warm. When fudge is firm, use foil to lift it out of pan. Cut fudge into squares. Store, tightly covered, at room temperature for up to 2 days or in the refrigerator for up to 1 month.

PER PIECE: 129 cal., 4 g fat (3 g sat. fat), 7 mg chol., 33 mg sodium, 24 g carb., 1 g fiber, 1 g pro.
EXCHANGES: 1½ Other Carb., 1 Fat

A FOIL LINING

When any recipe calls for lining a square or rectangular pan with foil, make it easy on yourself. Turn the pan over and press the foil around the botttom and sides of the pan. Remove the foil and drop the formed foil liner into the pan. Done!

4. ROLLING BOIL
Make sure your fudge boils at a steady rate across the entire surface of the pan to 236°F. This should take about 20 minutes.

5. DON'T TOUCH!
Remove pan from the heat, leaving the candy thermometer immersed in the pan. Add the butter and vanilla. Then DO NOT TOUCH! Do not move or bump the pan. There are millions of tiny sugar crystals in your fudge at this point. Any movement may agitate the mixture, encouraging large crystals to form.

6. BEAT IT
Once the fudge cools to 110°F, you're ready to beat it to thicken it slightly. If you beat it when the fudge is hotter than 110°F, large crystals will form and you will have a gritty fudge. Beat the fudge vigorously with a spoon until it loses its sheen and starts to turn opaque—or until a small bit dropped from the spoon holds its shape.

WHEN IT'S READY FOR THE PAN

Once the fudge is ready, pour the fudge QUICKLY into the foil-lined pan. Using a spatula, knife, or the back of a spoon, gently push it into the corners. DO NOT SCRAPE THE PAN; this might cause larger crystals to form rapidly and your fudge can turn grainy in the blink of an eye.

CANDY-BAR FUDGE

BEST-LOVED

Candy-Bar Fudge

PREP: 15 MINUTES **COOK:** 7 MINUTES
CHILL: 2 TO 3 HOURS
MAKES: ABOUT 2¾ POUNDS (64 PIECES)

- **½ cup butter**
- **⅓ cup unsweetened cocoa powder**
- **¼ cup packed brown sugar**
- **¼ cup milk**
- **3½ cups powdered sugar**
- **1 teaspoon vanilla**
- **30 vanilla caramels, unwrapped***
- **1 tablespoon water***
- **2 cups peanuts**
- **½ cup semisweet chocolate pieces**
- **½ cup milk chocolate pieces**

1 Line a 9×9×2-inch or 11×7×1½-inch baking pan with foil, extending the foil over the edges of the pan. Butter the foil; set pan aside (see photos, page 178).

2 In a large microwave-safe bowl microwave the butter, uncovered, on 100% power (high) for 1 to 1½ minutes or until butter melts. Stir in cocoa powder, brown sugar, and milk. Microwave, uncovered, on 100% power (high) for 1 to 1½ minutes or until mixture comes to a boil, stirring once. Stir again; microwave on high for 30 seconds more. Stir in powdered sugar and vanilla until smooth. Spread fudge in the prepared pan.

3 In a medium microwave-safe bowl combine caramels and the water. Microwave, uncovered, on 50% power (medium) for 2 to 2½ minutes or until caramels melt, stirring once. Stir in peanuts. Microwave, uncovered, on medium power for 45 to 60 seconds more or until mixture softens. Gently and quickly spread caramel mixture over fudge layer in pan.

4 In a 2-cup microwave-safe glass measure or small bowl combine semisweet and milk chocolate pieces. Microwave, uncovered, on 50% power (medium) for 2 to 2½ minutes or until chocolate melts, stirring once or twice. Spread over caramel layer. Cover and chill for 2 to 3 hours or until firm. When fudge is firm, use foil to lift it out of pan. Cut fudge into pieces. Store, tightly covered, in the refrigerator for up to 3 weeks.

***NOTE:** Or use 1 cup purchased refrigerated caramel dip (not ice cream topping) and omit the water. In a medium microwave-safe bowl microwave dip, uncovered, on 50% power (medium) for 2 minutes or until heated through, stirring once. Stir in peanuts and microwave, uncovered, on medium power for 45 to 60 seconds more. Spread over fudge layer and continue as directed in Step 4.

PER PIECE: 102 cal., 5 g total fat (2 g sat. fat), 5 mg chol., 24 mg sodium, 14 g carb., 1 g fiber, 2 g pro.
EXCHANGES: 1 Other Carb., 1 Fat

BEST-LOVED

Easy Fudge

PREP: 45 MINUTES **CHILL:** 2 TO 3 HOURS
MAKES: ABOUT 5 POUNDS (96 PIECES)

- **4½ cups sugar**
- **1 12-ounce can evaporated milk (1½ cups)**
- **½ teaspoon salt**
- **1 pound milk chocolate bars, chopped**
- **1 12-ounce package semisweet chocolate pieces (2 cups)**
- **1 7-ounce jar marshmallow crème**
- **1 cup chopped walnuts or pecans (optional)**
- **1 teaspoon vanilla**

1 Line a 13×9×2-inch baking pan with foil, extending the foil over the edges of the pan. Butter the foil; set pan aside (see photos, page 178).

2 Butter the sides of a 3-quart heavy saucepan. In the saucepan combine sugar, evaporated milk, and salt. Cook and stir over medium-high heat until mixture boils. Reduce heat to medium; continue cooking and stirring for 10 minutes.

3 Remove saucepan from heat. Add chopped chocolate, chocolate pieces, marshmallow crème, nuts (if desired), and vanilla. Stir until chocolate melts and mixture is combined. Beat mixture with a clean wooden spoon for 3 to 5 minutes or until mixture starts to become thicker.

4 Immediately pour fudge into the prepared pan; shake pan gently to spread fudge to edges of pan. Cover; chill for 2 to 3 hours or until firm. When fudge is firm, use foil to lift it out of pan. Cut fudge into squares. Store, tightly covered, at room temperature for up to 2 days or in the refrigerator for up to 1 month.

EASY CHOCOLATE-PEANUT BUTTER FUDGE: Prepare as directed, except stir ½ cup peanut butter into mixture in saucepan before bringing to boiling in Step 2 and substitute 1 cup chopped peanuts for the walnuts or pecans.

EASY MOCHA FUDGE: Prepare as directed, except stir 2 tablespoons instant espresso coffee powder or instant coffee crystals into the mixture with the vanilla in Step 3.

EASY ROCKY ROAD FUDGE: Prepare as directed, except after spreading fudge in pan in Step 4, sprinkle top with a mixture of 1 cup semisweet chocolate pieces, 1 cup tiny marshmallows, and ½ cup chopped walnuts, toasted (see tip, page 21). Press mixture lightly into fudge. Chill as directed.

PER PIECE PLAIN, CHOCOLATE-PEANUT BUTTER, MOCHA, OR ROCKY ROAD VARIATIONS: 90 cal., 3 g total fat (2 g sat. fat), 2 mg chol., 22 mg sodium, 16 g carb., 0 g fiber, 1 g pro. EXCHANGES: 1 Other Carb., ½ Fat

Peanut Butter Fudge

PREP: 15 MINUTES **COOK:** 12 MINUTES
STAND: 60 MINUTES
MAKES: ABOUT 1½ POUNDS (64 PIECES)

- **2 cups sugar**
- **1 5-ounce can evaporated milk (⅔ cup)**
- **½ cup butter**
- **¾ cup peanut butter**
- **½ of a 7-ounce jar marshmallow crème (about ¾ cup) or 2 cups tiny marshmallows**
- **½ cup finely chopped peanuts (optional)**
- **½ teaspoon vanilla**

1 Line a 9×9×2-inch baking pan with foil, extending the foil over the edges of the pan. Butter the foil; set pan aside (see photos, page 178).

2 Butter the sides of a 1½- to 2-quart heavy saucepan. In the saucepan combine the sugar, evaporated milk, and butter. Cook and stir over medium-high heat until mixture boils. Reduce heat to medium and continue boiling at a moderate, steady rate for 12 minutes, stirring occasionally.

3 Remove saucepan from heat. Add peanut butter, marshmallow crème, peanuts (if desired), and vanilla; stir until mixture is combined. Spread fudge evenly in the prepared pan. Let stand for 1 to 2 hours or until firm. When fudge is firm, use foil to lift it out of pan. Cut into squares. Store, tightly covered, at room temperature for up to 2 days or in the refrigerator for up to 1 month.

PER PIECE: 63 cal., 3 g total fat (1 g sat. fat), 4 mg chol., 28 mg sodium, 8 g carb., 0 g fiber, 1 g pro.
EXCHANGES: ½ Other Carb., ½ Fat

BEST-LOVED

Classic Truffles

PREP: 60 MINUTES **CHILL:** 1½ TO 2 HOURS
MAKES: 25 TO 30 TRUFFLES

- **1 12-ounce package semisweet chocolate pieces or one 11.5 ounce package milk chocolate pieces**
- **⅓ cup whipping cream**
- **4 teaspoons cherry brandy, hazelnut or orange liqueur, or milk**
- **3 tablespoons finely chopped candied cherries or candied orange peel**
- **Unsweetened cocoa powder; finely chopped nuts, toasted (see tip, page 21); and/or powdered sugar**

1 In a medium heavy saucepan combine chocolate pieces and whipping cream. Cook and stir constantly over low heat until the chocolate melts. Remove saucepan from heat; cool slightly. Sir in cherry brandy. Beat the truffle mixture with an electric mixer on low speed until mixture is smooth. Stir in candied cherries. Chill for 1½ to 2 hours or until mixture is firm.

2 Line a tray or baking sheet with waxed paper. Shape the chilled chocolate mixture into ¾- to 1-inch balls. Roll balls in cocoa powder, finely chopped nuts, and/or powdered sugar; place on prepared tray. Store in a single layer in an airtight container in the refrigerator for up to 2 weeks. Let stand at room temperature about 30 minutes before serving.

PER TRUFFLE: 85 cal., 5 g total fat (3 g sat. fat), 4 mg chol., 3 mg sodium, 11 g carb., 1 g fiber, 1 g pro. EXCHANGES: 1 Other Carb., 1 Fat

COOKIE TRUFFLES

Cookie Truffles

PREP: 50 MINUTES **CHILL:** 60 TO 90 MINUTES
FREEZE: 30 MINUTES **STAND:** 30 MINUTES
MAKES: ABOUT 50 TRUFFLES

- **1 12-ounce package semisweet chocolate pieces**
- **1 8-ounce package cream cheese, cut up and softened**
- **1 8-ounce package miniature chocolate sandwich cookies with white filling, finely chopped**
- **2¼ cups milk chocolate pieces or semisweet chocolate pieces**
- **2 tablespoons shortening**
- **Nonpareils or jimmies (optional)**

1 Line a tray or baking sheet with waxed paper; set aside. In a medium heavy saucepan heat and stir the 12 ounces semisweet chocolate pieces over low heat until chocolate melts. Remove from heat; stir in cream cheese until mixture is well combined (mixture will thicken). Stir in chopped chocolate cookies; chill for 30 to 60 minutes. Use a small cookie scoop to drop mounds of mixture onto the prepared tray. Cover and freeze for 30 minutes or until firm. Reshape into balls. Chill; reshape again as necessary.

2 In a small heavy saucepan combine the 2¼ cups milk chocolate pieces and shortening; stir over low heat until mixture melts and is smooth. Remove from heat.

3 Line another tray or baking sheet with waxed paper. Using a fork, dip balls into chocolate mixture, allowing excess chocolate to drip back into saucepan. Place dipped balls on prepared tray. If desired, sprinkle with nonpareils. Chill about 30 minutes or until firm. Store in a single layer in an airtight container in the refrigerator for up to 1 week or freeze for up to 1 month. Let stand at room temperature about 30 minutes before serving.

PER TRUFFLE: 115 cal., 7 g total fat (4 g sat. fat), 7 mg chol., 47 mg sodium, 12 g carb., 1 g fiber, 1 g pro.
EXCHANGES: 1 Other Carb., 1½ Fat

Chocolate-Covered Cherries

(photo, page 175)

PREP: 75 MINUTES **STAND:** 3 HOURS
CHILL: 1 TO 4 HOURS **MAKES:** 40 CHERRIES

- **2 10-ounce jars maraschino cherries with stems (40 cherries)**
- **3 tablespoons butter, softened**
- **3 tablespoons light-color corn syrup**
- **2 cups powdered sugar**
- **8 ounces chocolate-flavor candy coating (almond bark), cut up**
- **8 ounces bittersweet or semisweet chocolate, cut up**

1 Let cherries stand on paper towels for 2 hours to drain. Line a tray or baking sheet with waxed paper; set aside.

2 In a medium bowl combine butter and corn syrup; stir in powdered sugar. Knead until smooth (chill if mixture is too soft to handle). Shape about ¾ teaspoon mixture around each cherry. Place coated cherries, stem sides up, on the prepared tray. Chill for 1 to 4 hours or until firm.

3 In a medium heavy saucepan melt candy coating and chocolate over low heat, stirring constantly until smooth. Line another tray or baking sheet with waxed paper. Holding cherries by stems, dip, one at a time, into melted mixture. If necessary, spoon mixture over cherries to cover completely (to prevent juice from leaking). Let excess mixture drip off. Place coated cherries, stem sides up, on prepared tray. Let cherries stand until coating is set (1 to 2 hours). Store, tightly covered, in the refrigerator for up to 1 month. (The longer the cherries are stored, the more the mixture around the cherries will soften and liquify.)

PER CHERRY: 117 cal., 5 g total fat (3 g sat. fat), 2 mg chol., 7 mg sodium, 19 g carb., 1 g fiber, 0 g pro. **EXCHANGES:** 1 Other Carb., 1 Fat

8 to try

Basic Candy Bark

Have lingering, almost empty bags of mixed nuts, dried fruit, or trail mix in your pantry? Use them up in creative combinations of nuts, fruits, candies, and salty snacks.

PREP: 20 MINUTES **CHILL:** 30 MINUTES
MAKES: ABOUT 1½ POUNDS (36 SERVINGS)

- **6 ounces chocolate- or vanilla-flavor candy coating (almond bark), chopped (1 cup)**
- **6 ounces milk, semisweet, dark chocolate, or white chocolate, chopped (1 cup)**
- **1 tablespoon shortening**
- **1 to 2 teaspoons finely shredded orange or lemon peel (optional)**
- **1½ cups chopped pecans, walnuts, or almonds, toasted (see tip, page 21), or macadamia nuts**

1 Line a large baking sheet with heavy foil; grease foil and set aside.

2 In a large microwave-safe bowl combine candy coating, chocolate, and shortening. Microwave, uncovered, on 100% power (high) for 1½ to 2 minutes or until chocolate melts, stirring every 30 seconds. If desired, add citrus peel; mix in nuts.

3 Pour mixture onto the baking sheet. Spread about ¼ inch thick.

4 Chill candy about 30 minutes or until firm. Use foil to lift candy; carefully break into pieces. Store between sheets of waxed paper in an airtight container. Refrigerate for up to 2 weeks.

PER SERVING: 75 cal., 6 g total fat (2 g sat. fat), 1 mg chol., 6 mg sodium, 5 g carb., 1 g fiber, 1 g pro.
EXCHANGES: ½ Other Carb., 1 Fat

INGREDIENT KNOW-HOW

Use half candy coating and half chocolate for a smooth, rich texture. (Using only chocolate results in a finished bark with tacky texture.) Adding citrus peel for flavor—as opposed to a liquid extract—keeps the mixture from seizing into a grainy-textured bark.

SALTED CARAMEL: Before mixture sets, melt together half of a 14-ounce package vanilla caramels, unwrapped, and 1 tablespoon milk. Drizzle caramel mixture over chocolate mixture. Sprinkle with ¾ cup chopped almonds, toasted, and ¼ teaspoon sea salt.

MINT-CHOCOLATE: Arrange 9 chocolate wafer cookies in a single layer on the foil. Melt half of the vanilla coating with 3 ounces milk chocolate pieces and half the shortening. Melt remaining vanilla coating with 3 ounces green mint-flavor baking pieces. Drop spoonfuls of the mixtures over cookies. Use a narrow spatula to swirl.

MOCHA-ORANGE: Use ⅔ cup chopped chocolate-covered coffee beans in place of the nuts and use orange peel. Before mixture sets, drop spoonfuls of 4 ounces melted white baking chocolate over mixture. Use a narrow spatula to swirl.

COCONUT-MACADAMIA: Use vanilla-flavor candy coating, white baking chocolate, macadamia nuts, and lime peel in place of the citrus peel. Sprinkle with toasted flaked coconut after spreading the mixture.

PEANUT BUTTER: Use peanuts for the nuts. Before the mixture sets, sprinkle with chopped chocolate-covered peanut butter cups and/or candy-coated peanut butter-flavor pieces.

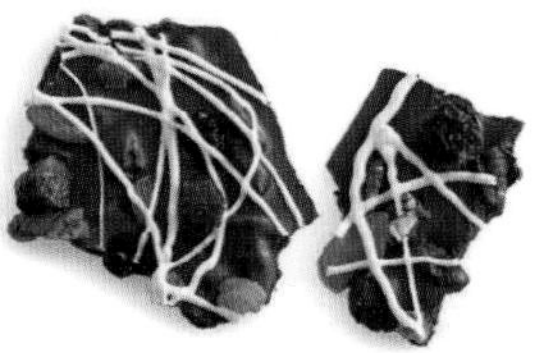

DRIED FRUIT: Use dried cherries, raisins, cranberries, and/or snipped dried apricots in place of the nuts. Drizzle with 2 ounces melted white chocolate after the mixture sets. Chill again until set.

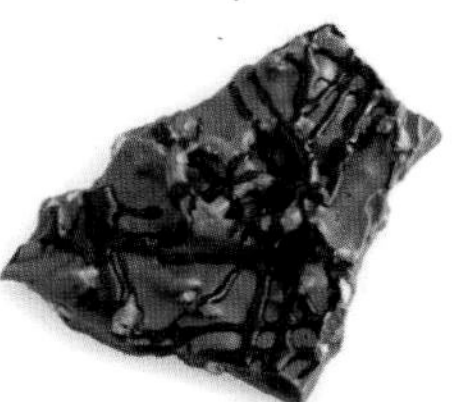

PRETZEL: Use broken pretzel twists in place of the nuts. Drizzle with 3 ounces melted bittersweet chocolate.

BUTTERSCOTCH TOFFEE: Use 6 ounces vanilla-flavor candy coating (almond bark) and 3 ounces butterscotch-flavor chips; replace half of the nuts with toffee pieces.

testing candy mixtures

When a candy thermometer isn't available, this cold-water test is the next best thing.

EQUIPMENT

- If candy making intrigues you, invest in a candy thermometer. There's simply no more accurate way to determine the stages of the hot candy mixture. (See "Essential Equipment," page 177, on how to use a candy thermometer.)
- If you do not have a candy thermometer, use the thread stage and cold-water test described here. All you need is a small bowl or cup and a spoon. You will want to use a wooden or high-heat-resistant spoon when stirring the mixture, but a kitchen spoon will work for the cold-water test.

THREAD STAGE

- Test the hot mixture in the pan. When testing for thread stage (see photo 1, right), you will not need a bowl of water.

COLD-WATER TEST

- Fill the small bowl or cup with cold (but not icy) water.
- Using the photos and captions to the right, you can determine the candy mixture's temperature by testing its firmness. If the mixture has not reached the desired stage, continue cooking and retesting, using fresh water at the same temperature you used in the previous test. Use a clean spoon each time.
- Start testing candy mixtures shortly before they reach minimum cooking times.
- To test, spoon a few drops of hot candy mixture into the bowl of water. Using your fingers, attempt to form the candy mixture into a ball; remove the ball from the water. For the soft-crack and hard-crack stages (see photos 5 and 6, right), the mixture won't form a ball but will separate into threads.

CANDY STAGE POINTERS

1. THREAD STAGE
(230°F to 233°F)
When a teaspoon is dipped into the hot mixture in the pan and lifted out, the candy falls off the spoon in a 2-inch-long, fine, thin thread.

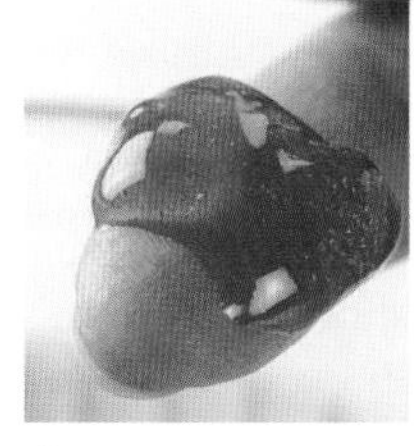

2. SOFT-BALL STAGE
(234°F to 240°F)
When the ball of candy is removed from the cold water, it instantly flattens and runs over your finger.

3. FIRM-BALL STAGE
(244°F to 248°F)
When the ball of candy is removed from the cold water, it is firm enough to hold its shape but quickly flattens.

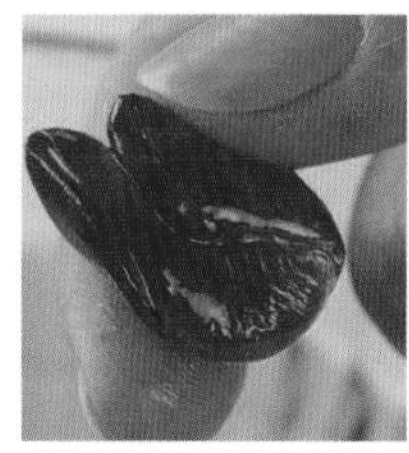

4. HARD-BALL STAGE
(250°F to 266°F)
When the ball of candy is removed from the cold water, it can be deformed by pressure, but it doesn't flatten until pressed.

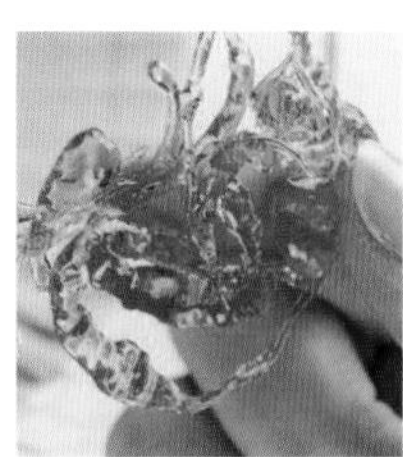

5. SOFT-CRACK STAGE
(270°F to 290°F)
When the hot mixture is dropped into the cold water, the candy separates into hard but pliable threads.

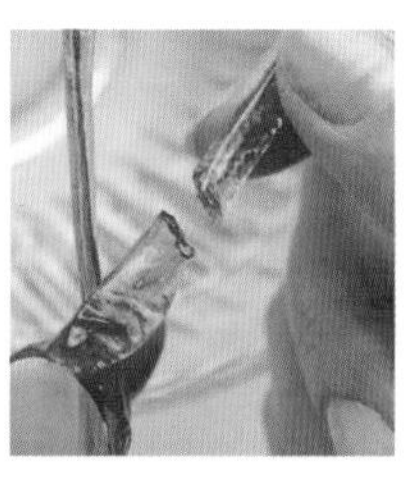

6. HARD-CRACK STAGE
(295°F to 310°F)
When the hot mixture is dropped into the cold water, it separates into hard, brittle threads that snap easily and cannot be shaped into a ball.

Cream Cheese Mints

PREP: 50 MINUTES **CHILL:** OVERNIGHT
MAKES: ABOUT 50 MINTS

- **1 3-ounce package cream cheese, softened**
- **½ teaspoon peppermint extract**
- **3 cups powdered sugar**
- **Few drops desired food coloring**
- **Granulated sugar**

1 In a large bowl stir together cream cheese and extract. Gradually add powdered sugar, stirring until mixture is smooth. (Knead in the last of the powdered sugar with your hands.) Add food coloring; knead until food coloring is evenly distributed.

2 Form cream cheese mixture into ¾-inch balls. Roll each ball in granulated sugar; place on waxed paper-lined tray. Flatten each ball with the bottom of a glass or with the tines of a fork. (Or sprinkle small candy molds lightly with sugar. Press ¾ to 1 teaspoon cream cheese mixture into each mold; remove from molds.) Cover mints with paper towels; chill overnight. Store, tightly covered, in the refrigerator up to 2 weeks or freeze for up to 1 month.

PER MINT: 36 cal., 1 g total fat (0 g sat. fat), 2 mg chol., 6 mg sodium, 8 g carb., 0 g fiber, 0 g pro.
EXCHANGES: ½ Other Carb.

Pralines

PREP: 15 MINUTES **COOK:** 15 MINUTES
COOL: 20 MINUTES **STAND:** 2 HOURS
MAKES: ABOUT 30 PRALINES

- **1½ cups granulated sugar**
- **1½ cups packed brown sugar**
- **1 cup evaporated milk**
- **2 tablespoons butter**
- **2 tablespoons dark-color corn syrup**
- **⅛ teaspoon salt**
- **2 cups pecan halves, toasted**
- **1 teaspoon vanilla**

1 Butter the sides of a 2-quart heavy saucepan. In saucepan combine granulated sugar, brown sugar, milk, butter, corn syrup, and salt. Cook and stir over medium-high heat until mixture boils. Clip a candy thermometer to side of pan. Reduce heat to medium-low; continue boiling at a moderate, steady rate, stirring occasionally, until the thermometer registers 236°F, soft-ball stage (15 to 20 minutes). Adjust heat as necessary to maintain a steady boil.

2 Remove saucepan from heat; remove thermometer. Cool, without stirring, for 20 minutes. Line two baking sheets with waxed paper; set aside.

3 Stir in pecans and vanilla. Beat vigorously with a clean wooden spoon until mixture thickens but is still glossy (7 to 8 minutes). Working quickly, drop candy by spoonfuls onto prepared baking sheets (mixture will spread). Let stand about 2 hours or until firm. Store, tightly covered, in the refrigerator for up to 1 week.

PER PRALINE: 153 cal., 7 g total fat (1 g sat. fat), 4 mg chol., 29 mg sodium, 24 g carb., 1 g fiber, 1 g pro.
EXCHANGES: 1½ Other Carb., 1½ Fat

Peanut Brittle *(photo, page 177)*

PREP: 10 MINUTES **COOK:** 45 MINUTES
MAKES: ABOUT 2¼ POUNDS (72 SERVINGS)

- **2 cups sugar**
- **1 cup light-color corn syrup**
- **½ cup water**
- **¼ cup butter**
- **2½ cups raw peanuts or raw cashews**
- **1½ teaspoons baking soda, sifted**

1 Butter two large baking sheets; set aside. Butter the sides of a 3-quart heavy saucepan. In saucepan combine sugar, corn syrup, water, and butter. Cook and stir over medium-high heat just until butter melts and sugar dissolves. Continue cooking over medium-high heat until mixture boils. Clip a candy thermometer to side of pan. Reduce heat to medium-low; continue boiling at a moderate, steady rate, stirring occasionally, until the thermometer registers 275°F, soft-crack stage (about 30 minutes). Adjust heat as necessary to maintain a steady boil.

2 Stir in raw nuts; continue cooking over medium-low heat, stirring frequently, until thermometer registers 295°F, hard-crack stage (15 to 20 minutes more).

3 Remove saucepan from heat; remove thermometer. Quickly sprinkle baking soda over corn syrup mixture, stirring constantly. Immediately pour onto prepared baking sheets. Allow both pans of brittle to cool for 2 minutes. Use two forks, like tongs, to lift and pull candy into an even, thin layer. Cool completely; break into pieces. Store, tightly covered, at room temperature for up to 1 week.

PER SERVING: 63 cal., 3 g total fat (1 g sat. fat), 2 mg chol., 33 mg sodium, 8 g carb., 0 g fiber, 1 g pro.
EXCHANGES: ½ Other Carb., ½ Fat

Homemade Marshmallows

(photo, page 175)

PREP: 30 MINUTES **COOK:** 12 MINUTES
CHILL: 5 HOURS **MAKES:** ABOUT 80 MARSHMALLOWS

- **Nonstick cooking spray**
- **2 envelopes unflavored gelatin (4¼ teaspoons)**
- **¾ cup cold water**
- **2 cups granulated sugar**
- **⅔ cup light-color corn syrup**
- **⅓ cup refrigerated egg white product* or 2 pasteurized liquid egg whites**
- **1 tablespoon vanilla**
- **¼ teaspoon salt**
- **⅔ cup powdered sugar**
- **3 tablespoons cornstarch**

1 Line a 13×9×2-inch baking pan with plastic wrap or line bottom of pan with waxed paper or parchment paper. Coat the plastic or paper with nonstick cooking spray; set pan aside. In a large metal or heatproof bowl sprinkle gelatin over ½ cup of the cold water; set aside.

2 In a 2-quart heavy saucepan stir together remaining ¼ cup water, 1¾ cups of the granulated sugar, and the corn syrup until combined. Bring to boiling over medium-high heat. Clip a candy thermometer to the side of the saucepan. Cook, without stirring, over medium-high heat until thermometer registers 260°F, hard-ball stage (12 to 15 minutes total). Remove from heat; pour over gelatin mixture in bowl and stir well to combine.

3 Meanwhile, in a clean large mixing bowl beat egg white product, vanilla, and salt with an electric mixer on high speed until foamy. Gradually add remaining ¼ cup granulated sugar, 1 tablespoon at a time, until stiff peaks form (tips stand straight). With the mixer running on high speed, gradually add gelatin mixture to egg white mixture, beating for 5 to 7 minutes or until thick (consistency of thick, pourable cake batter). Quickly and gently spread marshmallow mixture into prepared pan. Coat a piece of plastic wrap with nonstick spray; place, coated side down, over marshmallow mixture in pan. Chill at least 5 hours or until firm.

4 In a small bowl combine powdered sugar and cornstarch; sprinkle about one-fourth of the mixture evenly onto a large cutting board. Remove plastic wrap from top of marshmallows. Run a knife around the edge of pan to loosen sides of marshmallow mixture and carefully invert onto the cutting board. Remove plastic wrap or paper. Sprinkle top with some of the remaining powdered sugar mixture. Cut marshmallows into about 1-inch squares. Place squares, about one-third at a time, in a large resealable plastic bag. Add remaining powdered sugar mixture; seal bag. Toss to coat all sides with powdered sugar mixture. Store marshmallows between sheets of waxed paper or parchment paper in an airtight container in the refrigerator for up to 1 week or in the freezer for up to 1 month.

***NOTE:** Buy a product that is only egg whites. If you cannot find pasteurized egg whites, you can use regular eggs and pasteurize the whites following the tip on page 20.

PER MARSHMALLOW: 38 cal., 0 g total fat, 0 mg chol., 20 mg sodium, 9 g carb., 0 g fiber, 0 g pro.
EXCHANGES: ½ Other Carb.

COCONUT MARSHMALLOWS: Prepare as directed, except sprinkle 1½ cups toasted flaked coconut in the bottom of the 13×9×2-inch pan after coating wrap or paper with nonstick cooking spray. Add ¼ teaspoon coconut flavoring to the egg whites with the vanilla. Sprinkle top of marshmallow mixture in pan with an additional 1½ cups toasted flaked coconut. Cover and chill as directed in Step 3. Omit powdered sugar and cornstarch. Invert marshmallows onto a large cutting board. Cut into 1-inch squares. Place squares, about one-third at a time, in a large resealable plastic bag. Add 1¼ cups toasted flaked coconut. Seal bag and shake to coat all sides of marshmallows with coconut.

PER MARSHMALLOW: 62 cal., 2 g total fat (2 g sat. fat), 0 mg chol., 37 mg sodium, 11 g carb., 0 g fiber, 1 g pro.
EXCHANGES: 1 Other Carb., ½ Fat

MARSHMALLOWS STEP-BY-STEP

1. Use a long thin-bladed, sharp knife to cut marshmallow into strips, then into squares.

↓

↑

2. Shake a portion of squares at a time with powdered sugar mixture in a plastic bag until evenly coated.

make it mine

Chewy Popcorn Drops

Pantry staples come together in these delightfully salty-sweet treats. Mix and match what you have on hand to make this goodie your own.

START TO FINISH: 30 MINUTES
MAKES: ABOUT 50 DROPS

- 6 **cups popped** POPCORN
- 3 **cups** PRETZELS
- 2 **cups** NUTS
- 1 **cup** DRIED FRUIT
- 1 **20-ounce package** CANDY COATING **(almond bark), coarsely chopped**
- ⅔ **cup** NUT BUTTER

1 In an extra-large bowl combine Popcorn, Pretzels, Nuts, and Dried Fruit.

2 In a medium heavy saucepan cook and stir Candy Coating over low heat just until melted and smooth, being careful not to overheat. Remove from heat. Stir in Nut Butter just until combined (do not overstir).

3 Pour melted coating mixture over popcorn mixture. Stir gently to coat. Immediately drop mixture by rounded tablespoons (or use a medium cookie scoop) onto a tray lined with waxed paper, pressing mixture into the sides of the bowl as you scoop (this will help hold the mixture together). Let candy stand until set.

TO STORE: Place drops between sheets of waxed paper in an airtight container; cover. Store in the refrigerator for up to 2 days.

POPCORN *(pick one)*
Cheese popcorn
Kettle popcorn
Plain popcorn

PRETZELS *(pick one)*
Pretzel squares, broken
Pretzel sticks
Tiny pretzel twists, broken

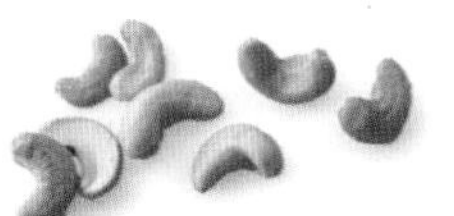

NUTS *(pick one)*
Toasted almonds, chopped
Roasted cashews, coarsely chopped
Roasted peanuts, coarsely chopped

DRIED FRUIT *(pick one)*
Snipped apricots
Cherries
Cranberries
Golden raisins

CANDY COATING *(pick one)*
Chocolate
Vanilla

NUT BUTTER *(pick one)*
Peanut butter
Chocolate-hazelnut spread

CARAMEL APPLES

BEST-LOVED

Caramel Apples

PREP: 25 MINUTES **MAKES:** 6 APPLES

- **6 small tart apples**
- **6 pop sticks or wooden skewers**
- **1 14-ounce package vanilla caramels, unwrapped**
- **2 tablespoons whipping cream, half-and-half, or light cream**
- **Toasted cashews, pecans, almonds, and/or walnuts, chopped (see tip, page 21) (optional)**
- **Miniature semisweet chocolate pieces (optional)**

1 Wash and dry apples; remove stems. Insert a pop stick into the stem end of each apple. Place apples on a buttered baking sheet.

2 In a medium saucepan combine caramels and whipping cream. Cook and stir over medium-low heat until caramels are completely melted, stirring constantly. Working quickly, dip each apple into hot caramel mixture; turn to coat (heat caramel again over low heat if it becomes too thick to easily coat apples). If desired, dip in chopped nuts or chocolate pieces. Set on prepared baking sheet and let stand until set. Serve the same day.

PER APPLE: 355 cal., 8 g total fat (4 g sat. fat), 15 mg chol., 189 mg sodium, 67 g carb., 3 g fiber, 4 g pro.
EXCHANGES: 1 Fruit, 3½ Other Carb., 1½ Fat

Caramels

PREP: 20 MINUTES **COOK:** 45 MINUTES
STAND: 2 HOURS **MAKES:** 64 CARAMELS

- **1 cup chopped walnuts, toasted (see tip, page 21) (optional)**
- **1 cup butter**
- **2¼ cups packed brown sugar**
- **2 cups half-and-half or light cream**
- **1 cup light-color corn syrup**
- **1 teaspoon vanilla**

1 Line an 8×8×2-inch or 9×9×2-inch baking pan with foil, extending foil over edges of pan. Butter the foil (see photos, page 178). If desired, sprinkle walnuts over bottom of pan. Set pan aside.

2 In a 3-quart heavy saucepan melt butter over low heat. Add brown sugar, half-and-half, and corn syrup; mix well. Cook and stir over medium-high heat until mixture boils. Clip a candy thermometer to the side of the pan. Reduce heat to medium; continue boiling at a moderate, steady rate, stirring frequently, until the thermometer registers 248°F, firm-ball stage (45 to 60 minutes). Adjust heat as necessary to maintain a steady boil and watch temperature carefully during the last 10 to 15 minutes of cooking as temperature can increase quickly at the end.

3 Remove saucepan from heat; remove thermometer. Stir in vanilla. Quickly pour mixture into prepared pan. Let stand about 2 hours or until firm. When firm, use foil to lift uncut caramels out of pan. Use a buttered knife to cut into 1-inch squares. Wrap each piece in waxed paper or plastic wrap. Store at room temperature for up to 2 weeks.

SHORTCUT CARAMELS: Prepare as directed, except substitute one 14-ounce can sweetened condensed milk (1¼ cups) for the half-and-half. Bring mixture to boiling over medium heat instead of medium-high heat. This mixture will take less time to reach 248°F, firm-ball stage (about 20 to 25 minutes).

PER CARAMEL REGULAR OR SHORTCUT VARIATION: 73 cal., 4 g total fat (2 g sat. fat), 10 mg chol., 27 mg sodium, 10 g carb., 0 g fiber, 0 g pro. EXCHANGES: ½ Other Carb., 1 Fat

BEST-LOVED

Caramel Corn

PREP: 20 MINUTES **BAKE:** 20 MINUTES AT 300°F
MAKES: 18 SERVINGS

- **14 cups popped popcorn**
- **2 cups whole almonds and/or roasted, salted cashews (optional)**
- **1½ cups packed brown sugar**
- **¾ cup butter**
- **⅓ cup light-color corn syrup**
- **½ teaspoon baking soda**
- **½ teaspoon vanilla**

1 Preheat oven to 300°F. Remove all unpopped kernels from popped popcorn. Put popcorn and, if desired, nuts into a 17×12×2-inch roasting pan. Keep warm in oven while preparing caramel.

2 Butter a large piece of foil; set aside. For caramel, in a medium saucepan combine brown sugar, butter, and corn syrup. Cook and stir over medium heat until mixture boils. Continue boiling at a moderate, steady rate, without stirring, for 5 minutes more.

3 Remove saucepan from heat. Stir in baking soda and vanilla. Pour caramel over popcorn; stir gently to coat. Bake for 15 minutes. Stir mixture; bake for 5 minutes more. Spread caramel corn on prepared foil; cool. Store, tightly covered, at room temperature for up to 1 week.

PER 1 CUP: 171 cal., 8 g total fat (5 g sat. fat), 20 mg chol., 97 mg sodium, 25 g carb., 1 g fiber, 1 g pro. EXCHANGES: ½ Starch, 1 Other Carb., 1½ Fat

Popcorn and Candy Balls *(photo, page 175)*

START TO FINISH: 45 MINUTES
OVEN: 300°F **MAKES:** 16 POPCORN BALLS

- **20 cups popped popcorn**
- **1½ cups light-color corn syrup**
- **1½ cups sugar**
- **1 7-ounce jar marshmallow crème**
- **2 tablespoons butter**
- **1 teaspoon vanilla**
- **1½ cups candy-coated milk chocolate pieces or candy-coated peanut butter-flavor pieces**

1 Preheat oven to 300°F. Remove all unpopped kernels from popped popcorn. Place popcorn in a buttered 17×12×2-inch baking pan or roasting pan. Keep popcorn warm in oven while preparing marshmallow mixture.

2 In a large saucepan bring corn syrup and sugar to boiling over medium-high heat, stirring constantly. Remove from heat. Stir in marshmallow crème, butter, and vanilla until combined.

3 Pour marshmallow mixture over popcorn; stir gently to coat. Cool until popcorn mixture can be handled easily. Stir in chocolate pieces. With buttered hands, quickly shape mixture into 3-inch-diameter balls. Wrap each ball in plastic wrap. Store at room temperature for up to 1 week.

PER POPCORN BALL: 307 cal., 6 g total fat (4 g sat. fat), 7 mg chol., 43 mg sodium, 63 g carb., 2 g fiber, 2 g pro. EXCHANGES: 1 Starch, 3 Other Carb., 1 Fat

SLICK MEASURING TRICK

Syrup, honey, and molasses cling to the inside of a measuring cup, making it necessary to scrape out the liquid with a spatula. Skip the sticky step by first spraying the empty measuring cup with nonstick cooking spray. The syrup, honey, or molasses will flow cleanly from the cup for a mess-free measure.

TOFFEE BUTTER CRUNCH

BEST-LOVED

Toffee Butter Crunch

PREP: 25 MINUTES **COOK:** 12 MINUTES
COOL: 4 MINUTES **STAND:** 3 HOURS
MAKES: 1¼ POUNDS (ABOUT 24 PIECES)

- **1 cup butter**
- **1 cup sugar**
- **3 tablespoons water**
- **1 tablespoon light-color corn syrup**
- **¾ cup milk chocolate pieces or semisweet chocolate pieces**
- **½ to ¾ cup chopped nuts, toasted (see tip, page 21)**

1 Line a 13×9×2-inch baking pan with foil, extending the foil over edges of pan; set aside.

2 In a 2-quart heavy saucepan melt butter over low heat. Stir in sugar, water, and corn syrup. Bring to boiling over medium-high heat, stirring until sugar is dissolved. Avoid splashing side of saucepan. Clip a candy thermometer to side of pan. Cook over medium heat, stirring frequently, until thermometer registers 290°F, soft-crack stage (about 12 minutes). Mixture should boil at a moderate, steady rate with bubbles over entire surface. Adjust heat as necessary to maintain a steady boil and watch temperature carefully during the last 5 minutes of cooking as temperature can increase quickly at the end. Remove from heat; remove thermometer.

3 Pour mixture into prepared pan; spread evenly. Cool 4 to 5 minutes or until top is just set. Sprinkle evenly with chocolate pieces; let stand for 2 minutes. Spread softened chocolate into an even layer over toffee layer. Sprinkle with nuts; lightly press into chocolate. Let stand at room temperature about 3 hours or until chocolate is set. Use foil to lift candy out of pan; break into pieces. Store between sheets of waxed paper in an airtight container at room temperature for up to 2 weeks.

PER PIECE: 141 cal., 10 g total fat (6 g sat. fat), 22 mg chol., 59 mg sodium, 12 g carb., 0 g fiber, 1 g pro. EXCHANGES: 1 Other Carb., 2 Fat

Peanut Clusters

PREP: 20 MINUTES **MAKES:** ABOUT 48 CLUSTERS

- **1 11.5-ounce package milk chocolate pieces or one 12-ounce package semisweet chocolate pieces**
- **12 ounces vanilla-flavor candy coating (almond bark), chopped**
- **1 pound (3 cups) cocktail peanuts**

1 Line a tray with waxed paper; set aside. In a medium heavy saucepan stir chocolate and candy coating over low heat until it melts and is smooth. Stir in peanuts. Drop from a teaspoon onto the prepared tray. Chill until set. Store, tightly covered, in the refrigerator for up to 1 week or freeze for up to 3 months.

PER CLUSTER: 133 cal., 9 g fat (4 g sat. fat), 1 mg chol., 23 mg sodium, 10 g carb., 1 g fiber, 3 g pro.
EXCHANGES: ½ Other Carb., 2 Fat

Peanut Butter Balls

PREP: 40 MINUTES **COOL:** 5 MINUTES
STAND: 10 MINUTES **MAKES:** ABOUT 40 CANDIES

- **1 cup peanut butter**
- **6 tablespoons butter, softened**
- **2 cups powdered sugar**
- **12 ounces chocolate-flavor candy coating (almond bark), cut up**

1 Line a tray with waxed paper; set aside. In a bowl stir together peanut butter and butter. Gradually add powdered sugar, stirring to combine. Knead with hands until smooth. Shape mixture into 1-inch balls; place on tray.

2 In a medium heavy saucepan melt candy coating over low heat, stirring constantly until smooth. Remove from heat; cool for 5 minutes. Dip balls, one at a time, into coating, allowing excess to drip off. Return to waxed paper; let stand about 10 minutes or until coating is set. Store, tightly covered, in the refrigerator for up to 1 month or freeze for up to 3 months.

PER CANDY: 124 cal., 8 g total fat (4 g sat. fat,), 5 mg chol., 42 mg sodium, 13 g carb., 0 g fiber, 2 g pro.
EXCHANGES: 1 Other Carb., 1½ Fat

205  209  204

200

canning & freezing

199

198

206

Apricot-Rosemary Jelly, page 211

essential rules of canning

Follow these basic rules exactly to ensure food safety and success.

KNOW WHICH CANNER TO USE: The boiling-water canner—basically a big pot with a lid and a rack in the bottom—is used for high-acid foods, which naturally resist bacteria growth. Pressure canners are used with low-acid foods and recipes that are especially prone to harboring harmful microorganisms. They heat food hotter than boiling-water canners.

The recipes will specify which type of canner is appropriate. In this book, all of the recipes use a boiling-water canner. (See page 194 for more information.)

CHOOSE THE RIGHT JARS: Use jars made specifically for canning. Don't use glass jars from purchased food, even if they look like canning jars. Don't use jars that look different from the canning jars currently on the market. And avoid jars with chipped edges because that can affect the seal.

Use the size jar specified in the recipe. (See page 195 for more information.)

USE LIDS PROPERLY: Use the special two-piece lids manufactured for canning. Reuse rings, but do not reuse lids, which have a sticky compound that seals the jar.

Don't screw lids on too tightly or they won't create a vacuum seal. Heat the lids in very hot but not boiling water or the compound won't seal. Test for sealing on each jar after it has cooled. (See page 198 for more information.)

CHOOSE THE RIGHT RECIPE: Modern canning recipes are safer than those from just 20 years ago. Foods may be processed longer or hotter. Always use tested recipes from reliable, current sources—and follow the recipes exactly. Don't alter ingredients. Alterations can compromise food safety. (See page 198 for more information.)

KEEP IT CLEAN AND KEEP IT HOT: Keep everything scrupulously clean. Wash and sterilize jars. Pack hot food into hot jars one at a time—not assembly-line style. Take only one sterilized jar out of the canner at a time. As soon as it is filled, place it back in the simmering water in the canner. (See pages 196–197 for more information.)

canning toolbox

Most of what you need for canning you already have in your kitchen, but a few specialty tools—such as a handy magnet to fish lids out of hot water with ease—make the job easier.

BOILING-WATER CANNER

1 BOILING-WATER CANNER: A boiling-water canner heats jars to 212°F, enough to kill microorganisms found in high-acid foods (see page 197). The rack allows water to flow beneath the jars for even heating. It also has handles that allow you to lower and lift jars easily into the hot water. Canners come in different sizes and finishes. A traditional speckled enameled finish resists chips and rust well. High-end boiling-water canners are available in sleek polished steel.

CANNING-SPECIFIC TOOLS

These few special tools make canning simpler and more efficient.

2 JAR LIFTER: This tool lifts jars firmly and securely in and out of hot water. Use two hands and squeeze firmly. You can use kitchen tongs, but they are not as secure.

3 JAR FUNNELS: Much wider and shorter than other funnels, these come in both wide-mouth and regular-mouth versions. They're invaluable for preventing spills when filling jars.

4 COMBINATION RULER/SPATULA: The notched end is calibrated to match the most common headspaces in jars (see page 195).

The tool is also somewhat flexible and has a tapered end, making it the ideal tool for slipping in along the sides of filled jars to release air bubbles.

5 MAGNETIC LID WAND: This wand enables you to drop lids and rings into the hot water of the canner to sterilize and soften them and easily lift them out from among jars and the racks; there's no need to heat them in a separate pan.

CREATE A CANNER

Today's boiling-water canners are sold with special racks that be filled and then submerged in the water or that can be lifted up to rest on the side and hold the jars partially submerged. But you don't have to buy a boiling-water canner to can. If you have a large stockpot that has a tight-fitting lid and holds several jars to a few inches deeper than their height, you can use that. You will need a rack to set jars up off the bottom to allow water to flow under them and heat the jars evenly.

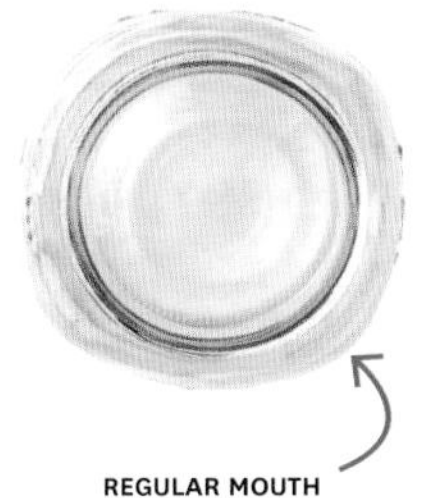

ALL ABOUT JARS

There are many different types of jars available for canning today. Take a look at the following guidelines for each.

QUART JARS: Use these large jars for any large food, such as whole tomatoes, or for a generous amount, such as spaghetti sauce and soup for a crowd. The jars come in wide-mouth and regular-mouth styles (see photo, above).

PINT JARS: The most versatile size jar, these containers hold nearly anything: smaller amounts of sauce, vegetables to serve a few people, and larger amounts of jam. The jars come in wide-mouth and regular-mouth styles.

8-OUNCE JELLY JARS: Usually with a quilt pattern or other design on their exteriors, these jars sport straight interior sides that allow you to get every last bit out of each jar.

4-OUNCE JARS: With no artificial preservatives, home-canned foods don't last as long in the refrigerator as commercial products. These small jars hold amounts you'll use up quickly.

DECORATIVE JARS: For refrigerator-pickled foods that don't require heat processing, decorative glass jars work fine. Just make sure you sterilize the jars in almost-boiling water before filling them.

VINTAGE JARS: Old canning jars with colored glass or spring-type lids are pretty collector pieces, but they shouldn't be used in modern canning. They have irregular sizes, might crack, and don't seal properly.

CHECKING HEADSPACE

The space between the top of the food and the container rim is the headspace. Leaving the correct amount of headspace is essential.

CANNING: Headspace allows a vacuum to form and the jar to seal. Use a ruler to make sure you have the right amount (see photo 3, page 196).

FREEZING: Headspace provides room for food to expand as it freezes. When using unsweetened or dry pack, leave a ½-inch headspace unless otherwise directed. When using a water, sugar, or syrup pack in freezer containers with wide tops, leave a ½-inch headspace for pints and a 1-inch headspace for quarts. For narrow-top containers, don't fill above the "shoulders."

THE ANATOMY OF A CANNING JAR

Wide-mouth canning jars are made for packing whole fruit and vegetables into a jar. Regular-mouth jars work well when transferring liquid contents—think jellies and sauces—to the jar.

1. The screw band *Bands may be reused; they secure lids to jars during processing. Removing the bands after processing is a matter of choice. Although they are no longer needed, the bands do provide some cushioning between jars when stacked on shelves.*

2. The lid *Lids are for onetime use only and are sized to fit regular-mouth and wide-mouth varieties. When purchasing new jars, lids and bands will be included, but you can also purchase new lids separately.*

3. The sealing compound *The red substance on the underside of the lid helps seal the lid onto the jar, ensuring a hermetic seal.*

4. The jar *Canning jars are molded from thick glass designed to withstand processing year after year. Jars are available in sizes from 4 ounces to 64 ounces, and you may choose between regular- and wide-mouth jars (see photo, above left).*

cook's secrets

canning basics

As a new generation discovers the joys of serving and sharing home-preserved food, canning is making a comeback. Follow these steps for safe, delicious results.

BOILING-WATER CANNING STEP-BY-STEP

1. HOT & CLEAN Kill any potential bacteria by sterilizing your jars first. Carefully place jars and lids separately in simmering water; remove jars from water with a jar lifter.

2. FUNNELS ARE KEY Clean wide-mouthed funnels make it easy to ladle prepared food into jars without making a mess.

Be sure to sterilize ladles and other utensils that will come into contact with the food.

3. CHECK HEADSPACE Double-check headspace called for in recipe with a ruler; measure from the top of the food to top of container rim. Headspace allows food to expand when heated and allows a vacuum seal to form.

BOILING-WATER CANNER: For a boiling-water canner, pack food into canning jars by the raw-pack (cold-pack) or hot-pack method.

RAW PACKING: In raw packing, uncooked food is packed into the canning jar and covered with boiling water, juice, or syrup (see Step 3, page 213, and chart introduction, page 217, for syrup information).

HOT PACKING: In hot packing, food is partially cooked, packed into jars, and covered with cooking liquid. The following guidelines apply to both methods.

1 Wash empty canning jars in hot, soapy water. Rinse thoroughly. Place jars in the boiling-water canner (or another large pot). Cover jars with hot water; bring to a simmer over medium heat. For food processed less than 10 minutes, boil the jars 10 minutes and keep warm in simmering water until needed. Set screw bands aside; place lids in another saucepan. Cover with water; bring to a simmer over medium heat (do not boil).

2 If using a different pot for sterilizing the jars, fill the boiling-water canner half full; bring to boiling. Heat additional water in another large pot (for topping off water in the canner); keep it hot but not boiling.

3 Prepare only as much food as needed to fill the maximum number of jars your canner will hold at one time. Keep the work area clean.

4 Remove sterilized jars from the hot water (see photo 1, left); place hot jars on cloth towels to prevent them from slipping during packing.

5 Pack food into jars using a wide-mouth funnel (see photo 2, left), allowing for adequate headspace (see tip, page 195). Ladle boiling liquid over the food, maintaining the adequate headspace.

6 Release trapped air bubbles by gently working a sterilized nonmetal utensil (such as the one provided in a canning kit) down the jars' sides. Add liquid, if needed, to maintain necessary headspace; double-check with a ruler (see photo 3, left).

7 Wipe jar rims with a clean, damp cloth; food on the rims prevents a perfect seal. Place prepared lids on jars; add screw bands and tighten according to manufacturer's directions (see photos 5 and 6, page 197).

8 Set each jar into the rack in the canner as it is filled and sealed. Jars should not touch each other. Replace canner cover each time you add a jar.

9 When all jars have been added, ladle hot water from the extra pot into the canner to cover jars by 1 inch (see photo 7, page 197).

10 Cover; heat to a full rolling boil. Begin processing time, following recipe procedures and timings exactly. (See tip, page 206, if necessary to adjust for altitude.) Keep water boiling gently during processing, adding boiling water if level drops. If water stops boiling when you add more, stop timing, turn up heat, and wait for a full boil before resuming counting.

11 At end of processing, remove jars (see photo 8, below right); place them on a rack or on towels in a draft-free area to cool. Leave at least 1 inch of space between jars to allow air to circulate.

12 After jars are completely cooled (12 to 24 hours), press center of each lid to check the seal (see tip, page 198). If the dip in the lid holds, the jar is sealed. If the lid bounces up and down, the jar isn't sealed. Check unsealed jars for flaws. Contents can be refrigerated and used within 2 to 3 days, frozen, or reprocessed within 24 hours. To reprocess, use a clean, sterilized jar and a new lid; process for full length of time specified. Mark label so you can use any recanned jars first. If jars have lost liquid but are sealed, the contents are safe. However, any food not covered by liquid can discolor, so use these jars first.

13 Wipe jars and lids. Remove, wash, and dry screw bands; store for future use. Label jars with contents and date; include batch number if you can more than a load a day (if a jar spoils, you can identify others from same batch). Store jars in cool (50°F to 70°F), dry, dark place. Use within 1 year.

Use a permanent marker to label jars. Once the ink dries, it resists fading and moisture.

HIGH-ACID AND LOW-ACID FOODS

In canning, the acidity level of foods is critical. High-acid foods are naturally less likely to harbor harmful microorganisms; low-acid foods require either more acid or more heat for safe canning.

Foods for canning are basically divided into two groups: low-acid and high-acid.

HIGH-ACID FOODS: These are the simplest to process. Their high acidity levels create a difficult environment for microorganisms and enzymes to thrive, so processing them in the lower heat of a boiling-water canner is safe. High-acid foods have a pH of 4.6 or lower. Lemon juice, lime juice, and vinegar are very acidic. For that reason, most pickles and most salsas are high-acid, even though they may contain foods that are otherwise low-acid, such as green beans and carrots.

LOW-ACID FOODS: These foods have a pH greater than 4.6. Most vegetables are low-acid, as are most soups, stews, and meat sauces. Unless large amounts of an acidic ingredient (such as vinegar) are added, these low-acid foods must be processed in the higher heat of a pressure canner.

ACIDITY BOOSTERS: Adding highly acidic elements such as lemon juice and vinegar to low-acid foods greatly broadens the types of foods you can process in a boiling-water canner because they control bacteria that can't thrive in acidic environments. That's why canning recipes for tomatoes, which have a fairly neutral pH, often call for adding a teaspoon of lemon juice. It's also why green beans in a vinegary brine can be processed in a boiling-water canner (which doesn't get as hot and doesn't kill microorganisms as effectively as a pressure canner). Plain green beans, on the other hand, must be processed in the higher heat of a pressure canner.

4. WIPE JAR RIMS
Use a clean, damp cloth to remove liquid or food from jar rims.

5. MAGNET MAGIC
Remove jar lids from hot water with a magnetic lid wand; place on the jars.

6. SCREW ON BANDS
Screw bands in place, but don't overtighten.

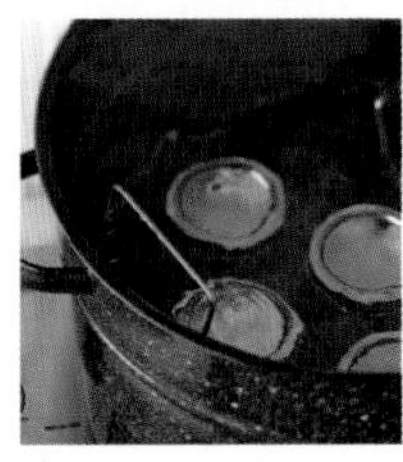

7. ONE INCH TO COVER THE LIDS
Once all the jars are in the canner, add additional hot water to cover jars by 1 inch. Process as directed.

8. REMOVE JARS
Remove jars from hot water; cool for 24 hours.

LOW-CALORIE

Zucchini Relish *(photo, page 191)*

PREP: 55 MINUTES **STAND:** 3 HOURS
COOK: 13 MINUTES **PROCESS:** 10 MINUTES
MAKES: 5 HALF-PINTS

- **5 cups finely chopped zucchini (about 4 medium)**
- **1½ cups finely chopped onion (3 medium)**
- **¾ cup finely chopped green sweet pepper (1 medium)**
- **¾ cup finely chopped red sweet pepper (1 medium)**
- **¼ cup pickling salt**
- **1¾ cups sugar**
- **1½ cups white vinegar**
- **¼ cup water**
- **1 teaspoon celery seeds**
- **1 teaspoon ground turmeric**
- **½ teaspoon mustard seeds**
- **1 to 2 drops green food coloring (optional)**

1 In a large nonmetal bowl combine zucchini, onion, and sweet peppers. Sprinkle salt over vegetables. Pour enough water (about 4 cups) over vegetables to cover. Cover; let stand for 3 hours. Transfer to a colander; rinse well.

2 In an 8- to 10-quart pot combine sugar, vinegar, the ¼ cup water, the celery seeds, turmeric, and mustard seeds. Bring to boiling; reduce heat. Simmer, uncovered, for 3 minutes. Stir in drained vegetables and, if desired, green food coloring. Return to boiling; reduce heat. Simmer, uncovered, for 10 minutes.

3 Ladle relish into hot, sterilized half-pint canning jars, leaving a ½-inch headspace. Wipe rims; adjust lids and screw bands. Process filled jars in a boiling-water canner for 10 minutes (start timing when water returns to boiling). Remove jars; cool on wire rack. (See "Canning Basics," pages 196–197.)

PER 1 TABLESPOON: 21 cal., 0 g total fat, 0 mg chol., 350 mg sodium, 5 g carb., 0 g fiber, 0 g pro. **EXCHANGES:** Free

TEST THE SEAL

After the jars have completely cooled, check the seal by pressing gently on the lids. If the lids are firm and slightly concave, the jars are properly sealed. If a lid bounces up and down, the jar is not sealed.

LOW-CALORIE

Sweet Pickle Relish

PREP: 60 MINUTES **STAND:** 2 HOURS
COOK: 10 MINUTES **PROCESS:** 10 MINUTES
MAKES: ABOUT 4 PINTS

- **6 cups finely chopped cucumbers, seeded if desired**
- **3 cups finely chopped green and/or red sweet peppers (3 medium)**
- **3 cups finely chopped onions (6 medium)**
- **¼ cup pickling salt**
- **3 cups sugar**
- **2 cups cider vinegar**
- **1 tablespoon mustard seeds**
- **2 teaspoons celery seeds**
- **½ teaspoon ground turmeric**

1 In a very large bowl combine cucumbers, sweet peppers, and onions. Sprinkle with salt; add cold water to cover. Let stand at room temperature for 2 hours.

2 Drain vegetable mixture through a colander. Rinse; drain well. In an 8-quart heavy pot combine sugar, vinegar, mustard seeds, celery seeds, and turmeric. Heat to boiling. Add vegetables; return to boiling. Cook, uncovered, over medium-high heat for 10 minutes, stirring occasionally.

3 Ladle relish into hot, sterilized pint canning jars, leaving a ½-inch headspace. Wipe the jar rims; adjust lids and screw bands. Process filled jars in a boiling-water canner for 10 minutes. Remove jars; cool on wire racks. (See "Canning Basics," pages 196–197.)

PER 1 TABLESPOON: 22 cal., 0 g total fat, 0 mg chol., 218 mg sodium, 5 g carb., 0 g fiber, 0 g pro.
EXCHANGES: ½ Other Carb.

PICKLES AND RELISHES

The right ingredients make all the difference.

CUCUMBERS: Pickling cucumbers, such as Kirby cucumbers, will make crunchier pickles than table or slicing varieties. Select unwaxed cucumbers and use them as soon as possible after harvest. Otherwise, refrigerate them or spread them out in a cool, well-ventilated area. Wash them just before canning; remove the blossoms and slice off the blossom ends.
PICKLING SALT: Use granulated pickling or canning salt as directed in recipes. Table salt might cause the pickles to darken or make the brine cloudy.
VINEGAR: Cider vinegar is often used for pickles and relishes; white vinegar can be used for a lighter-color product. Always use the vinegar specified in a recipe to ensure the proper acidity.
SPICES: Do not swap ground spices for whole spices.
WATER: Use soft or distilled water because hard water might prevent brined pickles from curing properly.

DILL PICKLES

LOW-CALORIE

Dill Pickles

PREP: 30 MINUTES **PROCESS:** 10 MINUTES
STAND: 1 WEEK **MAKES:** 6 PINTS

- **3 4-inch pickling cucumbers (about 36)**
- **3 cups water**
- **3 cups white vinegar**
- **¼ cup pickling salt**
- **¼ cup sugar**
- **6 to 12 heads fresh dill weed or 6 tablespoons dill seeds**

1 Thoroughly rinse cucumbers. Remove stems and cut off a slice from each blossom end. Leave cucumbers whole, cut into spears, or slice. In a large stainless-steel, enameled, or nonstick saucepan combine water, vinegar, salt, and sugar. Bring mixture to boiling.

2 Pack cucumbers loosely into hot, sterilized pint canning jars, leaving a ½-inch headspace. Add 1 to 2 heads of dill weed or 1 tablespoon dill seeds to each jar. Pour hot vinegar mixture over cucumbers, leaving a ½-inch headspace. Discard any remaining hot vinegar mixture. Wipe jar rims; adjust lids and screw bands.

3 Process in a boiling-water canner for 10 minutes (start timing when water returns to boil). Remove jars; cool on racks. (See "Canning Basics," pages 196–197.) Let stand 1 week.

SWEET-AND-SPICY DILL PICKLES: Prepare as directed, except substitute cider vinegar for the white vinegar and add 2 hot red chile peppers, seeded and minced, to the vinegar mixture in Step 1. When adding the heads of dill weed in Step 2, also add to each jar ½ tablespoon mustard seeds, 1 bay leaf, ½ tablespoon black peppercorns, and 1 clove garlic, halved.

DILL RELISH: Prepare as directed, except use 3 to 3¼ pounds cucumbers. Seed and finely chop enough cucumbers to equal 8 cups. Reduce water to 1½ cups and vinegar to 1½ cups. Use a 4- to 5-quart pot. Stir cucumbers into boiling vinegar mixture with 3 tablespoons dill seeds. Return to boiling. Cook, uncovered, for 5 minutes. Ladle into hot, sterilized pint canning jars, leaving ½-inch headspace. Wipe jar rims; adjust lids and screw bands. Process in a boiling-water canner for 10 minutes. Remove jars; cool on wire racks. Makes 4 pints.

PER PICKLE DILL OR SWEET-AND-SPICY VARIATION OR 1 TABLESPOON RELISH: 10 cal., 0 g total fat, 0 mg chol., 389 mg sodium, 2 g carb., 0 g fiber, 0 g pro. EXCHANGES: Free

LOW-CALORIE

Bread-and-Butter Pickles

PREP: 40 MINUTES **CHILL:** 3 HOURS
PROCESS: 10 MINUTES **MAKES:** 7 PINTS

- **4 quarts sliced medium cucumbers (16 cups)**
- **8 medium white onions, sliced**
- **⅓ cup pickling salt**
- **3 cloves garlic, halved**
- **Crushed ice**
- **4 cups sugar**
- **3 cups cider vinegar**
- **2 tablespoons mustard seeds**
- **1½ teaspoons ground turmeric**
- **1½ teaspoons celery seeds**

1 In a 6- to 8-quart stainless-steel, enameled, or nonstick pot combine cucumbers, onions, pickling salt, and garlic. Add 2 inches of crushed ice. Cover; chill for 3 to 12 hours. Remove any remaining ice. Drain mixture; remove garlic.

2 In the same pot combine sugar, vinegar, mustard seeds, turmeric, and celery seeds. Bring to boiling; add cucumber mixture. Return to boiling.

3 Pack hot cucumber mixture and liquid into hot, sterilized pint canning jars, leaving a ½-inch headspace. Wipe jar rims; adjust lids and screw bands. Process in a boiling-water canner for 10 minutes (start timing when water returns to boiling). Remove jars; cool on wire racks. (See "Canning Basics," pages 196–197.)

PER ¼ CUP: 33 cal., 0 g total fat, 0 mg chol., 200 mg sodium, 9 g carb., 0 g fiber, 0 g pro. EXCHANGES: ½ Other Carb.

Spicy-Sweet Pickled Three-Bean Salad

PREP: 60 MINUTES **STAND:** 60 MINUTES + 1 WEEK
COOK: 60 MINUTES **PROCESS:** 15 MINUTES
MAKES: 8 PINTS

- **1¼ cups dried dark red kidney beans**
- **1½ pounds green beans, trimmed and cut into 1½-inch pieces**
- **1½ pounds wax beans, trimmed and cut into 1½-inch pieces**
- **2 large onions, chopped**
- **2 large red sweet peppers, chopped**
- **2 jalapeño chile peppers, seeded and finely chopped (see tip, page 44)**
- **6 cups sugar**
- **4 cups white vinegar**
- **3 cups water**
- **1 cup cider vinegar**
- **1 cup red wine vinegar**
- **2 tablespoons pickling salt**

1 Rinse kidney beans. In a large saucepan combine kidney beans and enough water to cover. Bring to boiling; reduce heat. Simmer, uncovered, for 2 minutes. Remove from heat. Cover; let stand for 60 minutes. Drain and rinse beans. In the same saucepan combine the beans and enough water to cover. Bring to boiling; reduce heat. Cover and simmer 60 to 90 minutes or until beans are tender. Drain; let cool.

2 Fill a large pot about two-thirds full with water. Bring to boiling. Add green beans; blanch for 3 minutes. Transfer green beans to a large bowl of ice water. Repeat blanching process with wax beans. Drain green beans and wax beans from ice water. In a large bowl combine the green beans, wax beans, kidney beans, onions, sweet red peppers, and jalapeño peppers.

3 Meanwhile, in a large stainless-steel, enamel, or nonstick saucepan combine sugar, white vinegar, water, cider vinegar, red wine vinegar, and pickling salt. Bring to boiling, stirring until sugar and salt are dissolved.

4 Pack bean mixture into hot, sterilized pint jars, leaving a ½-inch headspace. Ladle hot vinegar mixture into jars, maintaining the ½-inch headspace. Discard any remaining vinegar mixture. Wipe jar rims; adjust lids and screw bands.

5 Process filled jars in a boiling-water canner for 15 minutes (start timing when water returns to boiling.) Remove jars from canner; cool on wire racks. (See "Canning Basics," pages 196–197.) Let stand at room temperature for 1 week before serving.

PER ½ CUP: 240 cal., 0 g total fat, 0 mg chol., 375 mg sodium, 53 g carb., 4 g fiber, 5 g pro. **EXCHANGES:** 1 Vegetable, ½ Starch, ½ Other Carb.

LOW-CALORIE

Pickled Garden Vegetables

PREP: 90 MINUTES **PROCESS:** 5 MINUTES
MAKES: 7 PINTS

- **1 pound carrots, peeled**
- **1 pound fresh green beans, trimmed and cut into 2-inch pieces**
- **3 cups cauliflower florets**
- **3 green and/or red sweet peppers, cut into strips**
- **2 zucchini and/or yellow summer squash, halved lengthwise and sliced ½ inch thick**
- **2 onions, cut into wedges**
- **3 cups water**
- **3 cups white wine vinegar**
- **2 tablespoons sugar**
- **1 tablespoon pickling salt**
- **3 tablespoons snipped fresh dill weed**
- **½ teaspoon crushed red pepper**
- **6 cloves garlic, minced**

1 Halve any large carrots lengthwise. Using a crinkle cutter or sharp knife, cut carrots into ¼-inch slices. In an 8-quart heavy pot combine carrots, green beans, cauliflower, sweet peppers, zucchini, and onions. Add enough water to cover. Bring to boiling. Cook, uncovered, about 3 minutes; drain.

2 In a large saucepan combine the 3 cups water, vinegar, sugar, salt, dill weed, crushed red pepper, and garlic. Bring to boiling.

3 Pack vegetables into hot, sterilized pint canning jars, leaving a ½-inch headspace. Pour vinegar mixture over vegetables, maintaining the ½-inch headspace. Wipe jar rims; adjust lids and screw bands. Process filled jars in a boiling-water canner for 5 minutes (start timing when water returns to boil). Remove jars; cool on racks. (See "Canning Basics," pages 196–197.)

PER ¼ CUP: 14 cal., 0 g total fat, 0 mg chol., 71 mg sodium, 3 g carb., 0 g fiber, 0 g pro. **EXCHANGES:** Free

BEST-LOVED LOW-CALORIE

Chunky Salsa

PREP: 2 HOURS **STAND:** 30 MINUTES
COOK: 100 MINUTES **PROCESS:** 15 MINUTES
MAKES: ABOUT 5 PINTS

- **8 pounds ripe tomatoes (about 16 medium)**
- **2 cups seeded and chopped fresh Anaheim or poblano chile peppers (2 to 3) (see tip, page 44)**
- **⅓ to ½ cup seeded and chopped fresh jalapeño chile peppers (2 large) (see tip, page 44)**
- **2 cups chopped onions (2 large)**

CHUNKY SALSA

- **½ cup snipped fresh cilantro**
- **½ cup lime juice**
- **½ cup white vinegar**
- **½ 6-ounce can tomato paste (⅓ cup)**
- **5 cloves garlic, minced**
- **1 teaspoon cumin seeds, toasted and crushed**
- **1 teaspoon salt**
- **1 teaspoon black pepper**

1 If desired, peel tomatoes (see photos 1–3, page 202). Seed, core, and coarsely chop tomatoes (you should have about 15 cups). Place tomatoes in a large colander. Let stand 30 minutes to drain.

2 Place drained tomatoes in a 7- to 8-quart stainless-steel, enameled, or nonstick heavy pot. Bring to boiling; reduce heat. Boil gently, uncovered, about 90 minutes or until desired consistency, stirring occasionally. Add chile peppers, onions, cilantro, lime juice, vinegar, tomato paste, garlic, crushed cumin, salt, and black pepper. Return mixture to boiling; reduce heat. Simmer, uncovered, for 10 minutes. Remove from heat.

3 Ladle hot salsa into hot, sterilized pint canning jars, leaving a ½-inch headspace. Wipe jar rims; adjust lids and screw bands. Process filled jars in a boiling-water canner for 15 minutes (start timing when water returns to boiling). Remove jars; cool on wire racks. (See "Canning Basics," pages 196–197.)

PER 2 TABLESPOONS: 13 cal., 0 g fat, 0 mg chol., 40 mg sodium, 3 g carb., 1 g fiber, 1 g pro. **EXCHANGES:** ½ Other Carb.

BEST-LOVED LOW-CALORIE

Triple-Pepper Hot Sauce

PREP: 45 MINUTES **COOK:** 30 MINUTES
PROCESS: 5 MINUTES **STAND:** 2 WEEKS
MAKES: FOUR 4-OUNCE JARS

- **2 cups white vinegar**
- **1½ cups finely chopped carrots (3 medium)**
- **1 cup finely chopped white onion (1 large)**
- **¼ cup lime juice**
- **3 cloves garlic, minced**
- **1 teaspoon salt**
- **½ cup finely chopped red sweet pepper (1 small)**
- **3 to 6 fresh habanero chile peppers,* seeded and finely chopped (see tip, page 44)**
- **3 fresh Fresno chile peppers, seeded and finely chopped (see tip, page 44)**
- **3 fresh Thai chile peppers, seeded and finely chopped (see tip, page 44)**

1 In a large stainless-steel, enameled, or nonstick heavy saucepan combine vinegar, carrots, onion, lime juice, garlic, and salt. Bring mixture to boiling; reduce heat. Simmer, uncovered, for 20 to 25 minutes or until carrots and onion are soft. Remove from heat; cool to room temperature.

2 Transfer carrot mixture to a blender or food processor. Add sweet pepper and habenero, Fresno, and Thai chile peppers. Cover and blend or process until smooth. Strain through a fine-mesh sieve; discard solids. Return strained mixture to saucepan. Bring to boiling over medium-high heat; reduce heat. Simmer, uncovered, for 10 minutes.

3 Ladle hot pepper sauce into hot, sterilized 4-ounce canning jars, leaving a ¼-inch headspace. Wipe jar rims; adjust lids and screw bands.

4 Process filled jars in a boiling-water canner for 5 minutes (start timing when water returns to boiling). Remove jars from canner; cool on wire racks. (See "Canning Basics," pages 196–197.) Let stand at room temperature for 2 weeks before serving.

***NOTE:** Using 3 habanero peppers will result in a medium-spice sauce, similar to a spicy Buffalo sauce. Using 6 habanero peppers will result in a much spicier sauce.

PER 1 TEASPOON: 4 cal., 0 g total fat, 0 mg chol., 23 mg sodium, 1 g carb., 0 g fiber, 0 g pro. **EXCHANGES:** Free

canning tomatoes

The Secret: Timing is everything! In late summer, when the tastiest, juiciest tomatoes appear in gardens and farmer's markets, capture their once-a-year flavor. When tomato season is over, you'll be glad you did. For more information, see the chart on page 216.

PEELING TOMATOES STEP-BY-STEP

While you're preparing the tomatoes, heat water in the canner and sterilize jars (see page 196 for more information).

1. SCORE BEFORE
With a small sharp knife, make an "X" in the blossom end of each tomato.

2. A HOT DIP
Heat a large pot of water to boiling. Gently drop in the tomatoes; simmer for 1 or 2 minutes.

3. THE EASY PEEL
Immediately plunge the tomatoes into icy water to loosen the skins. The skins will slip off easily. Cut out the stem ends with a small sharp knife.

It is best to use bottled lemon juice for canning. The pH level of bottled lemon juice is always spot-on; the pH level in fresh lemons might vary.

To ensure the skins soften evenly, gently stir the tomatoes while they are blanching.

PREP: 15 MINUTES **PROCESS:** 85 MINUTES **MAKES:** 8 PINTS OR 4 QUARTS

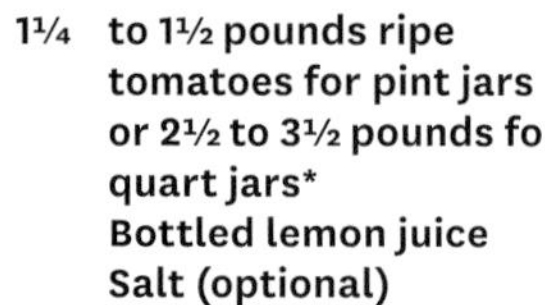

- $1\frac{1}{4}$ to $1\frac{1}{2}$ **pounds ripe tomatoes for pint jars or $2\frac{1}{2}$ to $3\frac{1}{2}$ pounds for quart jars***
- **Bottled lemon juice**
- **Salt (optional)**

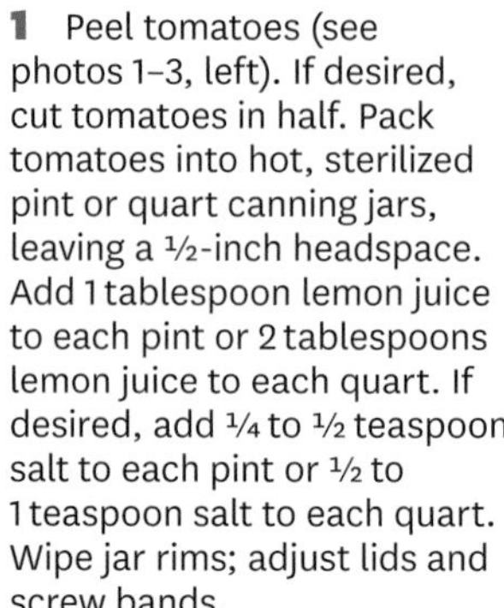

1 Peel tomatoes (see photos 1–3, left). If desired, cut tomatoes in half. Pack tomatoes into hot, sterilized pint or quart canning jars, leaving a ½-inch headspace. Add 1 tablespoon lemon juice to each pint or 2 tablespoons lemon juice to each quart. If desired, add ¼ to ½ teaspoon salt to each pint or ½ to 1 teaspoon salt to each quart. Wipe jar rims; adjust lids and screw bands.

2 Process filled pint or quart jars in a boiling-water canner for 85 minutes (start timing when water returns to boiling). Remove jars; cool on wire racks. (See "Canning Basics," pages 193–197.)

HOT-PACK TOMATOES IN WATER: Peel tomatoes (see photos 1–3, left) and, if desired, cut in half. In a pot combine tomatoes and enough water to cover. Bring to boiling; reduce heat. Simmer for 5 minutes. Pack jars with tomatoes and cooking liquid, leaving a ½-inch headspace. Add lemon juice and, if desired, salt. Wipe jar rims; adjust lids and screw bands. Process in a boiling-water canner for 40 minutes for pints, 45 minutes for quarts (start timing when water returns to boiling); remove and cool. (See "Canning Basics," pages 196–197.)

RAW-PACK TOMATOES IN WATER: Prepare tomatoes and fill jars as directed. Pour boiling water into each jar, maintaining the ½-inch headspace. Wipe jar rims; adjust lids and screw bands. Process in a boiling-water canner for 40 minutes for pints, 45 minutes for quarts (start timing when water returns to boiling); remove and cool. (See "Canning Basics," pages 196–197.)

CRUSHED TOMATOES: Peel tomatoes (see photos 1–3, left) and cut into quarters. Add enough quartered tomatoes to a large pot to cover the bottom. Crush with a wooden spoon. Bring to boiling, stirring constantly. Slowly add the remaining quartered tomatoes, stirring constantly. Simmer for 5 minutes. Pack jars with tomatoes, leaving a ½-inch headspace. Add lemon juice and, if desired, salt as directed. Wipe jar rims; adjust lids and screw bands. Process in a boiling-water canner for 35 minutes for pints, 45 minutes for quarts (start timing when water returns to boiling); remove and cool. (See "Canning Basics," pages 196–197.)

***NOTE:** Prepare only as many tomatoes as needed to fill the maximum number of jars your canner will hold at one time.

PER ¼ CUP: 13 cal., 0 g total fat, 0 mg chol., 4 mg sodium, 3 g carb., 1 g fiber, 1 g pro.
EXCHANGES: ½ Vegetable

CANNING TOMATOES STEP-BY-STEP

1. PACK, DON'T CRUSH
Pack the jar as tightly as you can with the food without crushing it. Top with any hot liquid as specified in the recipe.

2. REMOVE AIR BUBBLES
Insert a special canning tool or a thin, flexible spatula down the sides of the jar to remove air bubbles. Too many bubbles can make the headspace too large and interfere with the seal. Measure headspace (see page 195), adding or removing liquid as needed.

3. LIDS AND BANDS
Set lid on jar and screw on band no more than fingertip-tight, just tight enough that you could turn the band another 1/4 to 1/2 inch tighter. This is the key to a proper seal.

4. A CANNER RACK
As you fill each jar, set it back in the canner (filled with simmering water). This canner shown has a rack with handles to hang over the canner rim so the jars sit halfway in the water before processing them all.

5. TAKE A REST
When the processing time is up, turn off heat. Using pot holders, lift up the rack and rest handles on the sides of the canner (if your canner allows). Allow the jars to cool in place for a few minutes.

6. COOL DOWN
Remove jars from canner and set on a wire rack or towel on the countertop to cool (bare countertops can crack jars). Do not tighten bands. Allow to cool 12 to 24 hours. Test the seal (see photo, page 198).

ROASTED GARLIC PASTA SAUCE

LOW-CALORIE

Roasted Garlic Pasta Sauce

PREP: 2½ HOURS **ROAST:** 40 MINUTES AT 400°F
STAND: 15 MINUTES **COOK:** 60 MINUTES
PROCESS: 35 MINUTES **MAKES:** ABOUT 6 PINTS

- **6 bulbs garlic**
- **3 tablespoons olive oil**
- **4 medium red, yellow and/or green sweet peppers, halved and seeded**
- **12 pounds ripe tomatoes (about 25 tomatoes), peeled (see photos 1–3, page 202)**
- **3 tablespoons packed brown sugar**
- **2 tablespoons kosher salt or 4 teaspoons salt**
- **1 tablespoon balsamic vinegar**
- **1 teaspoon black pepper**
- **2 cups lightly packed fresh basil leaves, chopped**
- **1 cup lightly packed assorted fresh herbs (such as oregano, thyme, Italian parsley, or basil), chopped**
- **6 tablespoons bottled lemon juice**

1 Preheat oven to 400°F. Peel away the dry outer layers of skin from garlic bulbs, leaving skins and cloves intact. Cut off the pointed top portions (about ½ inch), leaving bulbs intact but exposing the individual cloves (see tip, page 600). Place the garlic bulbs, cut sides up, in a 1- to 1½-quart casserole. Drizzle with about 1 tablespoon of the olive oil; cover casserole. Arrange peppers, cut sides down, on a foil-lined baking sheet; brush with remaining olive oil. Roast garlic and peppers about 40 minutes or until pepper skins are charred and cloves of garlic are soft. Cool garlic on a wire rack until cool enough to handle. Pull up sides of foil and pinch together to fully enclose the peppers. Let peppers stand 15 to 20 minutes or until cool enough to handle. When peppers are cool enough to handle, peel off skins and discard. Chop peppers; set aside.

2 Remove garlic cloves from paper by squeezing the bottoms of the bulbs. Place garlic cloves in a food processor. Cut peeled tomatoes into chunks and add some of the chunks to the food processor with garlic. Cover and process until chopped. Transfer chopped garlic and tomatoes to a 7- to 8-quart stainless-steel, enameled, or nonstick heavy pot. Repeat chopping remaining tomatoes, in batches, in the food processor. Add all tomatoes to pot.

3 Add brown sugar, salt, vinegar, and black pepper to the tomato mixture. Bring to boiling. Boil steadily, uncovered, for 50 minutes, stirring occasionally. Add chopped, peeled peppers to tomato mixture. Continue boiling for 10 to 20 minutes more or until mixture is reduced to about 11 cups and reaches desired sauce consistency, stirring occasionally. Remove from heat; stir in basil and assorted herbs.

4 Spoon 1 tablespoon lemon juice into each of six hot, sterilized pint canning jars. Ladle sauce into jars with lemon juice, leaving a ½-inch headspace. Wipe the jar rims; adjust lids and screw bands. Process filled jars in a boiling-water canner for 35 minutes (start time when water returns to boiling). Remove jars; cool on wire racks. (See "Canning Basics," pages 196–197.)

PER ½ CUP: 95 cal., 3 g total fat (0 g sat. fat), 0 mg chol., 542 mg sodium, 17 g carb., 4 g fiber, 3 g pro.
EXCHANGES: 1½ Vegetable, ½ Other Carb., ½ Fat

BEST-LOVED

Lemony Tomato-Basil Soup

PREP: 45 MINUTES **COOK:** 85 MINUTES
PROCESS: 35 MINUTES **MAKES:** 5 PINTS

- **¼ cup butter**
- **2 tablespoons olive oil**
- **4 cups finely chopped onions (4 large) or leeks (12 medium)**
- **2¼ cups finely chopped carrots**
- **1 cup finely chopped celery (2 stalks)**
- **6 cloves garlic, minced**
- **10 pounds ripe roma tomatoes, chopped**
- **¼ cup sugar**

- 4 **teaspoons kosher salt**
- 1 **cup lightly packed fresh basil or Italian parsley leaves, snipped**
- 2 **tablespoons finely shredded lemon peel**
- ¾ **cup bottled lemon juice**

1 In a 7- to 8-quart stainless-steel, enameled, or nonstick heavy pot heat butter and oil over medium heat. Add onions, carrots, celery, and garlic. Cook about 20 minutes or until tender, stirring occasionally. Stir in tomatoes, sugar, and salt. Bring to boiling over medium-high heat, stirring occasionally; reduce heat. Simmer, uncovered, for 20 minutes.

2 Press tomato mixture through a food mill or sieve; discard skins and seeds. Return strained mixture to pot. Bring mixture to boiling; reduce heat. Simmer, uncovered, about 45 minutes or until reduced to about 10 cups. Remove from heat. Stir in basil, lemon peel, and lemon juice.

3 Ladle hot soup into hot, sterilized pint canning jars, leaving a ½-inch headspace. Wipe jar rims; adjust lids and screw bands.

4 Process filled jars in a boiling-water canner for 35 minutes (start timing when water returns to boiling). Remove jars from canner; cool on wire racks. (See "Canning Basics," pages 196–197.)

PER 1 CUP: 204 cal., 8 g total fat (3 g sat. fat), 12 mg chol., 875 mg sodium, 32 g carb., 7 g fiber, 5 g pro.
EXCHANGES: 5 Vegetable, 1½ Fat

Spicy Ginger Red-Hot Pears

(photo, page 191)

PREP: 20 MINUTES **PROCESS:** 20 MINUTES
MAKES: 6 PINTS

- 6 **pounds firm, ripe pears**
  Ascorbic acid color-keeper
- 4½ **cups water**
- 2 **cups sugar**
- 6 **cinnamon sticks**
- 6 **tablespoons chopped fresh ginger**
- 12 **teaspoons red cinnamon candies**

1 Peel, halve, core, and cut pears into wedges, placing wedges in an ascorbic acid solution (follow package directions) as you slice them to prevent browning.

2 In a 6- to 8-quart heavy pot combine the water and sugar. Cook and stir over medium heat until sugar is dissolved. Drain pears; add to syrup in pot. Return to boiling; reduce heat. Simmer, uncovered, about 4 minutes or until pears are nearly tender, stirring occasionally.

3 Place 1 cinnamon stick, 1 tablespoon ginger, and 2 teaspoons cinnamon candies in each of six hot, sterilized pint canning jars. Ladle hot pears and syrup into jars with spices, leaving a ½-inch headspace (there will be syrup left over). Wipe jar rims; adjust lids and screw bands.

4 Process filled jars in a boiling-water canner for 20 minutes (start timing when water returns to boiling). Remove jars from canner; cool on wire racks. (See "Canning Basics," pages 196–197.)

PER ½ CUP: 122 cal., 0 g total fat, 0 mg chol., 3 mg sodium, 32 g carb., 3 g fiber, 0 g pro. **EXCHANGES:** 1 Fruit, 1 Other Carb.

Honey-Lavender Peaches

PREP: 1 HOUR **PROCESS:** 25 MINUTES
MAKES: 8 QUARTS OR 12 PINTS

- 14 **to 15 pounds ripe peaches**
- 4 **cups water**
- 1¾ **cups honey**
- ⅔ **cup Riesling or other sweet white wine**
- 1 **tablespoon dried lavender buds**
- ½ **teaspoon salt**
- 1 **lemon**

1 Bring a large pan of water to boiling. Working in batches, carefully lower peaches into boiling water for 30 to 60 seconds or until skins start to split. Using a slotted spoon, transfer peaches to a large bowl of ice water. When cool enough to handle, remove peaches from ice water. Using a small sharp knife, peel skin off peaches. Cut peaches in half lengthwise; remove and discard pits (if using pint jars, quarter and pit peaches).

2 In a Dutch oven combine the 4 cups water, honey, wine, lavender, and salt. Cook and stir over medium heat until honey is dissolved.

3 Using a vegetable peeler, cut 2- to 3-inch strips of peel from lemon, scraping off any white portions with a paring knife. Reserve the lemon for another use.

4 Pack peaches, cut sides down, and lemon peel into hot, sterilized quart or pint canning jars, leaving a ½-inch headspace. Ladle hot syrup over peaches, distributing lavender buds evenly among jars and maintaining the ½-inch headspace. Wipe jar rims; adjust lids and screw bands.

5 Process filled jars in a boiling-water canner for 25 minutes for quarts, 20 minutes for pints (start timing when water returns to boiling). Remove jars from canner; cool on wire racks. (See "Canning Basics," pages 196–197.)

PER ½ CUP: 77 cal., 0 g total fat, 0 mg chol., 22 mg sodium, 19 g carb., 2 g fiber, 1 g pro. **EXCHANGES:** 1 Fruit, ½ Other Carb.

LOW-CALORIE

Rosy Fruit Cocktail

PREP: 1 HOUR **PROCESS:** 20 MINUTES
MAKES: 9 PINTS

- **5¼ cups Light Syrup**
- **1 2-pound pineapple**
- **3 pounds peaches**
- **3 pounds pears**
- **1 pound dark sweet cherries**
- **1 pound seedless green grapes**

1 Prepare Light Syrup (measure 5¼ cups; may not use all of the syrup); keep hot but not boiling.

2 Wash fruit. Using a large sharp knife, slice off the bottom stem end and the green top from the pineapple. Stand pineapple on one cut end and slice off the skin from top to bottom; discard skin. To remove the eyes, cut diagonally around the fruit, following the pattern of the eyes and making narrow wedge-shape grooves into the pineapple. Cut pineapple in half lengthwise; place pieces cut sides down and cut lengthwise again. Cut off and discard core from each quarter. Finely chop pineapple. Measure 3 cups pineapple. Peel, pit, and cut peaches into cubes. Measure 8½ cups peaches. Peel, core, and cut pears into cubes. Measure 6½ cups pears. Halve and pit cherries. Measure 2½ cups cherries. Remove stems from grapes. Measure 3 cups grapes.

3 In a 4- to 6-quart pot combine pineapple, peaches, pears, cherries, and grapes. Add hot syrup; bring to boiling.

4 Ladle hot fruit and syrup into hot, sterilized pint canning jars, leaving a ½-inch headspace. Wipe jar rims; adjust lids and screw bands. Process filled jars in a boiling-water canner for 20 minutes (start timing when water returns to boiling). Remove jars from canner; cool on wire racks. (See "Canning Basics," pages 196–197.)

LIGHT SYRUP: In a large saucepan cook and stir 1¼ cups sugar and 5 cups water over medium heat until sugar dissolves.

PER ½ CUP: 108 cal., 0 g total fat, 0 mg chol., 1 mg sodium, 27 g carb., 2 g fiber, 1 g pro. EXCHANGES: 1 Fruit, 1 Other Carb.

LOW-CALORIE

Applesauce *(photo, page 191)*

PREP: 1 HOUR **COOK:** 25 MINUTES
PROCESS: 15 MINUTES **MAKES:** ABOUT 6 PINTS

- **8 pounds cooking apples, cored and quartered (24 cups)**
- **2 cups water**
- **¼ cup fresh lemon juice, strained**
- **¾ to 1¼ cups granulated sugar**

1 In an 8- to 10-quart heavy pot combine apples, water, and lemon juice. Bring to boiling; reduce heat. Simmer, covered, for 25 to 30 minutes or until apples are very tender, stirring often.

2 Press apples through a food mill or sieve. Return pulp to pot; discard skins. Stir in sugar to taste. If necessary, add ½ to 1 cup water for desired consistency. Bring to boiling.

3 Ladle hot applesauce into hot, sterilized pint canning jars, leaving a ½-inch headspace. Wipe jar rims; adjust lids and screw bands. Process in a boiling-water canner for 15 minutes for pints and 20 minutes for quarts (start timing when water returns to boil). Remove jars; cool on racks. (See "Canning Basics," pages 196–197.)

SPICED APPLESAUCE: Prepare as directed, except add 10 inches stick cinnamon and 1½ teaspoons apple pie spice in Step 1. Simmer as directed; remove stick cinnamon and discard. Substitute ¾ cup packed brown sugar for the granulated sugar. Stir in enough additional brown sugar to taste (¼ to ¾ cup).

VERY BERRY APPLESAUCE: Prepare as directed, except replace 1 pound (4 cups) of the apples with 1 pound (4 cups) fresh or frozen thawed raspberries and/or strawberries and decrease water to 1½ cups in Step 1.

FREEZER DIRECTIONS: Place pot of applesauce in a sink filled with ice water; stir mixture to cool. Ladle into wide-mouth freezer containers, leaving a ½-inch headspace. Seal and label; freeze for up to 8 months. (See "Freezing Basics," pages 212–213.)

PER ½ CUP PLAIN, SPICED, OR BERRY VARIATIONS: 81 cal., 0 g total fat, 0 mg chol., 1 mg sodium, 21 g carb., 2 g fiber, 0 g pro. EXCHANGES: 1 Fruit, ½ Other Carb.

ALTITUDE ADJUSTMENT

The timings in these recipes are for altitudes up to 1,000 feet above sea level. Water boils at lower temperatures at higher altitudes, so follow these directions:

BLANCHING: Add 1 minute if you live 5,000 feet or more above sea level.

BOILING-WATER CANNING: Call your county extension service for detailed instructions.

JELLIES AND JAMS: Add 1 minute processing time for each additional 1,000 feet

STERILIZING JARS: Boil jars an additional 1 minute for each additional 1,000 feet.

Apple Butter

PREP: 45 MINUTES **COOK:** 2 HOURS
PROCESS: 5 MINUTES **MAKES:** 6 HALF-PINTS

- **4½ pounds tart cooking apples, cored and quartered (about 14 medium)**
- **3 cups apple cider or apple juice**
- **2 cups granulated sugar**
- **2 tablespoons fresh lemon juice, strained**
- **½ teaspoon ground cinnamon**

1 In an 8- to 10-quart heavy pot combine apples and cider. Bring to boiling; reduce heat. Simmer, covered, for 30 minutes, stirring occasionally. Press apple mixture through a food mill or sieve until you have 7½ cups. Return pulp to pot.

2 Stir in sugar, lemon juice, and cinnamon. Bring to boiling; reduce heat. Cook, uncovered, over very low heat for 1½ to 1¾ hours or until very thick and mixture mounds on a spoon, stirring often.

3 Ladle hot apple butter into hot, sterilized half-pint canning jars, leaving a ¼-inch headspace. Wipe jar rims; adjust lids and screw bands. Process filled jars in a boiling-water canner for 5 minutes (start timing when water returns to boiling). Remove jars from canner; cool on wire racks. (See "Canning Basics," pages 196–197.)

APPLE-PEAR BUTTER: Prepare as directed, except substitute 2 pounds cored, quartered ripe pears for 2 pounds of the apples.

CARAMEL APPLE BUTTER: Prepare as directed, except decrease granulated sugar to ½ cup and add 1½ cups packed brown sugar.

FREEZER DIRECTIONS: Place pot of apple butter in a sink filled with ice water; stir mixture to cool. Ladle into wide-top freezer containers, leaving a ½-inch headspace. Seal and label; freeze up to 10 months. Apple butter may darken slightly on freezing. (See "Freezing Basics," pages 212–213.)

PER 1 TABLESPOON PLAIN, APPLE-PEAR, OR CARAMEL APPLE VARIATIONS: 28 cal., 0 g total fat, 0 mg chol., 0 mg sodium, 7 g carb., 0 g fiber, 0 g pro. EXCHANGES: ½ Other Carb.

IS IT READY?

You'll know your fruit butter is finished simmering when it has thickened enough to mound on a spoon.

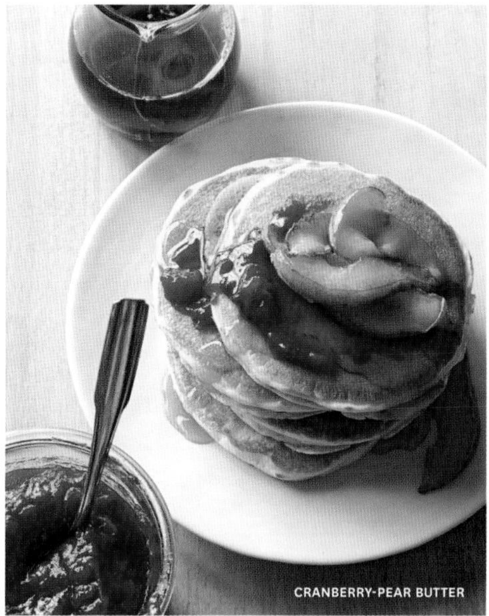
CRANBERRY-PEAR BUTTER

BEST-LOVED

Cranberry-Pear Butter

PREP: 25 MINUTES **COOK:** 35 MINUTES
PROCESS: 5 MINUTES **MAKES:** 6 HALF-PINTS

- **3 pounds ripe pears, peeled, cored, and cubed**
- **2 12-ounce packages cranberries**
- **¼ cup water**
- **2 cups sugar**
- **1 tablespoon ground cinnamon**
- **¼ teaspoon ground cloves**

1 In a 5- to 6-quart heavy pot combine pears, cranberries, and the water. Bring to boiling; reduce heat. Simmer, covered, about 15 minutes or until cranberry skins pop and pears are disintegrated, stirring occasionally.

2 Stir in sugar, cinnamon, and cloves. Return to boiling; reduce heat. Simmer, uncovered, for 20 to 22 minutes or until mixture is very thick and mounds on a spoon, stirring often.

3 Ladle into hot, sterilized half-pint canning jars, leaving a ¼-inch headspace. Wipe jar rims; adjust lids and screw bands.

4 Process filled jars in a boiling-water canner for 5 minutes (start timing when water returns to boiling). Remove jars from canner; cool on wire racks. (See "Canning Basics," pages 196–197.)

PER 2 TABLESPOONS: 48 cal., 0 g total fat, 0 mg chol., 0 mg sodium, 13 g carb., 1 g fiber, 0 g pro. EXCHANGES: ½ Fruit, ½ Other Carb.

cook's secrets

strawberry jam

The Secret: Use the right kind of pectin and the freshest, plumpest strawberries you can find.

PREP: 35 MINUTES **PROCESS:** 5 MINUTES **MAKES:** ABOUT 7 HALF-PINTS

- **12 cups fresh hulled strawberries**
- **1 1.75-ounce package regular powdered fruit pectin or 6 tablespoons classic powdered fruit pectin**
- **½ teaspoon butter**
- **7 cups sugar**

Be sure to use this type of pectin for this recipe. When making jams, always use the type of pectin specified in the recipe.

1 Place 1 cup of the strawberries in an 8-quart heavy pot. Using a potato masher, crush berries. Continue adding and crushing berries. Measure 5 cups crushed berries. Stir in pectin and butter. Place mixture over high heat, stirring constantly, until mixture comes to a full rolling boil. Add sugar all at once. Return to boiling; boil 1 minute, stirring constantly. Remove from heat; skim off foam with a metal spoon.

2 Ladle at once into hot, sterilized half-pint canning jars, leaving a ¼-inch headspace. Wipe jar rims; adjust lids and screw bands. Process in a boiling-water canner for 5 minutes (start timing when water returns to boiling). Remove jars; cool on racks. (See "Canning Basics," pages 196–197.) To distribute fruit, cool for 20 minutes; turn jars. Repeat as needed.

RASPBERRY JAM: Prepare as directed, except use 3 quarts fresh raspberries for the strawberries. If desired, press half of the 5 cups crushed berries through a sieve before stirring in the pectin and butter.

PER 1 TABLESPOON STRAWBERRY OR RASPBERRY VARIATION: 54 cal., 0 g total fat, 0 mg chol., 0 mg sodium, 14 g carb., 0 g fiber, 0 g pro. EXCHANGES: 1 Other Carb.

MAKING JAM STEP-BY-STEP

Making jam is fairly simple. Follow these steps when making a jam or jelly that calls for pectin.

1. BRING TO A ROLLING BOIL
Unless otherwise specified in the recipe, bring mixture to a full rolling boil. (This occurs when the bubbles break the surface so rapidly you can't stir them down.)

2. SKIM AWAY
To skim off foam, gently glide a metal spoon over the surface of the jam. Discard the foam.

3. AN EASY FILL
Ladle mixture into a wide-mouth funnel to cleanly fill the jars.

4. HEADSPACE IS KEY
When filling jars, leave the recommended headspace (the space between the top of the jam and the rim). Use a clean, damp cloth to wipe jar rims.

5. A MAGIC WAND
Using a magnetic wand, place hot sterilized lids on jars. Gently adjust screw bands over lids.

6. KEEP FRUIT IN EVERY BITE
After about 20 minutes of cooling, turn sealed jars over to help distribute fruit.

Grape Jam

PREP: 65 MINUTES **COOK:** 38 MINUTES
PROCESS: 5 MINUTES **MAKES:** ABOUT 6 HALF-PINTS

- **3 to 3½ pounds Concord grapes**
- **2 cups water**
- **4½ cups sugar**

1 Wash and stem grapes. Measure 8 cups. Remove skins from half of the grapes (see photo 1, below); set grape skins aside.

2 In an 8- to 10-quart heavy pot combine all the grapes. Cover and cook 10 minutes or until very soft. Press grapes through a sieve or food mill (see photo 2, below); discard seeds and cooked skins. Measure 3 cups strained pulp; return to pot. Stir in the uncooked grape skins and water. Cook, covered, for 10 minutes. Uncover; stir in sugar. Bring mixture to a full rolling boil, stirring often (see photo 3, below). Boil, uncovered, for 18 to 24 minutes or until jam sheets off a metal spoon (see photo 4, below).

3 Remove pot from heat; quickly skim off foam with a metal spoon (see photo 5, below). Ladle at once into hot, sterilized half-pint canning jars, leaving a ¼-inch headspace. Wipe jar rims; adjust lids and screw bands. Process in a boiling-water canner for 5 minutes (start timing when water returns to boiling). Remove jars; cool on wire racks until set. (See "Canning Basics," pages 196–197.)

PER 1 TABLESPOON: 42 cal., 0 g total fat, 0 mg chol., 0 mg sodium, 11 g carb., 0 g fiber, 0 g pro.
EXCHANGES: 1 Other Carb.

Peach Jam *(photo, page 191)*

PREP: 30 MINUTES **PROCESS:** 5 MINUTES
MAKES: ABOUT 7 HALF-PINTS

- **7 cups sugar**
- **4 cups finely chopped, peeled ripe peaches* (about 3 pounds fresh or 2 pounds frozen, thawed)**
- **¼ cup lemon juice**
- **½ of a 6-ounce package liquid fruit pectin (1 foil pouch)**

1 In a 6- to 8-quart heavy pot combine sugar, peaches, and lemon juice. Bring to boiling, stirring constantly until sugar dissolves. Quickly stir in pectin. Bring to a full rolling boil, stirring constantly. Boil hard for 1 minute, stirring constantly. Remove from heat. Quickly skim off foam with a metal spoon.

2 Ladle hot jam into hot, sterilized half-pint canning jars, leaving a ¼-inch headspace. Wipe jar rims; adjust lids and screw bands.

3 Process filled jars in a boiling-water canner for 5 minutes (start timing when water returns to boiling). Remove jars from canner; cool on wire racks. (See "Canning Basics," pages 196–197.) To distribute fruit, cool about 20 minutes; gently turn jars. Repeat as needed.

CARDAMOM-PEACH JAM: Prepare as directed, except stir in ¾ teaspoon freshly ground cardamom after skimming off foam.

***NOTE:** If desired, place small batches of peeled and cut-up peaches in a food processor. Cover and pulse until peaches are finely chopped.

PER 1 TABLESPOON PEACH OR CARDAMOM-PEACH VARIATION: 54 cal., 0 g total fat, 0 mg chol., 0 mg sodium, 14 g carb., 0 g fiber, 0 g pro. EXCHANGES: 1 Other Carb.

MAKING CONCORD GRAPE JAM STEP-BY-STEP

1. To remove skins from half of the grapes, squeeze grape until the pulp pops out. Set skins aside.

2. Press cooked grapes through a sieve or food mill to remove cooked skins and seeds.

3. A full rolling boil occurs when the bubbles break the surface so rapidly you can't stir them down.

4. When the mixture is ready, it will slide in sheets (rather than drips) from a metal spoon.

5. Gently scoop the foam off the top with a spoon.

Orange Marmalade

PREP: 55 MINUTES **COOK:** 31 MINUTES
PROCESS: 5 MINUTES **STAND:** 2 WEEKS
MAKES: 6 HALF-PINTS

- **4 medium oranges**
- **1 medium lemon**
- **1½ cups water**
- **⅛ teaspoon baking soda**
- **5 cups sugar**
- **½ of a 6-ounce package (1 foil pouch) liquid fruit pectin**

1 Score orange and lemon peels into four lengthwise sections; remove peels. Scrape off white portions; discard. Cut peels into thin strips. In a large saucepan bring peels, water, and baking soda to boiling. Cover; simmer for 20 minutes. Do not drain. Section fruits (see tip, page 19), reserving juices; discard seeds. Add fruits and juices to peels; return to boiling. Cover; simmer 10 minutes (should have about 3 cups mixture).

2 In a 10-quart heavy pot combine fruit mixture and sugar. Bring to a full rolling boil (see photo 3, page 209), stirring constantly. Quickly stir in pectin. Return to a full rolling boil; boil for 1 minute, stirring constantly. Remove from heat; skim off foam with a metal spoon (see photo 5, page 209).

3 Ladle marmalade into hot, sterilized half-pint canning jars, leaving a ¼-inch headspace. Wipe jar rims; adjust lids and screw bands. Process in a boiling-water canner for 5 minutes (start timing when water returns to boil). Remove jars; cool on wire racks. (See "Canning Basics," pages 196–197.) Allow the marmalade to stand for 2 weeks before serving.

STRAWBERRY-LEMON MARMALADE: Prepare as directed, except omit oranges and increase to 2 lemons. Reduce water to ½ cup. Measure 3 cups crushed hulled strawberries. Stir into mixture with the lemon sections in Step 1.

PER 1 TABLESPOON ORANGE OR STRAWBERRY-LEMON VARIATION: 44 cal., 0 g total fat, 0 mg chol., 2 mg sodium, 11 g carb., 0 g fiber, 0 g pro. EXCHANGES: 1 Other Carb.

Blueberry-Maple-Pecan Conserve

PREP: 20 MINUTES **COOK:** 35 MINUTES
PROCESS: 10 MINUTES **MAKES:** 5 HALF-PINTS

- **4 cups blueberries**
- **1 cup water**
- **1 cup pure maple syrup**
- **2 tablespoons lemon juice**
- **2 cups packed brown sugar**

BLUEBERRY-MAPLE-PECAN CONSERVE

- **1 cup dried currants**
- **1 cup chopped pecans**
- **1 teaspoon ground cinnamon**

1 In a 4- to 6-quart heavy pot combine blueberries, the water, maple syrup, and lemon juice. Using a potato masher, slightly crush the blueberries. Bring to boiling; reduce heat. Simmer, covered, for about 5 minutes or until blueberries are tender, stirring occasionally.

2 Stir the brown sugar and currants into blueberry mixture. Return to boiling, stirring until brown sugar dissolves; reduce heat. Simmer, uncovered, for about 30 minutes or until mixture thickens, stirring occasionally. Remove from heat. Stir in pecans and cinnamon.

3 Ladle hot conserve into hot, sterilized half-pint canning jars, leaving a ¼-inch headspace. Wipe jar rims; adjust lids and screw bands.

4 Process in a boiling-water canner for 10 minutes (start timing when water returns to boiling). Remove jars from canner; cool on wire racks. (See "Canning Basics," pages 196–197.)

PER 2 TABLESPOONS: 100 cal., 2 g total fat (0 g sat. fat), 0 mg chol., 4 mg sodium, 21 g carb., 1 g fiber, 1 g pro. EXCHANGES: ½ Fruit, 1 Other Carb., ½ Fat

Apricot-Rosemary Jelly *(photo, page 193)*

PREP: 50 MINUTES **COOK:** 20 MINUTES
PROCESS: 5 MINUTES **MAKES:** 8 HALF-PINTS

- **5 pounds ripe apricots**
- **4½ cups water**
- **3 3-inch sprigs fresh rosemary**
- **1 1.75-ounce package regular powdered fruit pectin or 6 tablespoons classic powdered fruit pectin**
- **7½ cups sugar**
- **8 small sprigs fresh rosemary (optional)**

1 Stem, pit, and coarsely chop apricots. Measure 18 cups chopped apricots. In a large pot combine the 18 cups chopped apricots, the water, and 3-inch rosemary sprigs. Bring mixture to simmering. Cook, covered, about 20 minutes or until apricots are soft; cool slightly. Strain mixture through a damp jelly bag or several layers of damp 100%-cotton cheesecloth to extract the juice; discard solids. Measure exactly 5½ cups juice, adding additional water if necessary.

2 Transfer the 5½ cups juice to a 6- to 8-quart heavy pot. Stir in pectin. Bring mixture to a full rolling boil (see photo 3, page 209), stirring constantly. Stir in sugar. Return to a full rolling boil, stirring constantly. Boil hard for 1 minute, stirring constantly. Remove from heat. Quickly skim off foam with a metal spoon (see photo 5, page 209).

3 Ladle hot jelly into hot, sterilized half-pint canning jars, leaving a ¼-inch headspace. If desired, add a small rosemary sprig to each jar. Wipe jar rims; adjust lids and screw bands.

4 Process filled jars in a boiling-water canner for 5 minutes (start timing when water returns to boiling). Remove jars from canner; cool on wire racks. (See "Canning Basics," pages 196–197.)

PER 1 TABLESPOON: 59 cal., 0 g total fat, 0 mg chol., 1 mg sodium, 15 g carb., 0 g fiber, 0 g pro.
EXCHANGES: 1 Other Carb.

PECTIN PRIMER

A natural substance found in many fruits, pectin gives jams, preserves, and jellies their desired thickness and body; without it, your jams and jellies would be more like fruit soup than something you could spread on a scone. Some fruits, such as apples and grapes, contain enough pectin to thicken jams on their own; others need a little boost. Pectin comes in both powdered and liquid forms. For the best results, use the exact type of pectin specified in recipes.

FRUIT JUICE JELLY

FAST

Fruit Juice Jelly

PREP: 25 MINUTES **PROCESS:** 5 MINUTES
MAKES: 5 HALF-PINTS

- **4 cups cranberry juice (not low-calorie) or unsweetened apple, grape, or orange juice**
- **¼ cup bottled lemon juice**
- **1 1.75-ounce package regular powdered fruit pectin or 6 tablespoons classic powdered fruit pectin**
- **4½ cups sugar**

1 Pour desired fruit juice and lemon juice into a 6- to 8-quart heavy kettle or pot. Sprinkle with pectin. Let stand for 1 to 2 minutes; stir to dissolve pectin. Bring to a full rolling boil over medium-high heat, stirring frequently. Stir in sugar. Return to a full rolling boil, stirring frequently. Boil hard for 1 minute, stirring constantly. Remove from heat; skim off foam with a metal spoon (see photo 5, page 209).

2 Ladle jelly at once into hot, sterilized half-pint canning jars, leaving a ¼-inch headspace. Wipe jar rims; adjust lids and screw bands. Process filled jars in a boiling-water canner for 5 minutes (start timing when water returns to boil). Remove jars from canner; cool on wire racks until set. (See "Canning Basics," pages 196–197.)

PER 1 TABLESPOON: 68 cal., 0 g fat, 0 mg chol., 2 mg sodium, 18 g carb., 0 g fiber, 0 g pro. **EXCHANGES:** 1 Other Carb.

freezing basics

Freezing is an easy way to enjoy fresh fruits and vegetables from gardens or farmer's markets well into the winter. For best results, use top-quality, garden-fresh produce and follow these guidelines.

EQUIPMENT

PANS AND UTENSILS: To freeze vegetables and fruits, you need a colander and a large pot or saucepan that has a wire basket. An accurate freezer thermometer will help you regulate your freezer temperature to 0°F or below.

FREEZER CONTAINERS

When freezing foods, use containers and packing materials that are durable, easy to seal, resistant to cracking at low temperatures, and moisture- and vapor-resistant. Choose the right size container for your volume of food; wasted space can lead to oxidation and freezer burn. Remember that foods containing water expand when frozen, so make sure the containers are expandable or leave enough headspace to allow for expansion. The following options are suitable for frozen foods.

RIGID CONTAINERS: Use sealable, rigid glass or plastic containers designed for freezing.

CANNING JARS: Select canning jars approved for freezing—this information is clearly noted on the jar packaging. Use only wide-mouth glass jars; jars with necks can crack more easily as contents expand. To allow for food expansion, do not fill jars above the 1-inch line.

PLASTIC FREEZER BAGS: Use bags designated for freezing, such as resealable bags and vacuum freezer bags. These are made of thicker material than regular plastic bags and are more resistant to moisture and oxygen. In lieu of a vacuum sealer, use a straw to suck air out of bags.

GENERAL FREEZING STEPS

1 For freezing, select fruits and vegetables that are at their peak of maturity. Hold produce in the refrigerator if it can't be frozen immediately. Rinse and drain small quantities through several changes of cold water. Lift fruits and vegetables out of the water; do not let them soak. Prepare cleaned produce for freezing as specified in the charts on pages 216–218.

2 Blanch vegetables (and fruits when directed) by scalding them in boiling water for specified time (see photo 1, page 213). This stops or slows enzymes that can cause loss of flavor and color and toughen the food. Do not blanch in the microwave because it might not inactivate some enzymes. Timings vary with vegetable type and size.

Blanching is a heat-and-cool process. First fill a large pot with water, using 1 gallon of water per 1 pound of prepared food. Heat to boiling. Add prepared food to the boiling water (or place it in a wire basket and lower it into the water); cover. Start timing immediately. Cook over high heat for the time specified in the charts (see pages 216–218). (Add 1 minute if you live 5,000 feet or higher above sea level.) Near the end of the time, fill your sink or a large container with ice water. When blanching time is complete, use a slotted spoon to remove the food from the boiling water (or lift the wire basket out of the water). Immediately plunge the food into the ice water. Chill for the same amount of time it was boiled; drain.

3 Spoon the cooled, drained food into freezer containers or bags (see photo 3, below), leaving specified headspace (see tip, page 195). Fruits often are frozen with added sugar or liquid for better texture and flavor. For more information, refer to the chart introduction on page 217. Pack as directed in recipes. Here are the packing methods referred to in the charts on pages 216–218.

UNSWEETENED OR DRY PACK: Do not add sugar or liquid to fruit; simply pack in a container. This is best for small whole fruits, such as berries.

WATER PACK: Cover the fruit with water or unsweetened fruit juice. Do not use glass jars. Maintain the recommended headspace.

SUGAR PACK: Place a small amount of fruit in the container and sprinkle lightly with sugar; repeat layering. Cover and let stand about 15 minutes or until juicy; seal.

SYRUP PACK: Cover fruit with a syrup of sugar and water. For a very thin syrup, use 1 cup sugar and 4 cups water to yield about 4 cups syrup. For a thin syrup, use 1⅔ cups sugar and 4 cups water to yield about 4¼ cups syrup. For a medium syrup, use 2⅔ cups sugar and 4 cups water to yield about 4⅔ cups syrup. For a heavy syrup, use 4 cups sugar and 4 cups water to yield about 5¾ cups syrup.

4 If using containers, wipe rims. Seal bags or containers according to manufacturer's directions, pressing out as much air as possible (see photo 4, below). If necessary, use freezer tape around container lid edges for a tight seal.

5 Label each container or bag with its contents, amount, and date (see photo 5, below). Lay bags flat; add packages to the freezer in batches to make sure food freezes quickly. Leave space between packages so air can circulate around them. When frozen solid, the packages can be placed closer together.

USING FROZEN FOODS

Vegetables are best cooked from a frozen state, without thawing them first. Thaw fruits in their containers either in the refrigerator or in a bowl of cold water. Meats, soups, and casseroles should be thawed in the refrigerator for a day or two, in the microwave oven on defrost, or in a leakproof plastic bag immersed in cold water (change water every 30 minutes). Use frozen fruits and vegetables within 8 to 10 months.

FREEZING CORN, STEP-BY-STEP

1. Place produce, a few pieces at a time, in a large pot of boiling water; cook for times specified in the charts on pages 216–218. Remove and plunge into a bowl of ice water.

2. When food is cool, remove from ice water and cut into small pieces. For corn, cut kernels from cob using a downward motion with a sharp knife.

3. Spoon produce into freezer-safe bags or containers.

4. Squeeze air from bags and seal.

5. Label each container with contents, amount, and date.

Strawberry Freezer Jam

When berries, peaches, pears, and other fresh fruits appear at farmer's markets, transform them into easy-to-make freezer jams.

PREP: 35 MINUTES **STAND:** 24 HOURS
MAKES: 80 SERVINGS

- **4 cups strawberries**
- **4 cups sugar**
- **$\frac{1}{2}$ teaspoon finely shredded lemon peel**
- **1 1.75-ounce package regular powdered fruit pectin or 6 tablespoons classic powdered fruit pectin**
- **$\frac{3}{4}$ cup water**

1 In a large bowl use a potato masher to crush the berries until you have 2 cups. Mix berries, sugar, and lemon peel. Let stand for 10 minutes, stirring occasionally. In a small saucepan combine pectin and water. Bring to boiling over high heat; boil 1 minute, stirring constantly. Remove from heat and add to berry mixture; stir about 3 minutes or until sugar dissolves and mixture is no longer grainy.

2 Ladle into half-pint freezer containers, leaving a $\frac{1}{2}$-inch headspace. Seal and label. Let stand at room temperature for 24 hours or until set. Store up to 3 weeks in the refrigerator or for up to 1 year in the freezer. (See "Freezing Basics," pages 212–213.)

PER 1 TABLESPOON: 41 cal., 0 g total fat, 0 mg chol., 0 mg sodium, 11 g carb., 0 g fiber, 0 g pro. **EXCHANGES:** 1 Other Carb.

8 to try

SPICED PEACH: Start with 6 peaches; peel, pit and finely chop. Measure 3 cups. Omit lemon peel and use 2 tablespoons lemon juice. Increase sugar to $4\frac{1}{2}$ cups and stir in $\frac{1}{2}$ teaspoon apple pie spice with the sugar. Makes 5 half-pints.

SPICED BLUEBERRY: Start with 5 cups blueberries; mash and measure 3 cups. Increase sugar to $5\frac{1}{4}$ cups. Stir in 1 teaspoon ground cinnamon with the sugar. Makes 7 half-pints.

BLACKBERRY-LIME: Start with 6 cups blackberries; mash and measure 3 cups. Increase sugar to $5\frac{1}{4}$ cups. Substitute lime peel for the lemon peel. Makes 7 half-pints.

RASPBERRY-ORANGE: Start with 6 cups raspberries; mash and measure 3 cups. Increase sugar to $5\frac{1}{4}$ cups. Substitute orange peel for the lemon peel. Makes 6 half-pints.

TROPICAL: Start with 4 mangoes; seed, peel and cube. Mash the mangoes and measure 3 cups. Omit lemon peel and use $\frac{1}{4}$ cup pineapple juice. Increase sugar to 5 cups. Makes 6 half-pints.

PEAR-BERRY: Core, peel, and finely chop 2 pounds ripe pears; measure 3 cups chopped pear. Add 1 cup crushed raspberries. Increase sugar to 5 cups. Makes 6 half-pints.

CHERRY-BERRY: Stem, pit, and finely chop 1 pound tart red cherries; measure $1\frac{1}{2}$ cups. Add 1 cup mashed blueberries. Increase sugar to $4\frac{1}{2}$ cups. Makes 5 half-pints.

STRAWBERRY-RHUBARB: Prepare as directed, except decrease strawberries to $1\frac{1}{2}$ cups mashed and add 1 cup finely chopped fresh rhubarb. Increase sugar to 5 cups. Makes 5 half-pints.

LOW-CALORIE

Freeze-Your-Own Herbed Vegetable Blend

PREP: 45 MINUTES **FREEZE:** 1 HOUR
MAKES: 4 (3-SERVING) PORTIONS

- **½ cup butter, softened**
  Desired Seasoning Mix
- **¼ teaspoon salt**
- **2 ears of corn, husks and silks removed**
- **2 cups broccoli and/or cauliflower florets**
- **3 medium carrots, bias-sliced ¼ inch thick**
- **1½ cups yellow summer squash and/or zucchini, bias-sliced ½ inch thick**
- **1 large red or yellow sweet pepper, seeded and cut into bite-size strips**
- **1 small sweet onion, cut into thin wedges**

1 In a medium bowl stir together butter, desired Seasoning Mix, and salt. Shape mixture into a 5-inch roll. Wrap in waxed paper or plastic wrap. Freeze about 1 hour or until firm. Cut butter into eight slices. Place in a freezer container and freeze until needed.

2 Meanwhile, in a covered 6-quart pot cook corn in enough boiling water to cover for 1 minute. Add broccoli, carrots, and squash. Cook, covered, for 2 minutes; drain. Plunge vegetables into an extra-large bowl of ice water. Let stand until chilled. Remove corn cobs (see photo 2, page 213). Cut kernels from cobs; do not scrape. Using a slotted spoon, transfer remaining vegetables to a paper towel-lined tray; pat dry.

3 Line a 15×10×1-inch baking pan with parchment paper or foil. In the prepared pan spread corn kernels, drained vegetables, sweet pepper, and onion in an even layer. Freeze about 1 hour or until nearly firm.

4 Spoon about 1½ cups vegetables into each quart freezer bag. Add 2 slices butter to each bag. Squeeze air from bag (see photo 4, page 213). Seal and label. Freeze for up to 6 months. (See "Freezing Basics," pages 212–213.)

SEASONING MIXES:

ITALIAN: Stir together 2 cloves minced garlic and ½ teaspoon dried Italian seasoning, crushed.

HERB AND CITRUS: Stir together 1 tablespoon finely shredded lemon peel; ½ teaspoon dried dill weed; ½ teaspoon dried basil, crushed; and ¼ teaspoon coarse-ground black pepper.

SOUTHWESTERN: Stir together 1 teaspoon ground ancho chile pepper; ½ teaspoon dried oregano, crushed; and ½ teaspoon finely shredded lime peel.

ASIAN: Stir together 1 tablespoon grated fresh ginger, 2 cloves minced garlic, and 3 drops toasted sesame oil.

FREEZE-YOUR-OWN HERBED VEGETABLE BLEND

SERVING DIRECTIONS: To reheat each portion, place frozen vegetable mixture in a medium saucepan or skillet. Cook, covered, over medium heat for 5 to 10 minutes or until butter is melted and vegetables are heated through, stirring occasionally. Season to taste with salt and black pepper.

PER ½ CUP: 107 cal., 8 g total fat (5 g sat. fat), 20 mg chol., 136 mg sodium, 8 g carb., 2 g fiber, 2 g pro.
EXCHANGES: 1½ Vegetable, 1½ fat

SAUCY VEGETABLES

To make a saucy vegetable dish, stir 2 tablespoons all-purpose flour into a reheated portion of the vegetable mixture. Stir in 1 cup reduced-sodium chicken broth. Cook and stir until thickened and bubbly. Cook and stir for 1 minute more. If desired, stir in 2 cups bite-size strips of cooked chicken breast, beef sirloin steak, or pork loin chops, or 2 cups peeled and cooked shrimp. Season to taste with salt and black pepper.

FAST

Freezer Pesto

START TO FINISH: 15 MINUTES **MAKES:** 1¼ CUPS

- **3 cups firmly packed fresh basil leaves (3 ounces)**
- **⅔ cup walnuts or almonds**
- **⅔ cup grated Parmesan or Romano cheese**
- **½ cup olive oil**
- **4 cloves garlic, quartered**
- **½ teaspoon salt**
- **¼ teaspoon black pepper**

1 In a food processor or blender combine basil, nuts, cheese, oil, garlic, salt, and pepper. Cover and process or blend until nearly smooth, stopping to scrape the sides as necessary.

2 Place 2 tablespoons of the pesto into each slot of a standard ice cube tray; cover tightly with foil. Freeze for up to 3 months. (See "Freezing Basics," pages 212–213.)

SERVING SUGGESTION: Use 2 tablespoons of the pesto to coat 1 cup hot cooked pasta.

PER 2 TABLESPOONS: 173 cal., 17 g total fat (3 g sat. fat), 5 mg chol., 199 mg sodium, 2 g carb., 1 g fiber, 4 g pro. EXCHANGES: ½ High-Fat Meat, 2½ Fat

LOW-CALORIE

Freezer Stewed Tomatoes

PREP: 50 MINUTES **COOK:** 10 MINUTES
MAKES: ABOUT 3 QUARTS

- **8 pounds ripe firm tomatoes, peeled (see photos 1–3, page 202) and cored**
- **1 cup chopped celery (2 stalks)**
- **½ cup chopped onion (1 medium)**
- **½ cup chopped green sweet pepper (1 small)**
- **2 teaspoons sugar**
- **2 teaspoons salt**

1 Chop tomatoes (you should have 17 cups). In an 8- to 10-quart heavy pot, combine chopped tomatoes, celery, onion, sweet pepper, sugar, and salt. Bring to boiling; reduce heat. Simmer, covered, for 10 minutes, stirring often to prevent sticking.

2 Place pot of stewed tomatoes in a sink filled with ice water; let tomatoes cool, stirring often. Ladle tomatoes into wide-mouth freezer containers, leaving a ½-inch headspace. Seal and label. Freeze for up to 10 months. (See "Freezing Basics," pages 212–213.)

PER ½ CUP: 37 cal., 0 g total fat, 0 mg chol., 246 mg sodium, 8 g carb., 2 g fiber, 2 g pro. EXCHANGES: 1½ Vegetable

CANNING & FREEZING TOMATOES

Read "Canning Basics," pages 196–197, "Canning Tomatoes," pages 202–203, and "Freezing Basics," pages 212–213. Allow 2½ to 3½ pounds unblemished tomatoes per quart. Wash and peel tomatoes, see photos 1–3, page 202.

Tomatoes	Preparation	Boiling-Water Canning	Freezing
Crushed	Wash and peel tomatoes. Cut into quarters; add enough to a large pan to cover bottom. Crush with a wooden spoon. Heat and stir until boiling. Slowly add remaining pieces, stirring constantly. Simmer for 5 minutes. Fill jars. Add bottled lemon juice* and salt.** Leave a ½-inch headspace.***	Process pints for 35 minutes and quarts for 45 minutes.	Set pan of tomatoes in ice water to cool. Fill freezer containers, leaving a 1-inch headspace.***
Whole or halved, no added liquid	Wash and peel tomatoes; halve if desired. Fill jars, pressing to fill spaces with juice. Add bottled lemon juice* and salt.** Leave a ½-inch headspace.***	Process pints and quarts for 85 minutes.	Fill freezer containers, leaving a 1-inch headspace.*** (Use only for cooking; freezing changes texture.)
Whole or halved, water pack	Wash and peel tomatoes; halve if desired. Fill jars. Add bottled lemon juice* and salt.** Add boiling water, leaving a ½-inch headspace.*** Or heat tomatoes in saucepan with enough water to cover; simmer for 5 minutes. Fill jars with tomatoes and cooking liquid. Add bottled lemon juice* and salt.** Leave a ½-inch headspace.***	Process pints for 40 minutes and quarts for 45 minutes.	If heated, set pan of tomatoes in cold water to cool. Fill freezer containers, leaving a 1-inch headspace.***

*Add 1 tablespoon bottled lemon juice for pints, 2 tablespoons for quarts.
**If desired, add salt: ¼ to ½ teaspoon for pints; ½ to 1 teaspoon for quarts.
***See tip, page 195.

CANNING & FREEZING FRUITS

Read "Canning Basics," pages 196–197, and "Freezing Basics," pages 213–213. Wash fresh fruits with cool, clear tap water but do not soak them; drain. Follow preparation directions, below. If you choose to can or freeze fruits with syrup, select the syrup that best suits the fruit and your taste. Generally, heavier syrups are used with sour fruits, and lighter syrups are recommended for mild fruits. To prepare a syrup, place the recommended amounts of sugar and water in a large saucepan (see page 213). Heat until the sugar dissolves. Skim off foam if necessary. Use the syrup hot for canned fruits and chilled for frozen fruits. Allow ½ to ⅔ cup syrup for each 2 cups fruit.

Food	Preparation	Boiling-Water Canning, Raw Pack	Boiling-Water Canning, Hot Pack	Freezing
Apples, Pears	Allow 2 to 3 pounds per quart. For apples, select varieties that are crisp, not mealy, in texture. Peel and core; halve, quarter, or slice. Dip into ascorbic acid color-keeper solution; drain.	Not recommended.	Simmer in syrup for 5 minutes, stirring occasionally. Fill jars with fruit and syrup, leaving a ½-inch headspace.* For apples, process pints and quarts for 20 minutes. For pears, process pints for 20 minutes and quarts for 25 minutes.	Use a syrup, sugar, or unsweetened pack (see Step 3, page 213), leaving the recommended headspace.*
Apricots, Nectarines, Peaches	Allow 2 to 3 pounds per quart. To peel peaches (peeling nectarines and apricots is not necessary), immerse in boiling water for 30 to 60 seconds or until skins start to split; remove and plunge into cold water. Halve and pit. If desired, slice. Treat with ascorbic acid color-keeper solution; drain.	Fill jars, placing fruit cut sides down. Add boiling syrup or water, leaving a ½-inch headspace.* Process pints for 25 minutes and quarts for 30 minutes. Do not raw-pack apricots. (Note: Hot-packing generally results in a better product.)	Add fruit to hot syrup; bring to boiling. Fill jars with fruit (placing cut sides down) and syrup, leaving a ½-inch headspace.* Process pints for 20 minutes and quarts for 25 minutes.	Use a syrup, sugar, or water pack (see Step 3, page 213), leaving the recommended headspace.*
Berries	Allow 1 to 3 pounds per quart. Can or freeze blackberries, blueberries, currants, elderberries, gooseberries, huckleberries, loganberries, and mulberries. Freeze (do not can) boysenberries, raspberries, and strawberries.	Fill jars with blackberries, loganberries, or mulberries. Shake down gently. Add boiling syrup, leaving a ½-inch headspace.* Process pints for 15 minutes and quarts for 20 minutes.	Simmer blueberries, currants, elderberries, gooseberries, and huckleberries in water for 30 seconds; drain. Fill jars with berries and hot syrup, leaving a ½-inch headspace.* Process pints and quarts for 15 minutes.	Slice strawberries, if desired. Freeze boysenberries and raspberries whole. Use a syrup, sugar, or unsweetened pack (see Step 3, page 213), leaving the recommended headspace.*
Cherries	Allow 2 to 3 pounds per quart. If desired, treat with ascorbic acid color-keeper solution; drain. If unpitted, prick skin on opposite sides to prevent splitting.	Fill jars, shaking down gently. Add boiling syrup or water, leaving a ½-inch headspace.* Process pints and quarts for 25 minutes.	Add cherries to hot syrup; bring to boiling. Fill jars with fruit and syrup, leaving a ½-inch headspace.* Process pints for 15 minutes and quarts for 20 minutes.	Use a syrup, sugar, or unsweetened pack (see Step 3, page 213), leaving the recommended headspace.*
Rhubarb	Allow 1½ pounds per quart. Discard leaves and woody ends. Cut into ½- to 1-inch pieces. Freeze for best quality.	Not recommended.	In a saucepan sprinkle ½ cup sugar over each 4 cups fruit; mix well. Let stand until juice appears. Bring slowly to boiling, stirring gently. Fill jars with hot fruit and juice, leaving a ½-inch headspace.* Process pints and quarts for 15 minutes.	Blanch for 1 minute; cool quickly and drain. Use a syrup or unsweetened pack (see Step 3, page 213) or use a sugar pack of ½ cup sugar to each 3 cups fruit, leaving the recommended headspace.*

*See tip, page 195.

FREEZING VEGETABLES

Read "Freezing Basics," pages 212–213. Wash fresh vegetables with cool, clear tap water; scrub firm vegetables with a clean produce brush to remove any dirt.

Vegetable	Preparation	Freezing
Asparagus	Allow 2½ to 4½ pounds per quart. Wash; scrape off scales. Break off woody bases where spears snap easily; wash again. Sort by thickness. Leave whole or cut into 1-inch lengths.	Blanch small spears for 2 minutes, medium for 3 minutes, and large for 4 minutes. Cool quickly by plunging into ice water; drain. Fill containers; shake down, leaving no headspace.
Beans: green, Italian, snap, or wax	Allow 1½ to 2½ pounds per quart. Wash; remove ends and strings. Leave whole or cut into 1-inch pieces.	Blanch for 3 minutes. Cool quickly by plunging into ice water; drain. Fill containers; shake down, leaving a ½-inch headspace.*
Beets	Allow 3 pounds (without tops) per quart. Trim off beet tops, leaving 1 inch of stem and roots, to reduce bleeding of color. Scrub well.	Cook unpeeled beets in boiling water until tender. (Allow 25 to 30 minutes for small beets; 45 to 50 minutes for medium beets.) Cool quickly by plunging into ice water; drain. Peel; remove stem and roots. Cut into slices or cubes. Fill containers, leaving a ½-inch headspace.*
Carrots	Use 1- to 1¼-inch-diameter carrots (larger carrots might be too fibrous). Allow 2 to 3 pounds per quart. Wash, trim, peel, and rinse again. Leave tiny ones whole; slice or dice the remainder.	Blanch tiny whole carrots for 5 minutes and cut-up carrots for 2 minutes. Cool quickly by plunging into ice water; drain. Pack tightly into containers, leaving a ½-inch headspace.*
Corn, whole kernel	Allow 4 to 5 pounds per quart. Remove husks. Scrub with a vegetable brush to remove silks. Wash and drain.	Cover ears with boiling water; return to boiling and boil 4 minutes. Cool by plunging into ice water; drain. Cut corn from cobs at two-thirds depth of kernels; do not scrape. Fill containers, leaving a ½-inch headspace.*
Peas: English or green	Allow 2 to 2½ pounds per pint. Wash, shell, rinse, and drain.	Blanch 1½ minutes. Cool quickly by plunging into ice water; drain. Fill containers; shake down, leaving a ½-inch headspace.*
Peppers, chile	Select firm jalapeño or other chile peppers; wash. Halve large peppers. Remove stems, seeds, and membranes (see tip, page 44). Place, cut sides down, on a foil-lined baking sheet. Roast in a 425°F oven for 20 to 25 minutes or until skins are bubbly and brown. Cover peppers or wrap in foil and let stand about 15 minutes or until cool. Pull skins off gently and slowly, using a paring knife.	Package in freezer containers, leaving no headspace.
Peppers, sweet	Select firm green, bright red, orange, or yellow peppers; wash. Remove stems, seeds, and membranes. Place, cut sides down, on a foil-lined baking sheet. Roast in a 425°F oven for 20 to 25 minutes or until skins are bubbly and brown. Cover peppers or wrap in foil and let stand about 15 minutes or until cool. Pull the skins off gently and slowly, using a paring knife.	Quarter large pepper pieces or cut into strips. Fill containers, leaving a ½-inch headspace.* Or spread peppers in a single layer on a baking sheet; freeze until firm. Fill containers; shake to pack closely, leaving no headspace.

*See tip, page 195.

236

228

234

casseroles

225

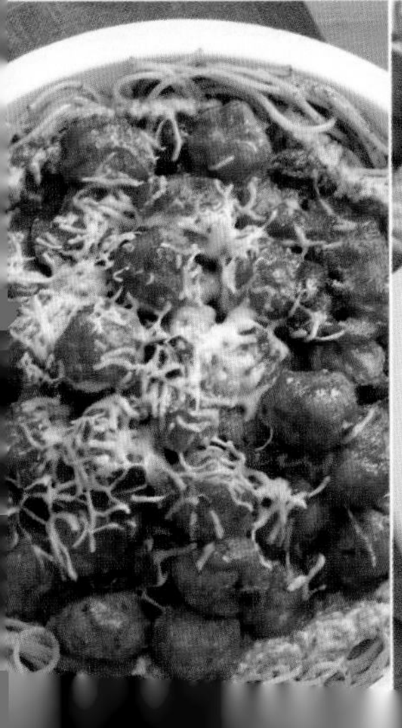

232

casseroles

Make your casseroles the best they can be with the right equipment plus some freezing and serving know-how.

EQUIPMENT

Casseroles and baking dishes can be made of glass, ceramic, stoneware, or enamel-coated cast iron. Here are the most versatile types of casserole bakeware and common sizes.

CASSEROLES: (1½-, 2-, and 3-quart) Usually round or oval, these casseroles often come with lids, which make them handy for storing leftovers. They have deeper sides than other baking dishes.

SQUARE BAKING DISHES: (2-quart) Look for 8- or 9-inch square baking dishes.

RECTANGULAR BAKING DISHES: (2- and 3-quart) More shallow than casseroles, (11×7×1½ inches and 9×13×2 inches in size, respectively), these increase the dish's surface area.

GRATIN DISHES: (1½-, 2-, and 3-quart) These round or oval dishes are more shallow and offer more surface area than a casserole. Gratin and rectangular baking dishes can generally be used interchangeably if the dish is of the volume specified in the recipe.

- For best results, use the type and size of bakeware your recipe calls for. To check a dish's capacity, fill it with water, 1 quart at a time.
- If you don't have the correct-size dish, use a larger dish. Note that because the food will be more spread out, it will take less time to cook, so reduce your baking time by about 25 percent.

METAL PANS: In a pinch a metal pan can be used for a casserole or baking dish if the recipe includes no acidic ingredients, such as tomatoes or lemons. These can react with metal, causing the foods to discolor.

FREEZING FOR FUTURE MEALS

Most casseroles freeze beautifully. Simply follow these tips.

- Make sure to use freezer-to-oven dishes. Line the dish with parchment paper, freezer paper, or foil.

- Prepare the casserole using the lined dish, but do not bake. Cover the dish with plastic freezer wrap or foil and freeze overnight. When frozen, lift out the paper- or foil-lined food and place it in a bag or container designed for freezer use. Freeze for up to 3 months.

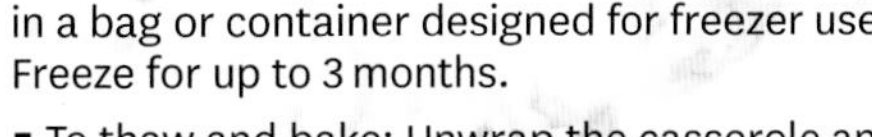

- To thaw and bake: Unwrap the casserole and place it in the original baking dish. Cover and thaw in the refrigerator for up to 2 days before baking. If you don't have time to thaw in the refrigerator, cover and heat the casserole in a 325°F oven for twice its normal baking time. To test for doneness, see tip, page 225.

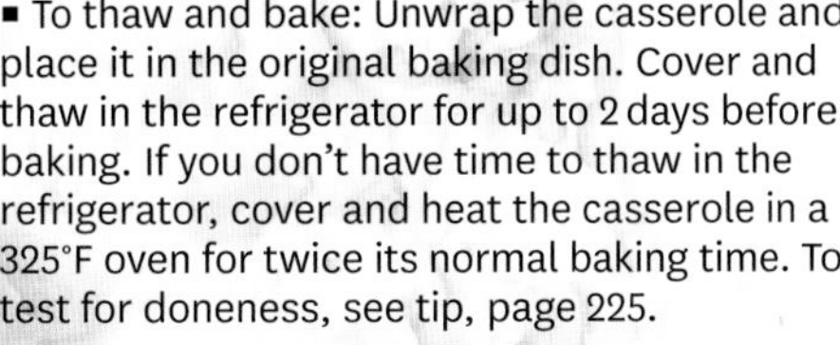

LET IT STAND

Allowing a casserole to stand for several minutes after it comes out of the oven improves texture and flavor and allows the food to firm and hold a cut edge. This is especially true with hot and cheesy dishes and layered casseroles.

Tuna Noodle Casserole, page 234

cook's secrets

four-cheese macaroni and cheese

The Secret: Whether you love this classic comfort food bubbly with a brown crusty topper or straight-from-the-saucepan creamy, the ultimate mac and cheese starts with a well-made white sauce.

PREP: 30 MINUTES **BAKE:** 20 MINUTES AT 350°F **MAKES:** 6 SERVINGS

- **Nonstick cooking spray**
- **5⅓ cups dried cavatappi or corkscrew-shape pasta (16 ounces)**
- **3 tablespoons butter**
- **⅓ cup finely chopped onion (1 small)**
- **3 tablespoons all-purpose flour**
- **½ teaspoon salt**
- **¼ teaspoon black pepper**
- **2½ cups milk**
- **2 cups Gouda cheese, shredded (8 ounces)**
- **1 cup sharp cheddar cheese, shredded (4 ounces)**
- **1 cup Swiss cheese, shredded (4 ounces)**
- **½ cup grated Parmesan cheese (2 ounces)**
- **1 teaspoon butter**
- **⅔ cup panko bread crumbs**

Because panko crumbs have a larger surface area than fine dry bread crumbs, when tossed with butter and baked, the texture is lighter and crispier too.

1 Preheat oven to 350°F. Coat a 2½- to 3-quart broiler-safe gratin or baking dish with cooking spray; set aside. Bring a large pot of lightly salted water to boiling. Add pasta and cook according to package directions. Drain and return to the warm pot.

2 Meanwhile, for the white sauce, in a large saucepan melt the 3 tablespoons butter over medium heat. Add onion; cook and stir for 3 minutes. Stir in flour, salt, and pepper. Gradually whisk in the milk. Cook, whisking constantly, until thickened and bubbly. Cook and whisk for 2 minutes more. Remove from heat.

3 Add Gouda, cheddar, Swiss, and ¼ cup of the Parmesan cheese, whisking until cheeses melt and sauce is smooth. Add the cheese sauce to cooked pasta; stir gently to coat.

4 Transfer mixture to the prepared dish. In a small microwave-safe bowl melt the 1 teaspoon butter. Stir in panko and the remaining ¼ cup Parmesan cheese; sprinkle over cheesy pasta. Bake for 20 to 25 minutes or until bubbly. Let stand for 10 minutes before serving.

PER 1¼ CUPS: 740 cal., 34 g total fat (20 g sat. fat), 111 mg chol., 888 mg sodium, 72 g carb., 3 g fiber, 36 g pro. **EXCHANGES:** ½ Milk, 4 Starch, 3 Lean Meat, 5 Fat

SAUCE TIPS

1. GRATE YOUR OWN CHEESE
Processed cheese is often key to the creamiest dishes, but we love the flavor of the four aged cheeses in this recipe. To make sure they melt into a smooth, creamy sauce, shred them by hand. Packaged shredded cheeses might contain added starches that affect the sauce's texture.

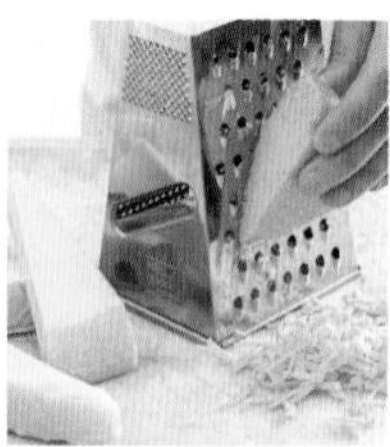

2. SAUCE SAVVY
Basic white sauce starts with a mixture of equal parts flour and butter. Whisk flour into melted butter, stirring constantly. The butter will coat the flour molecules, which prevents them from sticking together and forming lumps.

3. WHISKING IS KEY
Once the flour and butter are combined, gradually add the milk to the flour, whisking constantly. Keep whisking until you have a thickened and bubbly sauce. Don't skip the last 2 minutes of cooking; it finishes cooking the flour.

FROM STOVE TOP TO TABLE

Whether you're making the classic recipe above or the butternut squash or pumpkin variations on page 223, simply skip Step 4 if you prefer extra-creamy saucepan macaroni and cheese. Don't use the baking dish and omit the panko topping.

TRUFFLE MACARONI AND CHEESE: Prepare as directed, except drizzle panko topping with 1 to 2 tablespoons truffle oil before broiling.

PER 1¼ CUPS: 760 cal., 36 g total fat (20 g sat. fat), 111 mg chol, 888 mg sodium, 72 g carb., 3 g fiber, 36 g pro. EXCHANGES: ½ Milk, 4 Starch, 3 Lean Meat, 5 Fat

BACON-BLUE MACARONI AND CHEESE: Prepare as directed, except stir 3 slices crisp-cooked, drained, and crumbled bacon and ¼ cup crumbled blue cheese into panko mixture before sprinkling over pasta mixture.

PER 1¼ CUPS: 781 cal., 37 g total fat (22 g sat. fat), 120 mg chol, 1,035 mg sodium, 72 g carb., 3 g fiber, 39 g pro. EXCHANGES: ½ Milk, 4 Starch, 3 Lean Meat, 5½ Fat

BUTTERNUT SQUASH MACARONI AND CHEESE: Prepare as directed, except preheat oven to 450°F. Coat a 15×10×1-inch baking pan with nonstick cooking spray. Place 1½ pounds butternut squash, peeled, seeded, and cut into 1-inch cubes, in the prepared baking pan. Drizzle 2 tablespoons olive oil over squash pieces; toss to coat. Roast, uncovered, for 25 to 30 minutes or until tender, stirring occasionally. Stir cooked squash into pasta with the cheese sauce.

PER 1¼ CUPS: 823 cal., 38 g total fat (21 g sat. fat), 111 mg chol, 892 mg sodium, 83 g carb., 5 g fiber, 37 g pro. EXCHANGES: ½ Milk, 2 Vegetable, 4 Starch, 3 Lean Meat, 5½ Fat

PUMPKIN MACARONI AND CHEESE: Prepare as directed, except substitute white cheddar cheese for the sharp cheddar cheese and Fontina cheese for the Swiss cheese. Stir one 15-ounce can pumpkin and 1 tablespoon snipped fresh sage into cheese sauce.

PER 1¼ CUPS: 766 cal., 34 g total fat (21 g sat. fat), 116 mg chol, 1,007 mg sodium, 77 g carb., 5 g fiber, 37 g pro. EXCHANGES: ½ Milk, 2 Vegetable, 4 Starch, 3 Lean Meat, 5 Fat

Italian Polenta Casserole

PREP: 45 MINUTES **BAKE:** 20 MINUTES AT 400°F
MAKES: 8 SERVINGS

- **2½ cups chicken broth**
- **3 tablespoons butter or margarine**
- **2 cups milk**
- **1½ cups quick-cooking polenta mix**
- **1 3-ounce package cream cheese, cut up**
- **1 cup shredded mozzarella or provolone cheese (4 ounces)**
- **½ cup finely shredded or grated Parmesan cheese (2 ounces)**
- **12 ounces bulk Italian sausage**
- **1 cup fresh mushrooms, quartered**
- **1 medium onion, cut into thin wedges**
- **2 cloves garlic, minced**
- **2 cups purchased pasta sauce**

1 Preheat oven to 400°F. Lightly grease a 3-quart rectangular baking dish; set aside.

2 In a large saucepan bring broth and butter to boiling. Meanwhile, stir together milk and polenta. Add polenta mixture to boiling broth (see photo 1, below). Cook and stir until bubbly; cook and stir for 3 to 5 minutes more or until very thick. Stir in cream cheese, ¾ cup of the mozzarella cheese, and ¼ cup of the Parmesan cheese until well mixed (see photo 2, below). Spread two-thirds of the polenta mixture in the prepared baking dish; set aside.

3 In a large skillet cook sausage, mushrooms, onion, and garlic until meat is browned and onion is tender. Drain fat; discard. Stir pasta sauce into meat mixture; heat through. Spoon meat mixture over polenta in dish, spreading evenly. Spoon remaining polenta on sauce (see photo 3, below) and sprinkle with remaining mozzarella and Parmesan cheeses.

4 Bake, uncovered, about 20 minutes or until heated through and top is lightly golden.

PER 1 CUP: 584 cal., 34 g total fat (18 g sat. fat), 93 mg chol., 1,879 mg sodium, 36 g carb., 4 g fiber, 31 g pro.
EXCHANGES: 1 Vegetable, 2 Starch, 3 High-Fat Meat, 1½ Fat

LOW-CALORIE

Turkey and Sweet Potato Shepherd's Pie

PREP: 40 MINUTES **BAKE:** 20 MINUTES AT 375°F
MAKES: 4 SERVINGS

- **1½ pounds sweet potatoes, peeled and cut into 2-inch pieces**
- **2 cloves garlic, halved**
- **¼ cup fat-free milk**
- **½ teaspoon salt**
- **12 ounces uncooked ground turkey breast**
- **½ cup chopped onion (1 medium)**
- **1¼ cups coarsely chopped zucchini (1 medium)**
- **1 cup chopped carrots (2 medium)**
- **½ cup frozen whole kernel yellow corn**
- **¼ cup water**
- **1 8-ounce can tomato sauce**
- **2 tablespoons Worcestershire sauce**
- **2 teaspoons snipped fresh sage or ½ teaspoon dried sage, crushed**
- **⅛ teaspoon black pepper**
- **Snipped fresh sage (optional)**

1 Preheat the oven to 375°F. In a medium saucepan cook sweet potatoes and garlic, covered, in enough lightly salted boiling water to

ITALIAN POLENTA CASSEROLE STEP-BY-STEP

1. Slowly add the polenta mixture to the boiling broth in a steady stream, stirring constantly. Continue to cook and stir over low heat until polenta is very thick.

2. As soon as the polenta thickens, add the cheeses. Continue stirring until the cheeses melt.

3. Drop the polenta from a wooden spoon, scraping with a rubber spatula to make small mounds on top of the meat mixture.

cover for 15 to 20 minutes or until tender; drain. Mash with a potato masher or beat with an electric mixer on low speed. Gradually add milk and salt, mashing or beating to make potato mixture light and fluffy. Cover and keep warm.

2 Meanwhile, in a large skillet cook turkey and onion over medium heat until meat is browned, stirring to break up turkey as it cooks. Drain if necessary. Stir in zucchini, carrots, corn, and water. Bring to boiling; reduce heat. Simmer, covered, for 5 to 10 minutes or until vegetables are tender.

3 Add tomato sauce, Worcestershire sauce, sage, and pepper to turkey mixture; heat through. Spoon turkey mixture into a 1½-quart casserole, spreading evenly. Spoon mashed potato mixture in mounds on turkey mixture.

4 Bake, uncovered, for 20 to 25 minutes or until heated through. If desired, sprinkle with additional fresh sage before serving.

PER 1½ CUPS: 268 cal., 1 g total fat (0 g sat. fat), 42 mg chol., 824 mg sodium, 41 g carb., 7 g fiber, 24 g pro.
EXCHANGES: 1 Vegetable, 2½ Starch, 2 Lean Meat

HOT-SPICED PORK AND RICE

Hot-Spiced Pork and Rice

PREP: 45 MINUTES **BAKE:** 60 MINUTES AT 375°F
STAND: 10 MINUTES **MAKES:** 6 SERVINGS

- 1 **2- to 2¼-pound boneless pork shoulder roast**
- 2 **to 3 tablespoons vegetable oil**
- 2 **cups thinly sliced carrots (4 medium)**
- 1 **8-ounce can sliced water chestnuts, drained**
- 1 **cup yellow sweet pepper strips (1 medium)**
- ½ **cup chopped onion (1 medium)**
- 1 **cup uncooked long grain rice**
- 1 **14.5-ounce can reduced-sodium chicken broth**
- ½ **cup water**
- ¼ **cup soy sauce**
- 2 **tablespoons light-color corn syrup**
- 2 **tablespoons molasses**
- 1 **to 2 teaspoons red chili paste**
- 1 **teaspoon five-spice powder**
- 3 **green onions, cut into very thin strips**
- **Crushed red pepper (optional)**

1 Preheat oven to 375°F. Trim fat from meat. Cut meat into ¾-inch cubes. In a very large skillet cook half of the meat at a time in 2 tablespoons hot oil until browned. Transfer meat to a 3-quart rectangular baking dish. Add carrots, water chestnuts, and sweet pepper.

2 Add remaining tablespoon oil to skillet if necessary. Cook onion in hot oil until tender. Add uncooked rice to skillet; cook and stir for 1 minute. Stir in broth, water, soy sauce, corn syrup, molasses, chili paste, and five-spice powder. Cook and stir just until mixture comes to a boil. Remove from heat. Carefully add rice mixture to casserole; stir to combine. Cover dish with foil.

3 Bake about 60 minutes or until pork and rice are tender. Let stand, covered, for 10 minutes. Gently stir and sprinkle with green onions and, if desired, crushed red pepper before serving.

PER 2 CUPS: 439 cal., 14 g total fat (3 g sat. fat), 91 mg chol., 980 mg sodium, 47 g carb., 3 g fiber, 34 g pro.
EXCHANGES: ½ Vegetable, 3 Starch, 3½ Lean Meat

CASSEROLE DONENESS TEST

Check the temperature to make sure the dish is at its safest, tastiest best.

For the best flavor and food safety, a casserole needs to be heated to 160°F. When the casserole is bubbly around the edges, test the temperature by inserting an instant-read thermometer at an angle in the center, being careful not to touch the baking dish.

Baked Risotto with Sausage and Artichokes

PREP: 40 MINUTES **BAKE:** 70 MINUTES AT 350°F
STAND: 5 MINUTES **MAKES:** 6 SERVINGS

- **1 pound bulk Italian sausage**
- **1 cup chopped fennel bulb (1 medium)**
- **½ cup chopped onion (1 medium)**
- **2 cloves garlic, minced**
- **¾ cup uncooked Arborio or long grain rice**
- **2 9-ounce packages frozen artichoke hearts, thawed, drained, and halved**
- **1 cup coarsely shredded carrots (2 medium)**
- **2 teaspoons snipped fresh thyme or ½ teaspoon dried thyme, crushed**
- **½ teaspoon black pepper**
- **2 cups chicken broth**
- **⅓ cup dry white wine or chicken broth**
- **½ cup panko bread crumbs or soft bread crumbs**
- **¼ cup finely shredded Asiago or Parmesan cheese (1 ounce)**
- **1 tablespoon butter or margarine, melted**
- **½ teaspoon finely shredded lemon peel**

1 Preheat oven to 350°F. In a very large skillet cook and stir sausage, fennel, onion, and garlic over medium-high heat until vegetables are tender but not browned; drain fat and discard. Add rice; cook and stir 1 minute more.

2 Add artichoke hearts, carrots, thyme, and pepper. Stir in broth and wine. Bring just to boiling. Transfer to a 2½-quart casserole. Bake, covered, about 60 minutes or until rice is tender, stirring once.

3 Meanwhile, in a small bowl combine panko, cheese, butter, and lemon peel. Uncover casserole and top with panko mixture. Bake, uncovered, for 10 minutes more. Let stand for 5 minutes before serving.

PER 1⅓ CUPS: 476 cal., 28 g total fat (11 g sat. fat), 68 mg chol., 1,038 mg sodium, 36 g carb., 8 g fiber, 17 g pro.
EXCHANGES: 1½ Vegetable, 2 Starch, 1 High-Fat Meat, 3½ Fat

Beef Stroganoff Casserole

PREP: 35 MINUTES **BAKE:** 30 MINUTES AT 350°F
MAKES: 6 SERVINGS

- **4 cups dried campanelle or penne pasta (12 ounces)**
- **1 15-ounce package refrigerated cooked beef roast au jus**
- **2 large portobello mushrooms**
- **1 medium sweet onion, cut into thin wedges**
- **2 cloves garlic, minced**
- **2 tablespoons butter or margarine**
- **3 tablespoons all-purpose flour**
- **2 tablespoons tomato paste**
- **1 14.5-ounce can beef broth**
- **1 tablespoon Worcestershire sauce**
- **1 teaspoon smoked paprika or Spanish paprika**
- **¼ teaspoon salt**
- **¼ teaspoon black pepper**
- **Snipped fresh Italian parsley (optional)**
- **½ cup sour cream**
- **1 tablespoon prepared horseradish**
- **1 teaspoon snipped fresh dill weed or ¼ teaspoon dried dill weed**

1 Preheat oven to 350°F. Cook pasta according to package directions; drain. Return pasta to hot saucepan; cover and keep warm. Place roast on a cutting board; reserve juices. Using two forks, pull meat apart into bite-size pieces; set aside.

2 Remove stems and gills from mushrooms; coarsely chop (you should have about 4 cups). In a very large skillet cook mushrooms, onion, and garlic in hot butter over medium heat for 4 to 5 minutes or until tender. Stir in flour and tomato paste. Add reserved meat juices, beef broth, Worcestershire sauce, paprika, salt, and pepper. Cook and stir until thickened and bubbly. Remove from heat.

3 Add pasta and beef to mushroom mixture in skillet; stir to combine. Transfer meat mixture to a 3-quart casserole or rectangular baking dish. Bake, covered, about 30 minutes or until heated through. If desired, sprinkle with parsley. In a small bowl combine sour cream, horseradish, and dill. Spoon some of the mixture over each serving.

PER 1½ CUPS: 425 cal., 12 g total fat (6 g sat. fat), 54 mg chol., 737 mg sodium, 57 g carb., 4 g fiber, 23 g pro.
EXCHANGES: 1½ Vegetable, 3 Starch, 1½ Lean Meat, 1½ Fat

BEST-LOVED LOW-CALORIE

Potato and Ham Bake

PREP: 25 MINUTES **BAKE:** 30 MINUTES AT 400°F
STAND: 5 MINUTES **MAKES:** 4 SERVINGS

- 1 **pound Yukon gold potatoes, sliced**
- 1 **8-ounce tub light cream cheese spread with chive and onion**
- ¾ **cup milk**
- ¼ **cup finely shredded Parmesan cheese**
- ¼ **teaspoon black pepper**
- 1 **tablespoon snipped fresh tarragon or ½ teaspoon dried tarragon, crushed**
- 8 **ounces cooked boneless ham, cut into bite-size slices**
- 1 **pound fresh asparagus spears, trimmed and cut into 2- to 3-inch pieces**

1 Preheat oven to 400°F. Lightly grease a 1½-quart baking dish; set aside. In a medium saucepan cook potatoes, covered, in a small amount of lightly salted boiling water for 5 to 7 minutes or just until tender. Drain; transfer potatoes to a medium bowl and set aside.

2 For cheese sauce, in same saucepan combine cream cheese, milk, 2 tablespoons of the Parmesan cheese, and the pepper. Heat and whisk cream cheese mixture until cheese melts and mixture is smooth. Remove from heat and stir in tarragon.

3 Layer half of the potatoes, ham, asparagus, and sauce in the prepared baking dish. Repeat layers. Cover with foil.

4 Bake for 20 minutes. Remove foil; sprinkle with remaining Parmesan cheese. Return to oven and bake, uncovered, for 10 to 12 minutes more or until heated through. Let stand for 5 minutes before serving.

PER SERVING: 346 cal., 16 g total fat (9 g sat. fat), 67 mg chol., 1,162 mg sodium, 30 g carb., 5 g fiber, 22 g pro.
EXCHANGES: 1 Vegetable, 1½ Starch, 2 Medium-Fat Meat, 1 Fat

SPECIAL SPUDS

Yukon gold potatoes have a moist, waxy texture and a moderate starch content that make them work especially well for scalloped potato dishes. If they aren't readily available, you can substitute round red potatoes.

Eight-Layer Casserole *(photo, page 219)*

PREP: 30 MINUTES **BAKE:** 55 MINUTES AT 350°F
STAND: 10 MINUTES **MAKES:** 8 SERVINGS

- **3 cups packaged dried medium noodles (6 ounces)**
- **1 pound lean ground beef**
- **1 15-ounce can tomato sauce**
- **1 teaspoon dried basil, crushed**
- **½ teaspoon sugar**
- **½ teaspoon garlic powder**
- **¼ teaspoon salt**
- **¼ teaspoon black pepper**
- **1 8-ounce carton sour cream**
- **1 8-ounce package cream cheese, softened**
- **½ cup milk**
- **⅓ cup chopped onion (1 small)**
- **1 10-ounce package frozen chopped spinach, cooked and well drained**
- **1 cup shredded cheddar cheese (4 ounces)**
- **Snipped fresh parsley (optional)**

1 Preheat oven to 350°F. Lightly grease a 2-quart casserole or square baking dish; set aside. Cook noodles according to package directions; drain and set aside.

2 Meanwhile, in a large skillet cook beef over medium heat until browned; drain fat and discard. Stir tomato sauce, basil, sugar, garlic powder, salt, and pepper into skillet. Bring to boiling; reduce heat. Simmer, uncovered, for 5 minutes.

3 In a medium mixing bowl beat together sour cream and cream cheese with an electric mixer on medium speed until smooth. Stir in milk and onion.

4 In prepared casserole layer half of the noodles (about 2 cups), meat mixture (about 1½ cups), cream cheese mixture (about 1 cup), and all of the spinach. Top with the remaining meat mixture and noodles. Cover and chill remaining cream cheese mixture until needed.

5 Cover casserole with lightly greased foil. Bake about 45 minutes or until heated through. Uncover; spread with remaining cream cheese mixture. Sprinkle with cheddar cheese. Bake, uncovered, about 10 minutes more or until cheese melts. Let stand for 10 minutes. If desired, sprinkle with snipped fresh parsley before serving.

MAKE-AHEAD DIRECTIONS: Prepare as directed through Step 4. Cover with lightly greased foil and chill for up to 24 hours. Bake in a 350°F oven for 60 to 70 minutes or until heated through. Continue as directed in Step 5.

PER 1½ CUPS: 420 cal., 27 g total fat (14 g sat. fat), 116 mg chol., 627 mg sodium, 23 g carb., 3 g fiber, 23 g pro.
EXCHANGES: ½ Vegetable, 1 Starch, ½ Other Carb, 2½ Lean Meat, 4 Fat

Turkey Meatballs in Pesto Pasta Pie
(photo, page 219)

PREP: 30 MINUTES **BAKE:** 50 MINUTES AT 350°F
MAKES: 6 SERVINGS

- **1 egg**
- **¾ cup soft bread crumbs (1 slice bread)**
- **⅓ cup finely chopped onion**
- **3 tablespoons grated Parmesan cheese**
- **3 tablespoons finely chopped drained oil-packed dried tomatoes**
- **1 teaspoon dried Italian seasoning, crushed**
- **¼ teaspoon garlic salt**
- **⅛ teaspoon black pepper**
- **1 pound uncooked ground turkey**
- **5 ounces packaged dried spaghetti**
- **6 tablespoons purchased basil pesto**
- **1 egg, lightly beaten**
- **Nonstick cooking spray**
- **1 cup ricotta cheese**
- **1 cup purchased mushroom pasta sauce**
- **2 tablespoons water**
- **½ cup sliced pitted Kalamata olives (optional)**
- **½ cup shredded pizza cheese (2 ounces)**
- **Snipped fresh basil (optional)**

1 Preheat oven to 350°F. For the meatballs, in a large bowl combine the egg, bread crumbs, onion, Parmesan, tomatoes, Italian seasoning, garlic salt, and pepper. Add turkey and mix well. Shape into 1-inch meatballs. Place meatballs in a foil-lined 15×10×1-inch baking pan. Bake about 20 minutes or until no longer pink.

2 Meanwhile, cook spaghetti according to package directions; drain. Stir in 4 tablespoons of the pesto and the egg; set aside.

3 Coat a 9-inch pie plate with cooking spray. Press spaghetti mixture onto bottom and up sides of prepared pie plate, forming a crust. In a small bowl combine ricotta and the remaining 2 tablespoons pesto; spread over the bottom and up the sides of the pasta crust.

4 In a medium saucepan stir together the meatballs, pasta sauce, water, and, if desired, olives. Bring to boiling, stirring occasionally; reduce heat. Simmer, covered, about 5 minutes or until meatballs are heated through, stirring twice. Spoon meatball mixture into pasta crust. Cover pie loosely with foil.

5 Bake for 25 minutes. Sprinkle with pizza cheese. Bake, uncovered, about 5 minutes more or until heated through. If desired, sprinkle with snipped fresh basil.

PER SERVING: 460 cal., 24 g total fat (9 g sat. fat), 149 mg chol., 560 mg sodium, 29 g carb., 2 g fiber, 31 g pro.
EXCHANGES: 1 Vegetable, 1½ Starch, 3½ Lean Meat, 3½ Fat

make it mine

Noodle Casserole

Whether you're seeking a satisfying way to use up leftovers or you wish to create a one-of-a-kind house specialty, use this plan to design your own casserole.

PREP: 30 MINUTES
BAKE: 55 MINUTES AT 350°F
MAKES: 6 SERVINGS

- **8** **ounces packaged dried NOODLES or PASTA**
- **1** **pound GROUND MEAT or HAM or one 15-ounce can BEANS, rinsed and drained**
- **1** **10.75-ounce can CONDENSED SOUP**
- **1½** **cups FROZEN VEGETABLE**
- **1** **cup SHREDDED CHEESE (4 ounces)**
- **¾** **cup milk**
- **¼** **cup GOODIE**
- **1** **teaspoon SEASONING**
- **½** **cup TOPPER (optional)**

1 Preheat oven to 350°F. Grease a 2-quart casserole; set aside. Cook Noodles or Pasta according to package directions; drain and return to the pan.

2 In a large skillet cook Ground Meat (or sausage) until meat is browned; drain fat and discard. (If using Ham or Beans, skip this step.)

3 Add drained Ground Meat or Ham or Beans (if using), Condensed Soup, Frozen Vegetable, half of the Shredded Cheese, the milk, Goodie, and Seasoning to cooked pasta; stir well to combine. Transfer pasta mixture to the prepared casserole. Sprinkle with remaining cheese.

4 Bake, covered, for 45 minutes. Uncover; if desired, sprinkle with Topper. Return to oven and bake 10 to 15 minutes more or until heated through and Topper (if using) is light brown.

PASTA (whole grain or regular) *(pick one)*

Egg noodles
Farfalle
Macaroni
Penne
Rotini

GROUND MEAT OR HAM OR BEANS *(pick one)*

Lean ground beef
Ground turkey
Bulk pork sausage
Chopped ham
Canned beans

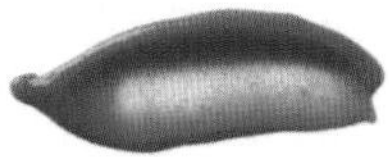

CONDENSED SOUP *(pick one)*

Broccoli cheese
Cream of chicken
Cream of mushroom
Tomato

FROZEN VEGETABLE *(pick one)*

Broccoli florets
Mixed vegetables
Peas
Whole kernel corn

SHREDDED CHEESE *(pick one)*

Cheddar
Italian or Mexican blend
Monterey Jack
Swiss

GOODIE *(pick one)*

Slivered almonds
Ripe or green olives, sliced
Canned sliced mushrooms, drained
Bottled roasted red peppers, drained and chopped

SEASONING *(pick one)*

Basil, dried, crushed
Cajun or Italian seasoning
Chili powder plus ¼ teaspoon ground cumin

TOPPER *(pick one)*

Bread crumbs tossed with 2 tablespoons melted butter
Chow mein noodles
Corn or potato chips, crushed

Bean-and-Beef Enchilada Casserole

PREP: 25 MINUTES **BAKE:** 35 MINUTES AT 350°F
MAKES: 6 SERVINGS

- **8 ounces lean ground beef**
- **½ cup chopped onion (1 medium)**
- **1 15-ounce can pinto beans, rinsed and drained**
- **1 4-ounce can diced green chile peppers, undrained**
- **1 teaspoon chili powder**
- **½ teaspoon ground cumin**
- **1 8-ounce carton sour cream or light sour cream**
- **2 tablespoons all-purpose flour**
- **¼ teaspoon garlic powder**
- **8 6-inch corn tortillas**
- **1 10-ounce can enchilada sauce**
- **1 cup shredded cheddar cheese (4 ounces)**

1 Preheat oven to 350°F. Lightly grease a 2-quart rectangular baking dish; set aside. In a large skillet cook beef and onion until meat is browned and onion is tender; drain fat and discard. Stir pinto beans, chiles, chili powder, and cumin into meat mixture; set aside.

2 In a small bowl stir together sour cream, flour, and garlic powder until combined; set aside.

3 Arrange half of the tortillas to cover bottom of prepared baking dish, overlapping to fit as necessary (see photo 1, below). Top with half of the meat mixture, sour cream mixture, and enchilada sauce (see photo 2, below). Repeat with remaining tortillas, meat mixture, sour cream mixture, and enchilada sauce.

4 Cover with foil. Bake about 30 minutes or until heated through. Remove foil; sprinkle casserole with cheese and bake 5 minutes more or until cheese melts.

MAKE-AHEAD DIRECTIONS: Prepare as directed through Step 3. Cover with plastic wrap and chill for up to 24 hours. Remove plastic wrap. Cover dish with foil. Bake in a 350°F oven for 35 minutes or until heated through. Uncover; sprinkle with cheese. Return to oven and bake 5 minutes more or until cheese melts.

PER SERVING: 345 cal., 19 g total fat (10 g sat. fat), 64 mg chol., 609 mg sodium, 25 g carb., 4 g fiber, 18 g pro.
EXCHANGES: 1½ Starch, 2 Lean Meat, 3 Fat

BEAN-AND-BEEF ENCHILADA CASSEROLE STEP-BY-STEP

1. Place 4 of the corn tortillas in the greased baking dish, overlapping as necessary to fit.

2. Arrange half of the meat mixture and sour cream mixture on top of the tortillas. Pour half of the enchilada sauce over top. Gently press down on the next layer of tortillas to help distribute the sauce evenly.

Cheeseburger and Fries Casserole

PREP: 20 MINUTES **BAKE:** 40 MINUTES AT 350°F
MAKES: 6 SERVINGS

- **1½ pounds lean ground beef**
- **¾ cup chopped green sweet pepper (1 medium)**
- **½ cup chopped onion (1 medium)**
- **2 cloves garlic, minced**
- **1 14.5-ounce can diced tomatoes, undrained**
- **1 6-ounce can tomato paste**
- **1 10.75-ounce can condensed cheddar cheese soup**
- **½ cup light sour cream**
- **4 cups frozen french-fried shoestring potatoes**
- **1 teaspoon seasoned salt (optional)**
- **Assorted toppers (ketchup, pickle slices, yellow mustard, and/or chopped fresh tomato) (optional)**

1 Preheat oven to 350°F. In a very large skillet cook ground beef, sweet pepper, onion, and garlic over medium heat until meat is browned and vegetables are tender; drain fat and discard. Stir tomatoes and tomato paste into beef mixture. Bring to boiling; reduce heat. Simmer, uncovered, for 5 minutes.

2 Spoon beef mixture into the bottom of an ungreased 2-quart rectangular baking dish. In a medium bowl stir together soup and sour cream; spread over meat mixture in baking dish. Sprinkle potatoes over top of soup mixture. If desired, sprinkle with seasoned salt.

3 Bake, uncovered, for 40 to 45 minutes or until heated through and potatoes are light brown. If desired, serve with assorted toppers.

PER 1 CUP: 493 cal., 26 g total fat (10 g sat. fat), 87 mg chol., 1,319 mg sodium, 46 g carb., 5 g fiber, 28 g pro.
EXCHANGES: ½ Vegetable, 3 Starch, 2½ Medium-Fat Meat, 2 Fat

BEST-LOVED

Upside-Down Pizza Casserole

PREP: 20 MINUTES
BAKE: 15 MINUTES AT 400°F
MAKES: 6 SERVINGS

- **1½ pounds lean ground beef or bulk Italian sausage**
- **1½ cups sliced fresh mushrooms**
- **1 15-ounce can tomato sauce with Italian seasonings**
- **¼ cup sliced pitted ripe olives (optional)**
- **1 to 1½ cups shredded mozzarella cheese or shredded Italian cheese blend (4 to 6 ounces)**
- **1 10-ounce package refrigerated biscuits (10 biscuits)**

1 Preheat oven to 400°F. In a large skillet cook beef and mushrooms until beef is browned; drain fat and discard. Stir in tomato sauce and, if desired, olives. Heat through. Transfer meat mixture to a 2-quart rectangular baking dish. Sprinkle with cheese.

2 Gently flatten each biscuit slightly with your hands. Arrange biscuits evenly on top of the cheese. Bake, uncovered, for 15 to 18 minutes or until biscuits are light brown.

PER ABOUT 1 CUP MEAT MIXTURE + 2 BISCUITS: 428 cal., 22 g total fat (9 g sat. fat), 84 mg chol., 1,036 mg sodium, 27 g carb., 2 g fiber, 32 g pro. EXCHANGES: ½ Vegetable, 1½ Starch, 3½ Lean Meat, 3 Fat

KEEP IT GOLDEN

If your casserole is perfectly golden on top before it's cooked through in the center (160°F), cover the baking dish loosely with foil for remaining baking time.

8 to try

WAFFLE FRIES: Arrange ⅓ of a 22-ounce package frozen waffle fries over hot mixture in dish. Bake about 28 minutes or until waffle fries are heated through and light brown.

BREADSTICK: Unroll one 11-ounce package refrigerated breadsticks. Separate at perforations. Twist each a few times and arrange over hot mixture in dish. Bake as directed.

FRENCH BREAD: Butter one side of each of eight ½-inch-thick slices French bread. Arrange over hot mixture, buttered sides up. Sprinkle with mozzarella cheese. Bake as directed.

TEXAS TOAST: Cut 4 slices purchased garlic Texas toast into 1-inch cubes. Scatter over hot mixture. Bake as directed.

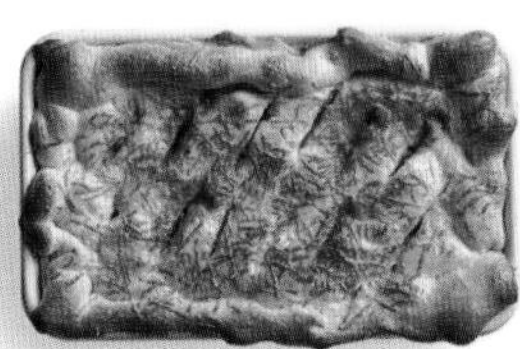

CRISPY CRUST: Unroll one 13.8-ounce package refrigerated pizza crust. Arrange over hot mixture in dish. Fold edges of crust under and pinch to seal along edge of dish. Cut ten 1-inch slits in the crust. Brush with milk and sprinkle with Parmesan cheese. Bake as directed.

GARLIC ROLLS: Thaw 6 frozen roll dough balls, snip into quarters, and toss in 2 tablespoons butter. Add 2 tablespoons Parmesan cheese and ¼ teaspoon garlic powder and toss to coat. Scatter over hot mixture in dish. Bake for 20 minutes.

MASHED POTATOES: Heat ½ of a 24-ounce package refrigerated garlic mashed potatoes. Spread over the hot mixture in dish. Drizzle with 2 tablespoons melted butter. Bake as directed. Top with snipped fresh chives.

EGG NOODLES: Cook 3 cups egg noodles according to package directions; drain and return to pan. Toss with 2 tablespoons melted butter. Spoon over hot mixture in dish. Bake for 20 minutes. Top with snipped fresh parsley.

Dilled Chicken-Orzo Casserole

PREP: 30 MINUTES **BAKE:** 35 MINUTES AT 350°F
MAKES: 6 TO 8 SERVINGS

- **1 cup packaged dried orzo pasta (8 ounces)**
- **1 2- to 2¼-pound purchased roasted chicken**
- **2 tablespoons butter or margarine**
- **2 tablespoons all-purpose flour**
- **1 14.5-ounce can chicken broth**
- **2 tablespoons capers, drained**
- **2 tablespoons snipped fresh dill weed**
- **1 tablespoon Dijon-style mustard**
- **1 teaspoon finely shredded lemon peel**
- **1 tablespoon lemon juice**
- **½ teaspoon salt**
- **¼ teaspoon black pepper**
- **1 medium yellow summer squash, halved lengthwise and sliced (1¼ cups)**
- **1 medium red sweet pepper, cut into bite-size strips (1 cup)**
- **½ of a small red onion, thinly sliced**
- **¼ cup pine nuts, toasted (see tip, page 21)**

1 Preheat oven to 350°F. In a large saucepan cook pasta according to package directions. Drain pasta; return to pan. Meanwhile, remove chicken from bones, discarding skin and bones. Using two forks, coarsely shred chicken.

2 In a medium saucepan melt butter over medium heat. Stir in flour. Gradually stir in broth. Cook and stir until thickened and bubbly. Stir in capers, dill weed, mustard, lemon peel, lemon juice, salt, and pepper.

3 Stir shredded chicken, dill mixture, squash, sweet pepper, and onion into pasta in saucepan. Transfer mixture to a 3-quart rectangular baking dish. Cover with foil.

4 Bake about 35 minutes or until heated through. Sprinkle with pine nuts.

PER 1⅔ CUPS: 598 cal., 33 g total fat (11 g sat. fat), 178 mg chol., 1,724 mg sodium, 37 g carb., 3 g fiber, 42 g pro.
EXCHANGES: ½ Vegetable, 2½ Starch, 5 Lean Meat, 3 Fat

BEST-LOVED

Chicken Enchiladas

PREP: 30 MINUTES **BAKE:** 40 MINUTES AT 350°F
MAKES: 6 SERVINGS

- **¼ cup slivered almonds, toasted (see tip, page 21)**
- **¼ cup chopped onion**
- **1 to 2 medium fresh jalapeño chile peppers, seeded and chopped (see tip, page 44) (optional)**
- **2 tablespoons butter or margarine**
- **1 4-ounce can diced green chiles, drained**
- **1 3-ounce package cream cheese, softened**
- **1 tablespoon milk**
- **1 teaspoon ground cumin**
- **3 cups chopped cooked chicken**
- **12 7-inch flour tortillas or 6-inch corn tortillas**
- **1 10.75-ounce can condensed cream of chicken or cream of mushroom soup**
- **1 8-ounce carton sour cream**
- **1 cup milk**
- **¾ cup shredded Monterey Jack or cheddar cheese (3 ounces)**
- **Finely chopped jalapeño chile peppers, snipped fresh cilantro, and/or sliced green onion (optional)**

1 Preheat oven to 350°F. Grease a 3-quart rectangular baking dish; set aside. In a medium skillet cook the ¼ cup almonds, the onion, and, if desired, jalapeño peppers in hot butter over medium heat until onion is tender. Remove from heat. Stir in 1 tablespoon of the canned chiles; reserve remaining chiles for sauce.

2 In a medium bowl combine cream cheese, the 1 tablespoon milk, and cumin; add nut mixture and chicken. Stir until combined. Spoon about ¼ cup of the chicken mixture onto each tortilla; roll up. Place filled tortillas, seam sides down, in prepared baking dish; set aside.

3 In a medium bowl combine soup, sour cream, 1 cup milk, and reserved chiles.* Pour over the tortillas in baking dish. Cover with foil.

4 Bake about 35 minutes or until heated through. Remove foil. Sprinkle enchiladas with cheese. Bake about 5 minutes more or until cheese melts. If desired, top with finely chopped jalapeño chile peppers, snipped fresh cilantro, and/or sliced green onion.

PER 2 ENCHILADAS: 668 cal., 37 g total fat (17 g sat. fat), 127 mg chol., 1,202 mg sodium, 47 g carb., 5 g fiber, 35 g pro
EXCHANGES: 2½ Starch, ½ Other Carb, 4 Medium-Fat Meat, 5½ Fat

***NOTE:** If you prefer a red sauce, omit the almonds, soup, sour cream, and 1 cup milk. Stir the reserved chiles into 2½ cups homemade enchilada sauce or two 10-ounce cans enchilada sauce. Bake as directed.

LIGHTENED-UP CHICKEN ENCHILADAS: Prepare as directed, except use fat-free or light cream cheese (4 ounces), reduced-sodium condensed soup, fat-free or light sour cream, fat-free milk, and reduced-fat Monterey Jack cheese. Top the baked enchiladas with ½ cup chopped tomato (1 medium).

PER 2 ENCHILADAS: 546 cal., 21 g total fat (8 g sat. fat,), 91 mg chol., 1,058 mg sodium, 51 g carb., 4 g fiber, 37 g pro.
EXCHANGES: 3½ Starch, 4 Lean Meat, 1½ Fat

Chicken Tetrazzini

PREP: 30 MINUTES **BAKE:** 15 MINUTES AT 350°F
MAKES: 6 SERVINGS

- **8 ounces packaged dried spaghetti or linguine**
- **2 cups sliced fresh mushrooms**
- **½ cup sliced green onions (4)**
- **2 tablespoons butter or margarine**
- **¼ cup all-purpose flour**
- **⅛ teaspoon black pepper**
- **⅛ teaspoon ground nutmeg**
- **1¼ cups chicken broth**
- **1¼ cups half-and-half, light cream, or milk**
- **2 cups chopped purchased roasted chicken (without skin), chopped cooked chicken, or chopped cooked turkey**
- **2 tablespoons dry sherry or milk**
- **¼ cup grated Parmesan cheese (1 ounce)**
- **¼ cup sliced almonds, toasted (see tip, page 21)**
- **2 tablespoons snipped fresh parsley (optional)**

1 Preheat oven to 350°F. Cook spaghetti according to package directions; drain.

2 Meanwhile, in a large saucepan cook mushrooms and green onions in hot butter over medium heat until tender. Stir in flour, pepper, and nutmeg. Add broth and half-and-half all at once. Cook and stir until thickened and bubbly. Stir in chicken, sherry, and half of the Parmesan cheese. Add cooked spaghetti; stir gently to coat.

3 Transfer pasta mixture to a 2-quart rectangular baking dish. Sprinkle with remaining cheese and the almonds. Bake, uncovered, about 15 minutes or until heated through. If desired, sprinkle with parsley.

PER 1 CUP: 421 cal., 21 g total fat (9 g sat. fat), 82 mg chol., 630 mg sodium, 38 g carb., 2 g fiber, 21 g pro.
EXCHANGES: ½ Vegetable, 2½ Starch, 2 Lean Meat, 2½ Fat

Classic Chicken Pot Pie *(photo, page 219)*

PREP: 30 MINUTES **BAKE:** 40 MINUTES AT 400°F
STAND: 10 MINUTES **MAKES:** 8 SERVINGS

- **½ cup butter**
- **½ cup all-purpose flour**
- **1 14.5-ounce can chicken broth**
- **1½ cups milk**
- **3 cups chopped cooked chicken**
- **1 16-ounce package frozen mixed vegetables**
- **½ of a 14.4-ounce package frozen pearl onions (1½ cups)**
- **1 teaspoon poultry seasoning**
- **½ teaspoon salt**
- **⅛ teaspoon black pepper**
- **1 recipe Pastry for Double-Crust Pie (page 442)**
- **1 tablespoon milk**
- **¼ cup grated Parmesan cheese**

1 Preheat oven to 400°F. In a large saucepan melt butter over medium heat. Stir in flour. Cook and stir for 1 minute. Stir in broth and the 1½ cups milk. Cook and stir until thickened and bubbly. Stir in chicken, vegetables, onions, poultry seasoning, salt, and pepper. Cook and stir until heated through. Set aside; keep warm.

2 Prepare Pastry for Double-Crust Pie, except do not divide pastry in half. On a lightly floured surface roll pastry from center to edges into an oval or rectangle 1 inch larger than a 3-quart oval or rectangular baking dish (about 14×10 inches). Transfer hot chicken mixture to baking dish. Cut pastry into 1½-inch-wide strips. Weave strips over hot filling in a wide lattice pattern. Trim pastry ½ inch beyond edge of dish. Brush top of pastry with the 1 tablespoon milk. Sprinkle with Parmesan cheese.

3 Bake, uncovered, about 40 minutes or until light brown and edges are bubbly. Let stand 10 minutes before serving.

PER 1 CUP: 618 cal., 37 g total fat (16 g sat. fat), 100 mg chol., 913 mg sodium, 48 g carb., 4 g fiber, 25 g pro.
EXCHANGES: 2 Vegetable, 2½ Starch, 2 Lean Meat, 6 Fat

BEST-LOVED

Tuna Noodle Casserole *(photo, page 221)*

PREP: 30 MINUTES **BAKE:** 25 MINUTES AT 375°F
STAND: 5 MINUTES **MAKES:** 4 SERVINGS

- **3 cups packaged dried wide egg noodles (about 5 ounces)**
- **1 cup chopped celery (2 stalks)**
- **¾ cup chopped sweet red pepper (1 medium)**
- **¼ cup chopped onion**
- **¼ cup butter or margarine**
- **¼ cup all-purpose flour**
- **1 to 2 tablespoons Dijon-style mustard**
- **½ teaspoon salt**
- **¼ teaspoon black pepper**
- **2¼ cups milk**
- **1 12-ounce can chunk white tuna (water pack), drained and broken into chunks; two 5-ounce pouches chunk light tuna in water, drained; or two 6-ounce cans skinless, boneless salmon, drained**
- **½ cup panko bread crumbs or soft bread crumbs**
- **¼ cup freshly grated Parmesan cheese**
- **1 tablespoon snipped fresh parsley**
- **1 tablespoon butter, melted**

1 Preheat oven to 375°F. Lightly grease a 1½-quart casserole; set aside. In a large saucepan cook noodles according to package directions. Drain; return noodles to pan.

2 Meanwhile, for sauce, in a medium saucepan cook celery, sweet pepper, and onion in ¼ cup hot butter over medium heat for 8 to 10 minutes or until vegetables are tender. Stir in flour, mustard, salt, and black pepper. Add milk all at once; cook and stir until slightly thickened and bubbly. Gently fold sauce and tuna into the cooked noodles. Transfer noodle mixture to prepared casserole.

3 In a small bowl combine panko bread crumbs, cheese, parsley, and melted butter. Sprinkle panko mixture over noodle mixture. Bake, uncovered, for 25 to 30 minutes or until heated through. Let stand about 5 minutes before serving.

PER 1½ CUPS: 495 cal., 23 g total fat (12 g sat. fat), 115 mg chol., 1,040 mg sodium, 42 g carb., 3 g fiber, 33 g pro.
EXCHANGES: ½ Vegetable, 2½ Starch, 3½ Lean Meat, 2 Fat

CHEESY TUNA NOODLE CASSEROLE: Prepare as directed, except add 1 cup cheddar cheese cubes (4 ounces) with the tuna.

PER 1½ CUPS: 609 cal., 31 g total fat (18 g sat. fat), 145 mg chol., 1,216 mg sodium, 42 g carb., 3 g fiber, 40 g pro.
EXCHANGES: 2½ Starch, ½ Vegetable, 4½ Medium-Fat Meat, 2 Fat

Quinoa Caprese Casserole

PREP: 35 MINUTES **STAND:** 5 MINUTES
BAKE: 30 MINUTES AT 350°F **MAKES:** 5 SERVINGS

- **Nonstick cooking spray**
- **2 cups water**
- **1 cup quinoa, rinsed and drained**
- **½ teaspoon salt**
- **1½ cups purchased marinara sauce**
- **2 tablespoons tomato paste**
- **⅔ cup finely shredded Parmesan cheese**
- **⅓ cup whipping cream**
- **½ teaspoon crushed red pepper**
- **¼ teaspoon black pepper**
- **1½ cups grape tomatoes or cherry tomatoes, halved**
- **1 cup shredded mozzarella cheese (4 ounces)**
- **¾ cup shredded fresh basil**
- **6 ounces fresh mozzarella, cut into ½-inch cubes**
- **Crusty Italian bread (optional)**

1 Preheat oven to 350°F. Lightly coat a 2-quart square baking dish with cooking spray; set aside. In a medium saucepan combine the water, the quinoa, and salt. Bring to boiling; reduce heat. Simmer, covered, about 15 minutes or until water is absorbed. Let stand for 5 minutes. Uncover and fluff quinoa with a fork; set aside.

QUINOA CAPRESE CASSEROLE

2 In a large saucepan combine marinara sauce and tomato paste. Stir over low heat until smooth. Stir in Parmesan cheese, cream, crushed red pepper, and black pepper. Bring to boiling; remove from heat. Add cooked quinoa; mix gently. Using a rubber spatula, fold in ¾ cup of the grape tomatoes, the shredded mozzarella cheese, and ¼ cup of the basil. Spoon quinoa mixture into the prepared baking dish, spreading evenly. Top with the fresh mozzarella cheese.

3 Bake, uncovered, about 30 minutes or until heated through. Top with the remaining ¾ cup grape tomatoes and the remaining ½ cup basil. If desired, serve with bread.

PER 1 CUP: 421 cal., 22 g total fat (12 g sat. fat), 70 mg chol., 1,043 mg sodium, 33 g carb., 5 g fiber, 23 g pro.
EXCHANGES: 1½ Vegetable, 1½ Starch, 2 Medium Fat Meat, 2 Fat

TOTING HOT CASSEROLES

Casseroles make perfect potluck fare. If you don't own an insulated casserole carrier, here are a few ideas to help keep your casserole hot as it travels.

- Fold an inch-deep thickness of old newspapers around the casserole.
- Wrap your casserole in a thick layer of clean, dry bath towels.
- Tuck microwavable hand warmers around the casserole before wrapping it up.

Farro, Cherry Tomato, and Carrot Gratin with Asiago

PREP: 20 MINUTES **COOK:** 30 MINUTES
BAKE: 20 MINUTES AT 400°F **STAND:** 15 MINUTES
MAKES: 4 SERVINGS

- **Olive oil cooking spray**
- **2 tablespoons olive oil**
- **3 large shallots, chopped**
- **1⅓ cups pearled farro or farro, rinsed and drained**
- **3 cups reduced-sodium chicken broth**
- **½ teaspoon salt**
- **¼ teaspoon black pepper**
- **1 cup shredded carrots (2 medium)**
- **1 cup cherry tomatoes, halved**
- **⅓ cup snipped fresh basil**
- **4 eggs, lightly beaten**
- **1 cup half-and-half or light cream**
- **½ cup grated Asiago cheese (2 ounces)**
- **⅓ cup soft whole wheat bread crumbs**
- **2 tablespoons coarsely snipped fresh Italian parsley**
- **6 ounces fresh asparagus spears, trimmed**

1 Lightly coat a 2-quart gratin or baking dish with olive oil cooking spray; set aside. In a medium saucepan heat oil over medium heat. Add shallots; reduce heat to medium-low. Cook 5 minutes or until tender. Add farro; stir to coat. Add broth, salt, and pepper. Return to boiling; reduce heat. Simmer, uncovered, for 25 minutes for pearled farro (or up to 45 minutes for regular farro) or until tender.

2 Remove farro mixture from heat. Stir in carrots, tomatoes, and basil. Cover; let stand for 5 minutes.

3 Preheat oven to 400°F. Scrape farro mixture into prepared dish; spread into a thin layer. In a medium bowl whisk together eggs, half-and-half, and cheese. Pour egg mixture over farro mixture; stir gently to combine.

4 In a small bowl combine bread crumbs and parsley; sprinkle over farro and egg mixture. Place asparagus spears in a crisscross pattern over the top of the dish. Lightly coat the asparagus and crumb mixture with additional olive oil cooking spray.

5 Bake, uncovered, for 20 to 25 minutes or until a knife inserted near center comes out clean. Let stand 10 minutes before serving.

PER 1 CUP: 557 cal., 24 g total fat (10 g sat. fat), 223 mg chol., 1,026 mg sodium, 57 g carb., 7 g fiber, 26 g pro.
EXCHANGES: 1 Vegetable, 3½ Starch, 1½ Medium Fat Meat, 2½ Fat

cookies & bars

cookies & bars

Follow these tips to make your cookies into perfect packages of pleasure the first and every time you bake them.

SHEET SMARTS

A quality cookie sheet in top-notch condition can make all the difference.

- Replace cookie sheets that have become warped or dark from years of baked-on grease.
- Purchase shiny, heavy-gauge cookie sheets that have very low or no sides.
- Choose cookie sheets that fit in your oven easily, allowing 1 to 2 inches of space around the pan.
- Avoid dark-color cookie sheets, which can cause cookies to overbrown.
- Use jelly-roll pans (four-sided 15×10×1-inch baking pans) for bar cookies only. The 1-inch sides prevent other types of cookies from browning evenly.

BUTTER BASICS

Nothing beats the flavor, richness, and texture that butter adds to cookies, so substitute another ingredient only if the option is offered. Make sure the butter you use has softened to room temperature. It should have lost its chill and be spreadable; 30 minutes should do the trick. Never use melted butter unless it is specifically called for.

Melt-in-Your-Mouth Sugar Cookies, page 244

SAVVY STORAGE

Proper storage keeps cookies fresh and appetizing.

- Cool cookies completely before storing.
- Layer cookies between waxed paper and use storage containers with tight-fitting lids.
- Store cookies or bars that have creamy or delicate toppings in a single layer.
- Avoid storing crisp cookies and soft cookies in the same container—one type can change the texture of another.
- Store cookies and bars at room temperature for up to 3 days or in the refrigerator as specified in the recipe.

FREEZE WITH EASE

Most cookies will freeze well if you keep these guidelines in mind.

- Freeze unfrosted, unfilled, and undrizzled cookies and bars layered between waxed paper in airtight containers up to 3 months.
- To thaw, leave the cookies in their storage containers and place the containers in the refrigerator or on the countertop. Frost or fill cookies after they have completely thawed.
- Most cookie doughs, with the exception of bar batters and meringue and macaroon doughs, can be frozen for up to 6 months. Thaw in the refrigerator.

COOKIE PACKAGING

To send cookies in the mail, choose crisp or firm cookies, such as sliced, drop, and bar cookies, not moist, frosted, or filled ones. Wrap cookies in plastic wrap back-to-back. Line a sturdy cardboard box with bubble wrap and pack cookies in layers of tissue paper. Fill the box completely so the cookies do not shift. Mark them “perishable.”

chocolate chip cookies

The Secret: Just a splash of corn syrup ensures the chewiest, most tender cookies that stay fresh for *days*.

PREP: 30 MINUTES **BAKE:** 6 MINUTES AT 375°F **COOL:** 2 MINUTES
MAKES: ABOUT 48 COOKIES

- **½ cup butter, softened**
- **½ cup shortening***
- **1 cup packed brown sugar**
- **½ cup granulated sugar**
- **1 teaspoon baking soda**
- **¾ teaspoon salt**
- **2 eggs**
- **2 tablespoons light-color corn syrup**
- **1 tablespoon vanilla**
- **2¾ cups all-purpose flour**
- **1 12-ounce package (2 cups) semisweet chocolate pieces or miniature candy-coated semisweet chocolate pieces**

Shortening melts at a higher temperature than butter, so it helps the cookie keep its structure for a longer time in the oven. A combo of butter and shortening is best: butter for flavor, shortening for texture.

1 Preheat oven to 375°F. In a large mixing bowl beat butter and shortening with an electric mixer on medium to high speed for 30 seconds. Add the brown sugar, granulated sugar, baking soda, and salt. Beat on medium speed for 2 minutes, scraping sides of bowl occasionally. Beat in eggs, corn syrup, and vanilla until combined. Beat in as much of the flour as you can with the mixer. Stir in any remaining flour. Stir in chocolate pieces.

2 Drop dough by rounded teaspoons or a small cookie scoop 2 inches apart onto ungreased cookie sheets. Bake for 6 to 8 minutes or until edges are just light brown (cookies may not appear set). Cool on cookie sheet for 2 minutes. Transfer to wire racks and let cool.

***NOTE:** You can substitute ½ cup vegetable oil for the shortening. Prepare as directed, except beat butter on medium to high speed for 30 seconds; gradually beat in the oil. Continue as directed.

WHOLE WHEAT CHOCOLATE CHIP COOKIES: Prepare as directed, except substitute 1 cup whole wheat flour for 1 cup of the all-purpose flour.

PER COOKIE PLAIN OR WHOLE WHEAT VARIATION: 128 cal., 6 g total fat (3 g sat. fat), 13 mg chol., 85 mg sodium, 17 g carb., 1 g fiber, 1 g pro.
EXCHANGES: 1 Starch, 1 Fat

COOKIE DOUGH POINTERS

1. SOFTEN IT UP
Softened butter is the perfect consistency to cream with sugar. To soften, leave butter on the counter at room temperature for 30 minutes or microwave on 50% power for 15-second intervals until you can press into it easily. Don't melt the butter; it won't behave the same in the batter.

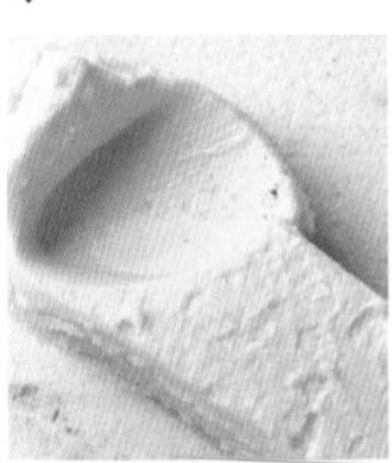

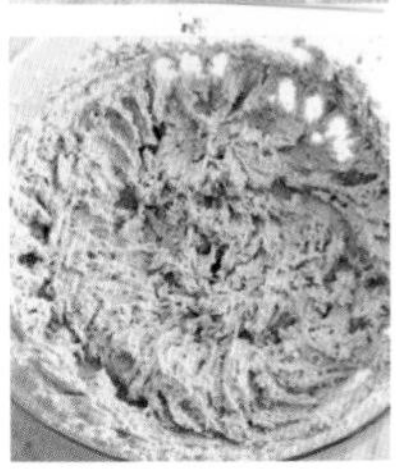

2. WHIP
Creaming the butter and sugar together traps tiny air bubbles, helping to leaven the cookies. Beat the butter and sugar together until the mixture is light in color and resembles whipped butter.

A LITTLE SUGAR
Although corn syrup is a form of sugar, it is not the same as high fructose corn syrup. In baked goods corn syrup acts as a liquid and a tenderizer.

NUTTY FLAVOR
The addition of whole wheat flour adds a nutty, rich flavor to this chocolate chip cookie. It's delicious without the whole wheat flour but exceptional with it.

ESSENTIAL COOKIE INGREDIENTS

FATS

Fats influence the cookie's flavor and how much the batter will spread while baking.

SHORTENING: It doesn't melt as quickly as butter during baking, so cookies keep their shape and won't be too crisp.

BUTTER: Adding a richer flavor to the baked cookies than shortening, butter also melts faster during baking, so the batter spreads more, resulting in thinner cookies.

FLOURS

Different types of flour contain different amounts of protein. The protein content may influence the shape, tenderness, and color of the final cookies.

CAKE FLOUR: This is low in protein, so cookies are tender and light in texture and color.

BREAD FLOUR: This high-protein flour makes the final cookies tuggier.

ALL-PURPOSE FLOUR: With a moderate amount of protein, this flour falls in the middle of the two.

LEAVENERS

BAKING SODA: This chemical leavener activates when it comes into contact with an acidic ingredient. Additional baking soda may contribute to browning.

BAKING POWDER: This is another chemical leavener. Most kinds are double-acting, so it first reacts when it comes into contact with liquid and again with heat.

SUGARS

GRANULATED SUGAR: It has a low moisture content, so the sugars crystallize when baked, creating a crisp texture.

BROWN SUGAR: This has a higher moisture content because it contains molasses. The brown sugar makes the cookies softer and is well suited for cakelike or chewy cookies.

make it mine

Oatmeal Cookies

What's the best recipe for oatmeal cookies? The one that's made with ingredients you like most! Start with the basics and play with tasty options for your own one-of-a-kind cookie.

PREP: 30 MINUTES
BAKE: 8 MINUTES AT 350°F
COOL: 2 MINUTES
MAKES: ABOUT 24 COOKIES

- FAT
- SUGAR
- 1 **teaspoon baking soda**
- SPICE
- ½ **teaspoon salt**
- 2 **eggs**
- FLAVORING
- FLOUR
- 3 **cups regular or quick rolled oats**
- 1 **cup STIR-IN (optional)**

1 Preheat oven to 350°F. In a large mixing bowl beat Fat with an electric mixer on medium to high speed for 30 seconds. Add Sugar, baking soda, Spice, and salt. Beat until combined, scraping sides of bowl. Beat in eggs and Flavoring. Beat in as much of the Flour as you can with the mixer. Stir in any remaining Flour and the oats. If desired, add Stir-In.*

2 Drop dough by rounded teaspoons or tablespoons or by a ¼-cup measure or cookie scoop 2 to 3 inches apart onto ungreased cookie sheets. Bake for 8 to 10 minutes for rounded teaspoons or tablespoons, or 12 to 14 minutes for ¼ cup or cookie scoop portions, or until light brown and centers appear set. Cool on cookie sheets for 2 minutes. Transfer cookies to wire racks and let cool completely.

***NOTE:** Instead of using just one Stir-In, you can use two or even three. Just be sure the total amount of the Stir-In equals 1 cup.

FAT *(pick one)*

1 cup butter
½ cup butter plus ½ cup shortening
½ cup butter plus ½ cup peanut butter

SUGAR *(pick one)*

1 cup packed brown sugar plus ½ cup granulated sugar
1½ cups packed brown sugar
1 cup granulated sugar plus ½ cup molasses (add ¼ cup additional all-purpose flour)
1 cup granulated sugar plus ½ cup honey

SPICE *(pick one)*

1 teaspoon ground cinnamon, pumpkin pie spice, or apple pie spice
½ teaspoon ground allspice

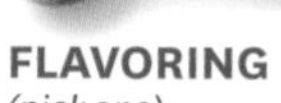

FLAVORING *(pick one)*

1 teaspoon vanilla
½ teaspoon coconut flavoring
½ teaspoon maple flavoring

FLOUR *(pick one)*

1½ cups all-purpose flour
¾ cup all-purpose flour plus ¾ cup whole wheat flour
1 cup all-purpose flour plus ½ cup oat bran
1¼ cups all-purpose flour plus ¼ cup toasted wheat germ

STIR-IN *(pick one)*

Raisins, dried cranberries or dried tart cherries
Semisweet or milk chocolate pieces
Butterscotch-flavor baking pieces
Flaked coconut
Candy-coated milk chocolate pieces

Triple-Chocolate Cookies

PREP: 40 MINUTES **COOL:** 10 MINUTES
STAND: 20 MINUTES **BAKE:** 9 MINUTES AT 350°F
MAKES: ABOUT 60 COOKIES

- **7 ounces bittersweet chocolate, chopped**
- **5 ounces unsweetened chocolate, chopped**
- **½ cup butter**
- **⅓ cup all-purpose flour**
- **¼ teaspoon baking powder**
- **¼ teaspoon salt**
- **1 cup granulated sugar**
- **¾ cup packed brown sugar**
- **4 eggs**
- **¼ cup finely chopped pecans, toasted (see tip, page 21)**
- **1 recipe Chocolate Drizzle**

1 In a 2-quart saucepan combine chocolates and butter. Heat and stir over low heat until chocolate melts and mixture is smooth. Remove from heat. Let cool for 10 minutes. In a small bowl stir together flour, baking powder, and salt; set aside.

2 In a large mixing bowl combine sugars and eggs. Beat with an electric mixer on medium to high speed for 2 to 3 minutes or until color lightens slightly. Beat in melted chocolate mixture. Add flour mixture to chocolate mixture; beat until combined. Stir in pecans (see photo 1, below). Cover surface of cookie dough with plastic wrap. Let stand for 20 minutes (dough thickens as it stands).

3 Preheat oven to 350°F. Line cookie sheets with parchment paper or foil. Drop dough by rounded teaspoons 2 inches apart on prepared cookie sheets (see photo 2, below). Bake about 9 minutes or just until tops are set. Cool on cookie sheet for 1 minute. Transfer to a wire rack and let cool. Spoon Chocolate Drizzle over cookies (see photo 3, below).

CHOCOLATE DRIZZLE: In a small saucepan heat and stir 1 cup semisweet chocolate pieces and 4 teaspoons shortening over low heat until chocolate melts and mixture is smooth. Remove from heat.

PER COOKIE: 92 cal., 6 g fat (3 g sat. fat), 18 mg chol., 19 mg sodium, 11 g carb., 1 g fiber, 1 g pro.
EXCHANGES: 2½ Other Carb., 4 Fat

BIG TRIPLE-CHOCOLATE COOKIES: Prepare as directed, except drop 3 tablespoons of dough per cookie in mounds 3 inches apart onto cookie sheets. Bake for 13 minutes. Makes about 18 cookies.

PER COOKIE: 307 cal., 19 g total fat (2 g sat. fat), 61 mg chol., 63 mg sodium, 37 g carb., 3 g fiber, 4 g pro.
EXCHANGES: 2½ Other Carb., 4 Fat

STORING CHOCOLATE

Maintain the quality of any leftover chocolate by storing it correctly. Place the chocolate in a tightly covered container or in a sealed plastic bag in a cool, dry place. If stored at higher than 70°F, chocolate may develop a "bloom"—a harmless gray surface film. Store chocolate for up to 1 year.

TRIPLE-CHOCOLATE COOKIES STEP-BY-STEP

1. Using a wooden spoon, gently stir in the chopped pecans. Note that before standing, the dough has a batterlike consistency.

2. After standing, the dough is thick enough to scoop.

3. For easy cleanup, place the cooling rack over parchment or waxed paper. To drizzle, dip a spoon into the melted chocolate and move it over the cookies as it streams off the spoon.

Sour Cream-Chocolate Drops

PREP: 25 MINUTES **BAKE:** 8 MINUTES AT 350°F
MAKES: ABOUT 42 COOKIES

- **½ cup butter, softened**
- **1 cup packed brown sugar**
- **½ teaspoon baking soda**
- **¼ teaspoon salt**
- **1 egg**
- **1 teaspoon vanilla**
- **2 ounces unsweetened chocolate, melted and cooled**
- **1 8-ounce carton sour cream**
- **2 cups all-purpose flour**
- **1 recipe Chocolate Buttercream Frosting**

1 Preheat oven to 350°F. In a large mixing bowl beat butter with an electric mixer on medium speed for 30 seconds. Add brown sugar, baking soda, and salt. Beat until combined, scraping sides of bowl occasionally. Beat in egg and vanilla. Add melted chocolate; beat until combined. Beat in sour cream. Beat in as much of the flour as you can with the mixer. Stir in any remaining flour.

2 Drop dough by rounded teaspoons 2 inches apart onto an ungreased cookie sheet. Bake for 8 to 10 minutes or until edges are firm. Transfer to a wire rack and let cool. Frost with Chocolate Buttercream Frosting.

CHOCOLATE BUTTERCREAM FROSTING: In a medium bowl beat ¼ cup butter until fluffy. Gradually add 1 cup powdered sugar and ⅓ cup unsweetened cocoa powder, beating well. Slowly beat in 3 tablespoons half-and-half and 1 teaspoon vanilla. Gradually beat in 1½ cups powdered sugar. If necessary, beat in additional half-and-half to make spreading consistency.

PER COOKIE: 120 cal., 5 g total fat (3 g sat. fat), 17 mg chol., 60 mg sodium, 18 g carb., 1 g fiber, 1 g pro.
EXCHANGES: 1 Other Carb., 1 Fat

BEST-LOVED

Coconut Macaroons

PREP: 30 MINUTES **BAKE:** 20 MINUTES AT 325°F
MAKES: ABOUT 60 MACAROONS

- **4 egg whites**
- **1 teaspoon vanilla**
- **¼ teaspoon cream of tartar**
- **⅛ teaspoon salt**
- **1⅓ cups sugar**
- **1 14-ounce package flaked coconut (5⅓ cups)**

1 Preheat oven to 325°F. Line two cookie sheets with parchment paper; set aside. In a very large mixing bowl beat egg whites, vanilla, cream of tartar, and salt with an electric mixer on high speed until soft peaks form (tips curl). Gradually add sugar, about 1 tablespoon at a time, beating until stiff peaks form (tips stand straight). Fold in coconut, half at a time.

2 Drop mixture from a teaspoon 1 inch apart into small mounds on prepared cookie sheets.* Bake for 20 to 25 minutes or until bottoms are light brown. Cool on wire racks.

***NOTE:** If you cannot use all the cookie mixture at once, cover and chill while first batch bakes.

PER MACAROON: 49 cal., 2 g total fat (2 g sat. fat), 0 mg chol., 0 mg sodium, 7 g carb., 0 g fiber, 1 g pro.
EXCHANGES: ½ Other Carb., ½ Fat

Melt-in-Your-Mouth Sugar Cookies

(photo, page 239)

PREP: 35 MINUTES **BAKE:** 12 MINUTES AT 300°F
COOL: 2 MINUTES **MAKES:** ABOUT 48 COOKIES

- **½ cup butter, softened**
- **½ cup shortening**
- **2 cups sugar**
- **1 teaspoon baking soda**
- **1 teaspoon cream of tartar**
- **⅛ teaspoon salt**
- **3 egg yolks**
- **½ teaspoon vanilla**
- **1¾ cups all-purpose flour**

1 Preheat oven to 300°F. In a large mixing bowl beat butter and shortening with an electric mixer on medium to high speed for 30 seconds. Add sugar, baking soda, cream of tartar, and salt. Beat mixture until combined, scraping sides of bowl occasionally. Beat in egg yolks and vanilla. Beat in as much of the flour as you can with the mixer. Stir in any remaining flour.

2 Shape dough into 1-inch balls. Place balls 2 inches apart on ungreased cookie sheets. Bake for 12 to 14 minutes or until edges are set; do not let edges brown. Cool cookies for 2 minutes on cookie sheet. Transfer cookies to wire racks and let cool.

PER COOKIE: 88 cal., 4 g total fat (2 g sat. fat), 18 mg chol., 47 mg sodium, 12 g carb., 0 g fiber, 1 g pro.
EXCHANGES: 1 Other Carb., 1 Fat

Frosted Maple Drops

PREP: 30 MINUTES **BAKE:** 8 MINUTES AT 350°F
MAKES: ABOUT 96 COOKIES

- **1 cup butter, softened**
- **1 cup packed brown sugar**
- **1 teaspoon baking soda**
- **1/8 teaspoon salt**
- **1 cup maple syrup**
- **1 egg**
- **1 teaspoon vanilla**
- **4 cups all-purpose flour**
- **1 recipe Maple Frosting**

1 Preheat oven to 350°F. Lightly grease a cookie sheet; set aside. In a large bowl beat 1 cup butter with an electric mixer on medium to high speed for 30 seconds. Add brown sugar, baking soda, and salt. Beat until combined, scraping sides of bowl occasionally. Add maple syrup, egg, and vanilla; beat until combined. Beat in as much of the flour as you can with the mixer. Stir in any remaining flour.

2 Drop dough by rounded teaspoons 2 inches apart onto prepared cookie sheet; flatten slightly. Bake for 8 to 10 minutes or until tops are set. Transfer cookies to a wire rack; let cool completely. Spread tops of cooled cookies with Maple Frosting.

MAPLE FROSTING: In a medium bowl whisk together 1/2 cup evaporated milk, 6 tablespoons melted butter, and 1 teaspoon maple flavoring until combined. Gradually stir in 3 to 4 cups powdered sugar until mixture is icing consistency.

PER COOKIE: 77 cal., 3 g total fat (2 g sat. fat), 10 mg chol., 38 mg sodium, 12 g carb., 0 g fiber, 1 g pro.
EXCHANGES: 1 Other Carb., 1/2 Fat

TWO WAYS TO DROP DOUGH

To drop dough from a spoon, fill a spoon with cookie dough and use another spoon to push the dough onto the cookie sheet. (Note that when a recipe calls for dropping dough from a teaspoon or tablespoon, it's referring to flatware spoons rather than measuring spoons.) A second way to drop dough is by using a small ice cream-style cookie scoop, available at kitchenware stores. This will help ensure uniform shape and size for every cookie in the batch.

Lemon Crinkles

PREP: 25 MINUTES **BAKE:** 7 MINUTES AT 375°F
COOL: 2 MINUTES **MAKES:** ABOUT 36 COOKIES

- **1 15.25-ounce package lemon cake mix (for moist cake)**
- **2 eggs**
- **⅓ cup all-purpose flour**
- **⅓ cup lemon-infused olive oil**
- **2 tablespoons finely shredded lemon peel**
- **2 tablespoons lemon juice**
- **1 teaspoon lemon extract**
- **½ teaspoon vanilla**
- **Granulated sugar**
- **Powdered sugar**

1 Preheat oven to 375°F. Line a cookie sheet with parchment paper; set aside. In a large bowl stir together cake mix, eggs, flour, oil, lemon peel, lemon juice, lemon extract, and vanilla until combined. (Dough will be soft.)

2 Place granulated sugar in one bowl and powdered sugar in another bowl. For each cookie, drop 1 tablespoon of the dough into the granulated sugar; roll to coat with sugar (dough will have a soft ball shape). Roll dough in the powdered sugar to coat. Place balls 2 inches apart on the prepared cookie sheet.

3 Bake for 7 to 9 minutes or until edges are light brown. Cool on cookie sheet for 2 minutes. Transfer cookies to a wire rack; let cool.

PER COOKIE: 86 cal., 3 g total fat (1 g sat. fat), 10 mg chol., 82 mg sodium, 14 g carb., 0 g fiber, 1 g pro.
EXCHANGES: ½ Other Carb., ½ Starch, ½ Fat

Snickerdoodles

PREP: 35 MINUTES **CHILL:** 60 MINUTES
BAKE: 10 MINUTES AT 375°F
MAKES: ABOUT 48 COOKIES

- **1 cup butter, softened**
- **1½ cups sugar**
- **1 teaspoon baking soda**
- **1 teaspoon cream of tartar**
- **¼ teaspoon salt**
- **2 eggs**
- **1 teaspoon vanilla**
- **3 cups all-purpose flour**
- **¼ cup sugar**
- **2 teaspoons ground cinnamon**

1 In a large mixing bowl beat butter with an electric mixer on medium to high speed for 30 seconds. Add the 1½ cups sugar, baking soda, cream of tartar, and salt. Beat until combined, scraping sides of bowl occasionally. Beat in eggs and vanilla until combined. Beat in as much of the flour as you can with the mixer. Stir in any remaining flour. Cover and chill dough about 60 minutes or until easy to handle.

2 Preheat oven to 375°F. In a small bowl combine the ¼ cup sugar and the cinnamon. Shape dough into 1¼-inch balls. Roll balls in sugar mixture to coat. Place 2 inches apart on ungreased cookie sheets.

3 Bake for 10 to 12 minutes or until bottoms are light brown. Transfer cookies to wire racks and let cool.

OLD-FASHIONED SUGAR COOKIES: Prepare as directed, except omit cinnamon and roll balls in ¼ cup sugar.

PER COOKIE PLAIN OR OLD-FASHIONED SUGAR COOKIE VARIATION: 94 cal., 4 g total fat (3 g sat. fat), 19 mg chol., 69 mg sodium, 13 g carb., 0 g fiber, 1 g pro.
EXCHANGES: 1 Other Carb., 1 Fat

Jam Thumbprints

PREP: 25 MINUTES **CHILL:** 60 MINUTES
BAKE: 10 MINUTES AT 375°F
MAKES: ABOUT 30 COOKIES

- **⅔ cup butter, softened**
- **½ cup sugar**
- **2 egg yolks**
- **1 teaspoon vanilla**
- **1½ cups all-purpose flour**
- **2 egg whites, lightly beaten**
- **1 cup finely chopped walnuts or pecans**
- **⅓ to ½ cup jam or preserves, chocolate-hazelnut spread, and/or desired-flavor fruit curd**

1 In a large mixing bowl beat butter with an electric mixer on medium to high speed for 30 seconds. Add sugar. Beat until combined, scraping sides of bowl occasionally. Beat in egg yolks and vanilla until combined. Beat in as much of the flour as you can with the mixer. Stir in any remaining flour. Cover and chill dough about 60 minutes or until easy to handle.

2 Preheat oven to 375°F. Grease cookie sheets; set aside. Shape dough into 1-inch balls. Roll balls in egg whites; roll balls in walnuts. Place 1 inch apart on the prepared cookie sheets. Press your thumb into the center of each ball (see photo 3, page 251). Bake for 10 to 12 minutes or until bottoms are light brown. If the cookie centers have puffed up during baking, re-press with the back of a small spoon. Transfer to a wire rack and let cool. Just before serving, fill centers with jam.

PER COOKIE: 112 cal., 7 g total fat (3 g sat. fat), 25 mg chol., 35 mg sodium, 11 g carb., 0 g fiber, 2 g pro.
EXCHANGES: 1 Other Carb., 1½ Fat

Peanut Butter Blossoms

PREP: 25 MINUTES **BAKE:** 10 MINUTES AT 350°F
MAKES: ABOUT 54 COOKIES

- ½ **cup shortening**
- ½ **cup peanut butter**
- ½ **cup granulated sugar**
- ½ **cup packed brown sugar**
- 1 **teaspoon baking powder**
- ⅛ **teaspoon baking soda**
- 1 **egg**
- 2 **tablespoons milk**
- 1 **teaspoon vanilla**
- 1¾ **cups all-purpose flour**
- ¼ **cup granulated sugar**
- **Milk chocolate kisses or stars**

1 Preheat oven to 350°F. In a large mixing bowl beat shortening and peanut butter with an electric mixer on medium to high speed for 30 seconds. Add the ½ cup granulated sugar, the brown sugar, baking powder, and baking soda. Beat until combined, scraping sides of bowl occasionally. Beat in egg, milk, and vanilla. Beat in as much of the flour as you can with the mixer. Stir in any remaining flour.

2 Shape dough into 1-inch balls. Roll balls in the ¼ cup granulated sugar. Place 2 inches apart on an ungreased cookie sheet. Bake for 10 to 12 minutes or until edges are firm and bottoms are light brown. Immediately press a chocolate kiss into each cookie's center. Transfer cookies to a wire rack and let cool.

PER COOKIE: 96 cal., 5 g total fat (2 g sat. fat), 5 mg chol., 27 mg sodium, 11 g carb., 0 g fiber, 2 g pro.
EXCHANGES: 1 Other Carb., 1 Fat.

Peanut Butter Cookies

PREP: 35 MINUTES **CHILL:** 60 MINUTES
BAKE: 7 MINUTES AT 375°F
COOL: 1 MINUTE **MAKES:** ABOUT 54 COOKIES

- 1 **cup peanut butter**
- ½ **cup butter, softened**
- ½ **cup shortening**
- 1 **cup granulated sugar**
- 1 **cup packed brown sugar or ½ cup honey**
- 1 **teaspoon baking soda**
- 1 **teaspoon baking powder**
- 2 **eggs**
- 1 **teaspoon vanilla**
- 2½ **cups all-purpose flour**
- 1 **cup honey-roasted peanuts, chopped (optional)**
- **Granulated sugar**

1 In a large mixing bowl beat peanut butter, butter, and shortening with an electric mixer on medium to high speed for 30 seconds. Add the 1 cup granulated sugar, the brown sugar, baking soda, and baking powder. Beat until combined, scraping sides of bowl occasionally. Beat in eggs and vanilla until combined. Beat in as much of the flour as you can with the mixer. Stir in any remaining flour. If desired, stir in nuts. Cover and chill dough about 60 minutes or until easy to handle.

2 Preheat oven to 375°F. Shape dough into 1¼-inch balls. Roll in additional granulated sugar to coat. Place 2 inches apart on ungreased cookie sheets. Flatten by making crisscross marks with the tines of a fork. Bake for 7 to 9 minutes or until bottoms are light brown. Let cool on cookie sheet for 1 minute. Transfer cookies to a wire rack and let cool.

PER COOKIE: 114 cal., 6 g total fat (2 g sat. fat), 12 mg chol., 63 mg sodium, 14 g carb., 0 g fiber, 2 g pro.
EXCHANGES: 1 Other Carb., 1 Fat

BEST-LOVED

Sandies *(photo, page 237)*

PREP: 35 MINUTES **CHILL:** 30 TO 60 MINUTES
BAKE: 15 MINUTES AT 325°F
MAKES: ABOUT 55 COOKIES

- **1 cup butter, softened**
- **½ cup powdered sugar**
- **1 tablespoon water**
- **1 teaspoon vanilla**
- **2 cups all-purpose flour**
- **1½ cups finely chopped pecans, toasted (see tip, page 21)**
- **1 cup powdered sugar**

1 In a large mixing bowl beat butter with an electric mixer on medium to high speed for 30 seconds. Add the ½ cup powdered sugar. Beat until combined, scraping sides of bowl occasionally. Beat in water and vanilla until combined. Beat in as much of the flour as you can with the mixer. Stir in any remaining flour and the pecans. Cover dough and chill for 30 to 60 minutes or until firm enough to shape.

2 Preheat oven to 325°F. Shape dough into 1-inch balls or 2×½-inch logs. Place 1 inch apart on ungreased cookie sheets. Bake about 15 minutes or until bottoms are light brown. Transfer to wire racks and let cool. Place the 1 cup powdered sugar in a large plastic bag. Add cooled cookies in batches to bag. Gently shake to coat.

CHOCOLATE-COVERED SANDIES: Prepare as directed, except decrease the 1 cup powdered sugar to ¾ cup and stir in ¼ cup unsweetened cocoa powder. Shake cooled cookies in cocoa powder mixture.

PER COOKIE PLAIN OR CHOCOLATE-COVERED VARIATION: 80 cal., 6 g total fat (2 g sat. fat), 9 mg chol., 24 mg sodium, 7 g carb., 0 g fiber, 1 g pro. EXCHANGES: ½ Other Carb., 1 Fat

READY OR NOT?

For the most tender cookies, do not overbake them. Check cookies for doneness after the minimum baking time called for in your recipe. If they meet the criteria for doneness as specified in the recipe, use a thin spatula to transfer the cookies to a wire cooling rack. Note that some cookies need to cool on the hot cookie sheet for 1 or 2 minutes before moving them.

Ginger Cookies

PREP: 40 MINUTES **BAKE:** 8 MINUTES AT 350°F
MAKES: ABOUT 120 COOKIES

- **4½ cups all-purpose flour**
- **4 teaspoons ground ginger**
- **2 teaspoons baking soda**
- **1½ teaspoons ground cinnamon**
- **1 teaspoon ground cloves**
- **¼ teaspoon salt**
- **1½ cups shortening**
- **2 cups sugar**
- **2 eggs**
- **½ cup molasses**
- **¾ cup sugar**

1 Preheat oven to 350°F. In a medium bowl stir together flour, ginger, baking soda, cinnamon, cloves, and salt; set aside. In a large mixing bowl beat shortening with an electric mixer on low speed for 30 seconds. Add the 2 cups sugar. Beat until combined, scraping sides of bowl occasionally. Beat in eggs and molasses until combined. Beat in as much of the flour mixture as you can with the mixer. Stir in any remaining flour mixture.

2 Shape dough into 1-inch balls. Roll balls in the ¾ cup sugar. Place 1½ inches apart on an ungreased cookie sheet. Bake for 8 to 9 minutes or until bottoms are light brown and tops are puffed (do not overbake). Cool on cookie sheet for 1 minute. Transfer to a wire rack and let cool.

PER COOKIE: 62 cal., 3 g total fat (1 g sat. fat), 4 mg chol., 28 mg sodium, 9 g carb., 0 g fiber, 1 g pro.
EXCHANGES: ½ Other Carb., ½ Fat.

BIG GINGER COOKIES: Prepare as directed, except shape dough into 2-inch balls by using a ¼-cup measure or scoop; roll in sugar. Place 2½ inches apart on an ungreased cookie sheet. Bake in a 350°F oven for 11 to 13 minutes or until bottoms are light brown and tops are puffed (do not overbake). Cool on cookie sheet for 2 minutes. Transfer to a wire rack and let cool. Makes about 24 cookies

PER COOKIE: 311 cal., 13 g total fat (3 g sat. fat), 18 mg chol., 138 mg sodium, 46 g carb., 1 g fiber, 3 g pro.
EXCHANGES: 3 Other Carb., 2½ Fat

CHOCOLATE CRINKLES

Chocolate Crinkles

PREP: 35 MINUTES **COOL:** 15 MINUTES
CHILL: 2 HOURS **BAKE:** 10 MINUTES AT 375°F
MAKES: ABOUT 60 COOKIES

- **4 ounces unsweetened chocolate**
- **½ cup shortening**
- **3 eggs, lightly beaten**
- **2 cups granulated sugar**
- **2 teaspoons baking powder**
- **2 teaspoons vanilla**
- **¼ teaspoon salt**
- **2 cups all-purpose flour**
- **⅔ cup powdered sugar**

1 In a small saucepan cook and stir chocolate and shortening over low heat until chocolate melts and mixture is smooth. Cool 15 minutes.

2 In a large bowl combine eggs, granulated sugar, baking powder, vanilla, and salt. Add chocolate mixture. Stir in flour. Cover; chill 2 hours or until easy to handle.

3 Preheat oven to 375°F. Lightly grease cookie sheets; set aside. Shape dough into 1-inch balls. Roll in powdered sugar to coat generously. Place 2 inches apart on prepared cookie sheets. Bake about 10 minutes or until edges are just set. Transfer to wire racks and let cool.

PER COOKIE: 74 cal., 3 g total fat (1 g sat. fat), 11 mg chol., 22 mg sodium, 12 g carb., 0 g fiber, 1 g pro.
EXCHANGES: 1 Other Carb., ½ Fat

BEST-LOVED

Chocolaty Caramel Thumbprints

PREP: 40 MINUTES **CHILL:** 2 HOURS
BAKE: 10 MINUTES AT 350°F
MAKES: ABOUT 32 COOKIES

- **1 egg**
- **½ cup butter, softened**
- **⅔ cup sugar**
- **2 tablespoons milk**
- **1 teaspoon vanilla**
- **1 cup all-purpose flour**
- **⅓ cup unsweetened cocoa powder**
- **¼ teaspoon salt**
- **16 vanilla caramels, unwrapped**
- **3 tablespoons whipping cream**
- **1¼ cups finely chopped pecans**
- **½ cup semisweet chocolate pieces (3 ounces)**
- **1 teaspoon shortening**

1 Separate egg; place yolk and white in separate bowls. Cover and chill egg white until needed. In a large mixing bowl beat butter with an electric mixer for 30 seconds. Add sugar and beat well. Beat in egg yolk, milk, and vanilla.

2 In another bowl combine the flour, cocoa powder, and salt. Add flour mixture to butter mixture and beat until well combined. Cover and chill dough about 2 hours or until easy to handle.

3 Preheat oven to 350°F. Lightly grease cookie sheets; set aside. In a small saucepan heat and stir caramels and whipping cream over low heat until caramels melt and mixture is smooth; set aside to cool slightly.

4 Lightly beat reserved egg white. Shape the dough into 1-inch balls. Roll the balls in egg white; roll in pecans to coat. Place balls 1 inch apart on prepared cookie sheets. Using your thumb, make an indentation in the center of each ball (see photo 3, page 251).

5 Bake about 10 minutes or until edges are firm. If cookie centers puff during baking, re-press with the back of a small spoon. Spoon melted caramel mixture into indentations of cookies. (If necessary, reheat caramel mixture to keep it spooning consistency.) Transfer cookies to wire racks; let cool.

6 In another saucepan heat and stir chocolate pieces and shortening over low heat until chocolate melts and mixture is smooth. Let cool slightly. Drizzle chocolate mixture over tops of cookies. Let stand until chocolate is set.

PER COOKIE: 127 cal., 8 g total fat (3 g sat. fat), 17 mg chol., 54 mg sodium, 14 g carb., 1 g fiber, 2 g pro.
EXCHANGES: 1 Other Carb., 1½ Fat

BEST-LOVED

Buried Cherry Cookies

PREP: 30 MINUTES **BAKE:** 10 MINUTES AT 350°F
COOL: 1 MINUTE **MAKES:** ABOUT 42 COOKIES

1 10-ounce jar maraschino cherries
½ cup butter, softened
1 cup sugar
¼ teaspoon baking powder
¼ teaspoon baking soda
¼ teaspoon salt
1 egg
1½ teaspoons vanilla
½ cup unsweetened cocoa powder
1½ cups all-purpose flour
1 cup semisweet chocolate pieces*
½ cup sweetened condensed milk

1 Preheat oven to 350°F. Drain cherries, reserving juice. Halve any large cherries. In a medium mixing bowl beat butter with an electric mixer on medium to high speed for 30 seconds. Add the sugar, baking powder, baking soda, and salt. Beat until combined, scraping sides of bowl occasionally. Beat in egg and vanilla until combined. Beat in cocoa powder and as much of the flour as you can with the mixer. Stir in any remaining flour.

2 Shape dough into 1-inch balls (see photos 1 and 2, below). Place balls 2 inches apart on an ungreased cookie sheet. Press your thumb into the center of each ball (see photo 3, below). Place a cherry in each center.

3 For frosting, in a small saucepan combine chocolate pieces and sweetened condensed milk. Cook and stir over low heat until chocolate melts and mixture is smooth. Stir in 4 teaspoons reserved cherry juice. (If necessary, frosting may be thinned with additional cherry juice.) Spoon 1 teaspoon frosting over each cherry, spreading to cover (see photo 4, below).

4 Bake about 10 minutes or until edges are firm. Cool on cookie sheet for 1 minute. Transfer cookies to a wire rack and let cool.

***NOTE:** Do not substitute imitation chocolate pieces for semisweet chocolate pieces.

BLONDIE BURIED CHERRY COOKIES: Prepare as directed, except increase baking powder to ½ teaspoon and omit baking soda. Substitute almond extract for the vanilla, omit the cocoa powder, and increase flour to 2 cups.

PER COOKIE PLAIN OR BLONDIE VARIATION: 101 cal., 4 g total fat (2 g sat. fat), 12 mg chol., 46 mg sodium, 16 g carb., 1 g fiber, 1 g pro. EXCHANGES: 1 Other Carb., 1 Fat

BLONDIE BURIED CHERRY COOKIES STEP-BY-STEP

1. To make the balls uniform in size, pat dough into a 6×7-inch rectangle on a lightly floured surface. Cut into 42 equal-size squares. Roll the squares into balls.

2. Or scoop dough using a small cookie scoop and roll into balls.

3. Gently press your thumb into each dough ball.

4. Place a cherry into each indentation and top each ball with frosting, spreading to completely cover the cherry.

Cherry Pie Bites

PREP: 30 MINUTES **BAKE:** 25 MINUTES AT 325°F
COOL: 5 MINUTES **MAKES:** 24 COOKIES

- **½ cup butter, softened**
- **1 3-ounce package cream cheese, softened**
- **1 cup all-purpose flour**
- **2 tablespoons all-purpose flour**
- **2 tablespoons chopped toasted walnuts or pecans (see tip, page 21)**
- **2 tablespoons packed brown sugar**
- **⅛ teaspoon ground nutmeg**
- **1½ tablespoons butter**
- **2 cups fresh or frozen unsweetened pitted tart red cherries, thawed**
- **⅓ cup granulated sugar**
- **2 teaspoons cornstarch**

1 Preheat oven to 325°F. For pastry, in a medium mixing bowl beat the ½ cup butter and the cream cheese with an electric mixer on medium to high speed until combined. Stir in the 1 cup flour. Shape dough into 24 balls (see photo 1, below). Press the balls into the bottoms and up the sides of 24 ungreased 1¾-inch muffin cups (see photo 2, below).

2 For streusel, in a small bowl stir together the 2 tablespoons flour, the walnuts, brown sugar, and nutmeg. Using a pastry blender, cut in the 1½ tablespoons butter until mixture is crumbly; set aside.

3 For filling, in a small saucepan combine the cherries, granulated sugar, and cornstarch. Cook over medium heat until cherries release juices, stirring occasionally. Continue to cook, stirring constantly, over medium heat until thick and bubbly. Spoon 1 heaping teaspoon of the filling into each pastry-lined cup (see photo 3, below). Sprinkle filled cups evenly with streusel (see photo 4, below).

4 Bake for 25 to 30 minutes or until edges are light brown. Cool bites in pan on a wire rack for 5 minutes. Carefully transfer to a wire rack and let cool.

PER COOKIE: 100 cal., 6 g total fat (4 g sat. fat), 16 mg chol., 52 mg sodium, 10 g carb., 0 g fiber, 1 g pro.
EXCHANGES: ½ Starch, 1 Fat

CHERRY PIE BITES STEP-BY-STEP

1. To make uniform-size balls, pat dough into a 6×4-inch rectangle on a lightly floured surface; cut into 24 equal-size squares. Roll each square into a ball.

2. Use a tassie tamper or your fingers to press the pastry dough balls into the bottom and up the sides of each muffin cup.

3. Carefully spoon a heaping tablespoon of the filling into each of the pastry dough-lined cups, being sure to get some cherries into each cup.

4. Spoon the streusel evenly over the filling. Be sure to clean up any streusel that drops onto the pan; it could burn during baking.

BEST-LOVED

Pecan Tassies

PREP: 30 MINUTES **BAKE:** 25 MINUTES AT 325°F
COOL: 5 MINUTES **MAKES:** 24 TASSIES

- **½ cup butter, softened**
- **1 3-ounce package cream cheese, softened**
- **1 cup all-purpose flour**
- **1 egg, lightly beaten**
- **¾ cup packed brown sugar**
- **1 tablespoon butter, melted**
- **⅔ cup coarsely chopped pecans**

1 Preheat oven to 325°F. For pastry, in a mixing bowl beat the ½ cup butter and cream cheese until combined. Stir in the flour. Shape dough into 24 balls (see photo 1, page 252). Press each ball into the bottom and up the sides of 24 ungreased 1¾-inch muffin cups (see photo 2, page 252).

2 For pecan filling, in a bowl stir together egg, brown sugar, and the 1 tablespoon melted butter. Stir in pecans. Spoon 1 heaping teaspoon of filling into each pastry-lined cup. Bake for 25 to 30 minutes or until pastry is light brown and filling is puffed. Cool tassies in pan on wire rack for 5 minutes. Carefully transfer to a wire rack and let cool.

FUDGY BROWNIE TASSIES: Prepare as directed, except instead of pecan filling, in a small saucepan heat and stir ½ cup semisweet chocolate pieces and 2 tablespoons butter or margarine over low heat until chocolate is melted and mixture is smooth; remove from heat. Stir in ⅓ cup granulated sugar, 1 beaten egg, and 1 teaspoon vanilla. If desired, place 1 hazelnut (filbert), almond, macadamia nut, or walnut piece in each pastry-lined muffin cup. Spoon about 1 teaspoon of the chocolate mixture into each pastry-lined muffin cup. Bake in a 325°F oven for 20 to 25 minutes or until pastry is light brown and filling is puffed. Continue as directed.

PER TASSIE PLAIN OR FUDGY BROWNIE VARIATION: 119 cal., 8 g total fat (4 g sat. fat), 24 mg chol., 47 mg sodium, 11 g carb., 0 g fiber, 1 g pro. EXCHANGES: 1 Other Carb., 1½ Fat

Chocolate Biscotti *(photo, page 237)*

PREP: 30 MINUTES **BAKE:** 20 MINUTES AT 375°F/ 15 MINUTES AT 325°F **COOL:** 60 MINUTES
MAKES: ABOUT 24 BISCOTTI

- **½ cup butter, softened**
- **⅔ cup sugar**
- **¼ cup unsweetened cocoa powder**
- **2 teaspoons baking powder**
- **2 eggs**
- **1¾ cups all-purpose flour**
- **2 cups bittersweet or semisweet chocolate pieces**
- **2 teaspoons shortening**

1 Preheat oven to 375°F. Lightly grease a cookie sheet; set aside. In a large mixing bowl beat butter with an electric mixer on medium to high speed for 30 seconds. Add sugar, cocoa powder, and baking powder. Beat until combined, scraping sides of bowl occasionally. Beat in eggs just until combined. Beat in as much of the flour as you can with the mixer. Stir in any remaining flour. Stir in 1 cup of the chocolate pieces.

2 Divide dough in half. Shape each half into a 9-inch-long roll. Place rolls about 3 inches apart on prepared cookie sheet; flatten slightly until about 2 inches wide.

3 Bake for 20 to 25 minutes or until a wooden toothpick inserted near center comes out clean. Cool on cookie sheet for 60 minutes. (For easier slicing, wrap cooled rolls in plastic wrap and let stand overnight at room temperature.)

4 Preheat oven to 325°F. Use a serrated knife to cut each roll diagonally into ½-inch-thick slices. Place slices, cut sides down, on an ungreased cookie sheet. Bake for 8 minutes. Turn slices over and bake for 7 to 9 minutes more or until dry and crisp. Transfer to a wire rack; let cool.

5 Microwave remaining chocolate pieces and the shortening, uncovered, in a small microwave-safe bowl on 50% power (medium) for 1 to 2 minutes or until chocolate melts and mixture is smooth, stirring twice. Dip one long side of each cookie into the melted chocolate; let excess drip back into bowl. Place cookies on waxed paper; let stand until set.

PER BISCOTTI: 173 cal., 10 g total fat (6 g sat. fat), 28 mg chol., 40 mg sodium, 21 g carb., 2 g fiber, 2 g pro.
EXCHANGES: 1½ Other Carb., 2 Fat

Salted Caramel-Ginger Macarons

PREP: 35 MINUTES **STAND:** 30 MINUTES
BAKE: 9 MINUTES AT 325°F
MAKES: ABOUT 30 COOKIES

- **1½ cups finely ground almonds (see tip, page 21)**
- **1¼ cups powdered sugar**
- **1½ teaspoons ground ginger**
- **3 egg whites**
- **½ teaspoon vanilla**
- **Dash salt**
- **¼ cup granulated sugar**
- **6 drops yellow food coloring**
- **½ of a 14-ounce package vanilla caramels, unwrapped**
- **2 tablespoons whipping cream**
- **Coarse sea salt**

1 Line three large cookie sheets with parchment paper; set aside. In a medium bowl stir together almonds, powdered sugar, and ginger; set aside.

2 In a large bowl combine egg whites, vanilla, and salt. Beat with an electric mixer on medium speed until frothy (see photo 1, below). Gradually add granulated sugar, about 1 tablespoon at a time, beating on high speed just until soft peaks form (tips curl) (see photo 2, below). Gradually fold in nut mixture and food coloring (see photo 3, below).

3 Spoon mixture into a large decorating bag fitted with a large (about ½-inch) round tip (see "In the Bag," below). Pipe 1½-inch circles 1 inch apart onto the prepared cookie sheets (see photo 4, below). Let stand for 30 minutes before baking.

4 Meanwhile, preheat oven to 325°F. Bake for 9 to 10 minutes or until set. Cool on cookie sheets on wire racks. Carefully peel cookies off parchment paper.

5 In a small saucepan combine caramels and cream; heat and stir over low heat until caramels melt and mixture is smooth. Spread a scant teaspoon of caramel mixture on bottoms of half of the cookies; immediately after spreading, sprinkle each with a little coarse sea salt. Top with the remaining cookies, bottom sides down.

PER COOKIE: 85 cal., 3 g total fat (1 g sat. fat), 1 mg chol., 40 mg sodium, 12 g carb., 1 g fiber, 2 g pro.
EXCHANGES: 1 Other Carb., ½ Fat

IN THE BAG

If you don't own a decorating bag, you can use a large resealable plastic bag. Spoon the cookie mixture into the bag and snip a ½-inch hole in the bottom corner of the bag. Gently push the mixture toward the corner hole from the top of the bag; twist the top of the bag to prevent the mixture from pushing upward.

SALTED CARAMEL-GINGER MACARONS STEP-BY-STEP

1. Before adding the granulated sugar, beat the egg white mixture until frothy. Bubbles should cover the surface of the mixture.

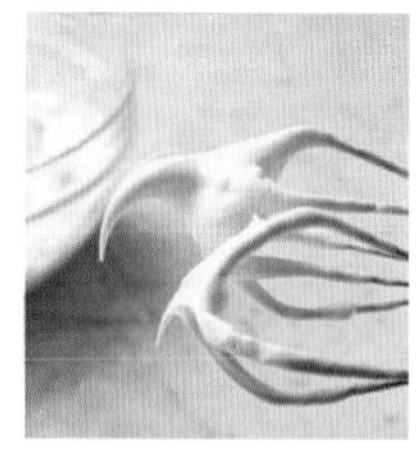

2. Gradually add the granulated sugar, beating on high speed just until soft peaks form (tips curl).

3. Use a rubber spatula to gently fold in nut mixture. To see if the batter is ready for piping, lift a spoonful about 2 inches above the surface and slowly streak it across the batter in the bowl. It should fall from the spoon in a thick ribbon and sit on the surface about 30 seconds before disappearing.

4. To pipe the cookies, use a pencil to draw 1½-inch circles 1 inch apart on the parchment paper. Flip paper over. Pipe the cookie mixture into each circle.

Chocolate-Mint Pinwheels

PREP: 40 MINUTES **CHILL:** 2 TO 3 HOURS
BAKE: 6 MINUTES AT 375°F
MAKES: ABOUT 72 COOKIES

- **1 cup butter, softened**
- **1 cup sugar**
- **1 teaspoon baking powder**
- **¼ teaspoon salt**
- **1 egg**
- **1 teaspoon vanilla**
- **2¼ cups all-purpose flour**
- **2 ounces semisweet chocolate, melted and slightly cooled***
- **1 4.67-ounce package layered chocolate-mint candies,** finely chopped (1 cup)**
- **¼ teaspoon peppermint extract**

1 In a large mixing bowl beat butter with an electric mixer on medium to high speed for 30 seconds. Add sugar, baking powder, and salt. Beat until mixture is combined, scraping sides of bowl occasionally. Beat in egg and vanilla until combined. Beat in as much flour as you can with the mixer. Stir in any remaining flour.

2 Divide dough in half. Stir melted chocolate into one dough portion. Stir chopped chocolate-mint candies and peppermint extract into remaining dough portion. Divide each dough portion in half. Cover and chill dough for at least 60 minutes or until easy to handle.

3 Roll each peppermint dough portion into a 9½×6-inch rectangle on a piece of waxed paper.*** Roll each chocolate dough portion into a 9½×6-inch rectangle on waxed paper. Invert one chocolate dough rectangle on top of one peppermint dough rectangle; remove waxed paper (see photo 1, left). Roll up dough (see photo 2, left). Pinch dough edges to seal; wrap in plastic wrap. Repeat with remaining chocolate and peppermint dough rectangles. Chill dough rolls for 60 minutes to 2 hours or until very firm.

4 Preheat oven to 375°F. Lightly grease cookie sheets; set aside. Unwrap dough rolls; reshape if necessary. Cut dough rolls crosswise into ¼-inch-thick slices. Place slices 2 inches apart on prepared cookie sheets.

5 Bake for 6 to 8 minutes or until edges are firm and just starting to brown. Transfer cookies to a wire rack and let cool.

***NOTE:** To melt the semisweet chocolate, chop chocolate and place in a small microwave-safe bowl. Microwave on 50% power (medium) about 1 to 2 minutes or until chocolate is melted and smooth, stirring once.

****NOTE:** If chocolate-mint candies aren't available, use one 4.67-ounce package of individually wrapped layered chocolate mint candies. Unwrap candies and finely chop.

*****NOTE:** To keep the waxed paper from sliding on the countertop while you roll out the cookie dough, lightly brush the countertop with shortening.

PER COOKIE: 65 cal., 4 g total fat (2 g sat. fat), 10 mg chol., 32 mg sodium, 8 g carb., 0 g fiber, 1 g pro.
EXCHANGES: ½ Other Carb., 1 Fat

CHOCOLATE-MINT PINWHEELS STEP-BY-STEP

1. Use the waxed paper and your hand to carefully invert chocolate dough rectangle onto peppermint dough rectangle.

2. Starting from a long side, roll up dough using bottom layer of waxed paper to help lift and guide the roll.

Cinnamon-Almond Slices *(photo, page 237)*

PREP: 25 MINUTES **CHILL:** 2 HOURS
BAKE: 8 MINUTES AT 350°F
MAKES: ABOUT 48 COOKIES

- **2/3 cup butter, softened**
- **1 8-ounce can almond paste**
- **1/4 cup packed brown sugar**
- **1 teaspoon baking powder**
- **1 teaspoon ground cinnamon**
- **1/2 teaspoon salt**
- **1 egg**
- **2 cups all-purpose flour**
- **1/4 cup toasted almonds, very finely chopped (see tip, page 21)**

1 In a large mixing bowl beat butter with an electric mixer on medium to high speed for 30 seconds. Add almond paste, brown sugar, baking powder, cinnamon, and salt. Beat until combined, scraping sides of bowl occasionally. Beat in egg until combined. Beat in as much of the flour as you can with the mixer. Stir in any remaining flour and the almonds.

2 Divide dough in half. Shape each half into an 8-inch roll. Wrap each roll in plastic wrap or waxed paper. Chill about 2 hours or until dough is firm enough to slice.

3 Preheat oven to 350°F. If necessary, reshape rolls to make them round. Use a serrated knife to cut rolls into 1/4-inch-thick slices. Place slices 1 inch apart on an ungreased cookie sheet.

4 Bake for 8 to 10 minutes or until edges are firm and centers are set. Transfer cookies to a wire rack; let cool.

PER COOKIE: 72 cal., 4 g total fat (2 g sat. fat), 11 mg chol., 59 mg sodium, 8 g carb., 0 g fiber, 1 g pro.
EXCHANGES: 1/2 Starch, 1/2 Other Carb., 1 Fat

BEST-LOVED

Lemony Glazed Shortbread Bars

PREP: 40 MINUTES **BAKE:** 40 MINUTES AT 300°F
MAKES: 32 BARS

- **3 cups all-purpose flour**
- **1/3 cup cornstarch**
- **1 1/4 cups powdered sugar**
- **1/4 cup finely shredded lemon peel (5 to 6 lemons)**
- **1 1/2 cups butter, softened**
- **1 tablespoon lemon juice**
- **1/2 teaspoon salt**
- **1/2 teaspoon vanilla**
- **1 recipe Lemony Glaze**

LEMONY GLAZED SHORTBREAD BARS

1 Preheat oven to 300°F. Line a 13×9×2-inch baking pan with heavy foil, extending foil over the edges of the pan (see photo 1, page 262). Lightly grease foil; set aside.

2 In a medium bowl combine flour and cornstarch; set aside. In a small bowl combine powdered sugar and lemon peel. Pressing against sides of bowl with a wooden spoon, work lemon peel into powdered sugar until mixture is yellow and very fragrant; set aside.

3 In a large mixing bowl beat butter, lemon juice, salt, and vanilla with an electric mixer on medium speed until combined. Gradually beat in powdered sugar mixture. Stir in flour mixture.

4 With lightly floured fingers, press dough evenly into the prepared pan. Bake about 40 minutes or until pale golden in color and edges begin to brown. Remove from oven. Immediately spoon Lemony Glaze over top and gently spread to evenly distribute the glaze. Let cool completely. Use the edges of the foil to lift uncut bars out of pan. Place on cutting board; cut into bars.

LEMONY GLAZE: In a medium bowl combine 2 1/2 cups powdered sugar, 2 teaspoons finely shredded lemon peel, 3 tablespoons lemon juice, 1 tablespoon light-color corn syrup, and 1/2 teaspoon vanilla.

PER BAR: 181 cal., 9 g total fat (5 g sat. fat), 23 mg chol., 98 mg sodium, 25 g carb., 0 g fiber, 1 g pro.
EXCHANGES: 1 1/2 Other Carb., 2 Fat

Shortbread

This classic cookie easily adapts into all shapes, sizes, and flavor profiles.

PREP: 15 MINUTES
BAKE: 25 MINUTES AT 325°F
COOL: 5 MINUTES
MAKES: ABOUT 16 COOKIES

1¼ cups all-purpose flour
3 tablespoons granulated sugar
½ cup butter, cut up

1 Preheat oven to 325°F. In a medium bowl combine flour and granulated sugar. Using a pastry blender, cut in butter until mixture resembles fine crumbs and starts to cling (see photo 1, page 259). Form the mixture into a ball and gently knead until smooth (see photo 2, page 259).

2 To make shortbread wedges,* on an ungreased cookie sheet pat or roll the dough into an 8-inch circle (see photo 3, page 259). Make a scalloped edge (see photo 4, page 259). Cut circle into 16 wedges. Leave wedges in the circle. Bake for 25 to 30 minutes or until bottom just starts to brown and center is set. Cut circle into wedges again while warm. Cool on cookie sheet 5 minutes. Transfer to a wire rack and let cool.

***NOTE:** To make different shortbread shapes, on a lightly floured surface roll or pat dough until ½ inch thick. Use cookie cutters or a knife to cut desired shapes. Place 1 inch apart on an ungreased cookie sheet. Bake for 20 to 25 minutes.

PER COOKIE: 96 cal., 6 g total fat (4 g sat. fat), 15 mg chol., 41 mg sodium, 10 g carb., 0 g fiber, 1 g pro. EXCHANGES: ½ Other Carb., 1½ Fat

BUTTER-PECAN: Prepare as directed, except substitute brown sugar for the granulated sugar. After cutting in butter, stir in 2 tablespoons finely chopped pecans. Press pecan halves into wedges before baking.

CHERRY-PISTACHIO: Prepare as directed, except after cutting in butter, stir in 2 tablespoons each snipped dried cherries and chopped pistachios. Drizzle cooled cookies with melted white chocolate. Sprinkle with pistachios.

CHOCOLATE-ORANGE: Prepare as directed, except add 1½ teaspoons finely shredded orange peel with the butter. After cutting in butter, stir in ⅓ cup miniature semisweet chocolate pieces.

SPICED: Prepare as directed, except substitute brown sugar for the granulated sugar and stir 1 teaspoon apple pie spice into the flour mixture. Brush with egg white and sprinkle with coarse sugar before baking.

LEMON-POPPY SEED: Prepare as directed, except stir in 1 tablespoon poppy seeds with the flour mixture and add 1 teaspoon finely shredded lemon peel with the butter. Before serving, sprinkle with powdered sugar.

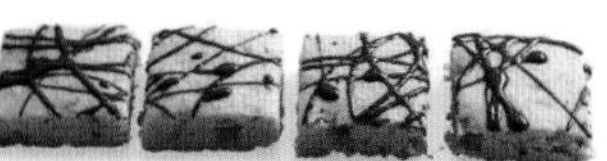

TOFFEE-ALMOND: Prepare as directed, except substitute brown sugar for the granulated sugar. After cutting in the butter, stir in 2 tablespoons each chopped almonds and crushed toffee pieces. Drizzle cooled cookies with melted chocolate.

ROSEMARY-CRANBERRY: Prepare as directed, except substitute ¼ cup cornmeal for ¼ cup of the all-purpose flour and stir in 1 teaspoon snipped fresh rosemary. After cutting in butter, stir in 2 tablespoons snipped dried cranberries.

HOLIDAY: Prepare as directed, except after cutting in butter, stir in ¼ cup finely chopped candied cherries. Dip one end of each cooled cookie in white chocolate, then in red and/or green candy sprinkles.

Chocolate-Peanut Butter Shortbread

PREP: 35 MINUTES **BAKE:** 20 MINUTES AT 325°F
COOL: 5 MINUTES **MAKES:** ABOUT 32 COOKIES

- **1½ cups all-purpose flour**
- **⅓ cup sugar**
- **¼ cup unsweetened cocoa powder**
- **⅔ cup butter, cut up**
- **¼ cup peanut butter**
- **½ cup semisweet chocolate pieces**
- **1 tablespoon shortening**
- **½ cup peanut butter-flavor pieces**

1 Preheat oven to 325°F. In a food processor combine flour, sugar, and cocoa powder. Cover and process with on/off pulses until well mixed. Add butter and peanut butter. Cover and process with on/off pulses until mixture starts to cling. Form the mixture into a ball and knead until smooth (see photo 2, below).

2 On a lightly floured surface roll dough until ½ inch thick. Using 1- to 2-inch cookie cutters, cut dough into desired shapes; place 1 inch apart on an ungreased large cookie sheet. Bake for 20 to 25 minutes or until centers are set. Cool on cookie sheet for 5 minutes. Transfer to a wire rack set over waxed paper; let cool.

3 In a small microwave-safe bowl microwave chocolate pieces and 1½ teaspoons of the shortening on 50% power (medium) about 2 minutes or until melted, stirring once. Repeat with remaining shortening and the peanut butter pieces. Drizzle cookies with the melted peanut butter and chocolate mixtures.

PER COOKIE: 113 cal., 7 g total fat (4 g sat. fat), 10 mg chol., 51 mg sodium, 11 g carb., 1 g fiber, 2 g pro.
EXCHANGES: 1 Other Carb., 1½ Fat

Blondies

PREP: 20 MINUTES **BAKE:** 25 MINUTES AT 350°F
MAKES: 36 BARS

- **2 cups packed brown sugar**
- **⅔ cup butter, cut up**
- **2 eggs**
- **2 teaspoons vanilla**
- **2 cups all-purpose flour**
- **1 teaspoon baking powder**
- **¼ teaspoon baking soda**
- **1½ cups chopped almonds**

1 Preheat oven to 350°F. Grease a 13×9×2-inch baking pan; set aside. In a medium saucepan cook and stir brown sugar and butter over medium heat until butter melts and mixture is smooth; cool slightly.

2 Stir in eggs, one at a time. Stir in vanilla. Stir in flour, baking powder, and baking soda until combined. Pour batter into the prepared baking pan; spread evenly. Sprinkle with almonds.

3 Bake for 25 to 30 minutes or until a wooden toothpick inserted near center comes out clean. Cool slightly in pan on a wire rack. Cut into bars while warm.

CHOCOLATE CHUNK BLONDIES: Prepare as directed, except reduce almonds to ¾ cup and add ¾ cup semisweet or white chocolate pieces at same time as almonds. When testing for doneness, be careful not to insert toothpick into the chocolate pieces.

PER BAR PLAIN OR CHOCOLATE CHUNK VARIATION: 129 cal., 6 g total fat (2 g sat. fat), 21 mg chol., 47 mg sodium, 18 g carb., 1 g fiber, 2 g pro. **EXCHANGES:** 1 Other Carb., 1 Fat

SHORTBREAD, STEP-BY-STEP

1. Cut the butter into the flour mixture just until the dough starts to cling.

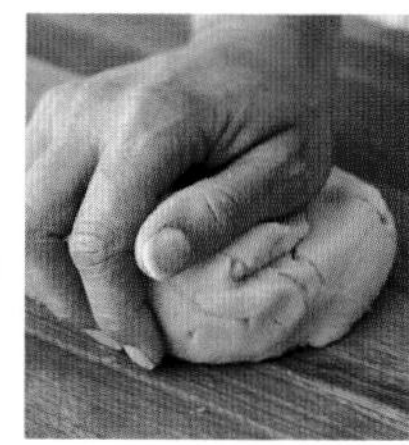

2. Gently knead the dough until smooth.

3. Use your fingers to pat dough into an 8-inch circle.

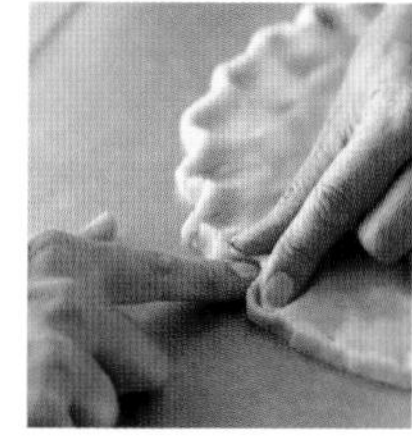

4. Make a scalloped edge by pinching the edge of the dough with your thumb and index finger while pressing into the pinched dough with your other index finger.

BEST-LOVED

White Chocolate Blondies with Macadamia Nuts and Figs *(photo, page 237)*

PREP: 20 MINUTES **BAKE:** 25 MINUTES AT 350°F
MAKES: 36 BARS

- **2 cups packed brown sugar**
- **2/3 cup butter**
- **2 eggs**
- **2 teaspoons vanilla**
- **2 cups all-purpose flour**
- **1 teaspoon baking powder**
- **1/4 teaspoon baking soda**
- **1/2 cup chopped macadamia nuts**
- **1/2 cup snipped dried figs**
- **3 ounces white baking chocolate with cocoa butter, cut into small chunks**
- **2 ounces white baking chocolate with cocoa butter, melted (optional)**

1 Preheat oven to 350°F. Grease a 13×9×2-inch baking pan; set aside. In a medium saucepan cook and stir brown sugar and butter over medium heat until butter melts and mixture is smooth; cool slightly.

2 Add eggs, one at a time, to the butter mixture, beating with a wooden spoon until combined. Stir in vanilla. Stir in flour, baking powder, and baking soda until combined. Stir in macadamia nuts, figs, and 3 ounces white chocolate chunks. Pour batter into the prepared baking pan; spread evenly.

3 Bake for 25 to 30 minutes or until a wooden toothpick inserted near the center comes out clean. If desired, drizzle 2 ounces melted white chocolate over uncut bars. Cut into bars while warm. Leave cut bars in pan; cool on a wire rack. If desired, drizzle bars with 2 ounces melted white chocolate.

PER BAR: 139 cal., 6 g total fat (3 g sat. fat), 19 mg chol., 62 mg sodium, 21 g carb., 1 g fiber, 2 g pro.
EXCHANGES: 1/2 Starch, 1 Other Carb., 1 Fat

BEST-LOVED

Chocolate Truffle Brownies

PREP: 25 MINUTES **BAKE:** 25 MINUTES AT 325°F
MAKES: 20 BROWNIES

- **Nonstick cooking spray**
- **2/3 cup all-purpose flour**
- **1/2 teaspoon baking powder**
- **1/2 teaspoon salt**
- **1/2 cup butter**
- **1/2 cup milk or dark chocolate pieces**
- **3 ounces unsweetened chocolate, chopped**

CHOCOLATE TRUFFLE BROWNIES

- **1 cup sugar**
- **1 1/2 teaspoons vanilla**
- **3 eggs**
- **1 4.63- to 5.25-ounce package (9 to 14 squares) truffle-filled chocolate squares or milk or dark chocolate squares**

1 Preheat oven to 325°F. Line a 9×9×2-inch baking pan with foil, extending foil over the edges of the pan (see photo 1, page 262). Coat foil with cooking spray; set pan aside. In a small bowl stir together flour, baking powder, and salt; set aside.

2 In a medium saucepan cook and stir butter, chocolate pieces, and unsweetened chocolate over low heat until chocolate melts and mixture is smooth; cool slightly. Stir in sugar and vanilla until combined. Add eggs one at a time, beating with a wooden spoon after each addition. Stir in flour mixture just until combined. Pour batter into the prepared baking pan; spread evenly. Bake for 25 minutes.

3 Break chocolate squares into irregular-shape pieces. Sprinkle over warm brownies. Cool in pan on a wire rack. Use the edges of the foil to lift uncut bars out of pan. Place on cutting board; cut into bars.

PER BROWNIE: 192 cal., 12 g total fat (7 g sat. fat), 44 mg chol., 131 mg sodium, 22 g carb., 1 g fiber, 3 g pro.
EXCHANGES: 1 1/2 Other Carb., 2 Fat

BEST-LOVED

Chocolate Revel Bars

PREP: 30 MINUTES **BAKE:** 25 MINUTES AT 350°F
MAKES: 60 BARS

- **1 cup butter, softened**
- **2 cups packed brown sugar**
- **1 teaspoon baking soda**
- **2 eggs**
- **2 teaspoons vanilla**
- **2½ cups all-purpose flour**
- **3 cups quick-cooking rolled oats**
- **1½ cups semisweet chocolate pieces**
- **1 14-ounce can sweetened condensed milk (1¼ cups)**
- **½ cup chopped walnuts or pecans**
- **2 teaspoons vanilla**

1 Preheat oven to 350°F. Line a 15×10×1-inch baking pan with foil, extending foil over the edges of the pan (see photo 1, page 262); set aside. Set aside 2 tablespoons of the butter.

2 In a large mixing bowl beat the remaining butter with an electric mixer on medium to high speed for 30 seconds. Add the brown sugar and baking soda. Beat until combined, scraping sides of bowl occasionally. Beat in eggs and 2 teaspoons vanilla until combined. Beat in as much of the flour as you can with the mixer. Stir in any remaining flour. Stir in the rolled oats.

3 For filling, in a medium saucepan combine the reserved 2 tablespoons butter, the chocolate pieces, and sweetened condensed milk. Cook over low heat until chocolate melts and mixture is smooth, stirring occasionally. Remove from heat. Stir in the nuts and 2 teaspoons vanilla.

4 Press two-thirds (about 3⅓ cups) of the oats mixture into the bottom of the prepared pan. Spread filling evenly over the oats mixture. Drop the remaining oats mixture by teaspoons on top of filling (see photo 2, page 262).

5 Bake about 25 minutes or until top is light brown (chocolate filling will look moist). Cool pan on a wire rack. Use foil to lift uncut bars out of pan; cut into bars.

PEANUT BUTTER-CHOCOLATE REVEL BARS: Prepare as directed, except substitute ½ cup peanut butter for the 2 tablespoons butter when making the chocolate filling in Step 2 and substitute peanuts for the walnuts.

WHOLE WHEAT CHOCOLATE REVEL BARS: Prepare as directed, except reduce the all-purpose flour to 1½ cups and add 1 cup whole wheat flour.

PER BAR PLAIN, PEANUT BUTTER-CHOCOLATE, OR WHOLE WHEAT-CHOCOLATE VARIATIONS: 145 cal., 6 g total fat (3 g sat. fat), 17 mg chol., 56 mg sodium, 21 g carb., 1 g fiber, 2 g pro. EXCHANGES: 1½ Other Carb., 1 Fat

BAR COOKIE YIELDS—MORE OR LESS

Although you should heed the pan sizes called for in each recipe, the number of bars you cut from a pan is up to you. To go up or down on the yield, make more or fewer horizontal and crosswise cuts using the guide below. Note that smaller is better when bars are especially rich.

Baking Pan Size	Number of Cuts		Approximate Size of Bar	Number of Bars
	Lengthwise	Crosswise		
13×9×2-inch	2	7	3×1⅝-inch	24
	3	7	2¼×1⅝-inch	32
	5	5	1½×2⅛-inch	36
	7	4	1⅛×2⅝-inch	40
	7	5	1⅛×2⅛-inch	48
15×10×1-inch	3	8	2½×1¾-inch	36
	3	11	2½×1¼-inch	48
	3	14	2½×1-inch	60
	7	7	1¼×1⅞-inch	64
	7	8	1¼×1¾-inch	72

Banana Bars

PREP: 30 MINUTES **BAKE:** 25 MINUTES AT 350°F
MAKES: 36 BARS

- **½ cup butter, softened**
- **1⅓ cups sugar**
- **1½ teaspoons baking powder**
- **½ teaspoon baking soda**
- **¼ teaspoon salt**
- **1 egg**
- **1 cup mashed bananas (2 to 3 medium)**
- **½ cup sour cream**
- **1 teaspoon vanilla**
- **2 cups all-purpose flour**
- **1 cup chopped pecans or walnuts, toasted (see tip, page 21)**
- **1 recipe Cream Cheese Frosting (page 173)**

1 Preheat oven to 350°F. Lightly grease a 15×10×1-inch baking pan; set aside. In a large mixing bowl beat butter with an electric mixer on medium to high speed for 30 seconds. Add sugar, baking powder, baking soda, and salt; beat until combined, scraping sides of bowl occasionally. Beat in the egg, mashed bananas, sour cream, and vanilla until combined. Beat or stir in the flour. Stir in pecans. Pour the batter into the prepared baking pan, spreading evenly.

2 Bake about 25 minutes or until a wooden toothpick inserted near center comes out clean. Cool completely in pan on a wire rack. Frost with Cream Cheese Frosting. Cut into bars.

PER BAR: 228 cal., 10 g total fat (5 g sat. fat), 28 mg chol., 105 mg sodium, 34 g carb., 1 g fiber, 2 g pro.
EXCHANGES: 2 Other Carb., 2 Fat

Oatmeal-Caramel Bars

PREP: 25 MINUTES **BAKE:** 22 MINUTES AT 350°F
MAKES: 60 BARS

- **1 cup butter, softened**
- **2 cups packed brown sugar**
- **2 eggs**
- **2 teaspoons vanilla**
- **1 teaspoon baking soda**
- **2½ cups all-purpose flour**
- **3 cups quick-cooking rolled oats**
- **1 cup miniature semisweet chocolate pieces**
- **½ cup chopped walnuts or pecans**
- **30 vanilla caramels (9 ounces), unwrapped**
- **3 tablespoons milk**

1 Preheat oven to 350°F. Line a 15×10×1-inch baking pan with foil, extending foil over the edges of the pan (see photo 1, below); set aside.

2 In a large mixing bowl beat butter with an electric mixer on medium to high speed for 30 seconds. Add the brown sugar. Beat until combined, scraping sides of bowl occasionally. Add eggs, vanilla, and baking soda; beat until combined. Beat or stir in the flour. Stir in the oats. Press two-thirds (about 3⅓ cups) of the oats mixture evenly into the bottom of the prepared pan. Sprinkle with chocolate pieces and nuts.

3 In a medium saucepan heat and stir the caramels and milk over low heat until caramels melt and mixture is smooth. Drizzle caramel mixture over chocolate and nuts in pan. Drop the remaining oats mixture by teaspoons on top of the caramel (see photo 2, below).

4 Bake for 22 to 25 minutes or until top is light brown. Cool in pan on a wire rack. Use foil to lift uncut bars out of pan. Place on cutting board; cut into bars.

PER BAR: 139 cal., 6 g total fat (3 g sat. fat), 16 mg chol., 60 mg sodium, 21 g carb., 1 g fiber, 2 g pro.
EXCHANGES: 1½ Other Carb., 1 Fat

OATMEAL-CARAMEL BARS STEP-BY-STEP

1. To line the pan with foil, turn pan upside down and shape the foil over the outside, extending foil about 1 inch past the pan's edges. Place the shaped foil, shiny side up, inside the pan.

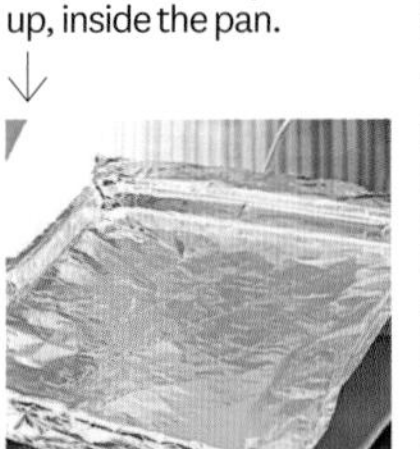

2. After drizzling caramel mixture over chocolate and nuts, use a spoon and a small spatula or table knife to drop remaining oats mixture over the surface of the caramel mixture.

Lemon Bars

PREP: 25 MINUTES **BAKE:** 33 MINUTES AT 350°F
MAKES: 36 BARS

- **2 cups all-purpose flour**
- **½ cup powdered sugar**
- **2 tablespoons cornstarch**
- **¼ teaspoon salt**
- **¾ cup butter, cut up**
- **4 eggs, lightly beaten**
- **1½ cups granulated sugar**
- **3 tablespoons all-purpose flour**
- **1 teaspoon finely shredded lemon peel**
- **¾ cup lemon juice**
- **¼ cup half-and-half, light cream, or milk**
- **Powdered sugar**

1 Preheat oven to 350°F. Line a 13×9×2-inch baking pan with foil, extending foil over edges of pan (see photo 1, page 262). Grease foil; set aside. In a large bowl combine the 2 cups flour, the ½ cup powdered sugar, the cornstarch, and salt. Use a pastry blender to cut in butter until mixture resembles coarse crumbs. Press into the bottom of prepared pan. Bake for 18 to 20 minutes or until edges are light brown.

2 Meanwhile, for filling, in a medium bowl stir together eggs, granulated sugar, the 3 tablespoons flour, the lemon peel, lemon juice, and half-and-half. Pour filling over hot crust. Bake for 15 to 20 minutes more or until center is set. Cool completely in pan on a wire rack. Use the edges of the foil to lift uncut bars out of pan. Place on cutting board; cut into bars. Just before serving, sift powdered sugar over tops. Cover and store in the refrigerator for up to 3 days.

BERRY-LEMON BARS: Prepare as directed, except sprinkle 1½ cups fresh raspberries or blueberries over filling before baking in Step 2. Bake for 20 to 25 minutes or until center is set.

PER BAR PLAIN OR BERRY VARIATION: 115 cal., 5 g total fat (3 g sat. fat), 34 mg chol., 52 mg sodium, 17 g carb., 0 g fiber, 2 g pro. EXCHANGES: 1 Other Carb., 1 Fat

BEST-LOVED

Pumpkin Bars

PREP: 25 MINUTES **BAKE:** 25 MINUTES AT 350°F
COOL: 2 HOURS **MAKES:** 36 BARS

- **2 cups all-purpose flour**
- **1½ cups sugar**
- **2 teaspoons baking powder**
- **2 teaspoons ground cinnamon**
- **1 teaspoon baking soda**
- **½ teaspoon salt**
- **¼ teaspoon ground cloves**
- **4 eggs, lightly beaten**
- **1 15-ounce can pumpkin**
- **1 cup vegetable oil**
- **2½ cups Cream Cheese Frosting (page 173)**

1 Preheat oven to 350°F. In a large bowl stir together the flour, sugar, baking powder, cinnamon, baking soda, salt, and cloves. Stir in the eggs, pumpkin, and oil until combined. Pour batter into an ungreased 15×10×1-inch baking pan, spreading evenly.

2 Bake for 25 to 30 minutes or until a wooden toothpick inserted near the center comes out clean. Cool in pan on a wire rack for 2 hours. Spread with Cream Cheese Frosting. Cut into bars. Cover and store in the refrigerator for up to 3 days.

APPLESAUCE BARS: Prepare as directed, except substitute one 15-ounce jar applesauce (1¾ cups) for the pumpkin.

PER BAR PLAIN OR APPLESAUCE VARIATION: 243 cal., 11 g total fat (3 g sat. fat), 37 mg chol., 135 mg sodium, 34 g carb., 1 g fiber, 2 g pro. EXCHANGES: 2 Other Carb., 2 Fat

ANY WAY YOU SLICE IT

Next time you serve bar cookies, go beyond squares with these fun shapes.

Unless your recipe directs otherwise, be sure to let the block of bars cool completely before cutting. To make clean, smudge-free cuts through chocolate or creamy bars, run your knife blade under hot water, dry it, and cut the bars. Repeat as necessary.

SHAPES: Use a 2- to 2½-inch round or desired-shape cookie cutter to cut the block.

TRIANGLES: Cut the block into 2½-inch squares. Cut the squares in half diagonally.

WEDGES: Cut the block lengthwise down the center. Cut each half into triangular wedges (you'll have half-triangles at ends of each strip).

DIAMONDS: Cut lines about 1½ inches apart down the length of the pan. Then cut straight lines 1½ inches apart diagonally across the pan.

CHERRY KUCHEN BARS

BEST-LOVED

Cherry Kuchen Bars

PREP: 25 MINUTES **BAKE:** 42 MINUTES AT 350°F
COOL: 10 MINUTES **MAKES:** 32 BARS

- **½ cup butter, softened**
- **½ cup shortening**
- **1¾ cups sugar**
- **1½ teaspoons baking powder**
- **½ teaspoon salt**
- **3 eggs**
- **1 teaspoon vanilla**
- **3 cups all-purpose flour**
- **1 21-ounce can cherry pie filling**
- **1 recipe Powdered Sugar Icing (page 173)**

1 Preheat oven to 350°F. In a large mixing bowl beat butter and shortening with an electric mixer on medium speed for 30 seconds. Add sugar, baking powder, and salt. Beat until well combined, scraping sides of bowl occasionally. Beat in eggs and vanilla. Beat in as much of the flour as you can with the mixer. Stir in any remaining flour. Reserve 1½ cups of the dough. Spread remaining dough in the bottom of an ungreased 15×10×1-inch baking pan.

2 Bake for 12 minutes. Remove from oven and spread cherry pie filling over the hot crust in pan. Drop the reserved dough by teaspoons into small mounds on top of the pie filling.

3 Bake about 30 minutes more or until top is light brown. Cool in pan on a wire rack for 10 minutes. Drizzle top with Powdered Sugar Icing; let cool. Cut into bars.

PER BAR: 190 cal., 7 g total fat (3 g sat. fat), 25 mg chol., 90 mg sodium, 31 g carb., 0 g fiber, 2 g pro.
EXCHANGES: ½ Starch, 1½ Other Carb., 1½ Fat

Danish Pastry Apple Bars

PREP: 30 MINUTES **BAKE:** 50 MINUTES AT 375°F
MAKES: 32 BARS

- **2½ cups all-purpose flour**
- **1 teaspoon salt**
- **1 cup shortening**
- **1 egg yolk**
- **Milk**
- **1 cup cornflakes**
- **8 cups tart cooking apples, peeled, cored, and sliced (8 to 10)**
- **¾ to 1 cup granulated sugar**
- **1 teaspoon ground cinnamon**

1 egg white, lightly beaten
1 cup powdered sugar
3 to 4 teaspoons milk

1 Preheat oven to 375°F. In a large bowl combine flour and salt. Use a pastry blender to cut in shortening until the mixture resembles coarse crumbs. In a liquid measuring cup beat egg yolk lightly. Add enough milk to make 2/3 cup liquid. Stir well to combine. Stir milk mixture into flour mixture with a fork until combined (dough will be slightly sticky). Divide dough in half.

2 On a well-floured surface roll one half of the dough to a 17×12-inch rectangle. Fold dough crosswise into thirds. Transfer to an ungreased 15×10×1-inch baking pan and unfold dough, pressing to fit into the bottom and up sides of the pan. Sprinkle with cornflakes. Top evenly with apples. In a small bowl combine granulated sugar and cinnamon; sprinkle over apples. Roll remaining dough to a 15×10-inch rectangle. Fold dough crosswise into thirds. Place on top of apples and unfold dough. Crimp edges or use the tines of a fork to seal. Cut slits in the top. Brush top with beaten egg white.

3 Bake about 50 minutes or until light brown and apples are tender, covering with foil after the first 25 minutes of baking time to prevent pastry from overbrowning.

4 In a small bowl combine powdered sugar and 3 to 4 teaspoons milk to make drizzling consistency. Drizzle over warm bars. Let cool completely in pan on a wire rack. Cut into bars.

PER BAR: 155 cal., 6 g total fat (2 g sat. fat), 7 mg chol., 83 mg sodium, 23 g carb., 1 g fiber, 2 g pro.
EXCHANGES: 1½ Other Carb., 1 Fat

Yummy No-Bake Bars

PREP: 30 MINUTES **CHILL:** 60 MINUTES
MAKES: 64 BARS

1 cup granulated sugar
1 cup light-color corn syrup
2 cups peanut butter
3 cups crisp rice cereal
3 cups cornflakes
3/4 cup butter
4 cups powdered sugar
2 4-serving-size packages vanilla instant pudding and pie filling mix
1/4 cup milk
1 12-ounce package semisweet chocolate pieces (2 cups)
1/2 cup butter

YUMMY NO-BAKE BARS

1 Line a 15×10×1-inch baking pan with foil, extending foil over the edges of the pan (see photo 1, page 262); set aside.

2 In a large saucepan combine granulated sugar and corn syrup; heat and stir just until mixture boils around edges. Heat and stir for 1 minute more. Remove from heat. Add peanut butter; stir until mixture is smooth. Use a wooden spoon to stir in rice cereal and cornflakes until coated. Press mixture into the bottom of prepared pan.

3 For pudding layer, in a medium saucepan melt the 3/4 cup butter. Stir in powdered sugar, pudding mix, and milk. Spread pudding mixture over cereal layer; set aside.

4 For frosting, in a small saucepan heat and stir chocolate pieces and the 1/2 cup butter over low heat until chocolate melts and mixture is smooth. Spread frosting over pudding layer. Loosely cover and chill about 60 minutes or until set. To serve, use foil to lift uncut bars out of pan. Place on cutting board; cut into bars.

PER BAR: 175 cal., 9 g total fat (4 g sat. fat), 10 mg chol., 133 mg sodium, 23 g carb., 1 g fiber, 2 g pro.
EXCHANGES: 1½ Other Carb., 2 Fat

NO-BAKE COCONUT-DATE BARS WITH BROWNED BUTTER GLAZE

No-Bake Coconut-Date Bars with Browned Butter Glaze

PREP: 30 MINUTES **CHILL:** 2 HOURS **MAKES:** 24 BARS

- **36 rich rectangular crackers**
- **¾ cup packed brown sugar**
- **½ cup whipping cream**
- **⅓ cup butter**
- **2 egg yolks**
- **½ teaspoon salt**
- **1 cup flaked coconut**
- **1 cup chopped pitted dates**
- **¾ cup chopped pecans or walnuts**
- **1 tablespoon dark rum**
- **1 teaspoon vanilla**
- **¼ cup butter**
- **1 cup powdered sugar**
- **1 tablespoon milk**
- **⅛ teaspoon salt**
- **⅓ cup chopped pecans or walnuts**

1 Line an 8×8×2-inch baking pan with foil, extending the foil over the edges of the pan (see photo 1, page 262). Lightly butter the foil. Arrange half of the crackers in a single layer that completely covers the bottom of the prepared pan, cutting some to fit if necessary; set aside.

2 For filling, in a medium saucepan combine brown sugar, cream, the ⅓ cup butter, the egg yolks, and ½ teaspoon salt. Cook over medium heat until butter melts and mixture is smooth, stirring constantly. Stir in coconut, dates, and the ¾ cup pecans. Cook about 8 minutes or until mixture is glossy and has turned a rich shade of brown, stirring constantly. Remove from heat. Stir in the rum and vanilla.

3 Pour filling over the cracker layer in the prepared pan, spreading gently to cover the crackers completely. Arrange the remaining crackers over the filling, pressing them lightly into the filling; set aside.

4 For the glaze, in a small saucepan melt the ¼ cup butter over medium heat. Cook until butter is light brown. Transfer to a small bowl. Whisk in the powdered sugar, milk, and the ⅛ teaspoon salt until smooth, adding additional milk as necessary to make a spreadable glaze. Pour the glaze over the cracker layer, spreading evenly. Sprinkle with the ⅓ cup pecans. Cover and chill about 2 hours or until set. Use foil to lift uncut bars out of pan. Place on a cutting board. Using a serrated knife, cut into bars.

PER BAR: 205 cal., 12 g fat (5 g sat. fat), 34 mg chol., 161 mg sodium, 23 g carb., 2 g fiber, 1 g pro.
EXCHANGES: 1 Other Carb., ½ Starch, 2½ Fat

Easy Monster Cookie Bars

PREP: 15 MINUTES **BAKE:** 20 MINUTES AT 350°F
MAKES: 16 BARS

- **1 16.5-ounce roll refrigerated peanut butter cookie dough**
- **¾ cup rolled oats**
- **1 cup candy-coated milk chocolate pieces**
- **½ cup semisweet chocolate pieces**
- **½ cup chopped peanuts (optional)**

1 Preheat oven to 350°F. Line a 9×9×2-inch baking pan with foil, extending foil over edges of pan (see photo 1, page 262). Lightly grease foil; set aside. Break up cookie dough into a large bowl. Stir in oats. Stir in milk chocolate pieces, semisweet chocolate pieces, and, if desired, nuts.

2 Pat mixture into the prepared baking pan. Bake about 20 minutes or until light brown. Cool in pan on a wire rack. Use foil to lift uncut bars out of pan. Place on a cutting board; cut into bars.

PER BAR: 241 cal., 12 g fat (4 g sat. fat), 9 mg chol., 123 mg sodium, 31 g carb., 2 g fiber, 4 g pro.
EXCHANGES: 2 Other Carb., 2½ Fat

desserts

desserts

Make life sweeter with these tips for better endings and a little advice on keeping goodies on hand in the freezer.

FINISHING FLOURISHES

Add something a little extra to your desserts with a few simple touches.

CANDIED NUTS: Preheat oven to 325°F. Grease a 15×10×1-inch baking pan; set pan aside. In a large bowl combine 1 egg white, 1 cup sugar, and ½ teaspoon salt. Add 5 cups walnut pieces and toss to coat. Spread evenly in the prepared pan. Bake for 20 minutes or until golden. Cool in pan on a wire rack. Break into pieces. Store in an airtight container at room temperature up to 1 week. Makes about 6 cups. Use as a topper for cakes or cheesecakes, toss in salads, mix into trail mixes, serve as a quick appetizer, and enjoy as a snack.

CHOCOLATE GARNISHES: Try one or more of these ideas to create the ultimate garnish:

- For shavings, make short strokes with a vegetable peeler across a solid piece of chocolate.
- For curls, draw a vegetable peeler across the narrow side of a chocolate bar (milk chocolate works best).
- To grate chocolate, rub a solid piece of chocolate across either the fine or the coarse side of a grater.

PROFESSIONAL PRESENTATION: Channel professional bakers and stylists with these tricks for turning heads with your desserts:

- Use a ruler to score and cut straight lines.
- Fill clean plastic squeeze bottles with dessert sauces. Drizzle over individual servings or use the bottle to pipe sauces onto dishes or dessert plate rims.
- Use a piping bag fitted with an icing tip (or a resealable bag with a snipped corner) to drizzle icing over finished desserts.
- Sprinkle coarse or turbinado sugar over individual pastries.
- Serve desserts with fresh sliced berries or fresh herbs, such as mint leaves.
- Sprinkle chopped candied or toasted nuts over finished desserts.

TO FREEZE OR NOT TO FREEZE

Some desserts freeze fabulously, making them terrific make-ahead options for entertaining (or allowing you to stash leftovers to savor later). Other desserts need to be enjoyed soon after they're made. Here are a few guidelines.

- Puddings and custard desserts, such as flan and panna cotta, do not freeze well. Refrigerate leftovers up to 2 days.
- Cheesecakes rank among the best desserts to freeze. Wrap in freezer wrap; freeze a whole cheesecake up to 1 month and pieces up to 2 weeks. Thaw in the refrigerator.
- The crumb topping for fruit crisps freezes well. Next time you make a crisp, consider preparing a double batch of the topping; place extra in a freezer bag and freeze up to 1 month. To use, prepare fruit as directed in the recipe and top with frozen crisp topping; bake—you might need to add a few minutes to the baking time.
- Freeze unfilled cream puffs up to 1 month. To thaw, place frozen cream puffs in a 350°F oven about 7 minutes or until crisp. Cool before filling.
- Unfrosted fruit- or nut-filled pastries such as baklava, turnovers, and strudel generally freeze well for up to 1 month.
- Freeze unfilled meringue shells up to 6 months.

Peach Turnovers, page 273

cook's secrets

strawberry shortcake

The Secret: Get your oven hot! Tender, flaky shortcake that's light and fluffy inside requires a high oven temp—it turns the liquid and butter in the batter to steam, which lightens the texture.

SHORTCAKE POINTERS

1. BATTER UP
Add the egg mixture to the flour mixture all at once and stir with a spatula or fork just until moistened. Stirring too long will cause the dough to become tough when baked. Stir wet and dry ingredients until they are just combined and the batter starts to pull away from the side of the bowl.

2. USE A SOFT TOUCH
A small offset metal spatula makes it easy to spread shortcake batter in the pan. Push the batter gently into the pan without pressing down and compacting the batter.

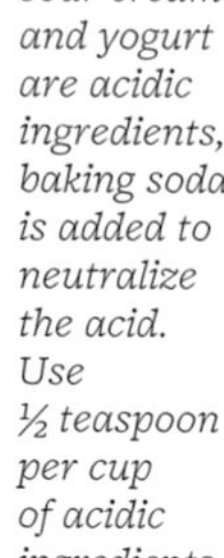

Because sour cream and yogurt are acidic ingredients, baking soda is added to neutralize the acid. Use ½ teaspoon per cup of acidic ingredients.

PREP: 25 MINUTES **BAKE:** 18 MINUTES AT 400°F **MAKES:** 8 SERVINGS

- **1½ cups all-purpose flour**
- **¼ cup sugar**
- **1 teaspoon baking powder**
- **¼ teaspoon salt**
- **¼ teaspoon baking soda**
- **⅓ cup cold butter**
- **1 egg, lightly beaten**
- **½ cup sour cream or plain yogurt**
- **3 tablespoons milk**
- **5 cups sliced strawberries**
- **3 tablespoons sugar**
- **1 recipe Sweetened Whipped Cream (below)**

1 Preheat oven to 400°F. Grease an 8×1½-inch round baking pan;* set aside. In a medium bowl combine flour, ¼ cup sugar, baking powder, salt, and baking soda. Using a pastry blender, cut in butter until mixture resembles coarse crumbs. Using the back of a spoon, make a well in the center of the flour mixture. In a small bowl stir together egg, sour cream, and milk. Add egg mixture to flour mixture, stirring with a fork just until moistened.

2 Using a small offset metal spatula, spread dough evenly in the prepared pan. Bake for 18 to 20 minutes or until a wooden pick inserted comes out clean. Cool in pan on wire rack for 10 minutes. Using a small metal spatula, loosen sides of shortcake. Place a wire rack on top of pan; place one hand on top of rack and other hand under pan with a hot pad and carefully invert pan with rack. Lift pan off shortcake. Cool completely.

3 Meanwhile, combine 4 cups of the strawberries and the 3 tablespoons sugar. If desired, mash berries slightly; set aside.

4 Transfer shortcake to a plate. To serve, cut shortcake in half horizontally. Spoon Sweetened Whipped Cream and half of the strawberry mixture over shortcake bottom. Replace the top. Top with the remaining strawberry mixture and remaining sliced strawberries.

***NOTE:** If you don't have an 8×1½-inch baking pan, spread the dough to an 8-inch circle on a parchment paper-lined baking sheet. Bake, split, and assemble as directed.

PER SERVING: 376 cal., 22 g fat (13 g sat. fat), 91 mg chol., 275 mg sodium, 41 g carb., 2 g fiber, 5 g pro. **EXCHANGES:** 1 Fruit, ½ Starch, 1 Other Carb., 4 Fat

WAY TO GO!

OOPS! OVERBEATEN

SWEETENED WHIPPED CREAM

In a chilled mixing bowl add 1 cup whipping cream, 2 tablespoons sugar, and ½ teaspoon vanilla. Beat with an electric mixer on medium speed until soft peaks form (tips curl). Cream whips up best when it's very cold, so use a chilled bowl and beaters in addition to chilled whipping cream. Letting them stand in the refrigerator for 15 to 20 minutes should do the trick. Watch carefully when whipping the cream. Once it starts to thicken, it can go from beautiful, soft peaks to curdled quickly.

individual shortcakes

Prepare Strawberry Shortcake as directed, except drop dough into eight mounds on a greased baking sheet. Bake for 12 to 15 minutes or until golden brown. Transfer to a wire rack. Cool completely. Makes 8 servings.

MIXED-BERRY OR MIXED-FRUIT SHORTCAKES: Prepare Individual Shortcakes as directed, except substitute 5 cups mixed fresh berries (blueberries, raspberries, and/or blackberries) or 5 cups mixed fresh fruit (sliced peaches, nectarines, bananas, blueberries, raspberries, and/or halved grapes) for the 5 cups sliced strawberries. Do not mash fruit. If desired, drizzle fruit mixture with honey.

PER MIXED-BERRY VARIATION: 393 cal., 22 g total fat (13 g sat. fat), 91 mg chol, 275 mg sodium, 45 g carb., 4 g fiber, 5 g pro. EXCHANGES: 1 Fruit, 1 Starch, 1 Other Carb., 4 Fat

APPLE-CRANBERRY SHORTCAKES: Prepare Individual Shortcakes as directed, except omit strawberries. In a large skillet heat 2 tablespoons butter over medium heat. Add 4 cups peeled and thinly sliced apples and 1 cup fresh or frozen cranberries. Cook about 4 minutes or until apples are tender, stirring occasionally. Add ⅓ cup sugar and stir to dissolve sugar. Cool slightly.

PER APPLE-CRANBERRY VARIATION: 440 cal., 25 g total fat (15 g sat. fat), 99 mg chol, 300 mg sodium, 51 g carb., 3 g fiber, 5 g pro. EXCHANGES: 1 Fruit, 1 Starch, 1½ Other Carb., 5 Fat

If you prefer, line your baking sheet with parchment paper instead of greasing the baking sheet.

CUTTING POINTER

GO SERRATED

Use a long, serrated knife to carefully cut the cooled shortcake in half horizontally. It won't compact the crumb of the shortcake while cutting.

PEACH CRISP

BEST-LOVED

Apple Crisp

PREP: 25 MINUTES **BAKE:** 35 MINUTES AT 375°F
MAKES: 6 SERVINGS

- **6 cups sliced, peeled cooking apples**
- **3 to 4 tablespoons granulated sugar**
- **½ cup regular rolled oats**
- **½ cup packed brown sugar**
- **¼ cup all-purpose flour**
- **¼ teaspoon ground cinnamon, ginger, or nutmeg**
- **¼ cup butter**
- **¼ cup chopped nuts or flaked coconut**
- **Vanilla ice cream (optional)**

1 Preheat oven to 375°F. In a large bowl combine apples and granulated sugar. Transfer apple mixture to a 1½- to 2-quart square baking dish; set aside.

2 For topping, in a medium bowl combine the oats, brown sugar, flour, and cinnamon. Cut in butter until mixture resembles coarse crumbs. Stir in nuts. Sprinkle topping over apple mixture in dish.

3 Bake for 35 to 40 minutes or until apples are tender and topping is golden. If desired, serve warm with ice cream.

PER SERVING: 298 cal., 12 g total fat (5 g sat. fat), 20 mg chol., 60 mg sodium, 49 g carb., 3 g fiber, 3 g pro. EXCHANGES: 1 Fruit, 2 Starch, 2 Fat

PEACH OR CHERRY CRISP: Prepare as directed, except substitute 6 cups sliced, peeled ripe peaches or fresh pitted tart red cherries (or two 16-ounce packages frozen unsweetened peach slices or frozen unsweetened pitted tart red cherries) for the apples. For the filling, increase granulated sugar to ½ cup and add 3 tablespoons all-purpose flour. If using frozen fruit, bake for 50 to 60 minutes or until filling is bubbly across entire surface (if necessary, cover with foil the last 10 minutes to prevent overbrowning).

RHUBARB CRISP: Prepare as directed, except substitute 6 cups fresh sliced rhubarb or two 16-ounce packages frozen unsweetened sliced rhubarb for the apples. For the filling, increase granulated sugar to ¾ cup and add 3 tablespoons all-purpose flour. If using frozen fruit, bake for 50 to 60 minutes or until filling is bubbly across entire surface (if necessary, cover with foil the last 10 minutes to prevent overbrowning).

PER ½ CUP PEACH, CHERRY, OR RHUBARB VARIATIONS: 358 cal., 12 g total fat (5 g sat. fat), 20 mg chol., 65 mg sodium, 62 g carb., 4 g fiber, 4 g pro. EXCHANGES: 3 Starch, 1 Fruit, ½ Other Carb., 2 Fat

Cherry Cobbler

PREP: 30 MINUTES **BAKE:** 20 MINUTES AT 400°F
COOL: 60 MINUTES **MAKES:** 6 SERVINGS

- **1 cup all-purpose flour**
- **2 tablespoons sugar**
- **1½ teaspoons baking powder**
- **¼ teaspoon salt**
- **½ teaspoon ground cinnamon (optional)**
- **¼ cup butter**
- **6 cups fresh or frozen unsweetened pitted tart red cherries (2 pounds)**
- **1 cup sugar**
- **3 tablespoons cornstarch**
- **1 egg**
- **¼ cup milk**
- **2 teaspoons sugar (optional)**
- **⅛ teaspoon ground cinnamon (optional)**

1 Preheat oven to 400°F. For biscuit topper, in a medium bowl stir together flour, the 2 tablespoons sugar, baking powder, salt, and, if desired, the ½ teaspoon cinnamon. Cut in butter until mixture resembles coarse crumbs; set aside.

2 For filling, in a large saucepan combine cherries, the 1 cup sugar, and cornstarch. Cook over medium heat until cherries release juices, stirring occasionally. Continue to cook, stirring constantly, over medium heat until thickened and bubbly. Keep the filling hot.

3 In a small bowl stir together egg and milk. Add to flour mixture, stirring to moisten (see photo 1, below). Transfer hot filling to a 2-quart square baking dish. Using two spoons, immediately drop batter into six mounds on top of filling (see photo 2, below). If desired, combine the 2 teaspoons sugar with ⅛ teaspoon cinnamon; sprinkle over biscuits.

4 Bake for 20 to 25 minutes or until biscuits are golden. Cool in dish on a wire rack for 60 minutes.

PER BISCUIT + ½ CUP FILLING: 400 cal., 9 g fat (5 g sat. fat), 56 mg chol., 233 mg sodium, 77 g carb., 3 g fiber, 5 g pro. EXCHANGES: 1 Fruit, 2 Starch, 2 Carb., 1½ Fat

BLUEBERRY COBBLER: Prepare as directed, except substitute 6 cups fresh or frozen blueberries for cherries, decrease sugar in filling to ¾ cup, and decrease cornstarch to 2 tablespoons.

PEACH COBBLER: Prepare as directed, except substitute 6 cups fresh or frozen unsweetened sliced peaches for cherries; decrease cornstarch to 2 tablespoons.

RHUBARB COBBLER: Prepare as directed, except substitute 6 cups fresh or frozen unsweetened sliced rhubarb for cherries and decrease cornstarch to 2 tablespoons.

PER BISCUIT + ½ CUP FILLING BLUEBERRY, PEACH, OR RHUBARB VARIATIONS: 367 cal., 9 g total fat (5 g sat. fat), 56 mg chol., 233 mg sodium, 69 g carb., 4 g fiber, 5 g pro. EXCHANGES: 1 Fruit, 2 Starch, 1½ Other Carb., 1½ Fat

COBBLER STEP-BY-STEP

1. Using a fork, stir the dry and wet ingredients together until the dry ingredients are just moistened.

2. Use two spoons to drop same-size spoonfuls of batter onto hot filling, spacing mounds equally on filling.

Peach Turnovers *(photo, page 269)*

PREP: 25 MINUTES **BAKE:** 15 MINUTES AT 400°F
MAKES: 4 TURNOVERS

- **2 tablespoons granulated sugar**
- **1 tablespoon all-purpose flour**
- **⅛ teaspoon ground cinnamon**
- **1⅓ cups chopped peach or nectarine or chopped peeled apple (1 large)**
- **½ of a 17.3-ounce package frozen puff pastry sheets (1 sheet), thawed**
- **3 to 4 teaspoons milk**
- **Coarse sugar (optional)**
- **¾ cup powdered sugar**
- **1 tablespoon butter, softened**
- **½ teaspoon vanilla**
- **Dash salt**

1 Preheat oven to 400°F. Line a large baking sheet with parchment paper; set aside. In a small bowl stir together granulated sugar, flour, and cinnamon. Add peach; toss to coat.

2 Unfold pastry. Cut pastry into four squares. Brush edges of squares with milk. Evenly spoon peach mixture onto centers of squares. Fold one corner of a square over filling to opposite corner. Press edges with the tines of a fork to seal. Place turnover on prepared baking sheet. Repeat with remaining dough squares. Prick tops of turnovers several times with a fork. Brush with additional milk and, if desired, sprinkle with coarse sugar.

3 Bake for 15 to 18 minutes or until puffed and golden brown. Cool slightly on baking sheet on a wire rack.

4 Meanwhile, stir together powdered sugar, butter, vanilla, and salt. Add enough additional milk to make thin icing. Drizzle over warm turnovers.

PER TURNOVER: 507 cal., 27 g fat (8 g sat. fat), 8 mg chol., 213 mg sodium, 63 g carb., 2 g fiber, 5 g pro. EXCHANGES: 2 Starch, 2 Other Carb., 5 Fat

PUFF PASTRY KNOW-HOW

Puff pastry is pastry dough layered with pieces of butter. When puff pastry bakes, the melting butter creates steam, which results in a flaky pastry with rich, buttery flavor. Bakers love the convenience and sophistication of purchased puff pastry. Look for it in the freezer section with the prepared piecrusts and desserts. You can buy puff pastry in sheets and in shells (to bake and fill with sweet or savory fillings). For the best results, store puff pastry in the freezer and thaw at room temperature for 30 minutes before using. Thaw only what you need; puff pastry does not refreeze well.

APPLE DUMPLINGS

BEST-LOVED

Apple Dumplings

PREP: 45 MINUTES **BAKE:** 55 MINUTES AT 350°F
MAKES: 6 DUMPLINGS

- **2 cups water**
- **1¼ cups sugar**
- **½ teaspoon ground cinnamon**
- **¼ cup butter, cut up**
- **2 cups all-purpose flour**
- **½ teaspoon salt**
- **⅔ cup shortening**
- **⅓ to ½ cup half-and-half or whole milk**
- **2 tablespoons chopped raisins**
- **2 tablespoons chopped walnuts**
- **1 tablespoon honey**
- **2 tablespoons sugar**
- **½ teaspoon ground cinnamon**
- **6 small cooking apples (about 1½ pounds)**
- **2 tablespoons butter**

1 Preheat oven to 350°F. For sauce, in a medium saucepan combine the water, the 1¼ cups sugar, and ½ teaspoon cinnamon. Bring to boiling; reduce heat. Simmer, uncovered, for 5 minutes. Add the ¼ cup butter; set aside.

2 Meanwhile, for pastry, in a medium bowl combine flour and salt. Using a pastry blender, cut in shortening until pieces are pea size. Sprinkle 1 tablespoon of the half-and-half over part of the mixture; gently toss with a fork. Push moistened dough to a side of the bowl. Repeat moistening dough, using 1 tablespoon of the half-and-half at a time, until all of the dough is moistened. Form dough into a ball. On a lightly floured surface roll dough to an 18×12-inch rectangle. Cut into six 6-inch squares (see photo 1, below).

3 In a small bowl combine raisins, walnuts, and honey. Stir together the 2 tablespoons sugar and ½ teaspoon cinnamon; set aside.

4 Core and peel apples (see photo 2, below). Place an apple on each pastry square. Fill apple with raisin mixture. Sprinkle with cinnamon mixture; dot with 1 teaspoon butter (see photo 3, below). Moisten edges of pastry squares with water; gather corners around apples (see photo 4, below). Pinch to seal. Place dumplings in a 13×9×2-inch baking pan. Heat sauce to boiling; pour over dumplings. Bake, uncovered, for 55 to 60 minutes or until apples are tender and pastry is golden. Spoon sauce over warm dumplings.

PER DUMPLING: 736 cal., 37 g total fat (14 g sat. fat), 35 mg chol., 286 mg sodium, 99 g carb., 4 g fiber, 6 g pro.
EXCHANGES: 1 Fruit, 5½ Other Carb., 6 Fat

APPLE DUMPLINGS STEP-BY-STEP

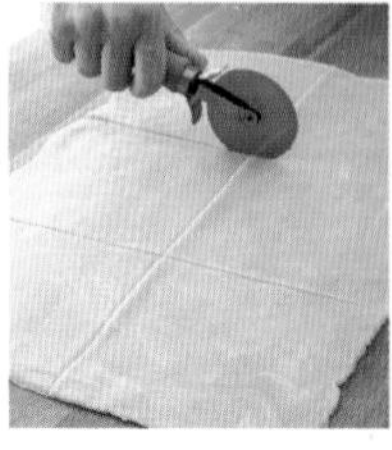

1. A pizza cutter makes it easy to cut the rectangle into 6-inch squares.

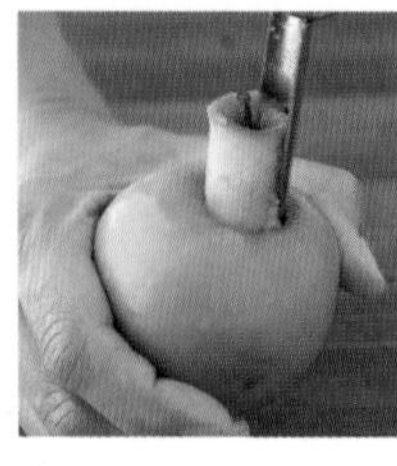

2. Using an apple corer, twist and pull up to remove each apple's core.

3. After filling the apples with the raisin mixture, top each with a small piece of butter.

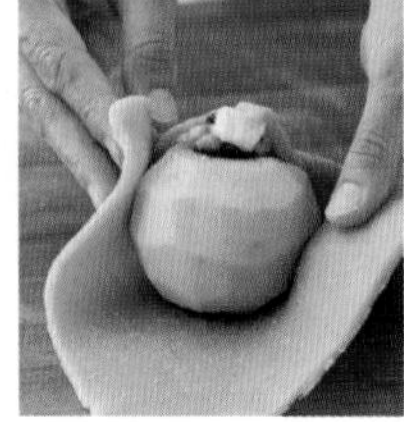

4. Gather the corners of dough squares at the apple tops; pinch to form a tight seal.

Baklava

PREP: 45 MINUTES **BAKE:** 35 MINUTES AT 325°F
MAKES: 32 TO 48 PIECES

- **3 cups walnuts, finely chopped**
- **1½ cups sugar**
- **1 teaspoon ground cinnamon**
- **¾ cup butter, melted**
- **½ of a 16-ounce package frozen phyllo dough (14×9-inch rectangles), thawed**
- **¾ cup water**
- **3 tablespoons honey**
- **½ teaspoon finely shredded lemon peel**
- **1 tablespoon lemon juice**
- **2 inches stick cinnamon**

1 Preheat oven to 325°F. In a large bowl stir together walnuts, ½ cup of the sugar, and the ground cinnamon; set aside.

2 Brush the bottom of a 13×9×2-inch baking pan with some melted butter. Unroll phyllo dough. Layer five or six phyllo sheets in the prepared baking pan, brushing each sheet generously with some melted butter (see photos 1 and 2, below). Sprinkle with about 1 cup of the nut mixture. Repeat layering phyllo sheets and sprinkling with nut mixture two more times, brushing each sheet with butter.

3 Layer the remaining phyllo sheets on top of filling, brushing each sheet with more butter. Drizzle with any remaining butter. Using a sharp knife, cut stacked layers into 32 to 48 diamond-shape, rectangle, or square pieces (see photo 3, below).

4 Bake for 35 to 45 minutes or until golden. Cool slightly in pan on a wire rack.

5 Meanwhile, in a medium saucepan stir together the remaining 1 cup sugar, the water, honey, lemon peel, lemon juice, and stick cinnamon. Bring to boiling; reduce heat. Simmer, uncovered, for 20 minutes. Remove cinnamon. Pour syrup evenly over warm baklava in pan (see photo 4, below). Cool completely.

PER PIECE: 174 cal., 12 g total fat (4 g sat. fat), 11 mg chol., 65 mg sodium, 16 g carb., 1 g fiber, 2 g pro. **EXCHANGES:** 1 Other Carb., 2½ Fat

PHYLLO DOUGH KNOW-HOW

It makes impressive desserts, and this paper-thin dough is easy to handle—perfect!

- Look for phyllo dough in the freezer section with the frozen prepared desserts. Sheets typically come in two sizes: 18×14 and 14×9 inches
- Thaw frozen phyllo dough in the refrigerator overnight or at room temperature for 2 hours as directed on the package.
- If you thaw a roll and don't need the whole thing, remove the number of sheets you need, roll up the remaining dough sheets, and refreeze (as long as the dough has not dried out).
- Because it's so thin, once unwrapped, phyllo dries out quickly and crumbles. As you work, keep the opened stack of dough covered with plastic wrap or a damp paper towel to prevent drying, removing only the number of sheets you need at a time.
- When brushed with butter, phyllo becomes pliable and easy to handle. Brush each sheet you layer with melted butter. Brushing with melted butter makes for crisp, flaky layers.
- If a sheet breaks, just piece it back together, brush it with butter, and stack another sheet on top. (Once stacked together, any torn pieces will be unnoticeable.)

BAKLAVA STEP-BY-STEP

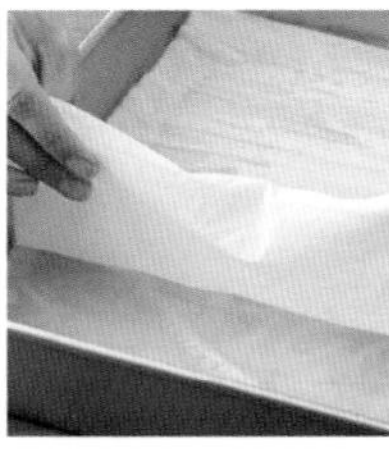

1. Each phyllo layer will consist of five or six sheets.

2. As you layer, brush each sheet to the edges with some of the melted butter.

3. Before baking, use a sharp knife to cut through all layers into desired shapes.

4. Pour syrup evenly over the still-warm baked baklava in the pan. Cool completely.

FRUIT PIZZA

Fruit Pizza

PREP: 30 MINUTES **BAKE:** 12 MINUTES AT 375°F
MAKES: 20 PIECES

- **1 recipe Sugar Cookie Cutouts dough** **(page 369)** **or 1½ 16.5-ounce packages refrigerated sugar cookie dough**
- **1 8-ounce package cream cheese, softened**
- **½ cup sugar**
- **1 teaspoon vanilla**
- **4 cups sliced or halved fresh strawberries; sliced or halved seedless red and/or green grapes; fresh blueberries or fresh raspberries; sliced kiwifruit; canned mandarin orange sections, drained; and/or fresh nectarine slices**
- **¼ cup apricot or seedless raspberry jam or orange marmalade, melted**

1 Preheat oven to 375°F. Pat dough into the bottom of an ungreased 15×10×1-inch baking pan. Bake for 12 to 14 minutes or until light golden brown (dough may puff while baking but will fall as it cools). Cool completely in pan on a wire rack.

2 In a medium bowl beat cream cheese with an electric mixer on medium to high speed for 30 seconds. Add sugar and vanilla; beat until fluffy. Spread cheese mixture over cooled crust. Arrange fruit on top. Brush or drizzle with jam. Serve immediately or cover and chill for up to 24 hours. To serve, cut into squares or triangles.

PER PIECE: 219 cal., 10 g total fat (6 g sat. fat), 39 mg chol., 127 mg sodium, 29 g carb., 1 g fiber, 3 g pro.
EXCHANGES: 1 Starch, 1 Other Carb., 2 Fat

Chocolate Soufflé

PREP: 25 MINUTES **BAKE:** 40 MINUTES AT 350°F
MAKES: 6 TO 8 SERVINGS

- **Butter**
- **Sugar**
- **4 ounces bittersweet or semisweet chocolate, chopped**
- **3 tablespoons all-purpose flour**
- **1 tablespoon unsweetened cocoa powder**
- **3 tablespoons butter**
- **1¼ cups half-and-half, light cream, or milk**
- **1 teaspoon vanilla**
- **4 egg yolks**
- **6 egg whites**
- **⅓ cup sugar**

1 Preheat oven to 350°F. Butter the sides of a 2-quart soufflé dish. Sprinkle inside of dish with sugar; set aside.

2 In a small saucepan cook and stir chocolate over low heat until melted; set aside.

3 In a small bowl combine the flour and cocoa powder. In a medium saucepan melt the 3 tablespoons butter over medium heat. Stir in flour mixture; gradually stir in half-and-half. Cook and stir over medium heat until thickened and bubbly. Remove from heat. Stir in vanilla. Stir the melted chocolate into the hot cream mixture. In a medium bowl beat the egg yolks with a fork just until combined. Gradually stir the chocolate mixture into egg yolks; set aside.

4 In a large bowl beat egg whites with an electric mixer on medium to high speed until soft peaks form (tips curl) (see photo 1, page 170). Gradually add the ⅓ cup sugar, 1 tablespoon at a time, beating until stiff peaks form (tips stand straight) (see photo 2, page 170).

5 Gently fold about one-fourth of the the beaten egg whites into the chocolate mixture to lighten. Fold chocolate mixture into remaining egg whites in bowl. Pour chocolate mixture into the prepared soufflé dish.

6 Bake for 40 to 45 minutes or until a knife inserted near the center comes out clean. Serve soufflé immediately. To serve, insert two forks back to back; gently pull soufflé apart into six to eight equal-size wedges. Use a spoon to transfer to plates.

PER SERVING: 333 cal., 23 g total fat (13 g sat. fat), 159 mg chol., 138 mg sodium, 28 g carb., 2 g fiber, 9 g pro.
EXCHANGES: ½ Starch, 1½ Other Carb., 1 Lean Meat, 4 Fat

Meringue Shells with Fruit

PREP: 45 MINUTES **BAKE:** 35 MINUTES AT 300°F
STAND: 60 MINUTES **MAKES:** 6 MERINGUES

- **2 egg whites**
- **½ teaspoon vanilla**
- **⅛ teaspoon cream of tartar**
- **½ cup sugar**
- **1 recipe Fluffy Lemon Filling or 1½ to 2 cups Lemon Curd (page 289), purchased lemon curd, or vanilla or lemon pudding**
- **2 to 3 cups assorted whole or cut-up fresh fruit**

1 Allow egg whites to stand at room temperature for 30 minutes. Line a large baking sheet with parchment paper or foil. Draw six 3- to 3½-inch circles 3 inches apart on the paper or foil; set aside.

2 Preheat oven to 300°F. For meringue, in a medium mixing bowl beat egg whites, vanilla, and cream of tartar with electric mixer on medium speed until soft peaks form (tips curl) (see photo 1, page 170). Add sugar, 1 tablespoon at a time, beating on high speed until stiff peaks form (tips stand straight) (see photo 2, page 170) and sugar is almost dissolved (5 to 6 minutes).

MERINGUE SHELLS WITH FRUIT

3 Spoon or pipe meringue over circles on paper, building up sides to form shells. Bake for 35 minutes. Turn off oven; let meringues dry in oven with door closed for 60 minutes. Lift meringues off paper. Transfer to a wire rack; cool completely.

4 Meanwhile, make Fluffy Lemon Filling. To serve, spoon lemon filling into shells. Arrange fruit on top of filling. Serve immediately.

FLUFFY LEMON FILLING: In a medium bowl stir together one 10-ounce jar purchased lemon curd and half of an 8-ounce carton frozen whipped topping, thawed.

MAKE-AHEAD DIRECTIONS: Carefully wrap meringue shells in foil or place in a freezer container. Freeze for up to 6 months.

PER FILLED MERINGUE: 293 cal., 6 g total fat (4 g sat. fat), 35 mg chol., 54 mg sodium, 30 g carb., 6 g fiber, 2 g pro.
EXCHANGES: ½ Fruit, 3½ Other Carb., 1 Fat

BREAD PUDDING

BEST-LOVED

Bread Pudding

PREP: 30 MINUTES **BAKE:** 50 MINUTES AT 350°F
MAKES: 8 SERVINGS

- **4 cups dried white or cinnamon swirl bread cubes* (6 to 7 slices)**
- **1/3 cup dried cranberries or raisins**
- **2 eggs, lightly beaten**
- **2 cups milk**
- **1/4 cup butter, melted**
- **1/2 cup sugar**
- **1 teaspoon ground cinnamon**
- **1/2 teaspoon ground nutmeg**
- **1 teaspoon vanilla**
- **1 recipe Salted Caramel Sauce (page 291) or Bourbon Sauce (page 292) (optional)**

1 Preheat oven to 350°F. Grease a 1½-quart casserole; set aside. In a large bowl combine bread cubes and dried cranberries.

2 In a medium bowl combine eggs, milk, butter, sugar, cinnamon, nutmeg, and vanilla. Stir into bread mixture. Pour into the casserole.

3 Bake, uncovered, for 50 to 55 minutes or until puffed and a knife inserted near the center comes out clean. Cool slightly. If desired, serve with Salted Caramel Sauce or Bourbon Sauce.

***NOTE:** To dry bread cubes, cut bread into ½-inch cubes and spread in a 15×10×1-inch baking pan. Bake in a 300°F oven for 10 to 15 minutes or until dry, stirring twice.

PEAR-GINGER BREAD PUDDING: Prepare as directed, except substitute snipped dried pears for the dried cranberries, 1 tablespoon finely chopped crystallized ginger for the cinnamon, and 1 teaspoon finely shredded orange peel for the nutmeg.

PER ¾ CUP PLAIN OR PEAR-GINGER VARIATION: 219 cal., 9 g total fat (5 g sat.fat), 73 mg chol., 212 mg sodium, 30 g carb., 1 g fiber, 5 g pro. EXCHANGES: 1 Starch, 1 Other Carb., 2 Fat

CHOCOLATE CHIP BREAD PUDDING: Prepare as directed, except substitute semisweet chocolate pieces for the dried cranberries and chocolate milk for the milk. Omit nutmeg; add ½ cup chopped pecans, toasted. Omit sauce.

PER ¾ CUP: 299 cal., 16 g total fat (7 g sat. fat), 73 mg chol., 228 mg sodium, 36 g carb., 2 g fiber, 6 g pro.
EXCHANGES: 1½ Starch, 1 Other Carb., 3 Fat

BEST-LOVED

Brownie Pudding Cake

PREP: 15 MINUTES **BAKE:** 40 MINUTES AT 350°F
COOL: 30 MINUTES **MAKES:** 6 SERVINGS

- **1 cup all-purpose flour**
- **3/4 cup granulated sugar**
- **2 tablespoons unsweetened cocoa powder**
- **2 teaspoons baking powder**
- **1/4 teaspoon salt**
- **1/2 cup milk**
- **2 tablespoons vegetable oil**
- **1 teaspoon vanilla**
- **1/2 cup chopped walnuts**
- **3/4 cup packed brown sugar**
- **1/4 cup unsweetened cocoa powder**
- **1½ cups boiling water**
- **Vanilla ice cream (optional)**

1 Preheat oven to 350°F. Grease an 8×8×2-inch baking pan; set aside. In a medium bowl stir together the flour, granulated sugar, the 2 tablespoons cocoa powder, baking powder, and salt. Stir in milk, oil, and vanilla. Stir in walnuts.

2 Pour batter into the prepared baking pan. In a small bowl stir together the brown sugar and the ¼ cup cocoa powder. Stir in the boiling water. Slowly pour brown sugar mixture over the batter.

3 Bake for 40 minutes. Transfer to a wire rack and cool for 30 to 45 minutes. Serve warm. Spoon cake into dessert bowls; spoon pudding from the bottom of the pan over cake. If desired, serve with vanilla ice cream.

PER SERVING: 406 cal., 12 g total fat (2 g sat. fat), 2 mg chol., 237 mg sodium, 74 g carb., 3 g fiber, 5 g pro.
EXCHANGES: 2 Starch, 3 Other Carb., 2 Fat

BEST-LOVED

Molten Chocolate Cakes

PREP: 30 MINUTES **COOL:** 15 MINUTES
CHILL: 2 HOURS **BAKE:** 15 MINUTES AT 375°F
STAND: 10 MINUTES **MAKES:** 8 CAKES

- **1¼ cups semisweet chocolate pieces**
- **½ cup whipping cream**
- **1 tablespoon butter**
- **¾ cup semisweet chocolate pieces**
- **½ cup butter, cut up**
- **4 eggs**
- **½ cup sugar**
- **½ cup all-purpose flour**
- **Unsweetened cocoa powder (optional)**
- **Fresh raspberries**

1 Generously butter eight 6-ounce ramekins or custard cups. For filling, in a small saucepan combine the 1¼ cups chocolate pieces, whipping cream, and the 1 tablespoon butter. Cook and stir over low heat until chocolate melts and mixture is smooth. Remove from heat. Cool for 15 minutes, stirring occasionally. Cover and chill about 2 hours or until it reaches a fudgelike consistency.

2 Preheat oven to 375°F. In a saucepan combine ¾ cup chocolate pieces and ½ cup butter. Cook and stir over low heat until chocolate melts; cool slightly.

3 In a large mixing bowl beat eggs and sugar with an electric mixer on medium to high speed for 5 minutes. Beat in flour and cooled chocolate mixture. Spoon enough batter into each ramekin to measure 1 inch in depth.

4 Form chilled filling into eight portions. Working quickly, use your hands to roll each portion into a ball. Place a ball of filling on top of the batter in each ramekin; do not allow the filling to touch the sides of the ramekins. Gently spoon remaining batter over filling to cover.

5 Bake for 15 minutes. Remove from oven; let stand for 10 minutes. Using a knife, loosen cakes from sides of ramekins. If desired, dust with unsweetened cocoa powder. If desired, invert onto dessert plates. Serve immediately with fresh raspberries. If desired, serve with small scoops of *vanilla ice cream*.

MAKE-AHEAD DIRECTIONS: Prepare as directed through Step 4. Cover; chill until ready to bake or up to 4 hours. Let stand at room temperature for 30 minutes before baking as directed.

PER CAKE: 490 cal., 34 g total fat (20 g sat. fat), 161 mg chol., 138 mg sodium, 47 g carb., 3 g fiber, 6 g pro.
EXCHANGES: 2 Starch, 1 Other Carb., 6½ Fat

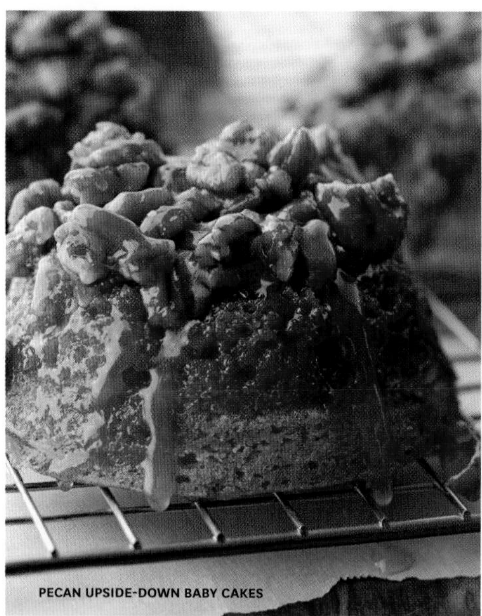
PECAN UPSIDE-DOWN BABY CAKES

Pecan Upside-Down Baby Cakes

PREP: 20 MINUTES **BAKE:** 25 MINUTES AT 350°F
COOL: 5 MINUTES **MAKES:** 12 CAKES

- **2½ cups all-purpose flour**
- **1 teaspoon baking powder**
- **½ teaspoon baking soda**
- **½ teaspoon salt**
- **⅔ cup packed brown sugar**
- **½ cup butter, cut up**
- **⅓ cup honey**
- **1½ cups coarsely chopped pecans**
- **1 teaspoon finely shredded orange peel**
- **3 eggs**
- **2 cups granulated sugar**
- **1 cup vegetable oil**
- **1 8-ounce carton sour cream**
- **2 teaspoons vanilla**

1 Preheat oven to 350°F. Lightly grease twelve 3½-inch (jumbo) muffin cups; set aside. In a medium bowl stir together flour, baking powder, baking soda, and salt; set aside.

2 In a medium saucepan combine brown sugar, butter, and honey. Cook and stir over medium heat about 2 minutes or until smooth; remove from heat. Stir in pecans and orange peel; set aside.

3 In a large bowl combine eggs and granulated sugar. Beat with an electric mixer about 3 minutes or until mixture is thick and lemon color. Add oil, sour cream, and vanilla; beat until combined. Gradually add flour mixture, beating on low speed until smooth.

4 Place 2 tablespoons of the pecan mixture in the bottom of each prepared muffin cup. Spoon a heaping ⅓ cup batter into each cup. Place muffin pans on a foil-lined large baking sheet.

5 Bake for 25 to 30 minutes or until a wooden toothpick comes out clean. Cool in pans for 5 minutes. Using a sharp knife, loosen cakes from sides of muffin cups. Invert onto wire rack. Spoon any pecan mixture remaining in the muffin cups onto cakes. Serve warm or cool.

PER CAKE: 679 cal., 41 g total fat (10 g sat. fat), 83 mg chol., 271 mg sodium, 76 g carb., 2 g fiber, 6 g pro.
EXCHANGES: 2 Starch, 3 Other Carb., 8 Fat

Caramel Flans

PREP: 25 MINUTES **STAND:** 10 MINUTES
BAKE: 30 MINUTES AT 325°F **MAKES:** 4 FLANS

- **⅓ cup sugar**
- **3 eggs, lightly beaten**
- **1½ cups half-and-half or light cream**
- **⅓ cup sugar**
- **1 teaspoon vanilla**
- **Ground nutmeg (optional)**

1 To caramelize sugar, in an small heavy skillet heat ⅓ cup sugar over medium-high heat until it begins to melt, shaking the skillet occasionally; do not stir (see photo 1, page 281). When the sugar starts to melt, reduce heat to low and cook about 5 minutes or until all of the sugar melts, stirring as needed with a wooden spoon (see photo 2, page 281). Immediately divide the caramelized sugar among four 6-ounce custard cups; tilt cups to coat bottoms. Let stand for 10 minutes.

2 Meanwhile, preheat oven to 325°F. Combine eggs, half-and-half, ⅓ cup sugar, and vanilla. Beat until well combined but not foamy. Place custard cups in a 2-quart square baking dish. Divide egg mixture among custard cups. If desired, sprinkle with nutmeg. Place baking dish on oven rack. Pour boiling water into baking dish around custard cups to a depth of 1 inch. Bake for 30 to 40 minutes or until a knife inserted near the centers comes out clean.

3 Remove custard cups from water. Cool slightly on a wire rack and unmold. (Or cool completely in cups. Cover; chill until serving time.) Using a sharp knife, loosen flan from sides of cups. Invert a plate over each cup; turn plate and cup over together. Remove custard cups.

PER FLAN: 304 cal., 14 g total fat (8 g sat. fat), 192 mg chol., 89 mg sodium, 38 g carb., 0 g fiber, 7 g pro.
EXCHANGES: 2½ Other Carb., 1 High-Fat Meat, 1 Fat

Crème Brûlée

PREP: 10 MINUTES **BAKE:** 30 MINUTES AT 325°F
CHILL: 1 TO 8 HOURS **STAND:** 20 MINUTES
MAKES: 6 SERVINGS

- **1¾ cups half-and-half or light cream**
- **5 egg yolks, lightly beaten**
- **⅓ cup sugar**
- **1 teaspoon vanilla**
- **⅛ teaspoon salt**
- **¼ cup sugar**

1 Preheat oven to 325°F. In a small heavy saucepan heat half-and-half over medium-low heat just until bubbly. Remove from heat; set aside.

2 Meanwhile, in a medium bowl combine egg yolks, the ⅓ cup sugar, the vanilla, and salt. Beat with a wire whisk just until combined. Slowly whisk the hot half-and-half into the custard.

3 Place six 4-ounce ramekins or 6-ounce custard cups in a 3-quart rectangular baking dish. Divide custard mixture evenly among ramekins. Place baking dish on oven rack. Pour enough boiling water into the baking dish to reach halfway up sides of ramekins.

4 Bake for 30 to 40 minutes or until a knife inserted near centers comes out clean (centers will still shake slightly). Remove ramekins from water; cool on a wire rack. Cover; chill for at least 1 to 8 hours.

5 Before serving, let custards stand at room temperature for 20 minutes. Meanwhile, in a medium heavy skillet heat the ¼ cup sugar over medium-high heat until sugar begins to melt, shaking skillet occasionally to heat sugar evenly (see photo 1, below). Do not stir. Once the sugar starts to melt, reduce heat to low and cook about 5 minutes or until all of the sugar melts and is golden, stirring as needed with a wooden spoon (see photo 2, below).

6 Quickly drizzle the caramelized sugar over custards.* (If sugar hardens in the skillet, return to heat; stir until melted.) Serve immediately.

***NOTE:** If you have a kitchen torch, prepare as directed through Step 4. Let custards stand at room temperature for 20 minutes. Spread the ¼ cup sugar equally among the tops of the custards. Using the torch, melt the sugar by evenly moving the tip of the flame across the top of the custards to form a crispy layer.

AMARETTO CRÈME BRÛLÉE: Prepare as directed, except stir 2 tablespoons amaretto or coffee liqueur into the custard mixture in Step 2.

PER SERVING PLAIN OR AMARETTO VARIATION: 214 cal., 12 g fat (6 g sat. fat), 201 mg chol., 84 mg sodium, 23 g carb., 0 g fiber, 4 g pro.
EXCHANGES: 1½ Other Carb., ½ Medium-Fat Meat, 1½ Fat

CRÈME BRÛLÉE

CARAMELIZING SUGAR STEP-BY-STEP

1. Spread sugar in an even layer in a heavy skillet. Shake the skillet occasionally for even melting, but don't stir it until the sugar starts to melt.

2. When sugar starts to melt, stir it occasionally with a wooden spoon, gradually incorporating the unmelted sugar until all is melted and golden brown. Reduce heat if syrup browns too rapidly.

VANILLA PANNA COTTA

Vanilla Panna Cotta

PREP: 20 MINUTES **CHILL:** 4 TO 24 HOURS
MAKES: 8 SERVINGS

- **1 envelope unflavored gelatin**
- **1/4 cup water**
- **1 1/2 cups whipping cream**
- **1 cup sugar**
- **1 vanilla bean, split lengthwise and seeds scraped, or 2 teaspoons vanilla**
- **2 cups buttermilk**
- **Blackberries, blueberries, raspberries, or strawberries**

1 Place eight 4- to 6-ounce ramekins, 6-ounce custard cups, or half-pint jars in a shallow baking pan; set aside. In a small bowl sprinkle gelatin over water. Do not stir. Let stand for 5 minutes.

2 Meanwhile, in a medium saucepan stir together the whipping cream, sugar, and, if using, the vanilla bean and seeds. Heat over medium heat until hot but not boiling. Add gelatin mixture; stir until gelatin is dissolved. Remove from heat. Remove and discard vanilla bean. Stir in buttermilk and, if using, vanilla. Pour into ramekins. Cover and chill for 4 to 24 hours or until set.

3 To serve, top with fresh berries.

PER PANNA COTTA + 1/8 CUP BERRIES: 294 cal., 17 g total fat (11 g sat. fat), 64 mg chol., 82 mg sodium, 32 g carb., 1 g fiber, 4 g pro. EXCHANGES: 1/2 Milk, 1 1/2 Other Carb., 3 Fat

LOW-CALORIE

Creamy Rice Pudding

PREP: 20 MINUTES **COOK:** 28 MINUTES
MAKES: 3 CUPS

- **1 cup water**
- **3/4 cup milk**
- **1/4 teaspoon salt**
- **1/2 cup Arborio or long grain rice**
- **1 teaspoon butter**
- **1 cup half-and-half or light cream**
- **1/2 of a vanilla bean, halved lengthwise or 1 teaspoon vanilla**
- **2 egg yolks**
- **1/3 cup sugar**

1 In a saucepan heat the water, milk, and salt over medium heat until nearly boiling. Stir in rice and butter. Bring to boiling; reduce heat. Cover; simmer over very low heat for 25 to 30 minutes or until thick and nearly all liquid is absorbed, stirring every 5 minutes at end of cooking. Transfer to a bowl.

2 Meanwhile, place half-and-half in a small saucepan. If using vanilla bean, use a paring knife to scrape seeds from inside of vanilla bean; add seeds to the cream. Heat just to boiling. In a medium bowl whisk together egg yolks and sugar. Gradually whisk in hot half-and-half; return all to saucepan. Cook and stir over medium-low heat for 3 to 5 minutes or until sauce thickens and coats the back of a spoon.

3 Stir sauce and, if using, vanilla into rice in bowl; serve warm. Or cover and chill for several hours or overnight. If desired, just before serving, stir in additional half-and-half until desired consistency.

PER ½ CUP: 189 cal., 7 g total fat (4 g sat. fat), 89 mg chol., 134 mg sodium, 27 g carb., 0 g fiber, 4 g pro.
EXCHANGES: 1 Starch, 1 Other Carb., 1 Fat

Cream Puffs

PREP: 25 MINUTES **COOL:** 10 MINUTES
BAKE: 30 MINUTES AT 400°F **MAKES:** 12 CREAM PUFFS

- **1 cup water**
- **½ cup butter**
- **⅛ teaspoon salt**
- **1 cup all-purpose flour**
- **4 eggs**
- **3 cups Sweetened Whipped Cream (page 270), Vanilla or Chocolate Pudding (page 285), or ice cream**

1 Preheat oven to 400°F. Grease a baking sheet. In a saucepan combine the water, butter, and salt. Bring to boiling. Immediately add flour all at once; stir vigorously. Cook and stir until mixture forms a ball (see photo 1, below).

CREAM PUFF DOUGH STEP-BY-STEP

1. Using a wooden spoon, vigorously stir dough in saucepan over heat until it forms a ball that doesn't separate.

2. Remove the pan from the heat. Let dough cool for 10 minutes. Beat in eggs, one at a time. Beat until the dough is smooth before adding the next egg.

CREAM PUFFS

Remove from heat. Cool for 10 minutes. Add eggs, one at a time, beating well after each addition (see photo 2, below).

2 Drop 12 heaping tablespoons of dough onto prepared baking sheet. Bake for 30 to 35 minutes or until golden brown and firm. Transfer to a wire rack; let cool.

3 Just before serving, cut tops from puffs; remove soft dough from inside. Fill with Sweetened Whipped Cream. Replace tops.

PER PUFF: 233 cal., 21 g total fat (12 g sat. fat), 132 mg chol., 114 mg sodium, 9 g carb., 0 g fiber, 4 g pro.
EXCHANGES: ½ Starch, ½ High-Fat Meat, 3½ Fat

MINI PUFFS: Prepare as directed, except drop dough by rounded teaspoons 2 inches apart onto greased baking sheets. Bake, one sheet at a time, in a preheated 400°F oven for 25 minutes (keep remaining dough covered while first batch bakes). Cool, split, and fill as directed. Makes about 30 mini puffs.

PER MINI PUFF: 93 cal., 8 g total fat (5 g sat. fat), 53 mg chol., 4 g carb., 46 mg sodium, 0 g fiber, 2 g pro. EXCHANGES: 2 Fat

make it mine

Cheesecake

Pumpkin-almond cheesecake, anyone? How about a mocha version with a touch of orange? With this master recipe, discover your own combination for a one-of-a-kind delight.

PREP: 30 MINUTES
BAKE: 40 MINUTES AT 350°F
COOL: 45 MINUTES **CHILL:** 4 HOURS
MAKES: 12 SERVINGS

- **1¾ cups CRUMBS, crushed**
- **¼ cup finely chopped NUTS**
- **1 tablespoon sugar**
- **½ teaspoon SPICE (optional)**
- **½ cup butter, melted**
- **DAIRY**
- **SWEETENER**
- **2 tablespoons all-purpose flour**
- **1 teaspoon FLAVORING**
- **¼ cup LIQUID**
- **3 eggs, lightly beaten**

1 Preheat oven to 350°F. For crust, in a bowl combine the Crumbs, Nuts, the 1 tablespoon sugar, and, if desired, the Spice. Stir in melted butter. Press the crumb mixture onto the bottom and about 1½ inches up the sides of a 9-inch springform pan; set aside.

2 For filling, in a large mixing bowl beat the Dairy, Sweetener, flour, and Flavoring with an electric mixer until combined. Beat in Liquid until smooth. Stir in eggs.

3 Pour filling into crust-lined pan. Place pan in a shallow baking pan (see optional water bath method, page 285). Bake for 40 to 50 minutes or until a 2½-inch area around the outside edge appears set when gently shaken.

4 Cool in pan on a wire rack for 15 minutes. Using a small sharp knife, loosen the crust from sides of pan; cool for 30 minutes more. Remove sides of pan; cool cheesecake completely on rack. Cover and chill at least 4 hours before serving.

CRUMBS *(pick one)*

Chocolate sandwich cookies (use 3 tablespoons butter, melted)
Gingersnaps
Graham crackers
Vanilla wafers

NUTS *(pick one)*

Almonds
Macadamia nuts
Pecans
Walnuts

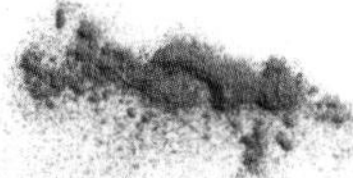

SPICE *(pick one)*

Ground allspice
Apple pie spice
Ground cinnamon
Ground ginger
Pumpkin pie spice

DAIRY *(pick one)*

Three 8-ounce packages cream cheese, softened
Two 8-ounce packages cream cheese, softened, plus one 8-ounce carton sour cream (omit Liquid)
Two 8-ounce packages cream cheese, softened, plus 1 cup canned pumpkin (omit Liquid)

SWEETENER *(pick one)*

1 cup granulated sugar
½ cup granulated sugar plus ½ cup packed brown sugar

FLAVORING *(pick one)*

Peppermint or almond extract
Shredded lemon or orange peel
Vanilla

LIQUID *(pick one)*

Brewed coffee
Milk
Orange or pineapple juice

LOW-CALORIE

Coconut Cream Squares

PREP: 30 MINUTES **BAKE:** 40 MINUTES AT 350°F
COOL: 60 MINUTES **CHILL:** 3 TO 6 HOURS
MAKES: 32 SQUARES

- **2 cups all-purpose flour**
- **¾ cup flaked coconut**
- **½ cup powdered sugar**
- **1 teaspoon finely shredded lime peel**
- **1 cup butter, softened**
- **1 cup granulated sugar**
- **¼ cup cornstarch**
- **¼ teaspoon salt**
- **3 cups whole milk**
- **⅔ cup cream of coconut***
- **5 egg yolks, lightly beaten**
- **1¼ teaspoons coconut extract**
- **1 teaspoon vanilla**
- **1 cup whipped cream**

1 Preheat oven to 350°F. Line a 13×9×2-inch baking pan with foil, extending the foil over edges of pan; set aside.

2 For crust, in a large bowl stir together flour, the ¾ cup flaked coconut, powdered sugar, and lime peel. Add butter, stirring until it comes together. Press evenly onto the bottom of the prepared baking pan. Bake about 20 minutes or until crust is light brown. Cool on a wire rack.

3 For filling, in a large saucepan stir together granulated sugar, cornstarch, and salt. Gradually stir in milk and cream of coconut. Cook and stir over medium-high heat until thickened and bubbly; reduce heat. Cook and stir for 2 minutes more. Remove from heat. Gradually stir about 1 cup of the hot mixture into egg yolks. Return egg yolk mixture to saucepan. Bring to a gentle boil, stirring constantly; reduce heat. Cook and stir for 2 minutes more. Remove from heat. Stir in coconut extract and vanilla. Pour warm mixture over crust.

4 Bake about 20 minutes more or until filling is set. Cool on a wire rack for 60 minutes. Cover and chill for 3 to 6 hours before serving. Using the edges of the foil, lift out of pan. Cut into 32 squares. If desired, garnish with whipped cream.

***NOTE:** Look for cream of coconut, such as Coco Lopez, among the drink mixers in liquor stores.

PER SQUARE: 183 cal., 10 g total fat (7 g sat. fat), 52 mg chol., 89 mg sodium, 21 g carb., 0 g fiber, 2 g pro.
EXCHANGES: ½ Starch, 1 Other Carb., 2 Fat

Vanilla Pudding

PREP: 10 MINUTES **COOK:** 20 MINUTES
MAKES: ABOUT 3 CUPS

- **¾ cup sugar**
- **3 tablespoons cornstarch**
- **3 cups milk**
- **4 egg yolks, lightly beaten**
- **1 tablespoon butter**
- **1½ teaspoons vanilla**

1 In a heavy saucepan combine sugar and cornstarch. Stir in milk. Cook and stir over medium heat until thickened and bubbly. Cook and stir 2 minutes more. Remove from heat. Gradually stir 1 cup of the milk mixture into yolks.

2 Add egg mixture to milk mixture in saucepan. Bring to a gentle boil; reduce heat. Cook and stir for 2 minutes more. Remove from heat. Stir in butter and vanilla. Pour pudding into a bowl. Cover surface with plastic wrap. Cool slightly and serve warm or chill. (Do not stir during chilling.)

CHOCOLATE PUDDING: Prepare as directed, except add ⅓ cup unsweetened cocoa powder with the sugar. (For most intense chocolate flavor, use Dutch-process cocoa.) Decrease cornstarch to 2 tablespoons and milk to 2⅔ cups.

PER ¾ CUP VANILLA OR CHOCOLATE VARIATION: 363 cal., 13 g total fat (7 g sat. fat), 236 mg chol., 102 mg sodium, 52 g carb., 0 g fiber, 9 g pro. EXCHANGES: 1 Milk, 2½ Other Carb., 2½ Fat

CHEESECAKE CHAT

Here are two tips for making this spectacular dessert:

- Always use a springform pan to make a cheesecake. Removing the cheesecake from any other type of pan is nearly impossible.
- For extra-creamy results, consider baking the cheesecake in a water bath: Prepare crust as directed. Place crust-lined springform on a double layer of 18×12-inch heavy-duty foil. Bring edges of foil up and mold around sides of pan to form a watertight seal. Pour prepared filling into pan. Place in a roasting pan. Pour enough boiling water into roasting pan to reach halfway up sides of the springform pan (see photo, right). Bake for 60 minutes. When done, cake edges will jiggle slightly when the pan is gently shaken. Turn oven off; allow cheesecake to sit in oven for 60 minutes (cheesecake will continue to set up). Carefully remove pan from water bath. Remove foil from pan. Cool and chill as directed on page 284.

ENGLISH TRIFLE

English Trifle

PREP: 30 MINUTES **CHILL:** 4 TO 24 HOURS
MAKES: 8 SERVINGS

- **1 recipe Vanilla Pudding (page 285)**
- **5½ cups 1-inch cubes pound cake***
- **6 tablespoons raspberry liqueur, orange liqueur, or orange juice**
- **3 cups fresh berries (raspberries, blueberries, and/or sliced strawberries)**
- **¼ cup toasted sliced almonds**
- **½ cup whipping cream**
- **1 tablespoon powdered sugar**
- **1 tablespoon raspberry liqueur, orange liqueur, or orange juice (optional)**
- **Fresh berries**

1 Prepare Vanilla Pudding and chill for 2 hours.

2 Arrange one-third of the cake cubes in the bottom of a 2-quart clear serving bowl. Drizzle with 2 tablespoons of the liqueur. Top with 1 cup of the berries. Spread one-third of the pudding over berries. Top with 1 tablespoon of the almonds. Repeat layers twice. Cover and chill for 4 to 24 hours.

3 To serve, in a medium mixing bowl beat whipping cream, powdered sugar, and, if desired, the 1 tablespoon liqueur with an electric mixer on medium speed until soft peaks form (tips curl). Spoon over top of trifle. Arrange additional berries over whipped cream and, if desired, sprinkle with remaining almonds.

***NOTE:** One 10¾-ounce frozen pound cake, thawed, yields 5½ cups of 1-inch cubes.

PER SERVING: 484 cal., 24 g total fat (13 g sat. fat), 218 mg chol., 240 mg sodium, 57 g carb., 4 g fiber, 8 g pro.
EXCHANGES: ½ Fruit, 1½ Starch, 1½ Other Carb., ½ Medium-Fat Meat, 4 Fat

Tiramisu

PREP: 45 MINUTES **CHILL:** 4 TO 24 HOURS
MAKES: 16 SERVINGS

- **½ cup sugar**
- **½ cup water**
- **2 tablespoons instant espresso coffee powder**
- **1 tablespoon amaretto**
- **1 tablespoon hazelnut liqueur**
- **2 8-ounce cartons mascarpone cheese**
- **¼ cup sugar**
- **1 teaspoon vanilla**
- **1½ cups whipping cream**
- **3 tablespoons sugar**
- **½ cup water**
- **3 tablespoons dried egg whites***
- **⅓ cup sugar**
- **2 3-ounce package ladyfingers, split**
- **2 tablespoons unsweetened cocoa powder**

1 For syrup, in a small saucepan combine the ½ cup sugar, ½ cup water, and the espresso powder. Bring to boiling over medium heat, stirring to dissolve sugar. Boil gently, uncovered, for 1 minute. Remove from heat. Stir in amaretto and hazelnut liqueur; cool.

2 In a medium bowl stir together mascarpone, the ¼ cup sugar, and vanilla. In a chilled large mixing bowl combine whipping cream and

TIRAMISU STEP-BY-STEP

1. Brush split ladyfingers evenly with coffee syrup.

2. To evenly spread egg white mixture, start by spooning mounds of the egg white mixture over the mascarpone mixture. Use an offset spatula to spread the egg white mixture evenly.

the 3 tablespoons sugar. Beat with an electric mixer on medium speed until soft peaks form (tips curl). Fold ½ cup whipped cream mixture into mascarpone mixture to lighten; set both mixtures aside.

3 Clean beaters thoroughly. In another large mixing bowl beat the ½ cup water and dried egg whites with an electric mixer on medium speed until soft peaks form (tips curl). Gradually beat in the ⅓ cup sugar, 1 tablespoon at a time, until stiff peaks form (tips stand straight).

4 Arrange half of the ladyfinger halves in the bottom of a 9×9×2-inch baking pan. Brush with half of the syrup (see photo 1, page 286). Spread with half of the mascarpone mixture. Spread with half of the egg white mixture (see photo 2, page 286). Top with half of the whipped cream mixture, spreading evenly. Sift half of the cocoa powder over the whipped cream layer. Repeat layers, except cocoa powder, once.

5 Cover and chill for 4 to 24 hours. Uncover and sift remaining cocoa powder over the top just before serving.

***NOTE:** Dried egg whites are a safe alternative to using raw whites. Find them in the baking aisle of grocery stores.

PER SERVING: 316 cal., 22 g total fat (13 g sat. fat), 90 mg chol., 57 mg sodium, 26 g carb., 0 g fiber, 9 g pro.
EXCHANGES: 1 Starch, 1 Other Carb., 1 High-Fat Meat, 2½ Fat

LOW-CALORIE

Orange Sherbet

PREP: 20 MINUTES **FREEZE:** PER MANUFACTURER'S DIRECTIONS **RIPEN:** 4 HOURS (OPTIONAL)
MAKES: 6 CUPS

- **1½ cups sugar**
- **1 envelope unflavored gelatin**
- **1 teaspoon finely shredded orange peel**
- **3¾ cups orange juice**
- **1 cup milk**
- **Few drops orange food coloring (optional)**

1 In a medium saucepan combine sugar and gelatin. Stir in 2 cups of the orange juice. Cook and stir until sugar and gelatin dissolve. Remove from heat. Stir in remaining orange juice, the orange peel, milk, and, if desired, food coloring (mixture may appear curdled).

2 Transfer mixture to a 4-quart ice cream freezer; freeze according to manufacturer's directions.* If desired, ripen 4 hours.

***NOTE:** If you don't have an ice cream freezer, transfer mixture to a 13×9×2-inch baking pan. Cover; freeze 2 to 3 hours or until almost firm. Break mixture into small chunks; transfer to a large mixing bowl. Beat with an electric mixer until smooth but not melted. Return to pan. Cover; freeze until firm.

LEMON SHERBET: In a saucepan combine sugar and gelatin as directed in Step 1. Stir in 1½ cups water instead of orange juice. Cook and stir until sugar and gelatin dissolve. Remove from heat. Stir in 1½ cups cold water, 1 cup milk, 1 teaspoon finely shredded lemon peel, and ¾ cup lemon juice. Freeze as directed.

PER ½ CUP ORANGE OR LEMON VARIATION: 150 cal., 1 g total fat (0 g sat. fat), 2 mg chol., 14 mg sodium, 34 g carb., 0 g fiber, 3 g pro. EXCHANGES: 2 Other Carb., ½ Lean Meat

LOW-CALORIE

Raspberry Sorbet

PREP: 20 MINUTES **CHILL:** 60 MINUTES
FREEZE: 10 TO 12 HOURS **STAND:** 5 MINUTES
MAKES: 3 CUPS

- **1 cup sugar**
- **1 cup water**
- **2 tablespoons lemon juice**
- **3 cups fresh raspberries**
- **2 tablespoons orange juice**

1 For syrup, in a medium saucepan heat and stir the sugar and water over medium heat until just simmering, stirring to dissolve sugar. Remove from heat; stir in lemon juice. Transfer to a medium bowl; cover and chill completely.

2 Place raspberries and orange juice in a food processor or blender. Cover and process until smooth. Press mixture through a fine-mesh sieve; discard seeds. Stir puree into chilled syrup.

3 Spread raspberry mixture into a 2-quart square baking dish. Cover; freeze 4 hours or until firm. Break up mixture with a fork; place in food processor or blender, half at a time if necessary. Cover and process for 30 to 60 seconds or until smooth. Spoon mixture back into the baking dish; cover and freeze for 6 to 8 hours or until firm. To serve, let stand at room temperature for 5 minutes before scooping.

MANGO SORBET: Prepare as directed, except substitute cut-up, peeled mango for raspberries. Omit pressing through sieve. Makes 4 cups.

PER ⅓ CUP RASPBERRY OR MANGO VARIATION: 110 cal., 0 g total fat, 0 mg chol., 1 mg sodium, 28 g carb., 3 g fiber, 1 g pro. EXCHANGES: ½ Fruit, 1½ Other Carb.

BUTTERSCOTCH CRUNCH SQUARES

BEST-LOVED

Butterscotch Crunch Squares

PREP: 40 MINUTES **BAKE:** 10 MINUTES AT 400°F
FREEZE: 6 HOURS **STAND:** 5 MINUTES
MAKES: 12 SQUARES

- **1 cup all-purpose flour**
- **¼ cup quick-cooking rolled oats**
- **¼ cup packed brown sugar**
- **½ cup butter**
- **½ cup chopped pecans or walnuts**
- **½ cup butterscotch-flavor ice cream topping**
- **½ gallon butter brickle or vanilla ice cream**

1 Preheat oven to 400°F. In a medium bowl combine flour, oats, and sugar. Cut in butter until mixture resembles coarse crumbs. Stir in nuts. Pat nut mixture lightly into an ungreased 13×9×2-inch baking pan. Bake for 10 to 15 minutes or until golden. While still warm, stir nut mixture to crumble; cool.

2 Spread half of the crumbs in a 9×9×2-inch pan; drizzle half of the ice cream topping over crumbs in pan. Place ice cream in a chilled bowl; stir to soften. Spread ice cream evenly over crumbs in pan. Top with remaining topping and crumbs. Cover; freeze about 6 hours or until firm. Let stand at room temperature 5 to 10 minutes before serving.

PER SQUARE: 404 cal., 25 g total fat (11 g sat. fat), 47 mg chol., 239 mg sodium, 43 g carb., 1 g fiber, 4 g pro.
EXCHANGES: 1 Starch, 2 Other Carb., 5 Fat

BEST-LOVED

Classic Vanilla Ice Cream

PREP: 50 MINUTES **CHILL:** 4 TO 24 HOURS
FREEZE: PER MANUFACTURER'S DIRECTIONS
RIPEN: 4 HOURS (OPTIONAL) **MAKES:** 6 CUPS

- **2 cups whole milk**
- **8 egg yolks**
- **¾ cup sugar**
- **2 cups whipping cream**
- **2 tablespoons vanilla**
- **½ teaspoon kosher salt or ¼ teaspoon salt**
- **Kosher or rock salt and crushed ice (for hand-crank or electric ice cream freezers)**

1 In a medium heavy saucepan whisk together milk, egg yolks, and sugar. Cook over medium heat, stirring constantly with a heatproof rubber scraper, until custard coats the back of the scraper (see photo 1, below).

2 Strain custard through a fine-mesh sieve into a bowl placed in a larger bowl of ice water (see photo 2, below). Stir custard until cooled. Stir in whipping cream, vanilla, and ½ teaspoon kosher salt. Cover and chill for 4 to 24 hours.

3 Freeze chilled mixture in a 4- to 5-quart ice cream freezer according to manufacturer's directions. If desired, ripen for at least 4 hours.*

***NOTE:** To ripen, for a traditional ice cream freezer, after churning remove lid and dasher. Cover the top with foil. Plug the lid hole wiht a cloth; replace lid on can and fill the outer freezer bucket with ice and rock salt (enough to cover top of the freezer can) in a ratio of 4 cups ice to 1 cup rock salt. Let stand at room temperature for 4 hours.

ICE CREAM CUSTARD STEP-BY-STEP

1. To check the custard for doneness, swipe a finger across the scraper. When the custard is done, the line made by your finger will remain without the custard running back together.

2. Place a bowl in a large bowl of ice. (The ice will help quickly cool the custard.) Strain custard into the bowl through a fine-mesh sieve to catch any bits of egg that might have overcooked.

FOR 1½- TO 2-QUART FREEZER: Prepare as directed, except in a small heavy saucepan whisk together 1 cup milk, 4 egg yolks, and ⅓ cup sugar. Cook over medium heat, stirring constantly with a heatproof rubber spatula, until custard coats the back of the scraper. Strain custard and chill in ice water as directed in Step 2. Stir in 1 cup whipping cream, 1 tablespoon vanilla, and ¼ teaspoon kosher salt. Cover and chill for 4 to 24 hours. Freeze chilled mixture in a 1½- to 2-quart ice cream freezer according to manufacturer's directions. Transfer to a freezer container and freeze until firm.

PER ½ CUP: 253 cal., 19 g total fat (11 g sat. fat), 182 mg chol., 120 mg sodium, 16 g carb., 0 g fiber, 4 g pro. EXCHANGES: 1 Other Carb., ½ High-Fat Meat, 3 Fat

STRAWBERRY ICE CREAM: Prepare as directed, except stir 4 cups hulled fresh strawberries, coarsely mashed, into the chilled mixture before freezing (use 2 cups strawberries for the 1½- to 2-quart freezer).

PER ½ CUP: 270 cal., 19 g total fat (11 g sat. fat), 182 chol., 121 mg sodium, 20 g carb., 1 g fiber, 4 g pro. EXCHANGES: ½ Fruit, 1½ Other Carb., ½ High-Fat Meat, 3 Fat

CHOCOLATE ICE CREAM: Prepare as directed, except increase sugar to 1 cup and stir ½ cup unsweetened cocoa powder with the sugar in the saucepan before adding the remaining ingredients. Continue cooking as directed. (Use ½ cup sugar and ¼ cup unsweetened cocoa powder for 1½-to 2-quart freezer.)

PER ½ CUP: 279 cal., 19 g total fat (11 g sat. fat), 182 chol., 121 mg sodium, 23 g carb., 1 g fiber, 5 g pro. EXCHANGES: 1½ Other Carb., ½ High-Fat Meat, 3 Fat

FAST

Chocolate Fondue

PREP: 15 MINUTES **MAKES:** 2 CUPS

- **8 ounces semisweet chocolate, chopped**
- **1 14-ounce can sweetened condensed milk (1¼ cups)**
- **⅓ cup milk**
- **Assorted dippers, such as angel food or pound cake cubes, brownie squares, marshmallows, strawberries, banana slices, or dried apricots**

1 In a medium heavy saucepan heat and stir chocolate over low heat until melted. Stir in sweetened condensed milk and milk; heat through. Transfer to a fondue pot; keep warm.

2 Serve fondue with dippers. Swirl pieces as you dip. If the fondue mixture thickens, stir in additional milk.

CHOCOLATE-LIQUEUR FONDUE: Prepare as directed, except stir 2 to 4 tablespoons amaretto or orange, hazelnut, or cherry liqueur into mixture after heating.

PER ¼ CUP PLAIN OR CHOCOLATE-LIQUEUR VARIATION: 306 cal., 14 g total fat (8 g sat. fat), 18 mg chol., 67 mg sodium, 44 g carb., 2 g fiber, 6 g pro. EXCHANGES: ½ Milk, 2½ Other Carb., 3 Fat

CHOCOLATE-PEANUT FONDUE: Prepare as directed, except stir ½ cup creamy peanut butter in with the milk.

PER ¼ CUP: 400 cal., 22 g total fat (10 g sat. fat), 18 mg chol., 141 mg sodium, 47 g carb., 3 g fiber, 10 g pro. EXCHANGES: ½ Milk, 2½ Other Carb., 1 High-Fat Meat, 2½ Fat

Lemon Curd

PREP: 5 MINUTES **COOK:** 8 MINUTES
CHILL: 60 MINUTES **MAKES:** 2 CUPS

- **1 cup sugar**
- **2 tablespoons cornstarch**
- **3 teaspoons finely shredded lemon peel**
- **6 tablespoons lemon juice**
- **6 tablespoons water**
- **6 egg yolks, lightly beaten**
- **½ cup butter, cut up**

1 In a medium saucepan stir together sugar and cornstarch. Stir in lemon peel, lemon juice, and water. Cook and stir over medium heat until thickened and bubbly.

2 Stir half of the lemon mixture into the egg yolks. Return egg mixture to the saucepan. Cook, stirring constantly, over medium heat until mixture comes to a gentle boil. Cook and stir for 2 minutes more. Remove from heat. Add butter pieces, stirring until melted. Remove from heat. Transfer to a bowl. Cover surface with plastic wrap. Chill for at least 60 minutes.

TO STORE: Cover and store prepared curd in refrigerator for up to 1 week or transfer to a freezer container and freeze for up to 2 months. Thaw in refrigerator before serving.

PER 2 TABLESPOONS: 125 cal., 7 g total fat (4 g sat. fat), 94 mg chol., 44 mg sodium, 14 g carb., 0 g fiber, 1 g pro. EXCHANGES: 1 Other Carb., 1½ Fat

ORANGE CURD: Prepare as directed, except decrease sugar to ¾ cup; substitute orange peel for the lemon peel and ¾ cup orange juice for the lemon juice and water. Makes about 1½ cups.

PER 2 TABLESPOONS: 156 cal., 10 g total fat (6 g sat. fat), 125 mg chol., 59 mg sodium, 16 g carb., 0 g fiber, 2 g pro. EXCHANGES: 1 Other Carb., 2 Fat

8 to try

Greek Frozen Yogurt

PREP: 15 MINUTES
FREEZE: PER MANUFACTURER'S DIRECTIONS **RIPEN:** 2 TO 4 HOURS
STAND: 5 MINUTES **MAKES:** 16 SERVINGS

- **3 cups plain low-fat Greek yogurt**
- **1 cup sugar**
- **¼ cup freshly squeezed lemon juice**
- **2 teaspoons vanilla**
- **⅛ teaspoon salt**

1 In a medium bowl combine yogurt, sugar, lemon juice, vanilla, and salt. Whisk until smooth.

2 Freeze the yogurt mixture in a 1½- to 2-quart ice cream maker according to the manufacturer's directions. Transfer to an airtight container and freeze for 2 to 4 hours to ripen before serving. Let stand at room temperature for 5 to 15 minutes before serving.

FROZEN YOGURT SANDWICHES: Spread prepared Greek Frozen Yogurt between oatmeal cookies. If desired, roll sides in chopped pistachio nuts.

FROZEN YOGURT POINTERS

1 Use the appropriate-size ice cream maker. Most countertop ice cream freezers are small-batch appliances. If you want to use a larger ice cream freezer, double the recipe.
2 It should take approximately 20 to 30 minutes for the yogurt to be adequately frozen. When checking for doneness, the mixture should be thickened like soft-serve ice cream, rich, and creamy.
3 Transfer the frozen yogurt from the ice cream maker to a freezer container with a tight-fitting lid. Freeze for 2 to 4 hours to ripen before serving. This improves the yogurt's consistency and flavor.

STRAWBERRY: Prepare as directed, except add 1 cup sliced strawberries during the last minute of mixing in the ice cream maker.

MINT: Prepare as directed, except stir in 2 tablespoons snipped fresh mint before placing in the airtight container and ripening.

BERRY: Prepare as directed, except add 1 cup blueberries, blackberries, and/or raspberries during the last minute of mixing in the ice cream maker.

PEACH: Prepare as directed, except puree 2 cups fresh or frozen, thawed, sliced peaches; swirl into yogurt before placing in airtight container and ripening.

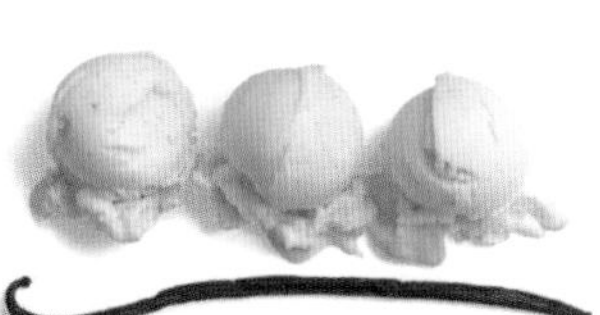

DOUBLE VANILLA: Prepare as directed, except omit lemon juice. Split 1 or 2 vanilla beans lengthwise; scrape seeds from beans. Stir seeds into yogurt mixture before freezing in the ice cream maker.

RASPBERRY FUDGE: Prepare as directed, except swirl in ¼ cup chocolate-flavor syrup and ¼ cup raspberry preserves before placing in airtight container and ripening. Serve topped with shaved chocolate and/or fresh red raspberries.

ALMOND-CHOCOLATE CHUNK: Prepare as directed, except omit the lemon juice and increase vanilla to 1 tablespoon. Add 1 cup chocolate chunks and ½ cup chopped toasted almonds before placing in airtight container and ripening.

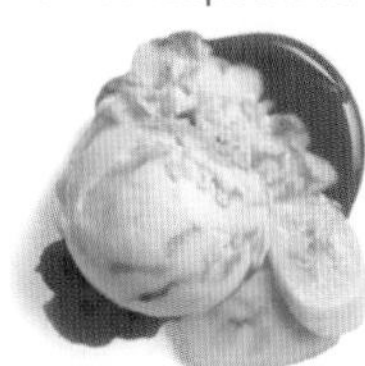

BANANA-CARAMEL: Prepare as directed, except omit the lemon juice and increase vanilla to 1 tablespoon. In a bowl combine 1 banana, sliced, and ½ cup caramel ice cream topping. Swirl into yogurt before placing in airtight container and ripening.

FAST

Heavenly Hot Fudge Sauce

START TO FINISH: 15 MINUTES **MAKES:** 2 CUPS

1 cup whipping cream
¼ cup light-color corn syrup
1 tablespoon coffee-flavor liqueur or 1 teaspoon vanilla
Dash salt
8 ounces semisweet or bittersweet chocolate, chopped

1 In a small saucepan combine cream, corn syrup, liqueur (if using), and salt. Cook over medium heat, until just simmering, stirring occasionally. Remove from heat. Add chocolate (do not stir); let stand 5 minutes (see photos 1 and 2, below). Stir until smooth. Stir in vanilla, if using (see photos 3 and 4, below). Serve warm.

TO STORE: Transfer to an airtight storage container. Cover and chill up to 2 weeks. Transfer to a microwave-safe container. Heat sauce on 100% power (high) at 20- to 30-second intervals; stir after each interval.

PER 2 TABLESPOONS: 142 cal., 10 g total fat (6 g sat. fat), 21 mg chol., 18 mg sodium, 13 g carb., 1 g fiber, 1 g pro. EXCHANGES: 1 Other Carb., 2 Fat

SALTED CARAMEL SAUCE

Salted Caramel Sauce

PREP: 10 MINUTES **COOK:** 5 MINUTES
COOL: 2 HOURS **MAKES:** 1½ CUPS

¾ cup packed brown sugar
½ cup butter, cut up
½ cup whipping cream
3 tablespoons light-color corn syrup
1 teaspoon vanilla
½ teaspoon sea salt or kosher salt

1 In a heavy 2-quart saucepan combine the brown sugar, butter, whipping cream, and corn syrup. Bring to boiling over medium-high heat, stirring to dissolve sugar and melt butter. Reduce heat to medium. Boil, uncovered, at a steady rate for 5 minutes (do not stir). Remove from heat; stir in vanilla. Transfer caramel to a small heatproof bowl. Cover and cool completely, about 2 hours (sauce will thicken as it cools). Sprinkle with ½ teaspoon sea salt before serving. To store, cover and chill up to 1 week. Warm before using.

PER 2 TABLESPOONS: 171 cal., 11 g total fat (7 g sat. fat), 34 mg chol., 170 mg sodium, 18 g carb., 0 g fiber, 0 g pro. EXCHANGES: 1 Other Carb., 2 Fat

HOT FUDGE SAUCE STEP-BY-STEP

1. Add chopped chocolate to the cream mixture, but do not stir.

2. Let the mixture stand for 5 minutes before stirring with a whisk to combine.

3. Continue stirring the mixture until smooth.

4. Stir in the vanilla (if using) and continue stirring the hot fudge until smooth. Serve warm.

FAST

Bourbon Sauce

PREP: 10 MINUTES **COOL:** 5 MINUTES **MAKES:** ¾ CUP

- **¼ cup butter, cut up**
- **½ cup sugar**
- **1 egg yolk, lightly beaten**
- **2 tablespoons water**
- **2 tablespoons bourbon**

1 In a small saucepan melt the butter. Stir in the sugar, egg yolk, and the water. Cook and stir over medium heat for 6 to 8 minutes or until mixture thickens and just boils. Remove from heat; stir in bourbon. Cool slightly. If desired, serve warm over bread pudding or ice cream.

PER 2 TABLESPOONS: 153 cal., 8 g total fat (5 g sat. fat), 55 mg chol., 56 mg sodium, 17 g carb., 0 g fiber, 1 g pro. EXCHANGES: 1 Other Carb., 2 Fat

FAST

Vanilla Sauce

START TO FINISH: 10 MINUTES **MAKES:** 1¼ CUPS

- **½ cup sugar**
- **1 tablespoon cornstarch**
- **1 cup boiling water**
- **2 tablespoons butter**
- **1 teaspoon vanilla paste or vanilla**
- **Dash salt**

1 In a medium saucepan stir together the sugar and cornstarch. Slowly stir in water. Bring to boiling over medium heat; reduce heat. Boil gently for 5 minutes; remove from heat. Stir in butter, vanilla paste, and salt. If desired, serve over gingerbread, apple dumplings, or berry pie. (Cover and chill any leftovers for up to 3 days.)

PER 2 TABLESPOONS: 64 cal., 2 g total fat (1 g sat. fat), 6 mg chol., 31 mg sodium, 11 g carb., 0 g fiber, 0 g pro. EXCHANGES: ½ Other Carb., ½ Fat

Custard Sauce

PREP: 15 MINUTES **CHILL:** 2 HOURS
MAKES: ABOUT 2 CUPS

- **5 egg yolks, lightly beaten**
- **1½ cups whole milk**
- **¼ cup sugar**
- **1½ teaspoons vanilla**

1 In a heavy medium saucepan stir together egg yolks, milk, and sugar. Cook and stir continuously with a wooden spoon or heatproof rubber spatula over medium heat until mixture thickens and just coats the back of a clean metal spoon (see photo 1, page 288). Remove pan from heat. Stir in vanilla. Quickly cool the custard mixture by placing the saucepan in a large bowl of ice water for 1 to 2 minutes, stirring constantly.

2 Pour custard sauce into a bowl. Cover the surface with plastic wrap to prevent a skin from forming. Chill for at least 2 hours, without stirring, before serving. If desired, serve over fresh fruit, baked fruit tarts, or dessert soufflés. (Cover and chill any leftovers for up to 3 days.)

CHOCOLATE CUSTARD SAUCE: Prepare as directed, except add ¼ cup unsweetened Dutch-process cocoa powder or unsweetened cocoa powder and, if desired, a dash ground cinnamon with the sugar. (If necessary, use a whisk to combine ingredients.)

PER 2 TABLESPOONS PLAIN OR CHOCOLATE VARIATION: 44 cal., 2 g total fat (1 g sat. fat), 68 mg chol., 12 mg sodium, 4 g carb., 0 g fiber, 2 g pro. EXCHANGES: ½ Fat

Raspberry Sauce *(photo, page 267)*

PREP: 20 MINUTES **CHILL:** 60 MINUTES
MAKES: 1 CUP

- **3 cups fresh or frozen raspberries**
- **⅓ cup sugar**
- **1 teaspoon cornstarch**

1 Thaw berries if frozen. Do not drain. Place half of the berries in a food processor or blender. Cover and process or blend until berries are smooth. Press berries through a fine-mesh sieve; discard seeds. Repeat with remaining berries. (You should have about 1¼ cups puree.)

2 In a small saucepan stir together the sugar and cornstarch. Add raspberry puree. Cook and stir over medium heat until thickened and bubbly. Cook and stir for 2 minutes more. Transfer to a small bowl. Cover and chill for at least 60 minutes before serving. If desired, serve over angel food cake, cheesecake, or ice cream. (Cover and chill any leftovers for up to 1 week.)

STRAWBERRY SAUCE: Prepare as directed, except substitute 3 cups fresh strawberries or one 16-ounce package frozen unsweetened whole strawberries, thawed, for the raspberries and do not use sieve; use a medium saucepan and reduce sugar to ¼ cup. (You should have 1¾ to 2 cups puree.) Makes about 2 cups.

PER 2 TABLESPOONS RASPBERRY OR STRAWBERRY VARIATION: 58 cal., 0 g total fat, 0 mg chol., 1 mg sodium, 14 g carb., 3 g fiber, 1 g pro. EXCHANGES: ½ Fruit, ½ Other Carb.

fish & shellfish

fish & shellfish

The trick to serving great seafood is to buy it at its best and avoid overcooking. Read here and pages 314–316 for purchasing and preparing tips.

COMMON FISH FORMS

DRAWN: Whole fish with internal organs removed; the scales might or might not be removed.

DRESSED: Ready-to-cook fish with organs, scales, gills, and fins removed.

PAN-DRESSED: Dressed fish with the heads and tails removed.

STEAK: A ready-to-cook crosscut slice from a large dressed fish; usually ½ to 1 inch thick.

FILLET: A ready-to-cook boneless piece of fish cut from the side and away from the backbone; it might or might not be skinned.

SELECTING FRESH FISH

Look for fish with the following characteristics:

- Clear, bright, bulging eyes with black pupils
- Shiny, taut, bright skin
- Red gills that are not slippery
- Flesh that feels firm, elastic, tight to the bone
- Moist, cleanly cut fillets and steaks

Avoid fish with the following characteristics:

- Strong "fishy" odor
- Dull, bloody, or sunken eyes
- Fading skin with bruises, red spots, or browning or yellowing flesh edges
- Ragged cuts in fillets and steaks

TO STORE: Plan to cook fresh fish the same day you buy it. If that's not possible, wrap fish loosely in plastic wrap and store in the coldest part of your refrigerator; use within 2 days. If not using fresh fish within 2 days, wrap it tightly in moisture- and vapor-proof wrap and store in the freezer (set at 0°F or lower) for up to 3 months. Leftover cooked fish can be covered and chilled up to 2 days.

TESTING FISH FOR DONENESS

The delicate texture of fish makes it easy to overcook. To test for doneness, insert a fork into the fish and gently twist. If fish easily begins to flake, it is done. Be sure to check at the minimum cooking time.

LIVE CRABS AND LOBSTERS

When purchasing, look for:

- Hard shells (except for soft-shell crabs)
- Vigorous activity; the lobster's or crab's legs should move when the body is touched
- Lobster tails that curl under body when lifted

TO STORE: Lobsters should be cooked live. Ideally, live lobsters and crabs should be cooked on the day they are purchased. Otherwise, place them in a shallow pan or large bowl and refrigerate them, covered with a damp towel. Or place them on damp newspapers in an insulated cooler half-filled with ice. Cook within 1 day.

LIVE CLAMS, MUSSELS, AND OYSTERS

When purchasing, look for:

- Tightly closed shells. Clams or mussels might gape slightly but should close when tapped; oysters should always be tightly closed.
- Clean, unbroken, moist shells
- Fresh scent, not a strong fishy odor

TO STORE: Refrigerate live clams, mussels, and oysters, covered with a moist cloth, in an open container for 1 to 2 days.

SHUCKED CLAMS, OYSTERS, AND SCALLOPS

When purchasing, look for:

- Plump meats in clear liquor (juices) without shell particles or grit; the liquor should not exceed 10 percent of total volume
- Fresh ocean scent (not sour or sulfurlike)
- Scallops that are firm and moist, retaining their shape when touched

TWO TYPES OF SCALLOPS: There are many species of scallops in the sea, but you'll find two general categories at the market. Sea scallops are about 1½ inches in diameter; on average, there are 20 to 30 per pound. Bay scallops are about ½ inch in diameter and average from 70 to 100 per pound. Be sure to use the type of scallop called for in each recipe; cooking times differ between the two.

TO STORE: Refrigerate shucked clams, oysters, and scallops, covered, in the liquor for up to 2 days or freeze for up to 3 months.

SHRIMP

When purchasing, look for:

- Firm meat
- Translucent, moist shells without black spots
- Fresh scent (not an ammonia odor, which indicates spoilage)

RAW, COOKED, AND CANNED EQUIVALENTS: Twelve ounces raw shrimp in the shell equals 8 ounces raw shelled shrimp or 1 cup cooked shelled shrimp.

TO STORE: Refrigerate shrimp in a covered container for up to 2 days. Keep frozen shrimp in freezer for up to 6 months.

GUIDE TO SHRIMP SIZE

Raw unshelled shrimp, available fresh or frozen, is sold by the pound. Use this list as a reference for market names and the number of shrimp per pound.

Market Name	Number Per Pound
Colossal	Fewer than 15
Extra Jumbo	16 to 20
Jumbo	21 to 25
Extra Large	26 to 30
Large	31 to 40
Medium	41 to 50
Small	51 to 60
Extra Small	61 to 70

THAWING FISH AND SHELLFISH

For the best flavor and for food safety, thaw fish or shellfish gradually by placing the unopened package in a container in the refrigerator. A 1-pound package will thaw in 1 to 2 days. If you must thaw seafood quickly, place it in a resealable plastic bag and immerse in cold water. Or microwave on the defrost setting until it is pliable but still icy. Fish and shellfish thawed in the microwave must be cooked immediately after thawing because some spots might become warm and begin to cook.

QUESTIONS ABOUT FOOD SAFETY?

Call the U.S. Food and Drug Administration's Center for Food Safety and Applied Nutrition Safe Food Information Line, 888/723-3366, weekdays from 10 a.m. to 4 p.m. (Eastern Standard Time).

Because most fish and shellfish contain small amounts of mercury, pregnant women and young children should monitor the fish they eat and restrict the amount. For this and more information, check out the website at *foodsafety.gov/keep/types/seafood.*

FAST **LOW-CALORIE**

Pan-Fried Fish

PREP: 10 MINUTES **COOK:** 6 MINUTES PER BATCH
MAKES: 4 SERVINGS

- **1 pound fresh or frozen skinless fish fillets, ½ to ¾ inch thick**
- **1 egg, lightly beaten**
- **2 tablespoons water**
- **⅔ cup cornmeal or fine dry bread crumbs**
- **½ teaspoon salt**
- **Dash black pepper**
- **Vegetable oil or shortening for frying**

1 Thaw fish if frozen. Rinse fish; pat dry with paper towels. Cut into four serving-size pieces. In a shallow dish combine egg and water. In another shallow dish stir together cornmeal, salt, and pepper. Dip fish into egg mixture; coat fish with cornmeal mixture (see photo 1, below).

2 Preheat oven to 300°F. In a large skillet heat ¼ inch oil or melted shortening. Add half of the fish in a single layer; fry on one side until golden. Turn carefully (see photo 2, below). Fry until second side is golden and fish flakes easily when tested with a fork. Allow 3 to 4 minutes per side. Drain on paper towels. Keep warm in oven while frying remaining fish.

PER FISH PORTION: 255 cal., 13 g total fat (2 g sat. fat), 101 mg chol., 230 mg sodium, 12 g carb., 1 g fiber, 23 g pro. EXCHANGES: 1 Starch, 3 Lean Meat, 1 Fat

SPICY HOT PAN-FRIED FISH: Prepare as directed, except omit black pepper. Reduce cornmeal to ¼ cup and combine with ¼ cup all-purpose flour, ¾ teaspoon cayenne pepper, ½ teaspoon chili powder, ½ teaspoon garlic powder, and ½ teaspoon paprika.

PER FISH PORTION: 244 cal., 12 g total fat (2 g sat. fat), 101 mg chol., 228 mg sodium, 9 g carb., 1 g fiber, 23 g pro. EXCHANGES: ½ Starch, 3 Lean Meat, 1½ Fat

POTATO CHIP PAN-FRIED FISH: Prepare as directed, except substitute 1⅓ cups finely crushed potato chips (about 4 cups chips) or saltine crackers for the cornmeal and omit salt.

PER FISH PORTION: 278 cal., 17 g total fat (3 g sat. fat), 101 mg chol., 153 mg sodium, 7 g carb., 1 g fiber, 23 g pro. EXCHANGES: ½ Starch, 3 Lean Meat, 2 Fat

PAN-FRIED FISH STEP-BY-STEP

1. Dip each egg-coated fish piece in the cornmeal mixture and press gently to help the mixture adhere to the fish; turn the piece over and repeat to coat the second side.

2. Once the first side is golden, flip the fish portion over using a large metal spatula and a fork to steady the fish. When turning the fish, be careful to avoid splattering fat. Cook until the second side is golden.

FAST

Hush Puppies

PREP: 15 MINUTES **COOK:** 3 MINUTES PER BATCH
MAKES: 14 HUSH PUPPIES

- **1 cup cornmeal**
- **¼ cup all-purpose flour**
- **2 teaspoons sugar**
- **¾ teaspoon baking powder**
- **¼ teaspoon baking soda**
- **½ teaspoon salt**
- **1 egg, lightly beaten**
- **½ cup buttermilk or sour milk (see tip, page 19)**
- **¼ cup sliced green onions (2)**
- **Vegetable oil or shortening for deep-fat frying**

1 In a medium bowl stir together cornmeal, flour, sugar, baking powder, baking soda, and salt. Make a well in the center of flour mixture.

2 In another bowl combine egg, buttermilk, and green onions. Add egg mixture all at once to flour mixture. Stir just until moistened (batter should be lumpy).

3 In a 3-quart saucepan or deep-fat fryer heat 2 inches vegetable oil to 375°F. For each hush puppy, drop a slightly rounded tablespoon batter into the hot oil. Fry three or four at a time about 3 minutes or until golden, turning once. Drain on paper towels. Serve warm.

PER HUSH PUPPY: 85 cal., 5 g total fat (1 g sat. fat), 15 mg chol., 136 mg sodium, 10 g carb., 1 g fiber, 2 g pro. EXCHANGES: ½ Starch, 1 Fat

thai green seafood curry

The Secret: As versatile as stir-fry but more complex, curry is not just another item on the take-out menu. The key to quality curry? Know your curry pastes—and know your palate. The rest is easy.

CURRY POINTERS

1. FRESH MAKES BEST
Buy fresh scallops if they are harvested locally or you have access to a reputable fish counter at your grocery store. Scallops have a tough bit of muscle on the side that helps them open and shut their shells. It's easy to remove. Just gently give it a tug to pull it off.

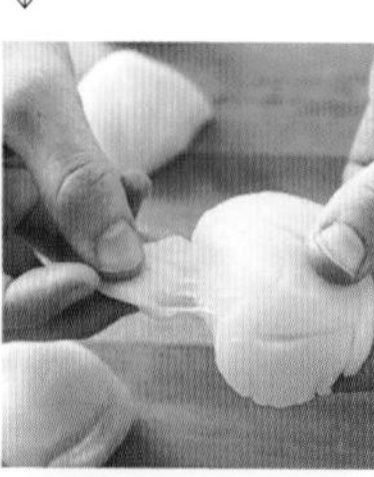

2. COOK AND STIR
Instead of browning the shrimp and scallops in a stir-fry, it's common to poach them in the coconut milk mixture. This moist-heat method allows the shrimp and scallops to take on the flavors of the curry paste and coconut milk.

Unsweetened coconut milk typically comes in a can. Don't confuse it with the sweetened product or with any coconut-flavor waters or beverages on the market today. Be sure to stir the milk before measuring; the solids and liquid separate in the can over time.

START TO FINISH: 35 MINUTES **MAKES:** 4 SERVINGS

- **1 pound medium shrimp in shells, peeled and deveined, and/or 12 ounces sea scallops**
- **1 tablespoon canola oil**
- **3 cloves garlic, minced**
- **1 cup unsweetened coconut milk**
- **1/3 cup reduced-sodium chicken broth**
- **1 tablespoon fish sauce**
- **2 teaspoons packed brown sugar**
- **2 tablespoons green or yellow curry paste or 3 tablespoons red curry paste**
- **1/2 of a small eggplant, peeled (if desired) and cut into bite-size pieces (2 cups)**
- **1 medium red or yellow sweet pepper, seeded and cut into thin bite-size strips**
- **1/4 cup thinly sliced fresh basil leaves**
- **1 teaspoon finely shredded lime peel**
- **1 recipe Jasmine Rice (page 299)**
- **Fresh basil leaves**
- **Lime wedges**

1 Thaw shrimp or scallops if frozen. Rinse and pat dry with paper towels; set aside. In a wok (see "Wok or Not," page 84) or large nonstick skillet heat oil over medium-high heat. Add garlic; cook for 30 seconds.

2 Stir in coconut milk, broth, fish sauce, and brown sugar. Whisk in curry paste. Bring mixture to boiling. Boil gently, uncovered, for 5 minutes, stirring occasionally. Stir in the shrimp or scallops, eggplant, and sweet pepper. Boil gently about 5 minutes more or until seafood turns opaque, vegetables are just tender, and sauce has thickened slightly, stirring occasionally.

3 Remove from heat. Stir the 1/4 cup thinly sliced basil leaves and the lime peel into seafood mixture. Serve over hot Jasmine Rice. Top with fresh basil leaves and serve with lime wedges.

PER 1 CUP STIR-FRY + 1/2 CUP RICE: 368 cal., 16 g total fat (11 g sat. fat), 137 mg chol., 887 mg sodium, 34 g carb., 4 g fiber, 22 g pro. **EXCHANGES:** 1/2 Vegetable, 1 1/2 Starch, 1/2 Other Carb., 2 1/2 Lean Meat, 2 Fat

CURRY PASTE COLORS

Because each type of curry paste is made with different chiles, aromatic herbs, and spices, the flavor of your dish will be greatly influenced by which paste you use. **Red curry paste**—the most versatile—is made from red chiles and often includes chili powder to deepen the flavor. **Green curry paste** is made with green chiles and may include some coriander, basil, and/or kaffir lime leaves. It is thought to be the hottest, followed by yellow curry paste. Turmeric is added to **yellow curry paste,** along with a much smaller amount of red chiles, to get the yellow color.

JASMINE RICE: In a medium saucepan combine 2 cups water and 1 cup uncooked jasmine rice. If desired, add a little salt. Bring to boiling; reduce heat. Simmer, covered, about 20 minutes or until liquid is absorbed and rice is tender. (Or preheat oven to 350°F. Place the 1 cup uncooked rice in a 2-quart square baking dish. Pour 2 cups boiling water over the rice. Cover tightly with foil and bake for 25 to 30 minutes or until tender; you can bake a double batch this same way using 2 cups rice and 4 cups water. Chill the extra rice for up to 3 days in the refrigerator.)

THAI CHICKEN CURRY: Prepare as directed, except substitute 12 ounces skinless, boneless chicken thighs cut into 1-inch strips for the seafood. Add after bringing to boiling with curry paste in Step 2.

PER 1 CUP STIR-FRY + ½ CUP RICE: 396 cal., 19 g total fat (12 g sat. fat), 81 mg chol., 846 mg sodium, 34 g carb., 4 g fiber, 21 g pro. EXCHANGES: ½ Vegetable, 1½ Starch, ½ Other Carb., 2½ Lean Meat, 3 Fat

If using chicken, cook the chicken until it is no longer pink.

3. KEEP IT HOT
This is where a wok pays off. You can cook and stir a lot of ingredients without losing them to your stove-top burner! Stir in the chopped eggplant and sweet pepper. Continue to cook about 5 minutes or until shrimp or scallops turn opaque or chicken is done. Vegetables should be just tender, and the sauce will have thickened.

4. SLIVERED BASIL
Thinly sliced basil is easy to achieve in just a few steps. After you've picked the basil leaves, stack them on top of one another and roll the stack into a small tubelike shape. Use a knife to cut thin slices from the basil roll, making sure to cut all the way through so strips detach from the roll.

INGREDIENTS YOU NEED TO KNOW

FISH SAUCE: Be prepared! The odor of fish sauce might deter you, but the flavor becomes incredible when combined with the rest of the ingredients. Fish sauce is made from the liquid of salted, fermented fish.

LIME PEEL: Traditional curries call for kaffir lime leaves. They're thick, dark green, and aromatic but hard to find. We used shredded lime peel here. Look for kaffir lime leaves in an Asian market.

EGGPLANT: Typically, Japanese or Thai eggplant is used in curry recipes. If you can't find these varieties, a regular eggplant will do. When cooked, the skin may become tough and bitter, so peel it if you like.

FISH AND CHIPS

BEST-LOVED

Fish and Chips

START TO FINISH: 60 MINUTES **MAKES:** 4 SERVINGS

- **1 pound fresh or frozen skinless fish fillets, about ½ inch thick**
- **1¼ pounds medium potatoes (about 4)**
- **Vegetable oil or shortening for deep-fat frying**
- **1 cup all-purpose flour**
- **½ cup beer**
- **1 egg**
- **¼ teaspoon baking powder**
- **¼ teaspoon salt**
- **¼ teaspoon black pepper**
- **Coarse salt**
- **Tartar Sauce (page 539) (optional)**
- **Malt vinegar or cider vinegar (optional)**
- **Lemon wedges (optional)**

1 Thaw fish if frozen. Preheat oven to 300°F. Cut fish into 3×2-inch pieces. Rinse fish; pat dry with paper towels. Cover and chill until needed.

2 For chips, cut the potatoes lengthwise into ½-inch-wide wedges. Pat dry with paper towels. In a 3-quart saucepan or deep-fat fryer heat 2 inches of vegetable oil to 375°F. Fry potatoes, one-fourth at a time, for 4 to 6 minutes or until tender and browned. Remove potatoes; drain on paper towels. Reserve oil in saucepan. Transfer potatoes to a wire rack set on a baking sheet, arranging them in a single layer. Keep warm in the oven.

3 Meanwhile, place ½ cup of the flour in a shallow dish. For batter, in a medium bowl combine remaining ½ cup flour, the beer, egg, baking powder, ¼ teaspoon salt, and the pepper. Whisk until smooth. Dip fish into the flour in dish, turning to coat all sides; shake off excess flour. Dip fish into batter, turning to coat all sides.

4 Fry fish, two or three pieces at a time, in the hot oil (375°F) for 4 to 6 minutes or until coating is golden brown and fish flakes easily when tested with a fork, turning once. Remove fish and drain on paper towels. Transfer fish to a second baking sheet; keep warm in the preheated oven while frying remaining fish. Sprinkle fish and chips with coarse salt. If desired, serve with Tartar Sauce or vinegar and lemon wedges.

PER 3 OUNCES FISH + 8 POTATO WEDGES: 552 cal., 29 g total fat (4 g sat. fat), 101 mg chol., 449 mg sodium, 43 g carb., 4 g fiber, 27 g pro. EXCHANGES: 3 Starch, 3 Lean Meat, 4 Fat

SESAME-CRUSTED COD

BEST-LOVED FAST LOW-CALORIE

Sesame-Crusted Cod

START TO FINISH: 30 MINUTES **MAKES:** 4 SERVINGS

- **1 pound fresh or frozen cod fillets, ¾ inch thick**
- **Salt and black pepper**
- **3 tablespoons butter or margarine, melted**
- **2 tablespoons sesame seeds**
- **12 ounces fresh tender young green beans**
- **1 medium orange, halved and sliced**
- **3 cloves garlic, thinly sliced**

1 Thaw fish if frozen. Rinse fish; pat dry with paper towels. Cut into four serving-size pieces if necessary. Place fish on the unheated rack of a broiler pan. Sprinkle fish with salt and pepper.

2 Preheat broiler. In a small bowl stir together butter and sesame seeds. Measure 1 tablespoon of the butter mixture; set aside for the vegetables. Brush fish with half of the remaining butter mixture. Broil 5 to 6 inches from the heat for 4 minutes; turn fish. Brush with remaining butter mixture. Broil 5 to 6 minutes more or until fish flakes easily when tested with a fork.

3 Meanwhile, in a covered very large skillet cook beans and orange in reserved butter mixture over medium-high heat for 2 minutes. Add garlic; cook, uncovered, for 5 to 6 minutes more or until beans are crisp-tender, stirring often. Serve fish on bean mixture.

PER 3 OUNCES FISH + ¾ CUP BEANS: 240 cal., 12 g total fat (6 g sat. fat), 71 mg chol., 274 mg sodium, 12 g carb., 4 g fiber, 23 g pro. EXCHANGES: 1 Vegetable, ½ Fruit, 3 Lean Meat, ½ Fat

make it mine

Baked Fish

Crumb-topped baked fish is a quick and healthful, family-pleasing main dish. Now you can make it just the way your family likes it, with everyone's favorite fish, seasonings, and toppings.

PREP: 20 MINUTES **BAKE:** 12 MINUTES AT 425°F **MAKES:** 4 SERVINGS

- **1½ pounds fresh or frozen skinless** FISH FILLETS
- **2 eggs or egg whites, lightly beaten**
- **1 tablespoon milk or water**
- CRUMBS
- SEASONING
- **Nonstick cooking spray**
- TOPPING

1 Thaw fish fillets if frozen. Preheat oven to 425°F. Line a large baking sheet with foil. Lightly grease foil; set aside.

2 Rinse fish; pat dry with paper towels. Cut fish into four serving-size pieces if necessary. In a shallow dish combine eggs and milk. In a second shallow dish combine Crumbs and Seasoning. Dip fish into egg mixture; coat fish with crumb mixture. Place on prepared baking sheet. Coat fish with cooking spray.

3 Bake for 12 to 15 minutes or until fish flakes easily when tested with a fork. Serve with Topping.

MAKING CRUMBS

To crush croutons or crackers for crumb topping, place ingredients in a resealable plastic bag and crush with a rolling pin.

FISH FILLETS *(pick one)*

Catfish
Grouper
Red snapper
Salmon
Tilapia

CRUMBS *(pick one)*

- **1 cup crushed Italian-seasoned or garlic croutons**
- **1 cup panko bread crumbs**
- **1 cup crushed saltine crackers**
- **1 cup crushed rich round crackers**
- **½ cup shredded coconut and ½ cup panko bread crumbs**

SEASONING *(pick one)*

Curry: **1 teaspoon curry powder, ¼ teaspoon salt, and ¼ teaspoon garlic salt**

Italian: **1 teaspoon dried Italian seasoning, ½ teaspoon salt, and ¼ teaspoon black pepper**

Ranch: **1 tablespoon dried ranch salad dressing mix and 1 teaspoon finely shredded lemon peel**

Taco: **1 tablespoon chopped fresh cilantro and 2 teaspoons taco seasoning mix**

TOPPING *(pick one)*

- **Honey**
- **Honey barbecue sauce**
- **Tartar sauce**
- **Purchased basil pesto**
- **¼ cup sour cream, ¼ cup mayonnaise, and ½ teaspoon grated fresh ginger**
- **Lemon wedges and horseradish sauce**
- **½ cup ranch dressing and 1 tablespoon finely chopped chipotle chile pepper in adobo sauce (see tip, page 44)**

BEST-LOVED   FAST   LOW-CALORIE

Tilapia Veracruz

START TO FINISH: 25 MINUTES   **MAKES:** 4 SERVINGS

- **4 6- to 8-ounce fresh or frozen skinless tilapia, red snapper, mahi mahi, or other fish fillets, about 1 inch thick**
- **1 tablespoon olive oil**
- **1 small onion, cut into thin wedges**
- **1 jalapeño chile pepper, seeded and finely chopped (see tip, page 44) (optional)**
- **1 clove garlic, minced**
- **1 14.5-ounce can diced tomatoes, undrained**
- **1 cup sliced fresh cremini or button mushrooms**
- **¾ cup pimiento-stuffed olives, coarsely chopped**
- **1 tablespoon snipped fresh oregano or ½ teaspoon dried oregano, crushed**
- **2 cups hot cooked rice**

1 Thaw fish if frozen. Rinse fish; pat dry with paper towels. Set fish aside.

2 For sauce, in a very large skillet heat olive oil over medium heat. Add onion, chile pepper (if desired), and garlic; cook and stir 2 to 3 minutes or until onion is tender. Add undrained tomatoes, mushrooms, olives, oregano, ¼ teaspoon *salt*, and ⅛ teaspoon *black pepper*. Bring to boiling.

3 Gently place fish in sauce in skillet, spooning sauce over fish. Return to boiling; reduce heat. Simmer, covered, 8 to 10 minutes or until fish flakes easily when tested with a fork. Using a wide spatula, carefully lift fish from skillet to a serving dish. Top with sauce; serve with rice.

PER FILLET + ½ CUP SAUCE + ½ CUP RICE: 363 cal., 10 g total fat (2 g sat. fat), 84 mg chol., 1,111 mg sodium, 31 g carb., 3 g fiber, 38 g pro. EXCHANGES: 1½ Vegetable, 1½ Starch, 4½ Lean Meat, ½ Fat

SHRIMP VERACRUZ: Prepare sauce; substitute 1 pound cooked, peeled, and deveined shrimp for the fish; heat through.

PER 4 OUNCES SHRIMP + ½ CUP SAUCE + ½ CUP RICE: 369 cal., 8 g total fat (1 g sat. fat), 321 mg chol., 1,211 mg sodium, 31 g carb., 3 g fiber, 45 g pro. EXCHANGES: 1½ Vegetable, 1½ Starch, 5 Lean Meat

SERVING SIZES

Use these amounts as a guide for how much fish or shellfish to purchase per person.

- 12 to 16 ounces whole fish
- 8 ounces drawn or dressed fish
- 4 to 5 ounces steaks or fillets
- 1 pound live crabs
- 3 to 4 ounces shelled shrimp
- One 1- to 1½-pound whole lobster, one 8-ounce lobster tail, or 4 to 5 ounces cooked lobster meat

FISH TACOS

FAST   LOW-CALORIE

Fish Tacos

PREP: 15 MINUTES   **BAKE:** 4 MINUTES PER ½-INCH THICKNESS AT 450°F   **MAKES:** 4 SERVINGS

- **12 ounces fresh or frozen skinless fish fillets**
- **1 tablespoon olive oil**
- **¼ teaspoon salt**
- **¼ teaspoon ground cumin**
- **⅛ teaspoon garlic powder**
- **1½ cups shredded lettuce**
- **8 corn tortillas or taco shells, warmed according to package directions**
- **1½ cups purchased pico de gallo**
- **Snipped fresh cilantro (optional)**

1 Thaw fish if frozen. Preheat oven to 450°F. Rinse fish; pat dry with paper towels. Cut fish crosswise into ¾-inch slices. Place fish in a single layer in a greased shallow baking pan. Combine olive oil, salt, cumin, and garlic powder. Brush over fish. Bake for 4 to 6 minutes or until fish flakes easily when tested with a fork.

2 To serve, spoon lettuce onto each tortilla; add fish slices. Top with pico de gallo and, if desired, cilantro.

PER 2 TACOS: 219 cal., 5 g total fat (1 g sat. fat), 37 mg chol., 226 mg sodium, 25 g carb., 4 g fiber, 18 g pro. EXCHANGES: ½ Vegetable, 1½ Starch, 2 Lean Meat

8 to try

FAST LOW-CALORIE

Basic Fish

For a new take on fish for dinner, start with the recipe below, choose the cooking method, and spice it up with a topper on the right.

PREP: 15 MINUTES **BAKE:** 4 MINUTES PER ½-INCH THICKNESS AT 450°F
MAKES: 4 SERVINGS

- **1 pound fresh or frozen skinless fish fillets, ½ to ¾ inch thick**
- **Salt and black pepper**

1 Thaw fish if frozen. Rinse fish; pat dry with paper towels. Cut into four serving-size pieces if necessary. Measure thickness of fish. Season with salt and pepper.

TO BAKE: Preheat oven to 450°F. Line a 15×10×1-inch baking pan with foil; coat foil with nonstick cooking spray. Arrange fish in pan. Bake for 4 to 6 minutes per ½-inch thickness of fish or until fish flakes easily when tested with a fork.

TO BROIL: Preheat broiler. Arrange fish on unheated, greased rack of a broiler pan. Broil 4 inches from heat for 4 to 6 minutes per ½-inch thickness of fish or until fish flakes easily when tested with a fork.

TO PAN SAUTÉ: In a very large skillet heat 1 tablespoon butter and 1 tablespoon vegetable oil over medium-high heat until butter melts. Add fish to skillet. Cook for 4 to 6 minutes per ½-inch thickness of fish or until fish flakes easily when tested with a fork, turning carefully halfway through cooking time.

GREEN ONION-GINGER: Stir together ¼ cup sliced green onions (2), ¼ cup slivered red sweet pepper, 2 teaspoons soy sauce, ½ teaspoon grated fresh ginger, and ½ teaspoon minced garlic.

BACON SLAW: Stir together 1 cup coleslaw mix; 2 tablespoons mayonnaise; 1 strip bacon, crisp cooked and crumbled; and 2 teaspoons cider vinegar.

AVOCADO SALSA: Stir together 1 ripe avocado, halved, seeded, peeled, and chopped; 2 tablespoons finely chopped red onion; 1 tablespoon snipped fresh cilantro; 1 tablespoon lime juice; and ¼ teaspoon salt.

LEMON-CAPER MAYO: Stir together ½ cup mayonnaise; 1 tablespoon capers, chopped; 2 teaspoons snipped fresh dill; 1 teaspoon Dijon-style mustard; 1 teaspoon grated lemon peel; and ¼ teaspoon pepper.

TAPENADE: Stir together ½ cup chopped pitted Kalamata olives; 1 tablespoon snipped parsley; 2 teaspoons capers; 2 teaspoons red wine vinegar; 2 teaspoons olive oil; 1 clove garlic, minced; ½ teaspoon shredded orange peel; and ¼ teaspoon black pepper.

PARMESAN-PANKO: In a skillet cook and stir ½ cup panko bread crumbs and 1 tablespoon olive oil over medium heat until toasted. Stir in ¼ cup grated Parmesan and 2 tablespoons snipped fresh parsley. Sprinkle over fish the last 1 minute of cooking.

MUSHROOM-SHALLOT: In skillet cook and stir 8 ounces sliced cremini mushrooms, ¼ teaspoon salt, and ¼ teaspoon black pepper in 2 tablespoons butter over medium heat 5 minutes. Add 1 shallot, sliced, and 1 garlic clove, minced. Cook and stir 3 to 4 minutes.

HAZELNUT: In a skillet cook ½ cup chopped hazelnuts in 2 tablespoons butter over medium heat until toasted. Stir in 1 tablespoon snipped fresh parsley and 1 teaspoon pure maple syrup. Cook about 1 minute or until slightly reduced. Serve with lemon wedges.

LOW-CALORIE

Red Snapper with Carrots and Fennel

(photo, page 293)

PREP: 25 MINUTES **BAKE:** 12 MINUTES AT 450°F
MAKES: 4 SERVINGS

- **1 pound fresh or frozen skinless red snapper, grouper, or ocean perch fillets, about ½ inch thick**
- **Salt and black pepper**
- **1 tablespoon olive oil**
- **2 cups sliced fennel bulb (1 large)**
- **1 cup chopped onion (1 large)**
- **1 cup chopped carrots (2 medium)**
- **2 cloves garlic, minced**
- **¼ cup dry white wine or reduced-sodium chicken broth**
- **2 tablespoons snipped fresh dill weed or 1½ teaspoons dried dill weed**
- **¼ teaspoon salt**
- **¼ teaspoon black pepper**

1 Thaw fish if frozen. Rinse fish; pat dry with paper towels. Sprinkle fish lightly with salt and pepper; set aside.

2 Preheat oven to 450°F. In a large skillet heat olive oil over medium heat. Add fennel, onion, carrots, and garlic to hot oil; cook for 7 to 9 minutes or until vegetables are tender and light brown. Remove from heat. Stir in wine, the dill, the ¼ teaspoon salt, and the ¼ teaspoon pepper.

3 Reserve ¼ cup of the vegetable mixture; spoon remaining vegetable mixture into a 2-quart square baking dish. Place fish on top of vegetables, tucking under any thin edges. Spoon reserved vegetable mixture on top of fish.

4 Bake, uncovered, about 12 minutes or until fish flakes easily when tested with a fork. To serve, transfer fish and vegetables to dinner plates. If desired, garnish with additional dill.

PER 3 OUNCES FISH + 1 CUP VEGETABLES: 199 cal., 5 g total fat (1 g sat. fat), 41 mg chol., 410 mg sodium, 11 g carb., 3 g fiber, 25 g pro. EXCHANGES: 1 Vegetable, 3 Lean Meat, ½ Fat

FAST LOW-CALORIE

Poached Salmon with Citrus Salad

START TO FINISH: 25 MINUTES **MAKES:** 4 SERVINGS

- **4 4-ounce fresh or frozen skinless salmon, cod, or haddock fillets, about 1 inch thick**
- **1 lime**
- **6 oranges (navel, blood, and/or Cara Cara) and/or tangerines**
- **½ cup water**
- **¼ cup olive oil**
- **1 teaspoon sugar**

POACHED SALMON WITH CITRUS SALAD

- **¼ teaspoon salt**
- **⅛ teaspoon ground black pepper**
- **1 7-ounce bunch watercress, trimmed, or 4 cups arugula or baby spinach**
- **Cracked black pepper (optional)**

1 Thaw fish if frozen. Rinse fish; pat dry with paper towels. Finely shred 1 teaspoon peel from lime; set aside. Squeeze juice from the lime and two of the oranges; combine juices. Measure ¼ cup juice for dressing and set aside. Pour the remaining juice into a large nonstick skillet; add water and the lime peel. Bring to boiling. Add salmon; reduce heat to medium. Simmer, covered, for 8 to 12 minutes or until fish flakes easily when tested with a fork.

2 Meanwhile, for dressing, in a small bowl whisk together the reserved ¼ cup juice, olive oil, sugar, salt, and ground pepper.

3 Peel, seed, and section or slice remaining oranges; arrange oranges, watercress, and salmon on dinner plates. Drizzle with dressing. If desired, sprinkle with cracked black pepper.

PER FILLET + 1½ ORANGES + 1 CUP SALAD + 2 TABLESPOONS DRESSING: 387 cal., 21 g total fat (3 g sat. fat), 62 mg chol., 217 mg sodium, 27 g carb., 5 g fiber, 26 g pro. EXCHANGES: ½ Vegetable, 1½ Fruit, 3 Lean Meat, 3 Fat

LOW-CALORIE

Salmon in Parchment

PREP: 30 MINUTES **BAKE:** 30 MINUTES AT 350°F
MAKES: 4 SERVINGS

- **1 pound fresh or frozen skinless salmon, halibut, cod, or arctic char fillets, ¾ to 1 inch thick**
- **4 cups fresh vegetables (such as sliced carrots,* trimmed fresh green beans,* sliced zucchini or yellow summer squash, and/or sliced red, yellow, and/or green sweet peppers)**
- **½ cup sliced green onions (4)**
- **1 tablespoon snipped fresh oregano or 1 teaspoon dried oregano, crushed**
- **2 teaspoons finely shredded orange peel**
- **¼ teaspoon salt**
- **¼ teaspoon black pepper**
- **4 cloves garlic, halved**
- **4 teaspoons olive oil**
- **Salt**
- **Black pepper**
- **1 medium orange, halved and thinly sliced**
- **4 sprigs fresh oregano (optional)**

1 Preheat oven to 350°F. Thaw fish if frozen. Rinse fish; pat dry with paper towels. Cut into four serving-size pieces if necessary; set aside. Tear off four 14-inch squares of parchment paper. (Or tear off four 24-inch pieces of 18-inch-wide heavy foil. Fold each in half to make four 18×12-inch pieces.)

2 In a large bowl combine carrots, green onions, snipped fresh or dried oregano, orange peel, the ¼ teaspoon salt, the ¼ teaspoon black pepper, and the garlic; toss gently.

SALMON IN PARCHMENT STEP-BY-STEP

1. To assemble, start with equal-size fish portions for the most even doneness. Place on top of vegetables on parchment.

2. Fold parchment over fish. Fold and pleat the paper from bottom to top to seal the edge.

SALMON IN PARCHMENT

3 Divide vegetable mixture among the four pieces of parchment or foil, placing vegetables to one side of parchment or in center of each foil piece. Place one fish piece on top of each vegetable portion. Drizzle 1 teaspoon of the oil over each fish piece. Sprinkle lightly with additional salt and black pepper; top with orange slices. Fold parchment over fish and vegetables; fold the open sides in several times to secure, curving the edge into a circular pattern (Step 2, left) to seal. (For foil, bring together two opposite foil edges and seal with a double fold. Fold the remaining edges together to completely enclose the food, allowing space for steam to build.) Place the packets in a single layer in a 15×10×1-inch baking pan.

4 Bake about 30 minutes or until carrots are tender and fish flakes when tested with a fork (cut an "X" in the top of the parchment packet to check for doneness or open a foil packet). To serve, transfer the packets to dinner plates. If desired, garnish with fresh oregano sprigs.

***NOTE:** If using carrots and/or green beans, precook them. In a covered medium saucepan cook the carrots and/or green beans in a small amount of boiling water for 2 minutes; drain.

PER PACKET: 262 cal., 12 g total fat (2 g sat. fat), 62 mg chol., 388 mg sodium, 14 g carb., 4 g fiber, 25 g pro.
EXCHANGES: 2 Vegetable, 3 Lean Meat, 1½ Fat

FAST LOW-CALORIE

Broiled Fish with Rosemary

PREP: 10 MINUTES **COOK:** 4 MINUTES PER ½-INCH THICKNESS **MAKES:** 4 SERVINGS

- **4 4-ounce fresh or frozen halibut or salmon steaks, cut ½ to 1 inch thick**
- **2 teaspoons olive oil**
- **2 teaspoons lemon juice**
- **⅛ teaspoon salt**
- **⅛ teaspoon black pepper**
- **2 teaspoons snipped fresh rosemary or tarragon or 1 teaspoon dried rosemary or tarragon, crushed**
- **2 cloves garlic, minced**
- **1 tablespoon capers, rinsed and drained**

1 Thaw fish if frozen. Preheat broiler. Rinse fish; pat dry with paper towels. Measure thickness of fish. Brush fish with oil and lemon juice; sprinkle with salt and pepper. Sprinkle rosemary and garlic on fish; rub in seasonings with your fingers.

2 Place fish on the greased unheated rack of a broiler pan. Broil 4 inches from heat until fish flakes easily when tested with a fork. Allow for 4 to 6 minutes per ½-inch thickness of fish, turning once if fish is 1 inch thick or more. Transfer fish to dinner plates; top with capers.

PER FISH STEAK: 145 cal., 3 g total fat (1 g sat. fat), 51 mg chol., 179 mg sodium, 1 g carb., 0 g fiber, 27 g pro.
EXCHANGES: 4 Lean Meat

Citrus-Marinated Fish

PREP: 25 MINUTES **MARINATE:** 15 MINUTES **COOK:** 4 MINUTES PER ½-INCH THICKNESS **MAKES:** 4 SERVINGS

- **4 6- to 8-ounce fresh or frozen skinless salmon, swordfish, or halibut fillets, ¾ to 1 inch thick**
- **¼ cup finely chopped green onions (2)**
- **¼ cup lime or lemon juice**
- **3 tablespoons snipped fresh cilantro, basil, or Italian parsley**
- **2 tablespoons olive oil**
- **½ teaspoon salt**
- **½ teaspoon ground cumin**
- **⅛ teaspoon cayenne pepper**
- **2 cloves garlic, minced**
- **Lime or lemon wedges (optional)**

1 Thaw fish if frozen. Rinse fish; pat dry with paper towels. Measure thickness of fish. Place fish in a shallow dish; set aside. In a small bowl combine green onions, lime juice, 2 tablespoons of the cilantro, the olive oil, salt, cumin, cayenne pepper, and garlic. Pour half of the lime juice mixture over the fish; turn fish to coat. Marinate for 15 minutes. Set remaining half of lime juice mixture aside.

2 Heat a lightly greased grill pan over medium-high heat. Transfer fish to the hot grill pan, allowing excess marinade to drip off fish. Discard any remaining marinade in dish. Cook until fish flakes easily when tested with a fork. Allow 4 to 6 minutes per ½-inch thickness of fish, turning once and brushing with reserved half of the lime juice mixture halfway through cooking. Discard any remaining lime juice mixture. Sprinkle with remaining 1 tablespoon cilantro. If desired, serve with lime wedges.

PER FILLET: 403 cal., 28 g total fat (6 g sat. fat), 92 mg chol., 247 mg sodium, 2 g carb., 0 g fiber, 35 g pro.
EXCHANGES: 5 Lean Meat, 4 Fat

LOW-CALORIE

Salmon with Roasted Tomatoes and Shallots

PREP: 20 MINUTES **ROAST:** 30 MINUTES AT 400°F **MAKES:** 4 SERVINGS

- **1 pound fresh or frozen salmon fillet(s), skinned (if desired)**
- **3 cups grape tomatoes**
- **2 shallots, thinly sliced**
- **4 teaspoons snipped fresh oregano or 1 teaspoon dried oregano, crushed**
- **1 tablespoon olive oil**
- **¼ teaspoon salt**
- **¼ teaspoon black pepper**
- **4 cloves garlic, minced**

1 Thaw fish if frozen. Rinse fish; pat dry with paper towels. Preheat oven to 400°F.

2 In a greased 3-quart rectangular baking dish combine tomatoes, shallots, oregano, olive oil, ¼ teaspoon salt, ¼ teaspoon pepper, and the garlic. Toss to coat.

3 Roast, uncovered, for 15 minutes. Place fish, skin sides down, on top of the tomato mixture. Season fish lightly with additional salt and pepper. Roast, uncovered, for 15 to 18 minutes or until fish flakes easily when tested with a fork. Using two large pancake turners, transfer the salmon to a cutting board. If desired, remove and discard skin. Serve salmon with the tomato mixture.

PER 3 OUNCES SALMON + ¾ CUP TOMATO MIXTURE: 228 cal., 11 g total fat (2 g sat. fat), 62 mg chol., 204 mg sodium, 8 g carb., 2 g fiber, 24 g pro. EXCHANGES: 1½ Vegetable, 3 Lean Meat, 1 Fat

Weeknight Salmon Cakes

PREP: 20 MINUTES **BROIL:** 14 MINUTES
MAKES: 4 SERVINGS

- **1 pound fresh or frozen skinless salmon fillet(s)**
- **¾ cup soft bread crumbs (1 to 2 slices)**
- **1 egg white**
- **¼ cup thinly sliced green onions (2)**
- **2 tablespoons chopped roasted red sweet pepper**
- **1 tablespoon snipped fresh basil**
- **¼ teaspoon salt**
- **¼ cup mayonnaise**
- **½ teaspoon smoked paprika or dash cayenne pepper**
- **⅛ teaspoon black pepper**

1 Thaw fish if frozen. Rinse fish; pat dry with paper towels. In a food processor or blender combine half of the salmon, the bread crumbs, egg white, green onions, roasted pepper, basil, and salt. Process or blend until combined. Chop the remaining salmon into ½-inch pieces. In a medium bowl combine salmon mixture and chopped salmon (mixture will be soft). Shape salmon mixture into four ¾-inch-thick cakes.

2 Preheat broiler. Arrange cakes on a greased foil-lined baking sheet. Broil 4 to 5 inches from heat for 14 to 18 minutes or until done (160°F), turning once halfway through broiling time.

3 Meanwhile, in a small bowl combine mayonnaise, paprika, and black pepper. Serve salmon cakes with mayonnaise mixture.

GRILLED SALMON CAKES: Prepare salmon cakes and mayonnaise mixture as directed. For a charcoal grill, grill cakes on the well-greased rack of an uncovered grill directly over medium coals for 14 to 18 minutes or until done (160°F), turning once halfway through grilling. (For a gas grill, preheat grill. Reduce heat to medium. Place cakes on well-greased grill rack over heat. Cover; grill as directed.)

PER CAKE: 359 cal., 26 g total fat (5 g sat. fat), 67 mg chol., 345 mg sodium, 4 g carb., 1 g fiber, 25 g pro.
EXCHANGES: 3½ Lean Meat, 4½ Fat

SALMON BURGERS: Prepare salmon cakes and mayonnaise mixture as directed. Serve on 4 whole wheat hamburger buns with mayonnaise mixture, shredded spinach, and/or sliced tomato.

PER BURGER: 475 cal., 27 g total fat (5 g sat. fat), 67 mg chol., 562 mg sodium, 26 g carb., 3 g fiber, 29 g pro. EXCHANGES: ½ Vegetable, 1½ Starch, 3½ Lean Meat, 4 Fat

Piri Piri Scallops with Spinach-Pineapple Salad

PREP: 35 MINUTES **MARINATE:** 2 TO 4 HOURS
BROIL: 5 MINUTES **MAKES:** 4 SERVINGS

- **16 fresh or frozen sea scallops**
- **½ cup lime juice**
- **2 tablespoons Asian chili sauce (Sriracha sauce)**
- **5 cloves garlic, minced**
- **2 teaspoons smoked paprika or Spanish paprika**
- **½ teaspoon salt**
- **¾ cup olive oil**
- **1 recipe Spinach-Pineapple Salad**

1 Thaw scallops if frozen. Rinse scallops; pat dry with paper towels and set aside. For piri piri sauce, in a food processor or blender combine lime juice, chili sauce, garlic, paprika, and salt. Cover and pulse with several on/off turns or blend until smooth. With processor or blender running, gradually add olive oil in a slow, steady stream through the opening in the lid; process or blend until oil is incorporated. Set aside ¼ cup of the piri piri sauce.

2 Place scallops in a resealable plastic bag set in a bowl; pour the remaining piri piri sauce over scallops. Seal bag; turn to coat scallops. Marinate in the refrigerator for 2 to 4 hours, turning bag occasionally. Drain scallops, discarding marinade. Thread four scallops on each of four skewers.*

3 Preheat broiler. Place skewers on unheated rack of a broiler pan. Broil 4 inches from heat for 5 to 6 minutes or until scallops are opaque, turning once halfway through broiling.

4 Prepare Spinach-Pineapple Salad. Serve scallops with salad and drizzle with the remaining reserved piri piri sauce.

SPINACH-PINEAPPLE SALAD: For dressing, in a small jar with a tight-fitting lid combine ⅓ cup olive oil, ¼ cup snipped fresh cilantro, 3 tablespoons white wine vinegar, 1 tablespoon chopped green onion, and 2 teaspoons of the reserved piri piri sauce. Cover; shake well to combine. In a large bowl combine 4 cups fresh baby spinach leaves, 1 cup fresh pineapple chunks, ½ cup slivered jicama, and

SEARING SCALLOPS

Higher-heat searing suits scallops. It browns the seafood quickly, locking in its sweet moisture while adding a delicate golden crust to the outside. For best results, pat scallops dry before using the searing technique to cook them.

4 slices bacon, crisp-cooked and coarsely chopped. Add the dressing and toss well. Serve immediately.

***NOTE:** If using wooden skewers, soak in enough water to cover at least 60 minutes before using.

PER SKEWER + 1¼ CUPS SALAD: 490 cal., 33 g total fat (5 g sat. fat), 65 mg chol., 553 mg sodium, 14 g carb., 3 g fiber, 33 g pro. EXCHANGES: 1 Vegetable, ½ Fruit, 3½ Lean Meat, 5½ Fat

FAST LOW-CALORIE

Seared Scallops with Ginger Sauce

START TO FINISH: 15 MINUTES **MAKES:** 4 SERVINGS

- **1 pound fresh or frozen sea scallops**
- **4 teaspoons butter**
- **⅓ cup chicken broth**
- **¼ cup frozen pineapple-orange juice concentrate, thawed**
- **1 teaspoon grated fresh ginger**

1 Thaw scallops if frozen. Rinse scallops; pat dry with paper towels. In a large skillet melt butter over medium-high heat. Add scallops to skillet. Cook for 2 to 3 minutes or until scallops are opaque, stirring frequently. Remove scallops from skillet; keep warm.

2 For sauce, add chicken broth, juice concentrate, and ginger to skillet. Bring to boiling. Boil, uncovered, until sauce is reduced by about half. Spoon over scallops.

PER 3 OUNCES SCALLOPS + 1 TABLESPOON SAUCE: 168 cal., 5 g total fat (3 g sat. fat), 48 mg chol., 262 mg sodium, 11 g carb., 0 g fiber, 19 g pro. EXCHANGES: ½ Fruit, 3 Lean Meat

LOW-CALORIE

Crab Cakes

PREP: 40 MINUTES **CHILL:** 60 MINUTES
COOK: 6 MINUTES PER BATCH **MAKES:** 4 SERVINGS

- **2 tablespoons chopped green onion (1)**
- **2 tablespoons butter**
- **1 tablespoon all-purpose flour**
- **¼ teaspoon seafood seasoning**
- **⅛ teaspoon black pepper**
- **½ cup milk**
- **1 6- to 8-ounce package frozen lump crabmeat, thawed; one 6-ounce can refrigerated lump crabmeat, drained and flaked; or 1 cup fresh crabmeat, flaked and cartilage removed**
- **2 tablespoons panko bread crumbs or fine dry bread crumbs**
- **¼ cup all-purpose flour**
- **1 egg**
- **1 teaspoon water**

CRAB CAKES

- **¾ cup panko bread crumbs or fine dry bread crumbs**
- **2 tablespoons vegetable oil**
- **¼ cup Mustard Chutney**

1 In a small saucepan cook onion in 1 tablespoon butter until tender. Stir in the 1 tablespoon flour, seafood seasoning, and pepper. Add milk all at once. Cook and stir until thickened and bubbly. Transfer to medium bowl. Cover and chill for 60 minutes or until cold.

2 Stir crabmeat and the 2 tablespoons panko into chilled sauce. Place the ¼ cup flour in a shallow dish. In a second shallow dish beat together egg and water. Place the ¾ cup panko in a third shallow dish.

3 Form about 2 tablespoons of crab mixture into a small patty. Dip patty into flour; carefully turn to coat. Dip in egg mixture; dip in panko. Set on a sheet of waxed paper. Repeat with remaining crab, flour, egg mixture, and panko.

4 In a large skillet heat oil and remaining 1 tablespoon butter over medium heat. Cook crab cakes, half at a time, about 3 minutes on each side or until golden brown and heated through. Serve with Mustard Chutney.

MUSTARD CHUTNEY: In a small bowl combine ½ cup purchased mango chutney (snip any large pieces), 1½ teaspoons Dijon-style mustard, and 1 teaspoon lemon juice (chill any leftovers).

PER 2 CAKES + 1 TABLESPOON CHUTNEY: 328 cal., 15 g total fat, (5 g sat. fat), 92 mg chol., 415 mg sodium, 39 g carb., 1 g fiber, 10 g pro. EXCHANGES: 1 Starch, 1½ Other Carb, 1 Lean Meat, 2½ Fat

FAST LOW-CALORIE

Steamed Crab Legs

START TO FINISH: 15 MINUTES **MAKES:** 4 SERVINGS

- **4** **4- to 8-ounce fresh or frozen crab legs**
- **1/4** **cup butter, melted**
- **1** **tablespoon snipped fresh basil or fresh Italian parsley**
- **1/2** **teaspoon finely shredded lemon peel**
- **1** **tablespoon lemon juice**

1 Thaw crab legs if frozen. Place crab legs in a steamer basket in a very large skillet. If necessary, bend crab legs at joints to fit in steamer basket (see photo 1, below). Add water to the skillet to just below the basket. Bring to boiling. Cover; steam for 5 to 6 minutes or until heated through.

2 For butter sauce, stir together butter, basil, lemon peel, and lemon juice.

3 To remove the meat, twist legs at joints (see photo 2, below) or split shell using kitchen shears (see photo 3, below). Peel back shell (see photo 4, below); remove meat. Serve with butter sauce.

BOILED CRAB LEGS: Thaw crab legs if frozen. Place crab legs in a large pot of boiling salted water. Return to boiling. Cook, uncovered, for 4 to 5 minutes or until heated through.

PER 4 OUNCES: 157 cal., 12 g total fat (7 g sat. fat), 58 mg chol., 622 mg sodium, 0 g carb., 0 g fiber, 12 g pro.
EXCHANGES: 2 Lean Meat, 1½ Fat

BEST-LOVED FAST

Shrimp Scampi

START TO FINISH: 20 MINUTES **MAKES:** 4 SERVINGS

- **1½** **pounds fresh or frozen large shrimp**
- **8** **ounces dried angel hair pasta**
- **1/4** **cup butter, melted**
- **1/4** **cup olive oil**
- **6** **cloves garlic, minced**
- **1/4** **teaspoon salt**
- **1/8** **teaspoon crushed red pepper**
- **2** **tablespoons snipped fresh parsley**
- **1** **teaspoon finely shredded lemon peel**
- **Lemon wedges (optional)**

1 Thaw shrimp if frozen. Peel and devein shrimp, leaving tails intact, if desired (see photos 1–3, page 311). Rinse shrimp; pat dry with paper towels. Set shrimp aside.

2 In a large pot cook pasta according to package directions; drain. Return pasta to pot.

3 Meanwhile, in a large skillet heat butter, olive oil, and garlic over medium-high heat. Add shrimp, salt, and crushed red pepper to skillet. Cook and stir about 3 minutes or until shrimp are opaque. Stir in parsley and lemon peel. Add shrimp mixture to pasta in pot; toss to combine. If desired, serve shrimp mixture with lemon wedges.

PER 7 SHRIMP + 3/4 CUP PASTA: 565 cal., 27 g total fat (9 g sat. fat), 269 mg chol., 428 mg sodium, 44 g carb., 2 g fiber, 38 g pro. EXCHANGES: 3 Starch, 4 Lean Meat, 3½ Fat

STEAMING AND CRACKING CRAB LEGS STEP-BY-STEP

1. Bend the legs at the joints to fit in the steamer basket. Steam until heated through.

2. To remove the meat, twist the legs at the joint. Often you can pull the meat from the shell as you twist.

3. You can also use kitchen shears to cut through the shell.

4. Pull the shell apart. Use a seafood fork to remove the meat.

FAST LOW-CALORIE

Spanish Shrimp and Scallop Sauté

START TO FINISH: 25 MINUTES **MAKES:** 4 SERVINGS

- **16 fresh or frozen medium shrimp (8 ounces)**
- **8 fresh or frozen sea scallops (8 ounces)**
- **1 tablespoon all-purpose flour**
- **2 teaspoons smoked paprika**
- **½ teaspoon salt**
- **¼ teaspoon sugar**
- **¼ teaspoon black pepper**
- **⅛ to ¼ teaspoon cayenne pepper**
- **2 tablespoons butter**
- **6 cloves garlic, thinly sliced**
- **1 cup grape or cherry tomatoes, halved**
- **¼ cup reduced-sodium chicken broth**
- **3 tablespoons dry vermouth or dry white wine**
- **1 tablespoon fresh lemon juice**
- **3 tablespoons finely snipped fresh Italian parsley**
- **3 tablespoons snipped fresh chives**
- **2 cups hot cooked brown rice**

1 Thaw shrimp and scallops if frozen. Peel and devein shrimp, leaving tails intact, if desired (see photos 1–3, below). Halve scallops horizontally. Rinse shrimp and scallops and pat dry with paper towels; set aside.

2 In a large resealable plastic bag combine the flour, paprika, ¼ teaspoon of the salt, the sugar, black pepper, and cayenne pepper. Seal bag; shake to combine. Add shrimp and scallops to the bag; seal bag. Shake to coat shrimp and scallops; set aside.

3 Melt 1 tablespoon of the butter in a large nonstick skillet over medium-high heat. Add garlic and remaining ¼ teaspoon salt; cook and stir for 30 seconds. Add shrimp and scallops to the pan in an even layer; cook for 2 minutes. Stir in tomatoes, broth, vermouth, and lemon juice; cook for 2 to 3 minutes or until shrimp and scallops are opaque, stirring occasionally. Remove from heat; stir in the remaining 1 tablespoon butter, the parsley, and chives. Serve in shallow bowls with hot cooked rice.

PER 1 CUP SEAFOOD + ½ CUP RICE: 276 cal., 7 g total fat (4 g sat. fat), 97 mg chol., 659 mg sodium, 31 g carb., 3 g fiber, 19 g pro. **EXCHANGES:** 2 Starch, 2 Lean Meat

HOW TO PEEL AND DEVEIN SHRIMP STEP-BY-STEP

1. Open shell down the underside of the shrimp. Starting at the head, pull off the shell.

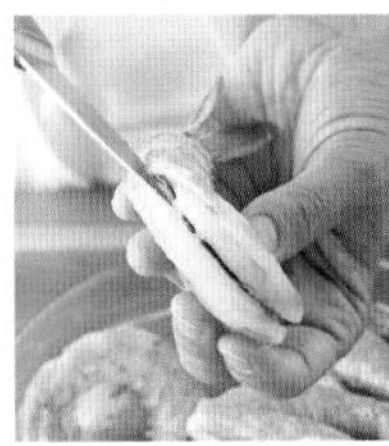

2. Use a sharp knife to cut down the center of the back to reveal the black vein.

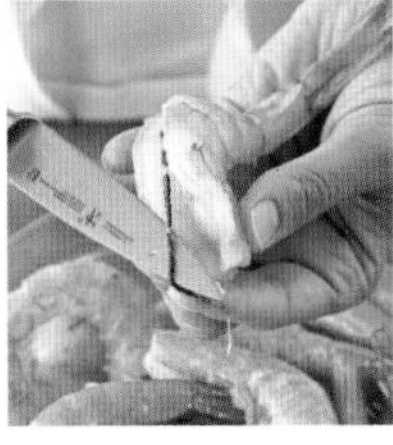

3. Use the tip of the knife to remove the vein. Rinse under cold running water.

FAST LOW-CALORIE

Boiled Lobster

PREP: 15 MINUTES **COOK:** 15 MINUTES
MAKES: 2 SERVINGS

- **8 quarts water**
- **½ cup coarse kosher salt or salt**
- **2 1- to 1½-pound live lobsters (cook same day as purchased)**
- **1 recipe Clarified Butter**

1 In a 20-quart or larger pot bring water and salt to boiling. Grasp lobsters just behind the eyes; rinse them under cold running water. Quickly plunge lobsters head first into boiling water. Cover; return to boiling. Boil 15 minutes, adjusting heat as necessary to maintain steady boil. Drain lobsters; remove bands on claws.

2 When cool enough to handle, place each lobster on its back. Separate the lobster tail from the body (see photo 1, below). Cut through the tail membrane to expose the meat (see photo 2, below). Remove and discard the black vein running through the tail. Remove meat from tail. Twist the large claws away from the body (see photo 3, below). Using a nutcracker, break open the claws (see photo 4, below). Remove the meat from the claws. Crack the shell on remaining part of the body; remove meat with a small fork. Discard the green tomalley (liver) and the coral roe (found in female lobsters). Serve lobster meat with Clarified Butter.

CLARIFIED BUTTER: Melt ¼ cup butter over very low heat without stirring; cool slightly. Strain through sieve lined with 100% cotton cheesecloth. Pour off clear top layer; discard milky layer.

PER LOBSTER + 2 TABLESPOONS BUTTER: 344 cal., 24 g total fat (15 g sat. fat), 209 mg chol., 1,894 mg sodium, 1 g carb., 0 g fiber, 30 g pro. EXCHANGES: 4 Lean Meat, 3½ Fat

FAST LOW-CALORIE

Lobster Tails with Garlic-Chili Butter

PREP: 15 MINUTES **BROIL:** 12 MINUTES
MAKES: 4 SERVINGS

- **4 8-ounce fresh or frozen lobster tails**
- **¼ cup butter**
- **1 teaspoon finely shredded orange peel**
- **½ teaspoon chili powder**
- **1 clove garlic, minced**
- **2 recipes Clarified Butter (left) (optional)**

1 Thaw lobster tails if frozen. Preheat broiler. Butterfly the lobster tails by using kitchen shears to cut lengthwise through centers of hard top shells and meat, cutting to but not through bottoms of shells. Spread the halves of tails apart. Place tails, meat sides up, on unheated rack of a broiler pan.

2 In a saucepan melt butter. Add orange peel, chili powder, and garlic; heat about 30 seconds or until garlic is tender. Brush mixture over lobster meat. Broil 4 inches from heat for 12 to 14 minutes or until lobster meat is opaque. If desired, serve with Clarified Butter.

LOBSTER TAILS WITH BASIL BUTTER: Prepare as directed, except omit orange peel and chili powder. Sprinkle on 2 tablespoons snipped fresh basil after cooking garlic.

LOBSTER TAILS WITH LEMON-CHIVE BUTTER: Prepare as directed, except substitute lemon peel for orange peel. Omit chili powder and garlic. Stir in 2 tablespoons snipped fresh chives after butter is melted.

PER TAIL WITH GARLIC-CHILI, BASIL, OR LEMON-CHIVE VARIATIONS: 149 cal., 12 g total fat (7 g sat. fat), 78 mg chol., 211 mg sodium, 1 g carb., 0 g fiber, 10 g pro.
EXCHANGES: 1½ Lean Meat, 2 Fat

REMOVING MEAT FROM LOBSTER STEP-BY-STEP

1. Remove the tail by twisting the tail and body in opposite directions.

2. Cut the membrane from the tail to expose the meat.

3. Twist the large claws where they join the body to remove them.

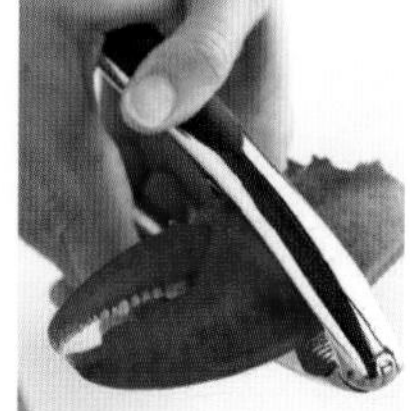

4. Break open the large claws with a nutcracker.

LOBSTER TAILS WITH BASIL BUTTER

PREPARING AND COOKING SHELLFISH

When you purchase shellfish at its top-quality best, you don't have to do a lot to make it taste great—simply follow these guidelines. If you like, serve with one of the sauces on pages 531–540.

Shellfish Type	Amount Per Serving	Preparation	Cooking
Clams	6 clams in the shell	Scrub live clams under cold running water. For 24 clams in shells, in an 8-quart pot combine 4 quarts cold water and ⅓ cup salt. Add clams and soak for 15 minutes; drain and rinse. Discard water; repeat.	For 24 clams in shells, add ½ inch water to an 8-quart pot; bring to boiling. Place clams in a steamer basket. Steam, covered, for 5 to 7 minutes or until clams open. Discard any that do not open.
Crabs, hard-shell	1 pound live crabs	Grasp live crabs from behind, firmly holding the back two legs on each side. Rinse under cold running water.	To boil 3 pounds live hard-shell blue crabs, in a 12- to 16-quart pot bring 8 quarts water and 2 teaspoons salt to boiling. Add crabs. Simmer, covered, about 10 minutes or until crabs turn pink; drain. (To crack and clean a crab, see page 315.)
Crawfish	1 pound live crawfish	Rinse live crawfish under cold running water. For 4 pounds crawfish, in a 12- to 16-quart pot combine 8 quarts cold water and ⅓ cup salt. Add crawfish. Soak for 15 minutes; rinse and drain.	For 4 pounds live crawfish, in a 12- to 16-quart pot bring 8 quarts water and 2 teaspoons salt to boiling. Add crawfish. Simmer, covered, for 5 to 8 minutes or until shells turn red; drain.
Lobster tails (To boil a live lobster, see page 312.)	One 8-ounce frozen lobster tail	Thaw frozen lobster tails in the refrigerator.	For four 8-ounce lobster tails, in a 3-quart saucepan bring 6 cups water and 1½ teaspoons salt to boiling; add tails. Simmer, uncovered, for 8 to 12 minutes or until shells turn bright red and meat is tender; drain.
Mussels	12 mussels in shells	Scrub live mussels under cold running water. Using your fingers, pull out beards that are visible between the shells.	For 24 mussels, add ½ inch water to an 8-quart pot; bring to boiling. Place mussels in a steamer basket. Steam, covered, for 5 to 7 minutes or until shells open. Discard any that do not open.
Oysters	6 oysters in shells	Scrub live oysters under cold running water. For easier shucking, chill. To shuck, hold oyster in heavy towel or mitt. Carefully insert oyster knife tip into hinge between shells. Move blade along inside of upper shell to free the muscle; twist knife to pry shell open. Slide knife under oyster to cut muscle from bottom shell.	For 2 pints shucked oysters, rinse oysters; pat dry with paper towels. In a large skillet cook and stir oysters in 1 tablespoon hot butter over medium heat for 3 to 4 minutes or until oyster edges curl; drain.
Shrimp	6 ounces shrimp in shells or 3 to 4 ounces peeled, deveined shrimp	To peel, open shell down the underside. Starting at head end, pull back the shell. Gently pull on the tail to remove. Use a sharp knife to remove the black vein that runs along center of back. Rinse under cold running water.	For 1 pound shrimp, in a 3-quart saucepan bring 4 cups water and 1 teaspoon salt to a boil. Add shrimp. Simmer, uncovered, 1 to 3 minutes or until shrimp turn opaque, stirring occasionally. Rinse under cold running water, drain, and chill (if desired).

CRACKING AND CLEANING COOKED CRAB

As any crab lover will tell you, the reward of cracking and cleaning hard-shell crabs, such as the Atlantic blue crab or the Pacific Dungeness (shown below), is well worth the effort. Follow these steps to get every last morsel of the rich, sweet-tasting meat, which is amazing simply dipped in butter. Or chill the meat and use it as an opulent extra in anything from salads and gazpacho to deviled eggs.

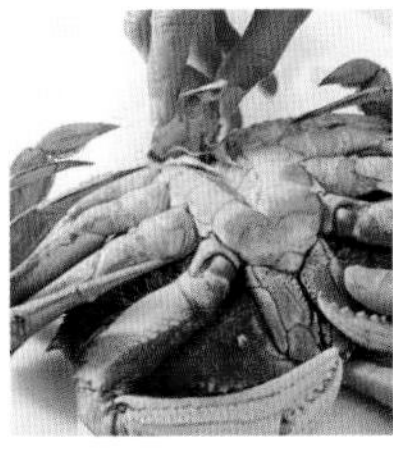

1. Turn the cooked, cooled crab on its back. Using your thumb, fold back the tail flap (apron), twist off, and discard.

2. Holding the crab with the top shell in one hand, grasp the bottom shell at the point where the apron was removed. Pull the top shell away from the body of the crab and discard.

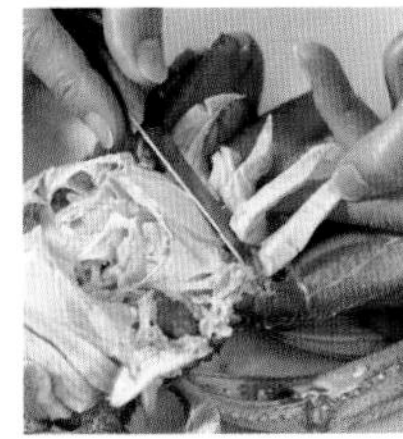

3. Discard the crab's internal organs, mouth, and appendages at the front; rinse crab. Using a small knife, remove the spongy gills from each side of the top of the crab.

4. Twist off the claws and legs. Use a nutcracker to crack each joint; pick out the meat. Cut the crab body into quarters. Use a small fork to remove the meat.

COOKING FISH

Minutes count when cooking fish. To best estimate the minimum cooking time, weigh dressed fish or use a ruler to measure the thickness of fillets and steaks before cooking. Properly cooked fish is opaque, flakes when tested with a fork, and readily comes away from the bones; the juices should be a milky white. If you like, serve with one of the sauces on pages 529–540.

Cooking Method	Preparation	Fresh or Thawed Fillets or Steaks	Dressed
Bake	Place in a single layer in a greased shallow baking pan. For fillets, tuck under any thin edges. Brush with olive oil or melted butter.	Bake, uncovered, in a 450°F oven for 4 to 6 minutes per ½-inch thickness of fish.	Bake, uncovered, in a 350°F oven for 6 to 9 minutes per 8 ounces of fish.
Broil	Preheat broiler. Place fish on greased unheated rack of a broiler pan. For fillets, tuck under any thin edges. Brush with vegetable oil or melted butter.	Broil 4 inches from the heat for 4 to 6 minutes per ½-inch thickness of fish. If fish is 1 inch or more thick, turn once halfway through broiling time.	Not recommended.
Grill	See Direct-Grilling and Indirect-Grilling Fish charts, page 349.		
Microwave	Arrange fish in a single layer in a shallow baking dish. For fillets, tuck under any thin edges. Cover with vented plastic wrap.	Cook on 100% power (high). For 8 ounces of ½-inch-thick fillets, allow 1½ to 2 minutes. For 1 pound of ½-inch-thick fillets, allow 2½ to 4 minutes. For 1 pound of ¾- to 1-inch-thick steaks, allow 3 to 5 minutes.	Not recommended.
Pan Sauté	In a very large skillet melt 1 tablespoon butter and 1 tablespoon vegetable oil over medium-high heat.	Add fish and cook for 4 to 6 minutes per ½-inch thickness of fish, turning carefully halfway through.	Not recommended.
Poach	Add 1½ cups water, broth, or wine to a large skillet. Bring to boiling. Add the fish. Return to boiling; reduce heat.	Simmer, uncovered, for 4 to 6 minutes per ½-inch thickness of fish.	Simmer, covered, for 6 to 9 minutes per 8 ounces.

GUIDE TO FISH TYPES

There are many fish in the sea—as well as in lakes and rivers—and they range greatly in flavor and texture. This chart describes the varieties that most often make their way to the market and offers appropriate substitutes for when you can't find a fish that's called for in a recipe.

Types	Market Forms	Texture	Flavor	Substitutions
FRESHWATER FISH				
Catfish	Whole, fillets, steaks	Firm	Mild	Grouper, rockfish, sea bass, tilapia
Lake trout (North American char)	Whole, fillets, steaks	Slightly firm	Moderate	Pike, sea trout, whitefish
Rainbow trout	Fillets	Slightly firm	Delicate	Salmon, sea trout
Tilapia	Whole, dressed, fillets	Slightly firm	Delicate	Catfish, flounder, orange roughy
Whitefish	Whole, fillets	Moderately firm	Delicate	Cod, lake trout, salmon, sea bass
SALTWATER FISH				
Atlantic ocean perch (redfish)	Whole, fillets	Slightly firm	Mild	Orange roughy, rockfish, snapper
Cod	Fillets, steaks	Moderately firm	Delicate	Flounder, haddock, pollock
Flounder	Whole, fillets	Fine	Delicate to mild	Cod, orange roughy, sea trout, sole, whitefish, whiting
Grouper	Whole, dressed, fillets	Moderately firm	Mild	Mahi mahi, sea bass
Haddock	Fillets	Moderately firm	Delicate	Cod, grouper, halibut, lake trout, sole, whitefish, whiting
Halibut	Fillets, steaks	Firm	Delicate	Cod, grouper, red snapper, sea bass
Mackerel	Whole	Delicate	Pronounced	Mahi mahi, swordfish, tuna
Mahi mahi (dolphinfish)	Whole, fillets	Firm	Mild to moderate	Grouper, orange roughy, red snapper
Orange roughy	Fillets	Moderately firm	Delicate	Cod, flounder, haddock, ocean perch, sea bass, sole
Red snapper	Whole, fillets	Moderately firm	Mild to moderate	Grouper, lake trout, ocean perch, rockfish, whitefish
Rockfish	Whole, fillets	Slightly firm	Mild to moderate	Cod, grouper, ocean perch, red snapper
Salmon	Whole, fillets, steaks	Moderately firm	Mild to moderate	Rainbow trout, swordfish, tuna, arctic char
Shark (mako)	Fillets, steaks	Firm, dense	Moderate	Swordfish, tuna
Sole	Fillets	Fine	Delicate	Flounder, haddock, halibut, pollock
Swordfish	Loins, steaks	Firm, dense	Mild to moderate	Halibut, shark, tuna
Tuna	Loins, steaks	Firm	Mild to moderate	Mackerel, salmon, shark, swordfish

332
322
335
338
grilling
324
326
342

grilling

No secret handshakes are needed to join the club of expert grillers—just good information. The instructions here and on page 320 are for grilling using charcoal and gas grills. To learn about smoking, see page 341.

DIRECT OR INDIRECT COOKING

Choose direct or indirect cooking depending on the foods you plan to cook on the grill.

DIRECT COOKING: This method works best for foods that cook in 30 minutes or less; these include tender, thin, and small foods such as burgers, steaks, chops, boneless chicken pieces, brats or frankfurters, and vegetables. With direct cooking, food cooks on the grill rack directly over the heat sources, with or without the grill lid closed (check the grill manufacturer's directions). For even cooking, turn foods only once during the cooking time.

INDIRECT COOKING: Recommended for large roasts, ribs, whole birds, and whole fish, this method positions the food on the grill rack away from or to the side of the heat source, with grill cover closed. Heat inside the grill reflects off the lid and other interior surfaces, cooking the food from all sides and eliminating the need to turn the food.

COOKING WITH GAS

Gas grills are clean, convenient, and easy to control to achieve best results.

- To light a gas grill, open the lid. Turn the gas valve to "on" and ignite grill as directed by the manufacturer. Turn burners on high. Close the lid and preheat the grill (usually with all burners on high for 10 to 15 minutes).
- For indirect cooking, turn off burners directly below where you place the food. Adjust burner controls to required temperature.

GRILLING WITH A CHARCOAL GRILL

Charcoal grills require more work than gas grills, but their fans love the smoky flavors they bring to food. Here's how to handle one.

- About 25 to 30 minutes prior to cooking, remove the grill cover and rack and open all of the vents.
- For direct cooking, use enough briquettes to cover the charcoal grate completely with one layer. Pile these briquettes into a pyramid in the center of the grate.
- For indirect cooking, the number of briquettes you need to use is based on your grill size. Refer to the following chart.

SETUP FOR INDIRECT COOKING

Grill diameter	Briquettes needed to start	Briquettes to add for longer cooking
26¾ inches	60	18
22½ inches	50	16
18½ inches	32	10

- Apply fire starter, use an electric starter, or place briquettes in a chimney starter. (If using a liquid starter, wait 1 minute before igniting the fire.) Let the fire burn for 25 to 30 minutes or until the coals are covered with a light coating of gray ash.
- For direct cooking, use long-handled tongs to spread coals evenly across the bottom of the grill, covering an area 3 inches larger on all sides of the food you are cooking.
- For indirect cooking, arrange coals to one side of the grill; place a drip pan on the other side. Or place the drip pan in the center; arrange the coals into two equal piles on two sides of the drip pan.
- Install grill rack and check temperature of coals using a built-in or separate flat grill thermometer. Or use the hand test (see chart, page 320).

HAND TEST

To judge how hot your grill is, carefully place the palm of your hand just above the grill rack and count the number of seconds you can hold it in that position. (For example, "One, I love grilling; two, I love grilling" and so on.) Note that when grilling indirectly, hot coals will provide medium-hot heat and medium-hot coals will provide medium heat.

Time	Temperature	Thermometer	Visual
2 seconds	Hot (high)	400°F to 450°F	Coals glowing and lightly covered with gray ash
3 seconds	Medium-high	375°F to 400°F	
4 seconds	Medium	350°F to 375°F	Coals glowing through a layer of ash
5 seconds	Medium-low	325°F to 350°F	
6 seconds	Low	300°F to 325°F	Coals burning down and covered with thick layer of ash

ADJUSTING THE HEAT

Weather conditions can affect coal temperature, and not everyone judges temperature alike. Therefore, use timings given with each recipe as a guideline and watch all foods on the grill closely. Adjust when the temperature isn't quite right.

CHARCOAL GRILLS: If the coals are too hot, raise the grill rack, spread the coals apart, close the air vents halfway, or remove some briquettes. If the coals are too cool, use long-handled tongs to tap ashes off the burning coals, move coals together, add briquettes, lower the rack, or open vents.

GAS OR ELECTRIC GRILL: Adjust burners to higher or lower settings as needed.

SAFETY PRECAUTIONS

Because grilling is cooking with fire, it requires its own set of safety rules.

- Use charcoal or gas grills outside only—never in a garage, porch, or enclosed area.
- Don't use lighter fluid, an electric starter, or a chimney starter with instant-lighting briquettes.
- Never leave a grill unattended or try to move it while it's in use or still hot.
- Periodically test your gas grill for leaks and clean the venturi tubes regularly according to the manufacturer's directions.
- Allow coals to burn completely and ashes to cool for 24 hours before disposing of them.
- Let the grill cool completely before covering or storing it.

REINING IN THOSE FLARE-UPS

Fat and meat juices dripping onto heat sources can cause flare-ups. To avoid them, clean a gas grill after each use as directed below. On a charcoal grill, raise the grill rack, cover the grill, space the hot coals farther apart, or remove a few coals. As a last resort, remove food from grill and mist the fire with water. When the flame subsides, return food to the grill.

KEEP IT CLEAN

For best results, clean your grill after each use.

CLEANING CHARCOAL GRILLS: Let the coals die down and the grill rack cool slightly. Brush off any debris using a brass-bristle grill brush. For a more thorough cleaning, wash the grill rack using mild soap and a steel-wool pad.

CLEANING GAS GRILLS: Burn off any residue by covering the grill and turning the grill on high until smoke subsides (about 10 to 15 minutes). Turn it off and allow it to cool slightly; brush the grill rack with a brass-bristle grill brush.

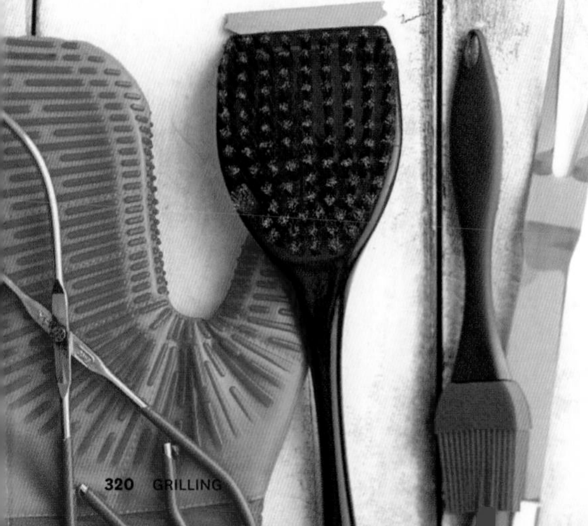

LOW-CALORIE

Spicy Soy Steak Noodle Bowl

PREP: 25 MINUTES **MARINATE:** 2 TO 4 HOURS
GRILL: 17 MINUTES **STAND:** 5 MINUTES
MAKES: 4 SERVINGS

- **1 1¼- to 1½-pound beef flank steak**
- **1 recipe Spicy Soy Marinade**
- **1 3-ounce package ramen noodles (any flavor)**
- **1 cup thin bite-size carrot strips**
- **1 cup lengthwise-sliced sugar snap peas**
- **¼ cup loosely packed fresh cilantro leaves**
- **2 tablespoons sliced almonds, toasted (see tip, page 21)**

1 Trim fat from steak. Score both sides of steak in a diamond pattern by making shallow diagonal cuts at 1-inch intervals (see photo 1, below). Place steak in a large resealable plastic bag set in a shallow dish. Reserve 3 tablespoons of Spicy Soy Marinade for noodles. Pour remaining marinade over steak in bag; seal bag (see photo 2, below). Turn to coat meat. Marinate in the refrigerator for 2 to 4 hours, turning bag occasionally.

2 Drain steak, discarding marinade. For a charcoal grill, grill steak on the rack of an uncovered grill directly over medium coals for 17 to 21 minutes for medium (160°F), turning once. (For a gas grill, preheat grill. Reduce heat to medium. Place steak on grill rack over heat. Cover and grill as directed.) Cover steak and let stand 5 minutes. Thinly slice steak diagonally across the grain into bite-size pieces.

3 Prepare ramen noodles according to package directions, omitting the seasoning packet. (Discard seasoning packet.) Drain noodles. If desired, snip noodles into short pieces. In a large bowl toss together noodles, steak, the 3 tablespoons reserved marinade, carrots, sugar snap peas, and cilantro. Sprinkle with almonds.

SPICY SOY MARINADE: In a small bowl combine ¼ cup soy sauce, 2 tablespoons rice vinegar, 2 tablespoons vegetable oil, 1 teaspoon finely shredded lime peel, 2 tablespoons lime juice, 1 tablespoon grated fresh ginger, 1 teaspoon Asian chili sauce, 1 teaspoon toasted sesame oil (if desired), ¼ teaspoon salt, ¼ teaspoon black pepper, and 2 cloves garlic, minced.

PER ¾ CUP: 373 cal., 16 g total fat (5 g sat. fat), 47 mg chol., 741 mg sodium, 20 g carb., 3 g fiber, 35 g pro.
EXCHANGES: ½ Vegetable, 1 Starch, 4½ Lean Meat, ½ Fat

MARINATING STEAK STEP-BY-STEP

1. Score the steak, making diagonal cuts. Make intersecting cuts in the opposite direction to form a diamond pattern.

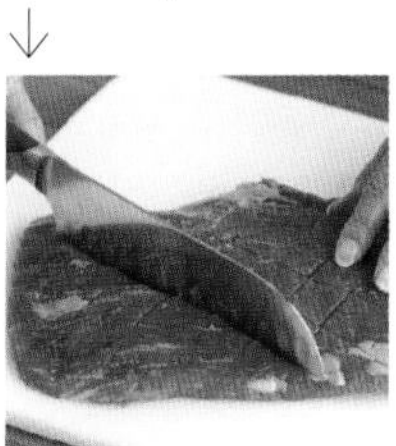

2. Pour the marinade over the meat in the bag. After sealing the bag, turn it a few times to be sure that all the meat is coated with marinade.

FAST LOW-CALORIE

Chipotle Steak and Tomatoes

PREP: 10 MINUTES **GRILL:** 10 MINUTES
STAND: 5 MINUTES **MAKES:** 4 SERVINGS

- **2 beef shoulder petite tenders or beef ribeye steaks, cut 1 inch thick (12 to 16 ounces)**
- **Salt and black pepper**
- **1 canned chipotle pepper in adobo sauce, finely chopped, plus 2 teaspoons adobo sauce (see tip, page 44)**
- **¼ cup olive oil**
- **¼ cup vinegar**
- **3 medium tomatoes, thickly sliced (1 pound)**
- **2 medium avocados, halved, seeded, peeled, and sliced**
- **½ of a small red onion, very thinly sliced**

1 Trim fat from steaks. Sprinkle steaks lightly with salt and black pepper. Spread the 2 teaspoons adobo sauce over steaks.

2 For a charcoal grill, grill steaks on the rack of an uncovered grill directly over medium coals. Allow 10 to 12 minutes for medium rare (145°F) and 12 to 15 minutes for medium (160°F). (For a gas grill, preheat grill. Reduce heat to medium. Place steaks on the grill rack over heat. Cover and grill as directed.) Cover steaks and let stand for 5 minutes.

3 Meanwhile, for dressing, in a screw-top jar combine the chopped chipotle pepper and sauce, oil, and vinegar. Cover and shake well.

4 To serve, slice steaks and arrange on four dinner plates with tomato and avocado slices. Top with onion slices; drizzle with dressing.

PER ½ STEAK + ¾ CUP VEGETABLES: 379 cal., 29 g total fat (5 g sat. fat), 48 mg chol., 223 mg sodium, 11 g carb., 6 g fiber, 20 g pro. **EXCHANGES:** 1 Vegetable, ½ Other Carb., 2½ Lean Meat, 4½ Fat

FLAT-IRON STEAKS WITH AVOCADO BUTTER

BEST-LOVED LOW-CALORIE

Flat-Iron Steaks with Avocado Butter

PREP: 20 MINUTES **GRILL:** 10 MINUTES
STAND: 5 MINUTES **MAKES:** 6 SERVINGS

- **6 beef shoulder top blade (flat-iron) steaks or boneless ribeye steaks, cut 1 inch thick**
- **1 tablespoon olive oil**
- **1 tablespoon herbes de Provence, crushed**
- **½ teaspoon salt**
- **½ teaspoon freshly ground black pepper**
- **1 recipe Avocado Butter**

1 Trim fat from steaks. Brush steaks with the oil. In a bowl combine herbes de Provence, salt, and pepper. Sprinkle evenly over both sides of each steak; rub in with your fingers. If desired, cover and chill steaks for up to 24 hours.

2 For a charcoal grill, grill steaks on the rack of an uncovered grill directly over medium coals to desired doneness, turning once halfway through grilling. Allow 10 to 12 minutes for medium rare (145°F) and 12 to 15 minutes for medium (160°F). (For a gas grill, preheat grill. Reduce heat to medium. Place steaks on the grill rack over heat. Cover and grill as directed.) Cover steaks and let stand for 5 minutes. Serve steaks with Avocado Butter.

AVOCADO BUTTER: Halve, seed, peel, and chop 1 ripe avocado. In a medium bowl combine the chopped avocado, ¼ cup softened butter, 3 tablespoons lime juice, 2 tablespoons snipped fresh chervil or parsley, 1 tablespoon snipped fresh tarragon, and ¼ teaspoon salt. Using a fork, gently mash the ingredients together until thoroughly combined. Chill until almost firm.

PER 1 STEAK + 3 TABLESPOONS AVOCADO BUTTER: 369 cal., 25 g total fat (10 g sat. fat), 109 mg chol., 463 mg sodium, 3 g carb., 2 g fiber, 33 g pro. EXCHANGES: 4½ Lean Meat, 2½ Fat

Tandoori Steaks with Summer Couscous

PREP: 15 MINUTES **MARINATE:** 1 TO 4 HOURS
GRILL: 10 MINUTES **STAND:** 5 MINUTES
MAKES: 4 SERVINGS

- **4 6-ounce boneless beef top loin steaks, about 1 inch thick**
- **½ cup plain low-fat yogurt**
- **¼ cup snipped fresh mint**
- **3 tablespoons lemon juice**
- **2 teaspoons packed brown sugar**
- **2 teaspoons curry powder**
- **2 teaspoons paprika**
- **6 cloves garlic, minced**
- **1 recipe Summer Couscous**

1 Trim fat from steaks. Place steaks in a large resealable plastic bag set in a shallow dish. For marinade, in a bowl combine yogurt, mint, lemon juice, brown sugar, curry powder, paprika, 1 teaspoon *salt*, and garlic. Pour over steaks in bag; seal bag (see photo 2, page 321). Marinate in refrigerator for 1 to 4 hours, turning occasionally.

2 Remove steaks from marinade (some marinade should cling to the steaks). Discard remaining marinade. For a charcoal grill, grill steaks on greased rack of uncovered grill directly over medium coals for 10 to 12 minutes for medium rare (145°F) and 12 to 15 minutes for medium (160°F), turning once. (For a gas grill, preheat grill. Reduce heat to medium. Place steaks on greased rack over heat. Cover; grill as directed.) Cover steaks; let stand for 5 minutes. Slice steaks and serve with Summer Couscous.

SUMMER COUSCOUS: In a saucepan bring ½ cup water to boiling. Stir in ½ cup couscous. Remove from heat. Cover; let stand 5 minutes. Fluff with a fork. In a bowl combine the couscous; ⅔ cup chopped tomato; ⅔ cup chopped cucumber; ⅔ cup chopped yellow summer squash; ½ cup snipped fresh parsley; ⅓ cup canned garbanzo beans, rinsed and drained; ⅓ cup crumbled feta cheese; 2 tablespoons olive oil; 2 tablespoons lemon juice; and ½ teaspoon ground cumin.

PER 1 STEAK + 1 CUP COUSCOUS: 471 cal., 19 g total fat (6 g sat. fat), 119 mg chol., 707 mg sodium, 29 g carb., 4 g fiber, 47 g pro. EXCHANGES: ½ Vegetable, 1½ Starch, 6 Lean Meat, 1½ Fat

make it mine

BEST-LOVED FAST

Burgers

Sizzle up all kinds of burgers, from straightforward yet satisfying to dashingly exotic.

PREP: 15 MINUTES **GRILL:** 14 MINUTES
MAKES: 4 BURGERS

- 1½ **pounds MEAT**
- **LIQUID (optional)**
- ½ **teaspoon salt**
- ¼ **teaspoon black pepper**
- **STUFFING (optional)**
- **BREAD**
- **Ketchup, mustard, and/or mayonnaise (optional)**

1 In a bowl combine Meat, Liquid (if desired), salt, and pepper; mix well. Shape meat mixture into four ¾-inch-thick patties. (To stuff, divide meat mixture into eight portions; shape into ¼-inch-thick patties. Place Stuffing on the center of four patties. Top with remaining patties; pinch edges together to seal.)

2 For a charcoal grill, grill unstuffed or stuffed patties on the rack of an uncovered grill directly over medium coals for 14 to 18 minutes or until done (160°F to 165°F), turning once. (For a gas grill, preheat grill. Reduce heat to medium. Place patties on grill rack over heat. Cover; grill as directed.) Serve burgers in Bread with ketchup, mustard and/or mayonnaise, if desired.

TOP IT

Add one or more of these toppers to finish the burgers: cheese slices, caramelized onion, cooked bacon, roasted peppers, fresh basil, tomato and onion slices, spinach or lettuce leaves, and/or pickle slices.

MEAT *(pick one)*

- **Ground beef**
- **Ground pork**
- **Ground lamb**
- **Ground turkey or chicken (use a Liquid, brush burgers with oil before grilling, and cook to 165°F)**
- **1 pound ground beef plus 8 ounces bulk Italian sausage**

LIQUID *(pick one)*

- **1 lightly beaten egg**
- **1 lightly beaten egg white**
- **2 tablespoons chutney**
- **2 tablespoons apricot preserves (snip large pieces)**
- **2 tablespoons barbecue sauce**
- **2 tablespoons milk**
- **2 tablespoons steak sauce**

STUFFING *(pick one or more)*

- **Crisp-cooked and crumbled bacon**
- **Crumbled feta or blue cheese**
- **Shredded provolone, mozzarella, smoked cheddar, cheddar, Monterey Jack cheese**
- **⅓ to ½ cup cooked sliced fresh mushrooms**
- **Chopped roasted red sweet peppers**

BREAD *(pick one)*

- **Kaiser rolls**
- **Onion rolls**
- **White or whole wheat hamburger buns**
- **White or whole wheat pita bread rounds, halved**

LOW-CALORIE

Grilled Chili-Garlic Tri-Tip

PREP: 25 MINUTES **MARINATE:** 2 TO 6 HOURS
GRILL: 35 MINUTES **STAND:** 15 MINUTES
MAKES: 6 SERVINGS

- **2 teaspoons caraway seeds**
- **2 teaspoons cumin seeds**
- **½ teaspoon coriander seeds**
- **2 tablespoons tomato sauce**
- **1 tablespoon red chili paste**
- **1 tablespoon olive oil**
- **1¼ teaspoons chili powder**
- **3 cloves garlic, minced**
- **1 2-pound boneless beef tri-tip roast (bottom sirloin)**
- **½ teaspoon salt**
- **¼ teaspoon black pepper**

1 In a large skillet combine caraway seeds, cumin seeds, and coriander seeds. Cook over medium-high heat for 2 to 3 minutes or until seeds are lightly toasted and fragrant, shaking the skillet constantly. Cool seeds completely. Transfer seeds to a clean coffee grinder; pulse to form a fine powder.

2 For spice paste, in a small bowl combine tomato sauce, chili paste, oil, chili powder, and garlic. Stir in the spice seed powder.

3 Trim fat from roast. Place meat in a shallow dish; sprinkle with salt and pepper. Spread spice paste over both sides of meat. Cover and marinate in the refrigerator for 2 to 6 hours.

4 For a charcoal grill, arrange medium-hot coals around a drip pan. Test for medium heat above pan. Place roast on grill rack over pan. Cover and grill to desired doneness, turning once halfway through grilling. Allow 35 to 40 minutes for medium rare (135°F) and 40 to 45 minutes for medium (150°F). (For a gas grill, preheat grill. Reduce heat to medium. Adjust for indirect cooking. Place roast in roasting pan; place pan on grill rack over the burner that is turned off. Grill as directed.)

5 Remove meat from grill. Cover meat with foil; let stand for 15 minutes. Temperature of meat will rise during standing.

PER 5 OUNCES MEAT: 280 cal., 16 g fat (5 g sat. fat), 100 mg chol., 365 mg sodium, 2 g carb., 1 g fiber, 32 g pro.
EXCHANGES: 4½ Lean Meat, 1½ Fat

DRY OR WET RUBS

Rubs can be either wet or dry. Both kinds add delicious flavor to meat. The spice paste in the Grilled Chili-Garlic Tri-Tip is a wet rub. Wet rubs contain oil and sometimes other liquids. The oil helps keep the meat moist. Dry rubs are a combination of herbs and spices. For dry rubs, see page 330.

Southwestern Beef Kabobs with Corn and Orzo Salad

PREP: 40 MINUTES **BROIL:** 8 MINUTES
MAKES: 8 SERVINGS

- **4 teaspoons chili powder**
- **2 teaspoons garlic salt**
- **1 teaspoon ground cumin**
- **1 teaspoon ground oregano**
- **2 pounds boneless beef sirloin, cut into 1-inch cubes**
- **1 recipe Corn and Orzo Salad**
- **Lime slices (optional)**

1 In a large resealable plastic bag combine chili powder, garlic salt, cumin, and oregano. Seal bag and shake to mix. Add beef cubes to bag. Seal bag and shake to coat. On eight 10-inch skewers (see tip, page 326) thread meat, leaving a ¼-inch space between pieces.

2 For a charcoal grill, grill kabobs on the rack of an uncovered grill directly over medium coals for 8 to 12 minutes or until desired doneness, turning once or twice. (For a gas grill, preheat grill. Reduce heat to medium. Place kabobs on grill rack over heat. Cover and grill as directed.)

3 Transfer Corn and Orzo Salad to a large platter; arrange beef kabobs on top. If desired, garnish with lime slices.

CORN AND ORZO SALAD: Cook ⅔ cup dried orzo (rosamarina) according to package directions, adding 2 cups fresh or frozen corn kernels for the last minute of cooking. Drain orzo and corn in a colander; rinse with cold water. In a large bowl combine orzo; corn; 1 medium orange or red sweet pepper, cut into bite-size pieces; ⅔ cup grape tomatoes, halved; one 14.5- to 15-ounce can kidney beans, rinsed and drained; ½ cup thinly sliced red onion; and 1 small zucchini, halved lengthwise and sliced. For dressing, in a screw-top jar combine 2 tablespoons olive oil; 2 tablespoons honey; 1 teaspoon finely shredded lime peel; ¼ cup lime juice; 1 fresh jalapeño chile pepper, seeded and finely chopped (see tip, page 44); 2 tablespoons snipped fresh cilantro; ½ teaspoon salt; and 3 cloves garlic, minced. Cover and shake well. Pour dressing over orzo mixture; mix well.

PER KABOB + 1 CUP SALAD: 413 cal., 19 g fat (6 g sat. fat), 82 mg chol., 537 mg sodium, 34 g carb., 5 g fiber, 29 g pro.
EXCHANGES: 1 Vegetable, 2 Starch, 3 Lean Meat, 2½ Fat

SOUTHWESTERN BEEF KABOBS WITH CORN AND ORZO SALAD

BEST-LOVED LOW-CALORIE

Lemon-Sage Pork Chops on a Stick

(photo, page 317)

PREP: 20 MINUTES **MARINATE:** 4 TO 6 HOURS
GRILL: 7 MINUTES **STAND:** 5 MINUTES
MAKES: 6 SERVINGS

- **6 6-ounce boneless pork loin chops, cut 1 inch thick**
- **2 teaspoons finely shredded lemon peel**
- **⅓ cup lemon juice**
- **⅓ cup olive oil**
- **3 tablespoons finely chopped shallots**
- **3 tablespoons coarse ground mustard**
- **2 tablespoons snipped fresh sage**
- **1 teaspoon coarse-ground black pepper**
- **½ teaspoon salt**
- **3 cloves garlic, minced**
- **6 8×¼-inch-thick bamboo chopsticks, wooden skewers, or dowels (see tip, below)**
- **Snipped fresh sage (optional)**
- **Lemon wedges (optional)**

1 Trim fat from chops. Place chops in a resealable plastic bag set in a shallow dish. For marinade, in a small bowl whisk together lemon peel, lemon juice, olive oil, shallots, mustard, 2 tablespoons sage, the pepper, salt, and garlic. Pour marinade over chops in bag (see photo 2, page 321); seal bag. Turn to coat chops. Marinate in the refrigerator for 4 to 6 hours, turning bag occasionally.

2 Drain chops, discarding marinade. Insert a wooden chopstick into a short side of each chop. For a charcoal grill, grill chops on the rack of an uncovered grill directly over medium coals for 7 to 9 minutes or until an instant-read thermometer inserted in chops registers 145°F, turning once halfway through grilling. (For a gas grill, preheat grill. Reduce heat to medium. Place chops on grill rack over heat. Cover and grill as directed.) Cover chops and let stand for 5 minutes before serving. Arrange chops on a platter. If desired, sprinkle with additional fresh sage and serve with lemon wedges.

PER SERVING: 427 cal., 29 g total fat (9 g sat. fat), 100 mg chol., 295 mg sodium, 2 g carb., 0 g fiber, 34 g pro.
EXCHANGES: 5 Medium-Fat Meat, 1 Fat

USING WOOD SKEWERS

When using wood or bamboo skewers , chopsticks, or dowels, soak them in water for at least 30 minutes before placing food on the skewers. A rectangular baking dish half-filled with water works well for soaking. The moist wood will not char or catch fire during grilling.

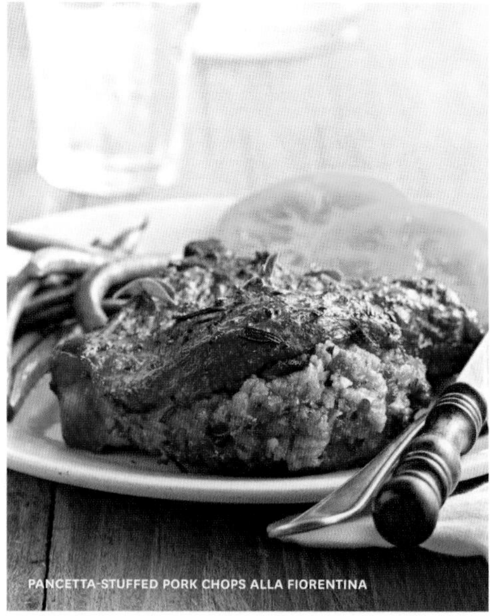

PANCETTA-STUFFED PORK CHOPS ALLA FIORENTINA

BEST-LOVED

Pancetta-Stuffed Pork Chops alla Fiorentina

PREP: 25 MINUTES **MARINATE:** 4 TO 6 HOURS
GRILL: 30 MINUTES **STAND:** 5 MINUTES
MAKES: 4 SERVINGS

- **4 bone-in pork loin chops or pork rib chops, cut 1¼ inches thick**
- **½ cup olive oil**
- **3 tablespoons finely shredded lemon peel**
- **2 tablespoons finely snipped fresh rosemary**
- **4 cloves garlic, minced**
- **½ teaspoon salt**
- **½ teaspoon freshly ground black pepper**
- **2 ounces pancetta, finely chopped**
- **1 cup chopped onion (1 large)**
- **½ cup soft bread crumbs**
- **2 teaspoons finely snipped fresh rosemary**
- **1 teaspoon snipped fresh oregano**
- **2 cloves garlic, minced**
- **1 tablespoon lemon juice**
- **Small fresh oregano leaves (optional)**

1 Trim fat from meat. Make a pocket in each chop by cutting horizontally from fat side almost to the bone. Place chops in a 2-gallon heavy resealable plastic bag set in extra-large bowl. For marinade, in a bowl combine oil, lemon peel, the 2 tablespoons rosemary, the four cloves garlic, the salt, and pepper; pour over pork in bag (see photo 2, page 321); seal bag. Turn to coat. Marinate in the refrigerator for 4 to 6 hours, turning bag occasionally.

2 In a large skillet cook and stir pancetta and onion over medium-high heat for 6 to 8 minutes or until pancetta is browned and crispy. Stir in bread crumbs, the 2 teaspoons rosemary, the snipped oregano, and the two cloves garlic. Stir in the lemon juice.

3 Drain chops, discarding marinade. Spoon one-fourth of the pancetta mixture into the pocket in each chop; press top of chop lightly with fingers to secure filling.

4 For a charcoal grill, arrange medium-hot coals around a drip pan. Test for medium heat above pan. Place chops on grill rack over drip pan. Cover and grill about 30 minutes or until chops are slightly pink in center (145°F). (For a gas grill, preheat grill. Reduce heat to medium. Adjust for indirect cooking. Place chops in a roasting pan on the rack over burner that is turned off. Cover and grill as directed.) Cover chops and let stand for 5 minutes before serving. If desired, garnish with oregano leaves.

PER SERVING: 493 cal., 33 g total fat (9 g sat. fat), 122 mg chol., 677 mg sodium, 8 g carb., 1 g fiber, 39 g pro.
EXCHANGES: ½ Starch, 5½ Lean Meat, 5 Fat

BEST-LOVED

Mojo Pork Fajitas

PREP: 45 MINUTES **MARINATE:** 8 TO 24 HOURS
GRILL: 40 MINUTES **STAND:** 10 MINUTES
MAKES: 4 SERVINGS

- **⅓ cup olive oil**
- **¼ cup chopped onion**
- **⅓ cup lime juice**
- **⅓ cup orange juice**
- **1 teaspoon ground cumin**
- **1 teaspoon dried oregano, crushed**
- **1 tablespoon minced garlic (6 cloves)**
- **1 1-pound pork tenderloin**
- **2 large red sweet peppers, quartered lengthwise and seeded**
- **2 medium onions, cut into thick slices**
- **8 8-inch flour tortillas, warmed***
- **1 recipe Orange-Avocado Salsa**
- **¼ cup sour cream**
- **Fresh cilantro leaves (optional)**
- **Lime wedges (optional)**

1 For marinade, in a small bowl combine olive oil, the ¼ cup chopped onion, lime juice, orange juice, cumin, oregano, and garlic. Trim fat from meat. Place meat in a resealable plastic bag set in a shallow dish. Pour marinade over meat (see photo 2, page 321); seal bag. Marinate in the refrigerator for 8 to 24 hours, turning bag occasionally.

2 Drain meat, reserving marinade. Brush sweet peppers and onion slices with some of the marinade; discard the remaining marinade.

3 For a charcoal grill, arrange hot coals around a drip pan. Test for medium-hot heat above pan. Place meat on grill rack over drip pan. Place pepper quarters and onion slices on grill rack directly over coals. Cover and grill for 10 to 12 minutes for onions and 8 to 10 minutes for peppers or until vegetables are crisp-tender, turning occasionally. Remove vegetables from grill. Cover and grill meat for 30 to 35 minutes or until an instant-read meat thermometer inserted in center of meat registers 145°F. (For a gas grill, preheat grill. Reduce heat to medium-high. Adjust for indirect cooking. Grill vegetables and meat as directed.)

4 Remove meat from grill. Cover with foil and let stand for 10 minutes. (The meat's temperature will rise during standing.) Meanwhile, if desired or if skin on peppers is too charred, peel skin from peppers. Cut peppers into thin strips and chop onions. Slice meat. Serve meat and vegetables on warm tortillas with Orange-Avocado Salsa and sour cream. If desired, sprinkle with cilantro and serve with lime wedges.

***NOTE:** To warm tortillas, wrap them tightly in foil. Place on edge of grill rack; heat for 10 minutes, turning once.

ORANGE-AVOCADO SALSA: In a medium bowl combine 2 medium oranges, peeled, sectioned, and chopped; 1 ripe large avocado, halved, seeded, peeled, and chopped; ¼ cup chopped red onion, ¼ cup snipped fresh cilantro; 2 tablespoons lime juice; ½ to 1 teaspoon bottled hot pepper sauce; and ¼ teaspoon salt. If desired, cover and chill for up to 4 hours.

PER 2 FAJITAS: 736 cal., 32 g total fat (6 g sat. fat), 80 mg chol., 729 mg sodium, 79 g carb., 8 g fiber, 36 g pro.
EXCHANGES: 1 Vegetable, 5 Starch, 2½ Lean Meat, 4 Fat

MOJO CHICKEN FAJITAS: Prepare as directed, except substitute 1 pound skinless, boneless chicken breast halves for the pork. Marinate for 2 to 4 hours. For a charcoal grill, grill chicken on the rack of an uncovered grill directly over medium coals for 15 to 18 minutes or until an instant-read thermometer inserted in chicken registers 165°F. Place peppers and onions on grill rack with chicken and grill as directed. (For gas grill, preheat grill. Reduce heat to medium. Add chicken to grill rack. Place peppers and onions on grill rack. Cover and grill as directed.)

PER 2 FAJITAS: 724 cal., 29 g total fat (5 g sat. fat), 72 mg chol., 744 mg sodium, 79 g carb., 8 g fiber, 39 g pro.
EXCHANGES: 1 Vegetable, 5 Starch, 3 Lean Meat, 3 Fat

cook's secrets

kansas city ribs

THE SECRET: Unlike the dry ribs from Memphis, Kansas City's version glistens with a glaze of molasses-base barbecue sauce. For the most luscious coat, brush the ribs occasionally with sauce as they grill over wood chips.

PREP: 25 MINUTES **BAKE:** 2 HOURS AT 350°F **SOAK:** 1 HOUR
COOK: 25 MINUTES **GRILL:** 10 MINUTES **MAKES:** 6 SERVINGS

- **4 to 5 pounds pork loin back ribs**
- **1 tablespoon packed brown sugar**
- **1 tablespoon paprika**
- **1 teaspoon garlic powder**
- **1 teaspoon celery salt**
- **½ teaspoon dry mustard**
- **½ teaspoon black pepper**
- **¼ teaspoon cayenne pepper**
- **½ cup finely chopped onion**
- **2 cloves garlic, minced**
- **1 tablespoon butter**
- **1 cup ketchup**
- **¼ cup molasses**
- **¼ cup cider vinegar**
- **¼ cup water**
- **2 tablespoons brown sugar**
- **1 tablespoon chili powder**
- **1 tablespoon yellow mustard**
- **1 tablespoon Worcestershire sauce**
- **½ teaspoon salt**
- **2 cups hickory chips***

Kansas City barbecue sauces call for molasses for a caramelized sweetness. Dark corn syrup can be used instead.

1 Preheat oven to 350°F. Trim fat from ribs; remove membrane. Place ribs in a shallow roasting pan. For rub, in a small bowl stir together 1 tablespoon brown sugar, the paprika, garlic powder, celery salt, dry mustard, black pepper, and cayenne pepper. Sprinkle rub evenly over both sides of ribs; rub in with your fingers. Cover pan with foil.

2 Bake ribs for 2 to 2½ hours or until very tender. Carefully drain off fat in roasting pan.

3 For sauce, in a saucepan cook onion and minced garlic in butter over medium heat until tender. Stir in ketchup, molasses, vinegar, the water, 2 tablespoons brown sugar, chili powder, yellow mustard, Worcestershire sauce, and salt. Bring to boiling; reduce heat. Simmer for 20 to 25 minutes or until desired consistency.

4 For a charcoal grill, sprinkle the wood chips over medium coals. Grill ribs on the rack of a covered grill directly over the coals for 10 to 15 minutes or until ribs are browned, turning once halfway through grilling and brushing occasionally with sauce. (For a gas grill, preheat grill. Reduce heat to medium. Add wood chips according to manufacturer's directions. Place ribs on grill rack over heat. Cover; grill as directed.) Serve with remaining sauce.

***NOTE:** Soak wood chips in enough water to cover for at least 1 hour before grilling. Drain wood chips before using.

PER ⅙ RIBS + ¼ CUP SAUCE: 553 cal., 30 g total fat (11 g sat. fat), 133 mg chol., 1,073 mg sodium, 31 g carb., 1 g fiber, 38 g pro. **EXCHANGES:** 2 Other Carb., 5 Medium-Fat Meat, 1 Fat

PREPARING RIBS STEP-BY-STEP

1. MEMBRANE
Remove the membrane that covers the bones by slipping a dull knife or the pointed end of a meat thermometer under the membrane. Use a paper towel to grip and pull it away from the bones.

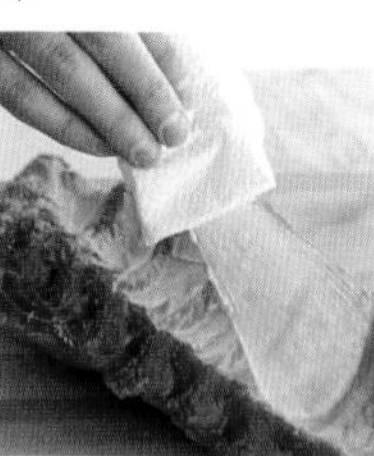

2. RUB
Place the ribs in a shallow roasting pan. Sprinkle the rub over the top of the meat and rub in with your fingers to form an even coating. Turn over and repeat.

3. SAUCE
Use a basting brush to spread the sauce onto the ribs before turning them. Turn the ribs and brush again with sauce. Continue brushing occasionally with sauce until ribs are done.

CHILI POWDER

Chili powder is usually made from dried New Mexican chiles, dried oregano, other seasonings, and salt. If you want to add a stronger chile pepper flavor to your rub, try ground ancho chile pepper—for spicier flavor try smoky ground chipotle chile pepper.

BASTING BRUSH-UPS

Grilling delicious ribs doesn't require special tools, but a simple basting brush is helpful to slather sauce over the ribs during the last 15 minutes of grilling. Traditional brushes are preferred by some because of how evenly they distribute the sauce. Silicone brushes are gaining favor because of their easy cleanup.

CHECKING RIBS FOR DONENESS

BONE TIPS
Once ribs are close to being finished, the meat will retract, exposing the rib tips.

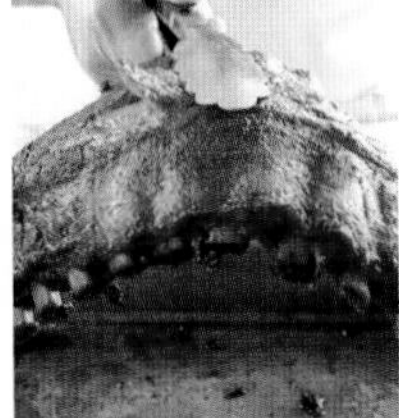

U SHAPE
Hold up the ribs in the middle with tongs. When they are ready, the rack will form a U shape. The meat may crack, too, which is a good sign.

RIB TWIST
Grab an exposed bone tip with your tongs and gently twist. If the bone turns easily, the ribs are done.

TOOTHPICK TEST
If a toothpick easily penetrates the meat between the ribs, they're ready to eat!

BEST-LOVED

Lamb Chops and Beans with Chile Butter

PREP: 25 MINUTES **CHILL:** 1 TO 24 HOURS
GRILL: 12 MINUTES **STAND:** 5 MINUTES
MAKES: 4 SERVINGS

- **1 recipe Chile Butter**
- **8 lamb loin chops, cut 1 inch thick**
- **1 15-ounce can cannellini (white kidney) beans or pinto beans, rinsed and drained**
- **½ cup chopped celery (1 stalk)**
- **¼ cup chopped green onions (2)**
- **1 tablespoon lime juice**

1 Prepare Chile Butter; chill until needed. Trim fat from chops. Sprinkle chops lightly with *salt* and *black pepper.* For a charcoal grill, grill chops on the rack of an uncovered grill directly over medium coals until desired doneness, turning once halfway through grilling. Allow 12 to 14 minutes for medium rare (145°F) and 15 to 17 minutes for medium (160°F). (For a gas grill, preheat grill. Reduce heat to medium. Place chops on grill rack over heat. Cover and grill as directed.) Cover chops and let stand for 5 minutes before serving

2 Meanwhile, in a medium saucepan combine beans, celery, green onions, and 2 tablespoons of the Chile Butter. Cook over medium heat until heated through, stirring occasionally. Stir in lime juice. Top each lamb chop with a slice of Chile Butter and serve with bean mixture.

CHILE BUTTER: In a bowl stir together ½ cup softened butter; ¼ cup snipped fresh cilantro; 2 fresh jalapeño chile peppers, seeded and finely chopped (see tip, page 44); 1 teaspoon chili powder; and 1 clove garlic, minced. Place on waxed paper; form into a log. Wrap well; chill for 1 hour or overnight. Store in refrigerator for up to 2 weeks or freeze for up to 1 month.

PER 2 CHOPS + ½ CUP BEANS: 445 cal., 30 g total fat (17 g sat. fat), 141 mg chol., 565 mg sodium, 17 g carb., 6 g fiber, 32 g pro. EXCHANGES: 1 Starch, 4 Lean Meat, 3½ Fat

Brats with Cucumber-Blueberry Slaw

PREP: 15 MINUTES **COOK:** 12 MINUTES
GRILL: 5 MINUTES **MAKES:** 6 SANDWICHES

- **6 uncooked bratwursts**
- **1½ cups apple juice**
- **3 cups shredded savoy cabbage**
- **½ cup thinly sliced cucumber**
- **⅓ cup fresh blueberries**
- **3 tablespoons sliced green onions**
- **⅓ cup buttermilk**
- **2 tablespoons mayonnaise**
- **1 tablespoon snipped fresh parsley**
- **1 tablespoon snipped fresh dill weed**
- **⅛ teaspoon salt**
- **⅛ teaspoon black pepper**
- **1 small clove garlic, minced**
- **6 bratwurst buns, split and toasted**

1 In a large saucepan combine bratwursts and apple juice. Bring to boiling; reduce heat. Simmer, covered, about 12 minutes or until an instant-read thermometer inserted in bratwursts registers 160°F, rearranging once.

2 Meanwhile, for slaw, in a medium bowl combine cabbage, cucumber, blueberries, and green onions. In a small bowl stir together buttermilk, mayonnaise, parsley, dill weed, salt, pepper, and garlic. Add buttermilk mixture to cabbage mixture; toss gently to coat.

3 For a charcoal grill, grill bratwursts on the rack of an uncovered grill directly over medium coals for 5 to 7 minutes or until browned, turning occasionally. (For a gas grill, preheat grill. Reduce heat to medium. Place bratwursts on grill rack over heat. Cover and grill as directed.) Serve bratwursts with slaw in buns.

PER SANDWICH: 464 cal., 26 g total fat (9 g sat. fat), 62 mg chol., 1,004 mg sodium, 36 g carb., 2 g fiber, 20 g pro. EXCHANGES: ½ Vegetable, ½ Fruit, 1½ Starch, 2 High-Fat Meat, 2 Fat

TRY A RUB

Use these rubs on meat and poultry. The Mediterranean rub is good for fish, too.

SMOKY RUB: In a small bowl mix 1 tablespoon smoked paprika, 1 tablespoon onion powder, 1½ teaspoons garlic powder, 1 teaspoon salt, 1 teaspoon dry mustard, and 1 teaspoon ground ginger.

BARBECUE RUB: In a small bowl mix 1 tablespoon chili powder, 1 tablespoon onion powder, 1 tablespoon brown sugar, 2 teaspoons ground cumin, 1¼ teaspoons cracked black pepper, 1½ teaspoons garlic powder, 1 teaspoon salt, 1 teaspoon dry mustard, and ¼ teaspoon ground cloves.

MEDITERRANEAN RUB: In a small bowl mix 1 tablespoon paprika, 1 tablespoon onion powder, 1½ teaspoons cracked black pepper, 1½ teaspoons each garlic powder and dried oregano, and 1 teaspoon each salt, snipped fresh mint, and finely shredded lemon peel.

8 to try

SUMMER: Layer on shredded lettuce, grilled corn kernels, chopped red onion, and chopped fresh tomato.

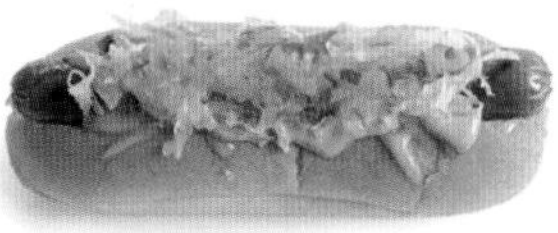

REUBEN: Layer on sauerkraut, dill pickle relish, and shredded Swiss cheese. Drizzle with Thousand Island salad dressing.

CHILI: Layer on hot chili, shredded cheddar cheese, corn chips, and, if desired, sour cream dip.

HAWAIIAN: Layer on chopped fresh pineapple, chopped green sweet peppers, and sliced onions. Drizzle with bottled teriyaki sauce.

CHICAGO-STYLE: Use poppy seed buns; layer on yellow mustard, chopped onion, sweet pickle relish, pickled peppers, and tomato slices.

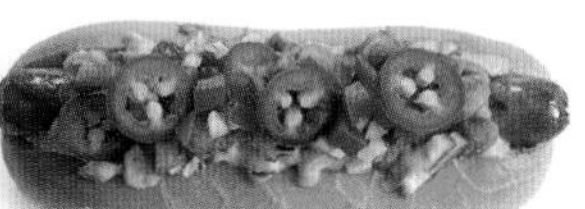

SONORAN: Layer on barbecue sauce, hot pinto beans, chopped tomatoes, and fresh jalapeño chile pepper slices (see tip, page 44).

CALIFORNIA: Layer on spring greens, chopped avocado, chopped tomatoes, and chopped hard-cooked eggs.

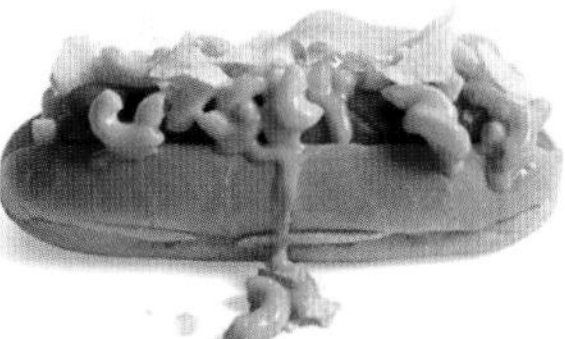

MAC AND CHEESE: Layer on hot macaroni and cheese and crushed potato chips.

Grilled Hot Dogs

START TO FINISH: 15 MINUTES
MAKES: 8 SANDWICHES

- 8 **frankfurters**
- 8 **frankfurter buns**
- **Desired toppers**

1 For a charcoal grill, grill frankfurters on the rack of a uncovered grill directly over medium coals for 3 to 7 minutes or until heated through, turning occasionally. (For a gas grill, preheat grill. Reduce heat to medium. Place frankfurters on grill rack over heat. Cover and grill as directed.)

2 If desired, during the last minute of grilling, place a frankfurter bun, cut side down, over each frankfurter on grill rack. Grill for 1 to 2 minutes or until buns are warmed and lightly toasted. Remove frankfurters and buns together. Top as desired.

PER SANDWICH: 260 cal., 14 g total fat (5 g sat. fat), 25 mg chol., 682 mg sodium, 23 g carb., 1 g fiber, 9 g pro.
EXCHANGES: 1½ Starch, ½ High-Fat Meat, 1½ Fat

SELECT A DOG

When it comes to frankfurters, you have more choices than ever.

FILLING: Choose beef, pork, poultry, or a combination. Kosher hot dogs are made without pork.

STUFFED: Look for franks stuffed with cheese or apple.

HEALTHY: Lean, vegetarian, and vegan options are available.
UNCURED: These contain no nitrates.

Chicken and Corn Skewers with Peanut Dipping Sauce

PREP: 30 MINUTES **MARINATE:** 2 TO 4 HOURS
GRILL: 8 MINUTES **MAKES:** 4 SERVINGS

- **1½ pounds skinless, boneless chicken thighs, cut into thin strips**
- **1 recipe Tare Sauce***
- **½ cup chicken broth**
- **¼ cup hoisin sauce**
- **2 tablespoons reduced-sodium soy sauce**
- **1 tablespoon rice vinegar**
- **1 teaspoon grated fresh ginger**
- **1 teaspoon Asian chili sauce (Sriracha sauce)**
- **½ teaspoon fish sauce**
- **3 tablespoons peanut butter**
- **1 teaspoon toasted sesame oil**
- **2 15-ounce cans whole baby corn, drained**
- **1 bunch green onions, cut into 3-inch pieces**
- **Snipped fresh cilantro (optional)**
- **Toasted sesame seeds (optional)**

1 Place chicken in a resealable plastic bag set in a shallow dish. Add ½ cup of the Tare Sauce; seal bag (see photo 2, page 321). Turn to coat chicken. Marinate in the refrigerator for 2 to 4 hours, turning bag occasionally. Cover and chill the remaining Tare Sauce until needed.

2 For peanut sauce, in a small saucepan combine broth, hoisin sauce, soy sauce, rice vinegar, ginger, chili sauce, and fish sauce. Bring to boiling over medium heat; reduce heat. Simmer, uncovered, for 5 minutes. Whisk in peanut butter until smooth. Remove from heat. Stir in sesame oil; cover to keep warm.

3 Drain chicken, discarding marinade. Thread chicken strips, accordion-style, onto skewers (see tip, page 326), leaving a ¼-inch space between pieces. Brush lightly with some of the remaining Tare Sauce.

4 Alternately thread corn and green onions onto sets of two parallel skewers, leaving a ¼-inch space between pieces. Brush lightly with some of the remaining Tare Sauce.

5 For a charcoal grill, place chicken skewers on the rack of an uncovered grill directly over medium coals. Grill for 8 to 10 minutes or until chicken is no longer pink, brushing both sides with some of the remaining Tare Sauce and turning once halfway through grilling. Add vegetable skewers to the grill for the last 4 to 5 minutes of grilling, brushing both sides with the remaining Tare Sauce and turning once. (For a gas grill, preheat grill. Reduce heat to medium. Place chicken skewers on grill rack over heat. Cover and grill as directed, adding vegetable skewers.)

6 If desired, sprinkle chicken and vegetables with cilantro and sesame seeds. Sprinkle peanut sauce with sesame seeds. Serve chicken and vegetables with peanut sauce.

TARE SAUCE: In a small saucepan combine 1 cup chicken or beef broth, ½ cup sweet rice wine (mirin), ¼ cup reduced-sodium soy sauce, 3 tablespoons sugar, 1 tablespoon grated fresh ginger, 1 teaspoon fish sauce, ½ teaspoon black pepper, and 1 tablespoon minced garlic (6 cloves). Bring to boiling; reduce heat. Simmer, uncovered, for 25 to 30 minutes or until reduced to 1 cup; cool. Strain sauce through a fine-mesh sieve; discard solids. Store, covered, in the refrigerator for up to 3 weeks.

***NOTE:** If you like, you may omit the Tare Sauce. If you do, omit the marinating step as well and season the food with salt and black pepper.

PER SERVING: 423 cal., 15 g total fat (3 g sat. fat), 163 mg chol., 1,840 mg sodium, 31 g carb., 5 g fiber, 40 g pro.
EXCHANGES: 2 Starch, 5 Lean Meat, 1 Fat

BEST-LOVED **LOW-CALORIE**

Chorizo-Chicken Burgers

PREP: 30 MINUTES **CHILL:** 30 MINUTES
GRILL: 34 MINUTES **STAND:** 15 MINUTES
MAKES: 6 BURGERS

- **8 ounces cooked chorizo sausage, casings removed and thinly sliced**
- **2 cloves garlic**
- **½ cup chopped onion (1 medium)**
- **1½ pounds uncooked ground chicken or uncooked ground turkey**
- **2 teaspoons ground ancho chile pepper**
- **¾ teaspoon kosher salt**
- **1 medium avocado, halved, seeded, and peeled**
- **⅓ cup mayonnaise**
- **2 fresh poblano chile peppers**
- **½ cup shredded Monterey Jack cheese with jalapeño chile peppers (2 ounces)**
- **6 hamburger buns, split and toasted**
- **Lettuce leaves, sliced tomato, and/or sliced onion (optional)**

1 In a food processor combine sausage and garlic. Cover and process with on/off pulses until sausage is finely chopped. Add ½ cup chopped onion; cover and process with on/off pulses until onion is finely chopped. Transfer sausage mixture to a large bowl. Add ground chicken, ground ancho pepper, and salt; mix gently until combined. Shape mixture into twelve ¼-inch-thick patties. Cover and chill patties for at least 30 minutes.

CHORIZO-CHICKEN BURGERS

2 Meanwhile, in a small bowl mash avocado with a fork. Stir in mayonnaise; set aside.

3 Trim a thin slice off the top of each poblano pepper to remove stem (see tip, page 44). Remove and discard seeds from inside peppers. For a charcoal grill, grill poblano peppers on the rack of an uncovered grill directly over medium coals about 20 minutes or until peppers are charred and very tender, turning occasionally. (For a gas grill, preheat grill. Reduce heat to medium. Place peppers on grill rack over heat. Cover and grill as directed.) Remove peppers from grill and wrap in foil. Let stand about 15 minutes or until cool enough to handle. Using a sharp knife, loosen edges of skins; gently pull off skins and discard. Cut peppers into strips.

4 Divide cheese and poblano peppers among six of the patties, being careful to arrange cheese and peppers in the center of each patty (see photo 1, right). Top with remaining six patties, pressing edges to seal well (see photo 2, right).

5 For charcoal grill, grill patties on the grill rack directly over medium coals for 14 to 18 minutes or until done (165°F), turning once halfway through grilling. (For gas grill, place patties on grill rack over medium heat. Cover and grill as directed.)

6 To serve, spread cut sides of buns with avocado mixture. Serve chicken burgers in buns and, if desired, with lettuce, tomato, and/or sliced onion.

PER BURGER: 632 cal., 41 g fat (12 g sat. fat), 144 mg chol., 1,126 mg sodium, 29 g carb., 3 g fiber, 36 g pro.
EXCHANGES: 1 Vegetable, 1½ Starch, 4 Medium-Fat Meat, 4 Fat

STUFFED BURGERS STEP-BY-STEP

1. Sprinkle the cheese on half of the patties. Leave the edge uncovered so you will have enough meat to make a seal with the top patty.

2. Place the grilled chiles on top of the cheese. Top with the remaining patties. Press the edges of the top and bottom patties together to enclose the cheese and peppers.

ALL-AMERICAN BARBECUED CHICKEN

BEST-LOVED

All-American Barbecued Chicken

PREP: 30 MINUTES **MARINATE:** 4 TO 6 HOURS
GRILL: 50 MINUTES **MAKES:** 4 SERVINGS

- **3 to 3½ pounds meaty chicken pieces (breast halves, thighs, and drumsticks)**
- **3 tablespoons lemon juice**
- **1 tablespoon vegetable oil**
- **1 teaspoon salt**
- **½ teaspoon black pepper**
- **1 clove garlic, minced**
- **1 cup Balsamic BBQ Sauce (page 536)**
- **Watermelon wedges (optional)**

1 Place chicken in a large resealable plastic bag set in a shallow dish. For marinade, stir together lemon juice, oil, salt, pepper, and garlic. Pour over chicken in bag (see photo 2, page 321); seal bag. Turn to coat chicken. Marinate in the refrigerator for 4 to 6 hours, turning bag occasionally.

2 Drain chicken, discarding marinade. For a charcoal grill, arrange medium-hot coals around a drip pan. Test for medium heat above the pan. Place chicken, bone sides down, on grill rack over drip pan. Cover and grill for 50 to 60 minutes or until chicken is done (170°F for breast halves and at least 175°F for thighs and drumsticks), brushing with half of the Balsamic BBQ Sauce during the last 15 minutes of grilling. (For a gas grill, preheat grill. Reduce heat to medium. Adjust for indirect cooking. Place chicken pieces on grill rack over burner that is off. Grill as directed.)

3 To serve, pass the remaining Balsamic BBQ Sauce with the chicken. If desired, serve with watermelon wedges.

PER 2 PIECES: 630 cal., 37 g total fat (10 g sat. fat), 173 mg chol., 900 mg sodium, 26 g carb., 1 g fiber, 44 g pro.
EXCHANGES: 2 Other Carb., 6 Lean Meat, 3½ Fat

Mozzarella- and Tomato-Stuffed Chicken Breasts

PREP: 20 MINUTES **MARINATE:** 2 TO 4 HOURS
GRILL: 50 MINUTES **MAKES:** 4 SERVINGS

- **4 6- to 8-ounce bone-in chicken breast halves**
- **½ cup bottled Italian salad dressing**
- **4 oil-packed dried tomatoes, undrained**
- **4 ounces fresh mozzarella cheese, sliced**
- **8 large fresh basil leaves**
- **¼ teaspoon salt**
- **⅛ teaspoon black pepper**

1 If desired, skin chicken. Using a sharp knife, cut a 2-inch pocket in the thickest part of each chicken breast half by cutting horizontally toward but not through the opposite side. Place chicken in a large resealable plastic bag set in a shallow dish. Pour salad dressing over chicken in bag (see photo 2, page 321); seal bag. Turn to coat chicken. Marinate in the refrigerator for 2 to 4 hours, turning bag occasionally.

2 Drain dried tomatoes, reserving 1 tablespoon of the oil. Slice tomatoes. Drain chicken, discarding dressing. Stuff tomatoes, cheese, and basil in pockets in chicken. If necessary, secure openings with wooden toothpicks. Brush chicken with the reserved 1 tablespoon oil; sprinkle with salt and pepper.

3 For a charcoal grill, arrange medium-hot coals around a drip pan. Test for medium heat above pan. Place chicken, bone sides down, on grill rack over drip pan. Cover and grill for 50 to 60 minutes or until chicken is done (170°F). (For a gas grill, preheat grill. Reduce heat to medium. Adjust for indirect cooking. Place chicken, bone sides down, on grill rack over the burner that is turned off. Grill as directed.) Remove and discard any toothpicks.

PER STUFFED BREAST HALF: 403 cal., 27 g total fat (8 g sat. fat), 106 mg chol., 599 mg sodium, 4 g carb., 0 g fiber, 34 g pro.
EXCHANGES: 4½ Medium-Fat Meat, 1 Fat

Ginger Peach Glazed Chicken

(photo, page 317)

PREP: 15 MINUTES **GRILL:** 50 MINUTES
MAKES: 4 SERVINGS

- **2½ to 3 pounds meaty chicken pieces (breast halves, thighs, and drumsticks)**
- **½ cup peach preserves**
- **1 tablespoon white wine vinegar**
- **1 tablespoon prepared horseradish**
- **1 teaspoon freshly grated ginger**

1 If desired, skin chicken. Sprinkle chicken with *salt* and *black pepper.* For a charcoal grill, arrange medium-hot coals around a drip pan. Test for medium heat above pan. Place chicken, bone sides down, on grill rack above drip pan. Cover and grill for 40 minutes. (For a gas grill, preheat grill. Reduce heat to medium. Adjust for indirect cooking. Place chicken on grill rack over burner that is off. Grill as directed.)

2 For glaze, place preserves in a microwave-safe bowl; snip any large pieces. Stir in vinegar, horseradish, ginger, ½ teaspoon *salt,* and ½ teaspoon *black pepper.* Microwave on 100% power (high) for 30 to 60 seconds or until preserves are melted, stirring once. Brush glaze over chicken. Cover; grill for 10 to 20 minutes more or until chicken is done (170°F for breast halves and at least 175°F for thighs and drumsticks), brushing occasionally with glaze. Spoon any remaining glaze over chicken.

PER 2 PIECES: 436 cal., 16 g total fat (4 g sat. fat), 130 mg chol., 575 mg sodium, 28 g carb., 1 g fiber, 42 g pro.
EXCHANGES: 2 Other Carb., 6 Lean Meat

BEST-LOVED

Beer Can Chicken

PREP: 25 MINUTES **GRILL:** 75 MINUTES
STAND: 10 MINUTES **MAKES:** 4 TO 6 SERVINGS

- **2 teaspoons salt**
- **2 teaspoons packed brown sugar**
- **2 teaspoons paprika**
- **1 teaspoon dry mustard**
- **½ teaspoon dried thyme, crushed**
- **½ teaspoon black pepper**
- **¼ teaspoon garlic powder**
- **1 12-ounce can beer***
- **1 3½- to 4-pound whole broiler-fryer chicken**
- **2 tablespoons butter or margarine, softened**
- **1 lemon wedge**

1 For rub, in a small bowl combine salt, brown sugar, paprika, dry mustard, thyme, pepper, and garlic powder. Discard about half of the beer from the can. Add 1 teaspoon of the spice mixture to the half-empty can (beer will foam up).

2 Remove neck and giblets from chicken; reserve for another use or discard. Rinse the body cavity; pat dry. Sprinkle 1 teaspoon of the rub inside the body cavity. Add the butter to the remaining spice mixture in bowl; mix well. Rub butter mixture over the outside of the chicken.

3 Hold the chicken upright and lower it onto the beer can; pull the legs forward (see photo 1, below). Twist wing tips behind back. Stuff the lemon wedge in the neck cavity.

4 For a charcoal grill, arrange medium-hot coals around a drip pan. Test for medium heat above pan. Stand chicken upright on grill rack over drip pan. Cover and grill for 75 to 105 minutes or until chicken is done (at least 170°F in thigh muscle). If necessary, tent chicken with foil to prevent overbrowning. (For a gas grill, preheat grill. Reduce heat to medium. Adjust for indirect cooking. Place chicken on grill rack as directed over burner that is turned off. If necessary, remove upper grill racks so chicken will stand upright. Grill as directed.) Carefully remove chicken from grill, holding it by the can with hot pads or oven mitts. Cover with foil; let stand for 10 minutes. To pull the can from the chicken, use sturdy tongs and a thick towel or hot pad to carefully remove the chicken (see photo 2, below).

***NOTE:** To grill the chicken without the beer can, prepare chicken through Step 3. Place the chicken, breast side up, on grill rack directly over drip pan. Cover and grill as directed.

PER ¼ CHICKEN: 670 cal., 47 g total fat (15 g sat. fat), 218 mg chol., 1,399 mg sodium, 6 g carb., 2 g fiber, 51 g pro.
EXCHANGES: ½ Other Carb., 7½ Lean Meat, 5 Fat.

BEER CAN CHICKEN STEP-BY-STEP

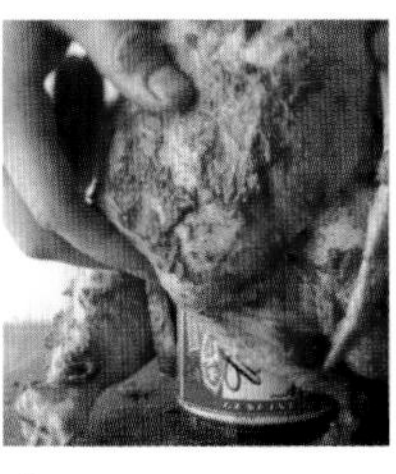

1. Position the chicken on the beer can so the can fits into the cavity. Pull the legs forward so the bird rests on its legs and the can.

2. Using large, sturdy tongs, grasp the chicken under the wings and use a thick towel to slide the beer can from the cavity.

BEST-LOVED FAST LOW-CALORIE

New England Grilled Turkey

PREP: 40 MINUTES **MARINATE:** 12 TO 24 HOURS
GRILL: 2½ HOURS **STAND:** 15 MINUTES
MAKES: 8 TO 12 SERVINGS

- **4 cups hot water**
- **1¼ cups kosher salt**
- **1 cup pure maple syrup**
- **1 6-ounce can apple juice concentrate, thawed**
- **16 cups cold water**
- **¼ teaspoon whole black peppercorns**
- **4 whole cloves**
- **3 cloves garlic, crushed**
- **1 8- to 10-pound whole turkey**
- **½ cup butter, softened**
- **1 teaspoon ground sage**
- **1 recipe Gingered Cranberry Sauce**

1 For brine, in a deep pot combine hot water, the 1¼ cups kosher salt, maple syrup, and juice concentrate. Stir until salt dissolves. Add cold water, peppercorns, cloves, and garlic. Remove neck and giblets from turkey; discard. Rinse turkey cavity. Add turkey to brine and weight it with a plate to keep it covered by brine. Cover; place in the refrigerator for 12 to 24 hours.

2 Drain turkey, discarding brine; pat dry. In a bowl combine butter and sage. Starting at the neck on one side of the breast, slip your fingers between skin and meat, loosening the skin as you work toward the tail end. Once your entire hand is under the skin, free the skin around the thigh and leg area up to but not around the tip of the drumstick. Repeat on the other side of the breast. Rub sage butter on meat under skin. Skewer neck skin to back. Twist wing tips behind back. Sprinkle surface and cavity of turkey with *salt* and *black pepper.* Tuck drumsticks under band of skin or tie to tail. Insert a meat thermometer into center of an inside thigh muscle. (The thermometer should not touch bone.)

3 For a charcoal grill, arrange medium-hot coals around a drip pan. Test for medium heat above the pan. Place turkey in a foil pan on grill rack over drip pan. Cover; grill for 2½ to 3 hours or until thermometer registers at least 175°F, adding fresh coals every 45 to 60 minutes and cutting band of skin or string the last hour of grilling. (For a gas grill, preheat grill; reduce heat to medium. Adjust for indirect cooking. Place turkey in foil pan on rack over burner that is turned off. Grill as directed.)Remove turkey from grill. Cover with foil; let stand for 15 minutes before carving. Serve with Gingered Cranberry Sauce.

GINGERED CRANBERRY SAUCE: In a medium saucepan combine 1 cup sugar and 1 cup water. Bring to boiling, stirring to dissolve sugar. Boil rapidly for 5 minutes. Add 2 cups fresh cranberries, ½ cup snipped dried apples, 1½ teaspoons grated fresh ginger, and 1 teaspoon finely shredded lemon peel. Return to boiling; reduce heat. Boil gently, uncovered, for 3 to 4 minutes or until cranberry skins pop, stirring occasionally. Serve warm or chilled.

PER 4 OUNCES TURKEY + ⅓ CUP SAUCE: 330 cal., 10 g total fat (4 g sat. fat), 111 mg chol., 463 mg sodium, 33 g carb., 2 g fiber, 28 g pro. **EXCHANGES:** ½ Fruit, 1½ Other Carb., 4 Lean Meat, 1 Fat

Buffalo-Style Turkey Wraps

PREP: 35 MINUTES **MARINATE:** 2 TO 3 HOURS
GRILL: 12 MINUTES **MAKES:** 6 WRAPS

- **2 turkey breast tenderloins (1 to 1½ pounds)**
- **3 tablespoons bottled hot pepper sauce**
- **2 tablespoons vegetable oil**
- **2 teaspoons paprika**
- **¼ teaspoon cayenne pepper**
- **6 10-inch flour tortillas**
- **1½ cups carrots cut into thin strips**
- **1½ cups thinly bias-sliced celery**
- **3 cups shredded lettuce**
- **1 recipe Blue Cheese Sauce**

1 Cut each turkey tenderloin in half horizontally to make 4 steaks. Place steaks in a resealable plastic bag set in a shallow dish. For marinade, in a bowl combine hot pepper sauce, oil, paprika, ¼ teaspoon *salt,* and cayenne pepper. Pour over turkey in bag; seal bag. Turn to coat turkey. Marinate in the refrigerator for 2 to 3 hours, turning bag occasionally.

2 Drain turkey, discarding marinade. For a charcoal grill, grill turkey on rack of an uncovered grill directly over medium coals for 12 to 15 minutes or until done (165°F), turning once. Wrap tortillas in foil. Place on the rack with turkey; heat for 10 minutes, turning once. (For a gas grill, preheat grill. Reduce heat to medium. Place turkey and wrapped tortillas on grill rack over heat. Cover; grill as directed.) Slice turkey. Divide turkey, carrots, celery, and lettuce among tortillas. Top with Blue Cheese Sauce. Roll up tortillas; serve immediately.

BLUE CHEESE SAUCE: In a food processor combine ½ cup sour cream, ¼ cup mayonnaise, ¼ cup crumbled blue cheese, 1 tablespoon lemon juice, ⅛ teaspoon salt, and 1 clove garlic, cut up. Cover and process until nearly smooth.

PER WRAP: 377 cal., 19 g total fat (5 g sat. fat), 63 mg chol., 513 mg sodium, 28 g carb., 3 g fiber, 24 g pro.
EXCHANGES: ½ Vegetable, 2 Starch, 2½ Lean Meat, 3 Fat

LOW-CALORIE

Grilled Scallops with Balsamic Syrup

PREP: 20 MINUTES **MARINATE:** 2 TO 4 HOURS
GRILL: 5 MINUTES **MAKES:** 4 SERVINGS

- **8 fresh or frozen sea scallops (about 1 pound total)**
- **1/4 cup olive oil**
- **2 tablespoons snipped fresh mint**
- **2 tablespoons snipped fresh Italian parsley**
- **2 tablespoons balsamic vinegar**
- **1 tablespoon freshly grated Parmesan cheese**
- **1 teaspoon finely shredded lemon peel**
- **1 clove garlic, minced**
- **4 slices prosciutto, halved lengthwise**
- **1/2 cup balsamic vinegar**
- **2 cups baby arugula**

1 Thaw scallops if frozen. Rinse scallops; pat dry. Place scallops in a resealable plastic bag set in a shallow dish. For marinade, in a bowl combine oil, mint, parsley, the 2 tablespoons vinegar, the cheese, lemon peel, and garlic. Pour marinade over scallops. Seal bag; turn to coat scallops. Marinate in the refrigerator for 2 to 4 hours, turning bag once or twice.

2 Drain scallops, discarding marinade. Wrap each scallop with a piece of prosciutto. Thread scallops onto four 6-inch skewers (see tip, page 326).

3 For a charcoal grill, place skewers on greased rack of an uncovered grill directly over medium-hot coals for 5 to 8 minutes or until scallops are opaque, turning once. (For a gas grill, preheat grill. Reduce heat to medium-high. Place skewers on greased grill rack over heat. Cover and grill as directed.)

4 For balsamic syrup, in a heavy saucepan bring the 1/2 cup vinegar to boiling; reduce heat. Simmer, uncovered, for 4 to 5 minutes or until reduced by half. Serve scallops with arugula. Drizzle with the balsamic syrup.

PER 2 SCALLOPS + 1 TABLESPOON SYRUP: 262 cal., 15 g total fat (2 g sat. fat), 35 mg chol., 726 mg sodium, 12 g carb., 0 g fiber, 17 g pro. EXCHANGES: 1 Starch, 2 Lean Meat, 2 Fat

BEST-LOVED LOW-CALORIE

Thai-Style Sea Bass

PREP: 25 MINUTES **MARINATE:** 60 MINUTES
GRILL: 4 MINUTES PER 1/2-INCH THICKNESS
MAKES: 4 SERVINGS

- **4 5- to 6-ounce fresh or frozen skinless sea bass fillets**
- **1/4 teaspoon salt**
- **1/2 cup lime juice**
- **2 tablespoons fish sauce or soy sauce**

THAI-STYLE SEA BASS

- **1 tablespoon toasted sesame oil**
- **1 teaspoon sugar**
- **1 teaspoon grated fresh ginger**
- **1/4 teaspoon crushed red pepper**
- **1 tablespoon minced fresh garlic (6 cloves)**
- **2 cups hot cooked rice noodles or rice**
- **Snipped fresh cilantro (optional)**

1 Thaw fish if frozen. Rinse fish; pat dry with paper towels. Measure thickness of fish. Sprinkle fish with salt. Place fish in a large resealable plastic bag set in a shallow dish; set aside.

2 In a bowl stir together lime juice, fish sauce, sesame oil, sugar, ginger, crushed red pepper, and garlic. Pour half of the marinade over fish in bag; seal bag. Turn to coat fish. Marinate in the refrigerator for 60 minutes, turning bag occasionally. Chill remaining lime juice mixture.

3 Drain fish, discarding marinade. For a charcoal grill, place fish on the greased rack of an uncovered grill directly over medium coals. Grill for 4 to 6 minutes per 1/2-inch thickness of fish or until fish begins to flake when tested with a fork. (For a gas grill, preheat grill. Reduce heat to medium. Place fish on greased grill rack over heat. Cover and grill as directed.)

4 Serve fish with rice noodles. Drizzle the remaining lime juice mixture over fish and noodles. If desired, sprinkle with cilantro.

PER FILLET + 1/2 CUP NOODLES: 270 cal., 6 g total fat (1 g sat. fat), 58 mg chol., 781 mg sodium, 26 g carb., 1 g fiber, 28 g pro. EXCHANGES: 2 Starch, 3 Lean Meat

BEST-LOVED FAST

Grilled Salmon and Asparagus with Garden Mayonnaise *(photo, page 317)*

PREP: 10 MINUTES **GRILL:** 8 MINUTES
MAKES: 4 SERVINGS

- **4 6- to 8-ounce fresh or frozen skinless salmon fillets, about 1 inch thick**
- **1 pound asparagus spears (20 spears)**
- **1 tablespoon olive oil**
- **Sea salt or salt**
- **Freshly ground black pepper**
- **½ cup finely chopped celery (1 stalk)**
- **⅓ cup mayonnaise**
- **¼ cup thinly sliced green onions (2)**
- **1 tablespoon lemon juice**
- **2 teaspoons snipped fresh tarragon or ½ teaspoon dried tarragon, crushed**
- **Lemon wedges (optional)**

1 Thaw fish if frozen. Rinse fish; pat dry with paper towels. Snap off and discard woody bases from asparagus (see tip, page 589). Brush both sides of fish and asparagus lightly with olive oil. Sprinkle fish and asparagus with sea salt and pepper.

2 For a charcoal grill, place fish on the greased rack of an uncovered grill directly over medium coals. Place asparagus on grill rack next to salmon. Grill for 8 to 12 minutes or until fish begins to flake when tested with a fork and asparagus is tender, turning fish once halfway through grilling and turning asparagus occasionally. (For a gas grill, preheat grill. Reduce heat to medium. Place fish and asparagus on a greased grill rack over heat. Cover and grill as directed.)

3 Meanwhile, for garden mayonnaise, in a small bowl combine celery, mayonnaise, green onions, lemon juice, and tarragon. Chill until serving time.

4 To serve, arrange fish and asparagus on four dinner plates. Top fish with garden mayonnaise. If desired, serve with lemon wedges.

BROILER METHOD: Prepare as directed, except preheat broiler. Place salmon and asparagus on the unheated greased rack of a broiler pan. Broil 4 to 5 inches from the heat for 8 to 12 minutes or until fish begins to flake when tested with a fork and asparagus is tender, turning fish once halfway through broiling and turning asparagus occasionally.

PER FILLET + 5 ASPARAGUS SPEARS + ¼ CUP MAYONNAISE: 545 cal., 41 g total fat (8 g sat. fat), 100 mg chol., 314 mg sodium, 6 g carb., 3 g fiber, 37 g pro. EXCHANGES: 1 Vegetable, 5 Lean Meat, 5 Fat

BEST-LOVED LOW-CALORIE

Planked Salmon with Grilled Tomato Salsa

PREP: 10 MINUTES **CHILL:** 8 TO 24 HOURS
GRILL: 18 MINUTES **MAKES:** 4 SERVINGS

- **1 1-pound fresh or frozen salmon fillet, 1 inch thick**
- **1 tablespoon packed brown sugar**
- **1 teaspoon salt**
- **¼ teaspoon black pepper**
- **1 cedar grill plank**
- **1 recipe Grilled Tomato Salsa**

1 Thaw fish if frozen. Rinse fish; pat dry with paper towels. Place fish, skin side down, in a shallow dish. For rub, in a small bowl stir together brown sugar, salt, and black pepper. Sprinkle rub evenly over salmon; rub in with your fingers. Cover and chill for 8 to 24 hours.

2 Soak plank in enough water to cover for 1 hour.

3 For a charcoal grill, arrange medium-hot coals around edge of grill. Place fish, skin side down, on cedar grill plank. Place plank in center of grill rack. Cover and grill for 18 to 22 minutes or until fish begins to flake when tested with a fork. (For a gas grill, preheat grill. Reduce heat to medium. Adjust heat for indirect cooking. Place plank on grill rack over the burner that is turned off. Grill as directed.)

4 To serve, cut salmon into four pieces. Slide a spatula between the fish and skin to release pieces from plank. Serve with Grilled Tomato Salsa.

GRILLED TOMATO SALSA: In a large bowl combine 2 cups red cherry tomatoes, 2 cups yellow cherry tomatoes, ¼ cup sliced garlic, ¼ cup olive oil, and 2 tablespoons snipped fresh thyme. Transfer tomato mixture to a grill basket. For a charcoal grill, grill tomato mixture in basket on the rack of an uncovered grill directly over medium coals about 10 minutes or until tomatoes are softened and slightly charred but still retain their shape, stirring occasionally. (For a gas grill, preheat grill. Reduce heat to medium. Place tomatoes in basket on grill rack over heat. Cover and grill as directed.) Season to taste with salt and black pepper.

PER SERVING: 334 cal., 21 g fat (3 g sat. fat), 62 mg chol., 727 mg sodium, 12 g carb., 2 g fiber, 25 g pro.
EXCHANGES: 1 Vegetable, ½ Other Carb., 3 Lean Meat, 3½ Fat

GRILLING ON A PLANK

Grilling the salmon fillet on a plank yields a double bonus: The plank flavors the fish and helps in placing the fish on the grill and removing it when it is done.

LOW-CALORIE

Shrimp-Olive Skewers with Orange Compote and Fennel

PREP: 30 MINUTES **GRILL:** 10 MINUTES
MAKES: 4 SERVINGS

32 fresh or frozen large shrimp in shells (about 1¾ pounds total)
2 large fennel bulbs
1 orange, quartered
½ cup sugar
1 tablespoon snipped fennel leaves
16 pimiento-stuffed green olives
Olive oil

1 Thaw shrimp if frozen. Peel and devein shrimp, leaving tails intact if desired. Rinse shrimp; pat dry. Cover and chill until needed. In a saucepan cook fennel bulbs in a small amount of boiling water for 10 minutes; drain. Cut each bulb into eight wedges; set aside.

2 For orange compote, place orange quarters in a food processor. Cover and process until finely chopped. Transfer to a saucepan. Stir in sugar and ¼ teaspoon *salt*. Cook over medium-low heat about 15 minutes or until thickened, stirring frequently. Remove from heat. Stir in snipped fennel leaves; set aside.

3 On four 12- to 15-inch skewers (see tip, page 326) alternately thread shrimp and olives, leaving a ¼-inch space between pieces. Brush with oil; sprinkle with additional salt and *black pepper*. Brush fennel wedges with oil; sprinkle with additional salt and *black pepper*.

4 For a charcoal grill, grill fennel wedges on the rack of an uncovered grill directly over medium coals for 10 to 12 minutes or just until fennel is tender, turning once halfway through grilling. Place skewers on the grill rack; grill for 5 to 8 minutes or until shrimp are opaque, turning once. (For a gas grill, preheat grill. Reduce heat to medium. Place fennel and skewers on grill rack over heat. Cover and grill as directed.) Serve skewers and fennel with orange compote.

PER SKEWER + 4 FENNEL WEDGES + 3 TABLESPOONS COMPOTE: 359 cal., 7 g total fat (1 g sat. fat), 277 mg chol., 793 mg sodium, 41 g carb., 6 g fiber, 37 g pro.
EXCHANGES: ½ Starch, 2 Other Carb., 5 Lean Meat

Spicy Grilled Mussels and Sausage

PREP: 20 MINUTES **SOAK:** 45 MINUTES
GRILL: 11 MINUTES **MAKES:** 4 SERVINGS

2 pounds mussels in shells
1 cup kosher salt
2 cups cherry tomatoes, halved

SPICY GRILLED MUSSELS AND SAUSAGE

¾ cup dry white wine or chicken broth
⅓ cup olive oil
½ to 1 teaspoon crushed red pepper
½ teaspoon kosher salt
½ teaspoon dried oregano, crushed
1 lemon, quartered
6 cloves garlic, thinly sliced
12 ounces spicy cooked smoked sausage or kielbasa, cut into four pieces
3 cups chopped fresh kale

1 To clean live mussels, scrub under cold running water; remove beards. Set mussels aside.

2 In a 15×11×3-inch disposable foil pan combine tomatoes, wine, oil, crushed red pepper, the ½ teaspoon salt, the oregano, lemon, and garlic.

3 For a charcoal grill, place foil pan and sausage on the rack of a covered grill directly over medium coals. Grill for 3 to 4 minutes or until sausage is heated through, turning sausage and stirring tomato mixture once. (For a gas grill, preheat grill. Reduce heat to medium. Place foil pan and sausage on grill rack over heat. Grill as directed.) Remove sausage from grill. Stir mussels into tomato mixture in pan. Cover; grill for 6 to 7 minutes or until shells open. Discard any that do not open. Stir in sausage pieces and kale. Cover and grill for 2 minutes more.

PER SERVING: 735 cal., 57 g total fat (14 g sat. fat), 144 mg chol., 1,571 mg sodium, 28 g carb., 4 g fiber, 24 g pro.
EXCHANGES: 2 Vegetable, 1 Starch, 2½ High-Fat Meat, 7 Fat

LOW-CALORIE

White Cheddar New Potatoes Hobo Pack

PREP: 15 MINUTES **GRILL:** 35 MINUTES
STAND: 2 MINUTES **MAKES:** 4 SERVINGS

- **Nonstick cooking spray**
- 1 **pound fingerling, new red, or tiny yellow-flesh potatoes, halved**
- 1/4 **cup chopped onion**
- 1 **teaspoon snipped fresh thyme**
- 1/4 **teaspoon salt**
- 1/4 **teaspoon black pepper**
- 1/4 **cup shredded white cheddar cheese (1 ounce)**

1 Fold a 36×18-inch piece of heavy foil in half to make an 18-inch square. Coat foil with cooking spray. Place potatoes and onion in center of foil. Sprinkle with thyme, salt, and pepper. Bring up two opposite edges of foil; seal with a double fold. Fold remaining edges to completely enclose vegetables, leaving space for steam to build.

2 For a charcoal grill, grill packet on the rack of an uncovered grill directly over medium coals for 35 to 40 minutes or until potatoes are tender, turning packet occasionally. (For a gas grill, preheat grill. Reduce heat to medium. Place packet on a grill rack over heat. Cover and grill as directed.)

3 Carefully open packet; sprinkle potatoes with cheese. Loosely pinch packet back together and let potatoes stand about 2 minutes or until cheese melts.

PER 3/4 CUP: 120 cal., 2 g total fat (2 g sat. fat), 7 mg chol., 197 mg sodium, 21 g carb., 3 g fiber, 4 g pro.
EXCHANGES: 1½ Starch

BEST-LOVED

Corn on the Cob with Herb Butter

PREP: 20 MINUTES **SOAK:** 60 MINUTES
GRILL: 25 MINUTES **MAKES:** 6 SERVINGS

- 6 **fresh ears corn (with husks)**
- 1 **recipe Herb Butter**
- **Salt and black pepper**

1 Place ears of corn with husks and silks intact in two very large bowls, two 13×9×2-inch pans, or a clean sink. Cover with water. Soak corn for 60 minutes; drain. Scrub and prepare ears for grilling (see photos 1 and 2, below).

2 For a charcoal grill, grill corn on the rack of an uncovered grill directly over medium coals for 25 to 30 minutes or until corn kernels are tender, turning and rearranging ears occasionally (see photos 3 and 4, below). (For a gas grill, preheat grill. Reduce heat to medium. Place corn on grill rack over heat. Cover and grill as directed.)

3 Cool slightly. Peel back cornhusks (see photo 5, below). Serve with Herb Butter, salt, and pepper.

HERB BUTTER: In a small bowl stir together 6 tablespoons softened butter and 2 tablespoons snipped fresh basil, cilantro, or thyme until combined. Serve immediately or cover and store in refrigerator up to 1 week. Let chilled butter stand at room temperature for 30 minutes or until spreadable before using.

PER EAR + 1 TABLESPOON BUTTER: 180 cal., 13 g total fat (7 g sat. fat), 31 mg chol., 192 mg sodium, 17 g carb., 2 g fiber, 3 g pro. EXCHANGES: 1 Starch, 2½ Fat

GRILLING CORN ON THE COB STEP-BY-STEP

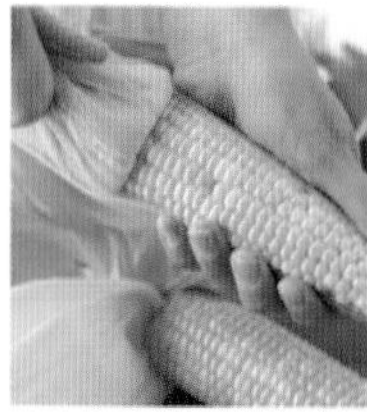

1. After soaking the ears, pull back the husks but leave them attached to the ear. Scrub the ears with a stiff brush to remove the silks.

2. Pull the husks back in place. Tear thin strips from one or two of the husks to make ties. Tie the husks at the top to hold them in place.

3. Grill the corn over medium heat. To ensure even cooking, turn the ears and rearrange them frequently.

4. To test for doneness, separate the husks and use a fork to check the kernels for tenderness.

5. To serve, peel back the husks and remove. Serve with Herb Butter, salt, and black pepper.

smoking essentials

Smoking is all about "low and slow." In smoking, foods cook at temperatures between 180°F and 220°F, with cooking times up to three times that of grilling. The results are legendary.

GENERAL SMOKING TIPS

Vertical water smokers are the most common type of smoker—follow manufacturer's directions for using. If you don't have a smoker, use your charcoal or gas grill. These hints help make for moist, smoke-imbued foods.

- Maintain temperatures by adding 8 to 10 briquettes every 45 to 60 minutes. Do not add instant-start charcoal briquettes during the smoking process.
- Keep the water pan filled to the recommended level, replenishing as needed with hot tap water. The water helps to keep the temperature steady and adds moisture to keep meats tender.
- Resist the temptation to peek. Heat and smoke escape each time you open the lid.
- Start with a small amount of wood (about four chunks) to see how you like the flavor. Add more as desired to maintain smoke as you cook. Don't overdo it, however, and don't add wood after the first half of smoking. Adding wood too late in the process can impart a bitter flavor to food.

USING A CHARCOAL GRILL FOR SMOKING

When using a charcoal grill to smoke foods, follow the tips at left, as well as these steps.

1 Arrange hot ash-covered coals around a foil pan that's filled with 1 inch of hot water.

2 Add the wood chips or chunks to coals.

3 Place food on the rack above water pan and cover grill.

4 Check food, temperature, and water pan every 45 to 60 minutes. Add briquettes as needed to maintain temperature.

USING A GAS GRILL FOR SMOKING

For a gas grill, follow these steps in addition to the tips at left.

1 Use wood chips rather than chunks.

2 If your gas grill is equipped with a smoker box attachment, before firing up the grill, fill the pan on the attachment with hot water. Place wood chips in the compartment following manufacturer's instructions. If you don't have the attachment, place wood chips in a foil pan; cover pan with foil and poke 10 holes in the foil. Before lighting the grill, place the pan on the flavorizer bars (beneath the grate) in a corner of the grill. You do not need a water pan for cooking times less than 2 hours. For longer cooking, fill a foil pan with 1 inch hot water; place on the grate over a lit burner.

3 Place food on rack over unlit burner; cover.

4 Check food, temperature, and water pan every 45 minutes. Do not replenish wood chips.

FOOD AND WOOD PAIRINGS

Smoke only foods that can handle an assertive smoke flavor. These include beef, lamb, pork, poultry, oily fish, and game.

Wood	Characteristics	Pairings
Alder	Delicate	Fish, pork, poultry
Apple or cherry	Delicate, slightly sweet and fruity	Veal, pork, poultry
Hickory	Strong and hearty, smoky	Beef brisket, ribs, pork chops, game
Mesquite	Light, sweet	Most meats
Oak	Assertive but versatile	Beef, pork, poultry
Pecan	Similar to hickory but more subtle	Pork, poultry, fish

Spicy-and-Sassy Beef Ribs

PREP: 30 MINUTES **CHILL:** 8 TO 24 HOURS
SMOKE: 3¼ HOURS **MAKES:** 4 SERVINGS

- **1 5-pound rack beef back ribs (7 ribs)**
- **1 tablespoon garlic salt**
- **1 tablespoon paprika**
- **1½ teaspoons ground black pepper**
- **½ teaspoon onion powder**
- **½ teaspoon ground cumin**
- **½ teaspoon dried thyme, crushed**
- **¼ teaspoon ground coriander**
- **⅛ teaspoon cayenne pepper**
- **⅛ teaspoon ground cardamom**
- **8 mesquite or hickory wood chunks**
- **¼ cup apple juice**
- **1 recipe Mustard Dipping Sauce**

1 Place ribs, meaty sides down, on a work surface. Work a table knife between a bone and the membrane; lift and pull membrane away. Repeat until all membrane is removed. Trim fat from ribs (see photo 1, below). In a bowl combine garlic salt, paprika, black pepper, onion powder, cumin, thyme, coriander, cayenne pepper, and cardamom. Sprinkle over ribs; rub in with your fingers (see photo 2, below). Wrap meat in plastic wrap; chill for 8 to 48 hours.

2 In a smoker arrange preheated coals, half of the wood chunks, and water pan according to manufacturer's directions. Pour water into pan. Place ribs, bone sides down, on grill rack over water pan. Cover; smoke for 1½ hours. Add additional coals and water as needed to maintain temperature and moisture during smoking. Add wood chunks as needed. Remove ribs and place on a double thickness of heavy foil. Drizzle with apple juice. Bring foil around ribs to enclose. Return ribs to smoker. Cover and smoke for 1½ hours. Do not add wood. Unwrap ribs, leaving ribs on foil. Brush with half of the Mustard Dipping Sauce. Cover and smoke about 15 minutes more or until ribs are tender. Serve with remaining sauce.

MUSTARD DIPPING SAUCE: In a saucepan mix ¼ cup Dijon-style mustard, ¼ cup honey, ¼ cup apple juice, 1 tablespoon cider vinegar, and ¼ teaspoon salt. Bring to boiling; reduce heat. Simmer, uncovered, about 10 minutes or until thickened, stirring occasionally.

PER 2 RIBS + ¼ CUP SAUCE: 592 cal., 37 g total fat (14 g sat. fat), 143 mg chol., 1,730 mg sodium, 24 g carb., 1 g fiber, 40 g pro. EXCHANGES: ½ Fruit, 1 Other Carb., 5 High-Fat Meat

PREPARING BEEF BACK RIBS STEP-BY-STEP

1. After removing the membrane from the back of the ribs, cut away any separable fat from front and back.

2. Sprinkle the spice rub evenly over the ribs. Using your fingers, rub the spices into the meat to keep it from falling off. Wrapping the meat and chilling it allows the meat to absorb the spicy flavor of the rub.

BEST-LOVED

Smoked Beef Brisket *(photo, page 317)*

PREP: 45 MINUTES **CHILL:** 8 TO 24 HOURS
SMOKE: 8 HOURS **STAND:** 15 MINUTES
MAKES: 10 TO 12 SANDWICHES

- **2 tablespoons paprika**
- **1 tablespoon chili powder**
- **1 teaspoon ground coriander**
- **1 teaspoon ground cumin**
- **1 teaspoon sugar**
- **½ teaspoon curry powder**
- **½ teaspoon dry mustard**
- **½ teaspoon cayenne pepper**
- **½ teaspoon dried thyme, crushed**
- **2 cups bottled barbecue sauce**
- **1 10- to 12-pound fresh beef brisket**
- **8 to 10 mesquite or hickory wood chunks**
- **10 to 12 kaiser rolls or hamburger buns**

1 For rub, in a bowl mix paprika, chili powder, coriander, cumin, sugar, 1 teaspoon *salt,* ½ teaspoon *black pepper,* curry powder, mustard, cayenne, and thyme. Stir 1 tablespoon rub into barbecue sauce; cover and chill. Do not trim fat from brisket. Sprinkle brisket with remaining rub. Wrap in plastic wrap; chill for 8 to 24 hours.

2 In a smoker arrange preheated coals, half of the wood chunks, and water pan according to manufacturer's directions. Pour water into pan. Place brisket, fat side up, on grill rack over water pan. Cover; smoke for 8 to 10 hours or until a fork can easily be inserted into center of meat. Add coals and water as needed to maintain temperature and moisture. Add wood chunks as needed during the first 3 hours. (Too much smoke can give a bitter taste.)

3 Remove brisket from smoker. Cover; let stand for 15 minutes. In a saucepan heat barbecue sauce. To serve, trim away crusty outer layer from brisket. Starting at widest end, cut along the seam of fat running through meat, slicing meat in half horizontally. Trim excess fat. Slice each section across the grain. Serve in rolls with sauce.

PER SANDWICH: 734 cal., 24 g total fat (7 g sat. fat), 194 mg chol., 1,283 mg sodium, 52 g carb., 3 g fiber, 72 g pro.
EXCHANGES: 3½ Starch., 9 Lean Meat, 1½ Fat

BEST-LOVED

Pulled Pork Shoulder

PREP: 15 MINUTES **SMOKE:** 4 HOURS
STAND: 15 MINUTES **MAKES:** 14 TO 18 SANDWICHES

- **1 tablespoon paprika**
- **2 teaspoons chili powder**
- **2 teaspoons ground cumin**
- **2 teaspoons packed brown sugar**
- **1 teaspoon granulated sugar**
- **1 teaspoon cayenne pepper**
- **1 5-pound boneless pork shoulder roast**
- **6 to 8 hickory wood chunks**
- **1 recipe Vinegar Barbecue Sauce**
- **14 to 18 hamburger buns**

1 For rub, in a bowl stir together paprika, 1 tablespoon *black pepper,* 2 teaspoons *salt,* chili powder, cumin, brown sugar, granulated sugar, and cayenne pepper. Sprinkle rub over meat; rub in with your fingers.

2 In a smoker arrange preheated coals, half of the wood chunks, and water pan according to the manufacturer's directions. Pour water into pan. Place meat on the grill rack over water pan. Cover; smoke for 4 to 5 hours or until meat is very tender. Add coals and water as needed to maintain temperature and moisture. Add wood chunks as needed. Do not add wood after first 2 hours of smoking. (Too much smoke can give a bitter taste.)

3 Remove meat from smoker. Cover; let stand for 15 minutes. Cut meat into pieces; using two forks, shred meat (see photos 1 and 2, below). Place pork in a bowl. Add 1½ cups of the Vinegar Barbecue Sauce. Stir until slightly moist, adding additional sauce if necessary. Serve meat in buns with remaining sauce.

VINEGAR BARBECUE SAUCE: In a 1-quart jar mix 3 cups cider vinegar, ⅓ cup sugar, 1 tablespoon dry mustard, 2 to 3 teaspoons crushed red pepper, 2 teaspoons bottled hot pepper sauce, 1½ teaspoons salt, and 1½ teaspoons black pepper. Cover and shake well.

PER SANDWICH: 390 cal., 17 g total fat (6 g sat. fat), 76 mg chol., 875 mg sodium, 29 g carb., 2 g fiber, 26 g pro.
EXCHANGES: 2 Starch, 3 Medium-Fat Meat

SHREDDING PORK STEP-BY-STEP

1. To shred the pork, first use a sharp carving knife to cut the smoked roast into large pieces.

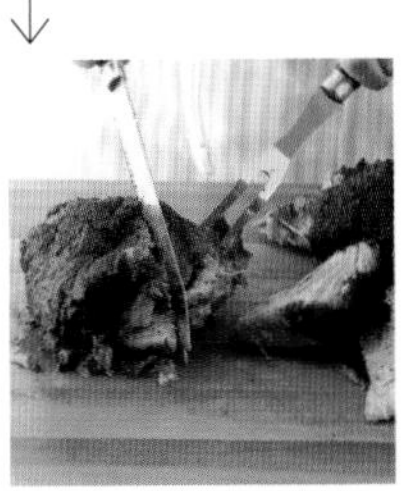

2. Insert two forks into a piece of pork and pull in opposite directions. The meat will easily form shreds that are perfect for a sandwich filling.

BEST-LOVED **LOW-CALORIE**

Jerk-Style Smoked Chicken

PREP: 15 MINUTES **MARINATE:** 1 TO 4 HOURS
SMOKE: 90 MINUTES **MAKES:** 6 SERVINGS

- **3 pounds meaty chicken pieces (breasts, thighs, and drumsticks)**
- **½ cup tomato juice**
- **⅓ cup finely chopped onion (1 small)**
- **2 tablespoons lime juice**
- **1 tablespoon vegetable oil**
- **4 cloves garlic, minced**
- **6 to 8 fruit wood chunks**
- **1 to 2 tablespoons Jamaican jerk seasoning**

1 Place chicken in a resealable plastic bag set in a dish. For marinade, in a bowl combine tomato juice, onion, 2 tablespoons *water,* lime juice, oil, ½ teaspoon *salt,* and garlic. Pour over chicken; seal bag. Marinate in the refrigerator for 1 to 4 hours, turning bag occasionally.

2 In a smoker arrange preheated coals, half of the wood chunks, and water pan according to the manufacturer's directions. Pour water into pan. Place chicken, bone sides down, on the grill rack over water pan. Cover; smoke for 1½ to 2 hours or until chicken is done (170°F for breasts; at least 175°F for thighs and drumsticks). Add coals and water as needed to maintain temperature and moisture. Add wood chunks as needed. Do not add wood after first hour of smoking. (Too much smoke can give a bitter taste.)

PER 2 PIECES: 363 cal., 26 g total fat (7 g sat. fat), 116 mg chol., 507 mg sodium, 3 g carb., 0 g fiber, 29 g pro.
EXCHANGES: 4 Lean Meat, 3 Fat

BEST-LOVED

Maple-Smoked Salmon Fillet

PREP: 15 MINUTES **MARINATE:** 60 MINUTES
SMOKE: 50 MINUTES **MAKES:** 4 SERVINGS

- **1 2-pound fresh or frozen salmon fillet (with skin), about 1 inch thick**
- **½ cup pure maple syrup**
- **1 tablespoon coarsely cracked mixed peppercorns**
- **6 to 8 alder or apple wood chunks**
- **2 tablespoons pure maple syrup**

1 Thaw salmon if frozen. Rinse fish; pat dry. Place fish in a resealable plastic bag set in a baking dish. For marinade, in a bowl mix the ½ cup maple syrup, 2 tablespoons *water,* peppercorns, and ¼ teaspoon *salt;* pour over fish; seal bag. Marinate in the refrigerator for 60 minutes, turning occasionally.

2 Drain fish, discarding marinade. Lightly sprinkle fish with additional salt.

3 In a smoker arrange preheated coals, wood chunks, and water pan according to the manufacturer's directions. Pour water into pan. Place fish, skin side down, on grill rack over water pan. Cover and smoke for 45 to 60 minutes or until fish begins to flake when tested with a fork. Brush fish with the 2 tablespoons maple syrup. Cover and smoke for 5 minutes more. To serve, cut salmon into four pieces, cutting to but not through the skin. Carefully slip a metal spatula between fish and skin, lifting fish away from skin.

PER ¼ FILLET: 516 cal., 30 g fat (7 g sat. fat), 123 mg chol., 310 mg sodium, 12 g carb., 0 g fiber, 46 g pro.
EXCHANGES: 1 Other Carb., 6½ Lean Meat, 2 Fat.

DIRECT-GRILLING POULTRY

If desired, remove skin from poultry. For a charcoal grill, place poultry on grill rack, bone side(s) up, directly over medium coals (see page 320). Grill, uncovered, for time given below or until the proper temperature is reached and done, turning once halfway through grilling. (For a gas grill, preheat grill. Reduce heat to medium. Place poultry on grill rack, bone side(s) down, over heat. Cover and grill as directed.) Test for doneness using a meat thermometer (use an instant-read thermometer to test small portions).

Type of Bird	Weight	Grilling Temperature	Approximate Direct-Grilling Time*	Doneness
CHICKEN				
Skinless, boneless breast halves	6 to 8 ounces	Medium	15 to 18 minutes	165°F
Skinless, boneless thighs	4 to 5 ounces	Medium	12 to 15 minutes	170°F
TURKEY				
Turkey breast tenderloin	8 to 10 ounces (¾ to 1 inch thick)	Medium	16 to 20 minutes	165°F
UNCOOKED GROUND TURKEY OR CHICKEN				
Patties (chicken or turkey	½ inch ¾ inch	Medium Medium	10 to 13 minutes 14 to 18 minutes	165°F 165°F

*All cooking times are based on poultry removed directly from refrigerator.

INDIRECT-GRILLING POULTRY

For a charcoal grill, arrange medium-hot coals around a drip pan. Test for medium heat above drip pan (see page 320). Place poultry on grill rack over drip pan (if whole, place breast side up and do not stuff). Cover; grill for the time given below or until poultry is done and proper temperature is reached, adding more charcoal as necessary. Or if desired, place whole birds on a rack in a roasting pan and omit the drip pan. (For a gas grill, preheat grill. Reduce heat to medium. Adjust heat for indirect cooking [see page 319].) Test for doneness using a meat or instant-read thermometer. For whole birds, insert meat thermometer into center of the inside thigh muscle, away from bone (see page 463). Poultry sizes vary; use these times as a general guide.

Type of Bird	Weight	Grilling Temperature	Approximate Indirect-Grilling Time*	Doneness
CHICKEN				
Chicken, broiler-fryer, half	1½ to 1¾ pounds	Medium	1 to 1¼ hours	170°F
Chicken, broiler-fryer, quarters	12 to 14 ounces each	Medium	50 to 60 minutes	175°F
Chicken, whole	2½ to 3 pounds 3½ to 4 pounds 4½ to 5 pounds	Medium Medium Medium	1 to 1¼ hours 1¼ to 1¾ hours 1¾ to 2 hours	170°F 170°F 170°F
Meaty chicken pieces (breast halves, thighs, and drumsticks)	2½ to 3 pounds total	Medium	50 to 60 minutes	170°F (breast halves); 175°F (thighs and drumsticks)
GAME				
Cornish game hen, halved lengthwise	10 to 12 ounces each	Medium	40 to 50 minutes	175°F
Cornish game hen, whole	1¼ to 1½ pounds	Medium	50 to 60 minutes	175°F
Pheasant, quarters	8 to 12 ounces each	Medium	50 to 60 minutes	180°F
Pheasant, whole	2 to 3 pounds	Medium	1 to 1½ hours	180°F
Quail, semiboneless	3 to 4 ounces	Medium	15 to 20 minutes	180°F
Squab	12 to 16 ounces	Medium	45 to 60 minutes	180°F
TURKEY				
Turkey breast, half	2 to 2½ pounds	Medium	1¼ to 2 hours	170°F
Turkey breast, whole	4 to 6 pounds 6 to 8 pounds	Medium Medium	1¾ to 2¼ hours 2½ to 3½ hours	170°F 170°F
Turkey breast tenderloin	8 to 10 ounces (¾ to 1 inch thick)	Medium	25 to 30 minutes	165°F
Turkey breast tenderloin steak (to make ½-inch-thick steaks, cut turkey tenderloin in half horizontally)	4 to 6 ounces	Medium	15 to 18 minutes	165°F
Turkey drumstick	8 to 16 ounces	Medium	¾ to 1¼ hours	175°F
Turkey thigh	1 to 1½ pounds	Medium	50 to 60 minutes	175°F
Turkey, whole	6 to 8 pounds 8 to 12 pounds 12 to 16 pounds	Medium Medium Medium	1¾ to 2¼ hours 2½ to 3½ hours 3 to 4 hours	175°F 175°F 175°F

*All cooking times are based on poultry removed directly from refrigerator.

INDIRECT-GRILLING MEAT

For a charcoal grill, arrange medium-hot coals (see page 320) around a drip pan. Test for medium heat above drip pan, unless chart says otherwise. Place meat, fat side up, on grill rack over drip pan. Cover and grill for the time given below or to desired temperature, adding more charcoal to maintain heat as necessary. (For a gas grill, preheat grill. Reduce heat to medium. Adjust heat for indirect cooking [see page 319].) To test for doneness, insert a meat thermometer (see tip, page 383), using an instant-read thermometer to test small portions. Thermometer should register temperature listed under Final Grilling Temperature. Remove meat from grill. For larger cuts, such as roasts, cover with foil and let stand for 15 minutes before slicing. The meat's temperature will rise during the time it stands. For thinner cuts, such as steaks, cover and let stand 5 minutes.

Cut	Thickness/Weight	Approximate Indirect-Grilling Time*	Final Grilling Temperature
BEEF			
Boneless top sirloin steak	1 inch 1 inch 1½ inches 1½ inches	22 to 26 minutes 26 to 30 minutes 32 to 36 minutes 36 to 40 minutes	145°F medium rare 160°F medium 145°F medium rare 160°F medium
Boneless tri-tip roast (bottom sirloin)	1½ to 2 pounds 1½ to 2 pounds	35 to 40 minutes 40 to 45 minutes	135°F medium rare 150°F medium
Flank steak	1¼ to 1¾ pounds	23 to 28 minutes	160°F medium
Rib roast (chine bone removed) (medium-low heat)	4 to 6 pounds 4 to 6 pounds	2 to 2¾ hours 2½ to 3¼ hours	135°F medium rare 150°F medium
Ribeye roast (medium-low heat)	4 to 6 pounds 4 to 6 pounds	1¼ to 1¾ hours 1½ to 2¼ hours	135°F medium rare 150°F medium
Steak (porterhouse, rib, ribeye, shoulder top blade [flat-iron], T-bone, tenderloin, top loin [strip])	1 inch 1 inch 1½ inches 1½ inches	16 to 20 minutes 20 to 24 minutes 22 to 25 minutes 25 to 28 minutes	145°F medium rare 160°F medium 145°F medium rare 160°F medium
Tenderloin roast (medium-high heat)	2 to 3 pounds 4 to 5 pounds	45 to 60 minutes 1 to 1¼ hours	135°F medium rare 135°F medium rare
GROUND MEAT			
Patties (beef, lamb, pork, or veal)	½ inch ¾ inch	15 to 18 minutes 20 to 24 minutes	160°F medium 160°F medium
LAMB			
Boneless leg roast (medium-low heat)	3 to 4 pounds 3 to 4 pounds 4 to 6 pounds 4 to 6 pounds	1½ to 2¼ hours 1¾ to 2½ hours 1¾ to 2½ hours 2 to 2¾ hours	135°F medium rare 150°F medium 135°F medium rare 150°F medium
Boneless sirloin roast (medium-low heat)	1½ to 2 pounds 1½ to 2 pounds	1 to 1¼ hours 1¼ to 1½ hours	135°F medium rare 150°F medium
Chop (loin or rib)	1 inch 1 inch	16 to 18 minutes 18 to 20 minutes	145°F medium rare 160°F medium
Leg of lamb (with bone) (medium-low heat)	5 to 7 pounds 5 to 7 pounds	1¾ to 2¼ hours 2¼ to 2¾ hours	135°F medium rare 150°F medium

*All cooking times are based on meat removed directly from refrigerator.

Cut	Thickness/Weight	Approximate Indirect-Grilling Time*	Final Grilling Temperature
PORK			
Boneless top loin roast (medium-low heat)	2 to 3 pounds (single loin) 3 to 5 pounds (double loin, tied)	1 to 1½ hours 1½ to 2¼ hours	145°F medium 145°F medium
Chop (boneless top loin)	¾ to 1 inch 1¼ to 1½ inch	20 to 24 minutes 30 to 35 minutes	145°F medium 145°F medium
Chop (loin or rib)	¾ to 1 inch 1¼ to 1½ inch	22 to 25 minutes 30 to 35 minutes	145°F medium 145°F medium
Country-style ribs		1½ to 2 hours	Tender (185°F)
Ham, cooked (boneless) (medium-low heat)	3 to 5 pounds 6 to 8 pounds	1¼ to 2 hours 2 to 2¾ hours	140°F 140°F
Ham steak, cooked (medium-high heat)	1 inch	20 to 24 minutes	140°F
Loin back ribs or spareribs		1½ to 1¾ hours	Tender
Loin center rib roast (backbone loosened) (medium-low heat)	3 to 4 pounds 4 to 6 pounds	1¼ to 2 hours 2 to 2¾ hours	145°F medium 145°F medium
Sausages, uncooked (bratwurst, Polish, or Italian sausage links)	about 4 per pound	20 to 30 minutes	160°F medium
Smoked shoulder picnic (with bone), cooked (medium-low heat)	4 to 6 pounds	1½ to 2¼ hours	140°F (heated through)
Tenderloin (medium-high heat)	¾ to 1 pound	30 to 35 minutes	145°F medium
VEAL			
Chop (loin or rib)	1 inch	19 to 23 minutes	160°F medium

*All cooking times are based on meat removed directly from refrigerator.

DIRECT-GRILLING MEAT

For a charcoal grill, place meat on grill rack directly over medium coals (see page 320). Grill, uncovered, for the time given below or to desired doneness, turning once halfway through grilling. (For a gas grill, preheat grill. Reduce heat to medium. Place meat on grill rack over heat. Cover the grill.) Test for doneness using a meat thermometer. For steaks, cover and let stand for 5 minutes.

Cut	Thickness/ Weight	Grilling Temperature	Approximate Direct-Grilling Time*	Doneness
BEEF				
Boneless steak (top loin [strip], ribeye, shoulder top blade [flat-iron], shoulder petite tenders, shoulder center [ranch], chuck eye, tenderloin)	1 inch 1 inch 1½ inches 1½ inches	Medium Medium Medium Medium	10 to 12 minutes 12 to 15 minutes 15 to 19 minutes 18 to 23 minutes	145°F medium rare 160°F medium 145°F medium rare 160°F medium
Boneless top sirloin steak	1 inch 1 inch 1½ inches 1½ inches	Medium Medium Medium Medium	14 to 18 minutes 18 to 22 minutes 20 to 24 minutes 24 to 28 minutes	145°F medium rare 160°F medium 145°F medium rare 160°F medium
Boneless tri-tip steak (bottom sirloin)	¾ inch ¾ inch 1 inch 1 inch	Medium Medium Medium Medium	9 to 11 minutes 11 to 13 minutes 13 to 15 minutes 15 to 17 minutes	145°F medium rare 160°F medium 145°F medium rare 160°F medium
Flank steak	1¼ to 1¾ pounds	Medium	17 to 21 minutes	160°F medium
Steak with bone (porterhouse, T-bone, rib)	1 inch 1 inch 1½ inches 1½ inches	Medium Medium Medium Medium	10 to 13 minutes 12 to 15 minutes 18 to 21 minutes 22 to 25 minutes	145°F medium rare 160°F medium 145°F medium rare 160°F medium
GROUND MEAT				
Patties (beef, lamb, pork, or veal)	½ inch ¾ inch	Medium Medium	10 to 13 minutes 14 to 18 minutes	160°F medium 160°F medium
LAMB				
Chop (loin or rib)	1 inch 1 inch	Medium Medium	12 to 14 minutes 15 to 17 minutes	145°F medium rare 160°F medium
Chop (sirloin)	¾ to 1 inch	Medium	14 to 17 minutes	160°F medium
MISCELLANEOUS				
Kabobs (beef or lamb)	1-inch cubes	Medium	8 to 12 minutes	160°F medium
Kabobs (veal)	1-inch cubes	Medium	10 to 14 minutes	160°F medium
Kabobs (pork)	1-inch cubes	Medium	10 to 14 minutes	145°F medium
Sausages, cooked (frankfurters, smoked bratwurst, etc.)		Medium	3 to 7 minutes	Heated through
PORK				
Chop (boneless top loin)	¾ to 1 inch 1¼ to 1½ inches	Medium Medium	7 to 9 minutes 14 to 18 minutes	145°F medium 145°F medium
Chop with bone (loin or rib)	¾ to 1 inch 1¼ to 1½ inches	Medium Medium	11 to 13 minutes 16 to 20 minutes	145°F medium 145°F medium
VEAL				
Chop (loin or rib)	1 inch	Medium	12 to 15 minutes	160°F medium

*All cooking times are based on meat removed directly from refrigerator.

DIRECT-GRILLING FISH AND SEAFOOD

Thaw fish or seafood if frozen. Rinse fish or seafood; pat dry. Place fish fillets in a well-greased grill basket. For fish steaks and whole fish, grease the grill rack. Thread scallops or shrimp on skewers, leaving a ¼-inch space between pieces. For a charcoal grill, place fish on the grill rack directly over medium coals (see page 320). Grill, uncovered, for the time given below or until fish begins to flake when tested with a fork (seafood should look opaque), turning once halfway through grilling. (For a gas grill, preheat grill. Reduce heat to medium. Place fish on grill rack over heat. Cover the grill.) If desired, brush with olive oil or melted butter after turning.

Form of Fish	Thickness, Weight, or Size	Grilling Temperature	Approximate Direct-Grilling Time*	Doneness
Dressed whole fish	½ to 1½ pounds	Medium	6 to 9 minutes per 8 ounces	Flakes
Fillets, steaks, cubes (for kabobs)	½ to 1 inch thick	Medium	4 to 6 minutes per ½-inch thickness	Flakes
Lobster tails	6 ounces 8 ounces	Medium Medium	10 to 12 minutes 12 to 15 minutes	Opaque Opaque
Sea scallops (for kabobs)	12 to 15 per pound	Medium	5 to 8 minutes	Opaque
Shrimp (for kabobs)	20 per pound 12 to 15 per pound	Medium Medium	5 to 8 minutes 7 to 9 minutes	Opaque Opaque

*All cooking times are based on fish or seafood removed directly from refrigerator.

INDIRECT-GRILLING FISH AND SEAFOOD

Thaw fish or seafood if frozen. Rinse fish or seafood; pat dry. Place fish fillets in a well-greased grill basket. For fish steaks and whole fish, grease the grill rack. Thread scallops or shrimp on skewers, leaving a ¼-inch space between pieces. For a charcoal grill, arrange medium-hot coals around drip pan. Test for medium heat above the pan (see page 320). Place fish on grill rack over drip pan. Cover and grill for the time given below or until fish begins to flake when tested with a fork (seafood should look opaque), turning once halfway through grilling if desired. (For a gas grill, preheat grill. Reduce heat to medium. Adjust heat for indirect cooking [see page 319].) If desired, brush with olive oil or melted butter halfway through grilling.

Form of Fish	Thickness, Weight, or Size	Grilling Temperature	Approximate Indirect-Grilling Time*	Doneness
Dressed fish	½ to 1½ pounds	Medium	15 to 20 minutes per 8 ounces	Flakes
Fillets, steaks, cubes (for kabobs)	½ to 1 inch thick	Medium	7 to 9 minutes per ½-inch thickness	Flakes
Sea scallops (for kabobs)	12 to 15 per pound	Medium	11 to 14 minutes	Opaque
Shrimp (for kabobs)	20 per pound 12 to 15 per pound	Medium Medium	8 to 10 minutes 9 to 11 minutes	Opaque Opaque

*All cooking times are based on fish or seafood removed directly from refrigerator.

DIRECT-GRILLING VEGETABLES

Before grilling, rinse, trim, cut up, and precook vegetables as directed below under Preparation. To precook vegetables, bring a small amount of water to boiling in a saucepan; add desired vegetable and simmer, covered, for the time specified in the chart; drain well. Generously brush vegetables with olive oil or melted butter before grilling to prevent vegetables from sticking to the grill rack. Place vegetables on a piece of heavy foil or directly on the grill rack. (If putting vegetables directly on grill rack, place them perpendicular to wires of the rack so they won't fall into the coals.) For a charcoal grill, place vegetables on rack directly over medium coals (see page 320). Grill, uncovered, for the time given below or until crisp-tender, turning occasionally. (For a gas grill, preheat grill. Reduce heat to medium. Place vegetables on grill rack directly over heat. Cover the grill.) Monitor the grilling closely so vegetables don't char.

Vegetable	Preparation	Precooking Time	Approximate Direct-Grilling Time
Asparagus	Snap off and discard tough bases of stems.	Do not precook.	7 to 10 minutes
Baby carrots	Cut off carrot tops. Wash and peel carrots.	3 to 5 minutes	3 to 5 minutes
Corn on the cob	Place corn with husks and silks intact in bowl or pan. Cover with water. Soak 1 hour; drain.	Do not precook.	25 to 30 minutes
Eggplant	Cut off top and blossom ends. Cut eggplant crosswise into 1-inch slices.	Do not precook.	8 minutes
Fennel	Snip off feathery leaves. Cut off stems.	10 minutes; then cut into 6 to 8 wedges	8 minutes
Mushrooms, portobello	Remove stems and scrape out gills. Grill; turn halfway through grilling.	Do not precook.	10 to 12 minutes
Onions, white, yellow, or red	Peel and cut into 1-inch crosswise slices. Grill; turn halfway through grilling.	Do not precook.	10 minutes
Potatoes, baking	Scrub potatoes; prick with a fork. Wrap individually in a double thickness of foil.	Do not precook.	1 to 1½ hours
Potatoes, new	Halve potatoes.	10 minutes or until almost tender	10 to 12 minutes
Sweet peppers	Remove stems. Halve peppers lengthwise. Remove seeds and membranes. Cut into 1-inch-wide strips.	Do not precook.	8 to 10 minutes
Tomatoes	Remove cores; cut in half crosswise.	Do not precook.	5 minutes
Zucchini or yellow summer squash	Wash; cut off ends and quarter lengthwise.	Do not precook.	5 to 6 minutes

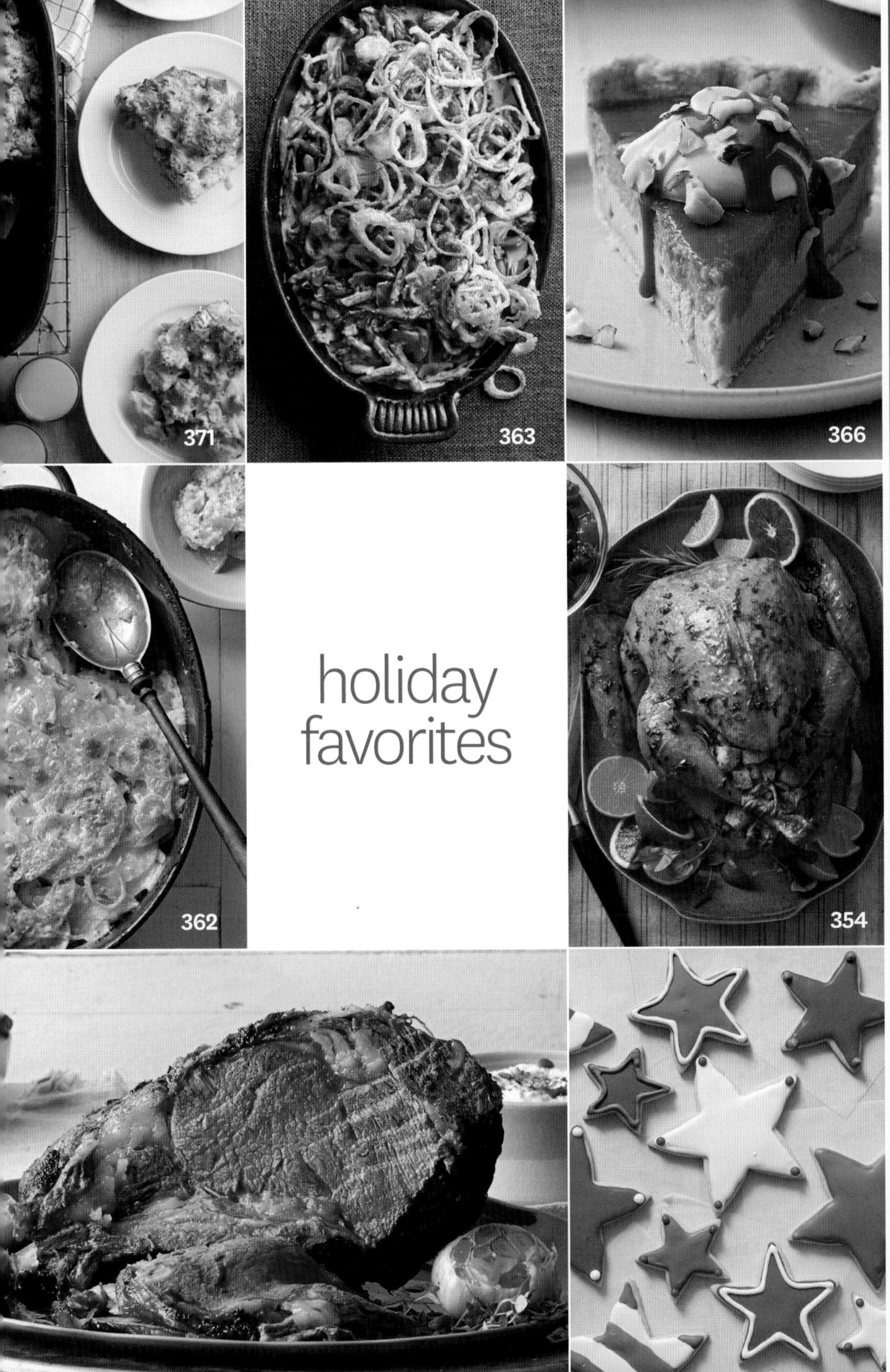

holiday favorites

basics

holiday favorites

Celebrate when feeding friends and family! Choose from show-stopping entrées, upscale sides, fabulous desserts, and delicious brunch dishes.

PLAN, PLAN, PLAN

Planning your holiday meals is half the battle. Stay organized and the big dinner will be as enjoyable for you as it is for your guests.

- Make the list for your menu and grocery shopping. Mix new and interesting recipes with tried-and-true standbys.
- Make sure you have enough. Purchase 1 pound of turkey per person or 4 to 6 ounces of meat per person.
- Plan on making ahead and freezing or storing. Avoid preparing everything the day of the meal.
- Let your appliances work for you. Look in the Slow Cooker chapter, pages 541–558, for some crowd-pleasing sides to take the pressure off any last-minute prep.

BUFFET FOR A CROWD

A thoughtfully set-up buffet helps guests glide through smoothly without having to backtrack.

- Put flatware on the dining table(s); stack plates at the head of the buffet line.
- Place the buffet table so people can go down both sides. Be sure to leave room so guests can set down their plates if they need both hands for serving.
- Put the main course next to the dinner plates. Arrange hot casseroles and side dishes after the main course. Cold sides and salads come next followed by condiments and rolls. You mashed potatoes, but put it at the end of the line for those folks who like to drizzle a little over everything.
- Small plates can be placed next to rolls, relishes, and cold sides so those items don't get soggy or hot from the hot dishes.

LEFTOVERS LOVE

If you are lucky enough to have leftovers, here are a few creative ways to put them to use.

- Add turkey to soup; layer beef in a sandwich with blue cheese, arugula, and whole grain mustard; put ham in egg dishes, mac and cheese, or a salad.
- Substitute stuffing for the veggies and meat in a frittata. Sauté onions in butter; add stuffing and serve it as hash with fried eggs on top.
- Form mashed potatoes into patties, dredge in flour, and fry in butter for crispy cakes. Or top individual servings in ramekins with cheese and bake in a 350°F oven for 15 minutes.
- Add cranberry sauce to a chicken salad or turkey sandwich. Stir it into plain or vanilla yogurt and top with granola or chopped toasted nuts for breakfast or a snack.

Classic Roast Turkey, page 354

cook's secrets

classic roast turkey

The Secret: Covering is the thing! To keep the lean breast meat juicy until the dark-meat thighs are done, tent the turkey breast with foil during the first 2¼ hours. Just as important, use a meat thermometer; don't rely on the pop-up timer that comes in the turkey—it often pops up too late.

TURKEY POINTERS

1. BUTTER IT
Applying butter rub between the meat and skin flavors the meat instead of just the skin. To loosen skin, work your fingers between skin and meat on breast as far as you can. Lift skin to rub butter on as much of meat as you can reach. Pull skin back over breast meat.

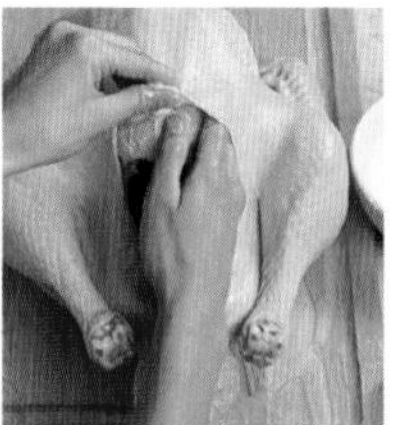

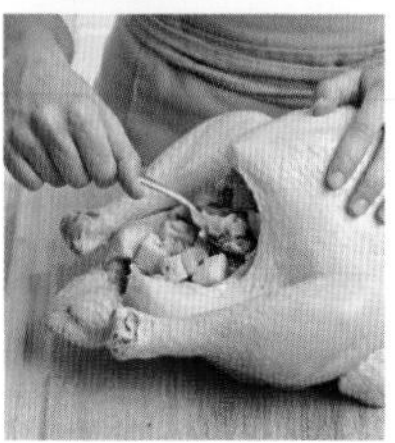

2. STUFF IT
If you choose to stuff the turkey, first pat the cavity dry with paper towels. Spoon the stuffing loosely into the body cavity of the turkey. Do not pack the stuffing in. Allow adequate air circulation so the stuffing cooks evenly and reaches a safe temperature at the same time as the turkey meat. (Bake any extra stuffing in a dish.)

If you purchased a frozen turkey, you will need to leave the turkey in the fridge for 1 day per 3½ pounds of weight to thaw completely. If it is still a little icy, run cold water over and through the cavity of the bird.

BEST-LOVED

PREP: 15 MINUTES **ROAST:** 2 HOURS 45 MINUTES AT 325°F
STAND: 15 MINUTES **MAKES:** 10 SERVINGS

- **1 10- to 12-pound turkey**
- **1 recipe Orange and Herb Butter Rub and Glaze (page 357) (optional)**
- **Salt and black pepper (optional)**
- **1 recipe Old-Fashioned Stuffing (page 365) or Turkey Aromatics (page 356) (optional)**
- **Vegetable oil**
- **1 recipe Perfect Turkey Gravy (page 358)**

1 Preheat oven to 325°F. Remove neck and giblets from turkey; reserve for another use or discard. Rinse turkey body cavity; pat dry with paper towels. Use Orange and Herb Butter Rub and Glaze as directed; sprinkle cavity with salt and pepper. If desired, spoon stuffing or Turkey Aromatics loosely into cavity. Skewer neck skin to back. Tuck drumstick ends under band of skin across tail (if present) or tie drumsticks to the tail using 100% cotton kitchen string. Twist wing tips under back.

2 Place turkey, breast side up, on a rack in a shallow roasting pan (see tip, page 357). Brush with oil; sprinkle with additional salt and pepper. Insert an oven-going meat thermometer into the center of an inside thigh muscle (thermometer should not touch bone). Cover turkey loosely with foil.

3 Roast turkey for 2¼ hours. Remove foil; cut band of skin or string between drumsticks so thighs cook evenly. Roast for 30 to 45 minutes more (60 to 75 minutes if stuffed) or until the meat thermometer registers at least 175°F in the thigh; if stuffed, the center of stuffing must register 165°F. Drumsticks should move easily in their sockets. If desired, during the last 15 minutes of roasting, brush turkey twice with glaze. Remove turkey from oven. Cover with foil; let stand for 15 to 20 minutes before carving. Transfer turkey to a cutting board and carve. If desired, garnish with *fresh fruit* and *herbs*. Serve with Turkey Gravy.

PER 7 OUNCES TURKEY: 517 cal., 24 g total fat (6 g sat. fat), 236 mg chol., 440 mg sodium, 3 g carb., 0 g fiber, 71 g pro. **EXCHANGES:** 10 Lean Meat, 1½ Fat

UNDER COVER

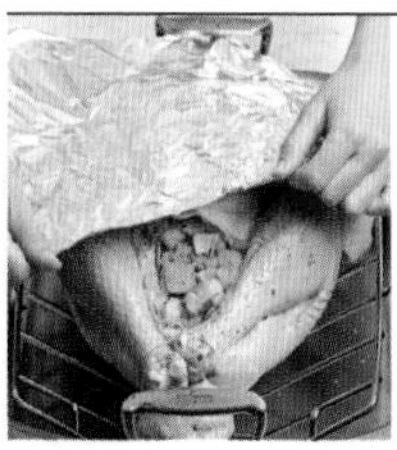

DRY TURKEY HAPPENS FOR THIS REASON: The lean white-meat breast cooks faster than the fattier dark-meat thighs. By the time the thighs are at the right temp, the breast is overcooked. Tenting with foil deflects a good portion of the heat from the breast, so it cooks more evenly with the thighs. To create the tent, form a large piece of foil loosely over the breast to allow for some air circulation.

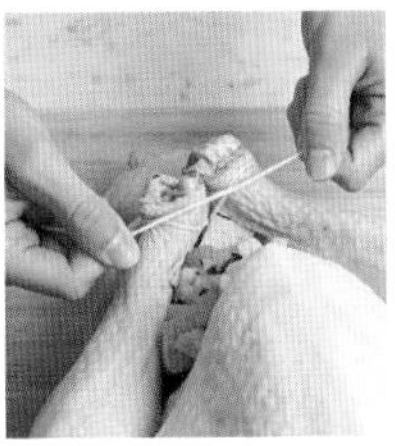

3. TIE IT

Use kitchen string to tie the legs together. If the tail is still on the turkey, secure legs to the tail. Wrap the string around the legs and tail, pull it tight, and tie a knot.

4. TUCK IT

Tuck the wing tips behind the back. Tucking the wings and tying the legs keeps them tight and secure against the body of the turkey, creating a uniform shape. This also helps the turkey roast at an even rate and prevents burning.

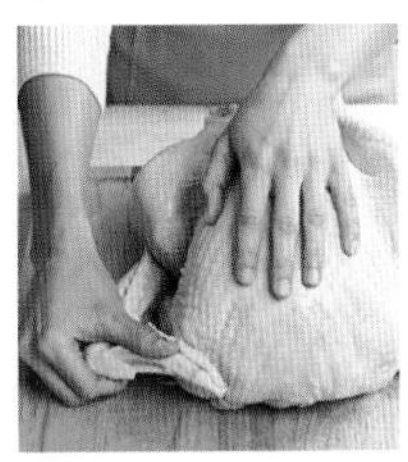

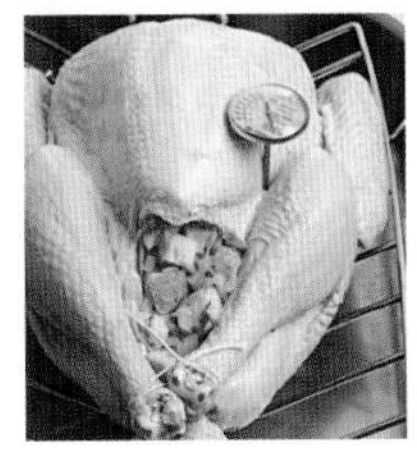

5. CHECK IT

According to the U.S. Department of Agriculture, turkey is safe to eat at 165°F. Our Test Kitchen thought the bird looked and tasted better when roasted to 175°F deep in the thigh muscle. Insert an oven-going meat thermometer into the thigh muscle, making sure the probe does not touch bone.

brine, rub, glazes & aromatics

Let's talk turkey flavoring for the Classic Roast Turkey recipe on page 354. Your options? Pick between a salty, flavorful brine and a buttery herb rub and glaze. With either option, you can fill the turkey cavity with simple aromatics to boost flavor.

FRUITED TURKEY BRINE: In a 16-quart stockpot combine 3 quarts water; 2 quarts apple cider; 1 cup kosher salt; ⅔ cup packed brown sugar; 2 oranges, sliced; 2 bay leaves; 2 tablespoons crystallized ginger; 1 tablespoon whole black peppercorns; and 2 teaspoons whole allspice. Cover; heat over high heat until brine is steaming, stirring occasionally to dissolve salt and brown sugar. Remove from heat. Add 12 cups ice; let stand until ice melts and brine is cool. Remove neck and giblets from turkey; reserve for another use or discard. Rinse the turkey body cavity. Place turkey in stockpot with cooled brine. Weight down turkey with several plates. Cover; chill for 12 to 16 hours. Remove turkey from brine, draining excess brine from cavity; discard brine. Pat turkey dry with paper towels. Continue preparing turkey for roasting as directed in Step 1 on page 354.

A POT TO BRINE IN

Before you start brining, make sure you have a pot that is big enough for the turkey but small enough to fit in your refrigerator. (If the pot isn't large enough, the liquid will overflow when you add the turkey to the brine.) The brine mixture is heated to dissolve the salt and sugar and to release the flavors of the aromatic ingredients. Adding ice helps quickly cool the brine so you can add the turkey. (Raw turkey in hot liquid is a food safety no-no!)

TURKEY AROMATICS

If you aren't stuffing the turkey, you will want to fill the cavity with Turkey Aromatics. These fruits, vegetables, and herbs release a lot of flavor and moisture into the turkey cavity and flavor the meat from within. The aromatics are not eaten, so it is not necessary to remove peels and stems. Once the cavity has been sprinkled with salt and black pepper, insert 1 medium orange, cut into wedges; 1 medium apple, cored and cut into wedges; 1 medium onion, cut into wedges; 1 small bulb garlic, top and bottom cut off to expose cloves; and 3 sprigs fresh sage, thyme, and/or rosemary into the cavity. Continue preparing turkey as directed in Step 1 on page 354. Discard aromatics after roasting.

ORANGE AND HERB BUTTER RUB AND GLAZE: In a bowl combine ½ cup softened butter; 2 teaspoons each snipped fresh sage, snipped fresh rosemary, and snipped fresh thyme; 1 teaspoon finely shredded orange peel; ½ teaspoon kosher salt; and ¼ teaspoon black pepper. Divide mixture in half.

For the butter rub, rub half of the mixture under skin from front to back of turkey (see photo 1, page 354). Continue as directed in Step 1.

For glaze, microwave remaining half of butter mixture on 100% power (high) until melted. Stir in ⅓ cup honey. Use to baste turkey the last 15 minutes of roasting.

Basting the turkey with glaze the last 15 minutes of roasting ensures the glaze won't burn.

CARVING POINTERS

1. CUTTING THE LEG
Pull the leg away from the body of the turkey and cut the joint that attaches the thigh to the body. On the cutting board cut the joint connecting the leg to the thigh. Slice meat from thigh.

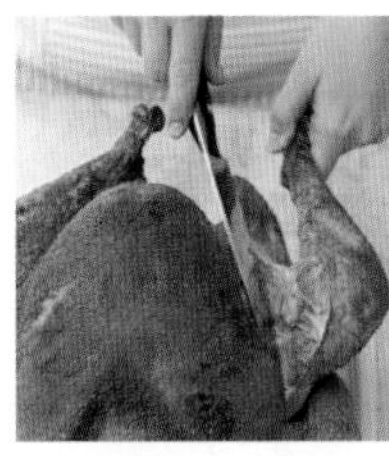

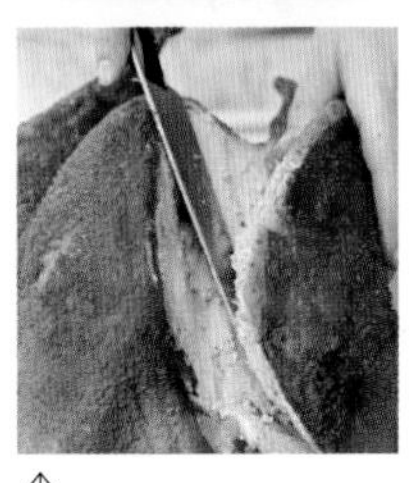

2. CUTTING THE BREAST
Holding a breast half with one hand or a meat fork, gently cut the meat from the bone, following as close to the rib cage bone as possible. Cut each breast half crosswise into slices.

ROAST IT RIGHT

Roasting pans and racks are great for turkeys because they're sturdy and have heavy-duty handles for easy maneuvering. But the price can be a detractor. If you don't have one, use a 13×9×2-inch pan and place vegetables under the turkey instead of a rack. Or purchase a large sturdy foil roasting pan at the grocery store.

Cooking the perfect turkey requires the correct combination of oven temperature and roasting time for the size of your bird. For a complete roasting chart, see page 485.

EASY GLAZES

Warm one of these condiments and brush on the turkey during the last 15 minutes of roasting.

- Orange marmalade
- Maple syrup
- Honey
- Apple jelly

perfect turkey gravy

The Secret: For lump-free gravy, use a roux as the thickener. Sounds fancy, but a roux is a simple mixture of flour and fat that is whisked together before the liquid is added. This prevents the flour from clumping, so the gravy is smooth as silk.

FAST

START TO FINISH: 15 MINUTES **MAKES:** 2 CUPS

- **Reduced-sodium chicken broth**
- **Pan drippings from roasted turkey**
- **Melted butter (optional)**
- 1/4 **cup all-purpose flour**
- **Salt and black pepper**

1 Stir 1 cup chicken broth into pan drippings in roasting pan, scraping up any browned bits from bottom of pan. Pour drippings into a 2-cup glass measuring cup. Skim and reserve fat from drippings. If necessary, add enough melted butter to the reserved fat to make 1/4 cup. Add enough additional broth to the drippings in the measuring cup to make 2 cups total liquid.

2 Pour the 1/4 cup fat into a medium saucepan (discard any remaining fat). Stir in flour with a whisk.

3 Add broth mixture to saucepan all at once, stirring until smooth. Cook and stir over medium heat until thickened and bubbly. Cook and stir 1 minute more. Season to taste with salt and pepper. Strain gravy into a bowl.

PER ABOUT 1/4 CUP: 76 cal., 6 g total fat (2 g sat. fat), 7 mg chol., 211 mg sodium, 3 g carb., 0 g fiber, 1 g pro.
EXCHANGES: 1 Fat

GRAVY POINTERS

1. GET THOSE BITS
The drippings are loaded with flavor—as are the browned bits stuck to the bottom of the pan—so you definitely want these to simmer in your gravy. That's where the rich turkey flavor comes into play. Make sure you scrape the bottom of the pan to loosen those up after adding the broth.

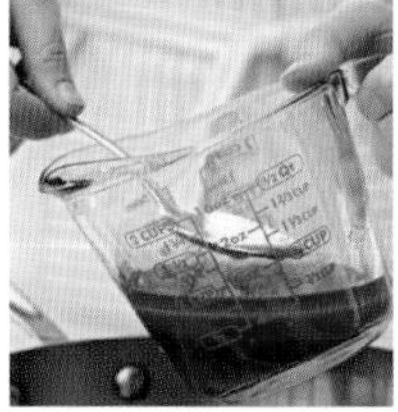

2. SKIM OFF THE FAT
Pour the broth and drippings into a glass measuring cup. The fat in the drippings will rise to the top, making it easy to skim off with a large shallow spoon. To make the roux, you must have equal parts flour and fat, so if the turkey didn't yield enough fat, add melted butter to get the right amount. If you skimp on the fat, you'll end up with a clumpy mess instead of a smooth roux. (Plus, butter adds richness and flavor!)

3. WHISKED AWAY
A whisk (versus a wooden spoon) works best for breaking up flour clumps so the flour and fat can be thoroughly combined. You want all the starch particles to be well coated with fat to prevent the flour molecules from sticking together once the broth is added (which would result in lumps). Continually whisk the roux while slowly adding 2 cups broth mixture. Once everything is added, heat the mixture until it's bubbly to cook out the raw flour taste and thicken the gravy.

GRAVY FOR EVERYONE

If 2 cups of gravy isn't enough, the recipe is easy to double. Use drippings as directed in Step 1 and add enough broth to make 4 cups total liquid. If there isn't 1/2 cup fat from the drippings, add melted butter. Stir 1/2 cup flour into fat in Step 2; continue as directed.

LOW-CALORIE

Stuffed Pork Loin

PREP: 55 MINUTES **ROAST:** 60 MINUTES AT 350°F
STAND: 10 MINUTES **MAKES:** 8 SERVINGS

- **1 recipe Spinach and Apricot Stuffing**
- **1 3-pound boneless pork top loin roast (single loin)**
- **1 teaspoon snipped fresh thyme or 1/4 teaspoon dried thyme, crushed**
- **1/4 teaspoon salt**
- **1/4 teaspoon ground black pepper**
- **1 cup water**
- **1/3 cup cold water**
- **2 tablespoons all-purpose flour**
- **Cracked black pepper (optional)**
- **Snipped fresh thyme sprigs (optional)**

1 Prepare Spinach and Apricot Stuffing; set aside. Trim fat from pork. Butterfly the meat by making a lengthwise cut down the center of the meat, cutting to within 1/2 inch of the other side; spread open (see photo 1, below). Place knife in the V and cut horizontally and away from the center cut to within 1/2 inch of the other side of the meat. Repeat on opposite side (see photos 2 and 3, below). Spread meat open. Cover roast with plastic wrap. Working from center (thicker part) to edges, pound with the flat side of a meat mallet until meat is an even thickness of 1/2 to 3/4 inch (see photo 4, below). Remove plastic wrap.

2 Preheat oven to 350°F. Spread stuffing evenly over meat. Roll meat into a spiral, starting from a short side (see photo 5, below). Tie roast in three or four places with heavy 100% cotton kitchen string. Place roast on a rack in a shallow roasting pan. Sprinkle with thyme, salt, and pepper. Insert an oven-going meat thermometer into center of roast. Roast, uncovered, for 60 to 90 minutes or until thermometer registers 145°F, covering ends of meat after 45 minutes to prevent stuffing from drying out. Transfer roast to a platter. Cover loosely with foil; let stand while preparing gravy.

3 For pan gravy, add the 1 cup water to roasting pan, using a wire whisk to stir and scrape up browned bits. In a small saucepan whisk together the 1/3 cup cold water and the flour. Whisk in pan juices. Cook and stir over medium heat until thickened and bubbly. Cook and stir for 1 minute more. Season to taste with additional salt and ground black pepper. If desired, sprinkle with cracked black pepper.

4 Remove string from pork roast; discard. Slice roast; serve with gravy. If desired, garnish slices with snipped fresh thyme sprigs.

SPINACH AND APRICOT STUFFING: In a large pot cook 12 cups loosely packed fresh spinach in boiling water for 1 minute. Drain well, squeezing out excess liquid. Pat dry with paper towels. Using kitchen shears, coarsely snip spinach; set aside. In a large skillet cook 1/2 cup finely chopped shallots or onion and 2 cloves garlic, minced, in 1 tablespoon hot olive oil about 3 minutes or until shallots are tender. Remove from heat. Cool for 5 minutes. Stir in spinach, 2 ounces chopped prosciutto, 1/2 cup snipped dried apricots, 1/3 cup chopped toasted pecans, and 1/2 cup shredded Gruyère cheese or Swiss cheese (2 ounces).

PER SERVING: 363 cal., 15 g total fat (4 g sat. fat), 123 mg chol., 372 mg sodium, 11 g carb., 3 g fiber, 45 g pro.
EXCHANGES: 1/2 Vegetable, 1/2 Fruit, 6 Lean Meat, 1 1/2 Fat

BUTTERFLYING AND STUFFING PORK ROAST STEP-BY-STEP

1. Make a lengthwise cut down the center of the roast. Stop when you are 1/2 inch from cutting all the way through.

2. Place the knife in the V you just made and lay it on its side. Cut horizontally into the meat, away from the center, so meat is about 1/2 inch thick.

3. Repeat cutting on the opposite side of the V, cutting the meat as evenly as you can.

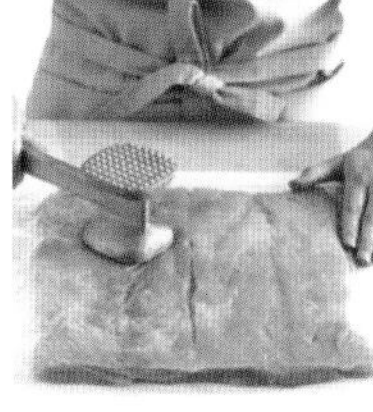

4. Spread the roast out so it is flat; cover with plastic wrap. Pound the meat until it is an even thickness of 1/2 to 3/4 inch thick.

5. Spread the stuffing evenly on the meat. Roll it into a spiral, tucking in any stuffing that falls out.

Holiday Ham

PREP: 15 MINUTES **BAKE:** 95 MINUTES AT 325°F
MAKES: 20 SERVINGS

- **1 6- to 8-pound cooked ham, rump half**
- **1 recipe Pomegranate BBQ Glaze or Cranberry-Orange Glaze**

1 Preheat oven to 325°F. Score ham by making shallow diagonal cuts in a diamond pattern at 1-inch intervals (see photo 1, below). Place ham on a rack in a shallow roasting pan. Insert an oven-going meat thermometer into center of ham (thermometer should not touch bone). Cover with foil.

2 Bake for 75 minutes. Uncover; bake for 20 to 60 minutes more or until thermometer registers 140°F. Meanwhile, prepare desired glaze. Brush ham with some of the glaze the last 20 minutes of baking. Carve ham (see photos 2–4, below). If desired, garnish with sliced *citrus fruit* and *fresh herbs*. Serve with remaining glaze.

POMEGRANATE BBQ GLAZE: In a medium saucepan cook ½ cup finely chopped onion (1 medium) and 2 cloves garlic, minced, in 1 tablespoon hot oil over medium heat about 2 minutes or until onion is tender. Stir in ¾ cup bottled chili sauce, ½ cup pomegranate juice, ¼ cup honey, 1 tablespoon white or regular balsamic vinegar, ½ teaspoon dry mustard, and ¼ teaspoon black pepper. Bring to boiling; reduce heat. Simmer, uncovered, about 20 minutes or until glazing consistency.

PER 3 OUNCES HAM + ABOUT 1 TABLESPOON GLAZE: 251 cal., 15 g total fat (5 g sat. fat), 72 mg chol., 1,015 mg sodium, 8 g carb., 0 g fiber, 21 g pro. EXCHANGES: ½ Starch, 3 Lean Meat, 2 Fat

CRANBERRY-ORANGE GLAZE: In a small saucepan combine 1 cup cranberry relish or orange-cranberry marmalade, ¼ cup orange juice, and 1 teaspoon snipped fresh thyme or sage. Bring to boiling; reduce heat. Simmer, uncovered, for 5 to 10 minutes or until thickened to glazing consistency.

PER 3 OUNCES HAM + ABOUT 1 TABLESPOON GLAZE: 241 cal., 14 g total fat (5 g sat. fat), 72 mg chol., 905 mg sodium, 7 g carb., 0 g fiber, 2 g pro. EXCHANGES: ½ Starch, 3 Lean Meat, 2 Fat

Standing Rib Roast *(photo, page 351)*

PREP: 10 MINUTES **ROAST:** 105 MINUTES AT 350°F
STAND: 15 MINUTES **MAKES:** 8 SERVINGS

- **1 4- to 6-pound beef rib roast**
- **Kosher salt and freshly ground black pepper**
- **2 to 3 cloves garlic, slivered**
- **1 recipe Oven-Browned Potatoes or Yorkshire Pudding (page 361) (optional)**
- **1 recipe Horseradish Sauce (page 537) (optional)**

1 Preheat oven to 350°F. Sprinkle meat with salt and pepper. Cut shallow slits all over meat and insert garlic slivers into slits. Place meat, fat side up, in a 15½×10½×2-inch roasting pan. Insert an oven-going meat thermometer into center of roast (thermometer should not touch bone).

2 Roast, uncovered, for 1¾ to 2¼ hours or until meat thermometer registers 135°F for medium-rare. (For medium, roast for 2¼ to 2¾ hours or until meat thermometer registers 150°F.) Add Oven-Browned Potatoes (if using)

SCORING AND CARVING HAM STEP-BY-STEP

1. Using a sharp knife, score the rind of the ham by making shallow diagonal cuts 1 inch apart and about ¼ inch deep. Score all sides of the rind.

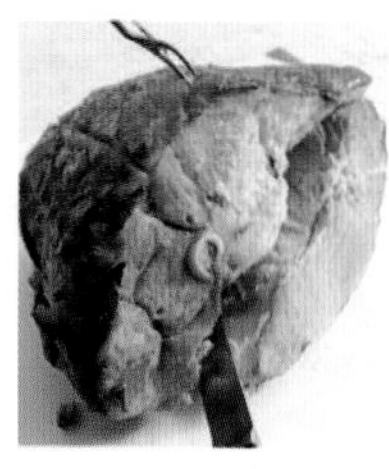

2. Using a long knife, make a horizontal cut just next to the leg bone. Cut straight through to remove the meaty portion.

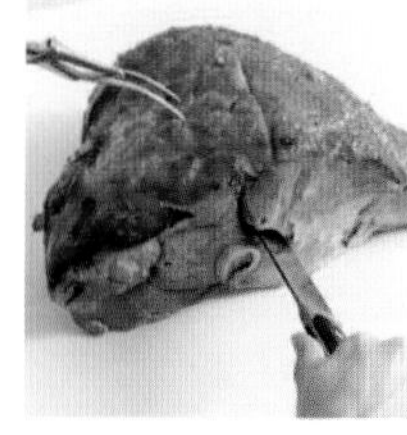

3. Place the cut side flat on the cutting board. Carve down perpendicular to the cutting board on the right side of the round bone.

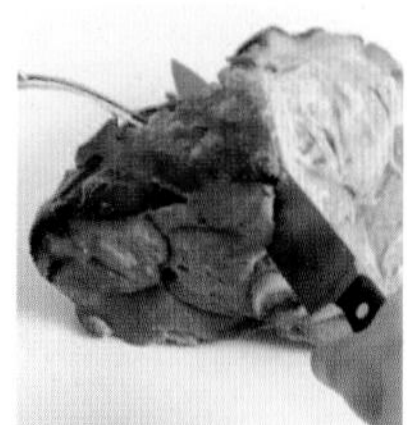

4. Cut the bone away from the remaining piece of meat. Slice the meaty pieces across the grain and arrange slices on a serving platter.

as directed. Cover with foil; let stand for 15 minutes.

3 While roast stands, prepare Yorkshire Pudding (if using). Slice meat. Serve with potatoes, pudding, and, if desired, Horseradish Sauce.

PER 7 OUNCES BEEF: 541 cal., 40 g fat (16 g sat. fat), 169 mg chol., 211 mg sodium, 0 g carb., 0 g fiber, 41 g pro. EXCHANGES: 6 High-Fat Meat

OVEN-BROWNED POTATOES: Halve or quarter 3 pounds assorted small potatoes (tiny new, fingerling, yellow). Cook potatoes and 1 large onion, cut into thin wedges, in boiling salted water for 10 minutes; drain. Toss hot potatoes and onion with 2 tablespoons olive oil and ½ teaspoon kosher salt. About 30 to 40 minutes before roast is done (the roast temperature should be about 100°F), arrange potatoes and onion around roast.

PER 1 CUP: 113 cal., 2 g total fat (0 g sat. fat), 0 mg chol., 136 mg sodium, 21 g carb., 3 g fiber, 2 g pro. EXCHANGES: 1½ Starch

YORKSHIRE PUDDING: After removing meat from the oven, increase oven temperature to 450°F. Measure pan drippings. If necessary, add enough vegetable oil to drippings to equal ¼ cup; return to pan. In a large mixing bowl combine 4 eggs and 2 cups milk. Add 2 cups all-purpose flour and ½ teaspoon salt. Beat with an electric mixer or whisk until smooth. Stir into drippings in roasting pan. Bake, uncovered, for 20 to 25 minutes or until puffy and golden. Cut into eight squares. Serve immediately.

PER SQUARE: 160 cal., 7 g total fat (2 g sat. fat), 74 mg chol., 137 mg sodium, 18 g carb., 1 g fiber, 6 g pro. EXCHANGES: 1 Starch, 1½ Fat

LOW-CALORIE

Oven-Roasted Beef Tenderloin

PREP: 30 MINUTES **ROAST:** 35 MINUTES AT 425°F
STAND: 15 MINUTES **MAKES:** 12 SERVINGS

- **1 tablespoon olive oil**
- **1 3-pound beef tenderloin roast, trimmed**
- **1½ teaspoons kosher salt**
- **1 teaspoon ground black pepper**
- **1 recipe Soy-Ginger Dipping Sauce, Peppercorn-Horseradish Sauce, or Mediterranean Dipping Sauce**
- **Fresh parsley sprigs (optional)**

1 Preheat oven to 425°F. Brush the olive oil over meat. For rub, in a small bowl stir together salt and pepper. Sprinkle mixture evenly over meat; rub in with your fingers.

2 Place roast on a rack set in a shallow roasting pan. Insert an oven-going meat thermometer into center of roast. Roast, uncovered, for 35 to 40 minutes or until meat thermometer registers 135°F for medium rare. (For medium, roast for 45 to 50 minutes or until meat thermometer registers 150°F.)

3 Transfer meat to a cutting board. Cover roast with foil; let stand for 15 minutes. Slice meat across the grain and arrange on a serving platter. Serve with sauce(s). If desired, garnish with fresh parsley sprigs.

SOY-GINGER DIPPING SAUCE: In a small bowl whisk together ½ cup reduced-sodium soy sauce; ¼ cup lime juice; 2 tablespoons thinly sliced green onion (1); 2 teaspoons grated fresh ginger; 2 teaspoons Asian sweet chili sauce; and 2 cloves garlic, minced. Gradually whisk in 2 tablespoons toasted sesame oil and 1 tablespoon canola oil.

PER 3 OUNCES MEAT + ABOUT 4 TEASPOONS SAUCE: 306 cal., 22 g total fat (7 g sat. fat), 91 mg chol, 668 mg sodium, 3 g carb., 0 g fiber, 23 g pro. EXCHANGES: 3 Medium-Fat Meat, 1½ Fat

PEPPERCORN-HORSERADISH SAUCE: In a small bowl stir together one 8-ounce carton sour cream, 3 tablespoons prepared horseradish, 1 tablespoon sipped fresh chives, 2 teaspoons white wine vinegar, and 1 teaspoon coarsely ground black peppercorns. Cover and chill at least 1 hour before serving.

PER 3 OUNCES MEAT + 2 TABLESPOONS SAUCE: 300 cal., 22 g total fat (9 g sat. fat), 101 mg chol, 324 mg sodium, 1 g carb., 0 g fiber, 22 g pro. EXCHANGES: 3 Medium-Fat Meat, 1½ Fat

MEDITERRANEAN DIPPING SAUCE: In a small bowl whisk together ¼ cup champagne vinegar or white wine vinegar, ¼ cup finely snipped fresh tarragon, 2 tablespoons finely chopped shallot (1 medium), 2 tablespoons chopped capers, 2 teaspoons Dijon-style mustard, and ½ teaspoon salt. Gradually whisk in ¼ cup olive oil.

PER 3 OUNCES MEAT + 1 TABLESPOON SAUCE: 305 cal., 23 g total fat (8 g sat. fat), 91 mg chol, 450 mg sodium, 1 g carb., 0 g fiber, 22 g pro. EXCHANGES: 3 Medium-Fat Meat, 1½ Fat

A CHEAPER CHOICE

Not feeling flush enough for a beef tenderloin? Try a 4-pound beef top round roast. Roast it in a 350°F oven for 1½ to 1¾ hours or until a meat thermometer registers 135°F for medium rare. Roasting past medium rare is not recommended for this cut because it is a tougher cut and cooking it beyond this doneness causes it to lose its tenderness.

AUTUMN POTATO GRATIN

Autumn Potato Gratin

PREP: 25 MINUTES **BAKE:** 110 MINUTES AT 350°F
STAND: 15 MINUTES **MAKES:** 10 SERVINGS

- **4 medium yellow-flesh potatoes (1½ pounds), thinly sliced (about 5 cups)**
- **1 small butternut squash (1½ pounds), peeled, halved, seeded, and thinly sliced crosswise**
- **½ cup thinly sliced leek (1 large) or green onions (4)**
- **1 tablespoon snipped fresh sage**
- **4 cloves garlic, minced**
- **1 teaspoon salt**
- **½ teaspoon ground nutmeg**
- **¼ teaspoon black pepper**
- **8 ounces Fontina cheese, shredded (2 cups)**
- **1½ cups whipping cream**

1 Preheat oven to 350°F. Grease a 3-quart baking dish or gratin dish. Layer half each of the sliced potatoes, butternut squash, and leek in prepared dish. Sprinkle with half each of the sage, garlic, salt, nutmeg, and pepper. Sprinkle with half of the cheese. Repeat layers. Pour whipping cream over top. Cover tightly with foil.

2 Bake, covered, for 80 minutes. Uncover; bake about 30 minutes more or until potatoes are tender when pierced with a fork and top is golden brown. Let stand for 15 minutes.

PER ABOUT ⅔ CUP: 279 cal., 21 g total fat (13 g sat. fat), 76 mg chol., 439 mg sodium, 17 g carb., 3 g fiber, 8 g pro.
EXCHANGES: 1 Starch, 1 Medium-Fat Meat, 3 Fat

Marshmallow Sweet Potato Casserole with Parsnips and Carrots

PREP: 20 MINUTES **COOK:** 15 MINUTES
BAKE: 15 MINUTES AT 400°F **MAKES:** 12 SERVINGS

- **2 pounds sweet potatoes, peeled and cut into 1-inch pieces (about 3 medium)**
- **1 pound parsnips, peeled and cut into 1-inch pieces (about 6 medium)**
- **1 pound carrots, peeled and cut into 1-inch pieces (about 6 medium)**
- **¾ cup whipping cream**
- **2 tablespoons butter, cut up**
- **2 tablespoons maple syrup**
- **1 tablespoon finely shredded lemon peel**
- **½ teaspoon salt**
- **1 13-ounce jar marshmallow crème**

1 In a 5- to 6-quart Dutch oven cook sweet potatoes, parsnips, and carrots, covered, in enough boiling salted water to cover for 15 to 20 minutes or until tender; drain. Return potato mixture to Dutch oven.

2 Meanwhile, preheat oven to 400°F. Mash potato mixture with a potato masher or an electric mixer on low speed until smooth. Gradually add whipping cream, butter, maple syrup, lemon peel, and salt, beating to make potato mixture light and fluffy. Transfer to a 2-quart square baking dish.

3 Spoon small spoonfuls of marshmallow crème onto potato mixture; spread evenly to cover surface. Bake for 15 to 20 minutes or until marshmallow crème is puffed and light brown.

PER ⅔ CUP: 257 cal., 8 g total fat (5 g sat. fat), 26 mg chol., 176 mg sodium, 49 g carb., 4 g fiber, 2 g pro.
EXCHANGES: 1½ Vegetable, ½ Starch, 2 Other Carb., 1½ Fat

EASY SPOONING & SPREADING

Using marshmallow crème instead of tiny marshmallows on this casserole ensures that every bite includes a toasted cloud of sweetness. To make it easier to spoon and spread the marshmallow crème over the casserole, spray the spoon and spatula you use with nonstick cooking spray. Or you can heat them under hot water and dry them off before spooning and spreading.

Homemade Green Bean Casserole

PREP: 40 MINUTES **BAKE:** 25 MINUTES AT 375°F
STAND: 10 MINUTES **MAKES:** 8 SERVINGS

- **1½ pounds haricots verts or thin green beans, trimmed and cut into 2-inch lengths**
- **4 ounces pancetta or bacon**
- **9 cups sliced stemmed shiitake mushrooms and/or sliced cremini or button mushrooms (1½ pounds)**
- **6 cloves garlic, minced**
- **½ teaspoon dried thyme, crushed**
- **½ teaspoon salt**
- **½ teaspoon black pepper**
- **2 tablespoons butter**
- **2 tablespoons all-purpose flour**
- **1½ cups half-and-half or light cream**
- **1 5.2-ounce package semisoft cheese with garlic and fines herbs, broken into pieces**
- **⅛ teaspoon salt**
- **⅛ teaspoon black pepper**
- **¼ cup dry white wine**
- **1 recipe Crispy Shallots or 1 cup canned french-fried onions**

1 Preheat oven to 375°F. Grease a 2½- to 3-quart gratin or baking dish; set aside. In a large skillet cook beans in enough lightly salted boiling water to cover for 3 to 5 minutes or until crisp-tender; drain. Transfer beans to a large bowl of ice water (see photo, below); drain.

2 In the same skillet cook pancetta over medium heat until crisp. Using a slotted spoon, transfer pancetta to paper towels to drain, reserving drippings. Finely crumble or chop pancetta; set aside.

3 Meanwhile, add mushrooms, garlic, and thyme to drippings in skillet (if there aren't many drippings, you may need to add up to 1 tablespoon vegetable oil); cook and stir for 5 to 6 minutes or until mushrooms are tender and liquid has evaporated. Stir in pancetta, the ½ teaspoon salt, and the ½ teaspoon pepper. Add mushroom mixture to beans, tossing gently to combine.

4 For sauce, in a small saucepan melt butter over medium heat. Stir in flour; cook and stir for 1 minute. Add half-and-half all at once. Cook and stir over medium heat until thickened and bubbly. Whisk in the cheese, the ⅛ teaspoon salt, and the ⅛ teaspoon pepper. Remove from heat; stir in wine. Pour sauce over green bean mixture, stirring gently just until combined. Transfer green bean mixture to the prepared baking dish.

5 Bake for 25 to 30 minutes or until bubbly and beans are tender. Top with the french-fried onions (if using) during the last 5 minutes of baking. Let stand for 10 minutes. Sprinkle with Crispy Shallots (if using).

CRISPY SHALLOTS: If desired, preheat oven to 375°F. In a small saucepan heat ¾ cup vegetable oil over medium-high heat. Thinly slice 4 large shallots or 1 large sweet onion (1 cup). Dip a small handful of sliced shallots in ½ cup milk, letting excess drip off. Toss shallots in 1 cup all-purpose flour; shake off excess flour. Place coated shallots in hot oil. Cook about 2 minutes or until golden and slightly crisp. Using a slotted spoon, transfer shallots to paper towels to drain; if desired, sprinkle lightly with salt. Repeat with remaining shallots, milk, and flour. If desired, line a baking sheet with foil; place shallots on prepared baking sheet. Reheat Crispy Shallots in hot oven for 10 minutes before topping casserole.

PER SERVING: 369 cal., 27 g total fat (13 g sat. fat), 49 mg chol., 436 mg sodium, 22 g carb., 4 g fiber, 12 g pro.
EXCHANGES: 2 Vegetable, 1 Starch, ½ High-Fat Meat, 4½ Fat

BLANCHING GREEN BEANS

Partially cooking the green beans and cooling them quickly in ice water (blanching) sets their color so they don't look washed out. It also gives them a jump-start on cooking so they get tender when baking.

BEST-LOVED LOW-CALORIE

Homemade Checkerboard Rolls

PREP: 45 MINUTES **RISE:** 90 MINUTES
STAND: 10 MINUTES **BAKE:** 12 MINUTES AT 400°F
MAKES: 24 ROLLS

- **1 cup milk**
- **¼ cup sugar**
- **¼ cup butter**
- **1 teaspoon salt**
- **1 package active dry yeast**
- **¼ cup warm water (105°F to 115°F)**
- **1 egg, lightly beaten**
- **3½ to 4 cups all-purpose flour**
- **2 tablespoons sesame seeds**
- **2 tablespoons poppy seeds**
- **2 teaspoons dried minced onion and/or dried minced garlic**
- **2 tablespoons yellow cornmeal**
- **2 tablespoons grated Romano or Parmesan cheese**
- **¼ cup butter, melted**

1 In a small saucepan heat and stir milk, sugar, ¼ cup butter, and the salt over medium-low heat just until warm (105°F to 115°F) and butter almost melts. Meanwhile, in a large bowl combine yeast and the warm water; stir to dissolve yeast. Add the milk mixture and egg to yeast mixture. Gradually stir in enough of the flour to make a soft dough.

2 Turn dough out onto a lightly floured surface. Knead in enough of the remaining flour to make a moderately soft dough that is smooth and elastic (3 to 5 minutes total). Shape dough into a ball. Place in a lightly greased bowl, turning once to grease surface of dough. Cover; let rise in a warm place until double in size (about 60 minutes).

3 Grease a 15×10×1-inch baking pan; set aside. Punch dough down; turn out onto a lightly floured surface. Cover and let rest for 10 minutes. Shape dough into 24 balls (see photo 1, below).

4 In a shallow dish combine sesame seeds, poppy seeds, and dried minced onion. In another shallow dish combine cornmeal and Romano cheese. Place ¼ cup melted butter in a third dish. Working quickly, roll dough pieces in butter, then in one of the seasoning mixtures to lightly coat. Coat half of the rolls with one seasoning mixture and the remaining rolls with the other seasoning mixture.* Alternate rolls in the prepared baking pan (see photo 2, below). Cover with lightly greased plastic wrap. Let rise in a warm place for 30 minutes.

5 Preheat oven to 400°F. Bake for 12 to 15 minutes or until golden. Remove from pan. Serve warm.

***NOTE:** To keep the poppy seed topping out of the butter and off the Romano cheese balls, coat all the Romano cheese balls first. Place balls in alternating spots in the pan. Coat the remaining balls with the poppy seed topping, filling in the remaining alternating spots in the pan (see photo 2, below).

PER ROLL: 129 cal., 5 g total fat (3 g sat. fat), 19 mg chol., 145 mg sodium, 18 g carb., 1 g fiber, 3 g pro.
EXCHANGES: 1 Starch, 1 Fat

CHECKERBOARD ROLLS STEP-BY-STEP

1. Divide dough into 24 equal pieces. Shape the pieces into balls by gently pulling edges and tucking them under until the tops are smooth and round.

2. Alternate the spots in the pan where you place the coated dough balls. The result should remind you of a checkerboard.

make it mine

Old-Fashioned Stuffing

Change the character of your stuffing by trying different bread and flavoring combinations.

PREP: 35 MINUTES
BAKE: 35 MINUTES AT 325°F
MAKES: 10 SERVINGS

- 1/2 **cup butter**
- 1 1/2 **cups VEGETABLES**
- **HERB**
- 1/4 **teaspoon black pepper**
- 1/8 **teaspoon salt**
- 8 **cups dry BREAD cubes**
- **MEAT (optional)**
- 1 **cup FRUIT (optional)**
- 1/4 **cup NUTS, toasted and chopped (optional)**
- 1 1/2 **to 2 cups LIQUID**

1 Preheat oven to 325°F. In a large skillet melt butter over medium heat. Add Vegetables; cook until tender but not brown, stirring occasionally. Remove from heat. Stir in Herb, pepper, and salt. Place the Bread cubes and, if desired, Meat, Fruit, and Nuts in an extra-large bowl. Add vegetable mixture. Drizzle with enough Liquid to moisten, tossing lightly to combine. Transfer bread mixture to a 2-quart casserole.*

2 Bake, covered, for 35 to 40 minutes or until heated through.

***NOTE:** Or use bread mixture to stuff a 10- to 12-pound turkey (see Classic Roast Turkey, page 354).

MAKING DRY BREAD CUBES STEP-BY-STEP

1. Slice loaf into 1/2-inch-thick slices; slice crosswise into 1/2-inch-wide strips. Cut the strips into 1/2-inch cubes.

2. Spread bread cubes in a single layer in a shallow pan. Let them sit overnight on the counter or bake in a 300°F oven for 10 to 15 minutes, stirring once or twice.

VEGETABLES *(pick a combination)*

Butternut squash, peeled and cubed
Celery, chopped
Fennel bulb, chopped
Mushrooms, sliced
Onions, chopped
Sweet peppers, chopped
Sweet potatoes, peeled and cubed

HERB *(pick one)*

1 teaspoon poultry seasoning
1 tablespoon snipped fresh sage or 1 teaspoon ground sage

BREAD *(pick one)*

Ciabatta bread
Corn bread
Focaccia bread
Italian bread
Multigrain bread
Sourdough bread
Wheat bread
White bread

MEAT *(pick one)*

1 pound pork, Italian, or chorizo sausage, cooked and drained
Turkey giblets, cooked, drained, and chopped
1 pint shucked oysters, drained, chopped, and cooked with Vegetables

FRUIT *(pick one)*

Apples or pears, cored and chopped
Snipped dried apricots
Dried cherries
Golden raisins

NUTS *(pick one)*

Almonds
Hazelnuts (filberts)
Pecans
Walnuts

LIQUID *(pick one)*

Apple juice or apple cider
Turkey or chicken broth
1 1/2 cups chicken broth + 1/2 cup dry white wine
Water

BEST-LOVED

Dulce de Leche-Hazelnut-Pumpkin Pie

PREP: 40 MINUTES **CHILL:** 30 MINUTES
BAKE: 50 MINUTES AT 350°F **MAKES:** 8 SERVINGS

- **1 recipe Hazelnut Pastry**
- **1 8-ounce package cream cheese, softened**
- **4 tablespoons dulce de leche**
- **1 egg**
- **1¼ cups canned pumpkin**
- **½ cup evaporated milk**
- **2 eggs**
- **⅓ cup sugar**
- **2 tablespoons hazelnut or almond liqueur (optional)**
- **1½ teaspoons pumpkin pie spice**
- **1 recipe Dulce de Leche-Hazelnut Whipped Cream**
- **Chopped hazelnuts (filberts), toasted (optional)**

1 On a floured surface roll Hazelnut Pastry into a 12-inch circle. Ease pastry circle into a 9-inch pie plate without stretching it; set aside.

2 In a small mixing bowl beat cream cheese and 2 tablespoons of the dulce de leche with an electric mixer on medium to high speed for 30 seconds. Add 1 egg; beat on medium speed until smooth. Spread evenly in the pastry-lined plate. Trim pastry to ½ inch beyond outside edge of pie plate. Fold under extra pastry. Crimp edge (see photo, page 441). Cover and chill for 30 minutes.

3 Preheat oven to 350°F. In a medium bowl whisk together pumpkin, evaporated milk, 2 eggs, sugar, the remaining 2 tablespoons dulce de leche, the hazelnut liqueur (if desired), and pumpkin pie spice. Carefully pour pumpkin mixture over cream cheese layer.

4 Cover edge of pie loosely with foil (see page 439). Bake for 25 minutes; remove foil. Bake about 25 minutes more or until filling is set in the center. Cool on a wire rack.

5 To serve, top pie with Dulce de Leche-Hazelnut Whipped Cream. If desired, drizzle with additional warmed dulce de leche and sprinkle with hazelnuts.

HAZELNUT PASTRY: In a medium bowl stir together 1 cup all-purpose flour; ¼ cup finely ground hazelnuts (filberts), almonds, or all-purpose flour; and ¼ teaspoon salt. Using a pastry blender, cut in ⅓ cup shortening until pieces are pea size. Sprinkle 1 tablespoon ice water over part of the flour mixture; toss with a fork. Push moistened pastry to one side of the bowl. Repeat moistening flour mixture, using 1 tablespoon ice water at a time, until all the flour mixture is moistened (4 to 5 tablespoons ice water total). Gather flour mixture into a ball, kneading gently until it holds together.

DULCE DE LECHE-HAZELNUT WHIPPED CREAM: Place 1 tablespoon dulce de leche in a chilled small mixing bowl. If desired, add 2 teaspoons hazelnut or almond liqueur. Beat with the chilled beaters of an electric mixer on medium to high speed until smooth. Add 1 cup whipping cream. Beat on medium speed just until stiff peaks begin to form (tips stand straight).

PER SERVING: 480 cal., 35 g total fat (17 g sat. fat), 150 mg chol., 237 mg sodium, 34 g carb., 2 g fiber, 9 g pro.
EXCHANGES: 1½ Starch, 1 Other Carb., ½ Medium-Fat Meat, 6½ Fat

DULCE DE LECHE

Dulce de leche is Spanish for "sweet milk." It is a thick, caramel-like mixture popular in Latin American cuisine and is made by cooking sugar and milk over low heat until the mixture becomes thick and golden. Look for it in the baking aisle or Mexican food aisle at the supermarket.

Red Velvet Cake

PREP: 50 MINUTES **BAKE:** 35 MINUTES AT 350°F
COOL: 1 HOUR **MAKES:** 16 SERVINGS

- **3 eggs**
- **3/4 cup butter**
- **3 cups all-purpose flour**
- **1 tablespoon unsweetened cocoa powder**
- **3/4 teaspoon salt**
- **2 1/4 cups sugar**
- **1 1-ounce bottle red food coloring (2 tablespoons)**
- **1 1/2 teaspoons vanilla**
- **1 1/2 cups buttermilk or sour milk (see tip, page 19)**
- **1 1/2 teaspoons baking soda**
- **1 1/2 teaspoons vinegar**
- **1 recipe Cooked White Frosting**

1 Allow eggs and butter to stand at room temperature for 30 minutes. Meanwhile, grease and lightly flour two 9×2-inch or three 9×1 1/2-inch round cake pans. Or grease one 13×9×2-inch baking pan. Set pan(s) aside. In a medium bowl stir together flour, cocoa powder, and salt; set aside.

2 Preheat oven to 350°F. In a very large mixing bowl beat butter with an electric mixer on medium to high speed for 30 seconds. Gradually add sugar, about 1/4 cup at time, beating on medium speed until well combined. Scrape sides of bowl; beat on medium speed for 2 minutes more. Add eggs, one at a time, beating well after each addition. Beat in red food coloring and vanilla. Alternately add flour mixture and buttermilk, beating on low speed after each addition just until combined. In a small bowl combine baking soda and vinegar; fold into batter. Spread batter evenly in the prepared pan(s).

3 Bake about 35 minutes for 9×2-inch pans (22 to 25 minutes for 9×1 1/2-inch pans or about 40 minutes for 13×9×2-inch pan) or until a wooden toothpick inserted near the centers comes out clean. Cool cake layers in pans on wire racks for 10 minutes. Remove layers from pans; cool thoroughly on wire racks. (Or place 13×9×2-inch cake in pan on wire rack; cool thoroughly.)

4 Prepare Cooked White Frosting (cut recipe in half for 13×9×2-inch cake). To assemble,* place one 9×2-inch cake layer, bottom side up, on serving platter. Spread with 1 1/2 cups of the frosting. Top with second cake layer, bottom side up. Spread top and sides with the remaining frosting. (If using 13×9×2-inch pan, spread frosting over cake in pan.) Cover cake and store in the refrigerator for up to 3 days. Before serving, let stand at room temperature for 30 to 60 minutes or until frosting is softened.

COOKED WHITE FROSTING: In a medium saucepan whisk together 1 1/2 cups sugar, 1 1/2 cups milk, 1/3 cup all-purpose flour, and a dash salt. Cook and stir over medium heat until thickened and bubbly. Reduce heat; cook and stir for 1 minute more. Remove from heat; stir in 2 teaspoons vanilla. Transfer to a large mixing bowl. Cover and cool completely at room temperature (2 1/2 to 3 hours). Gradually beat in 1 1/2 cups butter, softened, with an electric mixer on medium speed until mixture is well combined and smooth, scraping sides of bowl occasionally. (Frosting may look curdled until all the butter is incorporated.)

***NOTE:** To assemble three cake layers, spread one 9×1 1/2-inch cake layer with 1 cup frosting; add another layer and spread with 1 cup frosting. Add remaining layer and spread top and, if desired, sides with remaining frosting.

PER SERVING: 546 cal., 28 g total fat (17 g sat. fat), 112 mg chol., 467 mg sodium, 70 g carb., 1 g fiber, 6 g pro.
EXCHANGES: 2 Starch, 2 1/2 Carb., 5 1/2 Fat

RED VELVET CUPCAKES: Grease and flour twenty-eight 2 1/2-inch muffin cups or line with paper bake cups. Prepare batter as directed. Fill muffin cups two-thirds full with batter. Bake for 15 to 17 minutes or until a wooden toothpick inserted in centers comes out clean. Continue as directed.

PER CUPCAKE: 312 cal., 16 g total fat (10 g sat. fat), 64 mg chol., 267 mg sodium, 40 g carb., 0 g fiber, 3 g pro.
EXCHANGES: 1 Starch, 1 1/2 Other Carb., 3 Fat

COOKED WHITE FROSTING STEP-BY-STEP

1. To cool mixture completely, pour it from pan into a large mixing bowl. Place a piece of plastic wrap right on the surface so a "skin" doesn't form.

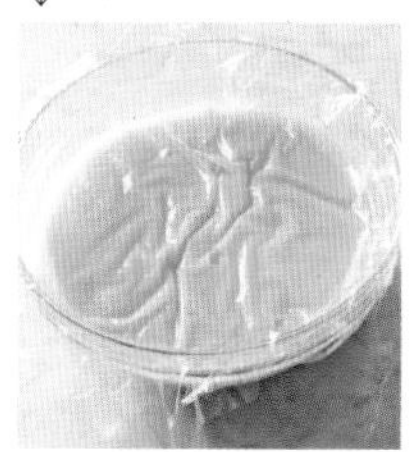

2. You need to add butter a little at a time, so cut room-temperature sticks into 1-tablespoon pieces. Add one piece at a time, beating until each is incorporated before adding more.

8 to try

Cake Pops

Use these flavor ideas to make cakey lollipops from a combo of crumbled cake and creamy frosting.

PREP: 60 MINUTES **FREEZE:** 60 MINUTES
STAND: 30 MINUTES
MAKES: 34 SERVINGS

- **1 package 2-layer-size cake mix**
- **1 to 1½ cups Butter Frosting (page 172)**
- **12 ounces vanilla- or chocolate-flavor candy coating, chopped**
- **12 ounces semisweet, dark, or white baking chocolate, chopped**
- **34 to 36 lollipop sticks**

1 Prepare desired-flavor cake mix according to package directions. Use any suggested pan size; bake according to package directions. Cool in pan on a wire rack. Line trays with waxed paper; set aside.

2 Remove cooled cake from pan and crumble into a very large mixing bowl. Add desired-flavor frosting. Beat with an electric mixer on low speed until combined. Using a small scoop, drop mixture into 1½-inch mounds onto prepared trays. Roll mounds into balls; freeze 30 minutes.

3 In a small microwave-safe bowl heat 1 ounce of the coating (about ¼ cup) on 50% power (medium) for 60 seconds until melted and smooth, stirring once. Dip one end of each lollipop stick into melted coating; poke sticks into balls (this keeps the balls on the sticks). Freeze for 30 to 60 minutes or until pops are firm.

4 Place remaining candy coating and chopped chocolate in a small saucepan. Heat and stir over medium-low heat until melted and smooth. Dip pops in coating mixture. Allow excess to drip off; place pops on clean waxed paper-lined trays.* After coating is set, transfer to storage containers; store in refrigerator. Before serving, let stand at room temperature for 30 minutes.

***NOTE:** For perfectly round pops, poke the lollipop sticks into foam to suspend the pops until coating is set.

CHOCOLATE-COVERED CHERRY: Use chocolate cake mix, Almond Frosting, chocolate-flavor candy coating, and semisweet or dark chocolate. Before freezing in Step 2, form each mound around a drained maraschino cherry.

COOKIES AND CREAM: Use white cake mix, plain Butter Frosting, vanilla-flavor candy coating, and white baking chocolate. Stir 1 cup crushed chocolate sandwich cookies with cream filling into crumbled cake. After dipping, sprinkle with more crushed cookies.

PEANUT BUTTER CUP: Use chocolate cake mix, Peanut Butter Frosting, chocolate-flavor candy coating, and dark chocolate. Stir 1 cup chopped chocolate-covered peanut butter cups into crumbled cake. After dipping, sprinkle with chopped peanuts.

CARROT CAKE: Use carrot cake mix, plain Butter Frosting, vanilla-flavor candy coating, and white baking chocolate. After dipping, sprinkle with finely chopped toasted pecans.

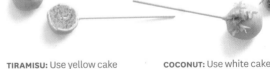

TIRAMISU: Use yellow cake mix, Coffee Frosting, vanilla-flavor candy coating, and white baking chocolate. After dipping pops, top each with a chocolate-covered espresso bean.

COCONUT: Use white cake mix, plain Butter Frosting, vanilla-flavor candy coating, and white baking chocolate. Stir 1 cup toasted flaked coconut into crumbled cake. After dipping, sprinkle with additional toasted coconut.

ULTIMATE CHOCOLATE: Use devil's food cake mix, Dark Chocolate Frosting, chocolate-flavor candy coating, and dark chocolate. After dipping, sprinkle with mini semisweet baking pieces.

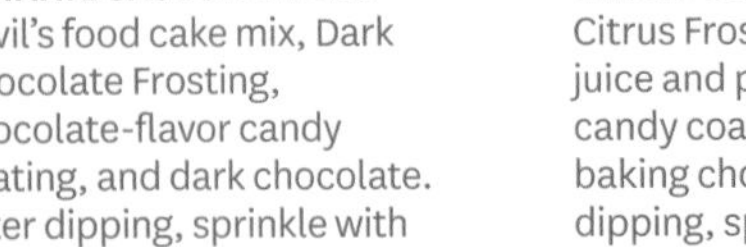

LEMON: Use lemon cake mix, Citrus Frosting (with lemon juice and peel), vanilla-flavor candy coating, and white baking chocolate. After dipping, sprinkle with finely crushed hard lemon candies.

Spritz

PREP: 25 MINUTES **BAKE:** 8 MINUTES AT 375°F
MAKES: 84 COOKIES

- **1½ cups butter, softened**
- **1 cup granulated sugar**
- **1 teaspoon baking powder**
- **1 egg**
- **1 teaspoon vanilla**
- **¼ teaspoon almond extract (optional)**
- **3½ cups all-purpose flour**
- **Colored sugar (optional)**
- **1 recipe Powdered Sugar Icing (page 173) (optional)**

1 Preheat oven to 375°F. In a large mixing bowl beat butter with an electric mixer on medium to high speed for 30 seconds. Add granulated sugar and baking powder. Beat until combined, scraping sides of bowl occasionally. Beat in egg, vanilla, and, if desired, almond extract until combined. Beat in as much of the flour as you can with the mixer. Stir in any remaining flour.

2 Force unchilled dough through a cookie press onto an ungreased cookie sheet. If desired, sprinkle cookies with colored sugar. Bake for 8 to 10 minutes or until edges are firm but not brown. Transfer to a wire rack and let cool. If desired, drizzle cookies with Powdered Sugar Icing.

CHOCOLATE SPRITZ: Prepare as directed, except reduce flour to 3¼ cups and add ¼ cup unsweetened cocoa powder with the sugar.

PEPPERMINT SPRITZ: Prepare as directed, except substitute 1 teaspoon peppermint extract or 14 drops peppermint oil for the vanilla and almond extract. If desired, drizzle cookies with Powdered Sugar Icing and immediately sprinkle with finely crushed striped round peppermint candies.

PER COOKIE PLAIN, CHOCOLATE, OR PEPPERMINT VARIATIONS: 58 cal., 3 g total fat (2 g sat. fat), 11 mg chol., 27 mg sodium, 6 g carb., 0 g fiber, 1 g pro.
EXCHANGES: ½ Starch, ½ Fat

NUTTY SPRITZ: Prepare as directed, except reduce sugar to ⅔ cup and flour to 3¼ cups. After adding flour, stir in 1 cup finely ground toasted almonds or hazelnuts (filberts).

PER COOKIE: 64 cal., 4 g total fat (2 g sat. fat), 12 mg chol., 29 mg sodium, 6 g carb., 0 g fiber, 1 g pro.
EXCHANGES: ½ Starch, 1 Fat

SUGAR COOKIE CUTOUTS

Sugar Cookie Cutouts

PREP: 40 MINUTES **CHILL:** 30 MINUTES
BAKE: 7 MINUTES AT 375°F **MAKES:** 52 COOKIES

- **1 cup butter, softened**
- **1¼ cups sugar**
- **1½ teaspoons baking powder**
- **2 eggs**
- **2 teaspoons vanilla**
- **3 cups all-purpose flour**
- **1 recipe Royal Icing (page 370) (optional)**

1 In a large mixing bowl beat butter on medium to high speed for 30 seconds. Add sugar, baking powder, and ½ teaspoon *salt*. Beat until combined, scraping sides of bowl occasionally. Beat in eggs and vanilla until combined. Beat in as much of the flour as you can with the mixer. Stir in any remaining flour. Divide dough in half. Cover and chill dough 30 minutes or until easy to handle.

2 Preheat oven to 375°F. On a floured surface roll half the dough at a time to ⅛- to ¼-inch thickness. Using a 2½-inch cookie cutter, cut into desired shapes. Place 1 inch apart on ungreased cookie sheets.

3 Bake about 7 minutes or until edges are firm and bottoms are very light brown. Transfer cookies to wire racks and let cool. If desired, frost with Royal Icing.

PER COOKIE: 80 cal., 4 g total fat (2 g sat. fat), 17 mg chol., 63 mg sodium, 10 g carb., 0 g fiber, 1 g pro.
EXCHANGES: ½ Other Carb., 1 Fat

Gingerbread Cutouts

PREP: 35 MINUTES **CHILL:** 3 HOURS
BAKE: 5 MINUTES AT 375°F **MAKES:** 36 COOKIES

- **½ cup shortening**
- **½ cup sugar**
- **1 teaspoon baking powder**
- **1 teaspoon ground ginger**
- **½ teaspoon baking soda**
- **½ teaspoon ground cinnamon**
- **½ teaspoon ground cloves**
- **½ cup molasses**
- **1 egg**
- **1 tablespoon vinegar**
- **2½ cups all-purpose flour**
- **1 recipe Royal Icing (right) (optional)**
- **Decorative candies (optional)**

1 In a large mixing bowl beat shortening with an electric mixer on medium to high speed for 30 seconds. Add sugar, baking powder, ginger, baking soda, cinnamon, and cloves. Beat until combined, scraping sides of bowl occasionally. Beat in molasses, egg, and vinegar until combined. Beat in as much of the flour as you can with the mixer. Stir in any remaining flour. Divide dough in half. Cover and chill dough about 3 hours or until easy to handle.

2 Preheat oven to 375°F. Grease a cookie sheet; set aside. On a lightly floured surface roll half of the dough at a time to ⅛ inch thick. Using a 2½-inch cookie cutter, cut into desired shapes. Place 1 inch apart on prepared cookie sheet.

3 Bake for 5 to 6 minutes or until bottoms are light brown. Cool on cookie sheet for 1 minute. Transfer cookies to a wire rack and let cool. If desired, decorate cookies with Royal Icing and decorative candies.

PER COOKIE: 82 cal., 3 g total fat (1 g sat. fat), 6 mg chol., 28 mg sodium, 13 g carb., 0 g fiber, 1 g pro.
EXCHANGES: 1 Other Carb., ½ Fat

GINGERBREAD PEOPLE CUTOUTS: Prepare as directed, except roll dough to ¼ inch thick. Cut with 4½- to 6-inch people-shape cookie cutters. Bake in a 375°F oven for 6 to 8 minutes or until edges are light brown. Makes about 18 cookies.

PER COOKIE: 164 cal., 6 g total fat (1 g sat. fat), 12 mg chol., 56 mg sodium, 26 g carb., 1 g fiber, 2 g pro.
EXCHANGES: 2 Other Carb., 1 Fat

FAST

Royal Icing

START TO FINISH: 15 MINUTES **MAKES:** 48 SERVINGS

- **1 16-ounce package powdered sugar (about 4 cups)**
- **3 tablespoons meringue powder**
- **½ teaspoon cream of tartar**
- **½ cup warm water**
- **1 teaspoon vanilla**
- **Paste food coloring (optional)**

1 In a large mixing bowl stir together powdered sugar, meringue powder, and cream of tartar. Add the ½ cup warm water and the vanilla. Beat with an electric mixer on low speed until combined. Beat on high speed for 7 to 10 minutes or until icing is very stiff. If not using immediately, cover bowl with a damp paper towel; cover tightly with plastic wrap (icing will dry out quickly when exposed to air). Chill for up to 48 hours. Stir before using. Tint as desired with paste food coloring.

PER SERVING: 37 cal., 0 g total fat, 0 mg chol., 0 mg sodium, 9 g carb., 0 g fiber, 0 g pro. EXCHANGES: ½ Other Carb.

FROSTING WITH ROYAL ICING

To apply icing, use a pastry bag fitted with a small round tip (or a resealable plastic bag with a very small hole snipped in a corner). Pipe an outline around cookie edge. Pipe thinned icing inside the outline; spread to edges with a spatula.

ROYAL ICING KNOW-HOW

MERINGUE POWDER: Meringue powder is a mixture of pasteurized egg whites, sugar, and edible gums. It makes Royal Icing dry quickly with a smooth, hard finish. Look for it in the baking aisle of large supermarkets or in the cake decorating department of hobby and crafts stores.
PASTE FOOD COLORING: Paste food coloring creates bright colors and doesn't thin icing like liquid coloring does. Use a clean toothpick to add coloring to icing until it's the desired color.

Goat Cheese, Artichoke, and Smoked Ham Strata *(photo, page 361)*

PREP: 30 MINUTES **STAND:** 20 MINUTES
CHILL: 2 TO 24 HOURS **BAKE:** 60 MINUTES AT 350°F
MAKES: 8 SERVINGS

- **2 cups whole milk**
- **2 tablespoons olive oil**
- **1 1-pound loaf sourdough bread, cut into 1-inch cubes (about 12 cups)**
- **5 eggs**
- **1½ cups half-and-half or light cream**
- **1 tablespoon minced garlic**
- **1½ teaspoons herbes de Provence**
- **¾ teaspoon black pepper**
- **½ teaspoon freshly ground nutmeg**
- **½ teaspoon dried sage, crushed**
- **½ teaspoon dried thyme, crushed**
- **8 ounces goat cheese (chèvre), crumbled**
- **12 ounces smoked ham, chopped**
- **3 6-ounce jars marinated artichoke hearts, drained and halved lengthwise**
- **6 ounces Parmesan cheese, finely shredded (1½ cups)**
- **4 ounces Fontina cheese, shredded (1 cup)**

1 Grease a 3-quart rectangular baking dish; set aside. In a very large bowl combine milk and olive oil. Add bread cubes, stirring to coat. Let stand for 10 minutes.

2 In a large bowl whisk together eggs, half-and-half, garlic, herbes de Provence, pepper, nutmeg, sage, and thyme. Whisk in goat cheese until combined; set aside.

3 Spread half of the bread cube mixture in the bottom of the prepared dish. Top with half each of the ham, artichoke hearts, and cheeses. Repeat layers. Drizzle egg mixture over all. Cover and chill for 2 to 24 hours.

4 Preheat oven to 350°F. Uncover and bake about 60 minutes or until set in the center and edges are browned. Let stand for 10 minutes before serving.

PER SERVING: 674 cal., 37 g fat (19 g sat. fat), 203 mg chol., 2,013 mg sodium, 45 g carb., 2 g fiber, 40 g pro.
EXCHANGES: ½ Vegetable, 3 Starch, 4 High-Fat Meat

BEST-LOVED

Fruit Coffee Cake

PREP: 30 MINUTES **BAKE:** 45 MINUTES AT 350°F
MAKES: 9 SERVINGS

- **2 cups blueberries and/or red raspberries; sliced, peeled apricots or peaches; or chopped, peeled apples**
- **⅓ cup water**
- **⅓ cup sugar**
- **2 tablespoons cornstarch**
- **¼ teaspoon ground cinnamon**
- **1¾ cups all-purpose flour**
- **¾ cup sugar**
- **¾ teaspoon baking powder**
- **¼ teaspoon baking soda**
- **5 tablespoons butter, cut up**
- **1 egg, lightly beaten**
- **¾ cup buttermilk or sour milk (see tip, page 19)**
- **1 teaspoon vanilla**
- **⅓ cup all-purpose flour**
- **⅓ cup sugar**
- **3 tablespoons butter, cut up**

1 For filling, in a medium saucepan combine fruit and water. Bring to boiling; reduce heat. Simmer (do not simmer if using all raspberries), covered, about 5 minutes or until fruit is tender. In a small bowl stir together the ⅓ cup sugar, the cornstarch, and cinnamon; stir into fruit. Cook and stir over medium heat until thickened and bubbly; set filling aside.

2 Preheat oven to 350°F. In a large bowl combine the 1¾ cups flour, the ¾ cup sugar, baking powder, and baking soda. Using a pastry blender, cut in the 5 tablespoons butter until mixture resembles coarse crumbs. Make a well in the center of the flour mixture; set aside.

3 In a medium bowl combine egg, buttermilk, and vanilla. Add egg mixture all at once to flour mixture. Stir just until moistened (batter should be lumpy). Remove 1 cup batter; set aside. Spread the remaining batter into an ungreased 9×9×2-inch or 8×8×2-inch baking pan. Spoon and gently spread filling over batter. Drop reserved 1 cup batter in small mounds onto filling.

4 In a small bowl stir together the ⅓ cup flour and ⅓ cup sugar. Cut in the 3 tablespoons butter until mixture resembles coarse crumbs. Sprinkle over coffee cake. Bake about 45 minutes or until golden. Serve warm.

RHUBARB-STRAWBERRY COFFEE CAKE: Prepare as directed, except substitute 1 cup fresh or frozen cut-up rhubarb and 1 cup frozen unsweetened whole strawberries for the fruit.

LARGER-SIZE FRUIT COFFEE CAKE: Prepare as directed, except double the recipe and use a 13×9×2-inch baking pan. Bake for 45 to 50 minutes.

PER SERVING FRUIT OR RHUBARB-STRAWBERRY VARIATION: 372 cal., 11 g total fat (7 g sat. fat), 49 mg chol., 197 mg sodium, 61 g carb., 2 g fiber, 5 g pro. EXCHANGES: ½ Fruit, 1½ Starch, 1 Other Carb., 2 Fat

GINGER-PEAR SCONES

BEST-LOVED LOW-CALORIE

Ginger-Pear Scones

PREP: 30 MINUTES **BAKE:** 8 MINUTES AT 400°F
MAKES: 32 SCONES

- **2½ cups all-purpose flour**
- **2 tablespoons packed brown sugar**
- **1 tablespoon baking powder**
- **1 tablespoon finely chopped crystallized ginger**
- **½ teaspoon freshly grated nutmeg or ¼ teaspoon ground nutmeg**
- **¼ teaspoon salt**
- **⅓ cup butter, cut up**
- **1 cup finely chopped Bosc pear**
- **2 eggs, lightly beaten**
- **⅔ cup whipping cream**
- **Whipping cream**
- **Freshly grated nutmeg and/or finely chopped crystallized ginger (optional)**
- **1 recipe Spiced Butter**

1 Preheat oven to 400°F. In a large bowl stir together flour, brown sugar, baking powder, 1 tablespoon ginger, ½ teaspoon grated nutmeg, and the salt. Using a pastry blender, cut in butter until mixture resembles coarse crumbs. Stir in pear. Make a well in center of flour mixture; set aside.

2 In a medium bowl combine eggs and the ⅔ cup whipping cream. Add egg mixture all at once to flour mixture. Using a fork, stir just until moistened.

3 Turn dough out onto a lightly floured surface. Knead dough by folding and gently pressing it for 10 to 12 strokes or until dough is nearly smooth. Divide dough in half. Pat or lightly roll each dough half into a 7-inch square. Using a pizza cutter or sharp knife, cut each square into 16 squares.

4 Place scones 2 inches apart on an ungreased baking sheet. Brush with additional whipping cream. If desired, sprinkle with additional grated nutmeg and/or ginger. Bake for 8 to 12 minutes or until golden. Serve warm with Spiced Butter.

SPICED BUTTER: In a small bowl stir together 1 tablespoon sugar, ½ teaspoon finely chopped crystallized ginger, ¼ teaspoon freshly grated nutmeg or ⅛ teaspoon ground nutmeg, and a dash ground cinnamon. Stir in ½ cup butter, softened, until combined. Cover and chill until ready to serve.

MAKE-AHEAD DIRECTIONS: Place cooled scones in a resealable plastic freezer bag; seal. Freeze for up to 2 months. To serve, thaw at room temperature. If desired, preheat oven to 350°F. Place scones on a baking sheet and bake for 5 to 6 minutes or until warm.

PER SCONE: 113 cal., 7 g total fat (5 g sat. fat), 32 mg chol., 102 mg sodium, 10 g carb., 0 g fiber, 2 g pro.
EXCHANGES: ½ Starch, 1½ Fat

BEST-LOVED

Cranberry-Clementine Sangria

PREP: 20 MINUTES **CHILL:** 3 TO 24 HOURS
MAKES: 12 SERVINGS

- **2 cups cranberry juice**
- **1 cup freshly squeezed clementine juice (8 clementines) or orange juice (3 oranges)**
- **2 750-milliliter bottles dry red wine**
- **½ to ⅔ cup sugar**
- **Orange slices, fresh or frozen thawed cranberries, fresh raspberries or halved strawberries, lemon slices, and/or other cut-up fruit**
- **Ice cubes**

1 In a large pitcher or punch bowl stir together cranberry juice and clementine juice. Add wine and sugar, stirring until sugar dissolves. Cover and refrigerate at least 3 hours or up to 24 hours to blend flavors. Before serving, stir in fruit. Serve in glasses over ice.

PER 6 OUNCES: 173 cal., 0 g total fat, 0 mg chol., 6 mg sodium, 20 g carb., 0 g fiber, 0 g pro. EXCHANGES: ½ Fruit, ½ Other Carb., 2 Fat

meat

basics

meat

Meats are the anchor to many satisfying meals. These tips will help you buy and keep meats at their best.

BUYING MEAT

WHAT TO LOOK FOR: When buying beef, veal, pork, and lamb, the meat should have good color and appear moist but not wet. Any cut edges should be even, not ragged. When buying packaged meats, avoid those with tears or with liquid in the bottom of the tray. The meat should feel firm and cold to the touch.

HOW MUCH TO BUY: Count on purchasing 3 to 4 ounces per serving for boneless roasts, steaks, and ground meat. For steaks and roasts with bones, each pound should yield 2 to 3 servings. For bony cuts such as ribs, each pound yields 1 or 2 servings.

GUIDE TO BEEF STEAKS

The names of meat cuts vary among shops and regions. Here is a quick reference.

Standard Name	Other Names You Might See
Flank steak	London broil
Ribeye steak	Delmonico steak
Round tip steak	Top sirloin steak
Shoulder top blade steak	Flat-iron
Tenderloin steak	Filet mignon
Top loin steak	Strip steak, Kansas City steak, New York strip steak
Tri-tip steak	Triangle steak

HANDLING MEAT SAFELY

Cooks should know and follow guidelines for the safe handling of meat and poultry. See pages 26–27.

STORING MEAT

REFRIGERATING TIMELINE: Store meat in the coldest part of the refrigerator as soon as possible after purchase. Use fresh ground and cubed meat within 2 days; use roasts, steaks, and chops within 3 days.

TO FREEZE MEATS: If you do not plan to use meats within the guidelines given above, you should freeze them. If you plan to use the meat within a week, you can freeze it in the transparent film-wrapped supermarket package. For longer storage, overwrap the meat with moistureproof, vaporproof wrap, such as freezer paper or heavy foil, or place it in a food-safe freezer bag. Label and date the package. Freeze the meat quickly and maintain freezer temperature at 0°F or below.

FREEZING TIMELINE: For best quality, freeze uncooked roasts, steaks, and chops no longer than 12 months, uncooked ground meat up to 4 months, and cooked meat up to 3 months.

TO THAW MEAT: Thaw meat in the refrigerator on a plate or in a pan to catch any juices. Never thaw meat on the counter at room temperature.

THE ROASTING PAN DEFINED

To roast meat and poultry, you need a pan specifically designed for roasting—a large, sturdy shallow pan with a rack. The pan's sides should be 2 to 3 inches high. The rack keeps the meat above the juices and allows the heat to circulate below the meat. If you don't have a roasting pan, you can place a wire rack in a 13×9×2-inch baking pan.

Beef and Sweet Potato Pan Roast, page 381

BEEF CUTS AND HOW TO COOK THEM

A surefire way to enjoy beef at its best is to use the cooking method that best suits each cut. The photos on these pages show the cuts that are the most widely available at supermarkets, along with the best recommended ways for cooking them. They correspond to the drawing, which shows where the cuts come from on the animal.

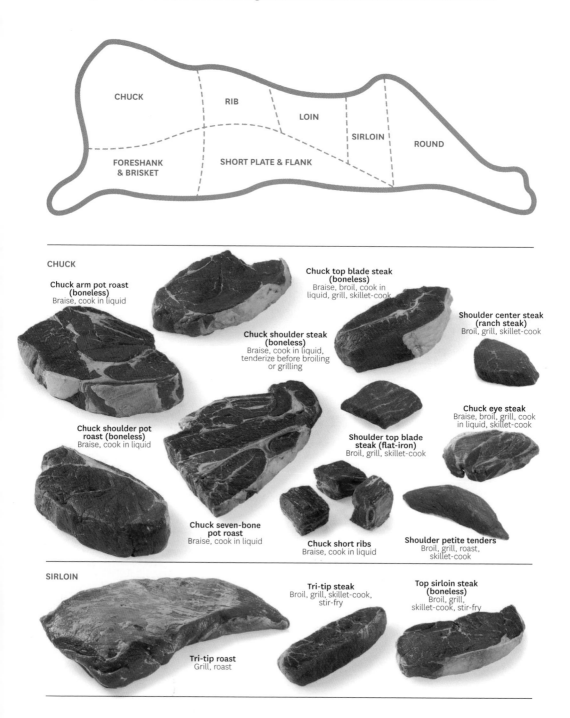

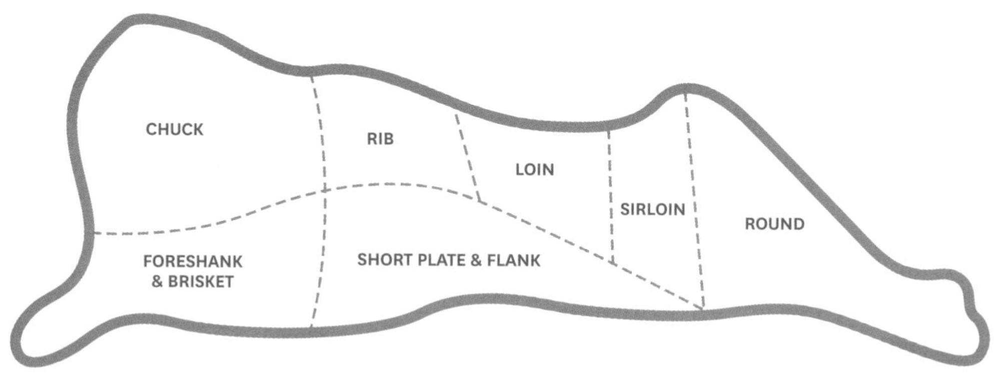

CHUCK

Chuck arm pot roast (boneless)
Braise, cook in liquid

Chuck top blade steak (boneless)
Braise, broil, cook in liquid, grill, skillet-cook

Shoulder center steak (ranch steak)
Broil, grill, skillet-cook

Chuck shoulder steak (boneless)
Braise, cook in liquid, tenderize before broiling or grilling

Chuck eye steak
Braise, broil, grill, cook in liquid, skillet-cook

Chuck shoulder pot roast (boneless)
Braise, cook in liquid

Shoulder top blade steak (flat-iron)
Broil, grill, skillet-cook

Chuck seven-bone pot roast
Braise, cook in liquid

Chuck short ribs
Braise, cook in liquid

Shoulder petite tenders
Broil, grill, roast, skillet-cook

SIRLOIN

Tri-tip steak
Broil, grill, skillet-cook, stir-fry

Top sirloin steak (boneless)
Broil, grill, skillet-cook, stir-fry

Tri-tip roast
Grill, roast

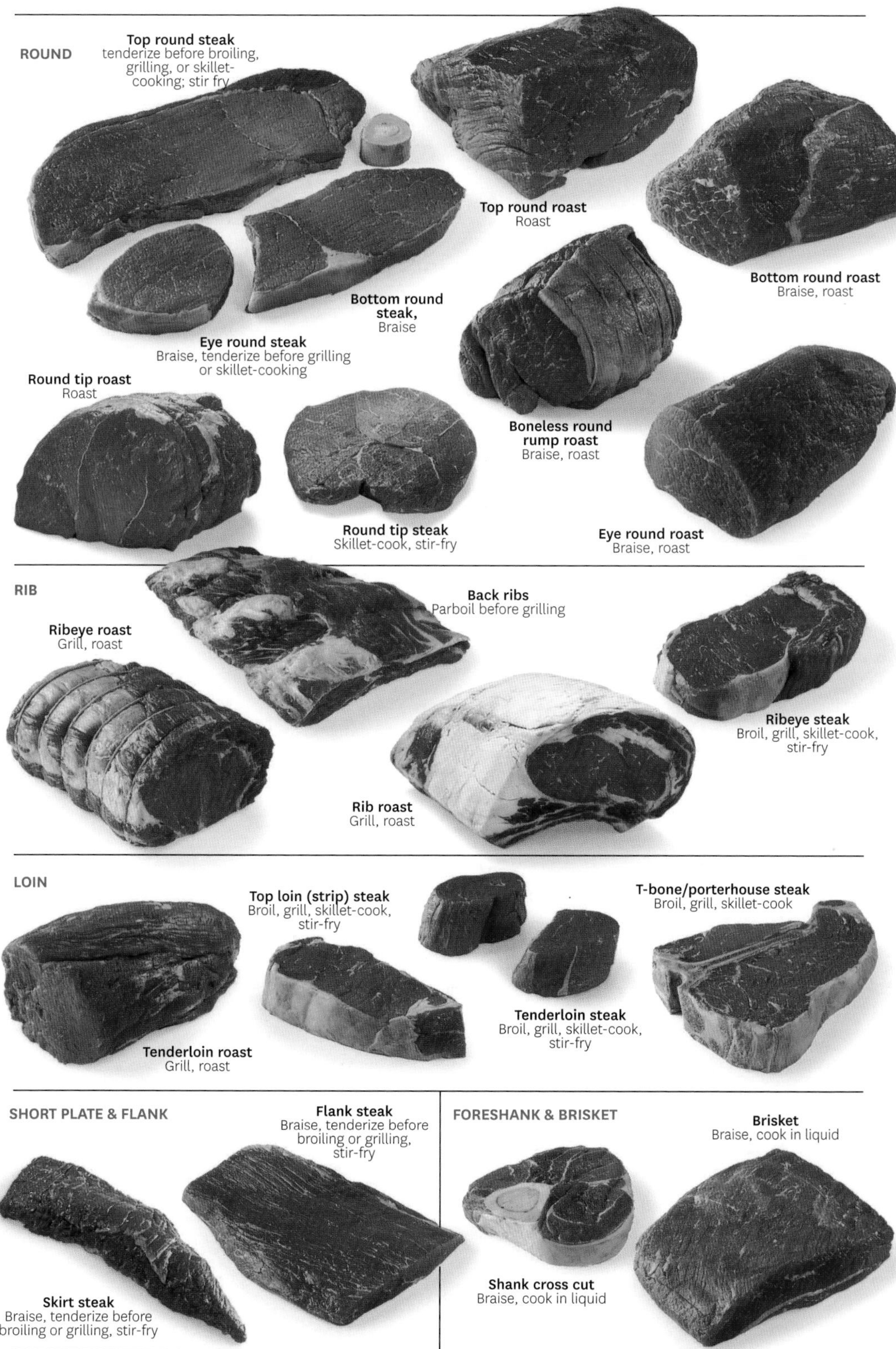
ROUND
Top round steak
tenderize before broiling, grilling, or skillet-cooking; stir fry
Top round roast
Roast
Bottom round roast
Braise, roast
Bottom round steak,
Braise
Eye round steak
Braise, tenderize before grilling or skillet-cooking
Round tip roast
Roast
Boneless round rump roast
Braise, roast
Round tip steak
Skillet-cook, stir-fry
Eye round roast
Braise, roast
RIB
Back ribs
Parboil before grilling
Ribeye roast
Grill, roast
Ribeye steak
Broil, grill, skillet-cook, stir-fry
Rib roast
Grill, roast
LOIN
Top loin (strip) steak
Broil, grill, skillet-cook, stir-fry
T-bone/porterhouse steak
Broil, grill, skillet-cook
Tenderloin steak
Broil, grill, skillet-cook, stir-fry
Tenderloin roast
Grill, roast
SHORT PLATE & FLANK
Flank steak
Braise, tenderize before broiling or grilling, stir-fry
Skirt steak
Braise, tenderize before broiling or grilling, stir-fry
FORESHANK & BRISKET
Brisket
Braise, cook in liquid
Shank cross cut
Braise, cook in liquid

cook's secrets

steak with pan sauce

The Secret: Searing steaks before roasting creates a crisp, caramelized exterior and develops flavorful browned bits that become the foundation for rich pan sauce. Wait until just before searing to season steaks with salt and pepper.

STEAK + PAN SAUCE POINTERS

1. THE SEAR
Make sure the pan is really hot before you add the steaks. If it's hot enough, the steak will brown instantly; if not, the meat will turn pale gray.

2. IS IT DONE YET?
Insert an instant-read thermometer into the thickest part of a steak at an angle. Cook steaks to 145°F for medium rare. Let steaks rest before serving to allow the juices to redistribute within the steak.

3. WHISKED AWAY
Deglaze the pan by adding wine and broth; scrape the bottom of the skillet to pick up the browned bits left behind by the steaks.

Using unsalted butter when preparing pan sauce lets you control the flavor while adding richness and body to the sauce.

The fat in whipping cream helps thicken the sauce and prevents it from curdling. Do not substitute a lower-fat cream.

PREP: 20 MINUTES **STAND:** 30 MINUTES **ROAST:** 10 MINUTES AT 400°F
MAKES: 4 SERVINGS

- 2 **beef top loin or ribeye steaks, cut 1 to 1½ inches thick, or 4 beef tenderloin steaks, cut 1 to 1½ inches thick (1½ to 2 pounds total)**
- 1 **tablespoon olive oil**
- 5 **tablespoons cold unsalted butter**
- ½ **teaspoon kosher salt**
- ½ **teaspoon freshly ground black pepper**
- ½ **cup dry red wine or apple juice**
- ⅓ **cup reduced-sodium beef broth**
- 3 **tablespoons finely chopped shallot or 2 cloves garlic, minced**
- 2 **tablespoons whipping cream**

1 Allow steaks to stand at room temperature for 30 minutes. Preheat oven to 400°F. Trim fat from steaks. Pat steaks dry with paper towels; set aside. Heat a large oven-going skillet over medium-high heat. Add oil and 1 tablespoon of the butter to skillet; reduce heat to medium. Sprinkle salt and pepper over steaks. Add steaks to skillet; cook about 4 minutes or until browned, turning once halfway through cooking time. Transfer skillet to oven. Roast, uncovered, for 10 to 13 minutes or until medium rare (an instant-read thermometer registers 145°F when inserted into centers of steaks). Transfer steaks to a platter. Cover with foil; let stand while preparing sauce.

2 For pan sauce, drain fat from skillet. Add wine, broth, and shallot to skillet. Bring to boiling, whisking constantly to scrape up any crusty browned bits from bottom of skillet. Boil gently, uncovered, over medium heat about 6 minutes or until liquid is reduced to about ¼ cup.

3 Whisk in whipping cream. Boil gently for 1 to 2 minutes more or until slightly thickened. Whisk in the remaining 4 tablespoons butter, 1 tablespoon at a time, whisking until butter is melted and sauce is thickened. Serve steaks with pan sauce.

PER ½ STEAK + 2 TABLESPOONS SAUCE: 450 cal., 29 g total fat (15 g sat. fat), 156 mg chol., 382 mg sodium, 3 g carb., 0 g fiber, 40 g pro.
EXCHANGES: 5½ Lean Meat, 4½ Fat

SAUCY FLAVOR BOOSTS

Vary the flavor of the sauce with one of these simple stir-ins:

HERBS: 1 teaspoon snipped fresh thyme, tarragon, or oregano added with the shallot

MUSTARD: 1 teaspoon Dijon-style mustard or balsamic vinegar added with the shallot

CAPERS: 1 teaspoon rinsed and drained capers stirred into the finished sauce

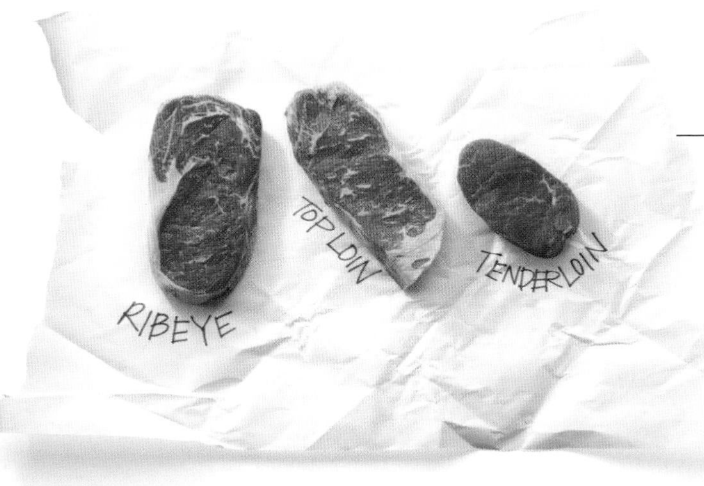

STEAK OUT!

Whether you choose ribeye, top loin, or tenderloin steaks, look for well-marbled meat with vibrant color and a moist (but not wet) surface. For more even cooking, let steaks stand at room temperature about 30 minutes before searing.

BEST-LOVED LOW-CALORIE

Steak with Creamy Onion Sauce

PREP: 20 MINUTES **STAND:** 35 MINUTES
BROIL: 12 MINUTES **MAKES:** 4 SERVINGS

- **4 beef ribeye steaks, cut about 1 inch thick**
- **1 tablespoon butter**
- **1 cup coarsely chopped sweet onion (such as Maui or Walla Walla) (1 large)**
- **½ cup light sour cream**
- **1 tablespoon capers, drained**
- **2 teaspoons Montreal steak seasoning**

1 Allow steaks to stand at room temperature for 30 minutes.

2 Meanwhile, for sauce, in a large skillet melt butter over medium-low heat. Add onion; cook, covered, for 13 to 15 minutes or until onion is tender, stirring occasionally. Uncover; increase heat to medium-high. Cook and stir for 3 to 5 minutes or until onion is golden. Reduce heat to medium-low. Stir in sour cream, capers, and ½ teaspoon of the steak seasoning. Cook until heated through (do not boil); set sauce aside.

3 Preheat broiler. Trim fat from steaks. Sprinkle steaks with the remaining 1½ teaspoons steak seasoning. Place steaks on the unheated rack of a broiler pan. Broil steaks 3 to 4 inches from the heat for 12 to 14 minutes for medium rare (145°F) or 15 to 18 minutes for medium (160°F), turning once halfway through broiling. Cover steaks with foil; let stand for 5 minutes before serving. Transfer steaks to serving plates. Spoon some of the sauce over steaks. Pass remaining sauce.

PER STEAK + ½ CUP SAUCE: 348 cal., 20 g total fat (9 g sat. fat), 116 mg chol., 550 mg sodium, 6 g carb., 1 g fiber, 36 g pro. EXCHANGES: ½ Other Carb., 5 Lean Meat, 1 Fat

LOW-CALORIE

Flat-Iron Steak with BBQ Beans

PREP: 10 MINUTES **STAND:** 35 MINUTES
COOK: 8 MINUTES **MAKES:** 4 SERVINGS

- **2 boneless beef shoulder top blade (flat-iron) steaks, halved (1 to 1¼ pounds)**
- **2 teaspoons fajita seasoning**
- **1 15-ounce can black beans, rinsed and drained**
- **⅓ cup bottled barbecue sauce**
- **2 to 3 medium tomatoes, sliced**
- **Pickled jalapeño chile pepper slices (optional)**

1 Allow steaks to stand at room temperature for 30 minutes. Lightly grease a grill pan; preheat the pan over medium-high heat. Sprinkle steaks with fajita seasoning. Place the steaks on the grill pan; grill for 8 to 12 minutes for medium rare (145°F) or 12 to 15 minutes for medium (160°F), turning once or twice. Remove steaks from pan. Cover with foil; let stand for 5 minutes.

2 Meanwhile, in a microwave-safe medium bowl stir together beans and barbecue sauce. Cover loosely with plastic wrap. Microwave on 100% power (high) about 3 minutes or until heated through, stirring once.

3 Serve steaks with beans, sliced tomatoes, and, if desired, pickled jalapeño slices.

PER ½ STEAK + ⅓ CUP BEANS: 305 cal., 11 g total fat (4 g sat. fat), 74 mg chol., 678 mg sodium, 25 g carb., 6 g fiber, 29 g pro. EXCHANGES: 1 Starch, ½ Other Carb., 3½ Lean Meat

BEST-LOVED LOW-CALORIE

Herbed Tri-Tip Beef Roast

PREP: 10 MINUTES **ROAST:** 30 MINUTES AT 425°F
STAND: 15 MINUTES **MAKES:** 8 SERVINGS

- **1 teaspoon dried thyme, crushed**
- **½ teaspoon salt**
- **½ teaspoon coarsely ground black pepper**
- **1 2-pound boneless beef tri-tip roast**
- **1 tablespoon olive oil**
- **1 recipe Demi-Glace Sauce (page 536)**

1 Preheat oven to 425°F. In a small bowl combine the thyme, ½ teaspoon salt, and ½ teaspoon pepper. Rub thyme mixture all over meat. Place roast on a rack in a shallow roasting pan. Drizzle with olive oil. Roast, uncovered, for 30 to 35 minutes or until an instant-read thermometer registers 135°F for medium rare or 150°F for medium.

2 Meanwhile, prepare Demi-Glace Sauce.

3 Remove roast from oven. Cover with foil; let stand for 15 minutes (temperature of meat will rise during standing time). Slice beef and serve with sauce.

PER 3 OUNCES MEAT + 2 TABLESPOONS SAUCE: 246 cal., 15 g total fat (6 g sat. fat), 84 mg chol., 366 mg sodium, 3 g carb., 0 g fiber, 24 g pro. EXCHANGES: 3½ Lean Meat, 2 Fat

TRY A TRI-TIP

A beef tri-tip roast is an economical, lean cut of meat from the sirloin section. It is a good choice for roasting and grilling. Because it contains so little fat, be sure not to cook it past medium doneness (150°F).

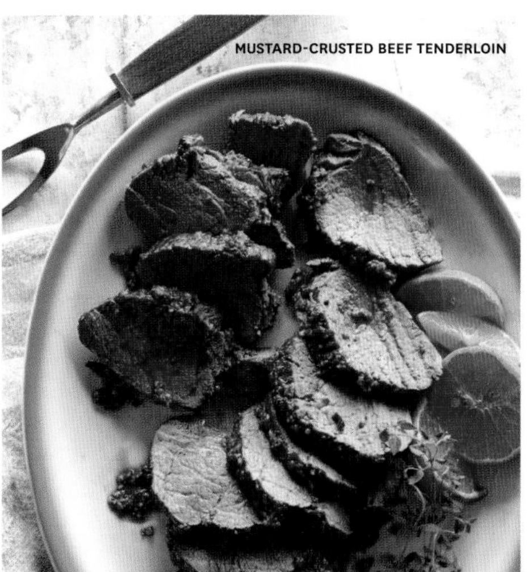
MUSTARD-CRUSTED BEEF TENDERLOIN

LOW-CALORIE

Mustard-Crusted Beef Tenderloin

PREP: 20 MINUTES **ROAST:** 35 MINUTES AT 425°F
STAND: 15 MINUTES **MAKES:** 8 SERVINGS

- **⅓ cup coarse-grain mustard**
- **1 tablespoon honey**
- **1 teaspoon black pepper**
- **1 teaspoon finely shredded orange peel**
- **½ teaspoon salt**
- **1 tablespoon olive oil**
- **1 2- to 3-pound beef tenderloin roast**
- **Orange wedges and/or slices (optional)**
- **Fresh thyme sprigs (optional)**

1 Preheat oven to 425°F. In a small bowl stir together mustard, honey, pepper, orange peel, and salt; set aside.

2 In a large heavy skillet heat oil over medium-high heat. Quickly brown roast on all sides in hot oil. Place roast on a rack set in a shallow roasting pan. Spread mustard mixture over top and sides of roast. Insert an oven-going meat thermometer into center of roast.

3 Roast, uncovered, for 35 to 40 minutes or until meat thermometer registers 135°F. Cover meat with foil; let stand for 15 minutes before slicing (temperature of the meat will rise during standing time). If desired, garnish with orange wedges and fresh thyme.

PER 3 OUNCES: 197 cal., 9 g total fat (3 g sat. fat), 74 mg chol., 339 mg sodium, 2 g carb., 0 g fiber, 25 g pro.
EXCHANGES: 3½ Lean Meat, ½ Fat

BEST-LOVED

Beef and Sweet Potato Pan Roast

PREP: 25 MINUTES **ROAST:** 30 MINUTES AT 425°F
STAND: 10 MINUTES **MAKES:** 6 SERVINGS

- **1 tablespoon dried Italian seasoning, crushed**
- **1 teaspoon salt**
- **½ teaspoon crushed red pepper**
- **1 tablespoon bottled roasted minced garlic**
- **3 tablespoons olive oil**
- **2 pounds medium sweet potatoes, cut into 1-inch wedges**
- **4 6- to 8-ounce beef shoulder petite tenders**
- **1 cup cherry tomatoes**
- **1 recipe Parsley Topping**

1 Preheat oven to 425°F. In a bowl mix Italian seasoning, salt, crushed red pepper, and garlic. Stir in oil. Divide seasoning mixture between two large resealable plastic bags. Place sweet potatoes in one bag; shake to coat. Spread potatoes in a single layer in a greased shallow roasting pan. Roast, uncovered, for 15 minutes.

2 Place beef tenders in remaining bag; shake to coat with seasoning mixture. In a very large skillet brown meat over medium-high heat, turning to brown evenly. Stir potatoes in roasting pan; push to edges of pan. Place meat in center of pan. Roast, uncovered, for 5 minutes. Add tomatoes; roast for 10 to 15 minutes more or until an instant-read thermometer inserted into meat registers 145°F for medium rare or 160°F for medium. Cover with foil; let stand for 10 minutes before slicing. Serve with Parsley Topping.

PARSLEY TOPPING: In a small bowl stir together ¼ cup snipped fresh parsley, 2 teaspoons finely shredded orange peel, ⅛ teaspoon salt, and 2 cloves garlic, minced.

PER 3 OUNCES MEAT + 1 CUP SWEET POTATOES: 365 cal., 14 g total fat (3 g sat. fat), 65 mg chol., 589 mg sodium, 33 g carb., 5 g fiber, 26 g pro. EXCHANGES: 2 Starch, 3 Lean Meat, ½ Fat

BEEF TENDERLOIN AND SWEET POTATO PAN ROAST: Substitute one 1½- to 2-pound beef tenderloin roast for the beef tenders. Prepare as directed, except do not roast sweet potatoes before adding beef. Place browned tenderloin in center of a greased roasting pan. Place sweet potato wedges around pan edges. Roast, uncovered, for 30 to 35 minutes for medium rare (135°F) or 40 to 45 minutes for medium (150°F). Cover with foil; let stand for 15 minutes before slicing (temperature of the meat will rise during standing). Serve as directed.

PER 3 OUNCES MEAT + 1 CUP SWEET POTATOES: 482 cal., 28 g total fat (9 g sat. fat, 0 g trans fat), 75 mg chol., 580 mg sodium, 33 g carb., 5 g fiber, 25 g pro. EXCHANGES: 2 Starch, 3 Medium-Fat Meat, 2½ Fat

BEST-LOVED FAST

Beef Stroganoff

START TO FINISH: 30 MINUTES **MAKES:** 4 SERVINGS

- **12 ounces boneless beef sirloin steak**
- **1 8-ounce carton sour cream**
- **2 tablespoons all-purpose flour**
- **½ cup water**
- **2 teaspoons instant beef bouillon granules**
- **¼ teaspoon black pepper**
- **2 tablespoons butter or margarine**
- **2 cups sliced mixed fresh mushrooms (button, cremini, and/or shiitake)**
- **½ cup chopped onion (1 medium)**
- **1 clove garlic, minced**
- **2 cups hot cooked noodles**

1 If desired, partially freeze beef for easier slicing. Trim fat from meat. Thinly slice meat across the grain into bite-size strips. In a small bowl stir together sour cream and flour. Stir in water, bouillon granules, and pepper; set aside.

2 In a large skillet melt butter over medium-high heat. Add meat, mushrooms, onion, and garlic; cook and stir about 5 minutes or until meat is desired doneness. Drain off fat.

3 Stir sour cream mixture into meat mixture. Cook and stir until thickened and bubbly. Cook and stir for 1 minute more. Serve over noodles.

PER 1 CUP MIXTURE + ½ CUP NOODLES: 486 cal., 30 g total fat (15 g sat. fat), 108 mg chol., 573 mg sodium, 30 g carb., 2 g fiber, 24 g pro. EXCHANGES: ½ Vegetable, 2 Starch, 2½ Medium-Fat Meat, 3 Fat

BEST-LOVED

Beef and Noodles

PREP: 25 MINUTES **COOK:** 80 MINUTES
MAKES: 4 SERVINGS

- **1 pound beef stew meat, trimmed and cut into ¾-inch cubes**
- **¼ cup all-purpose flour**
- **1 tablespoon vegetable oil**
- **½ cup chopped onion (1 medium)**
- **2 cloves garlic, minced**
- **3 cups beef broth**
- **1 teaspoon dried thyme or basil, crushed**
- **¼ teaspoon black pepper**
- **½ of a recipe Homemade Egg Noodles (page 418) or half of a 16-ounce package frozen egg noodles**

1 In a bowl toss meat with flour to coat. In a large saucepan brown half of the meat in hot oil over medium-high heat, stirring often. Remove meat from pan. Add remaining meat, the onion, and garlic. Cook until meat is browned and onion is tender, adding more oil if necessary. Drain off fat. Return all meat to saucepan. Stir in the 3 cups broth, the thyme, and pepper. Bring to boiling; reduce heat. Simmer, covered, for 75 to 90 minutes or until meat is tender.

2 Stir Homemade Egg Noodles into broth mixture. Bring to boiling; reduce heat. Cook, uncovered, about 5 minutes or until noodles are tender, stirring occasionally. (If using frozen noodles, cook about 25 minutes.) Add additional broth to reach desired consistency. If desired, sprinkle each serving with snipped *fresh parsley*.

PER 1½ CUPS: 411 cal., 14 g total fat (4 g sat. fat), 131 mg chol., 834 mg sodium, 37 g carb., 2 g fiber, 32 g pro.
EXCHANGES: 2½ Starch, 3½ Lean Meat, 1 Fat

Asian Short Ribs *(photo, page 373)*

PREP: 30 MINUTES **BAKE:** 2¾ HOURS AT 350°F
MAKES: 4 TO 5 SERVINGS

- **2½ cups reduced-sodium beef broth**
- **¾ cup hoisin sauce**
- **3 tablespoons reduced-sodium soy sauce**
- **2 teaspoons toasted sesame oil**
- **1½ teaspoons five-spice powder**
- **⅛ teaspoon cayenne pepper (optional)**
- **3½ to 4 pounds beef short ribs (about 8 to 10 ribs), cut into serving-size pieces**
- **¼ teaspoon black pepper**
- **1 tablespoon vegetable oil**
- **½ cup chopped onion (1 medium)**
- **1 teaspoon grated fresh ginger**
- **3 to 4 cloves garlic, minced**
- **1½ cups sliced fresh shiitake mushrooms (stems removed) or button mushrooms**
- **Hot cooked rice noodles (optional)**
- **Sliced green onions (optional)**

1 Preheat oven to 350°F. In a bowl combine broth, hoisin sauce, soy sauce, sesame oil, five-spice powder, and, if desired, cayenne pepper; set aside. Trim fat from ribs. Sprinkle ribs with the black pepper. In a 4- to 5-quart Dutch oven heat oil over medium-high heat. Add ribs, half at a time; cook until browned on all sides. Remove ribs to a large bowl. Add onion, ginger, and garlic to Dutch oven. Cook and stir for 1 to 2 minutes or until onion is lightly browned.

2 Return ribs to Dutch oven. Add broth mixture. Bring to boiling. Cover Dutch oven; transfer to oven. Bake, covered, for 2 hours, stirring once or twice. Add mushrooms; stir. Bake, covered, about 45 minutes more or until ribs are tender.

3 Transfer ribs to a deep serving platter; keep warm. Pour cooking liquid into a large glass measure. Skim fat from liquid. For sauce, return cooking liquid to pan; bring to boiling. Cook, uncovered, for 2 to 3 minutes or until thickened. Pour some of the sauce over ribs. Pass remaining sauce. If desired, serve with rice noodles and sprinkle with green onions.

PER 2 RIBS + ½ CUP SAUCE: 474 cal., 24 g total fat (8 g sat. fat), 97 mg chol., 1,565 mg sodium, 26 g carb., 2 g fiber, 37 g pro. EXCHANGES: ½ Vegetable, 1½ Other Carb., 5 Lean Meat, 3½ Fat

FAST LOW-CALORIE

Sweet and Spicy Edamame-Beef Stir-Fry

PREP: 20 MINUTES **COOK:** 10 MINUTES
MAKES: 4 SERVINGS

- **8 ounces boneless beef sirloin steak**
- **4 teaspoons vegetable oil**
- **2 teaspoons finely chopped fresh ginger**
- **2 cups fresh broccoli florets**
- **1 cup red and/or yellow sweet pepper strips**
- **1 cup frozen shelled sweet soybeans (edamame)**
- **3 tablespoons hoisin sauce**
- **2 tablespoons rice vinegar**
- **1 teaspoon red chili paste**
- **2 cups hot cooked brown or white rice**

1 If desired, partially freeze beef for easier slicing. Trim fat from meat. Thinly slice meat across the grain into bite-size strips; set aside.

2 In a nonstick wok or large skillet heat 2 teaspoons of the oil over medium-high heat. Add ginger; cook and stir for 15 seconds. Add broccoli and sweet pepper strips to wok. Cook and stir about 4 minutes or until crisp-tender. Remove vegetables from wok.

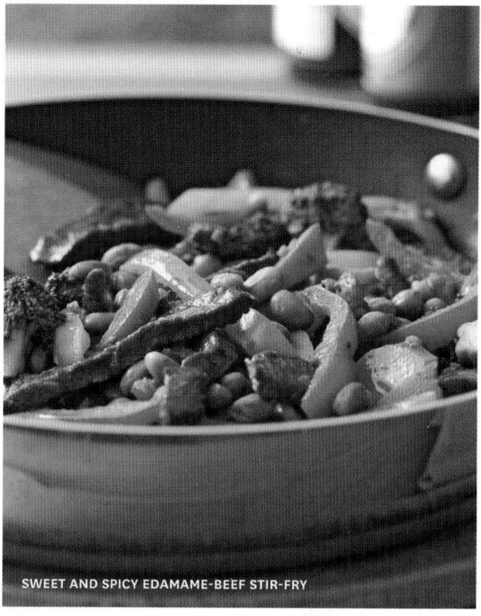
SWEET AND SPICY EDAMAME-BEEF STIR-FRY

3 Add the remaining 2 teaspoons oil to wok. Add beef and soybeans; cook and stir about 2 minutes or until beef is desired doneness. Return vegetables to wok.

4 In a small bowl combine hoisin sauce, vinegar, and chili paste. Add to beef mixture, tossing to coat. Heat through. Serve over rice.

PER ¾ CUP BEEF MIXTURE + ½ CUP RICE: 340 cal., 11 g total fat (2 g sat. fat), 24 mg chol., 262 mg sodium, 38 g carb., 6 g fiber, 22 g pro. EXCHANGES: 1 Vegetable, 2 Starch, 2 Lean Meat, 1 Fat

THERMOMETER CHOICES

Choose a model that's appropriate for the meat you are cooking. Be sure to insert the thermometer into the meat so it is not touching fat, bone, or the pan.

1. DIAL OVEN-GOING THERMOMETER: Use for roasts and larger cuts of meat; insert it into the meat before cooking.

2. INSTANT-READ THERMOMETER: This is used to check both larger and smaller cuts of meat toward the end of cooking time. These are not meant to be left in foods during cooking (unless the model you have is specifically designed to do so). For thin meats, such as burgers, steaks, and chops, insert into the side of the cut as shown.

3. PROBE THERMOMETER: Also for larger cuts, this model has a probe you insert into the meat before cooking. It's wired to a digital display that remains outside of the oven, allowing you to check the temperature of the meat without opening the oven door.

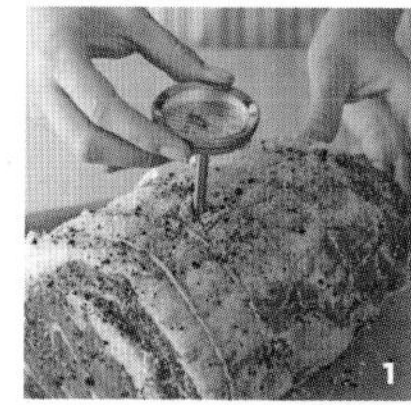
1

2

3

LOW-CALORIE

Swiss Steak

PREP: 25 MINUTES **COOK:** 75 MINUTES
MAKES: 4 SERVINGS

- **1 pound boneless beef round steak, cut ¾ inch thick; four 5-ounce beef cubed steaks; or two 10-ounce beef cubed steaks**
- **2 tablespoons all-purpose flour**
- **1 teaspoon smoked paprika or sweet paprika**
- **¼ teaspoon salt**
- **¼ teaspoon black pepper**
- **1 tablespoon vegetable oil**
- **1 14.5-ounce can diced tomatoes with basil, garlic, and oregano, undrained**
- **½ cup sliced celery (1 stalk)**
- **½ cup sliced carrot (1 medium)**
- **1 small onion, sliced and separated into rings**
- **¼ cup water**
- **1 recipe Mashed Potatoes (page 586)**

1 If using round steak, trim fat from meat. Cut meat into four serving-size pieces. With the notched side of a meat mallet, pound meat to about ½-inch thickness. (If using 10-ounce cubed steaks, cut each steak in half.) In a shallow dish combine the flour, paprika, salt, and pepper. Coat meat with flour mixture.

2 In a large skillet heat oil over medium-high heat. Add meat; brown meat on both sides in hot oil. Add tomatoes, celery, carrot, onion, and water. Bring to boiling; reduce heat. Simmer, covered, about 75 minutes or until meat is tender. Serve meat and vegetable mixture with Mashed Potatoes.

OVEN DIRECTIONS: Preheat oven to 350°F. Prepare and brown meat in skillet as directed. Transfer meat to a 2-quart square baking dish. In the same skillet combine tomatoes, celery, carrot, onion, and water. Bring to boiling, whisking constantly to scrape up any crusty browned bits from bottom of skillet. Pour over meat in dish. Cover with foil; bake about 75 minutes or until meat is tender. Serve as directed.

PER 4 OUNCES MEAT + ⅔ CUP VEGETABLES AND SAUCE + ½ CUP MASHED POTATOES: 332 cal., 9 g total fat (2 g sat. fat), 70 mg chol., 848 mg sodium, 33 g carb., 4 g fiber, 28 g pro. EXCHANGES: 2 Vegetable, 1½ Starch, 3 Lean Meat, ½ Fat

SMOKED PAPRIKA

Smoked paprika ranges from mild to hot and gives food a more intense flavor than regular sweet paprika.

Chicken Fried Steak

PREP: 20 MINUTES **COOK:** 60 MINUTES
MAKES: 4 SERVINGS

- **4 5-ounce beef cubed steaks or two 10-ounce beef cubed steaks**
- **¾ teaspoon salt**
- **¼ teaspoon black pepper**
- **¼ cup all-purpose flour**
- **1 egg, lightly beaten**
- **1 tablespoon milk**
- **¾ cup seasoned fine dry bread crumbs**
- **3 tablespoons vegetable oil**
- **2 tablespoons water**
- **1 small onion, halved, sliced, and separated into rings**
- **2 tablespoons all-purpose flour**
- **1½ cups milk**
- **Black pepper (optional)**

1 If using 10-ounce steaks, cut each steak in half. Sprinkle meat with ½ teaspoon of the salt and the ¼ teaspoon pepper.

2 Place the ¼ cup flour in a shallow dish. In a second shallow dish combine egg and the 1 tablespoon milk. In a third dish place bread crumbs. Dip meat pieces into the flour, then into the egg mixture. Coat with the bread crumbs.

3 In a very large skillet heat oil over medium-high heat. Cook meat, half at time, in hot oil about 8 minutes or until browned, turning once (add more oil if necessary). Return all of the meat to the skillet. Add water. Reduce heat to medium-low. Cook, covered, about 40 minutes more or until meat is tender, carefully turning with a spatula after 20 minutes. Transfer meat to a serving platter, reserving drippings in skillet. Keep warm.

4 For gravy, add onion to reserved drippings in skillet; cook until tender (add more oil if necessary). Stir in the 2 tablespoons flour and the remaining ¼ teaspoon salt. Gradually stir in the 1½ cups milk. Cook and stir over medium heat until thickened and bubbly. Cook and stir for 1 minute more. If desired, season to taste with additional pepper. Serve gravy with meat.

PER 4 OUNCES MEAT + ⅓ CUP GRAVY: 483 cal., 20 g total fat (5 g sat. fat), 139 mg chol., 976 mg sodium, 31 g carb., 2 g fiber, 42 g pro. EXCHANGES: 2 Starch, 5 Lean Meat, 1 Fat

make it mine

BEST-LOVED

Beef Pot Roast

There are thousands of recipes for pot roast in the world, but none will be better than the one you make with the combination of ingredients your family likes best.

PREP: 30 MINUTES **COOK:** 105 MINUTES
MAKES: 6 SERVINGS

- **1** **2½- to 3-pound beef chuck arm pot roast, chuck shoulder pot roast, or beef chuck seven-bone pot roast**
- **2** **tablespoons vegetable oil**
- **¾** **cup LIQUID**
- **1** **tablespoon LIQUID SEASONING**
- **1** **teaspoon DRIED HERB, crushed**
- **1** **pound POTATOES**
- **1** **pound VEGETABLES, cut into 1- to 2-inch pieces**
- **¼** **cup all-purpose flour**

1 Trim fat from meat. Sprinkle meat with *salt* and *black pepper.* In a 4- to 6-quart Dutch oven brown roast on all sides in hot oil. Drain off fat. Combine desired Liquid, Liquid Seasoning, Dried Herb, and ½ teaspoon *salt.* Pour over roast. Bring to boiling; reduce heat. Simmer, covered, for 1 hour.

2 Meanwhile, if using new potatoes, peel a strip of skin from the center of each. If using medium potatoes or sweet potatoes, peel and quarter. Add Potatoes and Vegetables to Dutch oven with meat. Return to boiling; reduce heat. Simmer, covered, for 45 to 60 minutes more or until meat and vegetables are tender. Using a slotted spoon, transfer meat and vegetables to a platter, reserving juices in Dutch oven. Keep warm.

3 For gravy, measure cooking juices; skim off fat. If necessary, add enough water to juices to equal 1½ cups. Return to Dutch oven. In a small bowl stir together ¼ cup *cold water* and flour until smooth. Stir into juices in pan. Cook and stir over medium heat until thickened and bubbly. Cook and stir for 1 minute more. Serve gravy with meat and vegetables.

LIQUID *(pick one)*

Apple juice
½ cup beef broth plus ¼ cup dry red wine
Beef broth
Cranberry juice
Tomato juice
Water

LIQUID SEASONING
(pick one)

Barbecue sauce
Dijon-style mustard
Soy sauce
Steak sauce
Worcestershire sauce

DRIED HERB *(pick one)*

Basil
Herbes de Provence
Italian seasoning
Mediterranean seasoning
Oregano
Rosemary
Thyme

POTATOES *(pick one)*

Fingerling
Red
Russet
Sweet
Tiny new
Yellow

VEGETABLES
(pick one or more)

Peeled butternut squash
Peeled carrots or parsnips
Celery
Trimmed fennel bulbs
Sliced leeks or shallots
Mushrooms
Onion wedges or peeled pearl onions
Peeled turnips or rutabaga

BALSAMIC-GLAZED FLANK STEAK WITH FALL FRUIT SALSA

LOW-CALORIE

Balsamic-Glazed Flank Steak with Fall Fruit Salsa

STAND: 35 MINUTES **PREP:** 20 MINUTES
BROIL: 17 MINUTES **MAKES:** 4 SERVINGS

- **1 pound beef flank steak**
- **3 tablespoons balsamic vinegar**
- **1⅓ cups chopped red and/or green apples**
- **1 cup chopped pear**
- **¼ cup dried cranberries**
- **2 teaspoons sugar**
- **¼ teaspoon ground cinnamon**

1 Allow steak to stand at room temperature for 30 minutes. Preheat broiler. Trim fat from steak. Score both sides of steak in a diamond pattern by making shallow diagonal cuts at 1-inch intervals. Sprinkle both sides of steak with *salt* and *black pepper.* Place steak on the unheated rack of broiler pan. Broil 3 to 4 inches from heat for 16 minutes, turning once. Brush both sides of steak with 1 tablespoon of the balsamic vinegar; broil for 1 to 5 minutes more or until medium (160°F). Cover with foil; let steak stand for 5 minutes before slicing.

2 For fruit salsa, in a bowl combine apples, pear, and cranberries. Stir in the remaining 2 tablespoons balsamic vinegar, the sugar, and cinnamon. Thinly slice steak; serve with salsa.

PER 3 OUNCES STEAK + ⅔ CUP SALSA: 261 cal., 8 g total fat (3 g sat. fat), 40 mg chol., 210 mg sodium, 22 g carb., 3 g fiber, 24 g pro. EXCHANGES: 1 Fruit, ½ Other Carb., 3½ Lean Meat

BEST-LOVED LOW-CALORIE

Fajitas

PREP: 15 MINUTES **CHILL:** 30 MINUTES
COOK: 6 MINUTES **MAKES:** 4 TO 6 SERVINGS

- **12 ounces beef skirt steak or flank steak, cut into thin bite-size strips**
- **1 recipe Homemade Fajita Seasoning**
- **1 medium red or green sweet pepper, cut into thin strips**
- **1 medium onion, thinly sliced and separated into rings**
- **2 tablespoons vegetable oil**
- **¾ cup chopped tomato (1 medium)**
- **1 tablespoon lime juice**
- **4 to six 8-inch flour tortillas, warmed**
- **1 recipe Fresh Tomato Salsa (page 44) (optional)**
- **1 recipe Chunky Guacamole (page 44) (optional)**
- **Sour cream (optional)**
- **Lime wedges (optional)**

1 Sprinkle beef with 2 teaspoons of the Homemade Fajita Seasoning; toss to coat. Cover and chill for 30 minutes.

2 In a very large skillet cook sweet pepper, onion, and the remaining fajita seasoning in 1 tablespoon of the oil until pepper and onion are crisp-tender. Remove pepper mixture from skillet. Add the remaining 1 tablespoon oil and the meat to the skillet. Cook and stir for 2 to 3 minutes or until desired doneness. Return pepper mixture to skillet. Stir in chopped tomato. Cook until heated through. Remove from heat; stir in lime juice.

3 To serve, fill warm tortillas with beef mixture. If desired, top with Fresh Tomato Salsa, Guacamole, and/or sour cream. Roll up tortillas; if desired, serve with lime wedges.

HOMEMADE FAJITA SEASONING: In a small bowl stir together 1½ teaspoons ground cumin; ½ teaspoon dried oregano, crushed; ¼ teaspoon salt; ¼ teaspoon cayenne pepper; ¼ teaspoon black pepper; ⅛ teaspoon garlic powder; and ⅛ teaspoon onion powder.

PER ¾ CUP BEEF MIXTURE + TORTILLA: 356 cal., 21 g total fat (6 g sat. fat), 51 mg chol., 326 mg sodium, 21 g carb., 2 g fiber, 20 g pro. EXCHANGES: 1 Vegetable, 1 Starch, 2 Lean Meat, 3 Fat

WEIGHING IN ON FLANK STEAK

Most flank steaks weigh about 2 pounds. If you don't need that much, cut it in half and freeze the extra for later. Flank steak is often marinated, and many recipes call for scoring the steak before marinating it. The shallow cuts on the steaks's surface allow the marinade to infuse the meat with added flavor and help tenderize the meat.

FAJITAS

Super Burritos

PREP: 40 MINUTES **BAKE:** 10 MINUTES AT 350°F
MAKES: 8 BURRITOS

- **1 pound lean ground beef**
- **1 cup chopped onion (1 large)**
- **½ cup chopped green sweet pepper (1 small)**
- **1 clove garlic, minced**
- **¼ cup water**
- **1 tablespoon medium or hot chili powder**
- **¼ teaspoon ground cumin**
- **¼ teaspoon salt**
- **1 cup cooked rice**
- **1 4-ounce can diced green chiles, drained**
- **8 10-inch flour tortillas, warmed**
- **1½ cups shredded Monterey Jack or cheddar cheese (6 ounces)**
- **1 cup chopped tomato (1 large)**
- **2 cups shredded lettuce**
- **1 recipe Chunky Guacamole (page 44)**

1 Preheat oven to 350°F. For filling, in a large skillet cook ground beef, onion, sweet pepper, and garlic until meat is browned and onion is tender. Drain off fat.

2 Stir water, chili powder, cumin, and salt into meat mixture in skillet. Cook about 5 minutes or until most of the water has evaporated. Remove from heat. Stir in cooked rice and chiles.

3 Spoon ½ cup filling onto each tortilla (see photo 1, below). Top with cheese and tomato. Fold bottom edge of tortillas over filling. Fold in opposite sides and roll up (see photo 2, below). Secure with wooden toothpicks.

SUPER BURRITOS STEP-BY-STEP

1. Spread about ½ cup of filling on a warmed tortilla so it's just below the center. Top the filling with cheese and tomato. Fold the bottom of the tortilla up and over the filling.

2. Fold the ends of the tortilla in and over the filling. Roll up from the bottom, completely enclosing the filling. Secure with wooden toothpicks.

4 Arrange burritos, seam sides down, on a baking sheet. Bake for 10 to 12 minutes or until heated through. Serve warm burritos on lettuce with Guacamole.

PER BURRITO: 449 cal., 25 g fat (9 g sat. fat), 63 mg chol., 528 mg sodium, 37 g carb., 5 g fiber, 21 g pro.
EXCHANGES: ½ Vegetable, 2½ Starch, 2 Lean Meat, 3 Fat

CHICKEN OR STEAK BURRITOS: Omit the ground beef. Partially freeze 1 pound skinless, boneless chicken breast halves or 1 pound beef flank steak for easier slicing. Cut chicken into thin bite-size strips or cut beef across the grain into thin, bite-size strips. For filling, in a large skillet cook chicken or beef, onion, sweet pepper, and garlic in 1 tablespoon hot vegetable oil until chicken is no longer pink or beef is desired doneness. Stir in water, chili powder, cumin, and salt. Cook about 5 minutes or until most of the water has evaporated. Remove from heat. Stir in rice and chiles. Continue as directed.

PER BURRITO: 415 cal., 20 g total fat (6 g sat. fat), 52 mg chol., 472 mg sodium, 37 g carb., 5 g fiber, 24 g pro.
EXCHANGES: ½ Vegetable, 2 Starch, 1 Lean Meat, 1 High-Fat Meat, 2 Fat

BEST-LOVED

Steak and Tomatoes on Toast

PREP: 20 MINUTES **COOK:** 17 MINUTES
MAKES: 6 OPEN-FACE SANDWICHES

- **2 tablespoons butter, softened**
- **2 tablespoons olive oil**
- **1 tablespoon snipped fresh oregano**
- **1 tablespoon snipped fresh rosemary**
- **2 cloves garlic, minced**
- **1 teaspoon smoked paprika**
- **½ teaspoon salt**
- **½ teaspoon cracked black pepper**
- **1 1-pound ciabatta loaf**
- **1½ pounds beef flank steak**
- **Salt and cracked black pepper**
- **3 cups cherry or grape tomatoes**

1 In a small bowl combine butter, oil, oregano, rosemary, garlic, paprika, ½ teaspoon salt, and cracked black pepper. Cut ciabatta loaf in half horizontally; cut each half crosswise into thirds to make six pieces. Very lightly brush cut sides of bread with some of the herb mixture. Set remaining herb mixture aside.

2 Score flank steak on both sides, making shallow cuts at 1-inch intervals diagonally across steak in a diamond pattern. Heat a very large skillet over medium-high heat until very hot. Sprinkle both sides of steak with additional salt and pepper.

3 Cook steak in hot skillet, uncovered, for 12 to 15 minutes or until medium rare (145°F), turning once halfway through cooking. Transfer steak to a plate. Cover; let stand for 5 minutes.

4 Meanwhile, place half of the bread, cut sides down, in the skillet; cook about 1 minute or until toasted. Remove from skillet. Repeat with remaining bread. Add remaining herb mixture to skillet. When mixture begins to bubble, add tomatoes for 4 to 6 minutes or until skins split. Remove from heat.

5 Thinly slice steak across the grain. Arrange thinly sliced steak on toasted bread; top with tomatoes. Serve immediately.

PER OPEN-FACE SANDWICH: 417 cal., 15 g total (6 g sat. fat), 88 mg chol., 723 mg sodium, 36 g carb., 3 g fiber, 32 g pro. EXCHANGES: 1 Vegetable, 2 Starch, 3½ Lean Meat, 1½ Fat

LOW-CALORIE

Wine-Braised Brisket with Onions

PREP: 30 MINUTES **MARINATE:** 12 TO 24 HOURS
BAKE: 3 HOURS AT 325°F **STAND:** 15 MINUTES
MAKES: 6 TO 8 SERVINGS + LEFTOVERS

- **1 3- to 3½-pound boneless beef brisket**
- **½ teaspoon kosher salt**
- **½ teaspoon freshly ground black pepper**
- **1 14.5-ounce can beef broth**
- **1½ cups dry red wine**
- **2 large red onions, sliced**
- **½ teaspoon dried thyme, crushed**
- **1 bay leaf**
- **6 cloves garlic, minced**
- **8 ounces fresh mushrooms, quartered**
- **2 tablespoons snipped fresh Italian parsley or chives**
- **Kosher salt and freshly ground black pepper**
- **1 recipe Mashed Potatoes (page 586) (optional)**

1 Pat brisket dry with paper towels. Sprinkle meat with the ½ teaspoon salt and the ½ teaspoon pepper. Transfer to a stainless-steel, enamel, or nonstick 6- to 8-quart Dutch oven. Add broth, wine, onions, thyme, bay leaf, and garlic. Cover with lid; marinate in refrigerator for 12 to 24 hours.

2 Preheat oven to 325°F. Place Dutch oven with meat over high heat; bring to boiling. Cover Dutch oven and transfer to oven. Bake for 1 hour; stir in mushrooms. Cover and bake for 2 to 2½ hours more or until meat is tender. Remove Dutch oven from oven; uncover. Let stand for 15 minutes.

WINE-BRAISED BRISKET WITH ONIONS

3 Transfer brisket to a cutting board; slice the meat across the grain. For sauce, skim fat from mushroom mixture. Discard bay leaf. Bring to boiling; reduce heat. Simmer, uncovered, until desired consistency. Stir in parsley. Season with additional salt and pepper. Serve brisket with the sauce and, if desired, Mashed Potatoes.

SLOW COOKER DIRECTIONS: Trim fat from meat. Sprinkle meat with ½ teaspoon salt and ½ teaspoon pepper. Cut brisket to fit into a 5- to 6-quart slow cooker. Place meat in removable liner of cooker. Pour wine and broth over brisket. Top with onions, thyme, bay leaf, and garlic. Cover; marinate in refrigerator 12 to 24 hours. Remove from refrigerator. Place liner in cooker; add mushrooms. Cover; cook on low-heat setting for 10 to 12 hours or on high-heat setting for 5 to 6 hours. Carefully remove brisket from cooker; slice across the grain. Discard bay leaf. Transfer mushroom mixture in cooker to a saucepan. Bring to boiling; reduce heat. Simmer, uncovered, until desired consistency.

PER 3½ OUNCES MEAT + ⅔ CUP VEGETABLES + ⅓ CUP SAUCE: 222 cal., 9 g total fat (3 g sat. fat), 120 mg chol., 337 mg sodium, 5 g carb., 1 g fiber, 25 g pro. EXCHANGES: 1 Vegetable, 3½ Lean Meat

THE RIGHT POT

When braising meat in wine, be sure to choose a Dutch oven with a stainless-steel, enamel, or nonstick interior. Other surfaces will react with the marinade, producing an unpleasant flavor. And for recipes that call for oven-braising be sure the pot is ovenproof.

cook's secrets

meat loaf

The Secret: A diner isn't the only place to get tender, moist meat loaf! A gentle hand is the key to success. Use your fingers to add air and lighten the mixture; resist packing it down as you mix.

PREP: 25 MINUTES **BAKE:** 60 MINUTES AT 350°F
STAND: 10 MINUTES **MAKES:** 8 SERVINGS

- **1 tablespoon vegetable oil**
- **½ cup finely chopped fresh mushrooms**
- **½ cup shredded carrot**
- **⅓ cup finely chopped onion**
- **2 cloves garlic, minced**
- **2 eggs, lightly beaten**
- **¼ cup milk**
- **3 tablespoons ketchup**
- **1 tablespoon Dijon-style mustard**
- **1 tablespoon Worcestershire sauce**
- **½ teaspoon kosher salt**
- **1 cup soft bread crumbs**
- **1 pound ground beef chuck (80% lean) (see tip, below)**
- **1 pound ground beef sirloin (90% lean) (see tip, below)**
- **½ cup ketchup**
- **¼ cup packed brown sugar**
- **2 teaspoons Dijon-style mustard**

Bread crumbs soak up some of the fat from the meat and lighten the mixture so it doesn't get too dense.

1 Preheat oven to 350°F. In a large skillet heat oil over medium-high heat. Add mushrooms, carrot, onion, and garlic; cook and stir for 4 to 5 minutes or until tender. In a large bowl combine eggs, milk, the 3 tablespoons ketchup, the 1 tablespoon mustard, the Worcestershire sauce, and kosher salt. Add vegetable mixture and bread crumbs, stirring until evenly moistened.

2 Add ground beef; using clean hands, mix lightly until combined. Line a 3-quart rectangular baking dish with foil. Lightly pat the mixture into a 9×5-inch loaf in the prepared dish.

3 For glaze, in a small bowl stir together the ½ cup ketchup, the brown sugar, and the 2 teaspoons mustard; set glaze aside.

4 Bake meat loaf about 60 minutes or until internal temperature registers 160°F on an instant-read thermometer, spooning glaze over meat loaf for the last 25 minutes of baking.

5 Let the meat loaf stand for 10 minutes before slicing. Using two spatulas, transfer loaf to a serving platter; cut into eight slices.

PER SERVING: 372 cal., 18 g total fat (6 g sat. fat), 123 mg chol., 606 mg sodium, 24 g carb., 1 g fiber, 26 g pro. **EXCHANGES:** ½ Starch, 1 Other Carb., 3½ Lean Meat, 2½ Fat

MEAT LOAF POINTERS

1. VEGGIE POWER
Mushrooms, carrots, onions, and garlic not only add nutrients, flavor, and moisture, but they also extend the meat loaf mixture. Cut or shred veggies in small, uniform pieces so they cook evenly and the mixture holds together when shaped. Briefly sautéing veggies first ensures they lose their crunch when baked.

2. MIX IT RIGHT
It's important to mix the wet and dry ingredients well before adding the meat. This ultimately reduces the amount of mixing you need to do. Be sure to use a bowl large enough to hold the entire mixture.

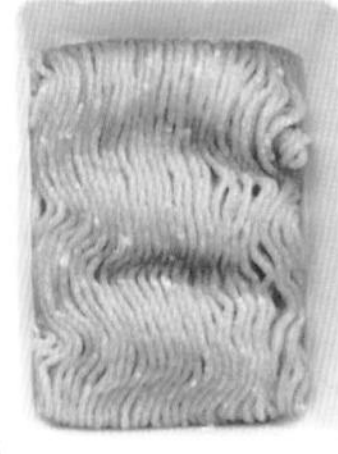

MEAT COMBOS

The best combination for meat loaf is a mixture of ground chuck (80% lean, 20% fat) and sirloin (90% lean, 10% fat). Because of its higher fat content, ground chuck adds flavor and moisture to the loaf; lean sirloin adds good structure. To change up your meat mixture, try the combos below. (If your meat mix is leaner, cover the meat loaf with foil for the first 35 minutes of baking.)

- ground beef + bulk sweet Italian sausage
- ground turkey breast + ground pork
- ground beef chuck + ground veal

↑

3. DON'T OVERMIX
Use your fingers to thoroughly but gently mix the ground meat into the egg-bread crumb mixture until just combined. Overmixing can make the meat loaf dense and tough.

4. SHAPE IT UP
To prevent the meat mixture from sticking to your hands, moisten hands with cold water before shaping. Gently pat and shape the meat mixture into an oblong loaf that is slightly smaller than the rectangular dish. This improves browning and lets some of the fat drain from the loaf into the dish.

↓

NEXT-DAY MEAT LOAF SANDWICHES!

Cut leftover meat loaf into ¾-inch slices and warm through on a lightly greased, preheated grill pan, carefully turning once. If you like, top each piece with a cheese slice and cook until melted. Serve between bread slices with mustard, ketchup, mayonnaise, arugula, and/or roasted red sweet pepper strips.

LOW-CALORIE

New England Boiled Dinner

PREP: 20 MINUTES **COOK:** 2 HOURS + 25 MINUTES
MAKES: 6 SERVINGS

- **1 2- to 2½-pound packaged corned beef brisket with spices***
- **12 ounces tiny new potatoes, quartered**
- **6 medium carrots and/or parsnips, peeled and quartered**
- **1 medium onion, cut into 6 wedges**
- **1 small cabbage, cut into 6 wedges**
- **Salt and black pepper (optional)**
- **Prepared horseradish or mustard (optional)**

1 Trim fat from meat. Place meat in a 5- to 6-quart Dutch oven; add juices and spices from package of corned beef.* Add enough water to cover meat in pot. Bring to boiling; reduce heat. Simmer, covered, about 2 hours or until meat is almost tender.

2 Add potatoes, carrots, and onion to meat in Dutch oven. Return to boiling; reduce heat. Simmer, covered, for 10 minutes. Add cabbage. Cook, covered, for 15 to 20 minutes more or until tender. Discard bay leaves (if using). Transfer meat to a cutting board. Thinly slice meat across the grain; arrange on a serving platter. Using a slotted spoon, remove vegetables from Dutch oven and arrange on platter with meat. Discard cooking liquid. If desired, season meat and vegetables with salt and pepper and serve with horseradish.

***NOTE:** If corned beef brisket does not come with a spice packet, add 1 teaspoon whole black peppercorns and 2 bay leaves with package juices and water in Step 1.

PER ABOUT 3½ OUNCES MEAT + 1 CUP VEGETABLES: 353 cal., 18 g total fat (5 g sat. fat), 77 mg chol., 1,081 mg sodium, 22 g carb., 6 g fiber, 25 g pro. EXCHANGES: 2½ Vegetable, ½ Starch, 3 Medium-Fat Meat, ½ Fat

CORNED BEEF AND CABBAGE: Prepare as directed, except omit the potatoes and carrots.

PER ABOUT 3½ OUNCES MEAT + 1 CABBAGE WEDGE: 289 cal., 18 g total fat (5 g sat. fat), 77 mg chol., 1,029 mg sodium, 7 g carb., 3 g fiber, 24 g pro. EXCHANGES: 1½ Vegetable, 3 Medium-Fat Meat, ½ Fat

CORNED BEEF LEFTOVERS

If you're lucky enough to have leftover corned beef brisket, save it to make hash. Cut the meat into small cubes or shred it. Melt butter or heat vegetable oil in a skillet. Cook the corned beef with cubed cooked potatoes and chopped onion until meat is browned and the potatoes are a little crispy. Serve with fried eggs for a hearty breakfast or quick supper.

BEST-LOVED LOW-CALORIE

Veal Piccata

START TO FINISH: 35 MINUTES **MAKES:** 4 SERVINGS

- **⅓ cup all-purpose flour**
- **½ teaspoon salt**
- **¼ teaspoon black pepper**
- **1 pound veal cutlets (thinly sliced boneless veal)**
- **2 tablespoons olive oil**
- **¾ cup dry white wine or chicken broth**
- **⅓ cup chicken broth**
- **3 tablespoons lemon juice**
- **3 tablespoons butter**
- **2 tablespoons drained capers**
- **1 lemon, thinly sliced**
- **2 tablespoons snipped fresh Italian parsley**

1 In a shallow dish combine flour, salt, and pepper. Cut veal into eight serving-size pieces. If necessary, use a meat mallet to pound veal to ⅛-inch thickness. Coat veal with flour mixture.

2 In a very large skillet heat oil over medium-high heat. Add veal slices, half at a time, to skillet. Cook about 4 minutes or until no longer pink, turning once. Remove from skillet; cover to keep warm while cooking remaining slices.

3 For sauce, remove skillet from heat. Add wine and broth. Return skillet to heat. Bring to boiling; reduce heat. Simmer, uncovered, for 6 minutes. Stir in lemon juice, butter, and capers. Stir until butter is melted. Return veal to skillet; add lemon slices. Heat through. Transfer veal and lemon to a serving platter. Spoon sauce over veal and lemon; sprinkle with parsley.

CHICKEN PICCATA: Prepare as directed, except use 4 small skinless, boneless chicken breast halves (1 to 1¼ pounds). Cut each chicken breast half in half crosswise. Place each chicken piece between two pieces of plastic wrap. Using the flat side of a meat mallet, lightly pound each piece to about ⅛-inch thickness, working from center to edges. Discard plastic wrap. Coat chicken with flour mixture and continue as directed.

PER 3 OUNCES VEAL OR CHICKEN + 3 TABLESPOONS SAUCE: 346 cal., 19 g total fat (7 g sat. fat), 117 mg chol., 640 mg sodium, 12 g carb., 1 g fiber, 25 g pro. EXCHANGES: ½ Starch, 3 Lean Meat, 2½ Fat

VEAL PICCATA

PORK CUTS AND HOW TO COOK THEM

A surefire way to enjoy pork at its best is to use the cooking method that best suits each cut. These photos show the cuts that are the most widely available at supermarkets, along with the best recommended ways for cooking them. They correspond to the drawing, which shows where the cuts come from on the animal.

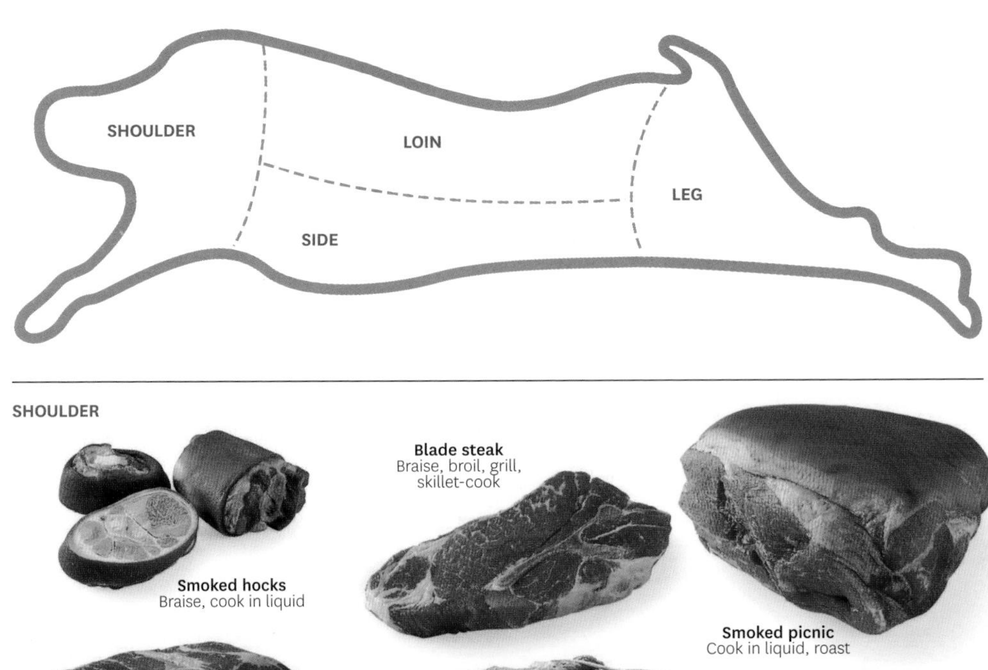

SHOULDER

Smoked hocks
Braise, cook in liquid

Blade steak
Braise, broil, grill, skillet-cook

Smoked picnic
Cook in liquid, roast

Blade roast
Braise, roast

Boneless blade roast
Braise, roast

Sausage links
Skillet-cook

LEG

Boneless cooked ham (whole muscle)
Grill, roast

Cutlet
Braise, skillet-cook

Ham (shank half)
Grill, roast

Ham steak
Broil, grill, skillet-cook

LOIN

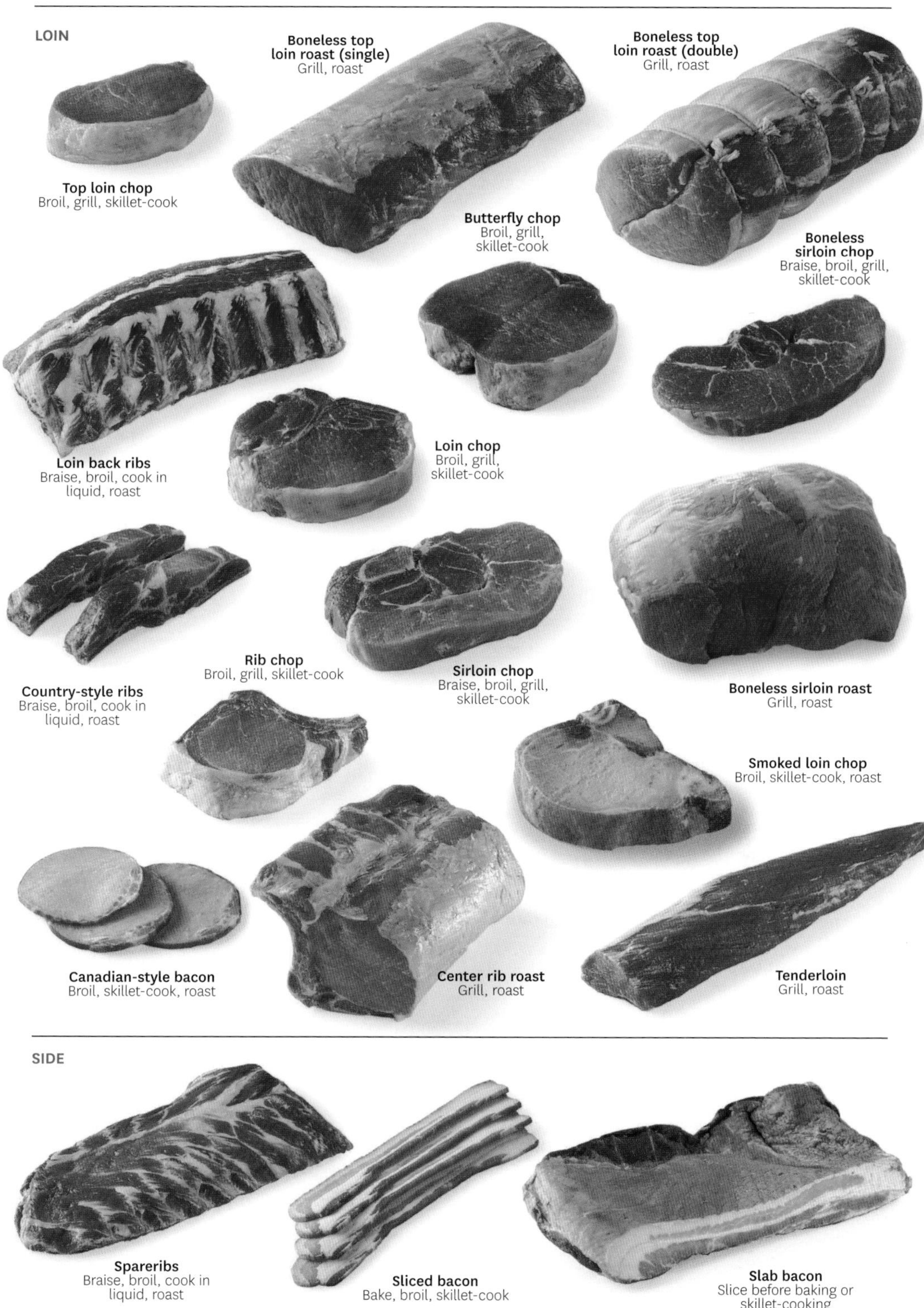

SIDE

Spareribs
Braise, broil, cook in liquid, roast

Sliced bacon
Bake, broil, skillet-cook

Slab bacon
Slice before baking or skillet-cooking

CASHEW PORK AND VEGETABLES

Cashew Pork and Vegetables

START TO FINISH: 45 MINUTES **MAKES:** 4 SERVINGS

- **1/4 cup orange juice**
- **2 tablespoons bottled hoisin sauce**
- **1/2 teaspoon ground ginger**
- **1/8 teaspoon crushed red pepper (optional)**
- **1 tablespoon vegetable oil**
- **3 medium carrots, bias-sliced, or 1 1/2 cups packaged fresh julienned carrots**
- **2 cups fresh pea pods, strings and tips removed, or one 6-ounce package frozen pea pods, thawed**
- **1/4 cup sliced green onions (2)**
- **1 pound lean boneless pork, cut into thin bite-size strips**
- **2 cups hot cooked rice**
- **1/2 cup cashews or peanuts**

1 For sauce, stir together orange juice, hoisin sauce, ginger, and, if desired, crushed red pepper; set aside.

2 Pour oil into a wok or large skillet (add more oil as necessary during cooking). Preheat wok over medium-high heat. Stir in carrots. Cook and stir for 2 minutes. Add pea pods and green onions. Cook and stir for 2 to 3 minutes or until vegetables are crisp-tender. Remove vegetables from wok.

3 Add half of the pork to hot wok. Cook and stir for 2 to 3 minutes or until no pink remains; remove from pan. Repeat with remaining strips. Return all meat and vegetables to wok. Stir sauce; add to center of wok. Cook and stir until heated through. Serve over rice; top with nuts.

PER 2 CUPS: 439 cal., 17 g total fat (3 g sat. fat), 60 mg chol., 204 mg sodium, 41 g carb., 4 g fiber, 32 g pro.
EXCHANGES: 1 Vegetable, 2 1/2 Starch, 3 Lean Meat, 1 Fat

LOW-CALORIE

Pork with Hot Pear Relish

PREP: 30 MINUTES **ROAST:** 75 MINUTES AT 325°F
STAND: 10 MINUTES **MAKES:** 8 SERVINGS

- **1 tablespoon olive oil**
- **1 cup finely chopped sweet onion (1 large)**
- **3/4 cup finely chopped red sweet pepper (1 medium)**
- **1 fresh jalapeño chile pepper, seeded and finely chopped (see tip, page 44)**
- **2 cups chopped, peeled pears (2 medium)**
- **1/2 cup sugar**
- **1/2 cup white balsamic vinegar**
- **1 teaspoon dry mustard**
- **1/4 teaspoon salt**
- **1 2- to 2 1/2-pound boneless pork top loin roast (single loin)**
- **Salt and black pepper**

1 For pear relish, in a large skillet heat oil over medium heat. Add onion, sweet pepper, and jalapeño pepper; cook and stir for 2 minutes. Stir in pears, sugar, vinegar, mustard, and the 1/4 teaspoon salt. Bring to boiling over medium-high heat, stirring occasionally; reduce heat. Simmer, uncovered, about 10 minutes or until pears are soft and transparent.

2 Meanwhile, preheat oven to 325°F. Place pork on a rack set in a shallow roasting pan. Sprinkle with additional salt and black pepper. Insert an oven-going meat thermometer into center of roast. Roast, uncovered, for 60 minutes. Top with 1/2 cup of the pear relish. Roast for 15 to 30 minutes more or until thermometer registers 145°F.

3 Remove roast from oven. Cover with foil and let stand for 10 minutes (temperature of the meat will rise during standing time). Slice meat and serve with remaining pear relish.

PER 4 OUNCES MEAT + 1/4 CUP RELISH: 309 cal., 11 g total fat (3 g sat. fat), 73 mg chol., 167 mg sodium, 25 g carb., 2 g fiber, 25 g pro. **EXCHANGES:** 1 1/2 Other Carb., 3 1/2 Lean Meat

LOW-CALORIE

Roasted Pork Tenderloin with Red Pepper Pesto

PREP: 30 MINUTES **ROAST:** 30 MINUTES AT 425°F
STAND: 10 MINUTES **MAKES:** 4 SERVINGS

- **3 cloves garlic, cut into thin slivers**
- **2 tablespoons snipped fresh oregano**
- **1 teaspoon smoked paprika**
- **1/4 teaspoon salt**
- **1/4 teaspoon black pepper**
- **1 1-pound pork tenderloin**
- **4 tablespoons olive oil**
- **3 large red sweet peppers, cut into wedges**
- **2 cloves garlic, minced**

1 Preheat oven to 425°F. In a small bowl combine slivered garlic, oregano, paprika, 1/4 teaspoon salt, and 1/4 teaspoon black pepper. Brush pork with 1 tablespoon of the olive oil; press garlic mixture onto all sides. Place on a rack in a shallow roasting pan.

2 Roast, uncovered, for 30 to 35 minutes or until an instant-read thermometer registers 145°F. Cover with foil; let stand for 10 minutes before slicing.

3 Meanwhile, heat a large nonstick skillet over medium-high heat. Add sweet pepper wedges. Cook for 8 to 10 minutes until peppers are well browned, turning occasionally. Remove from heat.

4 For red pepper pesto, transfer one-third of the peppers to a blender or food processor. Add the minced garlic and the remaining 3 tablespoons olive oil. Blend or process until almost smooth. If necessary, add additional oil to make pesto desired consistency. Season to taste with additional salt and black pepper. Serve pork with pesto and the remaining roasted pepper wedges.

PER 3½ OUNCES MEAT + 3 TABLESPOONS PESTO + ½ SWEET PEPPER: 302 cal., 18 g total fat (3 g sat. fat), 74 mg chol., 356 mg sodium, 9 g carb., 3 g fiber, 25 g pro.
EXCHANGES: 1½ Vegetable, 3 Lean Meat, 2½ Fat

BEST-LOVED FAST LOW-CALORIE

Pork Medallions with Fennel and Pancetta

START TO FINISH: 30 MINUTES **MAKES:** 4 SERVINGS

- **12 ounces pork tenderloin**
- **1/4 cup all-purpose flour**
- **Dash salt**
- **Dash black pepper**
- **2 tablespoons olive oil**
- **2 ounces pancetta (Italian bacon) or bacon, finely chopped**

PORK MEDALLIONS WITH FENNEL AND PANCETTA

- **2 fennel bulbs, trimmed and cut crosswise into 1/4-inch slices**
- **1 small onion, thinly sliced**
- **2 cloves garlic, minced**
- **2 tablespoons lemon juice**
- **1/2 cup whipping cream**

1 Trim fat from pork. Cut pork crosswise into 1-inch slices. Place each slice between two pieces of plastic wrap. Use the flat side of a meat mallet to lightly pound pork to 1/4-inch thickness. Discard plastic wrap.

2 In a shallow dish combine flour, salt, and pepper. Dip meat slices in flour mixture to coat. In a large heavy skillet heat oil over medium-high heat. Cook pork, half at a time, in hot oil for 2 to 3 minutes or until meat is slightly pink in center, turning once (add more oil during cooking if necessary). Remove meat from skillet; set aside.

3 In the same skillet cook pancetta over medium-high heat until crisp. Add fennel, onion, and garlic; cook and stir for 3 to 5 minutes or until crisp-tender. Add lemon juice; stir in whipping cream. Bring to boiling; return meat to skillet. Cook until meat is heated through and sauce is slightly thickened.

4 Transfer meat to a serving platter. Spoon vegetable mixture and sauce over meat.

PER 2½ OUNCES MEAT + ½ CUP VEGETABLES: 382 cal., 24 g total fat (10 g sat. fat), 106 mg chol., 416 mg sodium, 18 g carb., 4 g fiber, 23 g pro. EXCHANGES: ½ Vegetable, 1 Starch, 3 Lean Meat, 3 Fat

LOW-CALORIE

Pork Pot Roast in Cider

PREP: 15 MINUTES **COOK:** 20 MINUTES
ROAST: 55 MINUTES AT 325°F **MAKES:** 6 SERVINGS

- **1 2- to 2½-pound boneless pork sirloin roast**
- **2 tablespoons vegetable oil**
- **1 large onion, cut into wedges**
- **1 cup beef broth**
- **½ cup apple cider or apple juice**
- **1 teaspoon dried thyme, crushed**
- **¼ teaspoon crushed red pepper**
- **4 medium Yukon gold potatoes, quartered, or 2 medium sweet potatoes, peeled and cut into 2-inch pieces**
- **4 medium carrots and/or parsnips, peeled and cut into 2-inch pieces**
- **1 pound butternut squash, peeled, halved, seeded, and cut into 1-inch pieces**
- **2 tablespoons honey mustard**

1 Preheat oven to 325°F. Trim fat from meat. In a 5- to 6-quart Dutch oven heat oil over medium-high heat. Add roast to Dutch oven; brown meat on all sides in hot oil. Drain off fat. Add onion to meat in Dutch oven (see photo 1, below).

2 In a medium bowl stir together broth, apple cider, thyme, and crushed red pepper. Pour over meat and onions in Dutch oven. Add potatoes and carrots and/or parsnips. Roast, covered, for 30 minutes.

3 Add butternut squash to Dutch oven. Roast, covered, for 25 to 35 minutes more or until vegetables are tender and an instant-read thermometer inserted into the center of roast registers 145°F. Transfer meat and vegetables to a serving platter, reserving juices in pan. Cover meat and vegetables with foil to keep warm.

4 For sauce, bring juices in pan to boiling (see photo 2, left). Boil gently, uncovered, for 10 to 15 minutes or until slightly thickened, stirring occasionally. Stir in mustard. To serve, remove string from meat if present. Slice meat and serve with vegetables and sauce.

PORK POT ROAST IN CIDER

SLOW COOKER DIRECTIONS: Prepare meat as directed in Step 1. Place vegetables in a 3½- or 4-quart slow cooker. Cut meat to fit if necessary; place on top of vegetables. Stir together broth, apple cider, mustard, thyme, and crushed red pepper. Pour over meat and vegetables in cooker. Cover and cook on low-heat setting for 8 to 10 hours or on high-heat setting for 4 to 5 hours or until tender. Transfer meat and vegetables to a serving platter; keep warm. For sauce, transfer juices to a medium saucepan and cook on the stove top as in Step 3. Continue as directed.

PER 4 OUNCES PORK + 1 CUP VEGETABLES + 3 TABLESPOONS GRAVY: 310 cal., 9 g total fat (2 g sat. fat), 70 mg chol., 262 mg sodium, 32 g carb., 5 g fiber, 25 g pro.
EXCHANGES: 2½ Vegetable, 1 Starch, 2½ Lean Meat

PORK POT ROAST IN CIDER STEP-BY-STEP

1. Scatter the onion wedges around the roast in the bottom of the pot. They should be covered in liquid during cooking.

2. For the sauce, gently boil the cooking liquid on the stove top. As the liquid boils, some of it evaporates, thickening the sauce and concentrating the flavors.

BROWNING MEAT

Whether you are making a beef or pork pot roast, browning the roast is crucial to developing a rich flavor in both the meat and gravy. Be sure to brown the roast on all sides and use tongs to turn the meat without piercing the surface.

FAST

Thai Pork and Vegetable Curry

START TO FINISH: 30 MINUTES **MAKES:** 4 SERVINGS

1⅓ cups uncooked jasmine rice
12 ounces pork tenderloin or lean boneless pork
2 tablespoons vegetable oil
8 ounces green beans, bias-sliced into 1½-inch pieces (2 cups)
1 red sweet pepper, seeded and cut into thin bite-size strips
2 green onions, bias-sliced into ¼-inch pieces
1 14-ounce can unsweetened coconut milk
4 teaspoons bottled green curry paste
1 teaspoon sugar
⅛ teaspoon crushed red pepper
1 lime, cut into wedges

1 Cook rice according to package directions; drain. Keep warm.

2 Meanwhile, thinly slice pork into bite-size strips. Sprinkle with *salt* and *black pepper*. In a large nonstick skillet heat 1 tablespoon of the oil over medium-high heat. Add pork; cook and stir about 4 minutes or until no pink remains. Remove meat from skillet.

3 Add the remaining 1 tablespoon oil to skillet. Add green beans; cook and stir for 3 minutes. Add sweet pepper and green onions; cook and stir about 2 minutes more or until vegetables are crisp-tender. Remove vegetables from skillet. Add coconut milk, curry paste, sugar, and crushed red pepper to skillet. Bring mixture to boiling; reduce heat. Simmer, uncovered, about 2 minutes or until mixture is slightly thickened. Stir in pork and vegetables; heat through. Serve over hot cooked rice with lime wedges.

PER 1 CUP PORK MIXTURE: 490 cal., 16 g total fat (5 g sat. fat), 47 mg chol., 593 mg sodium, 63 g carb., 3 g fiber, 23 g pro.
EXCHANGES: 1 Vegetable, 2 Starch, 2 Other Carb., 2 Lean Meat, 1½ Fat

FAST LOW-CALORIE

Oven-Fried Pork Chops

PREP: 10 MINUTES **BAKE:** 20 MINUTES AT 425°F
STAND: 5 MINUTES **MAKES:** 4 SERVINGS

4 pork loin chops, cut ¾ inch thick
2 tablespoons butter, melted
1 egg, beaten
2 tablespoons milk
¼ teaspoon black pepper
1 cup herb-seasoned stuffing mix, finely crushed

1 Preheat oven to 425°F. Trim fat from meat. Pour butter into a 13×9×2-inch baking pan, tilting pan to coat the bottom. In a shallow dish combine egg, milk, and pepper. Place stuffing mix in second shallow dish. Dip chops into egg mixture. Coat both sides with stuffing mix. Place chops in the prepared pan.

2 Bake, uncovered, for 10 minutes; turn chops. Bake for 10 to 15 minutes more or until an instant-read thermometer inserted in chops registers 145°F. Transfer chops to serving plate. Cover with foil and let stand for 5 minutes before serving.

PER CHOP: 327 cal., 14 g total fat (6 g sat. fat), 147 mg chol., 383 mg sodium, 13 g carb., 2 g fiber, 35 g pro.
EXCHANGES: 1 Starch, 4½ Lean Meat, 2 Fat

Pesto-Stuffed Pork Chops

PREP: 20 MINUTES **BAKE:** 35 MINUTES AT 375°F
STAND: 5 MINUTES **MAKES:** 4 SERVINGS

3 tablespoons crumbled feta cheese
2 tablespoons refrigerated basil pesto
1 tablespoon pine nuts, toasted (see tip, page 21)
4 bone-in pork loin chops or boneless pork loin chops, cut 1¼ inches thick
1 teaspoon freshly ground black pepper
1 teaspoon dried oregano, crushed
¼ teaspoon crushed red pepper
¼ teaspoon dried thyme, crushed
2 cloves garlic, minced
1 tablespoon balsamic vinegar

1 Preheat oven to 375°F. For filling, in a small bowl stir together feta cheese, pesto, and pine nuts. Set filling aside.

2 Trim fat from meat. Make a pocket in each chop by cutting horizontally from the fat side almost to the bone or opposite side. Spoon filling into pockets. If necessary, secure the openings with wooden toothpicks.

3 For rub, in a small bowl combine black pepper, oregano, crushed red pepper, thyme, and garlic. Rub evenly onto all sides of meat. Place chops on a rack in a shallow roasting pan.

4 Bake for 35 to 45 minutes or until an instant-read thermometer inserted in chops registers 145°F. Brush vinegar onto chops the last 5 minutes of baking. Transfer chops to a serving platter. Cover with foil and let stand for 5 minutes. Discard toothpicks before serving.

PER CHOP: 415 cal., 20 g total fat (7 g sat. fat), 133 mg chol., 228 mg sodium, 3 g carb., 0 g fiber, 52 g pro.
EXCHANGES: 7½ Lean Meat

8 to try

LOW-CALORIE

Oven-Baked Pork Chops

Combine your favorite ingredients to make a flavorful fresh or cooked topping for easy baked pork chops.

PREP: 20 MINUTES
BAKE: 14 MINUTES AT 350°F
STAND: 5 MINUTES **MAKES:** 4 SERVINGS

4 bone-in pork loin chops, cut 1¼ inches thick (about 3 pounds total), or 4 boneless pork loin chops, cut 1¼ inches thick (about 2½ pounds total)
¼ teaspoon salt
¼ teaspoon black pepper
1 tablespoon olive oil
Salt and black pepper (optional)

1 Preheat oven to 350°F. Trim fat from chops. Pat chops dry with paper towels. Sprinkle chops with the ¼ teaspoon salt and the ¼ teaspoon pepper.

2 In a very large skillet heat the oil over medium-high heat. Add two bone-in chops or all of the boneless chops. Cook about 6 minutes or until browned, turning to brown evenly. Transfer chops to a 15×10×1-inch baking pan. Repeat with remaining bone-in chops.

3 Bake chops for 14 to 17 minutes or until an instant-read thermometer inserted in chops registers 145°F. Cover and let stand for 5 minutes. Serve chops with one of the toppings. If desired, sprinkle with additional salt and pepper.

PER CHOP: 271 cal., 10 g total fat (3 g sat. fat), 131 mg chol., 235 mg sodium, 0 g carb., 0 g fiber, 41 g pro. EXCHANGES: 6 Lean Meat

CRANBERRY-APPLE: Cook 1 cup chopped apple and 2 minced shallots in 2 tablespoons butter for 3 minutes. Stir in ⅓ cup dried cranberries. Cook 2 minutes. Stir in 1 tablespoon snipped fresh sage and 1 tablespoon cider vinegar.

SPINACH-FETA: In a skillet cook ½ cup finely chopped celery and ½ cup finely chopped onion in 1 tablespoon butter until tender. Stir in 4 cups chopped fresh spinach, 1 cup at a time. Stir in ¼ cup crumbled feta cheese.

OLIVE GREMOLATA: Combine ½ teaspoon lemon peel, 1 tablespoon lemon juice, 1 tablespoon olive oil, ⅛ teaspoon crushed red pepper, 1 clove minced garlic, and 2 tablespoons each snipped parsley, chopped olives, capers, and shredded Parmesan cheese.

BRUSSELS SPROUTS AND PEAR: In a skillet cook 2 slices chopped bacon; remove bacon, reserving drippings. Cook ¾ cup sliced Brussels sprouts, ½ cup chopped pear, and ⅓ cup chopped red onion in drippings until tender. Add bacon and 1 teaspoon snipped fresh thyme.

FRESH FRUIT SALSA: Combine ¾ cup chopped mango, ½ cup chopped red sweet pepper, 2 tablespoons finely chopped red onion, 1 tablespoon snipped cilantro, 1 tablespoon olive oil, and 1 tablespoon white wine vinegar.

GRAPES AND BLUE CHEESE: In a skillet cook 1 cup halved seedless grapes and 1 sliced shallot in 1 tablespoon butter until grapes soften. Stir in ¼ cup finely chopped toasted almonds or pistachio nuts and ¼ cup crumbled blue cheese.

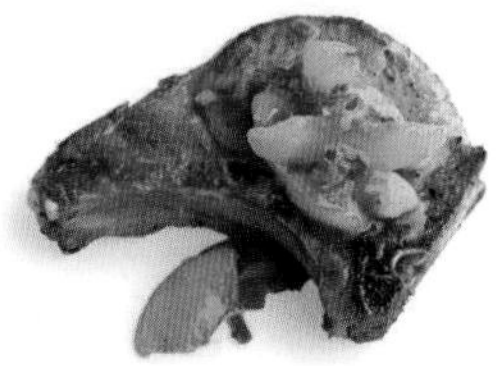

PEACH-HONEY: In a skillet cook 1½ cups sliced, peeled peaches and ½ cup finely chopped red onion in 1 tablespoon butter until tender. Stir in 2 tablespoons honey; cook until glazed. Stir in ⅛ teaspoon crushed red pepper.

CARAMELIZED ONION-WALNUT: In covered skillet cook 2 cups sliced sweet yellow onions in 1 tablespoon butter over medium-low heat 10 minutes. Uncover; cook 4 to 5 minutes more or until browned. Add ¼ cup chopped toasted walnuts and 1 tablespoon snipped fresh parsley.

FAST LOW-CALORIE

Smoked Pork Chops with Mustard-Dill Sauce

PREP: 10 MINUTES **BROIL:** 9 MINUTES
MAKES: 6 SERVINGS

- **6 smoked pork loin chops, cut 1 inch thick**
- **3 tablespoons packed brown sugar**
- **3 tablespoons cider vinegar or white wine vinegar**
- **½ cup Dijon-style mustard**
- **3 tablespoons olive oil**
- **½ teaspoon dried dill weed**
- **Dash black pepper**

1 Preheat broiler. Place chops on the unheated rack of a broiler pan. Broil 3 to 4 inches from the heat for 9 to 12 minutes or until heated through, turning once halfway through broiling.

2 Meanwhile, for sauce, in a small bowl stir together brown sugar and vinegar until sugar is dissolved. Using a wire whisk, beat in mustard, olive oil, dill weed, and pepper until combined. Transfer warm chops to a serving platter. To serve, spoon some of the sauce over chops. Pass remaining sauce.

PER CHOP + 2 TABLESPOONS SAUCE: 208 cal., 11 g total fat (2 g sat. fat), 45 mg chol., 1,453 mg sodium, 7 g carb., 0 g fiber, 15 g pro. EXCHANGES: ½ Other Carb., 2 Lean Meat, 1 Fat

BEST-LOVED

Oven-Barbecued Ribs

PREP: 25 MINUTES **BAKE:** 90 MINUTES AT 350°F
MAKES: 4 SERVINGS

- **3 to 4 pounds pork loin back ribs**
- **¾ cup ketchup**
- **¾ cup water**
- **2 tablespoons vinegar**
- **2 tablespoons Worcestershire sauce**
- **1 teaspoon paprika**
- **1 teaspoon chili powder**
- **½ teaspoon black pepper**
- **¼ teaspoon salt**
- **¼ to ½ teaspoon cayenne pepper**
- **1 cup finely chopped onion (1 large)**

1 Preheat oven to 350°F. If desired, cut ribs into serving-size pieces. Place the ribs, bone sides down, in a large shallow roasting pan. Bake, covered, for 60 minutes. Carefully drain off fat in roasting pan.

2 Meanwhile, for sauce, in a bowl combine ketchup, water, vinegar, Worcestershire sauce, paprika, chili powder, black pepper, salt, and cayenne pepper. Stir in onion.

3 Pour some sauce over ribs. Bake, uncovered, about 30 minutes more or until ribs are tender, basting once with sauce. In saucepan, bring remaining sauce to boiling; pass with ribs.

PER ¼ RIBS + ¼ CUP SAUCE: 675 cal., 50 g total fat (18 g sat. fat), 171 mg chol., 915 mg sodium, 18 g carb., 2 g fiber, 36 g pro. EXCHANGES: 5 High-Fat Meat, 2 Fat

Oven-Roasted Asian-Style Pork Ribs

PREP: 45 MINUTES **BAKE:** 15 MINUTES AT 350°F
MAKES: 4 SERVINGS

- **3 pounds pork loin back ribs or pork spareribs**
- **3 tablespoons pineapple, peach, or apricot preserves**
- **⅓ cup ketchup**
- **2 tablespoons soy sauce**
- **1 teaspoon grated fresh ginger or ¼ teaspoon ground ginger**
- **1 clove garlic, minced**

1 Cut ribs into serving-size pieces. Place ribs in a 4- to 6-quart Dutch oven. Add enough water to cover. Bring to boiling; reduce heat. Simmer, covered, for 25 to 30 minutes or until ribs are tender; drain.

2 Meanwhile, for sauce, cut up any large pieces of fruit in the preserves. In a small bowl stir together preserves, ketchup, soy sauce, ginger, and garlic.

3 Preheat oven to 350°F. Brush some sauce over both sides of the ribs. Place ribs, bone sides down, in a shallow roasting pan. Bake, uncovered, for 15 to 20 minutes or until glazed and heated through. Brush with the remaining sauce before serving.

PER ¼ RIBS + ¼ CUP SAUCE: 662 cal., 50 g total fat (18 g sat. fat), 171 mg chol., 893 mg sodium, 16 g carb., 0 g fiber, 35 g pro. EXCHANGES: 1 Other Carb., 5 High-Fat Meat, 2 Fat

ALL ABOUT RIBS

Although you might first think of ribs for grilling, you can cook both pork loin back ribs and spareribs indoors with delicious results. Loin back ribs, sometimes called baby back ribs, are located closest to the back of the pig and have more tender meat than spareribs; they are typically short, curvy, and meaty. Spareribs are from the side section of the pig and connect to the breast bone. The meat is leaner and the bones are straighter. Both types of ribs have a thin membrane that covers the bones. To remove it, slip the tip of a table knife under the membrane and use a paper towel to grab it and pull it away.

HONEY AND APPLE RIBS

Honey and Apple Ribs

PREP: 15 MINUTES **COOK:** 20 MINUTES
BAKE: 50 MINUTES AT 350°F **MAKES:** 6 SERVINGS

- **2 tablespoons vegetable oil**
- **2 cloves garlic, minced**
- **1 12-ounce bottle chili sauce**
- **½ cup apple juice or apple cider**
- **⅓ cup honey**
- **3 tablespoons Worcestershire sauce**
- **1 teaspoon dry mustard**
- **2½ pounds boneless pork country-style ribs (6 ribs), cut from the shoulder (see tip, right)**
- **1 large onion, cut into wedges (2 cups)**
- **2 apples, cored and cut into wedges**

1 Preheat oven to 350°F. For sauce, in a medium saucepan heat 1 tablespoon of the oil over medium heat. Add garlic; cook for 30 seconds. Stir in chili sauce, apple juice, honey, Worcestershire sauce, and dry mustard. Bring to boiling; reduce heat. Simmer, uncovered, for 20 minutes (should have 1¾ cups sauce). Remove from heat.

2 Meanwhile, in a very large skillet heat the remaining 1 tablespoon oil over medium-high heat. Add ribs; cook in hot oil about 5 minutes or until browned, turning to brown evenly on all sides; set aside.

3 Place onion wedges in a shallow roasting pan. Place browned ribs on top of onions. Spoon sauce over ribs and onions. Cover pan with foil. Bake, covered, for 20 minutes. Add apple wedges to pan and stir into sauce. Bake, covered, about 30 minutes more or until ribs are tender (185°F). Transfer ribs, onions, and apples to serving platter. Spoon sauce from pan over all.

PER RIB + ½ CUP APPLE MIXTURE + ¼ CUP SAUCE: 452 cal., 18 g total fat (3 g sat. fat), 90 mg chol., 783 mg sodium, 48 g carb., 3 g fiber, 25 g pro. **EXCHANGES:**, 1 Vegetable, ½ Fruit, 1 Starch, 1½ Other Carb., 3 Medium-Fat Meat, ½ Fat

BEST-LOVED

Ham Balls in Barbecue Sauce

(photo, page 373)

PREP: 20 MINUTES **BAKE:** 45 MINUTES AT 350°F
MAKES: 6 SERVINGS

- **2 eggs, lightly beaten**
- **1½ cups soft bread crumbs (2 slices)**
- **½ cup finely chopped onion (1 medium)**
- **2 tablespoons milk**
- **1 teaspoon dry mustard**
- **¼ teaspoon black pepper**
- **12 ounces ground cooked ham**
- **12 ounces ground pork or ground beef**
- **¾ cup packed brown sugar**
- **½ cup ketchup**
- **2 tablespoons vinegar**
- **1 teaspoon dry mustard**

1 Preheat oven to 350°F. Lightly grease a 2-quart rectangular baking dish; set aside. In a large bowl combine eggs, bread crumbs, onion, milk, 1 teaspoon mustard, and the pepper. Add ground ham and ground pork; mix well. Shape meat mixture into 12 balls, using about ⅓ cup mixture for each. Place ham balls in the prepared baking dish.

2 In a small bowl mix brown sugar, ketchup, vinegar, and 1 teaspoon mustard. Stir until the brown sugar dissolves. Pour ketchup mixture over meatballs. Bake, uncovered, about 45 minutes or until done (160°F).

PER 2 HAM BALLS: 429 cal., 19 g total fat (7 g sat. fat), 144 mg chol., 1,104 mg sodium, 42 g carb., 1 g fiber, 23 g pro. **EXCHANGES:** 1 Starch, 2 Carb., 3 Medium-Fat Meat, ½ Fat

COUNTRY-STYLE RIBS

Pork country-style ribs are the meatiest ribs and are cut from either the loin section or the shoulder (also known as the butt). Those cut from the loin require less cooking than those cut from the shoulder. You may find country-style ribs labeled loin, shoulder, or butt. If the cut doesn't appear on the label, ask the butcher so you will know how long to cook the ribs. You will need shoulder ribs for Honey and Apple Ribs. If you happen to buy loin ribs, reduce roasting time.

LOW-CALORIE

Apple Butter-Glazed Ham

PREP: 20 MINUTES **ROAST:** 20 MINUTES AT 425°F
MAKES: 4 SERVINGS

- **2 medium sweet potatoes, peeled and cut into 1-inch cubes (1 pound)**
- **12 ounces Brussels sprouts, halved**
- **2 tablespoons vegetable oil**
- **1/4 cup apple butter**
- **1/4 cup cider vinegar**
- **1 to 1 1/4 pounds center-cut ham slice, about 1 inch thick**

1 Preheat oven to 425°F. Line a 15×10×1-inch baking pan with foil; lightly coat with *nonstick cooking spray.* Set pan aside. In a bowl combine sweet potatoes and Brussels sprouts. Sprinkle with 1/2 teaspoon *salt* and 1/4 teaspoon *black pepper.* Add 1 tablespoon of the oil; toss to coat. Spread vegetables in a single layer in the prepared pan. Roast, uncovered, for 20 to 22 minutes or until tender, stirring once.

2 For vinaigrette, in a screw-top jar combine apple butter, vinegar, and the remaining 1 tablespoon oil. Cover; shake well. Set aside 2 tablespoons of the vinaigrette. Toss remaining vinaigrette with vegetables; keep warm.

3 Heat a grill pan over medium-high heat. Add ham slice to hot pan; cook about 8 minutes or until browned and heated through, turning once. Drizzle the 2 tablespoons reserved vinaigrette over ham. Serve with vegetables.

PER 4 OUNCES HAM + 1 CUP VEGETABLES: 396 cal., 11 g total fat (2 g sat. fat), 65 mg chol., 1,640 mg sodium, 48 g carb., 7 g fiber, 28 g pro. **EXCHANGES:** 1 1/2 Vegetable, 1 1/2 Other Carb., 3 Lean Meat, 1 Fat

FAST

Kielbasa and Orzo

START TO FINISH: 20 MINUTES **MAKES:** 4 SERVINGS

- **1 tablespoon vegetable oil**
- **1 pound cooked kielbasa, halved lengthwise and cut into 2-inch lengths**
- **1 cup dried orzo (rosamarina)**
- **1 14.5-ounce can beef broth**
- **1 teaspoon dried Italian seasoning, crushed**
- **2 1/2 cups coarsely chopped zucchini**
- **1/3 cup 1-inch pieces green onions (optional)**

1 In a large skillet heat oil over medium-high heat. Add kielbasa; cook about 2 minutes or until browned; stir in orzo. Cook and stir for 1 minute.

2 Stir in broth, 1/2 cup *water,* and Italian seasoning. Bring to boiling; reduce heat. Simmer, covered, about 8 minutes or until orzo is tender, adding the zucchini for the last 4 minutes of cooking, and stirring occasionally. If desired, stir in green onions. Season to taste with *salt* and *black pepper.*

PER 1 1/2 CUPS: 589 cal., 38 g total fat (16 g sat. fat), 50 mg chol., 1,373 mg sodium, 39 g carb., 2 g fiber, 21 g pro. **EXCHANGES:** 1/2 Vegetable, 2 1/2 Starch, 2 High-Fat Meat, 4 Fat

FAST LOW-CALORIE

Corn Dogs

START TO FINISH: 30 MINUTES
MAKES: 10 TO 12 CORN DOGS

- **1 cup all-purpose flour**
- **2/3 cup yellow cornmeal**
- **2 tablespoons sugar**
- **1 1/2 teaspoons baking powder**
- **1/2 teaspoon dry mustard**
- **1 tablespoon shortening**
- **1 egg, lightly beaten**
- **3/4 cup milk**
- **10 to 12 wooden skewers**
- **10 to 12 frankfurters or smoked frankfurters**
- **Vegetable oil for frying (about 8 cups)**

1 Preheat oven to 200°F. In a bowl combine flour, cornmeal, sugar, baking powder, mustard, and 1/4 teaspoon *salt.* Using a pastry blender, cut in shortening until fine crumbs form. Combine egg and milk. Stir egg mixture into flour mixture. Insert wooden skewers into ends of frankfurters. Pour oil into a very large skillet to a depth of 1 inch; heat over medium-high heat to 365°F. Spoon and spread the batter over frankfurters, coating completely (if batter is too thick, add 1 to 2 tablespoons additional milk).

2 Arrange batter-coated franks, three at a time, in hot oil. Turn franks after 10 seconds to prevent batter from sliding off (see photo, below). Cook for 2 to 3 minutes or until golden, turning halfway through cooking. Drain on paper towels; keep warm in oven while frying remaining franks.

PER CORN DOG: 315 cal., 22 g total fat (6 g sat. fat), 45 mg chol., 632 mg sodium, 21 g carb., 1 g fiber, 8 g pro. **EXCHANGES:** 1 1/2 Starch, 1/2 Medium-Fat Meat, 3 1/2 Fat

FRYING CORN DOGS

Using tongs to grab the skewer, turn the corn dog after 10 seconds of cooking. This prevents the batter from slipping off the frankfurter and ensures even cooking.

LAMB CUTS AND HOW TO COOK THEM

This page helps you identify lamb cuts and offers recommended ways to cook them. The photos show cuts available at markets. They correspond to the drawing, which shows where the cuts come from on the animal.

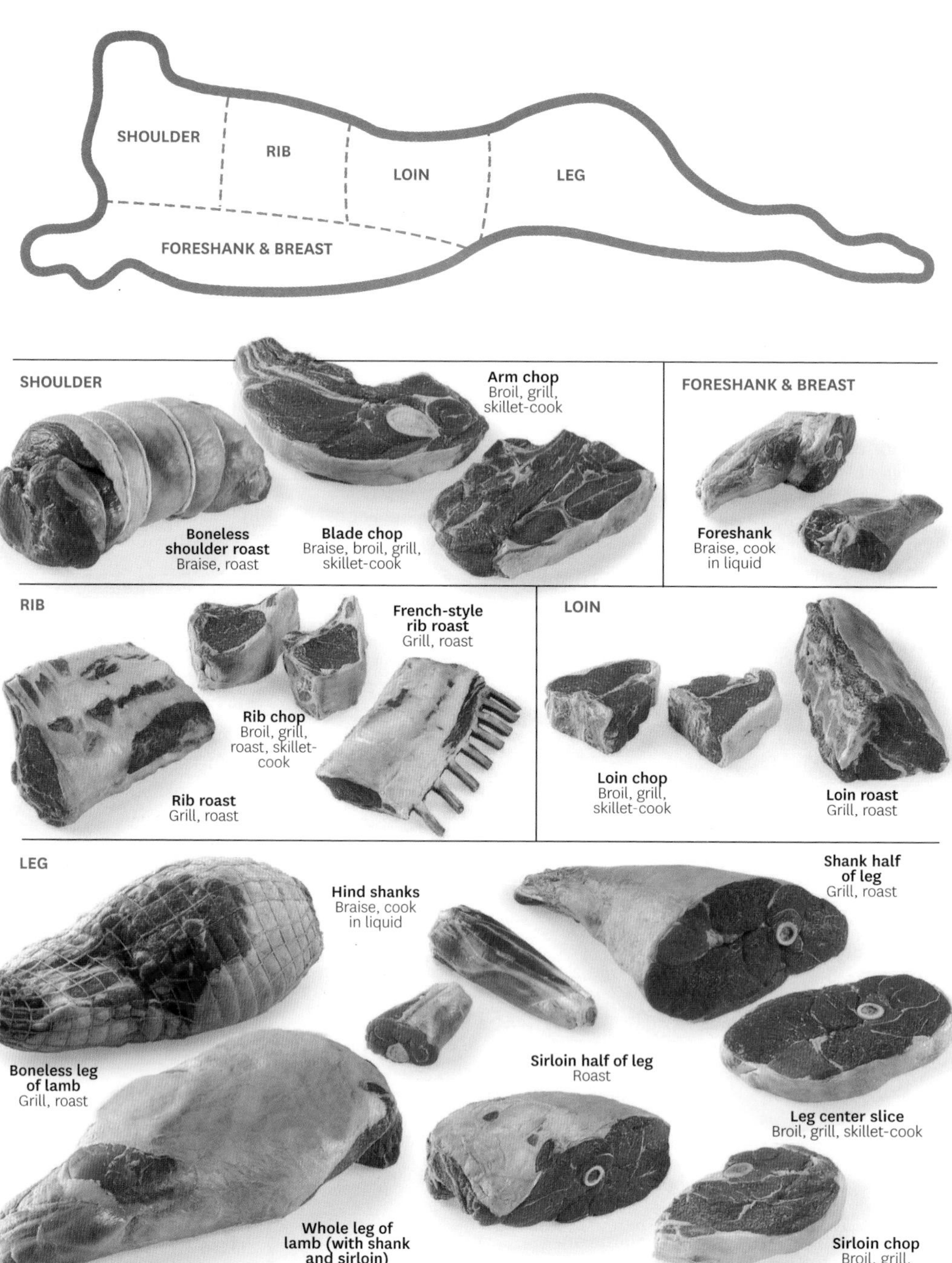

BEST-LOVED

Lamb Shanks with Beans

PREP: 30 MINUTES **STAND:** 60 MINUTES
COOK: 2 HOURS 35 MINUTES **MAKES:** 6 SERVINGS

1¼ cups dried navy beans
4 cups water
1 tablespoon vegetable oil
4 meaty lamb shanks (about 4 pounds), cut into 3- to 4-inch pieces, or meaty veal shank cross cuts (about 3 pounds)
1 medium onion, sliced and separated into rings
2 cloves garlic, minced
2 cups chicken broth
1 teaspoon dried thyme, crushed
½ teaspoon salt
¼ teaspoon black pepper
1 14.5-ounce can diced tomatoes, undrained

1 Rinse beans. In a 4- to 6-quart Dutch oven combine the beans and the water. Bring to boiling; reduce heat. Simmer, uncovered, for 2 minutes. Remove from heat. Do not drain. Cover and let stand for 60 minutes. (Or add water to cover beans. Cover and let stand overnight.)

2 Drain and rinse beans. In the same pan heat the oil over medium heat. Add lamb shanks and brown on all sides; remove from pan. Add onion and garlic to the same pan; cook until tender. Stir in beans, chicken broth, thyme, salt, and pepper. Add shanks. Bring to boiling; reduce heat. Simmer, covered, for 2 to 2½ hours or until meat and beans are tender. (If necessary, add more chicken broth to keep mixture moist.)

3 Remove meat from pan; cool slightly. When cool enough to handle, cut meat off bones and coarsely chop. Discard fat and bones. Skim fat from the top of the bean mixture. Stir in the meat and tomatoes. Bring to boiling; reduce heat. Simmer, covered, for 10 to 15 minutes or until heated through and flavors are blended.

PER 1½ CUPS MEAT-BEAN MIXTURE: 430 cal., 10 g total fat (2 g sat. fat), 132 mg chol., 785 mg sodium, 31 g carb., 12 g fiber, 53 g pro. EXCHANGES: ½ Vegetable, 2 Starch, 6½ Lean Meat, ½ Fat

A SPECIAL CUT

Think ahead if you're making a dish featuring lamb shanks or leg of lamb. You might need to special-order these cuts from a butcher at a supermarket or specialty meat market.

LOW-CALORIE

Roasted Lamb with Olive Tapenade

PREP: 30 MINUTES **ROAST:** 105 MINUTES AT 325°F
STAND: 15 MINUTES **MAKES:** 8 SERVINGS

1 cup pitted Kalamata olives
1 tablespoon snipped fresh Italian parsley
1 tablespoon olive oil
1 teaspoon finely shredded lemon peel
2 teaspoons lemon juice
1 teaspoon snipped fresh rosemary
1 teaspoon snipped fresh thyme
¼ teaspoon freshly ground black pepper
2 cloves garlic, minced
1 4- to 5-pound boneless leg of lamb, rolled and tied
⅓ cup dry red wine
1 teaspoon kosher salt
1 teaspoon freshly ground black pepper

1 Preheat oven to 325°F. For olive tapenade, in a food processor combine olives, parsley, olive oil, lemon peel, lemon juice, rosemary, thyme, the ¼ teaspoon pepper, and the garlic. Cover and process until finely chopped, stopping to scrape down sides of the food processor as necessary; set aside.

2 Untie and unroll roast; trim fat. If necessary, place meat, boned side up, between two pieces of plastic wrap and pound meat with a meat mallet to an even thickness. Spread tapenade over cut surface of meat. Roll up; tie securely with 100% cotton kitchen string.

3 Place roast, seam side down, on a rack set in a shallow roasting pan. Insert an oven-going meat thermometer into roast. In a small bowl combine wine, salt, and the 1 teaspoon pepper; set aside. Roast meat, uncovered, for 1¾ to 2¼ hours or until thermometer registers 135°F (medium rare), basting with red wine mixture several times until the last 10 minutes of roasting. Discard any remaining wine mixture.

4 Remove roast from oven. Cover with foil and let stand for 15 minutes before slicing (temperature of the meat will rise during standing time). Remove string and slice meat.

PER 5 OUNCES MEAT + 1½ TABLESPOONS TAPENADE: 320 cal., 14 g total fat (4 g sat. fat), 127 mg chol., 591 mg sodium, 2 g carb., 1 g fiber, 41 g pro. EXCHANGES: 6 Lean Meat

MEDITERRANEAN LAMB SKILLET

FAST LOW-CALORIE

Mediterranean Lamb Skillet

START TO FINISH: 25 MINUTES **MAKES:** 4 SERVINGS

- **½ cup dried orzo (rosamarina)**
- **8 lamb rib chops, cut 1 inch thick**
- **2 teaspoons olive oil**
- **3 cloves garlic, minced**
- **1 14.5-ounce can diced tomatoes with basil, garlic, and oregano, undrained**
- **1 tablespoon balsamic vinegar**
- **2 teaspoons snipped fresh rosemary**
- **⅓ cup halved, pitted Kalamata olives**

1 Cook orzo according to package directions; drain and keep warm. Meanwhile, trim fat from chops. Sprinkle chops with *salt* and *black pepper.* In a large skillet heat olive oil over medium heat. Add chops; cook in hot oil for 9 to 11 minutes for medium (160°F), turning once. Remove chops from skillet.

2 Stir garlic into drippings in skillet. Cook and stir for 1 minute. Stir in tomatoes, vinegar, and snipped rosemary. Bring to boiling; reduce heat. Simmer, uncovered, for 5 minutes. Stir in orzo and olives. Return chops to skillet; heat through.

PER 2 CHOPS + ¾ CUP ORZO MIXTURE: 303 cal., 11 g total fat (3 g sat. fat), 60 mg chol., 622 mg sodium, 27 g carb., 2 g fiber, 22 g pro. EXCHANGES: 2 Vegetable, 1 Starch, 2 Lean Meat, 1½ Fat

FAST LOW-CALORIE

Spicy Apricot Lamb Chops

PREP: 20 MINUTES **BROIL:** 10 MINUTES
MAKES: 4 SERVINGS

- **8 lamb rib chops, cut 1 inch thick**
- **1 tablespoon packed brown sugar**
- **1 teaspoon garlic salt**
- **1 teaspoon chili powder**
- **1 teaspoon paprika**
- **½ teaspoon dried oregano, crushed**
- **¼ teaspoon ground cinnamon**
- **¼ teaspoon ground allspice**
- **¼ teaspoon black pepper**
- **¼ cup apricot preserves**

1 Preheat broiler. Trim fat from chops. In a bowl combine brown sugar, garlic salt, chili powder, paprika, oregano, cinnamon, allspice, and pepper. Rub spice mixture on all sides of chops.

2 Place chops on the unheated rack of a broiler pan. Broil 4 to 5 inches from the heat for 10 to 15 minutes for medium (160°F), turning chops and brushing with preserves once.

PER 2 CHOPS: 311 cal., 8 g total fat (3 g sat. fat), 119 mg chol., 345 mg sodium, 18 g carb., 1 g fiber, 39 g pro. EXCHANGES: 1 Other Carb., 5½ Lean Meat, ½ Fat

LOW-CALORIE

Roast Rack of Lamb with Sweet Mango Chutney

PREP: 20 MINUTES **ROAST:** 45 MINUTES AT 325°F
STAND: 15 MINUTES **MAKES:** 6 SERVINGS

- **2 1- to 1½-pound lamb french-style rib roasts (6 to 8 ribs each), with or without backbone**
- **3 tablespoons Dijon-style mustard**
- **3 tablespoons lemon juice**
- **1 tablespoon snipped fresh rosemary or thyme**
- **½ teaspoon salt**
- **¾ cup soft bread crumbs (1 slice)**
- **1 tablespoon butter or margarine, melted**
- **1 recipe Sweet Mango Chutney (page 539)**

1 Preheat oven to 325°F. Trim fat from meat. Stir together mustard, lemon juice, rosemary, and salt. Rub onto meat. In a small bowl toss together crumbs and melted butter. Sprinkle onto meat.

2 Place meat on a rack set in a shallow roasting pan, arranging roasts to stand upright (see photo 1, below). Insert an oven-going meat thermometer into one roast. The thermometer should not touch bone. Roast, uncovered, for 45 to 60 minutes or until thermometer registers 135°F for medium rare. Cover with foil; let stand for 15 minutes. (For medium, roast for 1 to 1½ hours or until thermometer registers 150°F. Cover; let stand for 15 minutes.) Temperature of the meat will rise during standing. To carve, slice between ribs (see photo 2, below). Serve with Sweet Mango Chutney.

PER 2 RIBS + ¼ CUP CHUTNEY: 255 cal., 8 g total fat (3 g sat. fat), 48 mg chol., 540 mg sodium, 33 g carb., 2 g fiber, 14 g pro. EXCHANGES: ½ Fruit, ½ Starch, 1 Other Carb., 2 Lean Meat, 1 Fat

ROAST RACK OF LAMB STEP-BY-STEP

1. Stand roasts on long ends with ribs on top. Lean roasts against each other, fitting the ribs of one roast between ribs of the second roast.

2. To carve roasts, place one roast on a cutting board and slice between ribs. Repeat with the second roast. Allow two rib portions per serving.

LOW-CALORIE

Herb-Rubbed Bison Sirloin Tip Roast

PREP: 20 MINUTES **ROAST:** 75 MINUTES AT 375°F
STAND: 15 MINUTES **MAKES:** 8 SERVINGS

- **1 tablespoon paprika**
- **2 teaspoons kosher salt or sea salt, or 1 teaspoon salt**
- **1 teaspoon garlic powder**
- **½ teaspoon dried oregano, crushed**
- **½ teaspoon dried thyme, crushed**
- **½ teaspoon black pepper**
- **½ teaspoon onion powder**
- **½ teaspoon cayenne pepper**
- **2 tablespoons olive oil**
- **1 3- to 3½-pound boneless bison (buffalo) sirloin tip roast**

1 Preheat oven to 375°F. In a small bowl combine paprika, salt, garlic powder, oregano, thyme, black pepper, onion powder, and cayenne pepper. Stir in oil until well combined.

2 Trim fat from roast. Spread oil mixture over meat. Place meat on a rack in a shallow roasting pan. Insert an oven-going meat thermometer into center of roast.

3 Roast, uncovered, for 15 minutes. Reduce oven temperature to 300°F. Roast for 60 to 65 minutes more or until meat thermometer registers 135°F (medium rare). Cover with foil and let stand for 15 minutes. Temperature of the meat will rise during standing. Thinly slice meat across the grain to serve.

PER 4 OUNCES: 238 cal., 8 g total fat (2 g sat. fat), 121 mg chol., 573 mg sodium, 2 g carb., 1 g fiber, 37 g pro.
EXCHANGES: 5 Lean Meat

Apple-Bison Burgers

PREP: 45 MINUTES **COOK:** 8 MINUTES
MAKES: 4 BURGERS

- **1 recipe Cantaloupe and Strawberry Relish**
- **⅓ cup finely chopped Granny Smith apple**
- **¼ cup finely chopped celery**
- **¼ cup finely chopped onion**
- **1 tablespoon vegetable oil**
- **2 tablespoons ketchup**
- **¾ teaspoon Jamaican jerk seasoning**
- **⅛ teaspoon salt**
- **⅛ teaspoon black or cayenne pepper**
- **1 pound ground bison (buffalo)**
- **1 tablespoon olive oil**
- **¼ cup mayonnaise**
- **4 slices Texas toast or ¾-inch slices rustic Italian bread, toasted**
- **Red-tipped leaf lettuce**

APPLE-BISON BURGERS

1 Prepare Cantaloupe and Strawberry Relish. In a medium saucepan cook apple, celery, and onion in hot oil over medium heat for 6 to 8 minutes or until tender. Remove from heat; cool to room temperature.

2 In a large bowl combine the apple mixture, ketchup, ½ teaspoon of the Jamaican jerk seasoning, the salt, and pepper. Add bison; mix well. Shape mixture into four ¾-inch-thick patties.

3 Brush a grill pan or skillet with olive oil; heat pan over medium heat. Add patties to hot pan. Cook for 8 to 10 minutes or until done (160°F), turning once halfway through cooking.

4 In a small bowl stir together mayonnaise and the remaining ¼ teaspoon jerk seasoning; spread on Texas toast. Place toast slices on dinner plates. Top with leaf lettuce, burgers, and Cantaloupe and Strawberry Relish.

CANTALOUPE AND STRAWBERRY RELISH: In a bowl combine ½ cup chopped cantaloupe or peeled peaches; ½ cup chopped fresh strawberries; 2 tablespoons finely chopped red onion; 2 tablespoons finely chopped green sweet pepper; 1 tablespoon snipped fresh cilantro; 2 teaspoons snipped fresh mint; ½ teaspoon finely shredded lemon or lime peel; and 1 tablespoon lemon or lime juice. Toss lightly to mix. Let stand at room temperature for 30 minutes, stirring occasionally. (Or cover and chill for 4 to 24 hours.)

PER BURGER + ¼ CUP RELISH: 417 cal., 22 g total fat (3 g sat. fat), 71 mg chol., 559 mg sodium, 29 g carb., 2 g fiber, 29 g pro.
EXCHANGES: 1 Vegetable, 1½ Starch, 3½ Lean Meat, 3 Fat

BROILING MEAT

Preheat broiler. Place meat on the unheated rack of a broiler pan. For cuts less than 1½ inches thick, broil 3 to 4 inches from the heat. For 1½-inch-thick cuts, broil 4 to 5 inches from the heat. Broil for the time listed or until done, turning meat over after half of the broiling time. For steaks and chops, cover and let stand for 5 minutes.

Cut	Thickness/Weight	Approximate Broiling Time*	Doneness
BEEF			
Boneless steak (chuck eye, shoulder center [ranch], ribeye, shoulder top blade [flat-iron], tenderloin, top loin)	1 inch 1 inch 1½ inches 1½ inches	12 to 14 minutes 15 to 18 minutes 18 to 21 minutes 22 to 27 minutes	145°F medium rare 160°F medium 145°F medium rare 160°F medium
Boneless top sirloin steak	1 inch 1 inch 1½ inches 1½ inches	15 to 17 minutes 20 to 22 minutes 25 to 27 minutes 30 to 32 minutes	145°F medium rare 160°F medium 145°F medium rare 160°F medium
Boneless tri-tip steak (bottom sirloin)	¾ inch ¾ inch 1 inch 1 inch	6 to 7 minutes 8 to 9 minutes 9 to 10 minutes 11 to 12 minutes	145°F medium rare 160°F medium 145°F medium rare 160°F medium
Flank steak	1¼ to 1¾ pounds	17 to 21 minutes	160°F medium
Steak with bone (porterhouse, rib, T-bone)	1 inch 1 inch 1½ inches 1½ inches	12 to 15 minutes 15 to 20 minutes 20 to 25 minutes 25 to 30 minutes	145°F medium rare 160°F medium 145°F medium rare 160°F medium
GROUND MEAT			
Patties (beef, lamb, pork, or veal)	½ inch ¾ inch	10 to 12 minutes 12 to 14 minutes	160°F medium 160°F medium
LAMB			
Chop (loin or rib)	1 inch	10 to 15 minutes	160°F medium
Chop (sirloin)	1 inch	12 to 15 minutes	160°F medium
PORK			
Chop (boneless top loin)	¾ to 1 inch 1¼ to 1½ inches	4 to 6 minutes 11 to 13 minutes**	145°F medium 145°F medium
Chop with bone (loin or rib)	¾ to 1 inch 1¼ to 1½ inches	6 to 8 minutes 15 to 17 minutes**	145°F medium 145°F medium
Chop with bone (sirloin)	¾ to 1 inch	7 to 10 minutes	145°F medium
Ham steak, cooked	1 inch	12 to 15 minutes	140°F heated through
SAUSAGES			
Frankfurters and sausage links, cooked		3 to 7 minutes	140°F heated through
VEAL			
Chop (loin or rib)	¾ to 1 inch 1½ inches	14 to 16 minutes 21 to 25 minutes	160°F medium 160°F medium

*All broiling times are based on meat removed directly from refrigerator.
**Turn two to three times during broiling.

ROASTING MEAT

Place meat, fat side up, on a rack in a shallow roasting pan. (Roasts with a bone do not need a rack.) Insert a meat thermometer (see tip, page 383). Do not add water or liquid and do not cover. Roast in a 325°F oven (unless chart says otherwise) for the time listed and until the thermometer registers the temperature listed under Final Roasting Temperature. Remove the meat from the oven; cover with foil and let it stand 15 minutes before carving. The meat's temperature will rise to the standard for medium-rare (145°F) and medium (160°) during the time it stands.

Cut	Weight	Approximate Roasting Time*	Final Roasting Temperature
BEEF			
Boneless tri-tip roast (bottom sirloin) Roast at 425°F	1½ to 2 pounds	30 to 35 minutes 40 to 45 minutes	135°F 150°F
Eye round roast Roasting past medium rare is not recommended	2 to 3 pounds	1½ to 1¾ hours	135°F
Ribeye roast Roast at 350°F	3 to 4 pounds 4 to 6 pounds 6 to 8 pounds	1½ to 1¾ hours 1¾ to 2 hours 1¾ to 2 hours 2 to 2½ hours 2 to 2¼ hours 2½ to 2¾ hours	135°F 150°F 135°F 150°F 135°F 150°F
Rib roast (chine bone removed) Roast at 350°F	4 to 6 pounds 6 to 8 pounds 8 to 10 pounds**	1¾ to 2¼ hours 2¼ to 2¾ hours 2¼ to 2½ hours 2¾ to 3 hours 2½ to 3 hours 3 to 3½ hours	135°F 150°F 135°F 150°F 135°F 150°F
Round tip roast	3 to 4 pounds 4 to 6 pounds 6 to 8 pounds	1¾ to 2 hours 2¼ to 2½ hours 2 to 2½ hours 2½ to 3 hours 2½ to 3 hours 3 to 3½ hours	135°F 150°F 135°F 150°F 135°F 150°F
Tenderloin roast Roast at 425°F	2 to 3 pounds 4 to 5 pounds	35 to 40 minutes 45 to 50 minutes 50 to 60 minutes 60 to 70 minutes	135°F 150°F 135°F 150°F
Top round roast Roasting past medium rare is not recommended	4 to 6 pounds 6 to 8 pounds	1¾ to 2½ hours 2½ to 3 hours	135°F 135°F
LAMB			
Boneless leg of lamb	4 to 5 pounds 5 to 6 pounds	1¾ to 2¼ hours 2 to 2½ hours 2 to 2½ hours 2½ to 3 hours	135°F 150°F 135°F 150°F
Boneless shoulder roast	3 to 4 pounds 4 to 5 pounds	1½ to 2 hours 1¾ to 2¼ hours 2 to 2½ hours 2¼ to 3 hours	135°F 150°F 135°F 150°F

*All roasting times are based on meat removed directly from refrigerator.
**Roasts weighing more than 8 pounds should be loosely covered with foil halfway through roasting.

Cut	Weight	Approximate Roasting Time*	Final Roasting Temperature
LAMB *(CONTINUED)*			
Boneless sirloin roast	1½ to 2 pounds	1 to 1¼ hours 1¼ to 1½ hours	135°F 150°F
Leg of lamb (with bone)	5 to 7 pounds 7 to 8 pounds	1¾ to 2¼ hours 2¼ to 2¾ hours 2¼ to 2¾ hours 2½ to 3 hours	135°F 150°F 135°F 150°F
Leg of lamb, shank half (with bone)	3 to 4 pounds	1¾ to 2¼ hours 2 to 2½ hours	135°F 150°F
Leg of lamb, sirloin half (with bone)	3 to 4 pounds	1½ to 2 hours 1¾ to 2¼ hours	135°F 150°F
PORK			
Boneless sirloin roast	2 to 2½ pounds	1¼ to 1¾ hours	145°F
Boneless top loin roast (single loin)	2 to 3 pounds	1 to 1½ hours	145°F
Loin center rib roast (backbone loosened)	3 to 4 pounds 4 to 6 pounds	1¼ to 1½ hours 1½ to 2½ hours	145°F 145°F
Loin back ribs or spareribs		1½ to 1¾ hours	Tender
Boneless country-style ribs (loin) Brown in oil before roasting Roast at 350°F		30 minutes	145°F
Boneless country-style ribs (shoulder) Brown in oil before roasting Roast at 350°F		50 minutes	Tender (185°F)
Crown roast	6 to 8 pounds	1¾ to 2½ hours	145°F
Tenderloin Roast at 425°F	1 pound	30 to 35 minutes	145°F
Ham, cooked (boneless)	1½ to 3 pounds 3 to 5 pounds 6 to 8 pounds 8 to 10 pounds**	¾ to 1¼ hours 1 to 1¾ hours 1¾ to 2½ hours 2¼ to 2¾ hours	140°F 140°F 140°F 140°F
Ham, cooked (with bone) (half or whole)	6 to 8 pounds 14 to 16 pounds**	1½ to 2¼ hours 2¾ to 3¾ hours	140°F 140°F
Ham, cook before eating (with bone)	3 to 5 pounds 7 to 8 pounds 14 to 16 pounds**	1¾ to 3 hours 2½ to 3¼ hours 4 to 5¼ hours	150°F 150°F 150°F
Smoked shoulder picnic, cooked (with bone)	4 to 6 pounds	1¼ to 2 hours	140°F
VEAL			
Loin roast (with bone)	3 to 4 pounds	1¾ to 2¼ hours	150°F
Rib roast (chine bone removed)	4 to 5 pounds	1½ to 2¼ hours	150°F

*All roasting times are based on meat removed directly from refrigerator.

**Roasts weighing more than 8 pounds should be loosely covered with foil halfway through roasting.

SKILLET-COOKING MEAT

Select a heavy skillet that is the correct size for the amount of meat you are cooking. (If the skillet is too large, the pan juices can burn.) Lightly coat the skillet with nonstick cooking spray. (Or use a heavy nonstick skillet.) Preheat skillet over medium-high heat until very hot. Add meat. Do not add any liquid and do not cover the skillet. Reduce heat to medium and cook for the time listed or until done, turning meat occasionally. If meat browns too quickly, reduce heat to medium-low. For steaks and chops, cover and let meat stand for 5 minutes before serving.

Cut	Thickness	Approximate Cooking Time*	Doneness
BEEF			
Boneless chuck eye steak	¾ inch 1 inch	9 to 11 minutes 12 to 15 minutes	145°F med. rare to 160°F medium 145°F med. rare to 160°F medium
Boneless top sirloin steak	¾ inch 1 inch	10 to 13 minutes 15 to 20 minutes	145°F med. rare to 160°F medium 145°F med. rare to 160°F medium
Boneless tri-tip steak (bottom sirloin)	¾ inch 1 inch	6 to 9 minutes 9 to 12 minutes	145°F med. rare to 160°F medium 145°F med. rare to 160°F medium
Cubed steak	½ inch	5 to 8 minutes	160°F medium
Porterhouse or T-bone steak	¾ inch 1 inch	11 to 13 minutes 14 to 17 minutes	145°F med. rare to 160°F medium 145°F med. rare to 160°F medium
Ribeye steak	¾ inch 1 inch	8 to 10 minutes 12 to 15 minutes	145°F med. rare to 160°F medium 145°F med. rare to 160°F medium
Shoulder center steak (ranch steak)	¾ inch 1 inch	9 to 12 minutes (turn twice) 13 to 16 minutes (turn twice)	145°F med. rare to 160°F medium 145°F med. rare to 160°F medium
Shoulder top blade steak (flat-iron)	6 to 8 ounces	8 to 15 minutes (turn once or twice)	145°F med. rare to 160°F medium
Tenderloin steak	¾ inch 1 inch	7 to 9 minutes 10 to 13 minutes	145°F med. rare to 160°F medium 145°F med. rare to 160°F medium
Top loin steak	¾ inch 1 inch	10 to 12 minutes 12 to 15 minutes	145°F med. rare to 160°F medium 145°F med. rare to 160°F medium
GROUND MEAT			
Patties (beef, lamb, pork, or veal)	½ inch ¾ inch	9 to 12 minutes 12 to 15 minutes	160°F medium 160°F medium
LAMB			
Chop (loin or rib)	1 inch	9 to 11 minutes	160°F medium
PORK			
Canadian-style bacon	¼ inch	3 to 4 minutes	heated through
Chop (boneless) **Chop** (rib with bone) **Chop** (sirloin)	¾ to 1 inch ¾ to 1 inch ¾ to 1 inch	6 to 8 minutes 9 to 12 minutes 10 to 12 minutes	145°F medium 145°F medium 145°F medium
Cutlet	¼ inch	3 to 4 minutes	no longer pink
Ham slice, cooked	½ inch	9 to 11 minutes	140°F heated through
VEAL			
Chop (loin or rib)	¾ to 1 inch	10 to 14 minutes	160°F medium
Cutlet	⅛ inch ¼ inch	2 to 3 minutes 4 to 6 minutes	no longer pink no longer pink

*All cooking times are based on meat removed directly from refrigerator.

pasta

Fettuccine Alfredo, page 426

pasta

Few foods are as fast, easy, and versatile as pasta. These hints will help you make this pantry staple into meals your family and friends will love.

FRESH OR DRIED?

Most pasta comes in fresh and dried forms, and each has its advantages. For example, sometimes you'll appreciate the light egg flavor and tender, delicate texture of fresh homemade pasta; other times you may prefer the simpler flavor (and convenience) of dried. Here's an overview of each.

FRESH PASTA: Make your own from scratch (page 420) or purchase fresh ready-made pasta, which can be found in the refrigerated section of grocery stores.

- Choose fresh pasta with consistent color throughout; it should look dry without appearing brittle and crumbly.
- Plan on 3 ounces for each main-dish serving and 1½ to 2 ounces for each side-dish serving. To substitute fresh pasta for dried in a recipe, use 6 to 8 ounces fresh for each 4 ounces dried. Follow package directions for cooking times.
- Store unopened packages of fresh pasta in the refrigerator for up to 2 weeks or in the freezer for up to a month.

DRIED PASTA: Found in boxes or bags at the supermarket, this is the most readily available form of pasta.

- Plan on 2 ounces cooked pasta for each main-dish serving and 1 to 1½ ounces for each side-dish serving. In most cases, 8 ounces uncooked dried pasta will equal 4 main-dish servings (4 cups). An exception is uncooked egg noodles: 8 ounces uncooked dried egg noodles yields 2½ cups cooked.
- Store in a cool, dry place for up to 1 year.

COOKING DRIED PASTA

To cook dried pasta, follow package directions; cooking times vary by brand. Whichever brand you buy, keep the following in mind.

USE PLENTY OF WATER: In general, use about 3 quarts of water for 4 to 8 ounces of pasta.

NO OIL NEEDED: If you use plenty of water and stir the pasta occasionally during cooking, you won't need to add oil to the water to prevent the pasta from sticking together. Adding oil prevents the sauce from adhering to the pasta.

GO FOR AL DENTE: To bring out pasta's full, nutty flavor, cook it just until it has the firm, chewy texture known as al dente (Italian for "to the tooth"). Test near the end of cooking time by giving it a taste. When done, drain the cooked pasta in a colander and shake well to remove excess water.

TO RINSE OR NOT TO RINSE: Rinsing removes a light coating of starch that helps the sauce and seasonings cling; therefore, do not rinse pasta unless it will be baked or served cool in a salad.

SERVE ASAP: Pasta continues to cook after draining, so try to serve immediately. Or follow the instructions below to keep pasta warm until serving time.

KEEPING PASTA WARM

For best flavor and texture, serve pasta immediately after cooking.

If your pasta should get done before your sauce, here's how to keep it warm.

- Return the drained cooked pasta to the warm cooking pan. Stir in a little butter or olive oil to help prevent it from sticking together. Cover and let the pasta stand no more than 15 minutes.
- Fill a serving bowl with hot water and let it stand for a few minutes. Empty and dry the bowl. Add the hot pasta and cover; serve the pasta within 5 minutes.

EGG NOODLES
1
2
3
1
2
3
4
5
6
7
8
9
10
11
TUBE PASTA
LONG PASTA
1
2
3
4
5
6
7
8
FILLED PASTA
1
2
SHAPE PASTA
1
2
3
4
5
6
7
8
9
10
11
12
TINY PASTA
1
2
3
4

pasta 101

PAIRING PASTA

Pasta comes in scores of shapes, lengths, and thicknesses. When matching pasta with sauces, soups, and more, it's hard to go wrong. That being said, these are some particularly good pairings.

EGG NOODLES

Serve medium to wide egg noodles alongside rich or meaty sauces and braised meats. Fine egg noodles make a perfect addition to broth-base soups.

1. Fine egg noodles
2. Medium egg noodles
3. Extra-wide egg noodles

TUBE PASTA

The largest of the tube pastas, manicotti is perfect for stuffing. Other wide tubular shapes (especially those with ridges) pair best with chunky sauces and in baked dishes; smaller, more slender tubes go well with smooth sauces or in soups.

1. Manicotti
2. Long ziti
3. Bucatini
4. Campanelle
5. Ziti
6. Ditalini
7. Mostaccioli
8. Elbow
9. Cavatappi
10. Rigatoni
11. Penne

FILLED PASTA

Toss filled pastas with simple, light sauces and stir small ones into soups. Tortellini are also a good option for pasta salads.

1. Tortellini
2. Ravioli

LONG PASTA

Thin, delicate long pastas, such as angel hair, are best paired with light, thin sauces; thicker, sturdier pastas partner well with thick, hearty sauces. Lasagna noodles are best used for baked dishes.

1. Nested angel hair
2. Lasagna
3. Mafalda
4. Fettuccine
5. Linguine
6. Spaghetti
7. Vermicelli
8. Cappellini

SHAPE PASTA

Shape pastas are a great choice for baked pasta dishes, chunky sauces, and pasta salads. Jumbo shells are ideal for stuffing.

1. Wagon wheel
2. Farfalle (bow tie)
3. Farfallini
4. Gnocchi
5. Rotini
6. Tiny shells
7. Medium shells
8. Orecchiette
9. Radiatore
10. Gemelli
11. Cavatelli
12. Jumbo shells

TINY PASTA

Tiny pasta shapes work best stirred into soups or tossed with a few simple additions for a quick side dish.

1. Orzo (rosamarina)
2. Couscous
3. Israeli couscous
4. Acini di pepe

ALTERNATIVE PASTAS

GLUTEN-FREE PASTA: This type of pasta is made using a combination of rice, corn, potatoes, quinoa, and other gluten-free starches. Because brands of this product vary greatly, you might need to try a few before finding one you like.

MULTIGRAIN PASTA: Made from a mixture of grains, seeds, and sometime legumes, multigrain pasta has a high fiber and protein content and is often enriched with omaga-3 fatty acids and other essential nutrients.

VEGETABLE-BASE PASTA: Made with pureed vegetables such as spinach, tomatoes, beets, and zucchini, these types of pasta often boast a full serving of vegetables in each serving.

WHITE FIBER PASTA: This product contains similar amounts of fiber and protein as whole grain pasta, but it has the texture and appearance of regular pasta.

WHOLE WHEAT PASTA: This type of pasta offers a rich, nutty flavor and higher protein and fiber content than traditional pasta.

homemade egg noodles

The Secret: Four basic ingredients and about an hour—that's all it takes to make fresh noodles. The most strenuous requirement? Just 10 minutes of kneading. It's what makes the noodle a noodle. Don't cut the time by even a minute.

EGG NOODLE POINTERS

1. NEED TO KNEAD
Knead the pasta dough, adding flour as necessary to keep it from sticking, for 10 minutes or until dough is smooth and slightly elastic. Kneading creates a gluten structure that binds the dough and gives the noodles their slightly chewy texture.

2. PORTION IT OUT
After the dough rests for 10 minutes, use a knife to cut it into four equal portions. This is the most manageable portion for both rolling the dough by hand and for using in a pasta machine.

Fill a fine-mesh sieve with 1 to 2 tablespoons of flour. And keep it handy to apply a light, even dusting as you knead, roll, and cut the dough.

PREP: 50 MINUTES **STAND:** 20 MINUTES **MAKES:** 6 SERVINGS

- **2 cups all-purpose flour**
- **½ teaspoon salt**
- **2 egg yolks**
- **1 egg**
- **⅓ cup water**
- **1 teaspoon vegetable oil or olive oil**
- **All-purpose flour**

1 In a large bowl stir together 1¾ cups of the flour and the salt. Make a well in the center of the flour mixture. In a small bowl combine egg yolks, whole egg, the water, and oil. Add egg mixture to flour mixture; stir until mixture forms a dough.

2 Sprinkle a kneading surface with the remaining ¼ cup flour. Turn dough out onto the floured surface. Knead until dough is smooth and elastic (10 minutes total kneading time). Cover dough and let rest for 10 minutes; divide into four equal portions.

3 On a lightly floured surface roll each dough portion into a 12-inch square (about 1/16 inch thick). Lightly dust both sides of the dough square with additional flour. Let stand, uncovered, about 20 minutes. (If using a pasta machine, pass each dough portion through machine according to manufacturer's directions until dough is 1/16 inch thick, dusting dough with flour as needed. Let stand, uncovered, for 20 minutes.) Loosely roll dough into a spiral; cut crosswise into ¼-inch-wide strips. Unroll strips to separate; cut into 2- to 3-inch-long pieces. Cook noodles in a large amount of boiling lightly salted water for 2 to 3 minutes or until tender; drain well. (Or place noodle pieces in a resealable plastic bag or an airtight container and chill for up to 1 day before cooking.)

MAKE-AHEAD DIRECTIONS: Prepare as directed through Step 2. Wrap dough in plastic wrap and place in airtight freezer container; seal and freeze for up to 3 months. Thaw completely in the refrigerator; continue with Step 3.

PER SERVING: 207 cal., 4 g total fat (1 g sat. fat), 92 mg chol., 210 mg sodium, 36 g carb., 1 g fiber, 7 g pro. **EXCHANGES:** 2½ Starch

FOOD PROCESSOR DIRECTIONS

Place the steel blade in the food processor. Add all of the flour, salt, and eggs to food processor. Cover and process until mixture forms fine crumbs, about the consistency of cornmeal. With the food processor running, slowly pour the water and oil through the feed tube. Continue processing just until the dough forms a ball. Transfer dough to a lightly floured surface. Cover; let dough rest for 10 minutes. Divide the dough into four equal portions. Continue as directed in Step 3.

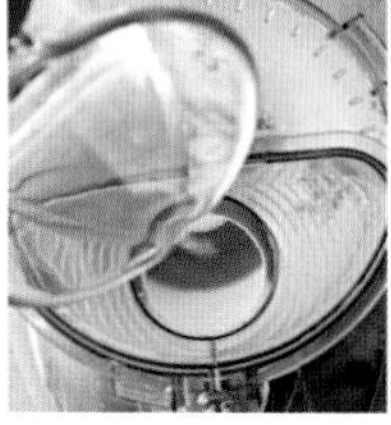

↑

3. ROLL FROM THE CENTER
A long rolling pin is helpful to roll each dough portion evenly. To begin, flatten each piece of dough from the center to the outer edge. Place one hand on the dough and roll away from yourself, pushing down and stretching the dough slightly as you roll. If your dough snaps back into place as you roll, let it rest a bit longer. Rotate occasionally and flip over once or twice. Dust with flour as necessary to keep it from sticking.

4. ROLL IT UP
Loosely roll each square of dough into a spiral shape. Use a sharp knife to cut the spirals crosswise into ¼-inch strips.

↓

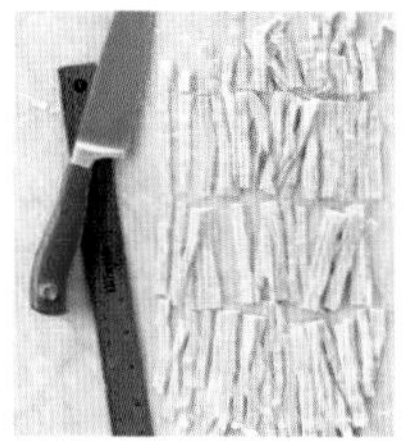

↑

5. CUT INTO PIECES
Unroll the ribbons of dough and use the knife to cut into 2- to 3-inch pieces.

DRYING DIRECTIONS

To dry the cut noodles, spread noodles on a wire rack or hang them from a pasta-drying rack or clothes hanger. Let pasta dry for up to 2 hours. Place in an airtight container and store in the refrigerator for up to 3 days before cooking. Or dry the noodles for at least 1 hour; place them in a plastic freezer bag or freezer container. Seal and freeze for up to 8 months before cooking. Add 1 to 2 minutes to cooking time for dried or frozen noodles.

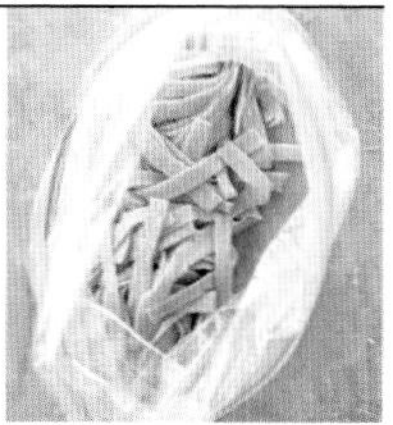

Homemade Pasta

PREP: 60 MINUTES **MAKES:** 5 SERVINGS

- **2⅓ cups all-purpose flour**
- **½ teaspoon salt**
- **2 eggs, lightly beaten**
- **⅓ cup water**
- **1 teaspoon vegetable or olive oil**
- **All-purpose flour**

1 In a large bowl stir together 2 cups of the flour and the salt. Make a well in the center of the flour mixture. In a small bowl combine eggs, water, and oil. Add egg mixture to flour mixture; stir to combine.

2 Sprinkle kneading surface with remaining ⅓ cup flour. Turn dough out onto floured surface; knead until smooth and elastic (8 to 10 minutes total). Cover; let rest for 10 minutes. Divide dough into four equal portions.

3 On a lightly floured surface roll each portion into a 12-inch square about 1/16 inch thick. Lightly dust both sides of dough square with additional flour. Let stand, uncovered, about 20 minutes; cut as desired. (If using a pasta machine, pass each portion through machine according to manufacturer's directions until dough is 1/16 inch thick, dusting dough with flour as needed. Let stand; cut as desired.)

4 To serve pasta immediately, cook according to the chart at right; drain.

5 To store cut pasta, spread it on a wire cooling rack or hang it from a pasta-drying rack or clothes hanger. Let pasta dry up to 2 hours. Place in an airtight container and chill for up to 3 days. Or dry the pasta for at least 1 hour; place in a freezer bag or freezer container and freeze for up to 8 months.

FOOD PROCESSOR DIRECTIONS: Place steel blade in food processor. Add all of the flour, salt, and eggs to food processor. Cover and process until mixture forms fine crumbs, about the consistency of cornmeal. With the processor running, slowly pour the water and oil through the feed tube. Continue processing just until the dough forms a ball. Transfer dough to a lightly floured surface. Cover; let dough rest for 10 minutes. Divide the dough into four equal portions. Continue as directed in Step 3.

MAKE-AHEAD DIRECTIONS: Prepare pasta dough through Step 2; wrap in plastic wrap. Transfer to an airtight container; freeze for up to 3 months. Thaw completely in the refrigerator; continue with Step 3.

FARFALLE (BOW TIE) PASTA: Cut rolled dough to 2×1-inch rectangles. Gently pinch centers to form bow tie shapes.

HERBED PASTA: Prepare as directed, except stir 2 tablespoons snipped fresh basil, thyme, or sage or 1 teaspoon dried basil, thyme, or sage, crushed, into the flour mixture before adding the liquid.

PER 1 CUP PLAIN, FARFALLE, OR HERBED VARIATIONS: 255 cal., 3 g total fat (1 g sat. fat), 85 mg chol., 262 mg sodium, 46 g carb., 2 g fiber, 8 g pro. EXCHANGES: 3 Starch

SPINACH PASTA: Prepare as directed, except increase flour to 2¾ cups, reduce water to ¼ cup, and stir ¼ cup cooked spinach, well drained and finely chopped, into water mixture before adding to flour mixture.

PER 1 CUP COOKED SPINACH PASTA: 294 cal., 10 g total fat (1 g sat. fat), 85 mg chol., 269 mg sodium, 54 g carb., 2 g fiber, 10 g pro. EXCHANGES: 3½ Starch

COOKING HOMEMADE PASTA

Cooking fresh pasta is as easy as boiling water. Fill a large pot with water (allow 3 quarts of water for 4 to 8 ounces pasta). Bring water to boiling. If desired, add 1 teaspoon salt. Add pasta a little at a time so the water does not stop boiling. This also helps keep the pasta from sticking together. Reduce heat slightly and boil, uncovered, stirring occasionally, for the time specified below or until the pasta is al dente. (For tip on testing pasta for doneness, see page 415.) Test often for doneness near the end of the cooking time. Drain in a colander, giving it a good shake to remove all the water.

Homemade Pasta	Cooking Time*
Bow ties	2 to 3 minutes
Egg noodles	1½ to 2 minutes
Fettuccine	1½ to 2 minutes
Lasagna	2 to 3 minutes
Linguine	1½ to 2 minutes
Ravioli	7 to 9 minutes
Tortellini	7 to 9 minutes

*Allow 1 to 2 minutes more for dried or frozen pasta.

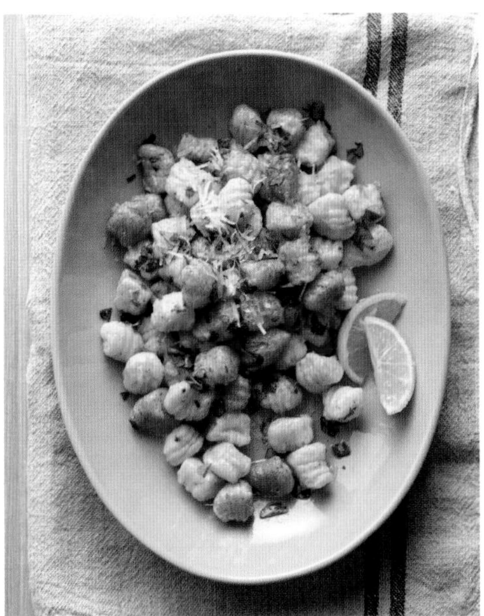

Potato Gnocchi

PREP: 65 MINUTES **BAKE:** 45 MINUTES AT 425°F
MAKES: 6 SERVINGS

- **1½ pounds russet potatoes**
- **2 egg yolks**
- **½ teaspoon salt**
- **⅛ teaspoon black pepper or white pepper**
- **¾ to 1 cup all-purpose flour**
- **¼ cup butter**
- **2 tablespoons snipped fresh parsley**
- **½ cup finely shredded Parmesan cheese (2 ounces)**
- **Lemon wedges**

1 Preheat oven to 425°F. Prick potatoes with a fork. Bake for 45 to 60 minutes or until tender and fork inserts easily. Holding each hot potato with an oven mitt or towel, peel quickly. Press the peeled hot potatoes through a ricer or food mill into a large bowl. Set aside.

2 In a small bowl whisk together egg yolks, salt, and pepper. Make a well in the center of the potatoes; add egg mixture to the well. Stir to combine. Add ¾ cup of the flour, stirring just until combined (use your hands if necessary to combine). Turn out onto a lightly floured surface. Knead in just enough of the remaining flour (may not need any) to make a smooth, fairly soft dough that is still slightly sticky. Do not overknead or add too much flour or the gnocchi will be heavy.

3 Divide dough into four portions. Roll each portion into a long, thin rope, ¾ to 1 inch thick. Cut ropes into ½-inch pieces (see photo 1, below). Roll each piece into a little ball. Add more flour to the work surface as needed. Roll balls over a lightly floured gnocchi paddle or a fork to create ovals with a pattern on one side (see photo 2, below). Place dough ovals on a clean kitchen towel or baking pan lightly dusted with flour. Set aside until ready to cook.

4 Place butter in a large skillet. Heat over medium-low heat for 15 to 17 minutes or until butter turns light brown (watch closely so it doesn't burn); set aside.

5 In a large pot or Dutch oven bring a large amount of lightly salted water to boiling; reduce heat to a slow simmer. Add half of the gnocchi, stirring to prevent them from sticking together. Cook about 2 minutes or until gnocchi rise to the top. Using a slotted spoon, transfer gnocchi to a tray or shallow baking pan. Repeat with the remaining gnocchi.

6 Return browned butter to medium heat. Stir all of the gnocchi and parsley into browned butter and toss gently until well coated. Cook and stir gently for 1 to 2 minutes or until heated through. Transfer to a serving dish. Sprinkle with Parmesan cheese. Serve with lemon wedges for squeezing.

PER SERVING: 249 cal., 12 g total fat (7 g sat. fat), 89 mg chol., 341 mg sodium, 28 g carb., 2 g fiber, 8 g pro.
EXCHANGES: 2 Starch, 2 Fat

POTATO GNOCCHI STEP-BY-STEP

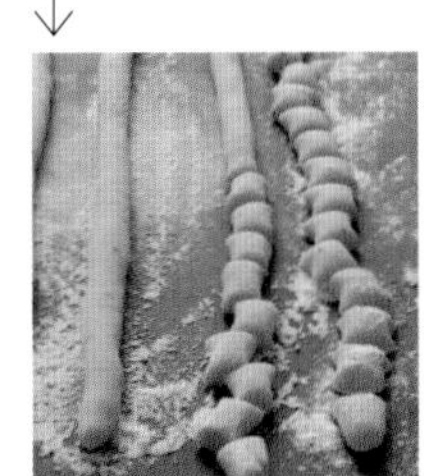

1. On a lightly floured surface use your hands to gently roll each dough portion into a long, thin rope. Use a table knife to cut each rope into 20 to 22 pieces, each about ½ inch in size.

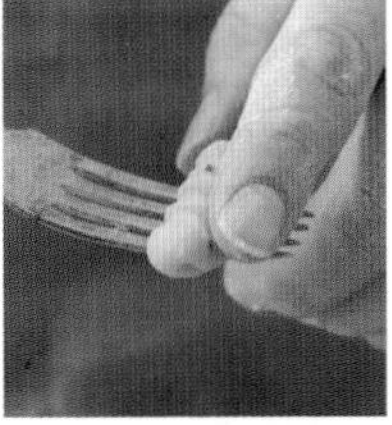

2. Roll each piece into a ball. Place one ball on a floured fork and press with your finger, rolling dough to make ridges. You will end up with ridges on one side and an indentation on the other side. Repeat with remaining dough.

LOW-CALORIE

Spaghetti with Marinara Sauce

PREP: 20 MINUTES **COOK:** 55 MINUTES
MAKES: 8 SERVINGS

- **2 tablespoons olive oil**
- **1 cup finely chopped onion (1 large)**
- **½ cup finely chopped carrot (1 medium)**
- **½ cup finely chopped celery (1 stalk)**
- **3 cloves garlic, minced**
- **2 15-ounce cans tomato sauce**
- **1 tablespoon tomato paste**
- **1 cup water**
- **1 cup dry red wine or cranberry juice**
- **3 tablespoons snipped fresh Italian parsley**
- **2 tablespoons snipped fresh basil**
- **1 tablespoon dried Italian seasoning**
- **2 to 3 teaspoons sugar**
- **¼ teaspoon crushed red pepper (optional)**
- **3 bay leaves**
- **½ teaspoon salt**
- **¼ teaspoon black pepper**
- **16 ounces packaged dried spaghetti or linguine**
- **Freshly grated Parmesan cheese**

1 In a large saucepan heat oil over medium heat. Add onion, carrot, celery, and garlic. Cook, uncovered, for 10 minutes or until vegetables are very tender but not browned, stirring occasionally.

2 Stir in tomato sauce, tomato paste, water, wine, parsley, basil, Italian seasoning, sugar, crushed red pepper (if desired), bay leaves, salt, and black pepper.

3 Bring sauce to boiling; reduce heat. Simmer sauce, uncovered, for 45 minutes, stirring occasionally, or until desired consistency.

4 In a large pot cook pasta according to package directions; drain. Remove and discard bay leaves from sauce. Serve sauce over pasta. Sprinkle each serving with Parmesan cheese.

MAKE-AHEAD DIRECTIONS: Place sauce in freezer containers. Cover and freeze for up to 3 months. To use, thaw overnight in the refrigerator. Transfer sauce to saucepan and heat through.

PER 1 CUP COOKED PASTA + ⅔ CUP SAUCE: 318 cal., 5 g total fat (1 g sat. fat), 2 mg chol., 762 mg sodium, 54 g carb., 4 g fiber, 10 g pro. EXCHANGES: 1½ Vegetable, 3 Starch, ½ Fat

SPAGHETTI WITH MARINARA MEAT SAUCE: Prepare as directed, except omit olive oil. In a large saucepan cook 12 ounces ground beef or bulk pork sausage with the onion, carrot, celery, and garlic until meat is browned; drain. Continue as directed in Step 2.

PER 1 CUP COOKED PASTA + ¾ CUP SAUCE: 396 cal., 10 g total fat (4 g sat. fat), 32 mg chol., 790 mg sodium, 54 g carb., 4 g fiber, 17 g pro. EXCHANGES: 3 Starch, 1½ Vegetable, 1 Medium Fat Meat, ½ Fat

SPAGHETTI WITH MARINARA MEATBALL SAUCE: Prepare sauce as directed through Step 3. Meanwhile, in a large bowl combine 2 eggs, lightly beaten; ⅓ cup soft bread crumbs; ¼ cup finely shredded Parmesan cheese; ¼ cup snipped fresh parsley; ¼ cup finely chopped onion; 1 teaspoon salt; ½ teaspoon crushed red pepper; and 1 clove garlic, minced. Add 1 pound lean ground beef and 8 ounces lean ground pork; mix well. Shape mixture into 16 meatballs (see tip, below left). In a very large skillet heat 1 tablespoon olive oil over medium heat. Add meatballs; cook about 10 minutes or until brown and cooked through (160°F), turning occasionally. Carefully drain fat. Stir meatballs into sauce. Serve as directed.

PER 1 CUP COOKED PASTA + 2 MEATBALLS + ⅔ CUP SAUCE: 530 cal., 19 g total fat (6 g sat. fat), 106 mg chol., 1,178 mg sodium, 55 g carb., 4 g fiber, 29 g pro. EXCHANGES: 2 Vegetable, 3 Starch, 2 medium Fat Meat, 1 Fat

SHAPING MEATBALLS

For 16 equal-size meatballs, shape the meat mixture into an 8-inch square on a cutting board. Cut the square into sixteen 2-inch squares. Roll each square into a ball.

FREEZER-READY MEATBALLS

Make a double batch of meatballs, as directed above, and freeze some for later meals.

- To freeze, place cooked meatballs in a single layer on a baking sheet. Freeze them overnight and repack in resealable freezer bags. Label with the date and return to the freezer. Use within 2 months.
- To use, thaw meatballs in the refrigerator or microwave oven. Serve meatballs whole in soups and sandwiches or sliced on top of pizza. Or simply add them to your favorite pasta sauce, heat through, and serve over pasta for an easy, quick spaghetti and meatball dinner.

BEST-LOVED

Pasta with Bolognese Sauce

PREP: 40 MINUTES **COOK:** 30 MINUTES
MAKES: 6 SERVINGS

- **1 pound bulk sweet Italian sausage or ground beef**
- **1 cup chopped onion (1 large)**
- **½ cup finely chopped carrot (1 medium)**
- **½ cup chopped green sweet pepper**
- **¼ cup celery, chopped**
- **4 cloves garlic, minced**
- **2 pounds roma tomatoes, peeled (if desired), seeded (see photos 1–4, below), and chopped (about 4 cups), or two 14.5 ounce cans diced tomatoes, undrained**
- **1 6-ounce can tomato paste**
- **½ cup dry red wine or beef broth**
- **2 tablespoons snipped fresh basil or 1½ teaspoons dried basil, crushed**
- **1 tablespoon snipped fresh oregano or 1 teaspoon dried oregano, crushed**
- **2 teaspoons snipped fresh marjoram or ½ teaspoon dried marjoram, crushed**
- **½ teaspoon salt**
- **¼ teaspoon black pepper**
- **¼ cup whipping cream**
- **2 tablespoons snipped fresh Italian parsley**
- **12 ounces packaged dried pasta, such as spaghetti, linguine, or penne**

1 In a large pot cook sausage, onion, carrot, sweet pepper, celery, and garlic until meat is browned and onion is tender; drain.

2 Stir in tomatoes, tomato paste, wine, dried herbs (if using), salt, and black pepper. Bring to boiling; reduce heat. Simmer, covered, for 30 minutes, stirring occasionally. If necessary, uncover and simmer about 10 minutes more or until desired consistency, stirring occasionally. Stir in whipping cream, parsley, and fresh herbs (if using); heat mixture through.

3 Meanwhile, in a large saucepan cook pasta according to package directions; drain. To serve, toss hot pasta with sauce to coat.

PER ¾ CUP COOKED PASTA AND 1 CUP SAUCE: 570 cal., 22 g total fat (10 g sat. fat), 66 mg chol., 652 mg sodium, 60 g carb., 6 g fiber, 22 g pro. EXCHANGES: 1 Vegetable, 3½ Starch, 1½ Medium-Fat Meat, 2½ Fat

PEELING AND SEEDING TOMATOES STEP-BY-STEP

1. To peel tomatoes, use a sharp knife to cut a shallow "X" on the bottom of each tomato.

2. Immerse tomatoes, in batches, in enough boiling water to cover. Cook for 30 to 60 seconds or until tomato skins begin to split open.

3. Using a slotted spoon, transfer tomatoes to a large bowl of ice water. When cool enough to handle, peel the skins off tomatoes.

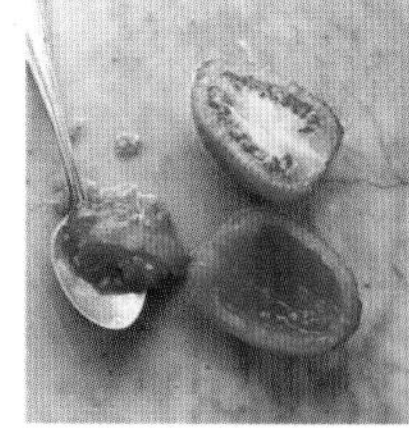

4. To remove the seeds, cut tomatoes in half lengthwise. Use a large spoon to scoop the seeds out of the tomato halves.

8 to try

Fresh Tomato Marinara Sauce

Enjoy the fresh simplicity of this sauce on its own or jazz it up with a few creative additions.

PREP: 30 MINUTES **COOK:** 23 MINUTES
MAKES: 6 SERVINGS

- **1 tablespoon olive oil**
- **1/3 cup finely chopped onion (1 small)**
- **4 cloves garlic, minced**
- **2 pounds fresh roma tomatoes,* peeled, seeded, and chopped (about 3 cups) (see photos 1–4, page 423)**
- **1/2 cup dry red wine, pomegranate juice, or cranberry juice**
- **1 to 2 teaspoons balsamic vinegar**
- **1/2 teaspoon salt***
- **1/2 teaspoon black pepper**
- **1/2 cup snipped fresh basil**

1 In a large saucepan heat oil over medium heat. Add onion and garlic; cook for 3 to 5 minutes or until onion is tender, stirring occasionally.

2 Stir in tomatoes, wine, vinegar, salt, and pepper. Bring to boiling; reduce heat. Simmer, uncovered, for 20 to 25 minutes or until sauce is slightly thickened, stirring occasionally. If desired, mash with a potato masher until desired consistency. Stir in basil.

***NOTE:** If fresh roma tomatoes are not available, substitute two 28-ounce cans Italian-style whole peeled tomatoes, drained and chopped (about 3 cups). Reduce the salt to 1/4 teaspoon.

TO STORE: Place sauce in an airtight container. Cover and chill in the refrigerator for up to 3 days or freeze for up to 3 months.

PER 1/2 CUP: 72 cal., 3 g total fat (0 g sat. fat), 0 mg chol., 203 mg sodium, 8 g carb., 2 g fiber, 2 g pro. EXCHANGES: 1 1/2 Vegetable, 1/2 Fat

CREAMY: Stir in 3/4 cup whipping cream with the fresh basil.

ARTICHOKE: Stir 1 cup quartered canned artichoke hearts into sauce. Top with shaved Parmesan cheese.

ARRABBIATA: Cook 3 ounces finely diced pancetta or prosciutto with the onion. Stir in 1/4 teaspoon crushed red pepper with the salt and black pepper. Top with additional crisp-cooked pancetta.

SAUSAGE: Cook 8 ounces bulk Italian sausage with onion and garlic until sausage is browned; drain. Top with thinly sliced pepperoncini salad peppers.

PUTTANESCA: Mash 3 or 4 anchovy fillets (rinsed and patted dry) into cooked onion mixture; cook about 30 seconds more. Stir 1/2 cup sliced pitted ripe olives and 2 tablespoons drained capers into sauce; substitute snipped fresh Italian parsley for the fresh basil.

EGGPLANT-MUSHROOM: Cook 2 cups chopped eggplant, 1 1/2 cups sliced fresh mushrooms, and 1/2 cup chopped yellow sweet pepper with the onion until tender. Increase the balsamic vinegar to 1 tablespoon and the salt to 3/4 teaspoon. Top with grated Parmesan cheese.

BASQUE CHICKEN: Stir 2 cups shredded or chopped cooked chicken, 1/2 cup sliced green olives with pimiento, and 1 teaspoon paprika into sauce; substitute snipped fresh Italian parsley for the basil.

SPINACH-BEAN: Omit basil. Stir one 15-ounce can cannellini (white kidney) beans, rinsed and drained, and 2 cups torn fresh spinach into sauce; heat through. Top with crumbled feta cheese.

Tortellini Emilia

PREP: 30 MINUTES **BAKE:** 20 MINUTES AT 400°F
STAND: 10 MINUTES **MAKES:** 8 SERVINGS

- **2** **8-ounce packages dried cheese-filled tortellini**
- **3** **tablespoons finely chopped red onion**
- **2** **tablespoons finely chopped shallots**
- **1** **tablespoon butter**
- **2** **cups half-and-half or light cream**
- **½** **cup milk**
- **2** **egg yolks**
- **¼** **cup grated Parmesan cheese (1 ounce)**
- **1** **tablespoon snipped fresh sage or 1 teaspoon dried sage, crushed**
- **¼** **teaspoon black pepper**
- **½** **cup shredded Gruyère or Swiss cheese (2 ounces)**
- **½** **cup walnut pieces**
- **2** **ounces prosciutto, snipped, or cooked ham, finely chopped**

1 Preheat oven to 400°F. Cook tortellini according to package directions. Drain and set aside.

2 For sauce, in a medium saucepan cook onion and shallots in hot butter over medium heat until tender. Stir in half-and-half and milk. Bring just to boiling. Remove from heat. In a small bowl lightly beat egg yolks. Slowly add about 1 cup of the hot milk mixture to the beaten yolks, beating until combined. Return all of the egg yolk mixture to saucepan. Cook and stir over medium-low heat about 10 minutes or until slightly thickened and just bubbly. Stir in Parmesan cheese, sage, and pepper.

3 Transfer half of the cooked tortellini to a 2-quart rectangular baking dish. Sprinkle with the Gruyère cheese. Pour half of the sauce over tortellini. Top with the remaining cooked tortellini, the walnuts, prosciutto, and the remaining sauce.

4 Bake, uncovered, about 20 minutes or until top is lightly browned and mixture is bubbly. Let stand for 10 minutes before serving.

PER SERVING: 457 cal., 27 g total fat (11 g sat. fat), 127 mg chol., 790 mg sodium, 38 g carb., 4 g fiber, 18 g pro.
EXCHANGES: 2½ Starch, 1½ Lean Meat, 4 Fat

WHITE BEAN AND SAUSAGE RIGATONI

FAST

White Bean and Sausage Rigatoni

START TO FINISH: 20 MINUTES **MAKES:** 4 SERVINGS

- **8** **ounces packaged dried rigatoni (2 cups)**
- **1** **15-ounce can cannellini (white kidney) beans, Great Northern beans, or navy beans, rinsed and drained**
- **1** **14.5-ounce can Italian-style stewed tomatoes, undrained**
- **1** **8-ounce can tomato sauce**
- **8** **ounces cooked smoked turkey sausage, halved lengthwise and cut into ½-inch slices**
- **⅓** **cup snipped fresh basil or 1 tablespoon dried basil, crushed**
- **¼** **cup shredded Asiago or Parmesan cheese (1 ounce)**

1 In a large saucepan cook pasta according to package directions; drain. Return the pasta to the saucepan.

2 Meanwhile, in another large saucepan combine beans, tomatoes, tomato sauce, sausage, and dried basil (if using). Cook and stir until heated through. Add bean mixture and fresh basil (if using) to pasta; stir gently to combine. To serve, sprinkle each serving with shredded cheese.

PER 2 CUPS: 460 cal., 9 g total fat (3 g sat. fat), 37 mg chol., 1,323 mg sodium, 69 g carb., 9 g fiber, 25 g pro.
EXCHANGES: 1½ Vegetable, 4 Starch, 1½ Lean Meat, ½ Fat

FARFALLE WITH MUSHROOMS AND SPINACH

FAST

Farfalle with Mushrooms and Spinach

START TO FINISH: 20 MINUTES **MAKES:** 4 SERVINGS

- **12 ounces packaged dried farfalle (bow tie) pasta (4 cups)**
- **2 tablespoons olive oil**
- **1 cup chopped onion (1 large)**
- **2 cups sliced portobello or other fresh mushrooms**
- **4 cloves garlic, minced**
- **8 cups fresh baby spinach**
- **2 teaspoons snipped fresh thyme**
- **¼ teaspoon black pepper**
- **¼ cup shredded Parmesan cheese (1 ounce)**
- **Crushed red pepper (optional)**

1 In a 4-quart pot cook farfalle according to package directions; drain.

2 Meanwhile, in a very large skillet heat oil over medium heat. Add onion, mushrooms, and garlic; cook and stir for 2 to 3 minutes or until mushrooms are nearly tender. Stir in spinach, thyme, and pepper; cook about 1 minute or until heated through and spinach is slightly wilted. Stir in cooked pasta; toss gently to mix. Sprinkle with cheese. If desired, sprinkle with crushed red pepper.

PER 1¾ CUPS: 451 cal., 11 g total fat (2 g sat. fat), 4 mg chol., 131 mg sodium, 74 g carb., 5 g fiber, 17 g pro.
EXCHANGES: 2 Vegetable, 4 Starch, 1½ Fat

Fettuccine Alfredo

START TO FINISH: 35 MINUTES **MAKES:** 4 SERVINGS

- **8 ounces packaged dried fettuccine**
- **2 cloves garlic, minced**
- **2 tablespoons butter**
- **1 cup whipping cream**
- **½ teaspoon salt**
- **⅛ teaspoon black pepper**
- **½ cup grated Parmesan cheese (2 ounces)**
- **Finely shredded or grated Parmesan cheese (optional)**

1 In a large saucepan cook pasta according to package directions; drain.

2 Meanwhile, in another large saucepan cook garlic in hot butter over medium-high heat for 1 minute. Add cream, salt, and pepper. Bring to boiling; reduce heat. Boil gently, uncovered, about 3 minutes or until mixture begins to thicken. Remove from heat and stir in the ½ cup Parmesan cheese. Drain pasta. Add pasta to hot sauce. Toss to combine. If desired, sprinkle each serving with additional cheese.

PER 1¼ CUPS: 514 cal., 32 g total fat (19 g sat. fat), 107 mg chol., 511 mg sodium, 45 g carb., 2 g fiber, 13 g pro.
EXCHANGES: 3 Starch, ½ High-Fat Meat, 5 Fat

LEMONY FETTUCCINE ALFREDO WITH SHRIMP AND PEAS: Prepare as directed, except add 8 ounces peeled, deveined uncooked shrimp (see photos 1–3, page 311) and 1 cup frozen peas to pasta the last 1 minute of cooking. Stir 1 teaspoon finely shredded lemon peel and 1 tablespoon lemon juice into sauce before adding pasta.

PER 1¼ CUPS: 603 cal., 33 g total fat (20 g sat. fat), 192 mg chol., 634 mg sodium, 51 g carb., 4 g fiber, 26 g pro.
EXCHANGES: 3½ Starch, 2 Lean Meat, 5 Fat

CREMINI FETTUCCINE ALFREDO: Prepare as directed, except cook 1½ cups sliced fresh cremini mushrooms in the hot butter for 4 to 5 minutes or until tender before adding the cream, salt, and pepper.

PER 1¼ CUPS: 544 cal., 32 g total fat (19 g sat. fat), 106 mg chol., 513 mg sodium, 53 g carb., 3 g fiber, 13 g pro.
EXCHANGES: ½ Vegetable, 3 Starch, ½ Meat, 5 Fat

GREAT GRATING CHEESES

To enjoy these cheeses at their full-flavored best, grate them as needed just before adding to recipes.
PARMIGIANO-REGGIANO: A granular texture and bold, snappy flavor are hallmarks of this time-honored cheese. Also try it thinly shaved in salads.
PECORINO ROMANO: This granular sheep's-milk cheese brings a sharp, peppery flavor to dishes.
AGED ASIAGO: Choose this one for its nutty, pleasantly salty flavor.

FETTUCCINE ALFREDO

FETTUCCINE ALLA CARBONARA

BEST-LOVED

Fettuccine alla Carbonara

START TO FINISH: 35 MINUTES **MAKES:** 6 SERVINGS

- **16 ounces packaged dried fettuccine**
- **8 slices bacon**
- **4 ounces sliced prosciutto**
- **2 tablespoons finely chopped onion**
- **¾ cup unsalted butter**
- **⅓ cup dry white wine**
- **½ cup whipping cream**
- **½ cup milk**
- **½ cup grated Parmesan cheese (2 ounces)**
- **1 tablespoon snipped fresh parsley**
- **Black pepper**

1 In a large pot cook pasta according to package directions; drain. Return pasta to pan; keep warm.

2 Meanwhile, for sauce, in a large skillet cook bacon over medium heat until crisp. Drain well on paper towels. Coarsely crumble bacon; set aside. Chop the prosciutto into ½-inch pieces; set aside.

3 In a medium saucepan cook onion in hot butter over medium heat about 4 minutes or until tender. Add prosciutto. Cook and stir over medium heat for 3 minutes. Remove pan from heat. Carefully add wine.

4 Return saucepan to heat and bring to boiling. Boil gently, uncovered, for 5 minutes. Stir in the bacon, cream, and milk; bring to boiling. Boil gently, uncovered, for 5 minutes.

5 Stir in ¼ cup of the Parmesan cheese and the parsley. Immediately pour sauce over pasta, stirring gently to coat. Sprinkle each serving with remaining cheese. Season to taste with pepper. Serve immediately.

PER 1⅓ CUPS: 722 cal., 43 g total fat (22 g sat. fat), 108 mg chol., 705 mg sodium, 59 g carb., 3 g fiber, 22 g pro.
EXCHANGES: 4 Starch, 1½ High-Fat Meat, 5½ Fat

FAST

Pasta Caprese

START TO FINISH: 30 MINUTES **MAKES:** 4 SERVINGS

- **12 ounces packaged dried fusilli or penne pasta (4 cups)**
- **3 tablespoons olive oil**
- **3 green onions, thinly sliced**
- **2 cloves garlic, minced**
- **1 teaspoon snipped fresh oregano or ½ teaspoon dried oregano, crushed**
- **3 ripe beefsteak tomatoes (about 2 pounds total), seeded and chopped**
- **1 tablespoon lemon juice**
- **¼ teaspoon salt**
- **¼ teaspoon black pepper**
- **¼ cup thinly sliced fresh basil**
- **8 ounces fresh mozzarella cheese, cut up**
- **½ cup grated Parmesan cheese (2 ounces)**

1 In a large saucepan cook pasta according to package directions. Drain pasta, reserving 1 cup of the cooking water. Return the cooked pasta to the hot saucepan.

2 Meanwhile, in a large skillet heat oil over medium-high heat. Add green onions, garlic, and oregano; cook and stir about 2 minutes or just until green onions are tender. Stir in tomatoes; heat through. Stir in lemon juice, salt, and pepper.

3 Pour tomato mixture over cooked pasta in saucepan. Add ½ cup of the reserved cooking liquid. Heat through. Stir in basil. If necessary, stir in enough of the remaining reserved cooking liquid to reach desired consistency.

4 Divide pasta among four to six shallow bowls. Top with mozzarella cheese; sprinkle with Parmesan cheese.

PER 1½ CUPS: 649 cal., 26 g total fat (10 g sat. fat), 50 mg chol., 574 mg sodium, 74 g carb., 6 g fiber, 29 g pro.
EXCHANGES: 2 Vegetable, 4 Starch, 2 Lean Meat, 3½ Fat

Fusilli with Garlic Pesto and Pecorino

START TO FINISH: 35 MINUTES **MAKES:** 6 SERVINGS

- **15 cloves garlic, peeled**
- **$\frac{1}{3}$ cup lightly packed fresh basil leaves**
- **16 ounces packaged dried fusilli, gemelli, or tagliatelle pasta ($5\frac{1}{4}$ cups)**
- **$\frac{1}{2}$ cup olive oil**
- **$\frac{1}{3}$ cup pine nuts, toasted (see tip, page 21)**
- **2 tablespoons finely shredded Pecorino Romano cheese ($\frac{1}{2}$ ounce)**
- **$\frac{3}{4}$ teaspoon salt**
- **$\frac{1}{8}$ teaspoon black pepper**
- **1 cup small fresh basil leaves**
- **$\frac{1}{4}$ cup finely shredded Pecorino Romano cheese (1 ounce)**

1 In a large pot cook garlic cloves in a large amount of boiling salted water for 8 minutes. Using a slotted spoon, transfer garlic to a blender. Add the $\frac{1}{3}$ cup basil leaves to the boiling water and cook for 5 seconds; remove with slotted spoon and drain well on paper towels. (Do not drain boiling water.) Add basil to blender.

2 Add pasta to boiling water and cook according to package directions. Before draining pasta, remove $\frac{1}{2}$ cup of cooking water; set aside. Drain pasta; return to pot.

3 Meanwhile, for pesto, add oil, 2 tablespoons of the pine nuts, the 2 tablespoons cheese, the salt, and pepper to blender or food processor. Cover and blend until nearly smooth (pesto will be thin).

4 Add pesto to cooked pasta; toss gently to coat. If necessary, toss in enough of the reserved cooking water to help coat the pasta evenly with pesto. Transfer pasta mixture to a serving bowl. Sprinkle with the 1 cup basil leaves, the $\frac{1}{4}$ cup cheese, and the remaining pine nuts. Serve immediately.

PER 1 CUP: 518 cal., 25 g total fat (4 g sat. fat), 5 mg chol., 264 mg sodium, 61 g carb., 3 g fiber, 14 g pro.
EXCHANGES: 4 Starch, $4\frac{1}{2}$ Fat

FUSILLI WITH GARLIC PESTO AND PECORINO

FAST

Pasta with White Clam Sauce

START TO FINISH: 30 MINUTES **MAKES:** 4 SERVINGS

- **10 ounces packaged dried linguine or fettuccine**
- **2 6.5-ounce cans chopped or minced clams**
- **2 cups half-and-half, light cream, or whole milk**
- **$\frac{1}{2}$ cup chopped onion (1 medium)**
- **2 cloves garlic, minced**
- **2 tablespoons butter**
- **$\frac{1}{4}$ cup all-purpose flour**
- **2 teaspoons snipped fresh oregano or $\frac{1}{2}$ teaspoon dried oregano, crushed**
- **$\frac{1}{4}$ teaspoon salt**
- **$\frac{1}{8}$ teaspoon black pepper**
- **$\frac{1}{4}$ cup snipped fresh parsley**
- **$\frac{1}{4}$ cup dry white wine, nonalcoholic dry white wine, or chicken broth**
- **$\frac{1}{4}$ cup finely shredded or grated Parmesan cheese (1 ounce)**

1 In a large saucepan cook pasta according to package directions; drain and keep warm.

2 Meanwhile, drain canned clams, reserving the juice from one of the cans (you should have about $\frac{1}{2}$ cup). Add enough half-and-half to reserved clam juice to equal $2\frac{1}{2}$ cups liquid. Set clams and clam juice mixture aside.

3 In a medium saucepan cook onion and garlic in hot butter over medium heat until tender but not browned. Stir in flour, dried oregano (if using), salt, and pepper. Add clam juice mixture all at once. Cook and stir until thickened and bubbly. Cook and stir for 1 minute more. Stir in drained clams, fresh oregano (if using), parsley, and wine. Heat through. Serve over hot pasta. Sprinkle with Parmesan cheese.

PER $1\frac{1}{2}$ CUPS: 680 cal., 24 g total fat (14 g sat. fat), 125 mg chol., 430 mg sodium, 72 g carb., 3 g fiber, 40 g pro.
EXCHANGES: 5 Starch, $3\frac{1}{2}$ Lean Meat, $1\frac{1}{2}$ Fat

FAST LOW-CALORIE

Shrimp Pasta Diavolo

START TO FINISH: 20 MINUTES **MAKES:** 4 SERVINGS

- **1 9-ounce package refrigerated linguine**
- **12 ounces medium fresh shrimp, peeled and deveined (see photos 1–3, page 311)**
- **1 medium onion, cut into thin wedges**
- **3 cloves garlic, minced**
- **¼ teaspoon crushed red pepper**
- **2 tablespoons olive oil**
- **1 14.5-ounce can diced tomatoes, undrained**
- **1 8-ounce can tomato sauce**
- **½ cup torn fresh basil**
- **2 cups fresh baby spinach**
- **½ cup finely shredded Parmesan cheese (2 ounces)**

1 In a large saucepan cook pasta according to package directions. Drain pasta and return to pan; set aside. Rinse shrimp; pat dry.

2 Meanwhile, in a large skillet cook onion, garlic, and crushed red pepper in hot oil until tender. Stir in tomatoes and tomato sauce. Bring to boiling; reduce heat. Simmer, uncovered, for 3 minutes. Add shrimp to skillet; cover and simmer for 3 minutes or until shrimp are opaque. Add shrimp mixture to pasta. Stir in basil and spinach. Top each serving with Parmesan cheese.

PER 2 CUPS: 390 cal., 12 g total fat (4 g sat. fat), 177 mg chol., 759 mg sodium, 45 g carb., 4 g fiber, 27 g pro.
EXCHANGES: 1½ Vegetable, 2½ Starch, 2 Lean Meat, 1 Fat

Seafood Pasta

PREP: 30 MINUTES **SOAK:** 45 MINUTES
COOK: 13 MINUTES **MAKES:** 6 SERVINGS

- **1 pound fresh or frozen medium shrimp in shells**
- **12 fresh mussels**
- **12 fresh small littleneck clams**
- **9 quarts water**
- **9 tablespoons salt**
- **12 ounces dried linguine or fettuccine**
- **1 tablespoon olive oil**
- **1 6.5-ounce can minced clams, drained**
- **1 cup dry white wine**
- **2 to 3 cloves garlic, minced**
- **1 8-ounce bottle clam juice**
- **¼ cup butter**
- **1 teaspoon finely shredded lemon peel**
- **2 tablespoons lemon juice**
- **¼ to ½ teaspoon crushed red pepper**
- **¼ cup snipped fresh Italian parsley**

1 Thaw shrimp if frozen. Peel and devein shrimp, leaving tails intact (see photos 1–3, page 311). Rinse shrimp; gently pat dry with paper towels. Cover and chill until ready to use.

2 Scrub the mussels and littleneck clams under cold running water. Using your fingers, pull out any beards that are visible between the mussel shells; discard. In a very large bowl, combine 3 quarts of the water and 3 tablespoons of the salt. Add clams and soak for 15 minutes. Drain and rinse thoroughly; drain. Repeat two more times with fresh water and salt. Drain and rinse clams thoroughly.

3 Meanwhile, cook pasta according to package directions; drain. Cover to keep warm.

4 In a 6- to 8-quart Dutch oven heat oil over medium-high heat. Add shrimp and minced clams. Cook and stir about 3 minutes or until shrimp are opaque. Remove pan from heat. Remove shrimp mixture; set aside. Add wine and garlic to pan. Return pan to heat. Bring to boiling; reduce heat and simmer, uncovered, 5 minutes or until liquid is reduced by about half. Add the mussels, clams, the clam juice, butter, lemon peel, lemon juice, and crushed red pepper. Bring to boiling; reduce heat. Cook, covered, for 5 to 9 minutes or until the mussels and clams open, discarding any unopened shells. Stir in drained pasta and shrimp and clam mixtures; heat through.

5 To serve, spoon pasta mixture onto a large serving platter, making sure most of the seafood is on top. Sprinkle with parsley.

PER 1½ CUPS: 497 cal., 13 g total fat (6 g sat. fat), 171 mg chol., 839 mg sodium, 48 g carb., 2 g fiber, 40 g pro.
EXCHANGES: 3 Starch, 4½ Lean Meat, 1½ Fat

FAST

Ravioli Skillet Lasagna

START TO FINISH: 25 MINUTES **MAKES:** 4 SERVINGS

- **2 cups chunky-style pasta sauce**
- **½ cup water**
- **4 cups packaged fresh baby spinach**
- **16 ounces frozen meat- or cheese-filled ravioli (4½ cups)**
- **1 egg, lightly beaten**
- **½ of a 15-ounce carton ricotta cheese**
- **¼ cup grated Romano or Parmesan cheese (1 ounce)**
- **Grated Romano or Parmesan cheese**

1 In a large skillet combine pasta sauce and water. Bring to boiling. Stir in spinach until it wilts. Stir in the ravioli. Return to boiling; reduce heat. Cover and cook mixture over medium heat about 5 minutes or until ravioli are nearly tender, stirring once to prevent sticking.

2 In a medium bowl combine the egg, ricotta cheese, and ¼ cup Romano cheese. Spoon ricotta mixture over the ravioli mixture in large mounds. Cover and cook over medium-low heat about 10 minutes more or until ricotta is set and pasta is just tender. Sprinkle each serving with additional Romano cheese.

PER 1¾ CUPS: 490 cal., 21 g total fat (10 g sat. fat), 146 mg chol., 1,061 mg sodium, 53 g carb., 7 g fiber, 23 g pro.
EXCHANGES: 1 Vegetable, 3 Starch, 1½ Medium-Fat Meat, 2 Fat

Baked Ziti with Three Cheeses

PREP: 30 MINUTES **BAKE:** 30 MINUTES AT 425°F
MAKES: 6 TO 8 SERVINGS

- **12 ounces packaged dried ziti or penne pasta (4 cups)**
- **1 14.5-ounce can fire-roasted diced tomatoes, undrained**
- **1 cup chopped onion (1 large)**
- **12 cloves garlic, minced (2 tablespoons)**
- **2 tablespoons olive oil**
- **½ cup dry white wine**
- **2 cups whipping cream**
- **1 cup finely shredded Parmesan cheese**
- **¾ cup Gorgonzola or other blue cheese, crumbled (3 ounces)**
- **½ cup Fontina cheese, shredded (2 ounces)**
- **½ teaspoon salt**
- **¼ teaspoon black pepper**
- **Snipped fresh Italian parsley (optional)**

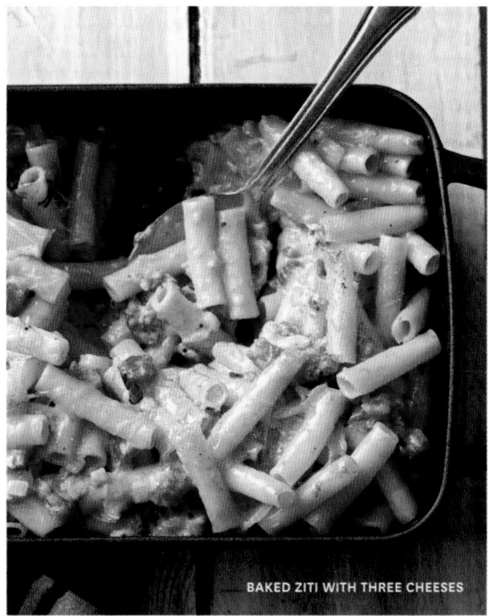
BAKED ZITI WITH THREE CHEESES

1 Preheat oven to 425°F. In a large saucepan cook pasta according to package directions; drain. Place in an ungreased 3-quart rectangular baking dish. Stir in tomatoes; set aside.

2 Meanwhile, in a large saucepan cook onion and garlic in hot oil over medium heat just until tender. Carefully stir in wine and cook about 3 minutes or until liquid reduces by half. Add cream; heat to boiling. Boil gently, uncovered, about 5 minutes or until mixture thickens slightly, stirring frequently. Remove from heat. Stir in Parmesan cheese, Gorgonzola cheese, Fontina cheese, salt, and pepper.

3 Pour cheese mixture over pasta. Bake, covered, for 30 to 35 minutes or until sauce is bubbly. Stir pasta to coat. If desired, sprinkle with parsley.

PER 2 CUPS: 717 cal., 46 g total fat (26 g sat. fat), 141 mg chol., 883 mg sodium, 54 g carb., 3 g fiber, 21 g pro.
EXCHANGES: 1½ Vegetable, 3 Starch, 1½ Medium-Fat Meat, 7 Fat

BEST-LOVED

Mile-High Lasagna Pie

PREP: 50 MINUTES **BAKE:** 60 MINUTES AT 375°F
STAND: 15 MINUTES **MAKES:** 10 SERVINGS

- **16 dried whole wheat or whole grain lasagna noodles**
- **2 tablespoons olive oil**
- **1½ cups finely chopped carrots (3 medium)**
- **2 cups finely chopped zucchini (1 medium)**
- **4 cloves garlic, minced**
- **3 cups sliced fresh button mushrooms (8 ounces)**
- **2 6-ounce packages fresh baby spinach**
- **2 tablespoons snipped fresh basil**
- **1 egg, beaten**
- **1 15-ounce carton ricotta cheese**
- **⅓ cup finely shredded Parmesan cheese**
- **½ teaspoon salt**
- **¼ teaspoon black pepper**
- **1 26-ounce jar tomato and basil pasta sauce (2½ cups)**
- **2 cups shredded Fontina or mozzarella cheese (8 ounces)**
- **Rosemary sprigs (optional)**

1 Preheat oven to 375°F. In a large saucepan cook noodles according to package directions. Drain noodles; rinse with cold water. Drain well; set aside.

2 Meanwhile, in a large skillet heat 1 tablespoon of the olive oil over medium-high heat. Add carrots, zucchini, and half of the garlic. Cook and stir about 5 minutes or until crisp-tender; transfer to a bowl. Add the remaining oil to the same skillet and heat over medium-high heat. Add mushrooms and remaining garlic. Cook and stir about 5 minutes or until tender. Gradually add spinach. Cook and stir for 1 to 2 minutes or until spinach is wilted. Remove from skillet with a slotted spoon. Stir in 2 tablespoons basil; set aside.

3 In a small bowl, stir together egg, ricotta cheese, Parmesan cheese, salt, and pepper; set aside.

4 To assemble pie, in the bottom of a 9×3-inch springform pan spread ½ cup of the pasta sauce. Arrange 3 to 4 of the cooked noodles over the sauce, overlapping and trimming as necessary to cover sauce with one layer (see photo 1, below). Top with half of the mushroom mixture. Spoon half of the ricotta cheese mixture over mushroom mixture. Top with another layer of noodles. Spread with 1 cup of the remaining pasta sauce. Top with all of the carrot mixture. Sprinkle with 1 cup of the Fontina cheese. Top with another layer of noodles. Layer with remaining mushroom mixture and remaining ricotta cheese mixture. Top with another layer of noodles and remaining sauce (might have extra noodles). Gently press down pie with the back of a large spatula (see photo 2, below).

5 Place springform pan on a foil-lined baking sheet. Bake about 60 minutes or until heated through, topping with remaining Fontina cheese for the last 15 minutes of baking. Cover and let stand on a wire rack for 15 minutes before serving. Cut around outside edge of pie and carefully remove pan ring (see photos 3 and 4, below). To serve, cut lasagna into wedges. If desired, garnish with rosemary sprigs.

PER SERVING: 463 cal., 23 g total fat (12 g sat. fat), 82 mg chol., 965 mg sodium, 38 g carb., 8 g fiber, 28 g pro.
EXCHANGES: 2 Vegetable, 2 Starch, 2½ Medium-Fat Meat, 1½ Fat

BUILDING THE LASAGNA PIE, STEP-BY-STEP

1. Allow lasagna noodles to overlap in pan for a firm base; trim noodles to fit the pan.

2. Using back of a spatula, gently press down the pie before baking it.

3. After baking, cut around outside edge of the pie to loosen the ring.

4. Carfeully remove the ring from pie.

make it mine

Lasagna

Use our easy-to-follow formula to adapt this classic baked pasta dish to suit your family's tastes.

PREP: 45 MINUTES **COOK:** 15 MINUTES
BAKE: 40 MINUTES AT 375°F
STAND: 10 MINUTES **MAKES:** 8 SERVINGS

NOODLES
12 ounces MEAT
1 cup chopped onion (1 large)
2 cloves garlic, minced
TOMATOES
SEASONING
1 egg, lightly beaten
DAIRY
¼ cup grated Parmesan cheese
1 cup jarred roasted red sweet peppers, drained and cut into strips (optional)
2 cups CHEESE **(8 ounces)**
Grated Parmesan cheese (optional)

1 Cook Noodles according to package directions or until tender but still firm. Drain noodles; rinse with cold water. Drain well; set aside.

2 Meanwhile, in a large saucepan cook desired Meat, onion, and garlic until meat is browned, stirring to break up meat as it cooks; drain.

3 Stir Tomatoes and Seasoning into meat mixture. Bring to boiling; reduce heat. Simmer, uncovered, for 15 minutes, stirring occasionally.

4 Preheat oven to 375°F. For filling, combine egg, Dairy, and the ¼ cup Parmesan cheese; set aside.

5 Spread about ½ cup of the meat sauce over the bottom of a 2-quart rectangular baking dish. Layer half of the Noodles in the dish, overlapping and trimming to fit. Spread with half of the cheese filling. Top with half of the remaining sauce, half of the roasted sweet peppers (if using), and half of the Cheese. Repeat layers. If desired, sprinkle with additional Parmesan.

6 Place baking dish on a baking sheet. Bake, uncovered, for 40 to 45 minutes or until heated through and bubbly. Let stand for 10 minutes before serving.

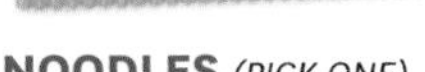

NOODLES *(PICK ONE)*

6 dried lasagna noodles
6 dried whole wheat lasagna noodles

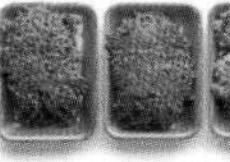

MEAT *(PICK ONE)*

12 ounces ground beef or ground turkey, or bulk pork sausage or bulk Italian sausage
8 ounces Italian sausage plus 4 ounces chopped pancetta or bacon

TOMATOES *(PICK ONE)*

One 14.5-ounce can diced tomatoes, undrained, plus one 8-ounce can tomato sauce plus ¼ cup tomato paste
4 fresh tomatoes, seeded and chopped (2 cups), plus one 8-ounce can tomato sauce plus ¼ cup tomato paste
2 cups purchased pasta sauce

SEASONING *(PICK ONE)*

1 tablespoon dried Italian seasoning, crushed
2 tablespoons snipped fresh basil or 2 teaspoons dried basil, crushed
1 tablespoon snipped fresh rosemary or 1 teaspoon dried rosemary, crushed

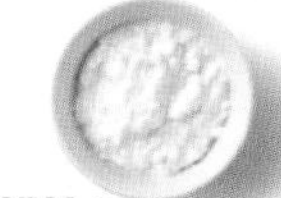

DAIRY *(PICK ONE)*

One 15-ounce carton regular or light ricotta cheese
2 cups cream-style cottage cheese, drained
1 cup bottled Alfredo pasta sauce
One 8-ounce package cream cheese, softened and cubed

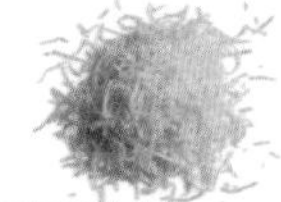

CHEESE *(pick one)*

Shredded mozzarella, provolone, Monterey Jack, and/or Fontina
Sliced fresh mozzarella cheese
Shredded Italian cheese blend

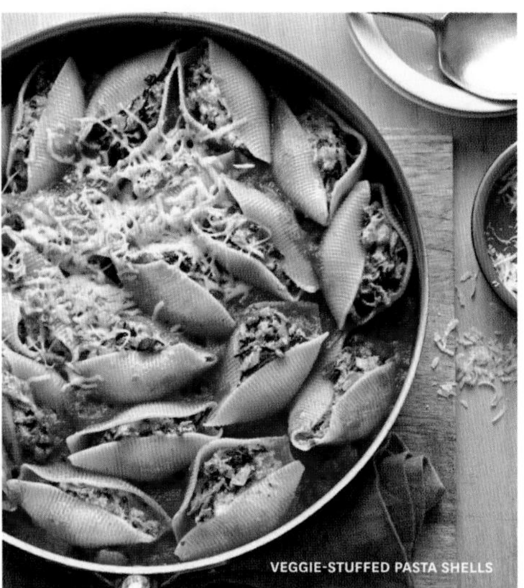
VEGGIE-STUFFED PASTA SHELLS

Stuffed Manicotti

PREP: 30 MINUTES **BAKE:** 35 MINUTES AT 350°F
MAKES: 6 SERVINGS

- **12 packaged dried manicotti**
- **8 ounces lean ground beef**
- **8 ounces bulk Italian sausage**
- **½ of a 15-ounce carton ricotta cheese (about 1 cup)**
- **2 cups shredded mozzarella cheese (8 ounces)**
- **½ cup finely shredded Parmesan cheese (2 ounces)**
- **1½ teaspoons dried Italian seasoning, crushed**
- **3 cups Marinara Sauce (page 422)**

1 Preheat oven to 350°F. Cook pasta according to package directions; drain. Place pasta in a single layer on a sheet of greased foil.

2 Meanwhile, in a large skillet cook ground beef and Italian sausage over medium heat until browned; drain fat and discard. In a medium bowl combine ricotta cheese, 1 cup of the mozzarella cheese, the Parmesan cheese, and Italian seasoning. Stir in meat mixture. Using a small spoon, fill pasta with meat mixture. Arrange filled pasta in a 3-quart rectangular baking dish. Pour Marinara Sauce over pasta. Sprinkle with remaining 1 cup mozzarella.

3 Bake, covered, for 25 minutes. Uncover and bake about 10 minutes more or until mixture heats through and cheese melts.

PER 2 MANICOTTI: 646 cal., 36 g total fat (16 g sat. fat), 109 mg chol., 1,203 mg sodium, 44 g carb., 3 g fiber, 34 g pro.
EXCHANGES: ½ Vegetable, 3 Starch, 3½ Medium-Fat Meat, 3 Fat

Veggie-Stuffed Pasta Shells *(photo, page 413)*

START TO FINISH: 40 MINUTES **MAKES:** 4 SERVINGS

- **12 packaged dried jumbo shell macaroni**
- **1½ cups shredded carrots (3)**
- **1⅓ cups shredded zucchini (1 medium)**
- **½ cup finely chopped onion (1 medium)**
- **1 tablespoon olive oil**
- **1 10-ounce package frozen chopped spinach, thawed and well drained**
- **½ of a 15-ounce carton ricotta cheese (about 1 cup)**
- **1½ cups shredded Italian cheese blend (6 ounces)**
- **¼ teaspoon salt**
- **1 24-ounce jar pasta sauce**

1 In a large saucepan cook pasta according to package directions; drain. Rinse pasta with cold water; drain again.

2 Meanwhile, in a large skillet cook carrots, zucchini, and onion in hot oil over medium-high heat for 3 to 5 minutes or until tender. Stir in spinach; cook and stir for 1 minute. Transfer spinach mixture to a large bowl.

3 Stir ricotta cheese, 1 cup of the Italian cheese blend, and the salt into spinach mixture. Spoon 2 rounded tablespoons filling into each pasta shell (see photo 1, below). Pour pasta sauce into skillet; place shells in sauce (see photo 2, below). Heat, covered, over medium heat about 10 minutes or until heated through. Sprinkle with remaining cheese before serving.

PER 3 SHELLS: 471 cal., 22 g total fat (11 g sat. fat), 57 mg chol., 1,219 mg sodium, 44 g carb., 8 g fiber, 25 g pro.
EXCHANGES: ½ Milk, 4½ Vegetable, 1 Starch, 1 Lean Meat, 4 Fat

VEGGIE-STUFFED PASTA SHELLS STEP-BY-STEP

1. Use a flatware tablespoon to fill each of the cooked jumbo shells with the vegetable mixture, using 2 rounded tablespoons for each pasta shell.

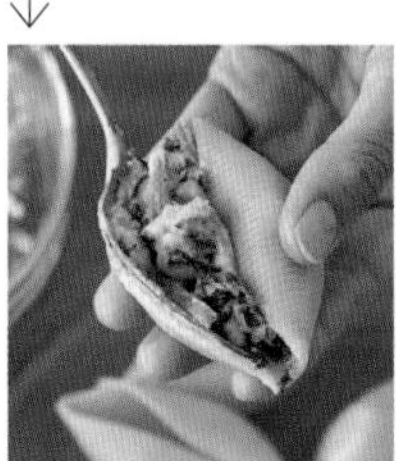

2. Place filled shells in sauce in skillet and cook over medium heat until heated through. You might need to gently lift and rearrange the shells with a large spoon during cooking to keep them from sticking.

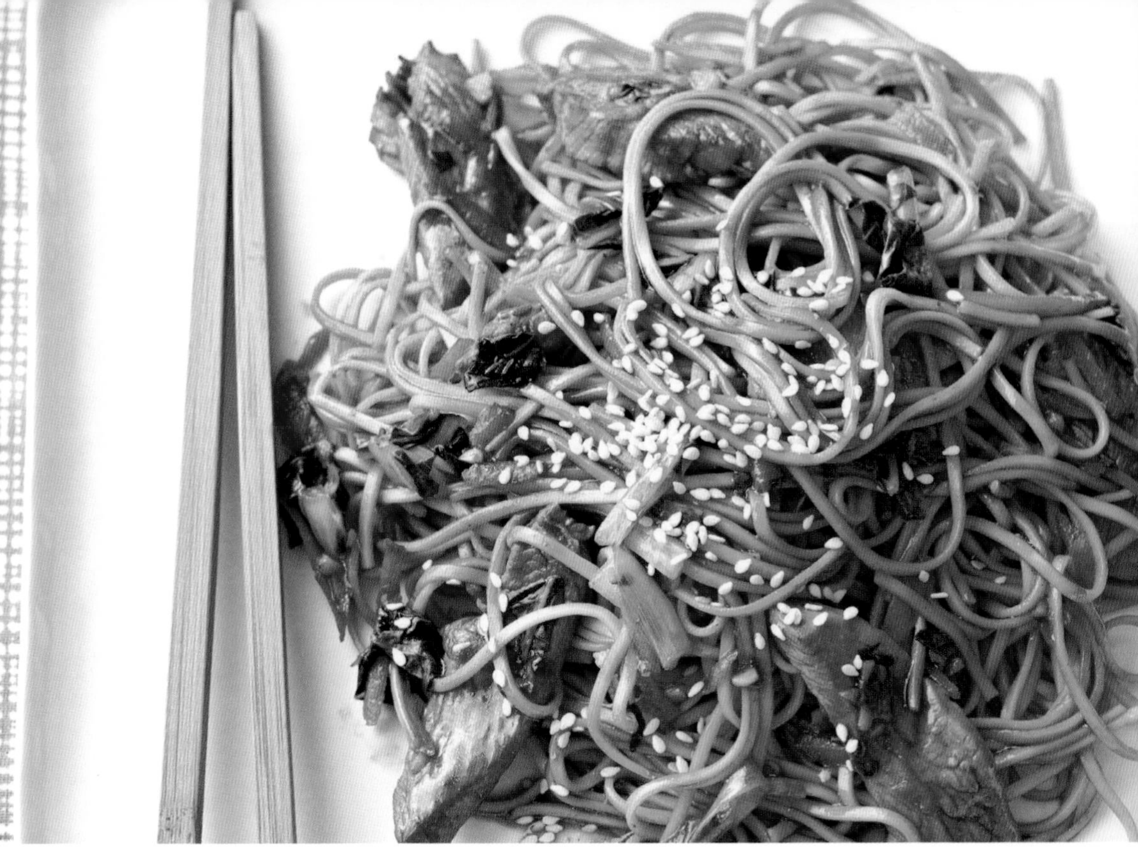

BEST-LOVED LOW-CALORIE

Chicken Lo Mein

PREP: 35 MINUTES **STAND:** 20 MINUTES
COOK: 8 MINUTES **MAKES:** 6 SERVINGS

- **12 ounces skinless, boneless chicken breast halves, beef sirloin steak, or lean boneless pork**
- **6 tablespoons reduced-sodium soy sauce**
- **1 tablespoon rice vinegar**
- **4 teaspoons sugar**
- **10 ounces dried Chinese egg noodles or linguine**
- **⅓ cup reduced-sodium chicken broth**
- **2 teaspoons cornstarch**
- **1 tablespoon vegetable oil**
- **1 tablespoon sesame oil**
- **4 cloves garlic, minced**
- **½ cup shredded carrot (1 medium)**
- **1 cup chopped bok choy**
- **4 green onions, cut into thin 2-inch strips**
- **Sesame seeds (optional)**

1 Cut chicken into bite-size strips. In a medium bowl combine 2 tablespoons of the soy sauce, the vinegar, and 2 teaspoons of the sugar. Add chicken; toss to coat. Let stand at room temperature for 20 minutes. Cook noodles according to package directions; drain. Rinse with cold water; drain well. Set noodles aside. For sauce, in a small bowl stir together chicken broth, the remaining 4 tablespoons soy sauce, the remaining 2 teaspoons sugar, and the cornstarch; set aside.

2 Pour vegetable oil and sesame oil into a wok or large nonstick skillet. Heat over medium-high heat. Add garlic; cook and stir for 30 seconds. Add carrot; cook and stir for 2 minutes. Add bok choy and green onions; cook and stir for 2 minutes more. Remove vegetables from wok.

3 Drain chicken; discard marinade. Add chicken to wok (add more oil if necessary); cook and stir for 3 to 4 minutes or until no longer pink (2 to 3 minutes for beef or pork). Push chicken to side of wok. Stir sauce; add to center of wok. Cook and stir until thickened and bubbly. Add the cooked noodles and vegetables. Gently toss mixture until combined and heated through. Transfer to a serving platter. If desired, sprinkle with sesame seeds.

SHRIMP LO MEIN: Substitute 1 pound peeled and deveined shrimp for the chicken breast halves. Rinse shrimp; pat dry with paper towels. Prepare as directed, except in Step 3 cook shrimp about 3 minutes or until opaque.

PER 1⅓ CUPS PLAIN OR SHRIMP VARIATION: 326 cal., 7 g total fat (1 g sat. fat), 73 mg chol., 615 mg sodium, 42 g carb., 2 g fiber, 22 g pro. **EXCHANGES:** 2½ Starch, 2 Lean Meat, 1 Fat

Chicken Pad Thai

START TO FINISH: 45 MINUTES **MAKES:** 4 SERVINGS

- **8 ounces dried linguine-style rice noodles**
- **¼ cup salted peanuts, finely chopped**
- **½ teaspoon finely shredded lime peel**
- **¼ cup fish sauce**
- **2 tablespoons packed brown sugar**
- **2 tablespoons lime juice**
- **2 tablespoons rice vinegar**
- **1 tablespoon water**
- **1 tablespoon Asian chili sauce with garlic**
- **3 tablespoons vegetable oil**
- **1 pound boneless, skinless chicken breast halves, patted dry and cut into bite-size strips**
- **6 cloves garlic, minced**
- **1 egg, lightly beaten**
- **1 cup fresh bean sprouts, rinsed and drained**
- **⅓ cup sliced green onions (3)**
- **2 tablespoons snipped fresh cilantro**
- **Lime wedges (optional)**

1 Place rice noodles in a large bowl. Add enough boiling water to cover; let stand for 10 to 15 minutes or until softened but still slightly chewy (al dente), stirring occasionally. Drain well in a colander set in a sink.

2 Meanwhile, for peanut topping, in a small bowl combine peanuts and lime peel; set aside. In another small bowl whisk together fish sauce, brown sugar, lime juice, rice vinegar, the water, and chili sauce until smooth; set aside.

3 In a very large nonstick skillet heat 1 tablespoon of the oil over medium-high heat. Add chicken and garlic to skillet. Cook and stir about 6 minutes or until chicken is tender and no pink remains; transfer mixture to a bowl.

4 Add egg to the hot skillet. Tilt skillet to spread egg in an even layer (egg may not fill bottom of skillet); cook, without stirring, for 30 seconds. Using a wide spatula, carefully turn egg round over; cook for 30 to 60 seconds more or just until set. Transfer egg round to a plate. Using a sharp knife, cut egg round into bite-size strips; set aside (see photos 1–3, page 85).

5 In same skillet heat the remaining 2 tablespoons oil over medium-high heat for 30 seconds. Add sprouts; stir-fry for 2 minutes. Add chicken and drained noodles (the noodles may clump together a bit, but they will separate when the sauce mixture is added). Stir in fish sauce mixture; cook for 1 to 2 minutes more or until heated through. Transfer chicken mixture to a serving plate. Top with egg strips and peanut topping. Sprinkle with green onions and cilantro. If desired, garnish with lime wedges.

PER 1¼ CUPS: 551 cal., 19 g total fat (3 g sat. fat), 119 mg chol., 1,790 mg sodium, 61 g carb., 2 g fiber, 32 g pro.
EXCHANGES: 1 Vegetable, 3 Starch, ½ Other Carb., 2½ Lean Meat, 2½ Fat

SHRIMP PAD THAI: Prepare as directed, except substitute 1 pound medium shrimp in shells for the chicken. Thaw shrimp if frozen. Peel and devein shrimp (see photos 1–3, page 311). Rinse shrimp; pat dry with paper towels. In Step 3 cook shrimp for 2 to 3 minutes or until shrimp are opaque.

PER 1¼ CUPS: 500 cal., 17 g total fat (2 g sat. fat), 189 mg chol., 1,816 mg sodium, 61 g carb., 2 g fiber, 23 g pro.
EXCHANGES: 1 Vegetable, 3 Starch, ½ Other Carb., 2½ Lean Meat, 2½ Fat

TOFU PAD THAI: Prepare as directed, except substitute one 16-ounce package extra-firm tub-style tofu (fresh bean curd) for the chicken. Drain tofu; cut into strips. Pat tofu strips dry with paper towels. In Step 3 cook tofu for 2 to 3 minutes or until browned.

PER 1¼ CUPS: 485 cal., 18 g total fat (3 g sat. fat), 47 mg chol., 1,757 mg sodium, 64 g carb., 3 g fiber, 16 g pro.
EXCHANGES: 1 Vegetable, 3 Starch, ½ Other Carb., 1 Lean Meat, 2½ Fat

INGREDIENT KNOW-HOW

ASIAN CHILI SAUCE: For the best, brightest flavor, look for an Asian chili sauce with chile peppers, garlic, and vinegar listed in the ingredients.
FRESH BEAN SPROUTS: To avoid any potential salmonella risk, be sure to rinse and drain bean sprouts well and stir-fry them for a full 2 minutes.
RICE NOODLES: Pad Thai is traditionally made with linguine-style rice noodles. If they aren't available, you can substitute thin rice-stick noodles (vermicelli-style) or wider straight-cut rice noodles.

pies & tarts

CHILLED & FROZEN PIES

CREAM & CUSTARD PIES

CRUSTS & PASTRY

FILLING, TOPPINGS & SAUCE

FRUIT PIES

NUT PIES & TARTS

TARTS

TIPS

pies & tarts

Once you've mastered a few basics, baking one of these yearned-for desserts is as easy as—well, pie!

THE ART OF THE PASTRY

You needn't be a pastry chef—or a grandmother—to pull off gorgeous homemade crusts. Yes, making piecrust is an art, but it's one that becomes second nature with know-how and practice.

USE EXACT MEASURES: Too much flour or water will make a crust tough, and too much shortening will make it crumbly. Also the water must be ice-cold to keep the shortening and butter from melting. Those bits of fat help separate the pastry into layers as it bakes—that's how your pastry gets flaky.

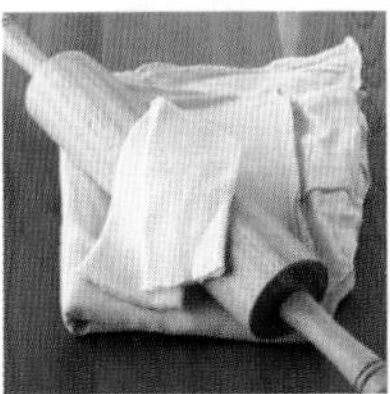

GO EASY ON THE FLOUR: You can roll out pastry on any smooth surface, such as a wooden cutting board. However, rolling it on top of a pastry cloth or a smooth lint-free towel (like a flour-sack towel) helps you avoid using excess flour, which can make pastry tough. You can also cover your rolling pin with a cotton stockinette designed for pastry; lightly flour both the cloth and stockinette. When rolling the dough, work it as little as possible because too much rolling also can make the pastry tough.

THE COVER-UP: To protect the crimped edge of the crust from overbrowning, fold a 12-inch square of foil into quarters. Cut 3½ inches off the folded corners; unfold to reveal a 7-inch hole in the center. Loosely mold foil over pie edge before baking. Or use a purchased pie shield to protect crust.

PLATES AND PANS

PIE PLATES: These can be made of glass, ceramic, stoneware, aluminum, and tin; the recipes in this chapter call for a 9-inch plate.

TART PANS: The fluted sides of these pans make your tarts pretty; the removable bottoms make it easy to transfer tarts to serving plates. Pans come in a variety of sizes, including 4-inch individual tartlet pans.

MASTERING MERINGUES

Follow these tips for airy, sweet meringues.

- Allow egg whites to stand at room temperature 30 minutes. It adds volume.
- Use a large bowl made of copper, stainless steel, or glass. Make sure the bowls, beaters, and other utensils are very clean and dry. Oil or grease residue prevents whites from beating properly. Also be sure no yolk gets into the whites when separating the eggs.
- Prevent shrinkage of baked meringue by beating whites until stiff peaks form (tips stand straight; see photo 3, page 451); spread meringue to the crust's edge (see photo, below).
- Prevent beading—small beads of moisture that can form on the surface of the baked meringue—by not overbaking the meringue.
- Prevent weeping—the watery layer that can form between the meringue and filling—by spreading the meringue over a hot filling.

TOPPING WITH MERINGUE

Mound the meringue onto the center of the hot filling. Using a spatula, quickly spread the meringue over the filling, sealing it against the edge of the crust.

cook's secrets

pastry for single-crust pie

The Secret: Pie pastry can be the most intimidating part of making a pie, but never fear! If you don't overwork your pastry, your piecrusts will be tender and flaky.

START TO FINISH: 15 MINUTES **MAKES:** 1 PIECRUST (8 SERVINGS)

- **1½ cups all-purpose flour**
- **½ teaspoon salt**
- **¼ cup shortening**
- **¼ cup butter, cut up, or shortening**
- **¼ to ⅓ cup cold water**

Some piecrust recipes call for pastry flour. Because it has a lower protein level than other flours, pastry flour helps create a very tender baked crust. To sub for all-purpose, use 1⅔ cups pastry flour.

1 In a medium bowl stir together flour and salt. Using a pastry blender, cut in shortening and butter until pieces are pea size (see photo 1, page 441).

2 Sprinkle 1 tablespoon of the water over part of the flour mixture; toss with a fork. Push moistened pastry to side of bowl. Repeat moistening flour mixture, using 1 tablespoon of the water at a time, until flour mixture is moist (see photo 2, page 441). Gather flour mixture into a ball, kneading gently until it holds together (see photo 3, page 441).

3 On a lightly floured surface use your hands to slightly flatten pastry. Roll pastry from center to edge into a circle 12 inches in diameter.

4 Fold pastry circle into fourths and place it in a 9-inch pie plate (see photo 5, page 441). Unfold pastry and ease it into pie plate without stretching it.

5 Trim pastry to ½ inch beyond edge of pie plate. Fold under extra pastry even with the plate's edge. Crimp edge as desired (see photo 7, page 441 and tip, page 441). Do not prick pastry. Fill and bake as directed in recipes.

BAKED PASTRY SHELL: Preheat oven to 450°F. Prepare as directed, except prick bottom and sides of pastry with a fork. Line pastry with a double thickness of foil. Bake for 8 minutes. Remove foil. Bake 6 to 8 minutes more or until golden. Cool on a wire rack.

BAKED PASTRY TART SHELL: Preheat oven to 450°F. Prepare as directed through Step 3. Wrap pastry circle around the rolling pin. Unroll it into a 10-inch tart pan with a removable bottom. Ease pastry into pan without stretching it. Press pastry into fluted sides of tart pan; trim edges. Prick pastry with a fork. Line pastry with a double thickness of foil. Bake for 8 minutes. Remove foil. Bake 6 to 8 minutes more or until golden. Cool on a wire rack.

PER SERVING: 191 cal., 12 g total fat (5 g sat. fat), 15 mg chol., 187 mg sodium, 18 g carb., 1 g fiber, 2 g pro.
EXCHANGES: 1 Starch, 2½ Fat

BUTTER OR SHORTENING?

All types of fat coat flour proteins so gluten doesn't form. This prevents a tough pastry. Because shortening has a higher melting point, it stays in pockets within your pastry dough in your oven longer than butter. When the shortening finally melts, steam forms in the pockets and the layers puff apart. This makes a flaky pastry. Butter, however, adds rich flavor to finished pastry. For the best pastry, this recipe uses both types of fat.

PASTRY POINTERS

1. PEA SIZE, PLEASE
Fat tenderizes and creates flakiness. When cutting shortening and butter into the flour, stop when the fat pieces are about the size of small peas. If they're too large, the fat melts and creates holes in the crust. If the pieces are too small, they melt too fast and you lose the flakiness.

2. ONE TABLESPOON AT A TIME
Add ice-cold water. This keeps the fat pieces cold so they don't melt during mixing, which creates a sandy texture. Add water, 1 tablespoon at a time, tossing gently with a fork. Push the moistened dough to the side of the bowl.

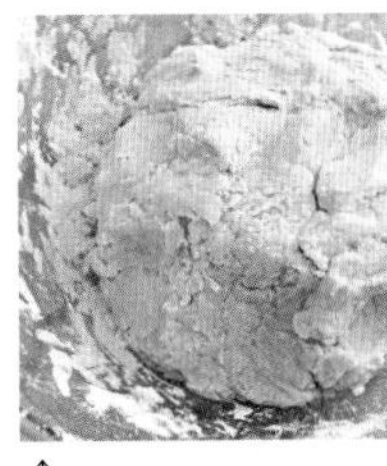

3. FORM A BALL
Once the dough is just moistened, gather it into a ball and knead gently just until it holds together. At this point you can wrap the dough in plastic wrap and refrigerate for up to 3 days or freeze for up to 3 months. Thaw at room temperature before using.

4. ROLL IT OUT
When rolling out pastry, add just enough flour to keep it from sticking. Adding too much flour or overworking the dough will make it tough. You can roll out the dough on a floured pastry cloth or cover your rolling pin with a cotton stockinette designed for pastry making—both will help prevent sticking.

5. FOLD IT
Once the pastry has been rolled to a circle, carefully fold it in half and then in half again to make quarters. Place the folded pastry on top of the pie plate with the folded tip in the center. Unfold the pastry and ease it into the plate, being careful not to stretch or tear the pastry.

6. TRIM & TUCK
Use a small sharp knife or kitchen shears to trim the pastry to ½ inch beyond the edge of the pie plate. After trimming, use your fingers to fold the pastry under, even with the edge of the pie plate.

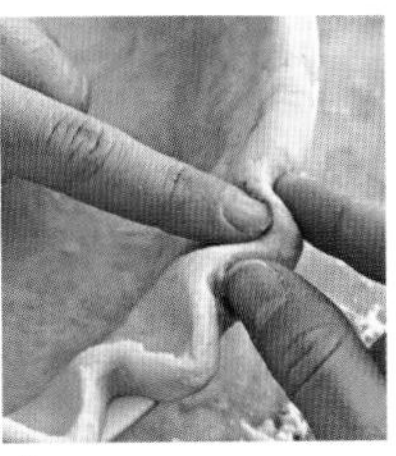

7. MAKE IT PRETTY
Crimping helps ensure the filling doesn't overflow. Crimp the edges high for pies with a lot of filling. To crimp edges, place an index finger against the inside edge of the pastry. Using the thumb and index finger of your other hand, press the pastry from the outside onto your finger to hold a crimp.

8. BLIND BAKING
Blind baking means baking a pastry shell before it is filled to create a stronger crust that can better hold moist filling. Before baking, line the inside of the shell with a double thickness of heavy-duty foil. The foil weights down the crust, which prevents it from bubbling up or blistering.

SPOON FINISH: Trim pastry even with edge of plate. Use a spoon to press design into edge.
PRESSED FLUTE: Crimp pastry (see photo 7, above); flatten flutes slightly. Press inside of flutes with tines of fork.
CRISSCROSS: Trim pastry even with edge of plate. Use tines of fork to make crisscross pattern.
THE WEAVE: Trim pastry even with edge of plate. Cut at ½-inch intervals. Fold every other section in.

cook's secrets

LATTICE STEP-BY-STEP

1. LATTICE WORK
For a lattice top, lay half of the pastry strips on top of the filling about 1 inch apart. Fold alternating pastry strips back halfway. Place a strip in the center of the pie across the strips already in place. Unfold the folded strips. Place another strip across the first set of strips parallel to the strip in the center. Repeat until lattice covers filling.

↓

pastry for double-crust pie

The Secret: Watch how you roll! Roll each pastry half from the center to the edge, working to create uniform circles. Achieving two nicely shaped circles makes trimming and crimping that much easier.

START TO FINISH: 15 MINUTES **MAKES:** 2 PIECRUSTS (8 SERVINGS)

- **2½ cups all-purpose flour**
- **1 teaspoon salt**
- **½ cup shortening**
- **¼ cup butter, cut up, or shortening**
- **½ to ⅔ cup cold water**

Salt actually enhances formation of gluten, which we don't want too much of in piecrust—but it's needed to bring out flavor in piecrust. Add it to the flour so it gets coated by the fats first to lessen gluten formation.

1 In a large bowl stir together flour and salt. Using a pastry blender, cut in shortening and butter until pieces are pea size (see photo 1, page 441).

2 Sprinkle 1 tablespoon of the water over part of the flour mixture; toss with a fork. Push moistened pastry to side of bowl. Repeat moistening flour mixture, 1 tablespoon of the water at a time, until flour mixture is moistened. Gather flour mixture into a ball, kneading gently until it holds together. Divide pastry in half; form halves into balls.

3 On a lightly floured surface use your hands to slightly flatten one pastry ball. Roll it from center to edges into a circle 12 inches in diameter.

4 Fold the pastry into quarters (see photo 5, page 441). Unfold pastry into a 9-inch pie plate. Ease pastry into plate without stretching it. Transfer desired filling to pastry-lined pie plate. Trim pastry even with pie plate rim (see photo 1, page 443).

5 Roll remaining ball into a 12-inch-diameter circle. Using a sharp knife, cut slits in pastry (see photo 2, page 443). Place pastry circle on filling (see photo 3, page 443); trim to ½ inch beyond edge of plate. Fold top pastry under bottom pastry (see photo 4, page 443). Crimp edge as desired (see page 441). Bake as directed in recipes.

NUT PASTRY: Prepare as directed, except substitute ¼ cup ground, toasted pecans or almonds for ¼ cup of flour.

PASTRY FOR LATTICE-TOP PIE: Prepare as directed, except trim bottom pastry to ½ inch beyond edge of pie plate. Roll out remaining pastry and cut into ½-inch-wide strips. Transfer desired filling to pastry-lined pie plate. Weave strips over filling in a lattice pattern (see photos, left). Trim any excess dough from the strips. Press strip ends into bottom pastry rim. Fold bottom pastry over strip ends; seal and crimp edge. Bake as directed in recipes.

PER SERVING PLAIN, NUT, OR LATTICE VARIATIONS: 303 cal., 18 g total fat (7 g sat. fat), 15 mg chol., 333 mg sodium, 30 g carb., 1 g fiber, 4 g pro.
EXCHANGES: 2 Starch, 3 Fat

WHY VENT?

Cutting slits in the top pastry of a double-crust pie allows steam to escape from the fruit pie so the filling does not bubble out or overflow. If you're feeling creative, use a small cookie cutter to cut a shape from the pastry and attach to the top with a dab of water.

Double-Crust Fruit Pie

PREP: 30 MINUTES **BAKE:** 65 MINUTES AT 375°F **MAKES:** 8 SLICES

- 1 **recipe Pastry for Double-Crust Pie (page 442)**
- 1 **recipe Fruit-Pie Filling (page 445)**
- **Milk (optional)**
- **Sugar (optional)**

1 Preheat oven to 375°F. Prepare and roll out Pastry for Double-Crust Pie. Line a 9-inch pie plate with a pastry circle; set aside.

2 In a very large bowl prepare desired Fruit-Pie Filling. Transfer the fruit mixture to the pastry-lined pie plate. Trim bottom pastry to edge of pie plate (see photo 1, below). Cut slits in remaining pastry circle; place on filling and seal (see photos 2–4, below). Crimp edge as desired (see page 441).

3 If desired, brush top pastry with milk and sprinkle with additional sugar. To prevent overbrowning, cover edge of pie with foil (see page 439). Place a foil-lined baking sheet on the rack below the pie in oven. Bake pie in the preheated oven for 30 minutes (50 minutes for frozen fruit). Remove foil. Bake for 35 to 40 minutes more or until fruit is tender and filling is bubbly in the center of the pie. Cool on a wire rack.

PER SLICE APPLE VARIATION: 399 cal., 18 g total fat (7 g sat. fat), 15 mg chol., 333 mg sodium, 54 g carb., 2 g fiber, 5 g pro. EXCHANGES: 1 Fruit, 2 Starch, ½ Other Carb., 3½ Fat

DOUBLE-CRUST PIE STEP-BY-STEP

1. After filling the pastry-lined pie plate with the desired filling, use kitchen shears or a sharp knife to trim the bottom pastry even with the plate's edge.

2. Roll out the remaining pie pastry. Use a sharp knife to cut slits or in the pastry. You can also use small cutters for a decorative look. This allows steam to escape from the filling while the pie bakes.

3. Gently fold the pastry in half and carefully place it on top of the filling, making sure to cover half of the filling. Unfold the pastry to cover other half of filling.

4. Using kitchen shears, trim the top pastry ½ inch beyond the edge of the plate. Fold the top pastry under the bottom pastry edge and crimp as desired (see page 441).

FAST

Oil Pastry for Single-Crust Pie

START TO FINISH: 10 MINUTES
MAKES: 1 PIECRUST (8 SERVINGS)

- **1⅓ cups all-purpose flour**
- **¼ teaspoon salt**
- **¼ cup vegetable oil**
- **3 to 4 tablespoons milk**

1 In a medium bowl stir together flour and salt. Add oil and 3 tablespoons milk all at once to flour. Stir lightly with a fork until combined. If necessary, stir in 1 tablespoon more milk to moisten (pastry will appear crumbly). Form pastry into a ball.

2 On a lightly floured surface use your hands to slightly flatten pastry ball. Roll dough from center to edges into a circle about 12 inches in diameter (press any cracks back together). Ease pastry circle into a 9-inch pie plate without stretching it. Trim pastry to ½ inch beyond edge of pie plate. Fold under extra pastry. Crimp edge as desired (see page 441). Do not prick pastry. Fill and bake pastry as directed in recipes.

BAKED OIL PASTRY SHELL: Preheat oven to 450°F. Prepare as directed, except prick bottom and sides of pastry with a fork. Line pastry with a double thickness of foil. Bake for 8 minutes. Remove foil. Bake for 5 to 6 minutes more or until crust is golden. Cool on a wire rack.

PER SERVING: 139 cal., 7 g total fat (1 g sat. fat), 0 mg chol., 75 mg sodium, 16 g carb., 1 g fiber, 2 g pro.
EXCHANGES: 1 Starch, 1 Fat

Rich Tart Pastry

PREP: 15 MINUTES **CHILL:** 30 TO 60 MINUTES
MAKES: 1 TART CRUST (8 SERVINGS)

- **1¼ cups all-purpose flour**
- **¼ cup sugar**
- **½ cup cold butter, cut up**
- **2 egg yolks, lightly beaten**
- **1 tablespoon cold water**

1 In a medium bowl stir together flour and sugar. Using a pastry blender, cut in butter until pieces are pea size (see photo 1, page 441). In a small bowl stir together egg yolks and water. Gradually stir egg yolk mixture into flour mixture. Using your fingers, gently knead the dough just until a ball forms. Cover pastry with plastic wrap and chill for 30 to 60 minutes or until dough is easy to handle.

2 On a floured surface use your hands to slightly flatten the pastry. Roll pastry from center to edges into a circle 12 inches in diameter.

3 Fold the pastry into quarters (see photo 5, page 441). Unfold pastry into a 10-inch tart pan with a removable bottom. Ease pastry into pan without stretching it. Press pastry into fluted sides of tart pan; trim edges. Do not prick pastry. Fill and bake as directed in recipes.

PER SERVING: 211 cal., 13 g total fat (8 g sat. fat), 83 mg chol., 84 mg sodium, 21 g carb., 1 g fiber, 3 g pro.
EXCHANGES: 1½ Starch, 2½ Fat

FAST

Graham Cracker Crust

PREP: 10 MINUTES **BAKE:** 5 MINUTES AT 375°F
MAKES: 1 PIECRUST (8 SERVINGS)

- **Nonstick cooking spray**
- **⅓ cup butter**
- **¼ cup sugar**
- **1¼ cups finely crushed graham crackers (about 18)**

1 Preheat oven to 375°F. Lightly coat a 9-inch pie plate with cooking spray; set aside. Melt butter; stir in sugar. Add crushed crackers; toss to mix well. Spread in the prepared pie plate; press evenly onto bottom and sides. Bake about 5 minutes or until edges are light brown. Cool completely on a wire rack. Fill and bake as directed in recipes.

GINGERSNAP CRUST: Prepare as directed, except omit sugar and substitute 1¼ cups finely crushed gingersnaps (20 to 22) for the graham crackers.

VANILLA WAFER CRUST: Prepare as directed, except omit sugar and substitute 1½ cups finely crushed vanilla wafers (about 44) for graham crackers.

CHOCOLATE WAFER CRUST: Prepare as directed, except omit sugar and substitute 1½ cups finely crushed chocolate wafers (about 25) for graham crackers. Do not bake; chill about 1 hour or until firm.

PER SERVING GRAHAM CRACKER, GINGERSNAP, OR VANILLA OR CHOCOLATE WAFER VARIATIONS: 159 cal., 9 g total fat (5 g sat. fat), 20 mg chol., 180 mg sodium, 17 g carb., 0 g fiber, 2 g pro. EXCHANGES: 1 Starch, 1½ Fat

DEEP-DISH GRAHAM CRACKER CRUST: Prepare as directed, except use ½ cup butter, ⅓ cup sugar, and 1½ cups crushed graham crackers (about 22 squares). Spread in a 9-inch deep-dish pie plate; press onto bottom and sides.

PER SERVING: 214 cal., 14 g total fat (8 g sat. fat), 31 mg chol., 232 mg sodium, 21 g carb., 1 g fiber, 2 g pro.
EXCHANGES: 1 Starch, ½ Other Carb., 2½ Fat

8 to try

Fruit-Pie Filling

These eight fruit-pie fillings can be used in the Double-Crust Fruit Pie (page 443) or Crumb-Topped Fruit Pie (page 446). Use the ingredient amounts specified with each photo for desired fruit.

PREP: 10 MINUTES **MAKES:** 6 CUPS

- **Sugar**
- **All-purpose flour or tapioca or cornstarch**
- 6 **cups desired fruit**

1 In a very large bowl combine the sugar* and flour or tapioca or cornstarch in amounts specified for desired fruit. Add the desired fruit;* gently toss fruit until coated. (If using frozen fruit, let mixture stand for 30 to 45 minutes or until the fruit is partially thawed but still icy.) Transfer fruit-pie filling to the pastry-lined pie plate.

***NOTE:** For added flavor, add one of the following to filling with the sugar: 1/8 teaspoon ground nutmeg, 1/4 teaspoon ground allspice, 1/4 to 1/2 teaspoon ground cinnamon or ground ginger, or 1/2 teaspoon finely shredded lemon peel. Or add 1/4 teaspoon almond extract to filling with the fruit.

FRESH OR FROZEN?

For the best pies, take advantage of fruit that is fresh and in season. If you have a craving for rhubarb pie in the winter, you CAN use frozen fruit. Don't thaw the fruit before measuring. Measure it frozen and let it stand at least 30 minutes once it is tossed with the sugar mixture.

APPLE: 1/2 to 3/4 cup sugar; 2 tablespoons flour; and 6 cups apples, peeled, cored, and thinly sliced

CHERRY: 1 1/4 to 1 1/2 cups sugar; 1/3 cup flour or 3 tablespoons quick-cooking tapioca or cornstarch; 6 cups pitted tart red cherries

RHUBARB: 1 1/4 to 1 1/2 cups sugar; 1/2 cup flour or 1/4 cup quick-cooking tapioca or cornstarch; and 6 cups 1-inch pieces rhubarb

BLACKBERRY: 1 to 1 1/4 cups sugar; 1/3 cup flour or 3 tablespoons cornstarch or quick-cooking tapioca; and 6 cups blackberries

GOOSEBERRY: 1 1/4 to 1 1/2 cups sugar; 1/3 cup flour or 3 tablespoons quick-cooking tapioca or cornstarch; 6 cups stemmed gooseberries

PEACH OR NECTARINE: 1/2 to 1 cup sugar; 3 tablespoons flour or 1 1/2 tablespoons cornstarch or quick-cooking tapioca; and 6 cups peaches or nectarines, peeled, pitted, and sliced

RASPBERRY: 3/4 to 1 cup sugar; 1/4 cup flour or 2 tablespoons quick-cooking tapioca or cornstarch; and 6 cups raspberries

BLUEBERRY: 1 to 1 1/4 cups sugar; 1/4 cup flour or 2 tablespoons quick-cooking tapioca or cornstarch; and 6 cups blueberries

MAPLE, APPLE, AND CHEDDAR PIE

Crumb-Topped Fruit Pie

PREP: 35 MINUTES **BAKE:** 65 MINUTES AT 375°F
MAKES: 8 SLICES

- **1 recipe Pastry for Single-Crust Pie (page 440)**
- **2/3 cup rolled oats**
- **2/3 cup all-purpose flour**
- **1/2 cup packed brown sugar**
- **1/4 teaspoon salt**
- **1/4 teaspoon ground cinnamon**
- **6 tablespoons butter**
- **1/4 cup chopped toasted pecans or walnuts (see tip, page 21) (optional)**
- **1 recipe Fruit-Pie Filling (page 445)**

1 Preheat oven to 375°F. Prepare and roll out Pastry for Single-Crust Pie. Line a 9-inch pie plate with the pastry circle and trim. Crimp edge as desired (see page 441). Set aside.

2 In a medium bowl stir together the oats, flour, brown sugar, salt, and cinnamon. Using a pastry blender, cut in butter until mixture resembles coarse crumbs. If desired, stir in nuts. Set aside.

3 In a very large bowl prepare desired Fruit-Pie Filling as directed. Transfer fruit filling to the pastry-lined pie plate. Sprinkle oats mixture over filling.

4 To prevent overbrowning, cover edge of pie with foil (see page 439). Bake for 30 minutes (50 minutes for frozen fruit). Remove foil. Bake for 35 to 40 minutes more or until fruit is tender and topping is golden (If necessary, loosely cover top of pie with foil the last 10 to 15 minutes of baking.) Cool on a wire rack.

PER SLICE APPLE VARIATION: 504 cal., 22 g total fat (11 g sat. fat), 38 mg chol., 325 mg sodium, 73 g carb., 3 g fiber, 6 g pro. **EXCHANGES:** 1 Fruit, 2 Starch, 2 Other Carb., 4 Fat

Maple, Apple, and Cheddar Pie

PREP: 30 MINUTES **BAKE:** 60 MINUTES AT 375°F
COOL: 60 MINUTES **MAKES:** 8 SLICES

- **1 recipe Pastry for Double-Crust Pie (page 442)**
- **1/2 cup sugar**
- **2 tablespoons all-purpose flour**
- **1/2 teaspoon ground cinnamon**
- **1/4 teaspoon salt**
- **5 cups thinly sliced, peeled tart apples (5 medium)**
- **1 1/2 cups shredded white cheddar cheese (6 ounces)**
- **1/4 cup maple syrup**
- **1 tablespoon whipping cream**
- **2 tablespoons maple syrup**
- **1/4 cup chopped pecans, toasted (see tip, page 21) (optional)**

1 Preheat oven to 375°F. Prepare and roll out Pastry for Double-Crust Pie. Line a 9-inch pie plate with a pastry circle (see photo 5, page 441); set aside.

2 For filling, in a large bowl stir together sugar, flour, cinnamon, and salt. Add apples; toss gently to coat. Add cheese and the 1/4 cup maple syrup; toss gently to combine. Transfer filling to the pastry-lined pie plate. Drizzle with cream. Trim bottom pastry to edge of pie plate (see photo 1, page 443).

3 Cut slits in remaining pastry circle; place on filling and seal (see photos 2–4, page 443). Crimp edge as desired (see page 441).

4 To prevent overbrowning, cover edge of pie with foil (see page 439). Bake pie for 40 minutes. Remove foil. Bake about 20 minutes more or until apples are tender and pastry is golden brown. Transfer to a wire rack. Brush pie with the 2 tablespoons maple syrup. If desired, sprinkle with pecans. Cool for 1 hour. Serve slightly warm.

PER SLICE: 523 cal., 26 g total fat (12 g sat. fat), 40 mg chol., 550 mg sodium, 63 g carb., 2 g fiber, 10 g pro.
EXCHANGES: 1/2 Fruit, 2 Starch, 1 1/2 Other Carb., 1/2 High-Fat Meat, 4 Fat

BEST-LOVED

Strawberry-Rhubarb Pie

PREP: 25 MINUTES **STAND:** 15 MINUTES
BAKE: 50 MINUTES AT 375°F **MAKES:** 8 SLICES

- **1¼ cups sugar**
- **3 tablespoons quick-cooking tapioca**
- **¼ teaspoon salt**
- **¼ teaspoon ground nutmeg**
- **1 pound fresh rhubarb, cut into 1-inch pieces (3 cups), or one 16-ounce package frozen cut rhubarb**
- **3 cups sliced fresh strawberries**
- **1 recipe Pastry for Double-Crust Pie (page 442)**

1 For filling, in a large bowl stir together sugar, tapioca, salt, and nutmeg. Add rhubarb and strawberries; gently toss until coated. Let rhubarb mixture stand for 15 minutes, stirring occasionally. (If using frozen rhubarb, let stand for 45 minutes.)

2 Preheat oven to 375°F. Prepare and roll out Pastry for Double-Crust Pie. Line 9-inch pie plate with pastry circle (see photo 5, page 441).

3 Stir rhubarb mixture; transfer to the pastry-lined pie plate. Trim bottom pastry to edge of the pie plate (see photo 1, page 443). Cut slits in remaining pastry; place on filling and seal (see photos 2–4, page 443). Crimp edge as desired (see page 441).

4 To prevent overbrowning, cover edge of pie with foil (see page 439). Place a foil-lined baking sheet on the rack below the pie in oven. Bake for 25 minutes. Remove foil; bake for 25 to 30 minutes more or until filling bubbles and crust is golden (45 to 50 minutes more if using frozen rhubarb). Cool on a wire rack.

PER SLICE: 467 cal., 18 g total fat (7 g sat. fat), 15 mg chol., 408 mg sodium, 71 g carb., 3 g fiber, 5 g pro.
EXCHANGES: 1 Fruit, 2 Starch, 2 Other Carb., 3 Fat

FRESH STRAWBERRY PIE

Fresh Strawberry Pie

PREP: 35 MINUTES **COOL:** 10 MINUTES
CHILL: 1 TO 3 HOURS **MAKES:** 8 SLICES

- **1 recipe Baked Pastry Shell (page 440)**
- **9 cups fresh strawberries, hulled and halved**
- **½ cup water**
- **⅔ cup sugar**
- **2 tablespoons cornstarch**
- **Several drops red food coloring (optional)**
- **Finely shredded lemon peel (optional)**
- **Fresh mint leaves (optional)**

1 Prepare Baked Pastry Shell;* set aside.

2 For glaze, in a blender or food processor combine 1½ cups of the strawberries and the water. Cover and blend or process until smooth. In a medium saucepan combine sugar and cornstarch; stir in blended strawberry mixture. Cook and stir over medium heat until mixture is thickened and bubbly. Cook and stir for 2 minutes more. If desired, stir in red food coloring. Remove from heat; cool for 10 minutes without stirring.

3 In a large bowl combine remaining strawberries and the strawberry glaze; toss gently to coat. Transfer strawberry mixture to the cooled pie shell.

4 Chill pie for at least 1 hour or up to 3 hours (after 3 hours, bottom of crust starts to soften). If desired, garnish with lemon peel and fresh mint leaves.

***NOTE:** Instead of crimping the edge of the pastry, roll out any dough scraps and cut into rectangles. Prick rectangles with a fork. Brush edge of piecrust with some water and attach rectangles to the edge, overlapping them, before baking.

PER SLICE: 316 cal., 12 g total fat (5 g sat. fat), 15 mg chol., 189 mg sodium, 49 g carb., 4 g fiber, 4 g pro.
EXCHANGES: 1 Fruit, 1 Starch, 1 Other Carb., 2½ Fat

TRI-BERRY PIE

BEST-LOVED

Tri-Berry Pie

PREP: 30 MINUTES **BAKE:** 65 MINUTES AT 375°F
MAKES: 8 SLICES

- **½ to ¾ cup sugar**
- **3 tablespoons cornstarch**
- **2 cups fresh or frozen red raspberries**
- **1½ cups fresh or frozen blueberries**
- **1½ cups fresh or frozen blackberries**
- **1 recipe Pastry for Lattice-Top Pie (page 442)**

1 For filling, in a large bowl stir together sugar and cornstarch. Add raspberries, blueberries, and blackberries. Gently toss berries until coated. (If using frozen fruit, let mixture stand for 45 minutes or until fruit is partially thawed but still icy.)

2 Preheat oven to 375°F. Prepare and roll out Pastry for Lattice-Top Pie. Line a 9-inch pie plate with a pastry circle (see photo 5, page 441).

3 Stir berry mixture. Transfer berry mixture to the pastry-lined pie plate. Trim bottom pastry to ½ inch beyond edge of pie plate. Continue as directed for Pastry for Lattice-Top Pie (see photos, page 442).

4 If desired, brush top pastry with *milk* and sprinkle with additional sugar. To prevent overbrowning, cover edge of pie with foil (see page 439). Place a foil-lined baking sheet on the rack below pie in the oven. Bake pie for 30 minutes (50 minutes for frozen fruit). Remove foil. Bake for 35 to 40 minutes more or until filling bubbles and pastry is golden. Cool on a wire rack.

PER SLICE: 406 cal., 19 g total fat (7 g sat. fat), 15 mg chol., 334 mg sodium, 55 g carb., 5 g fiber, 5 g pro.
EXCHANGES: ½ Fruit, 2 Starch, 1 Other Carb., 3½ Fat

Frozen Black Raspberry Cream Pie

PREP: 10 MINUTES **FREEZE:** 4 TO 24 HOURS
STAND: 5 MINUTES **MAKES:** 8 SLICES

- **1 recipe Graham Cracker Crust (page 444)**
- **1 cup whipping cream**
- **1 8-ounce package cream cheese, softened**
- **1 10-ounce jar seedless black raspberry spreadable fruit**
- **Fresh black raspberries (optional)**

1 Prepare Graham Cracker Crust; set aside.

2 In a medium mixing bowl beat whipping cream with an electric mixer on medium to high speed until stiff peaks form (tips stand straight); set aside.

3 In a large mixing bowl beat cream cheese with an electric mixer on medium speed until smooth. Add spreadable fruit; beat until combined. Fold in whipped cream. Spoon cream mixture into crust.

4 Cover and freeze pie for 4 to 24 hours or until firm. To serve, place pie plate on a warm, damp cloth and let pie stand for 5 minutes to loosen crust from bottom of plate before cutting. If desired, garnish with fresh black raspberries.

PER SERVING: 438 cal., 30 g total fat (18 g sat. fat), 93 mg chol., 282 mg sodium, 39 g carb., 0 g fiber, 4 g pro.
EXCHANGES: 1 Starch, 1½ Other Carb., 6 Fat

BEST-LOVED

Key Lime Pie *(photo, page 437)*

PREP: 20 MINUTES **BAKE:** 25 MINUTES AT 325°F
COOL: 60 MINUTES **CHILL:** 2 TO 24 HOURS
MAKES: 8 SLICES

- **1 recipe Baked Pastry Shell (page 440)**
- **3 egg yolks**
- **1 14-ounce can sweetened condensed milk**
- **½ teaspoon finely shredded Key lime or Persian lime peel**
- **½ cup Key lime or Persian lime juice**
- **1½ cups whipping cream**
- **2 drops green food coloring (optional)**
- **2 tablespoons sugar**
- **1 teaspoon vanilla**
- **Key lime or Persian lime slices (optional)**

1 Prepare Baked Pastry Shell; set aside. Preheat oven to 325°F.

2 For filling, in a medium mixing bowl beat egg yolks with a whisk or fork. Stir in sweetened condensed milk and the ½ teaspoon lime peel. Whisk in the lime juice until combined (mixture will thicken). Whisk in ½ cup of the cream and, if desired, the food coloring; mix well.

3 Spoon filling into crust. Bake about 25 minutes or until filling is firm when lightly touched. Cool on a wire rack for 60 minutes. Cover and chill for 2 to 24 hours.

4 In a chilled large mixing bowl beat the remaining 1 cup whipping cream, the sugar, and vanilla with an electric mixer on medium speed until stiff peaks form (tips stand straight). Spoon over chilled pie or spoon into a pastry bag fitted with an open star tip and pipe onto pie. If desired, top with lime slices.

PER SLICE: 544 cal., 35 g total fat (19 g sat. fat), 163 mg chol., 280 mg sodium, 51 g carb., 1 g fiber, 8 g pro.
EXCHANGES: 1 Starch, 2½ Other Carb., ½ Lean Meat, 6½ Fat

cook's secrets

lemon meringue pie

The Secret: A beautiful meringue should sit on top of a perfectly cooked, lemony filling that holds a nice cut edge. How? When cooking the filling, don't skip the last 2 minutes of cooking time—it's a make-or-break step!

FILLING POINTERS

1. EASY TEMPERED
If you don't temper the egg yolks before adding them to the filling, you'll have scrambled eggs! Gradually whisk half of the hot filling into the yolks. Don't stop whisking!

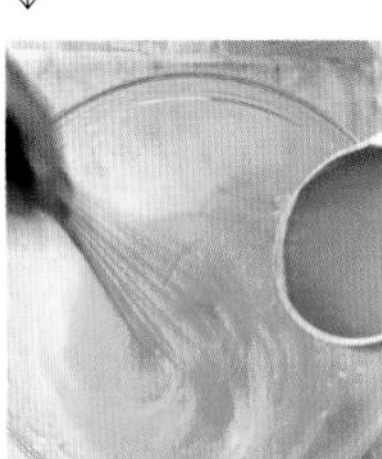

2. CRUCIAL MINUTES
After returning the tempered yolks to the lemon filling, simmer for the full 2 minutes, giving the eggs time to cook and the cornstarch time to reach its full thickening power.

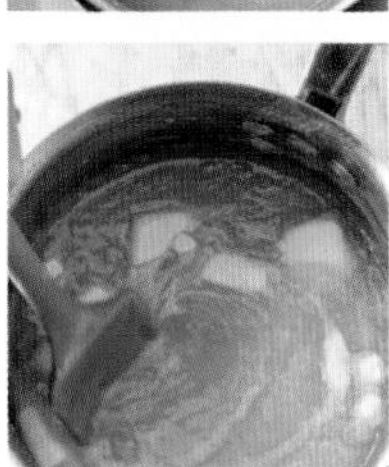

3. KEEP IT HOT!
A hot filling prevents meringue from weeping between the meringue layer and filling. If your filling is not piping hot before you pour it into your pastry, reheat it gently on the stove top.

BEST-LOVED

PREP: 40 MINUTES **BAKE:** 30 MINUTES AT 325°F **COOL:** 60 MINUTES
CHILL: 5 TO 6 HOURS **MAKES:** 8 SLICES

- **1 recipe Baked Pastry Shell (page 440)**
- **5 eggs**
- **2 cups sugar**
- **1/3 cup cornstarch**
- **2 teaspoons finely shredded lemon peel (optional)**
- **1 cup water**
- **3/4 cup lemon juice**
- **1/3 cup butter, cut up**
- **1 recipe Five-Egg White Meringue (page 451)**

Cornstarch must be added to a cold liquid and then heated for it to lose its starchy flavor and start the thickening process. Closely follow the timings in the recipe for perfectly thickened filling.

1 Prepare Baked Pastry Shell; set aside. Separate egg yolks from egg whites. Set aside yolks for filling and whites for Five-Egg White Meringue.

2 Preheat oven to 325°F. For filling, in a medium saucepan stir together sugar and cornstarch. Stir in lemon peel (if desired), the water, and lemon juice. Cook and stir over medium heat until thickened and bubbly. Remove from heat.

3 Lightly beat egg yolks with a whisk. Gradually whisk half of the hot lemon mixture into yolks. Return egg yolk mixture to saucepan. Bring to a gentle boil; reduce heat. Cook and whisk for 2 minutes more. Remove from heat. Add butter, whisking until melted. Cover filling with plastic wrap; keep warm.

4 Prepare Five-Egg White Meringue through Step 2. Pour the hot filling into Baked Pastry Shell. Immediately spoon meringue over filling; spread meringue evenly, sealing it to the edges of the pastry shell (see page 439). Using the back of a spoon, swirl meringue to form high, decorative peaks. Bake for 30 minutes. (Do not overbake. Overbaking causes beading on the surface of the meringue.) Cool on a wire rack for 60 minutes. Chill for 5 to 6 hours before serving; cover pie for longer storage.

PER SLICE: 623 cal., 23 g total fat (11 g sat. fat), 167 mg chol., 283 mg sodium, 101 g carb., 1 g fiber, 7 g pro. **EXCHANGES:** 1 Starch, 6 Other Carb., 1/2 Lean Meat, 4 Fat

LEMONS 101

PEEL: Use a Microplane grater or the fine shredding surface of a box grater. Remove only the yellow part (zest) of the rind—the white pith is bitter, so leave it on the lemon. An average lemon will yield 2 teaspoons finely shredded peel.

JUICE: To extract the most juice, roll room-temperature lemons on the countertop under your palm to break up pulp inside; halve and juice. You should get 3 tablespoons juice per average lemon.

Meringue for Pie

PREP: 15 MINUTES **STAND:** 30 MINUTES
MAKES: 8 SERVINGS (ENOUGH TO TOP ONE 9-INCH PIE)

- **4 egg whites**
- **1 teaspoon vanilla**
- **½ teaspoon cream of tartar**
- **½ cup sugar**

1 Allow egg whites to stand at room temperature for 30 minutes. In a large mixing bowl combine egg whites, vanilla, and cream of tartar. Beat with an electric mixer on medium speed about 1 minute or until soft peaks form (tips curl; see photo 1, below).

2 Gradually add sugar, 1 tablespoon at a time, beating on high speed about 5 minutes or until mixture forms stiff, glossy peaks (tips stand straight; see photos 2 and 3, below) and sugar dissolves (rub a small amount between two fingers; it should feel completely smooth) (see photo 4 below).

3 Immediately spread meringue over hot pie filling, carefully sealing to edge of pastry (see page 439) to prevent shrinkage. Bake as directed in recipes.

PER SERVING: 59 cal., 0 g total fat, 0 mg chol., 28 mg sodium, 13 g carb., 0 g fiber, 2 g pro.
EXCHANGES: 1 Other Carb.

FIVE-EGG WHITE MERINGUE: Prepare as directed, except use 5 egg whites and 1 cup sugar. In Step 2 beat about 6 minutes or until stiff peaks form. Continue as directed in Step 3.

PER SERVING: 109 cal., 0 g total fat, 0 mg chol., 34 mg sodium, 26 g carb., 0 g fiber, 2 g pro.
EXCHANGES: 1½ Other Carb.

CREAM OF TARTAR

Cream of tartar—found in the spice section of the grocery store—is an acid. It reinforces the air bubbles so they hold up until the heat sets the foam structure as it bakes.

MERINGUE STEP-BY-STEP

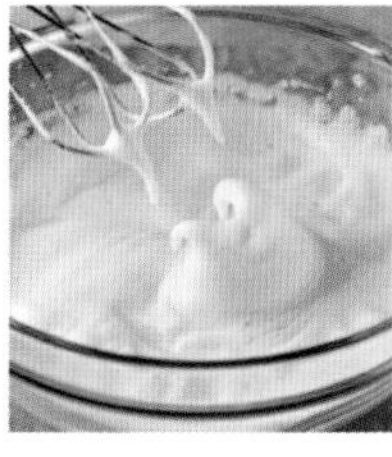

1. SOFT PEAKS
Use a clean bowl—squeaky clean! Even a little fat will hinder your meringue. Beat room-temperature egg whites, vanilla, and cream of tartar just until the tips curl over. The whites will move less like liquid in the bowl once you hit soft peak stage.

2. ONE TABLESPOON AT A TIME
Add sugar to egg white mixture, 1 tablespoon at a time, beating constantly. Go slowly because you want the sugar to dissolve completely as you incorporate it.

3. STIFF PEAKS
The meringue is ready when the mixture forms stiff, glossy peaks (the tips will stand straight) and all of the sugar has dissolved.

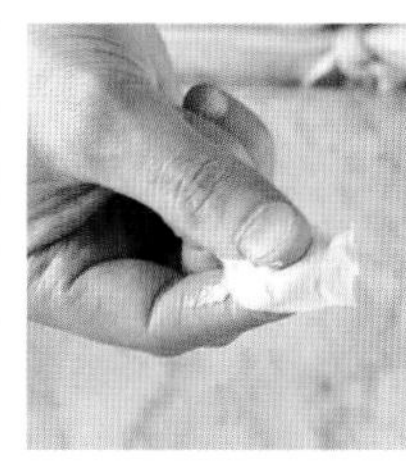

4. TEXTURE TEST
To test the texture of the meringue for doneness, rub a small amount between two fingers. It should feel completely smooth.

Vanilla Cream Pie

PREP: 50 MINUTES **BAKE:** 30 MINUTES AT 325°F
COOL: 60 MINUTES **CHILL:** 3 TO 6 HOURS
MAKES: 8 SLICES

- **1 recipe Baked Pastry Shell (page 440)**
- **4 eggs**
- **3/4 cup sugar**
- **3 tablespoons cornstarch**
- **2 1/2 cups half-and-half, light cream, or milk**
- **1 tablespoon butter**
- **1 1/2 teaspoons vanilla**
- **1 recipe Meringue for Pie (page 451)**

1 Prepare Baked Pastry Shell. Separate egg yolks from whites. Set aside yolks for filling and whites for Meringue for Pie.

2 Preheat oven to 325°F. For filling, in a saucepan combine sugar and cornstarch. Gradually stir in half-and-half. Cook and stir over medium-high heat until thickened and bubbly; reduce heat. Cook and stir for 2 minutes more. Remove from heat. Lightly beat egg yolks with a whisk. Gradually whisk about 1 cup of the hot filling into yolks (see photo 1, page 450). Add yolk mixture to saucepan. Bring to a gentle boil, stirring constantly; reduce heat. Cook and stir for 2 minutes more (see photo 2, page 450). Remove from heat. Stir in butter and vanilla. Keep filling warm. Prepare Meringue for Pie through Step 2.

3 Pour the warm filling into Baked Pastry Shell. Immediately spoon meringue over filling; spread meringue evenly, sealing it to the edges of the pastry shell (see page 439). Bake for 30 minutes. Cool on wire rack for 60 minutes. Chill for 3 to 6 hours before serving; cover for longer storage.

PER SLICE: 483 cal., 25 g total fat (12 g sat. fat), 152 mg chol., 291 mg sodium, 56 g carb., 1 g fiber, 10 g pro.
EXCHANGES: 1 Starch, 3 Other Carb., 1 Lean Meat, 4 1/2 Fat

BANANA CREAM PIE: *(photo, page 437)* Prepare as directed, except before adding filling, arrange 3 medium bananas, sliced (about 2 1/4 cups), on bottom of the pastry shell.

PER SLICE: 522 cal., 25 g total fat (12 g sat. fat), 152 mg chol., 291 mg sodium, 66 g carb., 2 g fiber, 10 g pro.
EXCHANGES: 1 Starch, 1/2 Fruit, 3 Other Carb., 1 Lean Meat, 4 1/2 Fat

COCONUT CREAM PIE: Prepare as directed, except stir in 1 cup flaked coconut with butter and vanilla. Sprinkle an additional 1/3 cup flaked coconut over meringue before baking.

PER SLICE: 576 cal., 31 g total fat (18 g sat. fat), 153 mg chol., 344 mg sodium, 64 g carb., 2 g fiber, 11 g pro.
EXCHANGES: 1 Starch, 3 Other Carb., 1 Lean Meat, 6 Fat

DARK CHOCOLATE CREAM PIE: Prepare as directed, except increase the sugar to 1 cup. Stir in 3 ounces chopped unsweetened chocolate with the half-and-half.

PER SLICE: 560 cal., 30 g total fat (16 g sat. fat), 153 mg chol., 293 mg sodium, 65 g carb., 2 g fiber, 11 g pro.
EXCHANGES: 1 Starch, 3 Other Carb., 1 Lean Meat, 5 1/2 Fat

SOUR CREAM-RAISIN PIE: Prepare as directed, except decrease the sugar to 2/3 cup and increase the cornstarch to 1/4 cup. Fold in 1 cup raisins and 1/2 cup sour cream with the butter and vanilla. Heat filling through but do not boil.

PER SLICE: 556 cal., 27 g total fat (14 g sat. fat), 159 mg chol., 302 mg sodium, 69 g carb., 1 g fiber, 10 g pro.
EXCHANGES: 1 Starch, 3 1/2 Other Carb., 1 Lean Meat, 5 Fat

BEST-LOVED

Pumpkin Pie

PREP: 30 MINUTES **BAKE:** 60 MINUTES AT 400°F
COOL: 60 MINUTES **MAKES:** 8 SLICES

- **1 recipe Pastry for Single-Crust Pie (page 440)**
- **1 15-ounce can pumpkin**
- **3/4 cup packed brown sugar**
- **1 1/4 teaspoons ground cinnamon**
- **1 teaspoon ground ginger**
- **1/2 teaspoon salt**
- **1/4 teaspoon ground cloves**
- **1/4 teaspoon finely shredded orange peel (optional)**
- **4 eggs, lightly beaten**
- **1 1/2 cups half-and-half or light cream**

1 Preheat oven to 400°F. Prepare and roll out Pastry for Single-Crust Pie. Line a 9-inch pie plate with pastry circle and trim. Crimp edge as desired (see page 441). Do not prick pastry. Line pastry with a double thickness of foil. Bake for 15 minutes. Remove foil.

2 Meanwhile, in a large bowl combine pumpkin, brown sugar, cinnamon, ginger, salt, cloves, and, if desired, orange peel. Add eggs; beat lightly with a fork until combined. Gradually add half-and-half; stir just until combined.

3 Place the partially baked piecrust on the oven rack. Carefully pour pumpkin mixture into pastry shell. To prevent overbrowning, cover edge of pie with foil (see page 439). Bake for 20 minutes. Remove foil. Bake 25 to 30 minutes more or until a knife inserted near center comes out clean. Cool on a wire rack for 60 minutes. Cover and chill within 2 hours.

PER SLICE: 449 cal., 25 g total fat (13 g sat. fat), 158 mg chol., 400 mg sodium, 49 g carb., 3 g fiber, 8 g pro.
EXCHANGES: 1 Starch, 2 Other Carb., 1/2 Lean Meat, 4 1/2 Fat

Bourbon-Sweet Potato Pie with Hazelnut Crumble

PREP: 35 MINUTES **BAKE:** 50 MINUTES AT 350°F
MAKES: 8 SLICES

- **1 recipe Baked Pastry Shell (page 440)**
- **1 cup packed brown sugar**
- **2 tablespoons all-purpose flour**
- **½ teaspoon ground cinnamon**
- **¼ teaspoon salt**
- **¼ teaspoon ground nutmeg**
- **3 eggs, lightly beaten**
- **½ cup milk**
- **½ cup sour cream**
- **2 tablespoons bourbon**
- **1 teaspoon vanilla**
- **2 cups mashed, cooked sweet potatoes (about 1½ pounds uncooked)**
- **2 tablespoons butter, melted**
- **1 recipe Hazelnut Crumble**
- **1 recipe Sweetened Whipped Cream (page 270) (optional)**
- **Ground cinnamon (optional)**

1 Prepare Baked Pastry Shell; set aside. Preheat oven to 350°F.

2 For filling, in a large bowl stir together brown sugar, flour, cinnamon, salt, and nutmeg; set aside. In a medium bowl combine eggs, milk, sour cream, bourbon, and vanilla. Stir in mashed sweet potatoes and melted butter. Add sweet potato mixture to brown sugar mixture, stirring just until combined.

3 Place the pastry shell on the oven rack. Carefully pour the filling into the pastry shell. Sprinkle with Hazelnut Crumble. Bake about 50 minutes or until the center is set. Cool on a wire rack. Cover and chill within 2 hours. If desired, top with a spoonful of Sweetened Whipped Cream and sprinkle with additional ground cinnamon.

HAZELNUT CRUMBLE: In a small bowl stir together ½ cup all-purpose flour; ½ cup toasted hazelnuts (filberts), chopped; and ¼ cup packed brown sugar. Drizzle with ¼ cup melted butter; toss with a fork until combined and crumbly.

PER SLICE: 610 cal., 30 g fat (13 g sat. fat), 115 mg chol., 421 mg sodium, 76 g carb., 4 g fiber, 9 g pro.
EXCHANGES: 3 Starch, 2 Other Carb., 5½ Fat

SNICKERDOODLE PIE

BEST-LOVED

Snickerdoodle Pie

PREP: 40 MINUTES **BAKE:** 45 MINUTES AT 350°F
COOL: 30 MINUTES **MAKES:** 10 SLICES

- **1 recipe Pastry for Single-Crust Pie (page 440)**
- **1 tablespoon granulated sugar, raw sugar, or coarse sugar**
- **3/4 teaspoon ground cinnamon**
- **2 teaspoons butter, melted**
- **1/2 cup packed brown sugar**
- **1/4 cup butter**
- **3 tablespoons water**
- **2 tablespoons light-color corn syrup**
- **1 1/2 teaspoons vanilla**
- **1/4 cup butter, softened**
- **1/2 cup granulated sugar**
- **1/4 cup powdered sugar**
- **1 teaspoon baking powder**
- **1/2 teaspoon salt**
- **1/4 teaspoon cream of tartar**
- **1 egg**
- **1/2 cup milk**
- **1 1/4 cups all-purpose flour**

1 Preheat oven to 350°F. Prepare and roll out Pastry for a Single-Crust Pie. Line 9-inch pie plate with the pastry circle and trim. Crimp edge as desired (see page 441). In a bowl combine the 1 tablespoon granulated sugar and 1/2 teaspoon of the cinnamon. Brush the 2 teaspoons melted butter over crust. Sprinkle with 1 teaspoon cinnamon-sugar mixture; set aside.

2 For syrup, in a small saucepan combine brown sugar, 1/4 cup butter, the water, corn syrup, and the remaining 1/4 teaspoon cinnamon. Bring to boiling over medium heat, stirring to dissolve brown sugar. Boil gently for 2 minutes. Remove from heat. Stir in 1/2 teaspoon of the vanilla. Set aside.

3 For filling, in a large mixing bowl beat 1/4 cup softened butter with an electric mixer on medium speed for 30 seconds. Beat in the 1/2 cup granulated sugar, the powdered sugar, baking powder, salt, and cream of tartar until well combined. Beat in egg and remaining 1 teaspoon vanilla. Gradually beat in milk until combined. Beat in flour. Spread evenly in pastry-lined pie plate. Slowly pour syrup over filling in pie plate. Sprinkle with remaining cinnamon-sugar mixture.

4 To prevent overbrowning, cover edge of pie with foil (see page 439). Bake pie for 25 minutes. Remove foil; bake about 20 minutes more or until top is puffed and golden brown and a wooden toothpick inserted near center comes out clean. Cool on a wire rack for at least 30 minutes. If desired, serve with *vanilla ice cream* dusted with *ground cinnamon* or *cinnamon ice cream*.

PER SLICE: 423 cal., 20 g total fat (11 g sat. fat), 61 mg chol., 380 mg sodium, 55 g carb., 1 g fiber, 5 g pro.
EXCHANGES: 2 Starch, 1 1/2 Other Carb., 3 1/2 Fat

Brownie-Walnut Pie

PREP: 40 MINUTES **COOL:** 20 MINUTES
BAKE: 50 MINUTES AT 350°F **MAKES:** 10 SLICES

- **1/2 cup butter**
- **3 ounces unsweetened chocolate, cut up**
- **1 Pastry for Single-Crust Pie (page 440)**
- **3 eggs, lightly beaten**
- **1 1/2 cups sugar**
- **1/2 cup all-purpose flour**
- **1 teaspoon vanilla**
- **1 cup chopped walnuts**
- **1 recipe Heavenly Hot Fudge Sauce (page 291); fresh fruit, such as raspberries, sliced strawberries, or sliced peaches; vanilla ice cream; and/or chopped walnuts (optional)**

1 For filling, in a small heavy saucepan melt butter and chocolate over low heat, stirring frequently. Remove from heat; cool for 20 minutes.

2 Preheat oven to 350°F. Prepare and roll out Pastry for Single-Crust Pie. Line a 9-inch pie plate with the pastry circle and trim. Crimp edge as desired (see page 441).

3 For filling, in a medium bowl combine eggs, sugar, flour, and vanilla; stir in the chocolate mixture and nuts.

4 Pour filling into a pastry-lined pie plate. Bake for 50 to 55 minutes or until a knife inserted near the center comes out clean. Cool on a wire rack. If desired, serve with Heavenly Hot Fudge Sauce, fresh fruit, vanilla ice cream, and/or additional chopped walnuts.

PER SLICE: 516 cal., 32 g total fat (14 g sat. fat), 92 mg chol., 263 mg sodium, 54 g carb., 3 g fiber, 7 g pro.
EXCHANGES: 1½ Starch, 2 Other Carb., ½ High-Fat Meat, 5½ Fat

Pecan Pie

PREP: 25 MINUTES **BAKE:** 45 MINUTES AT 350°F
MAKES: 8 SLICES

- **1 recipe Pastry for Single-Crust Pie (page 440)**
- **3 eggs, lightly beaten**
- **1 cup light-color corn syrup**
- **⅔ cup sugar**
- **⅓ cup butter, melted**
- **1 teaspoon vanilla**
- **1¼ cups pecan halves or chopped macadamia nuts**

1 Preheat oven to 350°F. Prepare and roll out Pastry for Single-Crust Pie. Line a 9-inch pie plate with the pastry circle and trim. Crimp edge as desired (see page 441).

2 For filling, in a medium bowl combine eggs, corn syrup, sugar, butter, and vanilla; mix well. Stir in pecan halves.

3 Pour the filling into the pastry-lined pie plate. To prevent overbrowning, cover edge of pie with foil (see page 439). Bake for 25 minutes. Remove foil. Bake for 20 to 25 minutes more or until filling is puffed and appears set. Cool on a wire rack. Cover and chill within 2 hours.

PER SLICE: 586 cal., 33 g total fat (12 g sat. fat), 105 mg chol., 319 mg sodium, 71 g carb., 2 g fiber, 6 g pro.
EXCHANGES: 1 Starch, 3½ Other Carb., ½ Lean Meat, 6½ Fat

CHOCOLATE PECAN PIE: Prepare as directed, except before adding the filling to the pastry-lined pie plate, evenly spread ¾ cup semisweet chocolate pieces on the bottom of pastry.

PER SLICE: 663 cal., 38 g total fat (15 g sat. fat), 105 mg chol., 321 mg sodium, 81 g carb., 3 g fiber, 7 g. pro.
EXCHANGES: 1 Starch, 4½ Other Carb., ½ Lean Meat, 7 Fat

Custard Pie

PREP: 25 MINUTES **BAKE:** 12 MINUTES AT 450°F/ 40 MINUTES AT 350°F **COOL:** 60 MINUTES
MAKES: 8 SLICES

- **1 recipe Pastry for Single-Crust Pie (page 440)**
- **4 eggs**
- **½ cup sugar**
- **2 teaspoons vanilla**
- **⅛ teaspoon salt**
- **⅛ teaspoon ground nutmeg**
- **2 cups half-and-half, light cream, or whole milk**

1 Preheat oven to 450°F. Prepare and roll out Pastry for Single-Crust Pie. Line a 9-inch pie plate with pastry circle and trim. Crimp edge as desired (see page 441). Line pastry with a double thickness of foil. Bake for 8 minutes. Remove foil. Bake for 4 to 5 minutes more or until set and dry. Remove from oven; reduce the oven temperature to 350°F.

2 Meanwhile, for filling, in a medium bowl lightly beat eggs with a fork. Stir in sugar, vanilla, salt, and nutmeg. Gradually stir in half-and-half until mixture is thoroughly combined.

3 Place the partially baked pastry-lined pie plate on the oven rack. Carefully pour filling into pastry shell. To prevent overbrowning, cover edge of pie with foil (see page 439). Bake for 25 minutes. Remove foil. Bake for 15 to 20 minutes more or until a knife inserted near the center comes out clean. To serve warm, cool on a wire rack for at least 60 minutes. Cover and chill within 2 hours. For longer storage, cover and chill for 2 days.

PER SLICE: 357 cal., 21 g total fat (10 g sat. fat), 143 mg chol., 283 mg sodium, 33 g carb., 1 g fiber, 7 g pro.
EXCHANGES: 1 Starch, 1 Other Carb., ½ Lean Meat, 4 Fat

PIECRUST NOT YOUR THING?

If you don't have the time or the inclination to make pastry crust from scratch, purchase rolled unbaked refrigerated piecrusts. They're the next best thing to homemade. And no one will be the wiser.

S'MORES ICE CREAM PIE

Strawberry Ice Cream Pie

PREP: 20 MINUTES **FREEZE:** 4 HOURS
STAND: 10 MINUTES **MAKES:** 8 SLICES

- **2 pints strawberry ice cream (4 cups)**
- **½ cup sliced almonds, toasted (see tip, page 21) (optional)**
- **1 purchased graham cracker crumb pie shell* or 1 recipe Graham Cracker Crust (page 444)**
- **¾ cup hot fudge ice cream topping, warmed**
- **Whole strawberries (optional)**
- **Whipped cream (optional)**
- **Sliced almonds, toasted (see tip, page 21) (optional)**

1 In a large chilled bowl stir ice cream until softened but not melted. If desired, stir in the ½ cup almonds. Spoon ice cream mixture into pie shell, spreading evenly. Cover; freeze about 4 hours or until firm.

2 To serve, let pie stand at room temperature for 10 to 15 minutes before cutting. Top each serving with hot fudge topping and, if desired, whole strawberries, whipped cream, and additional toasted almonds.

***NOTE:** Brushing the purchased crust with egg white and prebaking it makes it easier to cut. Preheat oven to 375°F. Brush pie shell with a lightly beaten egg white and bake for 5 minutes. Cool completely on a wire rack before filling.

PER SLICE: 323 cal., 14 g total fat (7 g sat. fat), 15 mg chol., 193 mg sodium, 44 g carb., 0 g fiber, 4 g pro.
EXCHANGES: 1 Starch, 2 Other Carb., 2½ Fat

CARAMEL-BUTTER PECAN ICE CREAM PIE: Prepare as directed, except use butter pecan ice cream. Omit the almonds, hot fudge topping, and strawberries. Drizzle slices with caramel ice cream topping. If desired, top with whipped cream and chopped, toasted pecans.

PER SLICE: 340 cal., 16 g total fat (6 g sat. fat), 20 mg chol., 304 mg sodium, 48 g carb., 0 g fiber, 3 g pro.
EXCHANGES: 1 Starch, 2 Other Carb., 3 Fat

PEPPERMINT STICK ICE CREAM PIE: Prepare as directed, except use peppermint ice cream and a purchased chocolate-flavor crumb pie shell.* Omit the almonds, strawberries, and whipped cream. Drizzle slices with the hot fudge topping. If desired, sprinkle with crushed peppermint candies.

PER SLICE: 345 cal., 15 g total fat (9 g sat. fat), 30 mg chol., 269 mg sodium, 47 g carb., 0 g fiber, 5 g pro.
EXCHANGES: 1 Starch, 2 Other Carb., 3 Fat

S'MORES ICE CREAM PIE: Prepare as directed, except use chocolate ice cream and a purchased graham cracker crumb or chocolate-flavor crumb pie shell.* Omit the almonds and strawberries. Stir 1 cup tiny marshmallows into ice cream. Sprinkle slices with additional marshmallows and drizzle with hot fudge topping. If desired, top with whipped cream, tiny marshmallows, and/or chopped honey-roasted peanuts.

PER SLICE: 376 cal., 16 g total fat (9 g sat. fat), 22 mg chol., 219 mg sodium, 54 g carb., 1 g fiber, 5 g pro.
EXCHANGES: 1 Starch, 2½ Other Carb., 3 Fat

French Silk Pie

PREP: 40 MINUTES **CHILL:** 5 TO 24 HOURS
MAKES: 8 SLICES

- **1 recipe Baked Pastry Shell (page 440)**
- **1 cup whipping cream**
- **1 cup semisweet chocolate pieces (6 ounces)**
- **⅓ cup butter**
- **⅓ cup sugar**
- **2 egg yolks, lightly beaten**
- **3 tablespoons crème de cacao or whipping cream**
- **1 cup Sweetened Whipped Cream (page 270)**

1 Prepare Baked Pastry Shell; set aside. In a medium heavy saucepan combine 1 cup whipping cream, the chocolate pieces, butter, and sugar. Cook over low heat, stirring constantly, until chocolate melts (about 10 minutes). Remove from heat. Gradually stir half of the hot mixture into beaten egg yolks. Return egg mixture to chocolate mixture in pan. Cook over medium-low heat, stirring constantly, until mixture is slightly thickened and begins to bubble (about 5 minutes). Remove from heat. (Mixture might appear slightly curdled.) Stir in crème de cacao. Place the saucepan in a bowl of ice water, stirring occasionally, until the mixture stiffens and becomes hard to stir (about 20 minutes).

2 Transfer the chocolate mixture to a medium mixing bowl. Beat chocolate mixture with an electric mixer on medium to high speed for 2 to 3 minutes or until light and fluffy. Spread filling in the Baked Pastry Shell. Cover and chill for 5 to 24 hours. To serve, top with Sweetened Whipped Cream.

PER SLICE: 583 cal., 44 g total fat (25 g sat. fat), 150 mg chol., 263 mg sodium, 44 g carb., 2 g fiber, 7 g pro.
EXCHANGES: ½ Milk, 1 Starch, 1½ Other Carb., 8½ Fat

Nut and Chocolate Chip Tart

PREP: 30 MINUTES **BAKE:** 40 MINUTES AT 350°F
MAKES: 10 SLICES

- **1 recipe Pastry for Single-Crust Pie (page 440)**
- **3 eggs**
- **1 cup light-color corn syrup**
- **½ cup packed brown sugar**
- **⅓ cup butter, melted and cooled**
- **1 teaspoon vanilla**
- **1 cup coarsely chopped salted mixed nuts**
- **½ cup miniature semisweet chocolate pieces**
- **⅓ cup miniature semisweet chocolate pieces (optional)**
- **1 tablespoon shortening (optional)**

1 Preheat oven to 350°F. Prepare and roll out Pastry for Single-Crust Pie. Transfer the pastry to an 11-inch tart pan with a removable bottom. Press pastry into fluted sides of tart pan and trim edge. Do not prick pastry.

2 For filling, in a large bowl beat eggs lightly with a fork. Stir in corn syrup. Add brown sugar, melted butter, and vanilla, stirring until sugar dissolves. Stir in nuts and the ½ cup chocolate pieces. Place pastry-lined tart pan on a baking sheet; place baking sheet on the oven rack. Carefully pour filling into tart pan. Bake tart about 40 minutes or until a knife inserted near the center comes out clean. Cool on a wire rack.

3 If desired, in a small heavy saucepan melt the ⅓ cup chocolate pieces and the shortening over very low heat. Immediately remove from heat; stir until smooth. Cool slightly; drizzle over tart. Let stand until chocolate is set. To serve, remove sides from tart pan and cut tart into slices. Cover and chill remaining tart for up to 2 days.

PER SLICE: 439 cal., 23 g total fat (8 g sat. fat), 80 mg chol., 210 mg sodium, 52 g carb., 2 g fiber, 6 g pro.
EXCHANGES: ½ Starch, 3 Other Carb., 5 Fat

HANDLE WITH CARE

If your tart pans are made of tinned steel, as many are, make sure they are completely dry before storing them so they don't rust.

Country Peach Tart

PREP: 30 MINUTES **BAKE:** 50 MINUTES AT 375°F
COOL: 30 MINUTES **MAKES:** 8 SLICES

- **1 recipe Pastry for Single-Crust Pie (page 440)**
- **¼ cup sugar**
- **4 teaspoons all-purpose flour**
- **¼ teaspoon ground nutmeg, cinnamon, or ginger**
- **3 cups sliced, peeled peaches or nectarines (about 1¼ pounds)**
- **1 tablespoon lemon juice**
- **1 tablespoon sliced almonds**
- **Milk**

1 Preheat oven to 375°F. Prepare pastry for Single-Crust Pie through Step 2; set aside. On a large piece of lightly floured parchment paper roll pastry into a 13-inch circle. Slide paper with pastry onto a baking sheet; set aside.

2 For filling, in a large bowl stir together ¼ cup sugar, the flour, and nutmeg. Add peaches and lemon juice; toss until coated. Mound filling in center of pastry, leaving the outer 2 inches uncovered (see photo 1, below). Fold uncovered pastry over filling, pleating as necessary and using paper to lift pastry border (see photo 2, below). Sprinkle filling with sliced almonds. Lightly brush pastry top and sides with milk and sprinkle with additional sugar.

3 Bake for 50 to 55 minutes or until filling is bubbly and crust is golden. If necessary to prevent overbrowning, cover edge of tart with foil the last 5 to 10 minutes of baking (see page 439). Cool for 30 minutes on the baking sheet on a wire rack.

PER SLICE: 253 cal., 13 g total fat (5 g sat. fat), 15 mg chol., 188 mg sodium, 32 g carb., 2 g fiber, 3 g pro.
EXCHANGES: ½ Fruit, 1 Starch, ½ Other Carb., 2½ Fat

COUNTRY PEAR TART: Prepare as directed, except increase sugar to ⅓ cup and substitute 4 cups sliced, peeled pears (1½ pounds) for the peaches; substitute 1 tablespoon finely chopped crystallized ginger or ¼ teaspoon ground ginger and ¼ teaspoon ground cinnamon for the nutmeg. Assemble tart as directed, except dot filling with 1 tablespoon butter before baking.

PER SLICE: 293 cal., 15 g total fat (5 g sat. fat), 15 mg chol., 189 mg sodium, 43 g carb., 3 g fiber, 3 g pro.
EXCHANGES: ½ Fruit, 1 Starch, 1½ Other Carb., 2½ Fat

COUNTRY TART STEP-BY-STEP

1. Spoon the filling in the center of the pastry circle. Leave a 2-inch pastry border around the filling.

2. Gently fold the pastry edge over the filling. Pleat the pastry as necessary to keep it flat against the fruit, using the parchment paper to lift pastry.

Fresh Fruit and Cream Tarts

PREP: 40 MINUTES **BAKE:** 13 MINUTES AT 450°F
CHILL: 4 HOURS **MAKES:** 8 TARTS

- **1 recipe Pastry Cream**
- **1 recipe Rich Tart Pastry (page 444)**
- **2 cups fresh fruit, such as sliced strawberries; raspberries; blackberries; peeled, sliced papaya; and/or peeled, sliced kiwifruit**

1 Prepare and chill Pastry Cream. Prepare Rich Tart Pastry through Step 1.

2 Preheat oven to 450°F. Divide pastry into eight portions. On a floured surface use your hands to slightly flatten each portion. Roll pastry from center to edges into circles about 5 inches in diameter. Transfer each pastry circle to a 4-inch tart pan with a removable bottom. Press pastry into fluted sides of tart pans; trim edge. Prick bottoms and sides of pastry shells. Line pastry shells with a double thickness of foil. Place on a large baking sheet. Bake for 8 minutes. Remove foil. Bake for 5 to 6 minutes more or until pastry shells are golden. Cool on a wire rack.

3 Divide the chilled Pastry Cream among the baked pastry shells. Arrange fruit on top of each tart.* To serve, remove sides of tart pans.

PASTRY CREAM: In a medium heavy saucepan stir together ½ cup sugar, 4 teaspoons cornstarch, and ¼ teaspoon salt. Gradually stir in 2 cups half-and-half. If desired, add 1 vanilla bean, split lengthwise. Cook and stir over medium heat until thickened and bubbly. Cook and stir for 1 minute more. Gradually stir half of the hot mixture into 4 beaten egg yolks. Return all of the egg yolk mixture to saucepan. Bring to a gentle boil; reduce heat. Cook and stir for 2 minutes. Remove from heat. Remove vanilla bean. Strain Pastry Cream into a bowl. If not using vanilla bean, stir in 1 teaspoon vanilla. Place Pastry Cream bowl in a bowl of ice water; let stand for 5 minutes, stirring occasionally. Cover surface with plastic wrap. Chill 4 hours or until cold; do not stir.

WHOLE FRESH FRUIT AND CREAM TART: Prepare Rich Tart Pastry as directed, except roll out pastry into a circle 12 inches in diameter; transfer pastry circle to a 10-inch tart pan with a removable bottom. Press pastry into fluted sides of tart pan and trim edge. Prick pastry. Bake and cool as directed. To serve, fill cooled shell with Pastry Cream and top with fruit.* To serve, remove sides of tart pan. Makes 8 slices.

***NOTE:** Filled tarts can be chilled up to 4 hours.

PER TART OR 1 SLICE WHOLE TART VARIATION: 383 cal., 22 g total fat (13 g sat. fat), 210 mg chol., 186 mg sodium, 41 g carb., 1 g fiber, 6 g pro. EXCHANGES: 1 Starch, 2 Other Carb., ½ Lean Meat, 4 Fat

CHERRY-ALMOND TART

Cherry-Almond Tart

PREP: 45 MINUTES **BAKE:** 50 MINUTES AT 350°F
COOL: 15 MINUTES **MAKES:** 12 SLICES

- **1 recipe Nut Pastry (page 442)**
- **2 12-ounce jars cherry preserves**
- **1 egg yolk**
- **1 teaspoon water**
- **¼ cup sliced almonds**

1 Preheat oven to 350°F. Lightly grease a 13×4-inch fluted rectangular tart pan or a 9- or 9½-inch fluted round or square tart pan with a removable bottom; set aside.

2 Prepare Nut Pastry as directed through Step 2. Press half of the pastry onto the bottom and up the sides of the prepared tart pan. Bake for 15 to 20 minutes or until crust is light brown.

3 Meanwhile, on a lightly floured surface roll the remaining pastry into a 13×10-inch oval. Using a fluted pastry wheel or pizza cutter, cut pastry crosswise into ¾- to 1-inch-wide strips.

4 Spread preserves evenly over hot crust. Arrange pastry strips on top of preserves in a lattice design, leaving about ¾ inch between each strip.

5 In a small bowl combine egg yolk and water; brush some of the mixture on pastry strips. Place tart on a baking sheet. Bake for 15 minutes. Remove from oven. Brush lattice strips with additional egg yolk mixture and sprinkle with sliced almonds. Bake about 20 minutes more or until top is golden brown.

6 Cool in pan on a wire rack for 15 minutes. Using a small sharp knife, gently loosen edge of crust from side of pan; cool completely. Remove sides from tart pan.

PER SLICE: 381 cal., 15 g total fat (5 g sat. fat), 28 mg chol., 241 mg sodium, 58 g carb., 2 g fiber, 4 g pro. EXCHANGES: 1½ Starch, 2½ Other Carb., 2½ Fat

STORING PIES AND TARTS

Keep your creations at their best.

1. SOME DON'T FREEZE: Do not freeze cream pies and tarts or certain ones that include eggs in the filling, such as custard pies or the Nut and Chocolate Chip Tart (page 457). To store, lightly cover in plastic wrap; refrigerate up to 2 days.

2. FREEZING BAKED FRUIT PIES: Let pie cool completely. Place in a freezer bag; seal, label, and freeze for up to 4 months. Thaw at room temperature.

3. FREEZING UNBAKED FRUIT PIES: Before assembling, treat light-color fruit with ascorbic acid color-keeper. Use a metal pie pan. Place in freezer bag; seal, label, and freeze up to 4 months. To bake, cover frozen pie with foil. Bake in a 450°F oven for 15 minutes. Reduce to 375°F; bake for 15 minutes. Remove foil; bake for 55 to 60 minutes more or until filling bubbles and crust is golden.

Butterscotch-Pecan Tart *(photo, page 437)*

PREP: 30 MINUTES **BAKE:** 15 MINUTES AT 400°F/ 15 MINUTES AT 350°F **MAKES:** 12 SLICES

- **1 recipe Rich Tart Pastry (page 444)**
- **3 cups pecan halves**
- **1¼ cups Creamy Butterscotch Sauce**
- **⅔ cup semisweet chocolate pieces**
- **⅓ cup butterscotch-flavor pieces**
- **Whipped cream (optional)**
- **Chocolate curls (see tip, page 269) (optional)**

1 Preheat oven to 400°F. Prepare Rich Tart Pastry; roll it into an 11-inch circle. Transfer the pastry circle to a 9-inch tart pan with a removable bottom. Press pastry into fluted sides of tart pan and trim edges. Line the pastry shell with a double thickness of foil. Bake for 10 minutes. Remove foil. Bake for 5 to 6 minutes more or until light brown. Cool slightly on a wire rack. Reduce oven temperature to 350°F.

2 For filling, toast pecans (see tip, page 21) in the oven. Meanwhile, prepare Creamy Butterscotch Sauce. Transfer 1¼ cups of the butterscotch sauce to a medium heatproof bowl. Stir in warm pecans, chocolate pieces, and butterscotch-flavor pieces, stirring until the pieces melt. Pour filling into pastry shell.

3 Bake about 15 minutes or until filling is bubbly at edge; cool on a wire rack. Remove sides from tart pan. If desired, serve with remaining Butterscotch Sauce, whipped cream, and/or chocolate curls.

CREAMY BUTTERSCOTCH SAUCE: In a medium heavy saucepan melt ½ cup butter over low heat, stirring frequently. Increase heat to medium. Stir in ¾ cup light-color corn syrup, ⅔ cup granulated sugar, ⅔ cup packed dark brown sugar, 2 tablespoons water, and ¼ teaspoon salt. Bring to boiling, stirring constantly; reduce heat. Simmer, uncovered, for 5 minutes, stirring frequently. Remove from heat. Carefully stir in ¾ cup whipping cream and 2 teaspoons vanilla. Cover and chill any remaining sauce for up to 2 weeks.

PER SLICE: 546 cal., 39 g total fat (14 g sat. fat), 76 mg chol., 127 mg sodium, 48 g carb., 4 g fiber, 5 g pro.
EXCHANGES: 1½ Starch, 1½ Other Carb., 7½ Fat

Ganache-Glazed Peanut Butter Tart

PREP: 30 MINUTES **BAKE:** 10 MINUTES AT 350°F **CHILL:** 4 TO 24 HOURS **COOL:** 10 MINUTES **STAND:** 10 MINUTES **MAKES:** 16 SLICES

- **1 cup crushed chocolate wafer cookies**
- **3 tablespoons sugar**
- **3 tablespoons butter, melted**
- **1½ cups half-and-half or light cream**
- **2 tablespoons all-purpose flour**
- **¼ teaspoon salt**
- **3 egg yolks**
- **⅓ cup sugar**
- **½ cup creamy peanut butter**
- **1 teaspoon vanilla**
- **4 ounces bittersweet chocolate, chopped**
- **5 tablespoons butter, cut into small pieces**
- **1 tablespoon light-color corn syrup**

1 Preheat oven to 350°F. For crust, in a medium bowl combine crushed chocolate cookies and the 3 tablespoons sugar. Stir in the melted butter. Press chocolate mixture onto the bottom of a 9-inch tart pan with a removable bottom. Bake about 10 minutes or until set. Cool on a wire rack.

2 For filling, in a medium saucepan combine half-and-half, flour, and salt. Cook over medium heat until simmering, stirring frequently.

3 In a small bowl combine egg yolks and the ⅓ cup sugar. Gradually whisk hot half-and-half mixture into egg yolk mixture. Return egg yolk mixture to saucepan. Cook and stir over medium heat until mixture is thickened and bubbly. Remove from heat. Whisk in peanut butter and vanilla until combined. Pour filling into crust, spreading evenly. Cover and chill for 3 hours.

4 For ganache, in a small saucepan combine chocolate and the 5 tablespoons butter. Cook and stir over low heat until melted. Remove from heat. Stir in corn syrup; cool for 10 minutes.

5 Pour ganache over filling; tilt pan to allow ganache to flow evenly over tart. Cover and chill for 1 to 24 hours.

6 Let stand at room temperature for 10 minutes before serving. Using a small sharp knife, gently loosen edge of tart from sides of pan; remove sides from tart pan. To cut, dip a sharp knife in hot water; dry the knife. Quickly score top of the tart into 16 slices with warm knife. Cut tart along score marks.

PER SLICE: 235 cal., 17 g total fat (8 g sat. fat), 63 mg chol., 166 mg sodium, 19 g carb., 1 g fiber, 4 g pro.
EXCHANGES: 1 Starch, 3½ Fat

poultry

poultry

There are many great ways to enjoy poultry. Before you try some, review a few basics to ensure food safety and best flavor.

BUYING POULTRY

Here's information you'll often find on the label:

- "Sell by" date: This tells you not to buy the package after a particular date.
- "Use by" date: A "use by" date indicates when raw poultry should be cooked or frozen. Precooked poultry will have a "use by" date.
- Note other information such as Nutrition Facts and handling and cooking tips.

STORING AND THAWING POULTRY

Store raw poultry in its original package in the coldest part of refrigerator; cook poultry pieces within 2 days of purchase. For longer storage, freeze poultry in its original package up to 2 months at 0°F. To freeze longer, wrap package with foil. Whole poultry will keep up to 1 year and cut-up pieces up to 9 months. Never freeze stuffed poultry.

Never thaw poultry at room temperature. Thaw it in the refrigerator in a dish to catch any drips. Allow at least 9 hours for parts and 24 hours per every 3½ to 4 pounds for whole birds.

For fast thawing, you can microwave poultry on the defrost setting; be sure to cook it right away. For a whole bird that doesn't fit in the microwave, place it in a resealable plastic bag in a sink full of cold water. Allow 30 minutes per pound, changing water every 30 minutes.

SAFE HANDLING OF POULTRY OR MEAT

- Set aside a cutting board to use exclusively for raw poultry, raw meat, and other foods that will be cooked. Have another cutting board for breads and foods that will not be cooked.
- Wash work surfaces and utensils in hot, soapy water before and right after handling poultry and meat to prevent the spread of bacteria. Never partially cook poultry and meat and then refrigerate and finish cooking later; bacteria might grow.
- Discard used marinades. If you wish to use some of the marinade for basting, set aside a little bit of it before adding it to poultry or meat.
- Serve cooked poultry and meat immediately; refrigerate leftovers within 2 hours.
- Rinsing poultry and meat is not necessary. The less they are handled the better. However, you should rinse cavities of whole birds that will be stuffed; pat dry with paper towels.

IS IT DONE?

A thermometer is the most accurate way to check if poultry is done. You shouldn't determine doneness by the color of the meat or juices. Doneness temperatures are given for recipes in this book that use poultry pieces or whole birds. For whole birds, it's important to insert the thermometer into the thickest part of the thigh muscle without touching bone.

Oven-Fried Chicken, page 467

cook's secrets

buttermilk-brined fried chicken

The Secret: What do you get when you give meaty chicken pieces a little soak in a buttermilk brine? Some of the most incredibly moist, tender fried chicken you'll ever taste.

FRIED CHICKEN POINTERS

1. SIZE MATTERS
When frying chicken, the pieces should be similar in size so they cook evenly in the same amount of time. You'll need to cut breast pieces in half using a sturdy, sharp chef's knife.

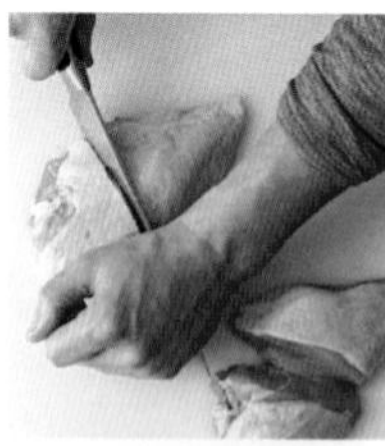

2. CLEAN COATING
A double dip in the seasoned flour mixture with a buttermilk bath in between ensures the chicken pieces are thoroughly coated with flavorful breading that won't fall off during frying. To keep the flour mixture from becoming overly messy and gummy during dipping, divide it evenly between two shallow bowls. Use one bowl for the first coating and the other only after the chicken has been dipped into the buttermilk.

BEST-LOVED

PREP: 30 MINUTES **CHILL:** 2 TO 4 HOURS **COOK:** 12 MINUTES PER BATCH
MAKES: 6 SERVINGS

- **3 cups buttermilk**
- **1/3 cup kosher salt**
- **2 tablespoons sugar**
- **2½ to 3 pounds meaty chicken pieces (breast halves, thighs, and drumsticks)**
- **2 cups all-purpose flour**
- **1/4 teaspoon salt**
- **1/4 teaspoon black pepper**
- **3/4 cup buttermilk**
- **Vegetable oil**
- **1 recipe Creamy Gravy (page 466)**

The salt and buttermilk help break down muscle fibers in the chicken, allowing the meat to absorb more moisture and flavor.

1 For brine, in a resealable plastic bag set in a bowl combine the 3 cups buttermilk, the kosher salt, and sugar. Using a chef's knife, cut chicken breast halves in half crosswise. Add all chicken pieces to the brine; seal bag. Turn bag to coat chicken. Chill for 2 to 4 hours; remove chicken from brine. Drain chicken; pat dry with paper towels. Discard brine.

2 In a large bowl combine flour, the 1/4 teaspoon salt, and the pepper. Place the 3/4 cup buttermilk in a shallow dish. Coat chicken with flour mixture; dip in buttermilk and coat again with flour mixture.

3 Meanwhile, in a deep, heavy pot or a deep-fat fryer heat 1½ inches oil to 350°F. Using tongs, carefully add a few pieces of chicken to hot oil. (Oil temperature will drop; adjust the heat to maintain temperature at 350°F.) Fry chicken for 12 to 15 minutes or until chicken is done (170°F for breasts; at least 175°F for thighs and drumsticks) and coating is golden, turning once. Drain on a wire rack or paper towels. If desired, keep fried chicken warm in a preheated 300°F oven while frying remaining chicken pieces and making the gravy. Serve the fried chicken with the Creamy Gravy.

SPICY BUTTERMILK-BRINED FRIED CHICKEN: Prepare as directed, except add 1½ teaspoons cayenne pepper to the flour mixture.

PER 3 OUNCES CHICKEN PLAIN OR SPICY VARIATION: 730 cal., 45 g total fat (10 g sat. fat), 135 mg chol., 1,382 mg sodium, 41 g carb., 1 g fiber, 39 g pro. EXCHANGES: ½ Milk, 2 Starch, 4 Medium-Fat Meat, 4½ Fat

OIL MATTERS

When deep-frying, choose a vegetable oil that has a smoking point above 400°F. Any of these oils work well for fried chicken:

- canola
- corn
- peanut
- safflower
- sunflower

3. KEEP IT HOT
To ensure chicken fries evenly without burning or becoming greasy, maintain the oil temperature as close to 350°F as possible at all times during the frying process. Use a deep-frying thermometer to monitor the temperature and adjust heat as necessary.

4. DON'T CROWD THE PAN
For the best results, fry chicken in smaller batches and don't crowd in the pan. As you finish each batch, drain on paper towels and place the fried pieces on a wire rack that has been set on a baking sheet; keep warm in a 300°F oven.

5. TESTING DONENESS
Unfortunately, you can't be sure your chicken is done inside just by looking at the outside. To be 100 percent certain, check the internal temperature with an instant-read thermometer (it is done when breasts are 170°F and thighs and drumsticks are 175°F). Insert thermometer into thickest part of the chicken without touching bone. Bone conducts heat faster than meat, so if the thermometer touches bone, the reading will be high.

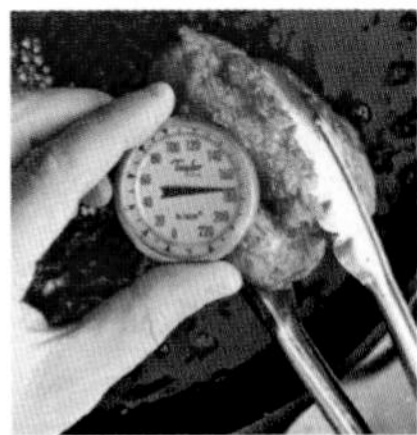

cook's secrets

creamy gravy

The Secret: No one loves lumpy gravy. By combining the right proportion of flour to drippings, you're on your way to making really good country-style gravy.

CREAMY GRAVY POINTERS

1. FAT + FLOUR
After heating drippings in the skillet, add flour and stir constantly with a wooden spoon until the mixture is bubbly and starts to turn a light golden brown. This step is important to prevent lumps. You're coating the flour particles with fat, which keeps them separated so they don't clump.

2. WHISK AWAY
When you add milk to the cooked flour mixture in the skillet, whisk constantly throughout the remaining cook time. The nonstop motion helps keep lumps from forming, and the heat ensures the flour gets fully cooked—important for thickening and eliminating any raw flour taste. Don't skip that last 1 minute of cook time—it ensures starch grains in the flour swell and cause the gravy to thicken properly. The gravy is done when it starts to thicken and coats the back of a spoon.

Fat adds flavor to gravy. It's important to use the amount called for. Too much fat makes for greasy gravy; too little yields lackluster results. If you don't have fried chicken drippings, use butter or bacon drippings.

START TO FINISH: 10 MINUTES **MAKES:** 1¾ CUPS

- **3 tablespoons fried chicken drippings, butter, or bacon drippings**
- **3 tablespoons all-purpose flour**
- **1¾ cups milk**
- **¼ teaspoon salt**
- **⅛ teaspoon black pepper**
- **Milk (optional)**

1 Place drippings in a large skillet. Heat drippings over medium heat. Using a wooden spoon, stir in flour until mixture is smooth, bubbly, and starting to brown. Whisk in the 1¾ cups milk, the salt, and pepper. Cook over medium heat, whisking constantly, until thickened and bubbly. Cook and whisk for 1 minute more. Reduce heat if gravy bubbles too hard. If desired, thin with additional milk.

MAKE-AHEAD DIRECTIONS: Store gravy in an airtight container in the refrigerator. Reheat in a saucepan over medium-low heat; if necessary, stir in milk to thin.

PER ABOUT ¼ CUP: 108 cal., 8 g total fat (3 g sat. fat), 12 mg chol., 140 mg sodium, 6 g carb., 0 g fiber, 3 g protein.
EXCHANGES: ½ Starch, 1½ Fat

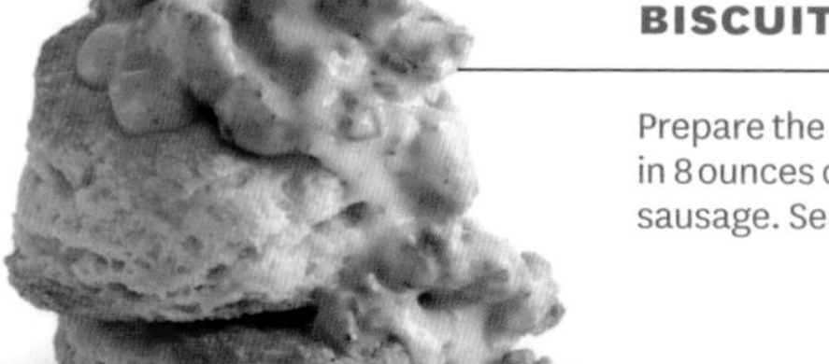

BISCUITS + GRAVY

Prepare the Creamy Gravy as directed, except stir in 8 ounces cooked and drained bulk pork sausage. Serve over Flaky Biscuits, page 123.

LOW-CALORIE

Oven-Fried Chicken *(photo, page 463)*

PREP: 20 MINUTES **BAKE:** 45 MINUTES AT 375°F
MAKES: 4 TO 6 SERVINGS

1 egg, lightly beaten
3 tablespoons milk
1¼ cups crushed cornflakes or finely crushed rich round crackers (about 35 crackers)
1 teaspoon dried thyme, crushed
½ teaspoon paprika
2 tablespoons butter, melted
2½ to 3 pounds meaty chicken pieces (breast halves, thighs, and drumsticks)

1 Preheat oven to 375°F. In a small bowl combine egg and milk. For coating, in a shallow dish combine crushed cornflakes, thyme, paprika, ¼ teaspoon *salt,* and ⅛ teaspoon *black pepper.* Stir in melted butter. Set aside. Skin chicken (see photos 1 and 2, page 468). Dip chicken pieces, one at a time, into egg mixture; coat with crumb mixture.

2 In a greased 15×10×1-inch baking pan arrange chicken, bone sides down, so pieces aren't touching. Sprinkle chicken pieces with any remaining crumb mixture.

3 Bake, uncovered, for 45 to 55 minutes or until chicken is done (170°F for breasts; at least 175°F for thighs and drumsticks). Do not turn chicken pieces while baking.

PER 5 OUNCES CHICKEN: 373 cal., 11 g total fat (5 g sat. fat), 187 mg chol., 522 mg sodium, 23 g carb., 0 g fiber, 43 g pro. EXCHANGES: 1½ Starch, 5½ Lean Meat, 1 Fat

OVEN-FRIED PARMESAN CHICKEN: Prepare as directed, except omit thyme and salt and reduce crushed cornflakes to ½ cup. For coating, combine cornflakes; ½ cup grated Parmesan cheese; 1 teaspoon dried oregano, crushed; the paprika; and pepper. Stir in melted butter.

PER 5 OUNCES CHICKEN: 398 cal., 14 g total fat (7 g sat. fat), 195 mg chol., 398 mg sodium, 10 g carb., 0 g fiber, 45 g protein. EXCHANGES: ½ Starch, 6 Lean Meat, 1½ Fat

LOW-CALORIE

Herb-Roasted Chicken

PREP: 20 MINUTES **ROAST:** 75 MINUTES AT 375°F
STAND: 10 MINUTES **MAKES:** 4 SERVINGS

1 3½- to 4-pound whole broiler chicken
2 tablespoons butter, melted
2 cloves garlic, minced
1 teaspoon dried basil, crushed
1 teaspoon dried sage, crushed
½ teaspoon dried thyme, crushed
¼ teaspoon salt
¼ teaspoon black pepper

HERB-ROASTED CHICKEN AND VEGETABLES

1 Preheat oven to 375°F. Rinse chicken body cavity; pat dry with paper towels. Skewer neck skin to back; tie legs to tail (see photo 3, page 355). Twist wing tips under back (see photo 4, page 355). Place chicken, breast side up, on a rack in a shallow roasting pan. Brush with melted butter; rub with garlic.

2 In a small bowl stir together basil, sage, thyme, salt, and pepper; rub onto chicken. Insert a meat thermometer into center of an inside thigh muscle (see photo 5, page 355). (Thermometer should not touch bone.)

3 Roast, uncovered, for 75 to 90 minutes or until drumsticks move easily in sockets and chicken is done (at least 170°F). Remove chicken from oven. Cover; let stand for 10 minutes before carving.

PER 4 OUNCES CHICKEN: 393 cal., 29 g total fat (10 g sat. fat), 186 mg chol., 313 mg sodium, 1 g carb., 0 g fiber, 32 g pro. EXCHANGES: 4½ Medium-Fat Meat, 1½ Fat

HERB-ROASTED CHICKEN AND VEGETABLES: Prepare as directed, except combine 1 pound red potatoes, cut into 1-inch pieces; 3 carrots, halved lengthwise and cut into 1-inch pieces; 1 medium turnip, peeled and cut into 1½-inch pieces; and 1 medium onion, cut into 1-inch chunks, in a large bowl. Add 2 tablespoons melted butter, 1 tablespoon vegetable oil, ¼ teaspoon salt, and ¼ teaspoon black pepper; toss to coat. Arrange vegetable mixture around chicken. Roast as directed, stirring vegetables once or twice during roasting.

PER 4 OUNCES CHICKEN + ⅔ CUP VEGETABLES: 590 cal., 39 g total fat (14 g sat. fat), 201 mg chol., 568 mg sodium, 27 g carb., 4 g fiber, 35 g pro. EXCHANGES: 1½ Vegetable, 1 Starch, 4½ Medium-Fat Meat, 3 Fat

BEST-LOVED

Oven-Barbecued Chicken

PREP: 25 MINUTES **BAKE:** 45 MINUTES AT 375°F
MAKES: 6 SERVINGS

- **4 pounds meaty chicken pieces (breast halves, thighs, and drumsticks)**
- **1 cup finely chopped onion**
- **1 tablespoon minced garlic**
- **2 tablespoons kosher salt**
- **¼ cup butter**
- **1 tablespoon paprika**
- **1 tablespoon chili powder**
- **1½ teaspoons crushed red pepper**
- **½ teaspoon freshly ground black pepper**
- **1½ cups water**
- **1 cup cider vinegar**
- **1 cup packed dark brown sugar**
- **2 tablespoons Worcestershire sauce**
- **1 cup tomato paste**
- **¼ cup molasses**

1 Preheat oven to 375°F. Line a 15×10×1-inch baking pan with parchment paper or foil; set aside. Skin chicken (see photos 1 and 2, below). Arrange chicken, bone sides up, in the prepared baking pan. Bake for 35 minutes.

2 Meanwhile, for sauce, in a large saucepan cook onion, garlic, and salt in hot butter over medium-low heat for 10 to 15 minutes or until onion is tender, stirring occasionally. Add paprika, chili powder, crushed red pepper, and black pepper; cook and stir for 1 minute more. Add water, vinegar, brown sugar, and Worcestershire sauce; bring to boiling. Whisk in tomato paste and molasses until smooth. Boil gently, uncovered, for 15 to 20 minutes or until sauce is thickened and reduced to about 4 cups, stirring occasionally.

REMOVING SKIN FROM DRUMSTICKS STEP-BY-STEP

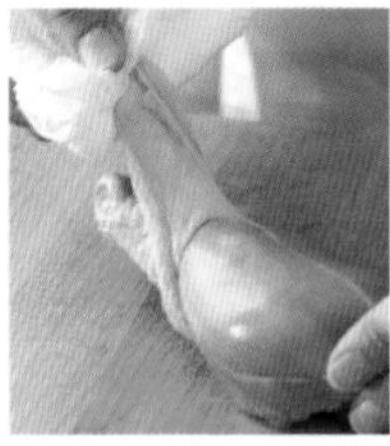

1. To remove skin from chicken pieces, use a paper towel to grip the skin and pull it away from the meat. For drumsticks, start at the meaty end and pull toward the bony end.

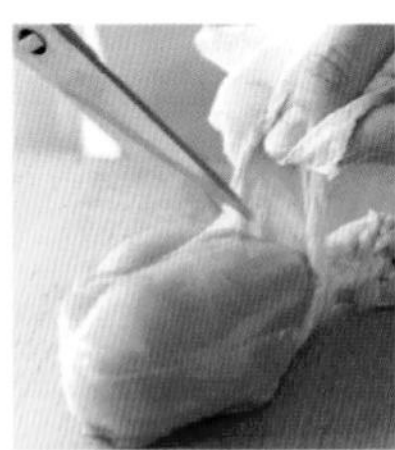

2. Use kitchen shears to cut the skin at the joint. Wash the shears in hot, soapy water when you are finished.

OVEN-BARBECUED CHICKEN

3 Turn chicken bone sides down. Brush about 1 cup of the sauce on chicken. Bake for 10 to 20 minutes more or until chicken is done (170°F for breasts; at least 175°F for thighs and drumsticks). Reheat the remaining sauce; pass with chicken. Refrigerate any leftover sauce in an airtight container for up to 1 week.

PER 4 OUNCES CHICKEN + ¼ CUP SAUCE: 420 cal., 10 g total fat (4 g sat. fat), 142 mg chol., 1,724 mg sodium, 40 g carb., 2 g fiber, 41 g pro. EXCHANGES: 2½ Other Carb., 6 Lean Meat, ½ Fat

LOW-CALORIE

Chicken and Dumplings

PREP: 30 MINUTES **COOK:** 47 MINUTES
MAKES: 6 SERVINGS

- **2½ to 3 pounds meaty chicken pieces (breast halves, thighs, and drumsticks), skinned**
- **3 cups water**
- **1 medium onion, cut into wedges**
- **¾ teaspoon salt**
- **½ teaspoon dried sage or marjoram, crushed**
- **¼ teaspoon black pepper**
- **1 bay leaf**
- **1 cup sliced celery (2 stalks)**
- **1 cup thinly sliced carrots (2 medium)**
- **1 cup sliced fresh mushrooms**
- **1 recipe Dumplings**
- **½ cup cold water**
- **¼ cup all-purpose flour**

1 In a 4-quart pot combine chicken, the 3 cups water, onion, salt, sage, pepper, and bay leaf. Bring to boiling; reduce heat. Simmer, covered, for 25 minutes. Add celery, carrots, and mushrooms. Return to boiling; reduce heat. Simmer, covered, about 10 minutes more or until vegetables are tender and chicken is done (170°F for breasts; at least 175°F for thighs and drumsticks). Discard bay leaf. Using tongs, arrange chicken pieces on top of vegetables in pot.

2 Prepare Dumplings. Spoon batter into six mounds on top of chicken. (Do not spoon into liquid.) Return to boiling; reduce heat. Simmer, covered, for 12 to 15 minutes or until a wooden toothpick inserted into dumplings comes out clean. Do not lift lid while simmering. With a slotted spoon, transfer chicken, dumplings, and vegetables to a bowl; keep warm.

3 For gravy, measure 2 cups cooking liquid. Skim fat from liquid (see photo 2, page 358); discard fat. Pour liquid into pot. Stir the ½ cup cold water into the flour; stir into liquid in pot. Cook and stir over medium heat until thickened and bubbly. Cook and stir for 1 minute more. Serve over chicken, dumplings, and vegetables.

DUMPLINGS: Combine 1 cup all-purpose flour, 1 teaspoon baking powder, and ½ teaspoon salt. Cut in 2 tablespoons shortening until mixture resembles coarse crumbs. Add ½ cup buttermilk, stirring just until moistened.

PER 3 OUNCES CHICKEN + ½ CUP VEGETABLE MIXTURE + 1 DUMPLING: 296 cal., 6 g total fat (2 g sat. fat), 72 mg chol., 644 mg sodium, 26 g carb., 2 g fiber, 33 g pro.
EXCHANGES: ½ Vegetable, 1½ Starch, 2½ Lean Meat, 1 Fat

LOW-CALORIE

Chicken and Noodles

PREP: 30 MINUTES **COOK:** 60 MINUTES
MAKES: 6 SERVINGS

- **1 3- to 3½-pound broiler-fryer chicken**
- **5 cups chicken broth**
- **½ teaspoon salt**
- **¼ teaspoon black pepper**
- **1 recipe Homemade Egg Noodles (page 418) or one 12-ounce package frozen noodles**
- **2 tablespoons all-purpose flour**
- **1 recipe Mashed Potatoes (page 586) (optional)**

1 In a 4- to 5-quart pot combine chicken, 4 cups of the broth, salt, and pepper. Bring to boiling; reduce heat. Simmer, covered, for 40 to 45 minutes or until chicken is very tender. Remove chicken from pot; cool slightly. Remove meat from bones; discard skin and bones. Chop chicken; set aside.

2 Strain broth; return to pot. Skim fat from broth (see photo 2, page 358). Bring to boiling. Add noodles; boil gently, uncovered, for 15 minutes, stirring occasionally. In a screw-top jar combine the remaining 1 cup broth and the flour; cover and shake until smooth. Stir into noodle mixture. Cook and stir until thickened and bubbly. Stir in chicken. Cook about 5 minutes more or until heated through, stirring occasionally. If necessary, stir in additional broth to make desired consistency. If desired, serve with Mashed Potatoes.

PER 1 CUP: 358 cal., 7 g total fat (2 g sat. fat), 183 mg chol., 1,270 mg sodium, 39 g carb., 1 g fiber, 31 g pro.
EXCHANGES: 2½ Starch, 3 Lean Meat, ½ Fat

Chicken Cacciatore *(photo, page 461)*

PREP: 30 MINUTES **COOK:** 20 MINUTES
MAKES: 4 SERVINGS

- **8 small bone-in chicken thighs (about 2 pounds total), skinned**
- **1 tablespoon olive oil**
- **3 cups sliced fresh cremini mushrooms**
- **1 large green sweet pepper, seeded and cut into bite-size strips**
- **⅓ cup finely chopped carrot (1 small)**
- **3 cloves garlic, minced**
- **½ cup dry white wine or chicken broth**
- **1 28-ounce can diced tomatoes, undrained**
- **1½ cups frozen small whole onions**
- **1 teaspoon dried oregano, crushed**
- **2 tablespoons balsamic vinegar**
- **Hot cooked broken lasagna noodles or desired pasta**
- **10 pitted Kalamata olives, halved (optional)**
- **⅓ cup snipped fresh Italian parsley (optional)**

1 Sprinkle chicken lightly with *salt* and *cracked black pepper*. In a large skillet heat oil over medium heat. Add chicken; cook just until browned, turning once. Remove from skillet.

2 Add mushrooms, sweet pepper, carrot, and garlic to the skillet. Cook over medium heat for 4 minutes, stirring occasionally. Remove from heat. Carefully add wine. Return to heat. Simmer, uncovered, until wine is nearly evaporated. Stir in tomatoes, onions, oregano, and 1 teaspoon *coarsely ground black pepper*.

3 Return chicken to skillet. Simmer, covered, about 20 minutes or until chicken is done (at least 175°F). Stir in vinegar. Season to taste with additional salt. Serve with hot cooked lasagna noodles. If desired, sprinkle with olives and parsley.

PER SERVING: 525 cal., 10 g total fat (2 g sat. fat), 129 mg chol., 611 mg sodium, 64 g carb., 6 g fiber, 39 g pro.
EXCHANGES: 3½ Vegetable, 3 Starch, 3 Lean Meat, ½ Fat

make it mine

Chicken Skillet

Put this simple and satisfyingly saucy dish in your recipe rotation and you'll never run out of ways to serve chicken.

PREP: 30 MINUTES **COOK:** 50 MINUTES
MAKES: 4 SERVINGS

- **¼ cup all-purpose flour**
- **1 teaspoon SEASONING**
- **½ teaspoon salt**
- **¼ teaspoon black pepper**
- **1 3- to 3½-pound broiler-fryer chicken, cut up and skinned, or 3 to 3½ pounds meaty chicken pieces, skinned**
- **2 tablespoons vegetable oil**
- **½ cup chopped onion (1 medium)**
- **2 cloves garlic, minced**
- **LIQUID**
- **SAUCE**
- **2 teaspoons cornstarch**
- **2 pounds VEGETABLES**
- **Hot cooked PASTA**
- **Snipped fresh parsley (optional)**
- **Cracked black pepper (optional)**

1 In a plastic or paper bag combine flour, Seasoning, salt, and pepper. Add chicken, a few pieces at a time; close bag and shake to coat well.

2 In a very large skillet cook chicken pieces in hot oil over medium heat about 10 minutes or until chicken is browned, turning to brown evenly; remove chicken from skillet.

3 If necessary, add 1 tablespoon additional vegetable oil to skillet. Add the chopped onion and garlic to skillet. Cook and stir for 4 to 5 minutes or until onion is tender. Carefully stir in Liquid. Return chicken to skillet. Bring to boiling; reduce heat. Simmer, covered, for 30 minutes.

4 Combine Sauce ingredients and cornstarch; stir into chicken mixture. Add Vegetables. Return to boiling; reduce heat. Simmer, covered, for 5 to 10 minutes more or until vegetables are crisp-tender and chicken is done (170°F for breasts; at least 175°F for thighs and drumsticks). Serve with Pasta. If desired, sprinkle with parsley and black pepper.

SEASONING *(pick one)*

Chili powder
Dry ranch salad dressing mix
Dried thyme, oregano, or basil, crushed
Garlic powder
Paprika

LIQUID *(pick one)*

¾ cup chicken broth
One 15-ounce can tomato sauce
½ cup chicken broth plus ¼ cup wine
One 10.75-ounce can condensed cream of mushroom or cream of chicken soup plus ½ cup milk

SAUCE *(pick one)*

⅓ cup sour cream, whipping cream, or milk
⅓ cup pasta sauce
¼ cup chicken broth plus 1 tablespoon Dijon-style mustard
¼ cup chicken broth plus 1 tablespoon soy sauce or hoisin sauce

VEGETABLES
(pick one or more)

Cut fresh asparagus
Cooked halved baby carrots
Broccoli or cauliflower florets
Quartered mushrooms
Sweet pepper strips

PASTA *(pick one)*

Bow ties
Egg noodles
Penne
Rotini

LOW-CALORIE

Coq au Vin

PREP: 35 MINUTES **COOK:** 50 MINUTES
MAKES: 6 SERVINGS

- **2½ to 3 pounds meaty chicken pieces (breast halves, thighs, and drumsticks)**
- **2 tablespoons vegetable oil**
- **Salt and black pepper**
- **12 to 18 pearl onions or shallots, peeled**
- **1¼ cups Pinot Noir or Burgundy**
- **1 cup whole fresh mushrooms**
- **1 cup thinly sliced carrots (2 medium)**
- **¼ cup chicken broth or water**
- **1 tablespoon snipped fresh parsley**
- **1½ teaspoons snipped fresh marjoram or ½ teaspoon dried marjoram, crushed**
- **1½ teaspoons snipped fresh thyme or ½ teaspoon dried thyme, crushed**
- **1 bay leaf**
- **2 cloves garlic, minced**
- **2 tablespoons all-purpose flour**
- **2 tablespoons butter or margarine, softened**
- **2 slices bacon, crisp-cooked, drained, and crumbled**
- **Snipped fresh parsley (optional)**
- **Hot cooked noodles (optional)**

1 Skin chicken. In a large skillet cook chicken in hot oil over medium heat about 15 minutes or until chicken is browned, turning to brown evenly; drain fat. Sprinkle chicken with salt and pepper. Add onions, wine, mushrooms, carrots, broth, the 1 tablespoon parsley, dried marjoram (if using), dried thyme (if using), bay leaf, and garlic. Bring to boiling; reduce heat. Simmer, covered, for 35 to 40 minutes or until chicken is done (170°F for breasts; at least 175°F for thighs and drumsticks). If using, add fresh marjoram and thyme. Discard bay leaf. Transfer chicken and vegetables to a serving platter; keep warm.

2 In a small bowl stir together flour and softened butter to make a smooth paste. Stir into wine mixture in skillet. Cook and stir until thickened and bubbly. Cook and stir for 1 minute more. Season to taste with additional salt and pepper.

3 Pour sauce over chicken and vegetables. Sprinkle with bacon. If desired, sprinkle with additional parsley and serve with hot cooked noodles.

PER 3 OUNCES CHICKEN + ½ CUP VEGETABLE MIXTURE: 288 cal., 12 g total fat (4 g sat. fat), 92 mg chol., 311 mg sodium, 7 g carb., 1 g fiber, 28 g pro. EXCHANGES: ½ Vegetable, 4 Lean Meat, 2 Fat

Drumsticks with Minty Rice and Peas

(photo, page 461)

PREP: 25 MINUTES **COOK:** 60 MINUTES
MAKES: 4 SERVINGS

- **8 chicken drumsticks, skinned if desired**
- **½ teaspoon salt**
- **3 tablespoons butter or margarine**
- **1 tablespoon olive or vegetable oil**
- **1 cup chopped onion (1 large)**
- **1 shallot, finely chopped**
- **2 cloves garlic, minced**
- **1 teaspoon dried thyme, crushed**
- **¼ teaspoon freshly ground black pepper**
- **1¼ cups reduced-sodium chicken broth**
- **1 tablespoon butter or margarine (optional)**
- **1 recipe Minty Rice and Peas**

1 Sprinkle chicken with salt. In a very large skillet heat butter and oil over medium heat until butter melts. Add chicken; cook for 10 minutes, turning often. Remove chicken, reserving butter and oil in skillet. Set the chicken aside.

2 Add onion, shallot, and garlic to skillet. Cook and stir about 5 minutes or until onion is tender, scraping up browned bits.

3 Return chicken to pan. Sprinkle with thyme and pepper. Add broth. Bring to boiling; reduce heat. Simmer, covered, for 35 to 40 minutes or until chicken is done (at least 175°F), spooning juices over chicken occasionally. Remove chicken to a serving platter; keep warm. (If chicken is skinned, add 1 tablespoon butter or margarine to onion mixture.) Simmer onion mixture in pan, uncovered, for 10 minutes, stirring occasionally.

4 To serve, spoon onion mixture over chicken and serve with Minty Rice and Peas.

MINTY RICE AND PEAS: In a medium saucepan combine 2½ cups water, 1 cup uncooked jasmine or long grain rice, 1 tablespoon butter or margarine, and ¼ teaspoon salt. Bring to boiling; reduce heat. Simmer, covered, for 15 to 18 minutes or until rice is tender and most of the liquid is absorbed. Stir in 1½ cups frozen peas, 2 tablespoons sliced green onion, and 2 tablespoons snipped fresh mint or 1 teaspoon dried thyme, crushed. Cover; let stand for 5 minutes. Stir before serving.

PER 2 DRUMSTICKS + 1 CUP RICE MIXTURE: 596 cal., 27 g total fat (11 g sat. fat), 149 mg chol., 915 mg sodium, 50 g carb., 3 g fiber, 35 g pro. EXCHANGES: 3 Starch, 3½ Medium-Fat Meat, 2 Fat

ORANGE-GINGER CHICKEN STIR-FRY

Orange-Ginger Chicken Stir-Fry

START TO FINISH: 45 MINUTES **MAKES:** 6 SERVINGS

- **1 pound skinless, boneless chicken breast halves**
- **2 tablespoons cornstarch**
- **2 tablespoons water**
- **3 tablespoons olive oil**
- **1 pound carrots, cut into bite-size strips**
- **1 medium red sweet pepper, seeded and cut into thin bite-size strips**
- **1 cup frozen shelled sweet soybeans (edamame), thawed**
- **1 tablespoon grated fresh ginger**
- **3 cloves garlic, minced**
- **½ teaspoon crushed red pepper (optional)**
- **1½ cups reduced-sodium chicken broth**
- **¼ cup frozen orange juice concentrate, thawed**
- **2 tablespoons reduced-sodium soy sauce**
- **3 cups hot cooked quinoa**
- **1 tablespoon sesame seeds, toasted**

1 Cut chicken into 1-inch pieces; set aside. In a small bowl combine cornstarch and the water; set aside.

2 In a wok or large skillet heat 1 tablespoon of the oil over medium heat. Add carrots; cook and stir for 5 minutes. Add sweet pepper; cook and stir about 3 minutes more or until carrots are tender. Transfer to a medium bowl. In the same wok heat 1 tablespoon of the oil over medium-high heat. Add chicken; cook and stir for 4 to 5 minutes or until chicken is no longer pink. Transfer to the bowl with carrot mixture. Stir in edamame.

3 In the same wok heat the remaining 1 tablespoon oil over medium heat. Add ginger, garlic, and, if desired, crushed red pepper; cook and stir for 30 seconds. Stir in broth, orange juice concentrate, and soy sauce. Bring to boiling. Stir cornstarch mixture; stir into wok. Simmer, uncovered, for 2 minutes. Stir in chicken mixture. Cook and stir until heated through. Serve with quinoa. Sprinkle with sesame seeds.

PER ⅔ CUP MIXTURE + ½ CUP QUINOA: 413 cal., 17 g total fat (3 g sat. fat), 48 mg chol., 423 mg sodium, 40 g carb., 7 g fiber, 25 g pro. EXCHANGES: 2 Vegetable, 2 Starch, 2 Lean Meat, 2½ Fat

LOW-CALORIE

Garlic Chicken Stir-Fry

PREP: 25 MINUTES **MARINATE:** 30 MINUTES
COOK: 5 MINUTES **MAKES:** 4 SERVINGS

- **12 ounces skinless, boneless chicken breast halves**
- **1 cup water**
- **3 tablespoons reduced-sodium soy sauce**
- **1 tablespoon rice vinegar or white wine vinegar**
- **1 tablespoon cornstarch**
- **2 tablespoons vegetable oil**
- **10 green onions, cut into 1-inch pieces**
- **1 cup thinly sliced fresh mushrooms**
- **12 cloves garlic, peeled and finely chopped**
- **½ cup sliced water chestnuts**
- **2 cups hot cooked rice**

1 Cut chicken into ½-inch pieces. Place chicken in a resealable plastic bag set in a shallow dish. For marinade, stir together water, soy sauce, and vinegar. Pour over chicken; seal bag. Marinate in the refrigerator for 30 minutes. Drain chicken, reserving the marinade. Stir cornstarch into reserved marinade; set aside.

2 In a wok or large skillet heat oil over medium-high heat. Add green onions, mushrooms, and garlic to wok; cook and stir for 1 to 2 minutes or until tender. Remove vegetables from wok.

3 If necessary, add more oil to wok. Add chicken to wok; cook and stir for 3 to 4 minutes or until no longer pink. Push chicken from center of wok. Stir marinade mixture; add to center of wok. Cook and stir until thickened and bubbly. Return cooked vegetables to wok. Add water chestnuts. Cook and stir about 1 minute more or until heated through. Serve with rice.

PER 1 CUP + ½ CUP RICE: 311 cal., 8 g total fat (1 g sat. fat), 49 mg chol., 755 mg sodium, 35 g carb., 2 g fiber, 25 g pro. EXCHANGES: ½ Vegetable, 2 Starch, 2½ Lean Meat, 1½ Fat

GARLIC CHICKEN STIR-FRY WITH CASHEWS: Prepare as directed, except stir ½ teaspoon crushed red pepper into marinade. Stir in 1 cup cashews with the water chestnuts.

PER 1 CUP + ½ CUP RICE: 508 cal., 24 g total fat (4 g sat. fat), 49 mg chol., 760 mg sodium, 46 g carb., 3 g fiber, 30 g pro. EXCHANGES: 3 Starch, 2½ Lean Meat, ½ Vegetable, 3 Fat

LOW-CALORIE

Chicken Parmigiana

PREP: 30 MINUTES **COOK:** 14 MINUTES
MAKES: 4 SERVINGS

- **1 tablespoon butter or margarine**
- **⅓ cup chopped onion (1 small)**
- **1 clove garlic, minced**
- **1 14.5-ounce can diced tomatoes, undrained**
- **½ teaspoon sugar**
- **⅛ teaspoon salt**
- **Dash black pepper**
- **¼ cup snipped fresh basil**
- **4 skinless, boneless chicken breast halves (6 to 8 ounces each)**
- **⅓ cup seasoned fine dry bread crumbs**
- **4 tablespoons grated Parmesan cheese**
- **½ teaspoon dried oregano, crushed**
- **1 egg, lightly beaten**
- **2 tablespoons milk**
- **3 tablespoons olive oil or vegetable oil**
- **¼ cup shredded mozzarella cheese (1 ounce)**

1 For sauce, in a medium saucepan melt butter over medium heat. Add onion and garlic; cook until tender. Carefully stir in the tomatoes, sugar, salt, and pepper. Bring to boiling; reduce heat. Simmer, uncovered, about 10 minutes or to desired consistency, stirring occasionally. Stir in basil. Set aside; keep warm.

2 Meanwhile, place each chicken breast half between two pieces of plastic wrap. Using the flat side of a meat mallet, pound chicken lightly to about ¼ inch thick (see photo 2, page 476). Discard plastic wrap.

3 In a shallow bowl stir together bread crumbs, 3 tablespoons of the Parmesan cheese, and the oregano. In a second bowl stir together the egg and milk. Dip chicken into egg mixture and into crumb mixture to coat.

4 In a very large skillet cook chicken in hot oil over medium heat for 2 to 3 minutes per side or until golden. Transfer chicken to platter.

5 Spoon sauce over chicken. Top with mozzarella cheese and the remaining 1 tablespoon Parmesan cheese. Let stand about 2 minutes or until cheese melts.

PER 3 OUNCES CHICKEN + ⅓ CUP SAUCE: 398 cal., 19 g fat (6 g sat. fat), 151 mg chol., 761 mg sodium, 15 g carb., 2 g fiber, 41 g pro. EXCHANGES: 1 Vegetable, ½ Starch, 4½ Lean Meat, 3 Fat

VEAL PARMIGIANA: Prepare as directed, except substitute 1 pound boneless veal sirloin steak or boneless veal leg round steak, cut ½ inch thick, for the chicken breast halves. Cut meat into four serving-size pieces and pound to ¼ inch thick.

PER 3 OUNCES VEAL + ⅓ CUP SAUCE: 366 cal., 20 g total fat (6 g sat. fat), 159 mg chol., 760 mg sodium, 15 g carb., 2 g fiber, 31 g pro. EXCHANGES: 1 Vegetable, ½ Starch, 4 Lean Meat, 3 Fat

LOW-CALORIE

Cheese-Stuffed Chicken Breasts

PREP: 20 MINUTES **COOK:** 18 MINUTES
MAKES: 4 SERVINGS

- **4 skinless, boneless chicken breast halves (6 to 8 ounces each)**
- **½ of an 8-ounce tub cream cheese**
- **2 tablespoons purchased dried tomato pesto**
- **¾ cup panko bread crumbs**
- **1 tablespoon grated Parmesan cheese**
- **½ teaspoon dried basil, crushed**
- **⅛ teaspoon garlic powder**
- **⅛ teaspoon black pepper**
- **¼ cup milk**
- **1 tablespoon olive oil or vegetable oil**
- **1 tablespoon butter or margarine**

1 Using a sharp knife, cut a pocket in each chicken breast by cutting horizontally through the thickest portion to, but not through, the opposite side. In a small bowl combine cream cheese and pesto. Spoon a rounded tablespoon of the cheese mixture into each pocket; set aside.

2 In a shallow bowl combine panko, Parmesan cheese, basil, garlic powder, and pepper. Place milk in a second shallow bowl. Dip stuffed chicken in milk to moisten and in panko mixture to coat.

3 In a large skillet heat oil and butter over medium heat. Add chicken. Cook for 18 to 20 minutes or until chicken is done (165°F) and is golden brown, turning once.

PER SERVING: 389 cal., 21 g total fat (9 g sat. fat), 124 mg chol., 299 mg sodium, 11 g carb., 1 g fiber, 38 g pro. EXCHANGES: ½ Starch, 5 Lean Meat, 2½ Fat

LOW-CALORIE

Baked Chicken Chiles Rellenos

PREP: 45 MINUTES **BAKE:** 30 MINUTES AT 375°F
MAKES: 6 CHICKEN ROLLS

- **6 skinless, boneless chicken breast halves (6 to 8 ounces each)**
- **1/3 cup all-purpose flour**
- **3 tablespoons cornmeal**
- **1/4 teaspoon salt**
- **1/4 teaspoon cayenne pepper**
- **1 egg, lightly beaten**
- **1 tablespoon water**
- **1 4-ounce can whole green chile peppers or whole jalapeño peppers, rinsed, stemmed, seeded, and halved lengthwise (6 pieces total) (see tip, page 44)**
- **2 ounces Monterey Jack cheese, cut into six 2×1/2-inch sticks**
- **2 tablespoons snipped fresh cilantro or fresh parsley**
- **1/4 teaspoon black pepper**
- **2 tablespoons butter or margarine, melted**
- **1 8-ounce jar green or red salsa**

1 Place each chicken breast half between two pieces of plastic wrap. Using the flat side of a meat mallet, pound chicken lightly into rectangles, 1/4 to 1/2 inch thick (see photo 2, page 476). Discard plastic wrap.

2 Preheat oven to 375°F. Line a shallow baking pan with foil; set aside. In a shallow bowl combine flour, cornmeal, salt, and cayenne pepper. In a second shallow bowl combine egg and the water.

3 Place a chile pepper half on each chicken piece near an edge. Place a stick of cheese on each chile pepper. Sprinkle with cilantro and black pepper. Fold in side edges; roll up from edge with cheese and chile pepper (see photo 3, page 476). Secure with wooden toothpicks.

4 Dip chicken rolls into egg mixture to coat; coat all sides with cornmeal mixture. Place rolls, seam sides down, in prepared baking pan. Brush with melted butter.

5 Bake, uncovered, for 30 to 35 minutes or until chicken is done (165°F). Remove toothpicks. Meanwhile, heat salsa; serve with the chicken.

PER CHICKEN ROLL: 299 cal., 10 g total fat (5 g sat. fat), 141 mg chol., 396 mg sodium, 11 g carb., 1 g fiber, 40 g pro.
EXCHANGES: 1/2 Starch, 5 1/2 Lean Meat, 1/2 Fat

LOW-CALORIE

Chicken with Pan Sauce

START TO FINISH: 35 MINUTES
MAKES: 4 SERVINGS

- **2 skinless, boneless chicken breast halves (6 to 8 ounces each)**
- **¼ teaspoon salt**
- **¼ teaspoon freshly ground black pepper**
- **1 tablespoon olive oil**
- **½ cup dry white wine or chicken broth**
- **½ cup chicken broth**
- **¼ cup finely chopped shallot or onion**
- **2 tablespoons whipping cream**
- **¼ cup cold butter, cut up**

1 Halve each chicken breast horizontally. Place each chicken breast piece between two pieces of plastic wrap. Using the flat side of a meat mallet, pound chicken lightly to about ¼ inch thick (see photo 2, page 476). Discard plastic wrap. Sprinkle chicken with salt and pepper.

2 In a very large skillet heat the oil over medium-high heat. Add chicken to skillet. Cook chicken for 5 to 6 minutes or until no longer pink, turning once. Transfer chicken to a platter; cover with foil to keep warm. Remove skillet from heat.

3 Add wine, broth, and shallot to the hot skillet. Return skillet to heat. Cook and stir to scrape up the browned bits from bottom of the pan. Bring to boiling. Boil gently, uncovered, about 10 minutes or until liquid is reduced to ¼ cup. Reduce heat to medium-low.

4 Stir in cream. Add butter, 1 tablespoon at a time, stirring until butter melts after each addition. Sauce should be slightly thickened. Season to taste with additional salt and pepper. Serve sauce over chicken.

PER BREAST HALF + 2 TABLESPOONS SAUCE: 287 cal., 20 g total fat (10 g sat. fat), 96 mg chol., 458 mg sodium, 3 g carb., 0 g fiber, 19 g pro. EXCHANGES: 2½ Lean Meat, 3 Fat

MUSHROOM: Add 1 cup sliced assorted fresh mushrooms with shallot; do not add wine and broth. Cook until tender and golden. Add wine and broth; continue as directed.

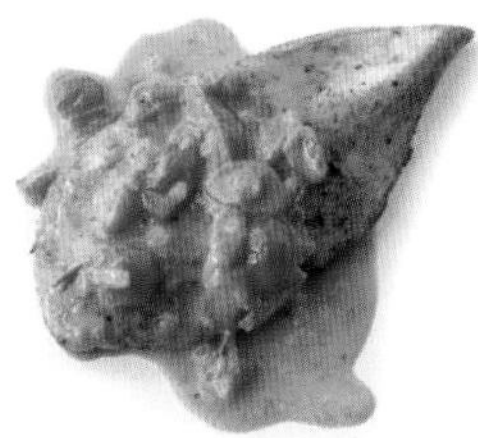

TOMATO-PARMESAN: Add ½ cup quartered grape tomatoes to skillet with shallot. Stir 2 tablespoons grated Parmesan into the finished sauce.

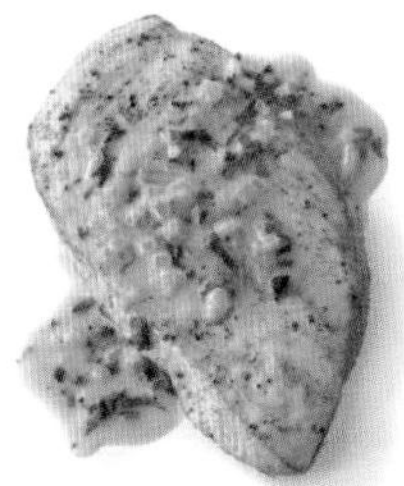

HERB: Stir 2 to 3 teaspoons snipped fresh basil, chervil, parsley, oregano, and/or dill weed into the finished sauce.

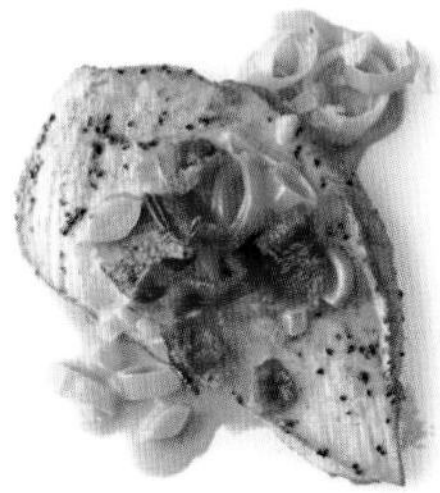

BACON-LEEK: Add ½ cup sliced leek to skillet with shallot. Top with 3 slices crumbled crisp-cooked bacon.

CILANTRO-CHIPOTLE: Stir 1 tablespoon snipped fresh cilantro and ½ teaspoon finely chopped chipotle chile pepper in adobo sauce into the finished sauce.

LEMON-THYME: Stir 2 teaspoons lemon juice and 2 teaspoons snipped fresh thyme into the finished sauce. Serve with lemon slices.

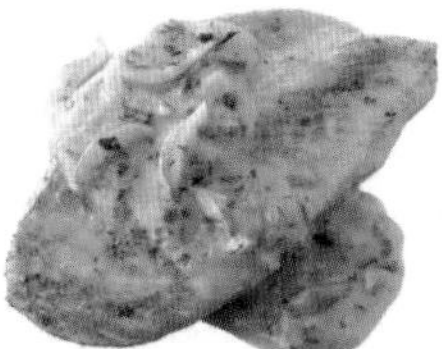

MUSTARD: Stir 1 tablespoon snipped fresh Italian parsley and 2 teaspoons Dijon-style mustard into finished sauce.

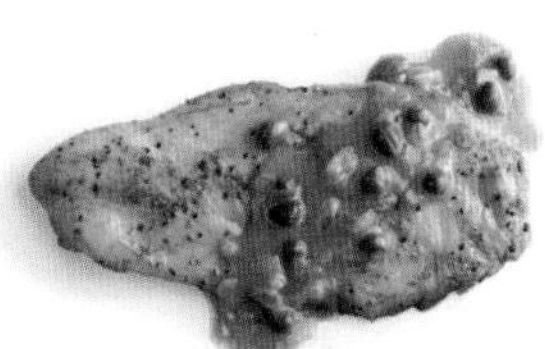

BALSAMIC-CAPER: Stir 2 teaspoons balsamic vinegar and 2 teaspoons drained capers into finished sauce.

Chicken Kiev

PREP: 20 MINUTES **CHILL:** 1 TO 24 HOURS
COOK: 5 MINUTES **BAKE:** 15 MINUTES AT 400°F
MAKES: 4 CHICKEN ROLLS

- **1 tablespoon chopped green onion**
- **1 tablespoon snipped fresh parsley**
- **1 clove garlic, minced**
- **½ of a ¼-pound stick of butter, chilled**
- **1 egg, lightly beaten**
- **1 tablespoon water**
- **¼ cup all-purpose flour**
- **½ cup fine dry bread crumbs**
- **4 skinless, boneless chicken breast halves (6 to 8 ounces each)**
- **Salt and black pepper**
- **1 tablespoon butter**
- **1 tablespoon vegetable oil**

1 In a small bowl combine green onion, parsley, and garlic; set aside. Cut chilled butter into four 2½×½-inch sticks (see photo 1, below). In a shallow bowl stir together egg and water. Place flour in a second shallow bowl. Place bread crumbs in a third shallow bowl. Set all three bowls aside.

2 Place each chicken breast half between two pieces of plastic wrap. Using the flat side of a meat mallet, pound chicken lightly into rectangles ¼ to ½ inch thick (see photo 2, below). Discard plastic wrap. Sprinkle chicken with salt and pepper. Divide green onion mixture among chicken pieces. Place a butter stick in center of each chicken piece. Fold in side edges; roll up from bottom edge (see photo 3, below).

3 Coat rolls with flour. Dip in egg mixture; coat with bread crumbs. Dip in egg mixture again; coat with additional bread crumbs (see photo 4, below). Coat ends well. Place chicken in a 2-quart baking dish. Cover; chill for 1 to 24 hours.

4 Preheat oven to 400°F. In a large skillet melt the 1 tablespoon butter over medium-high heat; add oil. Add chilled chicken rolls, seam sides down. Cook about 5 minutes or until golden brown, turning to brown on all sides (see photo 5, below). Return rolls to the baking dish. Bake, uncovered, for 15 to 18 minutes or until chicken is done (165°F). Spoon any drippings over rolls.

PER CHICKEN ROLL: 416 cal., 22 g total fat (11 g sat. fat), 173 mg chol., 450 mg sodium, 17 g carb., 1 g fiber, 37 g pro.
EXCHANGES: 1 Starch, 4½ Lean Meat, 3 Fat

CHEESY CHICKEN ROLLS: Prepare as directed, except substitute 2½×½-inch sticks of Gruyère or cheddar cheese for the butter. If using Gruyère cheese, substitute 2 teaspoons snipped fresh tarragon for the parsley. If using cheddar cheese, substitute 2 teaspoons snipped fresh thyme for the parsley.

PER CHICKEN ROLL: 420 cal., 18 g total fat (9 g sat. fat), 169 mg chol., 563 mg sodium, 17 g carb., 1 g fiber, 44 g pro.
EXCHANGES: 1 Starch, 4½ Lean Meat, 1 High-Fat Meat, 1 Fat

CHICKEN KIEV STEP-BY-STEP

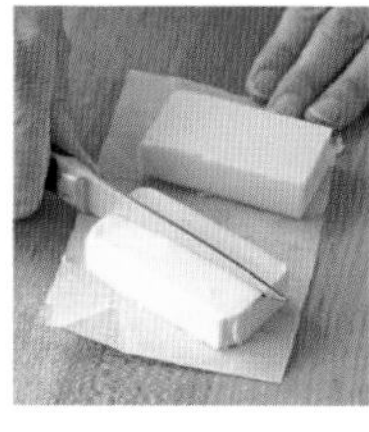

1. Cut the half stick of butter lengthwise into four pieces.

2. Starting from center, lightly pound chicken pieces with the flat side of a meat mallet to an even thickness of ¼ to ½ inch.

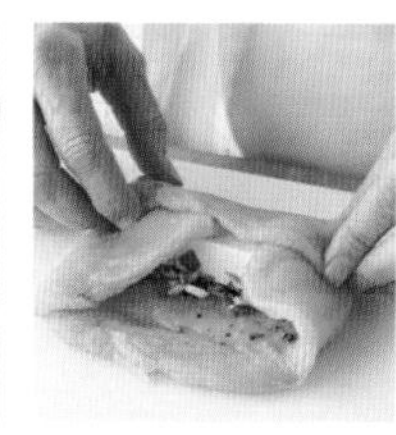

3. To enclose butter, fold in the side edges. Roll up chicken from bottom edge.

4. Completely cover chicken, including the ends, with flour, egg mixture, and the bread crumbs.

5. Cook chicken until golden, turning to brown evenly. Place rolls in baking dish.

FAST LOW-CALORIE

Coconut Chicken with Pineapple-Mango Salsa

START TO FINISH: 30 MINUTES **OVEN:** 400°F
MAKES: 4 SERVINGS

- **1 egg, lightly beaten**
- **1 tablespoon vegetable oil**
- **½ teaspoon salt**
- **⅛ teaspoon cayenne pepper**
- **1¼ cups flaked coconut**
- **14 to 16 ounces chicken breast tenderloins**
- **1 8-ounce can pineapple tidbits (juice pack), drained**
- **1 cup chopped refrigerated mango slices (about 10 slices)**
- **2 tablespoons snipped fresh cilantro (optional)**
- **1 tablespoon lime juice**

1 Preheat oven to 400°F. Line a large baking sheet with foil; lightly grease foil. Set pan aside.

2 In a shallow bowl whisk together egg, oil, ¼ teaspoon of the salt, and the cayenne pepper. Spread coconut in a second shallow bowl. Dip each chicken piece in egg mixture, allowing excess to drip off. Coat chicken with coconut. Arrange chicken on the prepared baking sheet. Bake for 10 to 12 minutes or until chicken is done (165°F).

3 Meanwhile, for salsa, in a medium bowl combine pineapple, mango, cilantro (if desired), lime juice, and the remaining ¼ teaspoon salt. Serve with chicken.

PER 3 OUNCES CHICKEN + ⅓ CUP SALSA: 393 cal., 18 g total fat (12 g sat. fat), 110 mg chol., 461 mg sodium, 31 g carb., 4 g fiber, 27 g pro. EXCHANGES: 1 Fruit, 1 Other Carb., 4 Lean Meat, 2 Fat

COCONUT CHICKEN WITH PINEAPPLE-MANGO SALSA

LOW-CALORIE

Chicken with Tomatoes and Spinach

PREP: 20 MINUTES **COOK:** 16 MINUTES
MAKES: 4 SERVINGS

- **¼ cup buttermilk**
- **½ cup all-purpose flour**
- **½ teaspoon salt**
- **½ teaspoon black pepper**
- **4 skinless, boneless chicken breast halves (6 to 8 ounces each)**
- **3 tablespoons vegetable oil**
- **2 cups grape tomatoes or cherry tomatoes**
- **1 tablespoon packed brown sugar**
- **1 9-ounce package fresh spinach Salt and black pepper**
- **1 recipe Polenta (page 88) (optional)**

1 Pour buttermilk into a shallow bowl. In a second shallow bowl combine flour, the ½ teaspoon salt, and the ½ teaspoon pepper. Dip chicken into buttermilk; dip into flour mixture, turning to coat both sides.

2 In a very large skillet heat oil over medium-high heat. Add chicken; cook for 15 to 20 minutes or until done (165°F), turning chicken halfway through cooking. Reduce heat to medium if chicken is browning too quickly.

3 Meanwhile, pierce tomatoes with a sharp knife. Place in a microwave-safe bowl; sprinkle with brown sugar. Cover loosely with plastic wrap. Microwave on 100% power (high) about 3 minutes or until skins burst and tomatoes are soft, stirring once; set aside.

4 Remove chicken from skillet; keep warm. Add spinach to drippings in skillet; cook and stir about 1 minute or until wilted. Season with additional salt and pepper. Serve chicken with spinach, tomatoes, and, if desired, Polenta.

PER CHICKEN PIECE + ½ CUP SPINACH + ⅓ CUP TOMATOES: 354 cal., 13 g total fat (1 g sat. fat), 83 mg chol., 528 mg sodium, 22 g carb., 3 g fiber, 38 g pro. EXCHANGES: 1½ Vegetable, 1 Starch, 4½ Lean Meat, 1½ Fat

CHICKEN MARSALA

LOW-CALORIE

Chicken Marsala

PREP: 25 MINUTES **COOK:** 11 MINUTES
MAKES: 4 SERVINGS

- **¼ cup all-purpose flour**
- **½ teaspoon dried thyme, crushed**
- **¼ teaspoon salt**
- **⅛ teaspoon black pepper**
- **4 skinless, boneless chicken breast halves (6 to 8 ounces each)**
- **1 cup chicken broth**
- **½ cup dry Marsala**
- **3 tablespoons butter**
- **1 tablespoon olive oil**
- **2 cups sliced fresh button or cremini mushrooms**
- **2 tablespoons finely chopped shallot**
- **Hot cooked pasta (optional)**
- **Snipped fresh Italian parsley**

1 In a shallow dish stir together flour, thyme, salt, and pepper; set aside. Place each chicken breast half between two pieces of plastic wrap. Using the flat side of a meat mallet, pound chicken lightly to about ¼ inch thick (see photo 2, page 476). Discard plastic wrap. Coat chicken pieces with flour mixture; shake off excess.

2 In a small bowl whisk together any remaining flour mixture, the broth, and Marsala; set aside.

3 In a very large skillet cook chicken in 1 tablespoon of the butter and the olive oil over medium-high heat for 4 to 6 minutes or until no longer pink, turning once. Transfer chicken to a platter; cover with foil to keep warm.

4 Add mushrooms and shallot to skillet; cook for 6 to 8 minutes until tender. Remove skillet from heat. Carefully add Marsala mixture to skillet. Return to heat. Cook and stir until slightly thickened and bubbly. Whisk in the remaining 2 tablespoons butter until incorporated. If desired, serve over pasta. Spoon mushroom sauce over chicken. Sprinkle with parsley.

PER BREAST HALF + ⅓ CUP SAUCE: 381 cal., 17 g total fat (7 g sat. fat), 133 mg chol., 638 mg sodium, 11 g carb., 1 g fiber, 39 g pro. **EXCHANGES:** ½ Starch, 5½ Lean Meat, 1½ Fat

LOW-CALORIE

Citrus-Herb Marinated Chicken

PREP: 20 MINUTES **MARINATE:** 2 TO 4 HOURS
BROIL: 12 MINUTES **MAKES:** 4 SERVINGS

- **4 skinless, boneless chicken breast halves (6 to 8 ounces each)**
- **⅓ cup lemon juice or orange juice**
- **1 tablespoon honey**
- **1 tablespoon olive oil**
- **1 tablespoon snipped fresh thyme or 1 teaspoon dried thyme, crushed**
- **2 teaspoons snipped fresh rosemary or ½ teaspoon dried rosemary, crushed**
- **2 tablespoons finely chopped shallot**
- **1 clove garlic, minced**
- **½ teaspoon salt**
- **¼ teaspoon freshly ground black pepper**
- **Lemon or orange wedges (optional)**

1 Place chicken breast halves in a resealable plastic bag set in a shallow bowl. For marinade, stir together lemon juice, honey, olive oil, thyme, rosemary, shallot, garlic, salt, and pepper. Pour over chicken; seal the bag. Marinate in the refrigerator for 2 to 4 hours, turning the bag occasionally.

2 Preheat broiler. Drain chicken, reserving marinade. Place chicken on the unheated rack of a broiler pan. Broil 4 to 5 inches from the heat about 6 minutes or until lightly browned.

3 Turn chicken and brush lightly with reserved marinade. Discard remaining marinade. Broil for 6 to 9 minutes more or until chicken is done (165°F). If desired, serve with lemon wedges.

PER BREAST HALF: 212 cal., 5 g total fat (1 g sat. fat), 82 mg chol., 366 mg sodium, 7 g carb., 0 g fiber, 33 g pro.
EXCHANGES: ½ Other Carb., 3½ Lean Meat, ½ Fat

BEST-LOVED **LOW-CALORIE**

Kalamata Lemon Chicken

PREP: 10 MINUTES **BAKE:** 35 MINUTES AT 400°F
MAKES: 4 SERVINGS

- **1 tablespoon olive oil**
- **4 large skinless, boneless chicken thighs (1 to 1¼ pounds)**
- **1 14.5-ounce can chicken broth**
- **⅔ cup dried orzo (rosamarina)**
- **½ cup pitted Kalamata olives, drained**
- **½ of a lemon, cut into wedges or chunks**
- **1 tablespoon lemon juice**
- **1 teaspoon dried Greek seasoning or dried oregano, crushed**
- **¼ teaspoon salt**
- **¼ teaspoon black pepper**
- **Hot chicken broth (optional)**
- **Snipped fresh oregano (optional)**

1 Preheat oven to 400°F. In a 4-quart Dutch oven heat oil over medium-high heat. Add chicken; cook about 5 minutes or until browned, turning once. Stir in broth, orzo, olives, lemon wedges, lemon juice, Greek seasoning, salt, and pepper. Bring to boiling. Transfer mixture to a 2-quart rectangular baking dish.

2 Bake, covered, about 35 minutes or until chicken is done (at least 170°F). If desired, serve in shallow bowls with additional hot broth and top with oregano.

PER 3 OUNCES CHICKEN + ½ CUP ORZO: 304 cal., 10 g total fat (2 g sat. fat), 95 mg chol., 830 mg sodium, 25 g carb., 2 g fiber, 27 g pro. **EXCHANGES:** 1½ Starch, 3 Lean Meat, 1 Fat

Chicken Thighs with Caramelized Onion and Bacon Dressing

(photo, page 461)

PREP: 40 MINUTES **BAKE:** 25 MINUTES AT 400°F
MAKES: 8 SERVINGS

- **6 slices bacon**
- **6 cups thinly sliced onions**
- **2 to 3 ciabatta rolls, cut into ½-inch cubes and dried (see tip, page 365) (about 7 ounces)**
- **2½ cups reduced-sodium chicken broth**
- **2 eggs, lightly beaten**
- **¼ cup snipped fresh parsley**
- **½ teaspoon black pepper**
- **8 large skinless, boneless chicken thighs (about 2 pounds)**
- **2 tablespoons olive oil**
- **1½ cups dry white wine**
- **¼ teaspoon salt**
- **3 tablespoons butter**
- **3 tablespoons whipping cream**
- **Snipped fresh parsley**

1 Preheat oven to 400°F. Heat a very large skillet over medium heat. Cook the bacon in hot skillet about 10 minutes or until browned and crispy, turning once. Transfer to paper towels to drain. Reserve 2 tablespoon of the drippings in skillet. Add onions. Reduce heat to medium-low. Cook, covered, for 13 to 15 minutes or until onions are tender, stirring occasionally. Uncover; cook and stir over medium-high heat for 3 to 5 minutes or until golden. Remove from heat.

2 Chop the bacon. In a medium bowl combine half of the bacon, the caramelized onions, bread cubes, 1 cup of the broth, eggs, ¼ cup parsley, and the pepper. Stir gently to combine. Spoon dressing into a 2-quart square or rectangular baking dish.

3 In the same skillet cook the chicken in hot oil over medium heat about 5 minutes or until browned, turning once. Place chicken on dressing mixture in baking dish. Bake, uncovered, for 25 to 35 minutes or until an instant-read thermometer inserted in dressing registers 165°F and registers at least 170°F in a thigh.

4 Meanwhile, whisk the 1½ cups remaining broth, the wine, and the salt into the skillet, scraping up browned bits from bottom of skillet. Return skillet to heat. Bring to boiling over medium-high heat. Boil gently, uncovered, about 12 minutes or until reduced to 1 cup. Whisk in the butter and cream. Simmer 5 minutes more or until reduced to ¾ cup. Stir in remaining bacon. Serve with chicken and dressing. If desired, sprinkle with additional parsley.

PER 1 THIGH + ⅔ CUP DRESSING: 440 cal., 22 g total fat (8 g sat. fat), 183 mg chol., 675 mg sodium, 24 g carb., 4 g fiber, 29 g pro. **EXCHANGES:** 2 Vegetable, 1 Starch, 3 Lean Meat, 3 Fat

DRESSING OR STUFFING?

When you read the title for Chicken Thighs with Caramelized Onion and Bacon Dressing, your first thought may have been of a dressing like those drizzled on salads. But this dressing has more in common with the bread mixtures used to stuff turkeys. Actually, this type of dressing and stuffing are the same thing. It's just called dressing when it's baked in a dish rather than stuffed in a bird. See Old-Fashioned Stuffing, page 365.

CHICKEN MEATBALL NOODLE BOWL

BEST-LOVED FAST LOW-CALORIE

Chicken Meatball Noodle Bowl

START TO FINISH: 25 MINUTES **MAKES:** 4 SERVINGS

- **4 ounces thin rice noodles**
- **12 ounces ground chicken**
- **1 tablespoon grated fresh ginger**
- **2 tablespoons snipped fresh cilantro**
- **3 tablespoons coconut oil or vegetable oil**
- **1 red Fresno chile pepper, seeded and finely chopped (see tip, page 44)**
- **⅓ cup rice vinegar**
- **2 tablespoons honey**
- **1 tablespoon lime juice**
- **3 cups shredded leaf lettuce**
- **½ cup finely shredded carrot (1 medium)**
- **Fresh cilantro, sliced Fresno peppers (see tip, page 44), lime wedges, and/or sliced green onions (optional)**

1 Prepare noodles according to package directions. Drain and set aside.

2 Meanwhile, in a large bowl combine ground chicken, ginger, cilantro, and ½ teaspoon *salt*. Shape mixture into 16 meatballs.

3 In a large skillet heat 1 tablespoon of the coconut oil over medium heat. Add meatballs. Cook about 10 minutes or until browned and cooked through (165°F), turning occasionally. Transfer meatballs to a plate; keep warm.

4 Remove skillet from heat. For sauce, add the remaining 2 tablespoons coconut oil and the chile pepper to the still-warm pan. Stir in vinegar, honey, and lime juice; set aside.

5 Divide noodles, lettuce, and carrot among bowls. Top with meatballs; drizzle with pan sauce. If desired, garnish with cilantro, Fresno peppers, lime wedges, and/or green onions.

PER SERVING: 368 cal., 17 g total fat (11 g sat. fat), 73 mg chol., 413 mg sodium, 36 g carb., 1 g fiber, 16 g pro.
EXCHANGES: ½ Vegetable, 1½ Starch, ½ Other Carb., 1½ Lean Meat, 2½ Fat

LOW-CALORIE

Chicken Burritos

PREP: 20 MINUTES **BAKE:** 30 MINUTES AT 350°F
MAKES: 8 BURRITOS

- **8 8- to 10-inch flour tortillas**
- **1½ cups shredded cooked chicken, turkey, beef, or pork**
- **1 cup bottled salsa**
- **1 3⅛-ounce can jalapeño-flavor bean dip**
- **1 teaspoon fajita seasoning**
- **8 ounces Monterey Jack cheese or cheddar cheese, cut into eight 5×½-inch sticks**
- **Shredded lettuce (optional)**
- **Sour cream (optional)**
- **Bottled salsa (optional)**

1 Preheat oven to 350°F. Wrap tortillas in foil; heat in oven about 10 minutes or until warm. Meanwhile, in a large bowl stir together chicken, the 1 cup salsa, bean dip, and fajita seasoning.

2 To assemble, place ⅓ cup chicken mixture onto each tortilla near one edge. Top chicken mixture with a stick of cheese. Fold in sides of tortilla; roll up, starting from edge with the filling. Place filled tortillas, seam sides down, in a greased 3-quart rectangular baking dish.

3 Bake, uncovered, about 30 minutes or until heated through. If desired, serve with lettuce, sour cream, and additional salsa.

PER BURRITO: 267 cal., 13 g total fat (7 g sat. fat), 49 mg chol., 589 mg sodium, 19 g carb., 1 g fiber, 18 g pro.
EXCHANGES: 1 Starch, 2 Lean Meat, 2 Fat

FAST LOW-CALORIE

Chile-Lime Turkey Patties

START TO FINISH: 30 MINUTES **MAKES:** 8 PATTIES

- **2 cups cut-up cooked oven-roasted turkey***
- **¼ cup fresh parsley**
- **2 tablespoons sliced celery**
- **2 tablespoons sliced green onion (1)**
- **1 cup panko bread crumbs**
- **¼ cup mayonnaise**
- **1 egg, lightly beaten**
- **1 tablespoon lime juice**
- **1 teaspoon Asian chili paste**
- **⅛ teaspoon Worcestershire sauce**
- **2 tablespoons butter**
- **1 recipe Lime-Butter Sauce**
- **Lime wedges**

1 In a food processor process turkey just until ground; transfer to a bowl. Process parsley, celery, and onion until finely chopped. Add to turkey with ½ cup of the panko, the mayonnaise, egg, lime juice, chili paste, and Worcestershire sauce; mix well. Shape mixture into eight 3-inch patties; coat patties with the remaining panko.

2 In a very large skillet heat 1 tablespoon of the butter over medium heat. Cook patties, half at a time, about 10 minutes or until browned and heated through (160°F), turning once. Repeat with the remaining butter and patties. Serve with Lime-Butter Sauce and lime wedges.

***NOTE:** Use leftover oven-roasted turkey. Avoid using purchased water-injected cooked turkey because the patties might fall apart during cooking.

LIME-BUTTER SAUCE: In a small heavy saucepan combine ⅓ cup white wine or reduced-sodium chicken broth; 1 tablespoon lime juice; ¾ teaspoon white wine vinegar; and 1 clove garlic, minced. Bring to boiling; reduce heat. Simmer, uncovered, about 5 minutes or until slightly reduced. Reduce heat to low. Whisk in 2 tablespoons whipping cream. Gradually whisk in ⅓ cup butter, cut up, cooking until melted and smooth. Stir in 1 tablespoon Asian sweet chili sauce, dash salt, and dash ground white pepper.

PER 1 PATTY + ABOUT 1 TABLESPOON SAUCE: 262 cal., 19 g total fat (9 g sat. fat), 95 mg chol., 260 mg sodium, 8 g carb., 1 g fiber, 12 g pro. EXCHANGES: ½ Starch, 1½ Lean Meat, 3½ Fat

LOW-CALORIE

Turkey Tenderloin with Bacon-Balsamic Glaze

PREP: 25 MINUTES **ROAST:** 20 MINUTES AT 400°F
MAKES: 6 SERVINGS

- **1½ pounds turkey breast tenderloins**
- **½ teaspoon salt**
- **¼ teaspoon black pepper**
- **1 tablespoon olive oil**
- **3 slices bacon, chopped**
- **½ cup finely chopped onion (1 medium)**
- **2 cloves garlic, minced**
- **½ cup balsamic vinegar**
- **¼ cup cranberry juice**
- **½ cup dried tart cherries**
- **2 teaspoons snipped fresh thyme**

1 Preheat oven to 400°F. Season turkey with salt and pepper. Heat oil in a large ovenproof skillet over medium-high heat. Cook turkey in hot oil about 3 minutes or until golden on one side. Turn turkey; transfer skillet to oven. Roast, uncovered, for 20 to 25 minutes or until done (165°F). Transfer the turkey to a cutting board; cover with foil and keep warm.

2 In the same skillet* cook the bacon, onion, and garlic over medium heat until bacon is browned and crisp. Add vinegar, cranberry juice, cherries, and thyme. Cook, uncovered, for 4 to 5 minutes or until slightly thickened, stirring to scrape up any browned bits. Slice the turkey. Spoon sauce over turkey.

***NOTE:** Skillet handle will still be hot from the oven. Be sure to use a hot pad to hold it.

PER 3 OUNCES TURKEY + 2½ TABLESPOONS SAUCE: 283 cal., 11 g total fat (3 g sat. fat), 58 mg chol., 393 mg sodium, 17 g carb., 1 g fiber, 31 g pro. EXCHANGES: ½ Fruit, ½ Other Carb., 4½ Lean Meat, 1 Fat

CITRUS-MARINATED TURKEY BREAST

BEST-LOVED

Citrus-Marinated Turkey Breast

PREP: 30 MINUTES **MARINATE:** 8 TO 24 HOURS
ROAST: 75 MINUTES AT 350°F **STAND:** 10 MINUTES
MAKES: 10 TO 12 SERVINGS

- **2 3- to 3½-pound turkey breast halves with bones**
- **2 cups lightly packed fresh cilantro leaves**
- **1⅓ cups orange juice**
- **½ cup lemon juice**
- **12 cloves garlic, halved**
- **1 fresh jalapeño chile pepper, seeded and cut up (see tip, page 44)**
- **2 teaspoons salt**
- **2 teaspoons ground cumin**
- **½ teaspoon freshly ground black pepper**
- **1½ cups olive oil**

1 Using a sharp knife, cut several slits in turkey breast halves. Place breast halves, skin sides down, in a very large resealable plastic bag set in a baking dish; set aside.

2 For cilantro sauce, in a food processor combine cilantro, orange juice, lemon juice, garlic, jalapeño pepper, salt, cumin, and black pepper. Cover and process until almost smooth. With processor running, add oil in a thin stream. Measure 2 cups sauce; cover and chill until serving time. Pour remaining sauce over breast halves; marinate in refrigerator for 8 to 24 hours, turning occasionally.

3 Preheat oven to 350°F. Remove turkey from marinade; discard marinade. Place turkey, bone sides down, on rack in roasting pan. Insert an oven-going meat thermometer into thickest part of one turkey breast half without touching bone. Roast, uncovered, for 75 to 90 minutes or until thermometer registers 170°F. If necessary, cover with foil the last 30 to 45 minutes to prevent overbrowning. Let stand, covered with foil, for 10 minutes before slicing. Stir reserved cilantro sauce; pass with turkey.

PER 7 OUNCES TURKEY: 685 cal., 49 g total fat (9 g sat. fat), 158 mg chol., 577 mg sodium, 6 g carb., 0 g fiber, 54 g pro. EXCHANGES: ½ Other Carb., 7½ Lean Meat, 7 Fat

PESTO TURKEY BREAST: Omit marinating turkey and the cilantro sauce. Combine two 7-ounce containers refrigerated basil pesto or one 10-ounce jar purchased basil pesto, ⅓ cup finely snipped fresh sage, ¼ cup finely chopped toasted walnuts, and ½ teaspoon black pepper. Set aside half of the pesto mixture. Starting at the breast bone, slip your fingers between skin and meat to loosen skin, leaving skin attached at top. Rub about two-thirds of the remaining pesto mixture under the skin over the meat. Rub remaining pesto mixture over skin. Insert an oven-going meat thermometer into thickest part of breast without touching bone. Roast as directed. Cover with foil the last 30 to 45 minutes to prevent overbrowning. Let stand, covered with foil, for 10 to 15 minutes before slicing. Serve with reserved pesto mixture.

PER 7 OUNCES TURKEY: 587 cal., 36 g total fat (8 g sat. fat), 171 mg chol., 454 mg sodium, 5 g carb., 2 g fiber, 59 g pro. EXCHANGES: 8 Lean Meat, 5 Fat

MAPLE BARBECUE-GLAZED TURKEY BREAST: Omit marinating turkey and the cilantro sauce. In a small saucepan stir together ½ cup pure maple syrup, 2 tablespoons bottled chili sauce, 2 tablespoons cider vinegar, 1 tablespoon Worcestershire sauce, ½ teaspoon dry mustard, and ¼ teaspoon black pepper. Heat and stir until slightly thickened. Brush on turkey the last 15 minutes of roasting.

PER 7 OUNCES TURKEY: 422 cal., 16 g total fat (4 g sat. fat), 158 mg chol., 223 mg sodium, 12 g carb., 0 g fiber, 54 g pro. EXCHANGES: 1 Other Carb., 7½ Lean Meat, ½ Fat

BEST-LOVED FAST

Zesty Skillet Turkey

START TO FINISH: 30 MINUTES **MAKES:** 4 SERVINGS

- **1 cup salsa**
- **¼ cup raisins**
- **1 tablespoon honey**
- **½ teaspoon ground cumin**
- **¼ teaspoon ground cinnamon**
- **2 turkey breast tenderloins**
- **1 tablespoon olive oil**
- **1 cup water**
- **¼ teaspoon salt**
- **¾ cup couscous**
- **¼ cup slivered almonds, toasted (see tip, page 21)**

1 In a medium bowl stir together salsa, raisins, honey, cumin, and cinnamon; set aside. Cut each turkey tenderloin in half horizontally.

2 In a large skillet heat oil over medium-high heat. Add turkey pieces; cook about 2 minutes per side or until browned. Add salsa mixture to skillet. Bring to boiling; reduce heat. Simmer, covered, for 10 to 12 minutes or until turkey is done (165°F).

3 Meanwhile, in a medium saucepan bring water and salt to boiling. Stir in couscous. Cover; remove from heat. Let stand for 5 minutes. Fluff with a fork before serving. Serve turkey and salsa mixture over couscous; sprinkle with almonds.

PER TURKEY PIECE + ⅓ CUP SAUCE + ½ CUP COUSCOUS: 447 cal., 8 g total fat (1 g sat. fat), 105 mg chol., 598 mg sodium, 44 g carb., 4 g fiber, 49 g pro. EXCHANGES: ½ Fruit, 2½ Starch, 5½ Lean Meat

Pan-Seared Duck with Apples

PREP: 30 MINUTES **ROAST:** 12 MINUTES AT 350°F
STAND: 10 MINUTES **MAKES:** 4 SERVINGS

- **4 boneless duck breast halves (with skin)**
- **1/4 cup butter or margarine**
- **4 Golden Delicious or Gala apples, sliced**
- **1/3 cup balsamic vinegar**
- **1/4 cup apple juice**
- **4 cups kale or broccoli rabe**

1 Preheat oven to 350°F. Trim excess fat from duck (do not remove skin). Score the skin in a diamond pattern (see photo 1, below). Sprinkle duck with *black pepper*.

2 Heat a very large ovenproof skillet over medium heat. Place duck pieces in hot skillet, skin sides down; cook for 5 minutes. Turn duck over and cook for 5 minutes more or until duck is browned (see photo 2, below). Drain off fat. Place the skillet in oven; roast for 12 to 18 minutes or until thermometer registers 155°F. Remove duck from skillet; cover and let stand for 10 minutes.

3 Meanwhile, in a large skillet melt butter over medium heat. Add apples; cook for 10 minutes or until tender, stirring frequently. Season apples to taste with *salt* and additional pepper; remove apples from skillet. Set aside and keep warm.

4 For sauce, reserve 1 tablespoon drippings in skillet used to cook the duck; discard remaining drippings. Add vinegar and apple juice to drippings in skillet, scraping up browned bits. Return skillet to stove top. Bring to boiling over medium-high heat. Cook for 3 to 5 minutes or until liquid is reduced by half.

PAN-SEARING DUCK BREASTS STEP-BY-STEP

1. Use a sharp knife to cut through the skin but not into the meat. Make parallel cuts about 1/2 inch apart; cut in the opposite direction to make a diamond pattern.

2. Place duck in the hot skillet, skin sides down. The duck will release enough fat to brown and crisp the skin. Cook until the skin is browned and crisp before turning.

5 In a large saucepan bring 4 cups water to boiling. Add broccoli rabe and cook for 1 minute. Drain in colander. To serve, arrange broccoli rabe, apples, and duck breast on a serving platter. Drizzle with sauce.

PER SERVING: 620 cal., 38 g total fat (16 g sat. fat), 185 mg chol., 332 mg sodium, 33 g carb., 5 g fiber, 36 g pro.
EXCHANGES: 1 Vegetable, 1½ Fruit, 5 Medium-Fat Meat, 3 Fat

CUT THE FAT

Duck skin from domestic ducks has a thick layer of fat under it. This fat renders into the pan when cooking the duck breast, allowing it to brown and crisp and keeping the duck from sticking. It also helps keep the duck breast moist while cooking. It is delicious, but if you want to cut back on the fat in this dish, remove some or all of the skin before eating the duck breast.

ROASTING POULTRY

Because birds vary in size and shape, use times as general guides. For stuffed birds, see page 354.

1 If desired, thoroughly rinse a whole bird's body and neck cavities. Pat dry with paper towels. If desired, sprinkle the body cavity with salt.

2 If desired, place quartered onions and celery in body cavity. Pull neck skin to back and fasten with a skewer. If a band of skin crosses tail, tuck drumsticks under band. If there is no band, tie drumsticks to tail with 100% cotton kitchen string. Twist wing tips under back.

3 Place bird, breast side up, on a rack in a shallow roasting pan; brush with vegetable oil and, if desired, sprinkle with a crushed dried herb, such as thyme or oregano. (When cooking a domestic duckling or goose, prick skin generously all over and omit oil.) For large birds, insert an oven-going meat thermometer into center of one of the inside thigh muscles. Thermometer should not touch the bone.

4 Cover Cornish game hen, pheasant, and whole turkey with foil, leaving air space between bird and foil. Lightly press foil to ends of drumsticks and neck to enclose bird. Leave other poultry uncovered.

5 Roast in an uncovered pan. Two-thirds through roasting time, cut band of skin or string between drumsticks. Uncover large birds last 45 minutes of roasting; uncover small birds last 30 minutes of roasting. Continue roasting until meat thermometer registers 175°F in thigh muscle (check temperature of thigh in several places) or until drumsticks move easily in sockets. (For a whole or half turkey breast, bone in, thermometer should register 170°F. For whole boneless breast, thermometer should register 165°F.) Remove bird from oven; cover. Allow whole birds and turkey portions to stand for 15 minutes before carving.

Type of Bird	Weight	Oven Temperature	Roasting Time
CHICKEN			
Capon	5 to 7 pounds	325°F	1¾ to 2½ hours
Meaty pieces (breast halves, drumsticks, and thighs with bone)	2½ to 3 pounds	375°F	45 to 55 minutes
Whole	2½ to 3 pounds 3½ to 4 pounds 4½ to 5 pounds	375°F 375°F 375°F	1 to 1¼ hours 1¼ to 1½ hours 1¾ to 2 hours
GAME			
Cornish game hen	1¼ to 1½ pounds	375°F	1 to 1¼ hours
Duckling, domestic	4 to 6 pounds	350°F	1¾ to 2½ hours
Goose, domestic	7 to 8 pounds 8 to 10 pounds	350°F 350°F	2 to 2½ hours 2½ to 3 hours
Pheasant	2 to 3 pounds	325°F	1½ to 2 hours
TURKEY			
Breast, whole	4 to 6 pounds 6 to 8 pounds	325°F 325°F	1½ to 2¼ hours 2¼ to 3¼ hours
Breast, boneless whole*	2½ to 3 pounds	325°F	40 to 60 minutes
Breast, half	2 to 2½ pounds	325°F	60 to 70 minutes
Breast, boneless half	1¼ to 1½ pounds	325°F	35 to 40 minutes
Drumstick	1 to 1½ pounds	325°F	1¼ to 1¾ hours
Thigh	1½ to 1¾ pounds	325°F	1½ to 1¾ hours
Whole (unstuffed)**	8 to 12 pounds 12 to 14 pounds 14 to 18 pounds 18 to 20 pounds 20 to 24 pounds	325°F 325°F 325°F 325°F 325°F	2¾ to 3 hours 3 to 3¾ hours 3¾ to 4¼ hours 4¼ to 4½ hours 4½ to 5 hours

*If you can't find a boneless whole turkey breast, have the butcher remove the bone.

**Stuffed birds generally require 15 to 45 minutes more roasting time than unstuffed birds. Always verify doneness temperatures of poultry and center of stuffing (165°F) with a meat thermometer.

BROILING POULTRY

If desired, remove poultry skin; sprinkle with salt and black pepper. Preheat broiler for 5 to 10 minutes. Arrange poultry on the unheated rack of broiler pan with the bone side(s) up. If desired, brush poultry with vegetable oil. Place pan under broiler so surface of the poultry is 4 to 5 inches from the heat; chicken and Cornish game hen halves should be 5 to 6 inches from the heat. Turn pieces over when browned on one side, usually after half of the broiling time. Chicken halves and quarters and meaty pieces should be turned after 20 minutes. Brush again with oil. The poultry is done when an instant-read thermometer registers at least 175°F for thighs and drumsticks, 170°F for bone-in breast meat, 165°F for boneless breast meat, and 160°F for duck breast. If desired, brush with a sauce the last 5 minutes of cooking.

Type of Bird	Weight	Broiling Time
CHICKEN		
Kabobs (boneless breast, cut into 2½-inch strips and threaded loosely onto skewers)*		8 to 10 minutes
Meaty pieces (breast halves, drumsticks, and thighs with bone)	2½ to 3 pounds	25 to 35 minutes
Skinless, boneless breast halves	6 to 8 ounces	15 to 18 minutes
GAME		
Boneless duck breast, skin removed	6 to 8 ounces	14 to 16 minutes
TURKEY		
Breast cutlet*	2 ounces	6 to 8 minutes
Breast tenderloin steaks (to make ½-inch-thick steaks, cut turkey tenderloin in half horizontally)	4 to 6 ounces	8 to 10 minutes

*Chicken strips and cutlets are too thin to get an accurate doneness temperature. Cook them until no longer pink.

SKILLET-COOKING POULTRY

Select a heavy skillet that is the right size for the amount of poultry being cooked. (If the skillet is too large, pan juices can burn. If it's too small, poultry will steam instead of brown.) If the skillet is not nonstick, lightly coat it with 2 to 3 teaspoons vegetable oil or nonstick cooking spray. Preheat skillet over medium-high heat until hot. Add poultry. Do not add any liquid and do not cover the skillet. Reduce heat to medium; cook for the time given or until done, turning poultry occasionally. (If poultry browns too quickly, reduce heat to medium-low.) Poultry is done when an instant-read thermometer registers 165°F for breast meat at least 175°F for thighs.

Type of Bird	Weight	Cooking Time
CHICKEN		
Breast tenders*	1 to 2 ounces	6 to 8 minutes
Skinless, boneless breast halves	6 to 8 ounces	15 to 18 minutes
Skinless, boneless thighs	3 to 4 ounces	14 to 18 minutes
TURKEY		
Breast tenderloin steaks (to make ½-inch-thick steaks, cut turkey tenderloin in half horizontally)	4 to 6 ounces	15 to 18 minutes

*Chicken tenders are too thin to get an accurate doneness temperature. Cook them until no longer pink.

498

501

503

salads & dressings

495

512

507

salads & dressings

Whether your salad is a first course, side, or the main attraction of the meal, here's how to make it shine.

PREPARING SALAD GREENS

Use these tips to showcase greens at their crispest and cleanest—and tastiest.

- Select greens that appear fresh and have no brown, bruised, or wilted leaves.
- To wash greens, remove and discard the root end; separate the leaves. Gently move the leaves around in a large bowl or sink filled with cold water about 30 seconds. Remove the leaves, gently shaking them to remove any dirt or debris. Repeat this process, using fresh water each time, until the water remains clear.
- To dry the greens, use a salad spinner or pat each leaf dry with paper towels.
- When ready to use the greens, tear them into bite-size pieces.
- Store washed and dried greens in the refrigerator in a resealable plastic bag lined with paper towels or in a fabric produce bag.
- Packaged prewashed greens are a realistic choice when you don't have time to prep them yourself. Because the packages are specifically designed to allow greens to breathe, store undressed leftovers in the original bag.

Bistro Salad, page 510

HOMEMADE DRESSING

French, honey mustard, creamy Parmesan—these are classic dressings you can get at the store or order off countless restaurant menus. Yet nothing beats a homemade version. Many start with oil and vinegar. Keep reading to find out about some of the varieties available to help you mix and match.

SALAD OILS

NUT OILS: Almond, hazelnut, and walnut oils can add rich flavor to dressings. Highly perishable, they should be stored after opening in the refrigerator.

OLIVE OIL: Choose pure olive oil for a milder flavor or extra virgin olive oil when you want the flavor of the oil to shine through. Store in a cool, dark place.

VEGETABLE OIL: With their neutral taste, vegetable oils, such as canola, safflower, and sunflower, bring body to dressings without impacting the flavor of other ingredients in the dressing or salad. Store at room temperature.

VINEGARS

CIDER VINEGAR: This tartly acidic vinegar is most often used for dressing cabbage and other hearty vegetables but can also be used for dressing greens. When a recipe simply calls for vinegar, cider vinegar works just fine.

DISTILLED WHITE VINEGAR: Mainly used for pickling, this is the sharpest of all vinegars. For something more subtle, use white wine vinegar.

FLAVORED VINEGARS: Infused with herbs, nuts, or fruits, these vinegars bring a subtle taste of the flavoring ingredient to dressings.

RICE VINEGAR: Made from fermented rice, this vinegar's mild flavor and subtle sweetness add an enticing contrast to spicy or bitter greens.

WINE VINEGARS: These are time-honored choices for classic vinaigrettes. Dark balsamic vinegar is a wine vinegar that has been aged in barrels, which imbues it with a deep color and sweetly pungent flavor.

GIVE IT A SHAKE

The key in making a vinaigrette is to combine oil and vinegar into one smooth mixture. An easy way to do this is to use a screw-top jar. Combine ingredients in the jar, shake, and serve.

Arugula
Spinach
Watercress
Endive
Mesclun
Romaine
Frisée
Savoy cabbage
Kale
Butterhead (Bibb or Boston)
Iceberg
Radicchio
Red cabbage
Red-tipped butterhead
Escarole
Napa cabbage
Green cabbage
Curly endive
Red-tipped leaf
Green leaf

GUIDE TO SALAD GREENS

Type	Weight at Purchase	Amount After Preparation	Preparation and Storage*
Arugula	1 ounce	1 cup torn	Rinse thoroughly in cold water to remove all sand; pat dry. Refrigerate in plastic bag for up to 2 days.
Cabbage	2 pounds (1 head)	12 cups shredded or 10 cups coarsely chopped	Refrigerate in plastic bag for up to 5 days. Rinse in cold water just before using; pat dry.
Cabbage, napa	2 pounds (1 head)	12 cups sliced stems and shredded leaves	Cut off bottom core. Rinse in cold water; pat dry. Refrigerate in plastic bag for up to 3 days.
Cabbage, savoy	1¾ pounds (1 head)	12 cups coarsely shredded	Refrigerate in plastic bag for up to 5 days. Rinse in cold water just before using; pat dry.
Endive, Belgian	4 ounces (1 head)	20 leaves	Cut off bottom core. Rinse in cold water; pat dry. Refrigerate in plastic bag and use within 1 day.
Endive, curly	12 ounces (1 head)	14 cups torn	Rinse in cold water; pat dry. Refrigerate, tightly wrapped, for up to 3 days.
Escarole	8 ounces (1 head)	7 cups torn	Rinse in cold water; pat dry. Refrigerate, tightly wrapped, for up to 3 days.
Frisée	8 ounces	7 cups torn	Rinse in cold water; pat dry. Refrigerate in plastic bag for up to 3 days.
Kale	10 ounces	6 cups torn	Remove and discard thick stems. Tear into bite-size pieces. Rinse in cold water; dry in salad spinner or pat dry. Refrigerate in plastic bag for up to 5 days.
Lettuce, butterhead (Bibb or Boston)	8 ounces (1 head)	6 cups torn	Cut off bottom core. Rinse in cold water; pat dry. Refrigerate in plastic bag for up to 3 days.
Lettuce, iceberg	1¼ pounds (1 head)	10 cups torn or 12 cups shredded	Remove core. Rinse (core side up) under cold running water; invert to drain. Refrigerate in plastic bag for up to 5 days.
Lettuce, leaf	12 ounces (1 head)	10 cups torn	Cut off bottom core. Rinse in cold water; pat dry. Refrigerate in plastic bag for up to 3 days.
Radicchio	8 ounces (1 head)	5½ cups torn	Rinse in cold water; pat dry. Refrigerate in plastic bag for up to 1 week.
Romaine	1 pound (1 head)	10 cups torn	Cut off bottom core. Rinse leaves in cold water; pat dry. Refrigerate in plastic bag for up to 5 days. Before using, remove fibrous rib from each leaf, if desired.
Spinach	1 pound	12 cups torn, stems removed	Rinse thoroughly in cold water to remove all sand; pat dry. Refrigerate in plastic bag for up to 3 days.
Watercress	4 ounces	2⅓ cups, stems removed	Rinse in cold water. Wrap in damp paper towels; refrigerate in plastic bag for up to 2 days.

*Line a resealable plastic bag with paper towels. For more information, see "Preparing Salad Greens," page 489.

CHOOSING GREENS

Vary the greens you choose depending on your tastes and how they will best complement the other ingredients in the salad. Follow these guidelines.

- Crunchy, mild-flavor greens, such as iceberg and romaine stand up to thick and/or creamy salad dressings.
- Soft and mild butterhead and red- or green-leaf lettuces are winning choices when you want the other salad ingredients, such as in-season fruits and vegetables, to stand out.
- Spicy and bitter greens, such as arugula, endive, frisée, radicchio, and watercress, make terrific choices when you want the flavor of the greens themselves to be a starring component of the salad.
- Rough, sturdy cabbages are best shredded. Perfect in coleslaw, they can also be added to green salads in smaller amounts for extra flavor and texture.

cook's secrets

classic potato salad

The Secret: If you're searching for a potato salad that is worthy of a family reunion, use a waxy potato variety and cook them with skins on.

POTATO SALAD POINTERS

1. SKINS ON
Boil potatoes, with skins on, about 15 minutes. Peeling the potatoes before cooking allows the starchy interior to absorb a lot of the liquid during boiling, resulting in a soggy, waterlogged salad.

↓

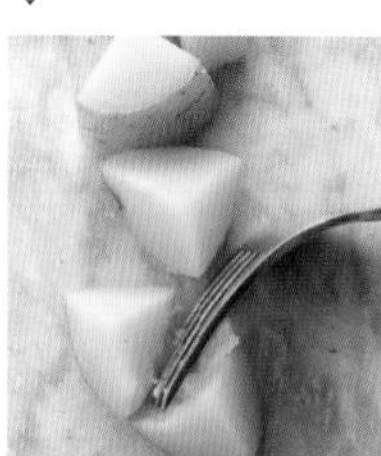

↑

2. LIFT & FOLD
Gently lift and fold ingredients until lightly coated. Folding together—as opposed to stirring—will keep the potato and egg pieces intact.

PREP: 40 MINUTES **CHILL:** 6 TO 24 HOURS **MAKES:** 12 SIDE-DISH SERVINGS

- **2 pounds red and/or yellow new potatoes, quartered**
- **1/4 teaspoon salt**
- **1 1/4 cups mayonnaise**
- **1 tablespoon yellow mustard**
- **1/2 teaspoon salt**
- **1/4 teaspoon black pepper**
- **1 cup thinly sliced celery (2 stalks)**
- **1/3 cup chopped onion (1 small)**
- **1/2 cup chopped sweet or dill pickles, or sweet or dill pickle relish**
- **6 Hard-Cooked Eggs, coarsely chopped**
- **Lettuce leaves (optional)**
- **Hard-Cooked Eggs, sliced (optional)**
- **Paprika (optional)**

For perfect Hard-Cooked Eggs, see page 130.

1 In a large saucepan combine potatoes, the 1/4 teaspoon salt, and enough cold water to cover. Bring to boiling; reduce heat. Simmer, covered, about 15 minutes or just until potatoes are tender. Drain well; cool slightly.

2 For dressing, in a large bowl combine mayonnaise, mustard, the 1/2 teaspoon salt, and pepper. Stir in celery, onion, and pickles. Fold in potatoes and eggs. Cover and chill for 6 to 24 hours.

3 To serve, if desired, line a salad bowl with lettuce leaves. Transfer the potato salad to the bowl. If desired, garnish with sliced eggs and/or sprinkle with paprika.

PER 1/2 CUP: 259 cal., 20 g total fat (4 g sat. fat), 103 mg chol., 389 mg sodium, 15 g carb., 2 g fiber, 5 g pro. EXCHANGES: 1 Starch, 1/2 Medium-Fat Meat, 3 1/2 Fat

TEX-MEX POTATO SALAD: Prepare Classic Potato Salad as directed, except reduce mayonnaise to 3/4 cup and omit yellow mustard, black pepper, and pickles. Stir 3/4 cup bottled ranch salad dressing and 1 canned chipotle chile pepper in adobo sauce, finely chopped (see tip, page 44), into dressing. Stir 1 cup rinsed and drained canned black beans and 1 cup frozen corn into salad with potatoes. Just before serving, garnish salad with tortilla chips.

PER 2/3 CUP: 300 cal., 21 g total fat (4 g sat. fat), 103 mg chol., 536 mg sodium, 23 g carb., 3 g fiber, 7 g pro. EXCHANGES: 1 1/2 Starch, 1/2 Medium-Fat Meat, 3 1/2 Fat

PICK THE RIGHT POTATO

There are hundreds of varieties of potatoes. The flesh of waxy potato varieties has a lower starch content and stays firm even after boiling, making waxy potatoes perfect for potato salad. They hold their shape but have a tender texture after cooking. Reds include Norland and Red La Soda; fingerlings, La Ratte and French fingerling; and yellows, Yukon gold.

HERB-GARLIC POTATO SALAD: Prepare Classic Potato Salad as directed, except omit pickles and use coarse ground mustard instead of yellow mustard. Preheat oven to 400°F. Cut off the top ½ inch of a garlic bulb to expose ends of individual cloves. Leaving garlic bulb whole, remove any loose, papery outer layers. Place garlic bulb in a custard cup. Drizzle with 1 teaspoon olive oil. Roast, covered, about 25 minutes or until garlic feels soft when squeezed; cool. Squeeze cloves from bulb into a small bowl, mash with a fork, and stir into dressing. Stir 1 tablespoon snipped fresh chives, parsley, or tarragon into the dressing. If desired, garnish with additional fresh herbs.

PER ½ CUP: 258 cal., 20 g total fat (4 g sat. fat), 103 mg chol., 360 mg sodium, 14 g carb., 2 g fiber, 5 g pro. **EXCHANGES:** 1 Starch, ½ Medium-Fat Meat, 3½ Fat

BLT POTATO SALAD: Prepare Classic Potato Salad as directed, except use ½ cup sliced green onions (4) instead of the ⅓ cup chopped onion. In a large skillet cook 6 slices bacon over medium heat until crisp. Remove bacon and drain on paper towels, reserving 1 tablespoon drippings in skillet. Crumble bacon; set aside. Add 1 clove garlic, minced, to the reserved drippings; cook and stir for 30 seconds. Stir garlic mixture into dressing. Stir crumbled bacon and 1 cup chopped tomato into salad with the potatoes. Serve in a lettuce-lined bowl or serve over shredded romaine lettuce.

PER ½ CUP: 294 cal., 23 g total fat (5 g sat. fat), 108 mg chol., 462 mg sodium, 16 g carb., 2 g fiber, 7 g pro. **EXCHANGES:** 1 Starch, ½ Medium-Fat Meat, 4 Fat

Top with summer-fresh tomatoes if you have them. If not, try cherry or grape tomatoes, halved.

LOWER CAL

To cut the fat and calories in any of these potato salad recipes, use reduced-fat mayonnaise, a combination of light sour cream and mayonnaise, or a combo of plain yogurt and mayonnaise.

Tex-Mex

Herb-Garlic

BLT

BLUE CHEESE DRESSING, CREAMY FRENCH DRESSING, AND PARMESAN DRESSING

Buttermilk Dressing

PREP: 10 MINUTES **CHILL:** 30 MINUTES
MAKES: 20 SERVINGS

- **3/4 cup buttermilk**
- **1/2 cup mayonnaise**
- **1 tablespoon snipped fresh Italian parsley**
- **1/4 teaspoon onion powder**
- **1/4 teaspoon dry mustard**
- **1/4 teaspoon black pepper**
- **1 clove garlic, minced**

1 In bowl mix 3/4 cup buttermilk, mayonnaise, parsley, onion powder, mustard, pepper, and garlic. If necessary, add additional buttermilk until dressing reaches desired consistency. Cover and chill dressing for 30 minutes to 1 week before serving. Stir or shake well to use.

PEPPERCORN-BUTTERMILK DRESSING: Prepare as directed, except omit ground black pepper and stir in 1/2 teaspoon cracked black pepper.

PER 1 TABLESPOON PLAIN OR PEPPERCORN VARIATION: 44 cal., 4 g total fat (1 g sat. fat), 2 mg chol., 40 mg sodium, 1 g carb., 0 g fiber, 0 g pro. EXCHANGES: 1 Fat

BACON-BUTTERMILK DRESSING: Prepare as directed, except cook 4 slices bacon until crisp; drain and crumble, reserving 1 tablespoon bacon drippings. Stir crumbled bacon and drippings into dressing just before serving. Cover; chill for up to 3 days.

PER 1 TABLESPOON: 55 cal., 6 g total fat (1 g sat. fat), 5 mg chol., 74 mg sodium, 1 g carb., 0 g fiber, 1 g pro. EXCHANGES: 1½ Fat

BEST-LOVED FAST

Blue Cheese Dressing

START TO FINISH: 10 MINUTES **MAKES:** 20 SERVINGS

- **1/2 cup plain yogurt or sour cream**
- **1/4 cup cottage cheese**
- **1/4 cup mayonnaise**
- **3/4 to 1 cup crumbled blue cheese (3 to 4 ounces)**
- **1/4 teaspoon salt**
- **1/4 teaspoon cracked black pepper**
- **1 to 2 tablespoons milk (optional)**

1 In a blender or food processor combine yogurt, cottage cheese, mayonnaise, 1/4 cup of the crumbled blue cheese, salt, and pepper. Cover and blend or process until smooth. Stir in remaining blue cheese. If necessary, stir in milk until dressing reaches desired consistency. Serve immediately or cover and chill for up to 2 weeks. Stir before using.

PER 1 TABLESPOON: 44 cal., 4 g total fat (2 g sat. fat), 6 mg chol., 127 mg sodium, 1 g carb., 0 g fiber, 2 g pro. EXCHANGES: 1 Fat

FAST

Creamy French Dressing

START TO FINISH: 15 MINUTES **MAKES:** 32 SERVINGS

- **1/3 cup water**
- **1/3 cup vinegar**
- **2 tablespoons sugar**
- **1 tablespoon lemon juice**
- **2 teaspoons paprika**
- **1 teaspoon salt**
- **1 teaspoon dry mustard**
- **1 teaspoon black pepper**
- **1 teaspoon Worcestershire sauce**
- **1 clove garlic, quartered**
- **1⅓ cups vegetable oil or olive oil**

1 In a blender combine water, vinegar, sugar, lemon juice, paprika, salt, mustard, pepper, Worcestershire sauce, and garlic. Cover and blend until combined. With blender running, slowly add oil in a thin, steady stream (dressing thickens as oil is added). Serve immediately or cover; chill up to 2 weeks. Stir before serving.

PER 1 TABLESPOON: 85 cal., 9 g total fat (1 g sat. fat), 0 mg chol., 75 mg sodium, 1 g carb., 0 g fiber, 0 g pro. EXCHANGES: 2 Fat

BEST MADE AHEAD

Mix up your homemade salad dressing a day ahead of serving if possible. The extra time allows the flavors to blend and intensify compared with dressing served immediately.

FAST

Creamy Parmesan Dressing

START TO FINISH: 10 MINUTES **MAKES:** 16 SERVINGS

- **½ cup mayonnaise**
- **¼ cup grated Parmesan cheese (1 ounce)**
- **¼ cup buttermilk**
- **3 cloves garlic, minced**
- **1 tablespoon snipped fresh Italian parsley**

1 In a small bowl stir together mayonnaise, cheese, buttermilk, garlic, and parsley. Cover and chill for up to 1 week. Stir before using. If necessary, add additional buttermilk if dressing thickens during chilling.

PER 1 TABLESPOON: 58 cal., 6 g total fat (1 g sat. fat), 4 mg chol., 61 mg sodium, 0 g carb., 0 g fiber, 1 g pro. EXCHANGES: 1 Fat

FAST

Creamy Italian Dressing

START TO FINISH: 15 MINUTES **MAKES:** 16 SERVINGS

- **¾ cup mayonnaise**
- **¼ cup sour cream**
- **2 teaspoons white wine vinegar or white vinegar**
- **1 clove garlic, minced**
- **½ teaspoon dried Italian seasoning**
- **¼ teaspoon dry mustard**
- **⅛ teaspoon salt**
- **1 to 2 tablespoons milk (optional)**

1 In a small bowl stir together mayonnaise, sour cream, vinegar, garlic, Italian seasoning, mustard, and salt. Serve immediately or cover and chill for up to 1 week. Before serving, if necessary, stir in milk until dressing reaches desired consistency.

CREAMY GARLIC DRESSING: Prepare as directed, except add 2 additional cloves garlic, minced.

PER 1 TABLESPOON PLAIN OR GARLIC VARIATION: 82 cal., 9 g total fat (2 g sat. fat), 5 mg chol., 77 mg sodium, 0 g carb., 0 g fiber, 0 g pro. EXCHANGES: 2 Fat

FAST

Thousand Island Dressing *(photo, page 487)*

START TO FINISH: 15 MINUTES **MAKES:** 24 SERVINGS

- **1 cup mayonnaise**
- **¼ cup bottled chili sauce**
- **2 tablespoons sweet pickle relish**
- **2 tablespoons finely chopped sweet pepper**
- **2 tablespoons finely chopped onion**
- **1 teaspoon Worcestershire sauce**
- **1 to 2 tablespoons milk (optional)**

1 In a small bowl combine mayonnaise and chili sauce. Stir in relish, sweet pepper, onion, and Worcestershire sauce. Serve immediately or cover and chill for up to 1 week. Before serving, if necessary, stir in milk until dressing reaches desired consistency.

PER 1 TABLESPOON: 71 cal., 7 g total fat (1 g sat. fat), 3 mg chol., 93 mg sodium, 1 g carb., 0 g fiber, 0 g pro. EXCHANGES: 1½ Fat

FAST

Honey-Mustard Dressing

START TO FINISH: 10 MINUTES **MAKES:** 16 SERVINGS

- **¼ cup stone-ground mustard**
- **¼ cup olive oil or vegetable oil**
- **¼ cup lemon juice**
- **¼ cup honey**
- **2 cloves garlic, minced**

1 In a screw-top jar combine mustard, oil, lemon juice, honey, and garlic. Cover and shake well. Serve immediately or cover and chill for up to 1 week. Stir or shake well before using.

PER 1 TABLESPOON: 51 cal., 4 g total fat (0 g sat. fat), 0 mg chol., 51 mg sodium, 5 g carb., 0 g fiber, 0 g pro. EXCHANGES: 1 Fat

FAST

Orange-Poppy Seed Dressing

START TO FINISH: 15 MINUTES **MAKES:** 10 SERVINGS

- **2 tablespoons honey**
- **1½ teaspoons finely shredded orange peel**
- **2 tablespoons orange juice**
- **2 tablespoons vinegar**
- **1 tablespoon finely chopped onion**
- **⅛ teaspoon salt**
- **Dash black pepper**
- **⅓ cup vegetable oil**
- **1 teaspoon poppy seeds**

1 In a small food processor or a blender combine honey, orange peel, orange juice, vinegar, onion, salt, and pepper. Cover and process or blend until combined. With processor or blender running, slowly add oil in a steady stream until mixture is thickened. Stir in the poppy seeds. Serve immediately or cover and chill for up to 1 week. Stir or shake well before using.

PER 1 TABLESPOON: 81 cal., 7 g total fat (1 g sat. fat), 0 mg chol., 30 mg sodium, 4 g carb., 0 g fiber, 0 g pro. EXCHANGES: 1½ Fat

FAST

Fresh Herb Vinaigrette

START TO FINISH: 10 MINUTES **MAKES:** 28 SERVINGS

- **1 cup olive oil or vegetable oil**
- **⅓ cup red wine vinegar, white wine vinegar, rice vinegar, or cider vinegar**
- **¼ cup finely chopped shallots**
- **2 tablespoons snipped fresh oregano, thyme, or basil; or 1 teaspoon dried oregano, thyme, or basil, crushed**
- **1 tablespoon Dijon-style mustard or ½ teaspoon dry mustard**
- **2 to 3 teaspoons sugar**
- **2 cloves garlic, minced**
- **¼ teaspoon salt**
- **¼ teaspoon black pepper**

1 In a screw-top jar combine oil, vinegar, shallots, herb, mustard, sugar, garlic, salt, and pepper. Cover; shake well. Serve immediately.

BALSAMIC VINAIGRETTE: Prepare as directed, except use regular or white balsamic vinegar.

TO STORE: If using fresh herbs, cover and chill for up to 3 days. If using dried herbs, cover and chill for up to 1 week. The olive oil will solidify when chilled, so let vinaigrette stand at room temperature for 1 hour before using. Stir or shake well before using.

PER TABLESPOON PLAIN OR BALSAMIC VARIATION: 72 cal., 8 g total fat (1 g sat. fat), 0 mg chol., 34 mg sodium, 1 g carb., 0 g fiber, 0 g pro. EXCHANGES: 1½ Fat

Like a classic vinaigrette, Fresh Herb Vinaigrette combines 3 parts oil to 1 part vinegar. Mustard adds the zing.

FAST

Chef's Salad

START TO FINISH: 30 MINUTES
MAKES: 4 MAIN-DISH SERVINGS

- **4 cups torn iceberg or leaf lettuce**
- **4 cups torn romaine or fresh spinach**
- **4 ounces cooked ham, chicken, turkey, or beef, cut into bite-size strips (1 cup)**
- **4 ounces Swiss, cheddar, American, or provolone cheese, cut into bite-size strips**
- **2 Hard-Cooked Eggs, sliced (page 130)**
- **2 medium tomatoes, cut into wedges, or 8 cherry tomatoes, halved**
- **1 small green or red sweet pepper, cut into bite-size strips (½ cup)**
- **1 cup Parmesan Croutons (page 500) or purchased croutons**
- **½ cup Creamy French Dressing (page 494), Buttermilk Dressing (page 494), Creamy Italian Dressing (page 495), or other salad dressing**

1 In a large bowl toss together greens. Divide among four large salad plates. Arrange meat, cheese, eggs, tomatoes, and sweet pepper strips on top of the greens. Sprinkle with croutons. Drizzle desired salad dressing over all, passing any remaining dressing.

PER 2 CUPS: 494 cal., 38 g total fat (12 g sat. fat), 165 mg chol., 775 mg sodium, 19 g carb., 4 g fiber, 20 g pro.
EXCHANGES: 2 Vegetable, ½ Starch, 2 Lean Meat, 6½ Fat

MEXICAN CHEF'S SALAD: Prepare as directed, except use chicken, beef, or pork, and cheddar cheese or Monterery Jack cheese. Omit eggs. Add one 4- to 4.5-ounce can diced green chile peppers, drained, and ¼ cup sliced ripe black olives. Substitute corn chips for croutons. For dressing, stir together ¼ cup bottled Thousand Island salad dressing and ¼ cup bottled salsa.

PER 2 CUPS: 358 cal., 23 g total fat (59 g sat. fat), 59 mg chol., 686 mg sodium, 20 g carb., 4 g fiber, 19 g pro.
EXCHANGES: 2 Vegetable, ½ Starch, 2 Very Lean Meat, 3½ Fat

ITALIAN CHEF'S SALAD: Prepare as directed, except use 2 ounces chicken and mozzarella cheese. Omit eggs. Add 2 ounces sliced pepperoni; a 6-ounce jar marinated artichoke heart quarters, drained; and ¼ cup sliced ripe black olives. For the dressing, use Creamy Italian Dressing or a bottled Italian vinaigrette.

PER 2 CUPS: 473 cal., 34 g total fat (13 g sat. fat), 67 mg chol., 1,184 mg sodium, 22 g carb., 3 g fiber, 18 g pro.
EXCHANGES: 1 Starch, 2 Vegetable, 1½ Very Lean Meat, 6 Fat

BEST-LOVED

Taco Salad

PREP: 40 MINUTES **BAKE:** 12 MINUTES AT 350°F
MAKES: 6 MAIN-DISH SERVINGS

- **1 recipe Tortilla Shells or 6 purchased taco salad shells**
- **8 ounces lean ground beef or uncooked ground turkey**
- **3 cloves garlic, minced**
- **1 15-ounce can dark red kidney beans or black beans, rinsed and drained**
- **1 cup bottled salsa**
- **¾ cup frozen whole kernel corn, thawed (optional)**
- **6 cups shredded leaf or iceberg lettuce**
- **1 cup chopped tomatoes (2 medium)**
- **1 cup chopped green sweet pepper (1 large)**
- **½ cup thinly sliced green onions (4)**
- **1 cup chopped avocado (1 medium)**
- **¾ cup shredded sharp cheddar cheese (3 ounces)**
- **Sour cream (optional)**

1 Prepare Tortilla Shells or heat taco salad shells according to package directions; set aside. In a medium saucepan cook ground beef and garlic until beef is browned. Drain off fat. Stir in kidney beans, 1 cup salsa, and, if desired, thawed corn. Bring to boiling; reduce heat. Simmer, covered, for 10 minutes.

2 Meanwhile, in a very large bowl combine lettuce, tomatoes, sweet pepper, and green onions. To serve, divide lettuce mixture among the salad shells. Top each serving with some of the meat mixture and avocado. Sprinkle with cheese. If desired, serve with sour cream and additional salsa.

TORTILLA SHELLS: Preheat oven to 350°F. Lightly coat six 8-inch flour tortillas with nonstick cooking spray. Coat the outside of six 6-ounce custard cups with nonstick cooking spray and place cups, sprayed sides up, on a baking sheet. Press tortillas, coated sides up, onto prepared custard cups, pleating as necessary. Bake for 12 to 15 minutes or until lightly browned. Remove and cool completely. Serve immediately or store in an airtight container for up to 5 days.

PER SALAD: 423 cal., 18 g total fat (6 g sat. fat), 23 mg chol., 1,005 mg sodium, 45 g carb., 7 g fiber, 21 g pro.
EXCHANGES: 2 Vegetable, 2 Starch, 1½ Medium-Fat Meat, 1½ Fat

TORTILLA SHELLS POINTERS

1. Carefully fit each tortilla over a 6-ounce oven-safe bowl coated with nonstick cooking spray, pleating edges as needed to fit. After lightly browned, let cool before removing.

2. No time to make tortilla shells? Build your Taco Salad on a bed of tortilla chips.

Tuna or Salmon Salad

PREP: 20 MINUTES **CHILL:** 60 MINUTES TO 24 HOURS
MAKES: 4 MAIN-DISH SERVINGS

- **1 12-ounce can solid white tuna or two 6-ounce pouches skinless, boneless pink salmon, drained and flaked**
- **½ cup celery, chopped (1 stalk)**
- **¼ cup thinly sliced green onions (2)**
- **3 tablespoons chopped sweet pickles**
- **½ cup mayonnaise**
- **1 tablespoon lemon juice**
- **2 teaspoons snipped fresh dill weed or ½ teaspoon dried dill weed**
- **Bread slices or mixed salad greens (optional)**

1 In a medium bowl combine tuna, celery, green onions, and chopped sweet pickle. For dressing, in a small bowl stir together mayonnaise, lemon juice, and dill weed. Add to tuna mixture; toss to coat. Cover and chill for 60 minutes to 24 hours before serving. Serve as a sandwich filling on bread slices or over mixed salad greens.

PER ½ CUP: 321 cal., 25 g total fat (5 g sat. fat), 46 mg chol., 518 mg sodium, 3 g carb., 0 g fiber, 20 g pro.
EXCHANGES: 3 Lean Meat, 3½ Fat

CHOPPED CHICKEN SALAD

Chopped Chicken Salad

START TO FINISH: 45 MINUTES
MAKES: 6 MAIN-DISH SERVINGS

- **6 thin slices prosciutto (about 4 ounces)**
- **½ cup olive oil**
- **4 skinless, boneless chicken breast halves (6 to 8 ounces each)**
- **Salt and black pepper**
- **Paprika**
- **2 lemons**
- **2 tablespoons finely chopped shallot (1)**
- **⅔ cup thinly sliced, peeled carrots**
- **2½ cups chopped zucchini (2 medium)**
- **¾ cup chopped red sweet pepper (1 medium)**
- **¾ cup chopped yellow sweet pepper (1 medium)**
- **¼ cup chopped red onion (½ small)**
- **5 ounces blue cheese, crumbled**
- **Romaine lettuce leaves**

1 Preheat oven to 400°F. Place prosciutto in single layer on large baking sheet. Bake for 8 to 10 minutes or until crisp; cool. Crumble and set aside.

2 In a large nonstick skillet heat 1 tablespoon olive oil over medium heat. Sprinkle chicken with salt, pepper, and paprika; add to skillet. Cook 15 to 18 minutes or until chicken is done (165°F), turning once. Cool slightly; slice.

3 For dressing, finely shred peel from one lemon; squeeze both lemons to make ⅓ cup juice. In a small bowl whisk together remaining olive oil, lemon juice, shredded peel, and shallot. Season to taste with salt and pepper.

4 In a large bowl combine sliced chicken, carrots, zucchini, sweet peppers, and onion. Toss with dressing. Add blue cheese. Line salad plates with romaine. Spoon in chicken mixture. Top with prosciutto.

PER 1½ CUPS: 434 cal., 28 g total fat (8 g sat. fat), 86 mg chol., 923 mg sodium, 14 g carb., 5 g fiber, 35 g pro.
EXCHANGES: 1 Vegetable, ½ Starch, 4½ Lean Meat, 3 Fat

Salad Niçoise

PREP: 40 MINUTES **CHILL:** 2 TO 24 HOURS
MAKES: 4 MAIN-DISH SERVINGS

- **8 ounces fresh green beans (2 cups)**
- **12 ounces tiny new potatoes, scrubbed and sliced (8)**
- **1 recipe Niçoise Dressing or ½ cup bottled balsamic vinaigrette salad dressing**
- **Spring greens and/or baby lettuce**
- **1½ cups flaked cooked tuna or salmon (8 ounces) or one 9.25-ounce can solid white tuna (water pack), drained and broken into chunks**
- **2 medium tomatoes, cut into wedges**
- **2 Hard-Cooked Eggs, sliced, halved, or quartered (page 130)**
- **½ cup niçoise or Kalamata olives**
- **¼ cup thinly sliced green onions (2)**
- **4 anchovy fillets, drained, rinsed, and patted dry (optional)**

1 Wash green beans; remove ends and strings. In a large saucepan cook green beans and potatoes, covered, in a small amount of lightly salted boiling water about 10 minutes or just until tender. Drain; place vegetables in a medium bowl. Cover and chill for 2 to 24 hours.

2 Prepare Niçoise Dressing. To serve, line four salad plates with greens. Arrange chilled vegetables, tuna, tomatoes, eggs, and olives over the greens. Sprinkle each serving with green onions. If desired, top each salad with an anchovy fillet. Shake dressing; drizzle over the salads.

NIÇOISE DRESSING: In a screw-top jar combine ¼ cup olive or vegetable oil, ¼ cup white wine vinegar, 1 teaspoon honey, 1 teaspoon snipped fresh tarragon or ¼ teaspoon crushed dried tarragon, 1 teaspoon Dijon-style mustard, ¼ teaspoon salt, and a dash black pepper. Cover and shake well.

PER 1½ CUPS: 473 cal., 28 g total fat (5 g sat. fat), 134 mg chol., 512 mg sodium, 32 g carb., 7 g fiber, 25 g pro.
EXCHANGES: 2 Vegetable, 1½ Starch, 2½ Lean Meat, 4 Fat

8 to try

BUFFALO: Omit basil. Stir in ½ cup crumbled blue cheese and ¼ to ½ teaspoon hot pepper sauce.

MEDITERRANEAN: Omit celery. Stir in ½ cup chopped marinated artichoke hearts and ¼ cup crumbled feta cheese.

Chicken Salad

Versatile chicken salad works as well on its own as in a sandwich. Pop the flavor with one of these stir-in blends.

PREP: 20 MINUTES
CHILL: 1 TO 4 HOURS
MAKES: 4 MAIN-DISH SERVINGS

- **2 cups chopped cooked chicken or turkey (8 ounces)**
- **½ cup chopped celery (1 stalk)**
- **¼ cup thinly sliced green onions (2)**
- **⅓ to ½ cup mayonnaise**
- **1 teaspoon snipped fresh basil or ¼ teaspoon dried basil, crushed**
- **½ teaspoon finely shredded lemon peel (optional)**
- **¼ teaspoon salt**
- **Bread slices or mixed salad greens (optional)**

1 In a medium bowl combine chicken, celery, and green onions. For dressing, in a small bowl stir together mayonnaise, basil, lemon peel (if desired), and salt. Pour dressing over chicken mixture; toss gently to coat. Cover and chill for 1 to 4 hours. If desired, serve on bread or over mixed salad greens.

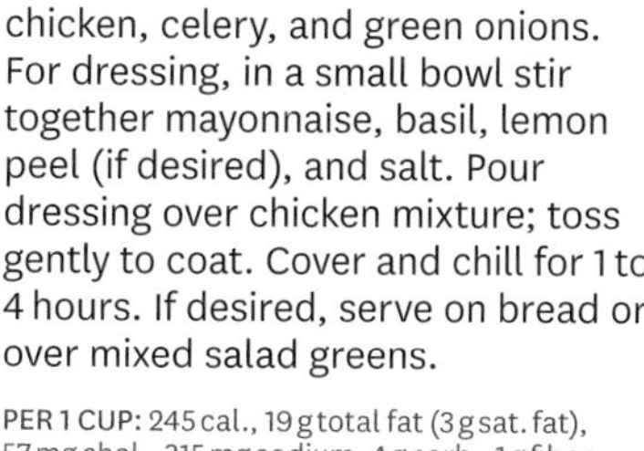

PER 1 CUP: 245 cal., 19 g total fat (3 g sat. fat), 57 mg chol., 315 mg sodium, 4 g carb., 1 g fiber, 16 g pro. EXCHANGES: 1 Vegetable, 2 Lean Meat, 2½ Fat

HAWAIIAN: Stir in ½ cup chopped pineapple. Before serving, stir in ¼ cup chopped macadamia nuts.

GRAPE-NUT: Stir in ¾ cup halved seedless grapes. Before serving, stir in ⅓ cup chopped toasted walnuts.

APPLE: Stir in ¾ cup chopped apple. Before serving, stir in ⅓ cup chopped toasted pecans.

CUCUMBER: Before serving, stir in ½ cup chopped cucumber.

CILANTRO-LIME: Omit basil and lemon peel. Stir in 1 tablespoon snipped cilantro and ½ teaspoon shredded lime peel. Top with toasted sesame seeds and cilantro.

CASHEW-CURRY: Stir in 1 to 2 teaspoons curry powder. Before serving, stir in 2 tablespoons chopped roasted cashews.

WHEN YOU NEED COOKED CHICKEN

Here are several ways to get cooked chicken. What fits your schedule?

1 Buy ready-to-use rotisserie chicken; remove meat and chop to make 2 cups total. Freeze the extra.

2 Grill two 6- to 8-ounce skinless, boneless chicken breast halves over medium heat 15 to 18 minutes; chop.

3 Skillet-cook two 6- to 8-ounce chicken breast halves in oil over medium heat for 15 to 18 minutes, turning once halfway through cooking; chop.

Note: Cook chicken until done (165°F).

CAESAR SALAD

BEST-LOVED

Caesar Salad

PREP: 30 MINUTES **BAKE:** 20 MINUTES AT 300°F
MAKES: 6 SIDE-DISH SERVINGS

- **3 cloves garlic**
- **3 anchovy fillets**
- **2 tablespoons lemon juice**
- **¼ cup olive oil**
- **1 teaspoon Dijon-style mustard**
- **½ teaspoon sugar**
- **1 Hard-Cooked Egg yolk (page 130)**
- **1 clove garlic, halved**
- **10 cups torn romaine lettuce (photo 1, right)**
- **¼ cup grated Parmesan cheese (1 ounce) or ½ cup Parmesan curls**
- **1 recipe Parmesan Croutons or 2 cups purchased garlic Parmesan croutons**
- **Freshly ground black pepper**
- **Lemon wedges**

1 For dressing, in a blender combine 3 garlic cloves, anchovy fillets, and lemon juice. Cover and blend until mixture is nearly smooth, stopping to scrape down sides as needed. Add oil, mustard, sugar, and cooked egg yolk. Cover and blend or process until smooth. Use immediately or cover and chill up to 24 hours.

2 To serve, rub inside of a wooden salad bowl with cut edges of halved garlic clove (photo 2, right); discard clove. Add romaine to bowl. Drizzle dressing over salad; toss lightly to coat. Sprinkle Parmesan cheese over top of salad; toss gently. Top with Parmesan Croutons; sprinkle with pepper. If desired, sprinkle with additional Parmesan cheese and serve with lemon wedges.

PARMESAN CROUTONS: Preheat oven to 300°F. Cut four ¾-inch-thick slices Italian bread or French bread into 1-inch pieces (you should have about 3½ cups bread pieces); set aside. In a small saucepan melt ¼ cup butter over medium heat. Transfer to a large bowl. Stir in 3 tablespoons grated Parmesan cheese and 2 cloves garlic, minced. Add bread pieces; stir to coat. Spread bread pieces in a single layer in a shallow baking pan. Bake about 20 minutes or until bread pieces are crisp and golden brown, stirring once. Cool completely. If desired, store in an airtight container at room temperature for up to 24 hours before using.

PER 1⅔ CUPS: 261 cal., 20 g fat (8 g sat. fat), 62 mg chol., 362 mg sodium, 15 g carb., 2 g fiber, 6 g pro.
EXCHANGES: 1 Vegetable, ½ Starch, ½ Medium-Fat Meat, 3½ Fat

CHICKEN CAESAR SALAD: Prepare the Caesar Salad as directed, except add 2 cups chopped cooked chicken with the romaine. Makes 6 main-dish servings.

PER 2 CUPS: 350 cal., 15 g total fat (9 g sat. fat), 104 mg chol., 402 mg sodium, 15 g carb., 2 g fiber, 20 g pro.
EXCHANGES: ½ Starch, 1 Vegetable, 2½ Very Lean Meat, 3 Fat

CAESAR SALAD POINTERS

1. You can remove the woody rib from the romaine by tearing away the outer leaves. Want the extra crunch? Leave the rib and tear leaves into pieces.

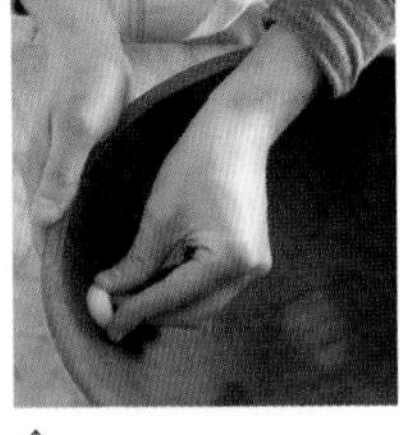

2. For a classic Caesar, use a wooden salad bowl and rub a raw, halved garlic clove around the inside. The wood soaks up the garlic oil, adding a subtle tang. Or use any bowl and add extra garlic to the dressing.

ROASTED ROOT VEGETABLE AND WILTED ROMAINE SALAD

LOW-CALORIE

Roasted Root Vegetable and Wilted Romaine Salad

PREP: 30 MINUTES
BAKE: 30 MINUTES AT 375°F/30 MINUTES AT 425°F
MAKES: 12 SIDE-DISH SERVINGS

- **2 medium fresh beets (about 12 ounces)**
- **7 tablespoons olive oil**
- **Salt and black pepper**
- **1¾ pounds fresh carrots, turnips, and/or parsnips**
- **4 medium shallots, peeled and quartered**
- **2 tablespoons white wine vinegar**
- **1 tablespoon snipped fresh thyme**
- **1 teaspoon Dijon-style mustard**
- **1 teaspoon honey**
- **1 clove garlic, minced**
- **8 cups torn romaine lettuce**
- **½ cup chopped pecans, toasted**
- **¼ cup chopped fresh Italian parsley**

1 Preheat the oven to 375°F. Wash and peel the beets; cut into 1-inch pieces. Place in a 2-quart baking dish. Toss with 1 tablespoon of the olive oil and salt and pepper to taste. Cover dish tightly with foil and bake for 30 minutes.

2 Meanwhile, peel the carrots, turnips, and/or parsnips. Cut carrots and turnips into irregular-shape 1-inch pieces. Cut parsnips into irregular ¾-inch pieces. Place the root vegetables in a 15×10×1-inch baking pan. Add shallots. Toss with 1 tablespoon of the olive oil. Sprinkle with additional salt and pepper.

3 Remove foil from dish with beets; stir beets gently. Increase oven temperature to 425°F. Return beets to oven and place pan with shallot mixture alongside beets. Roast both pans, uncovered, for 30 to 40 minutes or until tender.

4 Meanwhile, for dressing, in a screw-top jar combine the remaining 5 tablespoons olive oil, the white wine vinegar, thyme, Dijon-style mustard, honey, garlic, and additional salt and pepper to taste; cover and shake well.

5 To serve, in a large bowl toss the romaine with the dressing to coat. Place on a platter. Top with the hot roasted vegetables. Sprinkle with pecans and parsley. Serve immediately.

MAKE-AHEAD DIRECTIONS: Prepare dressing; chill for up to 3 days. To serve, bring dressing to room temperature; shake well before using.

PER 1 CUP: 158 cal., 13 g total fat (2 g sat. fat), 0 mg chol., 167 mg sodium, 11 g carb., 4 g fiber, 2 g pro.
EXCHANGES: 2 Vegetable, 2 Fat

FAST LOW-CALORIE

Wilted Spinach Salad

START TO FINISH: 25 MINUTES
MAKES: 4 SIDE-DISH SERVINGS

- **8 cups fresh baby spinach or torn spinach (5 ounces)**
- **1 cup sliced fresh mushrooms**
- **¼ cup thinly sliced green onions (2)**
- **Dash black pepper (optional)**
- **3 slices bacon**
- **Vegetable oil (optional)**
- **¼ cup vinegar**
- **2 teaspoons sugar**
- **½ teaspoon dry mustard**
- **1 Hard-Cooked Egg, chopped (page 130)**

1 In a large bowl combine spinach, mushrooms, and green onions. If desired, sprinkle with pepper; set aside.

2 For dressing, in a very large skillet cook bacon until crisp. Remove bacon, reserving 2 tablespoons drippings in skillet (add vegetable oil if necessary). (If desired, substitute 2 tablespoons vegetable oil for bacon drippings.) Crumble bacon; set aside. Stir vinegar, sugar, and dry mustard into drippings. Bring to boiling; remove from heat. Add the spinach mixture. Toss mixture in skillet for 30 to 60 seconds or until spinach just wilts.

3 Transfer spinach mixture to a serving dish. Add crumbled bacon and chopped egg; toss to combine. Serve salad immediately.

PER 1 CUP: 157 cal., 11 g total fat (4 g sat. fat), 66 mg chol., 253 mg sodium, 8 g carb., 3 g fiber, 7 g pro.
EXCHANGES: 2 Vegetable, ½ High-Fat Meat, 1½ Fat

WILTED GARDEN GREENS SALAD: Prepare as directed, except omit the spinach and use 8 cups arugula or torn leaf lettuce (5 ounces). Omit egg.

PER 1 CUP: 121 cal., 10 g total fat (3 g sat. fat), 13 mg chol., 162 mg sodium, 5 g carb., 1 g fiber, 4 g pro. EXCHANGES: 2 Vegetable, 2 Fat

FAST LOW-CALORIE

Greek Salad

START TO FINISH: 15 MINUTES
MAKES: 6 SIDE-DISH SERVINGS

- **6 cups torn mixed salad greens or romaine lettuce leaves**
- **2 medium tomatoes, cut into wedges, or 8 cherry tomatoes, halved**
- **1 small cucumber, halved lengthwise and thinly sliced**
- **1 small red onion, cut into thin wedges**
- **½ cup pitted Kalamata olives**
- **½ cup crumbled feta cheese (2 ounces)**
- **1 recipe Greek Vinaigrette**
- **2 small pita bread rounds, cut into wedges (optional)**

1 In a salad bowl combine salad greens, tomatoes, cucumber, onion, olives, and crumbled cheese. Add Greek Vinaigrette; toss to coat. If desired, serve salad with the pita bread wedges.

GREEK VINAIGRETTE: In a screw-top jar combine 2 tablespoons olive oil or vegetable oil, 2 tablespoons lemon juice, 2 teaspoons snipped fresh oregano or ½ teaspoon crushed dried oregano, ⅛ teaspoon salt, and ⅛ teaspoon black pepper. Cover and shake well.

PER 1⅔ CUPS: 112 cal., 8 g total fat (2 g sat. fat), 8 mg chol., 303 mg sodium, 8 g carb., 2 g fiber, 3 g pro.
EXCHANGES: 1½ Vegetable, 1½ Fat

LOW-CALORIE

Creamy Coleslaw

PREP: 20 MINUTES **CHILL:** 2 TO 24 HOURS
MAKES: 6 SIDE-DISH SERVINGS

- **½ cup mayonnaise**
- **1 tablespoon vinegar**
- **1 to 2 teaspoons sugar**
- **½ teaspoon celery seeds**
- **¼ teaspoon salt**
- **4 cups shredded green and/or red cabbage* (photos 1 and 2, below)**
- **1 cup shredded carrots* (2 medium)**
- **¼ cup thinly sliced green onions (2)**

SHREDDING CABBAGE STEP-BY-STEP

1. Using a large chef's knife, cut cabbage head into wedges; remove and discard the core from each.

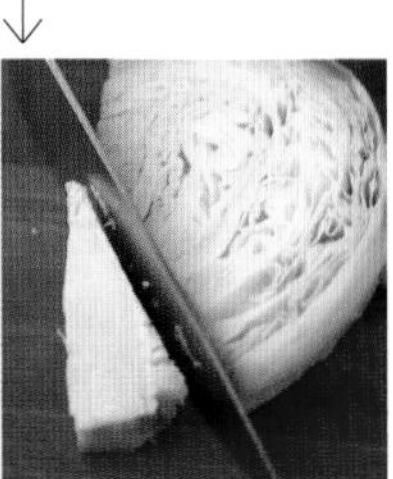

2. Thinly slice cored cabbage wedge into shreds, cutting across the grain of the leaves.

1 For dressing, in a large bowl stir together mayonnaise, vinegar, sugar, celery seeds, and salt. Add cabbage, carrots, and onions. Toss lightly to coat. Cover; chill 2 to 24 hours.

***NOTE:** If desired, substitute 5 cups packaged shredded cabbage with carrot (coleslaw mix) for cabbage and carrots.

PER 3/4 CUP: 159 cal., 15 g total fat (3 g sat. fat), 7 mg chol., 220 mg sodium, 6 g carb., 2 g fiber, 1 g pro.
EXCHANGES: 1 Vegetable, 3 Fat

LOW-CALORIE

Vinaigrette Coleslaw

PREP: 20 MINUTES **CHILL:** 2 TO 24 HOURS
MAKES: 6 SIDE-DISH SERVINGS

- **3 tablespoons cider vinegar**
- **2 tablespoons sugar**
- **2 tablespoons vegetable oil**
- **1/2 teaspoon celery or caraway seeds (optional)**
- **1/4 teaspoon salt**
- **1/4 teaspoon dry mustard**
- **1/8 to 1/4 teaspoon black pepper**
- **4 cups shredded green and/or red cabbage* (photos 1 and 2, page 502)**
- **1 cup shredded carrots* (2 medium)**
- **1/4 cup thinly sliced green onions (2)**

1 For vinaigrette, in a screw-top jar combine vinegar, sugar, oil, caraway seeds (if desired), salt, mustard, and pepper. Cover; shake well. In a large bowl combine cabbage, carrots, and green onions. Pour vinaigrette over cabbage mixture; toss lightly. Cover; chill 2 to 24 hours.

***NOTE:** If desired, substitute 5 cups packaged shredded cabbage with carrot (coleslaw mix) for the cabbage and carrots.

PER 3/4 CUP: 79 cal., 5 g total fat (0 g sat. fat), 0 mg chol., 120 mg sodium, 10 g carb., 2 g fiber, 1 g pro.
EXCHANGES: 1/2 Vegetable, 1/2 Other Carb., 1 Fat

FAST LOW-CALORIE

Winter Slaw

START TO FINISH: 25 MINUTES
MAKES: 10 SIDE-DISH SERVINGS

- **4 cups shredded kale, stems removed (4 ounces)**
- **1 teaspoon salt**
- **1 tablespoon olive oil**
- **4 cups shredded savoy cabbage**
- **1 cup shredded purple cabbage**
- **1 cup shredded carrots (2 medium)**
- **3/4 cup packed finely snipped Italian parsley**
- **1/3 cup mayonnaise**
- **3 tablespoons sour cream**
- **2 tablespoons sliced green onion (1)**
- **1 tablespoon white wine vinegar**
- **1 tablespoon snipped fresh tarragon or 1/4 teaspoon dried tarragon, crushed**
- **1 teaspoon sugar**
- **1 clove garlic, minced**
- **1/2 cup pepitas (pumpkin seeds), toasted**

WINTER SLAW

1 In an extra-large bowl combine the kale, salt, and olive oil. Using your hands, rub the kale to help soften it and brighten its color. Rinse the kale in a colander under cool running water; drain well and return to the bowl. Add the savoy cabbage, purple cabbage, and carrots; toss to combine. Set slaw aside.

2 For the dressing, in a food processor or blender combine the parsley, mayonnaise, sour cream, green onion, vinegar, tarragon, sugar, and garlic. Cover and process or blend to combine. Add the dressing to the kale mixture; toss to coat. Sprinkle with pepitas.

MAKE-AHEAD DIRECTIONS: Prepare the slaw as directed. Cover and chill for up to 24 hours.

PER 3/4 CUP: 159 cal., 13 g total fat (2 g sat. fat), 5 mg chol., 310 mg sodium, 7 g carb., 3 g fiber, 5 g pro.
EXCHANGES: 1 1/2 Vegetable, 2 1/2 Fat

BEST-LOVED LOW-CALORIE

Sesame Noodle Slaw

PREP: 20 MINUTES **BAKE:** 15 MINUTES AT 300°F
CHILL: 30 MINUTES TO 4 HOURS
MAKES: 8 SIDE-DISH SERVINGS

- **½ cup sliced almonds**
- **2 tablespoons sesame seeds**
- **⅓ cup vegetable oil**
- **3 tablespoons rice vinegar or cider vinegar**
- **2 tablespoons reduced-sodium soy sauce**
- **1 3-ounce package chicken-flavor ramen noodles**
- **1 tablespoon sugar**
- **¼ teaspoon black pepper**
- **½ of a medium head cabbage, cored and shredded (about 6 cups) (see photos 1 and 2, page 502); 6 cups packaged shredded cabbage with carrot (coleslaw mix); or 6 cups packaged shredded broccoli (broccoli slaw mix)**
- **⅓ to ½ cup thinly sliced green onions (3 or 4)**
- **⅓ cup golden raisins or raisins (optional)**

1 Preheat oven to 300°F. Spread almonds and sesame seeds in a shallow pan. Bake for 15 to 20 minutes or until toasted, stirring once; cool.

2 Meanwhile, for dressing, in a screw-top jar combine oil, vinegar, soy sauce, seasoning packet from noodles, sugar, and pepper. Cover and shake well.

3 In a large bowl combine almonds and sesame seeds, cabbage, green onions, and, if desired, raisins. Break ramen noodles into small pieces; add to salad. Add dressing; toss gently to coat. Cover and chill for 30 minutes to 4 hours.

PER 1 CUP: 205 cal., 16 g fat (1 g sat. fat), 0 mg chol., 349 mg sodium, 14 g carb., 3 g fiber, 4 g pro.
EXCHANGES: 1 Starch, 3 Fat

SESAME CHICKEN AND NOODLE SLAW: Prepare as directed, except add 1½ cups chopped cooked chicken or pork with the cabbage and onions. Makes 4 main-dish servings.

PER 1¼ CUPS: 510 cal., 28 g total fat (3 g sat. fat), 47 mg chol., 744 mg sodium, 28 g carb., 5 g fiber, 23 g pro.
EXCHANGES: 2 Starch, 2½ Lean Meat, 5 Fat

A DASH OF FLAVOR

If you're looking to add some extra kick to salads with bacon, try using peppered bacon in such recipes as the Creamy Broccoli-Bacon Salad or the Pea Salad on this page.

LOW-CALORIE

Creamy Broccoli-Bacon Salad

PREP: 20 MINUTES **CHILL:** 2 TO 24 HOURS
MAKES: 12 TO 16 SIDE-DISH SERVINGS

- **1 cup mayonnaise**
- **½ cup raisins**
- **¼ cup finely chopped red onion (1 small)**
- **3 tablespoons sugar**
- **2 tablespoons vinegar**
- **7 cups chopped fresh broccoli florets**
- **½ cup shelled sunflower kernels**
- **8 slices bacon, crisp-cooked, drained, and crumbled**

1 In a large bowl combine mayonnaise, raisins, onion, sugar, and vinegar. Add broccoli and stir to coat. Cover and chill for 2 to 24 hours. Before serving, stir in sunflower kernels and bacon.

PER ½ CUP: 247 cal., 20 g total fat (4 g sat. fat), 13 mg chol., 242 mg, 13 g carb., 2 g fiber, 5 g pro. **EXCHANGES:** ½ Vegetable, ½ Other Carb., ½ High-Fat Meat, 3 Fat

Pea Salad

PREP: 20 MINUTES **CHILL:** 4 TO 24 HOURS
MAKES: 6 TO 8 SIDE-DISH SERVINGS

- **1 16-ounce package frozen peas**
- **4 ounces cheddar cheese, cut into ½-inch cubes**
- **½ cup chopped celery**
- **½ cup mayonnaise**
- **½ cup sour cream**
- **1 small red onion, finely chopped**
- **1 teaspoon snipped fresh dill weed or ¼ teaspoon dried dill weed (optional)**
- **¼ teaspoon salt**
- **¼ teaspoon black pepper**
- **2 slices bacon, crisp-cooked, drained, and crumbled**

1 Place the peas in a colander and run under cold water just until thawed but still cold; drain well.

2 In a medium bowl stir together peas, cheese, and celery. In a small bowl stir together the mayonnaise, sour cream, onion, dill weed (if desired), salt, and pepper. Add to pea mixture. Stir to combine. Cover and chill for 4 to 24 hours. Just before serving, top with bacon.

PER ½ CUP: 321 cal., 25 g total fat (9 g sat. fat), 38 mg chol., 566 mg sodium, 12 g carb., 4 g fiber, 10 g pro.
EXCHANGES: 1 Starch, 1 High-Fat Meat, 3 Fat

LOW-CALORIE

Sweet and Tangy Four-Bean Salad

PREP: 30 MINUTES **CHILL:** 4 TO 48 HOURS
MAKES: 18 SIDE-DISH SERVINGS

- **8 ounces fresh green beans, trimmed**
- **1 12-ounce package frozen shelled sweet soybeans (edamame)**
- **¾ cup cider vinegar**
- **⅔ cup tomato juice**
- **½ cup sugar**
- **¼ cup vegetable oil**
- **3 tablespoons dry red wine or apple juice**
- **2 teaspoons Worcestershire sauce**
- **2 teaspoons Dijon-style mustard**
- **1 clove garlic, minced**
- **1 15-ounce can red kidney beans, rinsed and drained**
- **1 14.5-ounce can cut wax beans, rinsed and drained**
- **2 cups coarsely shredded carrots (4 medium)**
- **½ cup finely chopped green onions (1 bunch)**

1 In large saucepan cook green beans in boiling lightly salted water for 4 minutes. Add edamame and cook 6 minutes more or just until tender. Drain and rinse with cold water; set aside.

2 In an extra-large bowl combine vinegar, tomato juice, sugar, oil, wine, Worcestershire, mustard, and garlic. Stir in bean mixture, canned beans, carrots, and green onions. Cover and chill for 4 to 48 hours. Serve with a slotted spoon.

MAKE-AHEAD DIRECTIONS: Assemble and chill for 4 to 48 hours. The fresh green beans will lose some color as they marinate in the dressing. For brightly colored green beans, cook and chill as directed but do not add to salad. Cover and refrigerate separately; toss with the salad just before serving.

PER ½ CUP: 58 cal., 1 g total fat (0 g sat. fat), 0 mg chol., 100 mg sodium, 9 g carb., 3 g fiber, 4 g pro.
EXCHANGES: ½ Starch

ENJOY EDAMAME

Edamame, also called sweet or green soybeans, are great additions to salads.

Fresh edamame beans can be found in specialty markets. They are typically sold frozen, in and out of the pods, in 1-pound bags. Frozen shelled edamame are a great timesaver; prepare according to package directions. Edamame are easy to digest and very high in protein, fiber, zinc, calcium, iron, and B vitamins.

LOW-CALORIE

Creamy Cucumbers

PREP: 15 MINUTES **CHILL:** 4 HOURS TO 3 DAYS
MAKES: 6 SIDE-DISH SERVINGS

- **½ cup sour cream or plain yogurt**
- **1 tablespoon vinegar**
- **½ teaspoon salt**
- **¼ teaspoon dried dill weed**
- **Dash black pepper**
- **1 large cucumber, peeled (if desired), halved lengthwise, and thinly sliced (3 cups)**
- **⅓ cup thinly sliced onion**

1 In a medium bowl combine sour cream, vinegar, salt, dill, and pepper. Add cucumber and onion; toss to coat. Cover and chill for 4 hours or up to 3 days, stirring occasionally. Stir before serving.

PER ½ CUP: 45 cal., 3 g total fat (2 g sat. fat), 8 mg chol., 209 mg sodium, 4 g carb., 0 g fiber, 1 g pro.
EXCHANGES: ½ Vegetable, ½ Fat

LOW-CALORIE

Fresh Cucumber Salad

PREP: 20 MINUTES **CHILL:** 60 MINUTES TO 3 DAYS
MAKES: 8 SIDE-DISH SERVINGS

- **⅓ cup seasoned rice vinegar**
- **⅓ cup apple juice or sweet rice wine (mirin)**
- **⅓ cup packed brown sugar**
- **1 tablespoon grated fresh ginger (optional)**
- **2 large cucumbers (10 to 12 ounces each), peeled (if desired) and thinly sliced**
- **½ cup thinly sliced quartered red onion**

1 In a medium bowl combine rice vinegar, apple juice, brown sugar, and, if desired, ginger. Stir in cucumbers and onion slices to coat. Cover and chill for 60 minutes to 3 days, stirring occasionally. Serve with a slotted spoon.

PER SERVING: 62 cal., 0 g total fat, 0 mg chol., 6 mg sodium, 15 g carb., 1 g fiber, 1 g pro. EXCHANGES: 1 Vegetable, ½ Other Carb

BEST-LOVED FAST LOW-CALORIE

Fiesta Corn Salad

START TO FINISH: 30 MINUTES
MAKES: 16 SIDE-DISH SERVINGS

- **4 cups fresh or frozen whole kernel corn**
- **1 cup frozen shelled sweet soybeans (edamame)**
- **1 small red onion, cut into thin wedges**
- **¼ cup snipped fresh cilantro**
- **1 fresh jalapeño chile pepper, seeded and finely chopped (see tip, page 44)**
- **2 tablespoons olive oil**
- **½ teaspoon finely shredded lime peel**
- **3 tablespoons lime juice**
- **1 teaspoon cumin seeds, toasted***
- **1 teaspoon salt**
- **2 cloves garlic, minced**
- **¼ teaspoon chili powder**
- **2 cups cherry or grape tomatoes, halved**

1 In a large saucepan cook corn and edamame, covered, in enough boiling water to cover for 2 minutes; drain. Rinse with cold water and drain again.

2 In a large bowl stir together corn, edamame, red onion, snipped cilantro, and jalapeño pepper.

3 In a screw-top jar combine olive oil, lime peel, lime juice, cumin seeds, salt, garlic, and chili powder. Cover and shake well.

4 Pour dressing over corn mixture; toss to coat. Stir in tomatoes. If desired, garnish with additional cilantro. Serve immediately. (Or cover and chill for up to 24 hours, stirring in tomatoes just before serving. If chilled, let stand for 30 minutes before serving.)

***NOTE:** To toast cumin seeds, place seeds in a skillet over medium heat. Heat about 2 minutes or until aromatic, shaking skillet often.

PER ½ CUP: 75 cal., 3 g total fat (0 g sat. fat), 0 mg chol., 150 mg sodium, 12 g carb., 2 g fiber, 3 g pro.
EXCHANGES: 1 Starch, ½ Fat

BEST-LOVED

Layered Vegetable Salad

PREP: 35 MINUTES **CHILL:** 4 TO 24 HOURS
MAKES: 8 TO 10 SIDE-DISH SERVINGS

- **6 cups torn mixed salad greens**
- **1 15-ounce can garbanzo beans (chickpeas), rinsed and drained, or one 10-ounce package frozen peas, thawed**
- **1 cup cherry or grape tomatoes, quartered or halved**
- **1 cup small broccoli florets**
- **1 cup chopped yellow and/or red sweet pepper (1 large)**
- **6 ounces diced cooked chicken or ham (1 cup) (optional)**
- **¼ cup thinly sliced green onions (2)**
- **3 ounces smoked cheddar cheese or cheddar cheese, shredded (¾ cup)**
- **1 cup mayonnaise**
- **1 8-ounce carton sour cream**
- **2 tablespoons snipped fresh dill weed or 2 teaspoons dried dill weed**
- **⅛ teaspoon black pepper**

1 Place 3 cups of the mixed greens in the bottom of a 3-quart clear salad bowl. Layer in the following order: garbanzo beans, tomatoes, broccoli, sweet pepper, remaining greens, chicken (if desired), green onions, and cheese.

2 For dressing, stir together mayonnaise, sour cream, dill weed, and black pepper. Spoon dressing over salad. Cover tightly with plastic wrap. Chill for 4 to 24 hours before serving.

PER 1¼ CUPS: 405 cal., 34 g total fat (10 g sat. fat), 55 mg chol., 429 mg sodium, 13 g carb., 4 g fiber, 13 g pro.
EXCHANGES: 2 Vegetable, 1 Lean Meat, 6½ Fat

FAST LOW-CALORIE

Fresh Tomato Salad

START TO FINISH: 20 MINUTES
MAKES: 6 SIDE-DISH SERVINGS

- **5 roma tomatoes, sliced**
- **½ cup tiny fresh mozzarella balls or 1-inch mozzarella balls, quartered**
- **¼ cup sliced pitted olives (pimiento-stuffed, Kalamata, or ripe black)**
- **3 tablespoons olive oil**
- **3 tablespoons white wine vinegar**
- **2 cloves garlic, minced**
- **2 tablespoons snipped fresh basil**

1 Arrange tomatoes on serving plate. Scatter mozzarella balls and olives over tomatoes.

2 For dressing, in a screw-top jar combine oil, vinegar, garlic, ¼ teaspoon *salt*, and ⅛ teaspoon *black pepper*. Cover and shake well to combine; drizzle over tomatoes on serving plate. Sprinkle basil over tomatoes.

PER ⅔ CUP: 113 cal., 10 g total fat (2 g sat. fat), 7 mg chol., 242 mg sodium, 4 g carb., 1 g fiber, 3 g pro.
EXCHANGES: ½ Vegetable, 2 Fat

Market Stand Pasta Salad

PREP: 20 MINUTES **COOK:** 25 MINUTES
CHILL: 60 MINUTES **MAKES:** 4 MAIN-DISH SERVINGS

- **6 cloves garlic**
- **¼ cup olive oil**
- **2 tablespoons chopped shallot (1 medium)**
- **½ teaspoon salt**
- **¼ teaspoon black pepper**
- **2 teaspoons finely shredded lemon peel**
- **¼ cup lemon juice**
- **2 tablespoons agave syrup or honey**
- **8 ounces campanelle**
- **3 cups assorted fresh vegetables (such as carrots, wax or green beans, pattypan squash, and/or sugar snap pea pods), cut into bite-size pieces**

MARKET STAND PASTA SALAD

- **2 cups baby spinach, kale, or arugula**
- **1 cup grape or cherry tomatoes, halved**
- **½ cup fresh basil leaves, slivered**
- **6 ounces hard salami, cut into ¼-inch-thick cubes**

1 For dressing, on a work surface lightly smash garlic cloves; remove and discard skins. In a small saucepan combine the garlic, olive oil, shallot, salt, and pepper. Cook over medium-low heat about 15 minutes or until garlic and shallot are very tender and caramelized; let cool. Scrape garlic mixture into a blender. Add lemon peel, lemon juice, and agave syrup. Cover and blend until almost smooth. Set dressing aside.

2 In a large pot cook pasta in boiling salted water according to package directions, adding the 3 cups vegetables the last 5 to 7 minutes or until crisp-tender. Drain; rinse with cold water. Drain pasta and vegetables well; lightly pat pasta mixture with paper towels to remove excess moisture.

3 In a large bowl combine the pasta mixture, baby spinach, tomatoes, basil, and salami. Lightly toss the mixture to combine. Pour dressing over salad; toss to coat. Cover and chill for 60 minutes before serving.

PER 2 CUPS: 595 cal., 28 g total fat (7 g sat. fat), 43 mg chol., 1,200 mg sodium, 68 g carb., 6 g fiber, 21 g pro.
EXCHANGES: 3 Vegetable, 3 Starch, ½ Other Carb., 1 Medium-Fat Meat, 4 Fat

make it mine

Pasta Salad

A pasta salad is a great way to feed a crowd. Make your version really stand out on the picnic or potluck table with a mix of ingredients your family and friends like best.

PREP: 40 MINUTES **CHILL:** 4 TO 24 HOURS
MAKES: 16 SIDE-DISH SERVINGS

- **3 cups DRIED PASTA**
- **2 tablespoons olive oil**
- **1 tablespoon lemon juice**
- **2 teaspoons seasoned salt**
- **3 to 4 cups VEGETABLE**
- **8 ounces cubed CHEESE**
- **1 cup TOMATO**
- **1 cup cubed COOKED MEAT (optional)**
- **½ cup chopped red onion or sliced green onions (4)**
- **½ cup OLIVES (optional)**
- **Snipped FRESH HERB**
- **1½ cups bottled SALAD DRESSING**

1 Cook desired Dried Pasta according to package directions; drain. Rinse with cold water; drain. In a very large bowl whisk together olive oil, lemon juice, and salt. Add pasta; toss to coat. Cover and chill overnight.

2 Add the Vegetable, Cheese, Tomato, Meat (if desired), onion, Olives (if desired), and Fresh Herb to pasta. Add Salad Dressing; toss to coat. Cover and chill for 4 to 24 hours.

SEASONAL PASTA SALAD

It's easy to give salads a seasonal twist. For a taste of fall, swap beans and summer squash for part or all of the vegetable, use smoked cheese, and substitute some dried tomatoes for part of the tomato choice.

DRIED PASTA *(pick one)*

Bow ties
Cavatelli
Medium shells
Mostaccioli
Penne
Rotini
Wagon wheels

VEGETABLE *(pick one or more)*

Fresh broccoli florets
Fresh green beans, trimmed and cut into 2-inch pieces (cook in boiling water 5 minutes; drain and cool)
Frozen peas or whole kernel corn, thawed
Red, green, and/or yellow sweet peppers, cut into strips
Thinly sliced carrots
Yellow summer squash or zucchini, halved lengthwise and sliced

CHEESE *(pick one)*

Cheddar
Monterey Jack
Monterey Jack with jalapeño peppers
Provolone
Smoked cheddar
Swiss

TOMATO *(pick one)*

Chopped tomato
Halved cherry tomatoes
Halved grape tomatoes

COOKED MEAT *(pick one)*

Ham
Pepperoni or salami
Turkey or chicken

OLIVES *(pick one)*

Halved pitted Kalamata
Sliced pimiento-stuffed green
Sliced pitted ripe black

FRESH HERB *(pick one)*

2 tablespoons snipped fresh basil, oregano, or dill weed

DRESSING *(pick one)*

Balsamic vinaigrette
Caesar
Creamy garlic
Italian
Ranch
Vinaigrette

Honey-Quinoa Salad with Cherries and Cashews

PREP: 30 MINUTES **COOK:** 10 MINUTES
STAND: 10 MINUTES **MAKES:** 4 MAIN-DISH SERVINGS

- **¼ cup honey**
- **2 tablespoons grated fresh ginger**
- **2 tablespoons white wine vinegar**
- **2 tablespoons lime juice**
- **1 small clove garlic, minced**
- **¼ teaspoon black pepper**
- **¼ cup extra virgin olive oil**
- **1 cup water**
- **⅔ cup uncooked quinoa (rinsed)***
- **1 cup fresh dark sweet cherries, pitted (see photos 1–3, below) and halved, or red seedless grapes, halved**
- **½ cup coarsely chopped cashews**
- **½ cup dried apricots, cut into thin slivers**
- **¼ cup thinly sliced red onion**
- **4 cups torn butterhead lettuce (Boston or Bibb) (1 small head)**

1 For honey vinaigrette, in a bowl whisk together honey, ginger, vinegar, lime juice, garlic, ¼ teaspoon *salt*, and pepper. Drizzle in olive oil, whisking constantly, until well combined; set aside.

2 In a medium saucepan combine water, quinoa, and ¼ teaspoon *salt*. Bring to boiling; reduce heat. Simmer, covered, about 10 minutes or until liquid is absorbed. Remove from heat; let stand for 10 minutes.

3 Fluff quinoa with fork. In bowl toss quinoa, cherries, cashews, apricots, and onion. Add lettuce. Drizzle with ½ cup of honey vinaigrette; toss again. Pass remaining vinaigrette. Chill remaining vinaigrette up to 5 days.

***NOTE:** Place quinoa in fine-mesh strainer; hold under running water to remove any saponin, the natural coating, which can taste bitter.

PER 1 CUP: 456 cal., 23 g fat (4 g sat. fat), 0 mg chol., 303 mg sodium, 58 g carb., 5 g fiber, 8 g pro.
EXCHANGES: 1½ Fruit, 1½ Starch, 1 Other Carb., ½ Medium-Fat Meat, 4 Fat

COUSCOUS VARIATION: Substitute ¾ cup couscous or ⅔ cup Israeli couscous for the quinoa. Prepare according to package directions and add to salad with fruit.

PER 1 CUP: 481 cal., 22 g fat (4 g sat. fat), 0 mg chol., 306 mg sodium, 66 g carb., 5 g fiber, 9 g pro.
EXCHANGES: 1½ Fruit, 2 Starch, 1 Other Carb., ½ Medium-Fat Meat, 3½ Fat

PITTING WITH A PAPER CLIP STEP-BY-STEP

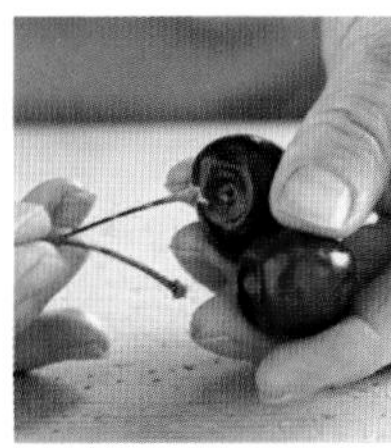

1. Remove the cherry stem.

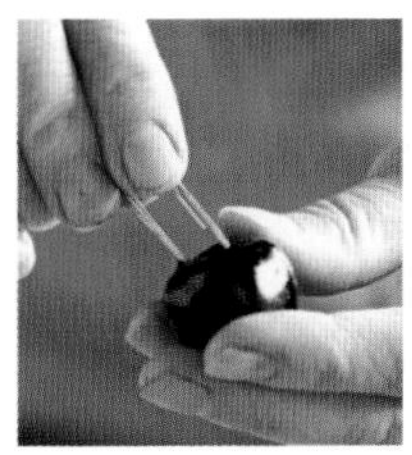

2. Insert a clean medium paper clip into the cherry. Twist it around the pit to loosen.

3. Pull out the pit. You can also use a cherry pitter.

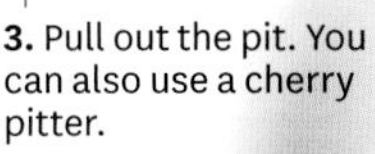

LOW-CALORIE

Curried Wild Rice Salad

PREP: 20 MINUTES **COOK:** 40 MINUTES
CHILL: 4 TO 24 HOURS **STAND:** 30 MINUTES
MAKES: 10 SIDE-DISH SERVINGS

- **3 cups water**
- **2/3 cup uncooked wild rice, rinsed and drained**
- **2/3 cup uncooked brown rice**
- **1/2 of a 10-ounce package frozen peas, thawed (1 cup)**
- **3/4 cup chopped red or yellow sweet pepper (1 medium)**
- **1/4 cup thinly sliced green onions (2)**
- **1/4 cup currants or raisins**
- **3 tablespoons canola oil**
- **1 teaspoon finely shredded orange peel**
- **3 tablespoons orange juice**
- **1 tablespoon honey**
- **1 teaspoon curry powder**
- **1/2 teaspoon salt**
- **1/2 cup chopped honey-roasted peanuts (optional)**

1 In a medium saucepan combine the water, wild rice, and brown rice. Bring to boiling; reduce heat. Simmer, covered, about 40 minutes or until rice is tender; drain if necessary. Transfer rice to a large bowl and let cool to room temperature. Add peas, sweet pepper, green onions, and currants to rice mixture.

2 In a screw-top jar combine oil, orange peel, orange juice, honey, curry powder, and salt. Cover and shake well. Pour dressing over rice mixture in bowl. Gently toss to combine. Cover and chill mixture for 4 to 24 hours.

3 Let salad stand at room temperature for 30 minutes before serving. If desired, sprinkle with chopped peanuts just before serving.

PER 1/2 CUP: 155 cal., 5 g total fat (0 g sat. fat), 0 mg chol., 153 mg sodium, 25 g carb., 2 g fiber, 4 g pro.
EXCHANGES: 1 1/2 Starch, 1 Fat

FAST LOW-CALORIE

Cucumber and Watermelon Salad with Arugula and Feta

START TO FINISH: 25 MINUTES
MAKES: 8 SIDE-DISH SERVINGS

- **4 cups chilled seedless watermelon cut into small chunks**
- **4 cups baby arugula**
- **1 medium seedless cucumber, halved lengthwise and thinly sliced**
- **1 cup thinly sliced red onion (1 large)**
- **1/2 cup snipped fresh mint**
- **3 tablespoons white wine vinegar**
- **3 tablespoons olive oil**
- **1/2 teaspoon salt**
- **1/2 teaspoon black pepper**
- **1/2 cup crumbled feta cheese (2 ounces)**
- **1/2 cup chopped walnuts, toasted (see tip, page 21)**

1 In a large bowl combine watermelon, arugula, cucumber, red onion, and mint. If desired, cover and chill for up to 60 minutes.

2 For vinaigrette, in a screw-top jar combine vinegar, oil, salt, and pepper. Cover and shake well. Pour vinaigrette over watermelon mixture and toss gently to coat. Sprinkle with cheese and walnuts.

PER 1 1/3 CUPS: 151 cal., 12 g total fat (2 g sat. fat), 6 mg chol., 231 mg sodium, 10 g carb., 2 g fiber, 3 g pro.
EXCHANGES: 1/2 Vegetable, 1/2 Fruit, 1/2 Medium-Fat Meat, 1 1/2 Fat

FAST LOW-CALORIE

Bistro Salad *(photo, page 489)*

START TO FINISH: 25 MINUTES
MAKES: 8 SIDE-DISH SERVINGS

- **10 cups mesclun, torn romaine lettuce, butterhead lettuce (Boston or Bibb), and/or spinach**
- **3 cups red and/or green pears, cored and thinly sliced; sliced strawberries; and/or blueberries**
- **1/4 cup olive oil**
- **1/4 cup balsamic vinegar**
- **1 tablespoon snipped fresh thyme, oregano, or basil; or 1/2 teaspoon dried thyme, oregano, or basil, crushed**
- **1 teaspoon sugar**
- **1 clove garlic, minced**
- **1/4 teaspoon dry mustard or 1 teaspoon Dijon-style mustard**
- **1/8 teaspoon black pepper**
- **1/2 cup broken walnuts, toasted (see tip, page 21) or 1/2 cup Candied Nuts (page 269)**
- **1/2 cup crumbled blue or feta cheese (2 ounces)**

1 In a large salad bowl place mesclun and fruit. Toss lightly to combine.

2 For dressing, in a screw-top jar combine oil, vinegar, herb, sugar, garlic, mustard, and pepper. Cover and shake well. Pour dressing over salad; toss lightly to coat. Divide evenly among salad plates. Sprinkle each serving with nuts and cheese.

PER 1 1/3 CUPS: 188 cal., 14 g total fat (3 g sat. fat), 6 mg chol., 125 mg sodium, 14 g carb., 3 g fiber, 4 g pro.
EXCHANGES: 1 Vegetable, 1/2 Fruit, 3 Fat

CUCUMBER AND WATERMELON SALAD WITH ARUGULA AND FETA

LOW-CALORIE

Melon and Berries Salad

PREP: 20 MINUTES **CHILL:** 3 TO 24 HOURS
MAKES: 4 TO 6 SIDE-DISH SERVINGS

- **2 cups chilled cantaloupe cubes or balls**
- **2 cups chilled honeydew melon cubes or balls**
- **1 tablespoon honey**
- **1 teaspoon fresh lime juice**
- **1 tablespoon snipped fresh mint**
- **1 cup fresh blueberries and/or red raspberries**

1 In a bowl combine cantaloupe and honeydew melon. Drizzle honey and lime juice over melon; gently toss to mix. Cover; chill for 3 to 24 hours. Just before serving, add mint and toss gently to mix. Sprinkle with berries.

PER 1 CUP: 97 cal., 0 g total fat, 0 mg chol., 30 mg sodium, 24 g carb., 2 g fiber, 1 g pro. EXCHANGES: 1 Fruit, ½ Other Carb.

Mandarin Cream Salad with Coconut-Crumb Crust *(photo, page 487)*

PREP: 30 MINUTES **BAKE:** 12 MINUTES AT 375°F
COOL: 60 MINUTES **CHILL:** 3½ TO 24½ HOURS
MAKES: 18 SIDE-DISH SERVINGS

- **2 cups finely crushed shortbread cookies (about 35 cookies)**
- **⅔ cup flaked coconut**
- **½ cup butter, melted**
- **1 teaspoon finely shredded orange peel**
- **2 3-ounce packages orange-flavor gelatin**
- **2 cups boiling water**
- **1 8-ounce package cream cheese, softened**
- **¾ cup sugar**
- **1 8-ounce container frozen whipped dessert topping, thawed**
- **2 11-ounce cans mandarin orange sections, drained**
- **Quartered fresh orange slices (optional)**

1 Preheat oven to 375°F. In a medium bowl stir together crushed cookies, coconut, melted butter, and orange peel. Pat mixture evenly into the bottom of a 3-quart rectangular baking dish. Bake for 12 to 14 minutes or until crust is lightly browned. Cool crust completely on a wire rack.

2 In a medium bowl stir together gelatin and boiling water until gelatin dissolves. Cool completely at room temperature.

3 Meanwhile, in a large mixing bowl beat cream cheese and sugar with an electric mixer on medium speed for 1 to 2 minutes or until light and fluffy. Fold in whipped topping. Spread cream cheese mixture evenly over cooled crust. Chill for at least 30 minutes.

4 Stir orange sections into gelatin mixture. Carefully pour orange mixture over chilled cream cheese layer. Cover and chill for 3 to 24 hours or until firm. To serve, cut into squares. If desired, garnish with quartered orange slices.

LIGHTEN UP: For a lighter recipe, substitute reduced-fat versions of the cream cheese and whipped dessert topping.

PER SQUARE: 283 cal., 16 g total fat (9 g sat. fat), 27 mg chol., 204 mg sodium, 34 g carb., 1 g fiber, 2 g pro.
EXCHANGES: 1 Starch, 1 Other Carb., 3 Fat

FAST LOW-CALORIE

Waldorf Salad

START TO FINISH: 20 MINUTES
MAKES: 8 TO 10 SIDE-DISH SERVINGS

- **4 cups chopped apples and/or pears**
- **4 teaspoons lemon juice**
- **½ cup chopped celery**
- **½ cup chopped walnuts or pecans, toasted (see tip, page 21)**
- **½ cup raisins, snipped pitted whole dates, or dried tart cherries**
- **½ cup seedless green grapes, halved**
- **⅔ cup mayonnaise**

1 In a medium bowl toss apples and/or pears with lemon juice. Stir in celery, nuts, raisins, and grapes. Stir in mayonnaise until combined. Serve salad immediately or cover and chill for up to 8 hours.

PER ½ CUP: 245 cal., 20 g fat (3 g sat. fat), 7 mg chol., 107 mg sodium, 18 g carb., 2 g fiber, 2 g pro.
EXCHANGES: 1 Fruit, 4 Fat

FLUFFY WALDORF SALAD: Prepare as directed, except substitute 1½ cups frozen whipped dessert topping, thawed, for the mayonnaise. Stir in 1 cup tiny marshmallows. Serve immediately or cover and chill for up to 8 hours.

PER ¾ CUP: 174 cal., 7 g total fat (3 g sat. fat), 0 mg chol., 16 mg sodium, 27 g carb., 2 g fiber, 2 g pro.
EXCHANGES: 1 Fruit, 1½ Other Carb., 1½ Fat

HEARTY WALDORF

If you like, turn your Waldorf into a main-dish salad by adding chopped cooked turkey or chicken. Stir in cooked wild rice to make it even more hearty. Add a little extra mayo as needed.

sandwiches & pizzas

COLD SANDWICHES

GRILLED SANDWICHES & PANINI

HOT SANDWICHES

PIZZAS & PIZZA DOUGHS

SAUCES & RELISHES

WRAPS

TIPS

sandwiches & pizzas

Sandwiches are more about choosing good ingredients than about mastering tricky techniques. This sandwich savvy will get you started.

BREAD

White and wheat, rye, pumpernickel, and more, sliced bread is your base for making sandwiches. If you want to shake up your sandwich routine, look for forms beyond sliced, such as baguettes (long, cylindrical French bread), bolillos (crusty Mexican sandwich rolls), croissants, ciabatta (crusty Italian bread that's perfect for panini), and tortillas for wraps.

TO TOAST SANDWICH BUNS: Toasting sandwich buns helps the bread stand up to the filling while adding a little crunch to the meal. The easiest way to toast rolls and hoagie buns is in a toaster oven; however, you can also use your broiler. Place the rolls and buns, cut sides up, on the unheated rack of a broiler pan and broil 4 to 5 inches from the heat for 1 to 2 minutes or until golden brown.

MEAT

Just about any cooked meat that can be sliced, chopped, shredded, or ground can be tucked into a sandwich. Select the best quality.

CHEESE

Choose a cheese depending on how it will be used.

MELTERS: For hot sandwiches, good melting cheeses include American, cheddar, Monterey Jack, Monterey Jack with jalapeño peppers, Colby-Jack, mozzarella, provolone, Muenster, Swiss, Gruyère, and Fontina.

STACKERS: For cold, stacked sandwiches, choose a semisoft cheese that slices easily and is moist and pliable. Most melters work fine in a cold sandwich (they're best sliced thin). Also try Brie, fresh mozzarella, and Havarti.

CRUMBLERS: Some cheeses, such as a few goat cheeses and most blue and feta cheeses, cannot be sliced; however, they pack plenty of flavor crumbled in a pita pocket or wrap.

CONDIMENTS AND MORE

Many a masterful sandwich is all in the details.

- A slather of something on the bread not only adds flavor and moisture, but it also does the important work of binding the bread and filling together. Mustard and mayonnaise are must-haves; also consider chutney, pesto, tapenade, cranberry sauce, apricot jam, and hummus.
- For a more healthful alternative to mayonnaise, combine minced garlic with olive oil and brush onto bread rolls.
- Add color, flavor, and crunch with a variety of extras, including thinly sliced cucumbers, radishes, sweet and hot peppers, and red onion; greens, such as mild spinach, bitter arugula, and peppery watercress; and pickles and relishes. Fruit can also add to sandwiches. Try sliced grapes in chicken salad and thinly sliced apple or pear in a turkey sandwich.

cook's secrets

homemade pizza

The Secret: For the chewy crispy crust, two things are imperative: a hot oven and a hot baking stone. If you don't have a stone in your kitchen, use a cornmeal-dusted baking sheet.

PREP: 20 MINUTES **RISE:** 2 HOURS **REST:** 10 MINUTES
BAKE: 7 MINUTES AT 500°F **MAKES:** 4 PIZZAS (8 SERVINGS)

5 cups bread flour
1 tablespoon sugar
1½ teaspoons salt
1 teaspoon active dry yeast
1¾ cups warm water (105°F to 115°F)
2 tablespoons olive oil
Cornmeal
½ cup pizza sauce
1 pound bulk Italian or pork sausage, cooked and drained, or one 3.5-ounce package sliced pepperoni (optional)
3 cups shredded mozzarella, Fontina, and/or Asiago cheese (12 ounces)

Because bread flour has a higher protein content than all-purpose flour, it will give your crust a better texture. If you don't have it in your pantry, all-purpose will work.

1 In a very large bowl stir together flour, sugar, salt, and yeast. Stir in water and oil until combined and all the flour is moistened.

2 Turn dough out onto a lightly floured surface. Knead dough until smooth and elastic, about 3 minutes. Place in a lightly greased bowl, turning to grease surface of dough. Cover; let rise at room temperature until double in size (2 hours). If not using right away, cover with plastic wrap coated with *nonstick cooking spray;* chill for up to 24 hours.

3 If chilled, let dough stand at room temperature for 30 minutes. Remove dough from bowl (do not punch down). Divide dough into four portions. Gently shape each portion into a ball. Cover; let rest for 10 minutes.

4 Preheat oven to 500°F. Place a pizza stone, if using, in the oven while it preheats. On a lightly floured surface roll or stretch each dough portion into a 10- to 11-inch circle. Transfer dough circles to a baking sheet that has been sprinkled generously with cornmeal. Spread 2 tablespoons pizza sauce on each dough circle. Top with meat, if desired, and cheese.

5 Gently slide one topped dough circle at a time to the heated baking stone (or place the baking sheet in the oven). Bake about 7 minutes for baking stone (about 10 minutes for the baking sheet) or until crust is golden.

HONEY-WHEAT PIZZA CRUST: Prepare as directed, except substitute 1 cup whole wheat flour for 1 cup of the bread flour and substitute 1 tablespoon honey for the sugar.

PER ½ BASIC PIZZA OR HONEY-WHEAT VARIATION: 492 cal., 14 g total fat (5 g sat. fat), 23 mg chol., 746 mg sodium, 69 g carb., 3 g fiber, 22 g pro.
EXCHANGES: 4½ Starch, 1½ Medium Fat Meat, ½ Fat

PIZZA DOUGH POINTERS

1. WATCH THE TEMP!
Yeast may seem fragile for some cooks, but if you watch the water temperature carefully, you won't kill the yeast. The best crusts rely on it.

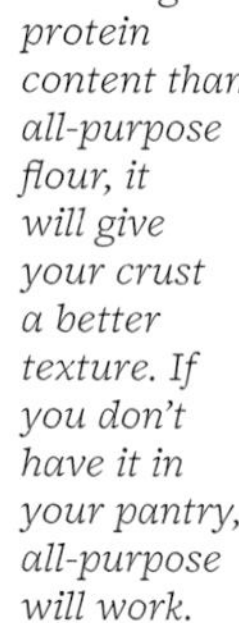

2. GATHER IT TOGETHER
It's usually impossible to get your dough uniformly mixed with a wooden spoon. Once most of the dough has come together to form a ball, use your hands to get it to come together completely before kneading.

BAKING STONES

Baking stones get hot, really hot! That heat makes your pizza crust crispy on the bottom yet chewy in the middle. Place the stone in the oven while it preheats and be careful when transferring your pizza to the hot stone (see photos 3 and 4, page 517). Manufacturers vary with care recommendations, so follow the instructions specific to your stone.

BARBECUE CHICKEN

BASIC HOMEMADE

VEGGIE

HAWAIIAN

PHILLY CHEESESTEAK

TACO

TACO: Prepare as directed, except substitute salsa for the pizza sauce, 1 pound cooked and drained ground beef for the sausage, and shredded cheddar cheese for the mozzarella. Stir ½ cup salsa into the cooked beef. Top pizzas with shredded lettuce, chopped tomatoes, and crushed tortilla chips.

PHILLY CHEESESTEAK: Prepare as directed, except substitute 8 ounces cream cheese and 3 tablespoons prepared horseradish for the pizza sauce and 8 ounces deli roast beef for the sausage. Add ¼ cup chopped sweet peppers and ¼ cup chopped onion per pizza. Substitute shredded Monterey Jack cheese for the mozzarella.

HAWAIIAN: Prepare as directed, except substitute 6 slices Canadian-style bacon per pizza for the sausage. Add one 20-ounce can pineapple tidbits, drained. Garnish with sliced green onions.

VEGGIE: Prepare as directed, except omit sausage and add 1½ cups assorted vegetables, such as chopped onion, sliced fresh mushrooms, sliced olives, chopped sweet peppers, and/or chopped tomatoes per pizza.

BARBECUE CHICKEN: Prepare as directed, except substitute barbecue sauce for the pizza sauce and 8 ounces chopped cooked chicken for the sausage. If desired, add sliced red onion, crumbled crisp-cooked bacon, and chopped tomato. Use a blend of cheddar and mozzarella cheeses.

↑

3. SPRINKLE AWAY
Generously dust a baking sheet with cornmeal. Gently transfer a dough circle to the sheet. If you have enough cornmeal on the sheet, the dough will transfer onto the hot stone easily.

4. THE BIG TRANSFER
Because the stone will be very hot, use the baking sheet to shimmy and shake the topped pizza dough onto the stone, gently pulling the baking sheet back toward you as the pizza settles on the stone.

↓

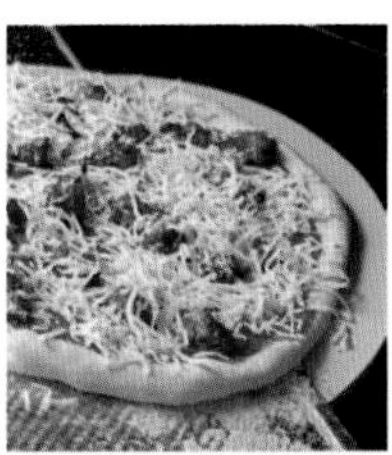

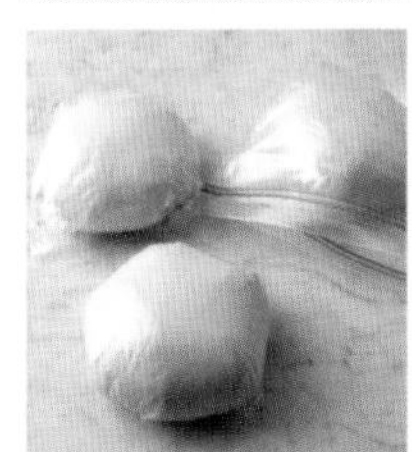

↑

MAKE IT AHEAD
After dividing dough into four portions (Step 3), wrap each portion in plastic wrap and place in airtight containers. Chill up to 24 hours or freeze up to 3 months. Thaw dough in refrigerator. Let it stand at room temperature for 30 minutes; continue with Steps 4 and 5.

DEEP-DISH PIZZA

Deep-Dish Pizza

PREP: 40 MINUTES **RISE:** 80 MINUTES
BAKE: 45 MINUTES AT 375°F **COOL:** 10 MINUTES
MAKES: 6 WEDGES

- **Olive oil or vegetable oil**
- **Cornmeal**
- **1 cup warm water (105°F to 115°F)**
- **1 package active dry yeast**
- **3 to 3½ cups all-purpose flour**
- **⅓ cup vegetable oil**
- **½ teaspoon salt**
- **6 ounces mild bulk Italian sausage**
- **1 14.5-ounce can diced tomatoes, drained**
- **1 tablespoon snipped fresh oregano or 1 teaspoon dried oregano, crushed**
- **1 tablespoon snipped fresh basil or 1 teaspoon dried basil, crushed**
- **12 ounces sliced mozzarella cheese**
- **¼ cup grated Parmesan or Romano cheese**
- **Grated Parmesan or Romano cheese (optional)**
- **Fresh basil leaves (optional)**

1 Generously grease a 10×2-inch heavy round cake pan or 10-inch springform pan with oil. Sprinkle bottom of pan with cornmeal; set pan aside.

2 In a large mixing bowl combine warm water and yeast, stirring to dissolve yeast. Let stand for 5 minutes. Stir in 1½ cups of the flour, the ⅓ cup oil, and salt. Beat with an electric mixer on low speed for 30 seconds, scraping sides of bowl constantly. Beat on high speed for 2 minutes. Using a wooden spoon, stir in as much of the remaining flour as you can.

3 Turn dough out onto a lightly floured surface. Knead in enough remaining flour to make a moderately stiff dough that is smooth and elastic (6 to 8 minutes total; see photo 2, page 99). Shape dough into a ball. Place in a lightly greased bowl, turning to grease surface of dough. Cover and let rise in a warm place until double in size (50 to 60 minutes). Punch dough down (see photos 3 and 4, page 99). Cover and let rest for 5 minutes.

4 Place dough in the prepared pan. Using oiled hands, press and spread dough evenly over the bottom and 1½ inches up sides of the pan. Cover and let rise in a warm place until nearly double in size (30 to 35 minutes).

5 Preheat oven to 375°F. For filling, in a medium skillet cook sausage over medium-high heat until browned; drain off fat. Using paper towels, pat sausage and wipe out skillet to remove additional fat. Stir in tomatoes, oregano, and basil. Cook and stir until heated through.

6 To assemble, arrange mozzarella slices over dough. Spoon filling over cheese; sprinkle with the ¼ cup Parmesan cheese.

7 Bake for 45 to 55 minutes or until edge of crust is crisp and golden brown and filling is heated through. If necessary, cover crust loosely with foil for the last 10 minutes of baking to prevent overbrowning. Cool on a wire rack for 10 minutes. If using a springform pan, remove the pan ring. If desired, sprinkle with additional Parmesan cheese and basil leaves. Cut into wedges.

PER WEDGE: 646 cal., 35 g total fat (12 g sat. fat), 51 mg chol., 956 mg sodium, 55 g carb., 3 g fiber, 26 g pro.
EXCHANGES: ½ Vegetable, 3½ Starch, 3½ Medium-Fat Meat, 2½ Fat

LOW-CALORIE

Enchilada Pizzas *(photo, page 513)*

PREP: 20 MINUTES **COOK:** 20 MINUTES
BAKE: 4 MINUTES PER PIZZA **MAKES:** 8 PIZZAS

- **1 recipe Easy Enchilada Sauce**
- **½ cup chopped onion (1 medium)**
- **6 cloves garlic, minced**
- **Pinch salt**
- **1 teaspoon olive oil**
- **2 teaspoons chili powder**
- **1 teaspoon ground cumin**
- **1 15.5-ounce can pinto beans, undrained**
- **3 to 4 tablespoons water**

8 **6-inch corn tortillas**
2 **cups shredded Oaxaca or Monterey Jack cheese (8 ounces)**
1 **ripe avocado, halved, seeded, peeled, and coarsely chopped (see photo 1, page 617)**
1 **cup crumbled queso fresco (4 ounces)**
½ **cup snipped fresh cilantro**
½ **cup red onion cut into slivers**

1 Prepare Enchilada Sauce; set aside. Place a pizza stone on the bottom rack of the oven. Preheat oven to 450°F.

2 In a small saucepan cook onion, garlic, and salt in hot oil over medium-high heat about 3 minutes or until onion and garlic are tender. Stir in chili powder and cumin; cook and stir for 1 minute more. Remove from heat; stir in beans and 3 tablespoons of the water. Transfer mixture to a food processor or blender. Cover and pulse with several on/off turns until bean mixture is spreadable but still chunky, adding more water if necessary.

3 Working with one tortilla at a time, evenly spread a thin layer of the bean mixture on the tortilla. Top with 1 to 2 tablespoons of the Easy Enchilada Sauce and ¼ cup of the Oaxaca cheese. Transfer topped tortilla to the pizza stone. Bake for 4 to 5 minutes or until cheese bubbles and edges are crisp.

4 Transfer pizza to a cutting board; let cool for 1 minute. Top with some of the avocado, 2 tablespoons of the queso fresco, 1 tablespoon of the cilantro, and 1 tablespoon of the red onion. Repeat to make eight pizzas total. (If desired, assemble and bake two pizzas at a time.)

EASY ENCHILADA SAUCE: In a large saucepan cook ½ cup chopped onion (1 medium), 1 tablespoon bottled minced garlic, and a pinch salt in 1 tablespoon hot vegetable oil over medium-high heat for 2 minutes. Stir in one 14.5-ounce can petite diced tomatoes, undrained, and ¼ teaspoon cayenne pepper. Cook, covered, for 4 to 5 minutes or until tomatoes can be easily mashed; cool slightly. Transfer tomato mixture to a food processor or blender. Cover and process or blend until smooth. Return mixture to saucepan. Stir in one 28-ounce can enchilada sauce; ¾ cup beef or vegetable broth; ½ ounce unsweetened chocolate, chopped; and 1 tablespoon honey. Bring to boiling; reduce heat. Simmer, uncovered, about 20 minutes or just until sauce thickens enough to coat the back of a spoon. Season to taste with additional salt.

PER PIZZA: 334 cal., 16 g total fat (4 g sat. fat), 34 mg chol., 1,494 mg sodium, 34 g carb., 10 g fiber, 14 g pro.
EXCHANGES: 1 Vegetable, 1 Starch, 1 High-Fat Meat, 1 Fat

BEEF AND BLUE CHEESE WRAPS

FAST LOW-CALORIE

Beef and Blue Cheese Wraps

START TO FINISH: 20 MINUTES **MAKES:** 4 WRAPS

3 **tablespoons mayonnaise**
1 **teaspoon dried thyme, crushed**
2 **tablespoons yellow mustard**
4 **8-inch flour tortillas**
12 **ounces thinly sliced cooked roast beef**
1 **12-ounce jar roasted red sweet peppers, drained**
⅓ **cup crumbled blue cheese (1½ ounces)**
4 **cups mixed greens**
Olive oil (optional)
Crumbled blue cheese (optional)

1 In a small bowl stir together mayonnaise and thyme. Set aside 1 tablespoon of the mayonnaise mixture. Stir mustard into remaining mayonnaise mixture.

2 Spread mustard mixture evenly over tortillas. Top evenly with roast beef, sweet peppers, and blue cheese. Roll up tortillas; brush with reserved 1 tablespoon mayonnaise mixture.

3 In a large skillet cook wraps over medium heat about 2 minutes per side or until lightly browned. Cut wraps in half and place on plates. Divide greens among plates. If desired, drizzle greens with olive oil and sprinkle with additional blue cheese.

PER WRAP: 330 cal., 17 g total fat (5 g sat. fat), 53 mg chol., 1,375 mg sodium, 23 g carb., 3 g fiber, 21 g pro.
EXCHANGES: 1½ Vegetable, 1 Starch, 2½ Medium-Fat Meat, ½ Fat

Lamb Meatball Flatbreads with Pickled Cucumber Salad *(photo, page 513)*

PREP: 35 MINUTES **COOK:** 12 MINUTES
MAKES: 4 SANDWICHES

- **3 tablespoons vegetable oil**
- **½ cup chopped pitted dates (6 to 8 whole)**
- **¼ cup finely chopped onion**
- **4 cloves garlic, minced**
- **1 pound ground lamb**
- **½ cup snipped fresh cilantro**
- **3 tablespoons snipped fresh mint**
- **3 teaspoons Asian chili sauce (Sriracha sauce) or harissa paste**
- **1 teaspoon salt**
- **1 teaspoon ground coriander**
- **½ teaspoon ground cumin**
- **¼ teaspoon ground cinnamon**
- **1 5- to 6-ounce container honey-flavor Greek yogurt**
- **4 flatbreads or naan, warmed**
- **1 recipe Pickled Cucumber Salad**

1 In a very large skillet heat 1 tablespoon of the oil over medium heat. Add dates, onion, and garlic. Cook and stir for 4 to 5 minutes or until onion is tender. Remove mixture from skillet; cool slightly.

2 For meatballs, in a large bowl combine lamb, cilantro, 2 tablespoons of the mint, 2 teaspoons of the chili sauce, the salt, coriander, cumin, cinnamon, and the cooled date mixture; mix well. Shape mixture into twenty 1-inch meatballs. Heat the remaining 2 tablespoons oil in the same skillet. Add meatballs; cook for 12 to 15 minutes or until browned and cooked through (160°F), turning frequently. Using a slotted spoon, transfer meatballs to paper towels to drain.

3 For yogurt sauce, in a small bowl stir together yogurt, the remaining 1 tablespoon mint, and the remaining 1 teaspoon chili sauce. Divide meatballs among flatbreads. Top with Pickled Cucumber Salad and the yogurt sauce.

PICKLED CUCUMBER SALAD: Thinly slice 1 small seedless cucumber and place in a medium bowl. Quarter 1 small white onion lengthwise; thinly slice each quarter. Add onion to bowl. In a small bowl combine ½ cup cider vinegar, 1 tablespoon snipped fresh cilantro, 2 teaspoons sugar, and ½ teaspoon salt. Stir the vinegar mixture into the cucumber mixture. Cover and chill for 1 to 6 hours.

PER SANDWICH: 736 cal., 38 g total fat (14 g sat. fat), 93 mg chol., 1,138 mg sodium, 71 g carb., 3 g fiber, 30 g pro.
EXCHANGES: 1 Fruit, 1 Vegetable, 3½ Starch, 2½ High-Fat Meat, 2½ Fat

FAST

Reuben Sandwiches

START TO FINISH: 18 MINUTES
MAKES: 4 SANDWICHES

- **3 tablespoons butter or margarine, softened**
- **8 slices dark rye or pumpernickel bread**
- **3 tablespoons bottled Thousand Island or Russian salad dressing**
- **6 ounces thinly sliced cooked corned beef**
- **4 slices Swiss cheese (3 ounces)**
- **1 cup sauerkraut, well drained**

1 Spread butter on one side of each bread slice and salad dressing on the other. Top four bread slices, buttered sides down, with meat, cheese, and sauerkraut. Top with remaining bread slices, buttered sides up.

2 Preheat a large skillet over medium heat. Reduce heat to medium-low. Cook two of the sandwiches at a time over medium-low heat for 4 to 6 minutes or until the bread is toasted and the cheese melts, turning once. Repeat with remaining sandwiches.

PER SANDWICH: 404 cal., 22 g total fat (10 g sat. fat), 64 mg chol., 2,508 mg sodium, 34 g carb., 8 g fiber, 20 g pro.
EXCHANGES: 2 Starch, 2 Medium-Fat Meat, 2 Fat

FAST LOW-CALORIE

Easy French Dip Sandwiches

START TO FINISH: 30 MINUTES
MAKES: 4 SANDWICHES

- **1 large onion, sliced and separated into rings (2 cups)**
- **1 clove garlic, minced**
- **1 tablespoon butter or margarine**
- **1 14.5-ounce can beef broth**
- **½ teaspoon dried thyme, marjoram, or oregano, crushed**
- **¼ teaspoon black pepper**
- **12 ounces thinly sliced cooked beef**
- **4 French-style rolls, split**

1 In a saucepan cook onion and garlic in hot butter until tender. Stir in broth, thyme, and pepper. Bring to boiling; reduce heat. Simmer, uncovered, for 10 minutes. Add beef. Return to boiling; reduce heat. Simmer, uncovered, about 5 minutes more or until beef is heated through.

2 If desired, toast rolls. Remove beef and onion from broth liquid. Arrange on rolls. If desired, serve with dishes of broth mixture for dipping.

PER SANDWICH: 346 cal., 10 g total fat (4 g sat. fat), 80 mg chol., 662 mg sodium, 27 g carb., 3 g fiber, 35 g pro.
EXCHANGES: 2 Starch, 4 Lean Meat

make it mine

Sloppy Joes

Sloppy Joes are an endlessly versatile, family-pleasing sandwich. You might think it's all about the sauce, but you can change this classic by mixing up your meat, vegetable, and even bread choices.

START TO FINISH: 25 MINUTES
MAKES: 6 SERVINGS

1½ **pounds** MEAT
VEGETABLE
SAUCE
SEASONING
BREAD, **split and toasted**

1 In a large skillet cook Meat and Vegetable until meat is browned and vegetable is tender; drain off fat. Stir in Sauce and Seasoning. Bring to boiling; reduce heat. Simmer, uncovered, for 5 minutes. Serve on toasted Bread.

GROUND MEAT TIPS

1 If cooking ground chicken or turkey for Sloppy Joes, pay attention to the label. If it specifies ground chicken breast or turkey breast, you will need to add 1 tablespoon vegetable oil to the skillet to keep the meat from sticking. If it just says "ground chicken" or "ground turkey," it likely contains some skin and fat, so you won't have to add oil.

2 When cooking ground meat, use a wooden spoon or potato masher to break it up as it cooks. A flat-edged spoon works better than one with a rounded bowl. Or you might be able to find a utensil specifically for cooking ground meat.

MEAT *(pick one)*

Ground beef, pork, turkey, or chicken
2 cups cooked brown rice plus one 15-ounce can kidney beans, rinsed and drained

VEGETABLE *(pick one)*

½ cup chopped onion and ½ cup chopped green sweet pepper
1 cup fresh or frozen corn kernels
1 cup chopped zucchini
1 cup chopped carrots

SAUCE *(pick one)*

One 8-ounce can tomato sauce plus 2 tablespoons water
One 14-ounce jar pizza sauce
1 cup bottled barbecue sauce
½ cup bottled barbecue sauce plus ⅓ cup orange marmalade
½ cup sweet-and-sour sauce plus ½ cup tomato sauce
1 cup bottled salsa plus ½ cup processed cheese dip

SEASONING *(pick one)*

2 teaspoons chili powder
2 teaspoons Worcestershire sauce and ½ teaspoon garlic salt
2 teaspoons barbecue spice
1 teaspoon finely chopped chipotle chile peppers in adobo sauce
1 teaspoon five-spice powder

BREAD *(pick one)*

6 bolillo rolls
6 ciabatta buns
1 focaccia bread round, cut into 6 wedges
6 kaiser rolls
6 pretzel buns
6 whole wheat or white hamburger buns

BEST-LOVED FAST

Pork Tenderloin Sandwiches

PREP: 20 MINUTES **COOK:** 6 MINUTES
MAKES: 4 SANDWICHES

- **1 pound pork tenderloin**
- **1/4 cup all-purpose flour**
- **1/4 teaspoon garlic salt**
- **1/4 teaspoon black pepper**
- **1 egg**
- **1 tablespoon milk**
- **1/2 cup seasoned fine dry bread crumbs**
- **2 tablespoons vegetable oil**
- **4 large hamburger buns or kaiser rolls, split and toasted**
- **Ketchup, mustard, onion slices, and/or dill pickle slices**

1 Trim fat from meat. Cut meat crosswise into four pieces (see photo 1, below). Place each piece between two pieces of plastic wrap. Using the flat side of a meat mallet, pound pork lightly to about 1/4 inch thick (see photos 2 and 3, below). Remove plastic wrap.

2 In a shallow bowl combine flour, garlic salt, and pepper. In another shallow bowl whisk together egg and milk. In a third bowl place bread crumbs. Dip pork into flour mixture to coat. Dip into egg mixture; coat with bread crumbs.

3 In a large heavy skillet cook pork in hot oil over medium heat for 6 to 8 minutes or until browned and meat is slightly pink in center, turning once (see photo 4, below).*

4 Serve tenderloins on warm buns with ketchup, mustard, onion slices, and/or dill pickle slices.

***NOTE:** If necessary, cook two tenderloin slices at a time. Keep warm on a baking sheet in a 300°F oven until all four are done. Add additional oil to the pan if necessary.

PER SANDWICH: 424 cal., 13 g total fat (3 g sat. fat), 127 mg chol., 776 mg sodium, 42 g carb., 2 g fiber, 33 g pro.
EXCHANGES: 2 1/2 Starch, 3 1/2 Lean Meat, 1 1/2 Fat

FAST LOW-CALORIE

Avocado BLT Sandwiches

START TO FINISH: 25 MINUTES
MAKES: 4 SANDWICHES

- **1 ripe avocado**
- **2 tablespoons light mayonnaise**
- **1 teaspoon lemon juice**
- **1 clove garlic, minced**
- **4 slices bacon, crisp-cooked and halved crosswise**
- **4 leaves romaine lettuce**
- **1 tomato, thinly sliced**
- **8 slices whole wheat bread, toasted**

1 Halve, seed, and peel avocado (see photo 1, page 617). Transfer one of the avocado halves to a small bowl; mash with a potato masher or the back of a wooden spoon. Stir in mayonnaise, lemon juice, and garlic; set aside. Thinly slice the remaining avocado half.

2 Arrange avocado slices, bacon, lettuce, and tomato on four of the toasted bread slices. Spread the mashed avocado mixture over the remaining four toasted bread slices; place on sandwiches, spread sides down.

PER SANDWICH: 257 cal., 14 g total fat (2 g sat. fat), 10 mg chol., 432 mg sodium, 27 g carb., 7 g fiber, 9 g pro.
EXCHANGES: 2 Starch, 2 1/2 Fat

MAKING PORK TENDERLOINS STEP-BY-STEP

1. Cut tenderloin crosswise into four equal pieces.

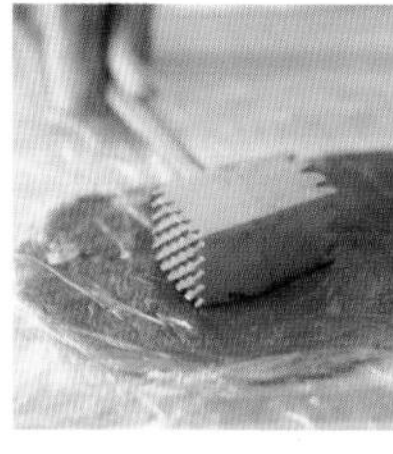

2. Working from center to edges, pound pork pieces into an even 1/4-inch thickness.

3. To make pieces rounder, fold any long edges toward the center and pound again until even.

4. Cook until coating is browned and pork is a little pink in the middle. Cut into a slice to check doneness.

BEST-LOVED FAST LOW-CALORIE

Thai Pork Wraps

START TO FINISH: 30 MINUTES **OVEN:** 350°F
MAKES: 6 WRAPS

- **6** **8- to 10-inch vegetable-flavor flour tortillas or plain flour tortillas**
- **½** **teaspoon garlic salt**
- **¼** **to ½ teaspoon black pepper**
- **12** **ounces pork tenderloin, cut into 1-inch strips**
- **1** **tablespoon vegetable oil**
- **4** **cups packaged shredded broccoli (broccoli slaw mix)**
- **1** **medium red onion, cut into thin wedges**
- **1** **teaspoon grated fresh ginger**
- **1** **recipe Peanut Sauce**

1 Preheat oven to 350°F. Wrap tortillas in foil. Bake about 10 minutes or until warm. Meanwhile, in a medium mixing bowl combine garlic salt and pepper. Add pork, tossing to coat.

2 In a large skillet cook and stir pork in hot oil over medium-high heat for 4 to 6 minutes or until no longer pink. (Reduce heat, if necessary, to prevent overbrowning.) Remove pork from skillet; keep warm. Add broccoli, onion, and ginger to skillet. Cook and stir for 4 to 6 minutes or until vegetables are crisp-tender. Remove from heat.

3 Spread Peanut Sauce evenly over tortillas. Top evenly with pork strips and vegetable mixture. Roll up tortillas, securing with wooden toothpicks. Serve immediately.

PEANUT SAUCE: In a small saucepan combine ¼ cup creamy peanut butter, 3 tablespoons water, 1 tablespoon sugar, 2 teaspoons soy sauce, and 1 clove garlic, minced. Heat over medium-low heat, whisking constantly, until smooth and warm. Use immediately or keep warm over very low heat, stirring occasionally.

THAI CHICKEN WRAPS: Prepare as directed, except substitute 12 ounces skinless, boneless chicken breast strips for the pork.

PER WRAP PORK OR CHICKEN VARIATION: 383 cal., 13 g total fat (3 g sat. fat), 37 mg chol., 661 mg sodium, 44 g carb., 5 g fiber, 22 g pro. EXCHANGES: 1 Vegetable, 2½ Starch, 2 Lean Meat, ½ High-Fat Meat, ½ Fat

Beer-Braised Brats

PREP: 15 MINUTES **COOK:** 25 MINUTES
MAKES: 5 SANDWICHES

- **½** **cup thinly sliced onion**
- **2** **tablespoons butter**
- **1** **12-ounce bottle dark German beer**
- **1** **tablespoon packed brown sugar**
- **1** **tablespoon vinegar**
- **½** **teaspoon caraway seeds**
- **½** **teaspoon dried thyme, crushed**
- **½** **teaspoon Worcestershire sauce**
- **5** **uncooked bratwurst links (1¼ pounds total)**
- **5** **hoagie buns, bratwurst buns, or other crusty rolls, split and toasted**
- **1** **recipe Easy Cranberry-Pickle Relish**

1 In a large saucepan cook and stir onion in hot butter over medium heat about 5 minutes or until tender. Add beer, brown sugar, vinegar, caraway seeds, thyme, and Worcestershire sauce. Bring to boiling; reduce heat. Add bratwursts. Cover and simmer for 10 minutes.

2 Remove bratwursts from cooking liquid; keep liquid warm. In a grill pan or skillet cook bratwursts over medium heat about 10 minutes or until browned and an instant-read thermometer inserted into bratwursts registers 160°F, turning occasionally. If desired, return bratwursts to cooking liquid to keep warm until serving time.

3 To serve, place grilled bratwursts in buns. Using a slotted spoon, top bratwursts with some cooked onion slices and the Easy Cranberry-Pickle Relish.

EASY CRANBERRY-PICKLE RELISH: In a small bowl stir together ½ cup canned whole cranberry sauce and ¼ cup sweet pickle relish.

PER SANDWICH: 600 cal., 26 g total fat (12 g sat. fat), 53 mg chol., 1,267 mg sodium, 69 g carb., 3 g fiber, 23 g pro. EXCHANGES: 4½ Starch, 2 High-Fat Meat, 1 Fat

PICKLED PEPPER SAUSAGE GRINDERS

Italian Sausage Grinders

PREP: 25 MINUTES **COOK:** 30 MINUTES
BROIL: 2 MINUTES **MAKES:** 4 SANDWICHES

- **1 pound bulk hot or sweet Italian sausage**
- **1 14.5-ounce can fire-roasted diced tomatoes, undrained**
- **1 14.5-ounce can crushed tomatoes, undrained**
- **2 cloves garlic, minced**
- **1 teaspoon balsamic vinegar**
- **1 teaspoon dried basil, crushed**
- **½ teaspoon dried oregano, crushed**
- **¼ teaspoon salt**
- **¼ teaspoon crushed red pepper**
- **1 small yellow onion, sliced**
- **1 small green sweet pepper, seeded and cut into strips**
- **2 tablespoons olive oil**
- **4 French-style rolls or hoagie buns, split**
- **4 slices provolone cheese**

1 In a large saucepan cook the sausage over medium heat until no longer pink; drain off fat. Stir in diced tomatoes, crushed tomatoes, the garlic, vinegar, basil, oregano, salt, and crushed red pepper. Bring to boiling; reduce heat. Simmer, uncovered, for 30 minutes or until thickened.

2 Meanwhile, in a large skillet cook onion and sweet pepper in the hot oil over medium heat until tender. Set aside and keep warm.

3 Preheat broiler. Place split rolls on a baking sheet. If desired, toast rolls. Spoon the meat mixture evenly into split rolls. Top with onion mixture. Top with cheese slices. Broil 4 to 5 inches from the heat for 2 to 3 minutes or until the cheese melts and bubbles.

BAKING DIRECTIONS: Prepare as directed, except do not broil. Preheat oven to 325°F. Wrap sandwiches with foil. Bake about 15 minutes or until heated through.

PER SANDWICH: 735 cal., 48 g total fat (21 g sat. fat), 96 mg chol., 2,121 mg sodium, 38 g carb., 4 g fiber, 37 g pro.
EXCHANGES: 1½ Vegetable, 2 Starch, 4 High-Fat Meat, 3 Fat

PICKLED PEPPER SAUSAGE GRINDERS: Prepare as directed, except omit onion, sweet pepper, and olive oil. Top meat mixture evenly with ½ cup bottled roasted red sweet peppers, drained, and ½ cup bottled sliced banana or pepperoncini peppers, drained.

PER SANDWICH: 672 cal., 41 g total fat (21 g sat. fat), 96 mg chol., 2,339 mg sodium, 37 g carb., 3 g fiber, 37 g pro.
EXCHANGES: 1½ Vegetable, 2 Starch, 4 High-Fat Meat, 1½ Fat

Ham Salad Sandwiches

PREP: 15 MINUTES **CHILL:** 1 TO 4 HOURS
MAKES: 4 SANDWICHES

- **2½ cups cubed cooked ham (10 ounces)**
- **½ cup finely chopped celery (1 stalk)**
- **¼ cup thinly sliced green onions (2)**
- **½ cup mayonnaise**
- **4 teaspoons sweet pickle relish**
- **8 slices bread**
- **Lettuce leaves**

1 Place ham cubes, celery, onions, mayonnaise, and relish in a food processor. Cover and process until creamy and finely chopped. Transfer to a small bowl. Cover and chill for 1 to 4 hours. Spread ham salad evenly on four slices of bread. Top with lettuce and the remaining bread slices.

PER SANDWICH: 416 cal., 26 g total fat (5 g sat. fat), 41 mg chol., 1,708 mg sodium, 28 g carb., 2 g fiber, 18 g pro.
EXCHANGES: 2 Starch, 2 Lean Meat, 3½ Fat

LIGHTEN UP

Cut the fat in sandwiches that call for mayo by choosing a reduced-fat or fat-free version. You'll still get all the flavor.

8 to try

ITALIAN BEEF: Sliced rare roast beef, mild giardiniera mix, and Colby-Jack cheese.

CHICKEN-BACON: Sliced or shredded smoked chicken, crisp-cooked bacon, corn relish, and shredded cheddar cheese.

Panini

Panini are the ultimate grilled sandwiches. Pressing them while cooking ensures crispy outsides and hot, melty insides. Try the Filling ideas given at right.

START TO FINISH: 20 MINUTES
MAKES: 4 SERVINGS

Filling
- **8 slices French, sourdough, or Italian bread, sliced ¾ inch thick**
- **2 tablespoons olive oil or butter, softened**

1 Preheat a covered indoor grill, panini press, grill pan, or large skillet. Layer desired amount of Filling ingredients on four slices of bread. Top with the remaining bread slices. Brush outsides of sandwiches with olive oil or spread with butter.

2 Place sandwiches (half at a time if necessary) in grill. Cover and cook about 6 minutes or until cheese melts (or until heated through) and bread is crisp. (If using a grill pan or skillet, place sandwiches on grill pan or skillet. Weight sandwiches down and grill about 2 minutes or until bread is toasted. Turn sandwiches over, weight them down, and grill until second side is toasted [see tip, below].)

VEGGIE: Thinly sliced cucumber, thinly sliced tomato, thinly sliced onion, fresh spinach, sliced provolone, and creamy ranch dressing.

APRICOT-TURKEY: Sliced roasted turkey or chicken, apricot preserves, Havarti or Brie cheese, and, if desired, leaf lettuce.

HAM AND APPLE: Thinly sliced cooked ham, sliced Taleggio or Brie cheese, and thinly sliced apple or pear.

BARBECUE: Barbecued shredded pork or chicken, smoked Gouda cheese, and dill pickle slices.

SOUTHWEST CHICKEN: Shredded rotisserie chicken, guacamole, sliced tomato, and Monterey Jack cheese with jalapeño peppers.

MEAT LOAF: Sliced leftover meat loaf, thinly sliced onion, dill pickle slices, cheddar or mozzarella cheese, and Dijon-style mustard.

NO PANINI PRESS NEEDED

You can get the packed-tight appeal of these sandwiches with two skillets.

1 Assemble sandwiches as directed; place in a heated skillet.

2 Place a large skillet on top of sandwiches; add a few unopened cans of food to top skillet.

3 Cook 2 minutes; turn. Replace skillet and cans; cook 2 minutes or until sandwiches are done.

4 These panini won't have classic grill marks, but they will have the well-loved crisp, melty goodness.

EGG SALAD SANDWICHES

BEST-LOVED FAST LOW-CALORIE

Egg Salad Sandwiches

START TO FINISH: 15 MINUTES **MAKES:** 4 SANDWICHES

- **8 Hard-Cooked Eggs (page 130), chopped**
- **¼ cup finely chopped green onions (2)**
- **¼ cup mayonnaise**
- **1 tablespoon yellow mustard**
- **1 tablespoon pickle relish (optional)**
- **1 teaspoon snipped fresh dill, tarragon, or chives (optional)**
- **¼ teaspoon salt**
- **⅛ teaspoon black pepper**
- **8 slices bread or 4 small croissants, split**
- **Lettuce leaves and/or tomato slices**

1 In a large bowl combine chopped eggs and green onions. Stir in mayonnaise, mustard, pickle relish (if desired), dill (if desired), salt, and pepper. Spread egg salad evenly on four slices of bread. Top with lettuce and/or tomato slices and the remaining bread slices.

PER SANDWICH: 394 cal., 23 g total fat (6 g sat. fat), 429 mg chol., 729 mg sodium, 27 g carb., 2 g fiber, 17 g pro. EXCHANGES: 2 Starch, 2 Medium-Fat Meat, 2 Fat

CALIFORNIA-STYLE EGG SALAD SANDWICHES: Prepare as directed, except omit mustard and pickle relish. Stir 1 avocado, halved, seeded, peeled, and chopped, and 2 slices crisp-cooked bacon, crumbled, into egg mixture.

PER SANDWICH: 471 cal., 30 g total fat (7 g sat. fat), 433 mg chol., 782 mg sodium, 31 g carb., 4 g fiber, 19 g pro. EXCHANGES: 2 Starch, 2 Medium-Fat Meat, 3½ Fat

GREEK-STYLE EGG SALAD SANDWICHES: Prepare as directed, except omit the mustard, pickle relish, and dill. Stir 1 cup crumbled feta cheese; ½ cup finely chopped, seeded tomato; and ¼ cup sliced pitted ripe olives into egg mixture.

PER SANDWICH: 504 cal., 32 g total fat (11 g sat. fat), 462 mg chol., 1,180 mg sodium, 30 g carb., 2 g fiber, 22 g pro. EXCHANGES: 2 Starch, 2½ Medium-Fat Meat, 3 Fat

BEST-LOVED LOW-CALORIE

New Orleans-Style Muffuletta

PREP: 10 MINUTES **CHILL:** 4 TO 24 HOURS
MAKES: 6 SANDWICHES

- **½ cup coarsely chopped pitted ripe olives**
- **½ cup chopped pimiento-stuffed green olives**
- **1 tablespoon snipped fresh parsley**
- **2 teaspoons lemon juice**
- **½ teaspoon dried oregano, crushed**
- **1 tablespoon olive oil**
- **1 clove garlic, minced**
- **1 16-ounce loaf ciabatta or unsliced French bread**
- **6 lettuce leaves**
- **3 ounces thinly sliced salami, pepperoni, or summer sausage**
- **3 ounces thinly sliced cooked ham or turkey**
- **6 ounces thinly sliced provolone, Swiss, or mozzarella cheese**
- **1 to 2 medium tomatoes, thinly sliced**
- **⅛ teaspoon coarsely ground black pepper**

1 For olive relish, in a small bowl combine the ripe olives, green olives, parsley, lemon juice, and oregano. Cover and chill for 4 to 24 hours.

2 Stir together olive oil and garlic. Split the loaf of bread horizontally and hollow out the inside of the top half, leaving a ¾-inch-thick shell.

3 Brush the bottom bread half with olive oil mixture. Top with lettuce, meats, cheese, and tomatoes; sprinkle with pepper. Stir olive relish; mound on top of tomatoes. Add top of the bread. To serve, cut into six portions.*

***NOTE:** For easiest slicing, use a serrated knife to gently saw through the sandwich.

PER SANDWICH: 398 cal., 19 g total fat (8 g sat. fat), 43 mg chol., 1,219 mg sodium, 39 g carb., 2 g fiber, 20 g pro. EXCHANGES: ½ Vegetable, 2½ Starch, 2 Medium-Fat Meat, 1 Fat

ITALIAN-STYLE MUFFULETTA: Prepare as directed, except omit the ripe and green olives, the parsley, lemon juice, and oregano. Drain a 16-ounce jar of pickled mixed vegetables (giardiniera), reserving the liquid. Chop the vegetables, removing any pepperoncini stems. In a medium bowl stir together the chopped vegetables; 2 tablespoons of the reserved liquid; ¼ cup chopped pimiento-stuffed green olives and/or pitted ripe olives; 1 clove garlic, minced; and 1 tablespoon olive oil. Assemble sandwich as directed, spooning the pickled vegetable mixture on top of the tomatoes.

PER SANDWICH: 409 cal., 19 g total fat (8 g sat. fat), 43 mg chol., 2,008 mg sodium, 41 g carb., 2 g fiber, 20 g pro.
EXCHANGES: 1 Vegetable, 2½ Starch, 2 Medium-Fat Meat, 1 Fat

FAST

Deluxe Grilled Cheese Sandwiches

START TO FINISH: 20 MINUTES
MAKES: 6 SANDWICHES

- **1 1-pound loaf unsliced bakery white bread**
- **6 slices cheddar cheese**
- **6 slices Swiss cheese**
- **2 tablespoons mayonnaise (optional)**
- **1 tablespoon desired mustard (optional)**
- **3 tablespoons olive oil**
- **3 tablespoons butter (optional)**

1 Slice bread ½ inch thick (you should have 12 slices; reserve end slices for another use). Top six of the bread slices with cheese slices.* If desired, spread remaining bread slices evenly with mayonnaise and mustard; place on top of cheese, spread sides down. Brush both sides of each sandwich with olive oil.

2 Heat a large skillet or griddle over medium heat. If desired, add 1 tablespoon of the butter; heat until butter melts. Add two sandwiches to skillet. Cook about 2 minutes or until bottoms are golden. Turn sandwiches over; cook for 2 to 3 minutes more or until bottoms are golden and cheese melts. (Adjust the heat as necessary to prevent overbrowning.) Repeat with the remaining sandwiches and butter (if using).

***NOTE:** If desired, add cooked bacon slices, cooked ham slices, tomato slices, or apple slices to sandwiches before grilling. Serve with purchased chutney or ketchup.

PER SANDWICH: 483 cal., 27 g total fat (12 g sat. fat), 56 mg chol., 745 mg sodium, 40 g carb., 2 g fiber, 20 g pro.
EXCHANGES: 2½ Starch, 2 High-Fat Meat, 1½ Fat

DELUXE GRILLED CHEESE SANDWICHES

FAST

Catfish Po'Boys

START TO FINISH: 20 MINUTES
MAKES: 4 SANDWICHES

- **1 to 1¼ pounds catfish fillets**
- **Salt and black pepper**
- **½ cup fine dry bread crumbs**
- **2 tablespoons olive oil**
- **4 hoagie buns, split and toasted**
- **2 medium red and/or yellow sweet peppers, cored and sliced into rings**
- **1 cup shredded Monterey Jack cheese with jalapeño peppers (4 ounces)**
- **1 cup purchased deli coleslaw**
- **Bottled hot pepper sauce (optional)**
- **Small hot peppers (optional)**

1 Cut catfish fillets into 3-inch pieces. Season catfish fillets lightly with salt and black pepper. Dredge fillets in bread crumbs to coat. In a very large skillet cook catfish in hot oil over medium heat for 6 to 8 minutes or until golden brown and fish flakes easily when tested with a fork, turning fillets over once.

2 Divide catfish among hoagie buns. Top with sweet pepper rings, cheese, and coleslaw. If desired, pass hot pepper sauce and serve with small hot peppers.

PER SANDWICH: 679 cal., 29 g total fat (10 g sat. fat), 85 mg chol., 1,025 mg sodium, 68 g carb., 4 g fiber, 35 g pro.
EXCHANGES: 1 Vegetable, 4 Starch, 3 Medium-Fat Meat, 2 Fat

Oven-Fried Fish Torta with Mexican Cocktail Sauce

PREP: 20 MINUTES **BAKE:** 11 MINUTES AT 425°F
MAKES: 4 SANDWICH HALVES

- **2** **8-ounce fresh or frozen skinless tilapia fillets, about ½ inch thick**
- **¼** **cup bottled cocktail sauce**
- **¼** **to ½ of a jalapeño chile pepper, seeded and finely chopped (see tip, page 44)**
- **1½** **teaspoons snipped fresh cilantro**
- **1½** **teaspoons lime juice**
- **¼** **teaspoon ground cumin**
- **¾** **cup cornflakes, crushed**
- **1** **teaspoon garlic powder**
- **1** **teaspoon chili powder**
- **⅛** **to ¼ teaspoon cayenne pepper**
- **1** **egg**
- **Salt**
- **1** **tablespoon all-purpose flour**
- **4** **1-ounce slices Monterey Jack cheese with jalapeño peppers or sharp cheddar cheese (optional)**
- **2** **8-inch Mexican sandwich rolls (bolillos) or hard rolls, split and toasted**
- **Mayonnaise**
- **Shredded lettuce, dill pickle slices, and/or sliced avocado**

1 Thaw fish if frozen. Rinse fish; pat dry with paper towels. Preheat oven to 425°F. Line a baking sheet with foil; set aside.

2 For sauce, in a small bowl stir together the cocktail sauce, jalapeño chile pepper, cilantro, lime juice, and cumin; set aside.

3 In a shallow dish stir together the crushed cornflakes, garlic powder, chili powder, and cayenne pepper. In a second shallow dish beat egg with a fork. Sprinkle fish with salt and flour; shake off excess flour. Dip fish into egg to coat; dip into cornflake mixture, pressing mixture lightly onto fish. Arrange fish on the prepared baking sheet.

4 Bake for 10 to 12 minutes or until fish begins to flake when tested with a fork. If desired, top each fish fillet with a slice of cheese; bake about 1 minute more or until cheese melts.

5 Spread cut sides of rolls evenly with mayonnaise and the sauce. Top bottoms of rolls with fish fillets, desired toppings, and tops of rolls. Cut sandwiches in half.

PER ½ SANDWICH: 481 cal., 20 g total fat (4 g sat. fat), 110 mg chol., 855 mg sodium, 45 g carb., 5 g fiber, 31 g pro.
EXCHANGES: 1½ Vegetable, 2½ Starch, 3 Lean Meat, 2½ Fat

534
539
sauces &
condiments
540
538
536
536
537

sauces & condiments

It's amazing how much flavor and finesse a sauce brings to a meal. Luckily, most are simple and quick to make—especially when you key into the basics. Find dessert sauces on pages 291–292.

PAN SAUCES

Pan sauces take advantage of the caramelized browned bits left in the pan after searing meats and poultry. With the simple addition of liquid, such as wine and/or broth, it's easy to scrape up these flavorful bits and create the foundation for a savory sauce. Once you master a basic pan sauce, you can create variations by adding ingredients that are fresh, in season, or on hand. Find tips and flavoring ideas for pan sauces on pages 378–379 and on page 475.

FLOUR-THICKENED SAUCES

Some sauces, such as White Sauce (page 532) and Demi-Glace Sauce (page 536), start with cooking flour and fat, such as butter, together before adding the liquid component of the sauce. The flour and fat provide the thickener for the finished sauce. This basic formula is the base for many dishes, including Classic Chicken Pot Pie (page 234), Baked Potato Soup (page 580), and Four-Cheese Macaroni and Cheese (page 222). For smooth, lump-free results, follow the tips on page 533.

TRICKY SAUCES

Hollandaise, Béarnaise, and Beurre Blanc, pages 534–535, require a little extra care. Be sure to cook each as specified in the recipe (in a double boiler over gently boiling water for the Hollandaise and Béarnaise; in a pan over medium-low heat to finish the Beurre Blanc). Excessive heat can cause the sauces to separate or curdle. Serve these classic sauces as soon as they're ready because they often separate upon reheating.

- **HOLLANDAISE SAUCE:** This rich, tangy emulsion of egg yolks, lemon juice, and butter is best served with foods that won't overpower its subtle flavor. Poached eggs, steamed vegetables, and simply seasoned meats and fish taste wonderful with a drizzle of this Sauce.
- **BÉARNAISE:** This traditional French sauce is made by reducing a mixture of vinegar, shallots, and herbs and emulsifying it with egg yolks and butter. It adds a bright flavor punch to steaks, pork chops, and chicken breasts.
- **BEURRE BLANC:** Literally meaning "white butter" in French, this rich sauce is simply a reduction of dry white wine, shallots, vinegar, and cream, with cold butter whisked in at the end of cooking. At this point, the sauce can either be strained to make a completely smooth mixture or left with bits of shallot in it. Spoon Beurre Blanc over vegetables, eggs, poultry, fish, and seafood.

CHUTNEYS & RELISHES

Chutney, such as Sweet Mango Chutney (page 539), is a thick spiced sauce made by simmering fruit, vinegar or citrus juice, and sugar. Its texture can range from chunky to smooth. Fruit relishes, such as Cranberry-Lime Relish (page 540), are mixtures of finely chopped fresh fruit. Because these mixtures are not cooked, be sure to give them time in the refrigerator before serving to allow their flavors to develop. Serve chutneys and relishes with roasted meats and poultry or with various cheeses and bread or crackers.

cook's secrets

basic white sauce

The Secret: So many delicious recipes start with a white sauce. To make sure you get it just right, you have to know the proportions of starch and liquid for the way you want to use the sauce.

FAST

White Sauce

START TO FINISH: 15 MINUTES **MAKES:** 8 SERVINGS

- **1 tablespoon butter**
- **1 tablespoon all-purpose flour**
- **¼ teaspoon salt**
- **Dash black pepper**
- **1 cup milk**

1 In a small saucepan melt butter over medium heat. Stir in flour, salt, and pepper. Stir in milk. Cook and stir over medium heat until thickened and bubbly. Cook and stir for 1 minute more.

CURRY SAUCE: Prepare as directed, except cook 1 teaspoon curry powder in the melted butter for 1 minute before adding the flour. Stir 2 tablespoons snipped chutney into the cooked sauce. Serve with poultry and fish.

HERB-GARLIC SAUCE: Prepare as directed, except cook 2 cloves garlic, minced, in the melted butter for 30 seconds. Stir in ½ teaspoon crushed dried basil with the flour, salt, and pepper. Serve with vegetables and poultry.

LEMON-CHIVE SAUCE: Prepare as directed, except stir in 2 tablespoons snipped fresh chives and 1 teaspoon finely shredded lemon peel with the flour, salt, and pepper. Serve with vegetables, poultry, or fish.

PER ¼ CUP PLAIN, CURRY, HERB-GARLIC, OR LEMON-CHIVE VARIATIONS: 32 cal., 2 g fat (1 g sat. fat), 21 mg chol., 100 mg sodium, 2 g carb., 0 g fiber, 1 g pro. EXCHANGES: ½ Fat

CHEESE SAUCE: Prepare as directed, except stir in 2 ounces cheddar cheese, shredded, and 2 ounces (3 slices) American cheese, torn, into sauce after thickening.

PER ¼ CUP CHEESE VARIATION: 86 cal., 7 g fat (4 g sat. fat), 21 mg chol., 262 mg sodium, 3 g carb., 0 g fiber, 4 g pro. EXCHANGES: ½ Fat

MEDIUM WHITE SAUCE: Prepare as directed, except increase butter and flour to 2 tablespoons each.

PER ¼ CUP: 47 cal., 4 g fat (4 g sat. fat), 10 mg chol., 112 mg sodium, 3 g carb., 0 g fiber, 1 g pro. EXCHANGES: ½ Fat

WHITE SAUCE POINTERS

1. COAT FLOUR WITH BUTTER
Flour coated with fat (butter) is called a roux. Melting the butter so it coats the flour particles prevents lumps from forming when milk is added. Cook and stir until the roux is just golden—not brown.

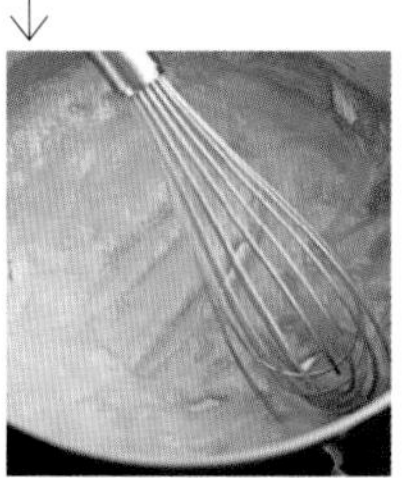

2. COLD MILK
Add cold milk to the roux, whisking constantly. Whisking in cold milk allows the flour particles to stay suspended—again preventing lumps. Warm milk may warm the flour particles quicker, potentially promoting formation of lumps.

3. GENTLY WHISK
A whisk is your best tool because it makes multiple points of contact as you stir the sauce. A whisk will also quickly get rid of any lumps if you see them begin to form. As the sauce thickens, whisk gently. You don't want to break down the starch particles at this point.

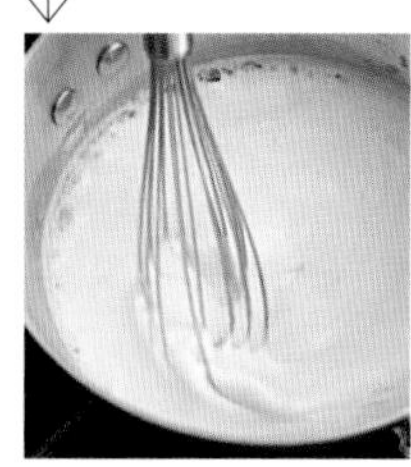

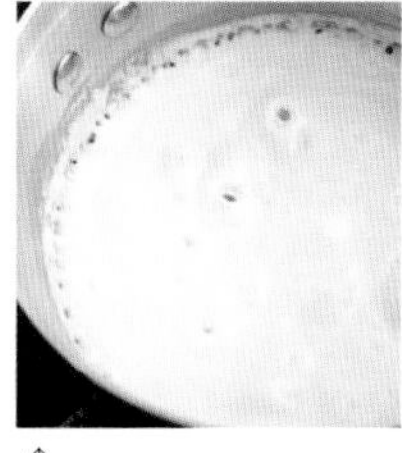

4. BUBBLES ACROSS THE SURFACE!
Cook until the white sauce shows bubbles across the entire surface. Thickening results when heat expands the starch particles in the flour. Cook 1 minute more to ensure the flour is fully cooked. Add cheeses or other flavors at this point.

THIN SAUCE

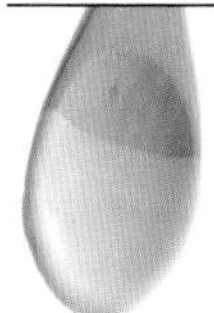

A thin white sauce is made with a low proportion of flour and butter to milk and can be poured rapidly. Most often thin white sauces are the base for creamed soups and cheese sauces for pasta.

CURRY SAUCE: Try the thin white sauce formula, using the curry variation, as the base for a creamy curry cauliflower soup (see Cream of Vegetable Soup, page 582, as a guide).

CHEESE SAUCE: Try the cheese variation, using the thin formula, to make a creamy stove-top macaroni and cheese. Double the cheese sauce recipe and toss with 6 cups cooked elbow macaroni (8 ounces or 2 cups dried elbow macaroni).

MEDIUM SAUCE

A medium white sauce is made with a higher proportion of flour and butter to milk. It will flow smoothly but should have more body to it. This sauce is the base for scalloped dishes and also makes a great dipping sauce.

HERB-GARLIC SAUCE: Try the Herb-Garlic variation, using the medium sauce formula, in scalloped potatoes. Simply double the sauce and follow the recipe for Scalloped Potatoes, page 609, as a guide.

LEMON-CHIVE SAUCE: Try this lemony variation, using the medium sauce formula, to serve with vegetables or as a topper for any fish or seafood. It's perfect drizzled over Crab Cakes, page 309.

FAST

Hollandaise Sauce

START TO FINISH: 12 MINUTES
MAKES: ¾ CUP

- **3 egg yolks, lightly beaten**
- **1 tablespoon lemon juice**
- **1 tablespoon water**
- **½ cup butter (1 stick), cut into thirds and softened**
- **Salt**
- **White or black pepper**

1 In the top of a double boiler combine egg yolks, lemon juice, and water. Add one piece of the butter (see photo 1, below). Place over gently boiling water (upper pan should not touch water). Cook, stirring rapidly with a whisk (see photo 2, below), until butter melts and sauce begins to thicken (see photo 3, below). (Sauce may appear to curdle at this point, but it will smooth out when the remaining butter is added.)

2 Add the remaining butter, one piece at a time, stirring constantly until melted (see photo 4, below). Continue to cook and stir for 2 to 2½ minutes more or until sauce thickens (see photo 5, below). Immediately remove from heat. If sauce is too thick or curdles, immediately whisk in 1 to 2 tablespoons hot water. Season to taste with salt and pepper. Serve with vegetables, poultry, fish, or eggs.

PER 2 TABLESPOONS: 163 cal., 18 g total fat (11 g sat. fat), 146 mg chol., 210 mg sodium, 1 g carb., 0 g fiber, 2 g pro.
EXCHANGES: 3½ Fat

HOLLANDAISE SAUCE

STIR IT UP

Give your Hollandaise Sauce a twist by finishing it off with one of these simple stir-ins:

- Paprika, cayenne pepper, or ground ancho chile
- Snipped fresh herbs, such as parsley, dill weed, or tarragon
- Finely shredded lemon or orange peel
- Chopped capers
- Finely chopped jarred pimientos or roasted red peppers

HOLLANDAISE SAUCE STEP-BY-STEP

1. Away from heat in the top of a double boiler, combine first three ingredients and first third of the butter.

2. Use a whisk to stir quickly so the sauce cooks evenly.

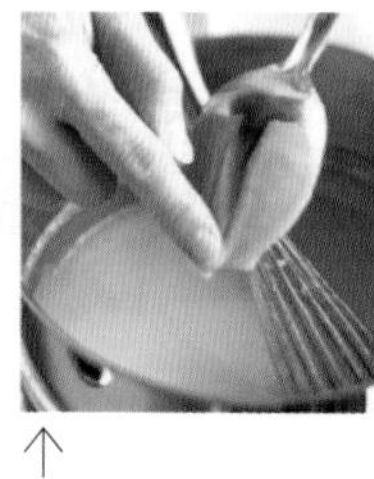

3. After adding the first third of butter, cook and stir until sauce thinly coats back of a spoon.

4. Melt each third of butter completely before adding more or the sauce will cool down too much.

5. Thickened sauce should "drape" from the spoon.

FAST

Béarnaise Sauce

START TO FINISH: 15 MINUTES
MAKES: ABOUT 1½ CUPS

- **5 tablespoons white wine vinegar**
- **1½ teaspoons finely chopped shallot**
- **1½ teaspoons snipped fresh tarragon or ¼ teaspoon dried tarragon, crushed**
- **¼ teaspoon snipped fresh chervil or dash dried chervil, crushed (optional)**
- **⅛ teaspoon white or black pepper**
- **6 egg yolks, lightly beaten**
- **2 tablespoons water**
- **¾ cup butter (1½ sticks), cut into thirds, softened**

1 In a small saucepan stir together vinegar, shallot, tarragon, chervil (if desired), and pepper. Bring to boiling. Boil gently, uncovered, about 2 minutes or until reduced by about half.

2 Place the egg yolks and water in the top of a double boiler. Whisk in vinegar mixture. Add one piece of the butter. Place over gently boiling water (upper pan should not touch water). Cook, stirring rapidly with a whisk, until butter melts and sauce begins to thicken. Add remaining butter, one piece at a time, stirring constantly until melted. Continue to cook and stir for 1½ to 2 minutes more or until sauce is thick (an instant-read thermometer inserted in sauce should register 160°F). Immediately remove from heat. If sauce is too thick or curdles, immediately whisk in 1 to 2 tablespoons hot water. Serve with beef, pork, or poultry.

PER 2 TABLESPOONS: 131 cal., 14 g total fat (8 g sat. fat), 135 mg chol., 86 mg sodium, 0 g carb., 0 g fiber, 1 g pro. EXCHANGES: 3 Fat

FAST

Beurre Blanc

START TO FINISH: 20 MINUTES
MAKES: 1 CUP (UNSTRAINED)

- **¼ cup dry white wine**
- **2 tablespoons finely chopped shallot**
- **1 tablespoon white wine vinegar**
- **2 tablespoons whipping cream**
- **¾ cup cold unsalted butter (1½ sticks), cut into 2-tablespoon pieces**
- **Salt and white pepper**

1 In a small stainless-steel, enamel, or nonstick saucepan combine the wine, shallot, and vinegar. Bring to boiling; reduce heat to medium. Boil gently, uncovered, for 7 to 9 minutes or until almost all of the liquid has evaporated. Stir in the cream. Bring to boiling and cook about 1 minute to reduce the cream slightly. Reduce heat to medium-low.

2 Using a wire whisk, stir in the butter, one piece at a time, allowing each piece to melt before adding the next. Allow about 8 minutes. If desired, strain sauce. Season to taste with salt and white pepper. Serve over fish or vegetables.

LEMONY BEURRE BLANC: Prepare as directed, except substitute lemon juice for the vinegar. If desired, top with finely shredded lemon peel.

CREAMY MUSTARD SAUCE: Prepare as directed, except whisk in 2 teaspoons Dijon-style mustard before serving.

PER 2 TABLESPOONS PLAIN, LEMONY, OR CREAMY MUSTARD VARIATIONS: 174 cal., 19 g total fat (12 g sat. fat), 51 mg chol., 41 mg sodium, 1 g carb., 0 g fiber, 0 g pro. EXCHANGES: 4 Fat

Bordelaise Sauce

START TO FINISH: 40 MINUTES **MAKES:** ABOUT 1 CUP

- **1¼ cups reduced-sodium beef broth**
- **¾ cup dry red wine**
- **2 tablespoons finely chopped shallot or onion**
- **3 tablespoons butter or margarine, softened**
- **1 tablespoon all-purpose flour**
- **¼ teaspoon salt**
- **1 tablespoon snipped fresh parsley (optional)**

1 In a medium saucepan combine broth, wine, and shallot. Bring just to boiling; reduce heat. Simmer, uncovered, skimming the surface often with a spoon, for 25 to 30 minutes or until reduced to 1 cup.

2 With a fork, in a small bowl stir together butter and flour. Whisk butter mixture into wine mixture, 1 teaspoon at a time, whisking constantly (mixture will thicken). Cook and stir for 1 minute more. Stir in salt and, if desired, parsley. Serve with beef or lamb.

PER 2 TABLESPOONS: 64 cal., 4 g total fat (3 g sat. fat), 11 mg chol., 173 mg sodium, 2 g carb., 0 g fiber, 1 g pro. EXCHANGES: 1 Fat

Demi-Glace Sauce

PREP: 15 MINUTES **COOK:** 40 MINUTES **MAKES:** 1 CUP

- **½ cup chopped onion (1 medium)**
- **½ cup sliced carrot (1 small)**
- **1 teaspoon sugar**
- **¼ cup butter**
- **4 teaspoons all-purpose flour**
- **1 14.5-ounce can beef broth**
- **2 tablespoons tomato paste**
- **½ teaspoon dried thyme, crushed**
- **1 bay leaf**
- **⅛ teaspoon black pepper**

1 In a medium saucepan cook onion, carrot, and sugar in hot butter over medium-low heat about 15 minutes or until tender and starting to brown, stirring occasionally. Stir in the flour. Cook and stir about 5 minutes more or until flour is brown. Add the beef broth, tomato paste, thyme, bay leaf, and pepper. Bring to boiling, stirring to incorporate the tomato paste. Reduce heat; simmer, uncovered, for 20 to 25 minutes or until mixture is reduced to about 1½ cups, stirring occasionally. Strain through a fine mesh sieve and discard vegetables and bay leaf. Serve with beef, pork, or lamb.

PER 2 TABLESPOONS: 36 cal., 3 g total fat (2 g sat. fat), 8 mg chol., 130 mg sodium, 2 g carb., 0 g fiber, 0 g pro. EXCHANGES: ½ Fat

FAST

Sauce Provençal

START TO FINISH: 25 MINUTES **MAKES:** 1¾ CUPS

- **¼ cup finely chopped onion**
- **1 clove garlic, minced**
- **2 tablespoons olive oil**
- **¼ cup dry white wine**
- **¼ cup chicken broth**
- **1½ cups chopped peeled, seeded tomatoes (3 medium)**
- **1 tablespoon snipped fresh parsley**
- **2 teaspoons snipped fresh thyme**
- **¼ teaspoon salt**

1 In a medium saucepan cook onion and garlic in hot oil over medium-high heat until tender but not browned. Stir in the wine and broth. Bring to boiling; reduce heat. Boil gently, uncovered, about 8 minutes or until reduced to ¼ cup. Stir in tomatoes, parsley, thyme, and salt; heat through. Serve over fish, chicken, couscous, or pasta.

PER 2 TABLESPOONS: 26 cal., 2 g total fat (0 g sat. fat), 0 mg chol., 60 mg sodium, 1 g carb., 0 g fiber, 0 g pro. EXCHANGES: ½ Fat

BEST-LOVED

Balsamic BBQ Sauce *(photo, page 529)*

PREP: 10 MINUTES **COOK:** 45 MINUTES
MAKES: 2 CUPS

- **1 cup lager beer**
- **1 cup ketchup**
- **½ cup packed brown sugar**
- **⅓ cup white balsamic vinegar**
- **6 cloves garlic, minced**
- **1 tablespoon honey**
- **1 teaspoon ground cumin**
- **1 teaspoon Asian chili sauce (optional)**
- **1 teaspoon chili powder**
- **½ teaspoon black pepper**

1 In a medium saucepan combine beer, ketchup, brown sugar, vinegar, garlic, honey, cumin, chili sauce (if desired), chili powder, and pepper. Bring to boiling; reduce heat. Simmer, uncovered, for 45 minutes to 1 hour or until mixture reaches desired consistency, stirring frequently. Serve with grilled poultry or pork. (Transfer any leftovers to a storage container. Cover and chill for up to 1 week. Before serving, warm sauce in saucepan.)

PER 2 TABLESPOONS: 60 cal., 0 g total fat, 0 mg chol., 172 mg sodium, 14 g carb., 0 g fiber, 0 g pro. EXCHANGES: 1 Other Carb.

FAST

Romesco Sauce *(photo, page 529)*

START TO FINISH: 20 MINUTES **MAKES:** 2 CUPS

- **4 medium roma tomatoes, peeled, seeded, and cut up**
- **⅔ cup bottled roasted red sweet peppers, cut up**
- **1 ¾-inch slice country-style bread, toasted and torn into pieces (2 ounces)**
- **½ cup blanched whole almonds, toasted (see tip, page 21)**
- **¼ cup sherry vinegar or red wine vinegar**
- **4 cloves garlic, smashed**
- **1 tablespoon snipped fresh Italian parsley**
- **1 teaspoon smoked paprika**
- **½ teaspoon ground ancho chile pepper**
- **⅛ teaspoon cayenne pepper**
- **¼ to ⅓ cup olive oil**
- **Salt**

1 In a food processor combine tomatoes, roasted red sweet peppers, torn bread pieces, almonds, vinegar, garlic, parsley, paprika, chile pepper, and cayenne. Cover and process until combined. With the motor running, add the olive oil through the opening in the lid in a thin, steady stream until combined and mixture is finely chopped. Season to taste with salt. Serve with fish, poultry, beef, pork, or vegetables. (Transfer any leftovers to a storage container. Cover and chill for up to 1 week. Before serving, let stand for 30 minutes at room temperature.)

PER 2 TABLESPOONS: 76 cal., 6 g total fat (1 g sat. fat), 0 mg chol., 61 mg sodium, 5 g carb., 1 g fiber, 2 g pro. **EXCHANGES:** 1½ Fat

BEST-LOVED

Classic Pesto

START TO FINISH: 20 MINUTES **MAKES:** ¾ CUP

- **⅓ cup olive oil**
- **2 cups firmly packed fresh basil leaves**
- **½ cup pine nuts**
- **½ cup grated Parmesan cheese (2 ounces)**
- **3 to 4 cloves garlic, peeled and quartered**
- **¼ teaspoon salt**
- **Olive oil**
- **Black pepper**

1 In a food processor or blender combine the ⅓ cup olive oil, basil, nuts, cheese, garlic, and salt. Cover and process or blend until nearly smooth, stopping and scraping sides as necessary and adding enough additional olive oil (about 2 tablespoons) to reach desired consistency. Season to taste with pepper. Serve with pasta, poultry, or fish.

PER TABLESPOON: 129 cal., 13 g total fat (0 g sat. fat), 3 mg chol., 100 mg sodium, 1 g carb., 0 g fiber, 2 g pro. **EXCHANGES:** 2½ Fat

Horseradish Sauce

PREP: 5 MINUTES **CHILL:** 60 MINUTES **MAKES:** 1 CUP

- **1 8-ounce carton sour cream**
- **3 tablespoons prepared horseradish**
- **⅛ teaspoon salt**

1 In a small bowl stir together sour cream, horseradish, and salt. Cover and chill for at least 60 minutes before serving. Serve with beef or pork.

MUSTARD-HORSERADISH SAUCE: Prepare as directed, except stir in 2 tablespoons chopped green onion (1) and 2 tablespoons Dijon-style mustard. Makes 1⅓ cups.

PER TABLESPOON PLAIN OR MUSTARD-HORSERADISH VARIATION: 57 cal., 6 g total fat (3 g sat. fat), 15 mg chol., 77 mg sodium, 1 g carb., 0 g fiber, 1 g pro. **EXCHANGES:** 1 Fat

CHIMICHURRI

Chimichurri

PREP: 15 MINUTES **CHILL:** 2 HOURS **MAKES:** ⅔ CUP

- **1¼ cups packed fresh Italian parsley leaves**
- **¼ cup olive oil**
- **2 tablespoons fresh oregano or basil leaves**
- **1 shallot, peeled**
- **3 to 4 cloves garlic, peeled**
- **2 tablespoons cider vinegar or red wine vinegar**
- **1 tablespoon lemon juice**
- **½ teaspoon salt**
- **¼ to ½ teaspoon crushed red pepper**

1 In a food processor or blender combine parsley, oil, oregano, shallot, garlic, vinegar, lemon juice, salt, and crushed red pepper. Cover and process or blend until just chopped and a few herb leaves are still visible. Cover and chill for 2 hours before serving. Serve with grilled meat or poultry. (Transfer any leftovers to a storage container. Cover and chill for up to 1 week. Before serving, let stand for 30 minutes at room temperature.)

PER TABLESPOON: 53 cal., 5 g total fat (1 g sat. fat), 0 mg chol., 114 mg sodium, 2 g carb., 0 g fiber, 0 g pro. **EXCHANGES:** 1 Fat

FAST

Tzatziki Sauce

START TO FINISH: 15 MINUTES **MAKES:** 1 CUP

- **1 6-ounce carton fat-free plain Greek or regular yogurt**
- **1 cup shredded, seeded cucumber**
- **1 tablespoon lemon juice**
- **1 tablespoon olive oil**
- **1 tablespoon snipped fresh mint**
- **1 clove garlic, minced**
- **¼ teaspoon salt**

1 In a small bowl stir together yogurt, cucumber, lemon juice, oil, mint, garlic, and salt. Serve immediately or cover and chill for up to 4 hours. Serve with lamb, pork, or vegetables.

PER 2 TABLESPOONS: 35 cal., 3 g total fat (1 g sat. fat), 6 mg chol., 66 mg sodium, 2 g carb., 0 g fiber, 1 g pro.
EXCHANGES: ½ Fat

TZATZIKI SAUCE

This go-to for gyros (Greek-style sandwiches) goes with many other foods, too.

This classic Greek sauce is creamy and refreshing (thanks to the yogurt and cucumber) yet pleasantly zippy (thanks to the garlic and lemon juice). It offers a cooling counterbalance to boldly spiced broiled and grilled meats and fish. In a pinch, substitute white wine vinegar for the lemon juice.

FAST

Sweet-and-Sour Sauce

START TO FINISH: 20 MINUTES **MAKES:** 1 CUP

- **½ cup packed brown sugar**
- **4 teaspoons cornstarch**
- **⅓ cup chicken broth**
- **⅓ cup red wine vinegar**
- **¼ cup finely chopped green sweet pepper**
- **2 tablespoons chopped pimientos or roasted red sweet pepper**
- **2 tablespoons soy sauce**
- **1½ teaspoons minced fresh ginger**
- **1 clove garlic, minced**
- **⅛ to ¼ teaspoon crushed red pepper**

1 In a small saucepan stir together brown sugar and cornstarch. Stir in broth, vinegar, sweet pepper, pimientos, soy sauce, ginger, garlic, and crushed red pepper. Cook and stir until thickened and bubbly. Cook and stir for 2 minutes more. Serve warm with egg rolls and wontons or use in recipes calling for sweet-and-sour sauce. (Transfer any leftovers to a storage container. Cover and chill for up to 3 days. Before serving, warm sauce in a saucepan.)

PER 2 TABLESPOONS: 65 cal., 0 g total fat, 0 mg chol., 298 mg sodium, 16 g carb., 0 g fiber, 0 g pro.
EXCHANGES: 1 Other Carb.

FAST

Cocktail Sauce

START TO FINISH: 10 MINUTES **MAKES:** 1 CUP

- **¾ cup bottled chili sauce**
- **2 tablespoons lemon juice**
- **2 tablespoons thinly sliced green onion (1)**
- **1 tablespoon prepared horseradish**
- **2 teaspoons Worcestershire sauce**
- **Several dashes bottled hot pepper sauce**

1 In a small bowl stir together chili sauce, lemon juice, green onion, horseradish, Worcestershire sauce, and hot pepper sauce. Serve with fish or seafood. (Transfer any leftovers to a storage container. Cover and chill for up to 2 weeks.)

PER 2 TABLESPOONS: 34 cal., 0 g total fat, 0 mg chol., 740 mg sodium, 9 g carb., 0 g fiber, 0 g pro.
EXCHANGES: ½ Other Carb.

Easy Aïoli

PREP: 10 MINUTES **CHILL:** 60 MINUTES
MAKES: 2/3 CUP

- **1/3 cup mayonnaise**
- **3 cloves garlic, minced**
- **1 teaspoon water**
- **1/2 teaspoon lemon juice**
- **1/8 teaspoon salt**
- **1/4 cup olive oil**

1 In a medium bowl combine the mayonnaise and garlic. Whisk in the water, lemon juice, and salt until the mixture is smooth. Slowly whisk in the olive oil until combined and smooth. Cover and chill for at least 60 minutes before serving. Serve with vegetables, shellfish, or beef.

PER TABLESPOON: 96 cal., 11 g total fat (2 g sat. fat), 2 mg chol., 60 mg sodium, 0 g carb., 0 g fiber, 0 g pro. **EXCHANGES:** 2 Fat

BEST-LOVED

Tartar Sauce

PREP: 10 MINUTES **CHILL:** 2 HOURS **MAKES:** 1 CUP

- **3/4 cup mayonnaise**
- **1/4 cup sweet or dill pickle relish**
- **2 tablespoons finely chopped onion**
- **1 tablespoon snipped fresh dill weed or 1 teaspoon dried dill weed**
- **1 teaspoon lemon juice**
- **2 teaspoons capers, drained (optional)**

1 In a small bowl stir together the mayonnaise, pickle relish, onion, dill, lemon juice, and, if desired, capers. Cover and chill for at least 2 hours before serving. Serve with fish or seafood. (Transfer any leftovers to a storage container. Cover and chill for up to 1 week.)

PER 2 TABLESPOONS: 161 cal., 17 g total fat (3 g sat. fat), 8 mg chol., 173 mg sodium, 3 g carb., 0 g fiber, 0 g pro. **EXCHANGES:** 3½ Fat

LOW-FAT TARTAR SAUCE: Prepare as directed, except substitute 1/2 cup light mayonnaise and 1/4 cup plain low-fat yogurt for the 3/4 cup mayonnaise.

PER 2 TABLESPOONS: 64 cal., 5 g total fat (1 g sat. fat), 6 mg chol., 167 mg sodium, 5 g carb., 0 g fiber, 1 g pro. **EXCHANGES:** 1 Fat

SWEET MANGO CHUTNEY

BEST-LOVED

Sweet Mango Chutney

PREP: 25 MINUTES **COOK:** 25 MINUTES
CHILL: 8 HOURS **MAKES:** 2 CUPS

- **2 mangoes, seeded, peeled, and chopped (2 cups)**
- **1 medium pear or tart apple, peeled, cored, and chopped (1 cup)**
- **1/2 cup chopped leek or onion (1 medium)**
- **1/3 cup honey**
- **1/3 cup rice vinegar, white wine vinegar, white balsamic vinegar, or apple cider vinegar**
- **1 tablespoon orange juice**
- **2 cloves garlic, minced**
- **1/4 teaspoon salt**
- **1/4 teaspoon crushed red pepper**
- **1/4 teaspoon ground ginger**

1 In a large saucepan stir together the mangoes, pear, leek, honey, vinegar, orange juice, garlic, salt, crushed red pepper, and ginger. Bring to boiling; reduce heat. Simmer, uncovered, about 25 minutes or until syrupy, stirring occasionally. Remove from heat; cool.

2 Cover and chill for at least 8 hours before serving. Serve with poultry, pork, or cheese. (Transfer any leftovers to a storage container. Cover and chill for up to 1 week. Before serving, let stand for 30 minutes at room temperature.)

PER 1/4 CUP: 89 cal., 0 g total fat, 0 mg chol., 76 mg sodium, 22 g carb., 1 g fiber, 1 g pro. **EXCHANGES:** ½ Fruit, 1 Other Carb.

FAST

Tapenade

START TO FINISH: 25 MINUTES **MAKES:** 1 CUP

- **½ cup pimiento-stuffed green olives**
- **½ cup pitted Kalamata olives**
- **1 tablespoon olive oil**
- **2 teaspoons balsamic vinegar**
- **1 teaspoon Dijon-style mustard**
- **2 cloves garlic, minced**
- **½ cup finely chopped, seeded tomato**
- **2 tablespoons thinly sliced green onion (1)**
- **1 teaspoon snipped fresh rosemary (optional)**
- **Toasted baguette slices or crackers**

1 In a blender or food processor combine green olives, Kalamata olives, olive oil, vinegar, mustard, and garlic. Cover and blend or process until nearly smooth, scraping down sides of container as necessary. Stir in tomato, green onion, and, if desired, rosemary. Serve with bread slices or crackers or as a sandwich spread. (Transfer any leftovers to a storage container. Cover and chill for up to 1 week.)

PER 2 TABLESPOONS: 43 cal., 2 g total fat (0 g sat. fat), 0 mg chol., 139 mg sodium, 6 g carb., 1 g fiber, 1 g pro.
EXCHANGES: ½ Starch

Cranberry-Lime Relish

PREP: 10 MINUTES **CHILL:** 2 HOURS
STAND: 30 MINUTES **MAKES:** 2½ CUPS

- **1 12-ounce bag fresh cranberries**
- **1 cup packed brown sugar**
- **2 teaspoons finely shredded lime peel**
- **¼ cup lime juice**
- **3 tablespoons bourbon, vodka, orange liqueur, or orange juice (optional)**

1 In a food processor combine cranberries, brown sugar, lime peel, lime juice, and, if desired, bourbon. Cover and process until cranberries are finely chopped. Chill for at least 2 hours. Let stand at room temperature for 30 minutes before serving. Serve with poultry or pork. (Transfer any leftovers to a storage container. Cover and chill for up to 1 week.)

PER ¼ CUP: 101 cal., 0 g total fat, 0 mg chol., 7 mg sodium, 26 g carb., 2 g fiber, 0 g pro. **EXCHANGES:** ½ Fruit, 1½ Other Carb.

CRANBERRY-LIME RELISH

FAST

Pear-Cranberry Chutney

PREP: 10 MINUTES **COOK:** 15 MINUTES
MAKES: ABOUT 4 CUPS

- **1 12-ounce bag fresh cranberries**
- **⅓ cup chopped onion (1 small)**
- **1 cup packed brown sugar**
- **½ cup water**
- **3 tablespoons lemon juice**
- **1 1-inch piece fresh ginger, peeled and grated**
- **¼ teaspoon ground cinnamon**
- **⅛ teaspoon ground cloves**
- **Dash cayenne pepper**
- **3 Bosc pears, cored and chopped**
- **Chopped walnuts (optional)**

1 In a medium saucepan combine cranberries, onion, brown sugar, water, lemon juice, ginger, cinnamon, cloves, and cayenne pepper. Bring to boiling; reduce heat. Simmer, uncovered, about 10 minutes or until cranberries soften. Add pears; cook for 5 to 10 minutes more or until pears are soft but still keep their shape. Serve chilled or at room temperature. If desired, top with chopped walnuts. Serve with poultry, pork, or cheese. (Transfer any leftovers to a storage container. Cover and chill for up to 1 week.)

PER ¼ CUP: 83 cal., 0 g total fat, 0 mg chol., 5 mg sodium, 22 g carb., 2 g fiber, 0 g pro. **EXCHANGES:** ½ Fruit, 1 Other Carb.

slow cooker recipes

slow cooker recipes

From party dips to family meals, slow-cooking gives you satisfying results with fix-now-savor-later ease.

COOKER CHOICES

Slow cookers range in size from 1 to 7 quarts. One-quart models generally provide one heat setting (low) and are best for making dips or meals for one or two. The most popular family sizes range from 3 to 6 quarts.

OVAL-SHAPE COOKERS: These models provide more space in the crockery insert for larger cuts of meat, such as brisket and ribs.

TIGHT-FITTING, SEE-THROUGH LIDS: These let you view the food as it cooks without lifting the lid, which allows heat to escape.

REMOVABLE INSERTS: These should have large, sturdy handles to make it easier (and safer) to remove them from the base. A stove-top-safe insert lets you brown meat and slow-cook it in one pan. Before washing the ceramic liner, let it cool to room temperature so it doesn't crack when it comes in contact with water.

DISPOSABLE PLASTIC BAG LINERS: Allowing for easy cleanup with no soaking or scrubbing, these fit most 3 to 6½ quart slow cookers. Look for liners where plastic storage bags are sold.

A PROGRAMMABLE TIMER: This allows you to set the cooker to start while you're out. (Note: The cooker should be set to start within 2 hours of filling.) Some timers can be programmed to cook on high for a set time, then switch to low. Newer programmable models automatically switch to a warm-heat setting once food is cooked to hold food at a safe temperature of 165°F.

WRAPAROUND HEATING ELEMENTS: Cookers with heating elements on the sides heat more evenly than those with the heating element below the food container. Recipes in this chapter require cookers with wraparound heating elements.

TIPS FOR SLOW-COOKED SUCCESS

- Always thaw frozen meat and poultry before cooking. If you're in a time crunch, use your microwave oven to thaw these foods before placing in a slow cooker.
- Trim excess fat from meat and skin poultry before cooking. Skim fat from cooking juices before serving (see tip, page 564).
- Take time to brown the meat before placing it in the cooker. Browning adds color and flavor and requires little fat when you use a nonstick skillet coated with nonstick cooking spray.
- Fill the cooker at least half full and no more than three-fourths full.
- Don't peek. Every time you lift the slow cooker lid, you release heat and add 30 minutes to the cooking time. If you need to lift the lid to stir in ingredients during cooking time, do so quickly.
- If you omit an ingredient because of family preferences, replace it with an equal amount of another ingredient. For example, if you decide to eliminate three parsnips in a pot roast recipe, replace them with three carrots.
- Allow your meals to cook as long as the recipe specifies for the most tender, juicy results.
- A touch of fresh herbs at the end of cooking will freshen the look of your finished dish.

Italian Braised Chicken with Fennel and Cannellini, page 558

PREPPING AHEAD

Here are a few ways to get a jump-start on preparing slow cooker meals.

- Chop vegetables and refrigerate in separate covered containers.
- Assemble, cover, and chill liquid ingredients or sauces in separate covered containers.
- Brown ground meat, ground poultry, and ground sausage the night before, making sure they're fully cooked before covering and refrigerating. (Do not brown other meats, such as chicken, beef, or pork cubes, or roasts; it is unsafe to partially cook meats and refrigerate them for later cooking.)

SAFETY POINTERS

- If you're concerned that your slow cooker is not heating properly, test it. Fill it half to three-fourths with cool tap water. Heat it on the low-heat setting, covered, for 2 to 3 hours; check the water temperature with an accurate food thermometer. It should be about 185°F. If it's not, replace your slow cooker with a new one.
- One of the nice things about slow-cooking is that many recipes make big batches, allowing you to freeze leftovers to reheat on busy days. Immediately after the meal, transfer leftover food to freezer containers and freeze up to 6 months. To serve, thaw the food in the refrigerator before reheating it on the stove top or in the microwave.
- A whole chicken or large cut of meat cooks safely in a slow cooker when it fits. If the chicken or meat extends over three-fourths of the way up the cooker, you need a bigger slow cooker. The other option is to cut up the chicken or trim the meat to fit.

MEET THE MEATS

These less tender (and less expensive) cuts of meat are ideal for long, slow, moist cooking.

BEEF: Arm pot roast, blade steak, brisket, chuck pot roast, chuck short ribs, flank steak, round steak, rump roast, shank cross cuts, shoulder steak, stew meat

PORK: Blade roast, boneless pork shoulder roast (butt roast), country-style ribs, sirloin chops, sirloin roast, smoked pork hocks

CHICKEN AND TURKEY: Breast halves (bone-in), drumsticks, thighs (bone-in or boneless).

SLOW-COOKING LONGTIME FAVORITES

Some of your family's favorite recipes might be good candidates for slow cooker meals. To adapt them, follow these guidelines:

- Choose recipes that feature one of the less-tender cuts (see "Meet the Meats," above) and find a recipe in this chapter similar to yours. Use it as a guide for quantities, piece sizes, liquid levels, and cooking times.
- Unless your dish contains long grain rice, reduce the liquids in the recipe you are adapting by about half.
- Trim the meat, cut it to the right size for a slow cooker, and, if desired, brown it.
- Cut vegetables into bite-size pieces; place them at the bottom of the slow cooker so they'll cook evenly and completely.
- Enhance the flavor of meat dishes by adding broth, wine, or juice for the liquid.

Chipotle, Chorizo, and Bean Dip

PREP: 30 MINUTES **COOK:** 4 HOURS (LOW) OR 2 HOURS (HIGH) **MAKES:** 4 CUPS

- **8 ounces uncooked chorizo sausage, casings removed if present**
- **½ cup chopped onion (1 medium)**
- **2 cloves garlic, minced**
- **1 15-ounce can black beans, rinsed and drained**
- **1 14.5-ounce can diced tomatoes, undrained**
- **¼ cup snipped fresh cilantro**
- **1 to 2 teaspoons chopped canned chipotle pepper in adobo sauce (see tip, page 44)**
- **1 15-ounce can pinto beans, rinsed and drained**
- **½ cup shredded Monterey Jack cheese with jalapeño chile peppers (2 ounces)**
- **Tortilla chips**

1 In skillet cook sausage, onion, and garlic over medium-high heat until sausage is browned. Remove from skillet; drain on paper towels.

2 In a bowl stir together sausage mixture, black beans, tomatoes, cilantro, and chipotle pepper. In a 1½-quart slow cooker mash pinto beans. Top with tomato mixture and sprinkle with cheese.

3 Cover and cook on low-heat setting about 4 hours or on high-heat setting about 2 hours or until bubbly. Serve immediately or keep covered on warm- or low-heat setting for up to 2 hours. Serve with tortilla chips.

PER ¼ CUP: 61 cal., 3 g total fat (1 g sat. fat), 8 mg chol., 206 mg sodium, 5 g carb., 1 g fiber, 4 g pro. EXCHANGES: ½ Starch, ½ High-Fat Meat

Crab and Horseradish Dip

PREP: 20 MINUTES **COOK:** 2 TO 3 HOURS (LOW) **MAKES:** 2½ CUPS

- **1 8-ounce package cream cheese, softened**
- **1¼ cups shredded Havarti cheese (5 ounces)**
- **⅓ cup sour cream**
- **¼ cup mayonnaise**
- **1 cup cooked crabmeat or one 6-ounce can crabmeat, drained, flaked, and cartilage removed**
- **1 cup shredded fresh spinach leaves**
- **⅓ cup thinly sliced green onions (3)**
- **1 tablespoon snipped chives**
- **2 teaspoons prepared horseradish**
- **Toasted flatbread, bagel chips, or crostini**

1 Combine cream cheese, 1 cup of the Havarti, sour cream, and mayonnaise; beat until well mixed. Stir in crabmeat and spinach. Transfer mixture to a 1½-quart slow cooker. Cover and cook on low-heat setting for 2 to 3 hours. Sprinkle

CRAB AND HORSERADISH DIP

with the remaining Havarti cheese, green onions, chives, and horseradish. Serve dip with toasted flatbread, bagel chips, or crostini.

PER ¼ CUP: 204 cal., 18 g total fat (9 g sat. fat), 52 mg chol., 387 mg sodium, 2 g carb., 0 g fiber, 8 g pro. EXCHANGES: 1 Medium-Fat Meat, 3 Fat

Spinach-Artichoke Dip *(photo, page 541)*

PREP: 25 MINUTES **COOK:** 3 TO 4 HOURS (LOW) **MAKES:** 6 CUPS

- **4 slices bacon**
- **1 cup coarsely chopped sweet onion**
- **2 14-ounce cans artichoke hearts, drained and coarsely chopped**
- **1 10-ounce package frozen chopped spinach, thawed and well drained**
- **1 cup chopped red sweet pepper (1 large)**
- **1 cup light mayonnaise**
- **1 8-ounce package cream cheese, cut up**
- **4 ounces blue cheese, crumbled**
- **3 cloves garlic, minced**
- **½ teaspoon dry mustard**

1 In a skillet cook bacon until crisp; drain and crumble. Chill bacon until ready to use. In skillet cook onion in 1 tablespoon bacon drippings about 5 minutes or until tender.

2 In 3½- or 4-quart slow cooker combine onion and remaining ingredients. Cover and cook on low-heat setting 3 to 4 hours or until heated. Stir in bacon. Serve with crackers.

PER ¼ CUP: 112 cal., 9 g total fat (4 g sat. fat), 19 mg chol., 323 mg sodium, 4 g carb., 1 g fiber, 3 g pro. EXCHANGES: 2 Fat

LOW-CALORIE

Sweet-Sour Meatballs

Take this perennial favorite and use our cutting-edge, alternative ideas for an all-new lineup on the party stage. Start with the recipe below and substitute ingredients for fresh flavors.

PREP: 35 MINUTES
BAKE: 25 MINUTES AT 375°F
COOK: 3 TO 4 HOURS (LOW) OR 90 MINUTES TO 2 HOURS (HIGH)
MAKES: 36 MEATBALLS

- **2 eggs**
- **½ cup fine dry bread crumbs**
- **½ cup finely chopped onion (1 medium)**
- **¼ cup milk**
- **½ teaspoon salt**
- **½ teaspoon black pepper**
- **1 pound bulk pork sausage**
- **1 pound ground beef**
- **¾ cup apple jelly**
- **⅓ cup spicy brown mustard**
- **⅓ cup whiskey or apple juice**
- **1½ teaspoons Worcestershire sauce**
- **Dash bottled hot pepper sauce**

1 Preheat oven to 375°F. In a large bowl beat eggs with a fork. Stir in bread crumbs, onion, milk, salt, and pepper. Add sausage and ground beef; mix well. Shape mixture into 36 meatballs. Place meatballs in a shallow baking pan. Bake for 25 to 30 minutes or until meatballs are cooked through (160°F). Drain off fat.

2 Place meatballs in a 3½- or 4-quart slow cooker. For the sauce, in a small bowl stir together jelly, mustard, whiskey, Worcestershire sauce, and hot pepper sauce; pour over meatballs.

3 Cover and cook on low-heat setting for 3 to 4 hours or on high-heat setting for 1½ to 2 hours. Serve immediately or keep warm, covered, on warm setting or low-heat setting for up to 2 hours. Serve with decorative toothpicks.

***NOTE:** See tip on handling chile peppers, page 44.

HAM BALLS WITH COLA GLAZE: Use 1 pound each ground ham and pork for the meats. Omit sauce ingredients. For sauce, use black cherry preserves for jelly and mix with ¾ cup cherry cola, ¼ cup Dijon-style mustard, and ¼ cup finely chopped onion.

PINEAPPLE MEATBALLS: Omit sauce ingredients. For sauce, mix 1 cup pineapple preserves; ¼ cup lime juice; 1 jalapeño pepper, seeded and chopped;* and 1 clove garlic, minced.

CHICKEN-CHORIZO MEATBALLS: Use 1 pound uncooked ground chicken and one 15-ounce package uncooked chorizo sausage for the meats. Omit sauce ingredients. For sauce, mix 1 cup salsa verde; 1 fresh poblano pepper, seeded and chopped;* ¼ cup chicken broth; 2 cloves garlic, minced; and 1 teaspoon ground cumin.

SHRIMP-PORK MEATBALLS: Use 1 pound each chopped shrimp and ground pork for meats. Use ¼ cup each chopped green onions and fresh cilantro for ½ cup onion. For sauce, mix ½ cup soy sauce, ⅓ cup rice vinegar, 2 tablespoons sugar, and 1 teaspoon minced fresh ginger; cook. Top with sesame seeds.

PEACH-TURKEY MEATBALLS: Use 1¼ pounds uncooked ground turkey and 12 ounces ground pork for the meats. Omit sauce ingredients. For sauce, mix 1½ cups peach preserves, 2 tablespoons white vinegar, 1 teaspoon smoked paprika, and 1 clove garlic, minced.

BEER-MUSTARD MEATBALLS: Use four 4-ounce uncooked bratwurst links, casings removed, for sausage. Omit sauce ingredients. For sauce, mix a 12-ounce bottle beer, ⅓ cup Dijon-style mustard, and ¼ cup chopped onion.

LAMB WITH HERBED FIG SAUCE: Use 1 pound ground pork and lamb for meats. Omit sauce ingredients. For sauce, mix 1¼ cups port, 2 tablespoons brown sugar, 8 chopped dried figs, and 1 tablespoon snipped fresh rosemary.

APRICOT-CURRY MEATBALLS: Use 1 pound ground pork for sausage. Omit sauce ingredients. For sauce, mix 1½ cups apricot preserves, ⅓ cup soy sauce, ¼ cup cider vinegar, 4 teaspoons grated fresh ginger, and 2 teaspoons curry powder.

LOW-CALORIE

Rosemary, Cherry, and Ham Stuffing

PREP: 40 MINUTES **COOK:** 3 TO 3½ HOURS (LOW)
MAKES: 12 SIDE-DISH SERVINGS

- **Nonstick cooking spray**
- **6 tablespoons butter**
- **½ of a medium butternut squash, peeled, seeded, and cut into ½-inch pieces**
- **1 cup chopped celery (2 stalks)**
- **1 cup chopped onion (1 large)**
- **1 cup slivered almonds**
- **¾ cup snipped dried cherries**
- **⅔ cup cubed cooked ham**
- **1 to 2 teaspoons snipped fresh rosemary or ½ teaspoon dried rosemary, crushed**
- **½ teaspoon cracked black pepper**
- **¼ teaspoon salt**
- **12 cups dry ½-inch cubes* country-style whole wheat or white bread**
- **1 14.5-ounce can reduced-sodium chicken broth**

1 Lightly coat a 4- to 6-quart slow cooker with cooking spray; set aside. In a large skillet heat butter over medium heat until melted. Add squash, celery, and onion; cook about 8 minutes or until onion is tender, stirring occasionally. Stir in almonds. Cook about 4 minutes more or until almonds start to brown. Stir in dried cherries, ham, rosemary, pepper, and salt. Cook about 3 minutes more or until heated through, stirring occasionally.

2 In an extra-large bowl combine bread cubes and squash mixture. Drizzle with broth to moisten, tossing lightly to combine. If desired, cover and chill for up to 24 hours.

3 Transfer bread mixture to the prepared cooker. Cover and cook on low-heat setting for 3 to 3½ hours.

***NOTE:** To make dry bread cubes, preheat oven to 300°F. Cut fresh bread slices into ½-inch cubes. (You'll need 18 to 21 slices of bread to yield 12 cups bread cubes.) Spread bread cubes in two 15×10×1-inch baking pans. Bake for 10 to 15 minutes or until bread is dry, stirring twice; cool (bread will continue to dry and crisp as it cools). Or let bread cubes stand, loosely covered, at room temperature for 8 to 12 hours.

PER ⅔ CUP: 243 cal., 12 g total fat (4 g sat. fat), 20 mg chol., 428 mg sodium, 29 g carb., 5 g fiber, 9 g pro.
EXCHANGES: ½ Fruit, 1½ Starch, ½ High-Fat Meat, 1 Fat

KEEP FOOD SAFE

Do not leave leftovers in the slow cooker to cool down; transfer warm leftovers to containers and refrigerate or freeze promptly. Also never reheat leftovers in the slow cooker because the temperature is not safe.

ORANGE-SAGE SWEET POTATOES WITH BACON

LOW-CALORIE

Orange-Sage Sweet Potatoes with Bacon

PREP: 25 MINUTES
COOK: 5 TO 6 HOURS (LOW) OR 2½ TO 3 HOURS (HIGH)
MAKES: 10 SIDE-DISH SERVINGS

- **4 pounds sweet potatoes, peeled and cut into ¼-inch-thick slices (about 10 cups)**
- **¼ cup frozen orange juice concentrate, thawed**
- **¼ cup water**
- **3 tablespoons packed brown sugar**
- **1½ teaspoons salt**
- **½ teaspoon dried leaf sage, crushed**
- **½ teaspoon dried thyme, crushed**
- **2 tablespoons butter or margarine, cut up**
- **4 slices bacon, crisp-cooked and crumbled**

1 Place sweet potato slices in a 5- or 6-quart slow cooker. In a small bowl stir together orange juice concentrate, water, brown sugar, salt, sage, and thyme. Pour over sweet potato slices; toss to coat. Dot with butter.

2 Cover and cook on low-heat setting for 5 to 6 hours or on high-heat setting for 2½ to 3 hours. Before serving, stir to coat with orange juice mixture and sprinkle with bacon.

PER 1 CUP: 177 cal., 4 g total fat (2 g sat. fat), 10 mg chol., 512 mg sodium, 33 g carb., 4 g fiber, 3 g pro.
EXCHANGES: 2 Starch, ½ Fat

HERBED WILD RICE

LOW-CALORIE

Herbed Wild Rice

PREP: 25 MINUTES
COOK: 6 TO 7 HOURS (LOW) OR 3 TO 3½ HOURS (HIGH)
MAKES: 12 SIDE-DISH SERVINGS

- **2 cups fresh button mushrooms, quartered**
- **1 cup sliced carrots (2 medium)**
- **1½ cups chopped onions (3 medium)**
- **1 cup uncooked wild rice, rinsed and drained**
- **1 cup uncooked brown rice**
- **1 teaspoon dried basil, crushed**
- **½ teaspoon dried thyme, crushed**
- **½ teaspoon dried rosemary, crushed**
- **¼ teaspoon black pepper**
- **4 cloves garlic, minced**
- **1 tablespoon butter or margarine**
- **1 14.5-ounce can diced tomatoes, undrained**
- **2 14.5-ounce cans vegetable or chicken broth**

1 In a 3½- or 4-quart slow cooker combine mushrooms, carrots, onions, wild rice, brown rice, basil, thyme, rosemary, pepper, garlic, and butter. Pour tomatoes and chicken broth over mixture in cooker.

2 Cover and cook on low-heat setting for 6 to 7 hours or on high-heat setting for 3 to 3½ hours. Stir before serving.

PER 1 CUP: 141 cal., 2 g total fat (1 g sat. fat), 3 mg chol., 345 mg sodium, 28 g carb., 3 g fiber, 4 g pro.
EXCHANGES: ½ Vegetable, 1½ Starch

LOW-CALORIE

Easy Cheesy Potatoes

PREP: 20 MINUTES **COOK:** 5 TO 6 HOURS (LOW)
STAND: 10 MINUTES **MAKES:** 12 SIDE-DISH SERVINGS

- **Nonstick cooking spray**
- **1 28-ounce package frozen diced hash brown potatoes with onion and peppers, thawed**
- **1 10.75-ounce can condensed cream of chicken with herbs soup**
- **4 ounces smoked Gouda cheese, shredded (1 cup)**
- **4 ounces American cheese slices, torn into 1-inch pieces**
- **¾ cup milk**
- **¼ cup thinly sliced leek or green onions**
- **½ teaspoon black pepper**
- **1 8-ounce package cream cheese, cut into cubes**
- **4 strips bacon, crisp-cooked and crumbled**

1 Coat a 3½- or 4-quart slow cooker with cooking spray. Combine thawed potatoes, condensed soup, Gouda and American cheeses, milk, leek, and pepper in the slow cooker.

2 Cover and cook on low-heat setting for 5 to 6 hours. Stir in cream cheese; cover and let stand 10 minutes. Just before serving, stir mixture. Sprinkle with bacon and, if desired, *sliced green onions.*

PER ½ CUP: 219 cal., 14 g total fat (8 g sat. fat), 44 mg chol., 626 mg sodium, 16 g carb., 2 g fiber, 8 g pro.
EXCHANGES: 1 Starch, 1 Other Carb., 1 High-Fat Meat, 1 Fat

LOW-CALORIE

Rustic Garlic Mashed Potatoes

PREP: 25 MINUTES
COOK: 6 TO 8 HOURS (LOW) OR 3 TO 4 HOURS (HIGH)
MAKES: 12 SIDE-DISH SERVINGS

- **3 pounds potatoes, peeled (if desired) and cut into 2-inch pieces**
- **6 cloves garlic, halved**
- **1 bay leaf**
- **2 14.5-ounce cans seasoned chicken broth with roasted garlic**
- **1 cup whole milk**
- **¼ cup butter**
- **1 teaspoon salt**

1 In 3½- or 4-quart slow cooker mix potatoes, garlic, and bay leaf. Pour broth over mixture in cooker. Cover; cook on low-heat setting 6 to 8 hours or on high-heat setting 3 to 4 hours.

2 Drain potatoes in a colander set over a bowl to catch the cooking liquid; set liquid aside. Discard bay leaf. Return potatoes to cooker. Mash with a potato masher.

3 In small saucepan heat milk and butter until milk is steaming and butter is almost melted. Add milk mixture and salt to mashed potatoes, beating to make potatoes light and fluffy. Stir in enough of the reserved cooking liquid to reach desired consistency. Transfer potatoes to a serving bowl. Sprinkle with *black pepper.*

MAKE-AHEAD DIRECTIONS: Prepare as directed through Step 3, except reserve remaining cooking liquid. Cover; keep warm on warm or low-heat setting for up to 2 hours. If potatoes thicken, stir in enough of the remaining cooking liquid to reach desired consistency.

PER ABOUT ½ CUP: 119 cal., 5 g total fat (3 g sat. fat), 12 mg chol., 544 mg sodium, 17 g carb., 2 g fiber, 3 g pro.
EXCHANGES: 1 Starch, ½ Fat

LOW-CALORIE

Loaded Creamed Corn with Tomato and Bacon *(photo, page 541)*

PREP: 25 MINUTES **COOK:** 3 TO 4 HOURS (LOW) OR 90 MINUTES TO 2 HOURS (HIGH) **STAND:** 5 MINUTES
MAKES: 16 SIDE-DISH SERVINGS

- **4 12-ounce packages frozen whole kernel corn, thawed**
- **1½ cups half-and-half or light cream**
- **1 cup chopped onion (1 large)**
- **½ cup grated Parmesan cheese (2 ounces)**
- **¼ cup butter, cut up**
- **1 teaspoon sugar**
- **½ teaspoon salt**
- **¼ teaspoon black pepper**
- **5 slices thick-sliced bacon or pancetta**
- **¾ cup shredded Monterey Jack cheese with jalapeño peppers or Monterey Jack cheese (3 ounces)**
- **½ cup chopped tomato (1 medium)**
- **2 tablespoons snipped fresh Italian parsley**
- **1 teaspoon red wine vinegar**
- **⅛ teaspoon sugar**

1 In a blender combine one package of corn and the half-and-half. Cover and blend until smooth. In a 3½- or 4-quart slow cooker combine pureed corn mixture, the remaining three packages of corn, onion, Parmesan cheese, butter, 1 teaspoon sugar, salt, and pepper. Cover; cook on low-heat setting for 3 to 4 hours or on high-heat setting for 90 minutes to 2 hours.

2 Meanwhile, in a large skillet cook bacon over medium heat until crisp. Remove bacon; drain on paper towels. Cut bacon into 1-inch pieces.

3 Sprinkle Monterey Jack cheese over corn mixture; top with bacon pieces. Cover and let stand about 5 minutes or until cheese is melted. In a small bowl stir together tomato, parsley, vinegar, and ⅛ teaspoon sugar. Spoon tomato mixture over corn mixture.

PER ABOUT ½ CUP: 186 cal., 10 g total fat (5 g sat. fat), 26 mg chol., 262 mg sodium, 20 g carb., 2 g fiber, 7 g pro.
EXCHANGES: ½ Vegetable, 1 Starch, ½ High-Fat Meat, 1 Fat

LOW-CALORIE

So-Easy Pepper Steak

PREP: 15 MINUTES
COOK: 9 TO 10 HOURS (LOW) OR 4½ TO 5 HOURS (HIGH)
MAKES: 6 MAIN-DISH SERVINGS

- **1 2-pound boneless beef round steak, cut ¾ to 1 inch thick**
- **½ teaspoon salt**
- **¼ teaspoon black pepper**
- **1 14.5-ounce can Cajun-, Mexican-, or Italian-style stewed tomatoes, undrained**
- **⅓ cup tomato paste**
- **½ teaspoon bottled hot pepper sauce (optional)**
- **1 16-ounce package frozen pepper stir-fry vegetables (green, red, and yellow peppers and onion)**
- **4 cups hot cooked whole wheat pasta (optional)**

1 Trim fat from steak. Cut steak into six serving-size pieces. Sprinkle meat with salt and black pepper. Place in a 3½- or 4-quart slow cooker. In a medium bowl combine tomatoes, tomato paste, and, if desired, hot pepper sauce. Pour over meat in cooker. Top with frozen vegetables.

2 Cover and cook on low-heat setting for 9 to 10 hours or on high-heat setting for 4½ to 5 hours. If desired, serve with hot cooked pasta.

PER 1 CUP MEAT + SAUCE: 258 cal., 6 g total fat (2 g sat. fat), 83 mg chol., 644 mg sodium, 12 g carb., 2 g fiber, 37 g pro.
EXCHANGES: 1½ Vegetable, 4½ Lean Meat

SIZING IT UP

Here's how to adapt a recipe to cook in a larger cooker than specified in recipe.

Most slow cookers with programmable features come in larger sizes than those called for in standard slow cooker recipes. When using these larger cookers, you'll need to adjust the recipe by increasing the amounts. For the best results, increase everything—from the meat and vegetables to the liquid and seasonings—proportionately. Be sure that the cooker is half to no more than three-fourths full. Cook for the same amount of time as you would in a smaller cooker.

cook's secrets

chipotle-coffee pot roast

The Secret: Pot roasts become meltingly tender in the slow cooker. Size matters when it comes to using the slow cooker, so choose the right-size roast and the right-size slow cooker, and fill it at least half full.

POT ROAST POINTERS

1. FIT AND TRIM
Most roasts have some visible fat that can be trimmed. Remove as much of it as you can to help reduce the fat in the cooking liquid. It won't affect the flavor, and you will have less to skim off.

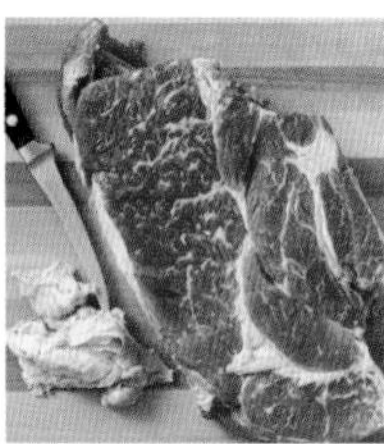

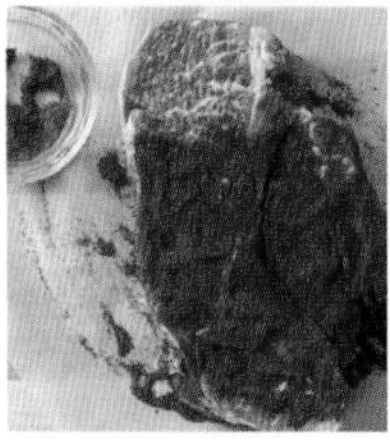

2. A GOOD RUB
Rubs aren't just for barbecue! Use your hands to REALLY rub this spice mixture into the muscle of the meat. Cover all sides of the roast.

BEEF ARM POT ROAST

BEEF CHUCK SHOULDER POT ROAST

BEEF CHUCK SEVEN-BONE POT ROAST

Ground chipotle chile pepper adds a distinct heat level. Ancho chile powder would be a fine substitute; it adds sweet, spicy flavor.

PREP: 35 MINUTES **COOK:** 8½ TO 9 HOURS (LOW) OR 4½ TO 5 HOURS (HIGH) **MAKES:** 6 MAIN-DISH SERVINGS

- 1 **2½- to 3-pound boneless beef chuck arm pot roast, beef chuck shoulder pot roast, or beef chuck seven-bone pot roast**
- 1 **tablespoon instant espresso coffee powder**
- 2 **teaspoons ground chipotle chile pepper**
- ⅛ **teaspoon salt**
- 2 **teaspoons vegetable oil**
- 3 **carrots, peeled and sliced ½ inch thick**
- 2 **parsnips, peeled and sliced ½ inch thick**
- 1 **red onion, cut into thick wedges**
- ¾ **cup reduced-sodium beef broth**
- 3 **tablespoons tomato paste**
- 2 **tablespoons balsamic vinegar**
- 3 **cloves garlic, minced**
- 12 **ounces Brussels sprouts, trimmed and halved lengthwise**
- 1 **sweet red pepper, seeded and cut into chunks**
- 1 **recipe Creamy Polenta (page 551)**

1 Trim fat from meat. Combine coffee powder, ground chipotle pepper, and salt. Sprinkle chipotle mixture evenly over meat; rub in with your fingers. Working in a well-ventilated area, cook meat in a large nonstick skillet in hot oil over medium-high heat until browned on all sides. Drain off fat.

2 In a 6-quart slow cooker combine carrots, parsnips, and red onion. In a small bowl stir together the broth, tomato paste, vinegar, and garlic. Add meat to cooker. Pour broth mixture over mixture in cooker.

3 Cover and cook on low-heat setting for 7 hours or on high-heat setting for 3 hours. Add Brussels sprouts and sweet pepper. Cover and cook on low- or high-heat setting for 1½ to 2 hours more. Using a slotted spoon, transfer meat and vegetables to a platter. Cover with foil and keep warm.

4 Transfer cooking liquid to a large skillet. Bring to boiling; reduce heat. Simmer, uncovered, 8 to 10 minutes or until reduced to about 1 cup. Slice meat or break into serving-size pieces. If desired, serve meat and vegetables over Creamy Polenta. Drizzle with the reduced cooking liquid.

PER 5 OUNCES MEAT, CUP COOKED VEGETABLES + ⅔ CUP POLENTA: 368 cal., 11 g total fat (3 g sat. fat), 123 mg chol., 344 mg sodium, 22 g carb., 6 g fiber, 46 g pro. EXCHANGES: 4 Vegetable, 5½ Lean Meat, ½ Fat

PICK A ROAST

Beef cuts from the shoulder or chuck are tough and filled with connective tissue. Moist heat or braising is best, which is why pot roasts LOVE the slow cooker. Choose one from the chuck and you'll be good to go.

perfect polenta

This recipe calls for regular cornmeal for the polenta. It's quick-cooking and has a smooth texture when compared to coarse-ground cornmeal. Take a look at the tip on page 88 for more info on cornmeal and grits.

CREAMY POLENTA: In a large saucepan bring 2¼ cups reduced-sodium chicken broth and one 12-ounce can evaporated milk just to boiling. Reduce heat to medium-low; slowly whisk in 1 cup cornmeal. Cook for 3 to 5 minutes or until mixture is thick, stirring frequently. Remove from heat. Stir in 3 tablespoons grated Parmesan cheese and 1 tablespoon unsalted butter. Season to taste with black pepper. Makes 4 cups.

POLENTA STEP-BY-STEP

↑
1. Use a whisk when adding the cornmeal to the hot milk and broth mixture. The whisk keeps everything in suspension before the grains begin to cook.

↑
2. A large saucepan is essential when making polenta. Be careful: it plops and spatters as it thickens, but don't let that stop you from stirring often.

↑
3. BROWN IS BEST
Browning the roast before adding it to the slow cooker helps create those rich caramelized flavors. Because of the spices on the roast, you'll want to turn your fan on over your stove.

4. VEGGIES FIRST
Place the veggies in the cooker first. This helps make sure they are submerged in the cooking liquid so they cook evenly. The meat sits on top braising, instead of in the liquid stewing.

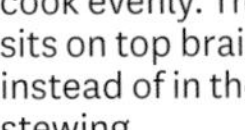

↓

WHEN YOU PEEK

We know you might have to open the lid to check on the progress of your meal. A little safety tip: Open the lid so it points away from you. That allows the steam to rise away from you instead of toward your arms and body or face.

LOW-CALORIE

Busy-Day Beef-Vegetable Soup

PREP: 20 MINUTES
COOK: 8 TO 10 HOURS (LOW) OR 4 TO 5 HOURS (HIGH)
MAKES: 4 MAIN-DISH SERVINGS

- **1 pound boneless beef chuck roast, trimmed and cut into bite-size pieces**
- **3 medium carrots, cut into ½-inch-thick slices**
- **2 small potatoes, peeled (if desired) and cut into ½-inch cubes**
- **½ cup chopped onion (1 medium)**
- **½ teaspoon salt**
- **½ teaspoon dried thyme, crushed**
- **1 bay leaf**
- **2 14.5-ounce cans diced tomatoes, undrained**
- **1 cup water**
- **½ cup frozen peas**

1 In a 3½- or 4-quart slow cooker combine beef, carrots, potatoes, and onion. Sprinkle with salt and thyme. Add bay leaf. Pour tomatoes and water over all.

2 Cover and cook on low-heat setting for 8 to 10 hours or on high-heat setting for 4 to 5 hours. Discard bay leaf. Stir in frozen peas.

PER 2 CUPS: 279 cal., 8 g total fat (3 g sat. fat), 72 mg chol., 860 mg sodium, 26 g carb., 7 g fiber, 26 g pro.
EXCHANGES: 1½ Vegetable, 1 Starch, 3 Lean Meat

Peppery Italian Beef Sandwiches

PREP: 30 MINUTES
COOK: 10 HOURS (LOW) OR 5 TO 6 HOURS (HIGH)
MAKES: 8 SANDWICHES

- **1 2½- to 3-pound boneless beef chuck pot roast**
- **4 teaspoons garlic pepper seasoning**
- **1 tablespoon vegetable oil**
- **1 14.5-ounce can beef broth**
- **1 0.6- to 1-ounce envelope Italian dry salad dressing mix**
- **1 teaspoon onion salt**
- **1 teaspoon dried oregano, crushed**
- **1 teaspoon dried basil, crushed**
- **1 teaspoon dried parsley**
- **1 12- to 16-ounce jar pepperoncini salad peppers, drained and sliced**
- **8 hoagie buns or kaiser rolls, split and toasted**
- **2 cups shredded mozzarella cheese (8 ounces)**

1 Trim fat from meat. Coat meat with garlic pepper seasoning. In a Dutch oven brown meat on all sides in hot oil. If necessary, cut meat in half to fit into a 3½- or 4-quart slow cooker.

PEPPERY ITALIAN BEEF SANDWICHES

2 Place meat in cooker. In a medium bowl whisk together beef broth, dressing mix, onion salt, oregano, basil, and parsley. Pour over meat in cooker. Top with pepperoncini peppers.

3 Cover and cook on low-heat setting about 10 hours or on high-heat setting for 5 to 6 hours. Transfer meat to a cutting board. Using two forks, pull meat apart into shreds. Using a slotted spoon, remove peppers from cooking liquid and transfer to a serving bowl. Skim fat from cooking liquid; transfer liquid to a bowl.

4 To serve, spoon some shredded meat on the bottom halves of buns. Sprinkle with cheese. Spoon desired amount of cooking liquid over meat. Top with peppers and bun tops.

PER SANDWICH: 579 cal., 21 g total fat (8 g sat. fat), 105 mg chol., 2,390 mg sodium, 54 g carb., 2 g fiber, 42 g pro.
EXCHANGES: 3½ Starch, 4½ Medium-Fat Meat

BEST-LOVED

Beef Chili Mac *(photo, page 541)*

PREP: 25 MINUTES
COOK: 4 TO 6 HOURS (LOW) OR 2 TO 3 HOURS (HIGH)
MAKES: 6 MAIN-DISH SERVINGS

- **1½ pounds ground beef**
- **1 cup chopped onion (1 large)**
- **3 cloves garlic, minced**
- **1 15-ounce can chili beans in chili gravy, undrained**
- **1 14.5-ounce can diced tomatoes and green chilies, undrained**

- **1 cup beef broth**
- **3/4 cup chopped green sweet pepper (1 medium)**
- **2 teaspoons chili powder**
- **1 teaspoon ground cumin**
- **1/4 teaspoon salt**
- **8 ounce package dried cavatappi or macaroni, cooked according to package directions**
- **Tortilla chips or corn chips**
- **Shredded cheddar cheese (optional)**

1 In a large skillet cook ground beef, onion, and garlic over medium heat until meat is browned and onion is tender. Drain fat; discard.

2 In a 3½- or 4-quart slow cooker combine meat mixture, chili beans, tomatoes and green chilies, broth, sweet pepper, chili powder, cumin, and salt.

3 Cover and cook on low-heat setting for 4 to 6 hours or on high-heat setting for 2 to 3 hours. Stir in cooked pasta. Serve with tortilla chips. If desired, top with cheese.

PER 1½ CUPS: 559 cal., 22 g total fat (7 g sat. fat), 77 mg chol., 871 mg sodium, 57 g carb., 8 g fiber, 33 g pro. EXCHANGES: 1 Vegetable, 3½ Starch, 3 Medium-Fat Meat, ½ Fat

Barbecued Brisket

PREP: 15 MINUTES
COOK: 12 TO 14 HOURS (LOW) OR 6 TO 7 HOURS (HIGH)
MAKES: 6 MAIN-DISH SERVINGS

- **1 4- to 4½-pound fresh beef brisket**
- **Black pepper**
- **1 16-ounce package peeled fresh baby carrots**
- **2 stalks celery, cut into ½-inch-thick slices**
- **1½ cups bottled smoke-flavor barbecue sauce**
- **2 tablespoons quick-cooking tapioca, crushed**
- **2 tablespoons Dijon-style mustard**
- **1 tablespoon Worcestershire sauce**
- **4 cups hot cooked mashed potatoes or noodles**

1 Trim fat from brisket. If necessary, cut brisket in half to fit into a 5- to 6-quart slow cooker. Season brisket with pepper. In the slow cooker combine carrots and celery. Place brisket on vegetables. In a small bowl combine barbecue sauce, tapioca, mustard, and Worcestershire sauce; pour over brisket.

2 Cover and cook on low-heat setting for 12 to 14 hours or on high-heat setting for 6 to 7 hours.

3 Transfer brisket to cutting board; cut brisket in half if necessary. Thinly slice half of the brisket across the grain. Skim fat from cooking liquid. Serve cooking liquid with brisket and vegetables over mashed potatoes. Slice remaining half of brisket and place in an airtight container; cover and chill for up to 24 hours or freeze for up to 1 month for a later use.

PER 3 OUNCES MEAT + 1 CUP VEGETABLES + SAUCE: 441 cal., 7 g total fat (3 g sat. fat), 65 mg chol., 1,580 mg sodium, 54 g carb., 5 g fiber, 37 g pro. EXCHANGES: 1 Vegetable, 1½ Starch, 2 Other Carb., 4½ Lean Meat

Spaghetti Sauce Italiano

PREP: 25 MINUTES
COOK: 8 TO 10 HOURS (LOW) OR 4 TO 5 HOURS (HIGH)
MAKES: 6 TO 8 MAIN-DISH SERVINGS

- **1 pound bulk Italian sausage or ground beef**
- **1 cup chopped onion (1 large)**
- **2 cloves garlic, minced**
- **2 14.5-ounce cans diced tomatoes, undrained**
- **1 6-ounce can tomato paste**
- **2 4-ounce cans mushroom stems and pieces, drained**
- **1 bay leaf**
- **2 teaspoons dried Italian seasoning, crushed**
- **½ teaspoon salt**
- **¼ teaspoon black pepper**
- **1 cup chopped green sweet pepper (1 large)**
- **12 to 16 ounce package dried spaghetti, cooked and drained**
- **Finely shredded or grated Parmesan cheese (optional)**

1 In a large skillet cook the sausage, onion, and garlic over medium heat until meat is browned and onion is tender. Drain fat; discard.

2 In a 3½- or 4-quart slow cooker stir together tomatoes, tomato paste, mushrooms, bay leaf, Italian seasoning, salt, and black pepper. Stir in meat mixture.

3 Cover and cook on low-heat setting for 8 to 10 hours or on high-heat setting for 4 to 5 hours. Stir in sweet pepper. Discard bay leaf. Serve meat mixture over hot cooked spaghetti. If desired, sprinkle with Parmesan cheese.

PER 1 CUP SAUCE + 1 CUP SPAGHETTI: 553 cal., 23 g total fat (10 g sat. fat), 51 mg chol., 1,506 mg sodium, 62 g carb., 6 g fiber, 27 g pro. EXCHANGES: 1 Vegetable, 3½ Starch, 2½ High-Fat Meat

SLOW COOKER DONENESS

For uniform doneness of a dish, cut the meat and vegetable(s) into the size of pieces specified in the recipe.

PORK, PORTOBELLO, AND MASHED ROOTS SHEPHERD'S PIE

Pork, Portobello, and Mashed Roots Shepherd's Pie

PREP: 35 MINUTES
COOK: 7 TO 8 HOURS (LOW) OR 3½ TO 4 HOURS + 30 MINUTES (HIGH) **MAKES:** 6 MAIN-DISH SERVINGS

- **1½ pounds lean ground pork**
- **6 cups stemmed and chopped fresh portobello mushrooms (16 ounces)**
- **1 cup chopped onion (1 large)**
- **6 cloves garlic, minced**
- **1¼ cups reduced-sodium chicken broth**
- **1 cup sliced celery (2 stalks)**
- **1 cup chopped carrots (2 medium)**
- **3 tablespoons quick-cooking tapioca**
- **2 tablespoons Worcestershire sauce**
- **1 teaspoon dried thyme, crushed**
- **½ teaspoon salt**
- **¼ teaspoon black pepper**
- **2 cups peeled and chopped rutabagas**
- **1 cup peeled and chopped potato (1 medium)**
- **1 cup peeled and chopped parsnips (2 medium)**
- **1 cup chopped carrots (2 medium)**
- **¼ cup low-fat milk**
- **½ teaspoon salt**
- **1 cup frozen peas**
- **Snipped fresh chives**

1 In a 4- to 5-quart Dutch oven cook ground pork, mushrooms, onion, and garlic over medium-high heat until meat is browned and mushrooms are tender, using a wooden spoon to break up meat as it cooks. Drain off fat.

2 In a 4-quart slow cooker combine meat mixture, broth, celery, 1 cup carrots, tapioca, Worcestershire sauce, thyme, the ½ teaspoon salt, and the pepper. Cover and cook on low-heat setting for 7 to 8 hours or on high-heat setting for 3½ to 4 hours.

3 About 1 hour before serving, in a covered large saucepan cook rutabagas, potato, parsnips, and remaining 1 cup carrots in enough boiling water to cover for 25 to 30 minutes or until vegetables are very tender; drain. Return vegetables to hot pan. Mash vegetables with a potato masher. Stir in milk and ½ teaspoon salt.

4 If using low-heat setting, turn cooker to high-heat setting. Stir frozen peas into mixture in cooker; spoon the mashed vegetable mixture evenly over pea mixture. Cover and cook for 30 minutes more. Before serving, sprinkle the mixture with some chives.

PER 1 CUP MEAT MIXTURE + ½ CUP MASH: 405 cal., 19 g total fat (6 g sat. fat), 78 mg chol., 713 mg sodium, 34 g carb., 7 g fiber, 27 g pro. **EXCHANGES:** 3½ Vegetable, 1 Starch, 2½ Medium-Fat Meat, 1 Fat

BEST-LOVED LOW-CALORIE

Spicy Pulled Pork

PREP: 15 MINUTES **COOK:** 8 TO 10 HOURS (LOW) OR 4 TO 5 HOURS (HIGH) **MAKES:** 8 SANDWICHES

- **2 to 2½ pounds boneless pork shoulder**
- **Salt and black pepper**
- **1 large sweet onion, cut into thin wedges**
- **1 18- to 20-ounce bottle hot and spicy barbecue sauce (about 1¾ cups)**
- **1 cup Dr Pepper carbonated beverage (not diet)**
- **8 hamburger buns or 16 baguette slices, toasted**

PORK-SHREDDING POINTER

Use two forks pulling in opposite directions but with the grain of the roast to shred the pork into long, thin pieces. The "grain" refers to the direction the bundles of muscle fibers are aligned on the meat.

1 Trim fat from meat. Cut meat into large chunks; sprinkle with salt and pepper.

2 Place onion wedges in a 4-quart slow cooker; top with meat. In a bowl stir together barbecue sauce and carbonated beverage; pour over meat. Cover and cook on low-heat setting for 8 to 10 hours or on high-heat setting for 4 to 5 hours.

3 Transfer meat to a cutting board. Using forks, shred meat; place in bowl. With a slotted spoon, remove onions from cooking liquid; add onions to meat. Skim fat from the cooking liquid. Add enough cooking liquid to meat mixture to moisten. Divide meat mixture among buns.

PER SANDWICH: 378 cal., 8 g total fat (3 g sat. fat), 73 mg chol., 1,355 mg sodium, 45 g carb., 1 g fiber, 27 g pro.
EXCHANGES: 2 Starch, 1 Other Carb., 3 Lean Meat, 1/2 Fat

Carnitas with Sweet Corn Polenta

PREP: 25 MINUTES
COOK: 8 TO 10 HOURS (LOW) OR 4 TO 5 HOURS (HIGH)
MAKES: 10 TO 12 MAIN-DISH SERVINGS

- **1½ teaspoons garlic powder**
- **¾ teaspoon dried oregano, crushed**
- **¾ teaspoon ground coriander**
- **¾ teaspoon ground ancho chile pepper**
- **¼ teaspoon ground cinnamon**
- **1 5-pound boneless pork shoulder roast**
- **2 tablespoons vegetable oil**
- **2 bay leaves**
- **1 cup chicken broth**
- **Sweet Corn Polenta**
- **Snipped fresh oregano (optional)**

1 In a large bowl combine garlic powder, 1 teaspoon *salt*, dried oregano, coriander, ground chile pepper, and cinnamon; set aside. Trim fat from meat. Cut meat into 2-inch pieces; add to spice mixture. Toss gently.

2 In a large skillet heat oil over medium-high heat. Cook meat, one-third at a time, in hot oil until browned. Using a slotted spoon, transfer meat to a 4- or 4½-quart slow cooker. Add bay leaves. Pour broth over meat.

3 Cover and cook on low-heat setting for 8 to 10 hours or on high-heat setting for 4 to 5 hours. Remove bay leaves. Serve meat and cooking liquid with Sweet Corn Polenta. If desired, sprinkle with fresh oregano.

SWEET CORN POLENTA: In a large saucepan combine 4 cups chicken broth; two 12-ounce cans evaporated milk; two 4-ounce cans diced green chiles, undrained; 2 teaspoons dried oregano, crushed; 2 teaspoons garlic powder; and 1 teaspoon salt. Bring to boiling. Gradually add 2 cups quick-cooking polenta mix or coarse cornmeal, stirring constantly. Reduce heat to low. Cook, uncovered, for 5 to 10 minutes or until thickened. Stir in 2 cups frozen whole kernel corn and, if desired, 1½ cups shredded Monterey Jack cheese (6 ounces). Remove from heat. Let polenta stand 5 minutes.

PER ¾ CUP MEAT + ¾ CUP POLENTA: 674 cal., 22 g total fat (8 g sat. fat), 168 mg chol., 1,270 mg sodium, 59 g carb., 7 g fiber, 56 g pro. EXCHANGES: ½ Milk, 3½ Starch, 6 Lean Meat, 1½ Fat

LOW-CALORIE

Teriyaki Pork with Asian Slaw

(photo, page 541)

PREP: 25 MINUTES
COOK: 5 TO 6 HOURS (LOW) OR 2½ TO 3 HOURS (HIGH)
MAKES: 8 MAIN-DISH SERVINGS

- **2 12-ounce pork tenderloins**
- **Nonstick cooking spray**
- **½ cup reduced-sodium soy sauce**
- **¼ cup rice vinegar**
- **3 tablespoons packed brown sugar**
- **2 tablespoons canola oil**
- **2 teaspoons grated fresh ginger**
- **2 cloves garlic, minced**
- **¼ teaspoon black pepper**
- **Asian Slaw**

1 Trim fat from meat. Coat an extra-large nonstick skillet with cooking spray; heat skillet over medium-high heat. Cook meat in hot skillet until browned on all sides. Transfer meat to a 3½- or 4-quart slow cooker. In a small bowl whisk together soy sauce, vinegar, brown sugar, oil, ginger, garlic, and pepper. Pour over meat.

2 Cover; cook on low-heat setting 5 to 6 hours or on high-heat setting for 2½ to 3 hours. Transfer meat to a cutting board, reserving cooking liquid. Cut meat into ½-inch slices.

3 To serve, drizzle meat with cooking liquid. If desired, sprinkle with *sliced green onions* and *sesame seeds*. Serve with Asian Slaw.

ASIAN SLAW: In a bowl mix 5 cups shredded napa cabbage; 1 cup yellow sweet pepper strips; ½ cup shredded carrot; ½ cup fresh snow pea pods sliced lengthwise; and ¼ cup sliced green onions. For dressing, in a screw-top jar combine 3 tablespoons rice vinegar, 2 tablespoons canola oil, 1 tablespoon toasted sesame oil, 1 tablespoon reduced-sodium soy sauce, ¼ teaspoon salt, and ¼ teaspoon black pepper; shake well. Toss slaw with dressing.

PER 3 OUNCES PORK + ¾ CUP SLAW: 238 cal., 11 g total fat (1 g sat. fat), 55 mg chol., 756 mg sodium, 14 g carb., 2 g fiber, 20 g pro. EXCHANGES: 1 Vegetable, ½ Other Carb., 2½ Lean Meat, 1½ Fat

HONEY-ROSEMARY ROAST LAMB

LOW-CALORIE

Honey-Rosemary Roast Lamb

PREP: 20 MINUTES
COOK: 5 TO 6 HOURS (LOW) OR 2½ TO 3 HOURS (HIGH)
MAKES: 5 MAIN-DISH SERVINGS

- **1¾ pounds boneless lamb leg roast**
- **Nonstick cooking spray**
- **2 medium Yukon gold potatoes, cut into 1-inch wedges**
- **1 large onion, cut into thin wedges**
- **3 cups green beans (12 ounces), trimmed (if desired)**
- **2 tablespoons quick-cooking tapioca**
- **2 tablespoons honey**
- **2 tablespoons lemon juice**
- **1 tablespoon snipped fresh rosemary**
- **4 cloves garlic, minced**
- **½ teaspoon salt**
- **¼ teaspoon black pepper**

1 Trim fat from meat. Coat a large nonstick skillet with cooking spray; heat skillet over medium-high heat. Cook meat in hot skillet until browned on all sides; set aside.

2 Coat a 3½- or 4-quart slow cooker with cooking spray. Place potatoes in bottom of the prepared cooker. Add onion; top with beans.

3 In a small bowl combine tapioca, honey, lemon juice, snipped rosemary, garlic, salt, and pepper. Pour mixture over vegetables. Top with meat. Cover and cook on low-heat setting for 5 to 6 hours or on high-heat setting for 2½ to 3 hours.

4 Remove meat from cooker; slice meat. Serve with vegetables and some of the cooking juices.

PER 2 TO 3 OUNCES LAMB + 1 CUP VEGETABLE MIXTURE: 343 cal., 7 g total fat (3 g sat. fat), 98 mg chol., 380 mg sodium, 34 g carb., 5 g fiber, 36 g pro. EXCHANGES: 1½ Vegetable, 1 Starch, ½ Other Carb., 4½ Lean Meat

LOW-CALORIE

Jambalaya *(photo, page 541)*

PREP: 30 MINUTES **COOK:** 6 TO 8 HOURS (LOW) OR 3 TO 4 HOURS + 30 MINUTES (HIGH)
MAKES: 6 MAIN-DISH SERVINGS

- **6 skinless, boneless chicken thighs, cut into bite-size pieces (1½ pounds)**
- **4 ounces cooked ham**
- **1 cup chopped onion (1 large)**
- **1 cup thinly sliced celery (2 stalks)**
- **1 14.5-ounce can fire-roasted diced tomatoes,* undrained**
- **1 cup chicken broth**
- **2 tablespoons tomato paste**
- **2 tablespoons quick-cooking tapioca, crushed**
- **1 tablespoon Worcestershire sauce**
- **1 tablespoon lemon juice**
- **1 serrano pepper, seeded and finely chopped (see tip, page 44)**
- **3 cloves garlic, minced**
- **½ teaspoon dried thyme, crushed**
- **½ teaspoon dried oregano, crushed**
- **¼ teaspoon cayenne pepper**
- **8 ounces fresh medium shrimp, peeled and deveined**
- **½ cup yellow sweet pepper, chopped**
- **2 cups frozen cut okra (optional)**
- **1 14.75- to 15-ounce package cooked long grain rice**

1 In a 3½- or 4-quart slow cooker combine chicken, ham, onion, and celery. Stir in undrained tomatoes, broth, tomato paste, tapioca, Worcestershire, lemon juice, serrano pepper, garlic, thyme, oregano, ¼ teaspoon *salt*, and cayenne pepper. Cover; cook on low-heat setting for 6 to 8 hours or on high-heat setting for 3 to 4 hours.

2 If using low-heat setting, turn cooker to high-heat setting. Stir in shrimp, sweet pepper, and, if desired, okra. Cover and cook about 30 minutes more or until shrimp turn opaque. Prepare rice according to package directions; serve with jambalaya.

***NOTE:** If you can't find fire-roasted diced tomatoes, use plain diced tomatoes and add ¼ teaspoon liquid smoke.

PER 1 CUP CHICKEN MIXTURE + ½ CUP RICE: 365 cal., 7 g total fat (1 g sat. fat), 160 mg chol., 941 mg sodium, 35 g carb., 2 g fiber, 37 g pro. EXCHANGES: 1½ Vegetable, 2 Starch, 4 Lean Meat

make it mine

One-Pot Meal

If you've ever looked at a cut of meat and wondered how to cook it in a slow cooker, this recipe is for you. Adapt the meats and ingredients you like best for a dish you'll love.

PREP: 25 MINUTES **COOK:** 8 TO 10 HOURS (LOW) OR 4 TO 5 HOURS (HIGH)
MAKES: 6 MAIN-DISH SERVINGS

- 2½ to 3 pounds MEAT
- 1½ to 2 pounds VEGETABLE
- 1½ teaspoons SEASONING
- ½ teaspoon salt
- ¼ teaspoon black pepper
- LIQUID
- SIDE (optional)
- 1 recipe Gravy

1 Trim any fat from desired Meat. If necessary, cut meat in half to fit into a 4- to 6-quart slow cooker.* Place Vegetable in slow cooker. Sprinkle with half of the Seasoning. Top with meat. Sprinkle with remaining Seasoning, salt, and pepper. Pour Liquid over top.

2 Cover and cook on low-heat setting for 8 to 10 hours or on high-heat setting for 4 to 5 hours. If desired, serve with a Side and Gravy.

GRAVY: If desired, make gravy with the cooking liquid. Remove meat and vegetables from cooker using a slotted spoon. Strain cooking liquid into a 4-cup glass measure. If necessary, add enough chicken or beef broth to equal 3 cups total. Pour into a medium saucepan. In a small bowl combine ⅓ cup all-purpose flour and ⅓ cup water until very smooth. Stir into cooking liquid. Cook and stir over medium heat until thickened and bubbly. Cook and stir for 1 minute more.

***NOTE:** When filling your slow cooker, make sure it is half to three-fourths full before you turn it on. Adjust the ingredient amounts as needed.

MEAT *(pick one)*

Beef chuck or bottom round roast
Chicken thighs and/or drumsticks (skinned)
Lamb shoulder roast
Pork shoulder or sirloin roast

VEGETABLE *(pick one)*

Brussels sprouts, halved**
Carrots, peeled and cut into 2-inch pieces, or packaged peeled baby carrots
Frozen stew vegetables**
Mushrooms, whole button
Onion wedges
Potatoes (russet, red, or peeled sweet potatoes), cut into 2-inch pieces
Sweet pepper, cut into thick slices
Zucchini, cut into slices**

SEASONING *(pick one)*

Chili powder
Dried basil, Italian seasoning, oregano, or thyme, crushed
Salt-free seasoning blend

LIQUID *(pick one)*

1 cup chicken or beef broth
One 10.75-ounce can condensed soup: tomato, cream of chicken, cream of mushroom, or cream of celery
½ cup each dry red or white wine plus ½ cup chicken or beef broth
1 cup tomato juice
One 8-ounce can tomato sauce

SIDE *(pick one)*

Hot cooked pasta (couscous, gnocchi, noodles, spaetzle)
Hot cooked rice (white, brown, or long grain)
Mashed potatoes

****NOTE:** Add to cooker the last hour of cooking.

LOW-CALORIE

Slow Cooker Moo Shu Chicken

PREP: 20 MINUTES
COOK: 6 HOURS (LOW) OR 4 HOURS (HIGH)
MAKES: 6 MAIN-DISH SERVINGS

- **½ cup hoisin sauce**
- **2 tablespoons water**
- **4 teaspoons toasted sesame oil**
- **1 tablespoon cornstarch**
- **1 tablespoon reduced-sodium soy sauce**
- **3 large cloves garlic, minced**
- **1 16-ounce package shredded cabbage with carrots (coleslaw mix)**
- **1 cup coarsely shredded carrots (2 medium)**
- **12 ounces skinless, boneless chicken thighs**
- **6 8-inch whole wheat flour tortillas**
- **Green onions (optional)**

1 In a small bowl stir together hoisin sauce, the water, sesame oil, cornstarch, soy sauce, and garlic; set aside.

2 In a 3½- or 4-quart slow cooker combine cabbage mixture and shredded carrots. Cut chicken into ⅛-inch slices; cut each slice in half lengthwise. Place the chicken on top of the cabbage mixture. Drizzle with ¼ cup of the hoisin mixture.

3 Cover and cook on low-heat setting for 6 hours or on high-heat setting for 4 hours. Stir in the remaining hoisin mixture.

4 To serve, heat the tortillas according to package directions. Spoon the chicken mixture onto tortillas. If desired, top each serving with green onions.

PER FILLED TORTILLA: 298 cal., 9 g total fat (2 g sat. fat), 54 mg chol., 736 mg sodium, 36 g carb., 5 g fiber, 17 g pro. EXCHANGES: 1 Vegetable, 1½ Starch, ½ Other Carb., 1½ Lean Meat, 1 Fat

LOW-CALORIE

Italian Braised Chicken with Fennel and Cannellini *(photo, page 543)*

PREP: 30 MINUTES
COOK: 5 TO 6 HOURS (LOW) OR 2½ TO 3 HOURS (HIGH)
MAKES: 6 MAIN-DISH SERVINGS

- **2 to 2½ pounds chicken drumsticks and/or thighs, skin removed**
- **¾ teaspoon salt**
- **¼ teaspoon black pepper**
- **1 15-ounce can cannellini beans (white kidney), rinsed and drained**
- **1 bulb fennel, cored and cut into thin wedges**
- **1 medium yellow sweet pepper, seeded and cut into 1-inch pieces**
- **1 medium onion, cut into thin wedges**
- **3 cloves garlic, minced**
- **1 teaspoon snipped fresh rosemary or ½ teaspoon dried rosemary, crushed**
- **1 teaspoon snipped fresh oregano or ½ teaspoon dried oregano, crushed**
- **¼ teaspoon crushed red pepper**
- **1 14.5-ounce can diced tomatoes, undrained**
- **½ cup dry white wine or reduced-sodium chicken broth**
- **¼ cup tomato paste**
- **¼ cup shaved Parmesan cheese (1 ounce)**
- **1 tablespoon snipped fresh Italian parsley**

1 Sprinkle chicken pieces with ¼ teaspoon of the salt and the black pepper. Place chicken in a 3½- or 4-quart slow cooker. Top with beans, fennel, sweet pepper, onion, garlic, rosemary, oregano, and crushed red pepper. In a medium bowl combine tomatoes, white wine, tomato paste, and remaining ½ teaspoon salt; pour over mixture in cooker.

2 Cover and cook on low-heat setting for 5 to 6 hours or on high-heat setting for 2½ to 3 hours. Sprinkle each serving with Parmesan cheese and parsley.

PER SERVING: 223 cal., 4 g total fat (1 g sat. fat), 68 mg chol., 762 mg sodium, 23 g carb., 7 g fiber, 25 g pro. EXCHANGES: 1½ Vegetable, 1 Starch, 2½ Lean Meat

LOW-CALORIE

Maple-Mustard-Sauced Turkey Thighs

PREP: 20 MINUTES
COOK: 6 TO 7 HOURS (LOW) OR 3 TO 3½ HOURS (HIGH)
MAKES: 4 MAIN-DISH SERVINGS

- **1 pound tiny new potatoes, quartered**
- **4 turkey thighs (2 to 2½ pounds total), skin removed**
- **⅓ cup coarse-ground brown mustard**
- **¼ cup maple syrup**
- **1 tablespoon quick-cooking tapioca**

1 Place potatoes in a 3½- or 4-quart slow cooker. Place turkey thighs on top of potatoes. In a small bowl stir together mustard, maple syrup, and tapioca. Pour mixture over turkey.

2 Cover and cook on low-heat setting for 6 to 7 hours or on high-heat setting for to 3 to 3½ hours. Serve the turkey thighs topped with the maple sauce.

PER TURKEY THIGH + ¾ CUP POTATOES: 330 cal., 6 g total fat (2 g sat. fat), 128 mg chol., 364 mg sodium, 35 g carb., 2 g fiber, 32 g pro. EXCHANGES: 1½ Starch, 1 Other Carb., 4 Lean Meat

soups & stews

soups & stews

From warm, hearty stews to creamy vegetable soups, many of the world's most beloved dishes are served up in a bowl. Here's some know-how.

TAKE STOCK

When you have the time, call on made-from-scratch broth to add extra homemade goodness to your soup recipes. When time is not on your side, these are the best options:

CANNED BROTH: Use this straight from the can or carton, unless it's a condensed broth, which you should dilute according to the label directions. Canned broths can be high in sodium; either pick a low-sodium version or adjust the salt in the recipe.

CHICKEN OR BEEF BASE: This pastelike ingredient comes in a jar and must be refrigerated after opening. When reconstituted in water, it makes a flavorful broth in recipes.

PERFECTLY PUREED

Some soups need to be pureed, and a handheld immersion blender provides an easy, safe, mess-free way to do this right in the pan (see photo, page 582). If using a traditional blender, follow these precautions.

- Cool the hot mixture slightly before blending.
- Fill the container no more than half full and make sure the blender lid is on tight.
- Remove the round plastic piece in the center of the blender lid and hold a kitchen towel over the opening to allow the steam to escape during blending.
- Blend on low speed to avoid an eruption.

SOUPS AND STEWS ON HAND

Soups and stews can often be made in larger batches—simply double a recipe that makes 4 to 6 servings and you'll likely have leftovers. The good news is they generally keep well. In fact, some even improve after a day in the fridge—extra time allows flavors to meld. Follow our pointers to keep leftovers at their best.

- Cool the soup or stew before freezing or refrigerating. Place the pot in a sink of ice water and stir the soup so it cools quickly.
- For short-term storage, divide the cooled soup or stew among shallow containers. Cover and refrigerate for up to 3 days.
- For long-term storage, divide the cooled soup or stew among shallow freezer-safe containers. Leave about ½ inch space between the top of the soup or stew and the rim of its container. This will provide room for the food to expand while it freezes without breaking the container or causing the lid to pop off. Freeze soups and stews for up to 3 months.

- Avoid freezing soups and stews thickened with cornstarch or flour; freezing causes them to lose their thickening capacity.

THAWING AND REHEATING LEFTOVERS

Be sure to bring leftovers safely to the table.

- If soup or stew has been frozen, thaw it for 1 to 2 days in the refrigerator before reheating.
- You can also thaw soup or stew in the microwave on 50% power (medium). Pop the soup or stew out of the freezer container into a microwave-safe dish. To prevent spattering, cover the dish with a microwave-safe lid or plastic wrap; loosen the lid or vent the wrap to allow steam to escape. Stir soup or stew once or twice as it thaws.
- Heat thawed soup or stew on the stove top, using medium-high heat for broth-based soups and medium heat for purees or stews. Stir often to keep it from burning; watch bean, potato, and flour-thickened mixtures closely.
- For food safety, soups and stews should be brought to a rolling boil before serving.

fresh tomato soup

The Secret: Exceptional tomato soup starts with sun-ripened, peak-of-the-season tomatoes. If you've got 'em, make this recipe to serve hot or cold. When tomatoes are not in season, use canned tomatoes or roast those you find in grocery stores to get that summer-sweet flavor.

TOMATO SOUP POINTERS

1. TO THE CORE
Coring a tomato is an easy process. Use a sharp paring knife. Holding the knife at an angle, remove the stem end. Cut the tomato into quarters and remove seeds with your fingers.

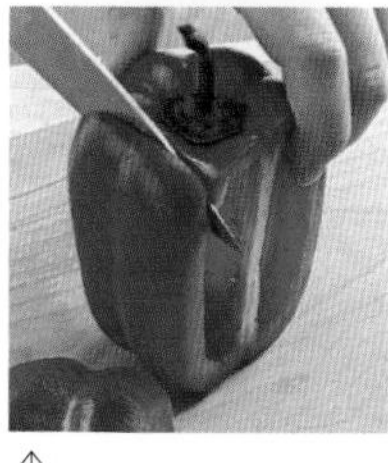

2. SLICK SLICING
Cut the four sides of the sweet pepper away from the stem. Cut the sides into slices and chop them. Discard the stem and core with the seeds.

Peak tomato season is typically July through September for most of the country. If fresh, in-season tomatoes aren't available, you can substitute two 14.5-ounce cans whole tomatoes.

START TO FINISH: 30 MINUTES **MAKES:** 6 SIDE-DISH SERVINGS

- **6 medium or 4 large tomatoes (2 pounds total), cored and seeded**
- **2 medium red sweet peppers, coarsely chopped (1½ cups)**
- **½ of a medium sweet onion (such as Vidalia or Maui), chopped (¼ cup)**
- **¼ cup snipped fresh basil**
- **1 cup reduced-sodium vegetable broth or chicken broth**
- **2 tablespoons whipping cream**
- **1 tablespoon honey**
- **Shredded fresh basil (optional)**
- **Grilled Cheese Croutons (page 563) (optional)**

1 In a food processor or blender combine half of the tomatoes, half of the sweet peppers, half of the onion, and half of the snipped basil. Add half of the broth. Cover and process or blend until smooth. Transfer to a large saucepan. Repeat with the remaining tomatoes, sweet peppers, onion, basil, and broth.

2 Cook soup over medium heat for 5 to 6 minutes or until heated through. Stir in whipping cream and honey. Serve warm. If desired, top each serving with shredded basil and serve with Grilled Cheese Croutons.

CHILLY TOMATO SOUP: Prepare as directed, except omit the whipping cream. If desired, increase honey to 2 tablespoons. Cover and chill for up to 24 hours before serving cold. If desired, garnish with quartered or halved yellow and/or red cherry tomatoes, fresh basil leaves, and a drizzle of honey.

PER 1 CUP PLAIN OR CHILLED VARIATION: 73 cal., 2 g total fat (1 g sat. fat), 7 mg chol., 35 mg sodium, 13 g carb., 3 g fiber, 2 g pro.
EXCHANGES: 2½ Vegetable, ½ Fat

TOMATO TALK

Tomatoes come in many shapes, sizes, and colors. Small cherry and grape tomatoes are sweet and best for eating out of hand (it's too time-consuming to seed these types of tomato). Medium-size vine-ripened tomatoes are usually sweeter and more evenly ripened compared with other commercial tomatoes. Large, standard slicing varieties, such as Big Boy and beefsteak, are a good size and shape for efficient coring and seeding. Heirloom tomatoes are more flavorful and juicy than commercial varieties. Although tomatoes are available in several hues, true red ones will give you the best color in this soup.

ROASTED TOMATO SOUP: Prepare as directed, except preheat oven to 450°F. Line two 15×10×1-inch baking pans with foil; set aside. Cut tomatoes in half crosswise. Seed tomatoes; arrange tomato halves, cut sides down, in one of the prepared pans. Set tomatoes aside. Cut sweet peppers in half; remove and discard stems, seeds, and membranes. Cut onion into ½-inch slices rather than chopping it. Arrange pepper halves (cut sides down) and onion slices in the remaining prepared pan. Drizzle tomatoes, peppers, and onion with 3 to 4 tablespoons olive oil. Roast peppers and onions, uncovered, about 20 minutes or until pepper skins are charred, turning onion slices once. Bring foil up around peppers and onions, folding edges together to enclose. Let stand for 15 to 20 minutes or until cool enough to handle. Using a sharp knife, loosen edges of pepper skins; gently pull off skins in strips and discard. Preheat broiler. Broil tomatoes 4 inches from the heat about 4 minutes or until skins are charred. Continue as directed in Step 1.

PER 1 CUP: 129 cal., 9 g total fat (2 g sat. fat), 7 mg chol., 105 mg sodium, 12 g carb. 3 g fiber, 2 g pro. Exchanges: 2 Vegetable, 2 Fat

GRILLED CHEESE CROUTONS

These croutons make the perfect Fresh Tomato Soup topper:

Just like a grilled cheese sandwich, these little bites of melty goodness are easy to make and easier to customize. Sandwich together any type of bread and a good melting cheese. Brush outsides of bread with butter or oil and toast in a hot skillet or griddle until browned. Cut into bite-size croutons.

LOW-CALORIE

Chicken Broth

PREP: 25 MINUTES **COOK:** 2½ HOURS
MAKES: ABOUT 5½ CUPS

- **3 pounds bony chicken pieces (wings, backs, and/or necks)**
- **3 stalks celery with leaves, cut up**
- **2 carrots, cut up**
- **1 large onion, unpeeled and cut up**
- **1 teaspoon salt**
- **1 teaspoon dried thyme, sage, or basil, crushed**
- **½ teaspoon whole black peppercorns or ¼ teaspoon black pepper**
- **4 sprigs fresh parsley**
- **2 bay leaves**
- **2 cloves garlic, unpeeled and halved**
- **6 cups cold water**

1 If using wings, cut each wing at joints into three pieces. Place chicken pieces in a large pot. Add celery, carrots, onion, salt, thyme, peppercorns, parsley, bay leaves, and garlic. Add water. Bring to boiling; reduce heat. Simmer, covered, for 2½ hours. Remove chicken pieces from broth; set aside.

2 Strain broth into a large bowl through a colander lined with two layers of 100% cotton cheesecloth. Discard vegetables and seasonings.

3 If using the broth while hot, skim fat. If storing, chill broth in a bowl for 6 hours; lift off fat. Place broth in a container. Cover and chill for up to 3 days or freeze for up to 6 months.

4 If desired, when chicken is cool enough to handle, remove meat from bones. Chop meat; discard bones. Place meat in a container. Cover and chill for up to 3 days or freeze for up to 6 months.

SLOW COOKER DIRECTIONS: Place chicken pieces in a 4- to 6-quart slow cooker. Add remaining ingredients. Cover and cook on low-heat setting for 10 to 12 hours or on high-heat setting for 5 to 6 hours. Continue as directed.

PER 1 CUP: 11 cal., 0 g total fat, 3 mg chol., 411 mg sodium, 1 g carb., 0 g fiber, 1 g pro. EXCHANGES: Free

SKIMMING FAT

The easiest way to remove fat from broth is to chill the broth until the fat becomes solid and you can lift it off. If you don't have time to chill the broth, use a metal spoon to skim the fat that rises to the top of the broth. Or pour the soup into a fat-separating pitcher. These pitchers are designed to easily pour off the fat that rises to the surface of the broth.

LOW-CALORIE

Beef Broth

PREP: 30 MINUTES **ROAST:** 30 MINUTES AT 450°F
COOK: 3½ HOURS **MAKES:** 6 TO 7 CUPS

- **4 pounds meaty beef soup bones (beef shank cross cuts or short ribs)**
- **½ cup water**
- **3 carrots, cut up**
- **2 medium onions, unpeeled and cut up**
- **2 stalks celery with leaves, cut up**
- **1 tablespoon dried basil or thyme, crushed**
- **1½ teaspoons salt**
- **10 whole black peppercorns**
- **8 sprigs fresh parsley**
- **4 bay leaves**
- **2 cloves garlic, unpeeled and halved**
- **8 cups water**

1 Preheat oven to 450°F. Place soup bones in a shallow roasting pan. Roast, uncovered, about 30 minutes or until well browned, turning once.

2 Place soup bones in a large pot. Pour the ½ cup water into the roasting pan; scrape up browned bits. Add water mixture to soup bones in pot. Stir in carrots, onions, celery, basil, salt, peppercorns, parsley, bay leaves, and garlic. Add the 8 cups water. Bring to boiling; reduce heat. Simmer, covered, for 3½ hours. Remove soup bones from broth; set aside.

3 Strain broth into a large bowl through a colander lined with two layers of 100% cotton cheesecloth. Discard vegetables and seasonings.

4 If using the broth while hot, skim fat. If storing broth for later use, chill in a bowl for 6 hours; lift off fat. Place broth in a container. Cover and chill for up to 3 days or freeze for up to 6 months.

5 If desired, when bones are cool enough to handle, remove meat from bones. Chop meat; discard bones. Place meat in a container. Cover and chill for up to 3 days or freeze for up to 6 months.

SLOW COOKER DIRECTIONS: Prepare as directed, except use 2 small onions and 7½ cups total water. Roast bones as directed. Place bones in a 4- to 6-quart slow cooker. Pour the ½ cup water into roasting pan and scrape up browned bits; add water mixture to slow cooker. Stir in carrots, onions, celery, basil, salt, peppercorns, parsley, bay leaves, and garlic. Add 7 cups water. Cover; cook on low-heat setting for 10 to 12 hours or on high-heat setting for 5 to 6 hours. Remove soup bones from broth; set aside. Continue as directed.

PER 1 CUP: 17 cal., 0 g total fat, 3 mg chol., 595 mg sodium, 2 g carb., 1 g fiber, 1 g pro. EXCHANGES: Free

LOW-CALORIE

Vegetable Broth

PREP: 25 MINUTES **COOK:** 2 HOURS **MAKES:** 6 CUPS

- **4 medium yellow onions**
- **4 medium carrots**
- **3 stalks celery with leaves**
- **2 medium parsnips or carrots**
- **2 medium potatoes**
- **1 medium sweet potato**
- **1 pound fresh button mushrooms**
- **8 cups water**
- **1½ teaspoons salt**
- **1 teaspoon dried dill weed, basil, rosemary, or marjoram, crushed**
- **½ teaspoon whole black peppercorns or ¼ teaspoon black pepper**

1 Do not peel the vegetables unless coated with wax. Cut the onions into wedges. Cut carrots, celery, parsnips, and potatoes into 2-inch pieces.

2 Place cut-up vegetables and mushrooms in a large pot. Add the water, salt, dill weed, and peppercorns. Bring to boiling; reduce heat. Simmer, covered, for 2 hours.

3 Strain broth into a large bowl through a colander lined with two layers of 100% cotton cheesecloth. Discard vegetables and seasonings. Place broth in a container. Cover and chill for up to 3 days or freeze for up to 6 months.

PER 1 CUP: 12 cal., 0 g total fat, 0 mg chol., 599 mg sodium, 3 g carb., 1 g fiber, 0 g pro. **EXCHANGES:** Free

BEST-LOVED

Old-Fashioned Beef Stew

PREP: 20 MINUTES **COOK:** 90 MINUTES
MAKES: 6 MAIN-DISH SERVINGS

- **2 pounds beef chuck roast or beef stew meat**
- **¼ cup all-purpose flour**
- **¼ teaspoon black pepper**
- **3 tablespoons vegetable oil**
- **3 cups vegetable juice**
- **3 cups reduced-sodium beef broth**
- **2 medium onions, cut into thin wedges**
- **1 cup thinly sliced celery (2 stalks)**
- **2 tablespoons Worcestershire sauce**
- **1 teaspoon dried oregano, crushed**
- **½ teaspoon dried marjoram, crushed**
- **1 bay leaf**
- **4 red potatoes, cut into 1-inch cubes**
- **4 carrots, bias-sliced ¼ inch thick**

OLD-FASHIONED BEEF STEW

1 Trim fat from meat; cut meat into ¾-inch pieces. In a large plastic bag combine flour and pepper. Add meat to bag; shake until evenly coated. In a large pot brown half of the meat in half of the oil over medium-high heat; remove meat from pot. Repeat with remaining meat and oil. Return all meat to pot. Stir in vegetable juice, broth, onions, celery, Worcestershire sauce, oregano, marjoram, and bay leaf. Bring to boiling; reduce heat. Simmer, covered, for 60 minutes.

2 Stir potatoes and carrots into stew. Return to boiling; reduce heat. Simmer, covered, for 30 to 40 minutes more or until meat and vegetables are tender. Discard bay leaf.

SLOW COOKER DIRECTIONS: Prepare and brown meat as directed. In a 4- to 6-quart slow cooker layer meat, onions, celery, potatoes, and carrots. Reduce vegetable juice to 2 cups. Combine vegetable juice, broth, Worcestershire sauce, oregano, marjoram, and bay leaf. Pour over meat and vegetables in slow cooker. Cover; cook on low-heat setting for 10 to 12 hours or on high-heat setting for 5 to 6 hours or until meat and vegetables are tender. Discard bay leaf

PER 1¾ CUPS: 476 cal., 20 g total fat (6 g sat. fat), 125 mg chol., 640 mg sodium, 30 g carb., 4 g fiber, 46 g pro.
EXCHANGES: 2 Vegetable, 1 Starch, 5½ Lean Meat, 2 Fat

All-American Cheeseburger Soup

START TO FINISH: 40 MINUTES
MAKES: 6 MAIN-DISH SERVINGS

1 pound ground beef
1/2 cup chopped onion (1 medium)
1/2 cup chopped celery (1 stalk)
2 cloves garlic, minced
2 tablespoons all-purpose flour
2 14.5-ounce cans reduced-sodium beef broth (3 1/2 cups)
2 medium potatoes, coarsely chopped
1 14.5-ounce can diced tomatoes, drained
1 8-ounce package shredded American-cheddar cheese blend (2 cups)
1 6-ounce can tomato paste
1/4 cup ketchup
2 tablespoons Dijon-style mustard
1 cup whole milk
6 cocktail buns, split and toasted*
Assorted condiments (pickles, chopped onions, shredded lettuce, mustard, and/or ketchup) (optional)

1 In a large pot cook beef, onion, celery, and garlic over medium heat until meat is browned and vegetables are tender, using a wooden spoon to break up meat as it cooks. Drain off fat. Sprinkle flour over beef mixture; cook and stir for 2 minutes. Stir in broth and potatoes. Bring to boiling, stirring occasionally. Reduce heat. Simmer, covered, about 10 minutes or until potatoes are tender.

2 Stir in tomatoes, cheese, tomato paste, ketchup, and mustard. Cook and stir until cheese melts and soup comes to a gentle boil. Stir in milk; heat through. Serve with toasted buns and, if desired, top with condiments.

***NOTE:** To toast buns, preheat the broiler. Place split buns, cut sides up, on a broiler pan. Brush lightly with 1 tablespoon melted butter or olive oil. Broil 3 to 4 inches from heat about 1 minute or until lightly toasted.

PER 1 1/2 CUPS + 1 COCKTAIL BUN: 528 cal., 27 g total fat (13 g sat. fat), 94 mg chol., 1,461 mg sodium, 39 g carb., 4 g fiber, 32 g pro. EXCHANGES: 1/2 Vegetable, 2 1/2 Starch, 3 1/2 Medium-Fat Meat, 1 1/2 Fat

TOP IT YOUR WAY

Any topping you enjoy on a cheeseburger will taste great with this soup. For added flavor, you also can use bacon, guacamole, jalapeño peppers, chopped tomatoes, and other faves.

LOW-CALORIE

Barley-Beef Soup

PREP: 25 MINUTES **COOK:** 105 MINUTES
MAKES: 8 MAIN-DISH SERVINGS

- **12 ounces beef or lamb stew meat, cut into 1-inch cubes**
- **1 tablespoon vegetable oil**
- **4 14.5-ounce cans beef broth (7 cups)**
- **1 cup chopped onion (1 large)**
- **½ cup chopped celery (1 stalk)**
- **1 teaspoon dried oregano or basil, crushed**
- **¼ teaspoon black pepper**
- **2 cloves garlic, minced**
- **1 bay leaf**
- **1 cup frozen mixed vegetables**
- **1 14.5-ounce can diced tomatoes, undrained**
- **1 cup ½-inch slices peeled parsnips or ½-inch cubes peeled potatoes**
- **⅔ cup quick-cooking barley**

1 In a large pot brown meat in hot oil. Drain off fat. Stir in broth, onion, celery, oregano, pepper, garlic, and bay leaf. Bring to boiling; reduce heat. Simmer, covered, for 1½ hours for beef (45 minutes for lamb).

2 Stir in frozen vegetables, tomatoes, parsnips, and barley. Return to boiling; reduce heat. Simmer, covered, about 15 minutes more or until meat and vegetables are tender. Discard bay leaf.

SLOW COOKER DIRECTIONS: Substitute regular barley for quick-cooking barley. Brown meat in hot oil; drain. In a 5- or 6-quart slow cooker combine beef and remaining ingredients. Cover; cook on low-heat setting for 8 to 10 hours or on high-heat setting for 4 to 5 hours.

PER 1⅓ CUPS: 188 cal., 5 g total fat (1 g sat. fat), 20 mg chol., 880 mg sodium, 23 g carb., 5 g fiber, 14 g pro.
EXCHANGES: 1 Vegetable, 1 Starch, 1½ Lean Meat

Philly Cheesesteak Soup

START TO FINISH: 50 MINUTES
MAKES: 6 MAIN-DISH SERVINGS

- **1 cup all-purpose flour**
- **1 tablespoon onion powder**
- **1 teaspoon garlic powder**
- **2½ pounds boneless beef top loin or ribeye steak, cut into ½-inch pieces**
- **1½ cups chopped onions (3 medium)**
- **¼ cup olive oil**
- **2½ cups coarsely chopped red sweet peppers**
- **1¼ cups coarsely chopped yellow sweet pepper**
- **4 cloves garlic, minced**
- **6 cups reduced-sodium beef broth**

PHILLY CHEESESTEAK SOUP

- **1 tablespoon Worcestershire sauce**
- **8 ounces process American cheese slices**
- **Cooked sweet pepper strips, onion slices, and/or mushroom slices (optional)**
- **2 hoagie rolls, split, toasted and cut into 2-inch strips**

1 In a large bowl stir together flour, onion powder, and garlic powder. Add meat pieces, stirring to coat; set aside.

2 In a 6- to 8-quart pot cook chopped onions in hot oil over medium-high heat for 6 to 8 minutes or until tender, stirring often. Add the chopped red and yellow sweet peppers; cook and stir for 3 to 4 minutes or until tender. Add garlic; cook and stir for 1 minute. Add meat and any remaining flour to vegetable mixture. Cook and stir over medium heat for 8 to 10 minutes or until meat is lightly browned.

3 Increase heat to high; add broth and Worcestershire sauce. Cook and stir until mixture begins to thicken; reduce heat slightly. Cook and stir until mixture is boiling. Remove from heat. Top with cheese slices; cover and let stand for 1 to 2 minutes or until cheese is melted. Stir to combine.

4 Ladle soup into bowls. If desired, garnish each serving with cooked sweet pepper strips, onion slices, and/or sliced mushrooms. Serve with toasted hoagie roll strips.

PER 2 CUPS: 685 cal., 32 g total fat (12 g sat. fat), 164 mg chol., 1,284 mg sodium, 44 g carb., 4 g fiber, 57 g pro.
EXCHANGES: 2 Vegetable, 2½ Starch, 6 Medium-Fat Meat

LOW-CALORIE

Vegetable Soup

This easy vegetable soup can be on the table in 30 minutes. With all the meat and flavor variations, you will want to make it often.

START TO FINISH: 45 MINUTES
MAKES: 4 MAIN-DISH SERVINGS

- **12 ounces ground beef**
- **1 cup chopped carrots (2 medium)**
- **1 cup chopped celery (2 stalks)**
- **½ cup chopped onion (1 medium)**
- **1 32-ounce carton reduced-sodium beef broth (4 cups)**
- **½ of a 6-ounce can tomato paste (⅓ cup)**
- **½ of a 2-ounce package (1 envelope) onion soup mix**
- **½ teaspoon dried thyme, crushed**
- **1 cup cooked medium shell pasta**

1 In a large saucepan cook beef, carrots, celery, and onion until meat is browned; drain off fat.

2 Stir in broth, tomato paste, soup mix, and thyme. Bring to boiling; reduce heat. Simmer, covered, for 15 minutes. Stir in pasta; heat through.

PER 1½ CUPS: 348 cal., 18 g fat (7 g sat. fat), 60 mg chol., 1,263 mg sodium, 25 g carb., 3 g fiber, 21 g pro. **EXCHANGES:** 2 Vegetable, 1 Starch, 2 High-Fat Meat

CHICKEN AND BEAN SOUP: Substitute skinless, boneless chicken thighs, cut into 1-inch pieces, for the beef and 1 cup each chopped zucchini, chopped potatoes, and whole kernel corn for carrots, celery, and onion. Cook chicken and vegetables in 1 tablespoon vegetable oil. Substitute chicken broth for beef broth, one 1.4-ounce envelope vegetable soup mix for onion soup mix, and one 15-ounce can cannellini beans, rinsed and drained, for the pasta.

KALE AND BEAN SOUP: Omit beef. Cook vegetables in 1 tablespoon vegetable oil until crisp-tender. Substitute vegetable broth for beef broth. Add 4 cups chopped, trimmed kale with the broth. Substitute one 15-ounce can black beans, rinsed and drained, for the pasta.

ASIAN PORK SOUP: Substitute pork tenderloin, cut into 1-inch cubes, for beef. Cook the pork in 1 tablespoon vegetable oil. Substitute 1½ cups each frozen stir-fry vegetables and frozen shelled sweet soybeans (edamame) for the carrots, celery, and onion; add to pork with broth. Omit tomato paste, soup mix, and thyme. Add 2 tablespoons reduced-sodium soy sauce with the broth. Substitute 3 ounces Asian noodles, cooked, for the pasta. Serve with Asian chili sauce.

TURKEY AND RICE SOUP: Substitute turkey breast tenderloin, cut into strips, for beef and 2 cups peeled, chopped sweet potatoes for carrots and celery. Cook turkey in 1 tablespoon vegetable oil until no longer pink; remove from pan. Cook onion in 1 tablespoon vegetable oil until crisp-tender. Return turkey to pan; add sweet potatoes. Substitute chicken broth for beef broth, one 1.4-ounce envelope vegetable soup mix for onion soup mix, 1 tablespoon snipped fresh basil for dried thyme, and 1 cup cooked rice for pasta.

SAUSAGE AND BEAN SOUP: Substitute bulk pork sausage for ground beef and one 15-ounce can red beans, rinsed and drained, for the pasta. Stir in 1 tablespoon finely chopped chipotle peppers in adobo sauce with the beans. Sprinkle with snipped fresh cilantro.

STEAK AND MUSHROOM SOUP: Substitute beef sirloin steak, cut into strips, for ground beef and 2 cups sliced mushrooms for carrots and celery. Cook beef in 1 tablespoon vegetable oil until desired doneness; remove from pan. Cook mushrooms and onion in 1 tablespoon butter until tender; return meat to pan. Substitute dried rosemary for thyme and cooked barley for the pasta.

CHICKEN AND QUINOA SOUP: Substitute skinless, boneless chicken breast halves, cut into strips, for beef and chopped fennel for celery. Cook the chicken in 1 tablespoon vegetable oil until no longer pink; remove from pan. Cook vegetables in 1 tablespoon vegetable oil until crisp-tender; return chicken to pan. Substitute chicken broth for beef broth, one 1.4-ounce envelope vegetable soup mix for onion soup mix, and 1½ cups cooked quinoa for the pasta. Omit tomato paste.

CHICKEN ALFREDO SOUP: Substitute skinless, boneless chicken thighs, cut into 1-inch pieces, for beef. Cook chicken in 1 tablespoon vegetable oil until no longer pink; remove from pan. Cook vegetables in 1 tablespoon vegetable oil until crisp-tender; return chicken to pan. Substitute 2 cups chicken broth plus one 15-ounce jar Alfredo sauce for beef broth, one 1.4-ounce envelope vegetable soup mix for onion soup mix, and dried basil for thyme. Omit tomato paste. Use cooked broken spaghetti for pasta.

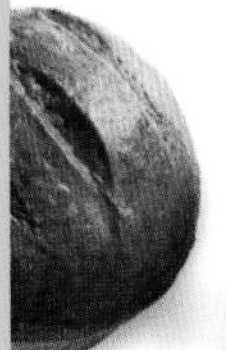

BREAD BOWLS

Serve soup in a bowl you can eat. Edible vessels are easy to make when you start with frozen bread dough.

Thaw two 1-pound loaves frozen white or wheat bread dough. Cut each into thirds crosswise to make six pieces total. Shape each piece into a ball. Grease a large baking sheet and sprinkle lightly with cornmeal. Arrange the dough balls on the baking sheet. Cover and let rise in a warm place until nearly double (about 40 minutes). Preheat oven to 400°F. In a small bowl combine 1 egg and 1 tablespoon water; brush dough balls with some of the egg mixture. Using a sharp knife, make two or three shallow cuts across the top of each ball. Bake for 15 minutes. Brush again with egg mixture. Bake for 8 to 10 minutes more or until golden and bread sounds hollow when lightly tapped. Remove and cool on a wire rack. To serve, cut a ½-inch-thick slice from the top of each bread round. Scoop out bread from the center of each round, leaving a ¾-inch shell. Fill bread bowls with hot soup; serve immediately.

GREEK LAMB SOUP WITH CUCUMBER-YOGURT TOPPING

Greek Lamb Soup with Cucumber-Yogurt Topping

PREP: 30 MINUTES **COOK:** 30 MINUTES
MAKES: 4 MAIN-DISH SERVINGS

- **2 pounds lean ground lamb or beef**
- **2 large onions, halved and thinly sliced**
- **2 tablespoons all-purpose flour**
- **1 tablespoon snipped fresh oregano or 1 teaspoon dried oregano, crushed**
- **1 tablespoon finely shredded lemon peel**
- **1½ teaspoons ground cumin**
- **¾ teaspoon salt**
- **½ teaspoon ground coriander**
- **6 cloves garlic, minced**
- **1 32-ounce carton reduced-sodium beef broth (4 cups)**
- **¼ cup tomato paste**
- **⅔ cup chopped roma tomatoes (2 medium)**
- **1 tablespoon snipped fresh mint**
- **1 recipe Yogurt-Cucumber Topping**
- **Purchased pita chips (optional)**

1 In a 4-quart pot cook meat over medium-high heat until browned, using a wooden spoon to break up meat as it cooks. Drain off fat.

2 Add onions, flour, oregano, lemon peel, cumin, salt, coriander, and garlic to meat. Cook over medium heat for 4 to 5 minutes or until onions are tender, stirring occasionally. Stir in broth and tomato paste. Bring to boiling; reduce heat. Simmer, covered, for 30 minutes, stirring occasionally.

3 Ladle soup into bowls. Top with chopped tomatoes and mint. Serve with Yogurt-Cucumber Topping and, if desired, pita chips.

YOGURT-CUCUMBER TOPPING: In a medium bowl combine ¾ cup plain Greek yogurt, ⅓ cup finely chopped English cucumber, 1½ teaspoons olive oil, 1 teaspoon red wine vinegar, and 1 clove garlic, minced. Cover and chill until needed.

PER 1¾ CUPS: 669 cal., 37 g total fat (16 g sat. fat), 150 mg chol., 1,263 mg sodium, 30 g carb., 4 g fiber, 51 g pro.
EXCHANGES: 2½ Vegetable, 1 Starch, 6 Medium-Fat Meat, 1½ Fat

Lamb Cassoulet

PREP: 30 MINUTES **STAND:** 60 MINUTES
COOK: 90 MINUTES **MAKES:** 6 MAIN-DISH SERVINGS

- **2 cups dried navy beans**
- **1 pound lean boneless lamb, cut into 1-inch cubes**
- **1 tablespoon vegetable oil**
- **1 cup chopped carrots (2 medium)**
- **½ cup chopped green sweet pepper**
- **½ cup chopped onion (1 medium)**
- **1 tablespoon instant beef bouillon granules**
- **1 tablespoon Worcestershire sauce**
- **1 teaspoon dried thyme, crushed**
- **½ teaspoon salt**
- **3 cloves garlic, minced**
- **2 bay leaves**
- **4 cups water**
- **8 ounces skinless, boneless chicken thighs, cut into 1-inch pieces**
- **1 14.5-ounce can diced tomatoes, undrained**

1 Rinse beans. In a large pot combine beans and 8 cups water. Bring to boiling; reduce heat. Simmer, uncovered, for 2 minutes. Remove from heat. Cover; let stand for 60 minutes. (Or place beans in water in pot. Cover; let stand in a cool place for 6 to 8 hours or overnight.) Drain and rinse beans. Wipe pot dry.

2 In the same pot brown lamb, half at a time, in hot oil; drain off fat. Return all lamb to pot. Add beans, carrots, sweet pepper, onion, bouillon granules, Worcestershire sauce, thyme, salt, garlic, and bay leaves. Add 4 cups fresh water. Bring to boiling; reduce heat. Simmer, covered, for 60 to 90 minutes or until beans are tender.

3 Add chicken and tomatoes. Return to boiling; reduce heat. Simmer, uncovered, for 30 minutes more. Discard bay leaves. Skim fat if necessary. Season to taste with additional salt and *black pepper.*

PER 1¾ CUPS: 417 cal., 8 g total fat (2 g sat. fat), 79 mg chol., 899 mg sodium, 49 g carb., 18 g fiber, 39 g pro.
EXCHANGES: 1 Vegetable, 3 Starch, 4 Lean Meat, ½ Fat

make it mine

BEST-LOVED

Chili

With so many possibilities for making great chili, why limit yourself to the usual formulas? With this recipe, you can mix and match your way to a true one-bowl wonder.

PREP: 25 MINUTES **COOK:** 20 MINUTES
MAKES: 8 MAIN-DISH SERVINGS

- 1½ pounds MEAT
- 3 cups CHOPPED VEGETABLE
- 4 cloves garlic, minced
- 1 tablespoon vegetable oil
- 2 15- to 16-ounce cans BEANS, rinsed and drained
- 2 14.5-ounce cans diced tomatoes, undrained
- 1 15-ounce can tomato sauce
- 1 cup LIQUID
- 2 tablespoons chili powder, ancho chili powder, or 1 teaspoon ground chipotle chile pepper
- 1 teaspoon DRIED HERB, crushed
- ½ teaspoon black pepper
- Shredded cheddar or Monterey Jack cheese (optional)
- Sliced green onions (optional)

1 In a large pot cook Meat, Chopped Vegetable, and garlic in hot oil until meat is browned. Drain off fat. Stir in Beans, tomatoes, tomato sauce, Liquid, chili powder, Dried Herb, and black pepper. Bring to boiling; reduce heat. Simmer, covered, for 20 minutes for ground meat (60 minutes or until tender for cubed meat), stirring occasionally. If desired, top each serving with cheese and green onions.

MEAT *(pick one)*
Ground beef or pork
Beef shoulder top blade steak (flat-iron), cut into ¾-inch cubes
Beef stew meat or pork shoulder, cut into ¾-inch cubes

CHOPPED VEGETABLE *(pick one)*
Carrots
Celery
Onions
Potatoes
Sweet peppers

BEANS *(pick one)*
Black
Cannellini (white kidney)
Garbanzo (chickpeas)
Pinto
Red kidney

LIQUID *(pick one)*
Apple juice
Beef broth
Chicken broth
Beer
Water

DRIED HERB *(pick one)*
Basil
Italian seasoning
Oregano
Thyme

LOW-CALORIE

Ham and Bean Soup

PREP: 30 MINUTES **STAND:** 60 MINUTES
COOK: 60 MINUTES **MAKES:** 8 MAIN-DISH SERVINGS

- **2 cups dried navy beans**
- **2 to 2½ pounds meaty smoked pork hocks or two 1- to 1½-pound meaty ham bones**
- **2 tablespoons butter or margarine**
- **3 cups sliced celery (6 stalks)**
- **3 cups chopped onion (6 medium)**
- **2 teaspoons dried thyme, crushed**
- **2 bay leaves**

1 Rinse beans. In a large pot combine beans and 8 cups water. Bring to boiling; reduce heat. Simmer, uncovered, for 2 minutes. Remove from heat. Cover and let stand for 60 minutes. (Or place beans in water in pot. Cover; let stand in a cool place for 6 to 8 hours or overnight.) Drain and rinse beans; set aside.

2 In the same pot brown pork hocks on all sides in hot butter over medium heat (see photo 1, below). Remove ham hocks from pot. Add celery and onion to drippings in pot. Cook and stir for 5 to 8 minutes or until tender. Add beans, hocks, thyme, ½ teaspoon *salt*, ½ teaspoon *black pepper*, bay leaves, and 8 cups fresh water. Bring to boiling; reduce heat. Simmer, covered, for 60 to 90 minutes or until beans are tender.

3 Remove pork hocks. When cool enough to handle, cut meat off bones; coarsely chop meat (see photo 2, below). Discard bones and bay leaves. Slightly mash beans in pot. Stir in chopped meat; heat through. Season to taste with additional salt and pepper.

PREPPING HAM STEP-BY-STEP

1. Brown the hocks over medium heat, turning as needed. Browning adds flavor to the meat; the browned bits left in the pan lend richness to the soup.

2. Use a chef's knife to cut the ham off the bones; discard bones and coarsely chop the meat into bite-size pieces.

SLOW COOKER DIRECTIONS: Rinse beans; drain. In a large pot combine the beans and 8 cups water. Bring to boiling; reduce heat. Simmer, uncovered, for 10 minutes. Cover; let stand for 60 minutes. Drain; rinse beans. Brown pork hocks as directed. In a 6-quart slow cooker combine pork hocks and the remaining ingredients. Stir in beans and 8 cups fresh water. Cover and cook on low-heat setting for 10 to 12 hours or on high-heat setting for 5 to 6 hours. Remove pork hocks. When cool enough to handle, cut meat off bones; coarsely chop meat. Discard bones and bay leaves. Slightly mash beans in cooker. Stir in meat. Season with additional salt and black pepper.

PER 1½ CUPS: 308 cal., 9 g total fat (4 g sat. fat), 38 mg chol., 377 mg sodium, 37 g carb., 14 g fiber, 21 g pro.
EXCHANGES: 1 Vegetable, 2 Starch, 2 Lean Meat ½ Fat

BEST-LOVED LOW-CALORIE

Split Pea Soup

PREP: 20 MINUTES **COOK:** 80 MINUTES
MAKES: 4 MAIN-DISH SERVINGS

- **1½ cups dried split peas, rinsed and drained**
- **1 14.5-ounce can reduced-sodium chicken broth (1¾ cups)**
- **1 to 1½ pounds meaty smoked pork hocks or one 1- to 1½-pound meaty ham bone**
- **¼ teaspoon dried marjoram, crushed**
- **1 bay leaf**
- **½ cup chopped carrot (1 medium)**
- **½ cup chopped celery (1 stalk)**
- **½ cup chopped onion (1 medium)**

1 In a large saucepan combine 2¾ cups *water*, split peas, broth, pork hocks, marjoram, bay leaf, and dash *black pepper*. Bring to boiling; reduce heat. Simmer, covered, for 60 minutes, stirring occasionally. Remove pork hocks.

2 When cool enough to handle, cut meat off bones; coarsely chop meat (see photo 2, left). Discard bones. Return meat to saucepan. Stir in carrot, celery, and onion. Return to boiling; reduce heat. Simmer, covered, for 20 to 30 minutes more or until vegetables are tender. Discard bay leaf.

SLOW COOKER DIRECTIONS: In a 3½- or 4-quart slow cooker combine peas, hocks, marjoram, pepper, bay leaf, carrot, celery, and onion. Pour water and broth over all. Cover; cook on low-heat setting for 8 to 10 hours or on high-heat setting for 4 to 5 hours. Discard bay leaf. Remove hocks, cut off meat, and add to soup.

PER 1½ CUPS: 307 cal., 3 g total fat (1 g sat. fat), 19 mg chol., 676 mg sodium, 47 g carb., 19 g fiber, 25 g pro.
EXCHANGES: ½ Vegetable, 3 Starch, 2½ Lean Meat

LOW-CALORIE

Caramelized Shallot-Bacon Soup

START TO FINISH: 40 MINUTES
MAKES: 4 MAIN-DISH SERVINGS

- **4 slices bacon**
- **1½ cups sliced shallots (12 medium)**
- **3 14.5-ounce cans reduced-sodium chicken broth (5¼ cups)**
- **1 cup chopped, seeded roma tomatoes**
- **2¼ cups coarsely chopped escarole or arugula**

1 In a large skillet cook bacon over medium heat until crisp. Transfer bacon to a plate lined with paper towels, reserving 1 tablespoon drippings in skillet. Set bacon aside.

2 Add shallots to reserved drippings in skillet. Cook, covered, over medium-low heat for 13 to 15 minutes or until tender, stirring occasionally. Cook, uncovered, over medium-high heat for 3 to 5 minutes or until golden, stirring often.

3 Transfer shallots to a large saucepan; add broth and tomatoes. Bring to boiling; reduce heat. Simmer, uncovered, for 5 minutes. Stir in escarole; cook for 5 minutes more. Crumble bacon and sprinkle over each serving.

PER 1½ CUPS: 143 cal., 6 g total fat (2 g sat. fat), 11 mg chol., 868 mg sodium, 14 g carb., 3 g fiber, 9 g pro.
EXCHANGES: 2½ Vegetable, ½ High-Fat Meat, ½ Fat

LOW-CALORIE

Lentil and Sausage Soup

PREP: 25 MINUTES **COOK:** 30 MINUTES
MAKES: 6 MAIN-DISH SERVINGS

- **1 medium fennel bulb, trimmed, cored, and thinly sliced**
- **1 cup thinly sliced carrots (2 medium)**
- **½ cup chopped onion (1 medium)**
- **2 cloves garlic, minced**
- **1 tablespoon olive oil**
- **2 uncooked sweet or hot Italian sausage links, sliced**
- **2 14.5-ounce cans reduced-sodium chicken broth (3½ cups)**
- **1 14.5-ounce can diced tomatoes with basil, garlic, and oregano, undrained**
- **1 cup brown lentils, rinsed and drained**
- **⅛ teaspoon crushed red pepper**

1 In a large saucepan cook fennel, carrots, onion, and garlic in hot oil over medium-high heat about 5 minutes or until vegetables are tender. Add sausage; cook for 2 to 3 minutes more or until browned.

2 Stir in broth, tomatoes, lentils, and crushed red pepper. Bring to boiling; reduce heat. Simmer, covered, for 30 to 35 minutes or until lentils are tender.

PER 1 CUP: 238 cal., 5 g total fat (1 g sat. fat), 9 mg chol., 866 mg sodium, 33 g carb., 12 g fiber, 16 g pro.
EXCHANGES: ½ Vegetable, 2 Starch, 1 Medium-Fat Meat

LOW-CALORIE

Supreme Pizza Soup

PREP: 35 MINUTES **COOK:** 35 MINUTES
MAKES: 6 MAIN-DISH SERVINGS

- **8 ounces bulk Italian sausage**
- **1 3.5-ounce package sliced pepperoni, chopped**
- **1 tablespoon olive oil**
- **1 8-ounce package fresh button mushrooms, coarsely chopped**
- **¾ cup chopped red and/or green sweet pepper (1 medium)**
- **½ cup chopped red onion (1 medium)**
- **6 cloves garlic, minced**
- **½ teaspoon crushed red pepper**
- **3 14.5-ounce cans diced tomatoes, undrained**
- **1 14.5-ounce can reduced-sodium chicken broth (1¾ cups)**
- **¼ cup pitted black olives, halved**
- **1½ teaspoons dried Italian seasoning, crushed**
- **Grated Parmesan cheese**
- **½ of a 5-ounce package croutons**

1 In a large pot cook sausage over medium heat about 10 minutes or until browned, using a wooden spoon to break up meat as it cooks. Remove sausage, reserving drippings in pot; drain sausage on a plate lined with paper towels. Add pepperoni to drippings. Cook and stir about 5 minutes or until pepperoni starts to crisp. Remove from pot; drain on a plate lined with paper towels.

2 In the same pot heat 1½ teaspoons of the oil over medium-low heat. Add mushrooms, sweet pepper, and onion; cook about 10 minutes or until tender. Remove vegetables; set aside. Add the remaining 1½ teaspoons olive oil to pot. Add garlic and crushed red pepper to the oil; cook about 30 seconds or until garlic is aromatic, stirring frequently. Add sausage, pepperoni, cooked vegetables, tomatoes, broth, olives, and Italian seasoning. Bring to boiling; reduce heat. Simmer, uncovered, for 20 minutes, stirring occasionally. Top servings with cheese and croutons.

PER 1½ CUPS: 350 cal., 21 g total fat (7 g sat. fat), 45 mg chol., 1,215 mg sodium, 22 g carb., 4 g fiber, 15 g pro.
EXCHANGES: 2½ Vegetable, ½ Starch, 1 High-Fat Meat, 2½ Fat

BEST-LOVED LOW-CALORIE

Old-Fashioned Chicken Noodle Soup

PREP: 25 MINUTES **COOK:** 100 MINUTES
MAKES: 8 MAIN-DISH SERVINGS

- **1 3½- to 4-pound broiler-fryer chicken, cut up, or 3 pounds meaty chicken pieces (breast halves, thighs, and/or drumsticks)**
- **½ cup chopped onion (1 medium)**
- **2 teaspoons salt**
- **1 teaspoon dried thyme, sage, or basil, crushed**
- **¼ teaspoon black pepper**
- **2 cloves garlic, peeled and halved**
- **2 bay leaves**
- **8 cups water**
- **1 cup chopped carrots (2 medium)**
- **1 cup chopped celery (2 stalks)**
- **2 cups Homemade Egg Noodles (page 418) or 6 ounces dried egg noodles**
- **1 tablespoon snipped fresh thyme, sage, or basil (optional)**

1 In a 6- to 8-quart pot combine chicken, onion, salt, dried thyme, pepper, garlic, and bay leaves. Pour the water over all. Bring to boiling; reduce heat. Simmer, covered, about 1½ hours or until chicken is very tender.

2 Remove chicken from broth. When cool enough to handle, remove meat from bones. Discard bones and skin. Cut meat into bite-size pieces; set meat aside. Discard bay leaves. Skim fat from broth.

3 Bring broth to boiling. Stir in carrots and celery. Return to boiling; reduce heat. Simmer, covered, for 7 minutes. Add noodles, stirring to combine. Simmer, covered, for 3 to 5 minutes more or until noodles are tender. Stir in chicken and, if desired, fresh thyme; heat through.

PER 1⅓ CUPS: 275 cal., 6 g total fat (1 g sat. fat), 136 mg chol., 826 mg sodium, 29 g carb., 2 g fiber, 26 g pro.
EXCHANGES: 2 Starch, 3 Lean Meat

MAKE-AHEAD NOODLE SOUP

Broth-base soups such as Old-Fashioned Chicken Noodle Soup are great for freezing, but the noodles need extra care.

Noodles and rice often lose texture and become mushy with freezing. To keep noodles and other starchy ingredients at their best, freeze the soup without them. Prepare the soup as the recipe directs, but leave the noodles out. Let the soup cool and freeze following the tips on page 561. If you are using homemade noodles, you can freeze them too. When ready to serve, thaw the soup and bring to boiling. Add the noodles and cook as directed.

LOW-CALORIE

Mexican Chicken-Tortilla Soup

PREP: 25 MINUTES **COOK:** 35 MINUTES
BAKE: 10 MINUTES AT 375°F
MAKES: 4 MAIN-DISH SERVINGS

- **2 medium chicken breast halves (with bone)**
- **1 14.5-ounce can reduced-sodium chicken broth (1¾ cups)**
- **½ cup chopped onion (1 medium)**
- **½ teaspoon ground cumin**
- **1 clove garlic, minced**
- **1 tablespoon vegetable oil**
- **1 14.5-ounce can no-salt-added diced tomatoes, undrained**
- **1 8-ounce can tomato sauce**
- **1 4-ounce can whole green chile peppers, rinsed, seeded, and cut into thin bite-size strips (see tip, page 44)**
- **¼ cup snipped fresh cilantro or parsley**
- **1 tablespoon snipped fresh oregano**
- **4 6-inch corn tortillas**
- **½ cup shredded cheddar cheese (2 ounces)**

1 In a large pot combine chicken, broth, and 1¾ cups *water*. Bring to boiling; reduce heat. Simmer, covered, about 15 minutes or until chicken is no longer pink. Remove chicken; cool slightly. Skin, bone, and finely shred chicken; set aside. Discard skin and bones. Strain broth; skim fat from broth and set broth aside.

2 In same saucepan cook onion, cumin, and garlic in hot oil until onion is tender. Stir in strained broth, tomatoes, tomato sauce, chiles, cilantro, and oregano. Bring to boiling; reduce heat. Simmer, covered, for 20 minutes. Stir in chicken; heat through.

3 Preheat oven to 375°F. Cut tortillas in half. Cut each half crosswise into ½-inch-wide strips. Place tortilla strips on a baking sheet. Bake about 10 minutes or until crisp. Top each serving with cheese and tortilla strips. Serve immediately.

PER 1½ CUPS: 313 cal., 11 g total fat (4 g sat. fat), 71 mg chol., 836 mg sodium, 24 g carb., 5 g fiber, 30 g pro.
EXCHANGES: 1 Vegetable, 1½ Starch, 3½ Lean Meat, 1 Fat

LOW-CALORIE

Thai Chicken Noodle Soup

START TO FINISH: 35 MINUTES
MAKES: 6 MAIN-DISH SERVINGS

- **1 cup canned crushed tomatoes**
- **½ cup chunky peanut butter**
- **1 pound skinless, boneless chicken thighs, cut into 1-inch pieces**
- **2 teaspoons grated fresh ginger**
- **4 cloves garlic, minced**

THAI CHICKEN NOODLE SOUP

- **1 tablespoon sesame oil (not toasted)**
- **6 cups reduced-sodium chicken broth**
- **2 teaspoons fish sauce**
- **1 serrano chile pepper, seeded and finely chopped (see tip, page 44) (optional)**
- **3 ounces dried rice noodles, broken if desired**
- **2 cups shredded green cabbage**
- **1 cup canned bean sprouts, rinsed and drained**
- **¼ cup chopped green onions (2)**
- **Snipped fresh cilantro (optional)**
- **Coarsely chopped peanuts (optional)**

1 In a bowl combine tomatoes and peanut butter; set aside. In a 4-quart pot cook chicken, ginger, and garlic in hot sesame oil over medium-high heat about 5 minutes or until chicken is browned.

2 Stir in tomato mixture, broth, fish sauce, and, if desired, serrano pepper. Bring to boiling. Stir in noodles; reduce heat. Simmer for 5 minutes. Stir in cabbage. Simmer about 5 minutes more or until cabbage is just tender. Remove from heat. Stir in bean sprouts and green onions. Ladle soup into bowls. If desired, top each serving with cilantro and peanuts.

PER 1⅓ CUPS: 334 cal., 16 g total fat (3 g sat. fat), 72 mg chol., 1,011 mg sodium, 24 g carb., 4 g fiber, 25 g pro.
EXCHANGES: 1 Vegetable, 1 Starch, 3 Lean Meat, 2 Fat

LOW-CALORIE

Wild Rice and Turkey Soup

START TO FINISH: 40 MINUTES
MAKES: 6 MAIN-DISH SERVINGS

- **1 6.2-ounce package quick-cooking long grain and wild rice mix**
- **2 tablespoons butter or margarine**
- **4 ounces fresh shiitake mushrooms, stems removed and sliced (about 1½ cups)**
- **1 cup sliced celery (2 stalks)**
- **2 14.5-ounce cans reduced-sodium chicken broth (3½ cups)**
- **¼ teaspoon black pepper**
- **2 cups chopped smoked turkey or chopped cooked turkey or chicken (about 10 ounces)**
- **1 cup whipping cream**
- **2 tablespoons dry sherry (optional)**

1 Prepare the rice mix (including the seasoning packet) according to package directions, except omit any butter or margarine.

2 In a large saucepan melt butter over medium heat. Add mushrooms and celery. Cook about 5 minutes or until vegetables are almost tender and most of the mushroom liquid evaporates, stirring occasionally. Add broth and pepper. Bring to boiling; reduce heat. Simmer, covered, for 5 minutes. Stir in cooked rice mixture, turkey, whipping cream, and, if desired, sherry. Heat through.

PER 1⅓ CUPS: 347 cal., 21 g total fat (12 g sat. fat), 90 mg chol., 1,301 mg sodium, 28 g carb., 1 g fiber, 15 g pro.
EXCHANGES: 2 Starch, 1½ Lean Meat, 3 Fat

FAST LOW-CALORIE

Quick Cioppino with Basil Gremolata

START TO FINISH: 25 MINUTES
MAKES: 4 MAIN-DISH SERVINGS

- **6 ounces fresh or frozen cod fillets**
- **6 ounces fresh or frozen peeled and deveined shrimp**
- **1 medium green sweet pepper, seeded and cut into bite-size strips**
- **1 cup chopped onion (1 large)**
- **2 cloves garlic, minced**
- **1 tablespoon olive oil or vegetable oil**
- **2 14.5-ounce cans Italian-style stewed tomatoes, undrained and cut up**
- **½ cup water**
- **¼ teaspoon salt**
- **¼ teaspoon black pepper**
- **3 tablespoons snipped fresh basil**
- **1 tablespoon finely shredded lemon peel**
- **2 cloves garlic, minced**

QUICK CIOPPINO WITH BASIL GREMOLATA

1 Thaw cod and shrimp if frozen. Rinse cod and shrimp; pat dry with paper towels. Cut cod into 1-inch pieces; set aside.

2 In a large pot cook and stir sweet pepper, onion, and 2 cloves minced garlic in hot oil until tender. Stir in tomatoes, the water, salt, and black pepper. Bring to boiling.

3 Stir in cod and shrimp. Return to boiling; reduce heat. Simmer, covered, for 2 to 3 minutes or until cod flakes easily when tested with a fork and shrimp are opaque.

4 For gremolata, in a small bowl combine basil, lemon peel, and 2 cloves minced garlic. Ladle cioppino into bowls. Sprinkle each serving with gremolata.

PER 1⅓ CUPS: 188 cal., 5 g total fat (1 g sat. fat), 83 mg chol., 921 mg sodium, 20 g carb., 5 g fiber, 19 g pro.
EXCHANGES: 1½ Vegetable, 1 Starch, 2 Lean Meat, ½ Fat

USE UP ALL THE GOOD STUFF

Give leftover foods a second life by stirring them into soups.

Soups are infinitely adaptable and can accommodate most leftover meats and vegetables you have on hand. For example, if you have fresh spinach or other sturdy greens in danger of wilting, toss them into a soup toward the end of cooking time for added color and nutrients. Extra cooked chicken or turkey can help turn a side-dish soup into a main dish.

FAST

Southwestern White Chili

START TO FINISH: 30 MINUTES
MAKES: 8 MAIN-DISH SERVINGS

- **1 cup chopped onion (1 large)**
- **4 cloves garlic, minced**
- **1 tablespoon olive oil**
- **2 teaspoons ground cumin**
- **1 teaspoon dried oregano, crushed**
- **¼ teaspoon cayenne pepper**
- **3 15.5-ounce cans Great Northern beans, rinsed and drained**
- **4 cups chicken broth or reduced-sodium chicken broth**
- **2 4.5-ounce cans diced green chiles or chopped jalapeño peppers**
- **3 cups chopped cooked chicken (1 pound)**
- **2 cups shredded Monterey Jack cheese (8 ounces)**
- **Sour cream (optional)**
- **Canned diced green chile peppers or chopped jalapeño peppers (optional)**

1 In a large pot cook onion and garlic in hot oil until onion is tender.

2 Stir in cumin, oregano, and cayenne pepper. Cook and stir for 2 minutes. Add one can of beans to the pot; mash with a potato masher or fork. Stir in remaining beans, chicken broth, and the two cans chiles. Bring to boiling; reduce heat. Simmer, uncovered, for 5 minutes. Stir in chicken; heat through.

3 Ladle chili into bowls. Top each serving with ¼ cup cheese. If desired, top with sour cream and additional canned chiles.

PER 1 CUP: 471 cal., 16 g total fat (7 g sat. fat), 76 mg chol., 468 mg sodium, 43 g carb., 9 g fiber, 38 g pro.
EXCHANGES: 3 Starch, 4 Lean Meat, ½ Fat

LOW-CALORIE

Salmon and Asparagus Chowder

PREP: 20 MINUTES **COOK:** 23 MINUTES
MAKES: 8 MAIN-DISH SERVINGS

- **1 pound fresh skinless salmon fillets or one 14.75-ounce can salmon, rinsed, drained, flaked, and skin and bones removed**
- **1½ cups water**
- **2 14.5-ounce cans vegetable broth (3½ cups)**
- **2 cups frozen whole small onions or 1 cup chopped onion (not frozen)**
- **2½ cups cubed red-skin potatoes (3 medium)**
- **1 tablespoon snipped fresh dill weed or ½ teaspoon dried dill weed**
- **1 teaspoon finely shredded lemon peel**
- **½ teaspoon salt**
- **½ teaspoon black pepper**
- **2½ cups whole milk, half-and-half, or light cream**
- **2 tablespoons cornstarch**
- **1 10-ounce package frozen cut asparagus, thawed and well drained, or 2 cups cut-up fresh trimmed asparagus**

1 Rinse fresh salmon (if using); pat dry. To poach fresh salmon, in a large skillet bring the water to boiling. Add salmon. Return to boiling; reduce heat. Simmer, covered, for 6 to 8 minutes or until the salmon flakes easily with a fork. Remove salmon from skillet, discarding poaching liquid. Flake salmon into ½-inch pieces; set aside.

2 In a large pot combine broth, onions, potatoes, dill weed, lemon peel, salt, and pepper. Bring to boiling; reduce heat. Simmer, covered, for 15 minutes or until vegetables are tender, stirring occasionally.

3 In a large screw-top jar combine milk and cornstarch. Cover and shake well; stir into soup (see photo 1, below). Stir in asparagus. Cook and stir until slightly thickened and bubbly. Cook and stir for 2 minutes more. Gently stir in poached or canned salmon (see photo 2, below); heat through.

PER 1⅓ CUPS: 235 cal., 10 g total fat (3 g sat. fat), 39 mg chol., 609 mg sodium, 19 g carb., 2 g fiber, 16 g pro.
EXCHANGES: ½ Vegetable, 1 Starch, 1½ Medium-Fat Meat, ½ Fat

FINISHING CHOWDER STEP-BY-STEP

1. Stir the hot soup continuously while adding the cornstarch mixture so the sauce thickens smoothly.

2. Add the salmon at the end of cooking and stir gently so the chowder retains the nice chunk-size pieces.

HOT-AND-SOUR SOUP WITH SHRIMP

LOW-CALORIE

Hot-and-Sour Soup with Shrimp

START TO FINISH: 35 MINUTES
MAKES: 4 MAIN-DISH SERVINGS

- **12 ounces fresh or frozen shrimp in shells**
- **4 ounces fresh shiitake mushrooms, stems removed and sliced, or button mushrooms, sliced**
- **1 tablespoon vegetable oil**
- **2 14.5-ounce cans chicken broth (3½ cups)**
- **¼ cup rice vinegar or white vinegar**
- **2 tablespoons soy sauce**
- **1 teaspoon sugar**
- **1 teaspoon grated fresh ginger or ¼ teaspoon ground ginger**
- **½ teaspoon black pepper**
- **1 tablespoon cornstarch**
- **1 tablespoon cold water**
- **½ cup frozen peas**
- **½ cup shredded carrot (1 medium)**
- **2 green onions, thinly slivered**
- **1 egg, lightly beaten**

1 Thaw shrimp if frozen. Peel and devein shrimp. Rinse shrimp and pat dry with paper towels; set aside. In a large saucepan cook and stir mushrooms in hot oil until tender. Add broth, vinegar, soy sauce, sugar, ginger, and pepper. Bring to boiling; reduce heat. Simmer, covered, for 2 minutes. Stir in shrimp. Return to boiling; reduce heat. Simmer, covered, for 1 minute more.

2 Stir together cornstarch and cold water; stir into broth mixture. Cook and stir until slightly thickened and bubbly. Cook and stir for 2 minutes more. Stir in peas, carrot, and green onions. Pour the egg into the soup in a steady stream, stirring a few times to create shreds.

PER 1⅔ CUPS: 212 cal., 7 g total fat (1 g sat. fat), 184 mg chol., 1,430 mg sodium, 13 g carb., 2 g fiber, 22 g pro.
EXCHANGES: ½ Vegetable, ½ Other Carb., 3 Lean Meat, 1 Fat

LOW-CALORIE

New England Clam Chowder

START TO FINISH: 45 MINUTES
MAKES: 4 MAIN-DISH SERVINGS

- **1 pint shucked clams or two 6.5-ounce cans minced clams**
- **2 slices bacon, halved**
- **2½ cups chopped, peeled potatoes (3 medium)**
- **1 cup chopped onion (1 large)**
- **1 teaspoon instant chicken bouillon granules**
- **1 teaspoon Worcestershire sauce**
- **¼ teaspoon dried thyme, crushed**
- **⅛ teaspoon black pepper**
- **2 cups milk**
- **1 cup half-and-half or light cream**
- **2 tablespoons all-purpose flour**
- **Snipped fresh parsley (optional)**

1 Chop fresh clams (if using), reserving juice; set clams aside. Strain clam juice to remove bits of shell. (Or drain canned clams, reserving the juice.) If necessary, add enough water to the reserved clam juice to equal 1 cup; set aside.

2 In a large saucepan cook bacon until crisp. Remove bacon, reserving 1 tablespoon drippings in pan. Drain bacon on paper towels; crumble bacon and set aside.

3 Stir the reserved 1 cup clam liquid, potatoes, onion, bouillon granules, Worcestershire sauce, thyme, and pepper into saucepan. Bring to boiling; reduce heat. Simmer, covered, about 15 minutes or until potatoes are tender. Using the back of a fork, mash potatoes slightly against the sides of the pan.

4 Stir together milk, half-and-half, and flour; add to potato mixture. Cook and stir until slightly thickened and bubbly. Stir in clams. Return to boiling; reduce heat. Cook for 1 to 2 minutes more or until heated through. Ladle chowder into bowls. Sprinkle each serving with crumbled bacon and, if desired, parsley.

PER 1½ CUPS: 378 cal., 15 g total fat (8 g sat. fat), 78 mg chol., 476 mg sodium, 35 g carb., 2 g fiber, 25 g pro.
EXCHANGES: 2 Starch, 2½ Lean Meat, 2 Fat

LOW-CALORIE

Manhattan Clam Chowder

START TO FINISH: 35 MINUTES
MAKES: 4 MAIN-DISH SERVINGS

- **1 pint shucked clams or two 6.5-ounce cans minced clams**
- **1 cup chopped celery (2 stalks)**
- **1/3 cup chopped onion (1 small)**
- **1/4 cup chopped carrot (1 small)**
- **2 tablespoons olive oil or vegetable oil**
- **1 8-ounce bottle clam juice or 1 cup chicken broth**
- **2 cups cubed red potatoes (2 medium)**
- **1 teaspoon dried thyme, crushed**
- **1/8 teaspoon cayenne pepper**
- **1/8 teaspoon black pepper**
- **1 14.5-ounce can diced tomatoes, undrained**
- **2 tablespoons cooked crumbled bacon**

1 Chop fresh clams (if using), reserving juice; set clams aside. Strain clam juice to remove bits of shell. (Or drain canned clams, reserving the juice.) If necessary, add enough water to the reserved clam juice to equal 1½ cups; set aside.

2 In a large saucepan cook celery, onion, and carrot in hot oil until tender. Stir in the reserved 1½ cups clam liquid and the bottle clam juice. Stir in potatoes, thyme, cayenne pepper, and black pepper. Bring to boiling; reduce heat. Simmer, covered, for 10 minutes. Stir in clams, tomatoes, and bacon. Return to boiling; reduce heat. Cook for 1 to 2 minutes more or until heated through.

PER 1½ CUPS: 252 cal., 9 g total fat (1 g sat. fat), 41 mg chol., 503 mg sodium, 24 g carb., 3 g fiber, 18 g pro.
EXCHANGES: 1 Vegetable, 1½ Starch, 1½ Lean Meat, 1 Fat

FAST LOW-CALORIE

Oyster Stew

START TO FINISH: 25 MINUTES
MAKES: 6 MAIN-DISH SERVINGS

- **1 pint (about 3 dozen) shucked oysters, undrained (about 1 pound)**
- **1 cup finely chopped onion (1 large)**
- **1/2 cup finely chopped celery (1 stalk)**
- **1/2 teaspoon salt**
- **1/4 cup butter or margarine**
- **2 tablespoons all-purpose flour**
- **1/4 teaspoon black pepper**
- **1/8 teaspoon cayenne pepper**
- **2 cups whole milk**
- **2 cups half-and-half or light cream**
- **Cream sherry (optional)**
- **Freshly ground nutmeg (optional)**
- **Snipped fresh Italian parsley (optional)**

1 Drain oysters, reserving liquor. Remove any shell pieces. Set oysters and liquor aside.

2 In a large saucepan cook onion, celery, and salt in hot butter over medium heat about 10 minutes or until tender. Stir in flour, black pepper, and cayenne pepper. Cook and stir for 2 minutes more. Slowly whisk in milk and half-and-half. Bring to a simmer.

3 Stir in the drained oysters. Cook for 3 to 5 minutes or until oysters curl around the edges. Stir in oyster liquor; heat through. If desired, add a splash of sherry, ground nutmeg, and/or parsley.

PER 1¾ CUPS: 294 cal., 21 g total fat (13 g sat. fat), 98 mg chol., 481 mg sodium, 15 g carb., 1 g fiber, 11 g pro.
EXCHANGES: 1 Starch, 1 Lean Meat, 4 Fat

BEST-LOVED FAST LOW-CALORIE

Minestrone *(photo, page 559)*

START TO FINISH: 25 MINUTES
MAKES: 6 MAIN-DISH SERVINGS

- **1/2 cup chopped onion (1 medium)**
- **2 cloves garlic, minced**
- **1 tablespoon olive oil**
- **1 cup chopped yellow sweet pepper (1 large)**
- **1¼ cups coarsely chopped zucchini (1 medium)**
- **2 14.5-ounce cans beef broth (3½ cups)**
- **2 cups water**
- **1 15- to 15.5-ounce can cannellini (white kidney) beans, rinsed and drained**
- **8 ounces green beans, trimmed and cut into 1½-inch pieces**
- **1 cup dried mostaccioli**
- **1/4 cup coarsely chopped fresh basil or 2 teaspoons dried basil, crushed**
- **2 medium tomatoes, coarsely chopped, or 1½ cups cherry tomatoes, halved**
- **2 cups packaged fresh baby spinach leaves**
- **Salt and black pepper**
- **Shaved Parmesan cheese (optional)**

1 In a large pot cook onion and garlic in hot oil until tender, stirring occasionally. Add sweet pepper, zucchini, broth, and water. Bring to boiling. Add cannellini beans, green beans, pasta, and, if using, dried basil. Return to boiling; reduce heat. Simmer, covered, for 10 to 12 minutes or until pasta is tender, stirring occasionally.

2 Stir in tomatoes, spinach, and, if using, fresh basil. Remove from heat. Season to taste with salt and black pepper. If desired, top each serving with Parmesan cheese.

PER 1¾ CUPS: 182 cal., 3 g total fat (0 g sat. fat), 0 mg chol., 717 mg sodium, 33 g carb., 7 g fiber, 10 g pro.
EXCHANGES: 1½ Vegetable, 1½ Starch, 1½ Lean Meat, ½ Fat

LOW-CALORIE

Bean Soup with Herbed Polenta Dumplings

PREP: 30 MINUTES **STAND:** 60 MINUTES
COOK: 2 HOURS 40 MINUTES
MAKES: 10 MAIN-DISH SERVINGS

- **8 ounces dried cranberry, red, or pinto beans**
- **12 cups water**
- **1 bay leaf**
- **1 tablespoon olive oil**
- **2 fennel bulbs, trimmed, cored, and thinly sliced**
- **1 cup chopped onion (1 large)**
- **1 cup chopped carrots (2 medium)**
- **1 cup chopped celery (2 stalks)**
- **3 cloves garlic, minced**
- **6 cups chicken broth or vegetable broth**
- **1 14.5-ounce can diced tomatoes, undrained**
- **2 cups shredded cabbage**
- **1 cup frozen cut green beans**
- **2 tablespoons finely shredded fresh basil**
- **1 recipe Herbed Polenta Dumplings**
- **Shredded Parmesan cheese (optional)**

1 Rinse dried beans. In a large pot combine beans and 6 cups of the water. Bring to boiling; reduce heat. Simmer, uncovered, for 2 minutes. Remove from heat. Cover and let stand for 60 minutes. (Or place beans and 6 cups of the water in the pot. Cover; let stand in a cool place for 6 to 8 hours or overnight.) Drain; rinse beans.

2 Return beans to pot; add the remaining 6 cups water and the bay leaf. Bring to boiling; reduce heat. Simmer, covered, about 90 minutes or until beans are tender. Drain; rinse beans and set aside. Discard bay leaf.

BEAN SOUP WITH HERBED POLENTA DUMPLINGS STEP-BY-STEP

1. Add ingredients and bring to boiling. Adjust the heat to keep soup at a simmer to blend flavors and tenderize the vegetables.

2. Be sure the soup is bubbling before topping with dumplings. Gently place the dumplings on the soup so they don't deflate.

3 In the same pot heat oil over medium heat. Add fennel, onion, carrots, celery, and garlic; cook until vegetables are tender, stirring occasionally. Stir in broth and tomatoes. Bring to boiling (see photo 1, left); reduce heat. Simmer, covered, for 30 minutes. Stir in cranberry beans, cabbage, and green beans. Return to boiling; reduce heat. Simmer, covered, for 30 minutes more. Stir in basil.

4 Prepare Herbed Polenta Dumplings. Drop dough mounds onto hot bubbling soup (see photo 2, left). Simmer, covered, for 10 minutes. (Do not lift lid during cooking.) If desired, sprinkle each serving with cheese.

HERBED POLENTA DUMPLINGS: In a large saucepan combine 2 cups chicken broth; ½ teaspoon dried Italian seasoning, crushed; and ¼ teaspoon salt. Bring to boiling. In a medium bowl stir together 1 cup quick-cooking polenta mix or cornmeal and 1 cup chicken broth. Gradually add polenta mixture to broth mixture, stirring constantly. Cook and stir until mixture returns to boiling. Reduce heat to low. Cook about 5 minutes or until thick, stirring frequently (mixture might spatter). Remove from heat. Stir in ⅓ cup grated Parmesan cheese and ¼ cup whipping cream. Using two spoons, drop mixture into 25 to 30 mounds onto a greased baking sheet. (If mixture is too soft to form mounds, cool about 15 minutes.) Cover; chill until ready to add to soup.

PER 1½ CUPS: 280 cal., 5 g total fat (2 g sat. fat), 13 mg chol., 1,102 mg sodium, 47 g carb., 10 g fiber, 11 g pro.
EXCHANGES: 1 Vegetable, 3 Starch, ½ Fat

BEST-LOVED

Baked Potato Soup

PREP: 20 MINUTES **BAKE:** 40 MINUTES AT 425°F
COOK: 20 MINUTES **MAKES:** 5 SIDE-DISH SERVINGS

- **2 large baking potatoes (8 ounces each)**
- **6 tablespoons thinly sliced green onions (3)**
- **3 tablespoons butter or margarine**
- **3 tablespoons all-purpose flour**
- **2 teaspoons snipped fresh dill weed or chives or ¼ teaspoon dried dill weed**
- **4 cups milk**
- **1¼ cups shredded American cheese (5 ounces)**
- **4 slices bacon, crisp-cooked, drained, and crumbled**

1 Preheat oven to 425°F. Scrub potatoes with a vegetable brush; pat dry. Prick potatoes with a fork. Bake for 40 to 60 minutes or until tender; cool. Cut each potato lengthwise. Scoop out white portion of each potato. Break up any large pieces of potato. Discard potato skins.

2 In a large saucepan cook 3 tablespoons of the green onions in butter over medium heat until tender. Stir in flour, dill weed, and 1/4 teaspoon each *salt* and *black pepper.* Add milk all at once. Cook and stir until thickened and bubbly. Add potatoes and 1 cup of the cheese; stir until cheese melts. Top each serving with remaining cheese, remaining green onions, and the bacon.

PER 1 CUP: 372 cal., 22 g total fat (13 g sat. fat), 68 mg chol., 821 mg sodium, 26 g carb., 1 g fiber, 17 g pro.
EXCHANGES: 2 Starch, 1½ High-Fat Meat, 1½ Fat

BEST-LOVED

Corn Chowder

START TO FINISH: 45 MINUTES
MAKES: 6 SIDE-DISH SERVINGS

- **6 ears fresh sweet corn or 3 cups frozen whole kernel corn**
- **½ cup chopped onion (1 medium)**
- **½ cup chopped green sweet pepper**
- **1 tablespoon vegetable oil**
- **1 14.5-ounce can chicken broth (1¾ cups)**
- **1 cup cubed, peeled potato (1 medium)**
- **2 tablespoons all-purpose flour**
- **½ teaspoon salt**
- **¼ teaspoon black pepper**
- **1½ cups half-and-half, light cream, or milk**
- **1 cup shredded white cheddar cheese (4 ounces)**
- **3 slices bacon, crisp-cooked, drained, and crumbled, or 2 tablespoons purchased cooked bacon pieces**
- **2 tablespoons snipped fresh parsley (optional)**

1 If using fresh corn, use a sharp knife to cut the kernels off the cobs (you should have about 3 cups corn kernels). Set corn kernels aside.

2 In a large saucepan cook onion and sweet pepper in hot oil until onion is tender but not browned. Stir in corn, broth, and potato. Bring to boiling; reduce heat. Simmer, covered, for 10 to 15 minutes or until vegetables are tender, stirring occasionally.

3 In a small bowl combine flour, salt, and pepper. Stir half-and-half into flour mixture; add to corn mixture in saucepan. Cook and stir until slightly thickened and bubbly. Cook and stir for 1 minute more. Stir in cheese; heat until melted and smooth. Top each serving with bacon, and, if desired, parsley and additional shredded white cheddar cheese.

PER 1 CUP: 314 cal., 18 g total fat (9 g sat. fat), 47 mg chol., 709 mg sodium, 29 g carb., 3 g fiber, 12 g pro.
EXCHANGES: 2 Starch, 1 High-Fat Meat, 1½ Fat

CORN CHOWDER

FAST

French Onion Soup *(photo, page 559)*

START TO FINISH: 30 MINUTES
MAKES: 4 SIDE-DISH SERVINGS

- **2 tablespoons butter or margarine**
- **2 cups thinly sliced yellow onions (2 large)**
- **4 cups beef broth**
- **2 tablespoons dry sherry or dry white wine (optional)**
- **1 teaspoon Worcestershire sauce**
- **Dash black pepper**
- **4 slices French bread, toasted**
- **¾ cup shredded Swiss, Gruyère, or Jarlsberg cheese (3 ounces)**

1 In a large saucepan melt butter; add onions. Cook, covered, over medium-low heat for 8 to 10 minutes or until tender and golden, stirring occasionally. Stir in broth, dry sherry (if desired), Worcestershire sauce, and pepper. Bring to boiling; reduce heat. Simmer, covered, for 10 minutes.

2 Meanwhile, preheat broiler. Arrange toasted bread on a baking sheet; sprinkle with cheese. Broil 3 to 4 inches from the heat about 1 minute or until cheese melts and is lightly browned. Ladle soup into bowls and top each serving with a toasted bread slice.

PER 1 CUP: 274 cal., 13 g total fat (7 g sat. fat), 34 mg chol., 1,201 mg sodium, 26 g carb., 2 g fiber, 13 g pro.
EXCHANGES: ½ Vegetable, 1½ Starch, 1 High-Fat Meat, 1 Fat

BEST-LOVED FAST LOW-CALORIE

Cream of Vegetable Soup *(photo, page 559)*

START TO FINISH: 25 MINUTES
MAKES: 4 SIDE-DISH SERVINGS

- **Desired vegetables (see variations)**
- **1½ cups chicken broth or vegetable broth**
- **1 tablespoon butter or margarine**
- **1 tablespoon all-purpose flour**
- **Seasoning (see variations)**
- **¼ teaspoon salt**
- **Dash black pepper**
- **1 cup milk, half-and-half, or light cream**
- **4 Bread Bowls (page 569) (optional)**

1 In a saucepan cook desired vegetables, covered, in a large amount of boiling water as directed. Drain well. Set aside 1 cup vegetables.

2 In a food processor or blender combine the remaining cooked vegetables and ¾ cup of the broth. Cover; process or blend until smooth.

3 In same saucepan melt butter. Stir in flour, seasoning, salt, and pepper. Add 1 cup milk all at once. Cook and stir until slightly thickened and bubbly. Cook and stir for 1 minute more.

4 Stir in the reserved 1 cup vegetables, blended vegetable mixture, and remaining ¾ cup broth. Cook and stir until heated through. If necessary, stir in additional milk to reach desired consistency. Season to taste with additional salt and pepper. If desired, serve soup in Bread Bowls.

CREAM OF POTATO SOUP: Cook 5 medium potatoes, peeled and cubed, and ½ cup chopped onion about 15 minutes or until tender. Set aside 1 cup potato mixture. Blend remaining mixture as directed in Step 2, except use all of the broth. For seasoning, use ¼ teaspoon dried dill weed or basil, crushed, in Step 3.

PER 1 CUP: 185 cal., 4 g total fat (3 g sat. fat), 13 mg chol., 560 mg sodium, 31 g carb., 3 g fiber, 6 g pro. EXCHANGES: 2 Starch, ½ Fat

CREAM OF BROCCOLI-CHEESE OR CAULIFLOWER-CHEESE SOUP: Cook 4 cups fresh or frozen chopped broccoli or cauliflower for 8 to 10 minutes or until tender (follow package directions if using frozen vegetable). Set aside 1 cup of vegetables. Blend remaining vegetables as directed in Step 2. For seasoning, use ½ teaspoon finely shredded lemon peel in Step 3. Stir ½ cup shredded American cheese into soup mixture after broth in Step 4. If desired, top with additional shredded American cheese.

PER 1 CUP: 153 cal., 9 g total fat (5 g sat. fat), 27 mg chol., 792 mg sodium, 11 g carb., 2 g fiber, 8 g pro.
EXCHANGES: 1 Vegetable, ½ Starch, ½ High-Fat Meat, 1 Fat

FAST LOW-CALORIE

Roasted Red Pepper Soup

PREP: 15 MINUTES **COOK:** 15 MINUTES
MAKES: 4 SIDE-DISH SERVINGS

- **1 cup chopped onion (1 large)**
- **4 cloves garlic, minced**
- **1 tablespoon olive oil**
- **3 14.5-ounce cans vegetable or chicken broth (5¼ cups)**
- **1 12-ounce jar roasted red sweet peppers, drained and sliced**
- **1 cup chopped, peeled potato (1 medium)**
- **1 tablespoon snipped fresh oregano or 1 teaspoon dried oregano, crushed**
- **1 teaspoon snipped fresh thyme or ½ teaspoon dried thyme, crushed**
- **¼ cup sour cream**
- **1 tablespoon minced fresh chives**

1 In a large saucepan cook and stir onion and garlic in hot oil for 3 to 4 minutes or until tender. Stir in broth, roasted sweet peppers, potato, oregano, and thyme. Bring to boiling; reduce heat. Simmer, covered, for 15 minutes. Cool mixture slightly.

2 Using a handheld immersion blender, blend soup until almost smooth (see photo, below); heat through. (Or let soup cool slightly. Transfer soup, one-third at a time, to a food processor or blender. Cover and process or blend until smooth. Return all the soup to the saucepan; heat through.)

3 In a small bowl combine sour cream and chives. To serve, ladle soup into bowls. Top each serving with a tablespoon of the sour cream mixture.

PER 1½ CUPS: 137 cal., 6 g total fat (2 g sat. fat), 5 mg chol., 1,181 mg sodium, 18 g carb., 3 g fiber, 2 g pro.
EXCHANGES: ½ Vegetable, 1 Starch, 1 Fat

ROASTED RED PEPPER SOUP

If you have an immersion blender, blend the soup right in the pan, which makes the task easy and safe. To use a traditional blender, see tips on page 561.

607
606
593
vegetables & fruits
618
595
590
598

vegetables &fruits

Count on vegetables and fruits to add color, sparkle, and other good things (like nutrients) to your meals.

VEGGIES ON THE QUICK

These methods are among the quickest ways to get veggies from the fridge to the table.

STIR-FRY: Cut vegetables into bite-size pieces. If you're cooking more than one type of vegetable, cut them into similar-size pieces so they cook at about the same rate. Heat oil in a wok or large skillet over medium-high heat. When hot, add the vegetables in small batches and cook, stirring constantly, until they are just crisp-tender. Note that stir-frying too many vegetables at once causes them to steam and become mushy. If necessary, you can return all cooked vegetables to the wok or skillet and cook them just long enough to reheat.

SAUTÉ: This method is much like stir-frying; the difference is that you generally use lower heat settings than for stir-frying, so you can stir occasionally rather than constantly. Sautéing works especially well for cooking vegetables in butter, which can burn quickly over medium-high heat.

STEAM, BOIL, MICROWAVE: For know-how on these methods, see the charts, pages 629–631.

ROAST TO BOOST FLAVOR

Roasting vegetables in the oven brings out their natural sweetness while giving them irresistible texture—crispy on the outside, tender on the inside. For this cooking technique, the vegetables are generally tossed with oil, seasoned with salt and pepper, and baked in a hot oven in a shallow pan. For a taste of this marvelous method, try the Roasted Beets with Golden Raisins and Pine Nuts, page 591, and the Roasted Tomato and Bread Toss, page 614. Once you get the hang of roasting, use it for other vegetables. Dense vegetables, such as potatoes, winter squash, and carrots, are particularly good candidates; tender vegetables, such as asparagus and mushrooms, also transform in the heat of the oven.

GETTING THE MOST FROM YOUR VEGGIES

To get the most nutrition from fresh vegetables, cook and enjoy them soon after purchasing. Frozen vegetables are also good sources of nutrition—they're flash-frozen soon after picking, which retains vitamins and minerals at levels equal to or sometimes greater than when fresh. Canned vegetables can be a good choice too; however, to keep sodium levels in check, look for canned products labeled "low sodium" or "no salt added."

RIPENING FRUITS

Some fruits are picked and shipped while still firm, so they might need additional ripening. To ripen fruit:

- Place it in a small, clean paper bag. (A plastic bag is not a good choice. It doesn't allow fruit to breathe, and the trapped moisture can cause the fruit to grow mold.)
- Loosely close the bag and store it at room temperature. To speed up the ripening, place an apple or ripe banana in the bag with the underripe fruit.
- Check the fruit daily and remove any that yield to gentle pressure. To check the fruit, cradle it in the palm of your hand and gently squeeze rather than prodding the fruit with your thumb or finger, which can bruise it.
- Enjoy the ripe fruit immediately or refrigerate it for a couple of days. Refrigeration will slow down further ripening.

cook's secrets

mashed potatoes

The Secret: Fluffiness is the goal with mashed potatoes, so here's how to get it: After draining, dry the potatoes in the pan for 2 minutes before mashing them to remove excess moisture. Don't overmash or you might get sticky rather than fluffy potatoes.

PREP: 30 MINUTES **COOK:** 20 MINUTES **MAKES:** 10 SERVINGS

- **3 pounds russet, Yukon gold, or red potatoes (9 medium), peeled (optional) and cut into 2-inch pieces**
- **¼ cup butter**
- **½ to ¾ cup milk, whipping cream, half-and-half, or light cream**
- **1 teaspoon salt**
- **½ teaspoon black pepper**
- **Butter, melted (optional)**
- **Snipped fresh chives (optional)**

1 In a 4- to 5-quart Dutch oven cook potatoes, covered, in enough boiling lightly salted water to cover for 20 to 25 minutes or until tender; drain. Return the hot, drained potatoes to the hot Dutch oven. Add the ¼ cup butter.* Let stand, uncovered, for 2 to 3 minutes. Meanwhile, in a small saucepan, heat the milk over low heat until very warm.

Start the potatoes in cold water. They will cook more evenly. (If you dump them into boiling water, the outsides will cook faster than the insides.)

2 Mash potatoes with a potato masher or ricer, or beat with an electric mixer on low speed just until light and fluffy.** Stir in the warm milk, salt, and pepper. Gradually stir in additional milk to make potatoes desired consistency. If desired, serve with additional butter and chives.

***NOTE:** If using a ricer (see photo, page 587), stir in melted butter after pressing potatoes through ricer.

****NOTE:** If you choose to leave the peel on the potatoes, use a potato masher rather than a mixer to mash the potatoes.

MAKE-AHEAD DIRECTIONS: Prepare Mashed Potatoes as directed. Transfer to a bowl; cool slightly. Cover tightly; chill for up to 48 hours. Place potato mixture in a greased 4- to 5-quart slow cooker. Cover and cook on low-heat setting for 3½ to 4 hours or until heated through. Stir before serving. Or place cooled potato mixture in a greased 2-quart rectangular baking dish. Cover tightly and chill for up to 48 hours. To serve, preheat oven to 350°F. Bake, covered with foil, for 45 minutes. Uncover; bake for 10 to 15 minutes more or until heated through.

PER SERVING: 118 cal., 5 g total fat (3 g sat. fat), 13 mg chol., 295 mg sodium, 17 g carb., 3 g fiber, 2 g pro.
EXCHANGES: 1 Starch, 1 Fat

MASHED POTATO POINTERS

1. DOUBLE COVER
Make sure there is enough cold water covering the potatoes so they have room for good boiling. An inch or 2 inches above the potatoes is good. When the water boils, cover the pan and reduce the heat so the water continues to simmer without bubbling over.

2. DRY 'EM OUT
After draining the potatoes, it's important to return them to the hot pan and let stand a couple minutes so the residual heat dries them out. Reducing this extra moisture creates lighter, fluffier potatoes.

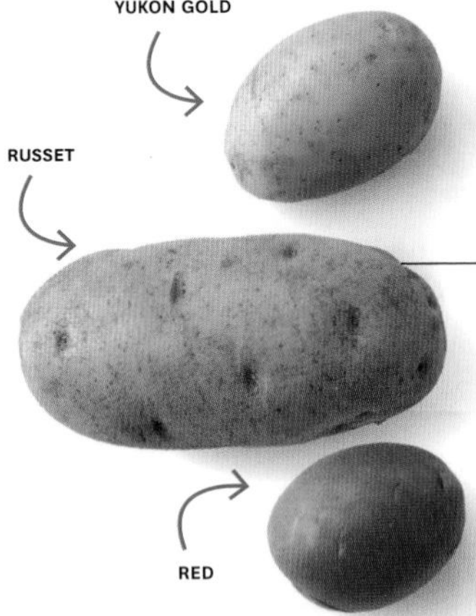

PICK A POTATO

YUKON GOLD: These waxy-texture potatoes with golden-yellow skin and flesh are great mashers. They have a rich, almost sweet flavor, and they mash to a creamy consistency. The skins are thin, so peeling is optional.
RUSSET: These potatoes contain more starch than the other two, so they create fluffier potatoes. The skin is thick—peeling is recommended.
RED: These fine-texture, white-flesh potatoes possess a mild flavor and creamy waxiness; peeling is optional.

↑

3. NOW FOR THE MILK Although it would be easy to pick up the jug and pour cold milk into the potatoes, it's worth the effort to heat it up. Hot milk keeps the potatoes hot until they get to the table. Some people like their potatoes fluffy and soft; others prefer them heavy and almost stiff. The amount of milk you add and how much you beat the potatoes determine the end product. Start by adding the least amount of milk in the range. Add additional milk gradually just until the potatoes reach your desired creaminess.

CHOOSE A MASHING METHOD

RICE 'EM: A ricer is a specialty tool made just for mashing potatoes. It produces very smooth, light, extra-fluffy potatoes. Press cooked, peeled potatoes through the ricer into a bowl. To maintain their lightness, be gentle when stirring additional ingredients into riced potatoes.

MASH 'EM: A hand masher is the simplest tool for mashing potatoes, and you can mash them directly in the pan. It produces a coarse-textured mashed potato with a homemade appearance. Mashers with the grid plate (versus the traditional wavy wire) produce an even texture.

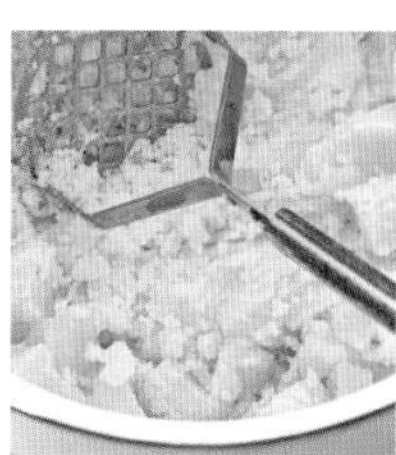

MIX 'EM: A hand mixer requires less muscle than a masher. It produces fluffier potatoes and minimizes lumps, but you have to be careful. Beat just until fluffy or creamy. Overbeating will break the cell walls of the starch and give your potatoes a sticky, gluelike texture.

Artichokes with Herb-Butter Sauce

START TO FINISH: 35 MINUTES **MAKES:** 2 SERVINGS

- **2 artichokes (about 10 ounces each)**
- **Lemon juice**
- **¼ cup butter**
- **1 tablespoon lemon juice**
- **1 teaspoon snipped fresh dill weed, tarragon, or oregano, or ¼ teaspoon dried dill weed, tarragon, or oregano, crushed**

1 Wash artichokes; trim stems and remove loose outer leaves (see photo 1, below). Cut 1 inch off the top of each artichoke (see photo 2, below) and snip off the sharp leaf tips. Brush the cut edges with a little lemon juice. In a large saucepan or Dutch oven bring a large amount of lightly salted water to boiling; add artichokes. Return to boiling; reduce heat. Simmer, covered, for 20 to 30 minutes or until a leaf pulls out easily. Drain artichokes upside down on paper towels.

2 Meanwhile, for sauce, melt butter. Stir in the 1 tablespoon lemon juice and the dill weed. Turn artichokes right sides up; serve with sauce.*

***NOTE:** To eat an artichoke, pull off one leaf and dip the leaf base into the sauce. Draw the leaf base through your teeth, scraping off only tender flesh. Discard remainder of leaf. Continue removing leaves until the fuzzy choke appears. Scoop out the choke with a grapefruit spoon and discard. Eat the remaining heart with a fork, dipping each piece into the sauce.

PER ARTICHOKE WITH 2 TABLESPOONS SAUCE: 268 cal., 23 g total fat (15 g sat. fat), 61 mg chol., 278 mg sodium, 15 g carb., 7 g fiber, 4 g pro. EXCHANGES: 2 Vegetable, 5 Fat

PREPARING ARTICHOKES STEP-BY-STEP

1. Use a large sharp knife to cut off the thick stem close to the base of the artichoke. Pull off any loose, dry outer leaves.

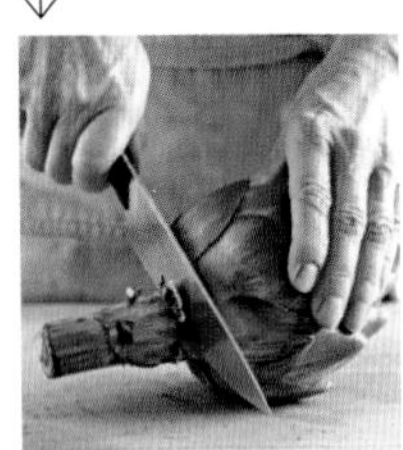

2. Place the artichoke on its side on a cutting board. Cut off the top inch or so of the artichoke. Use kitchen shears to snip the sharp tips off the leaves. This looks nicer and helps the leaves cook evenly.

ARTICHOKES WITH LEMON-MUSTARD MAYO: Prepare as directed, except chill artichokes after Step 1 and omit sauce. For Lemon-Mustard Mayo, combine ½ cup mayonnaise, ½ teaspoon finely shredded lemon peel, 2 teaspoons fresh lemon juice, and 1 teaspoon Dijon-style mustard. Season with black pepper. Makes 4 appetizer servings.

PER HALF ARTICHOKE WITH 2 TABLESPOONS MAYO: 466 cal., 44 g total fat (8 g sat. fat), 20 mg chol., 613 mg sodium, 15 g carb., 7 g fiber, 4 g pro. EXCHANGES: 2 Vegetable, 9 Fat

FAST LOW-CALORIE

Roasted Asparagus

PREP: 15 MINUTES **ROAST:** 15 MINUTES AT 400°F
MAKES: 6 SERVINGS

- **2 pounds asparagus spears**
- **1 tablespoon olive oil**
- **⅛ to ¼ teaspoon salt**
- **⅛ to ¼ teaspoon black pepper**
- **¼ cup shredded Parmesan or Asiago cheese (1 ounce)**

1 Preheat oven to 400°F. Snap off and discard woody bases from asparagus (see photo, page 589). If desired, scrape off scales. Place asparagus in a 15×10×1-inch baking pan. Drizzle with olive oil to coat. Spread in a single layer. Sprinkle with salt and pepper.

2 Roast, uncovered, for 15 to 20 minutes or until asparagus is crisp-tender, turning once. Transfer asparagus to a serving platter and sprinkle with cheese.

PER SERVING: 57 cal., 3 g total fat (1 g sat. fat), 2 mg chol., 107 mg sodium, 5 g carb., 2 g fiber, 4 g pro.
EXCHANGES: 1 Vegetable, ½ Fat

THICK AND THIN ASPARAGUS

Try to use aparagus spears that are uniform in diameter to ensure all are done at the same time. Bundles purchased at supermarkets are usually consistent, but offerings at farmer's markets might be varied. If some stalks are thicker than others, cut them in half lengthwise. If they are super thin, slightly reduce cooking time.

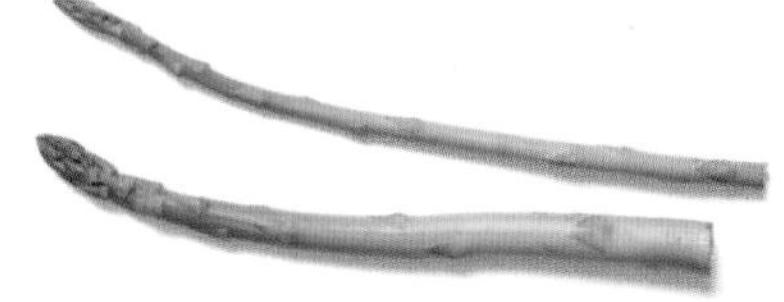

FAST LOW-CALORIE

Asparagus with Tarragon Sauce

START TO FINISH: 30 MINUTES **MAKES:** 6 SERVINGS

1¼ pounds asparagus spears
2 tablespoons butter
2 tablespoons finely chopped shallot (1 medium)
2 tablespoons snipped fresh tarragon
½ teaspoon kosher salt
¼ teaspoon cracked black pepper
¼ cup mayonnaise
2 tablespoons Dijon-style mustard
2 tablespoons cider vinegar
1 teaspoon lemon juice
2 ounces prosciutto, torn or cut into 2×1-inch pieces
2 Hard-Cooked Eggs (page 130), finely chopped
Snipped fresh tarragon
Kosher salt and cracked black pepper

1 Snap off and discard woody bases from asparagus (see photo, below). If desired, scrape off scales.

2 For tarragon sauce, in a small saucepan melt 1 tablespoon of the butter over medium heat. Add shallot; cook and stir about 2 minutes or until softened. Stir in the 2 tablespoons tarragon, ½ teaspoon salt, and ¼ teaspoon pepper. Stir in mayonnaise, mustard, vinegar, and lemon juice. Heat through, stirring frequently. Cover and keep warm.

3 In a medium skillet heat the remaining 1 tablespoon butter over medium-high heat; add prosciutto. Cook about 2 to 4 minutes or until just crisp, turning once halfway through cooking time. Transfer to paper towels to drain.

4 Bring a large saucepan of salted water to boiling. Add asparagus. Cook about 3 minutes or until crisp-tender; drain. Transfer asparagus to a serving platter. Drizzle with tarragon sauce. Sprinkle with prosciutto and eggs. Sprinkle with additional tarragon, salt, and pepper.

PER SERVING: 158 cal., 14 g total fat (4 g sat. fat), 86 mg chol., 697 mg sodium, 3 g carb., 1 g fiber, 6 g pro.
EXCHANGES: ½ Vegetable, ½ Medium-Fat Meat, 2 Fat

TRIMMING ASPARAGUS

Start at the base of each asparagus spear. Work toward the tip, bending the spear until you find a place where it is flexible. Snap off the woody base at that point.

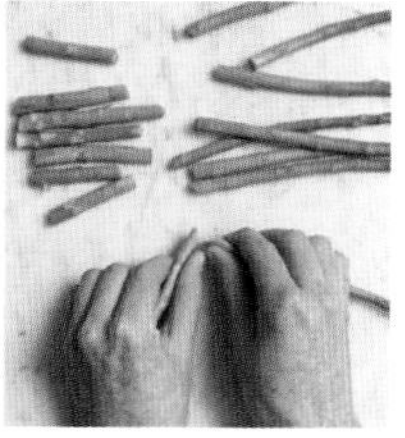

ASPARAGUS WITH TARRAGON SAUCE

FAST LOW-CALORIE

Sweet-and-Sour Cabbage

START TO FINISH: 15 MINUTES **MAKES:** 4 SERVINGS

3 tablespoons packed brown sugar
3 tablespoons vinegar
3 tablespoons water
4 teaspoons vegetable oil
¼ teaspoon caraway seeds
¼ teaspoon salt
Dash black pepper
3 cups shredded red or green cabbage
¾ cup chopped apple

1 In a large skillet combine brown sugar, vinegar, water, oil, caraway seeds, salt, and pepper. Cook for 2 to 3 minutes or until hot and brown sugar is dissolved, stirring occasionally.

2 Stir in the cabbage and apple. Cook, covered, over medium-low heat about 5 minutes or until cabbage is crisp-tender, stirring occasionally. Use a slotted spoon to serve cabbage.

PER ½ CUP: 109 cal., 5 g total fat (1 g sat. fat), 0 mg chol., 163 mg sodium, 17 g carb., 2 g fiber, 1 g pro.
EXCHANGES: 1 Vegetable, ½ Other Carb., 1 Fat

SESAME GREEN BEANS WITH TERIYAKI GLAZE

FAST LOW-CALORIE

Sesame Green Beans with Teriyaki Glaze

START TO FINISH: 30 MINUTES **MAKES:** 8 SERVINGS

- **1½ pounds green beans, trimmed**
- **1 cup julienned carrots (2 medium) or packaged fresh julienned carrots**
- **¾ cup chicken broth**
- **¼ cup soy sauce**
- **¼ cup hoisin sauce**
- **1 tablespoon cornstarch**
- **1 tablespoon toasted sesame oil**
- **3 tablespoons canola oil**
- **2 cups sliced stemmed fresh shiitake mushrooms**
- **1 tablespoon grated fresh ginger**
- **4 cloves garlic, minced**
- **2 tablespoons snipped fresh basil**
- **1 tablespoon toasted sesame seeds**
- **Fresh basil leaves**

1 Bring a large pot of salted water to boiling. Add green beans; return to boiling. Boil for 4 minutes. Add carrots and boil for 1 minute more; drain well.

2 In a small bowl stir together chicken broth, soy sauce, hoisin sauce, cornstarch, and sesame oil; set aside.

3 In a large wok or a very large nonstick skillet heat canola oil over high heat. Add mushrooms, ginger, and garlic; cook and stir about 3 minutes or until mushrooms are tender. Stir broth mixture and add to skillet; cook and stir about 1 minute or until just thickened and bubbly. Stir in green beans and carrots and the 2 tablespoons basil; heat through.

4 To serve, sprinkle with toasted sesame seeds and garnish with additional fresh basil leaves.

PER ABOUT 1 CUP: 131 cal., 8 g total fat (1 g sat. fat), 1 mg chol., 741 mg sodium, 14 g carb., 3 g fiber, 3 g pro.
EXCHANGES: 1½ Vegetable, ½ Starch, 1½ Fat

FAST LOW-CALORIE

Sea Salt-and-Vinegar Green Beans

(photo, page 583)

START TO FINISH: 25 MINUTES **MAKES:** 8 SERVINGS

- **1½ pounds green beans, trimmed**
- **1 cup chopped red sweet pepper (1 large)**
- **1 cup thinly sliced red onion**
- **⅓ cup white wine vinegar or champagne vinegar**
- **2 teaspoons sugar**
- **2 teaspoons seafood seasoning**
- **1½ teaspoons sea salt**
- **¼ teaspoon cayenne pepper**
- **¼ teaspoon cracked black pepper**
- **¼ cup olive oil**

1 In a large pot cook beans, covered, in a small amount of boiling salted water for 8 to 10 minutes or just until crisp-tender, adding sweet pepper and onion to the water for the last 3 minutes of cooking; drain. Rinse with cold water; drain again.

2 Meanwhile, in a medium bowl whisk together vinegar, sugar, seafood seasoning, 1 teaspoon of the salt, the cayenne pepper, and black pepper. Whisk in oil.

3 Transfer green bean mixture to a platter. Drizzle with vinegar mixture; toss gently to coat. Sprinkle with the remaining ½ teaspoon salt. Serve warm.

MAKE-AHEAD DIRECTIONS: Prepare as directed. Cover and chill for up to 24 hours. Serve chilled or at room temperature.

PER ABOUT 1 CUP: 105 cal., 7 g total fat (1 g sat. fat), 0 mg chol., 524 mg sodium, 9 g carb., 3 g fiber, 2 g pro.
EXCHANGES: 1½ Vegetable, 1½ Fat

Roasted Beets with Golden Raisins and Pine Nuts

PREP: 25 MINUTES **ROAST:** 55 MINUTES AT 450°F
MAKES: 4 SERVINGS

- **2 pounds fresh beets with tops**
- **2 sprigs fresh rosemary**
- **3 tablespoons olive oil**
- **Salt and black pepper**
- **½ cup golden raisins**
- **2 tablespoons pine nuts, toasted**
- **4 ounces Manchego cheese or ricotta salata, sliced**
- **Balsamic vinegar (optional)**

1 Preheat oven to 450°F. Cut tops from beets; if desired, set tops aside. Place beets and rosemary on a piece of heavy foil. Drizzle with 1 tablespoon of the oil. Bring up two opposite edges of foil (see photo 1, below); seal with a double fold. Fold in remaining edges to completely enclose. Roast beets about 55 minutes or until tender when pierced with a knife. Carefully open packet to release steam. Set aside until cool enough to handle. Peel skins from beets and cut into wedges. Discard rosemary.

2 Meanwhile, if desired, thoroughly wash and dry beet greens. Cut greens off beet tops, discarding stems (see photo 2, below); thinly slice greens.

3 In a large bowl gently toss together warm beets, beet greens (if using), and the remaining 2 tablespoons oil until greens are slightly wilted. Season to taste with salt and pepper.

4 On a large platter or four salad plates arrange beet mixture. Sprinkle with raisins and nuts. Top with cheese. If desired, drizzle with balsamic vinegar.

PER 1½ CUPS: 365 cal., 21 g total fat (7 g sat. fat), 20 mg chol., 748 mg sodium, 33 g carb., 5 g fiber, 14 g pro.
EXCHANGES: 3 Vegetable, 1 Fruit, 1 High-Fat Meat, 2½ Fat

PREPARING BEETS STEP-BY-STEP

1. Roasting beets in foil steams them for faster cooking. Make sure the foil is crimped and sealed well. The skin is easier to remove after the beets are roasted.

2. Cut greens off stems of beet tops. Pull tender greens off any thick veins. Discard stems and veins.

Blue Cheese Broccoli au Gratin

PREP: 35 MINUTES **BAKE:** 30 MINUTES AT 375°F
STAND: 15 MINUTES **MAKES:** 10 SERVINGS

- **10 cups broccoli florets (about 2½ pounds)**
- **¼ cup butter**
- **¼ cup all-purpose flour**
- **2 cups whole milk**
- **1 cup crumbled mild blue cheese (4 ounces)**
- **1 cup shredded Gruyère cheese (4 ounces)**
- **1 teaspoon salt**
- **½ teaspoon black pepper**
- **4 slices bacon, crisp-cooked and crumbled**
- **1½ cups coarse herbed focaccia bread crumbs (about 3 ounces)**
- **2 tablespoons butter, melted**
- **2 tablespoons snipped fresh chives**

1 Preheat oven to 375°F. Bring a large pot of water to boiling. Add broccoli; return to boil. Cook for 1 minute; drain well. Transfer broccoli to an extra-large bowl.

2 Meanwhile, in a large saucepan melt the ¼ cup butter over medium heat. Add the flour; cook and stir for 2 minutes. Slowly whisk in the milk; cook and stir until mixture bubbles. Reduce heat; simmer about 2 minutes or until slightly thickened. Remove from heat; stir in ½ cup of the blue cheese, ½ cup of the Gruyère cheese, ½ teaspoon of the salt, and ¼ teaspoon of the pepper. Pour over the broccoli, tossing to coat.

3 Transfer broccoli mixture to a 3-quart gratin dish or casserole. Sprinkle with bacon and the remaining blue cheese and Gruyère cheese.

4 In a small bowl stir together bread crumbs, 2 tablespoons melted butter, the remaining ½ teaspoon salt and ¼ teaspoon pepper, and the chives. Sprinkle over broccoli mixture.

5 Bake, uncovered, about 30 minutes or until bubbly and topping is browned. Let stand for 15 minutes before serving.

PER ½ CUP: 275 cal., 19 g total fat (11 g sat. fat), 51 mg chol., 692 mg sodium, 16 g carb., 3 g fiber, 13 g pro.
EXCHANGES: 1 Vegetable, ½ Starch, 1½ High-Fat Meat, 1½ Fat

BROCCOLINI WITH PEAS AND SEARED LEMONS

FAST **LOW-CALORIE**

Broccolini with Peas and Seared Lemons

START TO FINISH: 30 MINUTES **MAKES:** 12 SERVINGS

- **2 pounds Broccolini, trimmed**
- **8 ounces Swiss chard, trimmed and cut into 2- to 3-inch lengths**
- **1 cup frozen peas**
- **2 tablespoons butter**
- **1 lemon, thinly sliced**
- **¼ cup chicken broth**
- **¼ teaspoon crushed red pepper**
- **¼ cup snipped fresh chives**
- **½ teaspoon coarse salt**

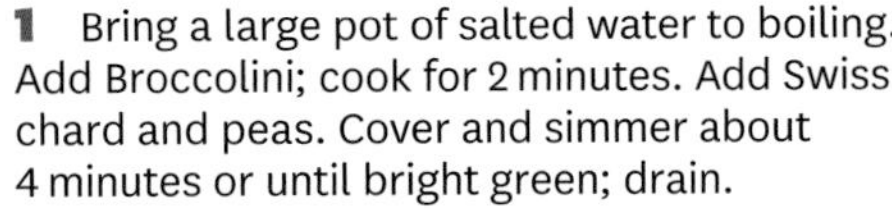

1 Bring a large pot of salted water to boiling. Add Broccolini; cook for 2 minutes. Add Swiss chard and peas. Cover and simmer about 4 minutes or until bright green; drain.

2 Meanwhile, melt butter in a large skillet. Add lemon slices; cook over medium to medium-high heat about 3 minutes per side or until lemons are soft and browned and butter is browned. (Do not move lemons around too much to ensure a nice sear.)

3 Return drained Broccolini, chard, and peas to the pot. Add broth and crushed red pepper; toss gently to coat. Transfer the Broccolini mixture to a serving platter. Top with the lemons, chives, and salt.

PER ½ CUP: 48 cal., 2 g total fat (1 g sat. fat), 5 mg chol., 185 mg sodium, 6 g carb., 2 g fiber, 2 g pro.
EXCHANGES: 1 Vegetable, ½ Fat

WHAT IS BROCCOLINI?

Although it looks like baby broccoli, it is not. This fully mature vegetable has long tender stalks and is topped with small florets. The sweet, bitter flavor is similar to broccoli. It cooks quickly because of the thin stem. Look for Broccolini that has firm stems and tight heads with no flowering.

LOW-CALORIE

Broccoli-Orzo Pilaf

PREP: 20 MINUTES **COOK:** 22 MINUTES
STAND: 5 MINUTES **MAKES:** 6 SERVINGS

- **2 teaspoons olive oil**
- **1 cup sliced fresh mushrooms**
- **½ cup chopped onion (1 medium)**
- **⅔ cup dried orzo**
- **1 14.5-ounce can reduced-sodium chicken broth**
- **1 teaspoon dried marjoram, crushed**
- **⅛ teaspoon black pepper**
- **2 cups small broccoli florets**
- **½ cup shredded carrot (1 medium)**

1 In a large saucepan heat olive oil over medium-high heat. Add mushrooms and onion; cook for 5 to 7 minutes or until onion is tender, stirring occasionally. Stir in orzo. Cook and stir about 2 minutes more or until orzo is lightly browned.

2 Stir in broth, marjoram, and pepper. Bring to boiling; reduce heat. Cover and simmer for 12 minutes. Stir in broccoli and carrot. Return to boiling; reduce heat. Cover and simmer about 3 minutes more or until orzo is just tender. Remove from heat. Let stand, covered, for 5 minutes.

PER ⅔ CUP: 111 cal., 2 g total fat (0 g sat. fat), 0 mg chol., 176 mg sodium, 19 g carb., 2 g fiber, 5 g pro.
EXCHANGES: ½ Vegetable, 1 Starch

Brussels Sprouts and Fennel over Bacon-Swiss Polenta *(photo, page 583)*

PREP: 25 MINUTES **ROAST:** 30 MINUTES AT 400°F
COOK: 25 MINUTES **MAKES:** 6 SERVINGS

- **1 pound fresh Brussels sprouts**
- **2 tablespoons olive oil**
- **½ teaspoon coarse salt**
- **¼ teaspoon coarsely ground black pepper**
- **2 tablespoons butter**
- **1 16-ounce package frozen pearl onions, thawed and patted dry**
- **1 teaspoon sugar**
- **2 large fennel bulbs, trimmed, cored, and thinly sliced**
- **2 cups chicken or vegetable broth**
- **2 bay leaves**
- **3 tablespoons snipped fresh Italian parsley**
- **2 teaspoons snipped fresh thyme**
- **½ cup chopped walnuts, toasted (see tip, page 21)**
- **2 tablespoons walnut oil**
- **1 recipe Bacon-Swiss Polenta**

1 Preheat oven to 400°F. Trim stems and remove any wilted outer leaves from Brussels sprouts (see photo 1, right). Halve any large sprouts. In a large bowl combine sprouts and olive oil; toss to coat. Spread sprouts in a 15×10×1-inch baking pan. Sprinkle with salt and pepper. Roast, uncovered, for 30 to 35 minutes or until tender and browned, stirring once.

2 Meanwhile, in a large skillet melt butter over medium heat. Add onions; sprinkle with sugar. Cook and stir just until onions begin to brown. Cover skillet; cook for 5 to 10 minutes more or until onions are almost tender. Add fennel. Cover skillet; cook for 8 to 10 minutes or until fennel is tender, stirring occasionally. Add broth, bay leaves, parsley, and thyme. Cook, uncovered, over medium heat until liquid is reduced to 2 to 3 tablespoons. Discard bay leaves. Stir in roasted sprouts, walnuts, and walnut oil. Serve over Bacon-Swiss Polenta. If desired, garnish with chopped *fennel leafy tops*.

BACON-SWISS POLENTA: In a medium saucepan bring 3¾ cups milk to boiling over medium-high heat. Stir in ¾ cup quick-cooking polenta or cornmeal; 3 tablespoons butter, softened; ½ teaspoon salt; and ¼ teaspoon black pepper. Cook over medium heat, whisking constantly, for 5 to 8 minutes or until mixture thickens. Stir in ½ cup shredded Swiss cheese (2 ounces) and 3 slices bacon, crisp-cooked and crumbled.

PER 1⅓ CUPS: 583 cal., 33 g total fat (12 g sat. fat), 52 mg chol., 969 mg sodium, 57 g carb., 11 g fiber, 18 g pro.
EXCHANGES: ½ Milk, 3½ Vegetable, 2 Starch, 6 Fat

FAST LOW-CALORIE

Brussels Sprouts and Noodle Stir-Fry

START TO FINISH: 30 MINUTES **MAKES:** 8 SERVINGS

- **3 ounces dried thin whole wheat spaghetti**
- **2 tablespoons olive oil**
- **1 cup thinly sliced red onion (1 large)**
- **3 cloves garlic, minced**
- **12 ounces fresh Brussels sprouts, trimmed and thinly sliced (see photos 1 and 2, below)**
- **1 tablespoon grated fresh ginger**
- **¼ to ½ teaspoon crushed red pepper**
- **½ cup reduced-sodium chicken broth**
- **2 tablespoons reduced-sodium soy sauce**
- **½ cup shredded carrot (1 medium)**
- **⅓ cup snipped fresh cilantro**
- **3 tablespoons slivered almonds, toasted (see tip, page 21)**

1 Break spaghetti into 1-inch pieces. Cook spaghetti according to package directions; drain. Return spaghetti to hot pan; cover and keep warm.

2 In a large skillet heat oil over medium-high heat. Add onion and garlic; cook and stir for 1 minute. Add Brussels sprouts, ginger, and crushed red pepper; cook and stir for 1 minute more. Add broth and soy sauce. Cook about 2 minutes more or until liquid is nearly evaporated, stirring occasionally. Remove from heat. Stir in cooked spaghetti, carrot, and cilantro. Sprinkle with almonds.

PER ¾ CUP: 115 cal., 5 g total fat (1 g sat. fat), 0 mg chol., 196 mg sodium, 15 g carb., 3 g fiber, 4 g pro.
EXCHANGES: 1 Vegetable, ½ Starch, 1 Fat

PREPARING BRUSSELS SPROUTS STEP-BY-STEP

1. Trim the stems of Brussels sprouts close to the bases. Pull off and discard any wilted outer leaves.

2. Thinly slice the Brussels sprouts lengthwise. The core helps keep the slices intact.

make it mine

FAST

Vegetable Stir-Fry

This quick stir-fry is a great way to use up bits of leftover vegetables so they don't go to waste. It can be different every time you make it.

START TO FINISH: 30 MINUTES
MAKES: 4 SERVINGS

- **1 tablespoon vegetable oil**
- **3 cups GROUP 1 VEGETABLES**
- **2 cloves garlic, minced**
- **3 cups GROUP 2 VEGETABLES**
- **SAUCE**
- **TOPPER**

1 In a very large skillet or wok heat oil over medium-high heat. Add Group 1 Vegetables and garlic. Cook and stir for 3 minutes. Add Group 2 Vegetables. Cook and stir for 3 to 5 minutes more or until vegetables are crisp-tender. Push vegetables to side of skillet or wok. Add Sauce to center of skillet or wok; bring to boiling. Cook and stir until slightly thickened. Toss to coat the vegetables; heat through.

2 Transfer vegetable mixture to a serving dish. Add desired Topper.

SPLASH-ONS

You can put more than a topper on the plated stir-fry to add a burst of flavor and aroma. Try splashing on Asian chili sauce (Sriracha sauce), chili garlic paste, fish sauce, reduced-sodium soy sauce, or toasted seame oil. Place them on the dinner table and let diners choose their own.

GROUP 1 VEGETABLES
(pick a combination)

Butternut squash, cubed
Carrots, thinly bias-sliced
Cauliflower florets
Celery, thinly bias-sliced
Green beans, cut into 1-inch pieces
Mushrooms, quartered
Onion wedges, thin
Sweet potatoes, cubed

GROUP 2 VEGETABLES
(pick a combination)

Asparagus, cut into 1-inch pieces
Broccoli florets
Snow pea pods
Sweet peppers, cut into bite-size strips
Zucchini or yellow summer squash, sliced

SAUCE *(pick one)*

Stir together 1/4 cup soy sauce, 1 tablespoon rice vinegar, 1 tablespoon packed brown sugar, 1 teaspoon ground ginger, and 1/4 teaspoon crushed red pepper
Stir together 1/3 cup orange juice, 2 tablespoons orange marmalade, 1 tablespoon soy sauce, and 1 teaspoon grated fresh ginger
1/3 cup Sweet-and-Sour Sauce (page 538) or bottled sweet-and-sour sauce
1/3 cup bottled stir-fry sauce, peanut sauce, or teriyaki sauce

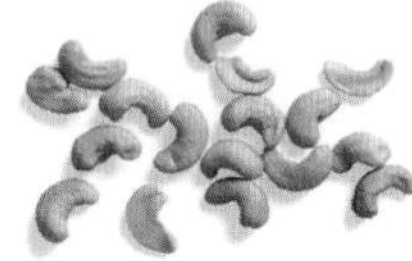

TOPPER *(pick one)*

Chopped peanuts, toasted almonds or hazelnuts, or roasted cashews
Chow mein noodles
Sesame seeds
Snipped fresh cilantro

BEST-LOVED FAST LOW-CALORIE

Pan-Roasted Brussels Sprouts

START TO FINISH: 30 MINUTES **MAKES:** 8 SERVINGS

2 pounds Brussels sprouts
7 cloves garlic, minced
1 tablespoon olive oil
3 tablespoons butter
12 sprigs fresh thyme
1 large sprig fresh rosemary, halved
2 teaspoons fennel seeds
1¼ teaspoons kosher salt or 1 teaspoon salt
1 tablespoon sherry vinegar or white wine vinegar

1 Trim stems and remove any wilted outer leaves from Brussels sprouts (see photo 1, page 593); wash. Halve any large sprouts. In a large pot cook sprouts, uncovered, in a large amount of boiling lightly salted water for 3 minutes; drain well. Pat dry with paper towels.

2 In a very large heavy skillet cook and stir garlic in hot oil over medium heat for 2 minutes. Add half of the butter, thyme, rosemary, fennel seeds, and salt. Increase heat to medium-high; using tongs, carefully arrange half of the Brussels sprouts, cut sides down, in the skillet. Cook, uncovered, for 4 to 6 minutes or until the sprouts are well browned. Remove sprouts from pan. Repeat with the remaining butter, thyme, rosemary, fennel seeds, salt, and Brussels sprouts. Return all sprouts to the skillet along with the vinegar; toss to coat.

PER ½ CUP: 108 cal., 6 g total fat (3 g sat. fat), 11 mg chol., 361 mg sodium, 11 g carb., 5 g fiber, 4 g pro. EXCHANGES: 1½ Vegetable, 1½ Fat

FAST LOW-CALORIE

Brown Sugar-Glazed Carrots

START TO FINISH: 25 MINUTES **MAKES:** 4 SERVINGS

1 pound packaged peeled fresh baby carrots or medium carrots, halved lengthwise and cut into 2-inch pieces
1 tablespoon butter or margarine
1 tablespoon packed brown sugar
Dash salt
Black pepper

1 In a medium saucepan cook carrots, covered, in a small amount of boiling salted water for 8 to 10 minutes or until crisp-tender; drain. Remove carrots from pan.

2 In the same saucepan combine butter, brown sugar, and salt. Cook and stir over medium heat until smooth. Add carrots. Cook and stir about 2 minutes or until glazed. Season to taste with pepper.

HERB-GLAZED CARROTS: Prepare as directed, except substitute 1 tablespoon honey for the brown sugar and add 1 tablespoon snipped fresh thyme or ½ teaspoon dried thyme, crushed, to the butter mixture. Sprinkle with snipped fresh Italian parsley before serving.

PER ¾ CUP BROWN SUGAR OR HERB VARIATION: 85 cal., 3 g total fat (2 g sat. fat), 8 mg chol., 135 mg sodium, 14 g carb., 3 g fiber, 1 g pro. EXCHANGES: 1½ Vegetable, ½ Other Carb., ½ Fat

LOW-CALORIE

Sweet Curry Carrots with Chive Yogurt *(photo, page 583)*

PREP: 20 MINUTES **ROAST:** 25 MINUTES AT 425°F
MAKES: 6 SERVINGS

1½ pounds carrots with tops, trimmed (about 10)
1 tablespoon olive oil
½ teaspoon salt
3 tablespoons honey
1 tablespoon curry powder
⅔ cup plain low-fat Greek yogurt
¼ cup snipped fresh chives

1 Preheat oven to 425°F. Scrub carrots and, if desired, peel. Halve any large carrots lengthwise. Line a 15×10×1-inch baking pan with foil. Toss carrots with olive oil. Spread carrots in the prepared pan. Sprinkle with ¼ teaspoon of the salt. Roast carrots for 15 minutes.

2 Meanwhile, in a small microwave-safe bowl microwave honey on 100% power (high) for 30 seconds. Whisk in curry powder; set aside.

3 Remove carrots from oven. Drizzle with honey mixture; toss to coat. Roast about 10 minutes more or until carrots are tender and glazed, turning occasionally. Transfer to a serving dish.

4 For chive yogurt, in a small bowl stir together yogurt, chives, and the remaining ¼ teaspoon salt. Serve with roasted carrots. If desired, sprinkle with additional snipped fresh chives.

PER SERVING: 116 cal., 3 g total fat (1 g sat. fat), 1 mg chol., 274 mg sodium, 20 g carb., 4 g fiber, 4 g pro. EXCHANGES: 2 Vegetable, ½ Other Carb., ½ Fat

CAULIFLOWER "COUSCOUS"

BEST-LOVED LOW-CALORIE

Cauliflower "Couscous"

START TO FINISH: 50 MINUTES **MAKES:** 8 SERVINGS

- **1/4 cup dried cranberries**
- **1/4 cup snipped dried apricots**
- **8 cups cauliflower florets (1 large head)**
- **2 tablespoons butter**
- **1 tablespoon olive oil**
- **1 medium onion, halved and thinly sliced**
- **2 cloves garlic, minced**
- **1 5-ounce package fresh baby spinach, chopped**
- **1/2 cup roasted pistachios, chopped**
- **1/2 teaspoon salt**
- **1/2 cup sliced green onions (4)**

1 Place the dried cranberries and apricots in a small bowl. Cover with boiling water; let stand about 10 minutes or until plump. Drain well; set aside.

2 Meanwhile, place the cauliflower, in batches, in a food processor. Cover and pulse, four to six times for each batch, until crumbly and mixture resembles the texture of couscous.

3 In a very large skillet heat 1 tablespoon of the butter and the olive oil over medium-high heat. Add the onion; cook and stir about 3 minutes or until tender and just starting to brown. Add garlic; cook and stir for 30 seconds more. Add the cauliflower, spreading in an even layer. Cook about 8 minutes or until cauliflower is evenly golden, stirring occasionally.

4 Stir in the drained cranberries and apricots, the spinach, pistachios, and salt. Cook and stir until well combined. Stir in the remaining 1 tablespoon butter and the green onions. Toss until butter melts. Transfer to a serving bowl.

MAKE-AHEAD DIRECTIONS: Prepare as directed through Step 3. Place in an airtight container; cover. Chill for up to 24 hours. To serve, reheat the cauliflower mixture in a very large lightly oiled skillet. Continue as directed.

PER ABOUT 1 CUP: 139 cal., 8 g total fat (3 g sat. fat), 8 mg chol., 217 mg sodium, 14 g carb., 4 g fiber, 4 g pro.
EXCHANGES: 1½ Vegetable, ½ Fruit, 1½ Fat

Skillet-Roasted Cauliflower Steaks

PREP: 30 MINUTES **ROAST:** 20 MINUTES AT 375°F
MAKES: 4 MAIN-DISH SERVINGS

- **1 to 2 large heads cauliflower (about 3 pounds total)**
- **1 tablespoon olive oil**
- **1/4 teaspoon salt**
- **1/4 teaspoon black pepper**
- **1/4 teaspoon ground cumin**
- **1 recipe Jalapeño Creamed Spinach**
- **1/4 cup roasted, salted pumpkin seeds (pepitas)**

1 Preheat oven to 375°F. Remove outer leaves from the cauliflower. Carefully trim stem end, leaving core intact so florets are still attached. Turn cauliflower head core side down; using a chef's knife or large serrated knife, cut cauliflower vertically into four 1- to 1¼-inch-thick "steaks" (reserve ends and loose pieces for another use).

2 In a very large oven-going skillet heat oil over medium heat. Add cauliflower steaks; cook for 4 to 6 minutes or until browned on both sides, turning once halfway through cooking time. Sprinkle with salt, pepper, and cumin. Transfer skillet to the oven; roast, uncovered, for 15 to 20 minutes or until tender. Remove cauliflower steaks from the skillet; keep warm. Carefully wipe out skillet.

3 In same skillet* prepare Jalapeño Creamed Spinach. Serve cauliflower steaks over the spinach mixture. Sprinkle with pumpkin seeds.

***NOTE:** The skillet will still be hot when making the spinach. Be sure to hold the handle with a hot-pan holder.

JALAPEÑO CREAMED SPINACH: In a very large skillet cook and stir two 5-ounce packages fresh baby spinach, half at a time, over medium heat until wilted. Transfer to a colander. Squeeze out excess liquid. Cook ½ cup chopped onion (1 medium) and 1 to 2 fresh jalapeño chile peppers, seeded and finely chopped (see tip, page 44), in 1 tablespoon hot oil about 5 minutes or until tender. Add 1 cup whipping cream, ¼ teaspoon salt, and ¼ teaspoon black pepper. Bring to boiling. Cook for 3 to 5 minutes or until cream starts to thicken. Stir in spinach. Simmer until mixture reaches desired consistency.

PER STEAK + ABOUT ⅓ CUP SPINACH: 408 cal., 36 g total fat (16 g sat. fat), 82 mg chol., 445 mg sodium, 15 g carb., 6 g fiber, 10 g pro. EXCHANGES: 2 Vegetable, 1 High-Fat Meat, 5½ Fat

FAST LOW-CALORIE

Corn on the Cob

START TO FINISH: 20 MINUTES **MAKES:** 8 SERVINGS

- **8 ears of corn**
- **Butter, margarine, or 1 recipe Chipotle-Lime Butter, Cajun Butter, or Herb Butter**
- **Salt**
- **Black pepper**

1 Remove husks from the ears of corn. Scrub with a stiff brush to remove silks; rinse. Cook, covered, in enough boiling lightly salted water to cover for 5 to 7 minutes or until tender. Serve with butter, salt, and pepper.

CHIPOTLE-LIME BUTTER: In a small mixing bowl beat ½ cup butter, softened; 1 teaspoon finely shredded lime peel; ½ teaspoon salt; ⅛ to ¼ teaspoon ground chipotle chile pepper; and dash cayenne pepper with electric mixer on low speed until combined. Cover; chill for 1 to 24 hours.

CAJUN BUTTER: In a small mixing bowl beat ½ cup butter, softened; 1 teaspoon garlic salt; ¼ teaspoon black pepper; ¼ teaspoon cayenne pepper; ⅛ teaspoon ground ginger; and ⅛ teaspoon ground cloves with an electric mixer on low speed until combined. Cover; chill for 1 to 24 hours.

HERB BUTTER: In a small mixing bowl beat ½ cup butter, softened; 2 teaspoons snipped fresh thyme; and 2 teaspoons snipped fresh marjoram or oregano with an electric mixer on low speed until combined. Cover; chill for 1 to 24 hours.

PER EAR + 1 TABLESPOON PLAIN OR FLAVORED BUTTER: 179 cal., 13 g total fat (7 g sat. fat), 31 mg chol., 168 mg sodium, 17 g carb., 2 g fiber, 3 g pro. EXCHANGES: 1 Starch, 2 Fat

FAST LOW-CALORIE

Skillet Scalloped Corn

START TO FINISH: 15 MINUTES **MAKES:** 4 SERVINGS

- **4 teaspoons butter**
- **¼ cup crushed rich round, wheat, or rye crackers**
- **1 11-ounce can whole kernel corn with sweet peppers, drained**
- **1 7- to 8.75-ounce can whole kernel corn with sweet peppers, whole kernel corn, or white (shoepeg) corn, drained**
- **2 1-ounce slices process Swiss cheese, torn**
- **⅓ cup crushed rich round, wheat, or rye crackers**
- **⅓ cup milk**
- **⅛ teaspoon onion powder**
- **Dash black pepper**

SKILLET SCALLOPED CORN

1 For topping, in a large skillet melt butter over medium heat. Add the ¼ cup crushed crackers to the skillet. Cook and stir until lightly browned; set aside.

2 In same skillet combine the corn, cheese, the ⅓ cup crushed crackers, the milk, onion powder, and pepper. Cook, stirring frequently, until cheese melts. Transfer to a serving dish; sprinkle with crumb topping.

PER ½ CUP: 220 cal., 12 g total fat (6 g sat. fat), 23 mg chol., 713 mg sodium, 24 g carb., 2 g fiber, 7 g pro. EXCHANGES: 1½ Starch, ½ Medium-Fat Meat, 1½ Fat

Corn Spoon Bread *(photo, page 583)*

PREP: 25 MINUTES **BAKE:** 55 MINUTES AT 325°F
STAND: 10 MINUTES **MAKES:** 8 SERVINGS

- **4 slices bacon, chopped**
- **½ cup chopped onion (1 medium)**
- **1 clove garlic, minced**
- **1 cup water**
- **½ cup yellow cornmeal**
- **¼ teaspoon salt**
- **1 cup shredded cheddar cheese (4 ounces)**
- **1 14.75-ounce can cream-style corn**
- **½ cup milk**
- **3 egg yolks**
- **1 teaspoon baking powder**
- **Dash cayenne pepper**
- **1 cup fresh or frozen whole corn kernels**
- **3 egg whites**

1 Preheat oven to 325°F. Grease a 2-quart square baking dish; set aside. In a large skillet cook bacon, onion, and garlic over medium heat until bacon is crisp; remove from heat and set aside (do not drain). In a medium saucepan combine the water, cornmeal, and salt. Bring to boiling; reduce heat. Cook and stir about 1 minute or until very thick. Remove from heat. Stir in cheese and cream-style corn. Stir until cheese almost melts. Stir in milk; set aside.

2 In a small mixing bowl beat egg yolks, baking powder, and cayenne pepper until well blended. Stir into cornmeal mixture along with bacon mixture and corn kernels; set aside.

3 In a medium mixing bowl beat egg whites with an electric mixer on medium speed until stiff peaks form (tips stand straight). Stir a small amount of the beaten egg whites into cornmeal mixture to lighten it. Fold in remaining egg whites. Pour into the prepared baking dish. Bake, uncovered, for 55 to 60 minutes or until puffed and golden. Let stand for 10 minutes before serving.

PER ¾ CUP: 255 cal., 15 g total fat (6 g sat. fat), 98 mg chol., 481 mg sodium, 20 g carb., 1 g fiber, 11 g pro.
EXCHANGES: 1 Starch, 1 Medium-Fat Meat, 1½ Fat

FAST LOW-CALORIE

Eggplant Parmigiana

START TO FINISH: 30 MINUTES **MAKES:** 4 SERVINGS

- **1 small eggplant (12 ounces)**
- **1 egg, lightly beaten**
- **1 tablespoon water**
- **¼ cup all-purpose flour**
- **2 tablespoons vegetable oil**
- **⅓ cup grated Parmesan cheese**
- **1 cup marinara sauce**
- **¾ cup shredded mozzarella cheese (3 ounces)**
- **Hot cooked pasta (optional)**
- **Shredded fresh basil (optional)**
- **Grated Parmesan cheese (optional)**

1 Wash and peel eggplant; cut crosswise into ½-inch slices. In a small bowl combine egg and water. Place flour in another small bowl. Dip eggplant slices into egg mixture; dip into flour, turning to coat both sides.

2 In a large skillet cook eggplant, half at a time, in hot oil over medium-high heat for 4 to 6 minutes or until golden, turning once. (If necessary, add additional oil and reduce heat to medium if eggplant browns too quickly.) Drain on paper towels.

EGGPLANT PARMIGIANA

3 Wipe the skillet with paper towels. Arrange the cooked eggplant slices in the skillet; sprinkle with the Parmesan cheese. Top with marinara sauce and mozzarella cheese. Cook, covered, over medium-low heat for 5 to 7 minutes or until heated through. If desired, serve with hot cooked pasta and top with basil and additional Parmesan cheese.

BAKED EGGPLANT PARMIGIANA: Preheat oven to 400°F. Prepare as directed, except in Step 2 place the eggplant slices in a single layer in an ungreased 2-quart rectangular baking dish, cutting slices to fit if necessary. Sprinkle with Parmesan cheese. Top with marinara sauce and mozzarella cheese. Bake, uncovered, for 12 to 15 minutes or until heated through. If desired, top with basil.

PER SERVING: 250 cal., 15 g total fat (5 g sat. fat), 70 mg chol., 563 mg sodium, 20 g carb., 5 g fiber, 12 g pro.
EXCHANGES: 2 Vegetable, ½ Other Carb., 1 Medium-Fat Meat, 2 Fat

KNOW YOUR EGGPLANT

Eggplants come in many colors, sizes, and shapes. Unless the recipe calls for a specific variety, look for the classic purple, egg-shape eggplant. These work especially well when slices are needed, as in the Eggplant Parmigiana and for grilling. Long, slender Japanese-type eggplants lend themselves to quick sautés and stir-fries.

cook's secrets

roasting garlic & peppers

The Secret: Rich, roasty flavor requires a hot oven to caramelize natural sugars in the raw veggies. The transformation is delicious.

ROASTING GARLIC POINTERS

1. BULBS & CLOVES
A garlic bulb is made up of 10 to 12 individual garlic cloves. For best results, remove the top ½ inch of the bulb to expose the cloves. Roast as many bulbs as you like. You should get about 1 tablespoon garlic from each roasted bulb.

ROASTING PEPPER POINTERS

1. FOIL ONCE
Place your peppers on a foil-lined pan. When it is time to wrap the roasted pepper in foil, just bring up the edges of the foil on the pan. This makes for easy cleanup too!

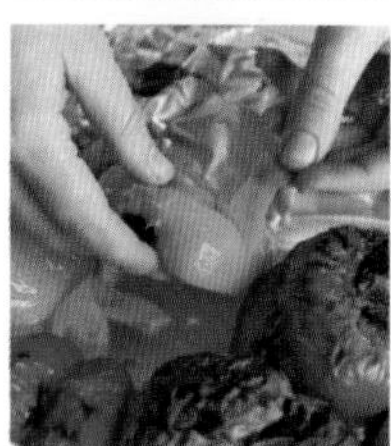

This roasting process works for chile peppers too (see tip, page 44). Poblanos are delicious roasted. Follow the steps for sweet peppers.

Roasted Garlic

MAKES: 1 TABLESPOON GARLIC PER BULB

1 Preheat oven to 400°F. Cut off the top ½ inch of a garlic bulb to expose the ends of the individual cloves. Leaving garlic bulb whole, remove any loose, papery outer layers.

2 Place bulb, cut end up, in a muffin or custard cup or on a double thickness of foil. Drizzle bulb with 1 tablespoon *olive oil*. Sprinkle with *salt* and *black pepper*.

3 Cover bulb with foil or bring foil up around bulb and fold edges together to loosely enclose.

4 Roast about 25 minutes or until the garlic feels soft when squeezed. Cool; squeeze bulb from the bottom of paper husk so cloves pop out.

5 To serve roasted garlic, simply spread on toasted crusty bread slices or crackers. Roasted garlic can also be used as a recipe ingredient—whisk it into soups and pan sauces. Or combine it with melted butter or olive oil and toss with vegetables, such as asparagus or hot cooked new potatoes.

Roasted Sweet Peppers

MAKES: ½ CUP STRIPS OR CHOPPED PER PEPPER

1 Preheat oven to 425°F. Cut sweet peppers in half lengthwise; remove stems, seeds, and membranes. Place pepper halves, cut sides down, on a foil-lined baking sheet. Roast for 20 to 25 minutes or until peppers are charred and very tender.

2 Bring the foil up around peppers and fold edges together to enclose. Let stand about 15 minutes or until cool enough to handle. Use a sharp knife to loosen edges of the skins; gently pull off skin in strips and discard.

3 To use roasted peppers, stir them into soups, casseroles, and pasta dishes. Add them to pizzas, scrambled eggs, and sandwiches.

FIRE-ROASTED PEPPERS

If you want to add a little smoky flavor to your roasted peppers, roast them on the grill. For a charcoal or gas grill, place whole sweet peppers on the grill rack directly over medium-high heat. Cover and grill for 13 to 15 minutes or until charred and very tender, turning occasionally. Wrap in foil and continue as directed in Step 2, above.

BEST-LOVED LOW-CALORIE

Braised Fennel with Dill

PREP: 10 MINUTES **COOK:** 30 MINUTES
MAKES: 6 SERVINGS

- **3 medium fennel bulbs**
- **2 tablespoons butter**
- **½ cup chicken broth**
- **¼ cup dry white wine**
- **¼ teaspoon salt**
- **⅛ to ¼ teaspoon black pepper**
- **3 tablespoons snipped fresh dill weed**

1 Cut a slice from base of each bulb (see photo 1, below). Cut off and discard fennel stalks (see photo 2, below). Remove any wilted outer layers from bulbs; Cut bulbs into quarters lengthwise and cut core out of each quarter (see photo 3, below). Cut quarters into 1-inch wedges.

2 In a large skillet melt butter over medium heat. Add fennel, broth, wine, salt, and pepper. Cook, covered, about 20 minutes or just until tender, stirring occasionally. Cook, uncovered, about 10 minutes more or until liquid evaporates. Stir in dill weed.

PER SERVING: 80 cal., 4 g total fat (2 g sat. fat), 10 mg chol., 266 mg sodium, 9 g carb., 4 g fiber, 2 g pro.
EXCHANGES: 1½ Vegetable, 1 Fat

PREP THE GREENS

You can't go wrong adding more leafy greens to your daily diet—the darker the better. Collard greens, mustard greens, kale, and Swiss chard are all nutritional powerhouses. The stems, or ribs, of these greens can be tough and chewy, so for best results in your recipes, pull the leafy parts off and discard the stems. Chop, tear, or shred the leaves. Swiss chard is an exception. You can slice the colorful stems and sauté them separately from the greens because they take longer to cook.

LOW-CALORIE

Collard Greens with Bacon

PREP: 30 MINUTES **COOK:** 60 MINUTES
MAKES: 6 SERVINGS

- **1 pound collard greens**
- **3 slices bacon, chopped**
- **2 cups water**
- **1 8- to 10-ounce smoked pork hock**
- **½ cup chopped onion (1 medium)**
- **½ cup chopped green sweet pepper (1 small)**
- **1 teaspoon sugar**
- **¼ teaspoon salt**
- **⅛ teaspoon cayenne pepper**
- **4 cloves garlic, minced**
- **Red wine vinegar (optional)**

1 Wash collard greens thoroughly in cold water; drain well. Remove and discard stems; trim bruised leaves. Coarsely chop leaves; lightly pack to measure 6 cups and set aside.

2 In a large saucepan cook bacon until crisp. Remove bacon, reserving drippings in saucepan. Drain bacon on paper towels and set aside. Add water, pork hock, onion, sweet pepper, sugar, salt, cayenne pepper, and garlic to saucepan. Bring to boiling; add chopped collard greens. Reduce heat. Simmer, covered, for 60 to 75 minutes or until greens are tender. Remove from heat. Remove pork hock. Cover greens; keep warm.

3 When cool enough to handle, cut meat off pork hock. Chop or shred meat; discard bone and fat. Return meat to greens mixture along with cooked bacon; heat through. Serve with a slotted spoon. If desired, drizzle each serving with a little vinegar.

PER SERVING: 176 cal., 13 g total fat (4 g sat. fat), 34 mg chol., 312 mg sodium, 6 g carb., 2 g fiber, 9 g pro.
EXCHANGES: 1 Vegetable, 1 High-Fat Meat, 1 Fat

PREPARING FENNEL BULBS STEP-BY-STEP

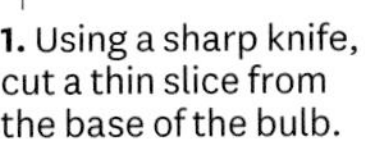

1. Using a sharp knife, cut a thin slice from the base of the bulb.

2. Cut stalks and root ends off fennel bulbs. If desired, save a few wispy fronds for a garnish.

3. Cut bulbs in half vertically. Cut halves in half again. Remove and discard tough core portion from each quarter.

LOW-CALORIE

Herbed Leek Gratin

PREP: 20 MINUTES **BAKE:** 50 MINUTES AT 375°F
STAND: 10 MINUTES **MAKES:** 6 SERVINGS

- **3 pounds slender leeks (about 6 leeks, each about 1¼ inches in diameter)**
- **½ cup whipping cream**
- **2 tablespoons chicken broth**
- **2 tablespoons snipped fresh marjoram or 1½ teaspoons dried marjoram, crushed**
- **½ teaspoon salt**
- **¼ to ½ teaspoon black pepper**
- **1½ cups soft French or Italian bread crumbs**
- **3 tablespoons grated Parmesan cheese**
- **3 tablespoons butter, melted**

1 Preheat oven to 375°F. Trim roots and wilted leaves from leeks (see photo 1, below). Cut leek pieces in half lengthwise; cut crosswise into ¼-inch-thick strips (see photo 2, below). Clean in cold water (see photo 3, below). Drain and dry leeks (see photo 4, below). Place in a 1½-quart gratin dish or casserole.

2 In a small bowl stir together whipping cream and broth; pour over leeks in dish. Sprinkle with half of the marjoram, the salt, and pepper. Cover tightly with foil. Bake for 20 minutes.

3 Meanwhile, in a small bowl stir together bread crumbs, Parmesan cheese, and the remaining marjoram. Drizzle with melted butter; toss to coat. Sprinkle partially baked leeks with bread crumb mixture. Bake, uncovered, about 30 minutes more or until leeks are tender and crumbs are golden. Let stand for 10 minutes before serving. If desired, garnish with *fresh marjoram leaves.*

ZUCCHINI AND SUMMER SQUASH GRATIN: Prepare as directed, except omit leeks and chicken broth. Pat dry 3 cups ¼-inch-thick slices zucchini (about 1 pound) and 3 cups ¼-inch-thick slices yellow summer squash (about 1 pound). Alternately layer the slices in the gratin dish. Bake, covered, for 10 minutes. Sprinkle with crumb mixture. Continue as directed.

PER SERVING LEEK OR ZUCCHINI VARIATION: 177 cal., 11 g total fat (9 g sat. fat), 45 mg chol., 373 mg sodium, 10 g carb., 1 g fiber, 3 g pro. EXCHANGES: ½ Vegetable, ½ Starch, 2½ Fat

BEST-LOVED LOW-CALORIE

Mushroom Medley au Gratin

PREP: 35 MINUTES **BAKE:** 15 MINUTES AT 350°F
MAKES: 6 SERVINGS

- **2 tablespoons grated Parmesan cheese**
- **2 tablespoons fine dry bread crumbs**
- **2 teaspoons butter, melted**
- **8 ounces fresh shiitake mushrooms**
- **4 ounces fresh oyster mushrooms**
- **1 pound fresh button mushrooms, sliced**
- **1 clove garlic, minced**
- **2 tablespoons butter**
- **2 tablespoons all-purpose flour**
- **2 teaspoons Dijon-style mustard**
- **1½ teaspoons snipped fresh thyme or ½ teaspoon dried thyme, crushed**
- **¼ teaspoon salt**
- **⅔ cup milk**

1 Preheat oven to 350°F. In a small bowl stir together Parmesan cheese, bread crumbs, and the 2 teaspoons melted butter; set aside.

PREPARING LEEKS STEP-BY-STEP

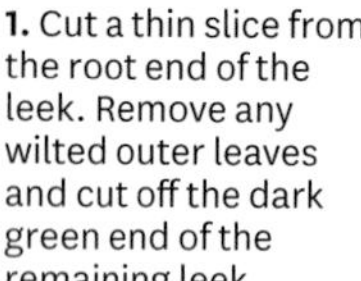

1. Cut a thin slice from the root end of the leek. Remove any wilted outer leaves and cut off the dark green end of the remaining leek.

2. Slice the leek in half lengthwise. Cut the halved leek crosswise into very thin (about ¼-inch) strips.

3. Fill a large bowl with cold water and add sliced leeks. Swish them with your hands to separate the layers and remove any dirt and sand.

4. Drain leeks in a colander and pat dry with paper towels. To dry leeks quickly and completely, use a salad spinner.

2 Separate caps and stems from shiitake and oyster mushrooms. (Reserve stems to use in stocks or discard.) Slice caps.

3 In a large skillet cook button mushrooms and garlic in the 2 tablespoons butter over medium-high heat about 5 minutes or until tender and most of the liquid evaporates, stirring occasionally. Remove mushrooms from skillet and set aside, reserving drippings in skillet.

4 Add shiitake and oyster mushrooms to the skillet. Cook for 7 to 8 minutes or until tender and most of the liquid evaporates, stirring occasionally. Stir in the flour, mustard, thyme, and salt. Add milk all at once. Cook and stir until thickened and bubbly. Stir in button mushroom mixture.

5 Transfer mushroom mixture to a 1-quart gratin dish or 1-quart casserole. Sprinkle with the bread crumb mixture. Bake, uncovered, about 15 minutes or until heated through.

PER SERVING: 120 cal., 7 g total fat (4 g sat. fat), 17 mg chol., 237 mg sodium, 10 g carb., 2 g fiber, 6 g pro.
EXCHANGES: 1½ Vegetable, 1½ Fat

LOW-CALORIE

Mushroom Fricassee with Fresh Herbs

PREP: 25 MINUTES COOK: 22 MINUTES
STAND: 5 MINUTES MAKES: 6 SERVINGS

- **2 pounds assorted fresh mushrooms, such as cremini, button, shiitake, chanterelle, porcini, oyster, and/or morels, cleaned and tough stems trimmed**
- **2 tablespoons walnut oil**
- **1 tablespoon butter**
- **½ cup finely chopped shallots (4 medium)**
- **2 cloves garlic, minced**
- **½ teaspoon coarse sea salt**
- **¼ teaspoon black pepper**
- **½ cup Madeira or chicken broth**
- **½ cup whipping cream**
- **1 tablespoon snipped fresh chives**
- **1 to 2 teaspoons snipped fresh rosemary or ¼ to ½ teaspoon dried rosemary, crushed**
- **¼ cup snipped fresh parsley**

1 Leave small mushrooms whole, halve medium-size mushrooms, and quarter large mushrooms to total 12 cups. In a very large skillet heat 1 tablespoon of the walnut oil and 1½ teaspoons of the butter over medium heat. Add 6 cups of the mushrooms; cook about 5 minutes or until the mushrooms begin to color, stirring occasionally. Using a slotted spoon, transfer cooked mushrooms to a large bowl. Repeat with the remaining mushrooms, oil, and butter. Add the shallots, garlic, and reserved cooked mushrooms to the skillet; cook and stir for 2 to 3 minutes more or until the mushrooms are golden and the shallots are tender. Stir in salt and pepper.

2 Remove from heat; add the Madeira. Return to heat; simmer about 3 minutes or until the liquid is nearly gone. Stir in the cream, chives, and rosemary. Cook about 2 minutes or until cream is slightly thickened. Remove from heat and let stand for 5 minutes. Transfer to a serving bowl and sprinkle with snipped fresh parsley; serve warm.

PER SERVING: 193 cal., 14 g total fat (6 g sat. fat), 32 mg chol., 231 mg sodium, 9 g carb., 2 g fiber, 6 g pro.
EXCHANGES: 1½ Vegetable, 3 Fat

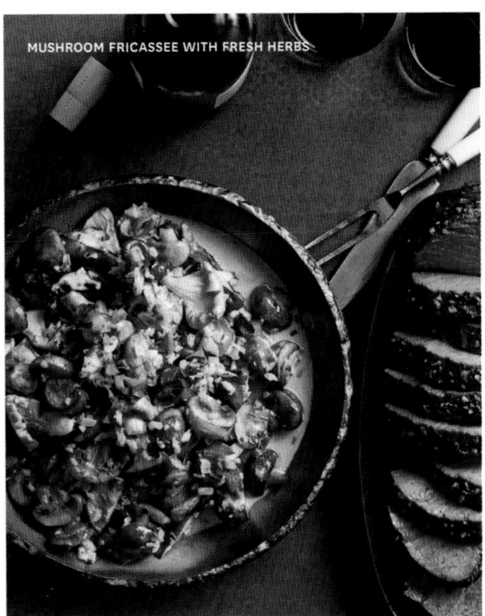
MUSHROOM FRICASSEE WITH FRESH HERBS

USING MUSHROOMS

Look for mushrooms with firm flesh and no blemishes or spots. They should have a clean, earthy smell. Store them in the refrigerator covered with paper towels or in a paper sack. Don't clean them until right before you use them. To clean, brush lightly with a damp paper towel. Don't soak them in water. It will make them mushy. If you have a lot and are using them immediately, you can rinse them quickly under cold running water and pat dry with paper towels. Morel mushrooms are the exception. If they are dirty, soak them in water to remove soil and bugs. Pat dry and use as soon as possible.

CRISPY FRIED OKRA WITH CREOLE REMOULADE

LOW-CALORIE

Crispy Fried Okra with Creole Remoulade

PREP: 20 MINUTES **FRY:** 4 MINUTES PER BATCH
MAKES: 16 SERVINGS

- **⅔ cup mayonnaise**
- **⅓ cup finely chopped cooked shrimp and/or andouille sausage**
- **1 tablespoon Creole mustard**
- **1 teaspoon prepared horseradish**
- **¼ teaspoon paprika**
- **⅛ teaspoon bottled hot pepper sauce**
- **16 whole fresh okra, stemmed and halved lengthwise or sliced ½ inch thick**
- **¼ cup all-purpose flour**
- **1 egg**
- **1 tablespoon water**
- **⅔ cup yellow cornmeal**
- **1 teaspoon seafood seasoning or celery salt**
- **2 cups peanut oil or other vegetable oil**

1 In a medium bowl stir together mayonnaise, shrimp and/or sausage, mustard, horseradish, paprika, and hot pepper sauce; chill remoulade until needed.

2 Pat okra dry with paper towels. Place flour in a shallow dish. In another shallow dish lightly beat egg and the water. In a third dish stir together cornmeal and seafood seasoning. Coat okra with flour, dip in egg mixture, and roll in cornmeal mixture to coat.

3 In a medium heavy saucepan heat oil over medium-high heat. Using a slotted spoon, carefully add okra, a few at a time, to hot oil. Fry about 4 minutes or until crisp and golden, turning once. Transfer okra to paper towels to drain. Repeat with remaining okra, adding more oil if necessary. Serve okra with remoulade.

PER 4 SLICES OKRA + 1 TABLESPOON REMOULADE: 165 cal., 14 g total fat (2 g sat. fat), 35 mg chol., 275 mg sodium, 6 g carb., 1 g fiber, 3 g pro. EXCHANGES: ½ Starch, 2½ Fat

FAST

Onion Rings

PREP: 15 MINUTES **COOK:** 2 MINUTES PER BATCH
MAKES: 6 SERVINGS

- **¾ cup all-purpose flour**
- **⅔ cup milk**
- **1 egg**
- **1 tablespoon vegetable oil**
- **¼ teaspoon salt**
- **Vegetable oil for deep-fat frying**
- **4 medium mild yellow or white onions, sliced ¼ inch thick and separated into rings (1¼ pounds)**
- **Salt**
- **1 recipe Chipotle Ketchup or Curried Aïoli**

1 For batter, in a medium mixing bowl combine flour, milk, egg, the 1 tablespoon oil, and the ¼ teaspoon salt. Using a whisk, beat just until smooth.

2 In a deep-fat fryer or large deep skillet heat 1 inch oil to 365°F. Using a fork, dip onion rings into batter;* drain off excess batter. Fry onion rings, a few at a time, in hot oil for 2 to 3 minutes or until golden, stirring once or twice with a fork to separate rings. Remove rings from oil; drain on paper towels. Repeat with remaining rings. Sprinkle with additional salt and serve with Chipotle Ketchup.

***NOTE:** You might need to stir the last few onion slices into batter to coat them well.

CHIPOTLE KETCHUP: In a small bowl stir together 1 cup ketchup and 2 teaspoons finely chopped chipotle chile peppers in adobo sauce.

PER SERVING WITH CHIPOTLE KETCHUP: 657 cal., 58 g total fat (5 g sat. fat), 37 mg chol., 771 mg sodium, 31 g carb., 2 g fiber, 5 g pro. EXCHANGES: 1 Vegetable, 1 Starch, 1 Other Carb., 11½ Fat

CURRIED AÏOLI: In a small bowl whisk together ½ cup mayonnaise; 2 cloves garlic, minced; 1 teaspoon lemon juice; and ½ teaspoon curry powder. Slowly drizzle in ⅓ cup olive oil in a thin stream, whisking constantly.

PER SERVING WITH CURRIED AÏOLI: 859 cal., 85 g total fat (9 g sat. fat), 44 mg chol., 418 mg sodium, 22 g carb., 2 g fiber, 5 g pro. EXCHANGES: 1 Starch, 1 Vegetable, 17 Fat

FAST LOW-CALORIE

Caramelized Onions

START TO FINISH: 21 MINUTES **MAKES:** 4 SERVINGS

- **2 tablespoons butter**
- **2 large sweet onions (such as Vidalia or Walla Walla), halved lengthwise and thinly sliced or cut into ¾-inch chunks**

1 In a large skillet melt butter over medium-low heat. Add onion. Cook, covered, for 13 to 15 minutes or until onions are tender, stirring occasionally. Uncover; cook and stir over medium-high heat for 3 to 5 minutes more or until golden.

PER ⅓ CUP: 104 cal., 6 g total fat (4 g sat. fat), 15 mg chol., 54 mg sodium, 13 g carb., 1 g fiber, 1 g pro.
EXCHANGES: 1½ Vegetable, 1½ Fat

LOW-CALORIE

Mashed Parsnips with Cauliflower and Carrots

PREP: 25 MINUTES **COOK:** 32 MINUTES
MAKES: 6 SERVINGS

- **3 cups peeled and chopped parsnips (3 medium)**
- **3 cups chopped cauliflower florets**
- **1 cup chopped carrots (2 medium)**
- **1 cup finely chopped onion (1 large)**
- **1 teaspoon salt**
- **4 cups water**
- **2 tablespoons snipped fresh chives**
- **2 tablespoons snipped fresh Italian parsley**
- **2 tablespoons grated Parmesan cheese**
- **2 tablespoons butter**
- **¼ teaspoon black pepper**

1 In a large pot combine the parsnips, cauliflower, carrots, onion, and ¾ teaspoon of the salt. Add the water. Bring to boiling; reduce heat. Simmer, covered, for 30 to 35 minutes or until vegetables are tender, stirring occasionally; drain well.

2 Return vegetables to the hot pan over low heat. Using a potato masher, mash vegetables until desired consistency. Cook and stir over low heat for 2 to 3 minutes or until any excess water has evaporated. Stir in chives, parsley, Parmesan cheese, butter, the remaining ¼ teaspoon salt, and the pepper.

PER ¾ CUP: 123 cal., 5 g total fat (3 g sat. fat), 12 mg chol., 483 mg sodium, 19 g carb., 5 g fiber, 3 g pro.
EXCHANGES: 3½ Vegetable, 1 Fat

LOW-CALORIE

Oven-Roasted Peas and Tomatoes

PREP: 15 MINUTES **ROAST:** 18 MINUTES AT 425°F
MAKES: 4 SERVINGS

- **Nonstick cooking spray**
- **2 cups frozen peas, thawed**
- **1 cup fresh button mushrooms, halved**
- **¾ cup grape tomatoes**
- **1 small onion, cut into very thin wedges**
- **1 tablespoon olive oil**
- **¼ teaspoon salt**
- **¼ teaspoon black pepper**
- **2 teaspoons snipped fresh dill weed or ½ teaspoon dried dill weed**

1 Preheat oven to 425°F. Lightly coat a 15×10×1-inch baking pan with cooking spray. Add peas, mushrooms, tomatoes, and onion to pan. Drizzle with olive oil; toss to coat. Sprinkle with salt and pepper. Roast, uncovered, for 18 to 20 minutes or until tender, stirring once. Sprinkle with dill weed.

PER ⅔ CUP: 103 cal., 4 g total fat (1 g sat. fat), 0 mg chol., 227 mg sodium, 13 g carb., 4 g fiber, 5 g pro.
EXCHANGES: 1 Vegetable, ½ Starch, 1 Fat

FAST LOW-CALORIE

Sugar Snap Peas with Orange-Ginger Butter

START TO FINISH: 25 MINUTES **MAKES:** 4 SERVINGS

- **3 cups fresh or frozen sugar snap peas**
- **1 teaspoon grated fresh ginger**
- **1 tablespoon butter or margarine**
- **1 tablespoon orange marmalade or peach preserves**
- **1 teaspoon cider vinegar**
- **⅛ teaspoon black pepper**

1 Remove strings and tips from peas. Cook fresh peas, covered, in a small amount of boiling salted water for 3 to 5 minutes or until crisp-tender. (Cook frozen peas according to the package directions.) Drain well.

2 Meanwhile, in a small saucepan cook ginger in hot butter for 1 minute. Stir in marmalade, vinegar, and pepper; cook and stir until marmalade melts. Pour marmalade mixture over hot cooked peas; toss to coat.

PER ⅔ CUP: 58 cal., 3 g total fat (2 g sat. fat), 8 mg chol., 25 mg sodium, 7 g carb., 1 g fiber, 1 g pro.
EXCHANGES: 1½ Vegetable, ½ Fat

FAST LOW-CALORIE

Lemon-Tarragon Peas *(photo, page 583)*

START TO FINISH: 30 MINUTES **MAKES:** 6 SERVINGS

- **½ cup water**
- **3½ cups shelled fresh English peas (see photos 1 and 2, below) or one 16-ounce package frozen peas**
- **1½ cups fresh sugar snap pea pods and/or snow pea pods**
- **1 tablespoon butter, softened**
- **1 tablespoon snipped fresh tarragon**
- **2 teaspoons finely shredded lemon peel**
- **½ teaspoon freshly cracked black pepper**
- **¼ teaspoon salt**

1 In a medium saucepan bring the water to boiling. Add shelled English peas. Return to boiling; reduce heat. Simmer, covered, for 8 minutes (2 minutes for frozen peas, if using). Add the sugar snap peas. Cook, covered, about 4 minutes or just until crisp-tender; drain.

2 Add butter, tarragon, lemon peel, pepper, and salt to the peas. Toss gently until the butter melts.

PER ½ CUP: 93 cal., 2 g total fat (1 g sat. fat), 5 mg chol., 119 mg sodium, 14 g carb., 5 g fiber, 5 g pro.
EXCHANGES: 1 Starch

SHELLING ENGLISH PEAS STEP-BY-STEP

1. Using a small paring knife, trim the stem end from each pea pod toward the flat side. Pull the "string" along the flat side to remove.

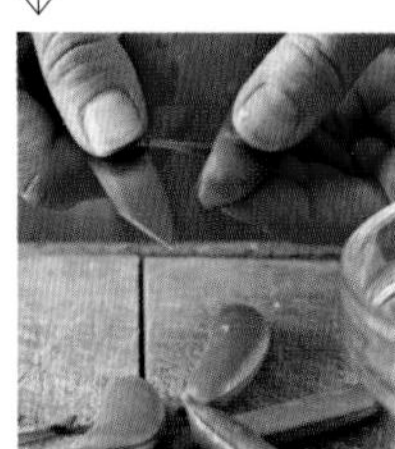

2. Split the pea pod open where you removed the string. Run your thumb along the inside of the pod to release the peas into a bowl.

LOW-CALORIE

Baked Potatoes

PREP: 5 MINUTES **BAKE:** 40 MINUTES AT 425°F
MAKES: 4 POTATOES

- **4 medium baking potatoes (6 to 8 ounces each)**
- **Shortening, butter, or margarine (optional)**

1 Preheat oven to 425°F. Scrub potatoes thoroughly with a brush; pat dry. Prick potatoes with a fork. (If desired, for soft skins, rub potatoes with shortening or wrap each potato in foil.)

2 Bake for 40 to 60 minutes (or in a 350°F oven for 70 to 80 minutes) or until tender. To serve, roll each potato gently under a towel. Using a knife, cut an "X" in the top of each potato. Press in and up on the ends of each potato.

SLOW COOKER POTATOES: Rub scrubbed potatoes lightly with olive oil. Place 4 potatoes in a 4-quart slow cooker (8 potatoes in a 6-quart slow cooker). Cover; cook on low-heat setting for 8 hours or high-heat setting for 4 hours or until potatoes are tender.

PER POTATO: 131 cal., 0 g total fat, 0 mg chol., 10 mg sodium, 30 g carb., 4 g fiber, 3 g pro. EXCHANGES: 2 Starch

BAKED SWEET POTATOES: Prepare as directed, except substitute sweet potatoes or yams for the baking potatoes. If desired, serve sweet potatoes with butter and brown sugar or cinnamon-sugar mixture.

PER SWEET POTATO: 146 cal., 0 g total fat, 0 mg chol., 94 mg sodium, 34 carb., 5 g fiber, 3 g pro.
EXCHANGES: 2 Starch

French Fries

START TO FINISH: 45 MINUTES **MAKES:** 6 SERVINGS

- **4 medium baking potatoes (6 to 8 ounces each)**
- **Peanut or vegetable oil for deep-fat frying**
- **Salt or seasoned salt (optional)**

1 If desired, peel potatoes. To prevent darkening, immerse peeled potatoes in a bowl of ice water until ready to cut. Cut potatoes lengthwise into ½-inch-wide strips. Return potato strips to ice water.

2 In a heavy, deep 3-quart saucepan or deep-fat fryer heat oil to 325°F over medium heat. Drain potatoes and place on paper towels; pat potatoes dry. Using a slotted spoon, carefully add potato strips, in about eight batches, to hot oil. Fry for 2 minutes. Using a slotted spoon, transfer potatoes to paper towels to drain.

3 Preheat oven to 300°F. Heat the oil to 375°F over medium-high heat. Add potatoes, in about eight batches, to hot oil and cook for 2 to 3 minutes or until crisp and golden. Using a slotted spoon, transfer potatoes to paper towels to drain. If desired, sprinkle with salt. Keep fries warm in a baking pan in oven while frying remaining potatoes.

PER SERVING: 487 cal., 45 g total fat (8 g sat. fat), 0 mg chol., 6 mg sodium, 20 g carb., 1 g fiber, 2 g pro.
EXCHANGES: 1 Starch, 9 Fat

SWEET POTATO FRIES: Prepare as directed, except use 4 medium sweet potatoes, peeled.

PER SERVING: 495 cal., 45 g total fat (8 g sat. fat), 0 mg chol., 62 mg sodium, 23 g carb., 3 g fiber, 2 g pro.
EXCHANGES: 1½ Starch, 9 Fat

LOW-CALORIE

Roasted Smashed Potatoes

PREP: 20 MINUTES **COOK:** 25 MINUTES
COOL: 10 MINUTES **BAKE:** 22 MINUTES AT 450°F
MAKES: 12 TO 16 SERVINGS

- **12 to 16 small red potatoes (1½ to 2 inches in diameter; 1½ to 2 pounds total)**
- **1 teaspoon salt**
- **¼ cup olive oil**
- **¾ teaspoon salt**
- **½ teaspoon black pepper**
- **¾ cup finely shredded Parmesan cheese**
- **2 tablespoons snipped fresh Italian parsley**

1 Place potatoes in a large saucepan and cover with at least 1 inch of water. Add the 1 teaspoon salt. Bring to boiling; reduce heat. Cover and simmer for 25 to 30 minutes or until potatoes are very tender; drain.

2 Preheat oven to 450°F. Transfer potatoes to a foil-lined 15×10×1-inch baking pan. Cool for 10 minutes. Using a potato masher or the palm of your hand (if potatoes are cool enough), press on each potato until about ½-inch thickness; keep each potato in one piece.

3 Brush half of the olive oil on potatoes. Sprinkle half of the ¾ teaspoon salt and ¼ teaspoon of the pepper on potatoes. Bake, uncovered, for 10 to 15 minutes or until bottoms are lightly browned and crisp. Turn potatoes; brush with the remaining olive oil and sprinkle with the remaining salt and pepper. Bake for 10 to 15 minutes more or until potatoes are lightly browned and crisp. In a bowl combine cheese and parsley. Sprinkle on potatoes. Bake for 2 to 3 minutes more or until cheese melts.

PER POTATO: 101 cal., 6 g total fat (2 g sat. fat), 4 mg chol., 232 mg sodium, 9 g carb., 1 g fiber, 3 g pro.
EXCHANGES: ½ Starch, 1 Fat

ROASTED SMASHED POTATOES

LOW-CALORIE

Easy Roasted Potatoes

PREP: 10 MINUTES **ROAST:** 25 MINUTES AT 425°F
MAKES: 4 SERVINGS

- **3 medium round red or white potatoes (1 pound), cut into eighths, or 10 to 12 tiny new potatoes (1 pound), halved**
- **2 tablespoons olive oil**
- **½ teaspoon onion powder**
- **¼ teaspoon salt**
- **¼ teaspoon black pepper**
- **⅛ teaspoon paprika**
- **1 clove garlic, minced**

1 Preheat oven to 425°F. Place potatoes in a greased 9×9×2-inch baking pan. In a small bowl combine oil, onion powder, salt, pepper, paprika, and garlic. Drizzle oil mixture over potatoes; toss to coat. Roast, uncovered, for 25 to 30 minutes or until potatoes are tender and brown on the edges, stirring occasionally.

CHIPOTLE ROASTED POTATOES: Prepare as directed, except omit paprika and add ½ teaspoon ground chipotle chile pepper with the salt and pepper.

PER PLAIN OR CHIPOTLE VARIATION: 150 cal., 7 g total fat (1 g sat. fat), 0 mg chol., 153 mg sodium, 20 g carb., 3 g fiber, 2 g pro. EXCHANGES: 1 Starch, 1 Fat

8 to try

Twice-Baked Potatoes

PREP: 20 MINUTES **STAND:** 10 MINUTES
BAKE: 22 MINUTES AT 425°F
MAKES: 4 POTATOES

- **1 recipe Baked Potatoes (page 606)**
- **½ cup sour cream or plain yogurt**
- **¼ teaspoon garlic salt**
- **⅛ teaspoon black pepper**
- **Milk (optional)**
- **¾ cup finely shredded cheddar cheese (3 ounces)**
- **1 tablespoon snipped fresh chives (optional)**

1 Bake potatoes as directed; let stand about 10 minutes. Cut a lengthwise slice off the top of each baked potato; discard skin from slices and place pulp in a bowl. Scoop out potato pulp (see photo, below); add to the bowl.

2 Mash the potato pulp with a potato masher or an electric mixer on low speed. Add sour cream, garlic salt, and pepper; beat until smooth. (If necessary, stir in 1 to 2 tablespoons milk to reach desired consistency.) Season to taste with salt and additional pepper. Stir in ½ cup of the cheddar cheese and, if desired, chives. Spoon the mashed potato mixture into the potato shells. Place in a 2-quart baking dish.

3 Bake, uncovered, in a 425°F oven for 20 to 25 minutes or until light brown. Sprinkle with remaining cheese. Bake for 2 to 3 minutes more or until cheese melts.

PER POTATO: 268 cal., 12 g total fat (7 g sat. fat), 35 mg chol., 221 mg sodium, 21 g carb., 2 g fiber, 10 g pro. EXCHANGES: 2 Starch, ½ High-Fat Meat, 1 Fat

THE SCOOP

Using a spoon, gently scoop out the cooked potato pulp, leaving ¼-inch shells. You want a shell that's thick enough to stay open by itself.

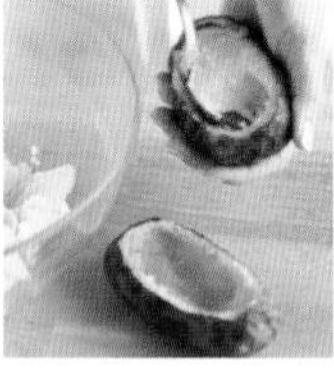

BACON-CHEDDAR: Prepare as directed, except stir in ⅓ cup crisp-cooked and crumbled bacon with sour cream.

BROCCOLI-CHEESE: Prepare as directed, except stir in 1 cup chopped cooked broccoli with cheese. Substitute dill weed for chives.

SOUTHWESTERN: Prepare as directed, except substitute Monterey Jack cheese with jalapeños for cheddar cheese and cilantro for chives. Top with purchased salsa.

GRUYÈRE-LEMON: Prepare as directed, except substitute Gruyère for cheddar cheese and add 2 teaspoons finely shredded lemon peel; omit chives. Top with lemon peel.

ROASTED GARLIC: Prepare as directed, except add 1 tablespoon Roasted Garlic (page 600). Substitute finely shredded Parmesan cheese for cheddar cheese. Garnish with Parmesan curls.

ROASTED POBLANO: Prepare as directed, except add 2 poblano chile peppers, roasted (see page 600) and chopped, with the cheese. Substitute cilantro for chives. Top with snipped cilantro.

MUSHROOM-SWISS: Prepare as directed, except cook and stir 2 cups sliced fresh mushrooms and 1 clove garlic, minced, in 1 tablespoon butter until tender; stir in with cheese. Substitute Swiss cheese for cheddar cheese and parsley for chives.

LEEK-CHEDDAR: Prepare as directed, except cook 2 leeks, halved and sliced, in 1 tablespoon olive oil until tender; stir in with cheese. Substitute crème fraîche for sour cream; substitute white cheddar cheese for cheddar. Top with crème fraîche.

LOW-CALORIE

Creamy Potluck Potatoes

PREP: 10 MINUTES **BAKE:** 75 MINUTES AT 350°F
STAND: 5 MINUTES **MAKES:** 12 SERVINGS

- **1 32-ounce package frozen diced hash brown potatoes, thawed (7½ cups)**
- **1 10.75-ounce can reduced-fat and reduced-sodium condensed cream of chicken soup**
- **1 8-ounce carton sour cream**
- **2 tablespoons butter or margarine, melted**
- **1 cup shredded cheddar cheese (4 ounces)**
- **¼ cup sliced green onions (2)**
- **¼ cup milk**
- **½ teaspoon garlic salt**
- **¼ teaspoon black pepper**

1 Preheat oven to 350°F. In a large bowl stir together potatoes, soup, sour cream, and butter. Stir in ½ cup of the shredded cheese, 3 tablespoons of the green onions, the milk, garlic salt, and pepper. Transfer potato mixture to a 2-quart rectangular baking dish.

2 Bake, covered, about 75 minutes or until potatoes are tender. Sprinkle with the remaining cheese. Let stand for 5 minutes. Sprinkle with the remaining green onion.

PER ¾ CUP: 173 cal., 10 g total fat (6 g sat. fat), 26 mg chol., 241 mg sodium, 17 g carb., 1 g fiber, 5 g pro.
EXCHANGES: 1 Starch, 2 Fat

LOW-CALORIE

Scalloped Potatoes

PREP: 30 MINUTES **BAKE:** 85 MINUTES AT 350°F
STAND: 10 MINUTES **MAKES:** 10 SERVINGS

- **1 cup chopped onion (1 large)**
- **2 cloves garlic, minced**
- **¼ cup butter or margarine**
- **¼ cup all-purpose flour**
- **½ teaspoon salt**
- **¼ teaspoon black pepper**
- **2½ cups milk**
- **8 cups thinly sliced red, white, long white, or yellow potatoes (about 2½ pounds)**

1 Preheat oven to 350°F. For sauce, in a medium saucepan cook onion and garlic in hot butter over medium heat until tender. Stir in flour, salt, and pepper. Add milk all at once. Cook and stir until thickened and bubbly. Remove from heat.

2 Place half of the potatoes in a greased 3-quart rectangular dish. Top with half of the sauce. Repeat layers.

3 Bake, covered, for 45 minutes. Uncover and bake for 40 to 50 minutes more or until potatoes are tender. Let stand, uncovered, for 10 minutes before serving.

PER ABOUT 1 CUP: 182 cal., 6 g total fat (4 g sat. fat), 17 mg chol., 182 mg sodium, 28 g carb., 3 g fiber, 5 g pro.
EXCHANGES: 2 Starch, 1 Fat

CHEESY SCALLOPED POTATOES: Prepare as directed, except gradually add 1½ cups shredded cheddar, Gruyère, or Swiss cheese (6 ounces) to the thickened sauce, stirring until cheese melts.

PER ABOUT 1 CUP: 251 cal., 12 g total fat (7 g sat. fat), 35 mg chol., 287 mg sodium, 28 g carb., 3 g fiber, 9 g pro.
EXCHANGES: 2 Starch, ½ High-Fat Meat, 1 Fat

Candied Sweet Potatoes

PREP: 30 MINUTES **BAKE:** 30 MINUTES AT 375°F
STAND: 5 MINUTES **MAKES:** 6 SERVINGS

- **4 medium sweet potatoes (about 2 pounds) or two 18-ounce cans sweet potatoes, drained**
- **¼ cup packed brown sugar or pure maple syrup**
- **¼ cup butter, melted**
- **¾ cup chopped pecans or walnuts, toasted if desired (see tip, page 21), and/or tiny marshmallows**

1 Preheat oven to 375°F. Peel fresh sweet potatoes; cut into 1½-inch chunks. Cook fresh sweet potatoes, covered, in enough boiling water to cover for 10 to 12 minutes or just until tender; drain. (Cut up canned sweet potatoes if using.)

2 Transfer potatoes to a 2-quart rectangular baking dish. Add brown sugar and melted butter; stir gently to combine.

3 Bake, uncovered, for 30 to 35 minutes or until potatoes are glazed, stirring gently twice. Sprinkle with nuts and/or marshmallows; let stand for 5 minutes before serving.

MAKE-AHEAD DIRECTIONS: Prepare as directed through Step 2. Cover and chill for up to 24 hours. Bake, uncovered, in a 375°F oven for 35 to 40 minutes or until potatoes are glazed, stirring gently twice. Continue as directed.

PER ¾ CUP: 327 cal., 18 g total fat (6 g sat. fat), 20 mg chol., 140 mg sodium, 41 g carb., 6 g fiber, 4 g pro.
EXCHANGES: 1½ Starch, 1 Other Carb., 3 Fat

BEST-LOVED LOW-CALORIE

Baked Sweet Potato Fries

PREP: 15 MINUTES **BAKE:** 25 MINUTES AT 400°F
MAKES: 6 SERVINGS

- **Nonstick cooking spray**
- **4 medium sweet potatoes (about 2 pounds), peeled if desired**
- **¼ cup olive oil**
- **1 teaspoon salt**
- **½ teaspoon black pepper**
- **Snipped fresh parsley (optional)**
- **Coarse salt (optional)**

1 Preheat oven to 400°F. If desired, line two baking sheets with foil. Lightly coat foil or unlined baking sheets with nonstick spray; set baking sheets aside.

2 Cut sweet potatoes lengthwise into ½-inch-thick strips. Place sweet potatoes in a large bowl. In a small bowl combine oil, salt, and pepper. Drizzle oil mixture over potatoes, tossing to coat. Arrange sweet potatoes in a single layer on prepared baking sheets.

3 Bake for 15 minutes. Turn potatoes over. Bake for 10 to 15 minutes more or until golden brown. If desired, sprinkle with parsley or coarse salt.

BROWN SUGAR-CINNAMON SWEET POTATO FRIES: Prepare as directed, except add 2 tablespoons packed brown sugar and ¼ teaspoon ground cinnamon with the oil.

GARLIC SWEET POTATO FRIES: Prepare as directed, except add 2 cloves garlic, minced, and ¼ teaspoon garlic powder with the oil.

SOUTHWESTERN SWEET POTATO FRIES: Prepare as directed, except before baking sprinkle with a mixture of 1 tablespoon sugar, 1 teaspoon ground cumin, 1 teaspoon chili powder, ¼ teaspoon onion powder, and ⅛ teaspoon cayenne pepper.

PER ⅔ CUP PLAIN, BROWN SUGAR, GARLIC, OR SOUTHWESTERN VARIATIONS: 178 cal., 9 g total fat (1 g sat. fat), 0 mg chol., 450 mg sodium, 23 g carb., 3 g fiber, 2 g pro.
EXCHANGES: 1½ Starch, 2 Fat

BEST-LOVED FAST

Creamy Spinach

START TO FINISH: 20 MINUTES **MAKES:** 4 SERVINGS

- 2 **9-ounce packages prewashed fresh spinach (large stems removed) or two 10-ounce packages frozen chopped spinach, thawed**
- ½ **cup chopped onion (1 medium)**
- 2 **to 3 cloves garlic, minced**
- 2 **tablespoons butter**
- 1 **cup whipping cream**
- ½ **teaspoon black pepper**
- ¼ **teaspoon salt**
- ¼ **teaspoon ground nutmeg**

1 In a large pot cook fresh spinach, if using, in rapidly boiling salted water for 1 minute. Drain well, squeezing out excess liquid. Pat dry with paper towels. Using kitchen shears, coarsely snip spinach; set aside. (If using frozen spinach, drain well after thawing, squeezing out excess liquid.)

2 In a large skillet cook onion and garlic in hot butter about 5 minutes or until onion is tender. Stir in whipping cream, pepper, salt, and nutmeg. Bring to boiling; cook for 3 to 5 minutes or until cream starts to thicken. Add spinach. Simmer until mixture reaches desired consistency, stirring occasionally. Serve immediately.

PER ¾ CUP: 312 cal., 29 g fat (18 g sat. fat), 97 mg chol., 345 mg sodium, 11 g carb., 4 g fiber, 7 g pro.
EXCHANGES: 2 Vegetable, 6 Fat

LOW-CALORIE

Maple Acorn Squash

PREP: 15 MINUTES **BAKE:** 65 MINUTES AT 350°F
MAKES: 4 SERVINGS

- 1 **medium acorn squash (about 1½ to 2 pounds)**
- ¼ **cup maple syrup**
- 2 **tablespoons butter or margarine, melted**
- ½ **teaspoon finely shredded orange peel (optional)**
- ⅛ **teaspoon ground cinnamon or ground nutmeg**

1 Preheat oven to 350°F. Cut squash in half lengthwise; remove and discard seeds (see photos 1 and 2, page 612). Arrange the squash halves, cut sides down, in a 2-quart rectangular baking dish. Bake, uncovered, for 45 minutes. Turn squash halves cut sides up.

2 Meanwhile, in a small bowl stir together maple syrup, butter, orange peel (if desired), and cinnamon. Spoon syrup mixture into centers of squash halves. Bake, uncovered, for 20 to 25 minutes more or until squash is tender. Cut squash halves in half and divide pieces among four serving plates. Spoon syrup mixture over squash pieces.

PER SERVING: 155 cal., 6 g total fat (4 g sat. fat), 15 mg chol., 47 mg sodium, 27 g carb., 2 g fiber, 1 g pro.
EXCHANGES: 1 Starch, 1 Other Carb., 1 Fat

LOW-CALORIE

Buttered Spaghetti Squash

PREP: 20 MINUTES **BAKE:** 30 MINUTES AT 350°F
MAKES: 6 SERVINGS

- 1 **medium spaghetti squash (2½ to 3 pounds)**
- ½ **cup finely shredded Parmesan cheese**
- 3 **tablespoons butter or margarine, cut up**
- 1 **tablespoon chopped fresh basil, oregano, or parsley**
- ¼ **teaspoon salt**

1 Preheat oven to 350°F. Halve squash lengthwise; remove and discard seeds. Place squash halves, cut sides down, in a large baking dish. Using a fork, prick the skin all over. Bake, uncovered, for 30 to 40 minutes or until tender.

2 Using a fork, remove the squash pulp from shell. Toss squash with ¼ cup of the Parmesan cheese, the butter, basil, and salt. Sprinkle with the remaining ¼ cup Parmesan cheese.

PER ¾ CUP: 120 cal., 8 g total fat (5 g sat. fat), 20 mg chol., 274 mg sodium, 10 g carb., 0 g fiber, 3 g pro.
EXCHANGES: 1½ Vegetable, 1½ Fat

SPAGHETTI SQUASH WITH MARINARA SAUCE: Bake squash as directed in Step 1. Omit Parmesan cheese, butter, basil, and salt. For marinara sauce, in a medium saucepan cook ¼ cup chopped onion and 2 cloves garlic, minced, in 1 tablespoon olive oil. Stir in one 14.5-ounce can diced tomatoes, undrained; 1 teaspoon dried Italian seasoning, crushed; ¼ teaspoon salt; ¼ teaspoon black pepper, and ⅛ teaspoon fennel seeds, crushed. Bring to boiling; reduce heat. Simmer, uncovered, for 10 to 15 minutes or until desired consistency, stirring often. Remove the squash pulp from shell. Spoon sauce over squash. If desired, sprinkle with grated Parmesan cheese.

PER ¾ CUP SQUASH + ¼ CUP SAUCE: 80 cal., 3 g total fat (0 g sat. fat), 0 mg chol., 256 mg sodium, 14 g carb., 1 g fiber, 2 g pro. EXCHANGES: 2 Vegetable, ½ Fat

Wild Rice-Stuffed Acorn Squash

PREP: 30 MINUTES **BAKE:** 70 MINUTES AT 400°F
MAKES: 6 MAIN-DISH SERVINGS

- **3 1½-pound acorn squash**
- **¼ cup butter, melted**
- **¼ cup packed brown sugar**
- **4 ounces pancetta, chopped**
- **½ cup chopped onion (1 medium)**
- **2 cups lightly packed baby spinach**
- **1 tablespoon snipped fresh sage**
- **2 cups cooked brown and/or wild rice**
- **⅔ cup pecans, toasted and chopped**
- **½ cup dried cranberries**

1 Preheat oven to 400°F. Cut squash in half; remove and discard seeds (see photos 1 and 2, below). Add ½ inch water to a large roasting pan. Arrange the squash halves, cut sides down, in the roasting pan. Bake, uncovered, for 30 minutes. Turn squash halves over. Brush cut sides with 2 tablespoons of the melted butter. Sprinkle evenly with brown sugar, ½ teaspoon *salt,* and ¼ teaspoon *black pepper.* Bake, uncovered, for 20 to 25 minutes or until tender.

2 Meanwhile, in a large skillet cook and stir pancetta over medium heat for 5 to 6 minutes or until crisp. Using a slotted spoon, transfer pancetta to paper towels to drain.

3 Add onion to drippings in skillet; cook for 4 to 5 minutes or until onion is tender, stirring occasionally. Add spinach, sage, and the crisped pancetta. Cook and stir for 2 minutes or until spinach wilts. Remove from heat. Add the cooked rice, pecans, and cranberries; mix well.

WILD RICE-STUFFED ACORN SQUASH

4 Spoon rice mixture into squash halves (about ⅔ cup rice mixture per half). Drizzle with remaining melted butter. Bake, uncovered, for 20 to 25 minutes more or until heated through.

PER SERVING: 462 cal., 23 g total fat (8 g sat. fat), 27 mg chol., 391 mg sodium, 63 g carb., 7 g fiber, 9 g pro.
EXCHANGES: ½ Fruit, 3 Starch, ½ Other Carb., 4 Fat

ACORN SQUASH STEP-BY-STEP

1. Securely hold the acorn squash on the cutting board so it will not roll. Using a large chef's knife, cut squash in half from the stem end to the blossom end.

2. Using a large spoon, scoop out and discard the seeds and membranes from squash halves.

FAST LOW-CALORIE

Summer Squash Toss

START TO FINISH: 25 MINUTES **MAKES:** 8 SERVINGS

- **1 medium red onion, cut into thin wedges**
- **1 tablespoon olive oil or vegetable oil**
- **3 medium zucchini and/or yellow summer squash, halved lengthwise and cut into ¼-inch slices (about 5 cups)**
- **½ teaspoon salt**
- **¼ teaspoon black pepper**
- **2 tablespoons snipped fresh basil, thyme, and/or Italian parsley**
- **2 ounces goat cheese, crumbled**

1 In a very large skillet cook onion in hot oil over medium-high heat for 7 minutes, stirring occasionally. Add zucchini, salt, and pepper to skillet; reduce heat to medium. Cook, uncovered, about 8 minutes or until vegetables are crisp-tender, stirring occasionally. Sprinkle with herb(s) and cheese.

PER ¾ CUP: 52 cal., 3 g total fat (1 g sat. fat), 3 mg chol., 179 mg sodium, 4 g carb., 1 g fiber, 2 g pro.
EXCHANGES: 1 Vegetable, ½ Fat

ZUCCHINI FRITTERS WITH CAPER MAYONNAISE

LOW-CALORIE

Zucchini Fritters with Caper Mayonnaise

PREP: 35 MINUTES **COOK:** 8 MINUTES PER BATCH
MAKES: 5 SERVINGS

- **8 ounces zucchini, coarsely shredded**
- **½ teaspoon salt**
- **⅓ cup mayonnaise**
- **1 teaspoon finely shredded lemon peel (set aside)**
- **2 teaspoons lemon juice**
- **1 tablespoon capers, drained and coarsely chopped**
- **1 teaspoon snipped fresh lemon thyme or thyme**
- **⅛ teaspoon black pepper**
- **8 ounces russet potatoes**
- **½ cup all-purpose flour**
- **½ teaspoon baking powder**
- **⅛ teaspoon cayenne pepper**
- **1 egg, lightly beaten**
- **2 tablespoons olive oil**

1 Line a 15×10×1-inch baking pan with several layers of paper towels. Spread zucchini on paper towels; sprinkle with salt. Top with another layer of paper towels. Let stand for 15 minutes, pressing occasionally to release moisture.

2 Meanwhile, for caper mayonnaise, in a small bowl stir together mayonnaise, lemon juice, capers, lemon thyme, and black pepper; set aside.

3 Transfer zucchini to a large bowl. Peel and finely shred the potatoes;* add to the zucchini. Add the lemon peel, flour, baking powder, and cayenne pepper; toss to mix well. Stir in egg until combined.

4 In a large nonstick skillet heat 2 teaspoons of the olive oil over medium-high heat. Working in batches, drop batter by slightly rounded tablespoons into the hot skillet. Use a spatula to flatten into patties. Cook for 4 to 5 minutes per side or until golden brown, decreasing heat to medium if necessary. Keep fritters warm in 200°F oven while cooking additional batches. Repeat with remaining batter, adding more oil as needed. Serve fritters with caper mayonnaise.

***NOTE:** Don't shred the potatoes ahead of time; they will darken.

PER 3 FRITTERS + 1 TABLESPOON MAYONNAISE: 243 cal., 18 g total fat (3 g sat. fat), 43 mg chol., 443 mg sodium, 18 g carb., 1 g fiber, 4 g pro. **EXCHANGES:** 1 Starch, 3½ Fat

LOW-CALORIE

Ratatouille

START TO FINISH: 40 MINUTES **MAKES:** 4 SERVINGS

- **½ cup chopped onion (1 medium)**
- **1 clove garlic, minced**
- **1 tablespoon olive oil or vegetable oil**
- **3 cups cubed, peeled eggplant**
- **1 medium zucchini or yellow summer squash, halved lengthwise and cut into ¼-inch slices (1½ cups)**
- **1 cup chopped, peeled tomatoes (2 medium) or one 14.5 ounce can diced tomatoes, drained**
- **¾ cup chopped green sweet pepper (1 medium)**
- **3 tablespoons dry white wine, chicken broth, or vegetable broth**
- **¼ teaspoon salt**
- **⅛ teaspoon black pepper**
- **1 tablespoon snipped fresh basil or oregano**

1 In a large skillet cook onion and garlic in hot oil over medium heat until onion is tender. Stir in eggplant, zucchini, tomatoes, sweet pepper, wine, salt, and black pepper. Bring to boiling; reduce heat. Simmer, covered, about 10 minutes or until vegetables are tender. Uncover; cook about 5 minutes more or until most of the liquid evaporates, stirring occasionally. Season with additional salt and pepper. Stir in basil.

PER ¾ CUP: 85 cal., 4 g total fat (1 g sat. fat), 0 mg chol., 156 mg sodium, 11 g carb., 4 g fiber, 2 g pro.
EXCHANGES: 1½ Vegetable, 1 Fat

Spicy Herb Fried Green Tomatoes

PREP: 30 MINUTES **COOK:** 8 MINUTES
MAKES: 6 SERVINGS

- **1 8-ounce carton sour cream**
- **6 cloves garlic, minced**
- **1 tablespoon snipped fresh cilantro**
- **⅛ teaspoon salt**
- **¼ cup milk**
- **2 cups crushed potato chips (about 5 ounces)**
- **1 tablespoon snipped fresh thyme**
- **½ teaspoon black pepper**
- **¼ teaspoon cayenne pepper**
- **½ cup all-purpose flour**
- **2 large firm green tomatoes (about 1 pound total), sliced ¼ inch thick**
- **3 tablespoons butter**
- **3 tablespoons olive oil**

1 In a small bowl combine sour cream, garlic, cilantro, and salt. Reserve half of the mixture to serve with fried tomatoes. Place the remaining mixture in a shallow dish and whisk in milk until combined. In another shallow dish combine crushed potato chips, thyme, black pepper, and cayenne pepper. Place flour in a third shallow dish.

2 Dip tomato slices in flour, turning to coat; shake off excess. Dip in milk mixture; dip in potato chip mixture.

3 In a very large skillet heat 2 tablespoons of the butter and 2 tablespoons of the oil over medium heat. Add half of the coated tomato slices; cook about 4 minutes or until crisp and golden, turning once halfway through cooking. Remove from pan; drain on paper towels. Repeat with remaining butter, olive oil, and tomato slices;. Serve with reserved sour cream mixture.

PER 2 SLICES: 376 cal., 29 g total fat (12 g sat. fat), 36 mg chol., 258 mg sodium, 26 g carb., 2 g fiber, 5 g pro.
EXCHANGES: 1 Vegetable, 1½ Starch, 5 Fat

LOW-CALORIE

Roasted Tomato and Bread Toss

PREP: 15 MINUTES **ROAST:** 20 MINUTES AT 400°F
MAKES: 8 SERVINGS

- **6 cups red and/or yellow cherry or grape tomatoes (2 pounds)**
- **6 cups torn baguette or Italian bread (12 ounces)**
- **2 to 3 tablespoons olive oil**
- **½ cup pitted Kalamata and/or green olives**

ROASTED TOMATO AND BREAD TOSS

- 2 tablespoons olive oil
- 2 tablespoons balsamic vinegar*
- 4 cloves garlic, minced
- ½ teaspoon kosher salt
- ½ teaspoon black pepper

1 Position one oven rack in the upper third of the oven. Preheat oven to 400°F. Line a 15×10×1-inch baking pan with parchment paper. Arrange tomatoes in a single layer in the prepared pan. Place bread in a large bowl. Drizzle 2 to 3 tablespoons oil over bread pieces. Toss to coat. In a second 15×10×1-inch baking pan arrange bread in a single layer.

2 Roast tomatoes on upper rack and bread on lower rack for 20 to 25 minutes or until tomato skins begin to split and wrinkle and bread is lightly toasted, stirring once.

3 Add bread and olives to tomatoes in pan; toss gently to mix. In a small bowl combine the 2 tablespoons olive oil, the balsamic vinegar, garlic, salt, and pepper. Drizzle over tomato mixture. Toss to coat.

***NOTE:** For a richer flavor, in a small saucepan heat ⅓ cup balsamic vinegar over medium heat until boiling. Boil gently, uncovered, for 6 to 8 minutes or until reduced to 2 tablespoons, watching carefully at the end because vinegar will reduce quickly.

PER 1 CUP: 215 cal., 10 g total fat (1 g sat. fat), 0 mg chol., 484 mg sodium, 28 g carb., 3 g fiber, 5 g pro.
EXCHANGES: 1 Vegetable, 1½ Starch, 1½ Fat

BEST-LOVED LOW-CALORIE

Oven-Fried Veggies

PREP: 25 MINUTES **BAKE:** 20 MINUTES AT 400°F
MAKES: 6 SERVINGS

- 1 cup panko bread crumbs
- ½ cup grated Parmesan cheese
- 1 teaspoon dried oregano, basil, or thyme, crushed
- ½ teaspoon garlic powder
- ½ teaspoon black pepper
- 1 egg, lightly beaten
- 1 tablespoon milk
- 4 cups cauliflower florets, broccoli florets, whole fresh button mushrooms, and/or packaged peeled baby carrots
- ¼ cup butter or margarine, melted
- Easy Aïoli (page 539) or bottled ranch dressing (optional)

1 Preheat oven to 400°F. Lightly grease a 15×10×1-inch baking pan; set aside. In a resealable plastic bag combine panko, Parmesan cheese, oregano, garlic powder, and pepper. In a small bowl combine egg and milk.

2 Toss 1 cup of the vegetables in the egg mixture. Using a slotted spoon, transfer vegetables to the plastic bag. Close bag and shake to coat with panko mixture. Place coated vegetables in the prepared baking pan. Repeat with remaining vegetables, egg mixture, and panko mixture. Drizzle melted butter over vegetables in pan.

3 Bake for 20 to 25 minutes or until golden, stirring twice. If desired, serve with Easy Aïoli.

PER ⅔ CUP: 169 cal., 11 g total fat (6 g sat. fat), 62 mg chol., 222 mg sodium, 12 g carb., 2 g fiber, 7 g pro.
EXCHANGES: 1 Vegetable, ½ Starch, ½ Lean Meat, 2 Fat

SIZE MATTERS

When you mix and match vegetables for the Oven-Fried Veggies, it's important that the pieces are all comparable in size. That way they will all get done at about the same time. You might need to halve or quarter large mushrooms.

APPLE-THYME SAUTÉ

FAST **LOW-CALORIE**

Fall Fruit Soup

START TO FINISH: 15 MINUTES **MAKES:** 6 SERVINGS

- **1 cup cranberries (4 ounces)**
- **3 plums, halved, pitted, and cut into thin slices**
- **1 medium pear, cored and cut into bite-size pieces**
- **1 medium cooking apple (such as Rome, Jonathan, or Fuji), cored and cut into bite-size pieces**
- **3 cups cranberry-apple juice**
- **¼ cup packed brown sugar**
- **1 tablespoon lemon juice**
- **2 3-inch pieces stick cinnamon**

1 In a large saucepan combine cranberries, plums, pear, and apple. Stir in cranberry-apple juice, brown sugar, lemon juice, and cinnamon stick. Bring to boiling; reduce heat. Simmer, covered, for 5 to 6 minutes or until fruit is tender and skins on cranberries pop. Remove cinnamon sticks; discard. Serve warm.

PER SERVING: 169 cal., 0 g total fat, 0 mg chol., 13 mg sodium, 45 g carb., 3 g fiber, 1 g pro. **EXCHANGES:** 2 Fruit, 1 Other Carb.

FAST **LOW-CALORIE**

Apple-Thyme Sauté

START TO FINISH: 15 MINUTES **MAKES:** 4 SERVINGS

- **1 tablespoon butter**
- **2 medium Granny Smith and/or Rome Beauty apples, cored and cut into ½-inch wedges (about 2½ cups)**
- **⅓ cup sliced shallots (3)**
- **1 tablespoon snipped fresh thyme or 1 teaspoon dried thyme, crushed**
- **1 tablespoon lemon juice**
- **¼ teaspoon salt**
- **⅛ teaspoon black pepper**

1 In a large skillet melt butter over medium heat. Add apples, shallots, and thyme. Cook, covered, about 5 minutes or just until apples are tender, stirring occasionally. Stir in lemon juice, salt, and pepper.

PER SERVING: 84 cal., 3 g total fat (2 g sat. fat), 8 mg chol., 168 mg sodium, 15 g carb., 2 g fiber, 1 g pro. **EXCHANGES:** 1 Fruit, ½ Fat

FAST

Avocado with Red Pepper Sauce

START TO FINISH: 20 MINUTES **MAKES:** 4 SERVINGS

- **½ cup red pepper jelly**
- **⅓ cup red wine vinegar**
- **2 medium avocados, halved, seeded, peeled, and sliced (see photos 1 and 2, below)**
- **¼ cup pitted ripe olives, coarsely chopped**
- **¼ cup chopped red or green sweet peppers**
- **Small sage leaves**
- **Red sweet pepper strips**

1 In a small saucepan combine jelly and vinegar. Cook and stir over medium-low heat until jelly melts. Spoon 2 tablespoons of the jelly mixture onto each of four salad plates. Arrange a few avocado slices on the jelly mixture on each plate. Top avocado slices with remaining jelly mixture. Sprinkle with chopped olives and sweet peppers. Garnish with sage and sweet pepper strips.

PER SERVING: 320 cal., 16 g total fat (3 g sat. fat), 0 mg chol., 92 mg sodium, 44 g carb., 10 g fiber, 4 g pro.
EXCHANGES: ½ Vegetable, 2½ Other Carb., 3½ Fat

SEEDING AND PEELING AVOCADOS STEP-BY-STEP

1. Starting from the stem end, cut the avocado in half, curving the blade around the seed. Twist the halves to separate them.

2. The seed will be in one of the halves. Use a small spoon to scoop gently around the seed and lift it out. You should be able to peel the skin back and away from the flesh with your fingers.

FAST

White Wine-Poached Pears
(photo, page 583)

START TO FINISH: 25 MINUTES **MAKES:** 4 SERVINGS

- **3 cups dry white wine**
- **1 cup sugar**
- **1 cup water**
- **4 strips orange peel**
- **3 inches stick cinnamon**
- **2 whole star anise**
- **4 firm ripe pears, peeled and cored**
- **¼ cup crème fraîche**
- **¼ cup whipping cream**
- **1 teaspoon vanilla bean paste or vanilla extract**

1 In a large heavy saucepan combine wine, sugar, water, orange peel, cinnamon, and star anise. Bring to boiling. Add pears. Return to boiling; reduce heat. Simmer, covered, for 15 to 20 minutes or until pears are tender.

2 For vanilla crème fraîche, in a small bowl whisk together crème fraîche, whipping cream, and vanilla bean paste until light.

3 Remove pears from syrup; reserve syrup. Cut pears in half lengthwise. Divide pear halves among four serving dishes. Spoon about ¼ cup syrup over each. Top with vanilla crème fraîche.

PER SERVING: 371 cal., 11 g total fat (7 g sat. fat), 41 mg chol., 18 mg sodium, 53 g carb., 5 g fiber, 1 g pro.
EXCHANGES: 1½ Fruit, ½ Starch, ½ Other Carb., 2 Fat

LOW-CALORIE

Honey-Berry Compote *(photo, page 583)*

PREP: 15 MINUTES **CHILL:** 2 TO 24 HOURS
MAKES: 8 SERVINGS

- **2 teaspoons finely shredded orange peel**
- **½ cup orange juice**
- **¼ cup honey**
- **1 tablespoon snipped fresh mint (optional)**
- **2 cups halved green or red seedless grapes**
- **2 cups fresh blueberries**
- **2 cups halved fresh strawberries**
- **2 cups fresh raspberries and/or blackberries**

1 In a medium bowl whisk together orange peel, orange juice, honey, and, if desired, mint.

2 In a large serving bowl combine grapes, blueberries, and strawberries. Gently stir in dressing. Cover; chill for 2 to 24 hours. To serve, stir in raspberries and/or blackberries.

PER SERVING: 103 cal., 1 g total fat (0 g sat. fat), 0 mg chol., 2 mg sodium, 26 g carb., 4 g fiber, 1 g pro. EXCHANGES: 1 Fruit, ½ Other Carb.

Persimmon, Blood Orange, and Pomegranate with Greens

START TO FINISH: 50 MINUTES **MAKES:** 6 SERVINGS

- **1 pomegranate**
- **2 large ripe Fuyu persimmons, mangoes, or papayas**
- **5 cups mesclun, arugula, baby arugula, or mixed salad greens**
- **6 tablespoons sliced green onions (3)**
- **1 recipe Pine Nut-Persimmon Vinaigrette**
- **4 medium blood and/or navel oranges, peeled and thinly sliced**

1 Score an "X" on the top of the pomegranate (see photo 1, below); break apart into quarters. Working in a bowl of cool water, immerse each quarter; loosen the seeds from the white membrane (see photo 2, below). Discard peel and membrane. Drain the seeds; set aside.

2 Cut each persimmon in half; remove core. Slice into ¼- to ½-inch-thick slices.

3 Combine mesclun and green onions. Drizzle ½ cup of the Pine Nut-Persimmon Vinaigrette over mesclun mixture; toss to coat.

4 To serve, arrange mesclun mixture on six plates. Arrange persimmons and oranges on top of greens, tucking a few in and under leaves. Sprinkle with the pomegranate seeds. Serve with remaining vinaigrette for drizzling.

PINE NUT-PERSIMMON VINAIGRETTE: Remove the core from 1 large ripe persimmon; cut in half. Scoop out pulp (should have ⅓ cup).

SEEDING A POMEGRANATE STEP-BY-STEP

1. Using a small sharp knife, make shallow cuts in an "X" pattern on the top of the pomegranate. Break the pomegranate into quarters.

2. Hold pomegranate quarters under water in a bowl to prevent juice from squirting. Gently loosen the seeds with your thumbs. Use a slotted spoon to remove white pith. Drain seeds.

Discard skin. Place pulp in a blender or food processor. Cover; blend or process until smooth. Add 1/3 cup olive oil; 1/4 cup red wine vinegar; 3 tablespoons pine nuts, toasted; 1½ teaspoons finely shredded blood orange peel; 2 tablespoons blood orange juice; 1 tablespoon honey; ½ of a large shallot, cut up; ½ teaspoon Dijon-style mustard; a dash ground cinnamon; and a dash black pepper. Cover and blend or process until smooth.

PER SERVING: 260 cal., 16 g total fat (2 g sat. fat), 0 mg chol., 20 mg sodium, 30 g carb., 5 g fiber, 3 g pro.
EXCHANGES: 1½ Fruit, ½ Vegetable, ½ Other Carb., 3 Fat

Stirred Custard with Fresh Figs

PREP: 25 MINUTES **CHILL:** 2 HOURS
COOL: 15 MINUTES **MAKES:** 8 SERVINGS

- **5 egg yolks, lightly beaten**
- **1½ cups whole milk**
- **1/4 cup granulated sugar**
- **1½ teaspoons vanilla**
- **3/4 cup packed brown sugar**
- **½ cup butter, cut up**
- **½ cup whipping cream**
- **2 tablespoons light-color corn syrup**
- **2 tablespoons dry sherry**
- **8 fresh figs or 4 peaches, halved, pitted, and sliced**

1 In a medium heavy saucepan combine egg yolks, milk, and granulated sugar. Cook and stir continuously with a heatproof rubber scraper over medium heat just until custard thickens and coats the back of the scraper (see photo 1, page 288). Remove from heat. Stir in vanilla.

2 Quickly cool custard by placing the saucepan in a large bowl of ice water for 1 to 2 minutes, stirring constantly. Pour custard into a medium bowl. Cover the surface with plastic wrap to prevent a skin from forming. Chill for at least 2 hours before serving; do not stir.

3 Meanwhile, for sherry-caramel sauce, in a medium heavy saucepan combine brown sugar, butter, whipping cream, and corn syrup. Bring to boiling over medium-high heat, whisking occasionally. Reduce heat to medium. Boil gently, uncovered, for 3 minutes more. Remove from heat. Stir in sherry. Let cool for 15 minutes.

4 To serve, halve figs. Spoon custard into eight dessert dishes. Top each with two fig halves. Drizzle with some of the sherry-caramel sauce.*

***NOTE:** Remaining sauce can be refrigerated in a covered container for up to 2 weeks.

PER SERVING: 379 cal., 22 g total fat (13 g sat. fat), 171 mg chol., 142 mg sodium, 44 g carb., 1 g fiber, 4 g pro.
EXCHANGES: ½ Fruit, 2½ Other Carb., ½ High-Fat Meat, 3½ Fat

FAST LOW-CALORIE

Warm Spiced Peaches

PREP: 15 MINUTES **BAKE:** 10 MINUTES AT 350°F
MAKES: 4 SERVINGS

- **3 cups peeled, pitted, and sliced peaches or pitted and sliced nectarines, plums, and/or apricots**
- **2 teaspoons sugar**
- **½ teaspoon finely shredded orange peel**
- **½ teaspoon vanilla**
- **1/4 teaspoon ground cinnamon**
- **1/8 teaspoon ground nutmeg**
- **2 teaspoons snipped fresh basil or 1 teaspoon snipped fresh mint**

1 Preheat oven to 350°F. In a medium bowl combine peaches, sugar, orange peel, vanilla, cinnamon, and nutmeg; toss gently to combine. Divide peach mixture among four 5-inch individual quiche dishes or 10-ounce custard cups.

2 Bake, covered, for 10 to 15 minutes or just until warm. Sprinkle with basil.

PER SERVING: 56 cal., 0 g total fat, 0 mg chol., 0 mg sodium, 13 g carb., 2 g fiber, 1 g pro. **EXCHANGES:** 1 Fruit

FRESH FIGS

ABOUT: Native to Turkey, figs are now grown and savored around the world. Fig varieties vary in color and texture, but they all have deliciously sweet flesh that surrounds nutty, crunchy seeds. You can eat figs fresh or dried. Dried figs can be used in muffins, cakes, oatmeal, and energy bars. Fresh figs are lovely in salads and poached in wine or fruit juice. Or just eat them in their purest form—fresh, out of hand.
VARIETIES: There are hundreds of fig varieties, and many are regionally supplied. California-grown Black Mission figs have purplish black skin and intensely sweet red flesh. Other common varieties include pale green-yellow Kadota figs; mild-tasting Brown Turkey figs; and large, gold-skin, nutty-flavor Calimyrna figs.
SELECTING: Figs come in many colors and types, so know what color your fig should be before you buy. Look for figs with smooth, dry skin and no blemishes or cracks. Ripe figs will be firm but give slightly to the touch. Avoid any overly soft or mushy fruit.
STORING: Use figs as soon as possible after purchase. You can place them in a plastic bag in your refrigerator to preserve them for a few days.

SELECTING FRESH VEGETABLES

These charts offer specific guidelines for selecting and storing a variety of fresh vegetables. In general, choose vegetables that are plump, crisp, bright in color, and heavy for their size. Avoid any that are bruised, shriveled, moldy, or blemished. Unless specified, do not wash produce before storing. For cooking information, see charts on pages 629–631.

Vegetable	Peak Season	How to Choose	How to Store
Asparagus	Available March through June with peak season in April and May; available year-round in some areas.	Choose crisp, firm, straight stalks with good color and compact, closed tips. If possible, select spears that are the same size for even cooking.	Wrap the bases of fresh asparagus spears in wet paper towels and place in a plastic bag in the refrigerator for up to 3 days.
Beans, green: snap or string	Available April through September; available year-round in some areas.	Select fresh beans that are brightly colored and crisp. Avoid those that are bruised, scarred, or rusty with brown spots or streaks. Bulging, leathery beans are old.	Refrigerate in a plastic bag in the crisper drawer of the refrigerator for up to 1 week.
Beets	Available year-round with peak season from June through October.	Select small or medium beets; large beets tend to be pithy, tough, and less sweet.	Trim beet greens, leaving 1 to 2 inches of stem. Do not cut the long root. Store unwashed beets in an open container in the refrigerator for up to 1 week.
Bok choy	Available year-round.	Look for firm, white, bulblike bases with deep green leaves. Avoid soft spots on bases or wilted, shriveled leaves.	Refrigerate in a plastic bag and use within 5 days.
Broccoli	Available year-round with peak season from October through May.	Look for firm stalks with tightly packed, deep green or purplish green heads. Avoid heads that are light green or yellowing.	Keep unwashed broccoli in a plastic bag in the refrigerator for up to 4 days.
Brussels sprouts	Available year-round with peak season from August through April.	Pick out the smaller sprouts that are vivid green; they will taste the sweetest. Large ones might be bitter.	Refrigerate in a plastic bag in the crisper drawer of the refrigerator for up to 5 days.
Cabbage: green, napa, red, or savoy	Available year-round.	The head should feel heavy for its size, and its leaves should be unwithered, brightly colored, and free of brown spots.	Refrigerate in a plastic bag for up to 5 days.
Carrots	Available year-round.	Select straight, rigid, bright orange carrots without cracks.	Refrigerate in a plastic bag for up to 2 weeks.
Cauliflower	Available year-round.	Look for solid, heavy heads with bright green leaves. Avoid those with brown bruises, yellowed leaves, or speckled appearance.	Refrigerate in a plastic bag in the crisper drawer of the refrigerator for up to 5 days. Keep away from ethylene-producing fruit, such as apples, mangoes, melons, pears, peaches, and plums.
Celery	Available year-round.	Look for crisp ribs that are firm, unwilted, and unblemished.	Refrigerate in a plastic bag for up to 2 weeks.
Cucumbers	Available year-round with peak season from late May through early September.	Select firm cucumbers without shriveled or soft spots. Edible wax sometimes is added to prevent moisture loss.	Keep cucumbers in a plastic bag in refrigerator for 3 to 5 days.

Vegetable	Peak Season	How to Choose	How to Store
Eggplant	Available year-round with peak season from August through September.	Look for plump, glossy eggplants that have fresh-looking, mold-free caps. Skip any that are scarred or bruised.	Refrigerate whole eggplants in a perforated plastic bag for 2 to 4 days.
Fennel	Available October through April; available year-round in some areas.	Look for crisp, clean bulbs without brown spots or blemishes. Tops should be bright green and fresh looking.	Refrigerate, tightly wrapped in a plastic bag, for up to 5 days.
Greens, cooking: beet, chard, collard, kale, mustard, or turnip	Most available year-round with peak season in winter months; peak season for chard is during the summer months.	Look for crisp or tender leaves that are brightly or richly colored. Avoid wilted or yellowing leaves.	Cut away center stalk of kale leaves. Refrigerate most greens in a plastic bag for up to 5 days; refrigerate mustard greens for up to 1 week.
Leeks	Available year-round.	Look for leeks that have clean white ends and fresh green tops.	Refrigerate, wrapped loosely in plastic, for 10 to 14 days.
Mushrooms (all varieties)	Available year-round; morel mushrooms available April through June.	Mushrooms should be firm, fresh, plump, and bruise-free. Size is a matter of preference. Avoid spotted or slimy mushrooms.	Store unwashed mushrooms in the refrigerator for up to 2 days in a paper bag. If in original packaging, remove plastic and wrap carton in barely damp paper towels.
Okra	Available year-round with peak season from May through September.	Look for small, crisp, brightly colored pods without brown spots or blemishes. Avoid shriveled pods.	Refrigerate, in a paper bag in crisper drawer of the refrigerator, for up to 3 days.
Onions (all varieties)	Variety determines availability. Some varieties, such as white, red, pearl, and boiling onions, are available year-round. Various sweet onion varieties, such as Vidalia and Walla Walla, are available on and off throughout the year.	Select dry bulb onions that are firm, free from blemishes, and not sprouting. They should have papery outer skins and short necks.	Keep in a cool, dry, well-ventilated place for several weeks.
Peas, Pea pods	Peas: Available January through June with peak season from March through May. Pea pods: Available February through August.	Select fresh, crisp, brightly colored peas, snow peas, or sugar snap peas. Avoid shriveled pods or those with brown spots.	Store, in a perforated plastic bag in the crisper drawer of the refrigerator, for 2 to 4 days.
Peppers: hot or sweet	Available year-round.	Fresh peppers, whether hot or sweet, should be brightly colored and have a good shape for the variety. Avoid shriveled, bruised, or broken peppers.	Refrigerate in a plastic bag for up to 5 days.
Potatoes	Available year-round.	Look for clean potatoes that have smooth, unblemished skins. They should be firm and have a typical shape for their variety. Avoid those that have green spots or are soft, moldy, or shriveled.	Store in an open paper bag or basket for several weeks in a dark, well-ventilated, cool place that is slightly humid but not wet. Do not refrigerate; potatoes tend to get sweet at cold temperatures.

Vegetable	Peak Season	How to Choose	How to Store
Root vegetables: parsnips, rutabagas, or turnips	Available year-round. Parsnips: Peak season from November through March. Rutabagas: Peak season from September through March. Turnips: Peak season from October through March.	Choose vegetables that are smooth-skinned and heavy for their size. Sometimes parsnips, rutabagas, and turnips are covered with a wax coating to extend storage; cut off this coating before cooking.	Refrigerate in a plastic bag for up to 2 weeks.
Spinach	Available year-round.	Leaves should be crisp and free of moisture. Avoid spinach with broken or bruised leaves.	Rinse leaves in cold water and thoroughly dry. Place the leaves in a storage container with a paper towel and refrigerate for up to 3 days.
Squash, winter	Some varieties available year-round with peak season from September through March.	Choose firm squash that are heavy for their size. Avoid those with soft spots.	Store whole squash in a cool, dry place for up to 2 months. Refrigerate cut squash, wrapped in plastic, for up to 4 days.
Sweet potatoes	Available year-round with peak season from October through January.	Choose small to medium smooth-skin potatoes that are firm and free of soft spots.	Store in an open paper bag or basket in a cool, dry, dark place for up to 1 week.
Tomatoes	Available year-round with peak season from June through early September.	Pick well-shaped, plump, fairly firm tomatoes. Ripe tomatoes yield to slight pressure and smell like a tomato.	Store at room temperature for up to 3 days. Do not store tomatoes in the refrigerator because they lose their flavor.
Zucchini, Summer squash	Some varieties available year-round with peak season from June through September.	It is almost impossible for tender-skin zucchini to be blemish-free, but look for small ones that are firm and free of cuts and soft spots.	Refrigerate squash, tightly wrapped, for up to 4 days.

SELECTING FRESH FRUITS

These charts offer specific guidelines for selecting and storing a variety of fresh fruits. In general, look for fruits that are plump, tender, and bright in color. Fruits should be heavy for their size and free from mold, mildew, bruises, cuts, or other blemishes. Some fruits are picked and shipped while still firm, so they might need additional ripening (see tip, page 585).

Fruit	Peak Season	How to Choose	How to Store
Apples	Available year-round with peak season September through November.	Select firm apples, free from bruises or soft spots. Apples are sold ready for eating. Select variety according to intended use.	Refrigerate for up to 6 weeks; store bulk apples in a cool, moist place. Don't store near foods with strong odors that can be absorbed.
Apricots	Available May through July.	Look for plump, fairly firm apricots with deep yellow or yellowish orange skin.	Ripen firm fruit as directed on page 585 until it yields to gentle pressure and is golden in color. Refrigerate ripened fruit for up to 2 days.
Avocados	Available year-round.	Avoid bruised fruit with gouges or broken skin. Soft avocados can be used immediately (and are especially good for guacamole).	Ripen firm fruit as directed on page 585 until it yields to gentle pressure in cradled hands. Store ripened fruit in the refrigerator for up to 5 days.
Bananas	Available year-round.	Choose bananas at any stage of ripeness, from green to yellow.	Ripen at room temperature until they have a bright yellow color. Overripe bananas are brown.

Fruit	Peak Season	How to Choose	How to Store
Berries	Blackberries: Available June through August. Blueberries: Available late May through October. Boysenberries: Available late June through early August. Raspberries: Available year-round with peak season from May through September. Strawberries: Available year-round with peak season from April through June.	If picking your own, select berries that separate easily from their stems.	Refrigerate berries in a single layer, loosely covered, for up to 3 days. Rinse just before using.
Cantaloupe	Available year-round with peak season from June through September.	Select cantaloupe that has a delicate, sweet, aromatic scent; look for cream-color netting over rind that is yellowish green or gray. Melon should feel heavy for its size.	Ripen as directed on page 585. Refrigerate ripened whole melon up to 4 days. Refrigerate cut fruit in a covered container or tightly wrapped for up to 3 days.
Carambolas (Star fruit)	Available late August through February.	Look for firm, shiny-skin golden fruit. Some brown on the edge of the fins is natural and does not affect the taste.	Ripen as directed on page 585. Refrigerate ripened fruit in a covered container or tightly wrapped for up to 1 week.
Cherries	Sweet: Available May through August with peak season in June and July. Tart: Available June through August with peak season in June and July.	Select firm, brightly colored fruit.	Refrigerate in a covered container for 2 to 3 days.
Cranberries	Available October through December with peak season in November.	Fruit is ripe when sold. Avoid soft, shriveled, or bruised cranberries.	Refrigerate for up to 2 weeks or freeze for up to 1 year.
Figs	Available mid-May through December.	Look for fruit with smooth, dry skin and no blemishes or cracks. Figs will be firm but give slightly to touch.	Use as soon as possible. Can refrigerate in a plastic bag for up to 3 days.
Grapefruit	Available year-round.	Choose brightly colored grapefruit with a nicely rounded shape. Juicy grapefruit will be heavy for its size.	Refrigerate for up to 2 weeks.
Grapes	Available year-round.	Look for plump grapes without bruises, soft spots, or mold. Bloom (a frosty white cast) is typical and doesn't affect quality.	Refrigerate in a perforated plastic bag for up to 1 week.
Honeydew melons	Available year-round with peak season from June through September.	Choose one that is firm and a creamy yellow color with a sweet, aromatic scent. Avoid wet, dented, bruised, or cracked ones.	Ripen as directed on page 585. Refrigerate ripened whole melons up to 4 days. Refrigerate cut fruit in a covered container or tightly wrapped for up to 3 days.
Kiwifruit	Available year-round.	Choose fruit that is free of wrinkles, bruises, and soft spots.	Ripen firm fruit as directed on page 585 until skin yields to gentle pressure; refrigerate ripened fruit for 3 to 5 days.
Lemons, Limes	Available year-round.	Look for firm, well-shaped fruit with smooth, brightly colored skin. Avoid fruit with shriveled skin.	Refrigerate for up to 2 weeks.
Mangoes	Available April through September with peak season from June through July.	Look for fully colored fruit that smells fruity and feels fairly firm when pressed.	Ripen firm fruit as directed on page 585. Refrigerate ripened fruit for up to 3 days.

Fruit	Peak Season	How to Choose	How to Store
Oranges	Available year-round.	Choose oranges that are firm and heavy for their size. Brown specks or a slight greenish tinge on the rind of an orange will not affect the eating quality.	Refrigerate for up to 2 weeks.
Papayas	Available year-round.	Choose fruit that is at least half yellow and feels somewhat soft when pressed. The skin should be smooth.	Ripen as directed on page 585 until yellow. Refrigerate ripened fruit, unwrapped, for 3 to 5 days.
Peaches, Nectarines	Peaches: Available May through September. Nectarines: Available May through September with peak season in July and August.	Look for fruit with a golden-yellow skin and no tinges of green. Ripe fruit should yield slightly to gentle pressure.	Ripen as directed on page 585. Refrigerate ripened fruit for up to 5 days.
Pears	Available year-round.	Skin color is not always an indicator of ripeness because the color of some varieties does not change much as the pears ripen. Look for pears without bruises or cuts. Choose a variety according to intended use.	Ripen as directed on page 585 until skin yields to gentle pressure at the stem end. Refrigerate ripened fruit for 5 to 7 days.
Persimmons (Hachiya and Fuyu)	Available October through February.	Hachiya persimmons should have a deep solid-orange color with no dark spots. Fuyu persimmons have a bright yellow-orange color and should be firm to the touch.	Ripen as directed on page 585 until soft. Hachiya persimmons can be stored for up to 1 week at room temperature. Fuyu persimmons will stay firm up to 3 weeks.
Pineapple	Available year-round with peak season from March through July.	Look for a plump pineapple with a sweet, aromatic smell. It should be slightly soft to the touch, heavy for its size, and have deep green leaves. Avoid those with soft spots.	Refrigerate for up to 2 days. Cut pineapple lasts a few more days if placed in a tightly covered container and refrigerated.
Plums	Available May through October with peak season in June and July.	Find firm, plump, well-shaped fresh plums. Fruit should give slightly when gently pressed. Bloom (light gray cast) on the skin is natural and doesn't affect quality.	Ripen as directed on page 585. Refrigerate ripened fruit for up to 3 days.
Rhubarb	Available February through June with peak season from April through June.	Look for crisp stalks that are firm and tender. Avoid rhubarb that looks wilted or has very thick stalks.	Wrap stalks tightly in plastic wrap and refrigerate for up to 5 days.
Watermelon	Available May through September with peak season from mid-June through late August.	Choose watermelon that has a hard, smooth rind and is heavy for its size. Avoid wet, dented, bruised, or cracked fruit.	Watermelon does not ripen after it is picked. Refrigerate whole melon for up to 4 days. Refrigerate cut fruit in a covered container or tightly wrapped for up to 3 days.

SPRING PRODUCE

1. **ARTICHOKE**
2. **RHUBARB**
3. **ASPARAGUS**
4. **CARROTS:** purple, white, and orange
5. **CAULIFLOWER**
6. **KOHLRABI:** white and purple
7. **LEEK**
8. **GREEN ONIONS:** also called scallions
9. **SUGAR SNAP PEAS**
10. **ENGLISH PEAS**
11. **BROCCOLI**
12. **BROCCO RABE**
13. **WHITE BUTTON MUSHROOMS**
14. **CREMINI MUSHROOMS**
15. **OYSTER MUSHROOMS**
16. **SHIITAKE MUSHROOM**
17. **PORTOBELLO MUSHROOM**

SUMMER PRODUCE

1. TOMATILLOS
2. CAMPARI TOMATOES
3. ROMA TOMATO
4. ENGLISH CUCUMBER
5. HOTHOUSE CUCUMBER
6. CUCUMBER
7. ZUCCHINI
8. YELLOW SUMMER SQUASH
9. EGGPLANT
10. HEIRLOOM TOMATO
11. GRAPE TOMATOES
12. CHERRY TOMATOES
13. AVOCADO
14. SWISS CHARD
15. GREEN SWEET PEPPER
16. RED SWEET PEPPER
17. SERRANO CHILE PEPPER
18. HABANERO CHILE PEPPER
19. GREEN BEANS
20. OKRA
21. JALAPEÑO CHILE PEPPER
22. ANAHEIM CHILE PEPPER
23. POBLANO CHILE PEPPER
24. CORN
25. BLACKBERRIES
26. RED RASPBERRIES
27. BLUEBERRIES
28. STRAWBERRIES
29. PLUM
30. PEACH
31. WATERMELON
32. CANTALOUPE
33. HONEYDEW MELON

FALL PRODUCE

1. BUTTERNUT SQUASH
2. BEETS: red and golden
3. CIPPOLINI ONIONS
4. PEARL ONIONS
5. SHALLOTS
6. WHITE ONION
7. RED ONION
8. RUSSET POTATO
9. ROUND WHITE POTATO
10. FINGERLING POTATO
11. PURPLE POTATO
12. ROUND RED POTATO
13. YUKON GOLD POTATO
14. YELLOW ONION
15. SPAGHETTI SQUASH
16. WHITE CABBAGE
17. RED CABBAGE
18. BOK CHOY
19. SAVOY CABBAGE
20. NAPA CABBAGE
21. ACORN SQUASH
22. RED DELICIOUS APPLE
23. BRAEBURN APPLE
24. GRANNY SMITH APPLE
25. GOLDEN DELICIOUS APPLE

WINTER PRODUCE

1. MUSTARD GREENS
2. COLLARD GREENS
3. KALE
4. SWEET POTATO
5. BARTLETT PEAR
6. ANJOU PEAR
7. FENNEL BULB
8. PINEAPPLE
9. CRANBERRIES
10. BRUSSELS SPROUTS
11. LEMON
12. LIME
13. CLEMENTINE
14. GRAPEFRUIT
15. BLOOD ORANGE
16. NAVEL ORANGE
17. TURNIP
18. RUTABAGA
19. PARSNIP

COOKING FRESH VEGETABLES

These charts offer basic cooking directions for fresh vegetables. The amounts given for each vegetable yield enough cooked vegetables for 4 servings, except where noted. To prepare fresh vegetables, wash with cool, clear tap water; scrub firm vegetables with a clean produce brush.

To steam vegetables, place a steamer basket in a saucepan. Add water to just below the bottom of the basket. Bring water to boiling. Add vegetables to steamer basket. Cover and reduce heat. Steam for the time specified in the chart or until vegetables reach desired doneness.

To microwave vegetables, use a microwave-safe baking dish or casserole and follow the directions in the chart, keeping in mind that times might vary depending on the microwave oven. Cover with waxed paper, vented plastic wrap, or the lid of the baking dish or casserole.

Vegetable and Amount	Preparation (Yield)	Conventional Cooking Directions	Microwave Cooking Directions
Artichokes 2 (10 ounces each) (2 servings)	Wash; trim stems. Cut off 1 inch from tops; snip off sharp leaf tips. Brush cut edges with lemon juice.	Cook, covered, in a large amount of boiling salted water for 20 to 30 minutes or until a leaf pulls out easily. (Or steam for 20 to 25 minutes.) Invert artichokes to drain.	Place in a casserole with 2 tablespoons water. Microwave, covered, on 100% power (high) for 7 to 9 minutes or until a leaf pulls out easily, rearranging artichokes once. Invert artichokes to drain.
Asparagus 1 pound (15 to 24 spears)	Wash and break off woody bases where spears snap easily. Leave spears whole or cut into 1-inch pieces (2 cups pieces).	Cook, covered, in a small amount of boiling salted water for 3 to 5 minutes or until crisp-tender. (Or steam for 3 to 5 minutes.)	Place in a baking dish or casserole with 2 tablespoons water. Microwave, covered, on 100% power (high) for 2 to 4 minutes or until crisp-tender.
Beans: green, French-cut, Italian green, purple, yellow wax 12 ounces	Wash; remove ends and strings. Leave whole or cut into 1-inch pieces (2½ cups pieces). For French-cut beans, slice lengthwise.	Cook, covered, in a small amount of boiling salted water for 10 to 15 minutes for whole or cut beans (5 to 10 minutes for French-cut beans) or until crisp-tender. (Or steam for 15 to 18 minutes.)	Place in a casserole with 2 tablespoons water. Microwave, covered, on 100% power (high) for 8 to 12 minutes for whole or cut beans (7 to 10 minutes for French-cut beans) or until crisp-tender, stirring once.
Beets 4 medium (1 pound)	For whole beets, cut off all but 1 inch of stems and roots; wash. Do not peel. Or peel beets; cube or slice (2¾ cups cubes).	Cook, covered, in enough boiling salted water to cover for 35 to 45 minutes for whole beets (about 20 minutes for cubed or sliced beets) or until tender. Slip skins off whole beets.	Place in a casserole with 2 tablespoons water. Microwave cubed or sliced beets, covered, on 100% power (high) for 9 to 12 minutes or until tender, stirring once.
Broccoli 1 pound	Wash; remove outer leaves and tough parts of stalks. Cut lengthwise into spears or into 1-inch florets (3½ cups florets).	Cook, covered, in a small amount of boiling salted water for 8 to 10 minutes or until crisp-tender. (Or steam for 8 to 10 minutes.)	Place in a baking dish with 2 tablespoons water. Microwave, covered, on 100% power (high) for 5 to 8 minutes or until crisp-tender, rearranging or stirring once.
Brussels sprouts 12 ounces	Trim stems and remove any wilted outer leaves; wash. Cut large sprouts in half lengthwise (3 cups).	Cook, covered, in enough boiling salted water to cover for 10 to 12 minutes or until crisp-tender. (Or steam for 10 to 15 minutes.)	Place in a casserole with ¼ cup water. Microwave, covered, on 100% power (high) for 5 to 7 minutes or until crisp-tender, stirring once.
Cabbage Half of a 1½-pound head	Remove wilted outer leaves; wash. Cut into 4 wedges or coarsely chop (3 cups coarsely chopped).	Cook, uncovered, in a small amount of boiling water for 2 minutes. Cover; cook 6 to 8 minutes more for wedges (3 to 5 minutes for pieces) or until crisp-tender. (Or steam wedges for 10 to 12 minutes.)	Place in a baking dish or casserole with 2 tablespoons water. Microwave, covered, on 100% power (high) for 9 to 11 minutes for wedges (4 to 6 minutes for pieces) or until crisp-tender, rearranging or stirring once.

Vegetable and Amount	Preparation (Yield)	Conventional Cooking Directions	Microwave Cooking Directions
Carrots 1 pound	Wash, trim, and peel or scrub if necessary. Cut standard-size carrots into ¼-inch slices or into strips (2½ cups slices) or measure 3½ cups packaged peeled baby carrots.	Cook, covered, in a small amount of boiling salted water for 7 to 9 minutes for slices (4 to 6 minutes for strips; 8 to 10 minutes for baby carrots) or until crisp-tender. (Or steam slices or baby carrots for 8 to 10 minutes or strips for 5 to 7 minutes.)	Place in a casserole with 2 tablespoons water. Microwave, covered, on 100% power (high) for 6 to 9 minutes for slices (5 to 7 minutes for strips; 7 to 9 minutes for baby carrots) or until crisp-tender, stirring once.
Cauliflower 12 ounces florets or 1½-pound head	Wash; remove leaves and woody stem. Leave whole or break into florets (3 cups florets).	Cook, covered, in a small amount of boiling salted water for 10 to 15 minutes for head (8 to 10 minutes for florets) or until crisp-tender. (Or steam head or florets for 8 to 12 minutes.)	Place in a casserole with 2 tablespoons water. Microwave, covered, on 100% power (high) for 9 to 11 minutes for head (7 to 10 minutes for florets) or until crisp-tender, turning or stirring once.
Corn 4 ears	Remove husks. Scrub with a stiff brush to remove silks; rinse. Cut kernels from cob (2 cups kernels).	Cook, covered, in a small amount of boiling salted water for 4 minutes. (Or steam for 4 to 5 minutes.)	Place in a casserole with 2 tablespoons water. Microwave, covered, on 100% power (high) for 5 to 6 minutes, stirring once.
Corn on the cob (1 ear equals 1 serving)	Remove husks from fresh ears of corn. Scrub with a stiff brush to remove silks; rinse.	Cook, covered, in enough boiling lightly salted water to cover for 5 to 7 minutes or until kernels are tender.	Wrap each ear in waxed paper; place on paper towels in microwave. Microwave on 100% power (high) for 3 to 5 minutes for 1 ear, 5 to 7 minutes for 2 ears, or 9 to 12 minutes for 4 ears; rearrange once.
Greens: beet or chard 12 ounces	Wash thoroughly in cold water; drain well. Remove stems; trim bruised leaves. Tear into pieces (12 cups torn).	Cook, covered, in a small amount of boiling salted water for 8 to 10 minutes or until tender.	Not recommended.
Greens: kale, mustard, or turnip 12 ounces	Wash thoroughly in cold water; drain well. Remove stems; trim bruised leaves. Tear into pieces (12 cups torn).	Cook, covered, in a small amount of boiling salted water for 20 to 25 minutes or until tender.	Not recommended.
Kohlrabi 1 pound	Cut off leaves; wash. Peel; chop or cut into strips (3 cups strips).	Cook, covered, in a small amount of boiling salted water for 4 to 6 minutes or until crisp-tender. (Or steam about 6 minutes.)	Place in a casserole with 2 tablespoons water. Microwave, covered, on 100% power (high) for 5 to 7 minutes or until crisp-tender, stirring once.
Mushrooms 1 pound	Wipe mushrooms with a damp towel or paper towel. Leave whole or slice (6 cups slices).	Cook sliced mushrooms in 2 tablespoons butter or margarine about 5 minutes. (Or steam whole mushrooms for 10 to 12 minutes.)	Place in a casserole with 2 tablespoons butter or margarine. Microwave, covered, on 100% power (high) for 4 to 6 minutes, stirring twice.
Okra 8 ounces	Wash; cut off stems. Cut into ½-inch slices (2 cups slices).	Cook, covered, in a small amount of boiling salted water for 8 to 10 minutes or until tender.	Place in a casserole with 2 tablespoons water. Microwave, covered, on 100% power (high) for 4 to 6 minutes or until tender, stirring once.
Onions: boiling or pearl 8 ounces boiling onions (10 to 12) 8 ounces pearl onions (24 to 30)	Peel boiling onions before cooking; peel pearl onions after cooking (2 cups).	Cook, covered, in a small amount of boiling salted water for 10 to 12 minutes (boiling onions) or 8 to 10 minutes (pearl onions). (Or steam boiling onions 12 to 15 minutes or pearl onions 10 to 12 minutes.)	Place in a casserole with 2 tablespoons water. Microwave, covered, on 100% power (high) for 3 to 5 minutes.

Vegetable and Amount	**Preparation** (Yield)	Conventional Cooking Directions	Microwave Cooking Directions
Parsnips 12 ounces	Wash, trim, and peel or scrub. Cut into ¼-inch slices (2 cups slices).	Cook, covered, in a small amount of boiling salted water for 7 to 9 minutes or until tender. (Or steam for 8 to 10 minutes.)	Place in a casserole with 2 tablespoons water. Microwave, covered, on 100% power (high) for 4 to 6 minutes or until tender, stirring once.
Peas, edible pod: snow peas or sugar snap peas 6 ounces	Remove strings and tips; wash (2 cups).	Cook, covered, in a small amount of boiling salted water for 2 to 4 minutes or until crisp-tender. (Or steam for 2 to 4 minutes.)	Place in a casserole with 2 tablespoons water. Microwave, covered, on 100% power (high) for 2 to 4 minutes or until crisp-tender.
Peas, green 2 pounds	Shell and wash (3 cups shelled).	Cook, covered, in a small amount of boiling salted water for 10 to 12 minutes or until crisp-tender. (Or steam for 12 to 15 minutes.)	Place in a casserole with 2 tablespoons water. Microwave, covered, on 100% power (high) 6 to 8 minutes or until crisp-tender, stirring once.
Potatoes 1 pound	Wash, peel, and remove eyes, sprouts, or green areas. Cut into quarters or cubes (2¾ cups cubes).	Cook, covered, in enough boiling salted water to cover for 20 to 25 minutes for quarters (15 minutes for cubes) or until tender. (Or steam about 20 minutes.)	Place in a casserole with 2 tablespoons water. Microwave, covered, on 100% power (high) for 8 to 10 minutes or until tender, stirring once.
Rutabagas 1 pound	Wash and peel. Cut into ½-inch cubes (3 cups cubes).	Cook, covered, in a small amount of boiling salted water for 18 to 20 minutes or until tender. (Or steam for 18 to 20 minutes.)	Place in a casserole with 2 tablespoons water. Microwave, covered, on 100% power (high) 11 to 13 minutes or until tender, stirring 3 times.
Spinach 1 pound	Wash and drain; remove stems and tear into pieces (12 cups torn).	Cook, covered, in a small amount of boiling salted water for 3 to 5 minutes or until tender. (Or steam for 3 to 5 minutes.)	Not recommended.
Squash: acorn or delicata One 1¼ pounds (2 servings)	Wash, halve, and remove seeds.	Place squash halves, cut sides down, in a baking dish. Bake in a 350°F oven for 45 to 50 minutes or until tender.	Place, cut sides down, in a baking dish with 2 tablespoons water. Microwave, covered, on 100% power (high) for 7 to 10 minutes or until tender, rearranging once. Let stand, covered, for 5 minutes.
Squash: buttercup or butternut One 1½ pounds or a 1½-pound piece	Wash, halve lengthwise, and remove seeds.	Place squash halves, cut sides down, in a baking dish. Bake in a 350°F oven for 45 to 50 minutes or until tender.	Place, cut sides down, in a baking dish with 2 tablespoons water. Microwave, covered, on 100% power (high) for 9 to 12 minutes or until tender, rearranging once.
Squash: pattypan, yellow summer, or zucchini 12 ounces	Wash; do not peel. Cut off ends. Cut into ¼-inch slices (3 cups slices) or leave pattypan whole.	Cook, covered, in a small amount of boiling salted water for 3 to 5 minutes or until crisp-tender. (Or steam for 4 to 6 minutes.)	Place in a casserole with 2 tablespoons water. Microwave, covered, on 100% power (high) for 4 to 5 minutes or until crisp-tender, stirring twice.
Squash, spaghetti Half of one 3 pounds or a 1½-pound piece	Wash and remove seeds.	Place, cut sides down, in a baking dish. Bake in a 350°F oven for 45 to 50 minutes or until tender.	Place, cut sides down, in a baking dish with ¼ cup water. Microwave, covered, on 100% power (high) for about 15 minutes or until tender.
Sweet potatoes 1 pound	Wash, peel, and cut off woody portions and ends. Cut into quarters for microwave) or into cubes (2¾ cups cubes).	Cook, covered, in enough boiling salted water to cover for 25 to 30 minutes or until tender. (Or steam for 20 to 25 minutes.)	Place in a casserole with ½ cup water. Microwave, covered, on 100% power (high) for 10 to 13 minutes or until tender, stirring once.
Turnips 1 pound	Wash and peel. Cut into ½-inch cubes or strips (2¾ cups cubes).	Cook, covered, in a small amount of boiling salted water for 10 to 12 minutes or until tender. (Or steam for 10 to 15 minutes.)	Place in a casserole with 2 tablespoons water. Microwave, covered, on 100% power (high) 10 to 12 minutes or until tender; stir once.

EQUIVALENTS

Use these guidelines to help determine how much you will need to purchase when a recipe calls for a measurement of food or fresh produce.

Food	Beginning Size or Amount	Yield and Cut
Apple	1 medium	1 cup sliced or ⅔ cup chopped
Apricots	1 pound (8 to 12 whole)	2½ cups sliced
Asparagus	1 pound (15 to 24 spears)	2 cups 1-inch pieces
Banana	1 medium	⅓ cup mashed or ¾ cup sliced
Beans, green	1 pound	3 to 3½ cups 1-inch pieces
Blueberries	1 pound	3 cups
Broccoli	1 pound	3½ cups florets
Cabbage	1 medium head (1½ pounds)	7 to 10 cups shredded or 6 cups coarsely chopped
Carrot	1 medium	½ cup sliced, chopped, julienned, or finely shredded
Cauliflower	1 head (2½ pounds)	1½ pounds florets or 6 cups florets
Celery	1 stalk	½ cup sliced or chopped
Cherries	1 pound	3 cups whole or 2½ cups halved
Cranberries	1 pound	4 cups
Garlic	1 clove	½ teaspoon minced
Grapes	1 pound	2½ cups
Greens, cooking	12 ounces	12 cups torn
Greens, salad (see page 491)		
Leek	1 medium	⅓ cup sliced
Lemon	1 medium	2 teaspoons finely shredded peel or 3 tablespoons juice
Lime	1 medium	1½ teaspoons finely shredded peel or 2 tablespoons juice
Mango	1 medium	1 cup sliced
Melon (cantaloupe, honeydew)	1 medium (2½ pounds)	6 cups cubed or 5½ cups balls
Mushrooms	8 ounces	3 cups sliced or chopped
Nectarine	1 medium	1 cup sliced or ¾ cup chopped
Onion	1 medium	½ cup chopped
Onion, green	1 medium	2 tablespoons sliced
Orange	1 medium	1 tablespoon finely shredded peel or ⅓ cup juice or ⅓ cup sections
Papaya	1 medium (1 pound)	1¼ cups sliced
Parsnip	1 medium	¾ to 1 cup sliced or chopped
Peach	1 medium	1 cup sliced or ¾ cup chopped
Pear	1 medium	1 cup sliced or chopped
Pepper, sweet	1 medium	1 cup strips or ¾ cup chopped
Pineapple	1 medium (4 pounds)	4½ cups peeled and cubed
Potatoes	1 pound	3 cups cubed (unpeeled) or 2¾ cups cubed (peeled)
Raspberries	1 pound	4 cups
Rhubarb	1 pound	4 cups sliced
Shallot	1 medium	2 tablespoons finely chopped
Squash		
Summer (zucchini, yellow)	1 medium	1¼ cups sliced
Winter (acorn, butternut)	2 pounds	4 cups chopped or 2 cups mashed
Strawberries	1 pint (about 1 pound)	3 cups whole or 2½ cups sliced
Tomato	1 medium	½ cup peeled, seeded, and chopped

index

Note: Page references in *italics* indicate photo pages for finished dishes.

A

B

D

E

F

G

M

S

EMERGENCY SUBSTITUTIONS

If you don't have:	Substitute:
Bacon, 1 slice, crisp-cooked, crumbled	1 tablespoon cooked bacon pieces
Baking powder, 1 teaspoon	½ teaspoon cream of tartar plus ¼ teaspoon baking soda
Balsamic vinegar, 1 tablespoon	1 tablespoon cider vinegar or red wine vinegar plus ½ teaspoon sugar
Bread crumbs, fine dry, ¼ cup	¾ cup soft bread crumbs, or ¼ cup cracker crumbs, or ¼ cup cornflake crumbs
Broth, beef or chicken, 1 cup	1 teaspoon or 1 cube instant beef or chicken bouillon plus 1 cup hot water
Butter, 1 cup	1 cup shortening plus, if desired, ¼ teaspoon salt
Buttermilk, 1 cup	1 tablespoon lemon juice or vinegar plus enough milk to make 1 cup (let stand 5 minutes before using) or 1 cup plain yogurt
Chocolate, semisweet or bittersweet, 1 ounce	3 tablespoons semisweet chocolate pieces, or 1 ounce unsweetened chocolate plus 1 tablespoon granulated sugar, or 1 tablespoon unsweetened cocoa powder plus 2 teaspoons sugar and 2 teaspoons shortening
Chocolate, sweet baking, 4 ounces	¼ cup unsweetened cocoa powder plus ⅓ cup granulated sugar and 3 tablespoons shortening
Chocolate, unsweetened, 1 ounce	3 tablespoons unsweetened cocoa powder plus 1 tablespoon cooking oil or shortening, melted
Corn syrup (light), 1 cup	1 cup granulated sugar plus ¼ cup water
Cornstarch, 1 tablespoon (for thickening)	2 tablespoons all-purpose flour
Egg, 1 whole	¼ cup refrigerated or frozen egg product, thawed
Flour, cake, 1 cup	1 cup minus 2 tablespoons all-purpose flour
Flour, self-rising, 1 cup	1 cup all-purpose flour plus 1 teaspoon baking powder, ½ teaspoon salt, and ¼ teaspoon baking soda
Garlic, 1 clove	½ teaspoon bottled minced garlic or ⅛ teaspoon garlic powder
Ginger, grated fresh, 1 teaspoon	¼ teaspoon ground ginger
Half-and-half or light cream, 1 cup	1 tablespoon melted butter or margarine plus enough whole milk to make 1 cup
Mustard, dry, 1 teaspoon	1 tablespoon prepared (in cooked mixtures)
Mustard, yellow, 1 tablespoon	½ teaspoon dry mustard plus 2 teaspoons vinegar
Onion, chopped, ½ cup	2 tablespoons dried minced onion or ½ teaspoon onion powder
Sour cream, dairy, 1 cup	1 cup plain yogurt or 1 cup light sour cream
Sugar, brown, 1 cup packed	1 cup granulated sugar plus 2 tablespoons molasses
Sugar, granulated, 1 cup	1 cup packed brown sugar or 2 cups sifted powdered sugar
Tomato juice, 1 cup	½ cup tomato sauce plus ½ cup water
Tomato sauce, 2 cups	¾ cup tomato paste plus 1 cup water
Vanilla bean, 1 whole	1 tablespoon vanilla
Wine, red, 1 cup	1 cup beef or chicken broth or cranberry juice in savory recipes; cranberry juice in desserts
Wine, white, 1 cup	1 cup chicken broth in savory recipes; apple juice or white grape juice in desserts

SEASONINGS*

Apple pie spice, 1 teaspoon	½ teaspoon ground cinnamon plus ¼ teaspoon ground nutmeg, ⅛ teaspoon ground allspice, and dash ground cloves or ginger
Cajun seasoning, 1 tablespoon	½ teaspoon white pepper plus ½ teaspoon garlic powder, ½ teaspoon onion powder, ½ teaspoon cayenne pepper, ½ teaspoon paprika, and ½ teaspoon black pepper
Fajita seasoning, 1 tablespoon	1½ teaspoons ground cumin plus ½ teaspoon dried oregano, crushed; ¼ teaspoon salt; ¼ teaspoon cayenne pepper; ¼ teaspoon black pepper; ⅛ teaspoon garlic powder; and ⅛ teaspoon onion powder
Herbs, snipped fresh, 1 tablespoon	½ to 1 teaspoon dried herb, crushed, or ½ teaspoon ground herb
Poultry seasoning, 1 teaspoon	¾ teaspoon dried sage, crushed, plus ¼ teaspoon dried thyme or marjoram, crushed
Pumpkin pie spice, 1 teaspoon	½ teaspoon ground cinnamon plus ¼ teaspoon ground ginger, ¼ teaspoon ground allspice, and ⅛ teaspoon ground nutmeg
Thai seasoning, 1 tablespoon	1 teaspoon ground coriander plus 1 teaspoon crushed red pepper, ¼ teaspoon salt, ¼ teaspoon ground ginger, ¼ teaspoon garlic powder, and ¼ teaspoon onion powder

*For information on spice and herb substitutions, see page 26.

REFRIGERATOR/FREEZER STORAGE

Use these short but safe guidelines to keep your refrigerated foods fresh. Freezer guidelines are for quality only. Frozen foods are safe indefinitely.

Product:	To store:	**Refrigerate** (40°F) up to:	**Freeze** (0°F) up to:
Dairy			
Butter	Refrigerate in original packaging. Overwrap with moistureproof and vaporproof wrap to freeze.	1 month	6 months
Buttermilk	Refrigerate in original packaging. To freeze, transfer to freezer containers; allow for headspace.	7 days	Up to 3 months Use for baking and cooking only.
Cheese, cottage and ricotta	Refrigerate in original packaging.	Use by date on container or within 5 days of purchase.	Not recommended.
Cheese, hard and semihard	Wrap in plastic wrap. Overwrap in freezer wrap to freeze.	4 to 6 weeks If cheese molds, cut ½ inch below the mold and discard molded portion.	1 month Use only for cooking.
Sour Cream and Yogurt	Refrigerate in original packaging.	Use by date on container or within 5 days of purchase	Not recommended.
Eggs			
Hard-cooked, in shells	Refrigerate.	7 days	Not recommended.
Whites	Refrigerate in tightly covered containers; transfer to freezer containers to freeze.	4 days	6 months
Whole, in shells	Store whole eggs in carton placed in coldest part of refrigerator. Do not wash; do not store in refrigerator door.	5 weeks after packing date.	Do not freeze eggs in shells.
Cooked Meats			
Bacon, Ham, Hot dogs, Sausage, smoked links and patties	Refrigerate in original wrapping. Overwrap in freezer wrap to freeze.	opened package: 7 days	1 month
Deli Meat	Refrigerate in original packaging.	opened package: 3 to 5 days	1 month
Uncooked Meat, Poultry, and Fish			
Meat (roasts, steaks, chops), **Poultry** (whole and pieces)	Refrigerate in original wrapping. Overwrap in freezer wrap to freeze.	3 days	3 to 6 months
Meat (including sausage) and **Poultry** (ground)	Refrigerate in original wrapping. Overwrap in freezer wrap to freeze.	1 to 2 days	3 months
Fish and Shellfish	Store in moisture- and vaporproof wrap in coldest part of refrigerator. Overwrap in freezer wrap to freeze.	1 to 2 days	3 months

cooking at high altitudes

When you cook at high altitudes, recipe adjustments need to be made to ensure the best results possible.

Unfortunately, no simple formula exists for converting all recipes to high altitude recipes. If you live more than 1,000 feet above sea level, it will help you to become familiar with common cooking adjustments.

GENERAL HIGH-ALTITUDE ISSUES

Higher than 3,000 feet above sea level:

- Water boils at lower temperatures, causing moisture to evaporate more quickly. This can cause food to dry out during cooking and baking.
- Because of a lower boiling point, foods cooked in steam or boiling liquids take longer to cook.
- Lower air pressure may cause baked goods that use yeast, baking powder, baking soda, egg whites, or steam to rise excessively, then fall.

SUGGESTIONS FOR BAKING

- For cakes leavened by air, such as angel food, beat the egg whites only to soft peaks; otherwise, the batter may expand too much.
- For cakes made with shortening, you may want to decrease the baking powder (start by decreasing it by 1/8 teaspoon per teaspoon called for); decrease the sugar (start by decreasing by about 1 tablespoon for each cup called for); and increase the liquid (start by increasing it 1 to 2 tablespoons for each cup called for). These estimates are based on an altitude of 3,000 feet above sea level—at higher altitudes you may need to alter these measures proportionately. You can also try increasing the baking temperature by 15°F to 25°F to help set the batter.
- When making a rich cake, reduce the shortening by 1 to 2 tablespoons per cup and add one egg (for a 2-layer cake) to prevent cake from falling.
- Cookies generally yield acceptable results, but if you're not satisfied, try slightly increasing baking temperature; slightly decreasing the baking powder or soda, fat, and/or sugar; and/or slightly increasing the liquid ingredients and flour.
- Muffinlike quick breads and biscuits generally need little adjustment, but if you find that these goods develop a bitter flavor, decrease the baking soda or powder slightly. Because cakelike quick breads are more delicate, you may need to follow guidelines for cakes.
- Yeast breads will rise more quickly at high altitudes. Allow unshaped dough to rise only until double in size, then punch the dough down. Repeat this rising step once more before shaping dough. Flour tends to be drier at high altitudes and sometimes absorbs more liquid. If your yeast dough seems dry, add more liquid and reduce the amount of flour the next time you make the recipe.
- Large cuts of meat may take longer to cook. Be sure to use a meat thermometer to determine proper doneness.

SUGGESTIONS FOR RANGE-TOP COOKING

CANDY-MAKING: Rapid evaporation caused by cooking at high altitudes can cause candies to cook down more quickly. Therefore, decrease the final cooking temperature by the difference in boiling water temperature at your altitude and that of sea level (212°F). This is an approximate decrease of 2°F for every increase of 1,000 feet in elevation above sea level.

CANNING AND FREEZING FOODS: When canning at high altitudes, adjustments in processing time or pressure are needed to guard against contamination; when freezing, an adjustment in the blanching time is needed. See the Canning and Freezing chapter, especially the tip on page 206.

DEEP-FAT FRYING: At high altitudes, deep-fried foods can overbrown but remain underdone inside. While foods vary, a rough guideline is to lower the temperature of the fat about 3°F for every 1,000 feet in elevation above sea level.

COOKING ABOVE 6,000 FEET

Cooking at altitudes higher than 6,000 feet above sea level poses further challenges because the dry air found at such elevations influences cooking. Call your local United States Department of Agriculture Extension Service Office for advice.

FURTHER INFORMATION

For more information on cooking at high altitudes, contact your county extension office or write to Colorado State University, Department of Food Science and Human Nutrition Cooperative Extension, Fort Collins, CO 80523-1571. Please use this contact only for queries regarding high-altitude cooking.

metric information

PRODUCT DIFFERENCES

Most of the ingredients called for in the recipes in this book are available in most countries. However, some are known by different names. Here are some common American ingredients and their possible counterparts:

- Sugar (white) is granulated, fine granulated, or castor sugar.
- Powdered sugar is icing sugar.
- All-purpose flour is enriched, bleached or unbleached white household flour. When self-rising flour is used in place of all-purpose flour in a recipe that calls for leavening, omit the leavening agent (baking soda or baking powder) and salt.
- Light-color corn syrup is golden syrup.
- Cornstarch is cornflour.
- Baking soda is bicarbonate of soda.
- Vanilla or vanilla extract is vanilla essence.
- Green, red, or yellow sweet peppers are capsicums or bell peppers.
- Golden raisins are sultanas.

VOLUME AND WEIGHT

The United States traditionally uses cup measures for liquid and solid ingredients. The chart below shows the approximate imperial and metric equivalents. If you are accustomed to weighing solid ingredients, the following approximate equivalents will be helpful.

- 1 cup butter, castor sugar, or rice = 8 ounces = ½ pound = 250 grams
- 1 cup flour = 4 ounces = ¼ pound = 125 grams
- 1 cup icing sugar = 5 ounces = 150 grams
- Canadian and U.S. volume for a cup measure is 8 fluid ounces (237 ml), but the standard metric equivalent is 250 ml.
- 1 British imperial cup is 10 fluid ounces.
- In Australia, 1 tablespoon equals 20 ml, and there are 4 teaspoons in the Australian tablespoon.
- Spoon measures are used for smaller amounts of ingredients. Although the size of the tablespoon varies slightly in different countries, for practical purposes and for recipes in this book, a straight substitution is all that's necessary. Measurements made using cups or spoons always should be level unless stated otherwise.

COMMON WEIGHT RANGE REPLACEMENTS

Imperial / U.S.	Metric
½ ounce	15 g
1 ounce	25 g or 30 g
4 ounces (¼ pound)	115 g or 125 g
8 ounces (½ pound)	225 g or 250 g
16 ounces (1 pound)	450 g or 500 g
1¼ pounds	625 g
1½ pounds	750 g
2 pounds or 2¼ pounds	1,000 g or 1 Kg

OVEN TEMPERATURE EQUIVALENTS

Fahrenheit Setting	Celsius Setting	Gas Setting
300°F	150°C	Gas Mark 2 (very low)
325°F	160°C	Gas Mark 3 (low)
350°F	180°C	Gas Mark 4 (moderate)
375°F	190°C	Gas Mark 5 (moderate)
400°F	200°C	Gas Mark 6 (hot)
425°F	220°C	Gas Mark 7 (hot)
450°F	230°C	Gas Mark 8 (very hot)
475°F	240°C	Gas Mark 9 (very hot)
500°F	260°C	Gas Mark 10 (extremely hot)
Broil	Broil	Grill

*Electric and gas ovens may be calibrated using celsius. However, for an electric oven, increase celsius setting 10 to 20 degrees when cooking above 160°C. For convection or forced air ovens (gas or electric), lower the temperature setting 25°F/10°C when cooking at all heat levels.

BAKING PAN SIZES

Imperial / U.S.	Metric
9×1½-inch round cake pan	22- or 23×4-cm (1.5 L)
9×1½-inch pie plate	22- or 23×4-cm (1 L)
8×8×2-inch square cake pan	20×5-cm (2 L)
9×9×2-inch square cake pan	22- or 23×4.5-cm (2.5 L)
11×7×1½-inch baking pan	28×17×4-cm (2 L)
2-quart rectangular baking pan	30×19×4.5-cm (3 L)
13×9×2-inch baking pan	34×22×4.5-cm (3.5 L)
15×10×1-inch jelly roll pan	40×25×2-cm
9×5×3-inch loaf pan	23×13×8-cm (2 L)
2-quart casserole	2 L

U.S. / STANDARD METRIC EQUIVALENTS

⅛ teaspoon = 0.5 ml
¼ teaspoon = 1 ml
½ teaspoon = 2 ml
1 teaspoon = 5 ml
1 tablespoon = 15 ml
2 tablespoons = 25 ml
¼ cup = 2 fluid ounces = 50 ml
⅓ cup = 3 fluid ounces = 75 ml
½ cup = 4 fluid ounces = 125 ml
⅔ cup = 5 fluid ounces = 150 ml
¾ cup = 6 fluid ounces = 175 ml
1 cup = 8 fluid ounces = 250 ml
2 cups = 1 pint = 500 ml
1 quart = 1 litre